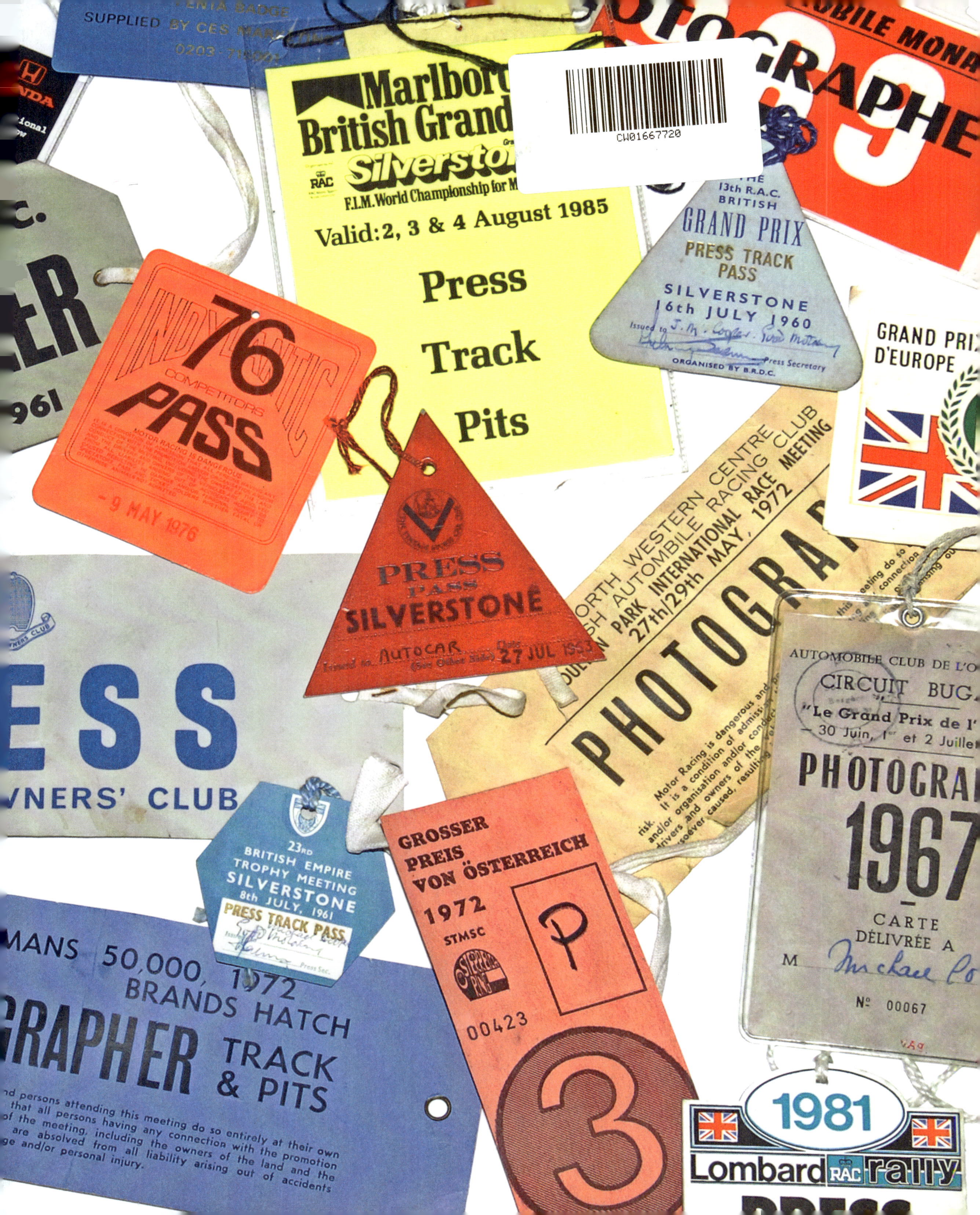
SUPPLIED BY CES
Marlboro
British Grand
Silverstone
RAC
F.I.M. World Championship for M
Valid: 2, 3 & 4 August 1985
Press
Track
Pits
13th R.A.C. BRITISH
GRAND PRIX
PRESS TRACK PASS
SILVERSTONE
16th JULY 1960
Issued to
Press Secretary
ORGANISED BY B.R.D.C.
GRAPHE
GRAND PRI
D'EUROPE
76
COMPETITORS
PASS
MOTOR RACING IS DANGEROUS
9 MAY 1976
961
PRESS
PASS
SILVERSTONE
Issued to AUTOCAR
27 JUL 1963
NORTH WESTERN CENTRE
BRITISH AUTOMOBILE RACING CLUB
INTERNATIONAL RACE MEETING
27th/29th MAY, 1972
PHOTOGRA
AUTOMOBILE CLUB DE L'O
CIRCUIT BUG
"Le Grand Prix de l'
30 Juin, 1er et 2 Juille
PHOTOGRA
1967
CARTE
DÉLIVRÉE A
M
Nº 00067
ESS
VNERS' CLUB
23RD
BRITISH EMPIRE
TROPHY MEETING
SILVERSTONE
8th JULY, 1961
PRESS TRACK PASS
Press Sec.
GROSSER
PREIS
VON ÖSTERREICH
1972
STMSC
P
00423
3
MANS 50,000, 1972
BRANDS HATCH
GRAPHER TRACK
& PITS
1981
Lombard RAC rally

CW01667720

RACES FACES PLACES

© Paul Parker, 2009

All rights reserved. No part of this publication may be reproduced, stored in a retrieval system or transmitted, in any form or by any means, electronic, mechanical, photocopying, recording or otherwise, without prior permission in writing from the publisher.

First published in June 2009

A catalogue record for this book is available
from the British Library

ISBN 978 184425 508 5

Library of Congress catalog card no. 2009923194

Haynes North America Inc., 861 Lawrence Drive,
Newbury Park, California 91320, USA.

Published by Haynes Publishing,
Sparkford, Yeovil, Somerset BA22 7JJ, UK
Tel: 01963 442030 Fax: 01963 440001
Int. tel: +44 1963 442030
Int. fax: +44 1963 440001
E-mail: sales@haynes.co.uk
Website: www.haynes.co.uk

Design and layout by Richard Parsons

Printed and bound in the UK

RACES FACES PLACES

The motor racing photography of Michael Cooper

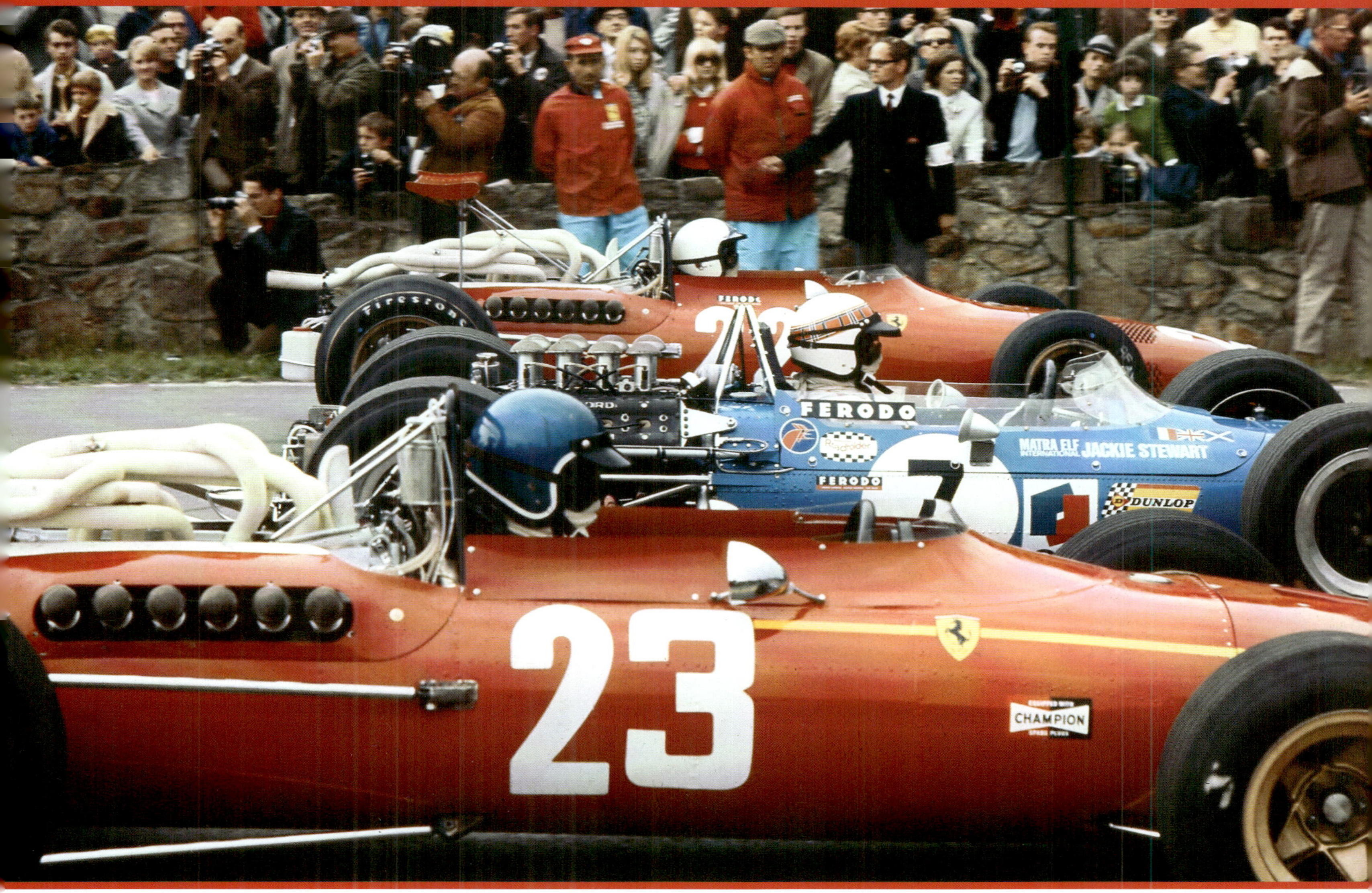

Paul Parker

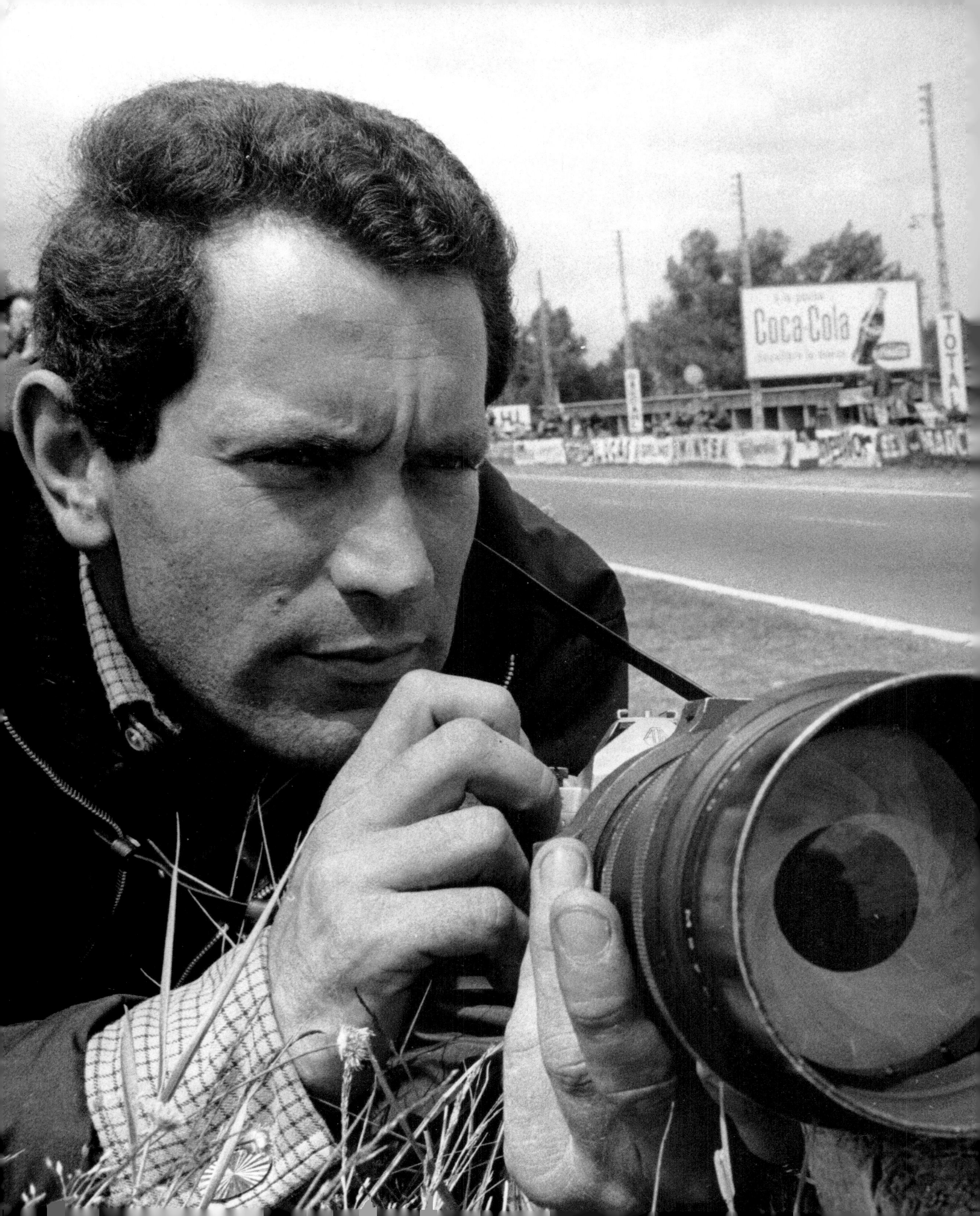
Coca-Cola
TOTAL

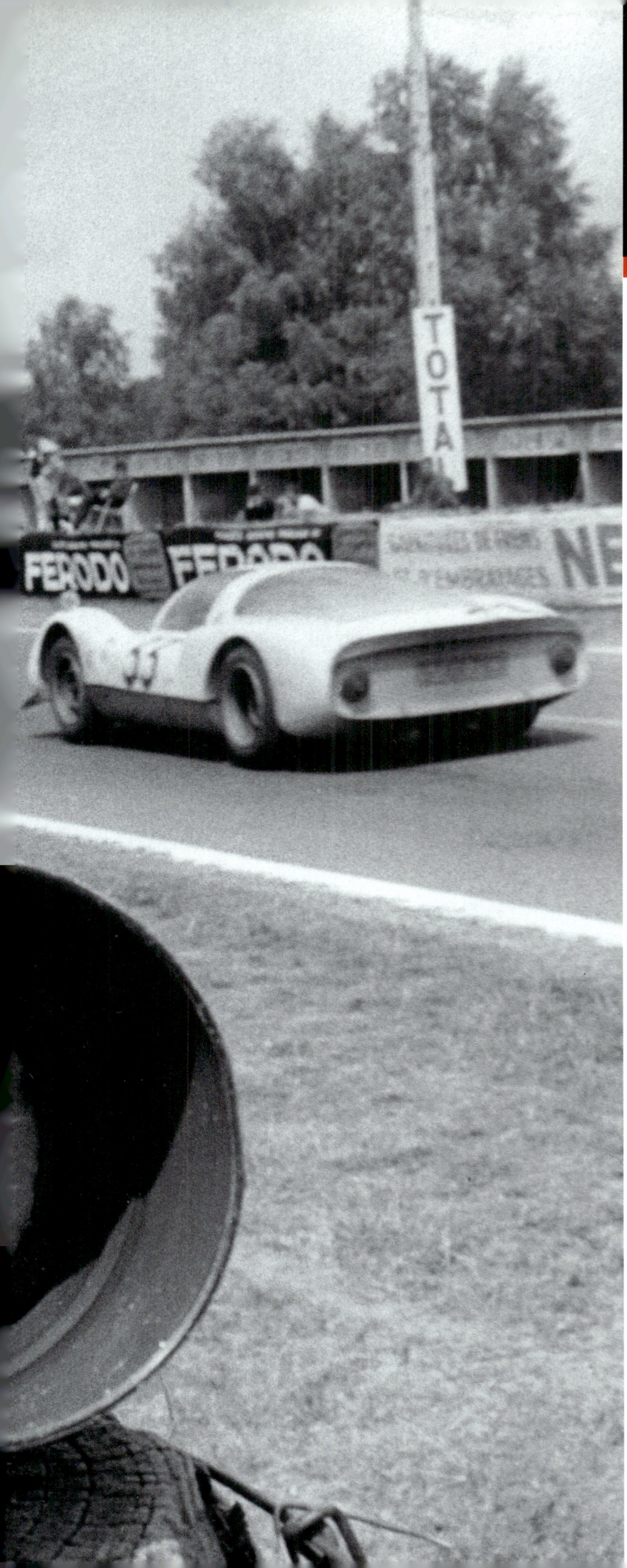

CONTENTS

INTRODUCTION 7
Liz Cooper 9

1956–1961 10
Michael Turner 53

1962–1964 54
Anthony Hussey 109

1965–1969 110
Dexter Brown 197

1970s 198

CINEMATIC OVERTURES 270
Jo Cooper 287

MORE TO CONSIDER 288
Ben Cooper 347

Final thoughts 348
Acknowledgements 349
Bibliography 349
Index 350

← A picture of Mike just past Mulsanne corner at Le Mans 1966, possibly taken by Geoff Goddard, as the Peter Gregg/Sten Axelsson Porsche 906 (112) that was eighth overall on distance but not running at the finish passes.

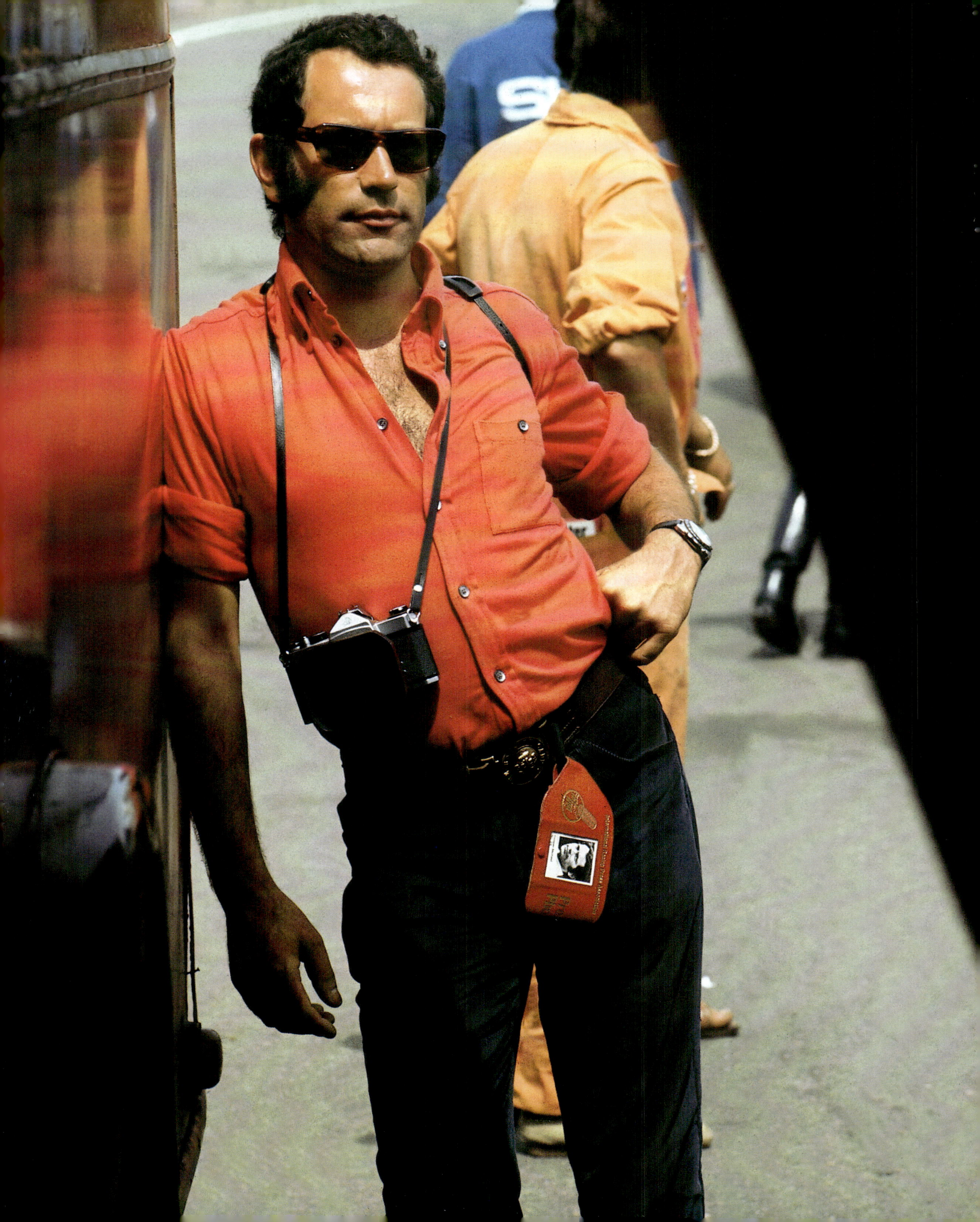

INTRODUCTION

Michael Cooper's career as a motorsport photographer was preceded by his work for ad agencies, record labels, and by general commercial work that in turn had been nurtured by National Service.

Years later, during the early 1970s, when he decided that F1 was becoming too commercialised and politicised, he returned to his roots, but continued covering the odd race or three. In latter times he was a regular at the Goodwood Festival of Speed and Revival meetings.

As a jobbing photographer for various magazines, including *Power Slide*, *Autovisie*, *Motor Racing*, and others, he covered most of the European GPs during 1962–70, plus assorted British national events and more. I collaborated with Michael on his first book *Sixties Motor Racing*, which was published in 2000, and this time I have used a selection from Michael's lesser-known work which is more varied than the usual action shots genre, hence the title *Races, Faces, Places*. Like all professional 'snappers' he took a whole series of shots at the same corner, some of which I have used for comparative purposes to illustrate the subtle differences 'twixt cars and drivers. When it came to actual 'people' shots there was often a touch of humour, unintended or otherwise, and you sometimes get the impression that Michael was encouraging them to play up. There was always a whiff of anarchy in the air.

These begin in the 1950s and end in the 1970s, and are not separated, bar the studies at the end of the book, as some fall into all three categories – so we leave you to simply enjoy the images. Many of them are in black and white, as was the custom at the time, but they are interspersed with some of his rarely, sometimes never seen, colour work. I have also included those that are not to a standard that Mike would have approved of, but these do illustrate an interesting story.

In a perfect world, this book would/could have featured 1,000 images and more, but practicality intrudes. So this is a selection of just some of Michael's oeuvre, and, as some wretched politician once said of taxpayers' money, 'There's plenty more where that came from.'

I beg your indulgence for the copious colour images of Monaco, but then this always has been the most picturesque of motor racing backdrops. Also, like many, he had his favourites, and NGH, always a splendid subject after all, is never far away.

Those of you who know my *In Camera* books will already be familiar with some of the caption details, and I hope you will bear with me as I also write for those coming to this genre for the first time. I have attempted to keep the contents in an approximate chronological order, but in some cases this proved diff cult. Alas, when Michael died in 2005 he had not yet started the huge task of setting the archive in order, and many images were not readily identifiable as to time and place, so I offer my apologies if some of the chronology is askew.

Unlike today's rigidly controlled accreditation, and access restrictions, Mike's busiest motor racing period coincided with the relatively easy working conditions and unfettered trackside access that so defines this era. He was also present during the making of *Grand Prix*, and became friends with John Frankenheimer. Four years later his attendance at Steve McQueen's *Le Mans* project provided further opportunity to capture celebrity with its guard down.

It has been my great good fortune to have known Michael and his wonderful family, and, although he has departed, h s work lives on in perpetuity, a record of a very different world and very different attitudes.

Paul Parker, Summer 2009

← Mike hamming it up – the very epitome of period style: shades, tight shirt, jeans, and an attitude.

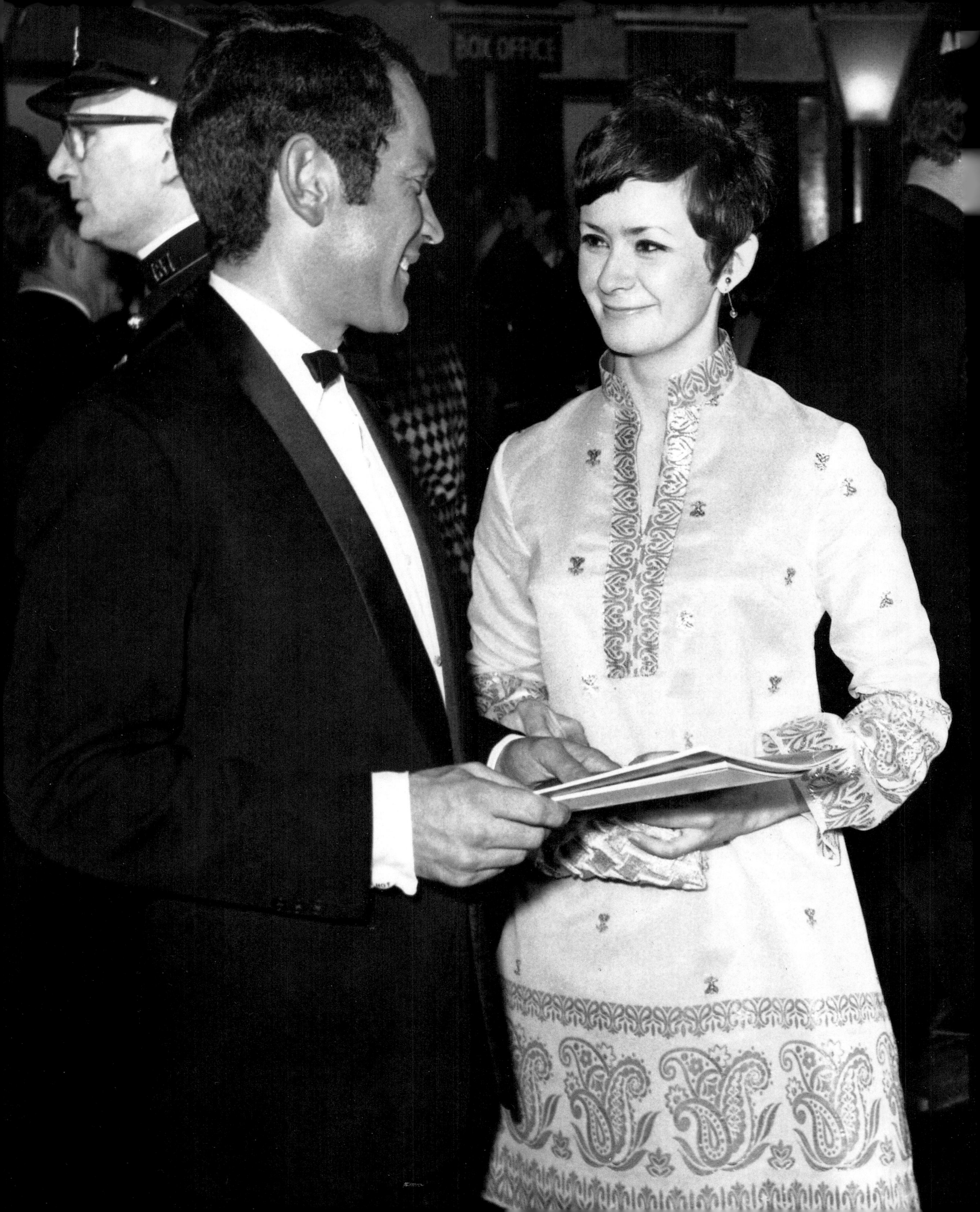
BOX OFFICE

Liz Cooper

My interest in motorsport had begun a few years before I met Mike, when my father, stationed with the army in Germany, took his family to watch Grand Prix racing at European circuits in the early sixties.

In 1965 I was working as a receptionist in an art gallery just off Carnaby Street, in London, and my boss introduced me to the new tenant of the top floor artist's studio. It was not long before I discovered that motorsport was one aspect of Mike's photographic business. Our first 'dates' soon followed – dinner at the Steering Wheel Club, a Bonfire Night party in the rain at Brands Hatch with a few beers in the Kentagon, and a Press 'function' at a motor show – he knew how to impress a girl!

London was already 'swinging', and Mike's photographic business was taking off in a similar style. Not only was he covering European Grands Prix at weekends, regularly contributing to various motor-racing publications on a freelance basis, but also other (paid) photographic commissions had to be fitted in during the week. He would return home immediately after races to process and print films, and (with my help glazing and captioning) post the prints off that night. If a dramatic incident had been captured on film, this usually meant delivering by hand for the next morning's newspapers.

Many a Vesta curry was 'created' in the darkroom on a Sunday night, and washed down with sweet sherry. Then, preparations for the following week's assignments had to be made, involving several trips up and down five flights of stairs with equipment, cameras, and plenty of film. These assignments could have been on location, such as on board an oil tanker in the North Sea or aerial photography of rice fields over Texas, or studio photography on a diverse range of subjects from antique furniture, works of art, and priceless jewellery at the V&A, to portraits of pop groups for LP record covers, car accessories, and standard 'product' shots for advertising agencies.

Every assignment was undertaken with enthusiasm and creativity, and in spite of such a hectic lifestyle he always found the time to 'surprise' – a New Year's Eve in Paris flying first class (my first ever flight); a room at the Hotel Metropole for the Monaco Grand Prix; arriving to pick me up in his newly-purchased Sunbeam Tiger. Nothing was ever planned; I never knew exactly where or when I would see him, but this was just the start of 40 years of humour, laughter, and being prepared for the unexpected. 'Free' weekends were spent at home with his parents in the country, where his other passion – gardening – had developed from an early age, along with music, and playing the piano. He was never without a camera, and so often captured the unusual and bizarre; every family event and occasion was recorded on film with two major exceptions – the births of our children – he fell fast asleep whilst waiting for a call from the hospital. In hindsight, maybe this was a good thing – he was never very good in 'medical' situations.

After the hustle of the sixties, the seventies saw us married (I eventually had to propose) and moving into our cottage in Surrey during its restoration, with every detail recorded for posterity. We survived with the minimum of home comforts, but with the maximum of garden produce – enough to feed an army. Initially, we both commuted daily to London, leaving before 6am to beat the rush hour, but in busy times camping out overnight on the studio floor. Facilities were basic, but there was always tea and a tin of baked beans for emergency sustenance. After Ben and Jo were born, Mike was always anxious to get home early at the end of a busy week, and any discipline I might have instilled in the children went completely out of the window when their Daddy arrived. It was always a riotous occasion, with silly presents, mad games, and much larking around, and of course the camera never far from reach.

The pressure of work over the next 30 years gradually eased. With interest in photographing 'modern' Grands Prix waning, and being more selective in the commissions undertaken, Mike was able to spend more time with us and enjoy country living. As a family we treasure our memories of our years with Mike – he was a very special, unique person.

In preparing the material for this book with Paul, it has been a revelation searching through the hundreds of rolls of film containing unseen historical and evocative images – the races, the faces, and the places. It has been fun, with help from friends, piecing together the stories behind some of the images, although too often we could only guess, and will never know the true story of why a particular photograph was taken. Of course, none of this would have been possible without Paul's prodigious enthusiasm for archival photographs, and his keen and knowledgeable eye for detail in those captured moments. I think Mike would have approved wholeheartedly.

← Michael and Liz at the premiere of John Frankenheimer's *Grand Prix* at Leicester Square on 10 March 1967.

1956–1961

The decade was over before Michael Cooper developed a serious involvement in motor racing photography and it was about to change irrevocably.

Meanwhile the hegemony of traditional GP cars was rapidly overtaken by the rear-engined Coventry Climax powered Coopers that, having finally acquired a full size 2.5-litre engine in 1959, were now in the ascendant. Within the space of just under three seasons Maserati disappeared, Vanwall went from being race winners and 1958 Constructors' Champion to obscurity and obsolescence whilst BRM and Ferrari had to join the new orthodoxy, the latter most reluctantly. Colin Chapman's featherweight but underdeveloped and fragile Lotus 12s and later 16 gave little indication of the innovative genius that was to follow, even if the fragility did linger on in the succeeding years.

Notwithstanding this necessary evolution most larger capacity sports racing cars were still stubbornly front-engined and more robustly constructed to cope with the long distances of championship endurance racing but this too would ultimately change. The last vestiges of this DNA survived into the mid-1960s amongst the big-engined GT racers, some derivatives of road cars, others true competition machines.

As Mike's wanderings took him from Goodwood to a bigger world, his interest and attitude hardened into a combination of personal enthusiasm combined with a determination to make it pay. These opening images travel from the streets of London to Goodwood, Silverstone, Snetterton, Oulton Park, Aintree, Zandvoort and beyond.

During this period he came to know the already established stars of his profession including Geoffrey Goddard, Maurice Rowe and Bernard Cahier. He frequently travelled to the continental races with Geoff by car whilst the renowned Bernard was the founder of the International Racing Press Association (IRPA) in 1968, the first organised media representation in F1. Other regular companions were Anthony Hussey of Connolly Leather and famed automotive artist Michael Turner who shared some of Mike's European-wide wanderings in a variety of often-unsuitable motor cars and light aircraft.

In the past I have noted that this era coincided with an almost complete dominance of Grand Prix racing by English speaking drivers and indeed from 1959 to 1969 inclusive every World Champion was thus. It was almost matched by the cars (with the notable exception of the 1961 season and the introduction of the much derided 1.5-litre F1 formula) and Mike was certainly very patriotic as his pictures perhaps reflect.

Latter day perceptions of 'F1' cars are inevitably coloured by the wide-wheeled be-spoilered and occasionally grotesque creations of the previous decade or two, so the toy-like dimensions of post-1959 single seaters must seem strange to those born after 1980. Ditto their all too obvious lack of protection, no belts and still in most cases tubular construction. But all this was normal for period racers and anybody who took their chances regardless of the consequences, the very antithesis of modern attitudes.

Looking at these images it is manifest that many have been shot with a short focal length lens (up to 125mm) due to the unrestricted access. This in turn shows the cars as they really were with all the body roll, wheel bending and suspension movement clearly perceptible. None of the telescoped, two dimensional, sterile, depth-of-field-compromised pictures taken with 300mm and longer pieces obligatory due to the ever more limited access at most modern circuits.

So we begin at the beginning, a very proper place to do so.

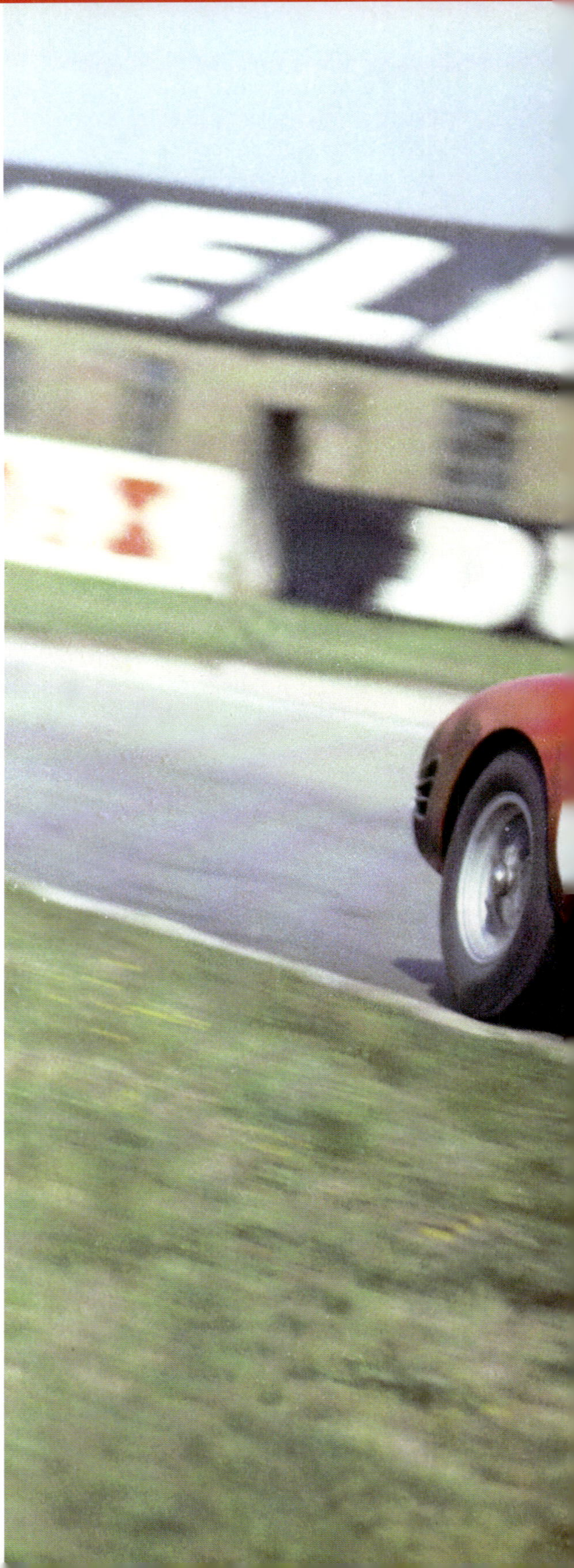

Phil Hill clips the first apex at Woodcote in the Fantuzzi-bodied Ferrari Testa Rossa (0776R) that he took over after his own car retired. This Ferrari was also driven by Olivier Gendebien, Tony Brooks (who drove the third team car to fifth with Dan Gurney despite a rear suspension failure late in the race) and Cliff Allison, and ultimately finished third just two seconds behind the von Trips/Bonnier Porsche RSK. Note the unprotected persons sitting on the earth bank in the background close to where Gregory will crash the Tojeiro.

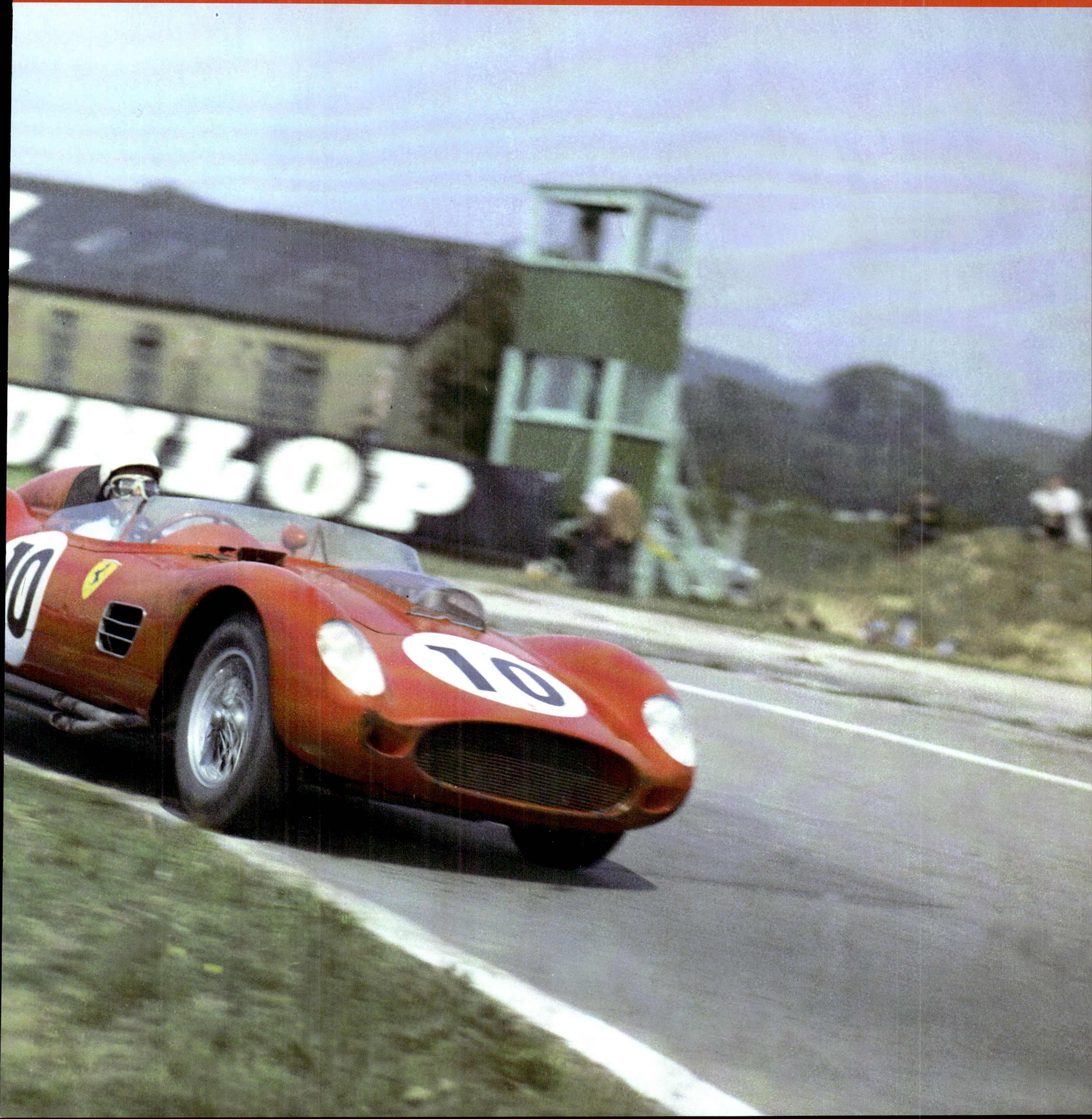

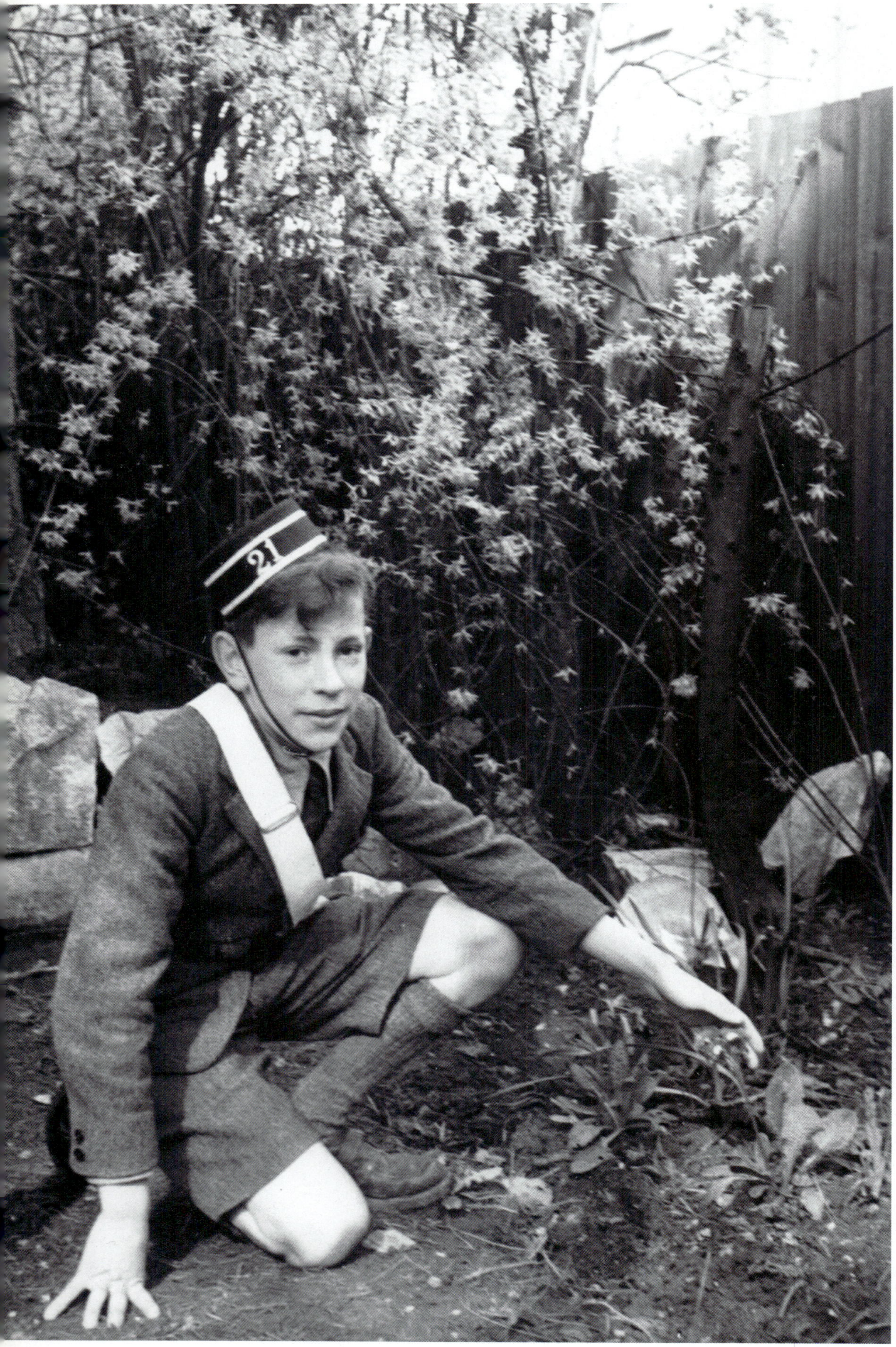

← Like so many of his generation, Mike was a member of the Boy's Brigade, hence the rather novel headwear. One cannot imagine any latter-day adolescent wearing such a thing now. Having had close contact with rural Surrey it was perhaps no surprise that, despite his later interest and involvement in things noisy, fast, and furious, he was more than anything a 'son of the soil'.

→ Having left school at 15, our future intrepid adventurer found himself working for Coltman Displays who provided the front of house film stills for cinemas. Never knowingly without a camera, Mike took this picture of a young Diana Dors receiving some ad hoc attention to her hair in a London street *circa* 1956. The onlookers, especially the woman nearest the camera, seem mesmerised by this close brush with 'movie' fame.

→ Also present was Michael Craig (real name Michael Gregson), a regular British movie star of the era, and they are together here promoting their film *Yield to the Night* that was made in 1956. Of Scots heritage but born in India (27 January 1928), Craig was a prolific stage, television, and screen actor who has long resided in Australia.

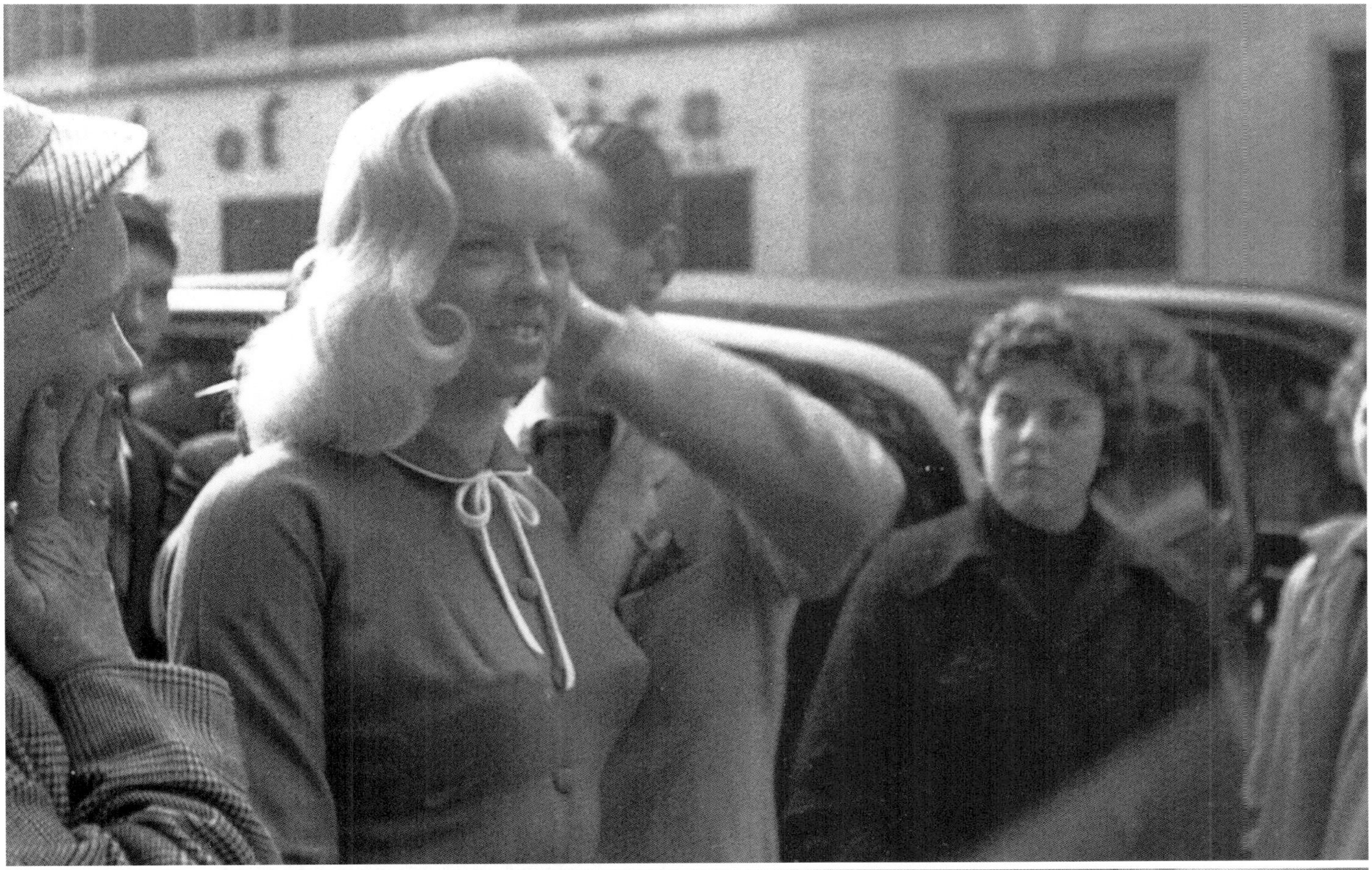

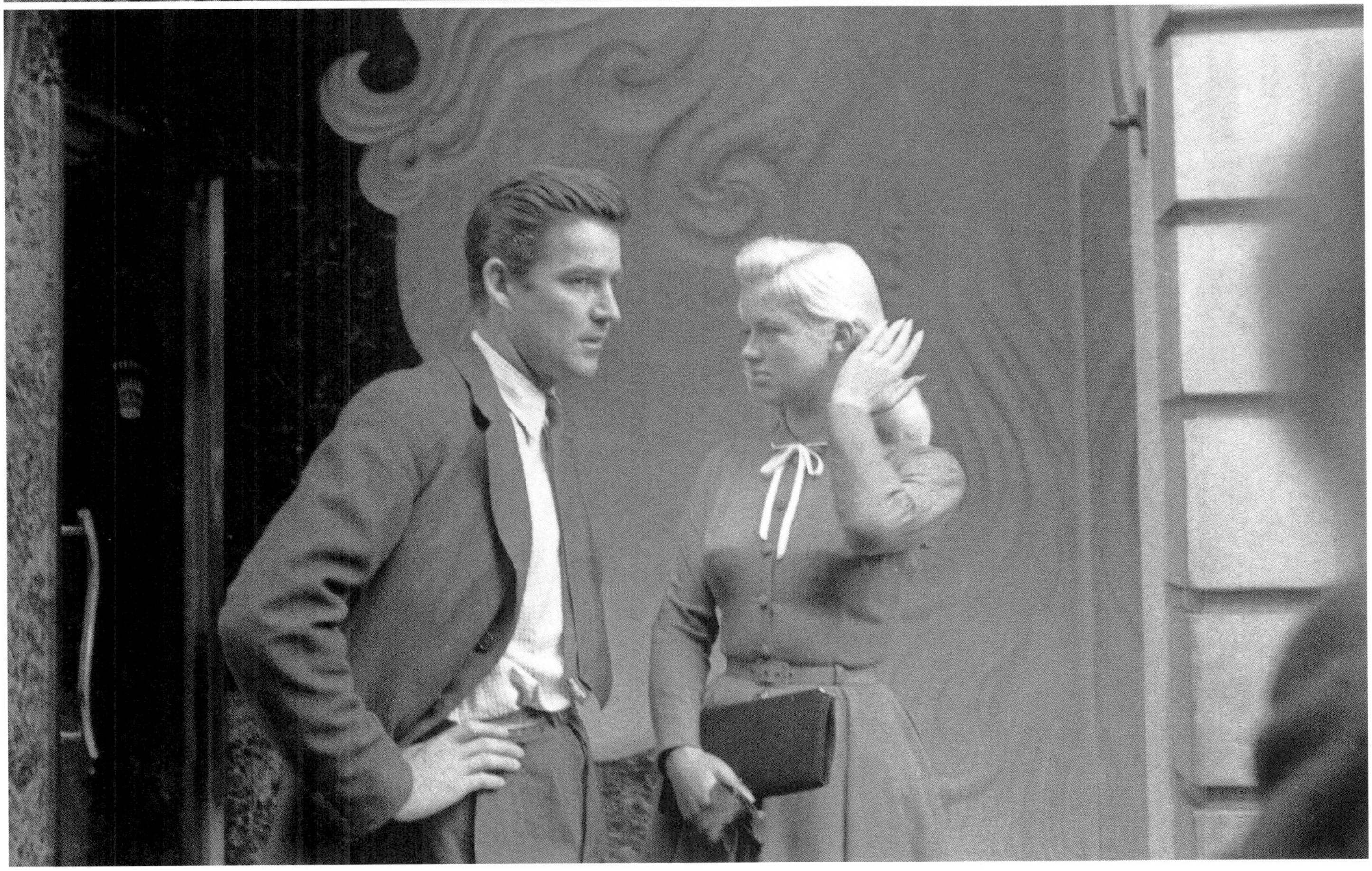

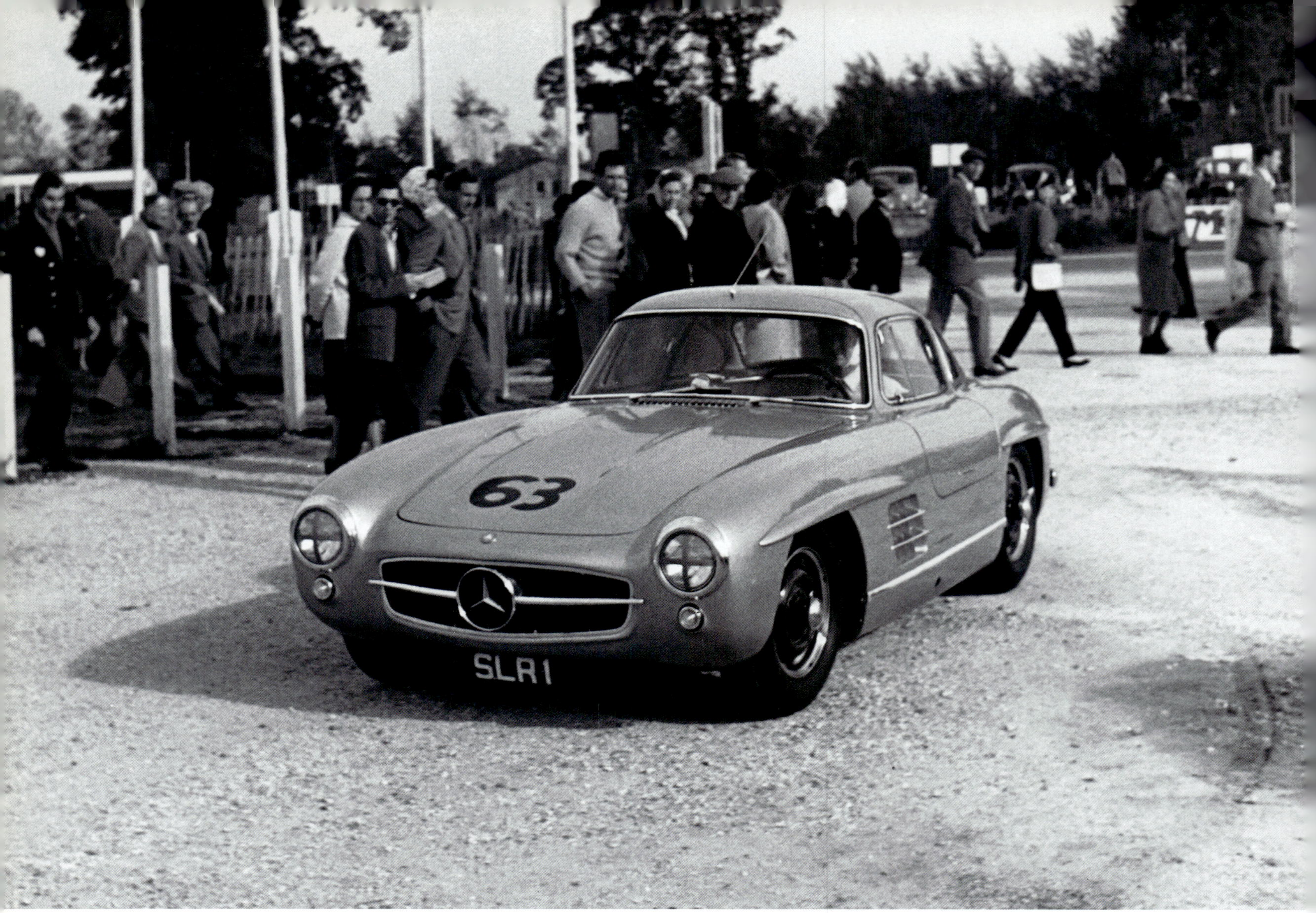

↑ Dennis Barthel's Mercedes Benz 300SL 'gullwing' lightweight sports an almost appropriate number plate after winning the Closed Cars Handicap race over five laps at Goodwood on 27 September 1958. This is the paddock entrance between the chicane exit and the pits that was then a dirt surface. Unlike the latter-day Revival evocation, there are no uniforms anywhere to be seen. Barthel bought the ex-works Aston Martin DB3S/5 (one of the 1953 cars that had been used originally on the road by David Brown) in late 1957. He had it prepared at Rob Walker's Pippbrook Garage by Alan Overton, and allowed Overton to drive it at the Gosport Speed Trials, Easter 1958. Allegedly, Barthel was having an affair with Overton's fiancée, and after crossing the finish line Overton never lifted off and drove straight into the sea with fatal results. The car was rebuilt and re-registered PAP 625, and it appeared in the film *School for Scoundrels* as a 'Bellini' driven by the film's lecherous cad Terry-Thomas. Today it resides in Switzerland with its 9046 H registration mark reinstated.

↗ Mike's early motor racing photography centred on Goodwood because his father was a member of the British Automobile Racing Club, and here is a shot of Dick Milne's HWM 1 after losing a wheel during practice for the 33rd BARC Members Meeting on 14 March 1959. Note the archetypal coach transporters, Austin A90 tow car, and the MG TF being attended to. I wonder what became of Peter Gordon & Co., Vauxhall dealers in Edinburgh. The casual setting reminds us of how relaxed and au naturel such things were in post-war England.

→ A sunnier day at Goodwood, and the car park includes Mike's father's Jensen 541 YBH 505. This is a typical mix of period transport, the already quite old XK120 (LXO 127), a split screen Morris Minor, Riley 1.5, AC Ace, the drophead SS Jaguar, a more modern Morris Minor, MGA coupé, convertible Hillman Minx, Sunbeam Rapier, an immaculate Aston Martin DB2 (chassis LML-50-99 that now lives in Canada) and another Minor, the ever-popular estate version. In the background can be discerned an Austin Healey, an XK140 dhc, an Austin A35, a Jowett Jupiter, et al, and hardly a foreign car in obvious sight.

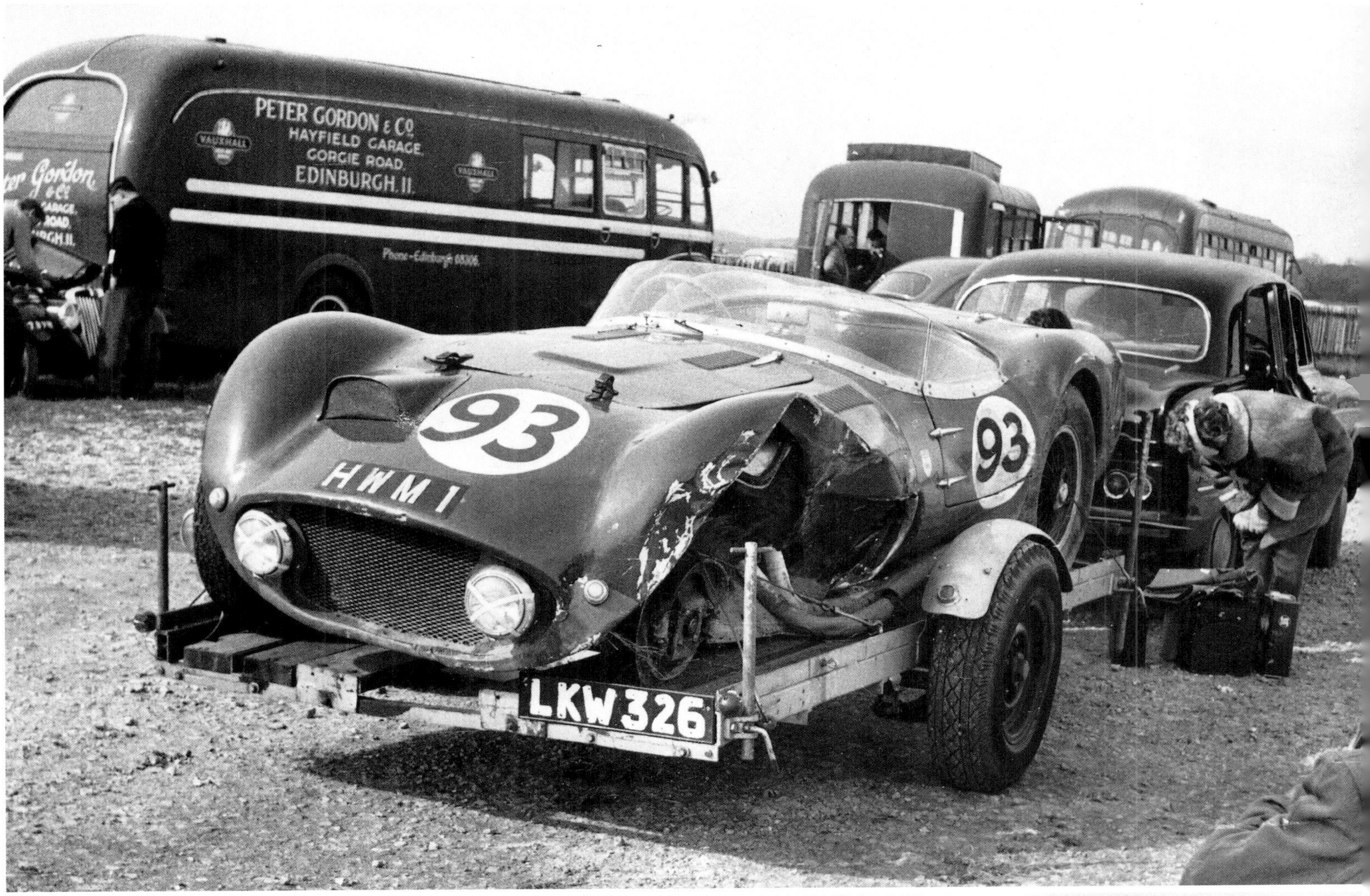
PETER GORDON & Co.
HAYFIELD GARAGE.
GORGIE ROAD.
EDINBURGH. 11.
93
HWM 1
LKW 326

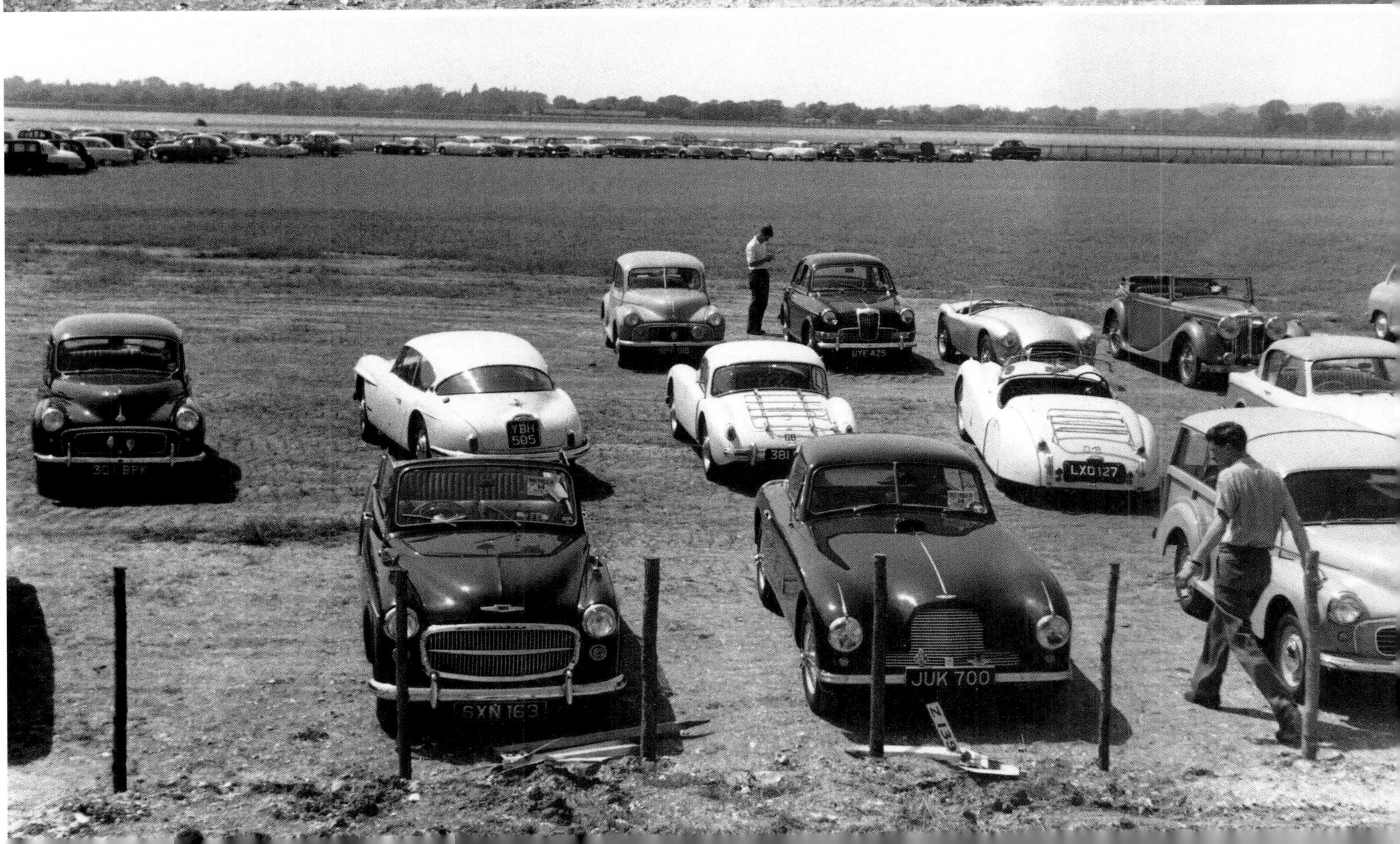
301 BPK
YBH 505
UYF 425
LXO 127
JUK 700
SXN 163

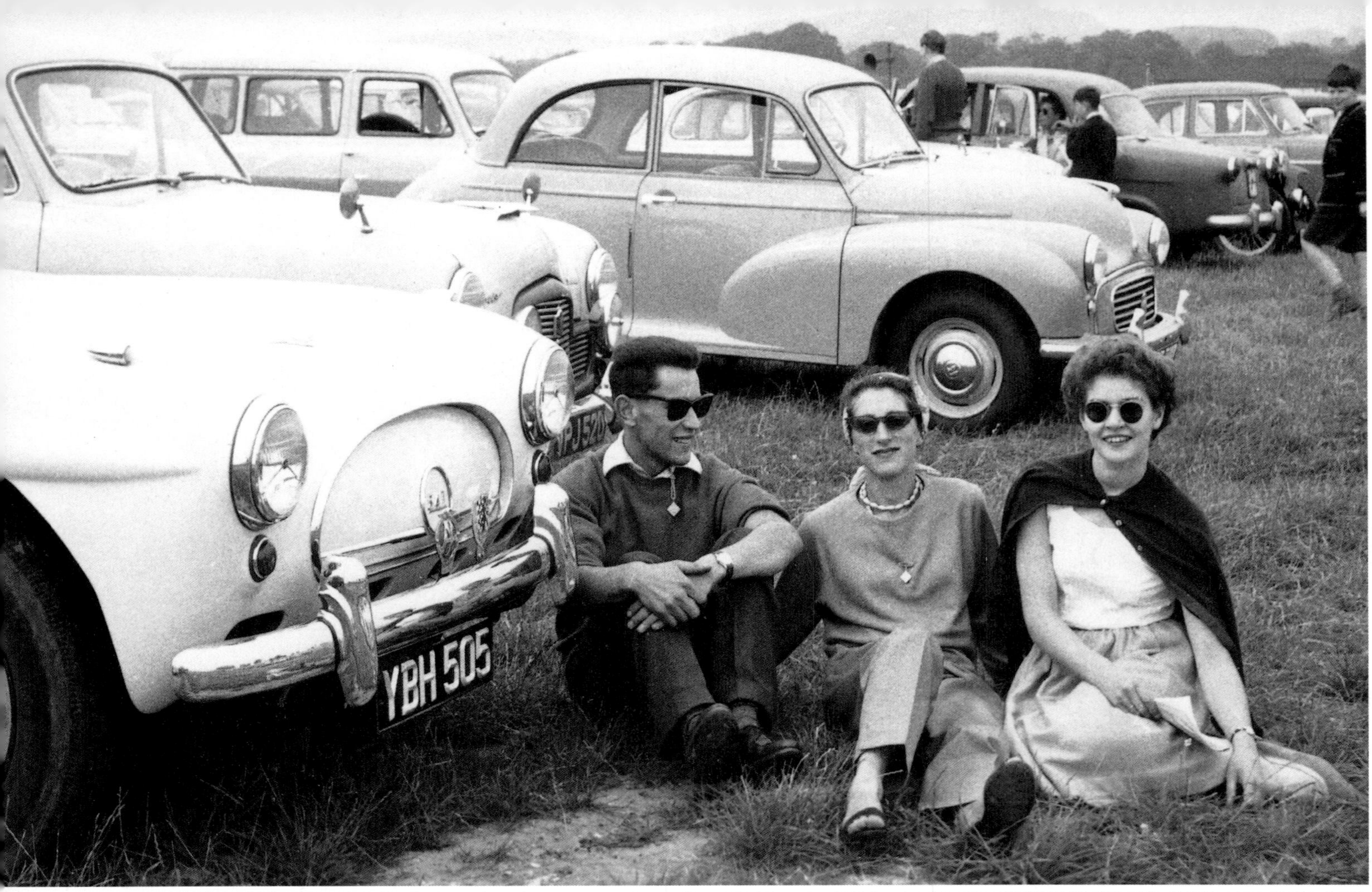
YBH 505

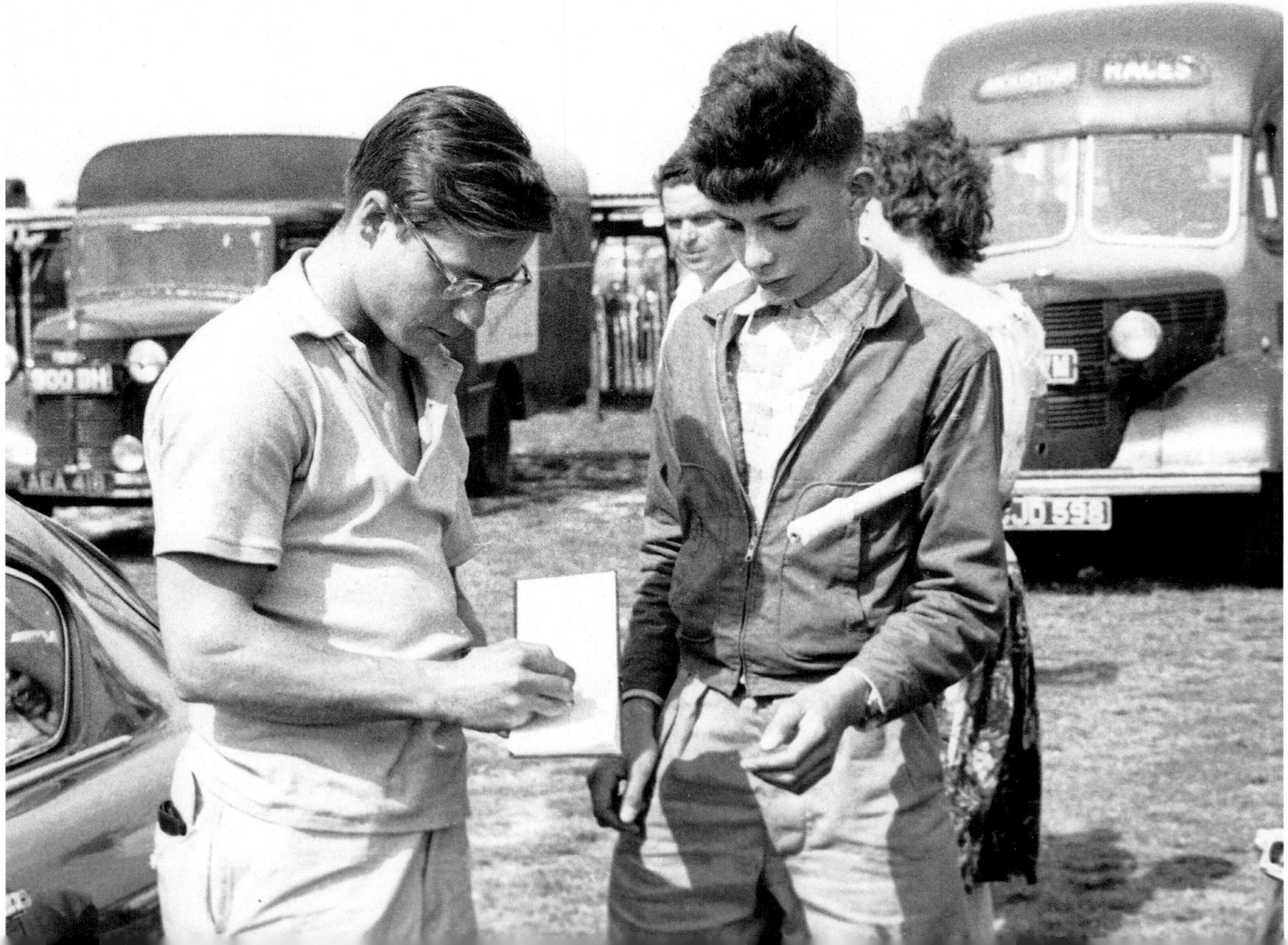
HALLS
JD 598

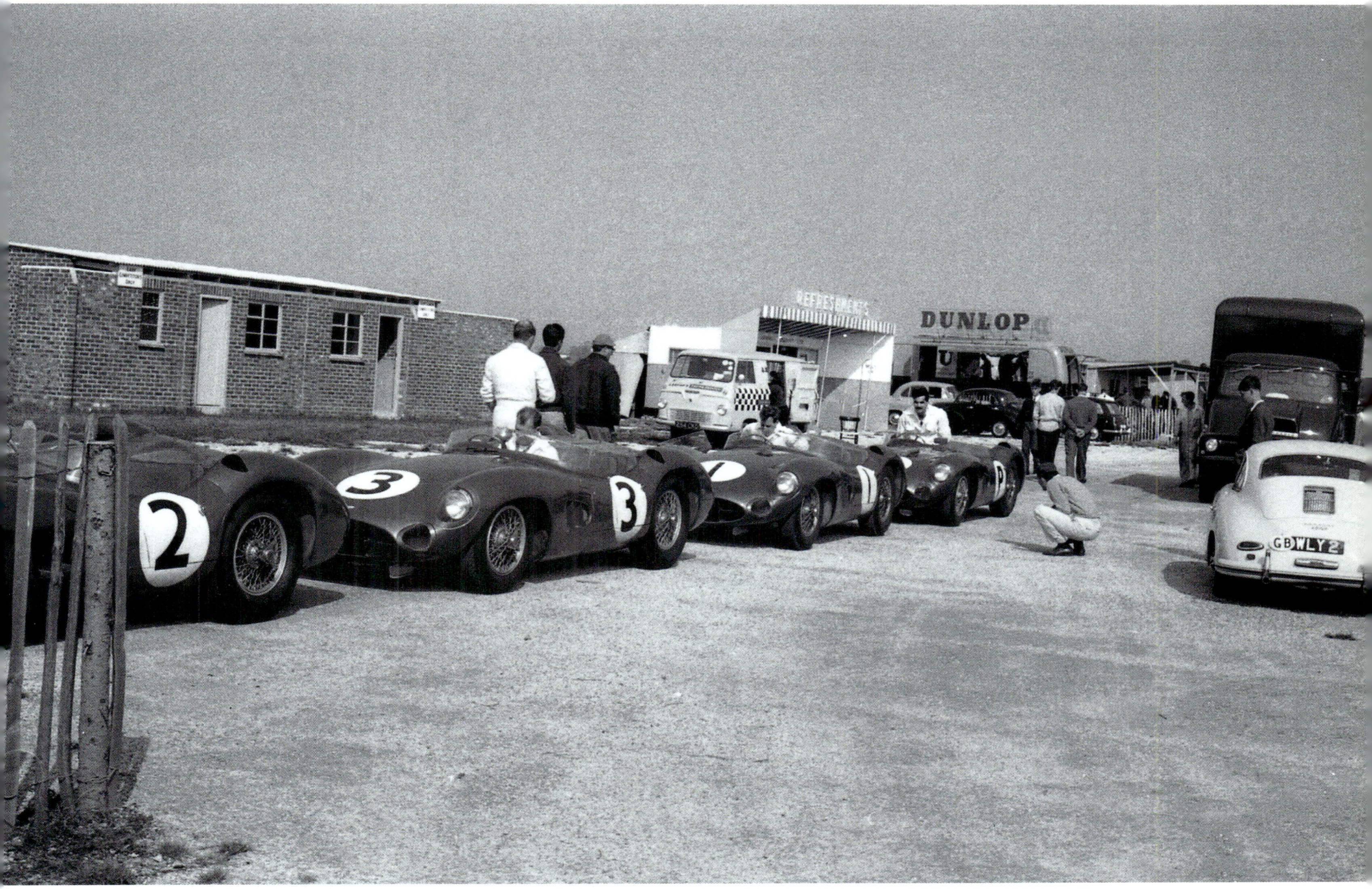

↑The Aston Martin DBR1/300s are still immaculate pre-race at the 1959 Tourist Trophy. No. 2 (DBR1/2) is the winning car that started with Carroll Shelby/Jack Fairman and was then taken over by Stirling Moss, No. 3 (DBR1/4) is the Paul Frère/Maurice Trintignant car, and No. 1 (DBR1/3) is the car for Stirling Moss/Roy Salvadori that was retired after the now notorious pit stop fire, and the spare car (DBR1/1) is bringing up the rear.

↖ Mike, with his sister Margaret and friend, in front of the Jensen with its AA and BARC membership badges. George Cooper had learnt to drive rather late in life, apparently at Mike's suggestion, being content thereafter with a Hillman Minx. Having joined the BARC (British Automobile Racing Club) he had taken to attending Goodwood meetings with his son, who became enthused about Jensens. One day, to Mike's delight, he turned up with this brand new white 541.

← Perhaps inevitably, Cooper junior crashed the beloved Jensen during some high speed motoring with his sister and father on board, in 1959. If you are going to do it, then do it properly! The car was towed to John Coombs of Guildford, where Mike espied an Ecurie Ecosse D-type Jaguar being prepared for the forthcoming Tourist Trophy at Goodwood. He met John Coombs, who promised to provide a pass for the event, but this did not materialise. Undismayed, Mike turned up at the TT, and Mr Coombs gave him a track pass that enabled Mike to take this and many other images. Here we see American sports car ace and Cooper works driver Masten Gregory standing by his lhd Aston Martin DB2/4 MkIII, providing an autograph for a young admirer (with bicycle pump tucked under his left arm) who is apparently taller than Masten! Some 10 years ago Mike recalled to the author that when he went to Masten's London Marble Arch apartment during the 1960s he had occasion to visit the bathroom. As he took a pee something landed on his left shoulder with a soft thud causing Mike's aim to veer wildly off course. Instantaneous panic quickly dissolved into amazement when he found himself staring into the large limpid eyes of a bush baby that Masten kept as a pet!

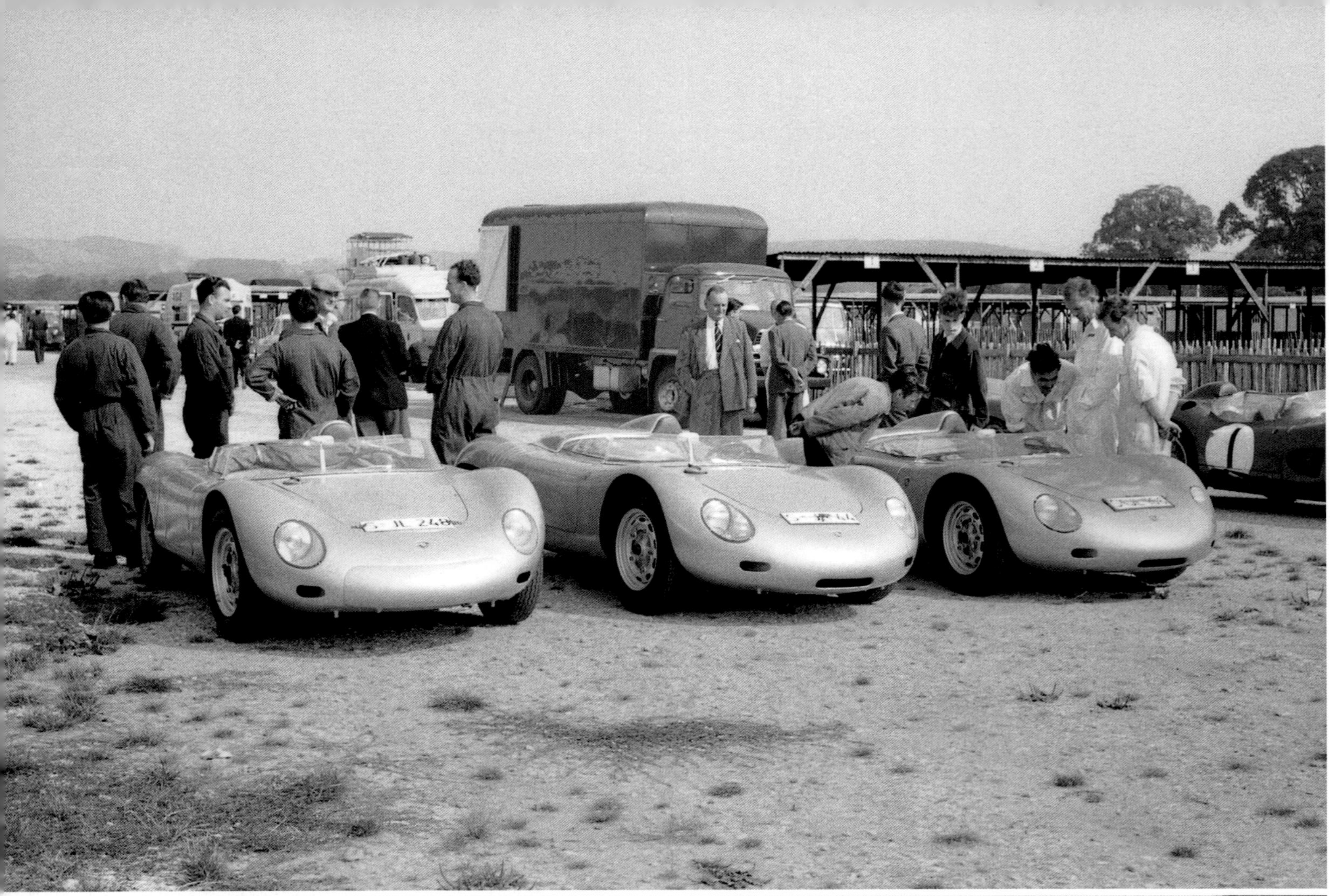

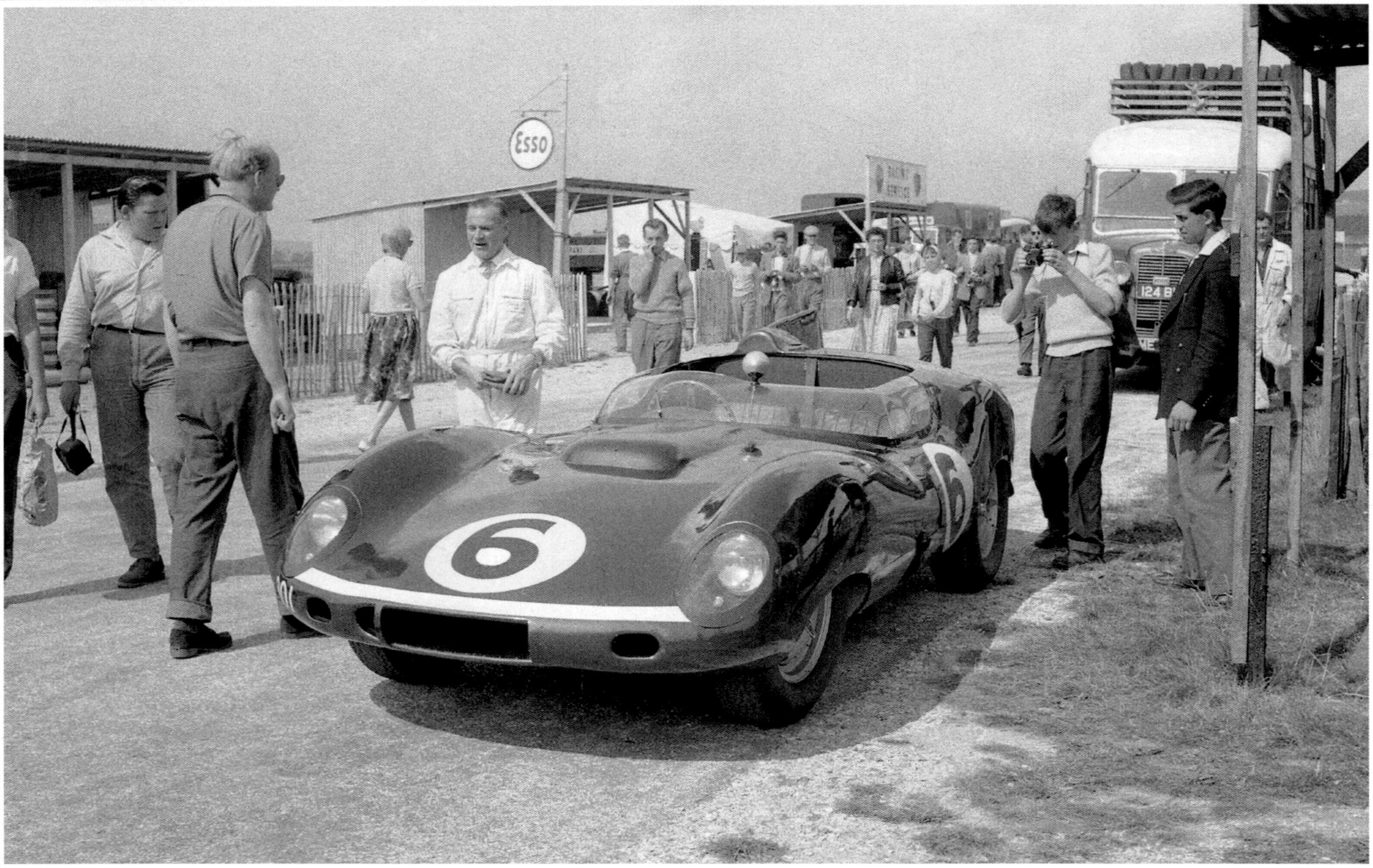
Esso

← Nearby are the works Porsche 718RSKs, as yet unnumbered and along with Ferrari and Aston Martin still in contention for the sports car championship. With its stalls, wooden picket fencing, and the Downs visible in the background, this could only be Goodwood, on 3 September 1959.

→ Refuelling the works Porsche 718 RSK that was driven to second place at the Tourist Trophy by German aristocrat Count Wolfgang von Trips and Swede Jo Bonnier.

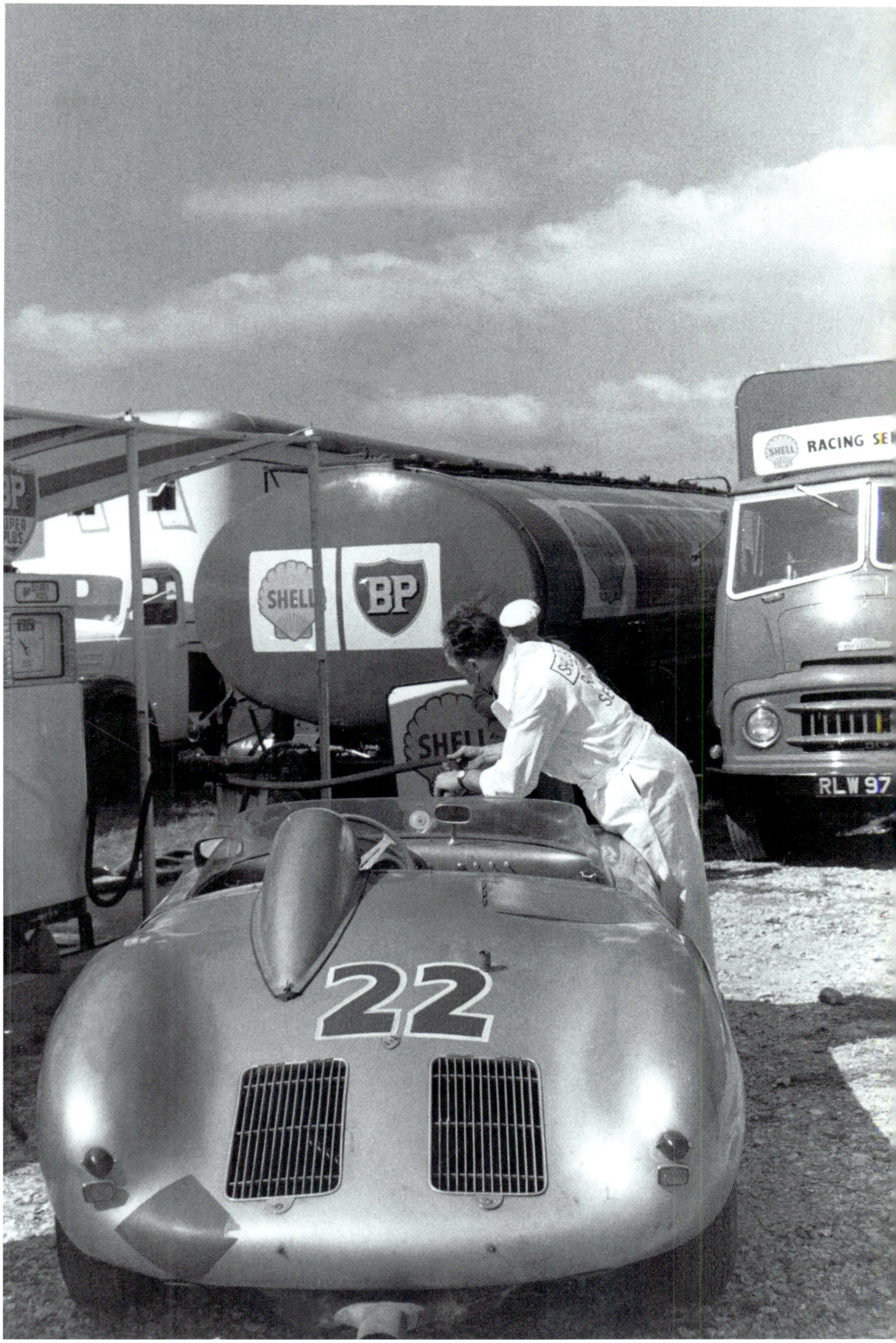

← Ecurie Ecosse's ill-fated 1959 Tojeiro Jaguar that Masten Gregory will hit the Woodcote bank with during the TT after a possible steering failure. Gregory's co-driver was Jim Clark, and the Tojeiro was the fastest Jaguar-powered entry but was only 14th quickest in practice. Ecosse's legendary 'Wilkie' Wilkinson stands by the driver's door as Mike Salmon strides towards him, whilst the inevitable teenager grabs a shot. Behind, a lorry sports trade plates, a trick at the time for avoiding paying the licence disc fee. How simple life was then (and a lot cheaper too).

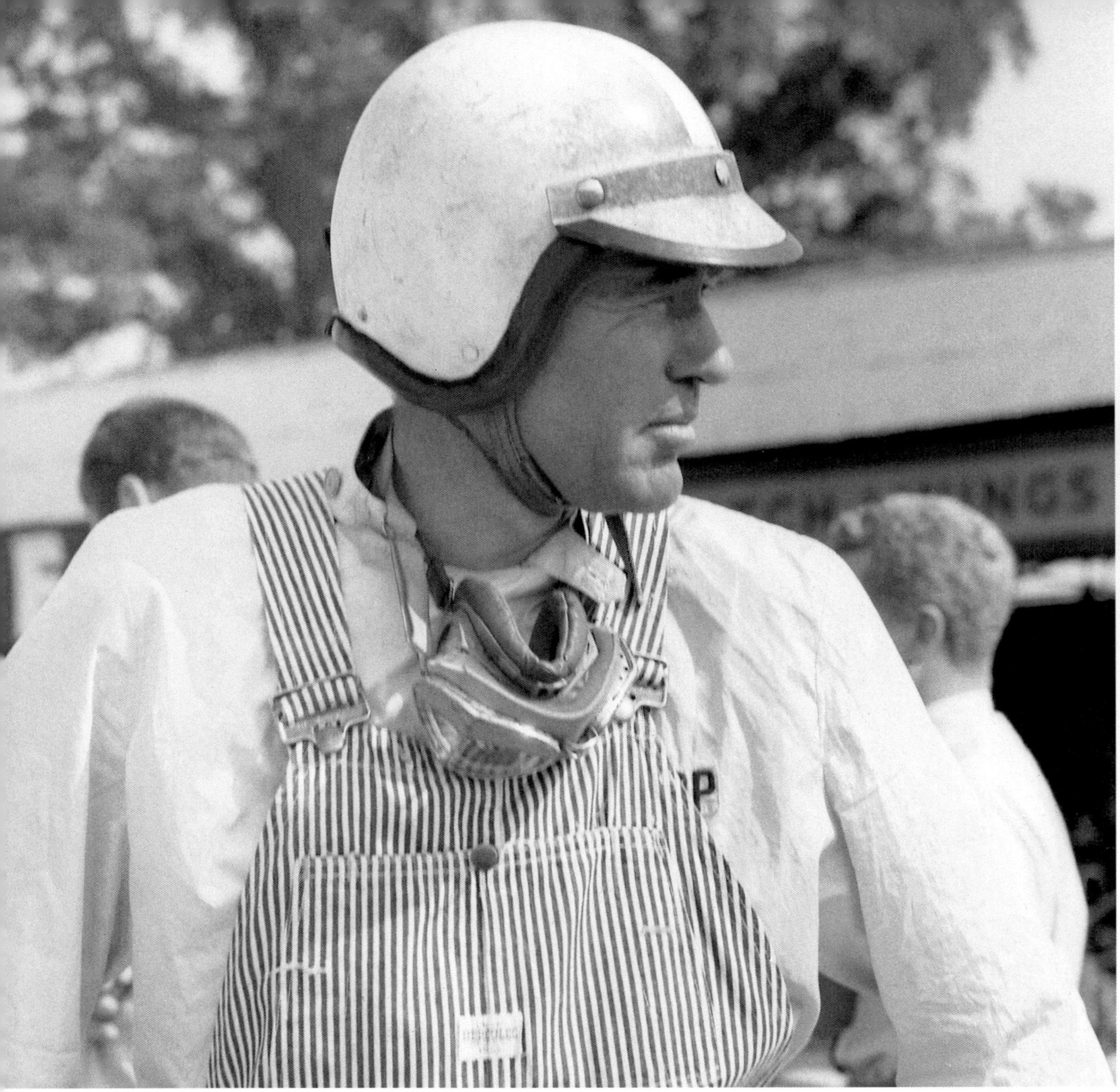

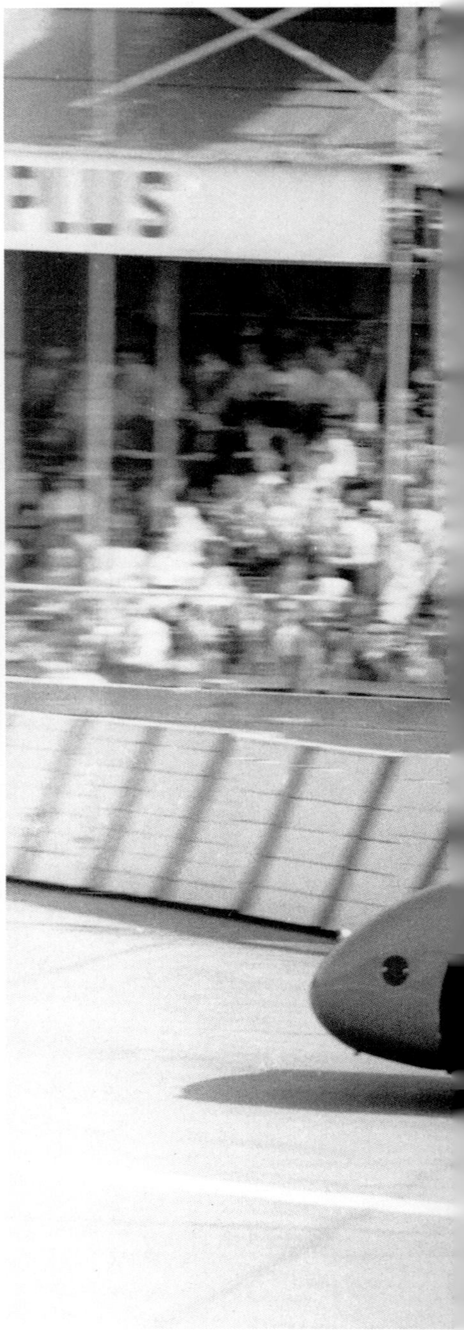

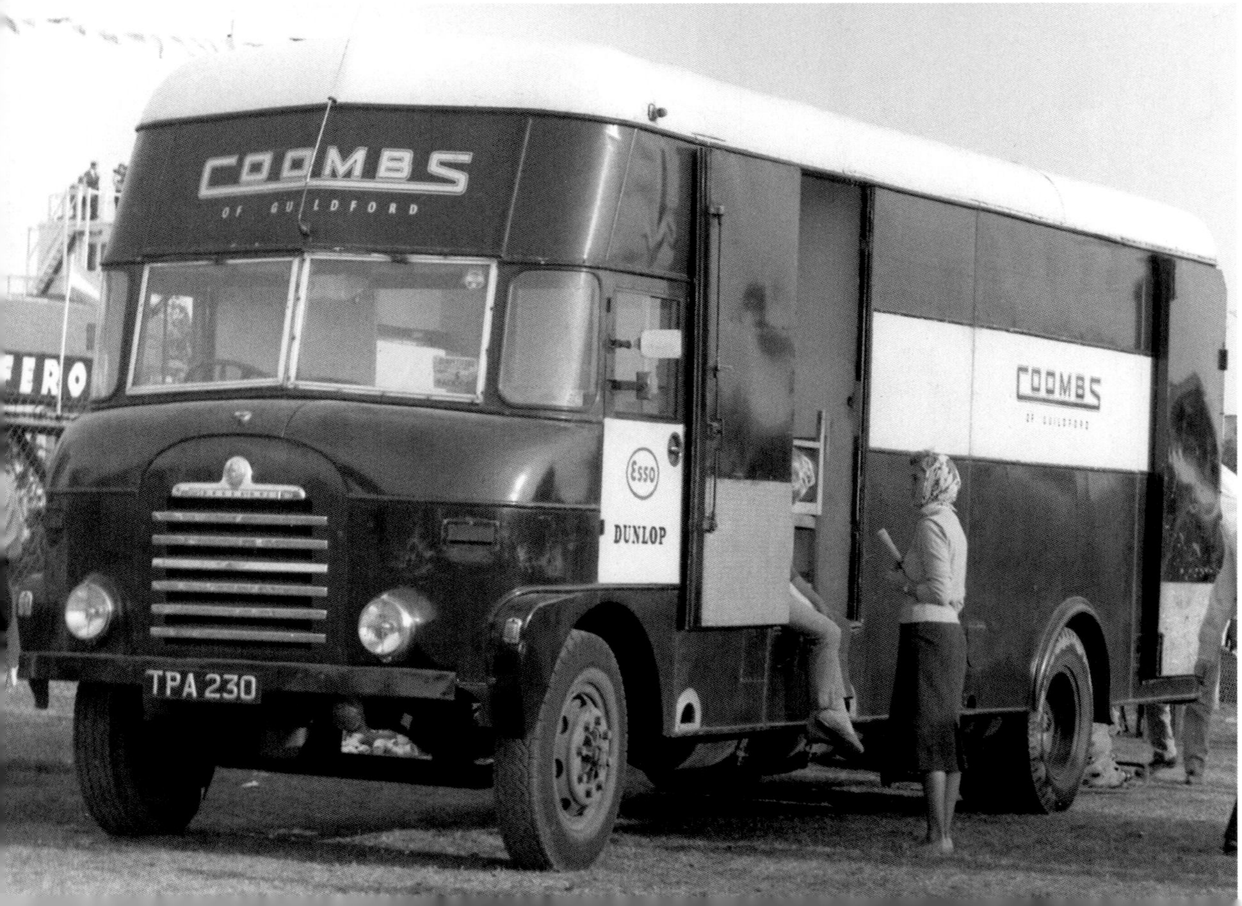

COOMBS
OF GUILDFORD
ESSO
DUNLOP
TPA 230
COOMBS
OF GUILDFORD

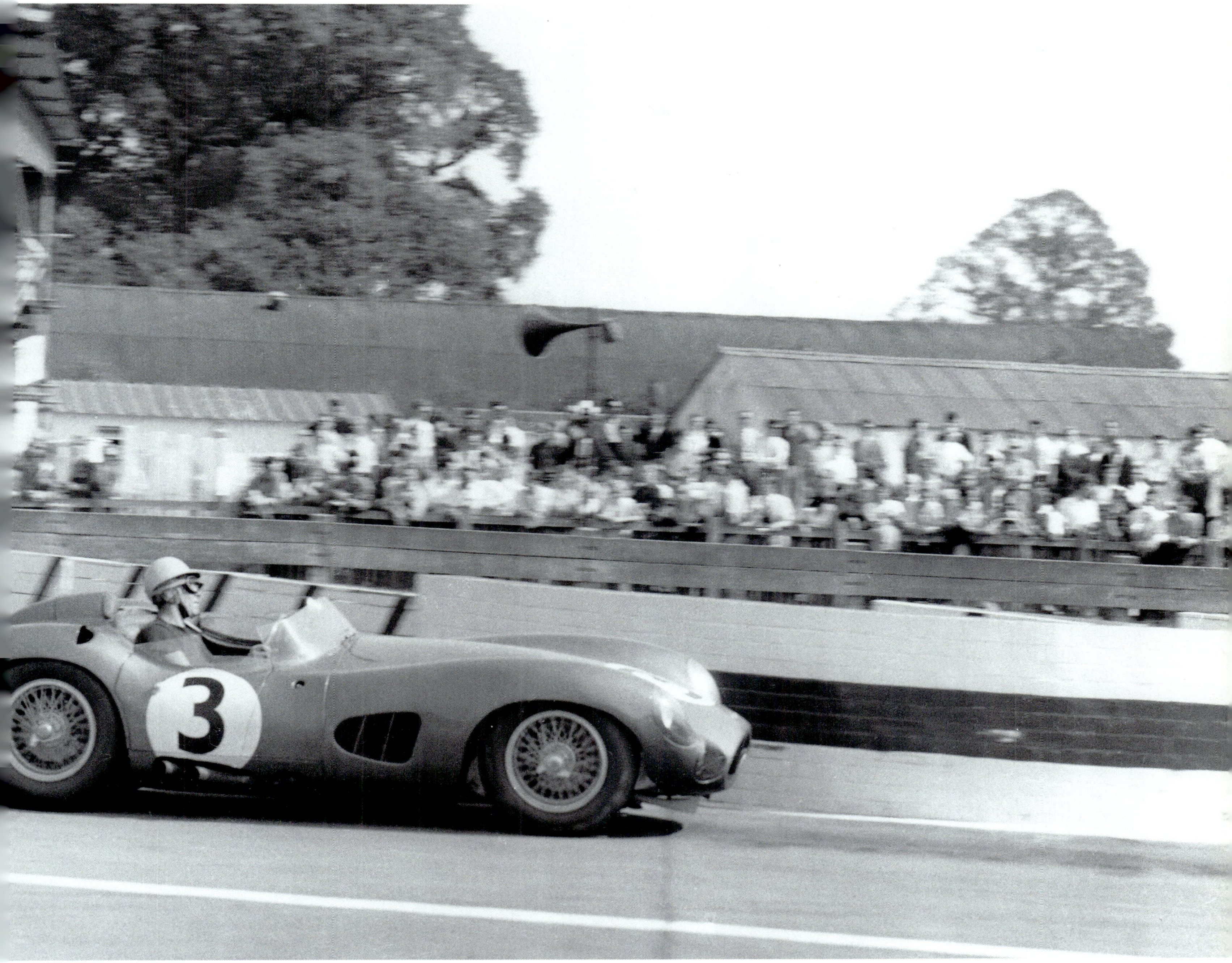

↑ Paul Frère threads through the chicane in the Aston Martin DBR1/300 (DBR1/4) he shared with Maurice Trintignant en route to fourth place in the 1959 TT. Writing in his book *Starting Grid to Chequered Flag*, the famous auto journalist, author, and 1960 Le Mans winner, who died aged 91 in 2008, gave an insight into just how fast Stirling Moss was when he lapped Frère during the race: 'Stirling lapped me and, despite all my efforts in trying not to drop back too quickly, I saw the gap between my car and his increase after every corner. In two laps he had gone out of sight. It was absolutely fantastic.'

↖ Carroll Shelby enjoyed a successful 1959 season with Aston Martin, winning Le Mans with Roy Salvadori, and the TT with Jack Fairman after Moss took over their car following a pit stop fire. The striped bib overalls were a Shelby trademark, and note the early pattern one-piece Bell helmet at a time when most Europeans were typically wearing the Herbert Johnson or Les Leston shellac lids with leather ear flaps.

← The John Coombs transporter; a pretty impressive vehicle by the standards of the day. Converted ancient coaches and assorted obsolete panel vans or trailers were the more usual offering outside of the factory teams.

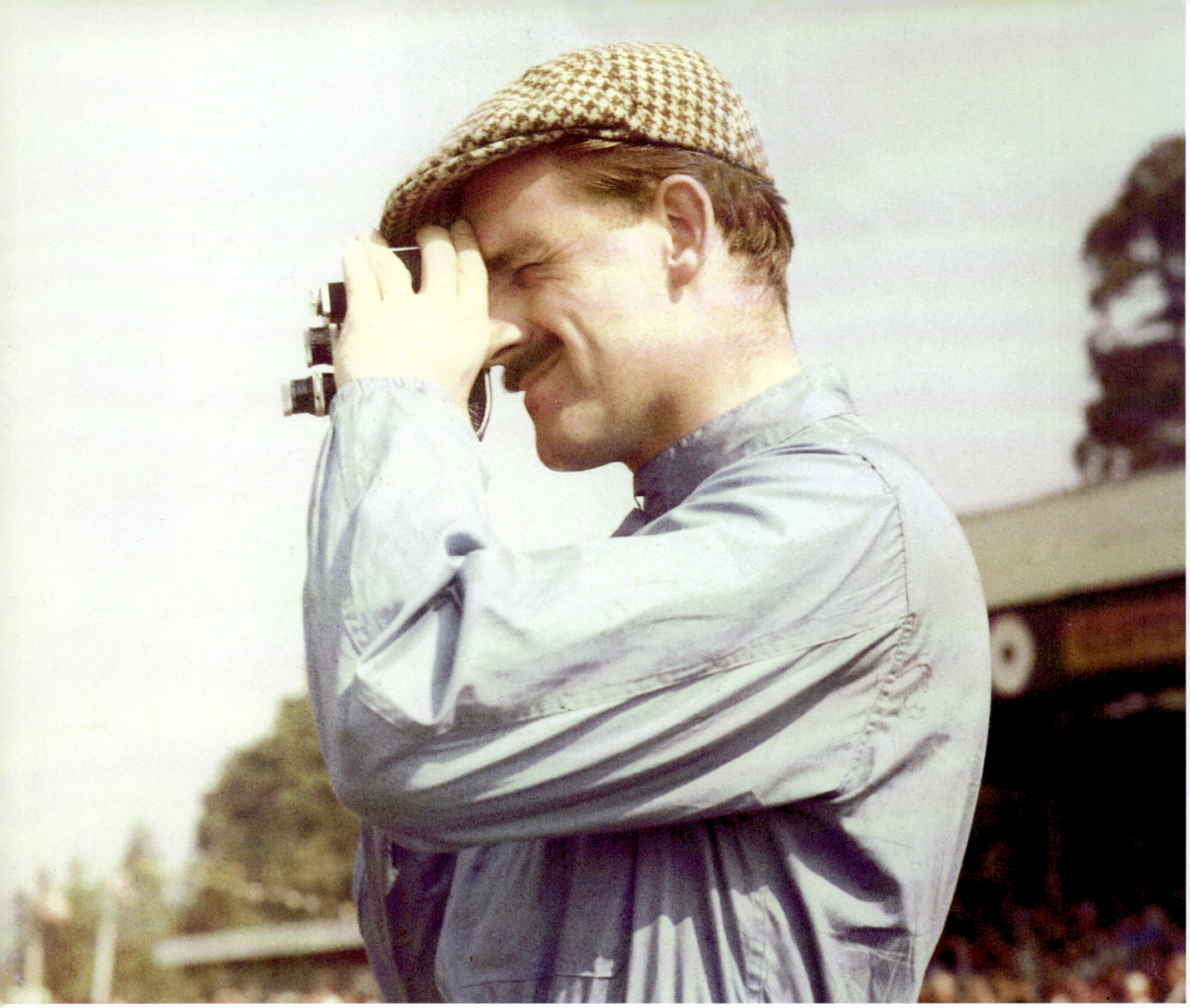

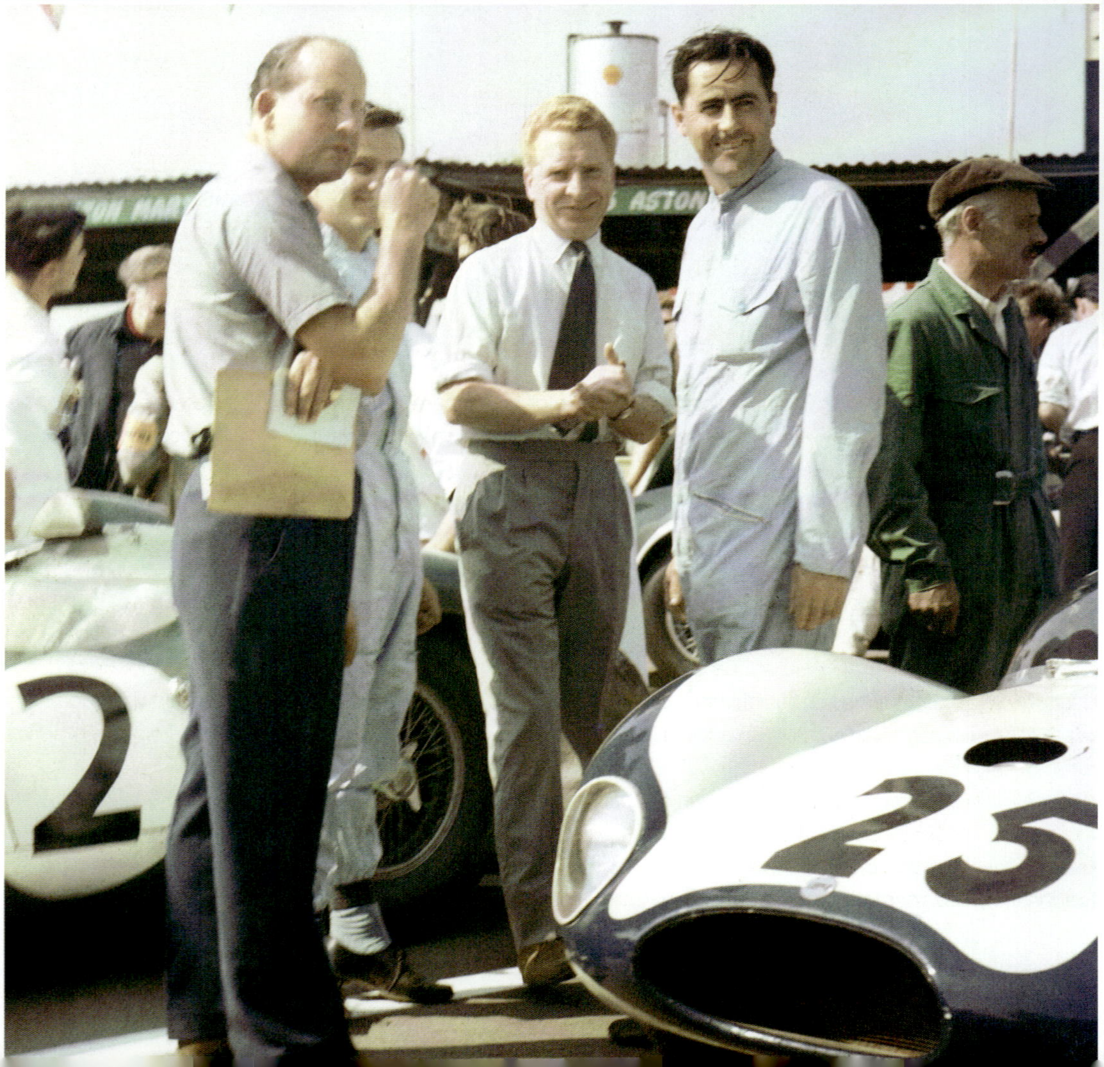
ASTON
25

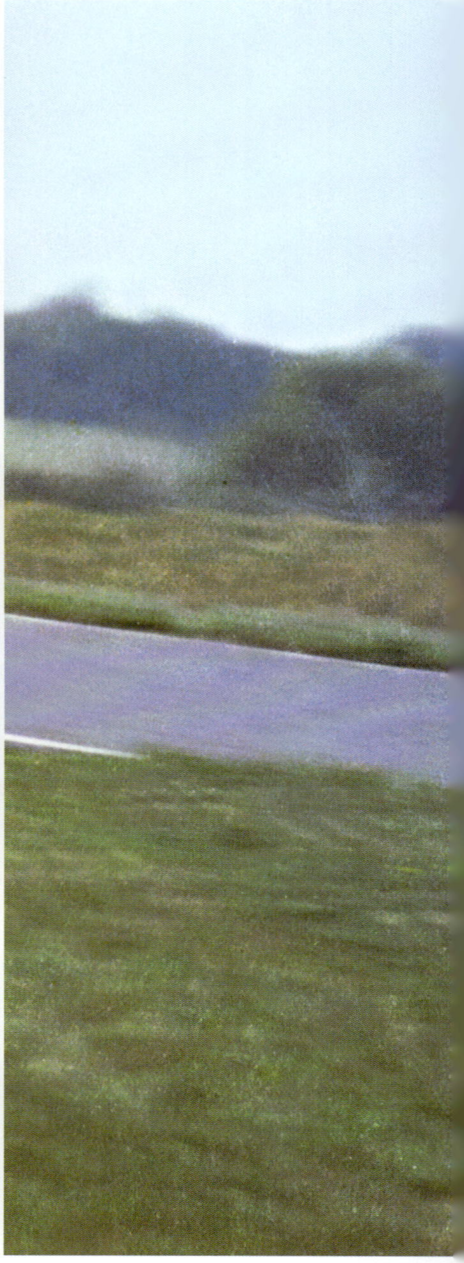

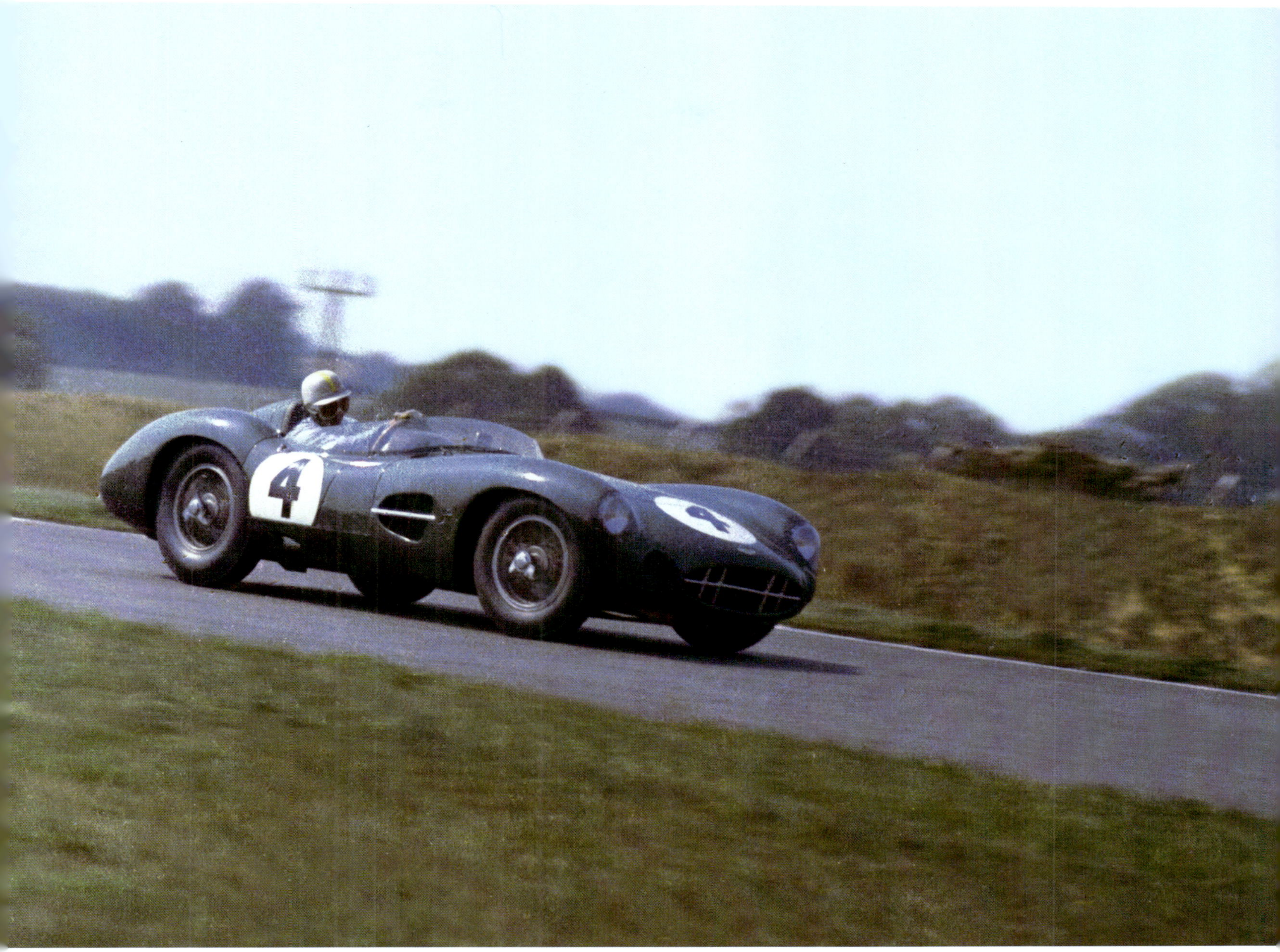

↑ Former merchant seaman Brian Naylor began his motor racing career in 1954, and went on to enter his own JBW-Maserati, later Coventry Climax-powered, car in assorted F1 races from 1959. He also raced a F2 Cooper and was active elsewhere, as here sharing Graham Whitehead's Aston Martin DBR1/300 (5) at the TT, the last and only DBR1/300 sold to a private owner during Aston's championship factory participation. Naylor indulges in some opposite lock, but his efforts were wasted when Whitehead gave up his pit to Aston Martin, following their fire dramas, and the car was withdrawn. Born on 24 March 1923, he retired from racing at the end of 1961 and died in Marbella, Spain, on 8 August 1989.

↖ Graham Hill, sporting a typical 1950s short-back-and-sides haircut, tries his hand at filming at Goodwood during practice for the TT. He was driving the works 2-litre Lotus 15 Climax with Alan Stacey, and lined up an impressive fourth, but retired after an accident.

← Jack Brabham (right), John Coombs, and Bruce McLaren with the Coombs Cooper Monaco CM/4/59 before the start of the 1959 Tourist Trophy. They started eighth, but retired early on apparently due to the fitment of knock-off wire wheels that were faster to remove during tyre changes than the normal bolt-on magnesium rims. But the extra weight of the wires wore out the wheel bearings on Goodwood's constant right-handers.

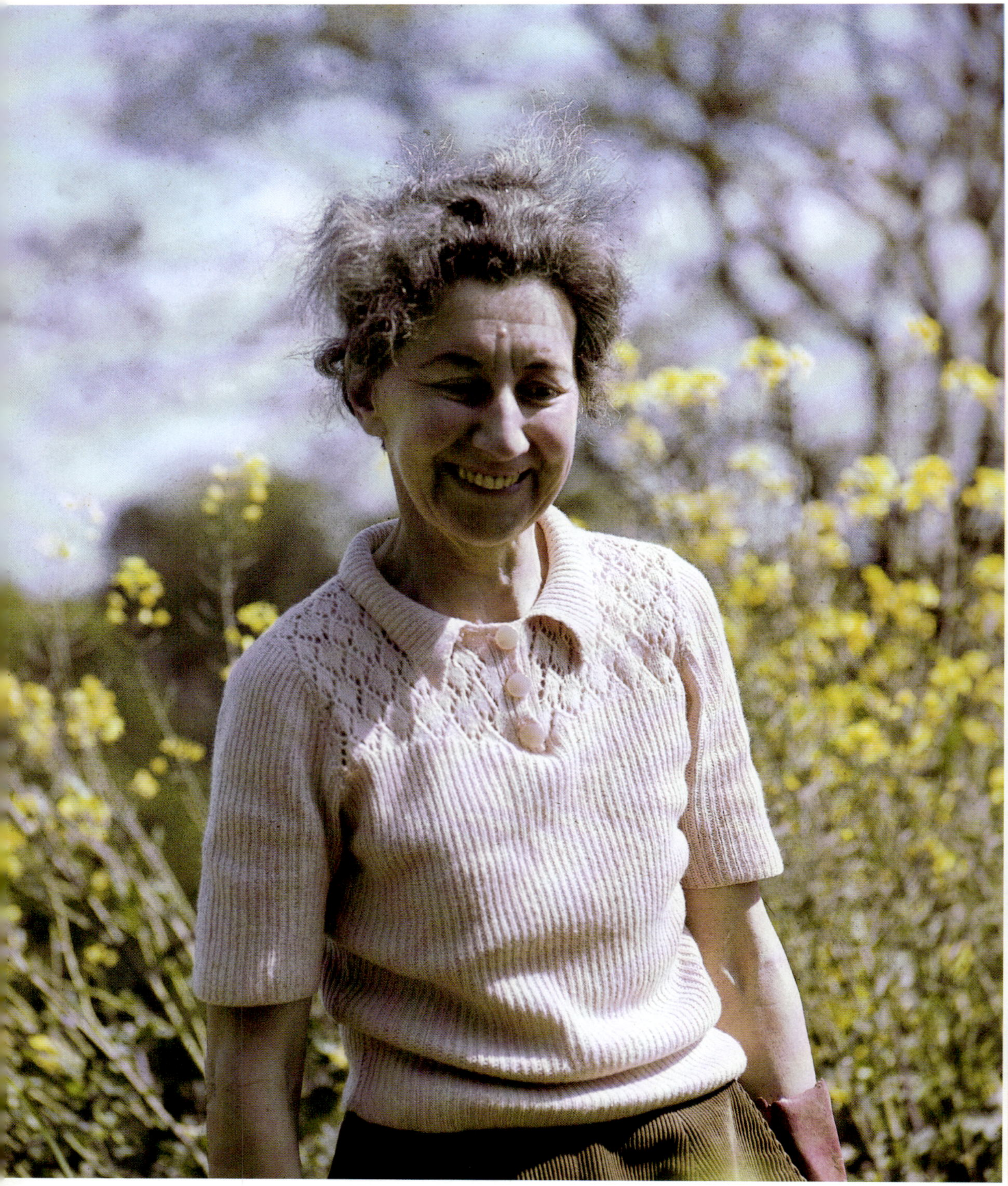

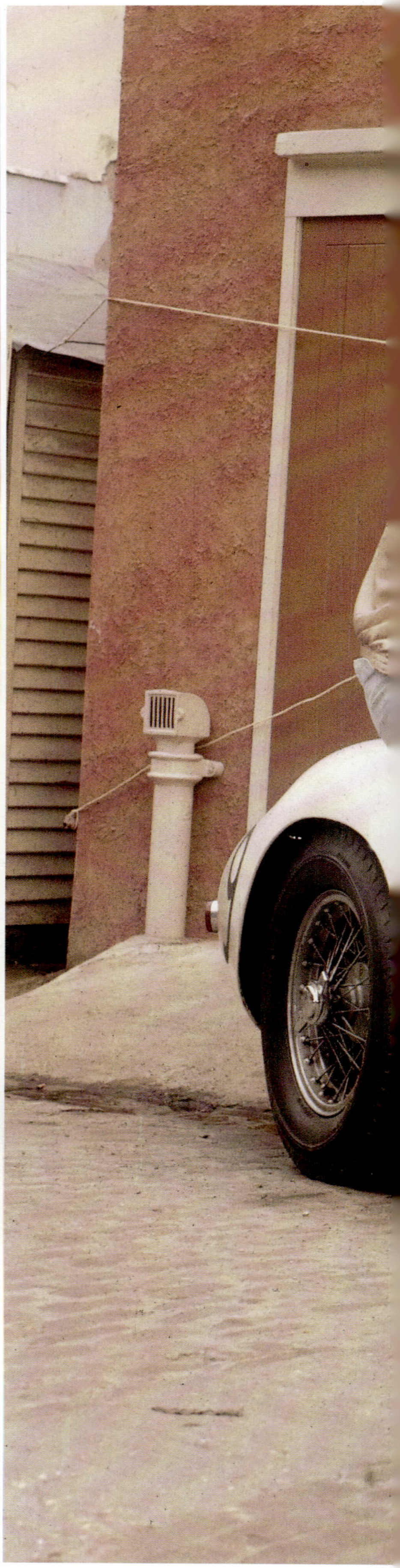

↑ Alice Cooper in the garden of her cottage next door to Rose Cottage where Mike later lived.

→ Masten Gregory in red cap and glasses, and Dan Gurney striking a distinctly boyish pose with one of Lloyd 'Lucky' Casner's Maserati Birdcages during 1960. Sadly, without Mike, I cannot say where or even precisely when this was taken, but given that the Maser is wearing a long tail I would guess pre-Le Mans 1960, even though Gurney drove the Cunningham E-type there. Note the Goodyear tyres and the BP Super Plus promotional banner.

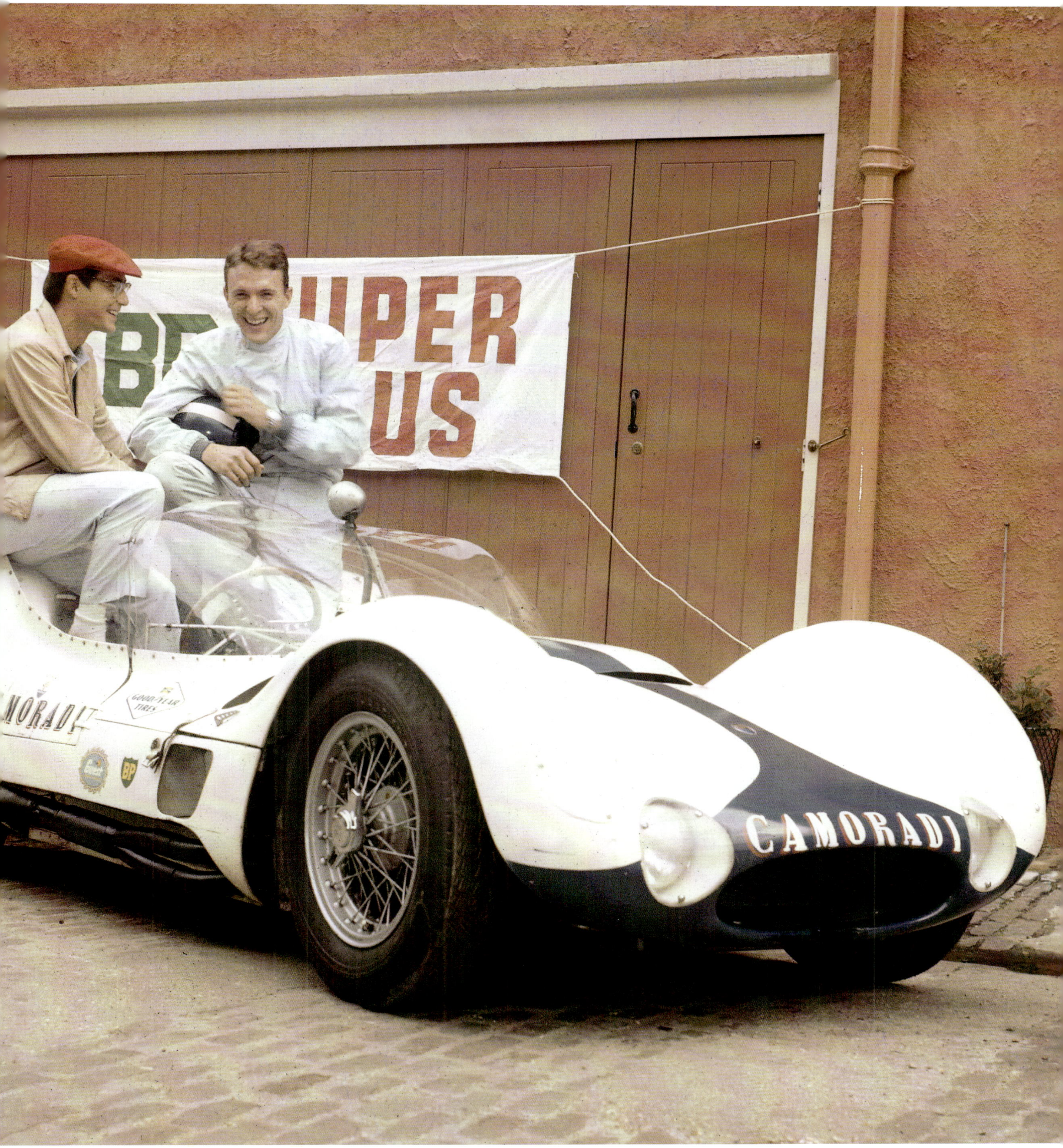
UPER
US
MORADI
CAMORADI

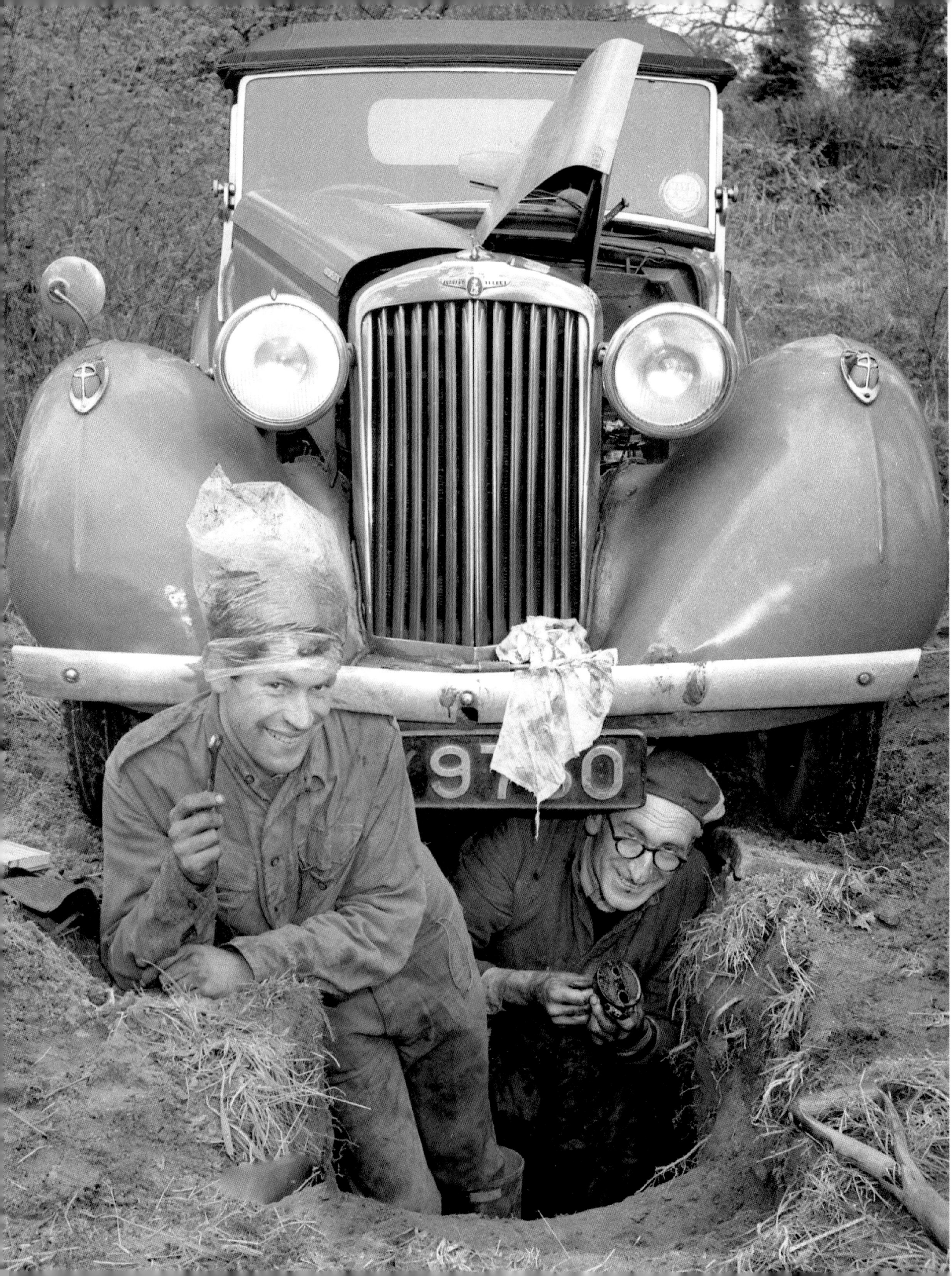

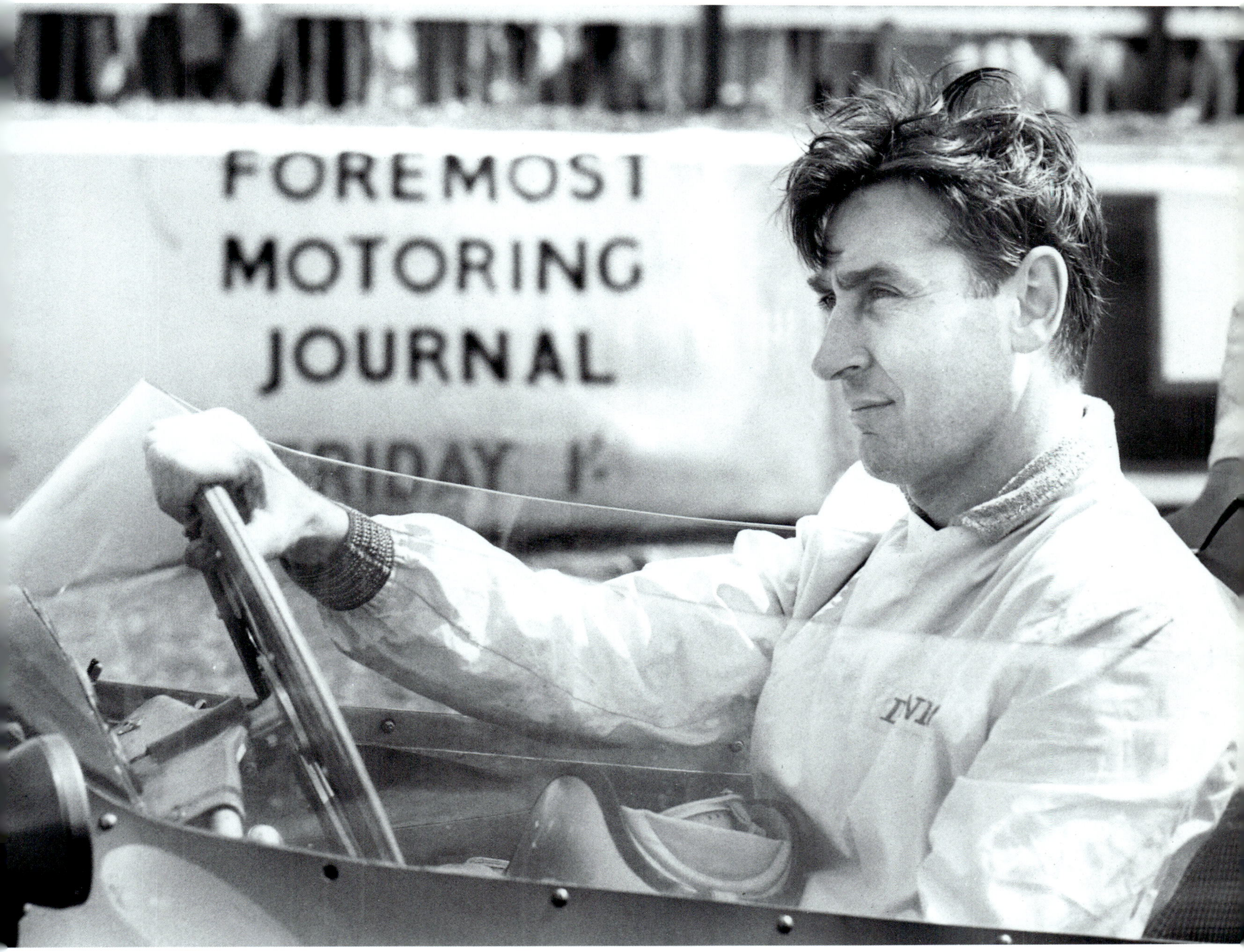

↑ The archetypal 1950s/60s racing driver, Roy Salvadori in the Aston Martin DBR4/250 at Silverstone. In the background can be seen a banner advertising *The Autocar* magazine as it then was, styled with the definite article.

← A picture taken by Alice shows Mike and his father George working on his sister's aged Sunbeam Talbot, with an improvised inspection pit, striking a typically anarchic pose.

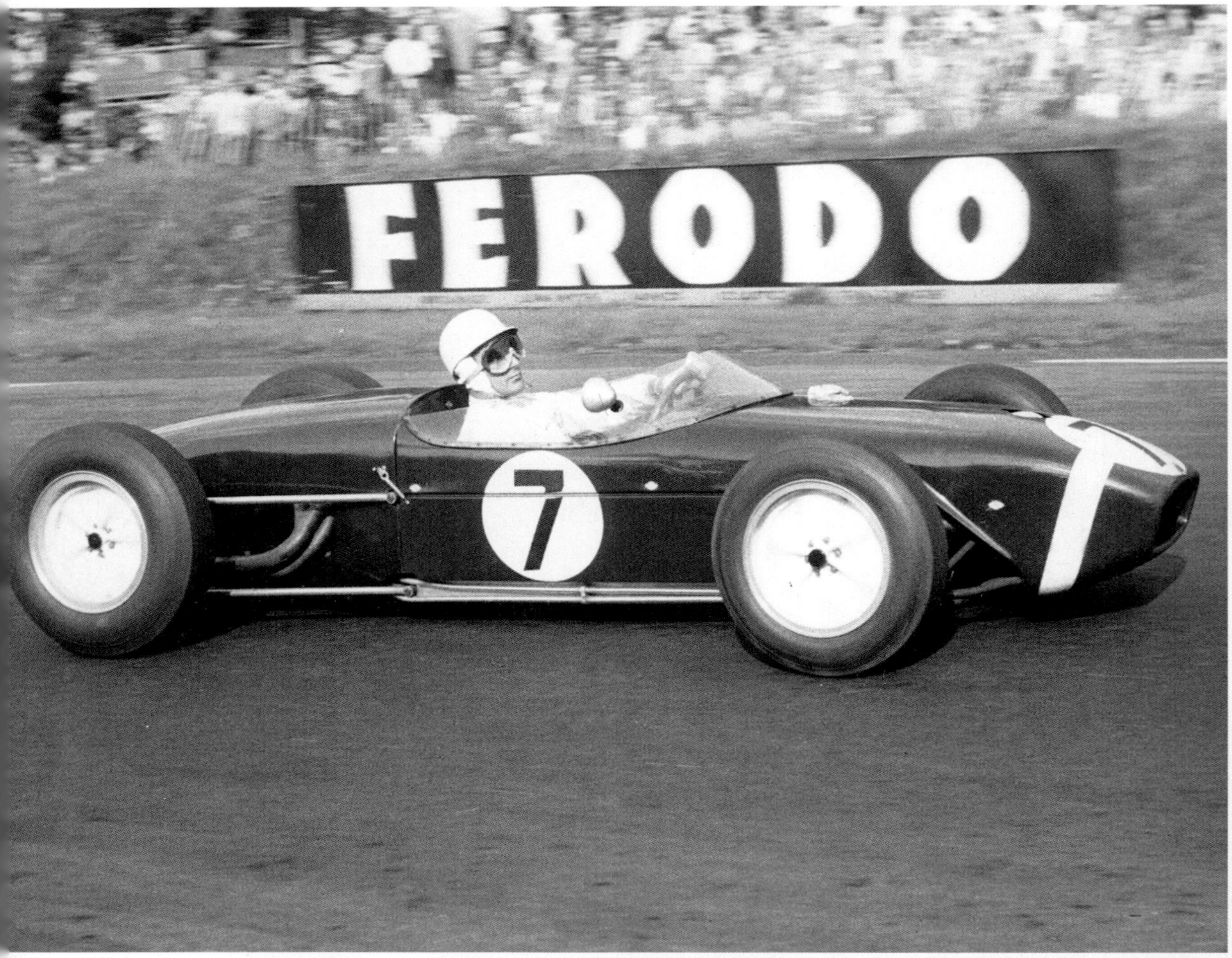
FERODO
7

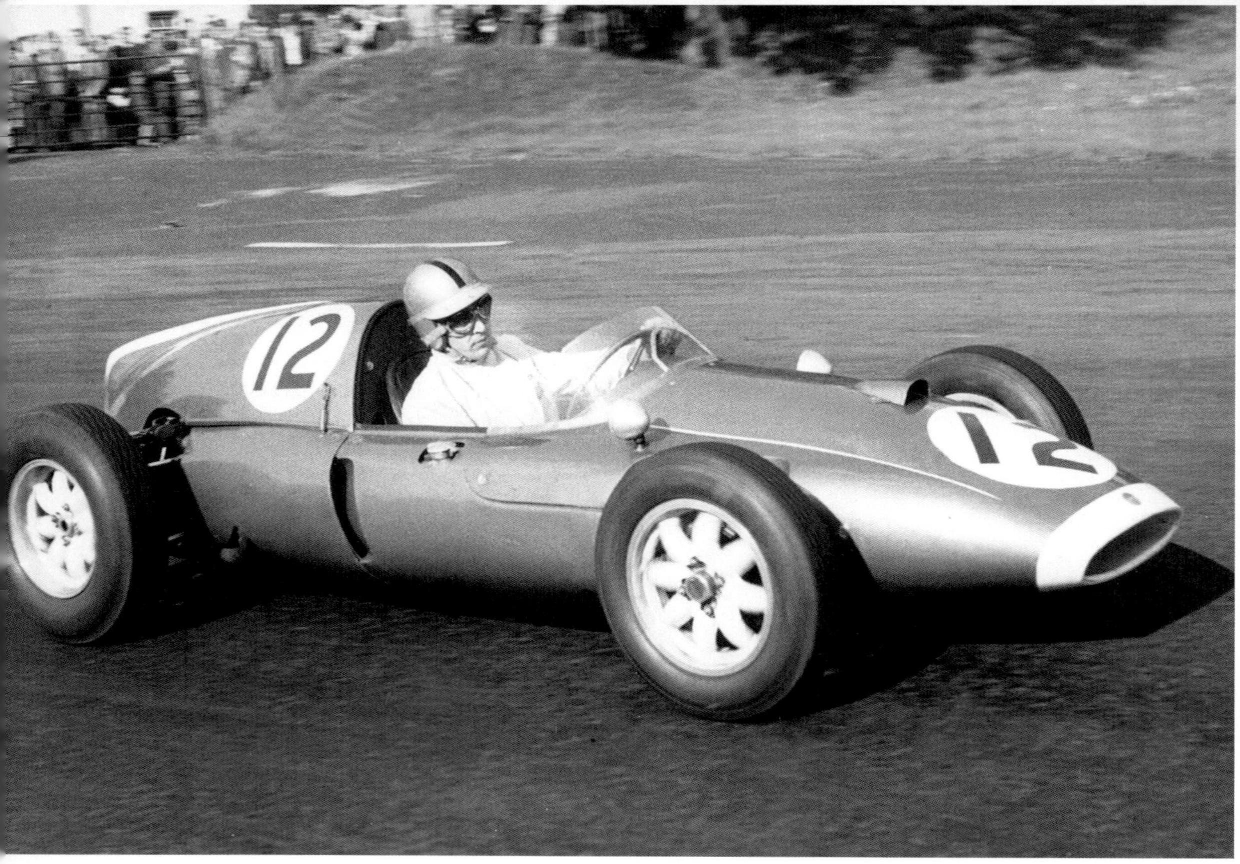
12

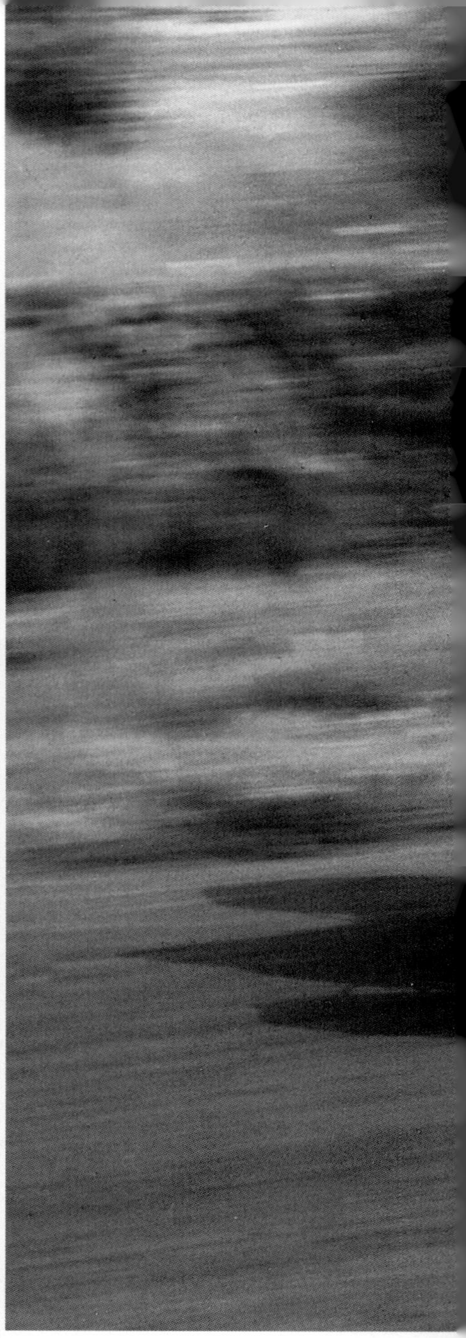

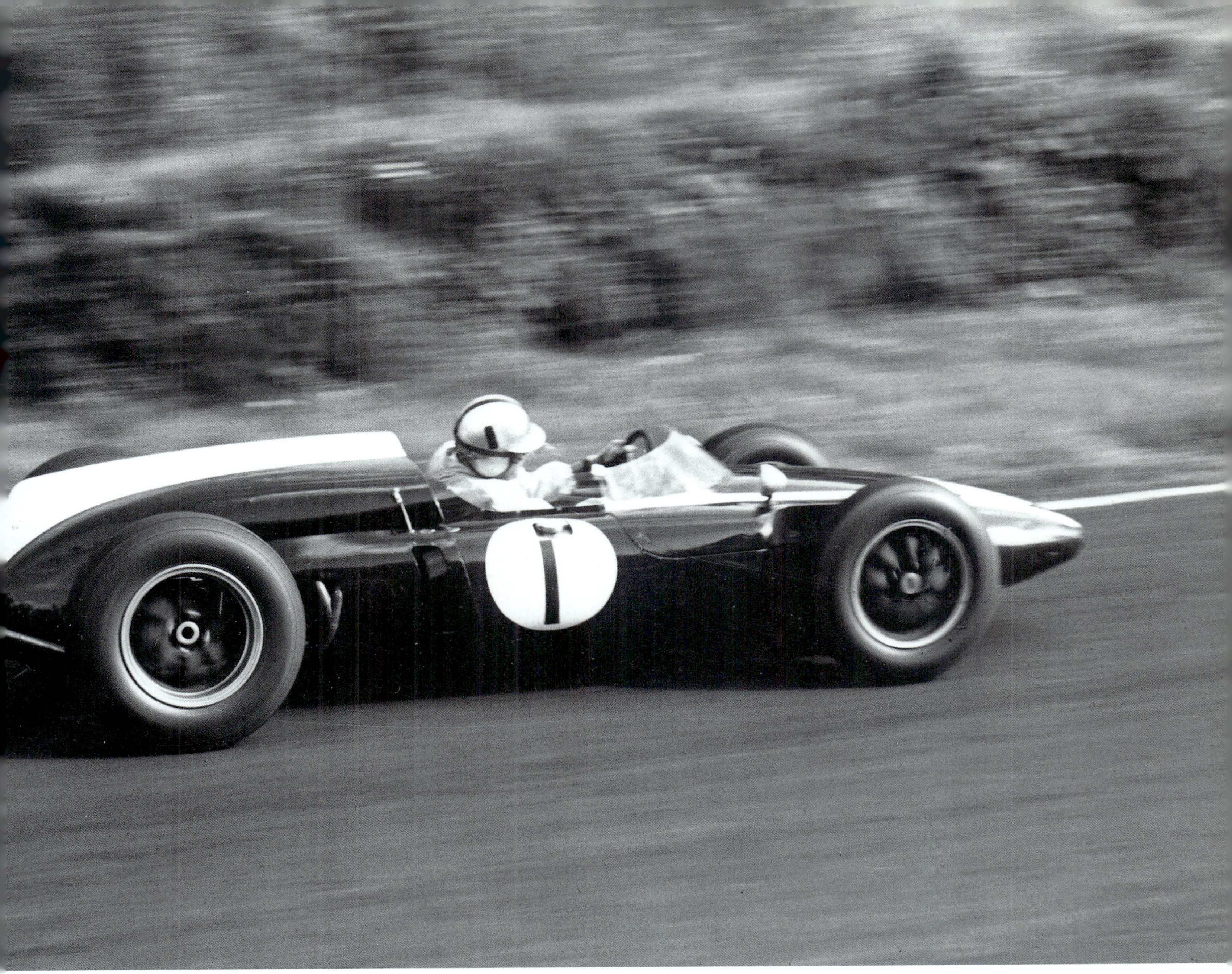

↑ 'Black Jack' in best press on, dirt track style in the works Cooper Climax T53 (F2-8-60) on his way to finishing second, 22.8sec behind Moss after 60 laps at Oulton Park. Brabham started third quickest on the front row alongside Jim Clark's factory Lotus 18. This was his regular championship-winning car and he led the race from laps 1–4 and later 17–19, dicing with Innes Ireland in the other works Lotus 18.

↖ Mike took a series of pictures at the seventh Oulton Park Gold Cup on 23 September 1960 and we start, fittingly, with serial Gold Cup winner Stirling Moss in the Rob Walker Lotus 18 (906), the replacement for the 18 wrecked at Spa after it lost a rear wheel and seriously injured SCM. Sadly, it was in this car, further modified as an 18/21 hybrid, that Moss had his career-ending Goodwood crash 18 months later. Note how remarkably plain and unadorned the Lotus appears, with no roll-over bar, no scoops, holes or other visible flaws outside of the two forward-mounted filler caps. The rear engine cover is secured courtesy of spring-loaded clips, and the upper cockpit/nose panel with Dzus fasteners. Moss, as ever with his number 7, won from pole, although the race was led by the works Lotuses of Innes Ireland and Jim Clark until they retired chased by Jack Brabham until lap 31. Stirling then took over, winning his fourth of five Gold Cup victories in front of a crowd of 30,000 and televised by the BBC.

← Compare the older T51 Cooper with its 'lowline' T53 successor above. Roy Salvadori in Tommy Atkins' Cooper Climax T51 (F2-7-59), which had a transverse leaf spring rear end, was a full 4.4sec slower in qualifying than pole-sitter Stirling Moss, although he was only two tenths slower than Gurney's BRM, and quicker than Bonnier's third BRM. He retired on lap 29 with steering failure. Tommy Atkins usually appears in the entry lists as C. T. Atkins, but also at times as High Efficiency Motors. Sadly, he committed suicide in 1965.

15
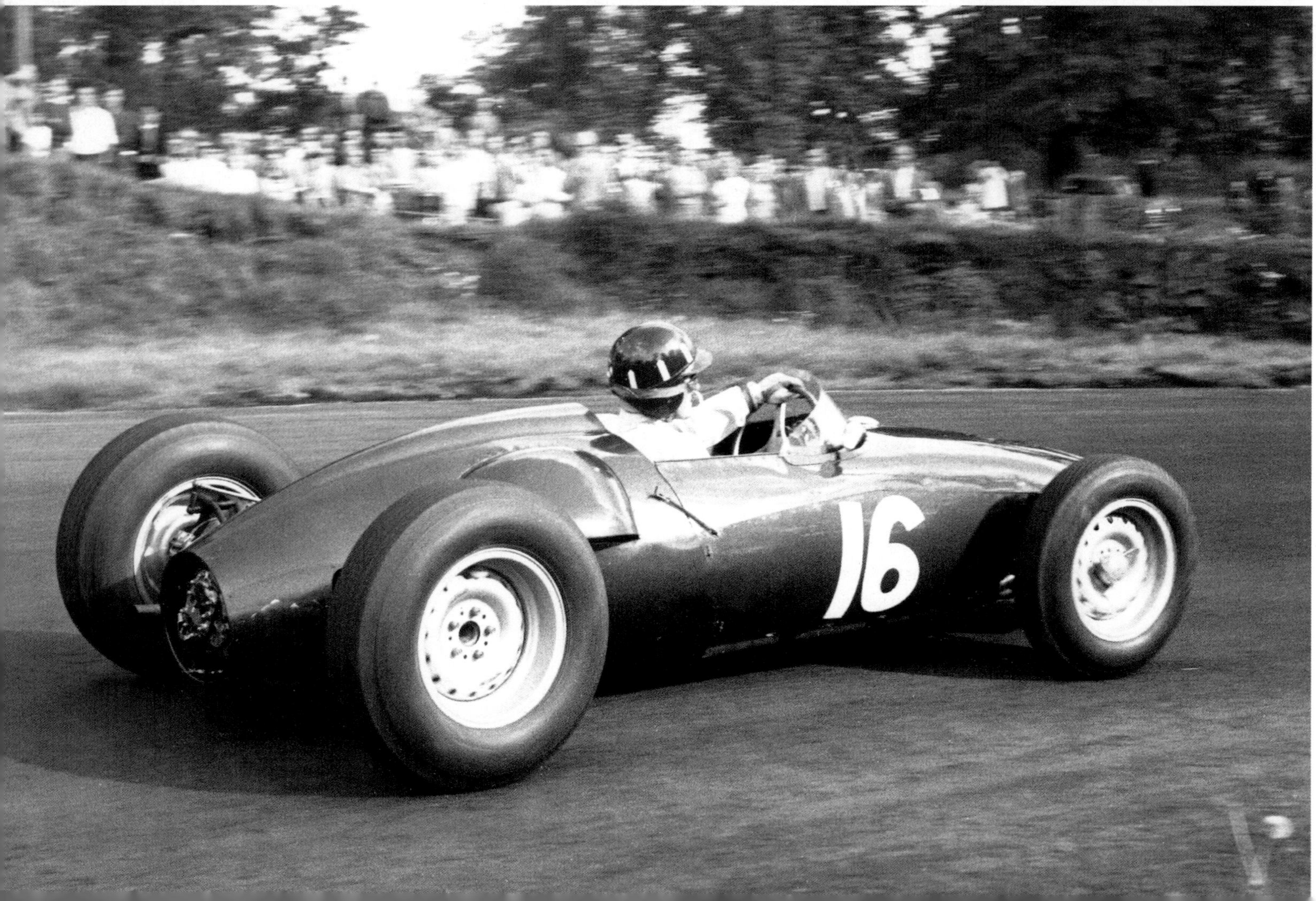
16

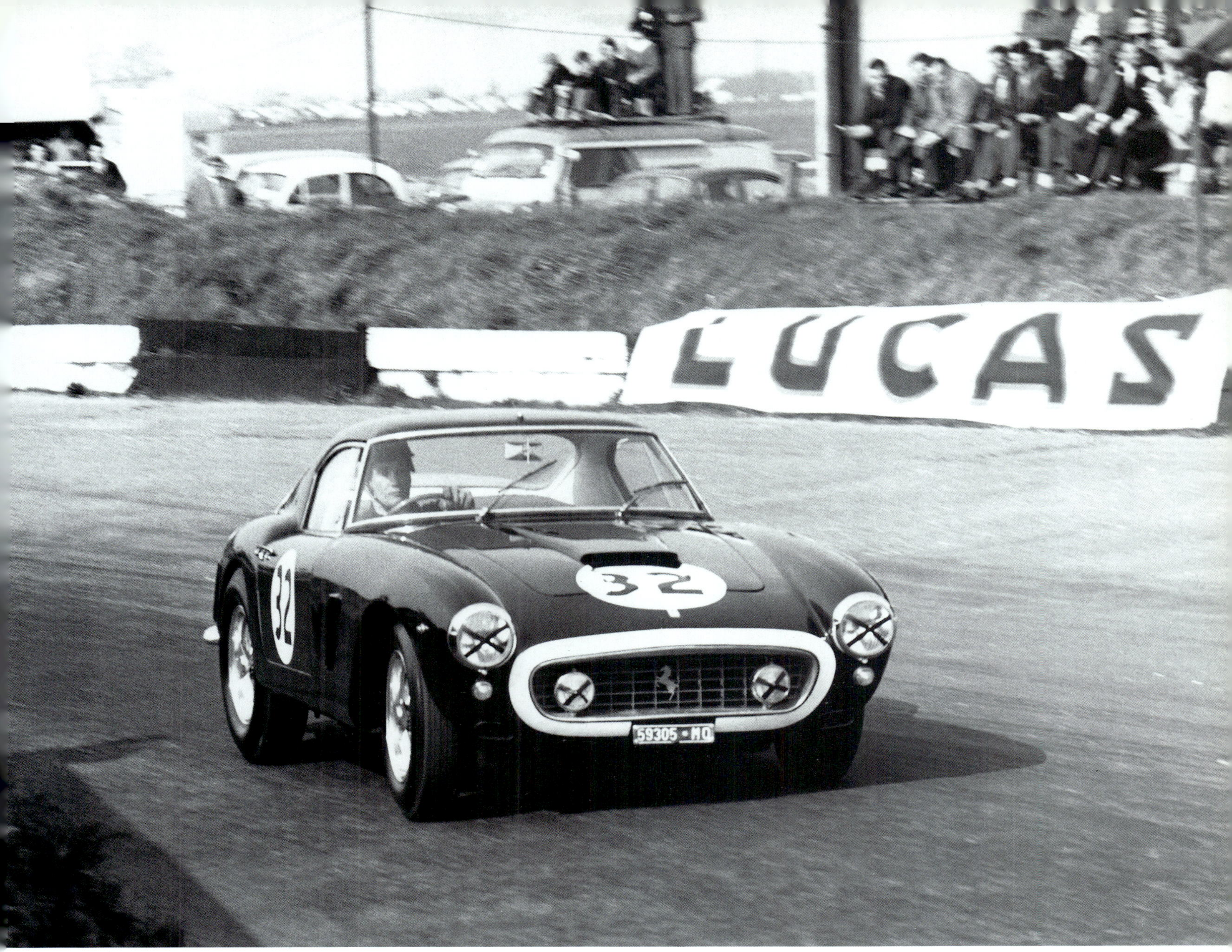

↑ Michael Johnston Parkes (24 September 1931–28 August 1977) on his way to winning at Snetterton on 3 March 1961 in his friend Tommy Sopwith's Equipe Endeavour Ferrari 250GT SWB (2119 GT), the 1960 TT-winning car bought jointly by Sopwith and Col. Ronnie Hoare. Parkes, whose father was the MD of Alvis, had joined the Rootes Group in 1949, aged 18, and later helped design and develop the Hillman Imp with Tim Fry. He raced Lotus, Gemini, and assorted other machines, including the Fry F2 project, during this period. Extremely tall at 6ft 4in, he was a very, very quick, press on type driver with a flamboyant style, and went on to become a Ferrari development engineer as well as successful team driver. During 1961/2 he raced for Sopwith and also Maranello Concessionaires, the English Ferrari distributor run by Col. Ronnie Hoare, and was almost unbeatable in British saloon and GT events in Jaguars and Ferraris.

↖ Dan Gurney's BRM P48 (486) finished sixth at Oulton Park, with team-mates Graham Hill third and Jo Bonnier fifth. It was something of a novelty for BRM to finish all three cars, although it must be noted that Gurney's race was compromised by misfiring. Note too that Dan is not wearing any gloves; the abbreviated screen; the riveted body panels, and the Dunlop cast magnesium alloy knock-off wheels, so typical of period BRMs.

← Graham Hill's sister car (chassis 487) en route to third place, 25sec adrift of Brabham's second-placed Cooper. Unlike Gurney's P48, chassis 487 is now a sleeker, lower Mk II P48 with wishbone rear suspension. Gone is the eccentric cheese-cutter central-mounted rear disc, the car now having four orthodox outboard disc brakes and bolt-on rear wheels.

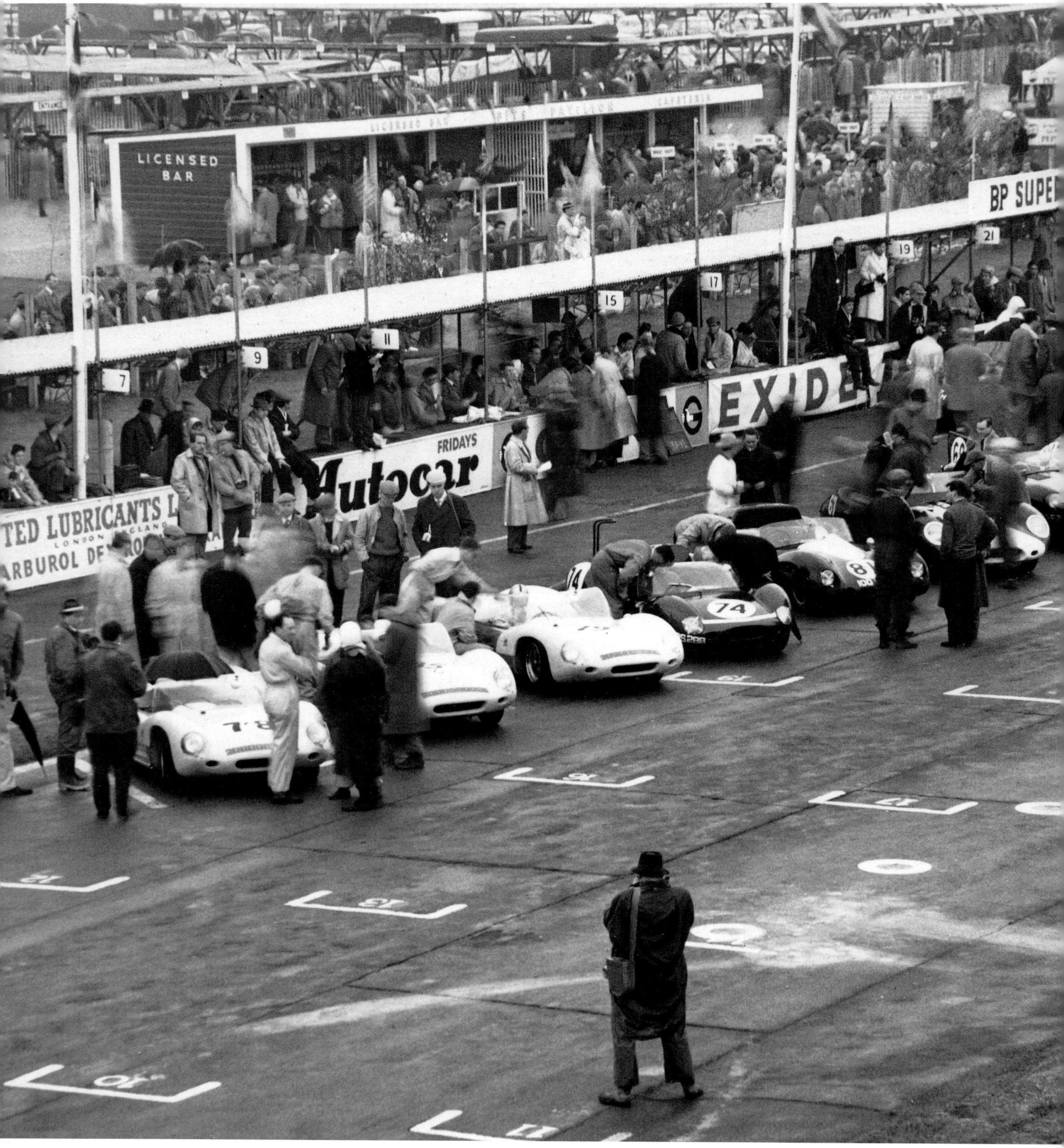
LICENSED
BAR
BP SUPE
EXIDE
FRIDAYS
Autocar
TED LUBRICANTS L
LONDON ENGLAND
ARBUROL DE

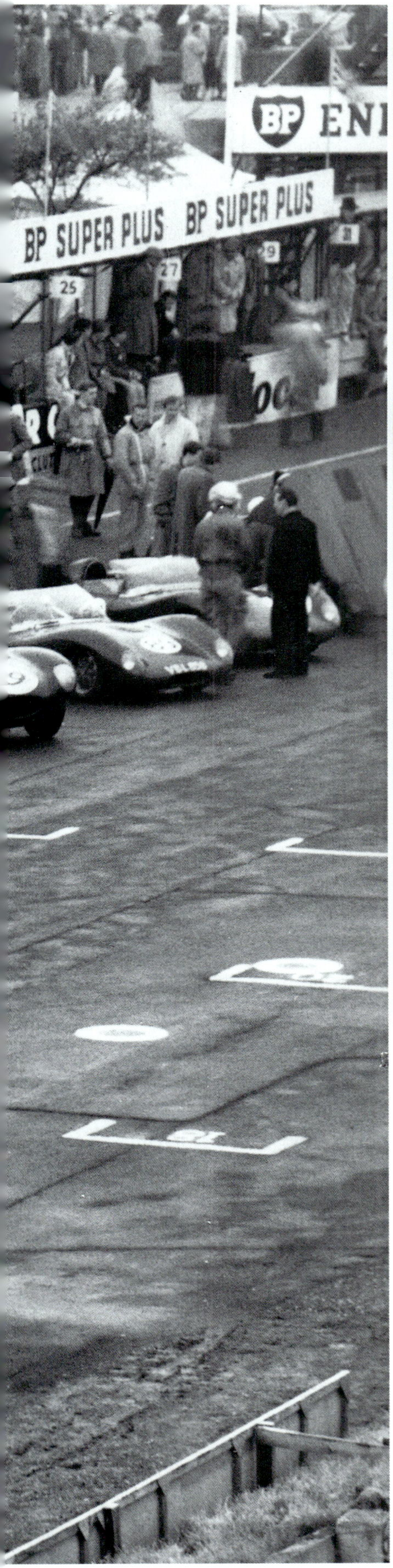

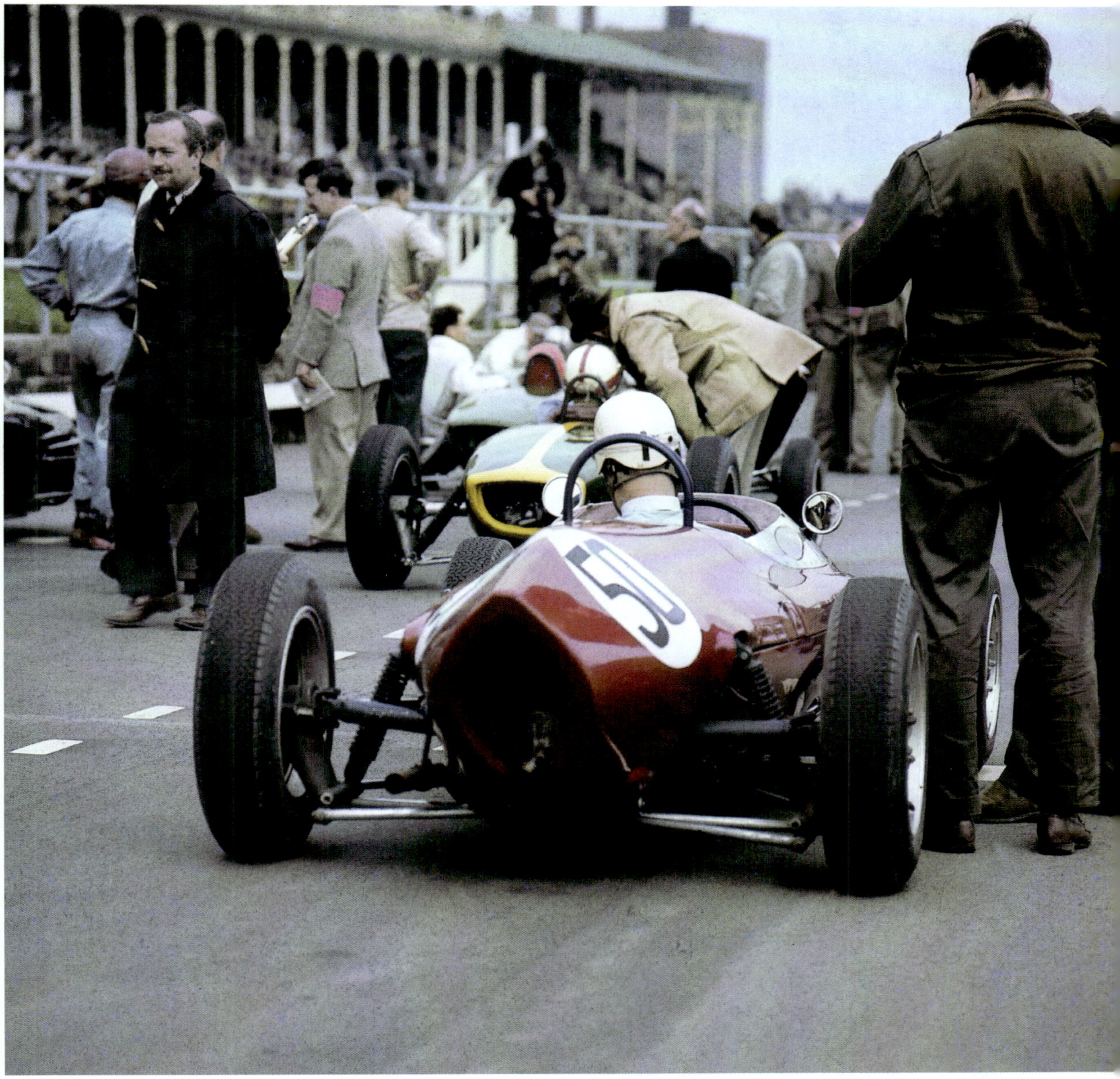

↑ The grid for the Formula Junior race at the BARC 200 Aintree meeting on 22 April 1961. Mike was apparently addicted to grid shots taken from behind, and in this one we see Dennis Taylor's Lola-Ford Mk3 (No. 50) that finished well down the field. Colin Chapman strolls through the picture in his typically British duffel coat with hood.

← The ridiculous Appendix C sports car regulations that begat the hideous high windscreens, and even in some cases luggage boxes, are all too obvious at Goodwood. This is the Sussex Trophy on 3 April 1961 and we see the UDT Laystall Lotus XIXs, or Monte Carlos if you prefer, with Moss's car on pole lined up ahead of the Ecurie Ecosse Cooper Monaco and the rest, including John Coundley's Lister Jaguar (No. 67) alongside Mike Salmon's ex-Ecosse 'long nose' Jaguar D-type (XKD 504). Moss, who can be seen with his back to the camera in dark overalls in front of the pole car, won ahead of team-mate Henry Taylor, with Tom Dickson third in the Cooper Monaco. This shot illustrates how the pits were separated from the track by a narrow grass strip – nothing as posh as a proper pit wall then.

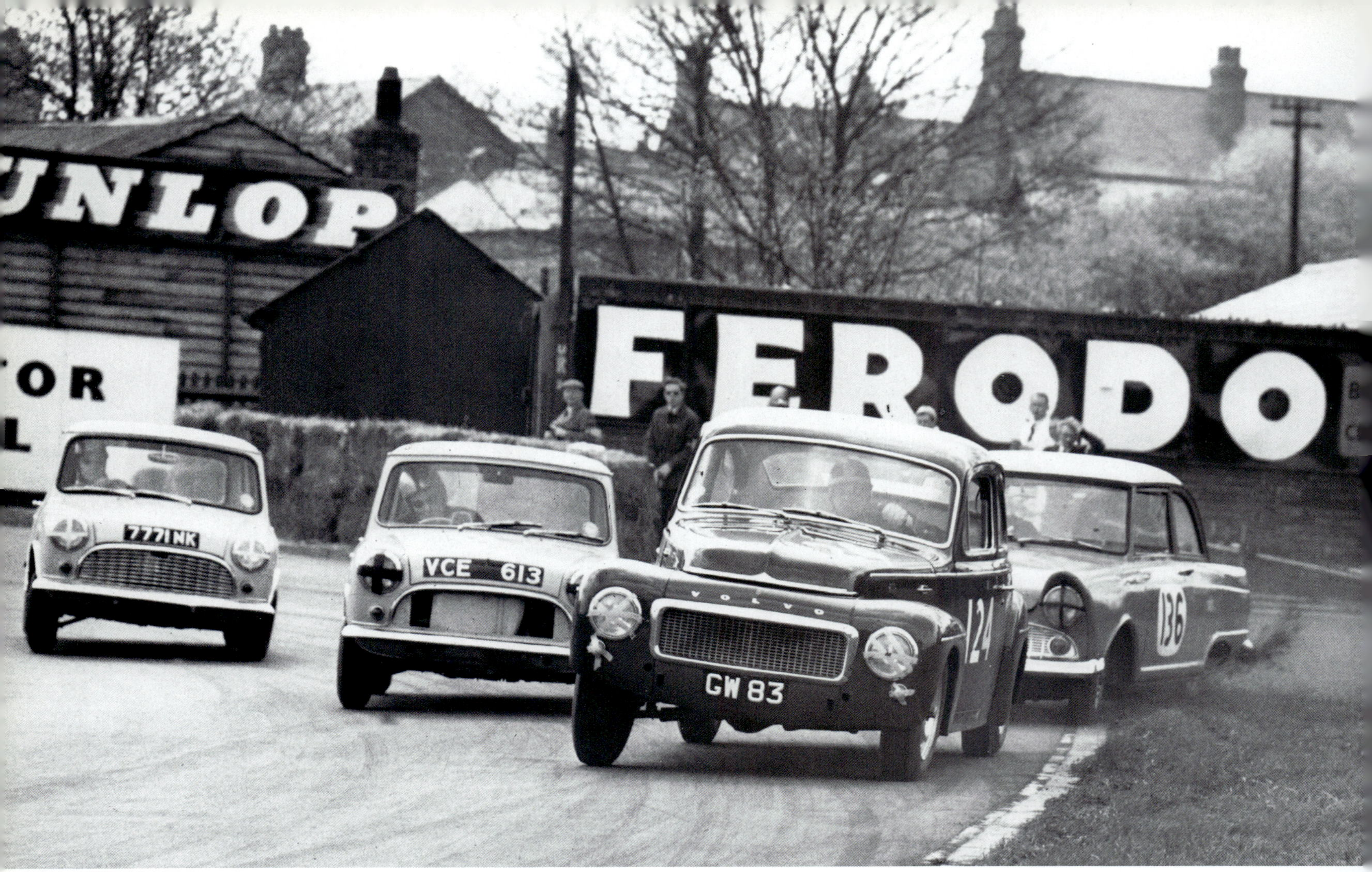

↑ G. Wood's Volvo P544 leads a real bun fight in the BSCC round at Aintree on 22 April 1961. He is pursued by 'Doc' Shepherd in his Mini VCE 613, the spectacular Nicky Byrne (Auto Union 1000S), and John Aley's Mini 7771 NK. Wood finished ninth o/a and third in class, Shepherd turned his Mini over at the Melling Crossing, Byrne was twelfth o/a and also third in class, and Aley came home eleventh o/a and second in class.

↗ Class leaders Alan Hutcheson (Riley 1.5) and Bill Blydenstein (Borgward Isabella TS) really having a go, with Hutcheson ultimately winning the battle finishing seventh o/a behind six Jaguar 3.8 Mk2s led by Roy Salvadori in the Coombs car. In an age of high-tech, über-modified electronic trickery, ultra sticky tyres, and hooligan driving, this image and the preceding one really illustrate just how different, entertaining, and far more apposite to the showroom product saloon car racing was in those far-off days.

→ Dan Gurney and the Chevrolet Impala gave Jaguar a rude shock at the May International Trophy Silverstone meeting in 1961, seriously threatening the Coventry concern's hegemony in British saloon car racing. Gurney, who started from pole and would have won the race had he not lost a wheel, is shown here being closely pursued by Graham Hill in one of the Equipe Endeavour Mk2 Jaguars who went on to win and set fastest lap. There was an unfortunate postscript when Gurney entered the Impala at the British Empire Trophy meeting in July, only to discover just two days before the race that apparently the car was not homologated (even though Gurney was accepted at the May meeting and held the necessary acceptance papers from the FIA committee in the US). The papers had been sent to the CSI of the FIA in Paris, who admitted they had the documents but now claimed it was too late to act. (Bureaucracy never fails to frustrate and deny.) This prompted Gurney to contact John Eason Gibson at the BRDC, but one hour later Eason Gibson received a telegram from Paris saying 'Chevrolet not homologated'. According to a letter from Dan Gurney published in *Autosport* magazine on 21 July 1961, the RAC knew ten days beforehand about the homologation problem but failed to inform Gurney in time. Unsurprisingly, Gurney was very upset and stated in print that 'I will in time get over the fact that I had spent a lot of time and money in bringing the Impala to Great Britain, but I will not readily forget the suspicion that there may have been some behind-the-scenes sabotage to prevent the Chevrolet from running at Silverstone.' He ended the letter by stating, 'I say again that our car is very standard and that it does comply with the rules and regulations.' No official response appears to have graced the pages of *Autosport*, and it was left to a Wim Hoeksma of Purley, Surrey, who wrote in the following week to state that Mr Gibson owed the paying public and Mr Gurney an explanation.

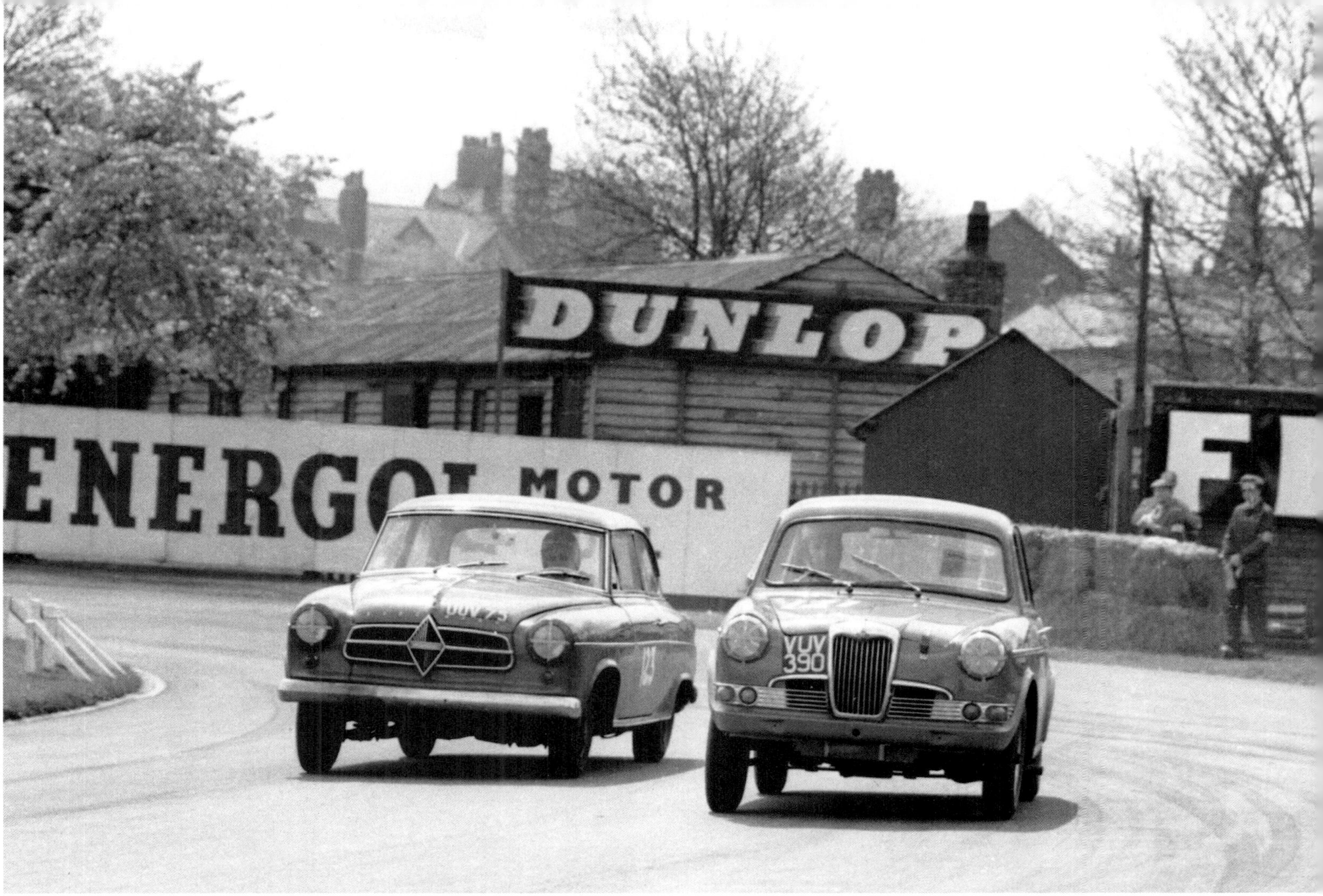
DUNLOP
MOTOR
VUV
390
123

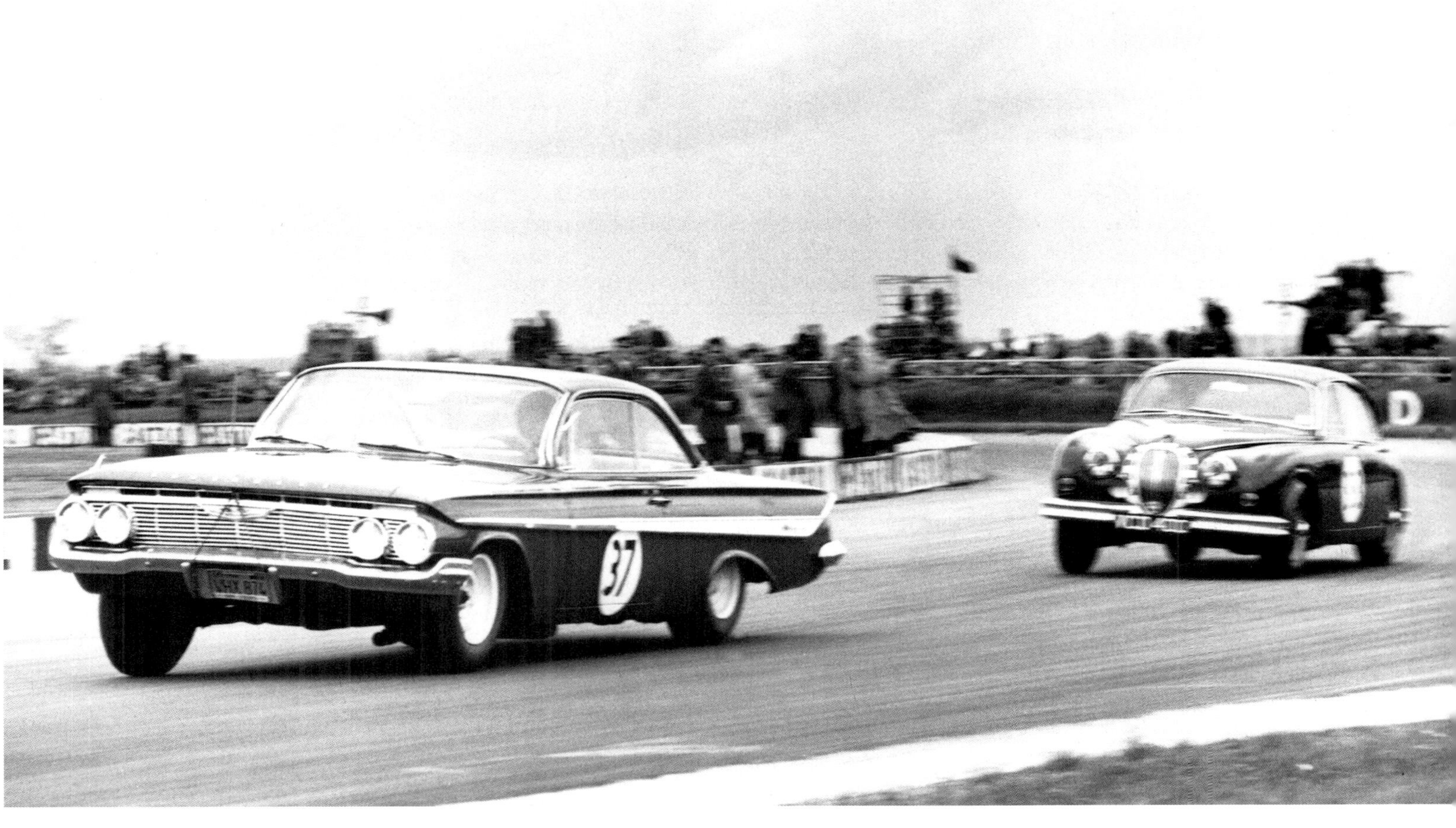
37

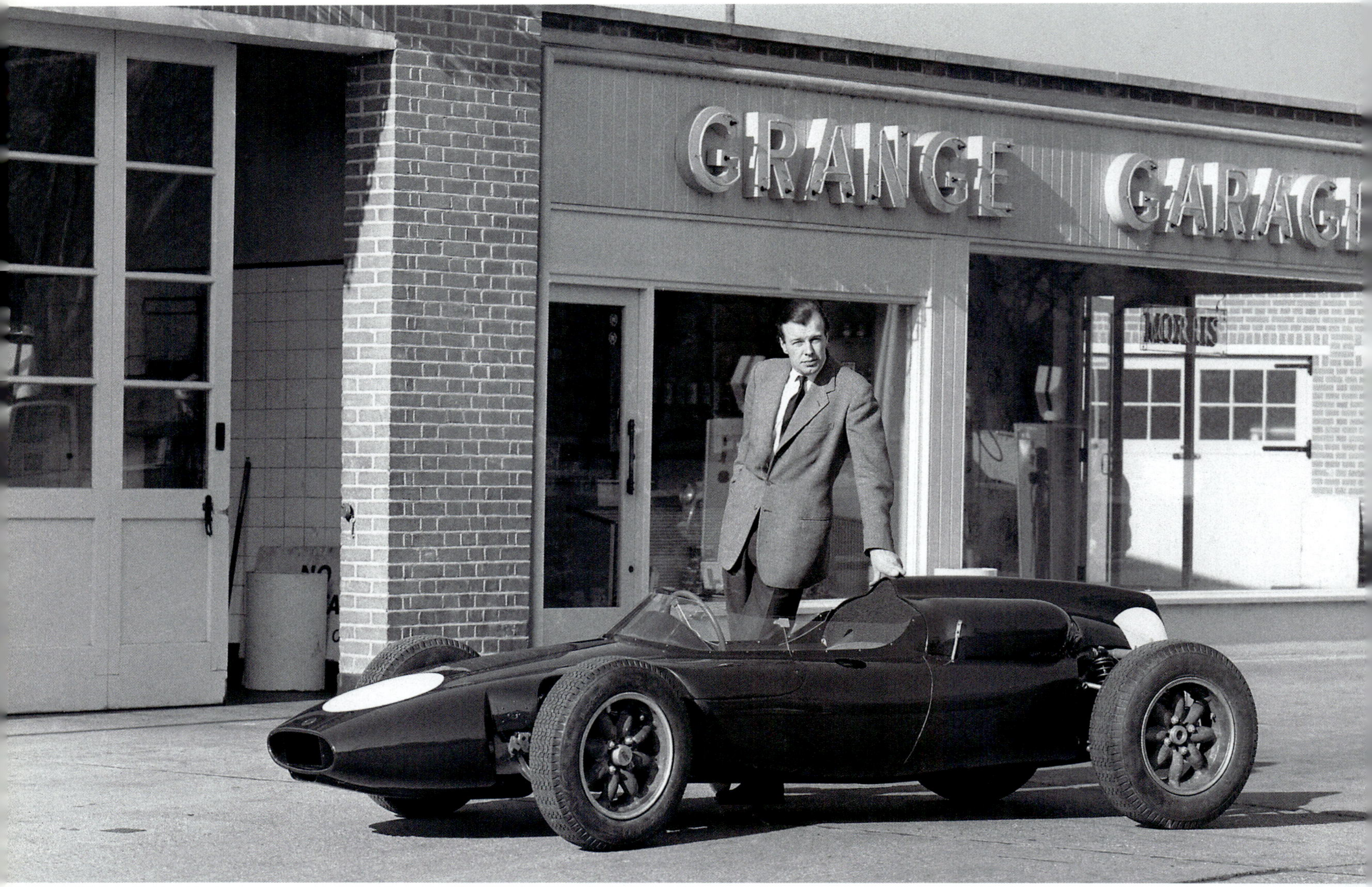

↑ The photo was captioned R. M. (Rick) Bartram, but the period entry lists referred to Terry Bartram of Cheyne Walk, Chelsea, London SW3. He was the mentor of the up-and-coming Shane Summers, for whom he had provided a Lotus 15 (the ex-Innes Ireland car) during 1960. In 1961 he bought this Cooper-Climax T53 (F1-8-61) for his protégé, but tragically Summers was killed in it during practice for the Silver City Trophy on 3 June 1961, and the car reportedly destroyed. Thereafter, Bartram disappeared from motor racing. This is the forecourt of Grange Motors, but where? Does anybody know?

→ Tony Brooks' Grand Prix career began in 1955 with a victory at Syracuse, Sicily, and ended at Watkins Glen in 1961. He drove for Connaught in 1955, BRM in 1956, Vanwall in 1957/58 and briefly in 1959 and 1960, Ferrari in 1959, BRP in 1960 and finally back to BRM in 1961. He won six Grands Prix and was most effective on high-speed circuits such as Spa, where he won the 1957 sports car race (Aston Martin) and the 1958 Belgian GP (Vanwall), and Reims (1959 French GP for Ferrari). He also won the 1957 Nürburgring 1,000km with Noel Cunningham-Reid (Aston Martin), and famously pitted during the final 1959 World Championship round at Sebring after a first lap collision despite being a championship contender, ultimately finishing third and losing any chance of becoming World Champion. Following an indifferent 1960 season he returned to BRM in 1961, but although his skill and finesse were still apparent, he effectively played second fiddle to the rapidly improving Graham Hill whom he outqualified only twice, at Aintree and the Nürburgring. He retired at the end of 1961 having survived an era of extreme risk with only a few relatively minor injuries. The legendary 'Wilkie' Wilkinson fiddles with the rear of the BRM P48/57, before the Lavant Cup at Goodwood Easter 1961, that displays the usual riveted body panels so characteristic of the Bourne cars. Brooks first drove for BRM in 1956 and this was his return drive.

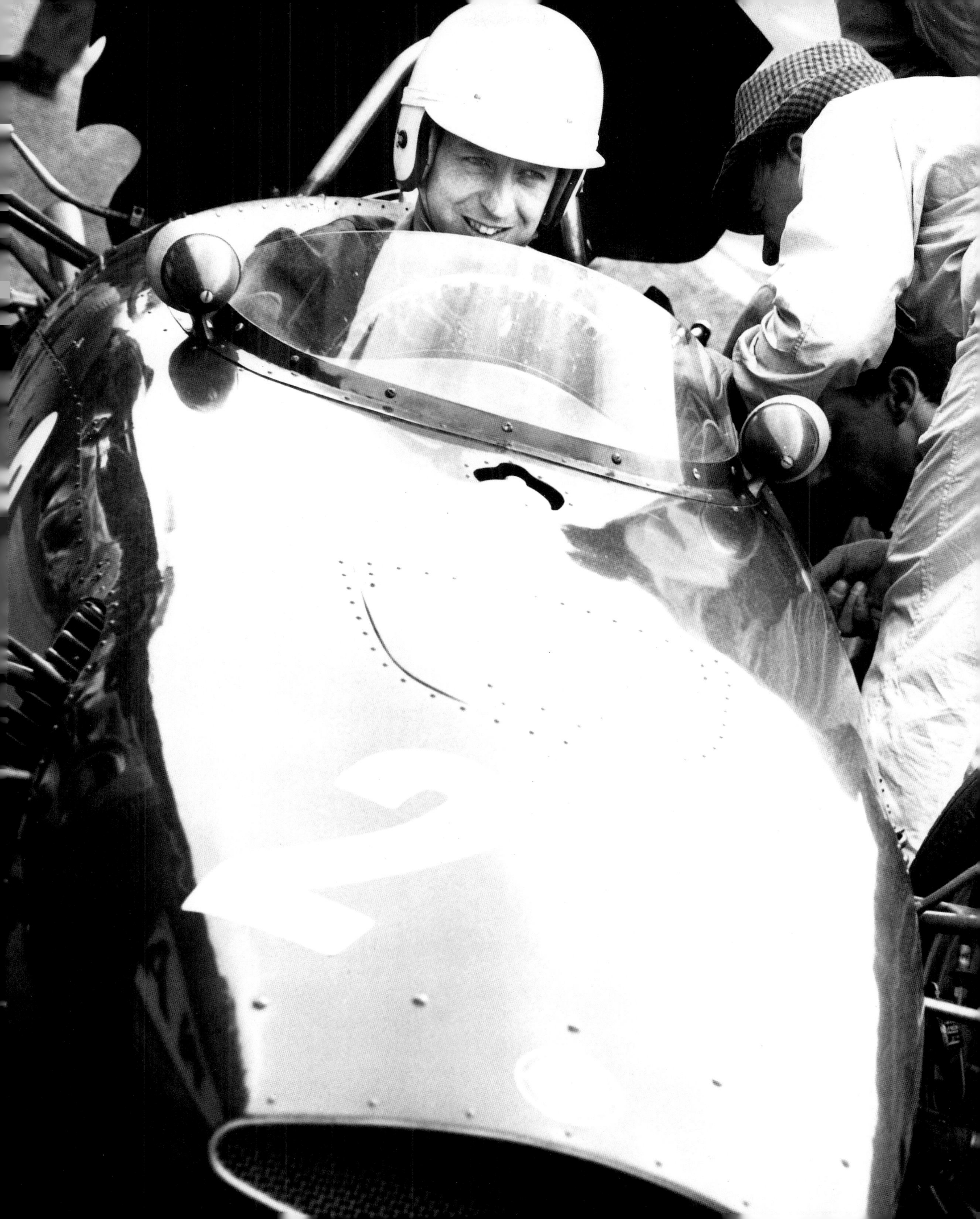

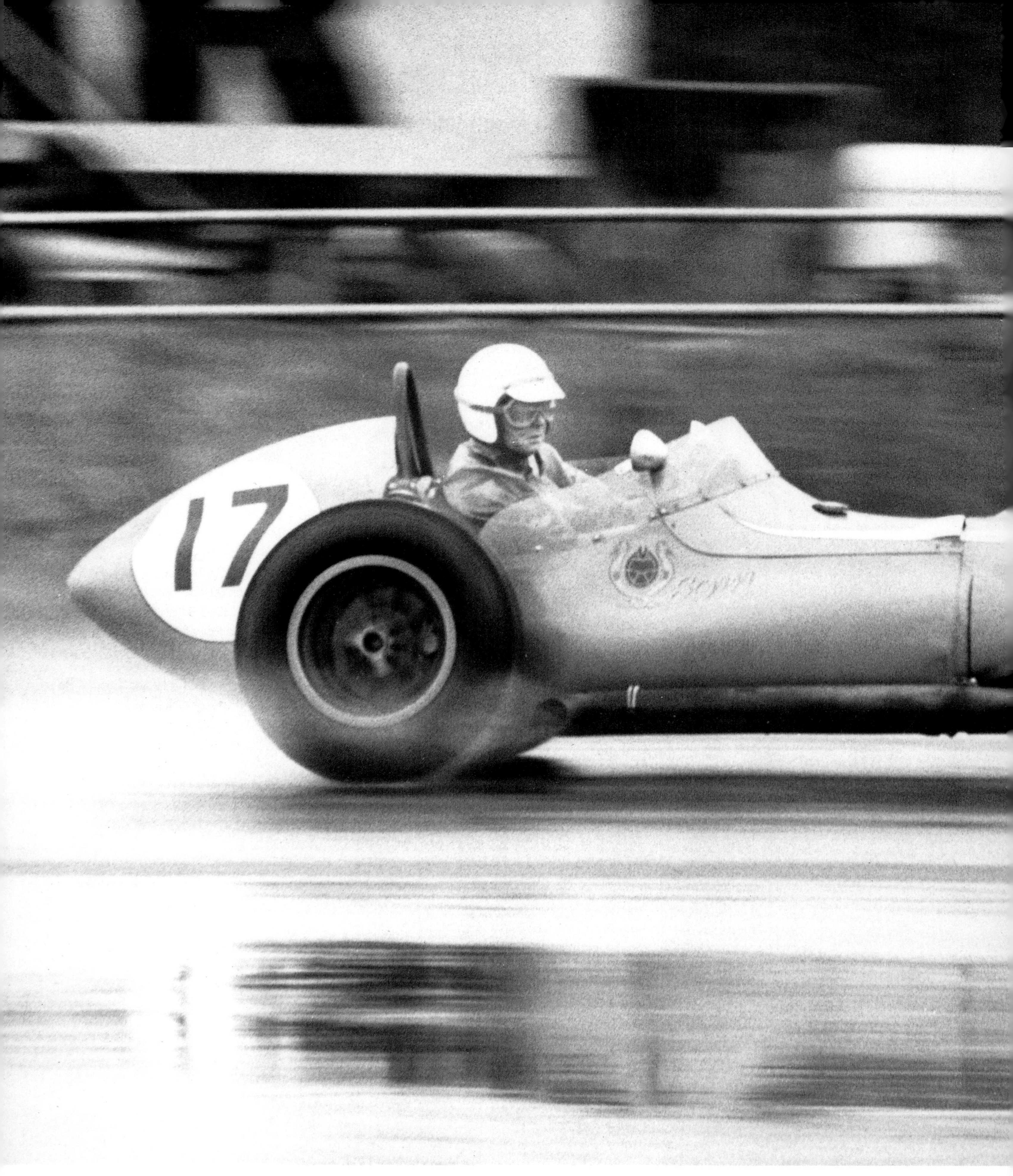
17

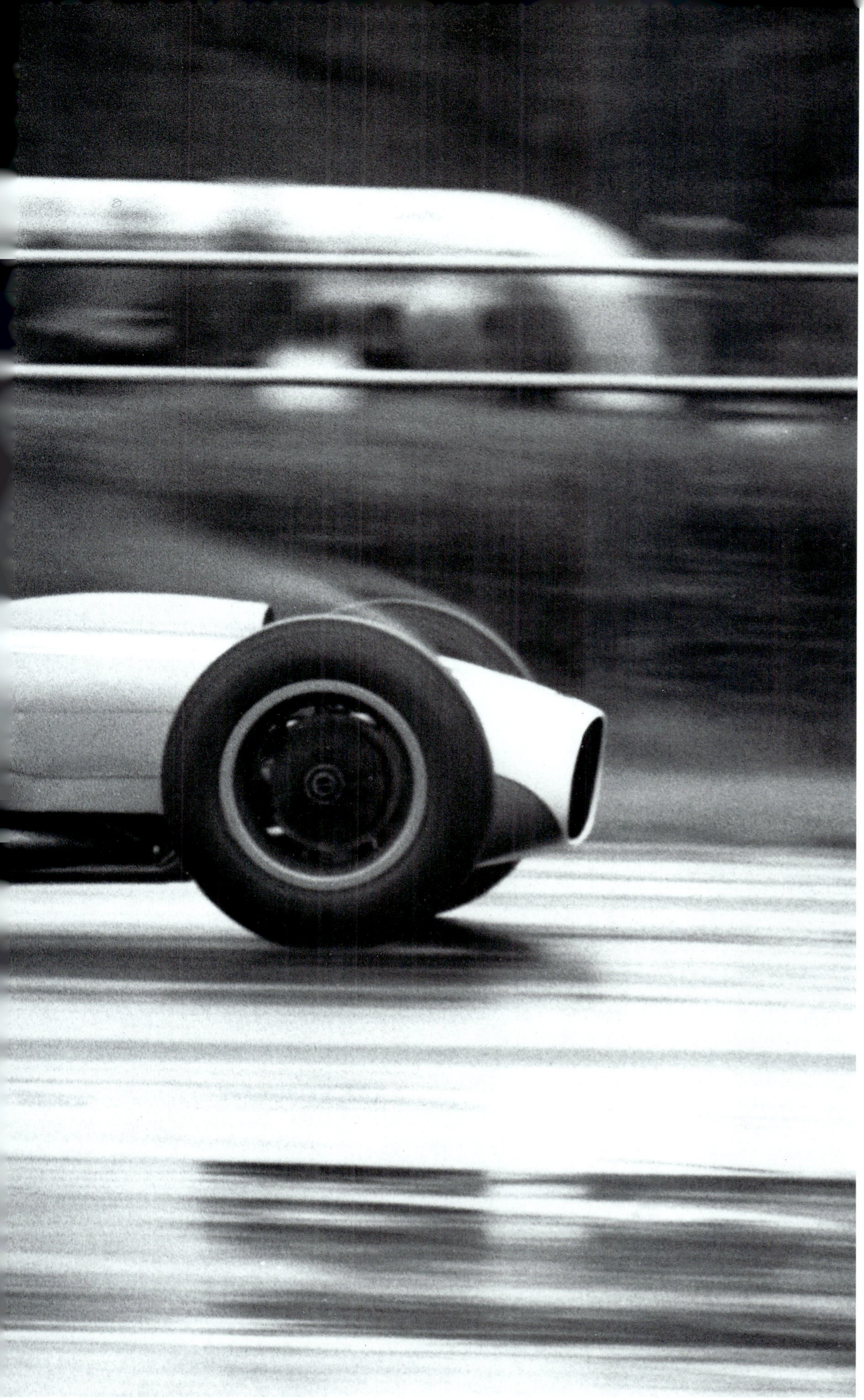

The very underrated and multi-talented Chuck Daigh (29 November 1923 – 29 April 2008), who won the 1959 Sebring 12 Hours and raced a multitude of cars and categories, here at sea in one of Lance Reventlow's Scarabs (01) at the wet Silverstone International Trophy on 6 May 1961. Carroll Shelby was quoted as saying, 'There are only two people I can think of who could sit down, take a welding torch, build their own chassis, go out to test it, and then win races with it. They are Jack Brabham and Chuck Daigh. I put Chuck in the same category as Jack.' He finished a very worthy seventh at Silverstone against the rear-engined machines, the race predictably being won by Stirling Moss who lapped everybody else at least once in his Rob Walker Cooper T53. The race was no less than 80 laps long, three more than the 1960 British Grand Prix here. The Scarab was raced again at Silverstone that year, also in wet conditions, in the British Empire Trophy (8 July), but Daigh crashed the car at this final European appearance.

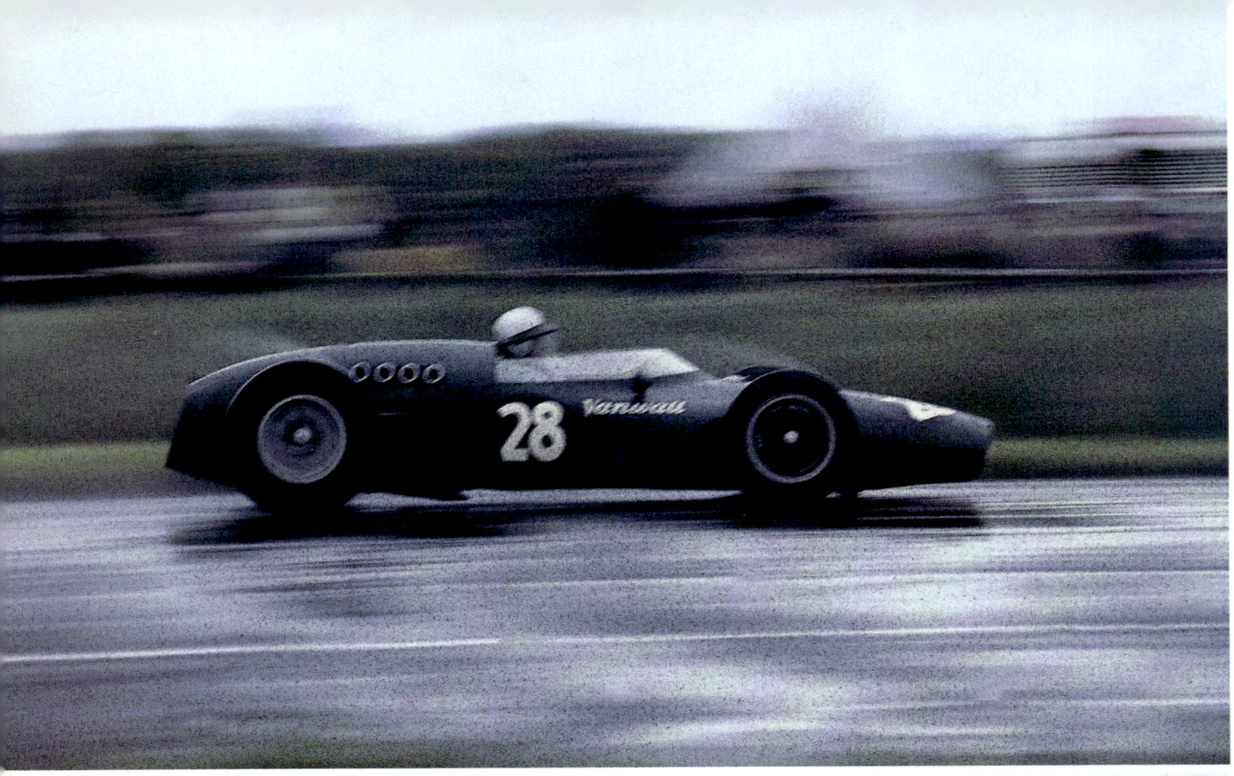
28
Vanwall

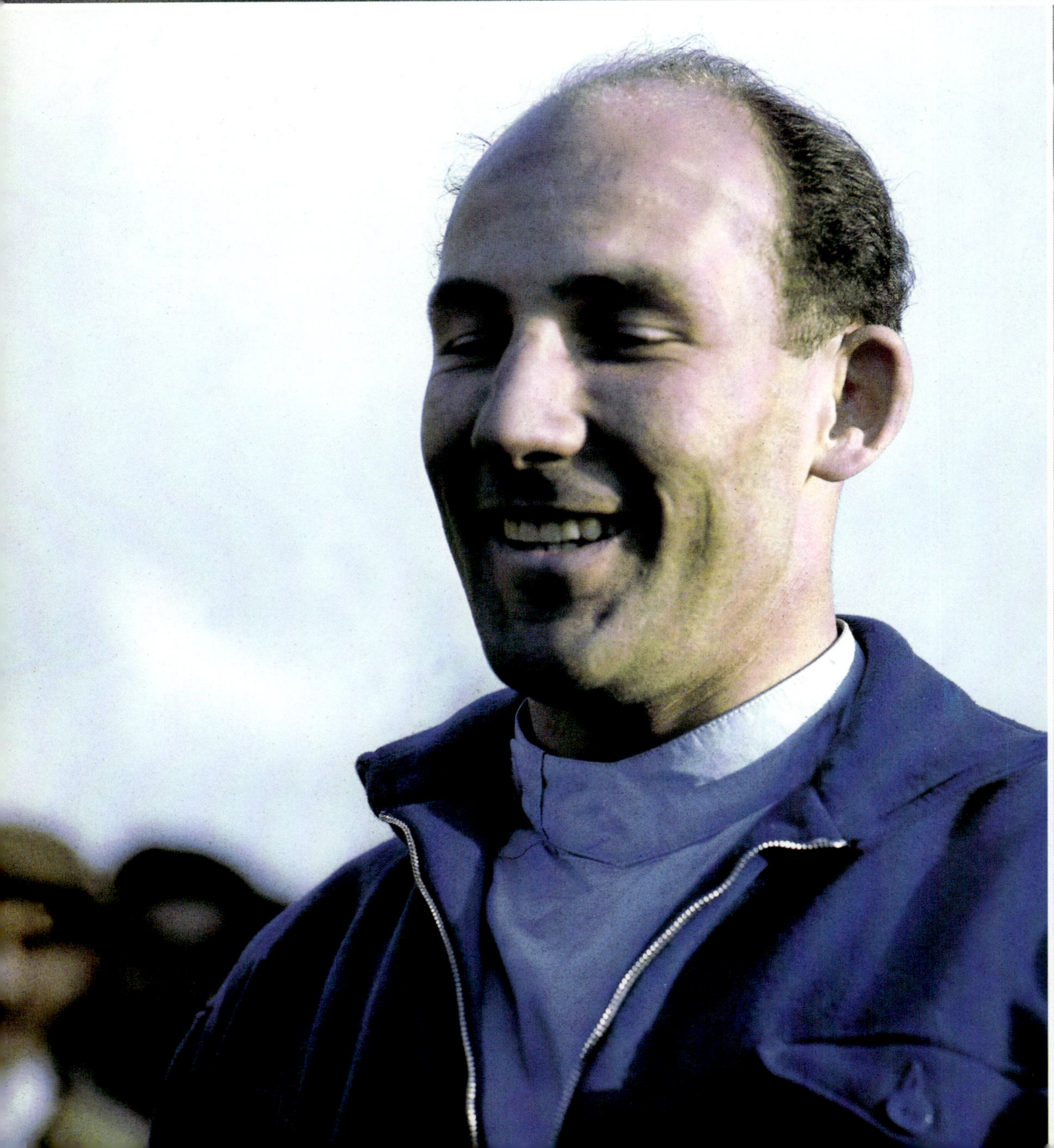

← Dark, wet, and horrible at Silverstone's International Trophy that was run under the short-lived Intercontinental formula, which was supposed to offer an alternative to the new and very unpopular 1.5-litre F1. John Surtees displays the unique rear-engined Vanwall VW14, with its long rear overhang, in which he finished fifth on the car's debut. It was only entered in one more race, the British Empire Trophy, also at Silverstone, but Surtees raced a Yeoman Credit Cooper instead, whilst Jack Brabham practised the Vanwall, setting a respectable time, but did not start. Alas, the failure of the Intercontinental series (five races in total) and economics doomed the VW14 to oblivion.

↙ Stirling Craufurd Moss at Silverstone 1961. Stirling was the place of his mother Aileen's birth, and Craufurd her maiden name.

↓ Another perfect illustration of Jack Brabham's robust driving style in the Cooper-Climax T55 (F1-10-61) during the 1961 Dutch GP. This was the year when the British teams found themselves unprepared and had to manage with Coventry Climax's underpowered four-cylinder FPF that gave at best 145–150bhp – no match for the 180–190bhp V6 Dino Ferraris. Imagine that, a F1 car with hardly more power than a 1980s 16-valve VW Golf GTI! Following his back-to-back World Championships of 1959/60, Brabham's 1961 season was a real let down, and sixth place here and fourth in the British round were his only points-scoring finishes of the year, and the last with Cooper before setting out to create his own team.

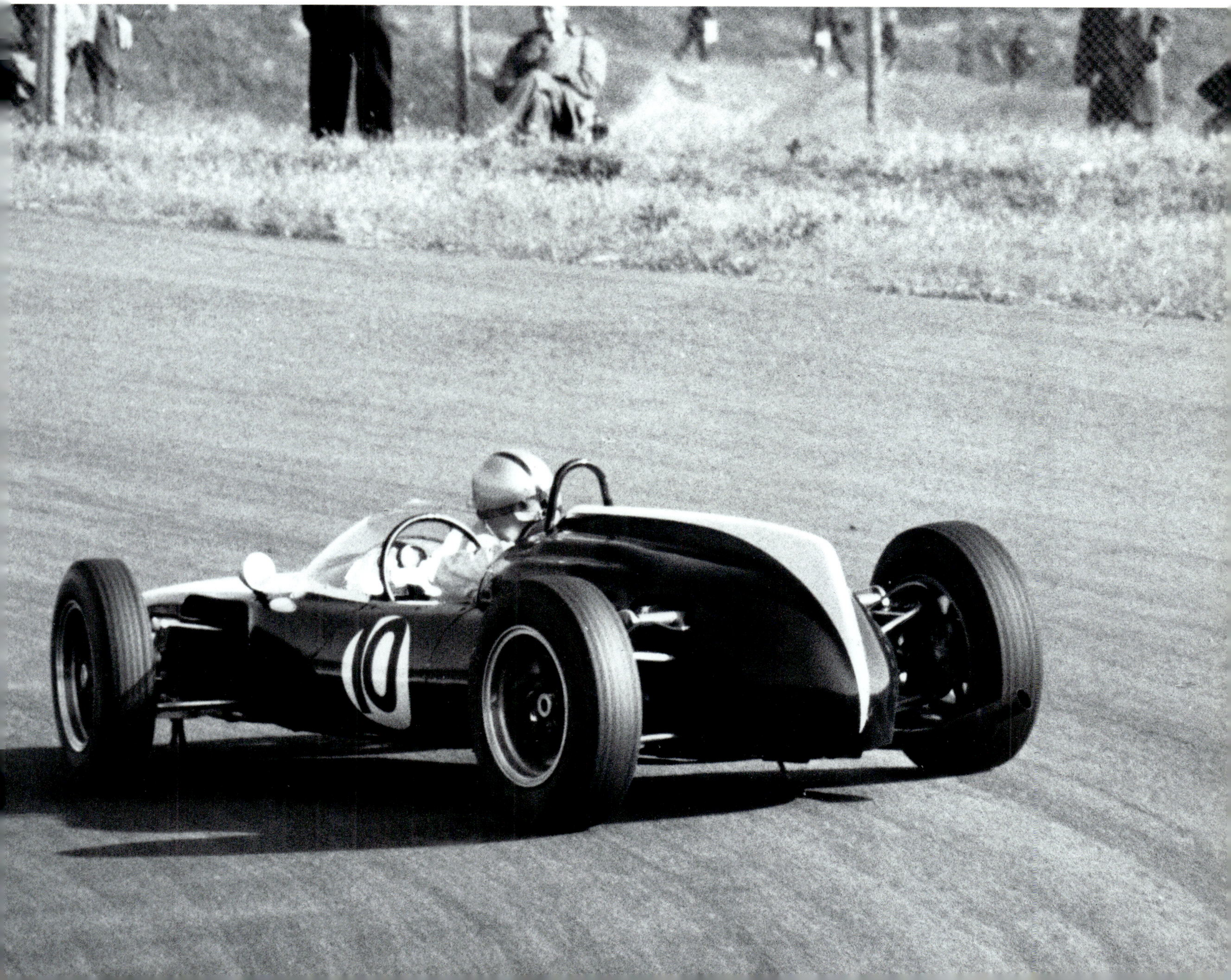

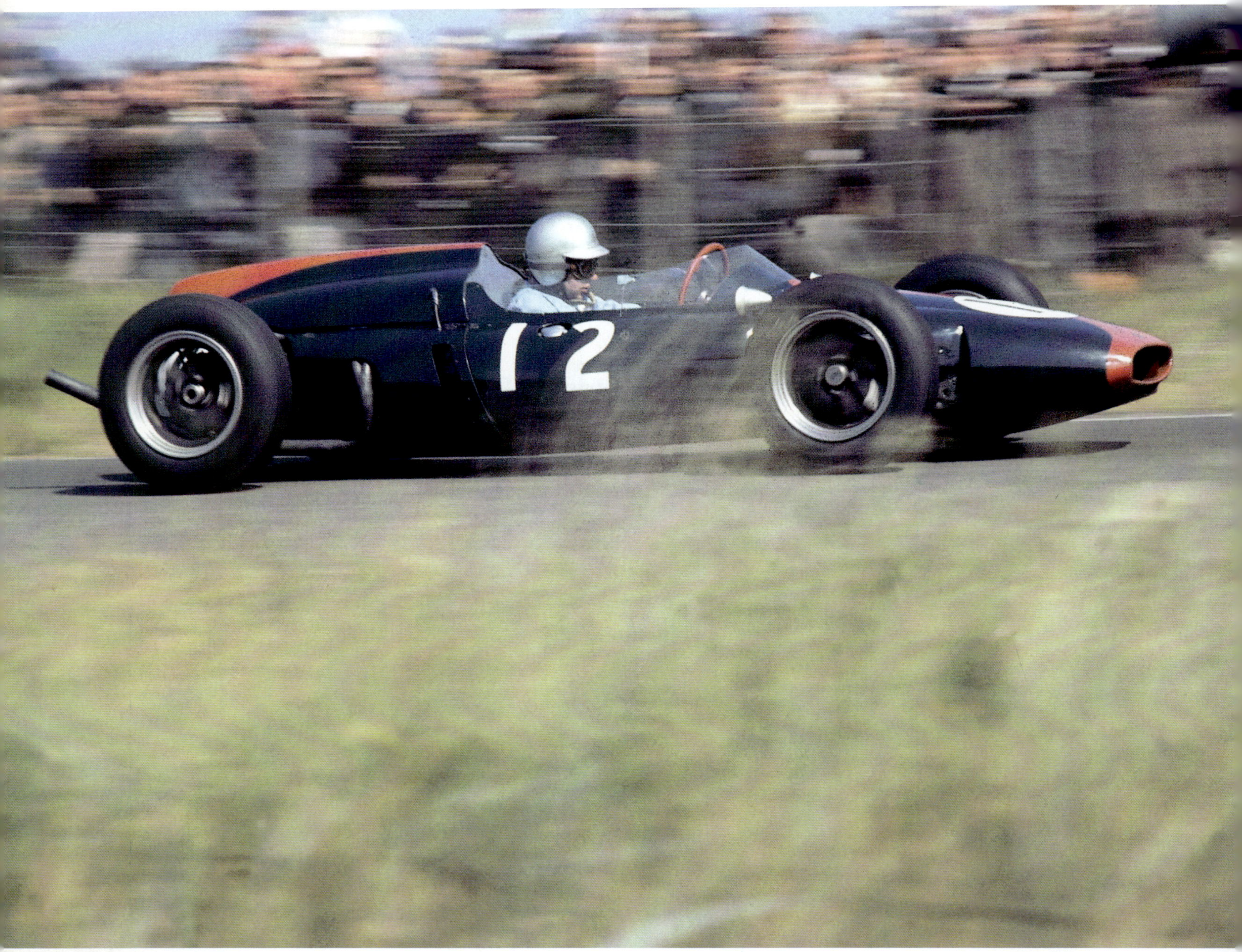

↑ The coastal location of Zandvoort not only featured nearby sand dunes but also the long grasses found in such areas. Mike's picture captures the green stuff as well as John Surtees, head down in the Yeoman Credit Cooper-Climax T53 (F1-4-61) on his way to seventh place. Apparently Yeoman Credit were supposed to have the latest T55 versions for 1961, but never got them.

↗ Look at this, an almost completely unadorned racing car – no stickers, garish colour schemes, names or any other commercial graffiti to spoil the lines, not even a race number on this side. For the record, Phil Hill's Ferrari Dino 156 (02) was No. 1 and he finished second, right behind team-mate Wolfgang von Trips, having spent some of the race battling with Jim Clark's Lotus 21. Perhaps the most notable, and to date unique, feature of this Grand Prix (Dutch 1961) was that every car that started, finished without a single pit stop between them.

→ This is Race 2 for Formula Junior cars at the British Empire Trophy at Silverstone on 8 July 1961, and Peter Arundell winning by nearly a minute in the Team Lotus-Cosworth 20 in his trademark orange helmet ahead of Ken Tyrrell's Cooper-BMC T56 driven by Tony Maggs.

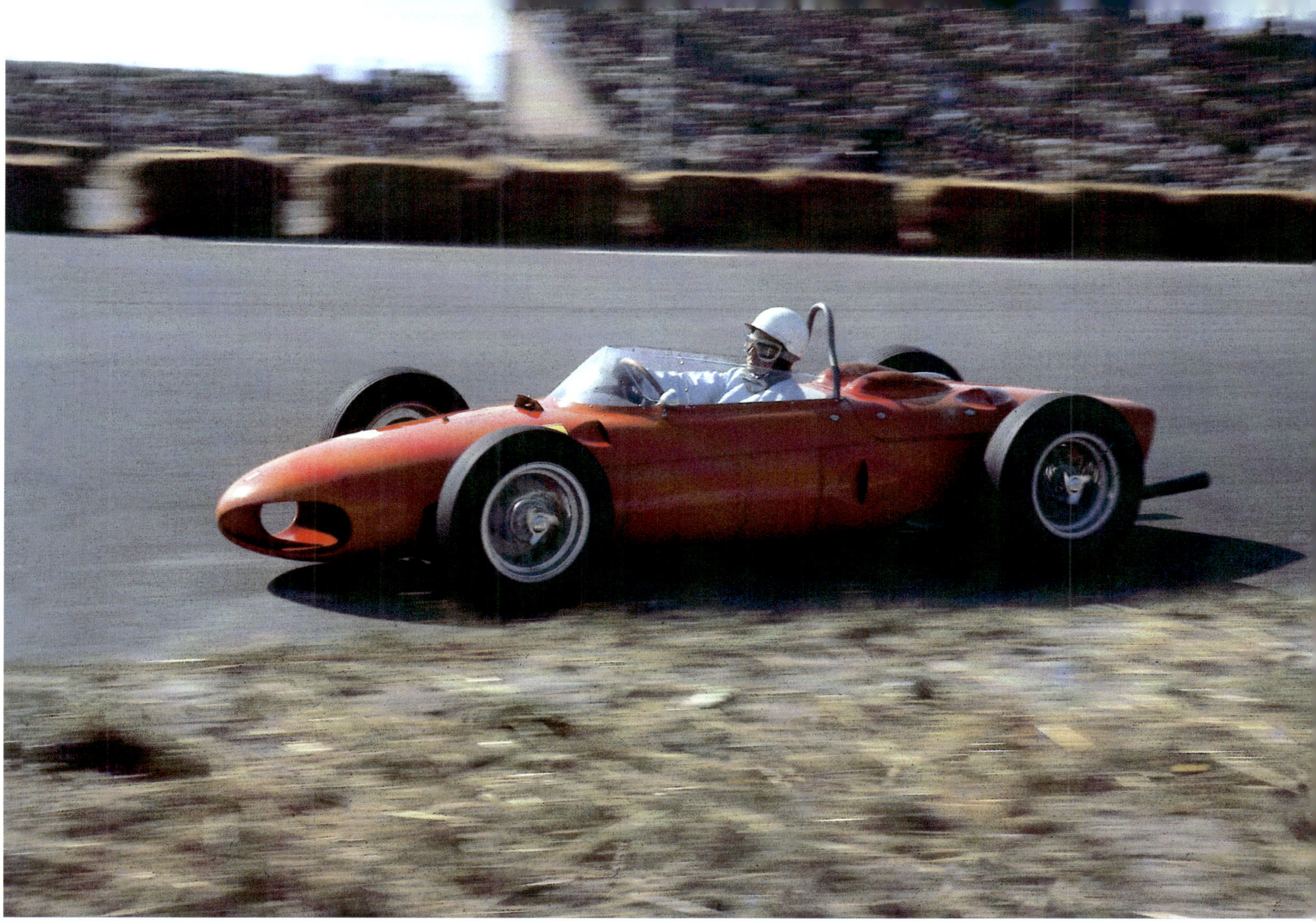

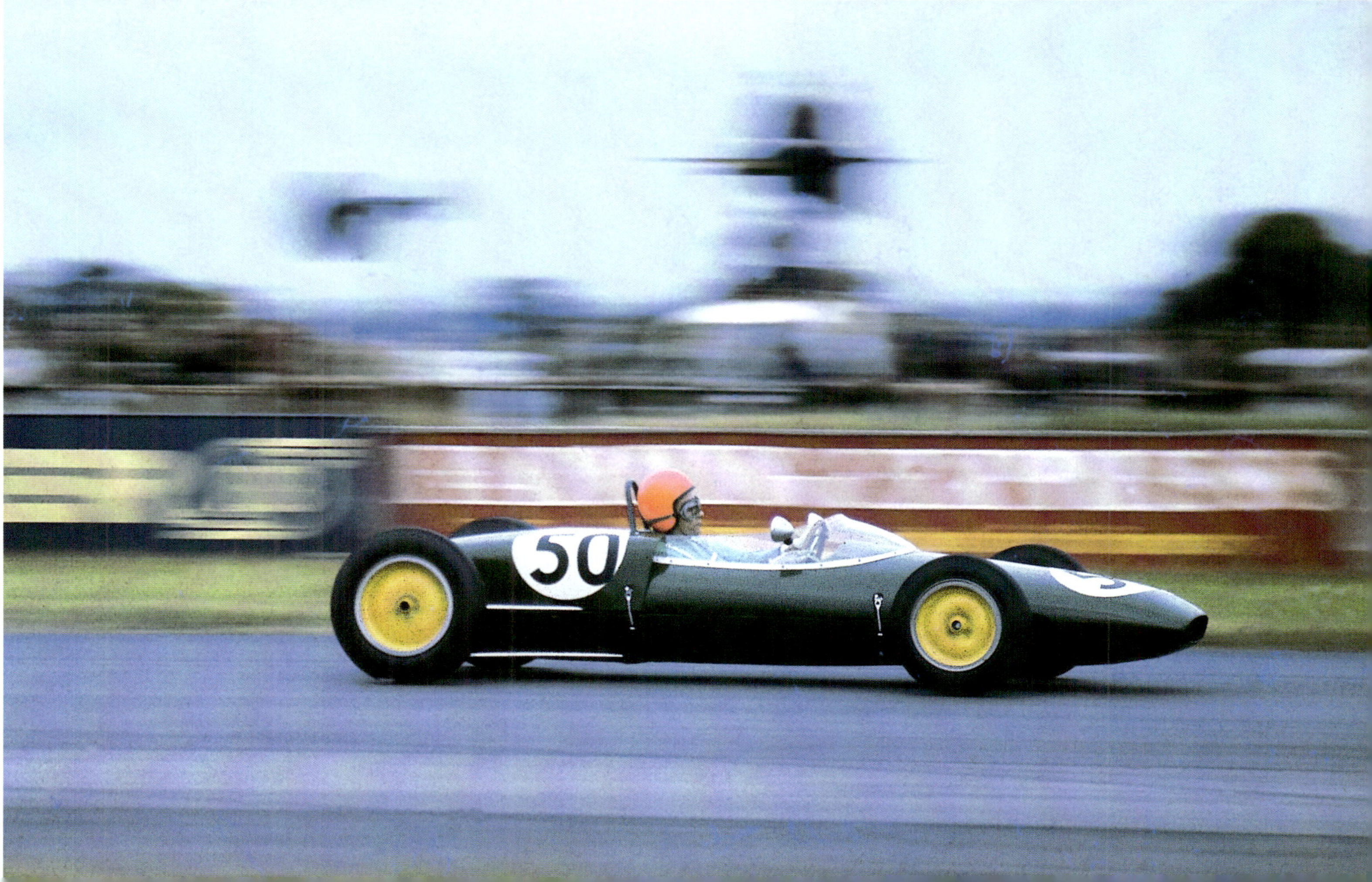
50

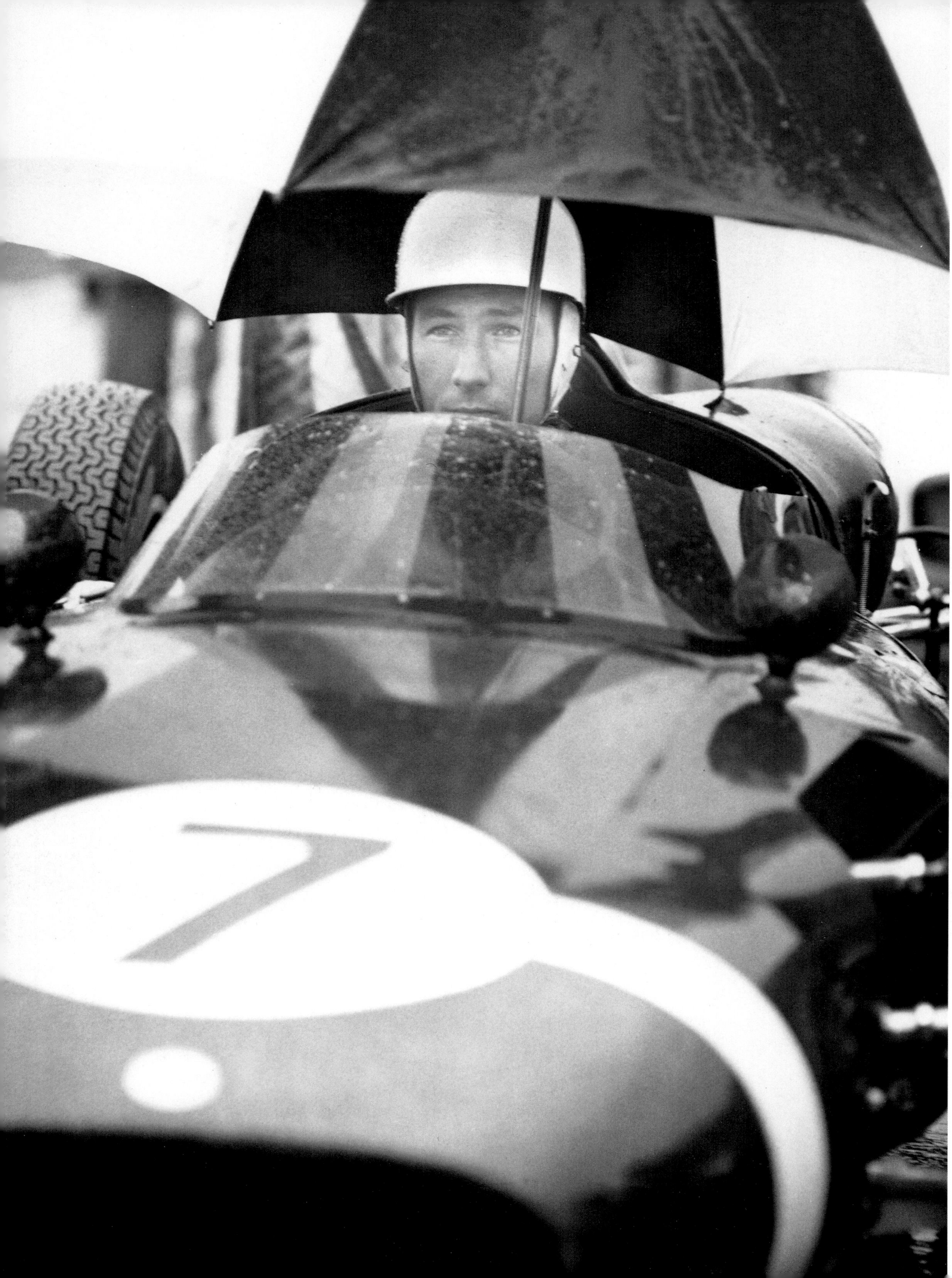

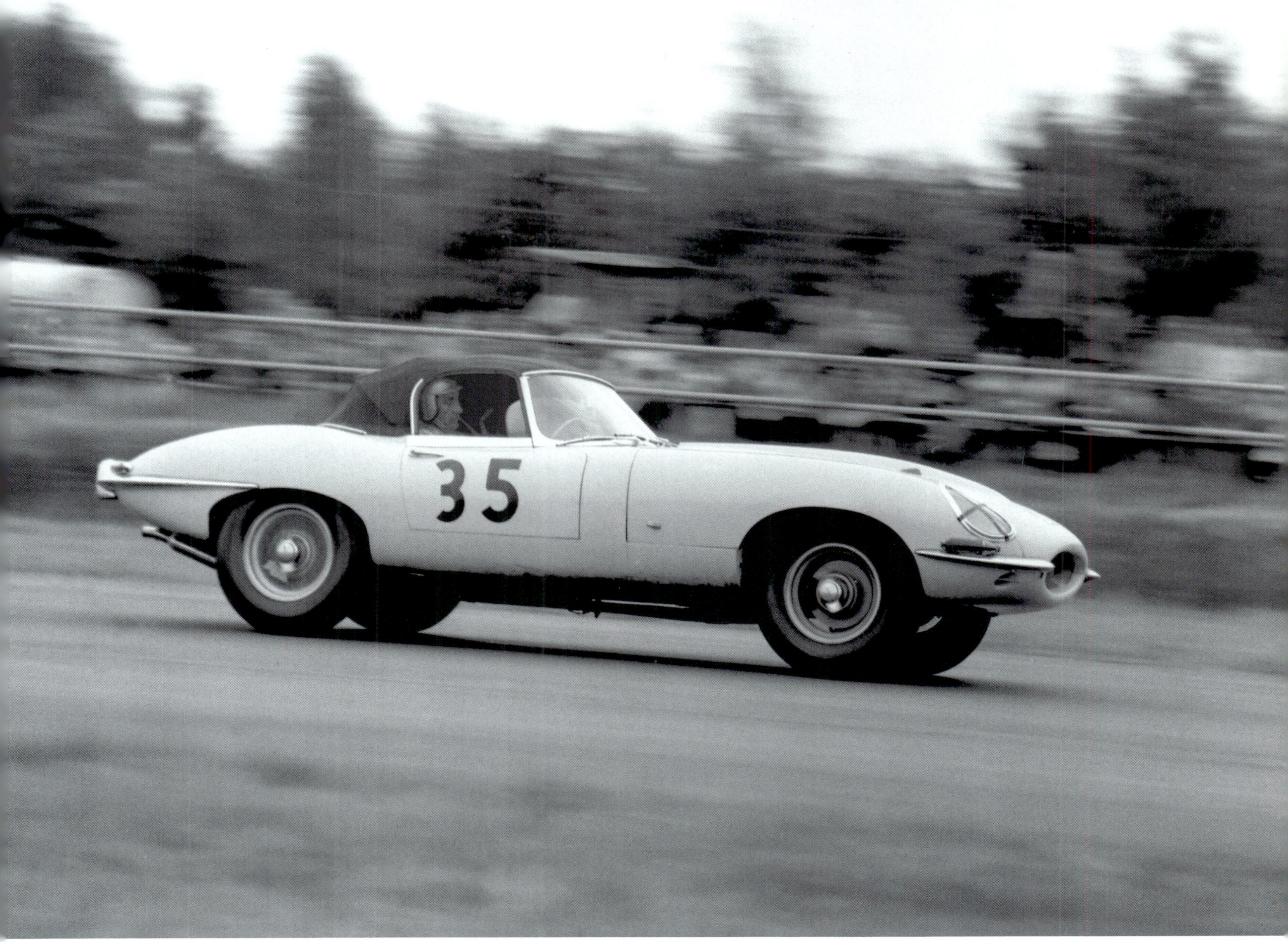

↑ Roy Salvadori in the pearl grey John Coombs Jaguar E-type S850006 at the British Empire Trophy Silverstone 8 July 1961. Front-end lift was a real problem with E-types, and at this embryonic stage it suffered from inadequate brakes, overheating, and other gremlins. In due course BUY 1 ceased to exist, as the car metamorphosed into a proper racer in 1962, now registered 4 WPD, via a thinner gauge steel monocoque after a major shunt at Goodwood, then the fitment of Dunlop cast magnesium alloy D-type pattern wheels, wide angle head engine, and much else. Ultimately it became a true 'lightweight' in 1963, with alloy monocoque and body panels, an aluminium block, and a ZF five-speed gearbox.

← Stirling Moss sits impassively in the Rob Walker Cooper-Climax T53 at Silverstone, wearing No. 7 as ever (even the chassis number F1-7-61 matches). He won the 1961 wet/dry British Empire Trophy by over 50sec from John Surtees in a similar Yeoman Credit Cooper.

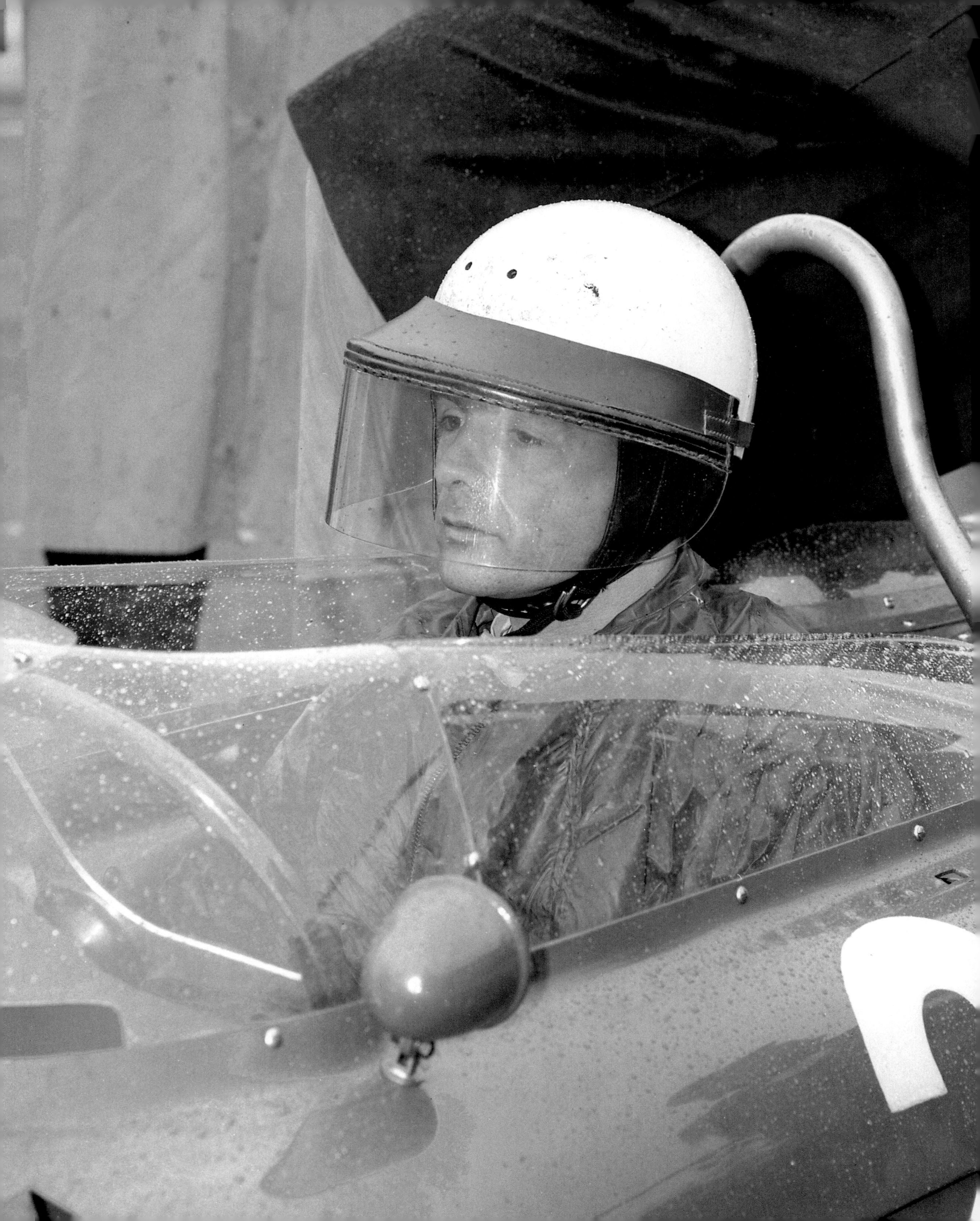

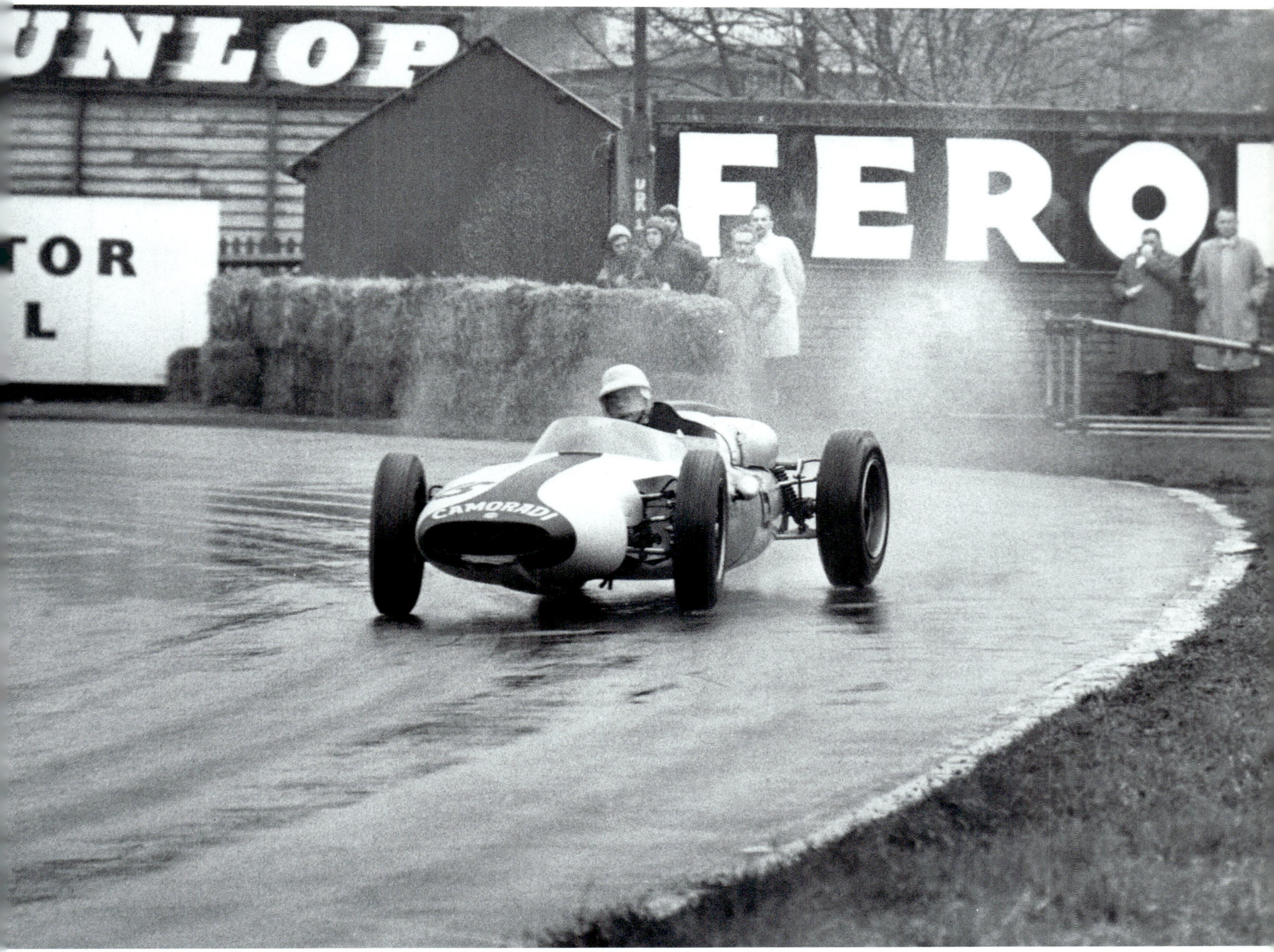

↑ 'Lucky' Casner's Camoradi team were better known for their Maserati Birdcage and Corvette exploits, but they also tried F1 in 1961 with this Cooper Climax T53 (F1-6-61). Having qualified 16th, Camoradi regular Masten Gregory finished 11th three laps down despite trying hard, as is apparent here. For those weened on latter-day F1, with its media dependency and regulatory fascism, it is worth noting that no less than 30 cars started, with the first 19 covered by 3.2sec over a 2min or so lap, not bad by the standards of the day and machinery.

← A tense looking Phil Hill, and well he might be given the miserable wet conditions at Aintree for the British GP. The leather peak and visor were standard wet weather wear for the era, and note that his Bell helmet (recognisable by its almost perfectly round symmetry as compared to the more upright Herbert Johnson hat) has two ventilation holes drilled in it. This was a perfect result for Scuderia Ferrari, with von Trips winning, Hill second, and Richie Ginther third.

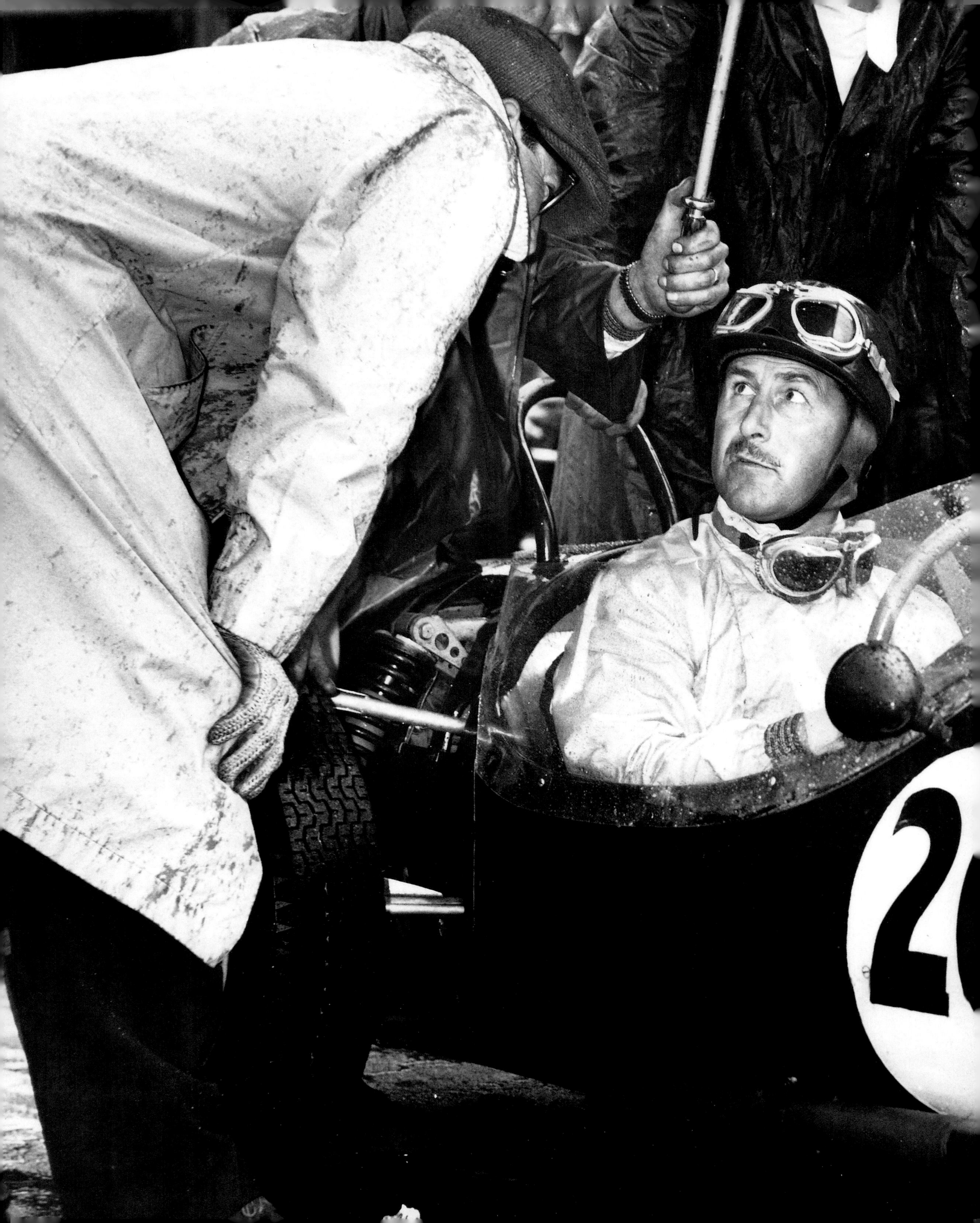

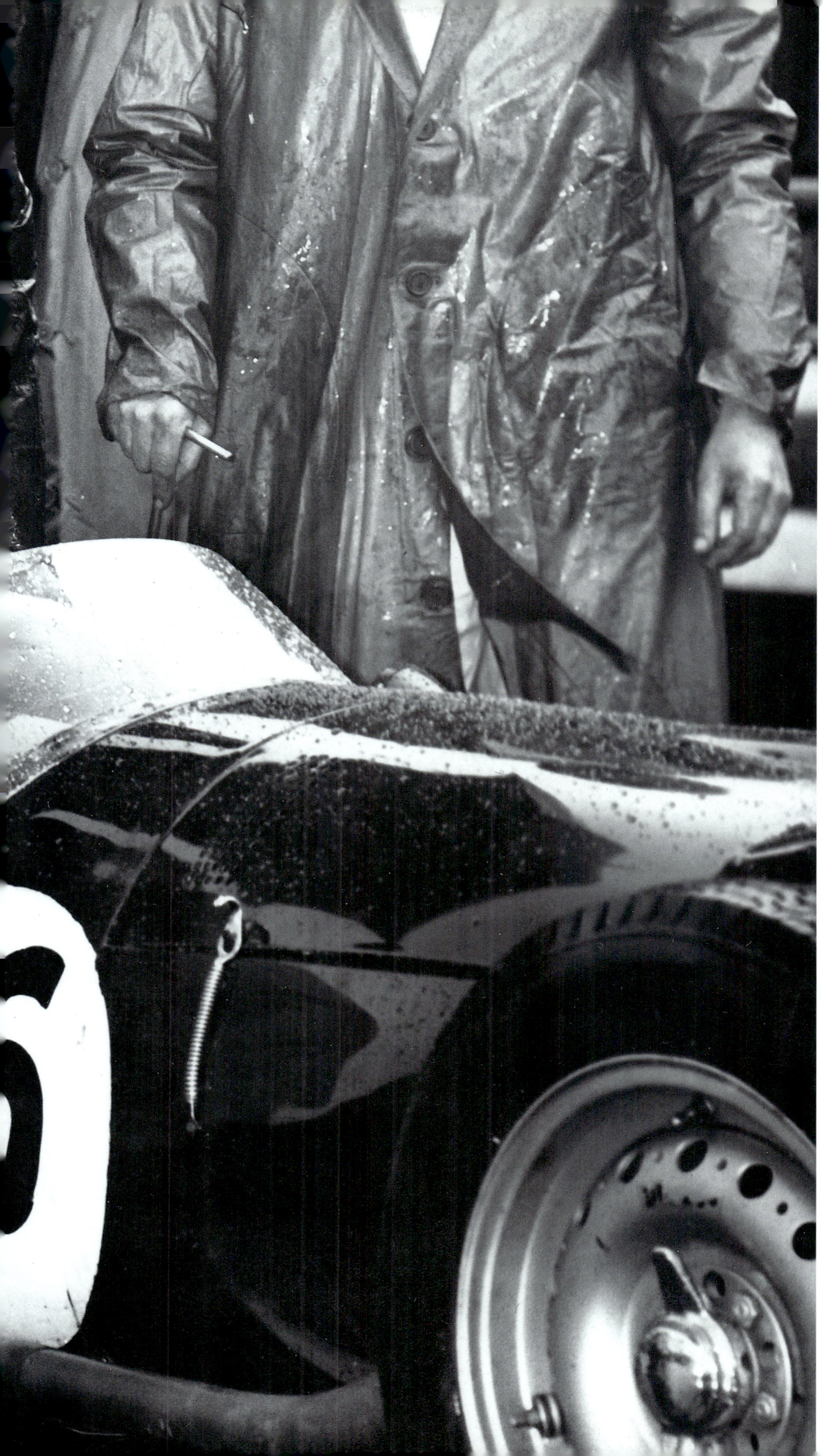

← Jack Fairman (15 March 1913 – 7 February 2002) raced anything and everything he could during the 1940s, '50s, and early '60s, including Ecurie Ecosse and works Jaguars, Bristols, and Aston Martins, the latter during 1959 with Stirling Moss. This pairing gave Jack perhaps his most impressive result when, mainly thanks to Stirling, they won the Nürburgring 1,000km despite Jack having had to extricate the Aston from a ditch during his stint. In single-seaters he drove for HWM, Connaught, BRM, Cooper, Tommy Atkins, Bernie Ecclestone, Fred Tuck, and here for Rob Walker in the unique Ferguson P99 4WD in the 1961 British GP at Aintree. Jack talks to Alfred Moss, but after Moss's Walker Lotus retired Stirling took over the Ferguson only to be disqualified for a push start. Fairman's career began in 1934 in trials events, moving on to Brooklands until the intervention of the Second World War, which he spent in the Tank Corps, and finally ended at the 1963 non-Championship City of Imola Grand Prix, driving a Porsche for Carel de Beaufort's Ecurie Maarsbergen team, where he finished seventh. A now almost forgotten episode was the abortive attempt to qualify the de Villiers Special (aka Connaught C-type C8 in supercharged form) entered by Pierre de Villiers of Santa Monica for the 1962 Indianapolis 500. In a final surprising nod to fame, bar chain Wetherspoons opened a pub named 'The Jack Fairman' on 12 February 2007 on the site of Fairman's former garage in Horley, Surrey.

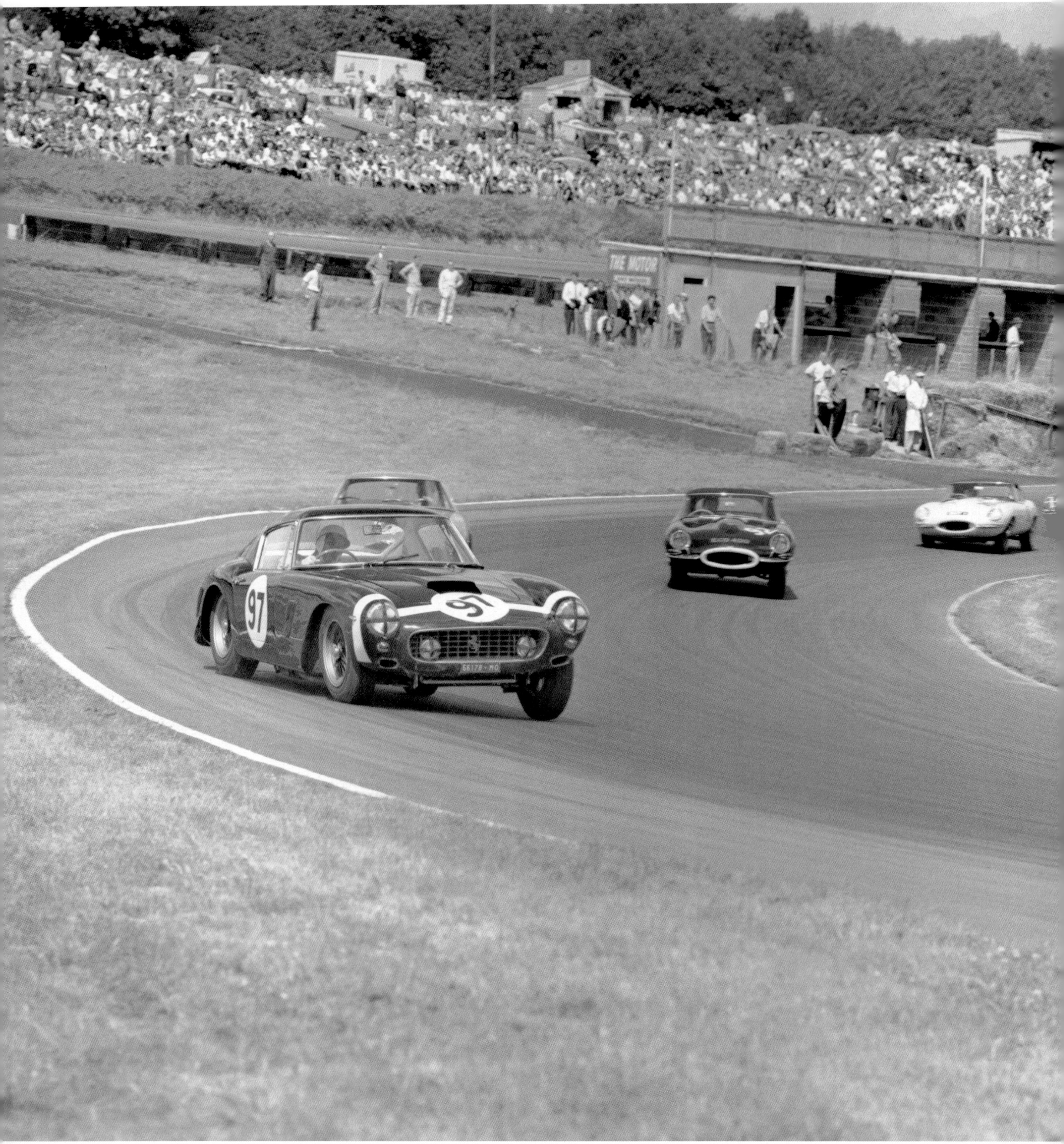
THE MOTOR
97

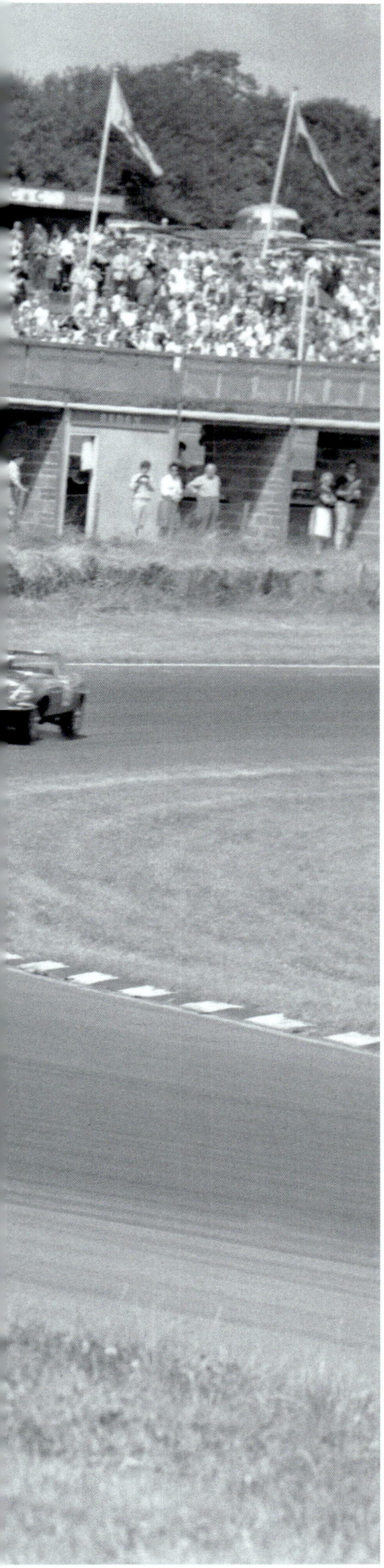

← The Peco GT Trophy at Brands Hatch on August Bank Holiday Monday (7 August 1961) and the Ferraris and Jaguars, especially Roy Salvadori in the Coombs E-type (S850006), fourth in picture, show a considerable amount of body roll. Leading is Stirling Moss in the Rob Walker/Dick Wilkins Ferrari 250GT SWB (2735 GT) who won ahead of the similar but lhd Maranello Concessionaires 2417 GT of Mike Parkes, followed by Graham Hill in the Equipe Endeavour Jaguar E-type (S850005) both of whom retired, then Salvadori who ultimately finished third after spinning at Druids, and Bruce McLaren in Peter Berry's E-type (S850010) that finished second. Note the differing lines and the front offside wheel camber of the Moss Ferrari.

↓ The Duke and Duchess of Kent arrive in remarkably low-key style at Goodwood, probably for the 1961 Tourist Trophy. Today any such Royal attendance at a public event would excite media and public hysteria. Note the Antone public address van, the providers of Tannoy systems for many motor racing/horse racing venues of the time, and the very new and shiny Jaguar Mk2, probably a 3.8 version, in bright red with black or beige leather, chrome wire wheels, and o/d, very much the vehicle of choice for those who wanted a high-performance, four-door, four-seater at the time.

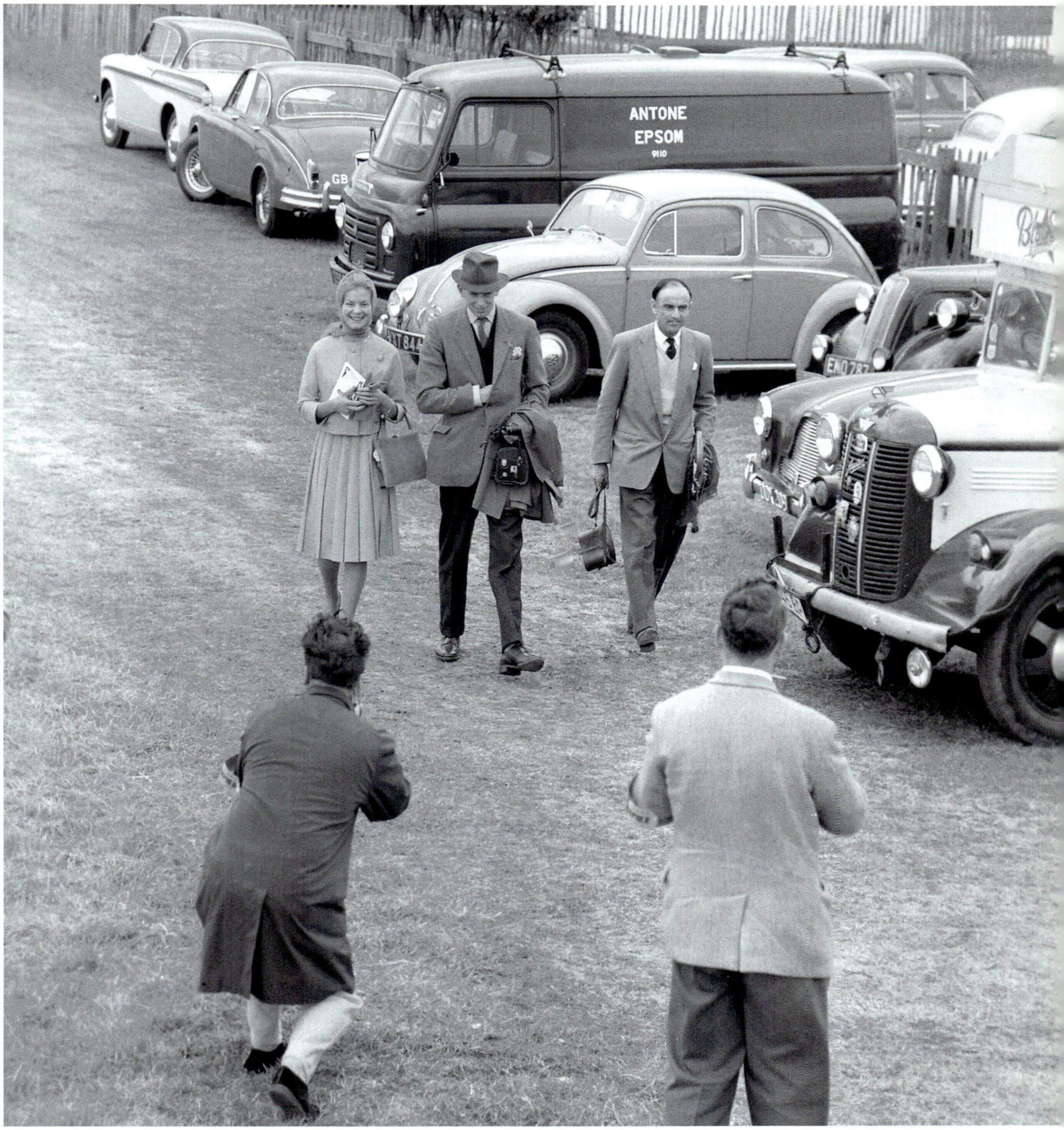

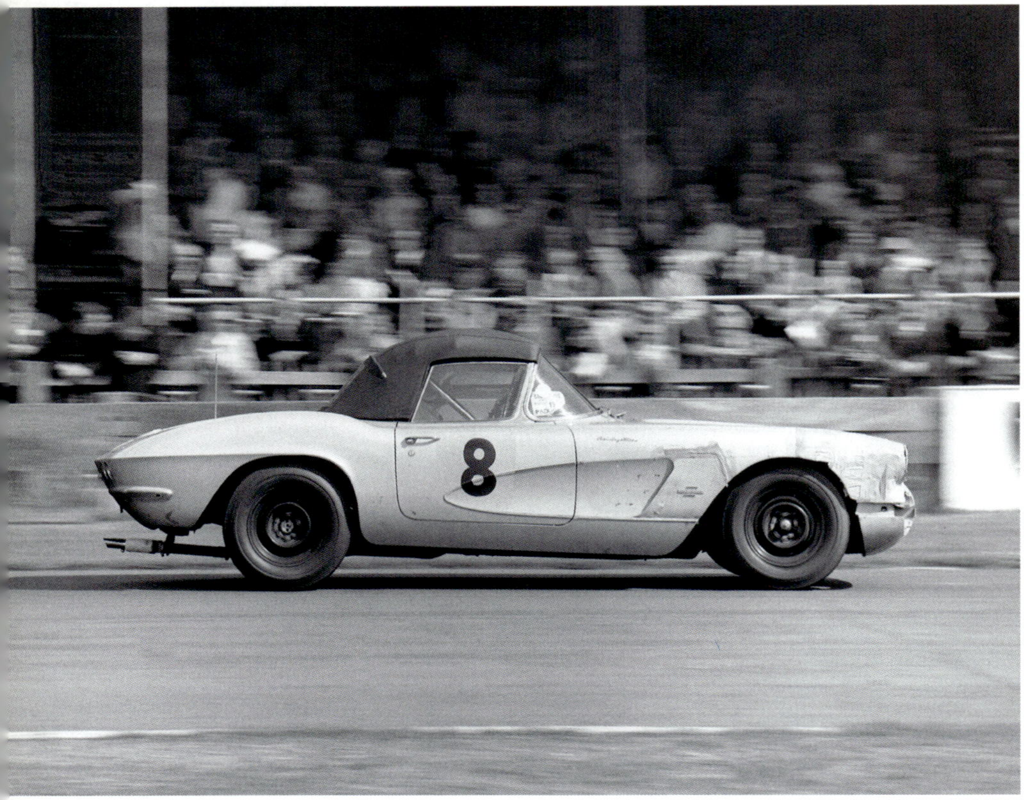

The 1961 Tourist Trophy was dominated by the Ferrari 250GT SWBs of Stirling Moss and Mike Parkes, followed at a distance by the John Ogier Aston Martins, with no Jaguar E-types attending. So this left just one other over 2000cc GT car, the Alan Markelson Chevrolet Corvette that ran unevenly and rumbled around at the back of the field for 42 laps before retiring with engine problems. Pity. The slightly tatty looking car with its steel wheels and interior roll cage brakes for the chicane in front of a typically large Goodwood crowd.

Yes the Goodwood chicane really was built of bricks, at least in part. Mike Parkes in the ex-works Maranello Concessionaires lhd Ferrari 250GT SWB (2417 GT) leads Stirling Moss by a lap after Parkes was further delayed by a loose undertray. The dreaded wattle fencing panels were still in use and if you drifted wide here they frequently became wrapped around your wheels and axles or trapped under the car. Note the large cantilever crane and camera at Woodcote and the light breeze disturbing the flags on this sunny August day nearly 48 years ago.

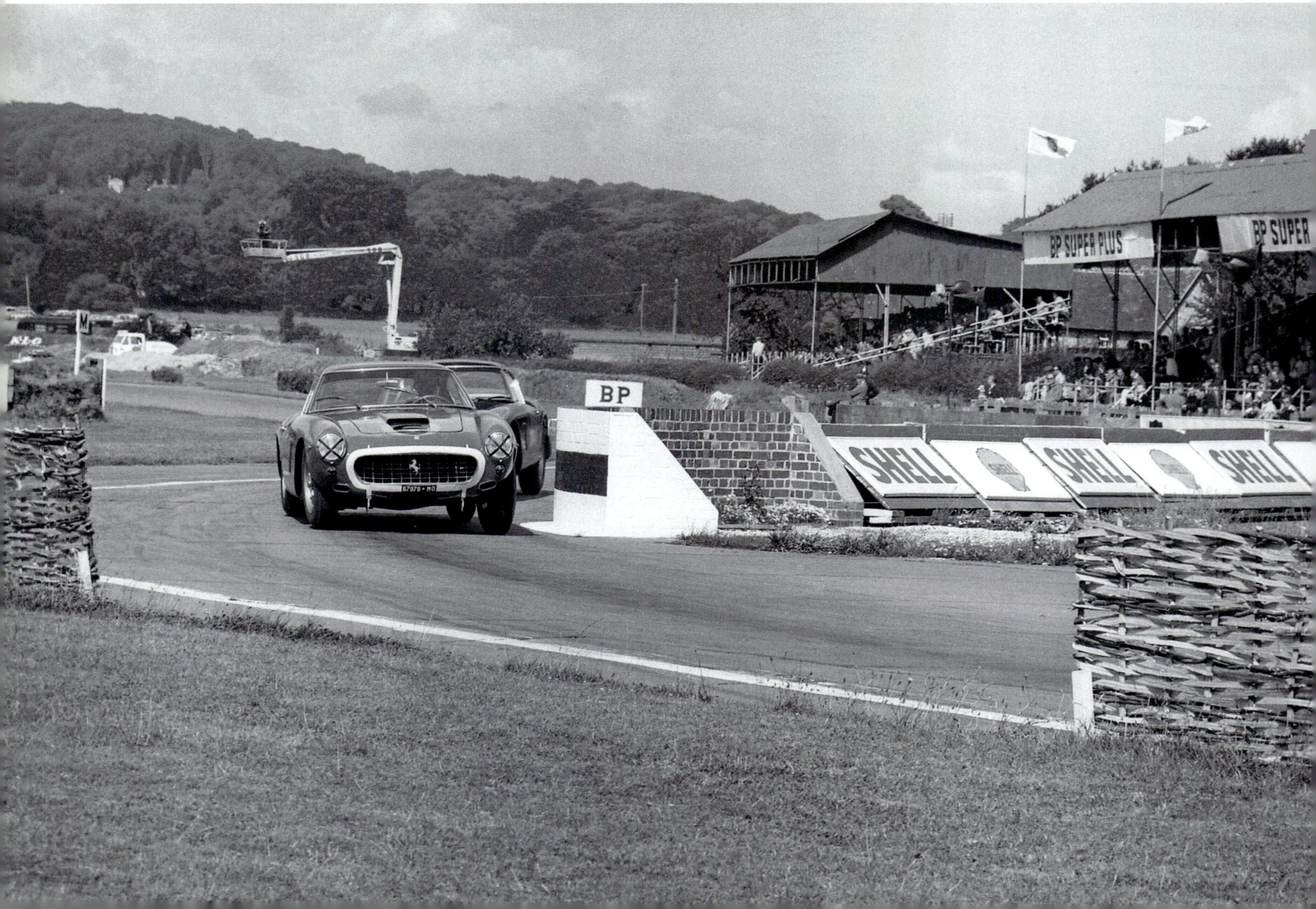

Michael Turner

I can't remember exactly where or when I first met Mike: it would have been at a motor race meeting, and probably Goodwood or Oulton Park in the late 1950s.

Working with a track pass at circuits in the UK, there was often time between races to strike up a conversation with those around, and, in spite of the differences in height and temperament, we quickly discovered a shared sense of humour, no doubt seen by some as childish, or at least somewhat obscure. However, we obviously got on well and enjoyed each other's company, often travelling to events in convoy at high speed, Mike in his Ford Cortina and Helen and I in my SS100 Jaguar.

I got to know most of the regular picture snappers, sharing as I did their 'modus operandi' (Mike would have seized on that sort of terminology, and we would soon have been convulsed in waves of laughter as a theme developed), and I often travelled to European events with Geoff Goddard, who was substantial and, on the surface, belligerent by nature.

It was not long before Mike joined us on trips to share expenses, and Geoff seemed happy to tolerate us most of the time. We usually had to leave promptly at the finish of a Grand Prix to get to the nearest ferry terminal and catch the evening boat home – the others having films to develop and print for magazine deadlines.

On one occasion, Mike and I were sharing the back seat because Maurice Rowe was with us and sat at the front. We had left Rouen and were making good time on a long straight stretch of undulating French road, and Mike realised that by bouncing gently up and down in harmony with the undulations in the road, we could maximise the reaction of the car's suspension movement. This was very effective, and Geoff commented to Maurice on the behaviour of the car, but it was not long before he realised what was causing it. 'All right, children,' he growled, 'jack it in – you've had your little joke', or words to that effect, and we pressed on for the coast with suppressed giggles coming from the back.

Mike hated pomposity, and wasted no time in pricking inflated egos with an appropriate comment, and could be disarmingly direct. He also took some mischievous pleasure in causing me embarrassment if an opportunity presented itself in company, but such moves were usually countered swiftly and turned into a joke. There was one occasion, however, when he overstepped the mark.

I was on friendly terms with General Motors Styling in Detroit, and their deputy head, Chuck Jordan, had come over to Opel in Germany for a spell. Chuck was a keen Formula 1 fan, and I had arranged a visit to the Opel Styling Department for Eoin Young, Mike and myself en route to the German Grand Prix.

The trip got off on the wrong foot when I missed final check-in at Heathrow, and watched the plane take off for Cologne with Eoin and Mike on board. Arriving by the next available flight and reaching Russelsheim in time for after-lunch coffee was embarrassing, but Chuck had loaned me a car for the weekend, and we set off for the Nürburgring with me driving.

As we toured an unfamiliar village looking for our digs, Eoin suddenly reached forward from the back seat and put his hands over my eyes, and Mike's foot stamped on the accelerator. The incident was momentary, but my reaction to this as stupid and irresponsible behaviour was greeted with gales of laughter, which rather set the tone for the weekend.

However, all went well until we left the circuit some time after the finish of the Grand Prix, and joined a traffic queue, which hardly moved. It got dark, and we were getting hungry, tired, and frustrated by the delay. Without warning, Mike reached over and sounded a long blast on the horn, which was pointless and merely irritating for the car in front. I asked him not to do it again, whereupon he launched into a series of random attacks on the horn button. I finally snapped, and lashed out with my fist, catching Mike full in the mouth. As the blood started to trickle down his face a look of astonishment came over him, and he subsided into silent bewilderment that I had actually struck him. We eventually reached a local inn in a subdued mood, but during our meal the frosty silence gradually gave way to normality, and bonhomie won through. Mike never quite forgot the incident, but neither did he push his luck that far again!

In 1962, Mike travelled to Aintree with Helen and I in our Austin Countryman. Arriving in Liverpool after dark with nowhere to stay – not even the Adelphi – we parked by a bus shelter on the prom' at Southsea. It was cramped in the back for two, even with the seats down, and Mike gallantly, if somewhat reluctantly, agreed to sleep on a bench in the shelter. A tap on the misted-up window by a passing Bobby woke us as dawn was breaking, and, satisfied that all was well, he asked about the vagrant in the shelter. This was no time to play jokes, so we admitted that he was with us.

Working weekends away could be, like show biz, periods of absorbing activity interspersed with tedious hanging about, but, with Mike around, there was seldom a dull moment. He did, however, take his work seriously, and was always keen to look for a different angle or location, an objective we shared, going to considerable lengths to find fresh inspiration.

Mike was motivated by his enthusiasm to record on film the excitement of motor sport – an honest and dedicated professional who also had time to enjoy life.

1962-1964

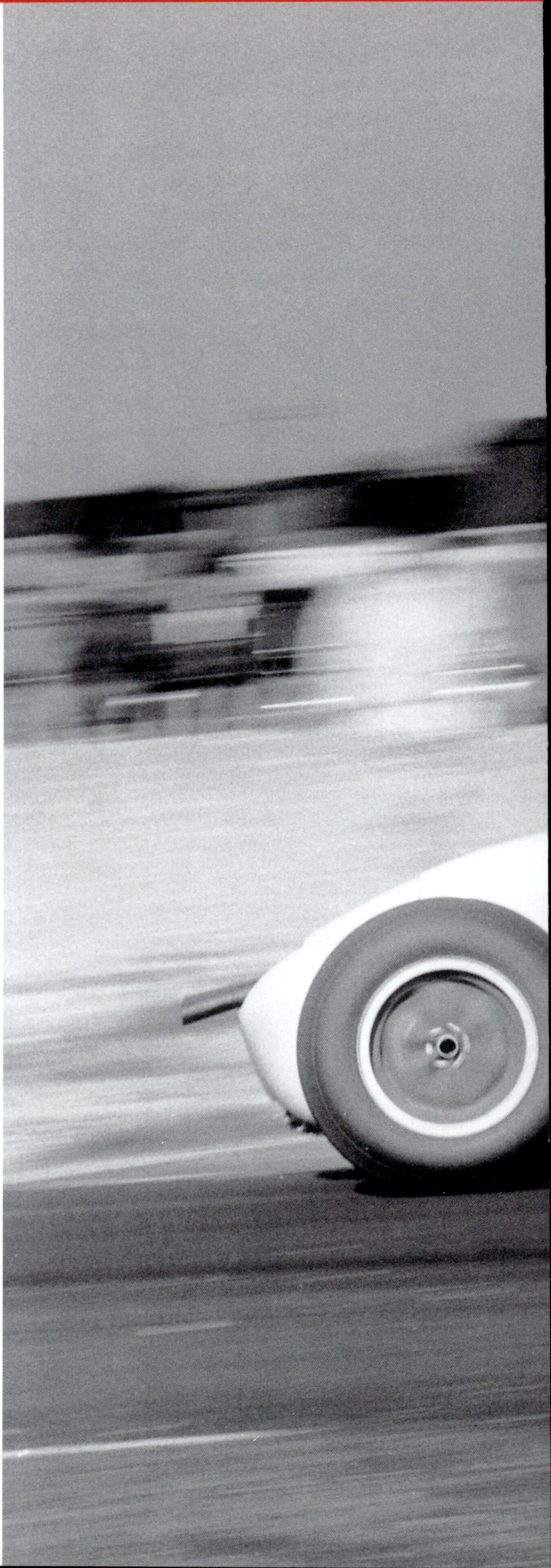

This time in contemporary terms represented a change in the driver status quo and could be realistically described as the post-Moss era following his career-ending Goodwood smash.

Jim Clark assumed Stirling's mantle, his dominance further enhanced by Chapman's masterpiece, the monocoque Lotus 25. However, had John Surtees (Lola) and Dan Gurney (Porsche) enjoyed machinery with equal potential in 1962 then Clark's ascendancy would have been less complete. In fact it was Graham Hill who mounted the most consistent challenge to the Scotsman, BRM under Tony Rudd combining with Hill's extreme determination (and Lotus unreliability) resulted in the team winning the Constructors' title and Graham his first World Championship.

With only sporadic Aston Martin, Jaguar and Maserati opposition the prototype and GT championships were Ferrari's absolute domain in the bigger class whilst Porsche, now free of F1 were runners up in the overall points table with their assorted machinery.

The following year was an almost complete Team Lotus/Clark benefit with everybody else left trailing as the pairing won 7 out of 10 Grands Prix. This left Graham Hill to win at Monaco and Watkins Glen and Surtees at the Nürburgring.

Ferrari however continued their prototype and GT dominance despite Aston Martin's last fling, the fast but fragile Project 215 and 214 devices. Carroll Shelby's Cobra was to prove a serious threat in due course and Jaguar joined in with their new 'lightweight' E-type which showed promise in British events, but ultimately proved disappointing. A one off factory 'low drag' E-type was built but never raced until it was sold to well known privateer Dick Protheroe who trounced the Ferrari GTOs at Reims, but this was a rare result.

Despite inconclusive results at its 1963 Silverstone debut and later at Le Mans, Eric Broadley's Lola Mk6 GT was probably the most significant new competition car of the year, as it was to be the basis of Ford's new GT40.

1964 proved to be a quixotic season with the World Championship finally falling to John Surtees and Ferrari in the last round at Mexico, a result that the Scuderia were not to repeat for another 11 years.

En route Honda made its F1 debut and Dan Gurney lost the extraordinary Belgian GP but won the French GP and then retired in Mexico whilst leading, but only after Clark, who would have been champion otherwise, retired on the last lap! Winner at Monaco and Watkins Glen again, Graham Hill was on his way to the title until Bandini's Ferrari punted him off in Mexico, leaving Surtees as the eventual beneficiary.

Ferrari also cleaned up in the sports car/GT stakes, the new Ford GT40 proving very fast but equally unreliable whilst the evergreen 250GTOs continued winning although outpaced at Spa and Le Mans by the new Daytona Cobra coupés that won the GT class at the Sarthe.

By now the advent of wider tyres/rims/accompanying increased grip was beginning to influence chassis and especially brake design, and before long the elegant, almost graceful look of many racing cars would soon evolve into something more aggressive and more substantial.

Mike's activities for the year had also included the Monte Carlo Rally and the British motor sport cavalcade at the Lord Mayor's Show.

This is Snetterton on 14 April 1962, and Stirling Moss is just nine days away from his career-ending crash at Goodwood in this car. The UDT Laystall Lotus is actually Rob Walker's hybrid 18/21 (906) repainted in UDT's pale green colours that had first appeared at the Grand Prix de Bruxelles 13 days previously. Stirling started from pole and went even faster in the race, but was delayed by throttle problems and finished seventh, five laps adrift in a race won by Jim Clark's Lotus 24 from Graham Hill in the BRM P578, setting a precedent for the year. Mike has captured the perfectly composed, flowing Moss driving style, Herbert Johnson helmet just tilted over in the familiar relaxed manner, the whole thing apparently so natural, so easy, so smooth.

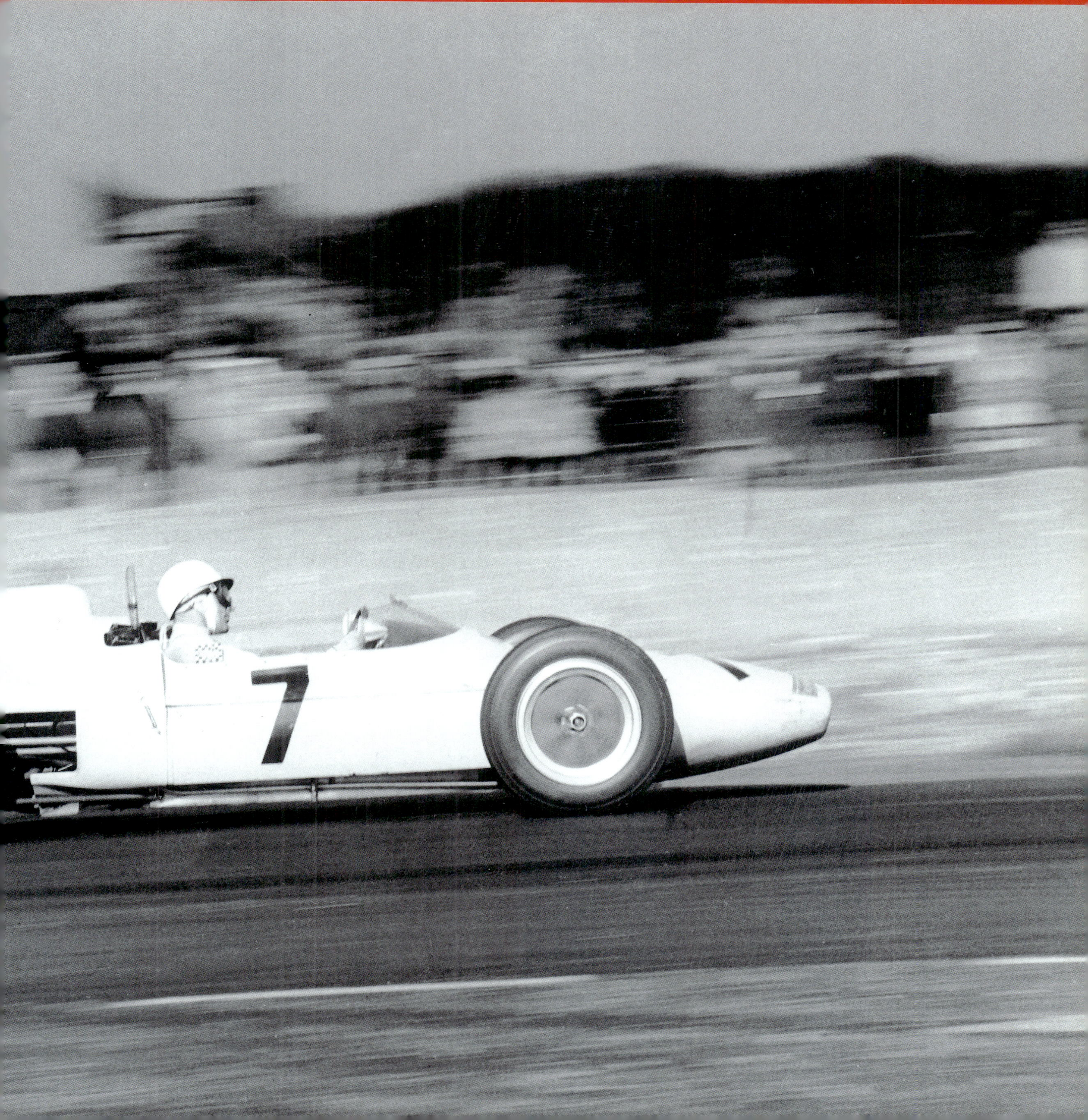

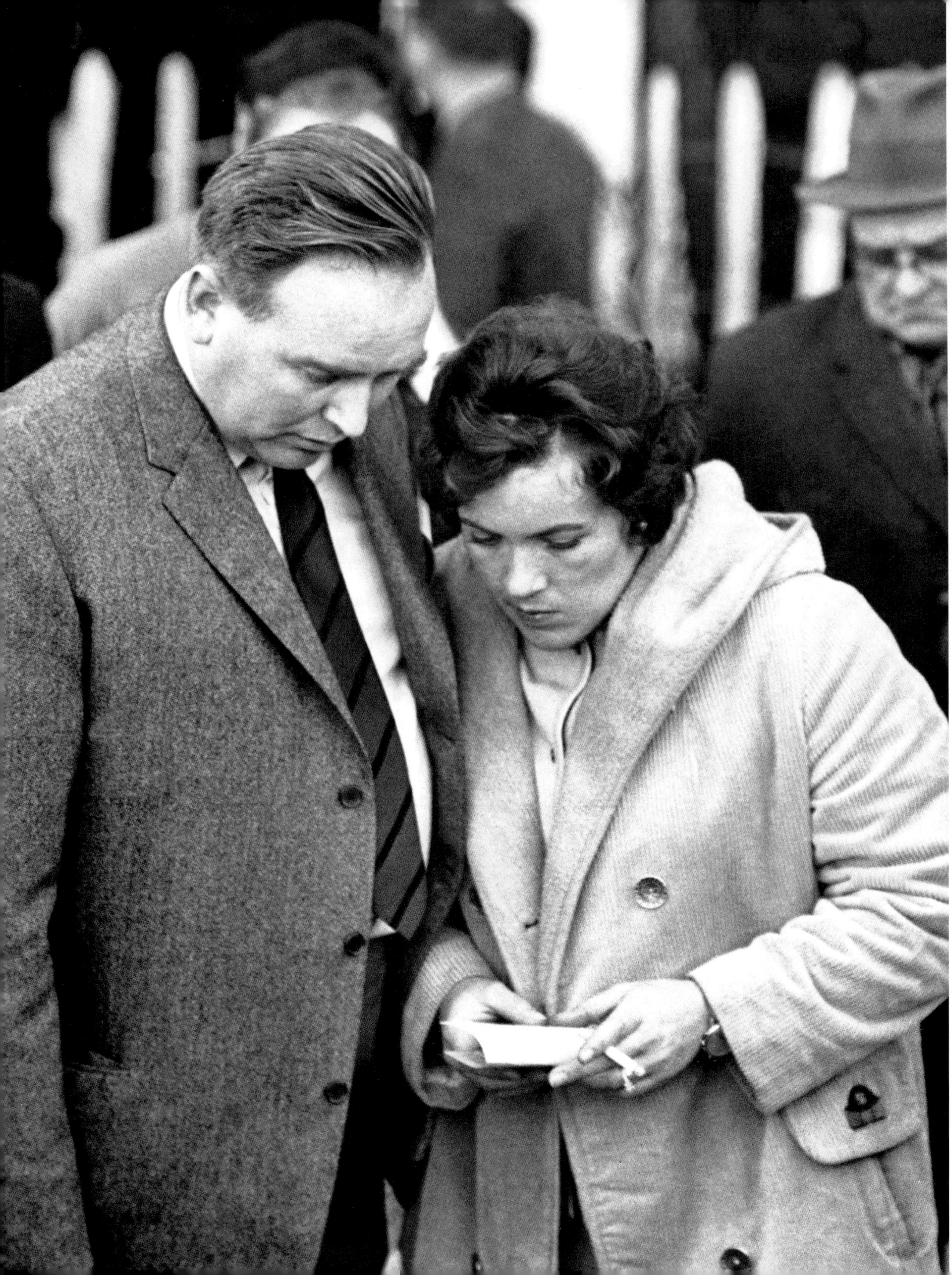

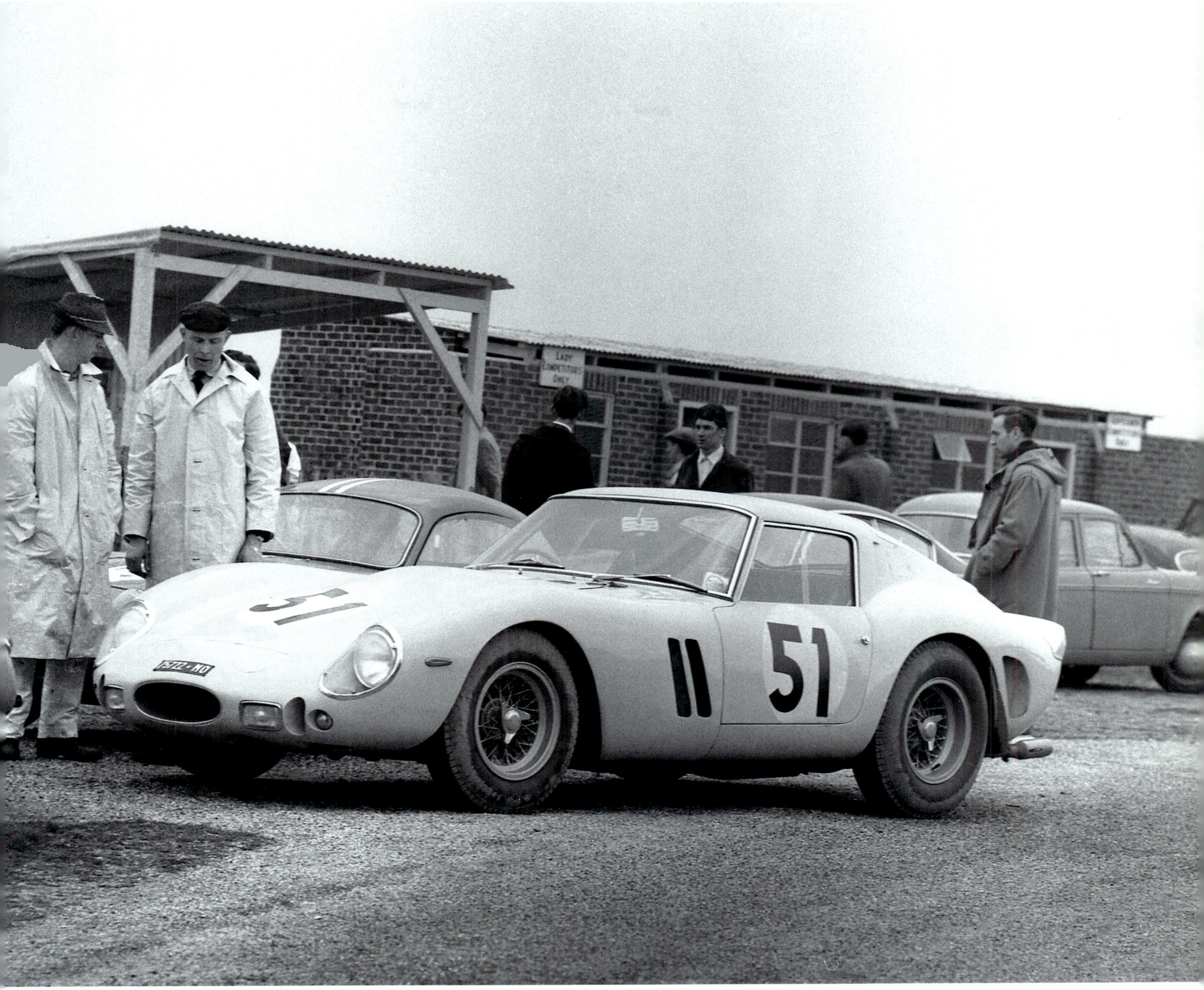

↑The UDT Laystall Ferrari 250GTO (3505 GT) was handed over to Innes Ireland at Maranello on 20 April 1962, together with the Equipe Endeavour car (3589 GT), and driven back to England in tandem with Col. Ronnie Hoare, the first British customer GTOs. Two days later it was at Goodwood, but remained unraced as the accident that befell Stirling Moss decreed that Innes Ireland would use the team's Lotus 19, and he duly won the Sussex Trophy ahead of Mike Parkes in the Endeavour GTO. The uneven race numbers and wonky wing extractor vents rather spoil the aesthetics. Les Leston's famous DAD 10 Lotus Elite can be glimpsed behind the GTC.

← Unlike the virtual reality fantasy of latter-day life, back then actions had consequences, often serious or fatal. This is Goodwood on Easter Monday 1962 following Stirling Moss's accident, and the obvious distress and body language of legendary Saab driver Erik Carlsson and his wife Pat Moss, Stirling's sister, remind us that the 'good old days' frequently had very sharp teeth.

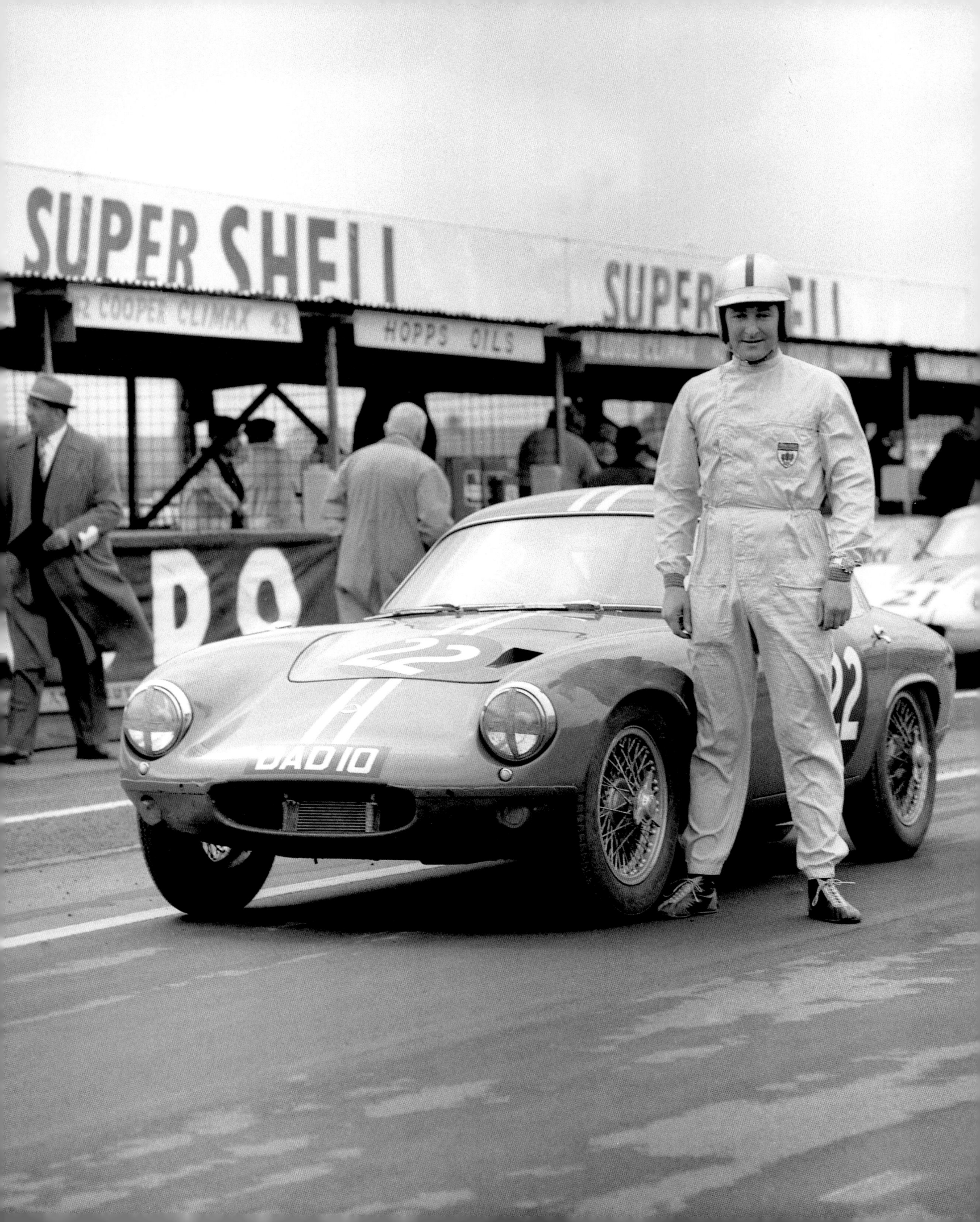

SUPER SHELL
COOPER CLIMAX 42
HOPPS OILS
22
DAD 10

← Les Leston, occasional 1950s Cooper, Connaught, BRM, and Aston Martin works driver, later the eponymous purveyor of racing apparel and accessories (helmets, overalls, gloves, steering wheels, etc.) and a formidable competitor in his Lotus Elite with its 'hip' registration number DAD 10 (dadio) and rival to Graham Warner's similar Chequered Flag Elite LOV 1. Even before this, in the 1950s, he was the proprietor of what his advertisement declared was the 'Modern Motorist's Store', the Aero-Spares Co. that was situated at 16 High Holborn, London WC1. His long and varied career began in 1949 with an SS100 Jaguar, and progressed via the 500cc F3 category to Cooper in 1953. Later, success in saloon and GT cars followed, and he also competed in the Monte Carlo and Alpine Rally, the Tour de France, and much else for various factory teams. During the 1970s he moved to Hong Kong where he took up broadcasting, but returned to England in the mid-1980s and now lives in Kent. He was born Alfred Lazarus Fingleston on 16 December 1920.

↓ Surely there never was a better looking early 1960s F1 car than the original Lotus 25 – beautiful, elegant, perfectly proportioned and formed. Mike captures Jim Clark at his best (pole position, fastest lap, and victory) on one of his peakless helmet days as he wins the 1962 British GP in chassis R2 at Aintree, 49.2 seconds ahead of John Surtees in the Bowmaker Racing Lola.

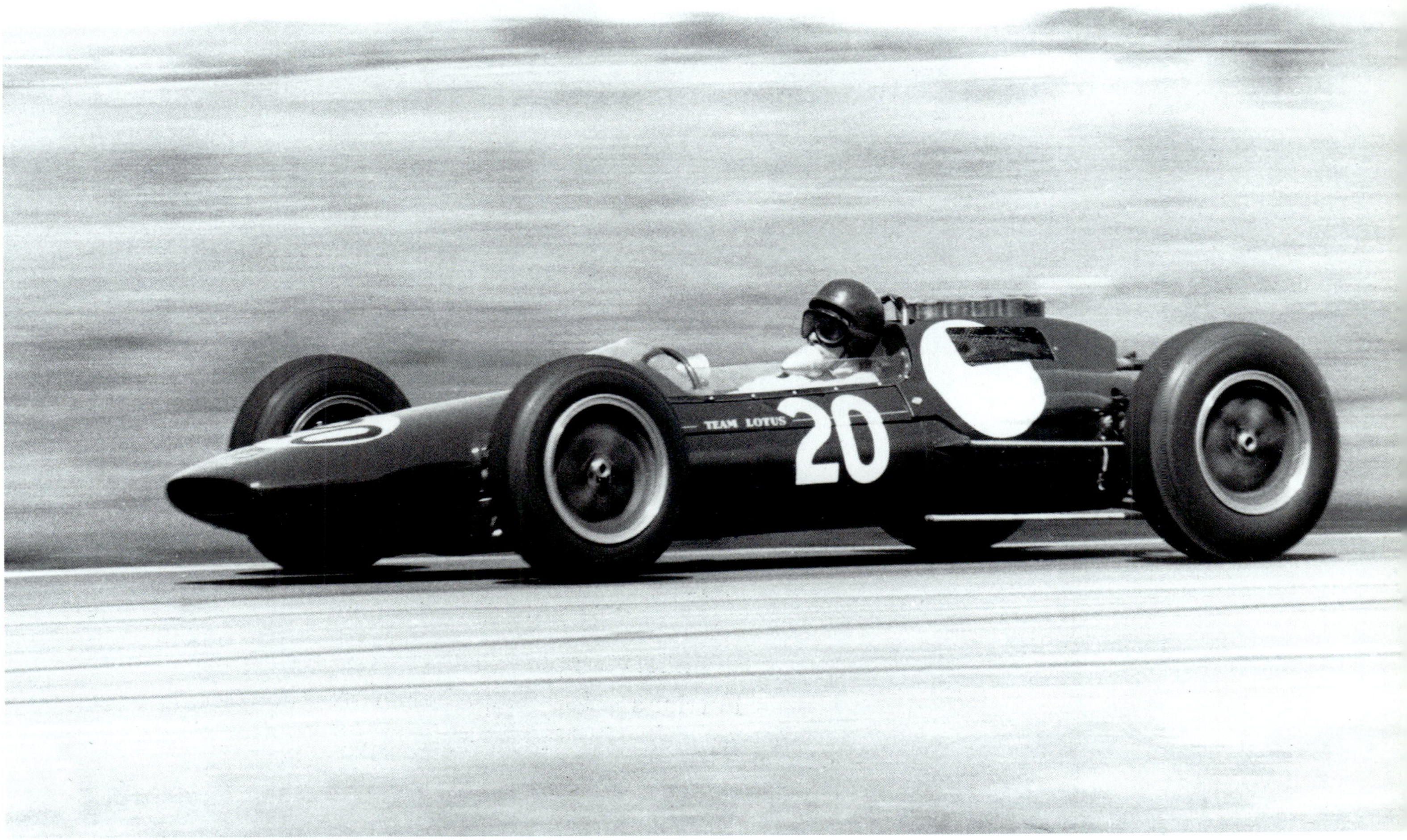

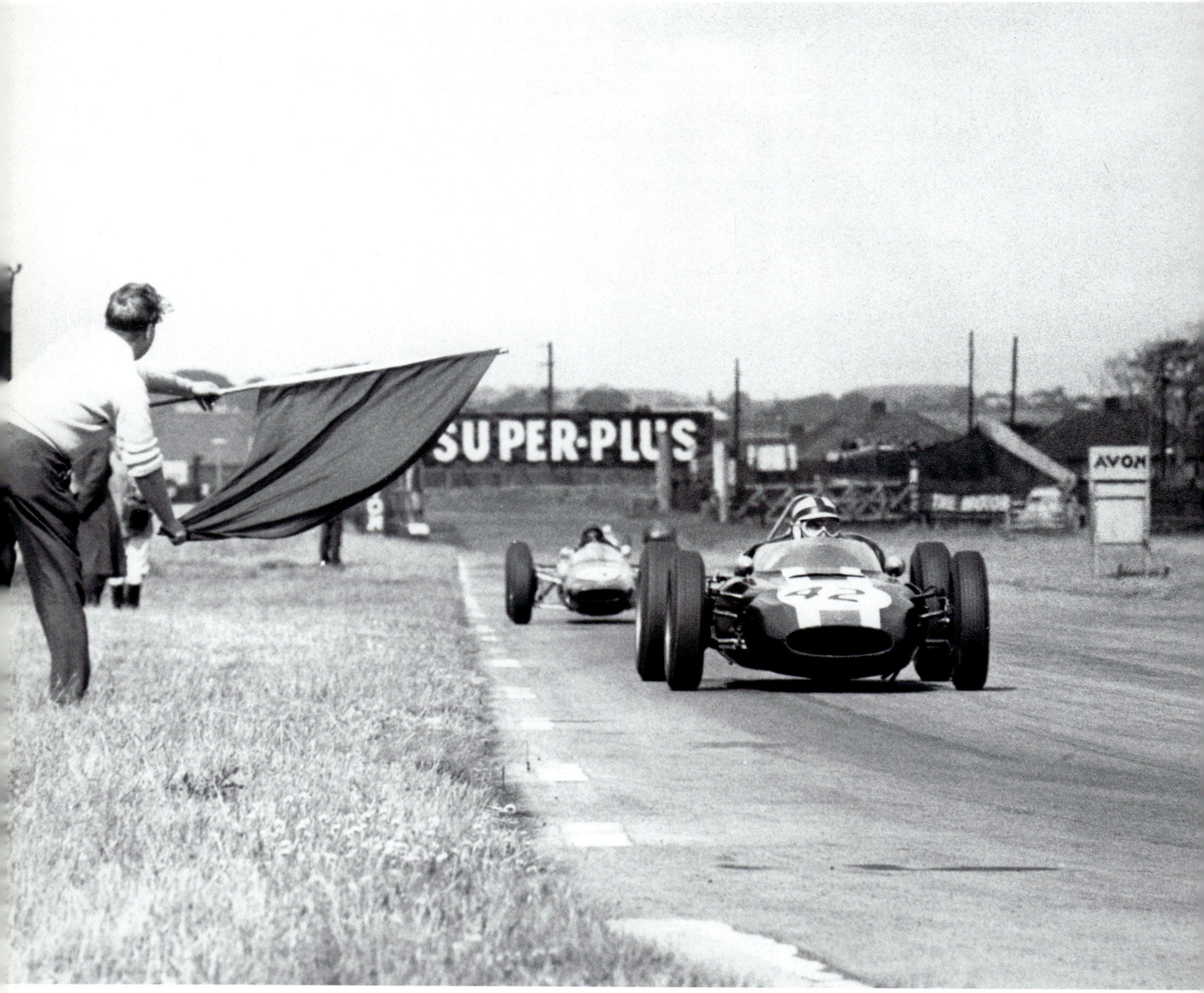

The Ecurie Galloise Cooper-Climax T53 (F1-6-61) of Welshman Jack Lewis is about to be swallowed up by Clark's dominant Lotus 25 at Aintree. Lewis finished tenth in his outdated, underpowered car, and his F1 career ended following the German GP after only five starts; a loss of a considerable but under-utilised talent. He went on to farm sheep for many years, an occupation not unknown to the man following. In the background Aintree's urban soul intrudes.

Peter Jopp's Alan Fraser-entered Sunbeam Rapier leads Edward Lewis's Riley 1.5, with Elizabeth Jones (Downton Engineering Mini) pursued by John Whitmore's works Mini, and Peter Pilsworth in another Sunbeam Rapier with a further two Minis following. This is the British GP saloon car support race at Aintree on 21 July 1962. They finished respectively eighth o/a and second in class, ninth o/a and third in class, twelfth o/a and fourth in class, tenth o/a and third in class and eleventh o/a and fourth in class. Predictably, the Jaguars dominated, finishing in the first four places led by Jack Sears for Equipe Endeavour.

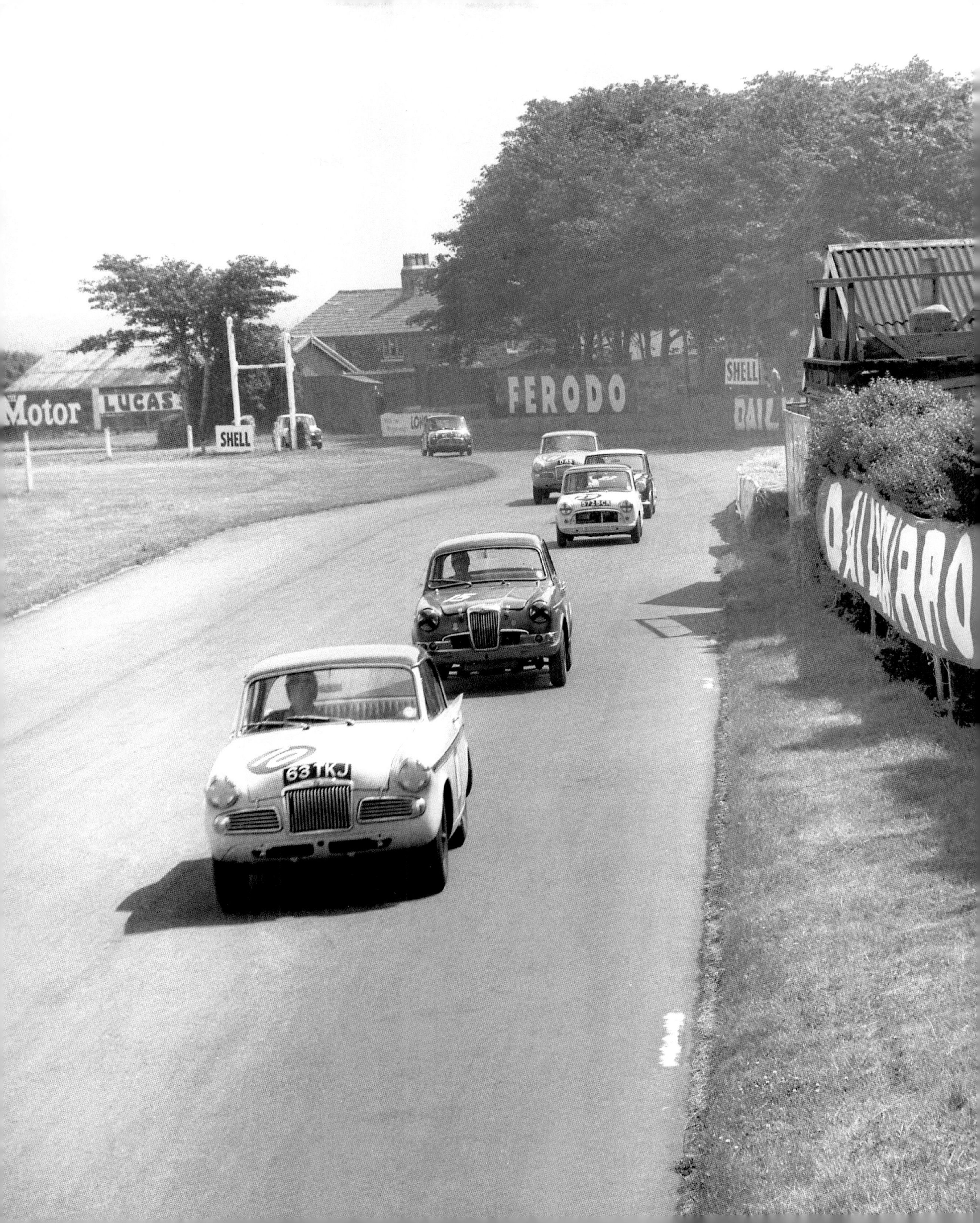
Motor
LUCAS
SHELL
FERODO
SHELL
631 TKJ

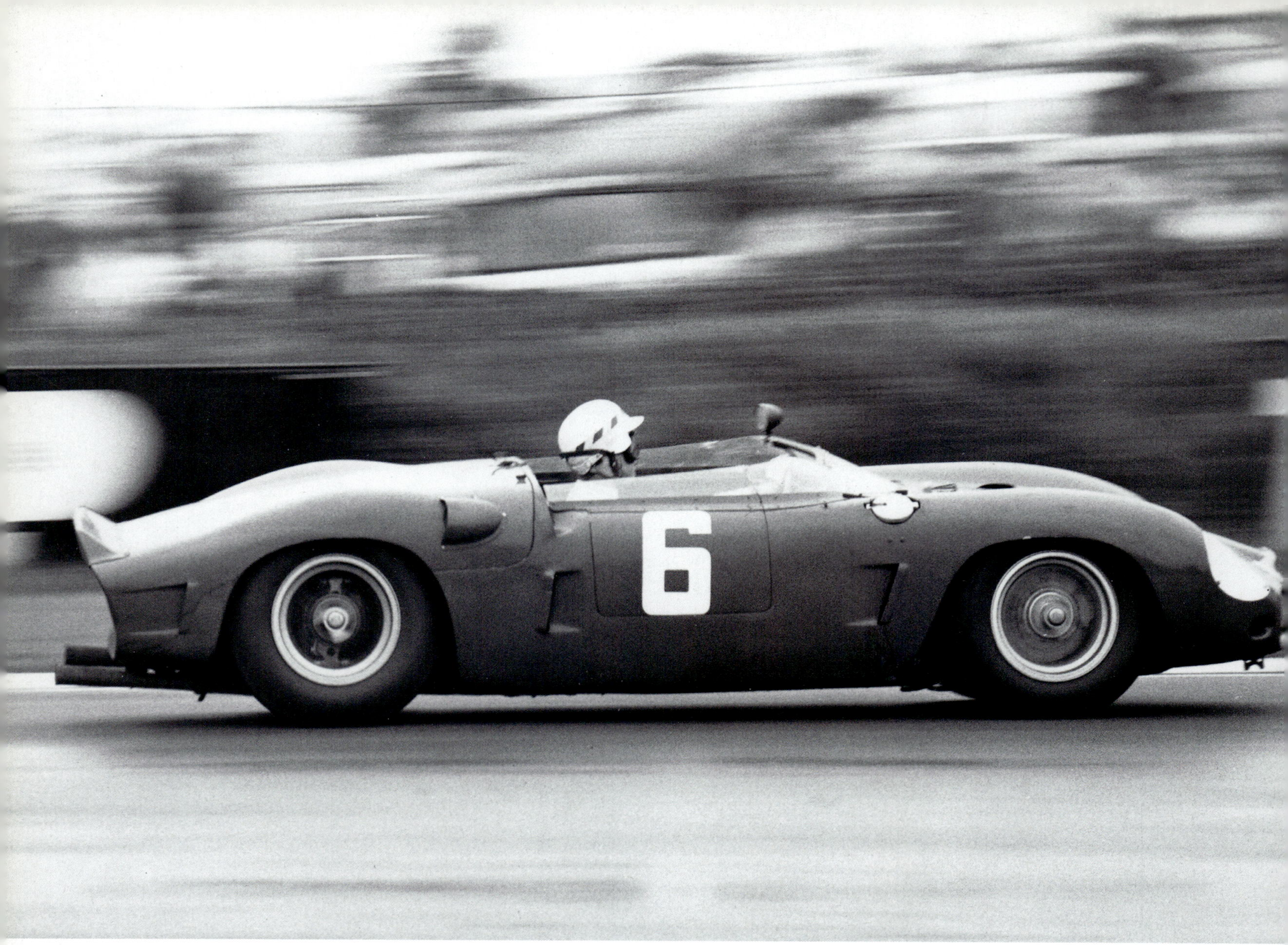

↑ Mike Parkes at the August Bank Holiday Brands Hatch meeting where he won the saloon car race in the Equipe Endeavour Jaguar 3.8 Mk2, the GT race in the Equipe Endeavour Ferrari 250GTO, and the Guards Trophy in this Ferrari 246SP (0790) entered by Maranello Concessionaires. It was a wet, miserable day until the racing ended, when miraculously the rain stopped and the weather brightened up.

↗ As Mike Parkes ran away with the Peco Trophy GT race at Brands Hatch in the Equipe Endeavour Ferrari 250GTO, Innes Ireland and Roy Salvadori battled over second place, with Salvo emerging victorious in the John Coombs 250GTO (3729 GT) seen here ahead of the UDT Laystall-entered GTO (3505 GT). This race featured no fewer than six Ferrari 250GTOs, the other three being the Bowmaker/Maranello Concessionaires car driven by John Surtees that spun here but finished fourth, David Piper's BP green car that finished sixth, and the Scuderia Serinissima car driven by Colin Davis who went straight on at Druids because of locked brakes, watched by the then adolescent author. The only interloper was the misfiring John Coombs E-type driven by Graham Hill that finished fifth.

→ The Molyslip Trophy for saloon cars was held in horrible conditions and was a Jaguar Mk2 benefit, with Mike Parkes leading home Endeavour team-mate Jack Sears from Roy Salvadori in the Coombs Jaguar, and the similar cars of Gawaine Baillie and David Hobbs. Further back, Peter Jopp won his class in the Sunbeam Rapier, whilst Bill Aston in the Tourist Trophy Garage Vauxhall VX 4/90, with its grille removed, held off Peter Harper in another Rapier to finish second in class and twelfth o/a. This eclectic field also included a works Ford Zodiac for David Haynes (ninth o/a), a Vauxhall Velox driven by John Sutton to tenth o/a, and Nicky Byrne's Equipe Rouge Mercedes Benz 220SE.

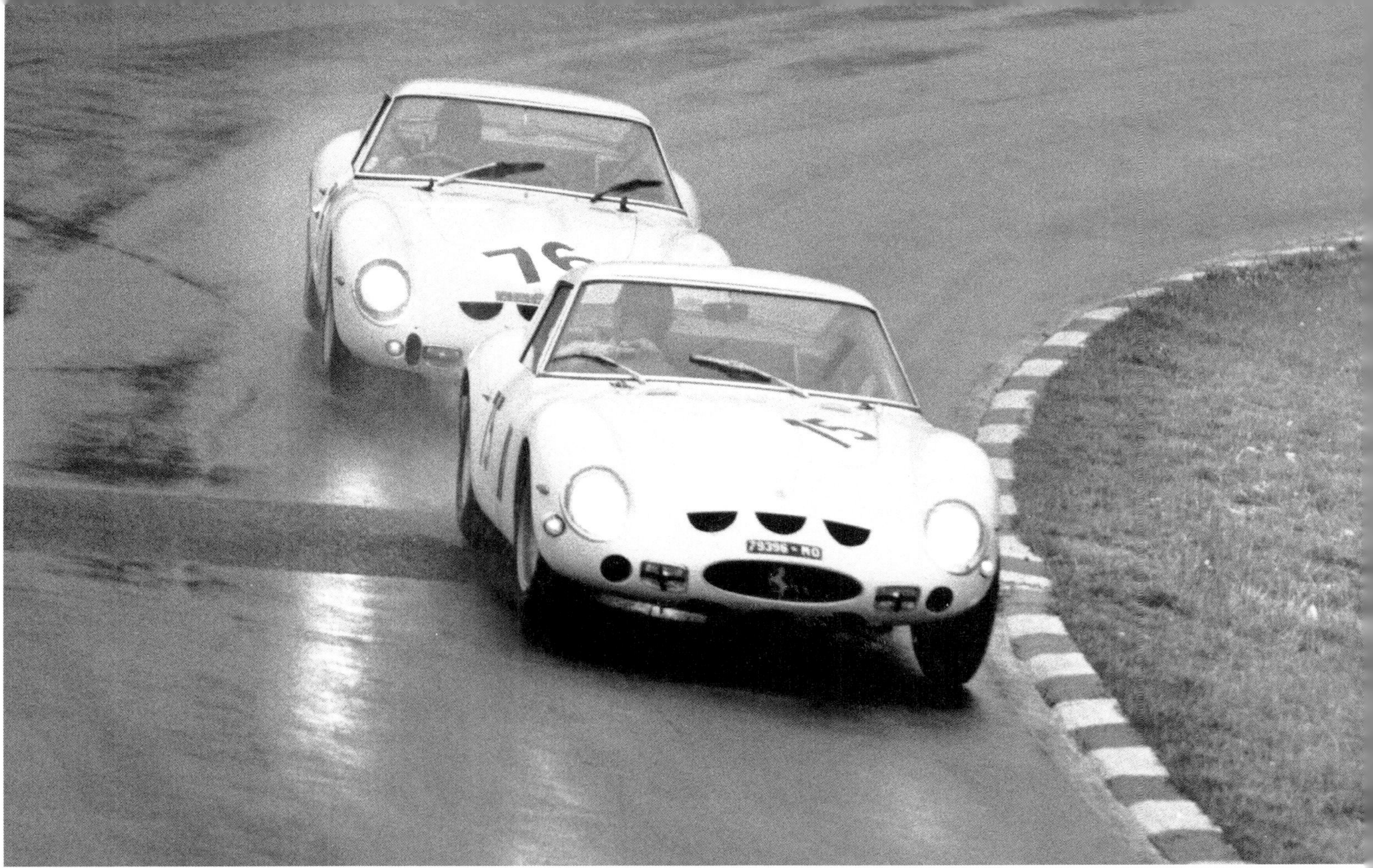

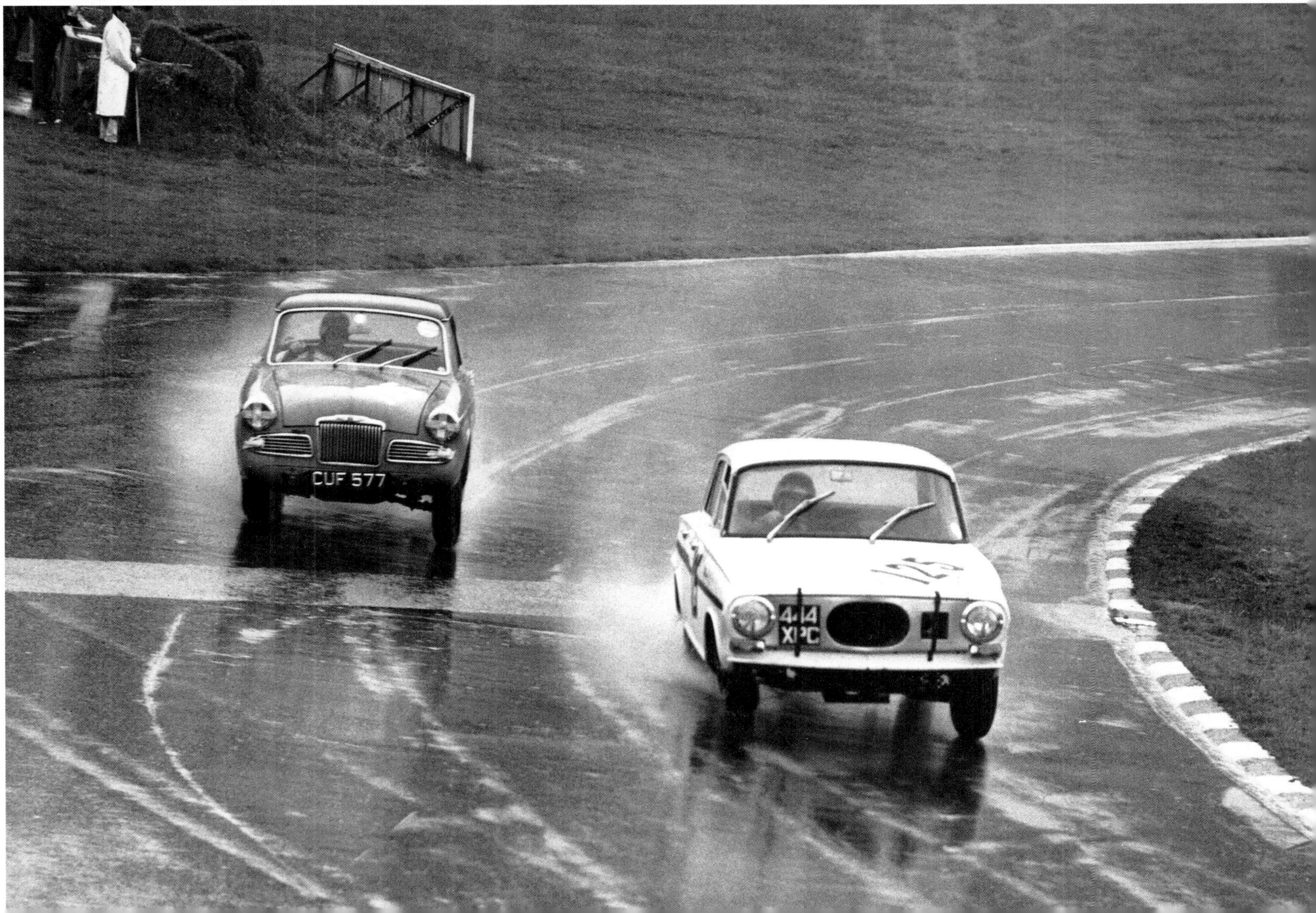
CUF 577
444
XPC

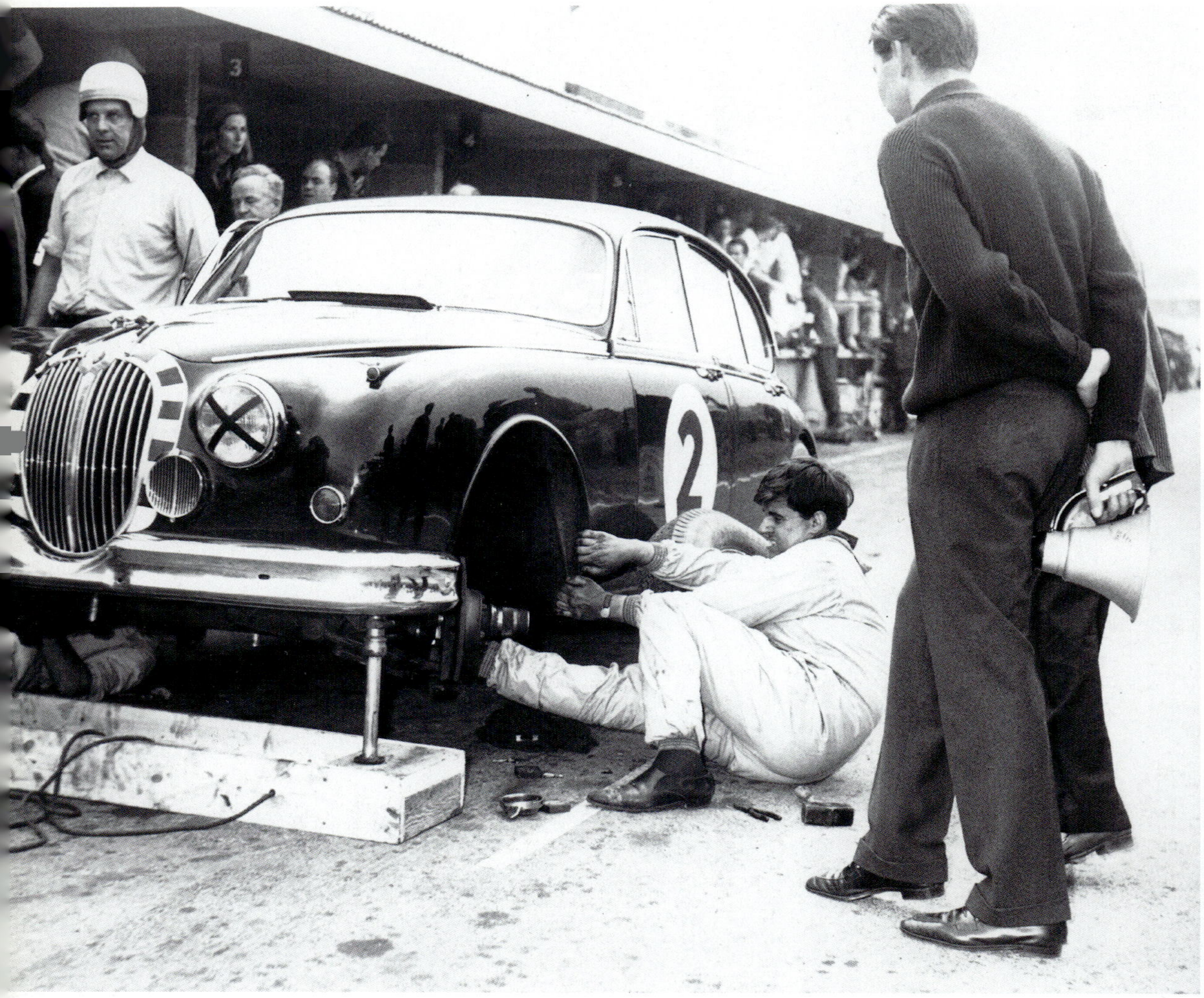

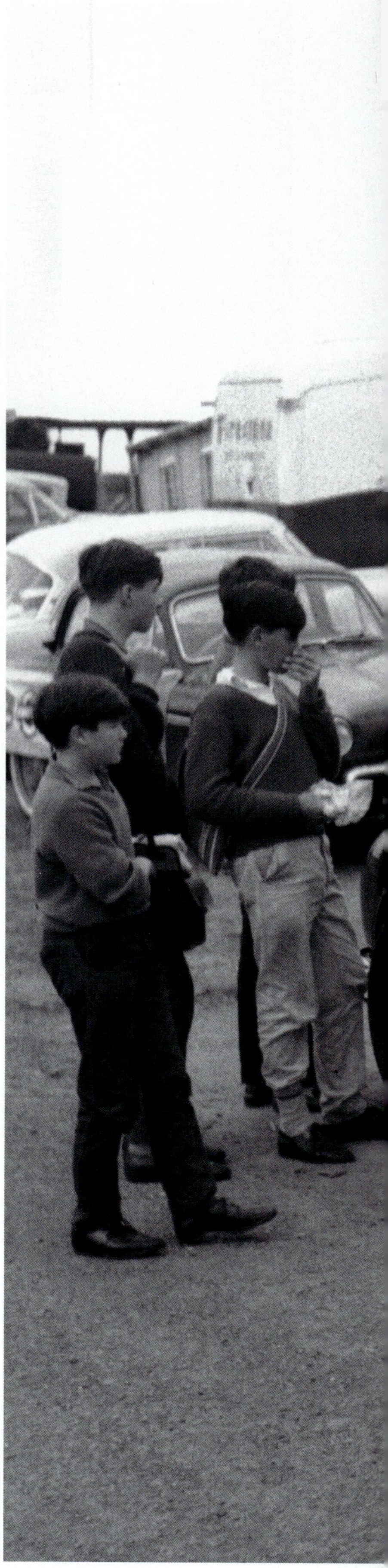

↑ On 6 October 1962 Brands Hatch hosted the *Motor* 6 Hours race for saloon cars with a field of 35 starters. The status quo at this time more or less guaranteed a Jaguar victory, mechanical mishaps or accidents aside, and Equipe Endeavour duly obliged, with Mike Parkes and Jimmy Blumer winning despite the car being stuck in o/d third for a long time, whilst the sister car (Bruce Halford/Roy Pierpoint), seen here retired with transmission troubles, and their main rival the Mike Salmon/Peter Sutcliffe Coombs Jaguar, that was second fastest in practice, suffered a front wheel bearing failure. Note the improvised timber base for the jacks, the hands- and feet-on activity of the mechanic (no lightweight panels here), and Roy Pierpoint's racing apparel, 'pudding basin' helmet, open shirt, and rolled up sleeves! Pierpoint first competed in 1949 at Goodwood, but did not race consistently until 1961. He went on to race the Attila sports cars in 1963/64 before winning the 1965 British Saloon Car Championship in an Alan Mann-prepared Ford Mustang. Thereafter he competed in a variety of cars, including Lola T70, Ferrari 250LM, Ford Falcon, GT40, Escort, and Chevrolet Camaro before gradually decreasing his racing in 1971, although he did participate in some historic racing during the 1980s. The man with the megaphone and expensive shoes is team patron Tommy Sopwith.

→ The Peter Lindner/Peter Nöcker Jaguar 3.8 Mk2 (winner of the Nürburgring 6 Hours that June), entered by Frankfurt Jaguar distributor Lindner, had to be content with second place at the Brands Hatch 6 Hours. It is receiving the attentions of the Krypton electronic tuning service in the Brands Hatch paddock, as witnessed by the exhaust gas sensor attached to the inside tail pipe. Note also the twin 'Monza' quick-release filler caps, one orthodox large size, the other smaller, perhaps for oil? The figures on the far right include at least one driver, possibly two, looking at the footwear of the man in the foreground.

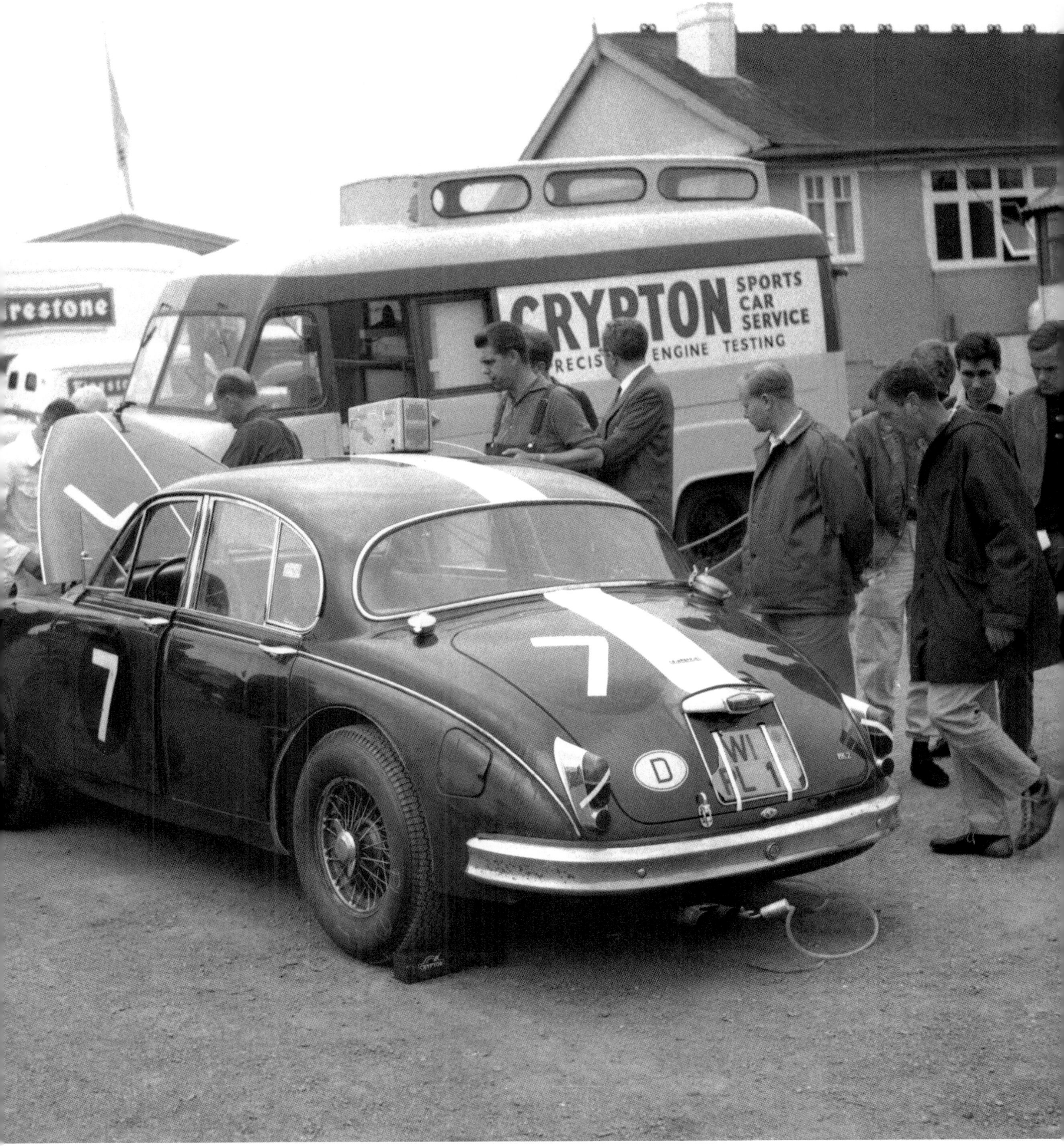
CRYPTON SPORTS CAR SERVICE
ENGINE TESTING

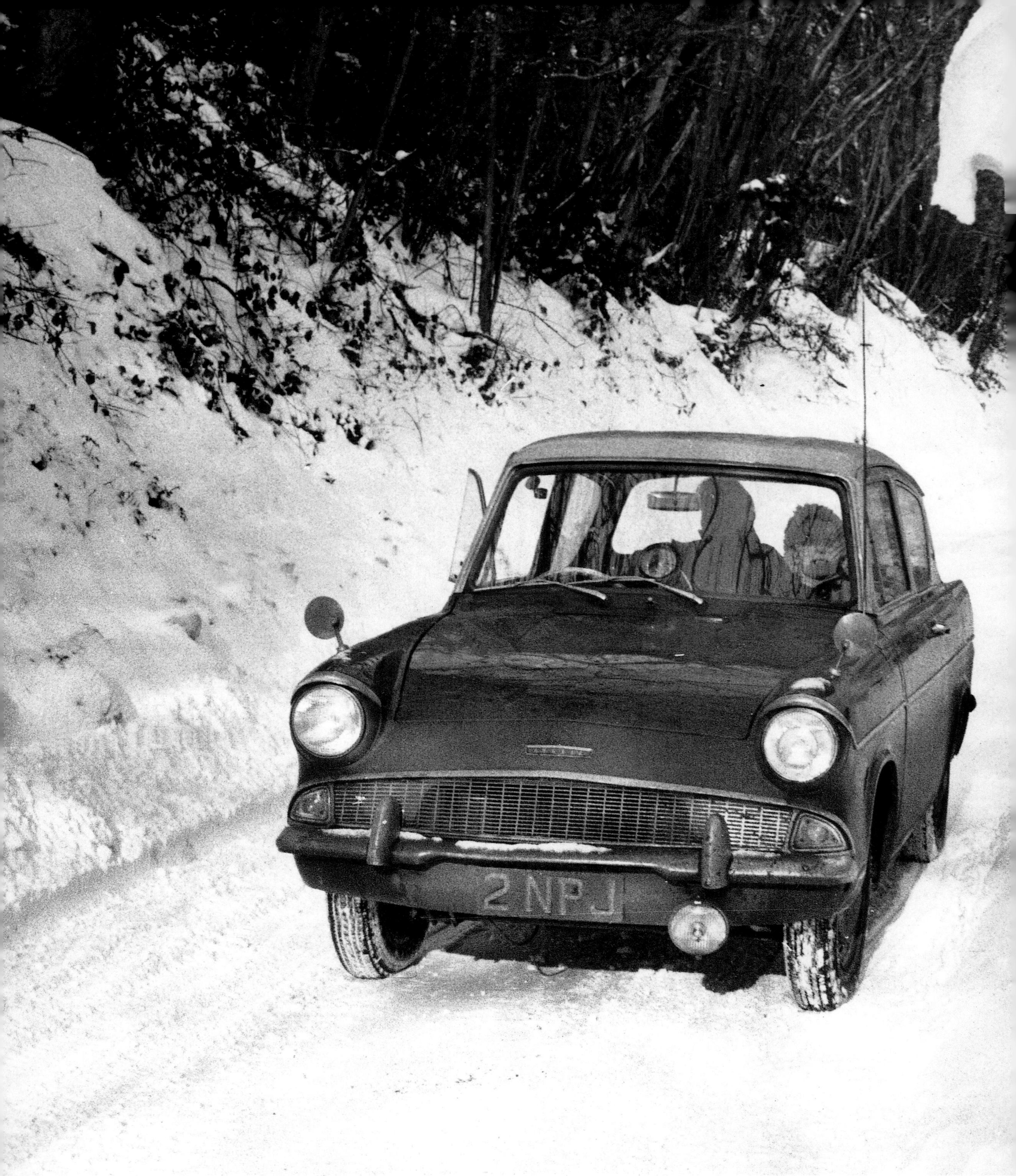
2 NPJ

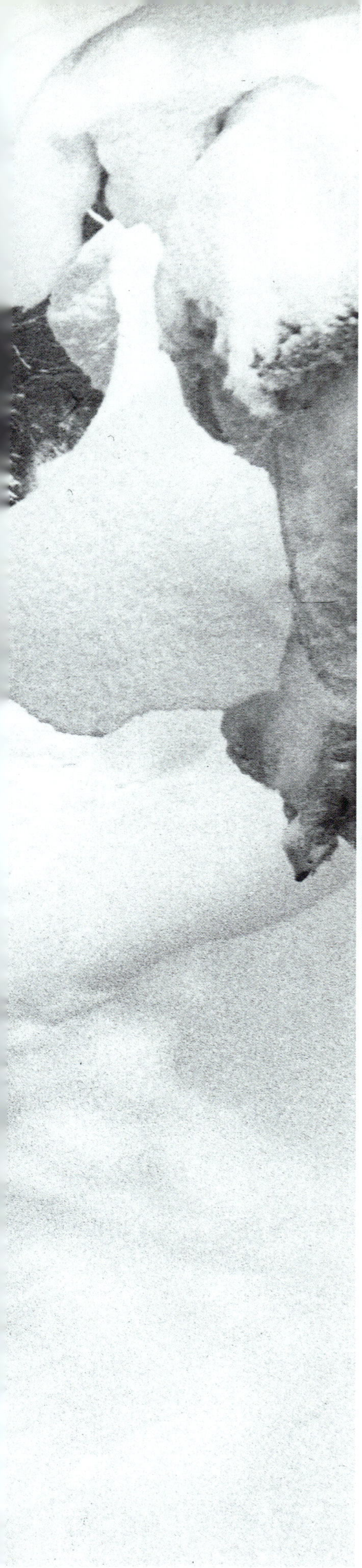

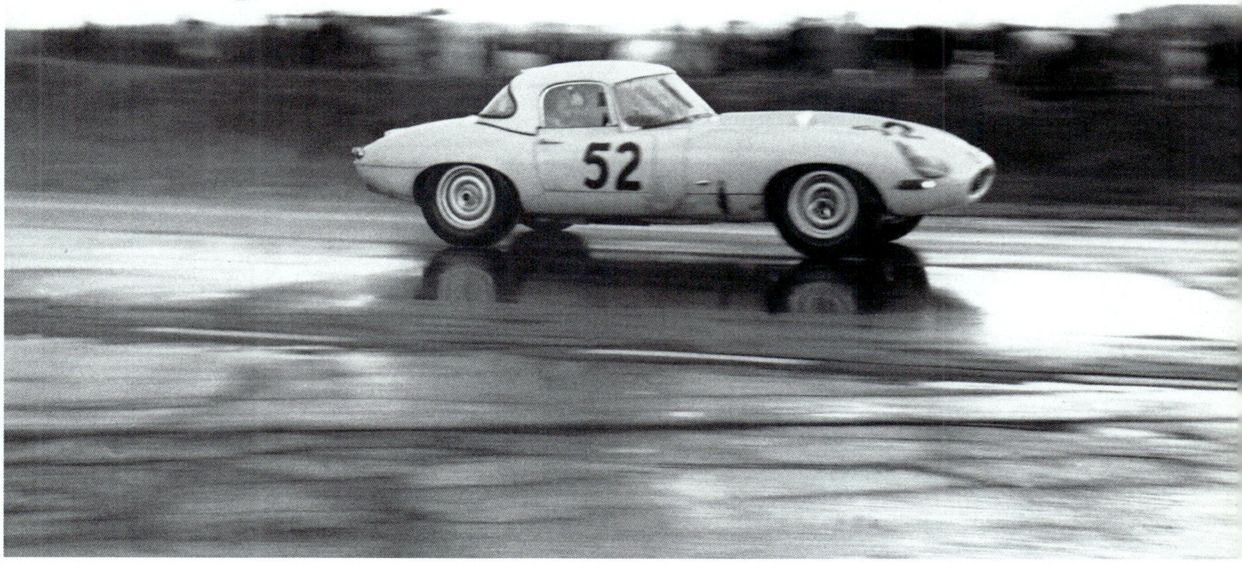

↑ The dreadful conditions and very poor light explain why this is not one of Mike's better pictures. Taken at Snetterton on 30 March 1963, not one of his favourite places where it was liable to rain horizontally, this nevertheless captures the official debut of the all-alloy 'lightweight' Jaguar E-type 4 WPD (S850006), entered by John Coombs and driven by Graham Hill, on its way to victory ahead of Roy Salvadori's Cooper Monaco. Look carefully and you can discern the small bug deflector mounted halfway down the bonnet.

← Michael's first car, a souped-up Ford Anglia with his own registration number sold to him by John Coombs, during the very snowy winter of 1962/63 near Shere in Surrey. It sports a typically period bolt-on spot or fog light in the usual ultra vulnerable position. Unlike modern cars that have one-piece door windows that create hurricane blasts even if opened only slightly, vehicles of this era sported quarter-lights that enabled one to let in a moderate amount of fresh air – manufacturers/cost accountants/designers please note.

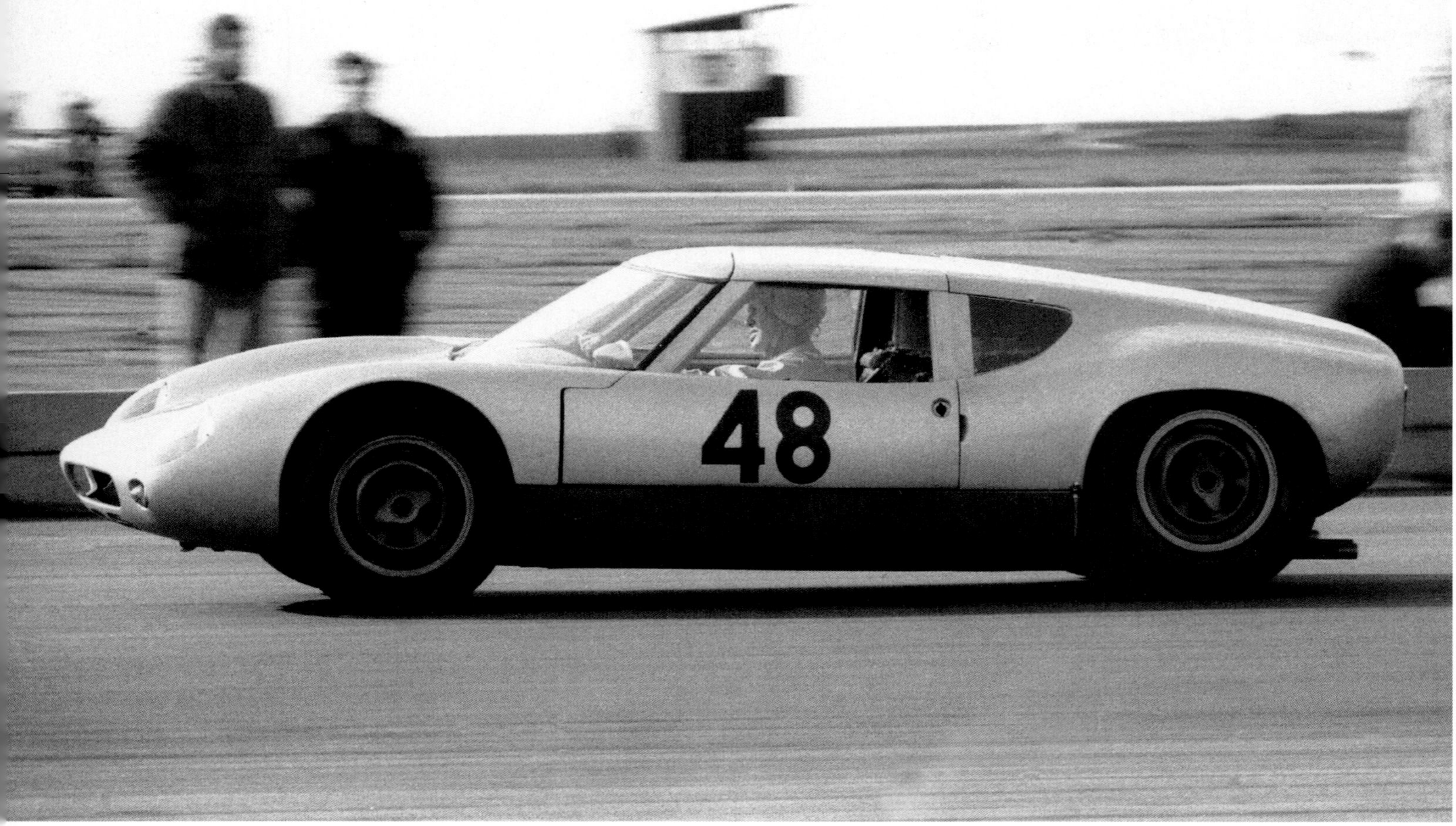
48

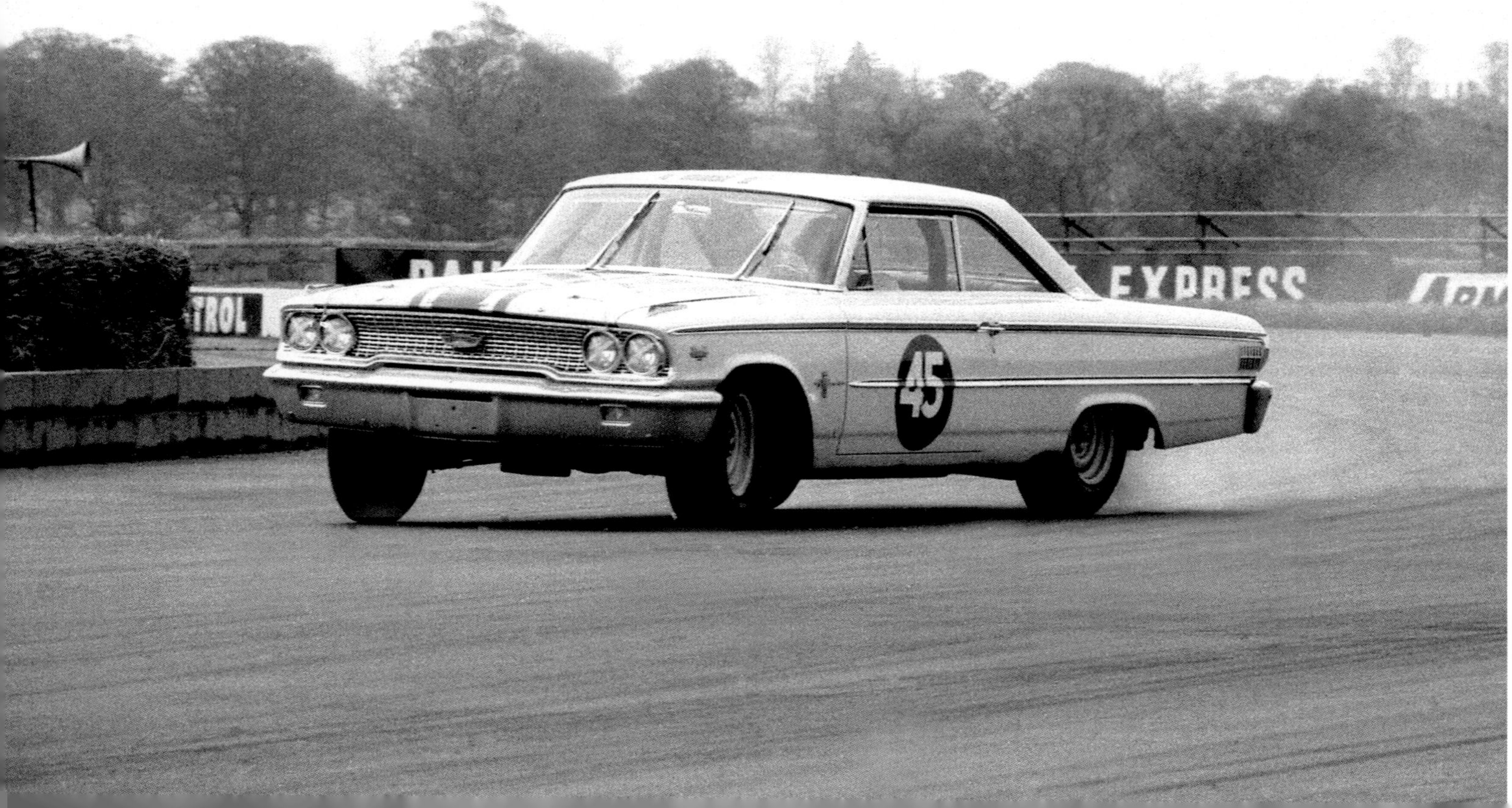
EXPRESS
45

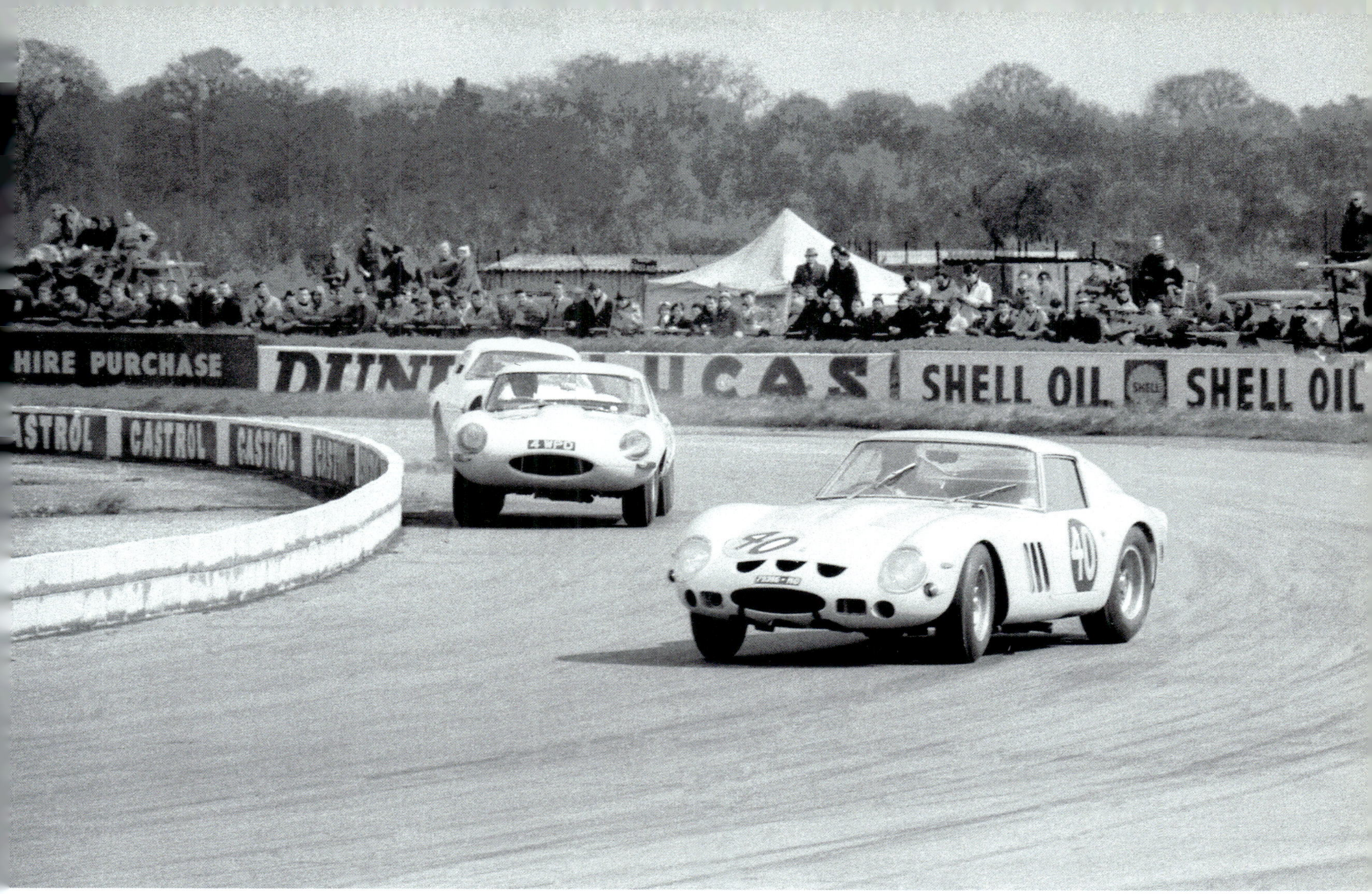

↑The GT race at Silverstone was dominated by the two 'lightweight' E-types of Graham Hill (John Coombs) and Roy Salvadori (Tommy Atkins) plus the John Coombs Ferrari 250GTO driven by Mike Parkes. Although Graham Hill finally won in the Coombs car pictured, he was led by Salvadori who set a new GT lap record (he was always super fast at Silverstone) but had an off at Becketts to finish second. Parkes, seen here in characteristic oversteer mode, had led but also crashed the GTO (3729 GT) at Becketts. Hill's Jaguar displays the characteristic 'off road' ride height of period E-types, whilst the Ferrari is now sporting a side exhaust. Latter-day Silverstone spectators, note the view on offer in 1963.

↖Tony Maggs finished ninth with the new Ford V8-powered Lola GT at the *Daily Express* Silverstone meeting, a performance that reflected its unsorted and embryonic state and also the single downdraught carburettor it was running rather than the proper four-barrel competition set-up. Once again we can observe the nose lift that so defined this pre-spoiler era and the clean, uncluttered profile.

←Following the threat from Chevrolet in 1961/62, Jaguar's hegemony in British saloon car racing finally ended in 1963 with the appearance of the 6997cc Ford Galaxies entered by John Willment, joined later by Alan Brown and Gawaine Baillie. Jack Sears, at his absolute best, demonstrates just how this vast and apparently unwieldy machine could be successfully thrown around to win the Silverstone saloon car race, ahead of Roy Salvadori's Tommy Atkins Jaguar 3.8 Mk2. Presumably the smoke visible is caused by wheelspin. In Graham Gauld's biography *Gentleman Jack*, Sears recalled that during practice 'On the second standing start the clutch began slipping.' Jeff Uren phoned Holman & Moody and was told that the Galaxie had a very high bottom gear for the NASCAR rolling starts, and that the clutch would not tolerate being 'dumped' for a quick getaway. So Sears, on pole, let in the clutch very gently before giving the Ford full throttle, enabling the Jaguars to briefly lead, but he overtook them on Hangar Straight and drew away to win easily, despite staying in fourth gear from lap 3 onwards. The car was equipped with drum brakes, and Sears noted that 'In that first race I had drum brakes with metal to metal lining so they didn't fade, and were actually quite good, better than you would believe.' Willment also entered three Ford Cortina GTs, one driven by BRM No. 2 Richie Ginther, but he retired because of a broken half-shaft.

→ The more polite end of the grid (not!) at Zandvoort for the XI Grote Prijs van Nederland on 23 June 1963 before the start. On the penultimate row of the grid, Jo Siffert grapples with his helmet strap in between the wheels of his Lotus-BRM 24 (944), whilst tall Texan Jim Hall (back to camera) adopts a combative stance. To Siffert's right is a wheel of Gurney's unseen Brabham BT7, and in front is the back of the Reg Parnell (Racing) Lola-Climax 4A (BRGP44) driven by Chris Amon. No. 26 is Giancarlo Baghetti's ATS 100 (02), and to the left on the next row is team-mate Phil Hill's sister ATS (01). Siffert finished seventh, Hall eighth, and Gurney second – Amon, Baghetti, and Phil Hill retired. Jim Clark, of course, won from pole with fastest lap, and led all the way, a lap or more ahead of the field.

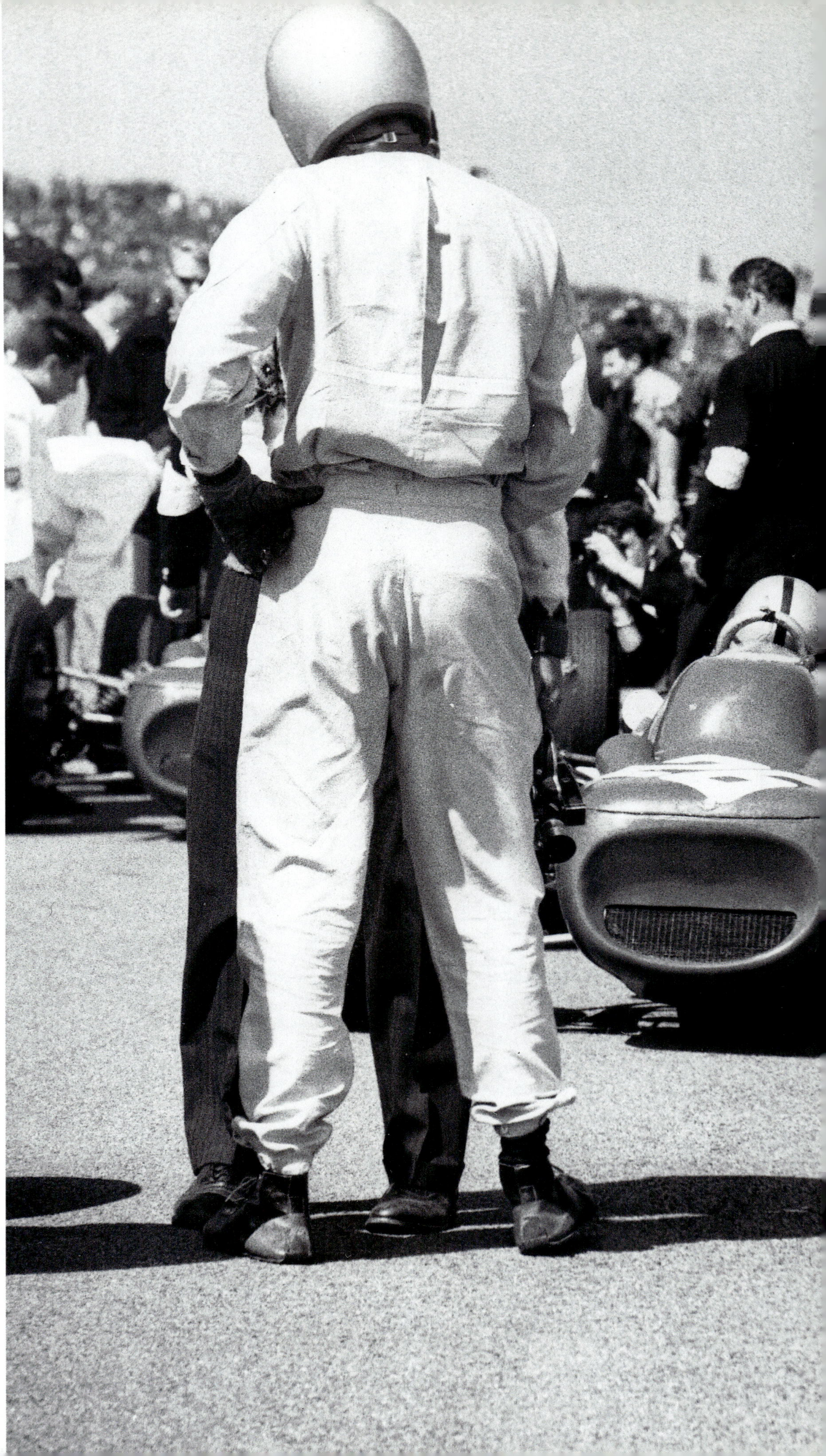

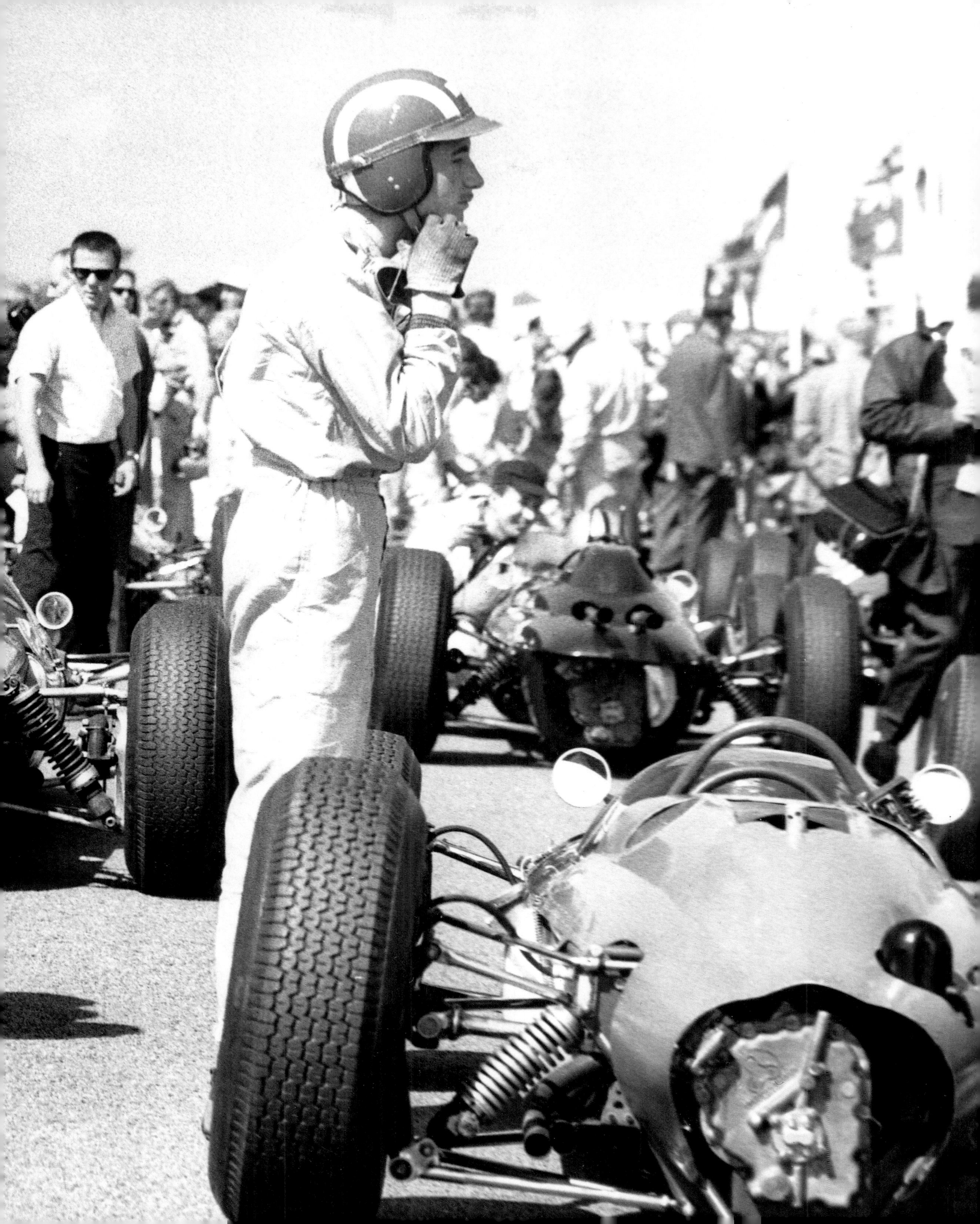

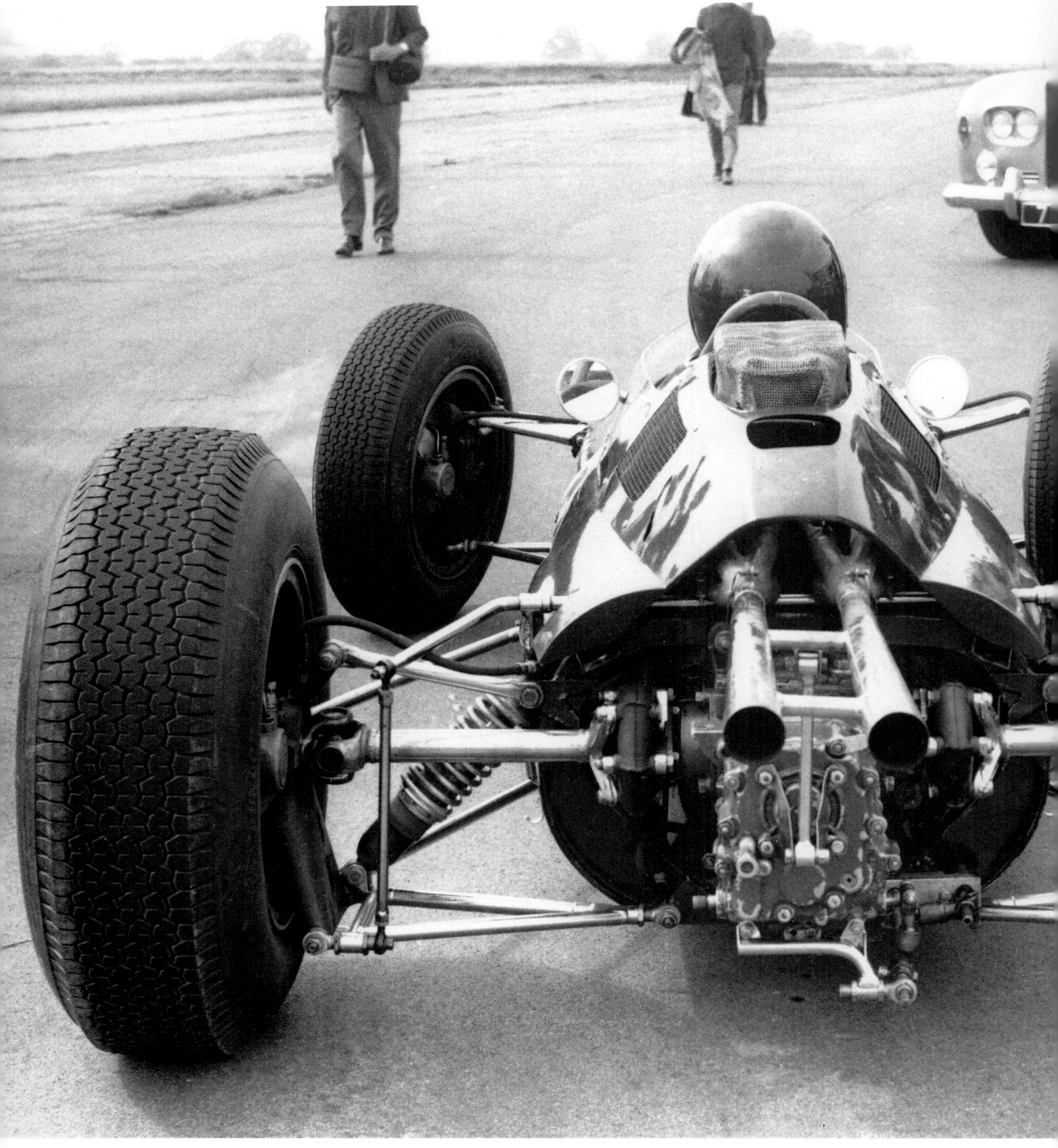

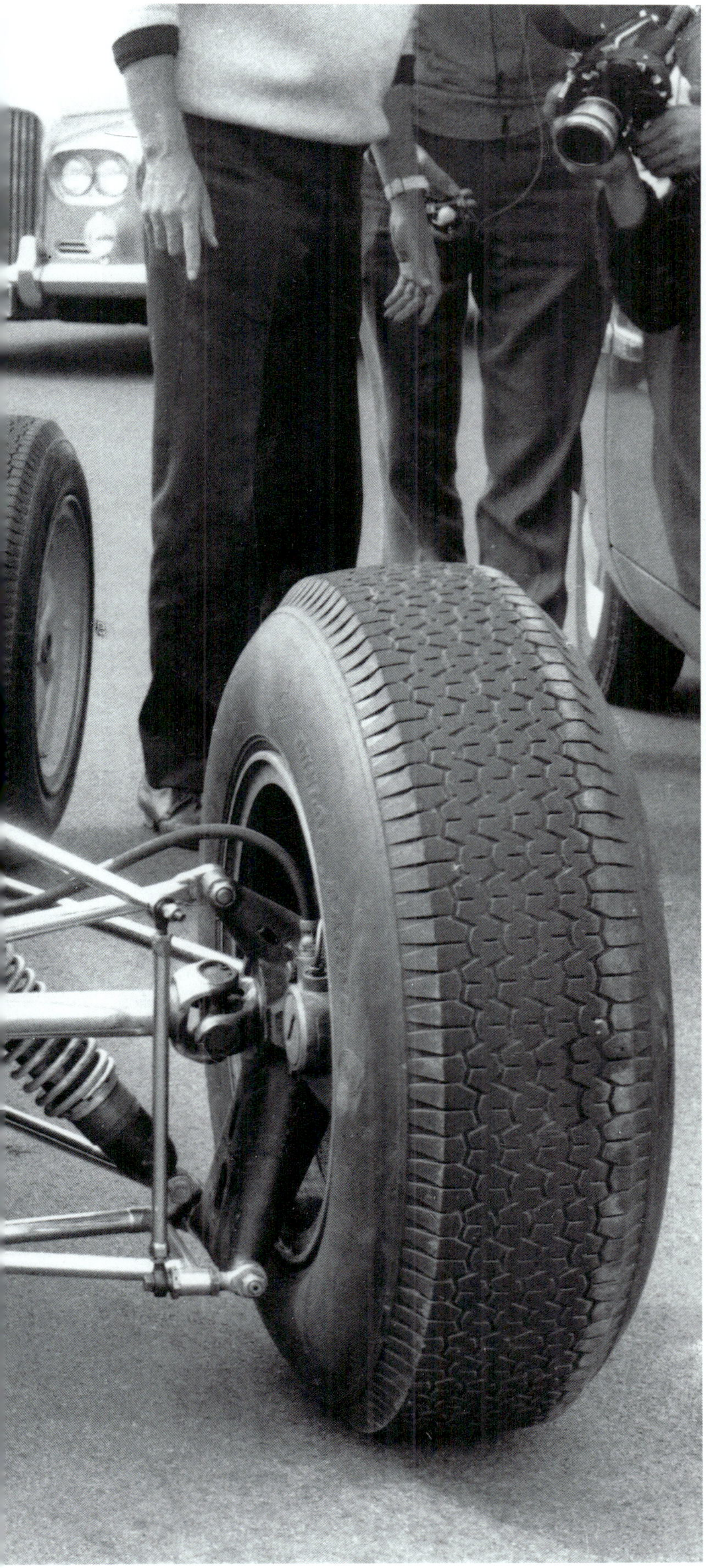

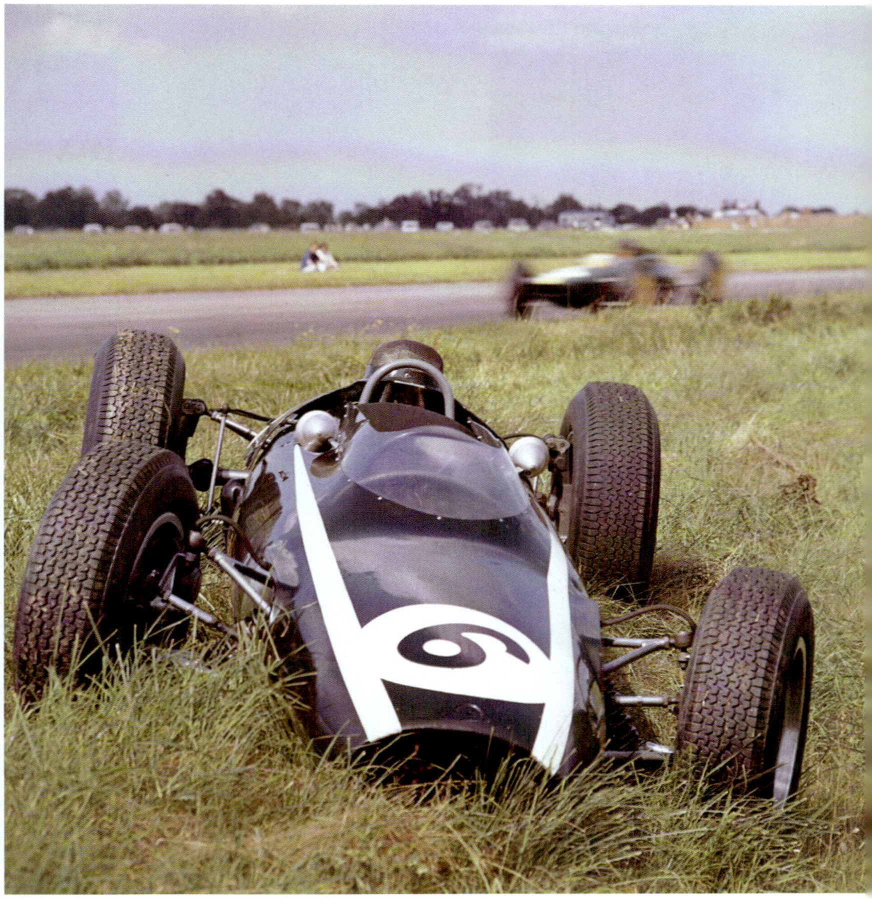

↑ In those days a photographer's track pass was literally that, and you could inhabit the roadside verges in many places, and even cross the track at the marshal's discretion. Here, Mike has found Bruce McLaren's abandoned Cooper-Climax T66 (F1-4-63) in the long grass alongside the Hangar Straight at Silverstone after engine failure on lap 6 of the 1963 British GP. Note the spindly suspension and how small single-seater racing cars of this period seem to modern eyes, like a two-thirds scale model. The blur behind is Jim Clark's Lotus 25 (R4) on his way to winning one of seven out of ten Grands Prix and the 1963 World Championship. On the other side of the track are two observers(?) enjoying the view.

← The rear of Jim Clark's race-winning Lotus-Climax 25 (F4) on Club Straight at Silverstone prior to the 1963 British GP. Those of a mechanical bent will appreciate this perfect illustration of period suspension, coil springs, shocks, drive shafts, gearbox/linkage, et al. Worthy of note is that the grid featured 16 cars with six-speed gearboxes, including Clark's team-mate Trevor Taylor, but JC made do with a ZF five-speed and won anyway. Sitting in the rear seat of the standard steel-bodied Bentley S2 in the background, with the rather inappropriate number plate, was a three-year-old Damon Hill.

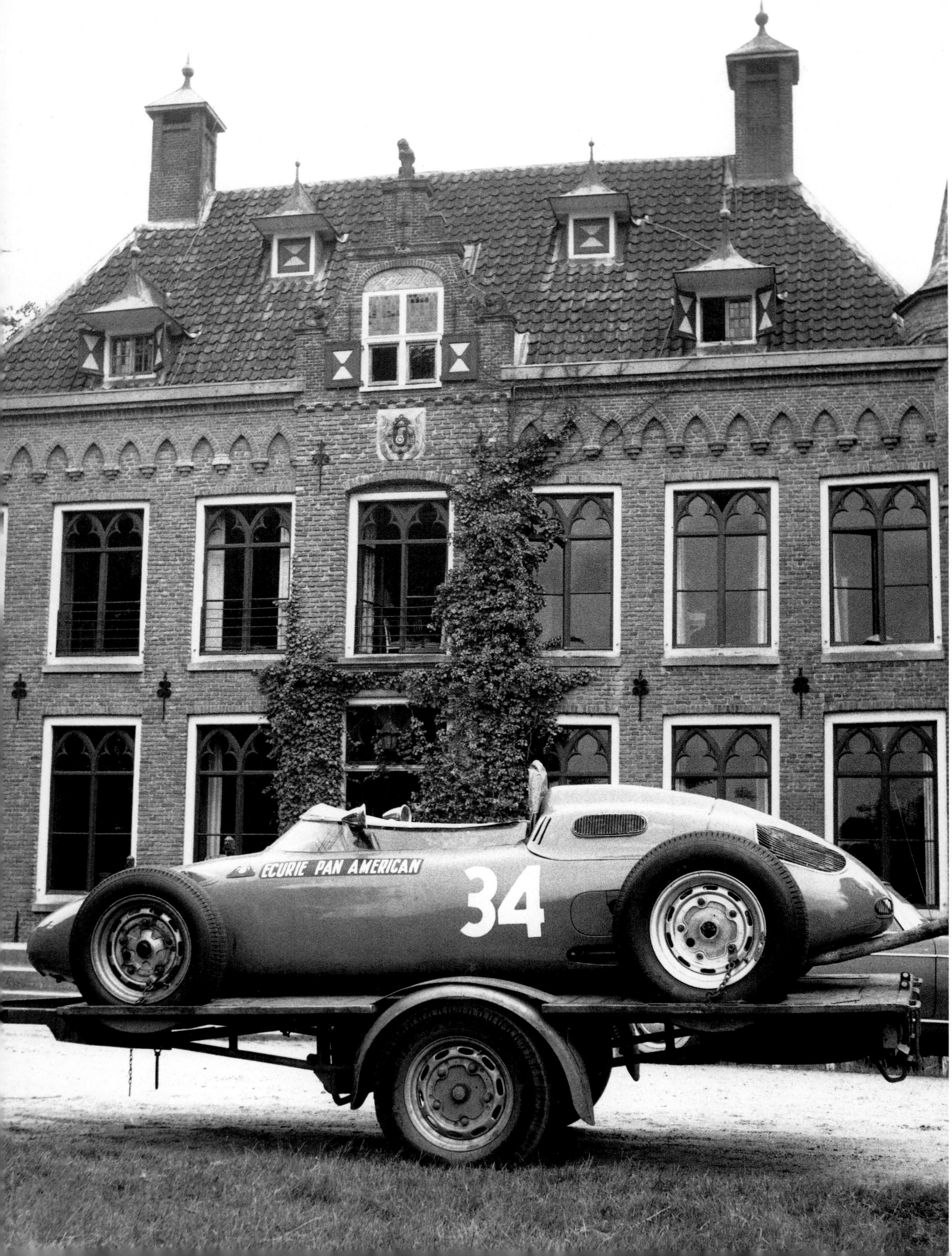
ECURIE PAN AMERICAN
34

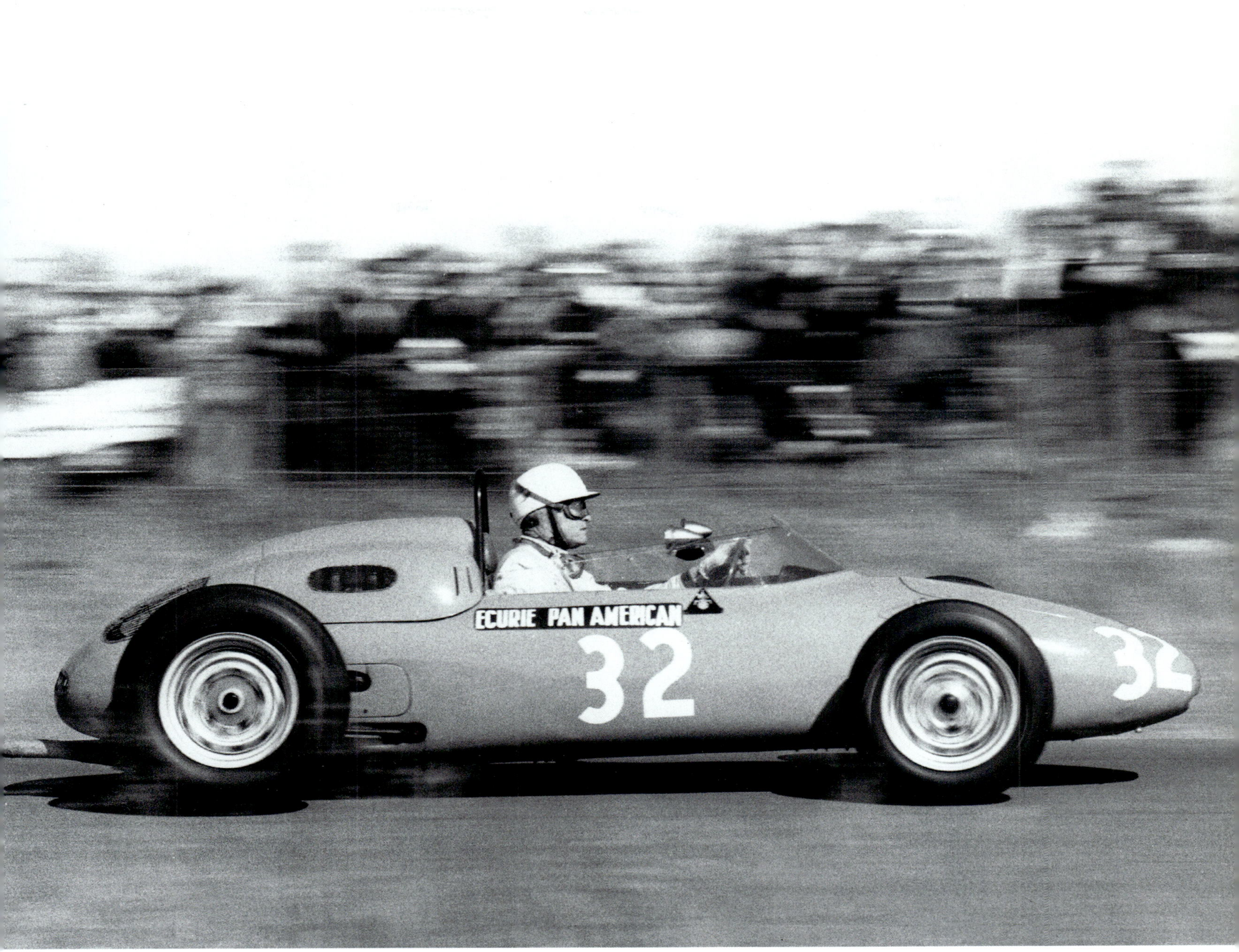

↑ Dutch aristocrat Carel Godin de Beaufort (10 April 1934 – 3 August 1964) in his long-serving Porsche 718/2 at Zandvoort. The usual front-end lift, either due to weight transference, as the relatively soft period suspension reacts under acceleration, or air building up under the nose, is very apparent here. The Porsche's cockpit had to be big to accommodate the rather large de Beaufort. He died from injuries received after crashing during practice for the 1964 German GP.

← Maarsbergen, home to Dutch aristocrat Carel Godin de Beaufort with his long serving Porsche 718 (201) adorned with Ecurie Pan American decal, apparently after securing sponsorship during 1963, although the entry lists continued to show the original Ecurie Maarsbergen name. He achieved some notoriety with this car when an onboard film camera fell off it during practising for the 1962 German GP causing a following Graham Hill (BRM) and Tony Maggs (Cooper) to run over it and crash, fortunately without personal harm. Bought from Rob Walker and first raced by him at the 1962 Dutch GP where he finished sixth. He was fatally injured in the 718 during practice for the 1964 German GP. Later the car was restored and displayed and is still owned by the family. Although forever associated with this car, de Beaufort also competed in a variety of other machinery, starting with a Dutch rally in 1952 driving a BMW. Later he went on to race Porsche 550 Spyders, RSKs, Carreras, 904GTS, a Maserati 250F at the 1959 French GP, and a F2 Cooper T51. A polished and precise driver, he was rather better than the results indicate, and his three seasons of F1 in an obsolete, underpowered car did not do him justice. Very tall and large, Carel raced in his socks, and he was the last descendant of the Beaufort family of statesmen and politicians.

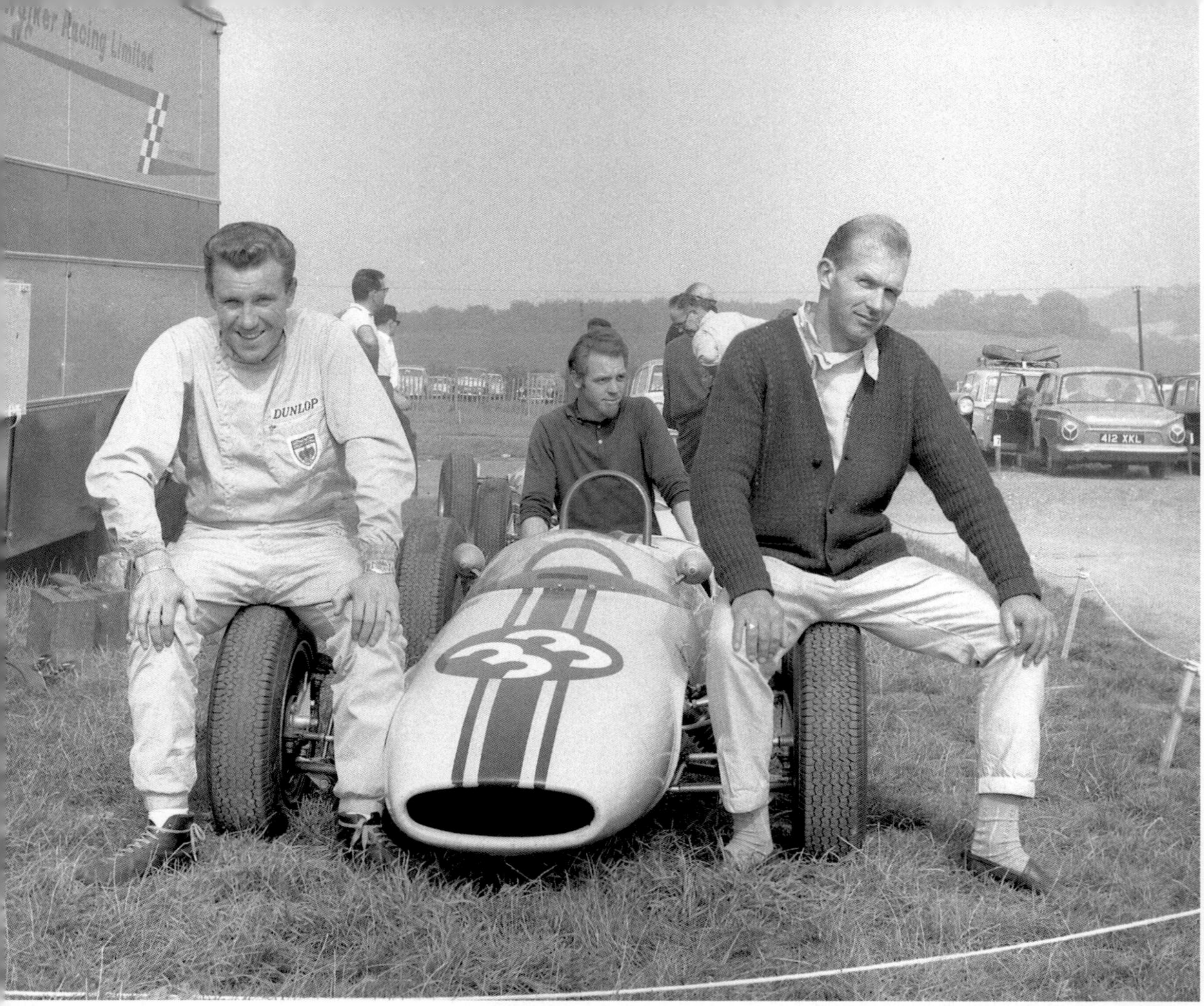
DUNLOP
33
412 XKL

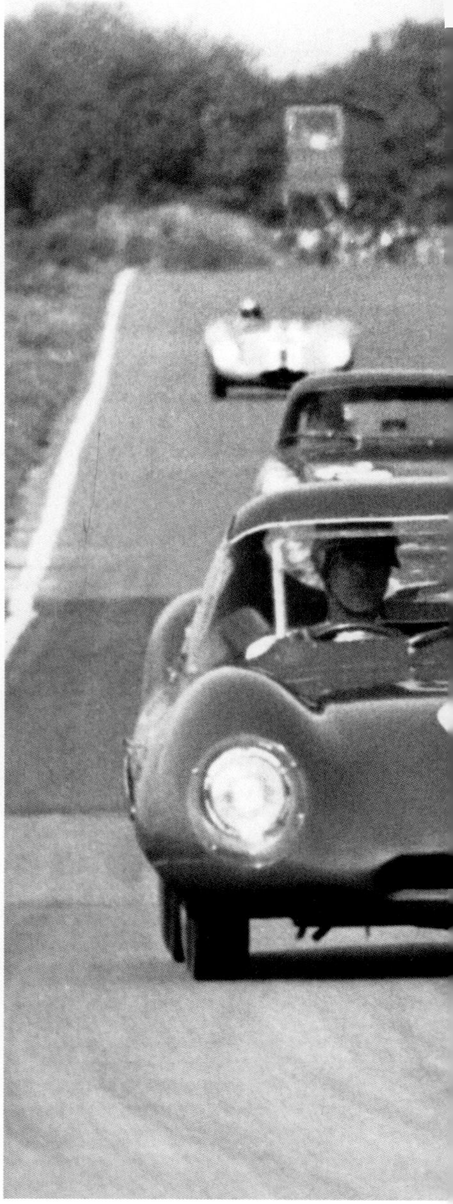

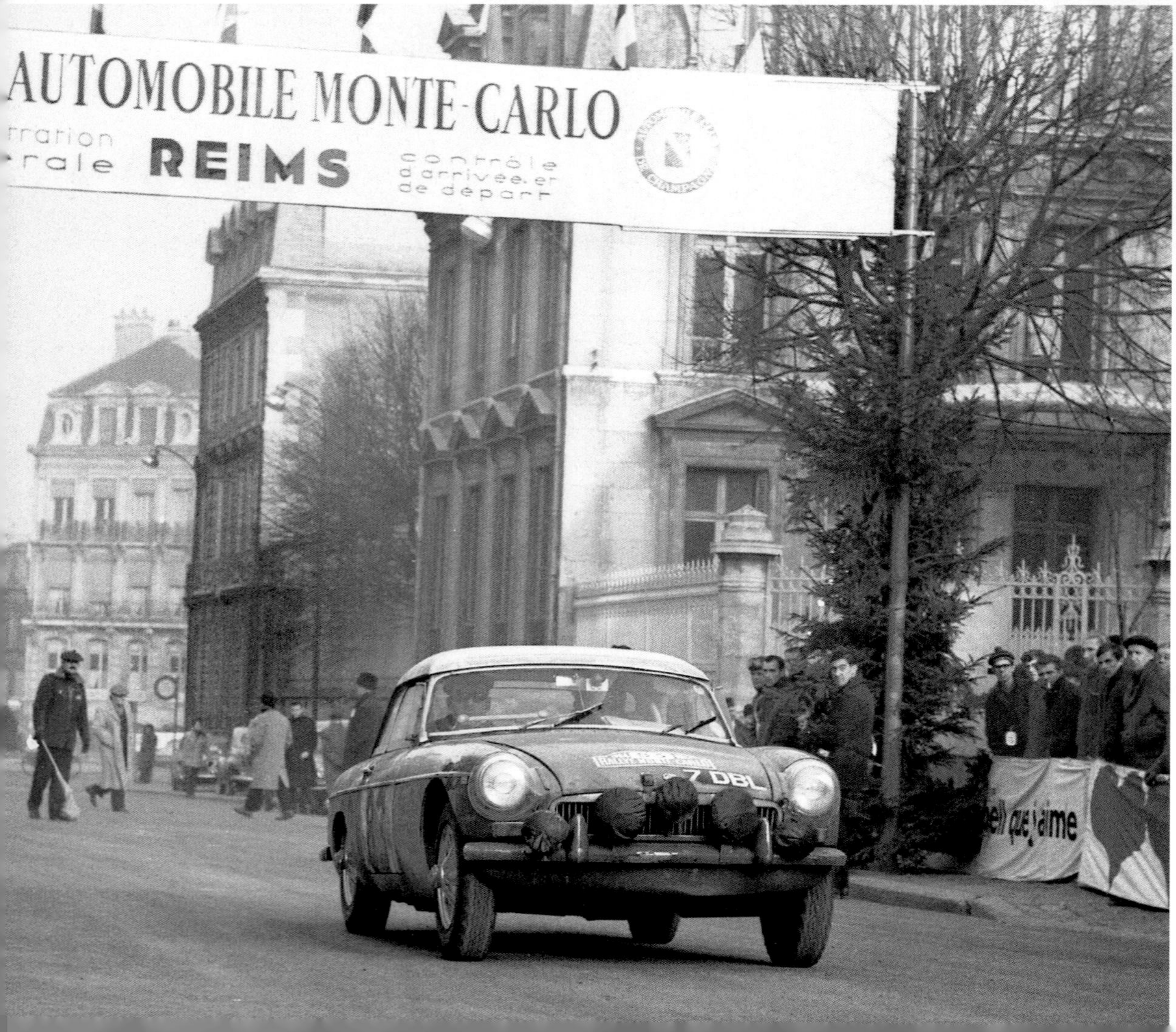
AUTOMOBILE MONTE-CARLO
REIMS
contrôle
d'arrivée et
de départ
7 DBL

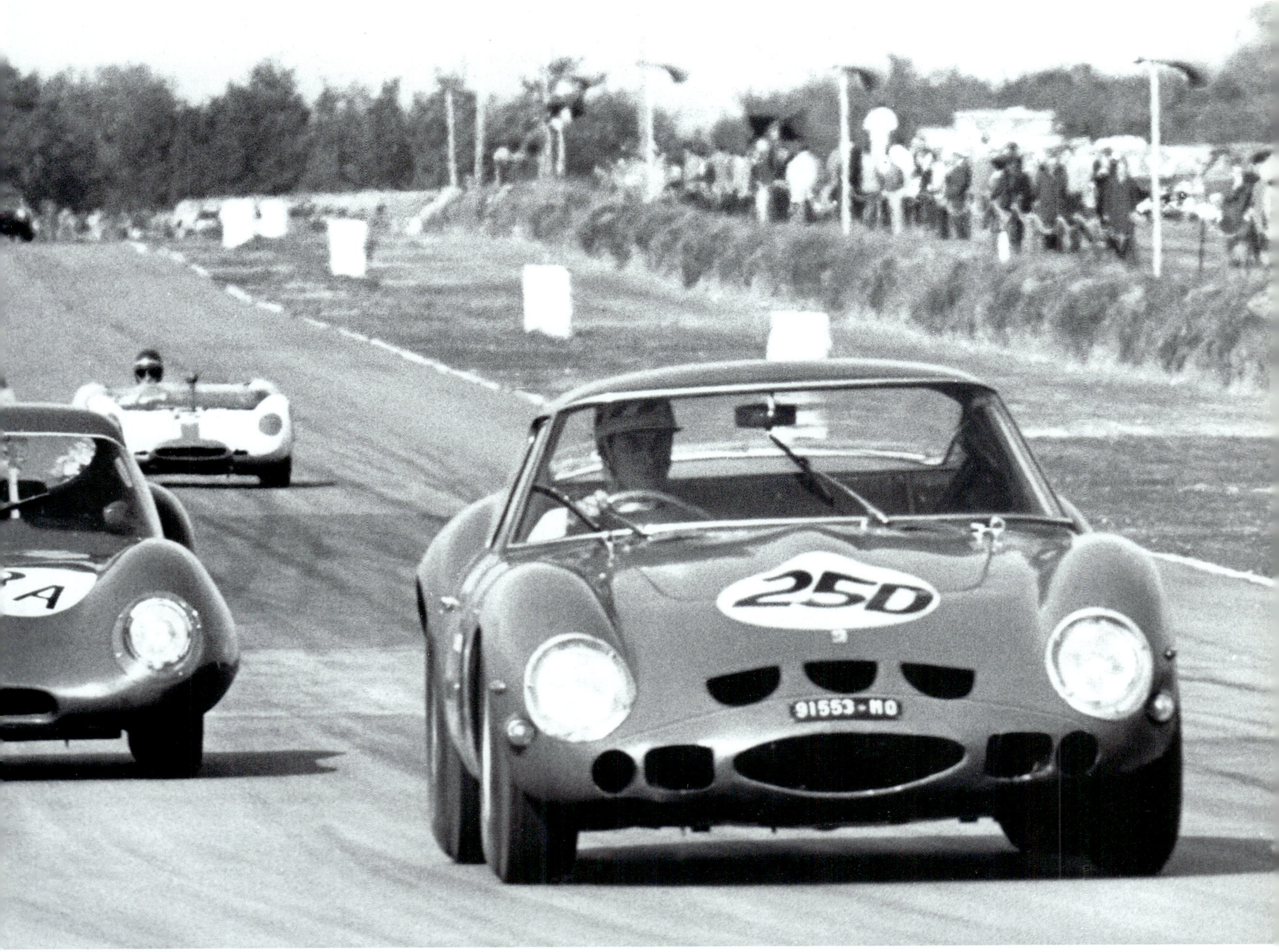

↑The *Autosport* Snetterton 3 Hours on 29 September 1963, with Mike Parkes in the class-winning and second overall Maranello Concessionaires Ferrari 250 GTO (4399 GT) lapping the unique Lotus-Climax XI GT (553) of John Dickinson. Following is one of the Mill Garage MG Midget coupés, with Tony Hegbourne (Normand Lotus-Ford 23B) alongside, then a Lola Mk1, and Peter Sutcliffe's 'lightweight' E-type in the distance. The race was won by Jim Clark in another Normand Lotus 23B after Roy Salvadori's Atkins much quicker Cooper Monaco retired.

↖ A brace of Aussies and Ian Walker Racing Brabham BT6s at the Anglo-European Trophy at Brands Hatch on 14 September 1963. The mischievous looking Paul Hawkins (left) and the laconic Frank Gardner (right) perch uncomfortably on the front wheels (no doubt at Mike's request) of Hawkins' mount, in which he will finish fifth, whilst Gardner, wearing his usual 'loafers', came in third in a race won by the omnipotent Peter Arundel 's Ron Harris Lotus 27, followed by Denny Hulme's works Brabham BT6.

← Competitors in the 1964 Monte Carlo Rally had a choice of several starting points, and Suffolk farming brothers Don and Erle Morley began in Oslo with the BMC works MGB 7 DBL. They are leaving the Reims control en route to finishing 17th overall and first GT car in the now filthy MG. The Morley brothers were well-known Healey 3000 exponents and won the 1961 and 1962 Alpine Rally, amongst many other successes.

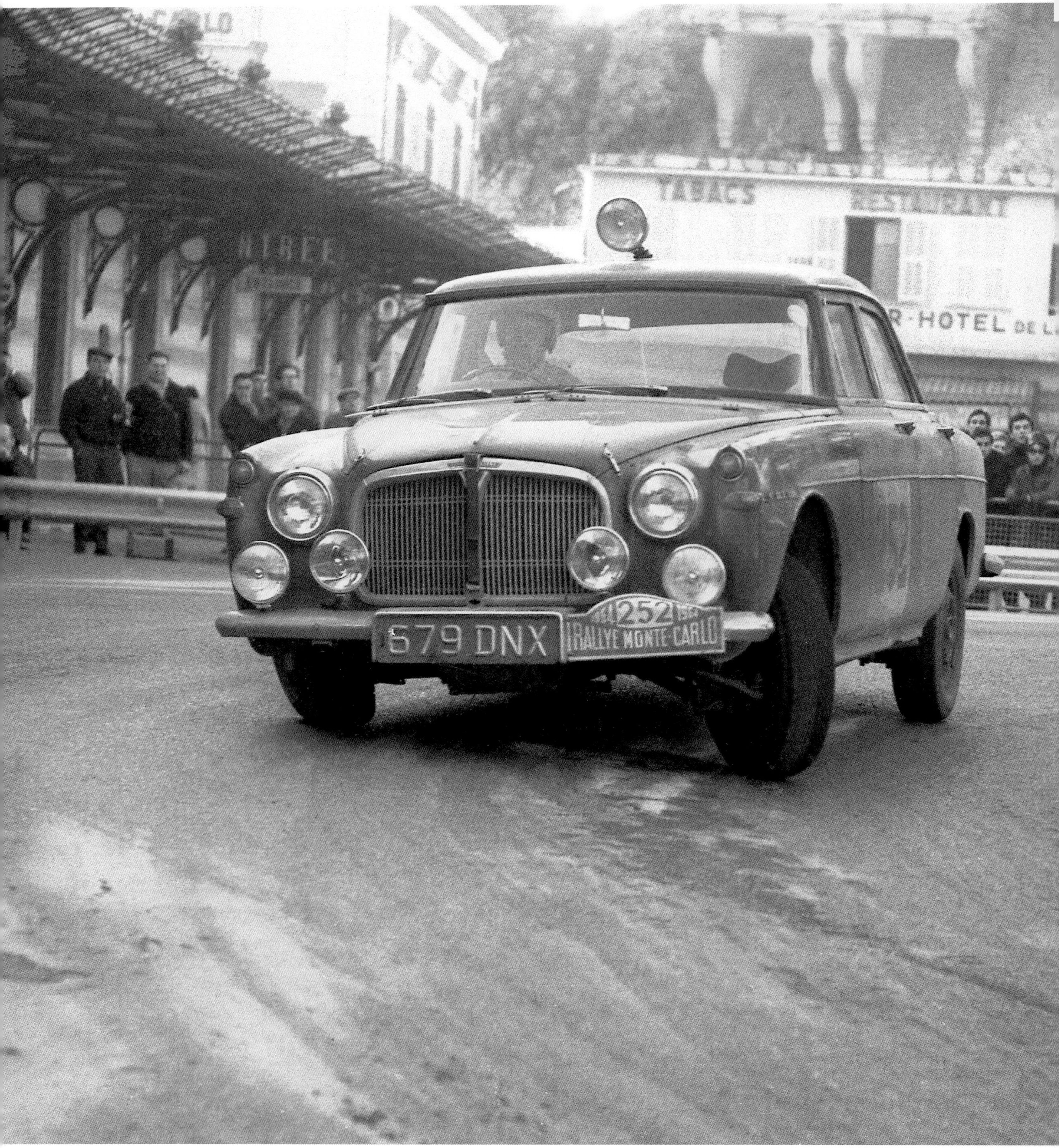
TABACS
RESTAURANT
HOTEL DE L
679 DNX
252
RALLYE MONTE-CARLO

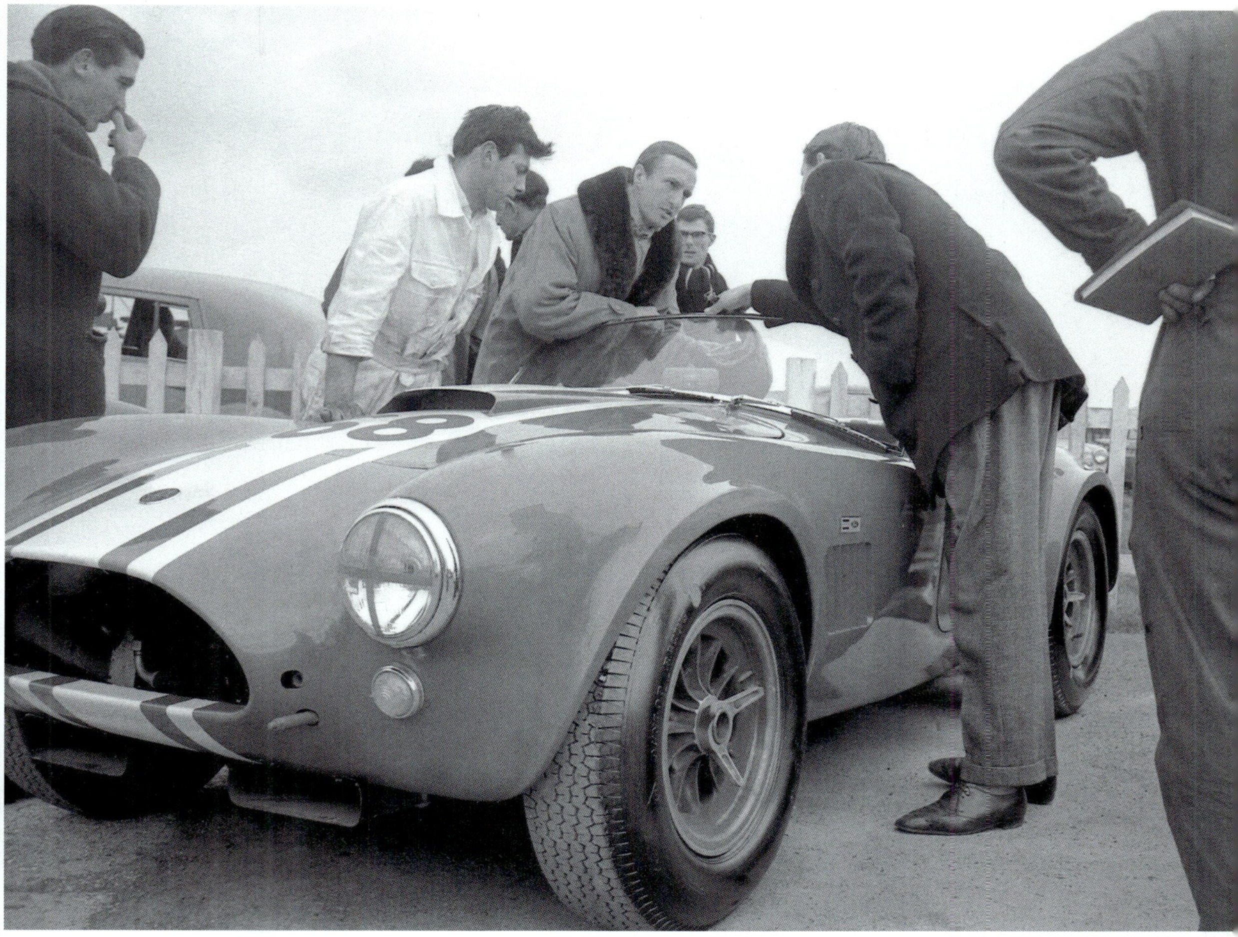

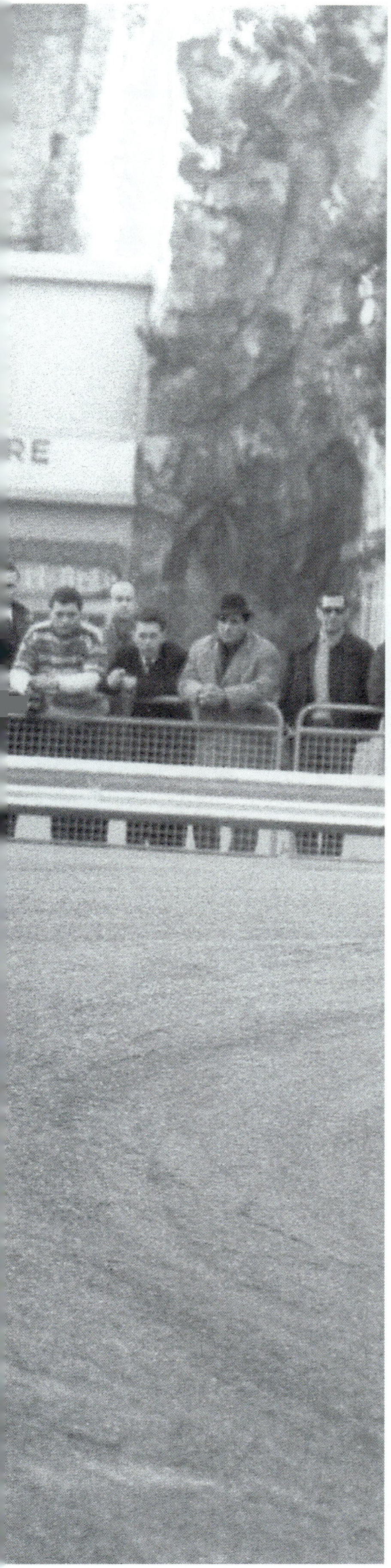

↑ A distinguished looking Jack Sears talking to Tommy Sopwith in the assembly area at Goodwood before the Easter Monday Sussex Trophy. The John Willment Cobra is still brand new, and looks it. Sears led the race for the first four laps from Graham Hill in the Maranello Concessionaires Ferrari 250GTO 64, and held on to finish second just eight tenths of a second adrift of the GTO on a cold 30 March 1964.

← A familiar setting, but an unlikely car on a cold winter's day in Monte Carlo 1964. Here is another reminder of our now-departed motoring heritage: Rover, once an independent purveyor of extremely well-made but modestly priced luxury cars. The works Rover 3-litre of Ken James/ Mike Hughes started from Glasgow and is pictured rounding the station hairpin on the GP circuit, with the station entrance on the left and the Hotel de la Gare in the background, both now long gone. The driver's side front wheel/tyre/suspension is being subjected to unknown forces, but the car survived and James/Hughes finished a very worthy 69th, despite their various problems, out of approximately 300 starters.

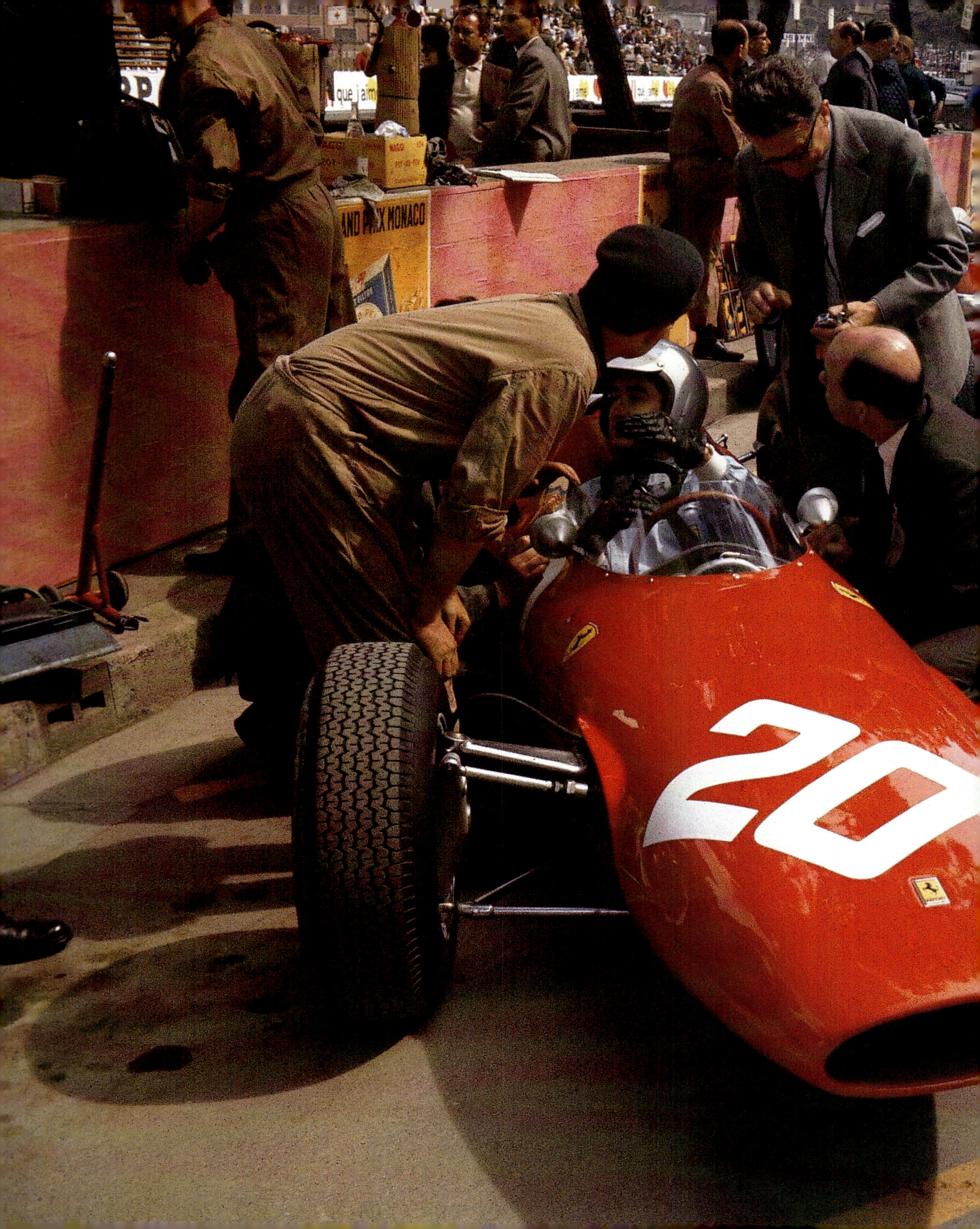
AND PRIX MONACO
20

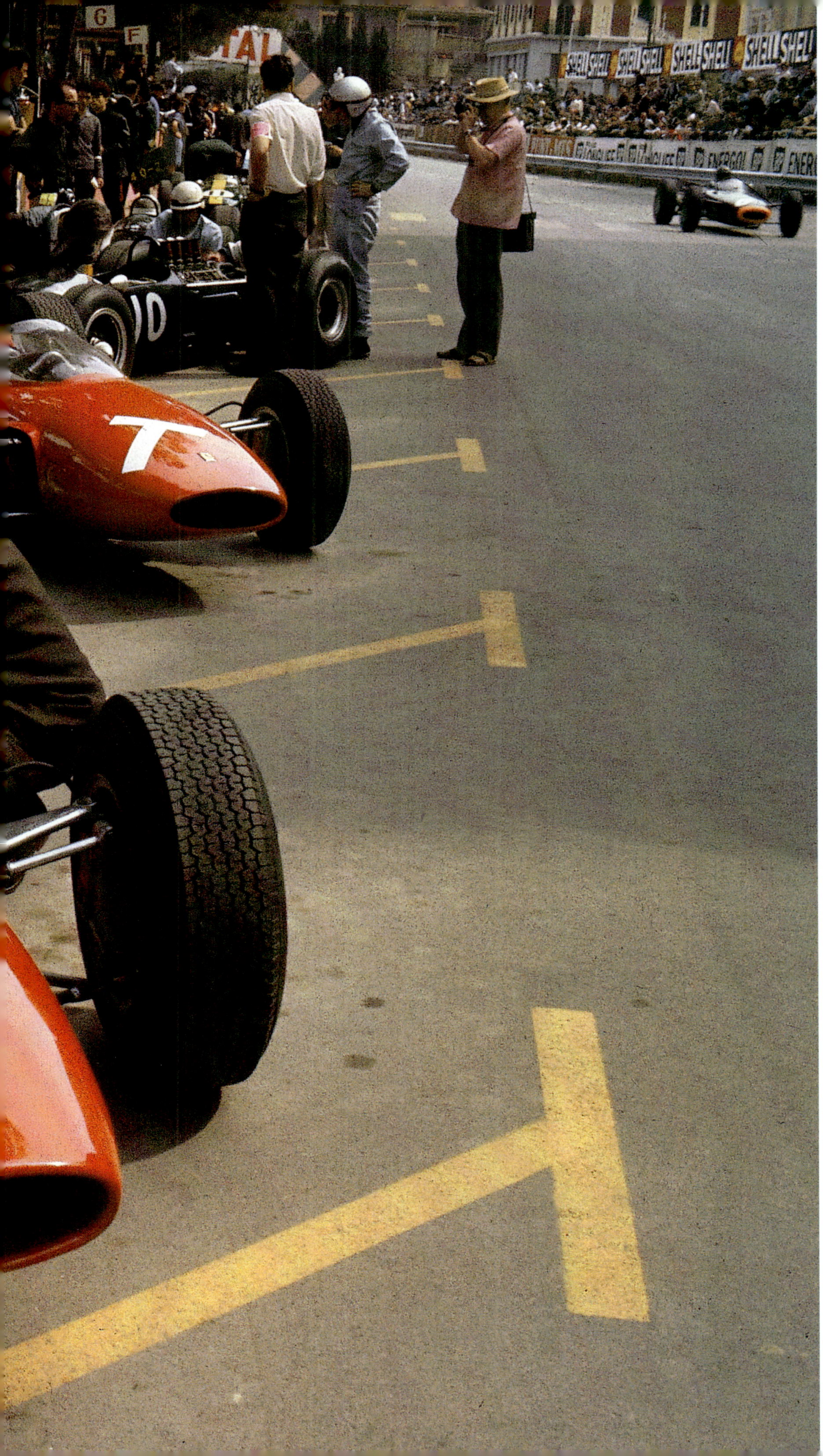

← They might have seemed little more than aluminium or plastic cigar tubes on wheels, but how beautiful and elegant these cars were. Lorenzo Bandini sits in the Ferrari 156 (0003) during practice for the XXII Grand Prix de Monaco on 9 May 1964. He is attended by team personnel, including team manager Eugenio Dragoni (on the right bending forward wearing suit and glasses) who was also a perfume manufacturer. In the background can be seen the Ferrari training car (chassis 0004) that was used by John Surtees but not raced, and No. 10 Bruce McLaren's Cooper-Climax T73 (F1-1-64), but this suffered steering failure and Bruce had to race a 1963 T66. McLaren stands, hands on hips. Phil Hill, in white helmet, is crouched behind the T73 as an intent photographer, back to the totally open track, takes a picture, and Norman Graham Hill zooms by in the race-winning BRM P261 (2614).

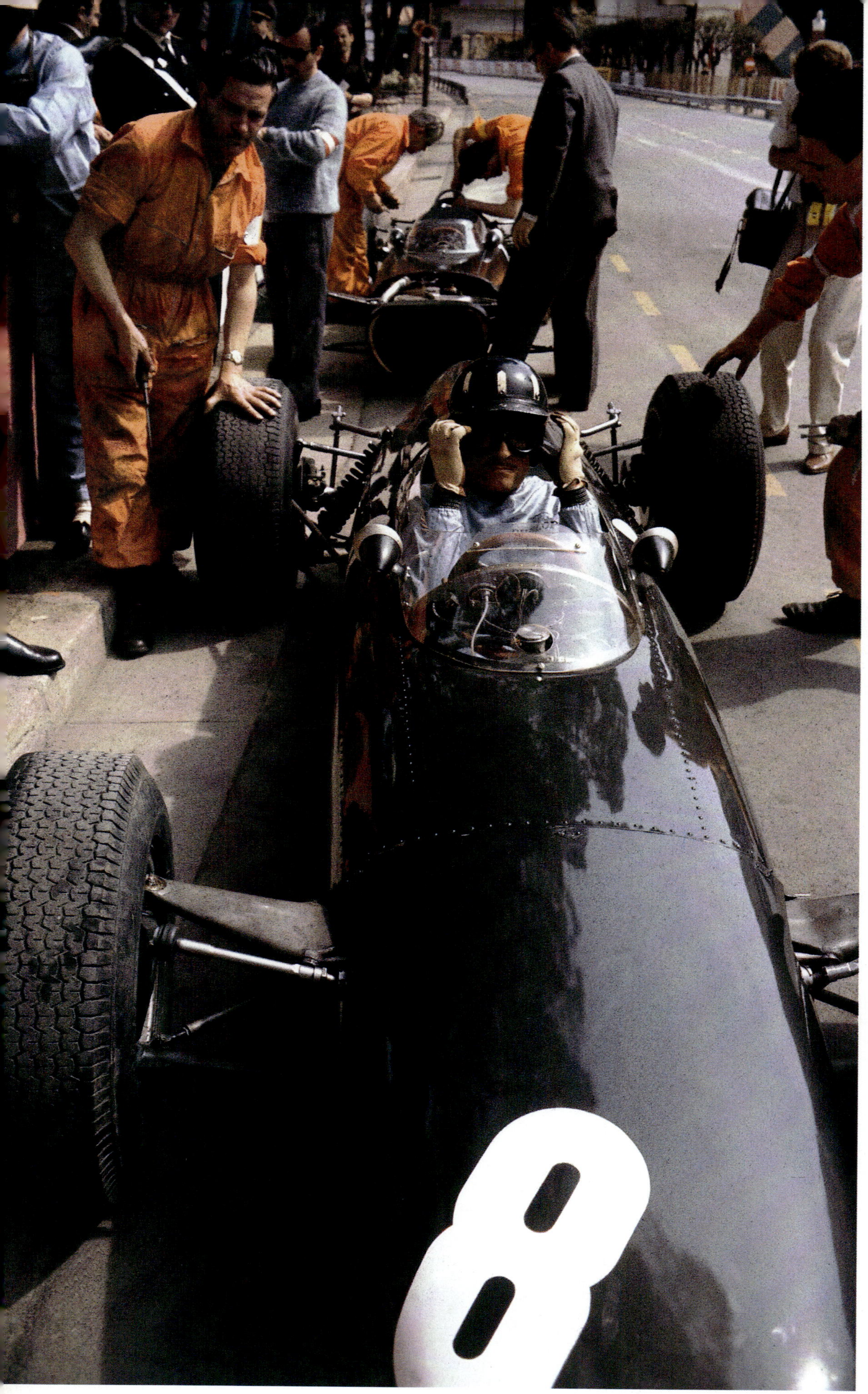

← Monaco and Graham Hill were two of Mike's favourite subjects, and here is a typically in your face (literally) picture as NGH is either about to, or has just finished adjusting, his goggles sitting in chassis 2614. Richie Ginther's 2613, with nose removed, sits behind and Richie is just visible, in helmet, at the top left. Hill, of course, won the race, his second consecutive victory here after a tense scrap with Clark's Lotus (that led despite a broken rear anti-roll bar) and Gurney's Brabham, both of which retired. Ginther finished second, a perfect result for Bourne. BRM chief mechanic Cyril Atkins rests his left hand on 2614's rear tyre.

→ Same treatment for Peter Arundell, who will finish third at Monaco in the Team Lotus 25 (R4) which looks almost new compared to Hill's grubby BRM in the other picture. Former FJ star Arundell subsequently finished third at Zandvoort and fourth at Rouen, but a dreadful accident at the Reims F2 race wrecked his career, and when he returned to F1 in 1966, as promised by Colin Chapman, his speed had gone and he drove his last of 11 Grands Prix at Mexico that year. Later he emigrated to Florida, but eventually returned to the UK. Sadly, he is now in ill health.

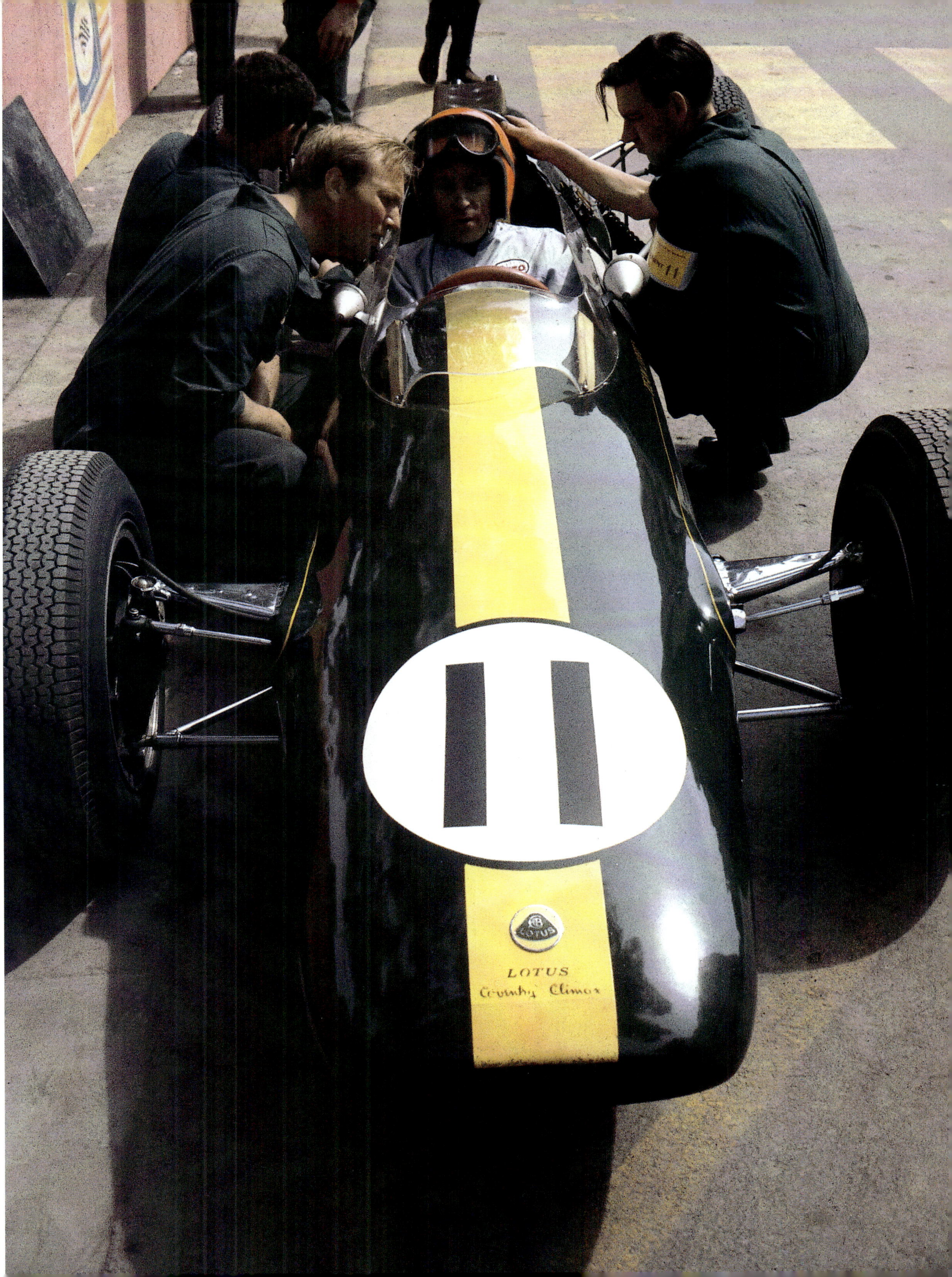
11
LOTUS
Coventry Climax

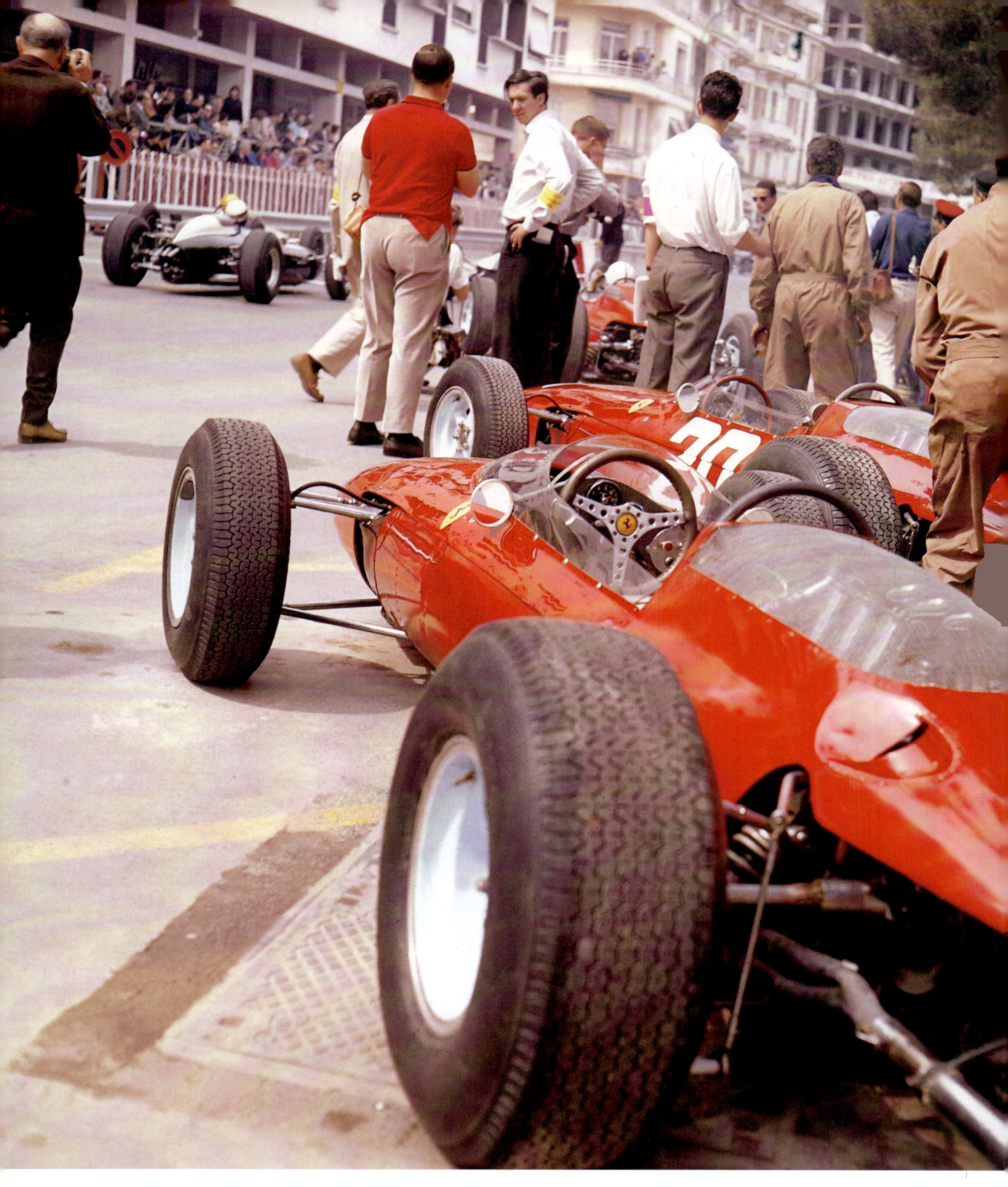

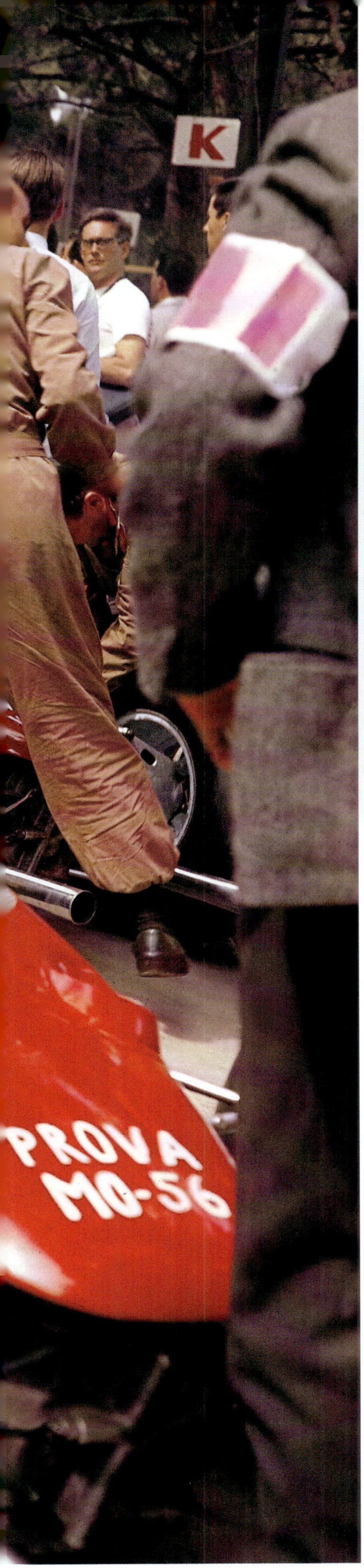

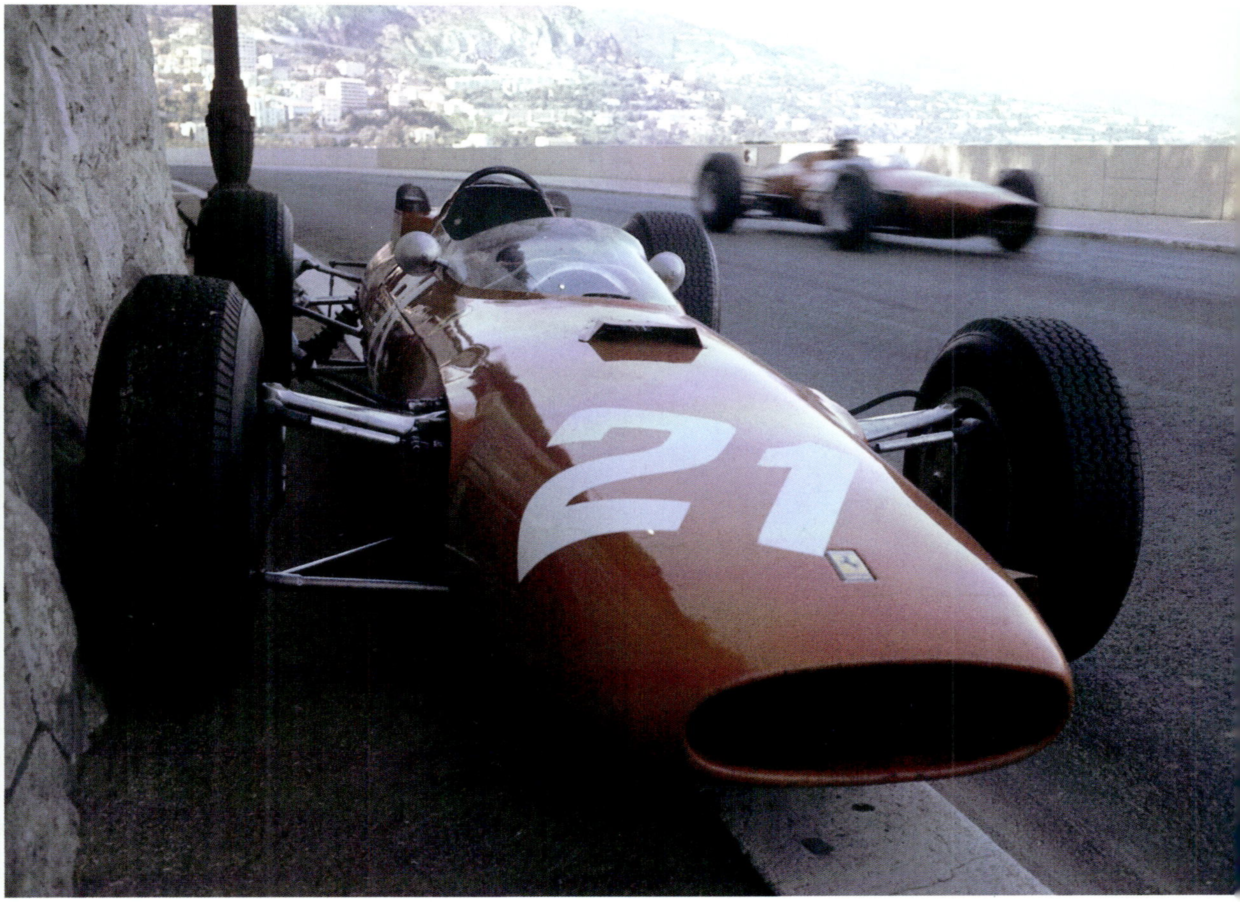

↑ At the approach to the old tunnel at Monaco, John Surtees' broken Ferrari 156 (0005) has been pushed over as far a possible into the rock face, whilst his team-mate Lorenzo Bandini races by only feet away. The casual abandonment of cars on track would nowadays bring on an attack of hives to any seat polisher, bureaucrat, or official within 20 square miles, but in those days such things were commonplace. Note the enamel Prancing Horse Ferrari badge in the nose of 0005.

← Another view of the Ferrari line up at Monaco 1964. The 156 nearest the camera is the 'T' car (0004) with its inboard rear brakes plainly visible, No. 20 is Bandini's 0003, Phil Hill has taken to the track in his Cooper-Climax T73 (F1-2-64), and John Surtees, with his distinctive white and blue stripe helmet, in his 156 race car (0005) can just be seen joining the throng between the onlookers.

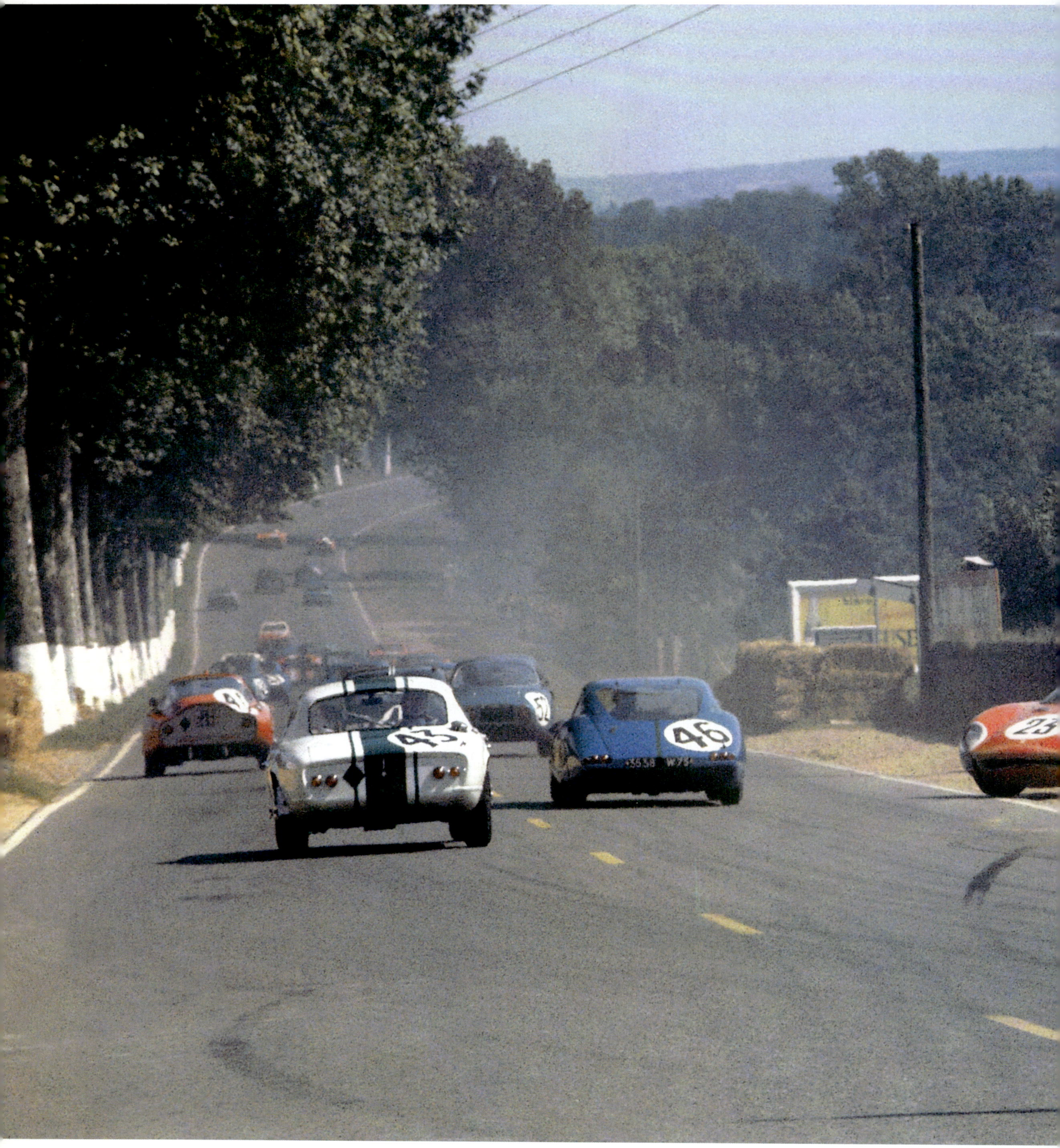

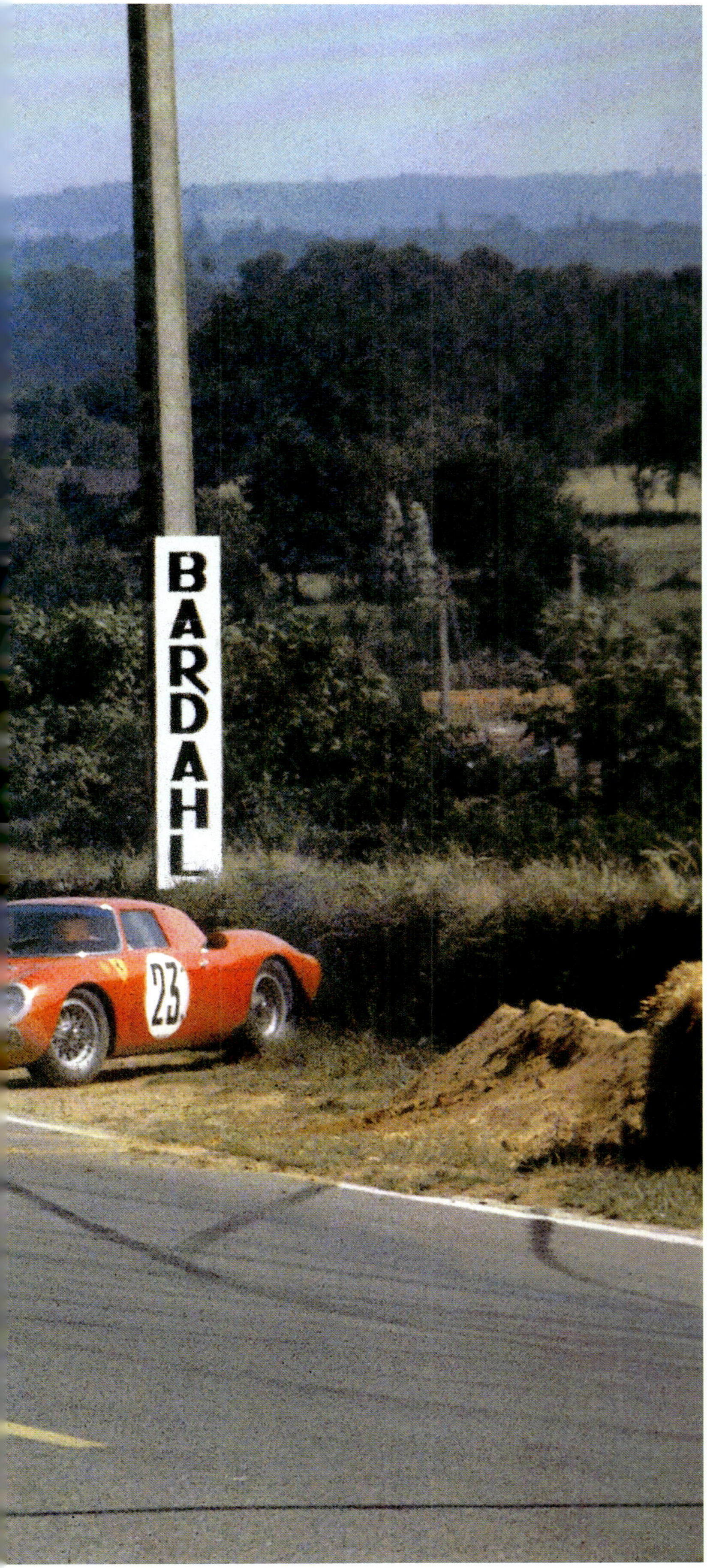

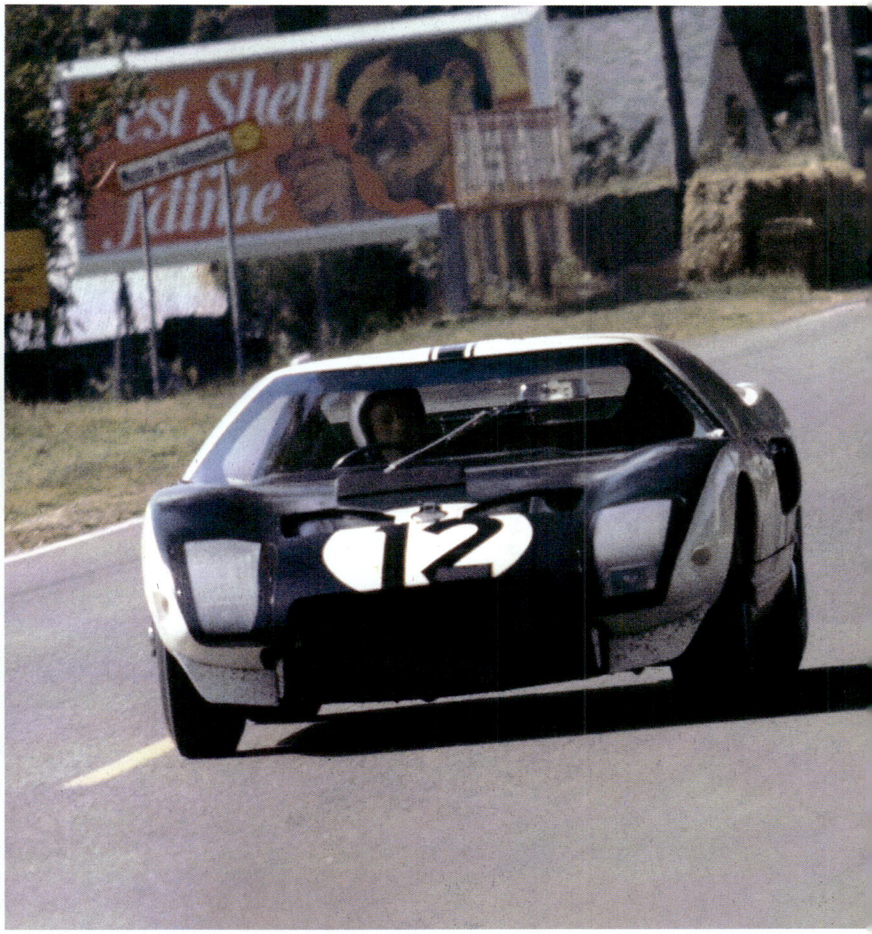

↑ Three Ford GT40s were entered for Le Mans. None finished – they were as fast as the Ferraris, but mechanically fragile. The slowest of the trio was driven By Richard Attwood/Jo Schlesser (chassis 104) and was the first to retire after catching fire in the pits, whilst the other two broke their Colotti transmissions that Ford had failed to develop from its Lola GT origins. At this stage the Ford was still using the special all alloy Indy 4.2-litre Fairlane engine and the omnipresent Borrani wire wheels.

← It is easy to assume that Mike started this sequence of shots at Tertre Rouge before walking up the Mulsanne Straight at Le Mans 1964. The No. 23 Ecurie Francorchamps Ferrari 250LM (5843) of Pierre Dumay/Gerard Langlois von Ophem has a 'which way am I supposed to be going?' moment as the Delageneste/Morrogh Alpine M64 Renault (1711) No. 46, the Hunt/Wagstaff Lotus Elite (41-10391) No. 43, the Farjon/Lelong Rene Bonnet Aerojet No. 52, the Sala/Biscald Alfa Romeo TZ No. 41, and the rest head off up the road. This is towards the back of the field, and is probably the opening lap. Those mentioned finished 16th, 17th, 22nd, 23rd, and 15th respectively.

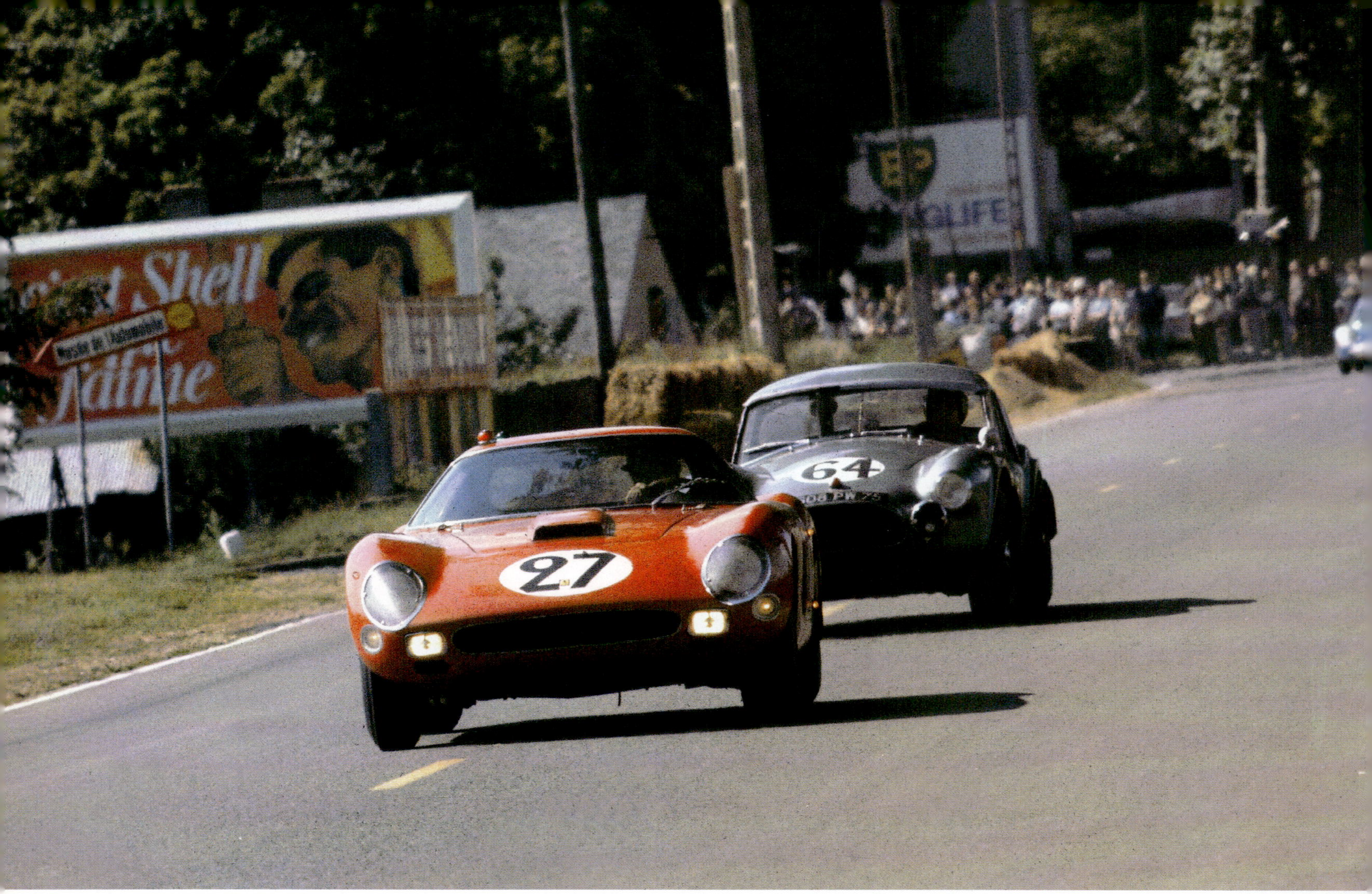

↑ Auguste Veuillet's Porsche 904GTS (021) was driven by Robert Buchet and later F1 racer/entrant Guy Ligier to 7th place and a class win at Le Mans in 1964. Buchet is followed by another 904GTS and the Peter Procter/ Jimmy Blumer Sunbeam Tiger as the cars begin the long flat-out thrash up the Mulsanne Straight watched, by the trackside observers (sic) at Tertre Rouge. The Lister constructed Sunbeam Tigers were a disaster. The Carroll Shelby-supplied 4.2-litre (260 cubic inch) V8 Fords were underpowered (260bhp rather than the 350 odd of the proper 289 Cobra V8 units) and the underdeveloped cars also suffered handling and cooling problems. The other Tiger was driven by Keith Ballisat and ex-Equipe National Belge driver Claud Dubois. It was the slower of the two and only survived 37 laps whilst its quicker sister seen here managed 118 laps. Later on when fitted with a proper Cobra engine, and properly sorted by Bernard Unett, the Tiger revealed its true potential and became a race winner, albeit at British national level.

↗ The NART (North American Racing Team) Fernand Tavano/Bob Grossman Ferrari 250GTO 64 (5573 GT) with its Le Mans roof light, one of the last GTOs built wearing the 1964 style LM bodywork, accelerates away from Tertre Rouge along the nearly 3.5-mile Mulsanne Straight (no chicanes then). It is followed by the Jean de Mortemart/Régis Fraissinet AC Cobra (COX6010) entered by Société Chardonnet. Both cars finished, the GTO 9th and the slower Cobra 18th.

→ Giancarlo Baghetti, Phil Hill, Bruce McLaren with book, and Jack Brabham wearing his half-finger gloves, chew the cud before the 1964 Belgian GP at Spa-Francorchamps. The Antipodeans are wearing boxing style boots, whilst Phil Hill favours lace-up shoes. Baghetti and Hill are wasting their time with the ancient Centro Sud BRM P57 and the second works Cooper respectively (ironically just as they did as team-mates for the woeful ATS team in 1963), but McLaren will finish second in the works Cooper Climax T73 behind omnipotent Jim Clark's Lotus 25 who won after Gurney (leading), Graham Hill, and McLaren all ran out of fuel. As his car ran dry, Bruce was caught and passed within sight of the flag by Clark who had earlier stopped for water and who then ran out of fuel on his slowing down lap! You could not make it up. Brabham finished third.

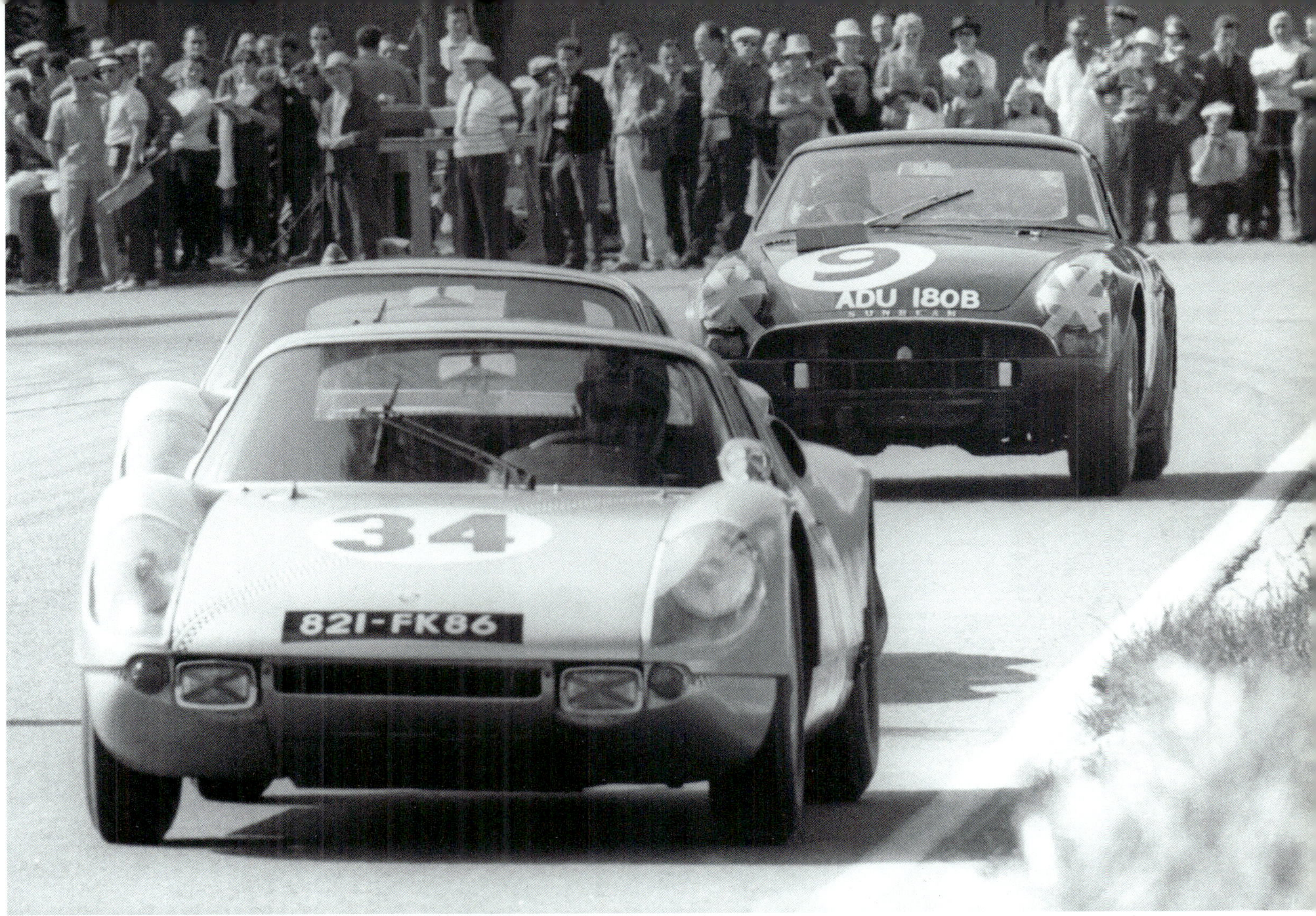
34
821-FK86
9
ADU 180B

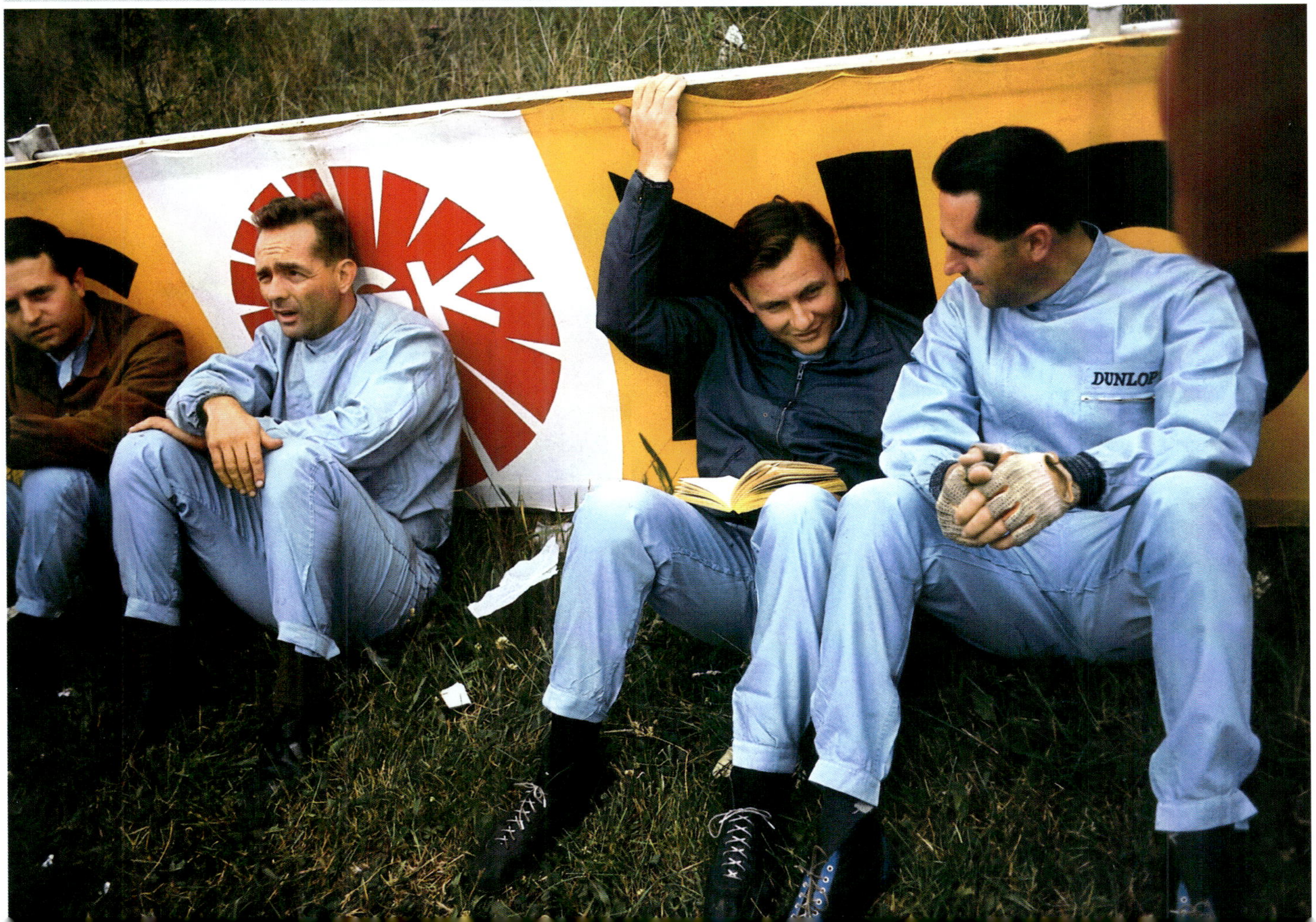
DUNLOP

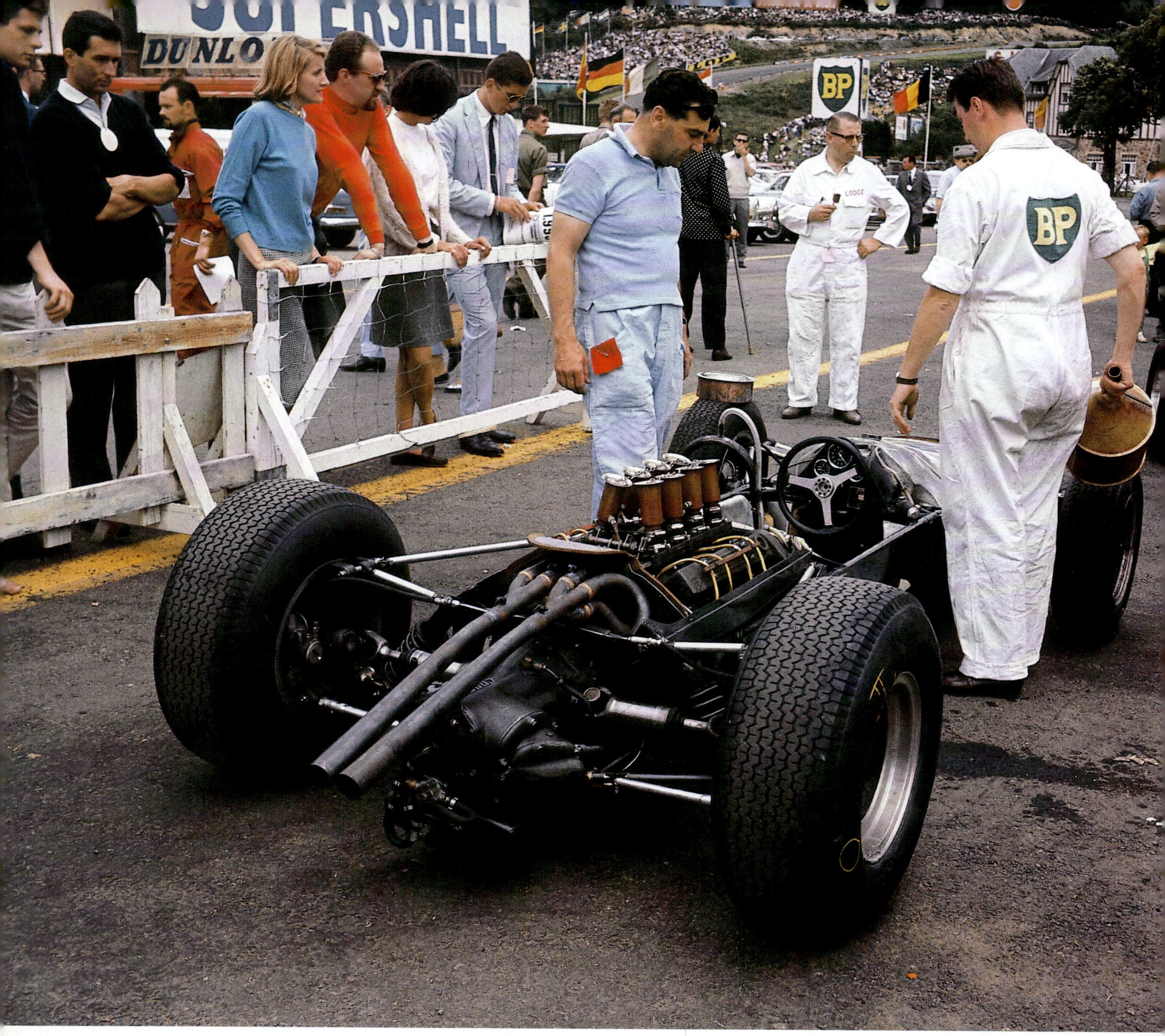

↑ The Spa paddock in 1964, with Eau Rouge visible in the background. Bruce McLaren's Cooper-Climax T73 (F1-1-64), with top panels removed and displaying its downswept exhaust system, alongside Jo Siffert's red Brabham-BRM BT11 (F1-6-64). John Cooper looks on, and the BP fuel man awaits. The chassis numbering for the works Coopers and customer Brabhams used an identical nomenclature – very confusing.

↗ With his cotton wool earplugs in place, John Surtees is focusing hard on the forthcoming Belgian GP, but he will retire. Ferrari engineer Mauro Foghieri holds his helmet.

→ Jim Clark's 1962 Lotus 25 (R6) was actually a preferred substitute at Spa for the proposed 33 (R8) that had been rebuilt after his Aintree 200 shunt. Note that this now 'old' car is still using the taller 1963 Dunlop R6 tyres, and narrower, larger diameter wheels, rather than the latest R7 rubber and wider rims.

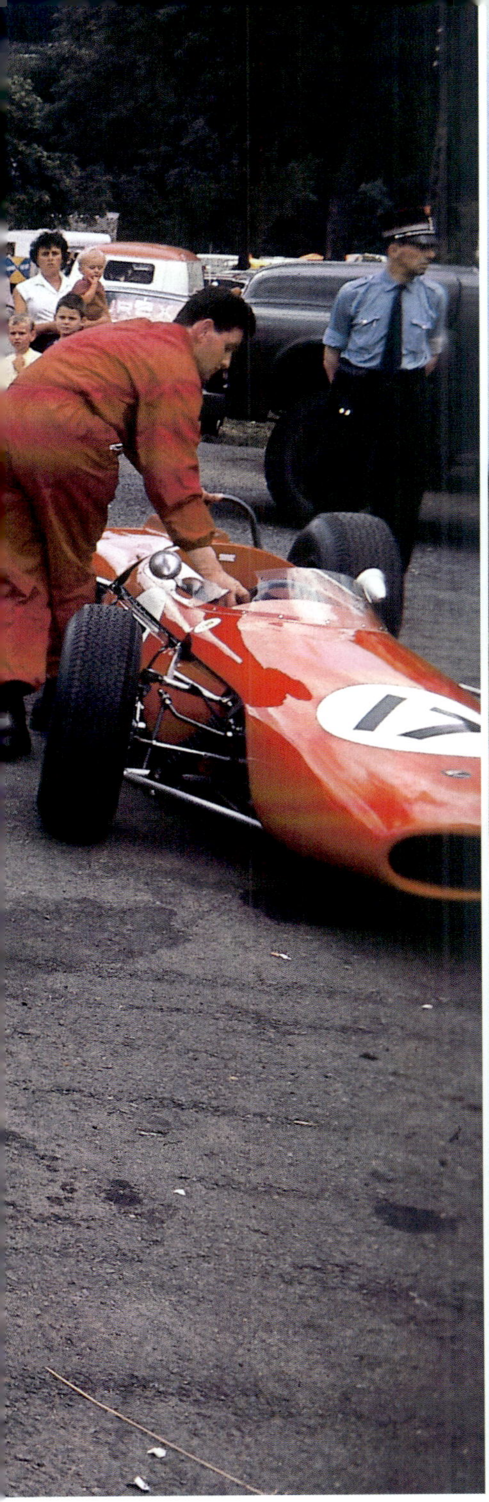
17

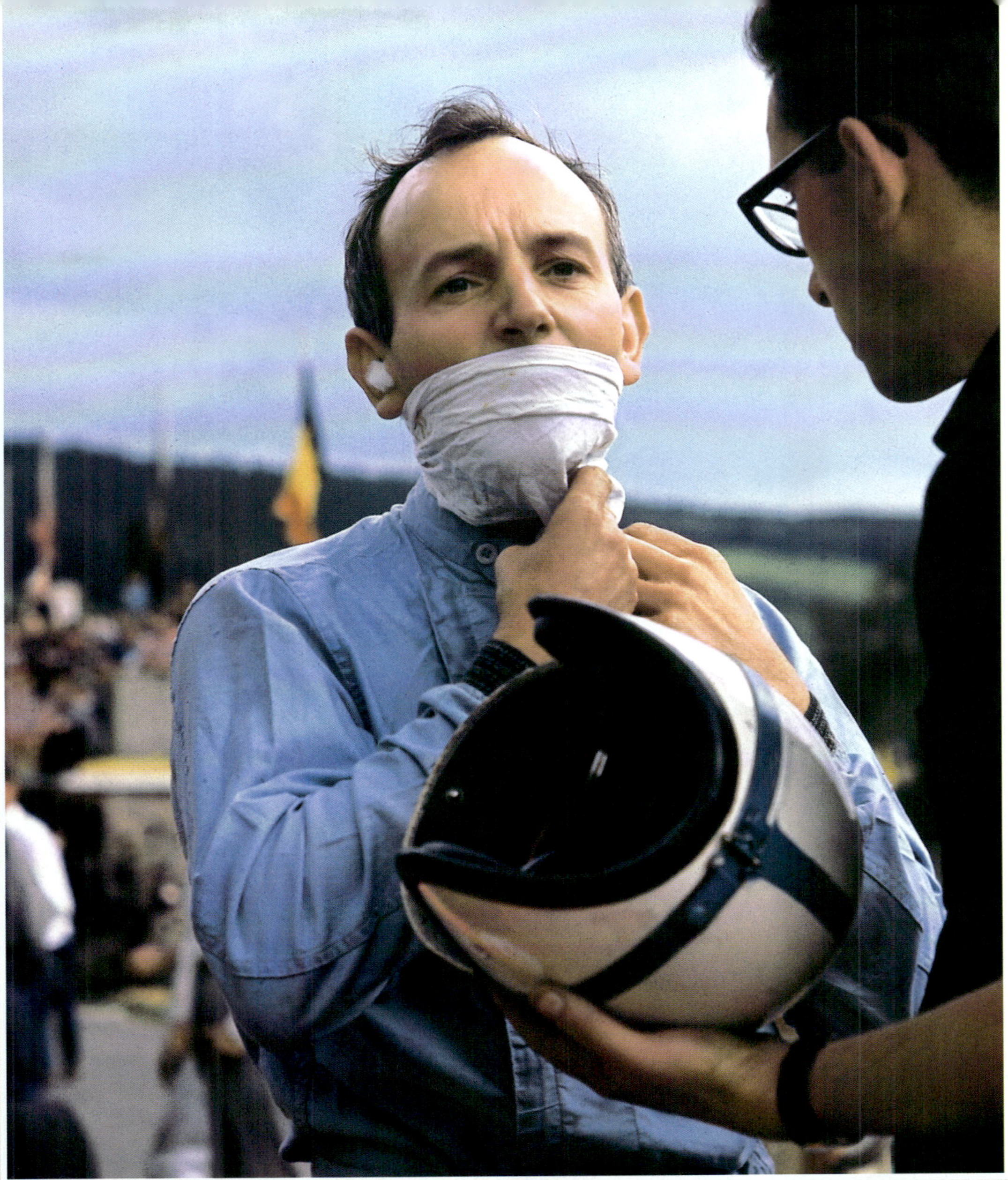

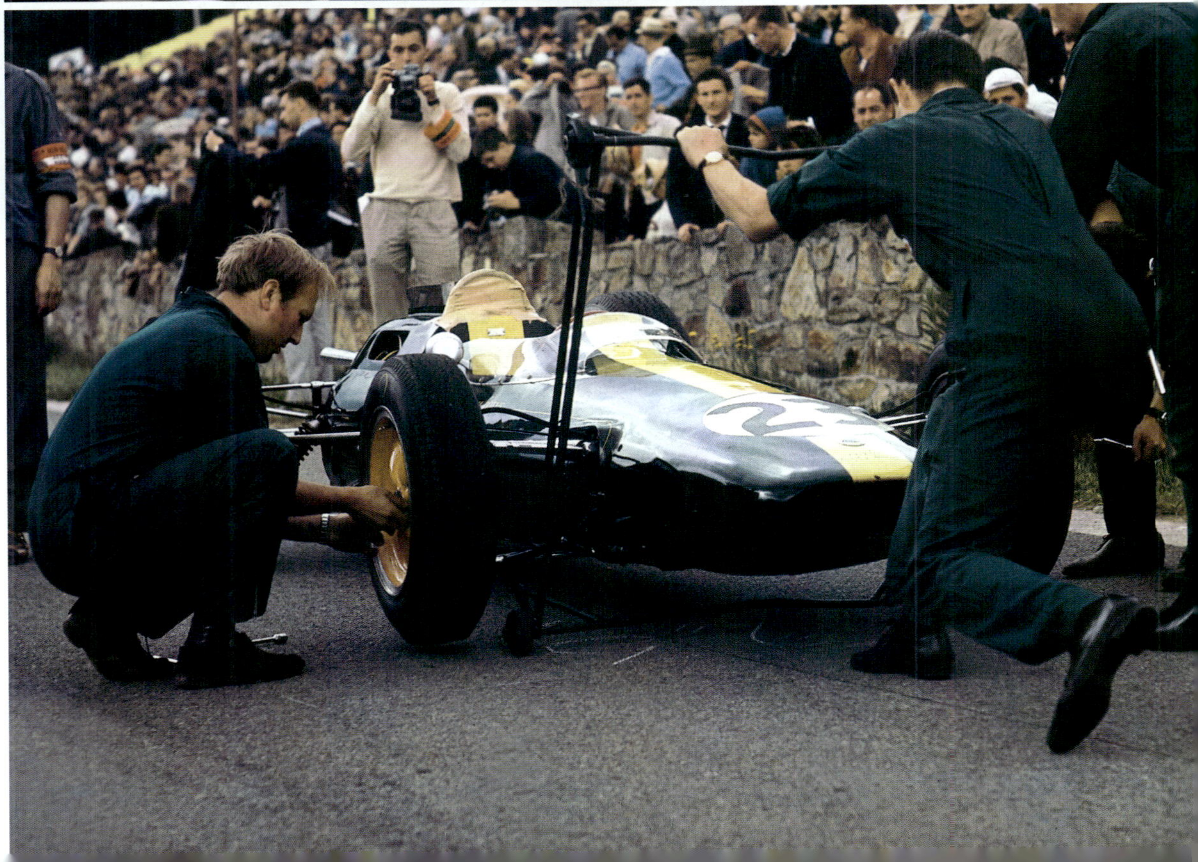

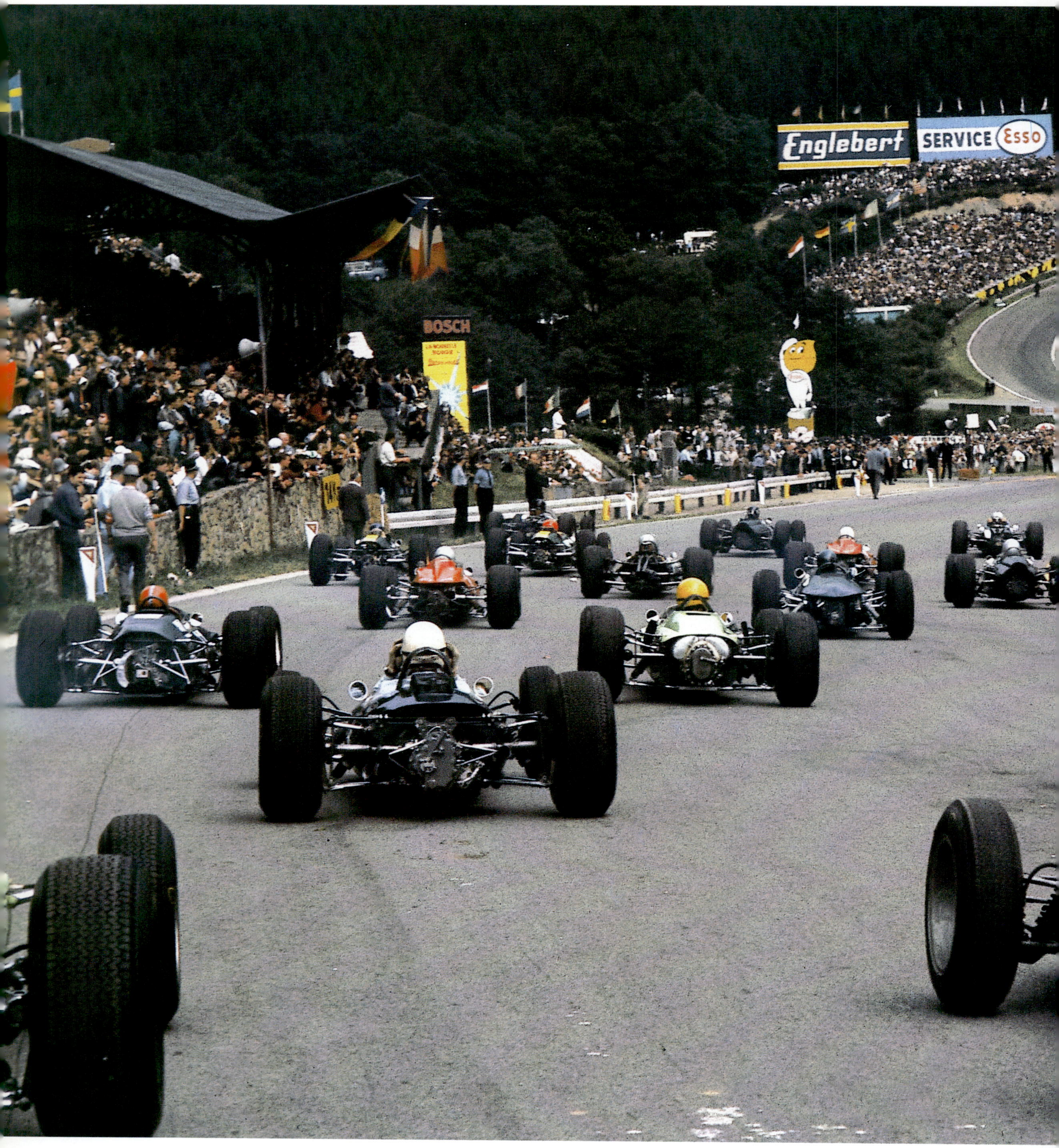
Englebert
SERVICE
Esso
BOSCH

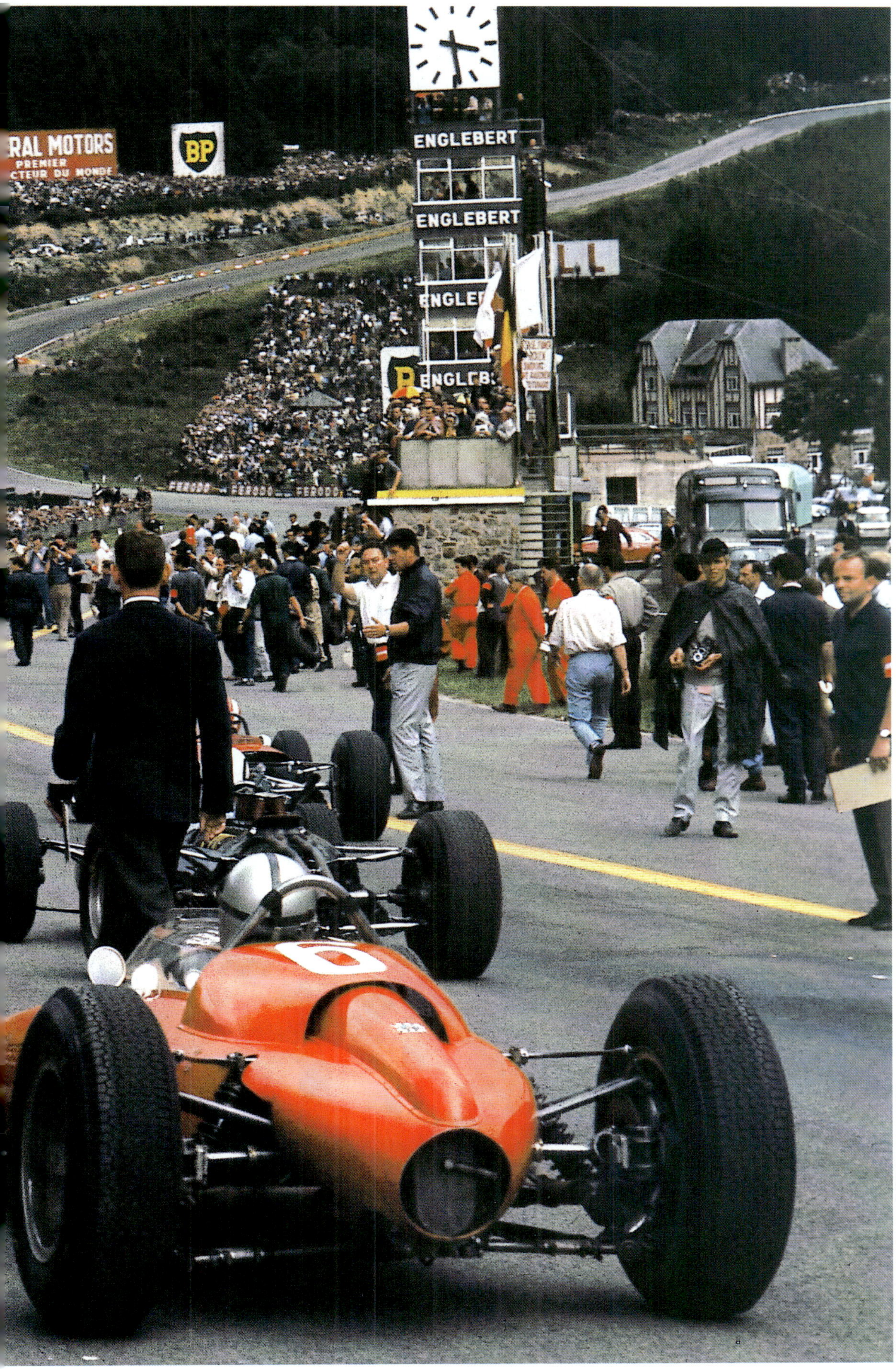

← In the distance the long sweeping curves of Eau Rouge await the unwary as Graham Hill's BRM sits flanked by the two Brabhams of Gurney (left on pole) and Brabham to his right. At the other end of the grid, once-budding Italian superstar Giancarlo Baghetti (who won his first three F1 races in 1961: Syracuse, Naples, and the French GP at Reims) sits in his Centro Sud BRM P578 (5785) no. 6, one of the 1963 works team cars. He will finish eighth, one lap down. Note the control tower clock reading 3.29pm – none of the TV schedule diktats to worry about then.

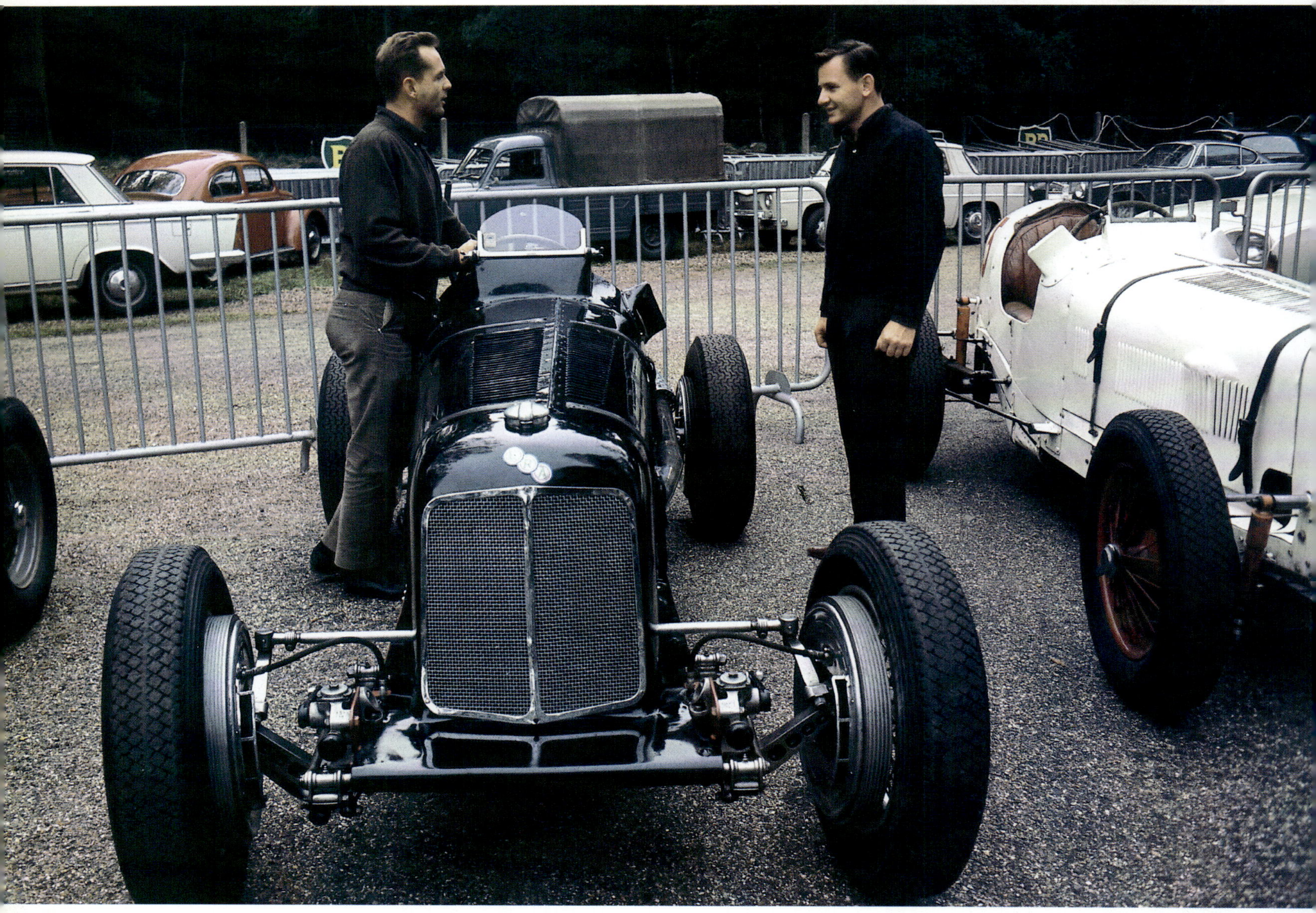

↑ At Rouen the organisers held a bona fide historic race, which was won by Patrick Lindsay's ERA R5B 'Remus' which Jim Clark drove for the first time during practice and lapped faster than the owner! Here, a couple of genuine car enthusiasts take an interest in the machinery during practice. Phil Hill leans against Alan Cottam's ERA R1B, as Bruce McLaren, back to R9B driven by Peter Waller, looks on.

↗ Tony Ellis demonstrates the fwd Derby-Maserati's lack of traction at Rouen. The Derby was based upon the American Miller 91 owned by 1920s driver Douglas Hawkes (1893–1974) who had a financial stake in the French Derby concern. It was progressively modified during the early 1930s, fitted with a Maserati 4CM engine and raced by Englishwoman Gwenda Stewart (1894–1990), later Mrs Douglas Hawkes. She had raced motorcycles and Morgan three-wheelers, amongst others, setting a three-wheeler world speed record at 118mph in France, plus the absolute Brooklands Ladies Outer Circuit lap record at 135.95mph, and the outright record at Montlhéry, near Paris, in the Derby Special at 145.94mph. Born Gwenda Mary Glubb, daughter of Sir Frederick Manley Glubb and sister of Lieutenant-General Sir John Bagot Glubb KCB, CMG, DSO, OBE (the famous soldier better known as Glubb Pasha), she drove ambulances on the Russian and Rumanian fronts in the First World War and was decorated with the Crosses of St George and St Stanislaus.

→ Renowned Connaught racer Alan Cottam has the same problem as Tony Ellis, but this time from the other end, as R1B scrabbles for grip at Rouen. Drivers of modern machinery will be unfamiliar with the sensation of an exposed, furiously spinning wheel just over or alongside their shoulder.

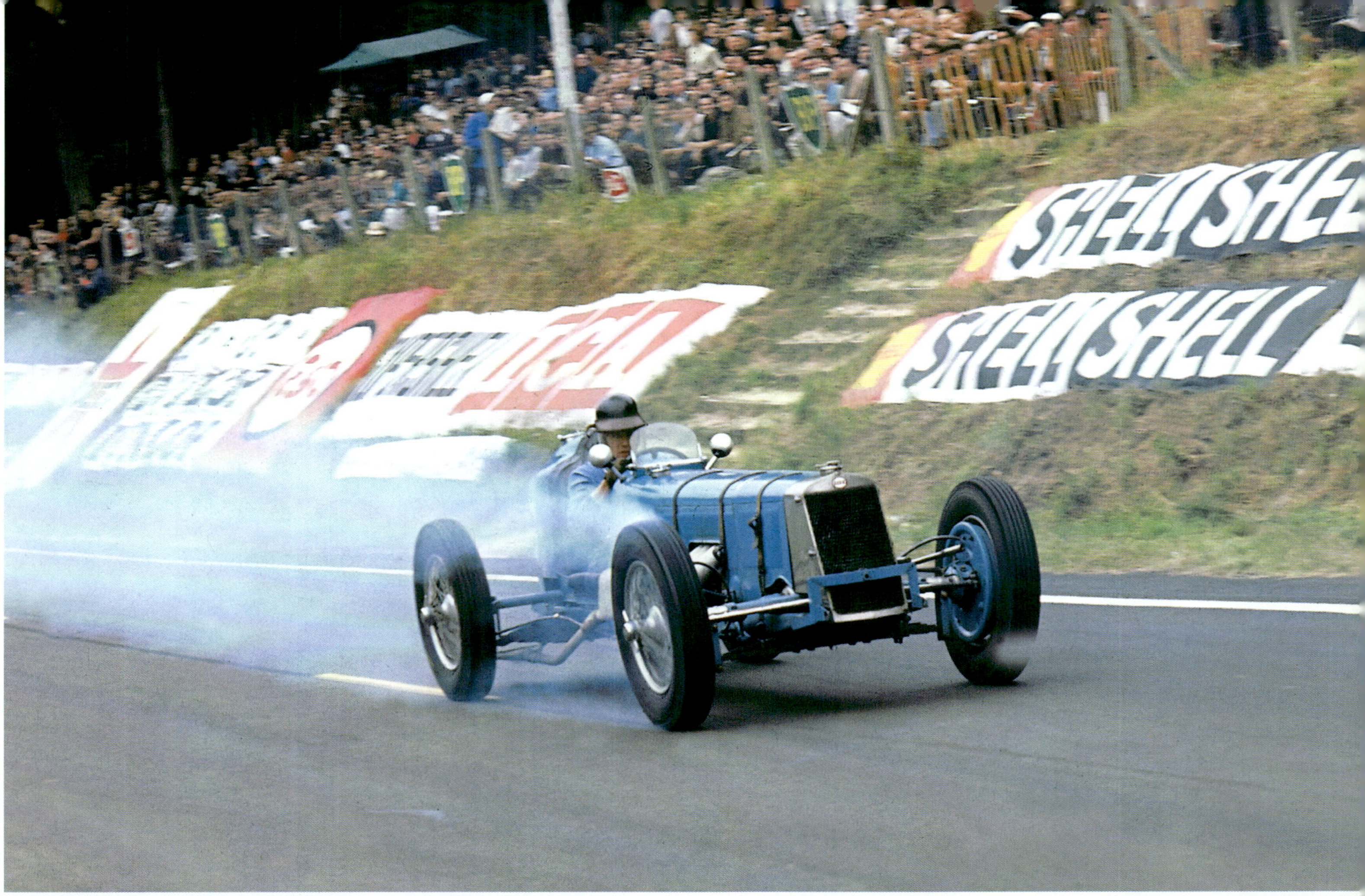
SHELL

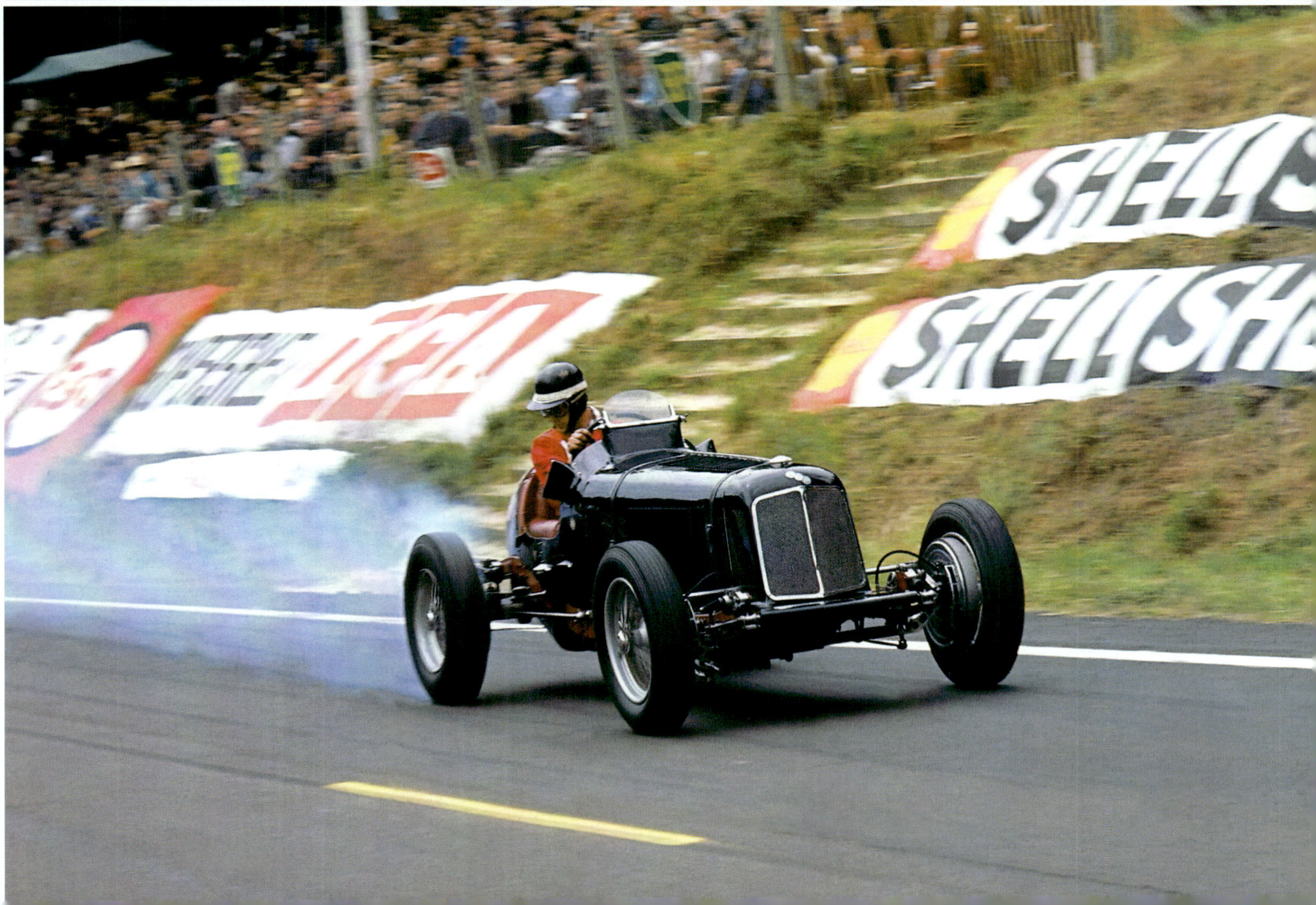
SHELL

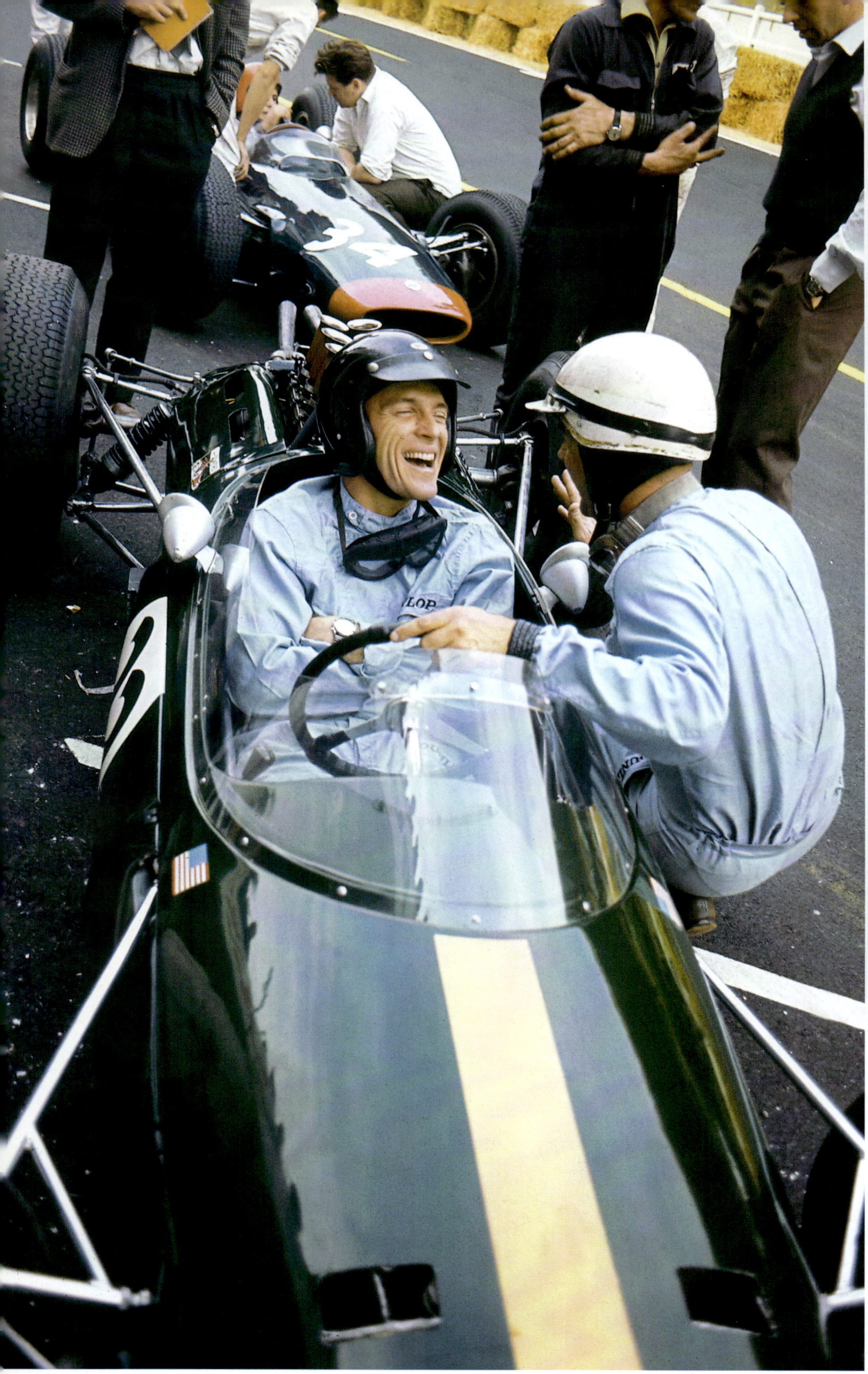

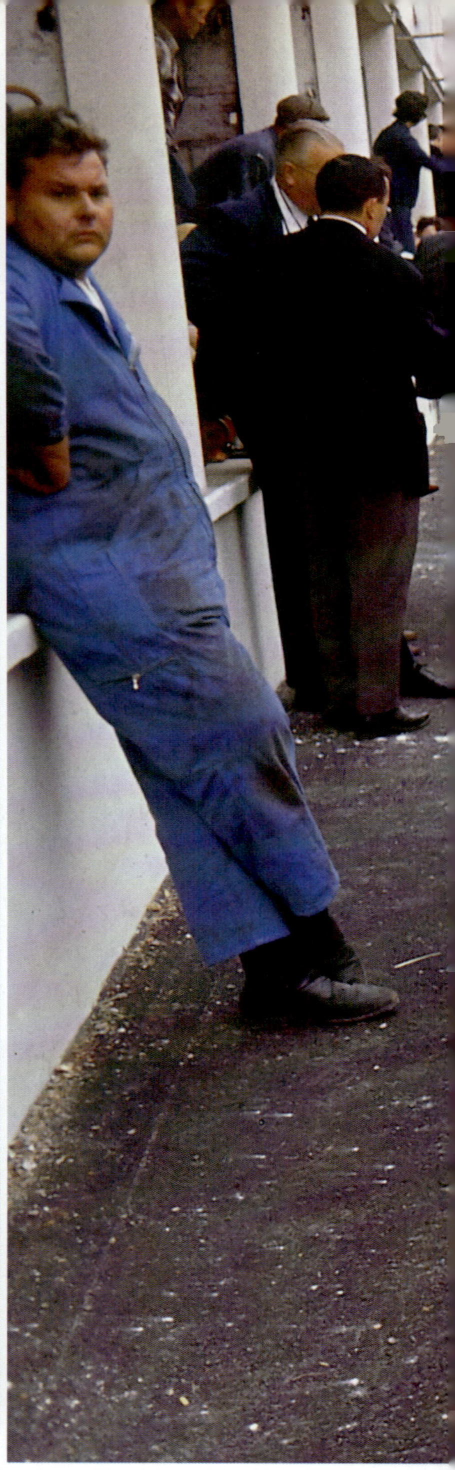

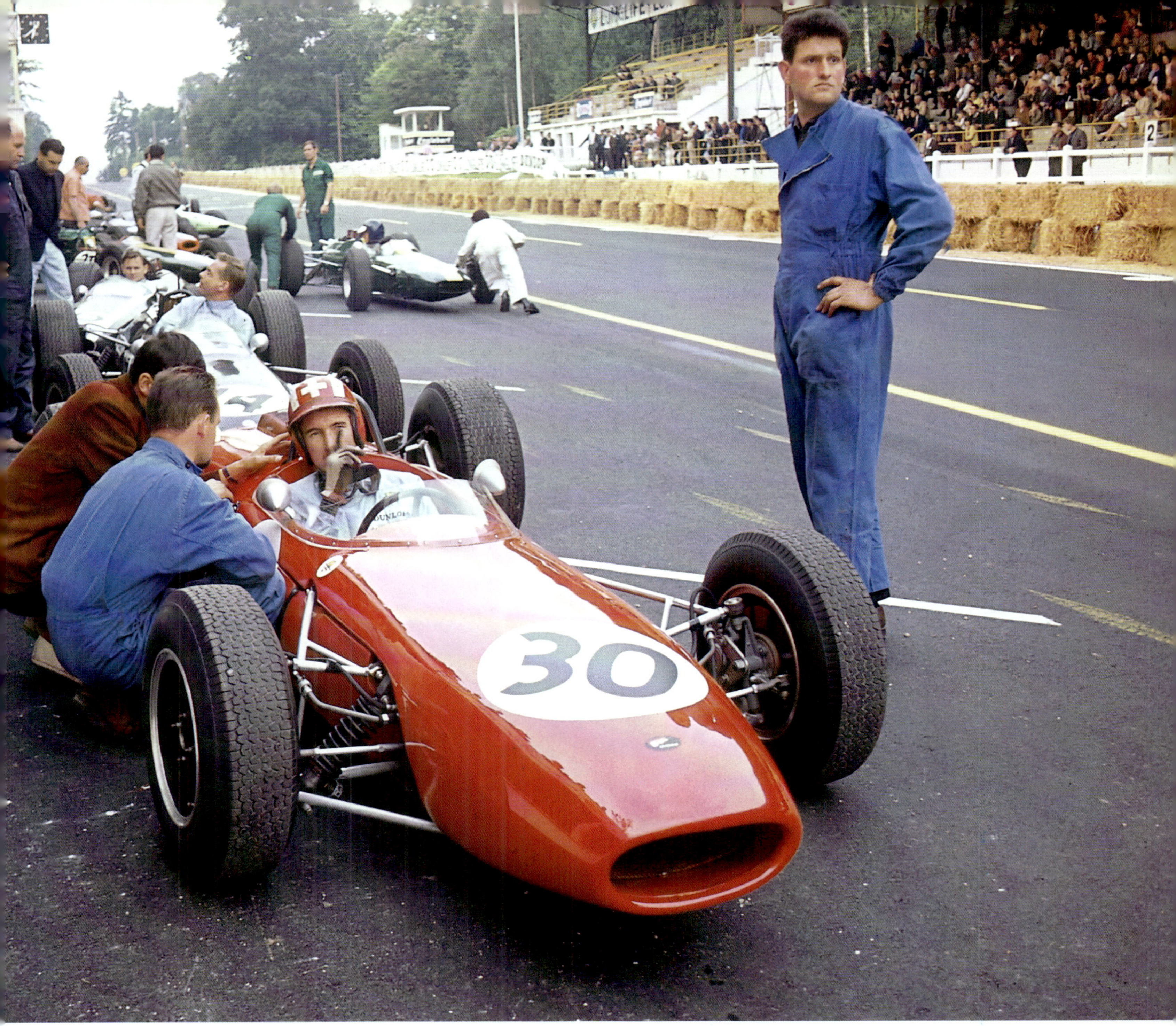

↑ The totally open and unprotected pits at Rouen-les-Essarts are typical of the period, and the straw bales on the spectator side would maximise the conflagration if a car crashed and caught fire. A young-looking Jo Siffert makes a point as he awaits the action in his very smart Brabham-BRM BT11 (F1-6-64), and behind, Phil Hill in his No. 14 Cooper-Climax T73 (F1-2-64) talks to an apparently unsympathetic mechanic. Hill's final full season in F1 was blighted by an unrecognised faulty throttle installation which meant he could not get full response at the pedal end. Beyond is Bruce McLaren in the sister T73 (F1-1-64), as Jim Clark's Lotus 25 (R6) is pushed back to its pit. Siffert only lasted four laps before his clutch failed, Hill finished seventh, McLaren sixth, and Clark retired.

← Following the extraordinary events at Spa, fate took a day off and Dan Gurney won the French GP at Rouen-les-Essarts in his Brabham BT7 (F1-1-63) after Clark's Lotus 25 (substituted for his newer 33 that was rejected due to a suspect engine) developed piston trouble. He seems very happy talking to fellow-American Phil Hill, whilst behind, Tim Parnell crouches down to talk to Chris Amon in the Reg Parnell Racing Lotus-BRM 25 (R3) who will finish tenth.

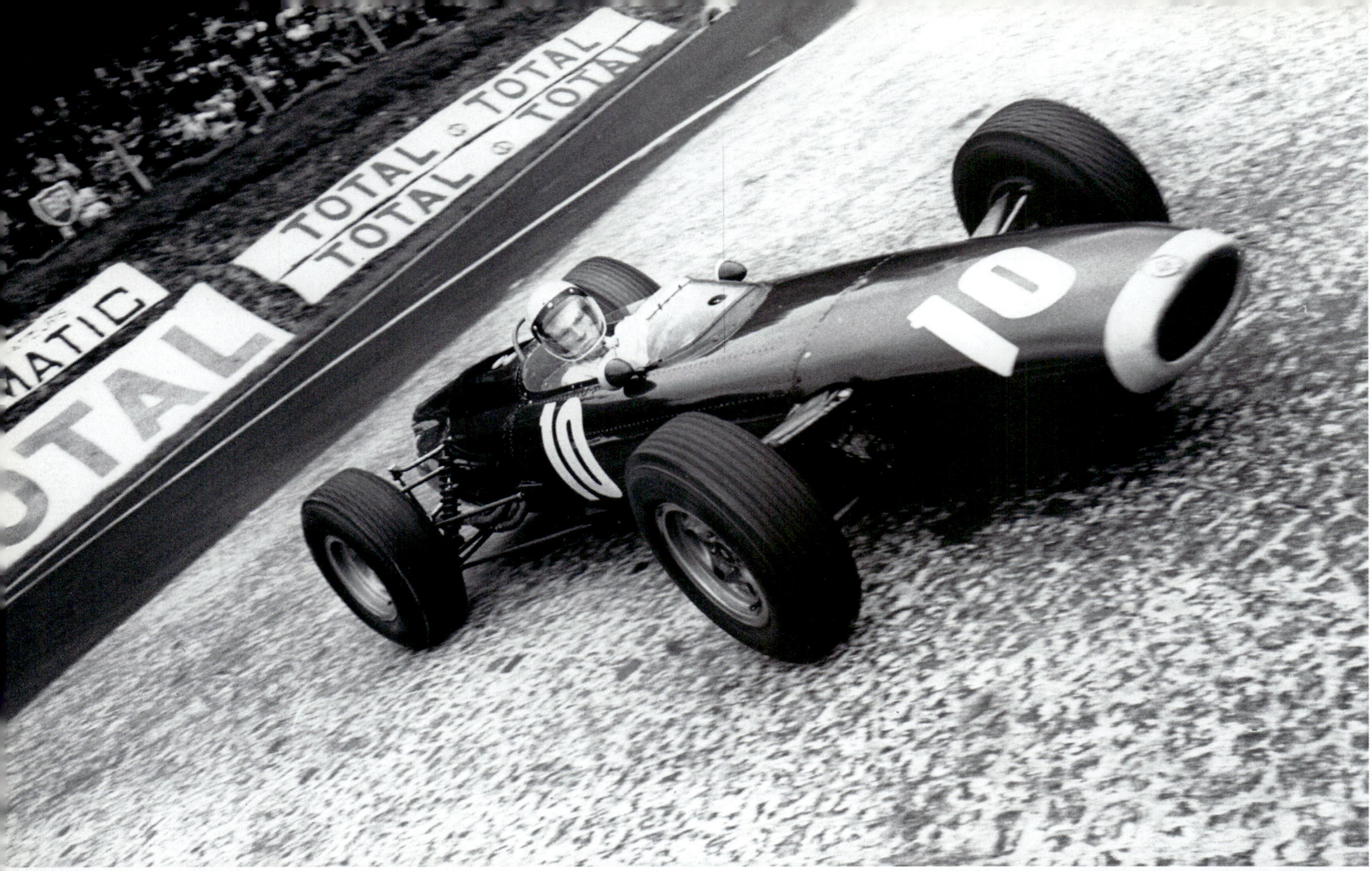
TOTAL
TOTAL
TOTAL
MATIC
OTAL
10
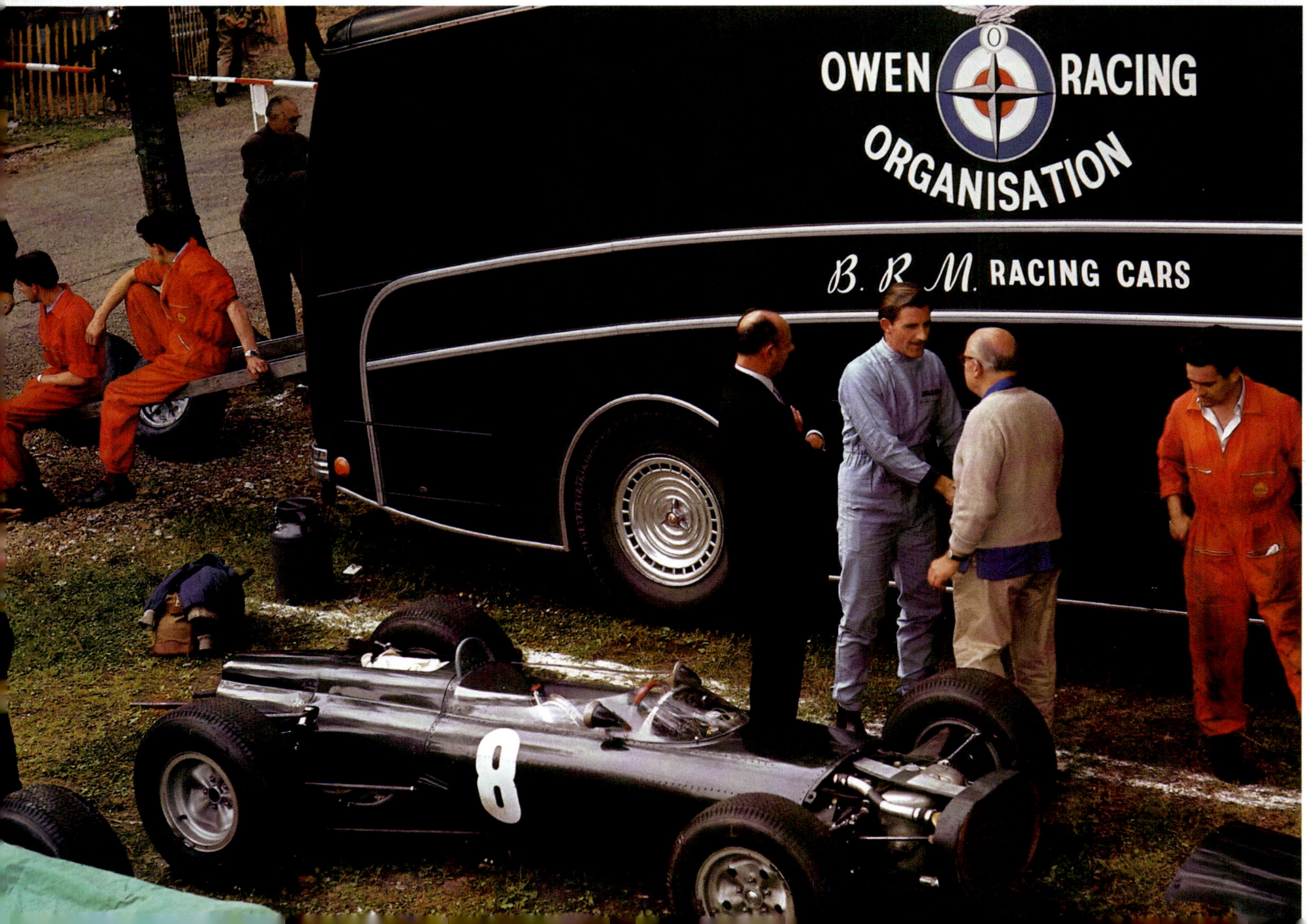
OWEN RACING ORGANISATION
B.R.M. RACING CARS
8

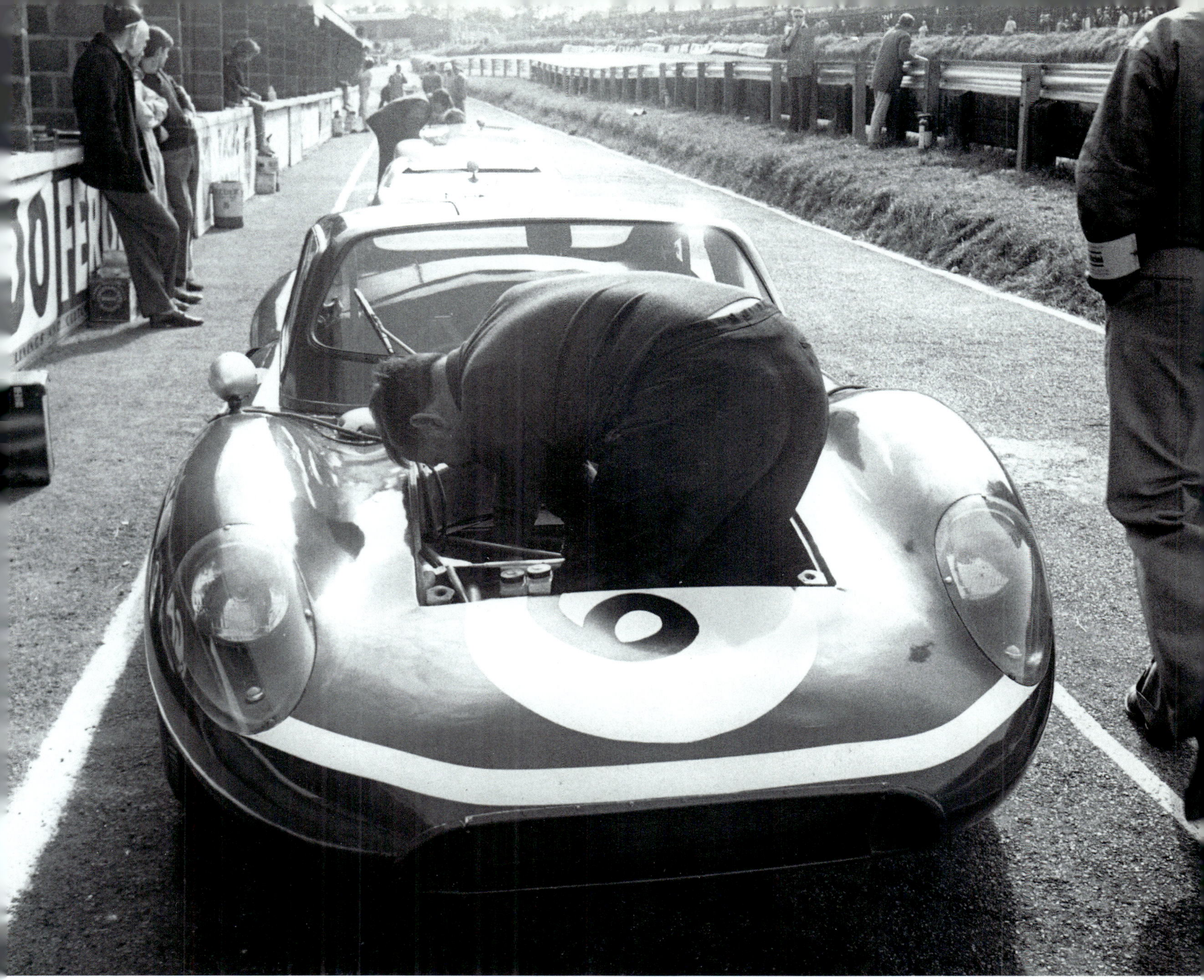

↑ The Brands Hatch pit lane, and Jackie Stewart's Ecurie Ecosse-Ford is being fettled for the sports car support race at the 1964 British GP. This is the second of these cars recognisable by its shallower screen that began life with a Coventry Climax FPF in 1962, then a Buick V8, and by 1964 a Ford 289 Cobra engine. Graham Gauld recalls that team patron David Murray was unsure of the car, but after Stewart finished eighth conceded that the Tojeiro (originally TAD/1/63 but renumbered TAD/1/64 after the Ford unit was fitted) needed more testing. The race was won by Hugh Dibley's Brabham-Climax BT8 run under the aegis of SMART (Stirling Moss Automobile Racing Team). EE's chief mechanic Stan Sproat is looking for something, the brake pedal perhaps, and has presumably removed the front undertray.

↖ Richie Ginther and goldfish bowl at the Nouveau Monde hairpin during the French GP in his BRM P261 (2613) where he came in fifth. He finished all ten Grands Prix during the 1964 season, including six points-scoring finishes and two podiums (second in Monaco and Austria), but this was to be the end of his three-year period with the Bourne team, and in 1965 he moved to Honda.

← I chose this picture not because it was Graham Hill with Raymond Mays in the paddock at Rouen-les-Essarts but because it shows the team's impressive logo in wonderfully clear, sharp colour. Hill finished second in the No. 8 BRM P261 (2615) at the French GP after a tremendous tussle with Jack Brabham.

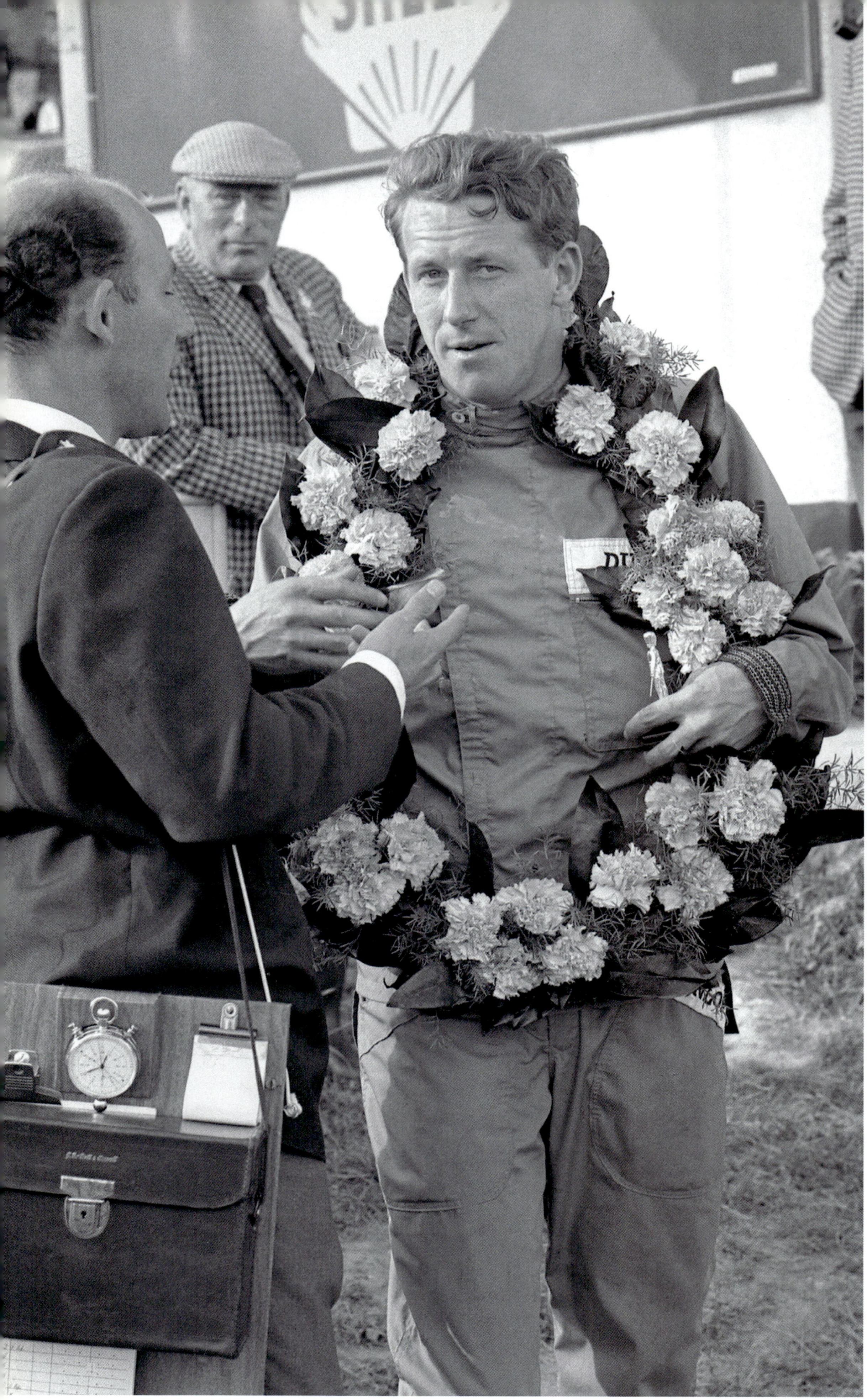

← Race winner being interviewed by team owner. Hugh Dibley, the first driver to lap Goodwood at over 100mph during a race, and Stirling Moss, with the microphone, after Dibley's sports car victory at the sports car support race at Brands Hatch on 11 July 1964. He had a very successful year in this car, winning five races and setting four lap records during the season.

→ John Mecom's Lotus 19, now powered by the ubiquitous Oldsmobile V8 and driven by renowned American Walt Hansgen, cruises along the Brands Hatch pits entrance road for the 1964 August Bank Holiday Monday Guards Trophy. Houston-based oil tycoon John Mecom had three entries at Brands, a Chevy-powered Lola Mk6 GT for Augie Pabst, a MkIV Scarab-Chevrolet for A. J. Foyt, and the Lotus. Only Walt excelled, at one point holding second place despite a collision with Frank Gardner's Elva-BMW before retiring on lap 34. The race was won by another Olds-powered car, the ex-Penske Zerex Special that had won here in 1963, albeit with Coventry Climax propulsion.

→ Here is the Chevrolet-powered Mecom Lola Mk6 GT (LGT 2) driven to 11th place in the Guards Trophy by Augie Pabst as it trundles along the narrow access road from the Paddock Bend tunnel toward the pits. It is a very chunky, muscular looking thing with myriad air scoops/outlets, but not quick enough here. Note also our old friends the Ford Cortina Mk1 rear light clusters.

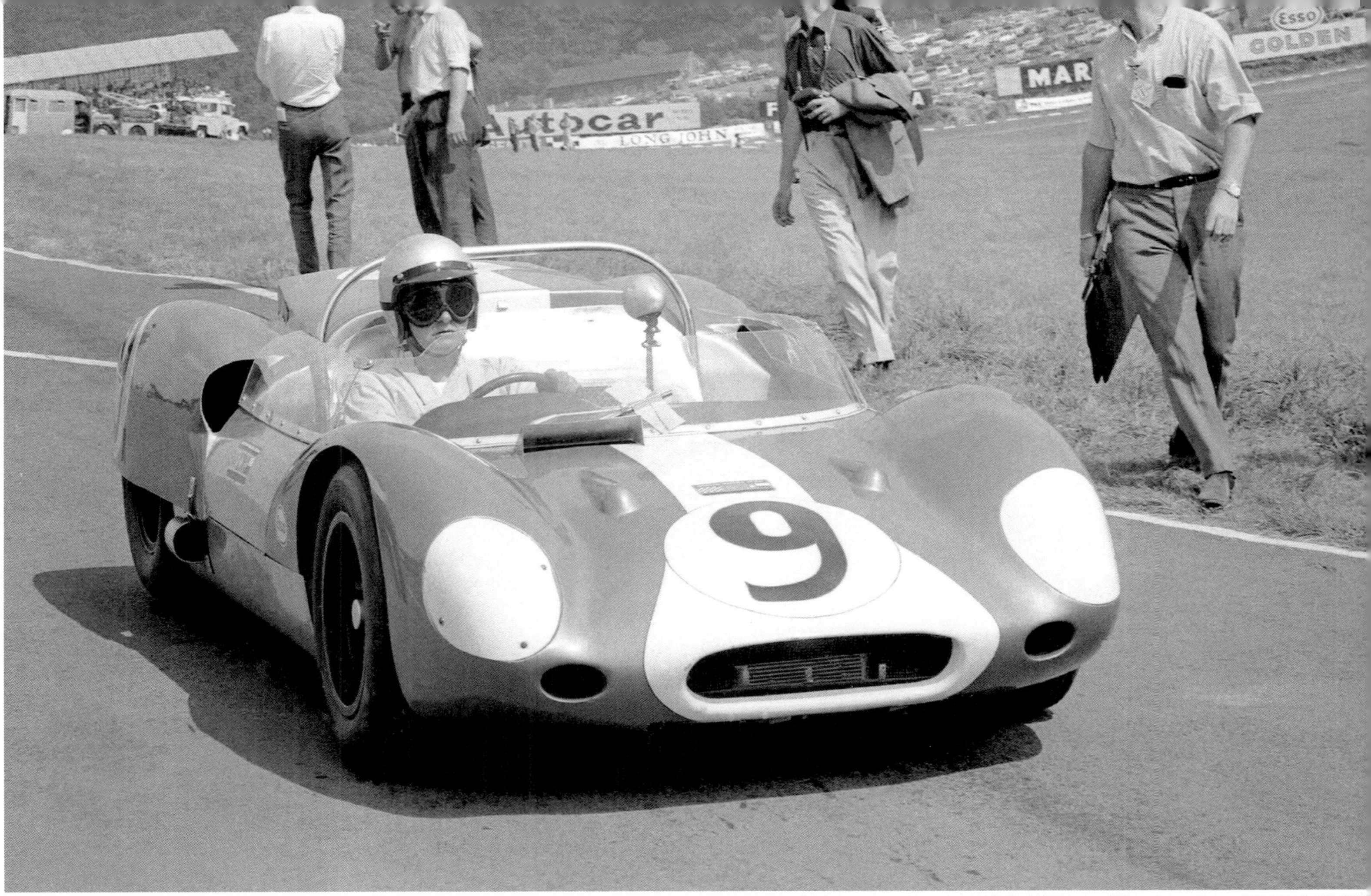
Esso
GOLDEN
Autocar
LONG JOHN
9

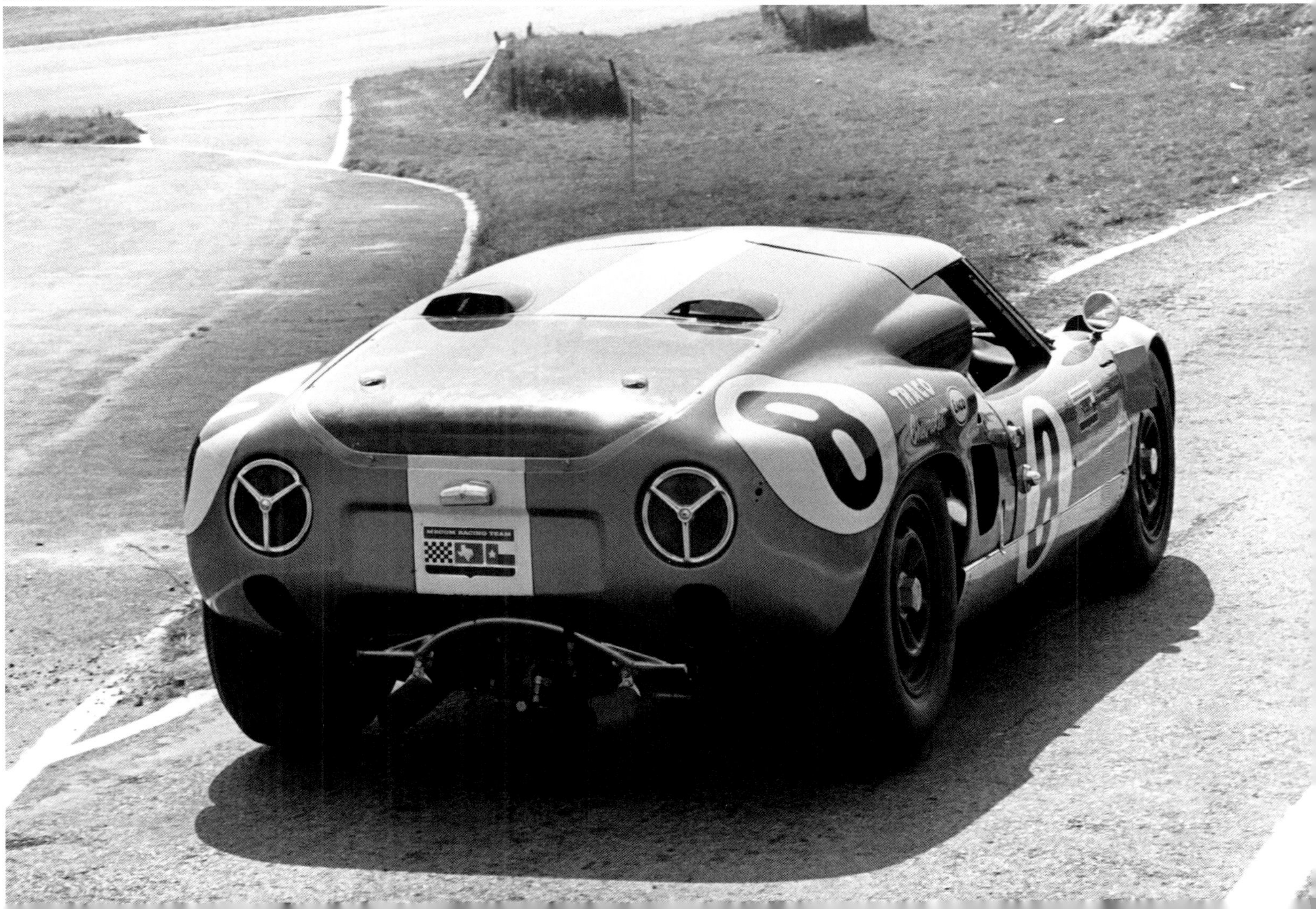

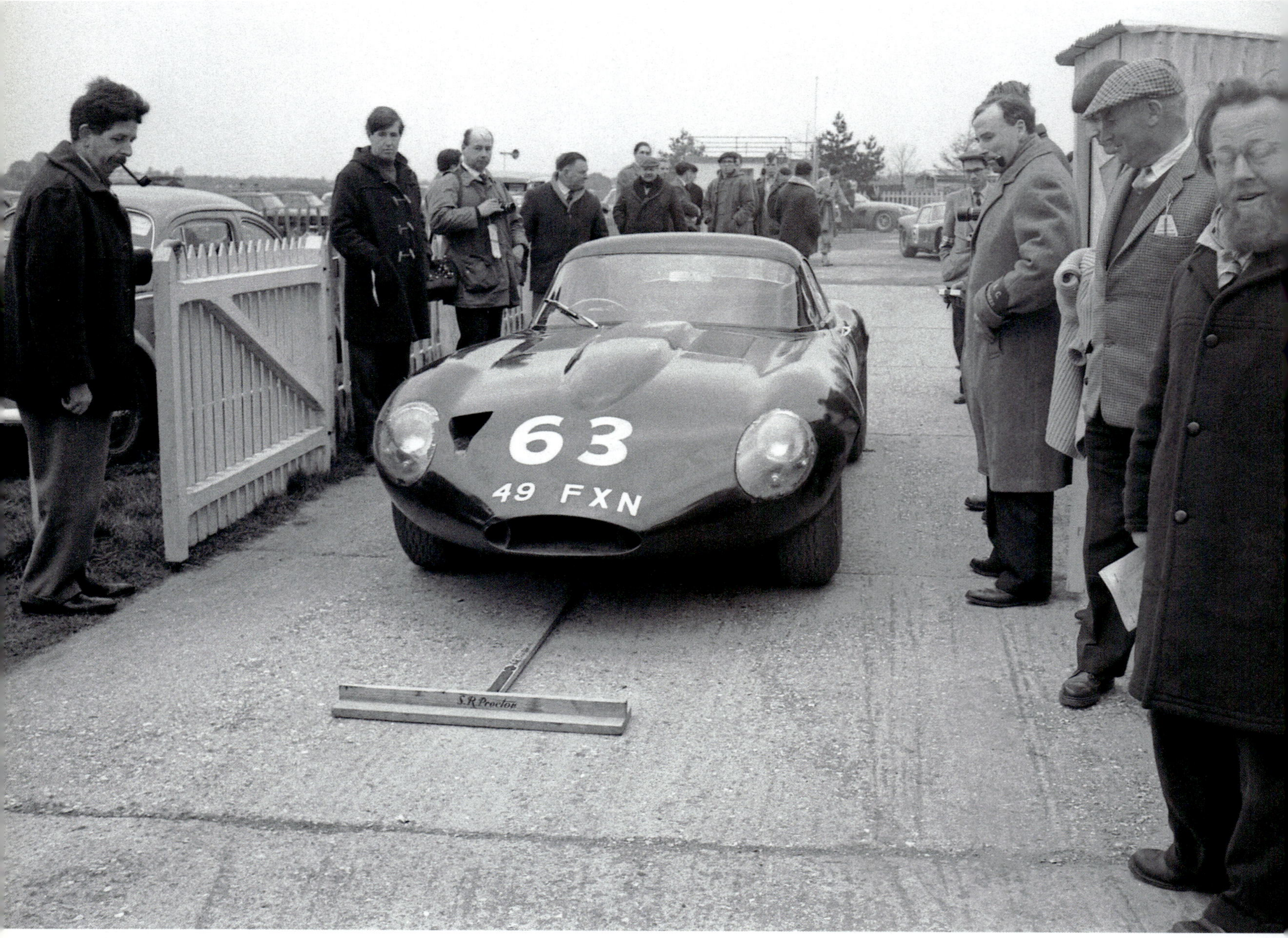

↑ Peter Sargent edges his low drag 'lightweight' E-type (S850663), that he shared with Peter Lumsden, with its NACA duct and Vanwall-like snout towards the ground clearance test at the 1964 Tourist Trophy, Goodwood. Note that the measuring device is marked S. R. Proctor, who was the eligibility scrutineer and the man responsible for denying Aston Martin the use of wider rear rims for their 214s in 1963 which almost certainly cost Aston a victory. He appears at the top of the list of officials in the race programme and is described as being 'in charge'. Right front foreground is *Motor Sport*'s fearless reporter Denis Jenkinson ('Jenks' or D. S. J. depending upon preference), the camera having caught him blinking. Standing by the offside rear of the E-type, right hand on camera, is the redoubtable Geoff Goddard, one of the greatest motor racing photographers of all, and noted Francophobe. Just visible in the background is Chris Kerrison's Drogo-bodied Ferrari 250GT SWB (2735 GT), the 1961 TT winner, and Mike Salmon's Aston Martin 214 (0194/R). The E-type finished eighth; the Ferrari was a reserve and did not race, whilst the Aston finished a delayed 13th.

→ The *Mr Bibendum Michelin Man* collar neck brace was a legacy of Graham's BRM Snetterton shunt during March, but he seems happy enough on a sunny 29 August 1964 at Goodwood. Following the demise of McLaren's Cooper-Oldsmobile T53 (née Penske/Mecom F1-based Zerex Special) and Clark's Lotus 30, Hill won his second consecutive TT driving the Maranello Concessionaires Ferrari 330P.

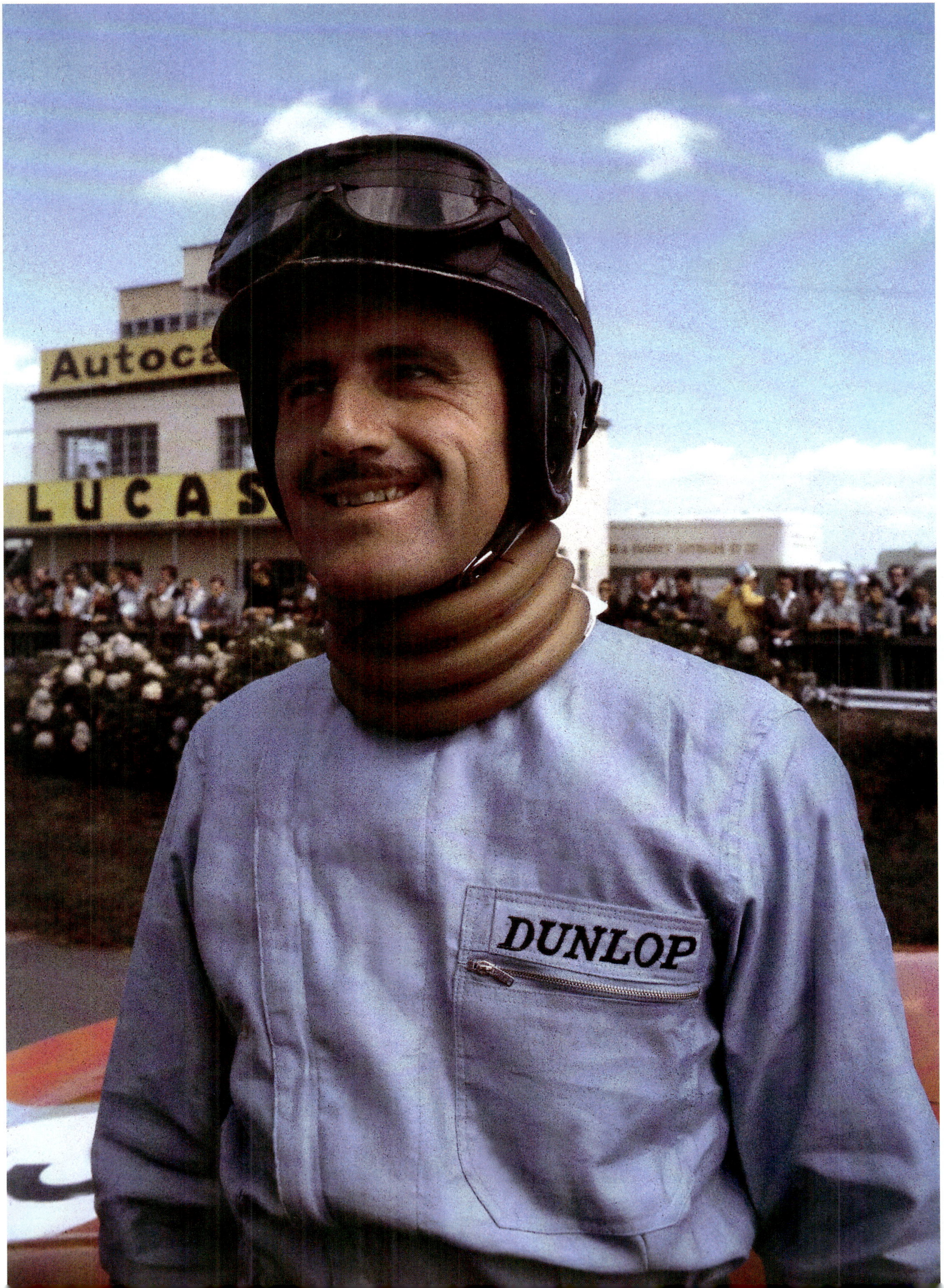
LUCAS
DUNLOP

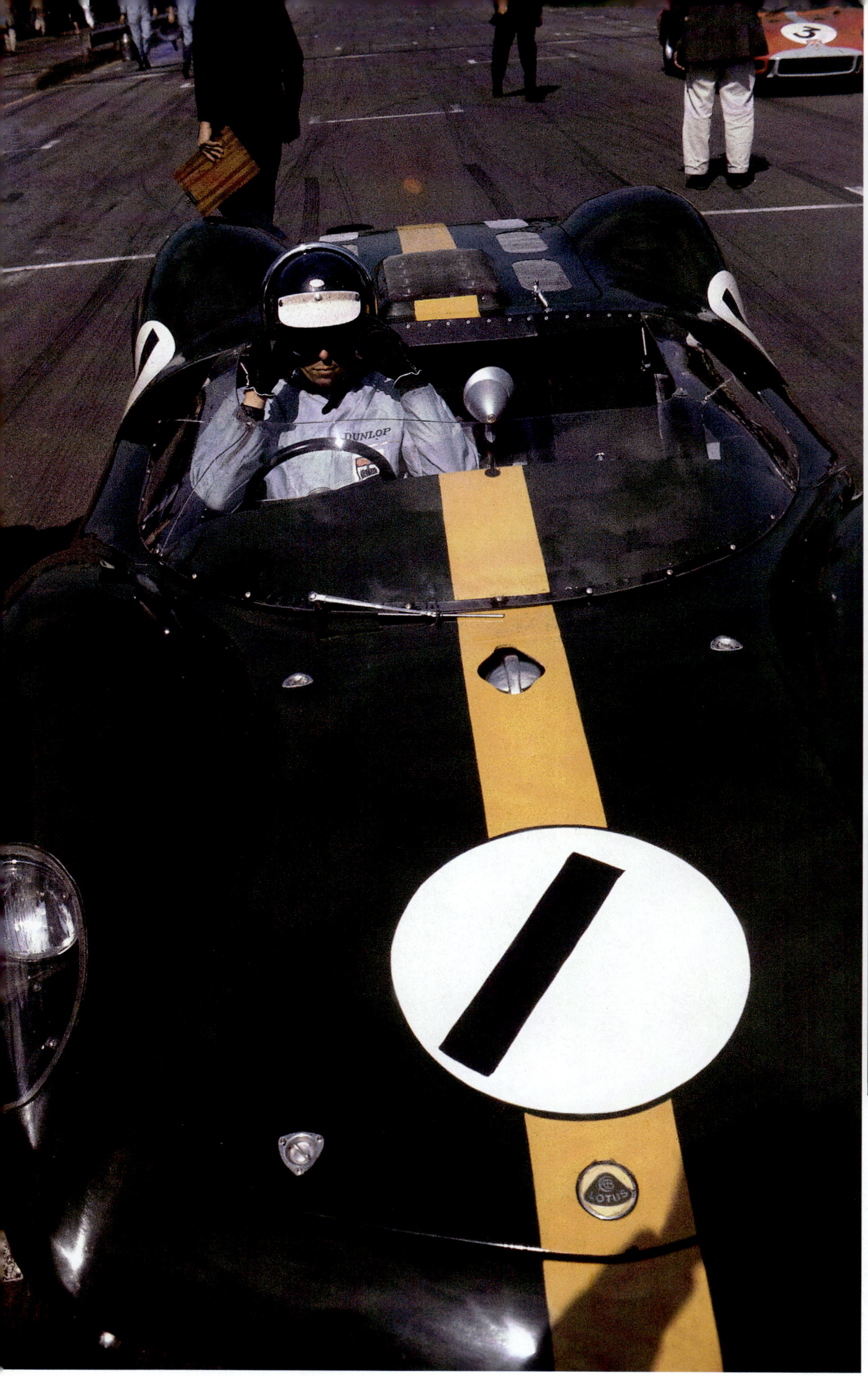
DUNLOP
LOTUS

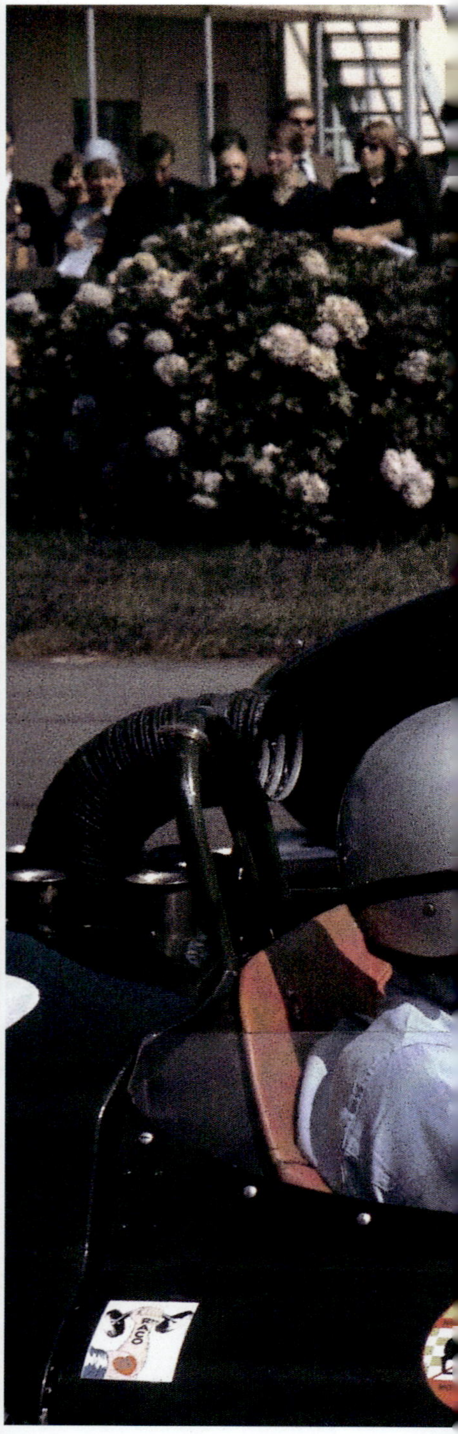

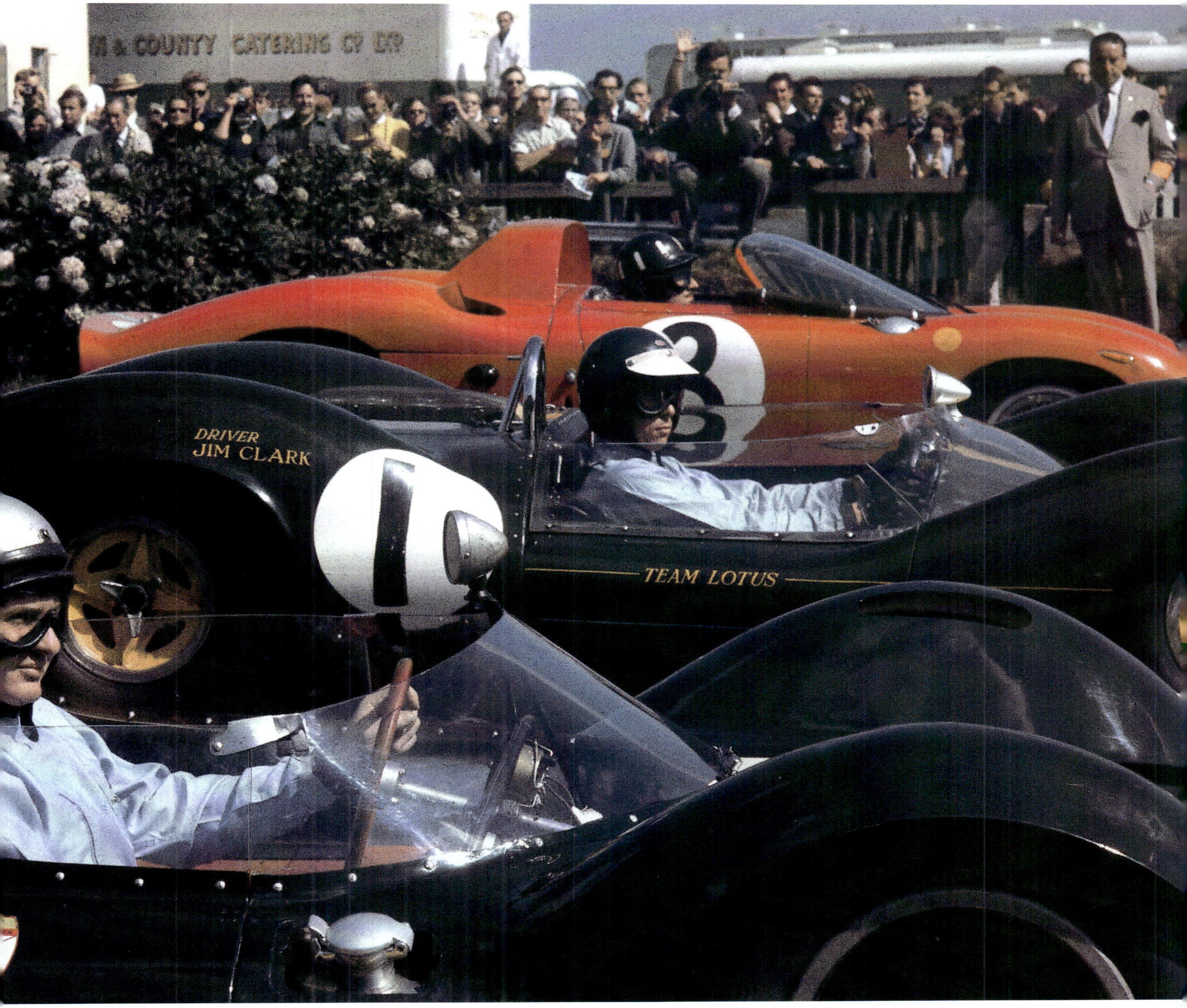

↑ The Goodwood hydrangeas have a ringside view of Bruce McLaren, Jim Clark, and Graham Hill before the off. Note that Bruce has neither belts nor gloves, and period steering wheel rims really were that thin. Hill's endurance racing Ferrari 330P (0818) looks positively porcine by comparison, and was much heavier than the lightweight Lotus and Cooper-based opposition, being a second or more per lap slower. However, McLaren retired with clutch failure early on, and the Lotus was first delayed by battery problems before a failed wheel bearing spelled *finis*, leaving Hill to win easily despite a spin. Both McLaren and Clark are obviously concentrating on the starter, but NGH appears to be staring straight ahead.

← Jim Clark, in the Team Lotus Lotus 30, adjusts his goggles from the middle of the front row of a still otherwise empty grid at the Goodwood TT, with Graham Hill's Ferrari just cruising up to the outside slot. The race numbers were painted on and dissolved when splashed by petrol during refuelling, while the daft regulatory windscreen wiper was no doubt very good at swatting flies. Note the lack of belts.

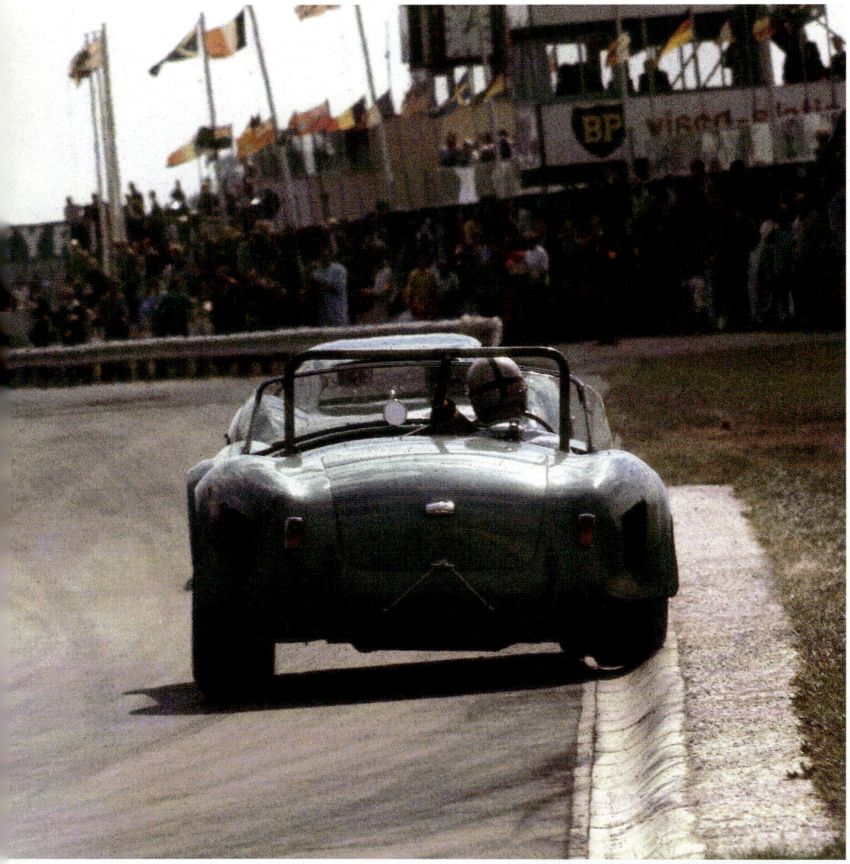

← Although Dan Gurney won the GT class at the TT, finishing third overall, he was nevertheless led by Roy Salvadori in Tommy Atkins' Cobra (HEM-6) seen here chasing David Piper's Ferrari 250LM (5897) out of Goodwood's chicane. Alas, 'Salvo' retired with clutch failure on lap 80. This picture shows that the pits were now protected by a single layer of Armco, the amount of body roll displayed by the Cobra, and the bungee cord securing its boot lid via the handle.

→ The inestimable and sometimes curmudgeonly Denis Jenkinson was a keen competitor as well as a 'scribbler', and here he is having a go at drag racing at Blackbushe aerodrome in October 1964. Note the motorcycle 'pudding basin' helmet (none of your FIA-approved red tape then) and the pleased expression upon his bearded visage.

↘ Obviously the driver of the Shelby Cobra is not superstitious with that number on his car as it rockets away from the start at Blackbushe, leaving behind the acrid smell of burning rubber for the standing start quarter-mile sprint.

↓ Phil Hill drove the other Shelby American Daytona Cobra and practised just two tenths slower than team-mate Dan Gurney, but ended up 11th in the TT following problems. It is 2.05pm by the control tower clock and mere mortals who stray this far on to the green stuff exiting the chicane nearly always ended up spinning like a marionette, but not the likes of Philip Toll Hill (1927–2008).

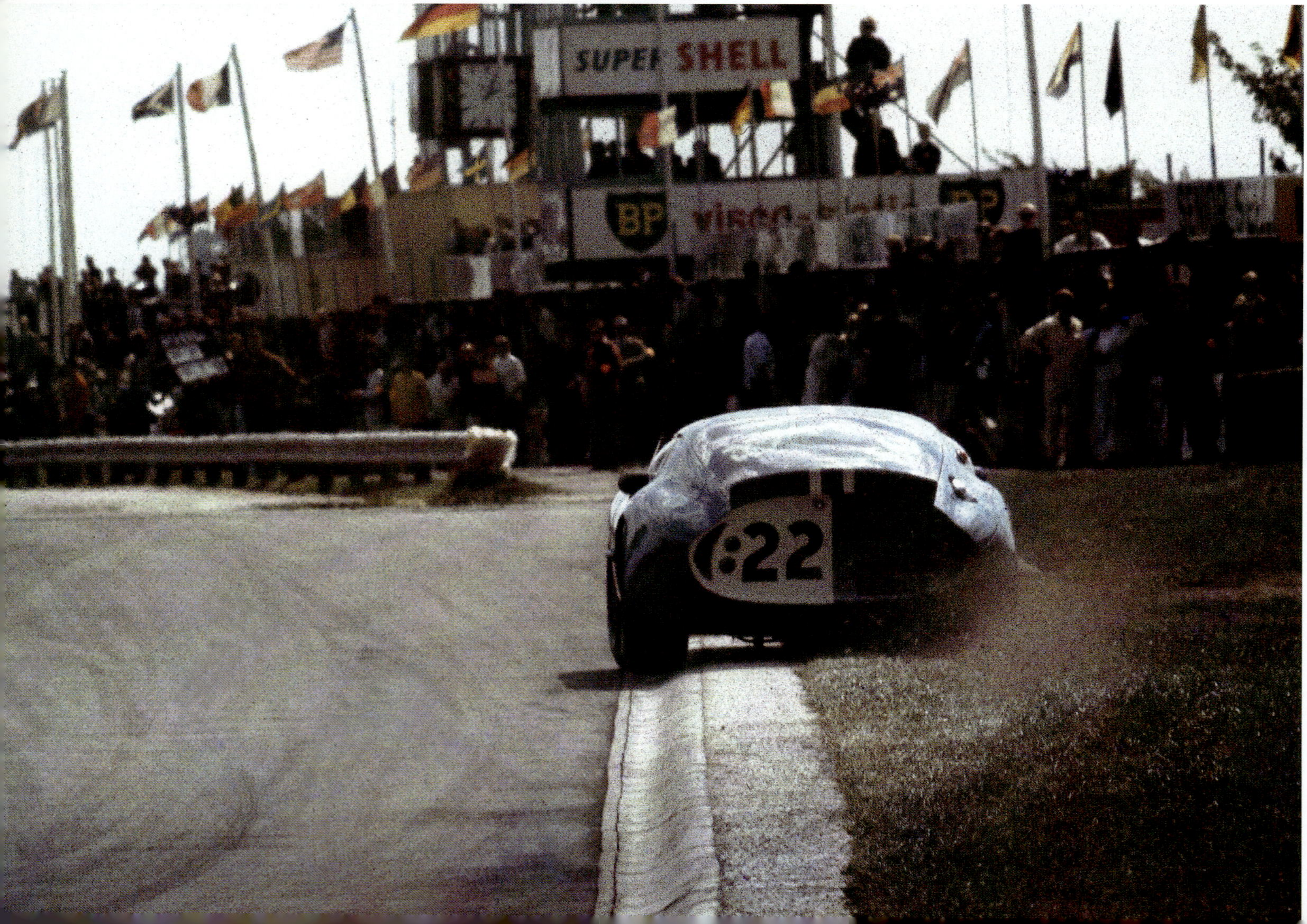

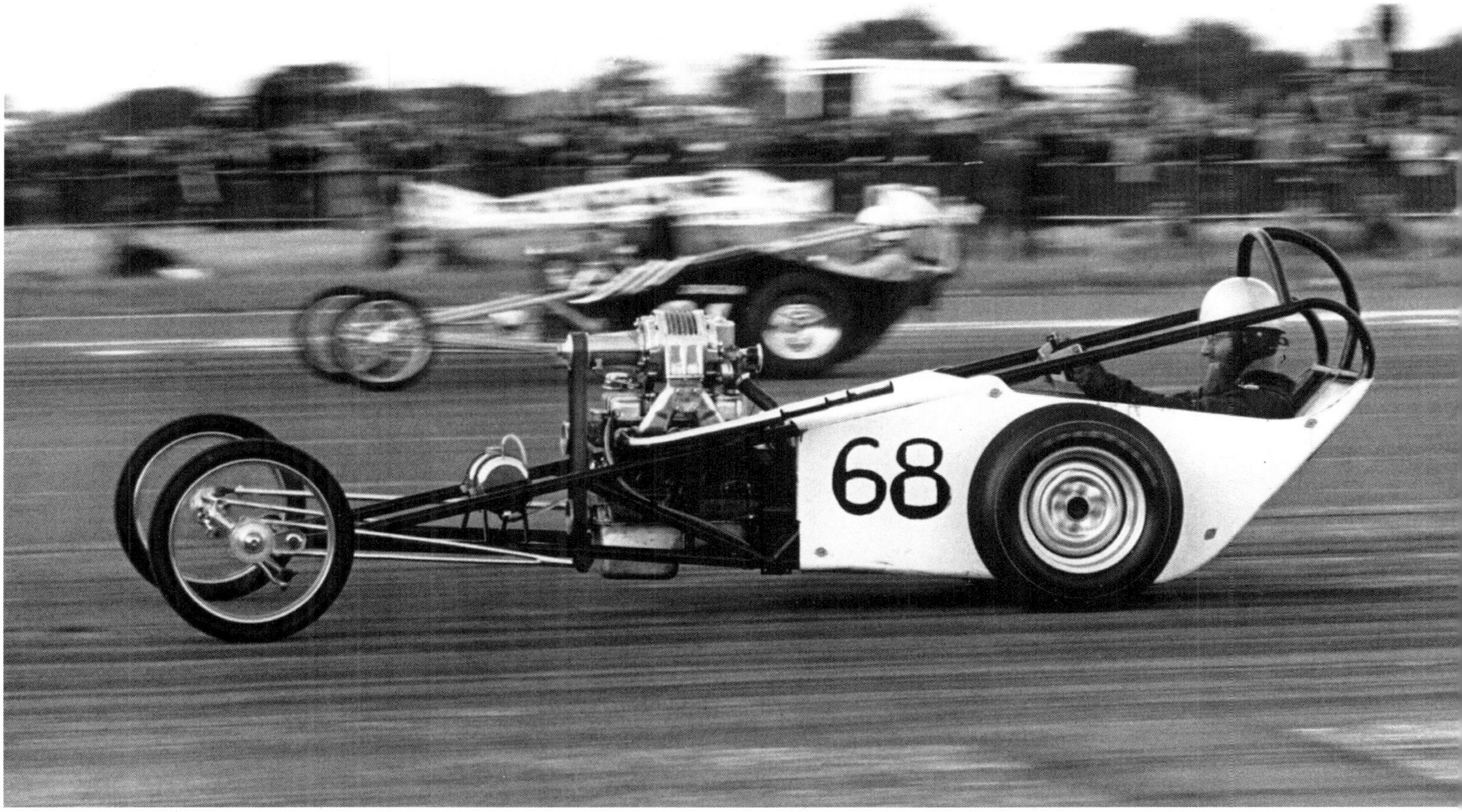
68

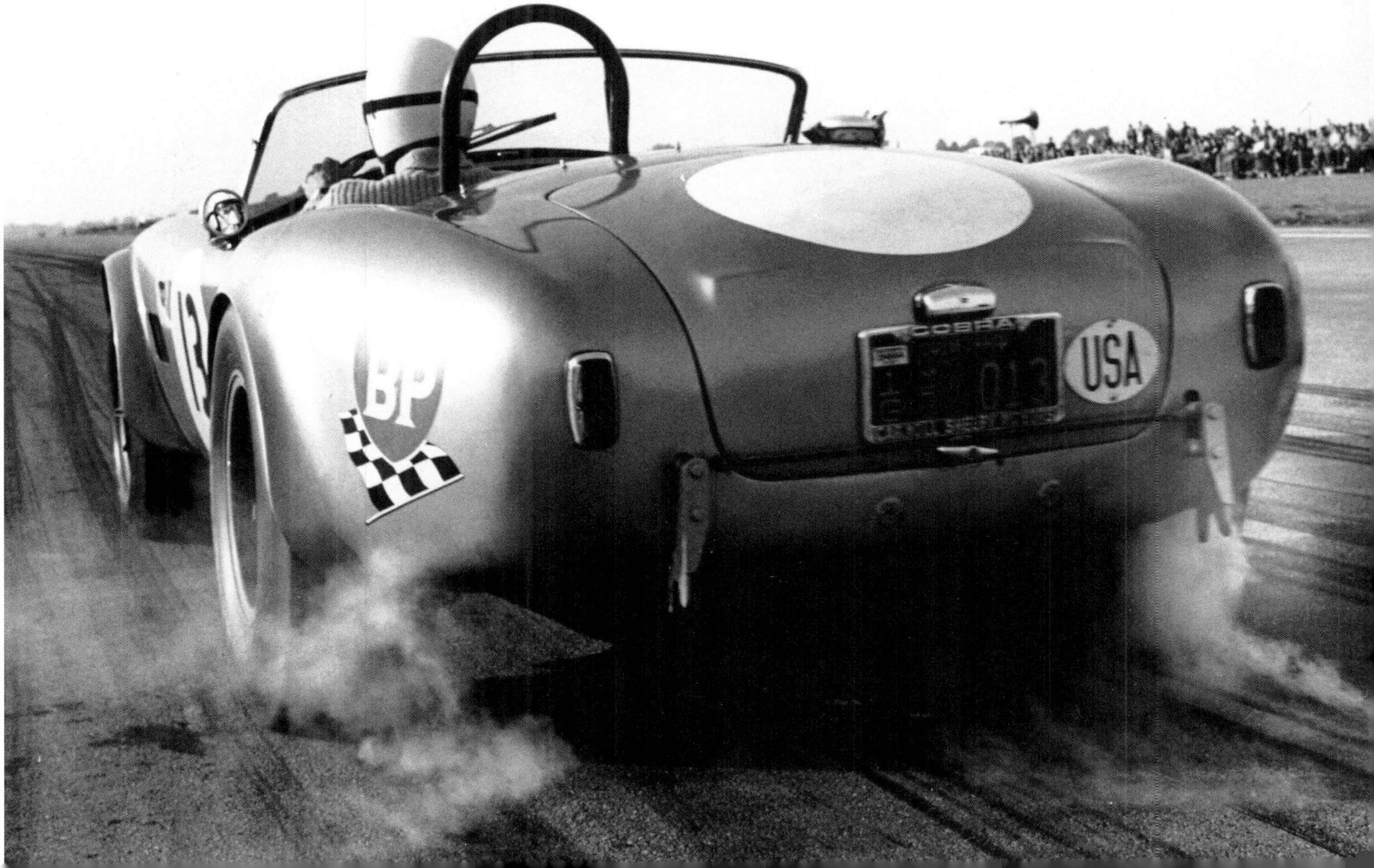
BP
COBRA
USA

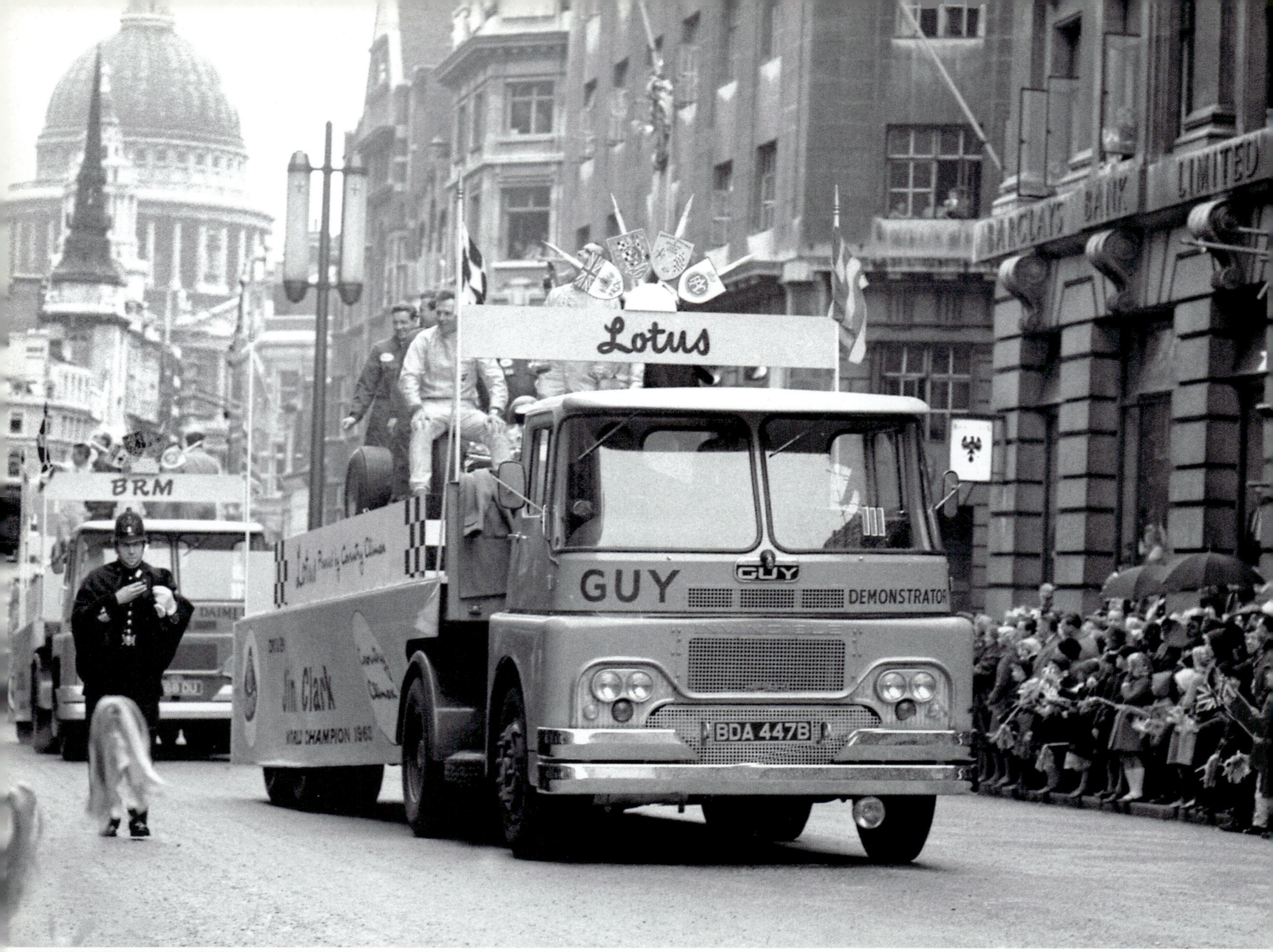

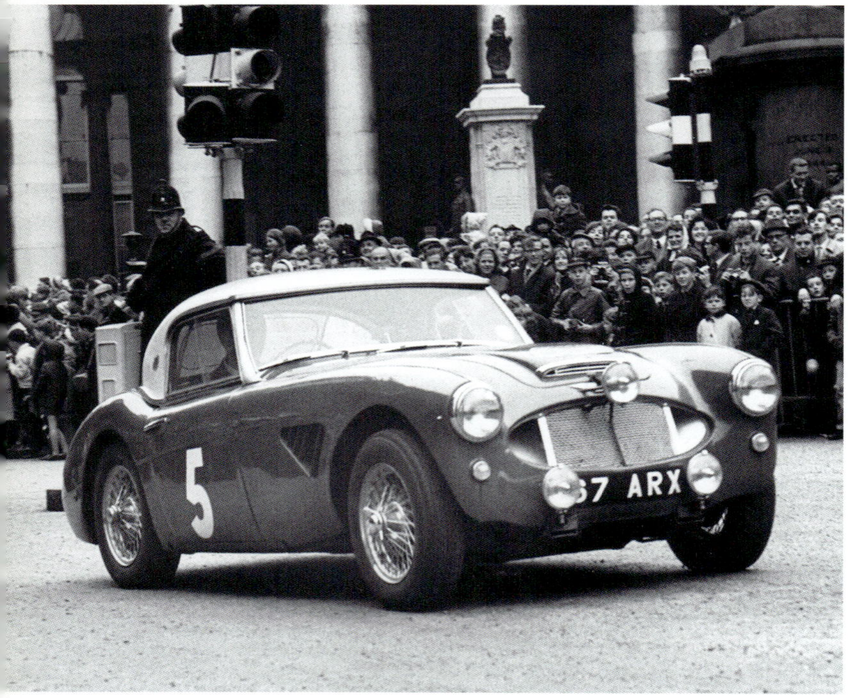

↑ As part of the Lord Mayor's Show in London in 1964, the British motorsport industry was fêted for its ongoing successes, and various competition cars and associated floats drove through the City. This picture shows one of the now long gone British commercial manufacturers GUY, which is carrying Jim Clark's Lotus, followed by a similar vehicle bearing BRM. St Paul's dominates the skyline, and is that Peter Arundell staring down from the Lotus display? GUY was founded by Sydney Slater Guy in 1913, became a public company one year later, and manufactured commercial vehicles, buses, and trolley buses over the next several decades, but ultimately went bust in 1961 when it was acquired by Jaguar, who had also hoovered up Daimler (see the Daimler name on the following BRM float). In 1968 the company was subsumed into the fatal clutches of British Leyland, and production ceased in 1979.

← One of the BMC works Austin Healeys braves the crowds under the stern gaze of a member of the Constabulary. 67 ARX was one of five Healey 3000s built in 1962 and driven by Paddy Hopkirk, Don and Erle Morley, and others, with Hopkirk finishing second in the RAC Rally. It was sold at the end of 1963 to make way for the next batch of big Healeys, and at this point the car was probably owned by Tony Ambrose.

Anthony Hussey

What a colourful character. Sideways driving, hard drinking, impatient (particularly with the pretentious), totally relaxed with, but aware of, social etiquette and the bits he wasn't familiar with.

He came to dinner with my mother and sisters just after I met him in 1960, appalled one sister by scratching his head while holding his fork, and entranced my garden-loving mother with his countryman's knowledge of nature.

He and I arrived back in London one night and went to my girlfriend's flat, both of us damp and bedraggled after a wet day at Brands. She had not met him before, and he was left emanating wet wool in the living room while we went into the kitchen to make coffee. We heard the piano and she looked at me with a raised eyebrow. 'You didn't tell me he could play.' 'I didn't know he could play.'

She sang with the London Choral Society and was rehearsing Bach's St Matthew Passion. In the following discussion he stopped the conversation. 'Drifting a car is a big buzz particularly when it's a really fast corner, sex is always great and every now and then sublime, but Nothing, I repeat Nothing, is as good as trying to play Bach on a really good organ. It's far too difficult for me, but every now and then I feel that I've got a bit right, and then it is transcendent.'

On a warm July night before the 1961 Reims GP we took two girls to a lakeside barbecue outside Guildford and, lying there, one of the eager ladies made a romantic comment about the stars. She was Mike's for the evening and he had really lost out for she was an overweight ten point moose. What she got was an astronomy lesson, in which looking back, was ironic as she was Australian, and the night sky out there is a squillion times more starry than here.

We left at about 5am from Biggin Hill and flew in a Proctor to the Reims GP on a boiling hot day, and Mike shot tigers [threw up] out of the plane window across the Channel. He recovered in time to capture the Baghetti/Gurney slipstreaming battle. The flight back was a mite hazardous as we had to circumnavigate a huge summer storm, got lost, and had to fly along a railway line low enough to read the name of a station to locate ourselves. We touched down and the engine cut. No fuel! I've had a soft spot for Petts Wood station ever since.

Mike was a great photographer, an innovative one. Rainer Schegelmilch, no less, acknowledges his influence, and there are many others who paid similar homage. His skill, allied to his rich humour, made him a much loved personality in the pits and paddocks of the time. Drivers trusted him so much that they would wave him into position on the apex of a corner, and then drift past, providing the opportunity for some wonderful shots. Jim Clark indulged himself so much at Goodwood practising for the TT that he got a bollocking from John Wyer for scrubbing his tyres.

In those pre-drink drive days when speed limits were optional, the journeys to and from the circuits were always part of the event, and the battles between my Downton Conversion Mini and Mike's John Coombs modified 105E Anglia were always hilarious and hard fought.

He nearly always won, for he was much faster and braver, but I would somehow contrive to be leading as we came down Duncton Hill from Goodwood, late at night, after a session in the Goodwood Arms. He would always try to overtake into the left-hander at the bottom, but I never gave way, resulting in him taking the escape road towards Duncton. I would drive on gleefully and he would switch off all lights and steal back up to blast past with a derisive blare of horn as Michael Turner watched from a discreet distance in his car. We would spend evenings pub crawling round Shere, and one day in 2002 as we drove together down the hobbit lanes of that pretty area he said, 'Did we really drive as fast here as we think we did, because if so we must have been mad.'

After Brands Hatch meetings, The White Horse at Shere, Mike's local, became a great meeting place, and we played wild games of bar football while eating pheasant. James Hunt and Gerry Birrell, then F3 racers, were regular attendees and the motoring press arrived in droves. I have a memory of Mike, James Hunt, and I chasing a bar football down Shere High Street being cheered on by journalists Maxwell Boyd and Colin Dryden.

And, talking of Shere, there was the time when Mike, eager to impress a new client, meant to say, 'We must hit Shere by 9 o'clock' but Spoonerised it.

And the time when he first went to his solicitor, found it a bit august, became a trifle flustered, and chose the wrong door to leave by. Backing out of the broom cupboard…! He did it again on his second visit.

He told these stories against himself because, for all his success, Mike's feet never left the ground. And in his case the ground was also his garden. After Liz, Ben and Jo it was his next great love, and his gardening diaries bear witness to the care he took and his deep interest.

Mike's outgoing fun-loving personality hid a person of real worth, humanitarian deep beliefs and a set of ethics to admire. I once told a puzzled, and obnoxious, American who couldn't understand why Mike wouldn't accept a good offer for his photographic collection, that if he wished to acquire it he should stop thinking of cash and offer Mike a telescope, organ and/or garden. So that would be Mount Palomar, the organ from the church in Stoke d'Abernon, and Kew Gardens. He gave up.

1965–1969

Jim Clark was the final 1.5-litre F1 champion and the two teams Lotus (6) and BRM (3) won every round bar Mexico where Richie Ginther (Honda) was victorious in the final race of the formula.

In endurance racing Ferrari triumphed but they were fortunate that Ford suffered serious unreliability problems although Carroll Shelby's Daytona Coupés did annex the GT category.

Maranello were favourites for the new 3-litre F1 era but after a promising start internal politics caused John Surtees to depart to Cooper where he won the Mexican GP. Ultimately Jack Brabham's Repco-powered machines would produce a third World Championship for the Australian. Ferrari did win Monza and Clark the US GP for Lotus using BRM's recalcitrant H-16 but most struggled with uncompetitive machinery.

Ford finally ended Ferrari's long reign at Le Mans with their 7-litre behemoths and Chaparral triumphed at the Nürburgring with Porsche inevitably winning the smaller classes.

Cosworth's Ford financed DFV V8 in the Lotus 49 changed F1 irrevocably driven by Jim Clark and a returning Graham Hill, with a debut victory at Zandvoort. Only development issues prevented the Lotus duo from dominating but it was Brabham who won a second championship (with Denny Hulme) whilst strong but inconsistent challenges from Dan Gurney's AAR Eagle-Weslake (winner at Spa) and Ferrari were not enough and the rest were usually outclassed.

Back on the sports car trail Ferrari mounted an all-out effort and won the championship but Ford's MkIV was too fast for them at Le Mans whilst Chaparral's bewinged 2F won the BOAC 500 at Brands Hatch.

1968 was a dreadful year with Jim Clark, Mike Spence, Ludovico Scarfiotti and Jo Schlesser all perishing behind the wheel, leaving Graham Hill to lead Lotus and win the F1 championship. Jackie Stewart, now returned to Ken Tyrrell for their inaugural F1 attempt with Matra, suffered a wrist injury that compromised his season. Ferrari appeared with the first vestigial wings (in F1) at Spa, and their latest signing Jacky Ickx won the French GP.

Ford officially withdrew from endurance racing, but despite rule changes they won the pot (and Le Mans) with John Wyer's GT40s despite growing Porsche presence and their new 908. Ferrari absented although Alfa Romeo held up the Italian end and the Howmet Continental TX gas turbine came and went.

In 1969 the evermore outrageous wings on F1 cars began to collapse regularly with near disastrous results. Both GLTL Lotus 49s (Jochen Rindt had now joined Hill) crashed at Barcelona and at Monaco all suspension mounted devices that were not part of the bodywork were banned where Hill, who was badly injured at Watkins Glen as Rindt won his first GP, scored his fifth and final victory here.

Cooper closed down and Jackie Stewart was the latest F1 champion with Tyrrell and Matra, Brabham with Jacky Ickx (winner in Germany and Canada) were championship runners up but BRM and Ferrari won nothing. Meanwhile the 4WD F1 fad was finally dumped.

Ferrari returned to sports car racing and once again Ford won Le Mans (the fourth in a row) and Sebring whilst Roger Penske's Lola T70 took Daytona. Porsche won everything else including the season's finale at Zeltweg with their new 917.

The shape of things to come had arrived.

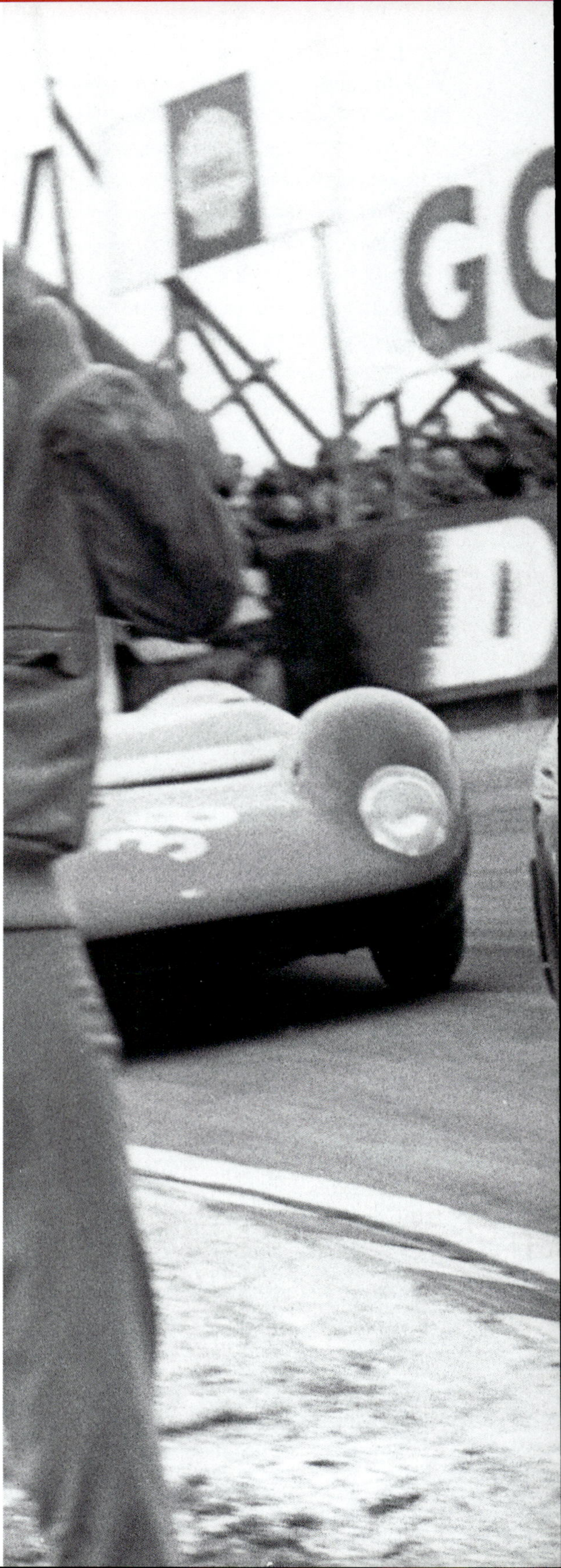

At Paddock Bend, Brands Hatch, in the Guards Trophy on 30 August 1965, are Maranello Concessionaires Ferrari 365P2 (0826), driven by Mike Parkes, and the Kay Racing Brabham BT8 (SC-2-65) driven by Peter Revson. In a two-heat race dominated by the Group 7 racers (British pre-cursor to the Can-Am series) John Surtees won in his Lola-Chevrolet T70. Parkes could only manage sixth in his overweight, albeit pared down, endurance racer, for once displaying understeer rather than his usual oversteer. The piece of flimsy water piping masquerading as a roll-bar is self evidently superfluous, as is the windscreen wiper. Revson finished fifth. This is how you used to photograph cars, from mere feet away, as the figure on the left who has his back to the action proves, and MJP aims the 365P2 directly at Mike. You needed to have confidence in the driver(s) and (preferably) no nerves, but what a difference it made.

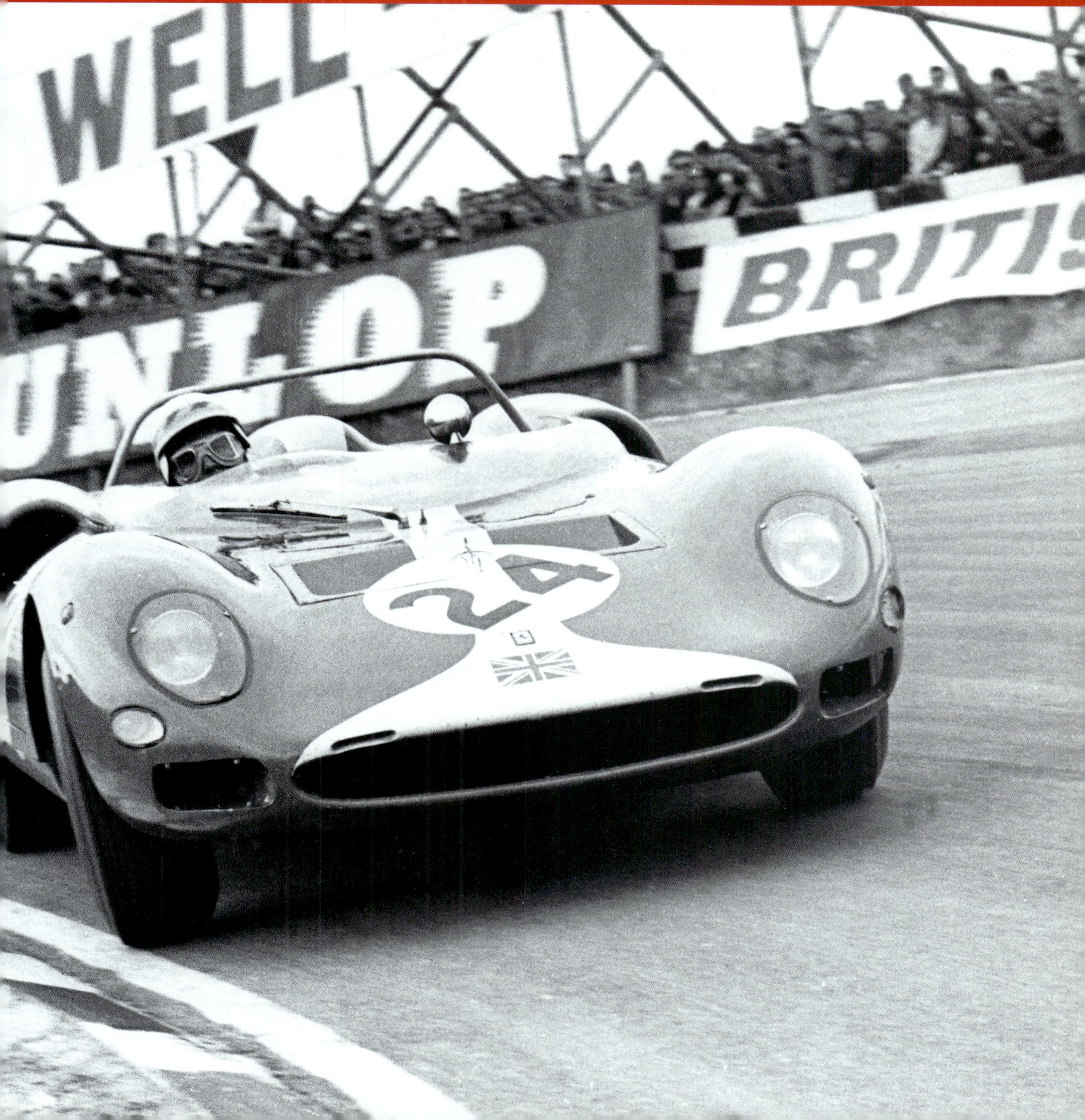

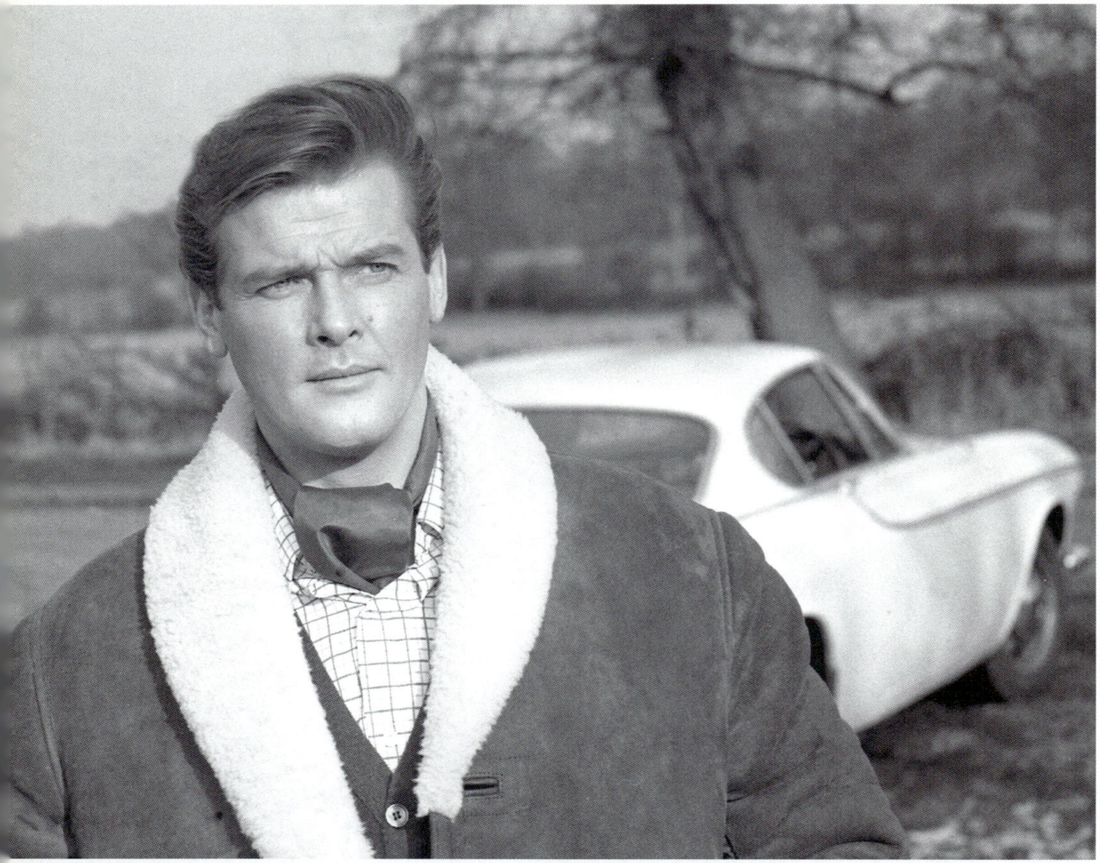

🡐 One of Mike's other existences was photographing various 'stars', artistes, and the like, and Roger Moore duly obliged as his *Saint* alter ego. The sheepskin coat, cardigan, Van Heusen shirt and cravat are so redolent of the time, whilst the now famous Volvo P1800 was in fact one of probably 12 such cars, including a cutaway cockpit section for interior shots. Producer Monty Berman had originally wanted a Jaguar E-type but when they approached Jaguar, dangling the guaranteed television exposure as a carrot, the manufacturer was uninterested, claiming they had sold all the cars they could make and did not need the publicity. Volvo, of course, was only too happy to oblige.

🡓 The Chequered Flag Shelby Cobra of Roger Mac retired for an obvious reason at the Oulton Park TT. This is the ex-Tommy Atkins car from 1964 and the Cobra might have a tiger in its tank but it has not got four functioning wheels apparently. The Esso tiger ad was a period piece of marketing familiar to British TV viewers and motorists.

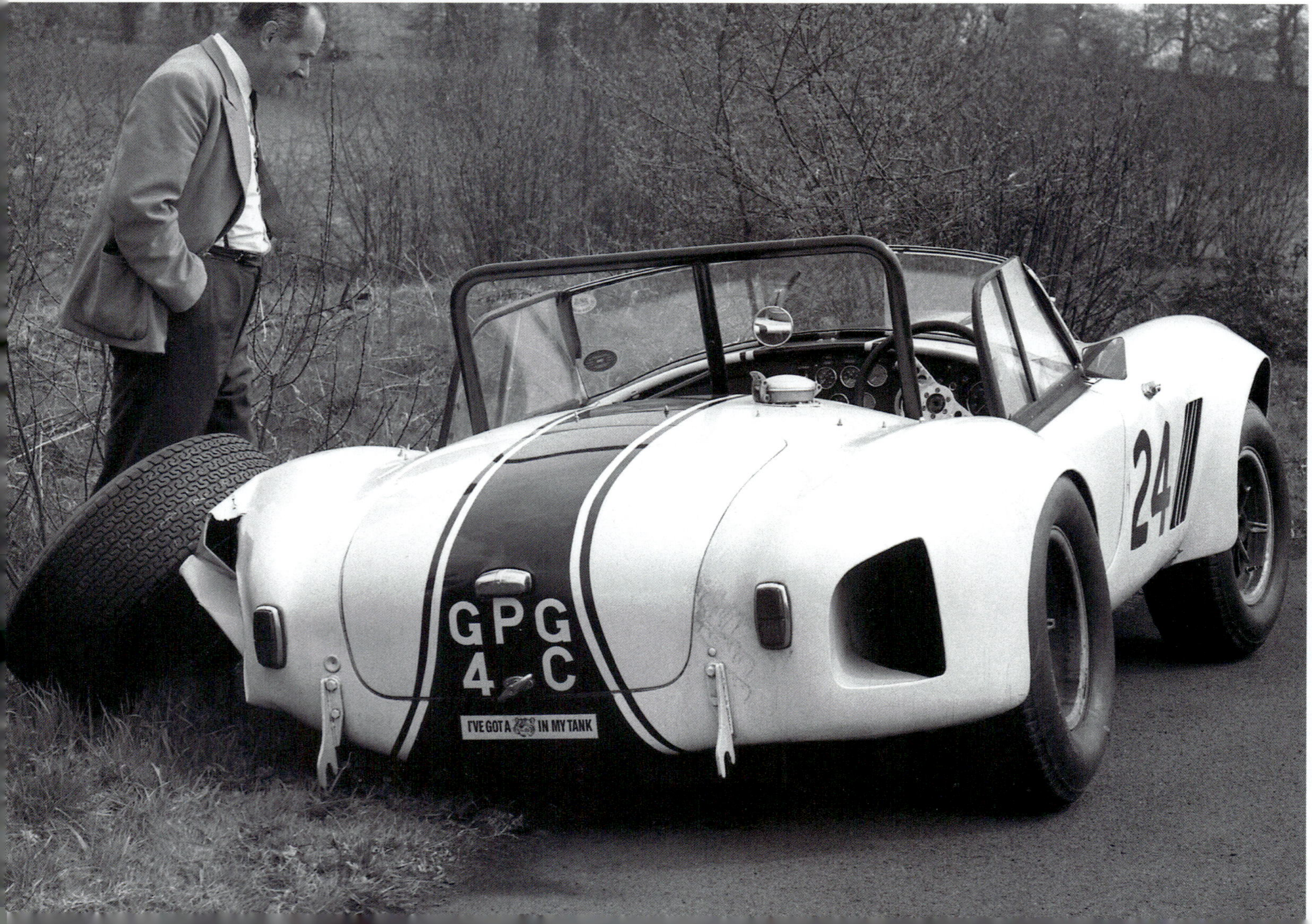

→ By 1965 the Tourist Trophy had passed from Goodwood to Oulton Park in Cheshire. This is the proper 2.76-mile circuit and Peter Sutcliffe races his unique 'lowline' Ferrari 250GTO (4491 GT) past the Neil Dangerfield/John Sparrow Radford Racing Cobra (CSX2301) approaching Esso with the notorious Oulton lake in the background. David Piper had modified this car during his ownership, lowering the roofline by nearly 6in, and it was faster than any other GTO, including the later LM-bodied cars. Sutcliffe was placed fifth overall and second in class to John Whitmore's Alan Mann Cobra roadster in the two-heat race.

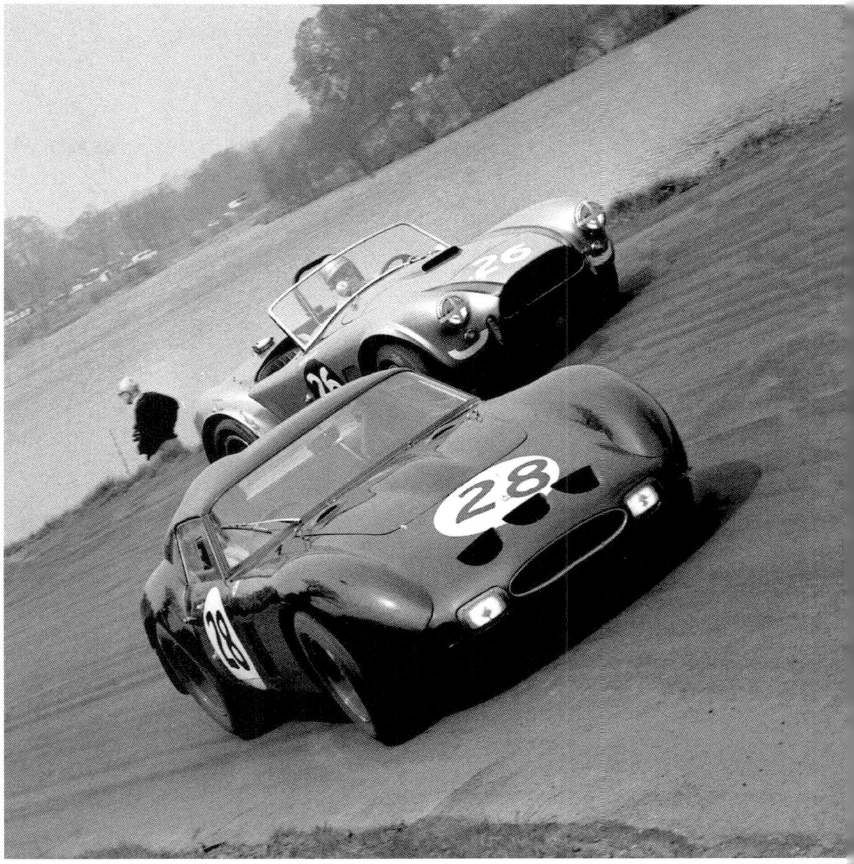

↓ Frank Gardner in the John Willment Cobra coupé (CSX2131) leads Jack Sears at Oulton in the official Peter Brock-designed 'Daytona' version (CSX2299) entered here by Alan Mann. Sears was delayed at the start of the first two-hour race and, despite his winning the GT class in the second heat, he ended up seventh overall and fourth in class because of his problems in race one. The Willment coupé was created by John Ohlsen (who had helped build the original Daytona) and Brian Waite, and constructed by Ted Richard, Frank Shattock, and Geoff Gilbert, all three ex-Aston Martin. It was driven to tenth overall by Frank Gardner. The high windscreen/roof line of the Sears car denotes that this was one of five built in Modena by Carrozziera Gransport. The roof-mounted rear-facing bust of the head and shoulders of a man was a cunning British device that hid a camera for keeping an eye on who was creeping up on you from behind.

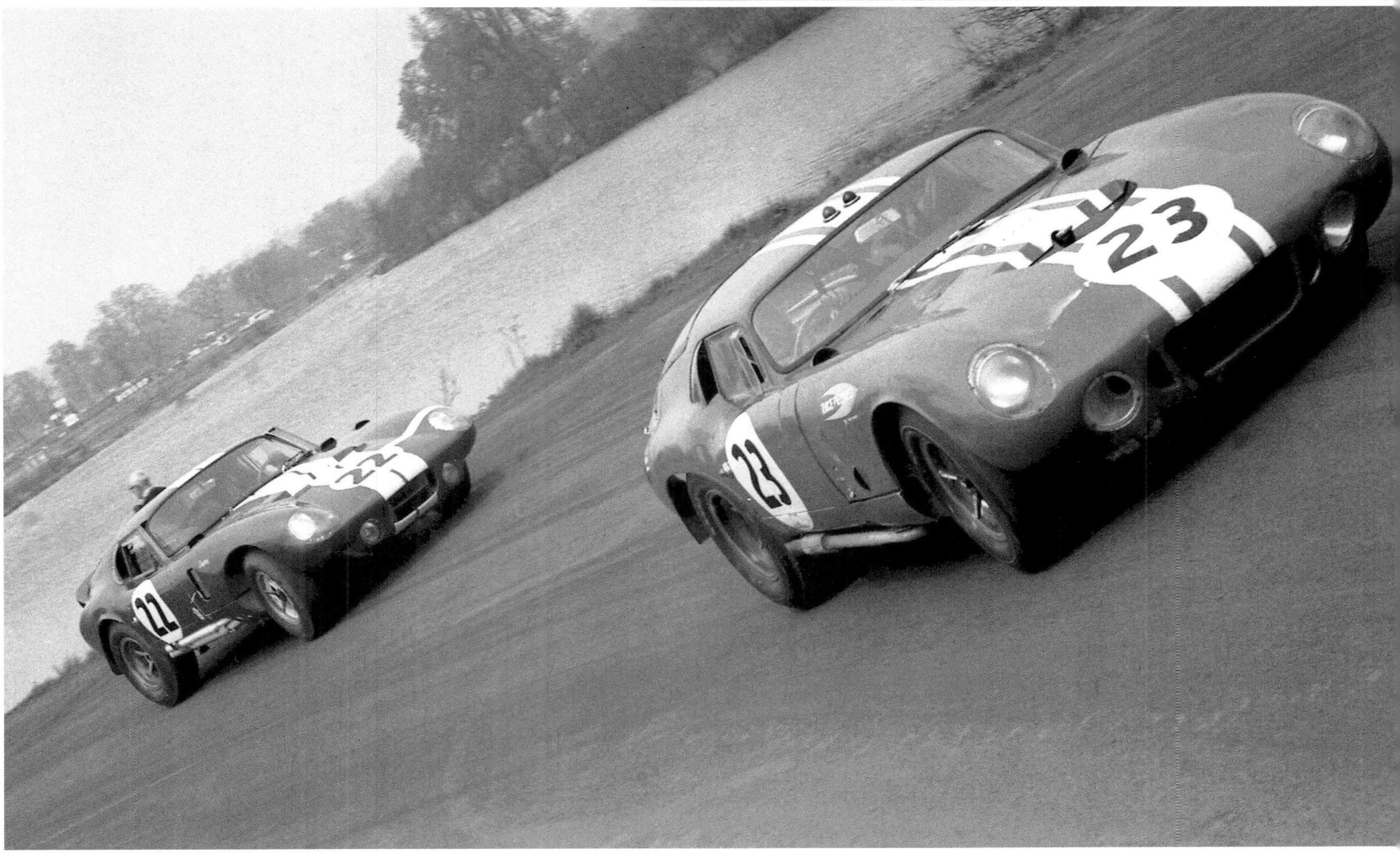

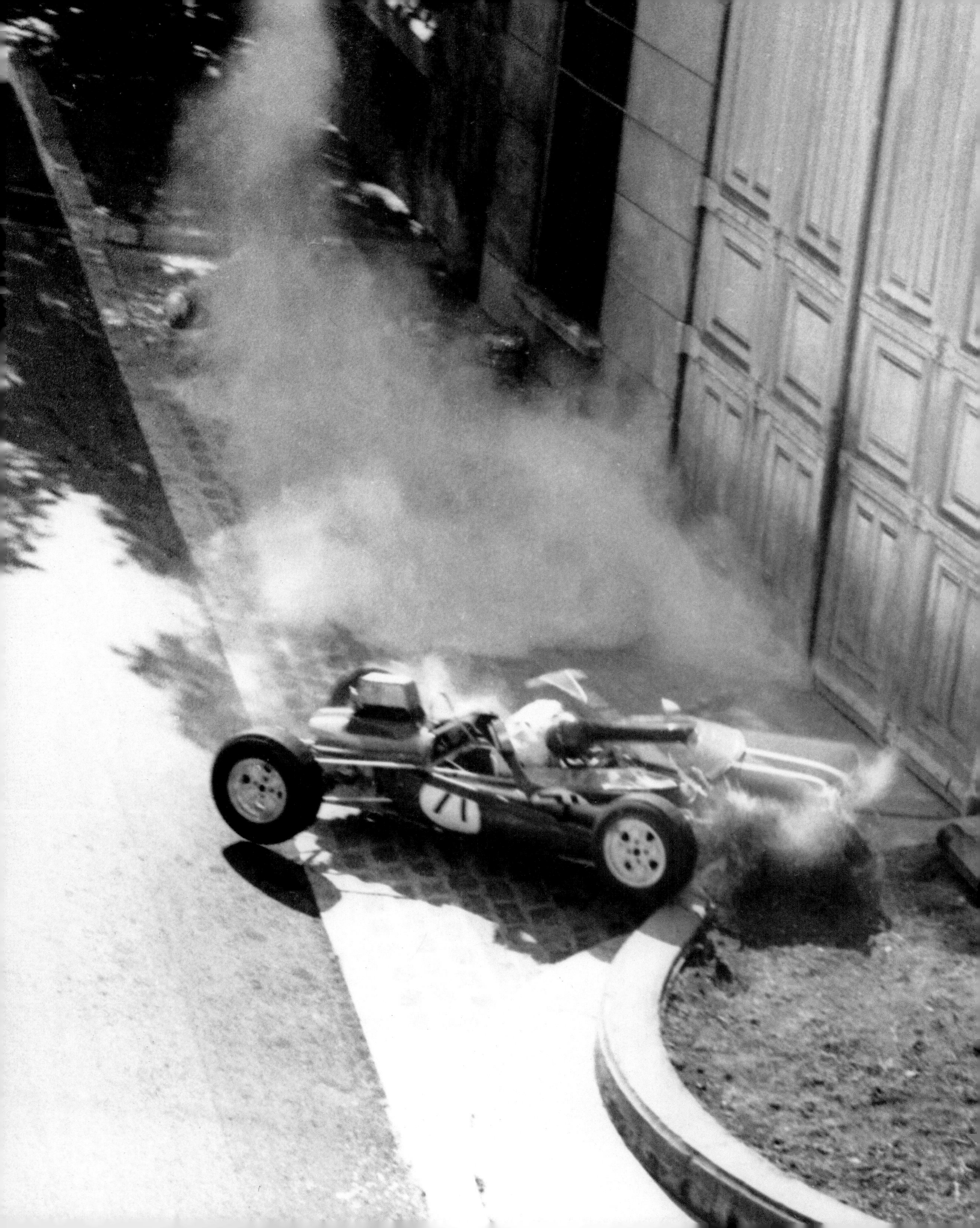

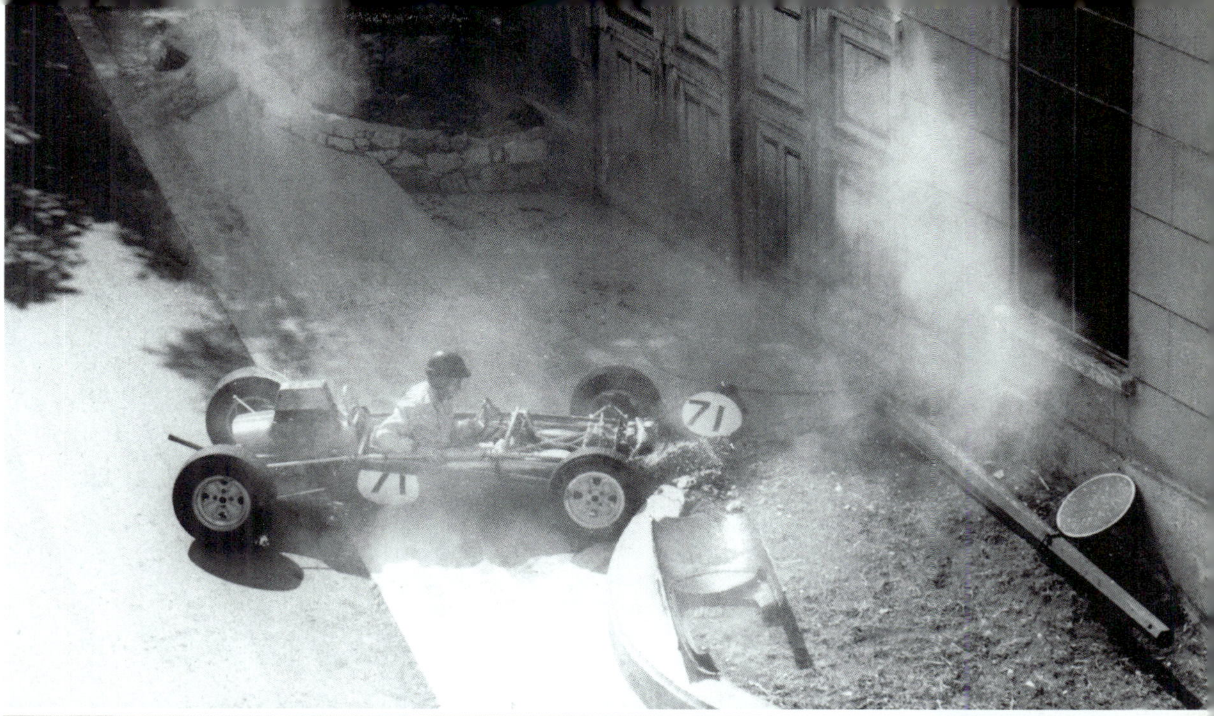

← The perils of street circuits are many and various; above all there is nowhere to go when you overdo it or suffer a problem. This is qualifying for the 1965 Monaco F3 race, and the sequence illustrates perfectly the relative fragility of period racing cars and potentially dire consequences thereof. In this picture, Denis O'Sullivan in the Baldyne Engineering Brabham BT10 attacks the stonework, and with no belts the driver is propelled forward as the nose comes off and the radiator splits, spraying water everywhere.

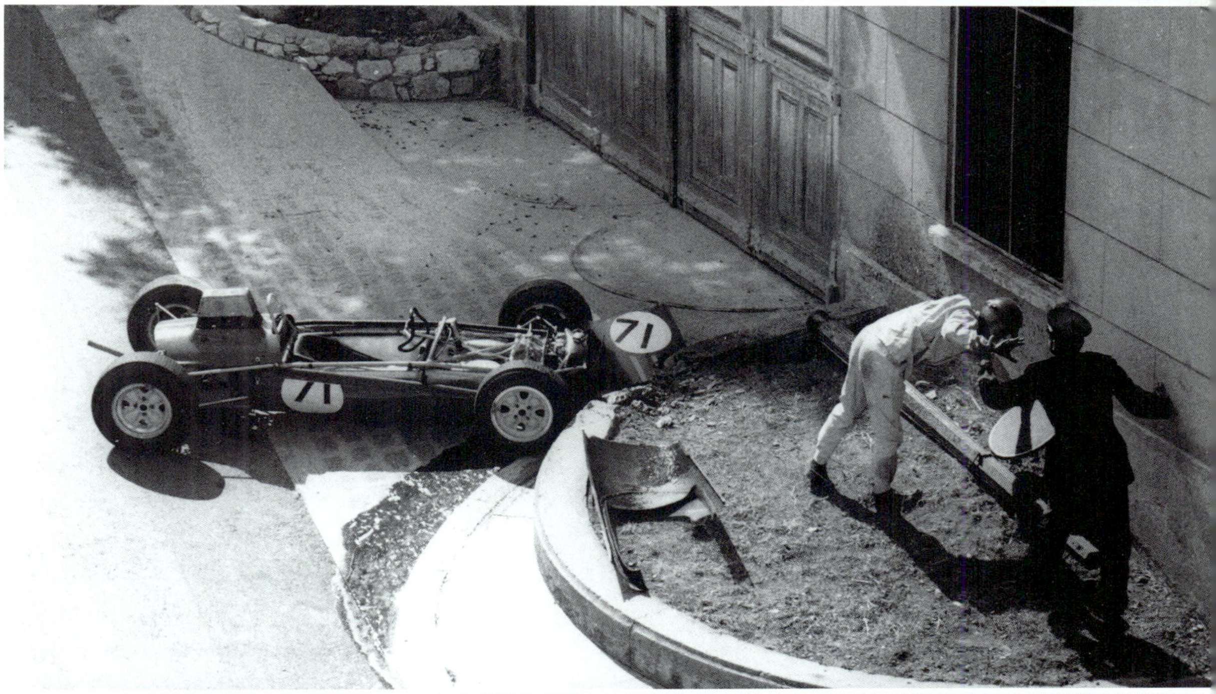

↗ Everything has stopped, bar the water still spewing forth, and our driver is happy to have survived, as is the car that seems remarkably sound, although its flimsy scuttle panel and screen surround lie upside down on the dirt whilst the nose rests on the stone surround.

→ The sudden adrenalin surge and shock have predictable results, and the driver is probably about to be sick or at least thinking about it as he waves away uniform man, presumably a medical officer. The Brabham's grotesquely distorted and buckled steering wheel bears witness to the driver's desperate grip at the moment of impact, and then his wholly unrestrained body flying forward.

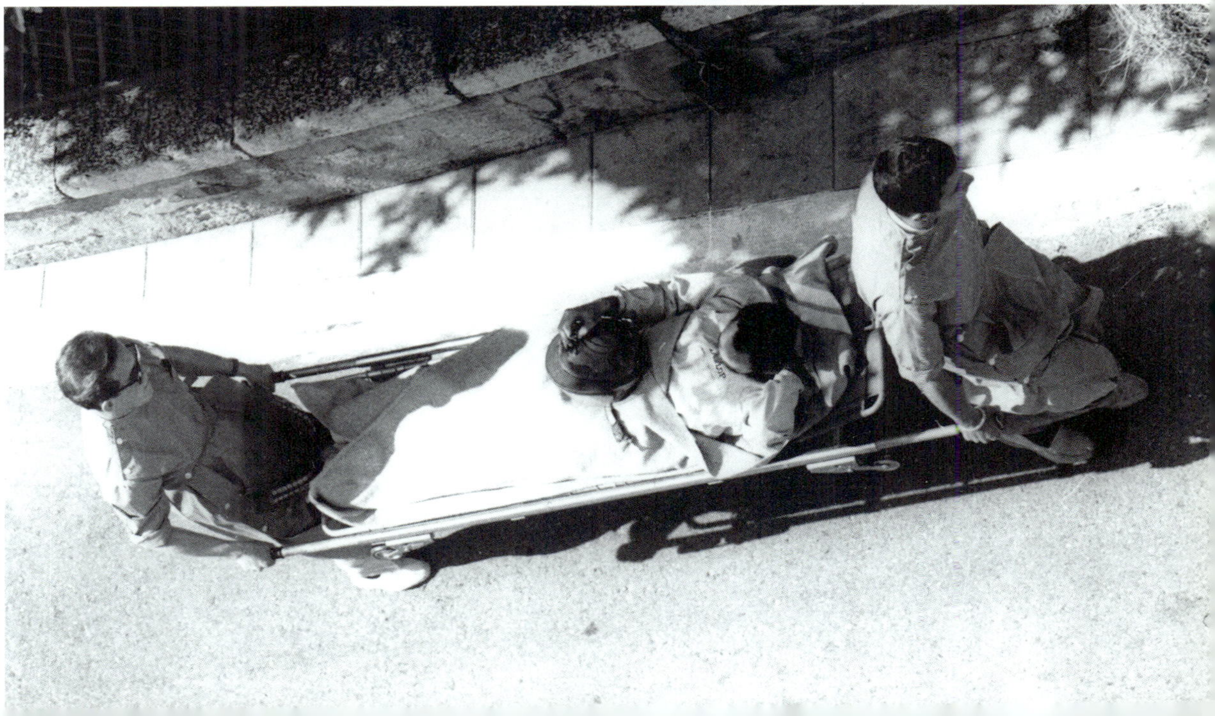

→ The medicos stretcher Mr O'Sullivan away, probably bruised and battered under his overalls, but glad to be alive and bloody furious in equal measure, no doubt. History does not record whether he was actually 'injured' but this looks like a happy outcome.

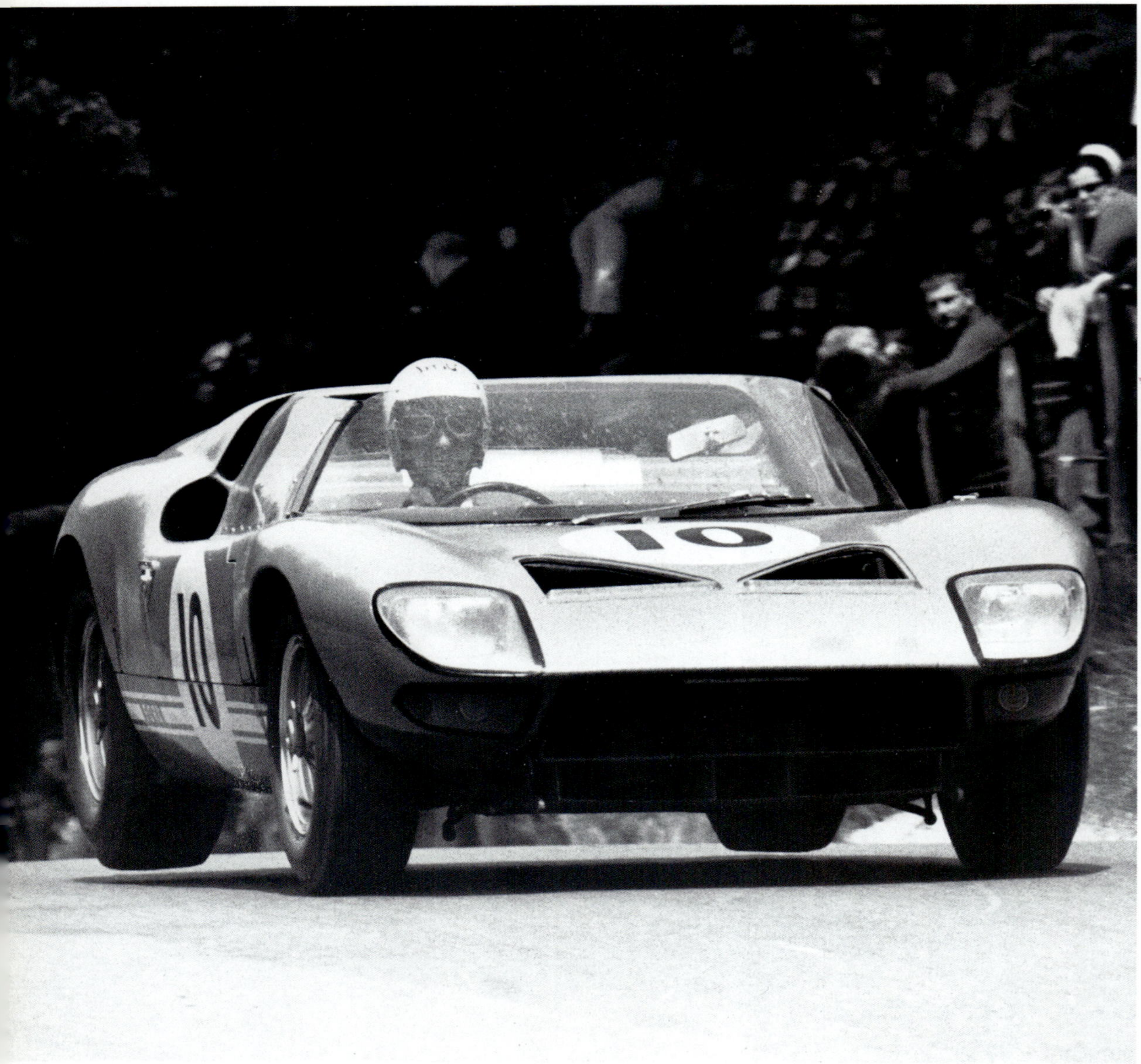

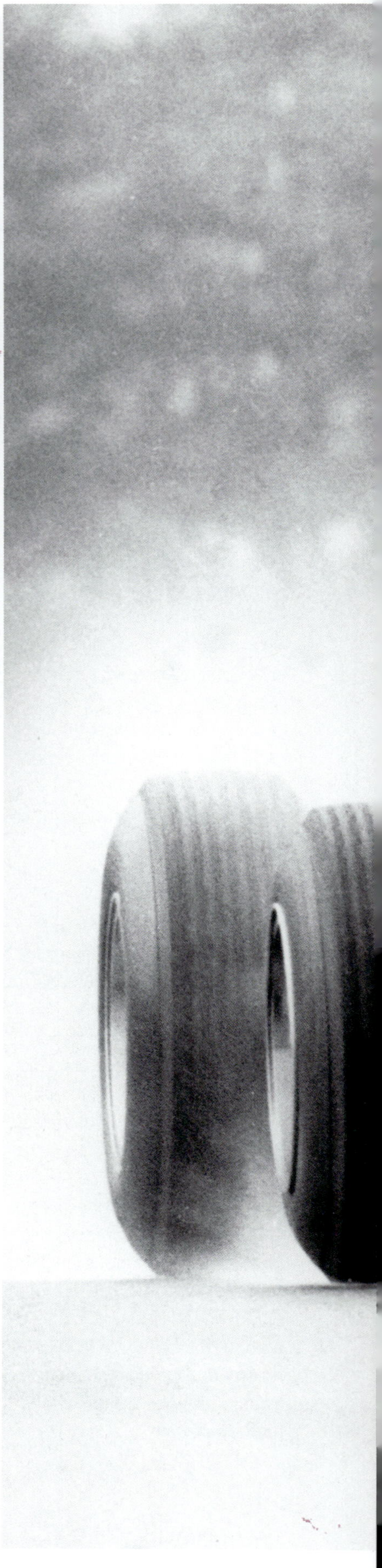

↑ John Whitmore aviates the Ford Advanced Vehicles Ford GT40 (112) at the Nürburgring 1,000km. This was the second such 'roadster', the first one having been badly damaged at the Targa Florio. Together with Richard Attwood, the car ran third at one point but ultimately retired with a broken engine mounting. Note the use of the now antiquated Borrani wire wheels. Rather surprisingly, some of the fastest 'prototype' racers of this time were still only slightly quicker than Stirling Moss's 1958 Vanwall lap here, this GT40 recording 9m 7.1sec against 9m 9.2sec for the Vanwall during the German GP on a then more difficult and less sanitised track.

→ Jim Clark, eyes staring, on his way to a third consecutive win at the Belgian GP at Spa-Francorchamps on 13 June 1965. Clark, as is well documented, hated Spa ever since he witnessed the aftermath of Archie Scott Brown's fatal accident in 1958, and the 1960 tragedies, yet his consummate skill was not to be denied, especially in conditions such as these. Clark exits Eau Rouge in the Lotus 33 (R11), and Mike's shot captures the period flat-bottomed single-seater as the inside front wheel lifts and the rain water builds up under the outer front tyre.

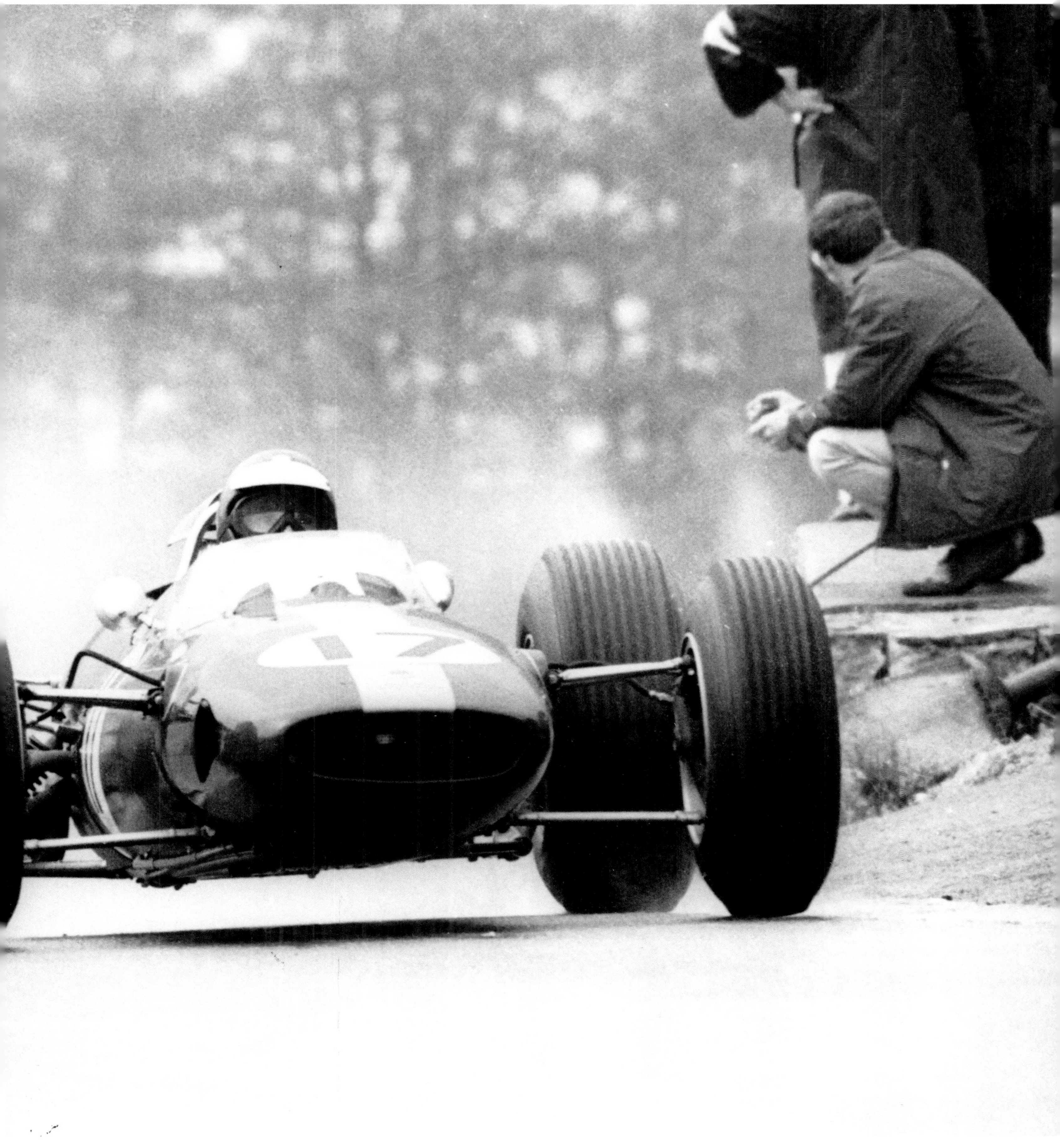

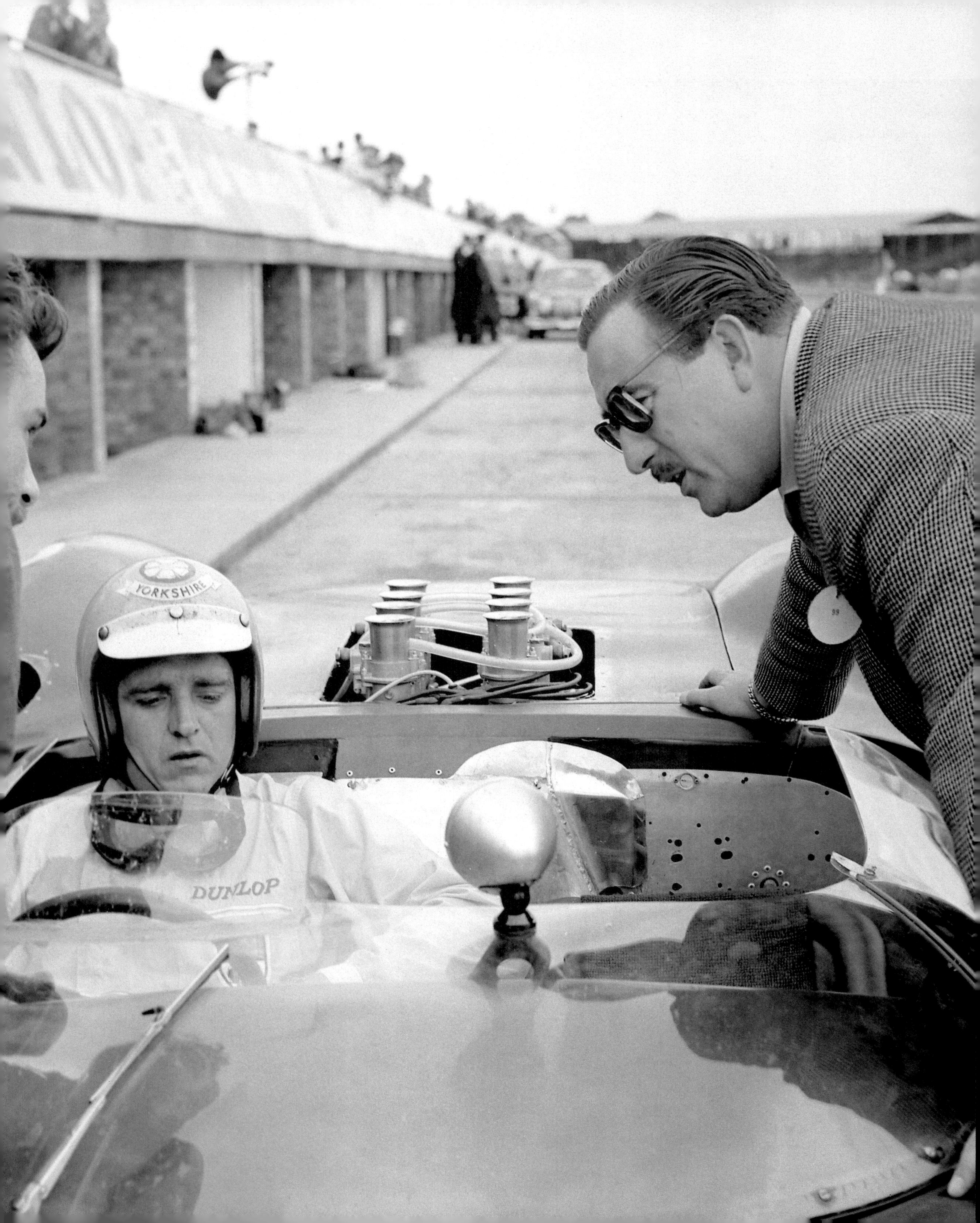
YORKSHIRE
DUNLOP

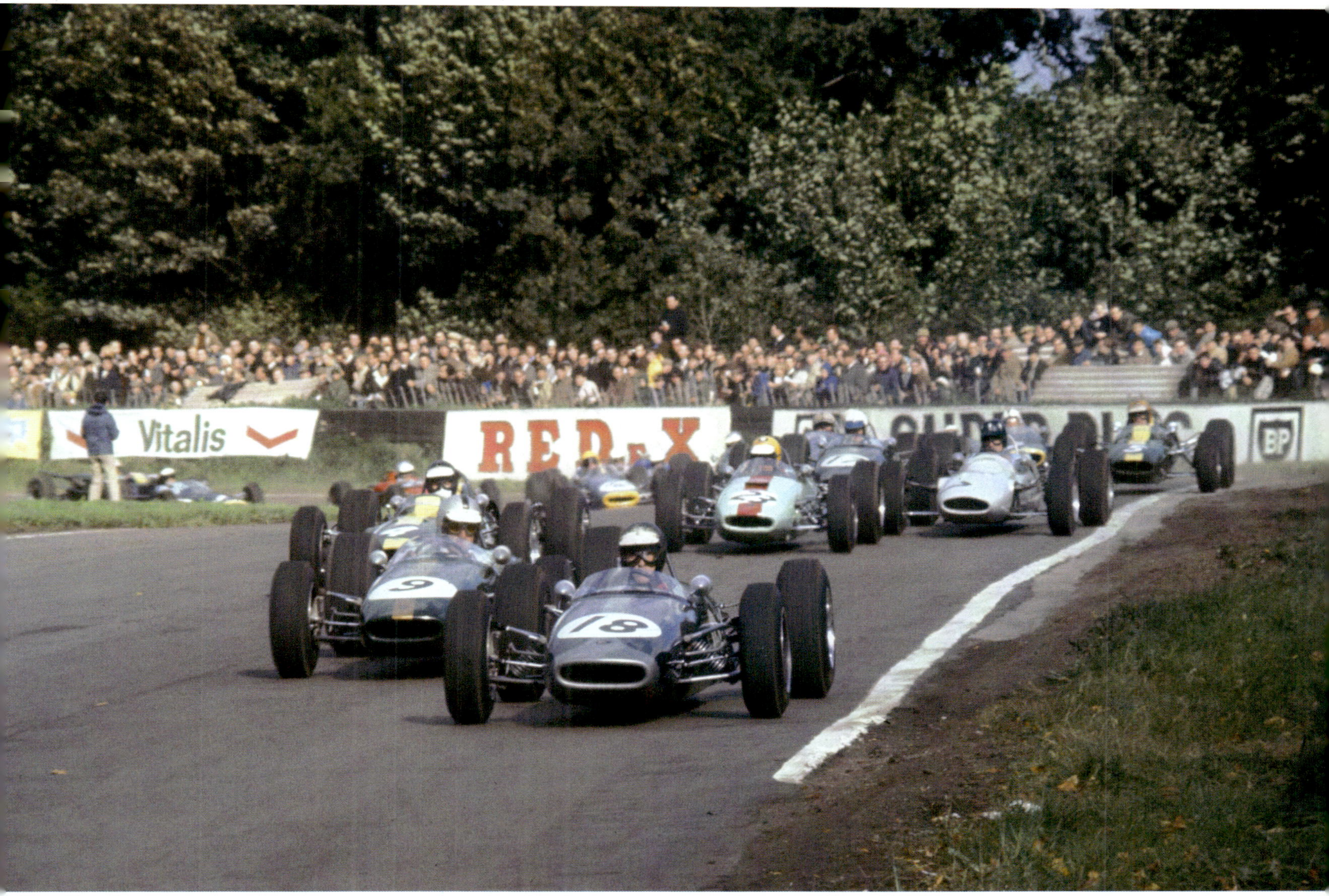

↑The XII Gold Cup at Oulton Park on 18 September 1965 is a perfect example of how fiercely contested these F2 races were. Jochen Rindt leads the pack in his Roy Winkelmann Racing Brabham-Cosworth SCA BT16, with Denny Hulme (No. 9) keeping a wary eye on Jochen's offside rear tyre with the works Brabham-Cosworth SCA BT16. No. 4 is Jim Clark in the Ron Harris Lotus-Cosworth SCA 35, No. 23 Trevor Taylor with his familiar yellow helmet in the Aurora Gear Racing Brabham-Cosworth SCA BT16, followed by Graham Hill (No. 7) in the pearl grey John Coombs Lotus-BRM 35. Also identifiable are Alan Rees in the second Winkelmann Brabham (No. 17) behind which can be seen John Surtees' crash helmet driving the Midland Racing Partnership Lola-Cosworth SCA T60, Mike Spence in the other Ron Harris Lotus (No. 5), and behind him Richard Attwood in another MRP Lola. Rindt was not classified, Hulme finished second, Clark sixth, Taylor fourth, Hill third, Rees fifth, Surtees first. Spence crashed and Attwood retired. The first three were separated by only six tenths of a second after 40 laps.

←This is probably the second of Ian Walker's two Lotus 30s, the first having been destroyed in a catastrophic accident at Brands Hatch during 1964 when driven by Tony Hegbourne. So this should be the series 2 30/S2/4 with Trevor Taylor (note the Yorkshire decal on his helmet) in the Silverstone pits with the boss. Ian Walker began his driving career in 1956 and retired in 1962 to form Ian Walker Racing. During the 1960s he employed many top drivers, including Mike Spence, Paul Hawkins, Frank Gardner, Jim Clark, and Graham Hill (whom he partnered in the 1964 Monte Carlo Rally in a Ford Falcon), but the deaths of Hegbourne, Doug Revson, and others caused him to close the team in 1966. In later life he supported his son Sean in historic racing. Sadly, he passed away on 7 July 2008 aged 82.

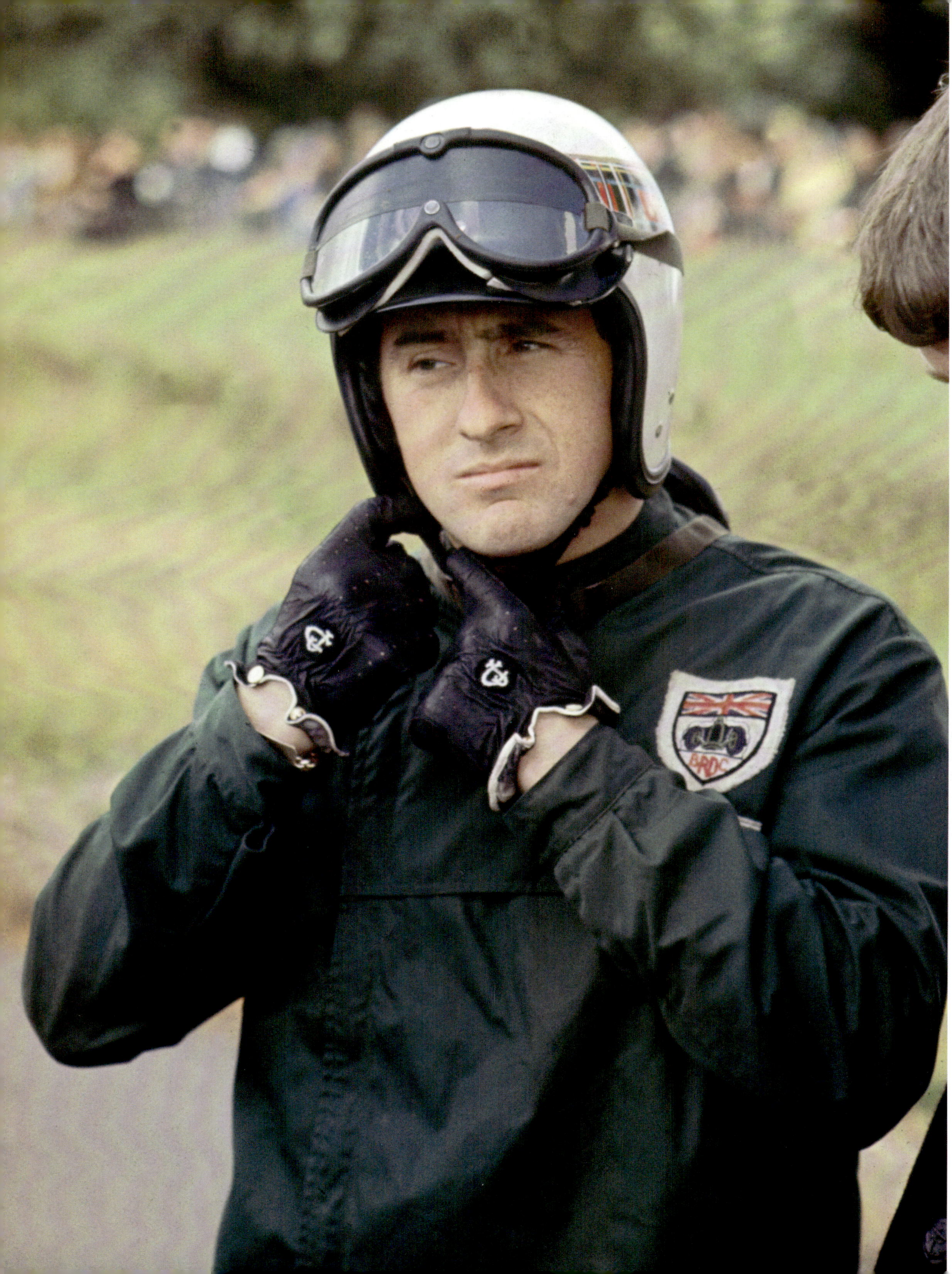
BRDC

🡐 Jackie Stewart drove the Ken Tyrrell Coopers in 1964, first in F3 and then in F2 for 1965, as well as for BRM in F1. At the Oulton Park Gold Cup he fiddles with his helmet strap. JYS's leather driving gloves are the JC (Jim Clark) branded product that originally cost three guineas (£3-3s-0d or, if you prefer, £3.15).

🡒 Most serious F2 cars in 1965 used the Cosworth SCA engine, but the Tyrrell Coopers and John Coombs used BRM's type 71 unit. Jackie Stewart was unclassified at Oulton Park in the Cooper-BRM T75, completing only 29 laps, whilst his team-mate American Bob Bondurant crashed on the first lap.

🡓 Gold Cup winner John Surtees in the MRP Lola T60 leads Alan Rees in the Winkelmann Brabham BT16, Denny Hulme in the BRD Brabham BT16, Graham Hill in John Coombs' Lotus 35, and Jochen Rindt in the other Winkelmann Brabham BT16. Even allowing for ancient colour film stock, John Surtees' helmet looks a trifle dirty.

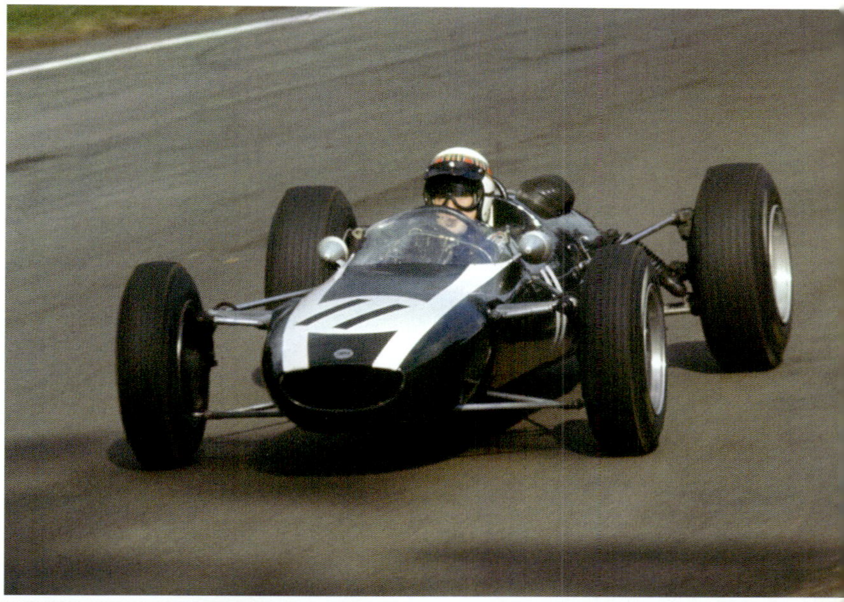

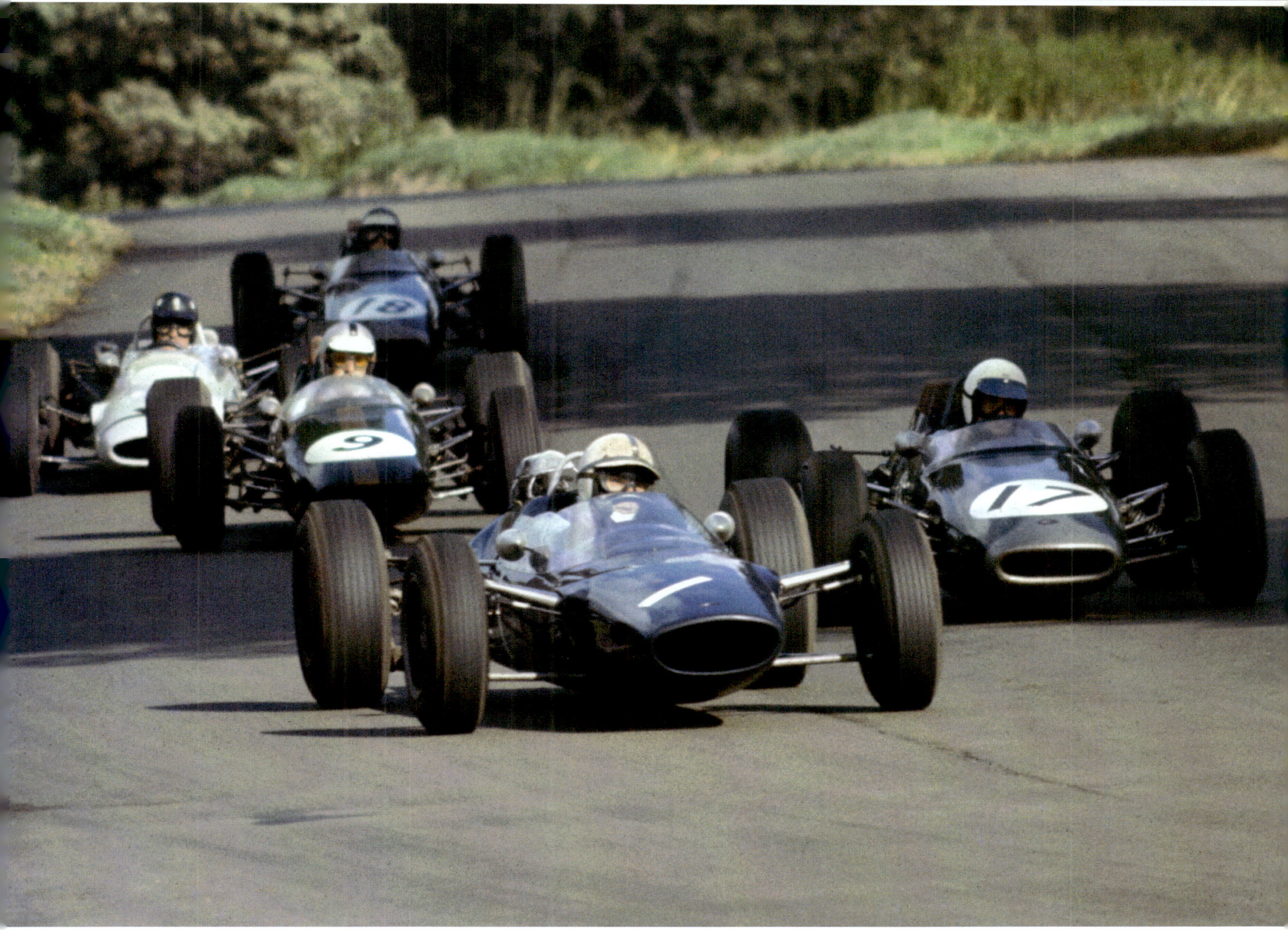

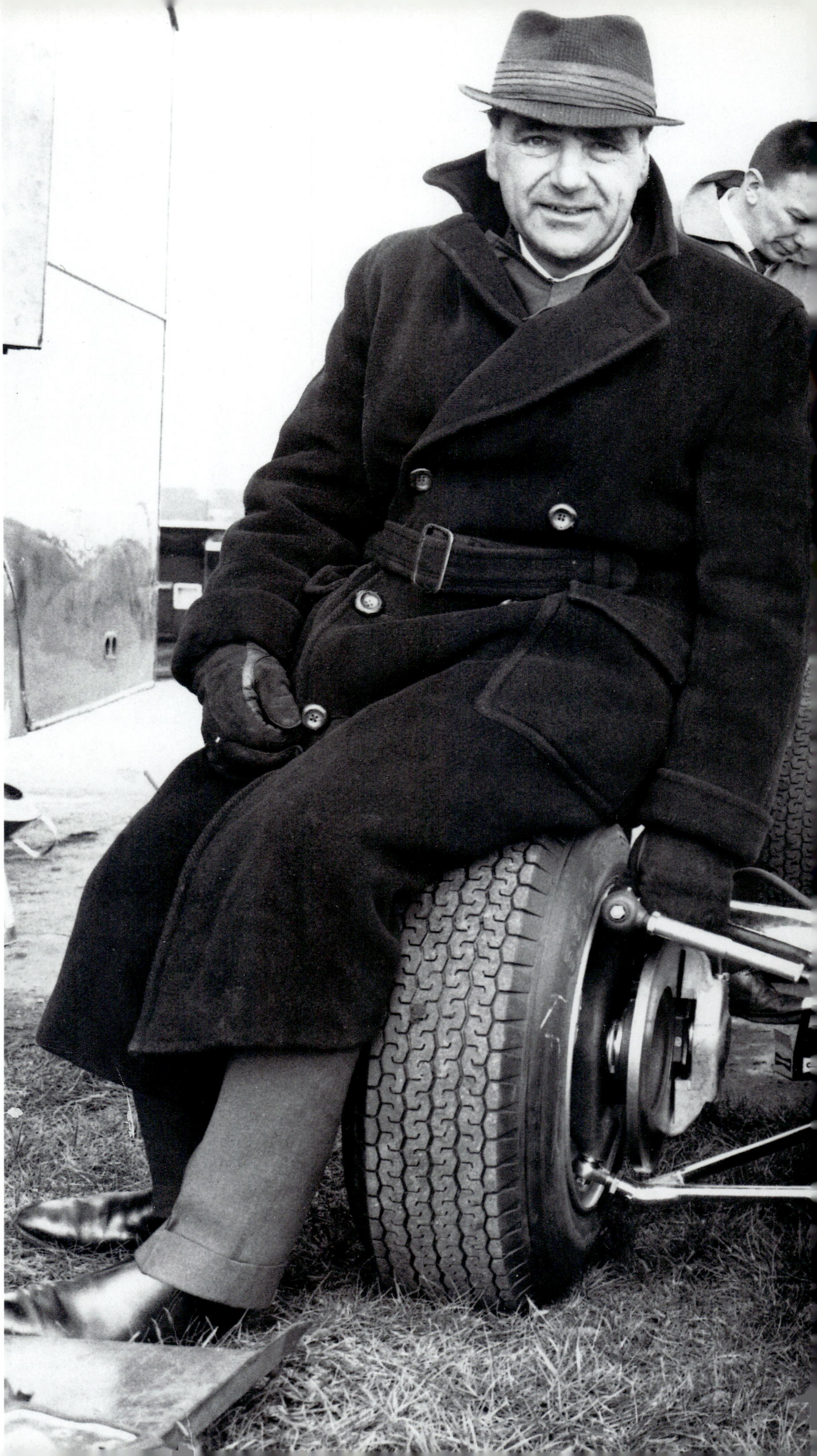

➔ John Cooper had sold Cooper to the Chipstead Motor Group in early 1965, but retained title to the property and continued working for the new company. Late in the year a prototype 'hack' first built for the redundant Climax flat 16 engine appeared using Maserati's rejuvenated 1957 V12 unit, now of 3 litres. Mike has obviously prevailed upon John Cooper to adopt one of his posed seated-on-a-front-wheel shots. Note the cranked lower wishbones, the exposed discs and, in the background, a favourite barge *du jour*, an old Mk 7 Jaguar with its rear wheel spats removed.

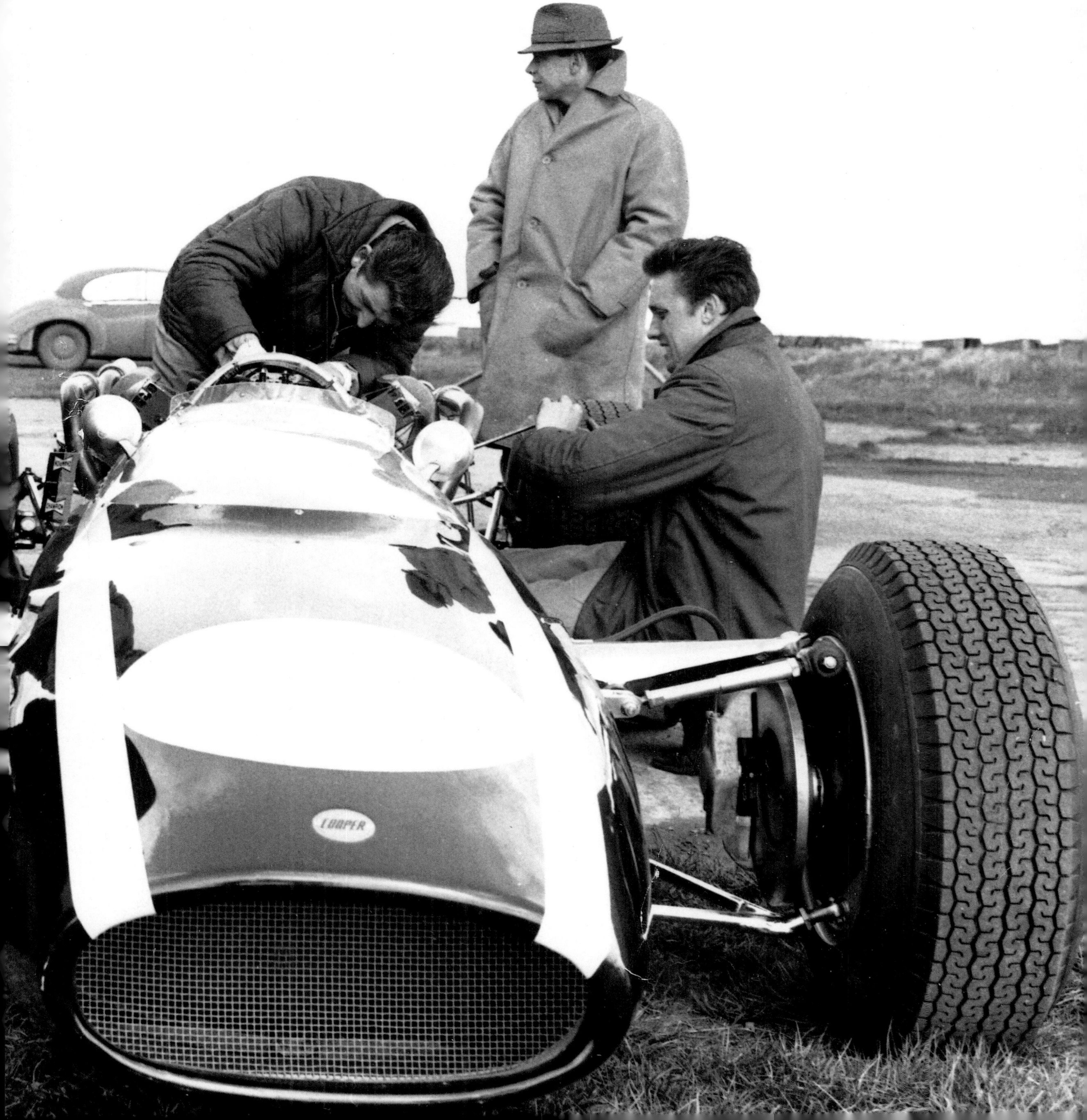
COOPER

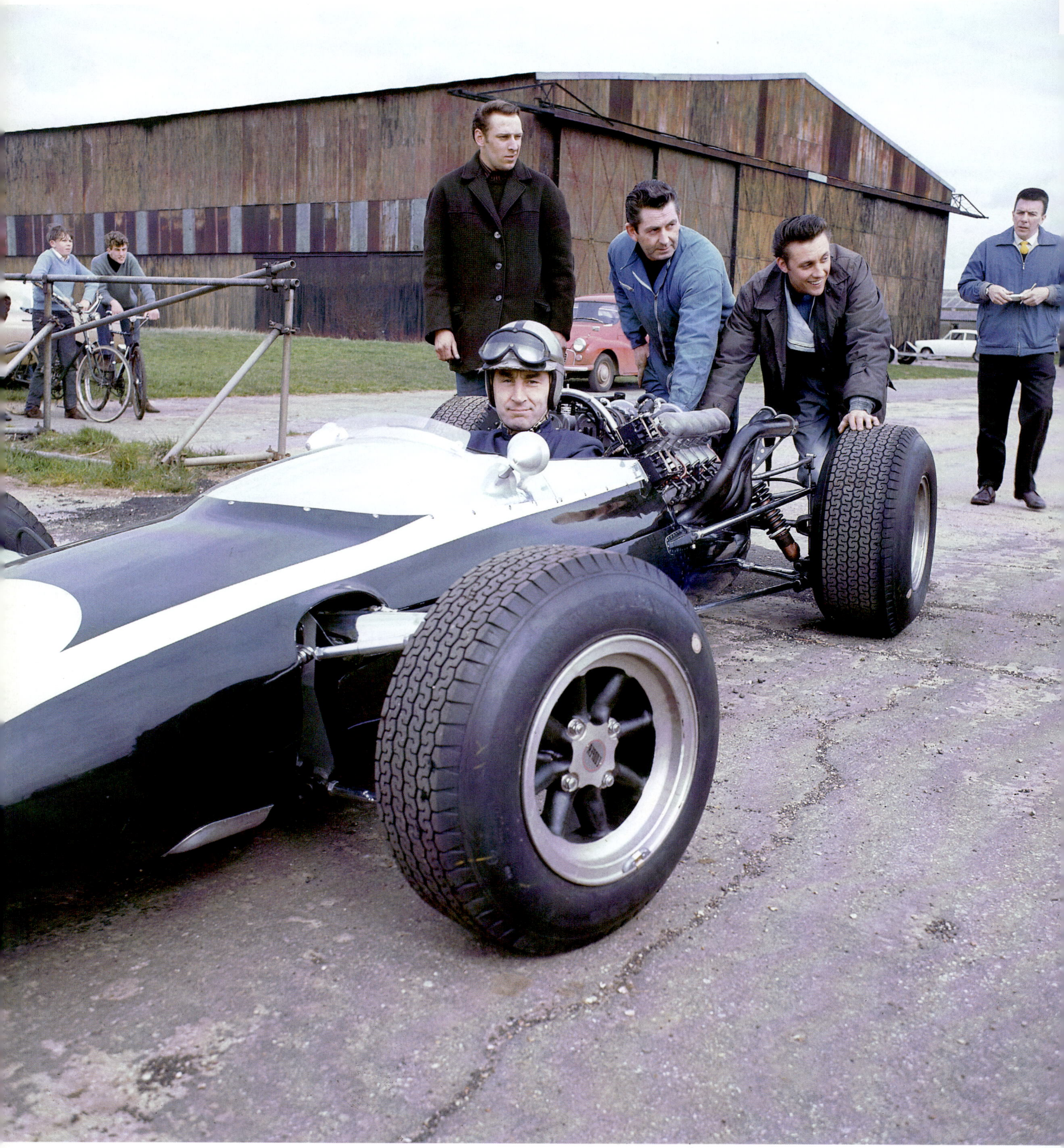

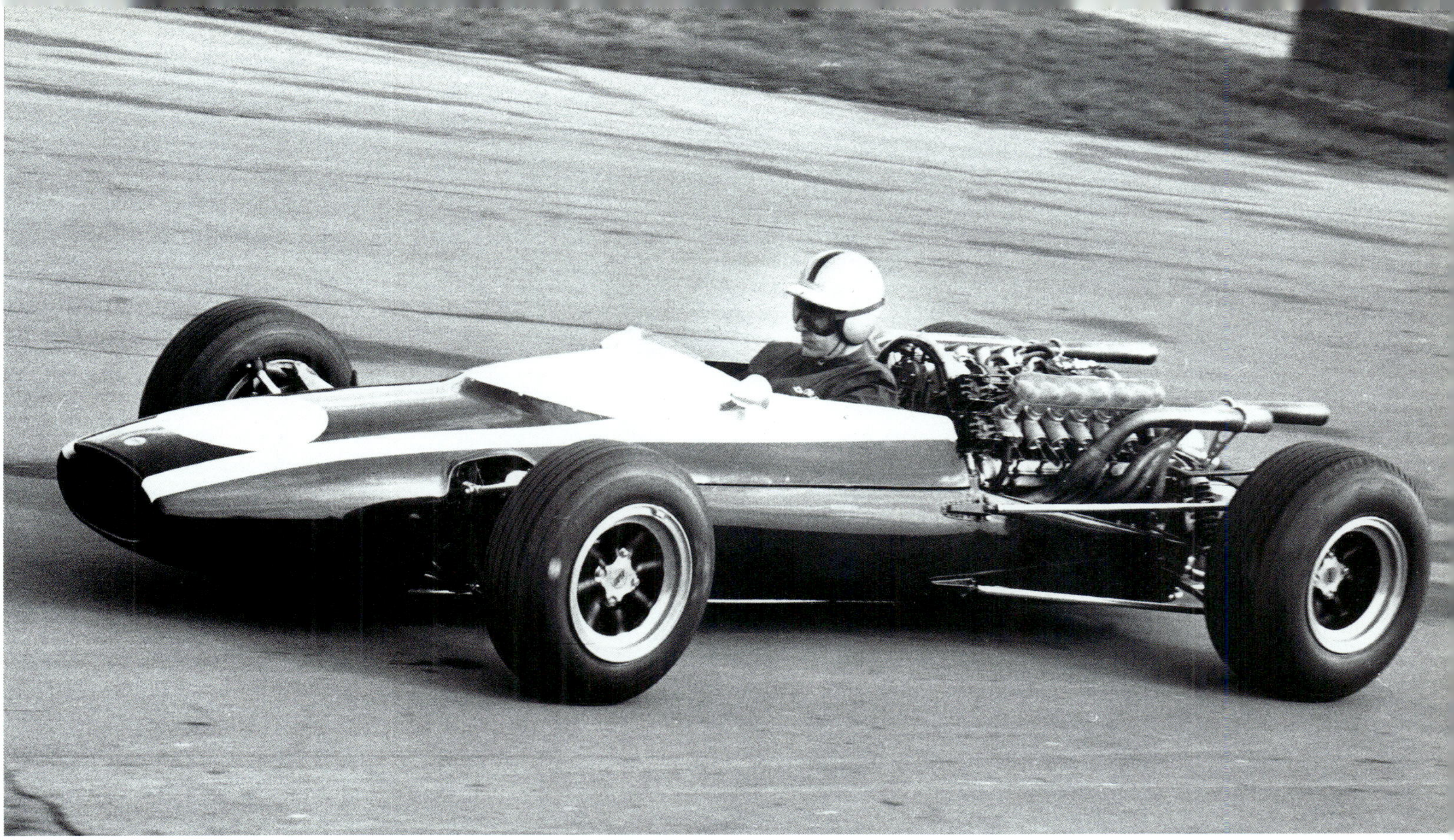

↑ Ironically, the T80 mule looks sleeker than the actual T81 racecar, and it is obviously not built to accommodate the rather tall Mr Salvadori.

← Roy Salvadori was an executive of the Chipstead Motor Group and, of course, an experienced, successful ex-Cooper driver, so his appointment as team manager and administrator of the new venture was an obvious step. A slightly quizzical-looking Roy is pushed off in the embryonic Maserati-powered device at Silverstone on a dull day, watched by the inevitable young boys (something that is no longer possible for mere bystanders). Ex-Jaguar designer Derrick White, who was employed to design the new car's monocoque, follows up at right rear.

→ There is no record as to whether Jo Siffert drove the fledgling Cooper-Maserati T80 at Silverstone, but he certainly tried the cockpit. Roy Salvadori looks on.

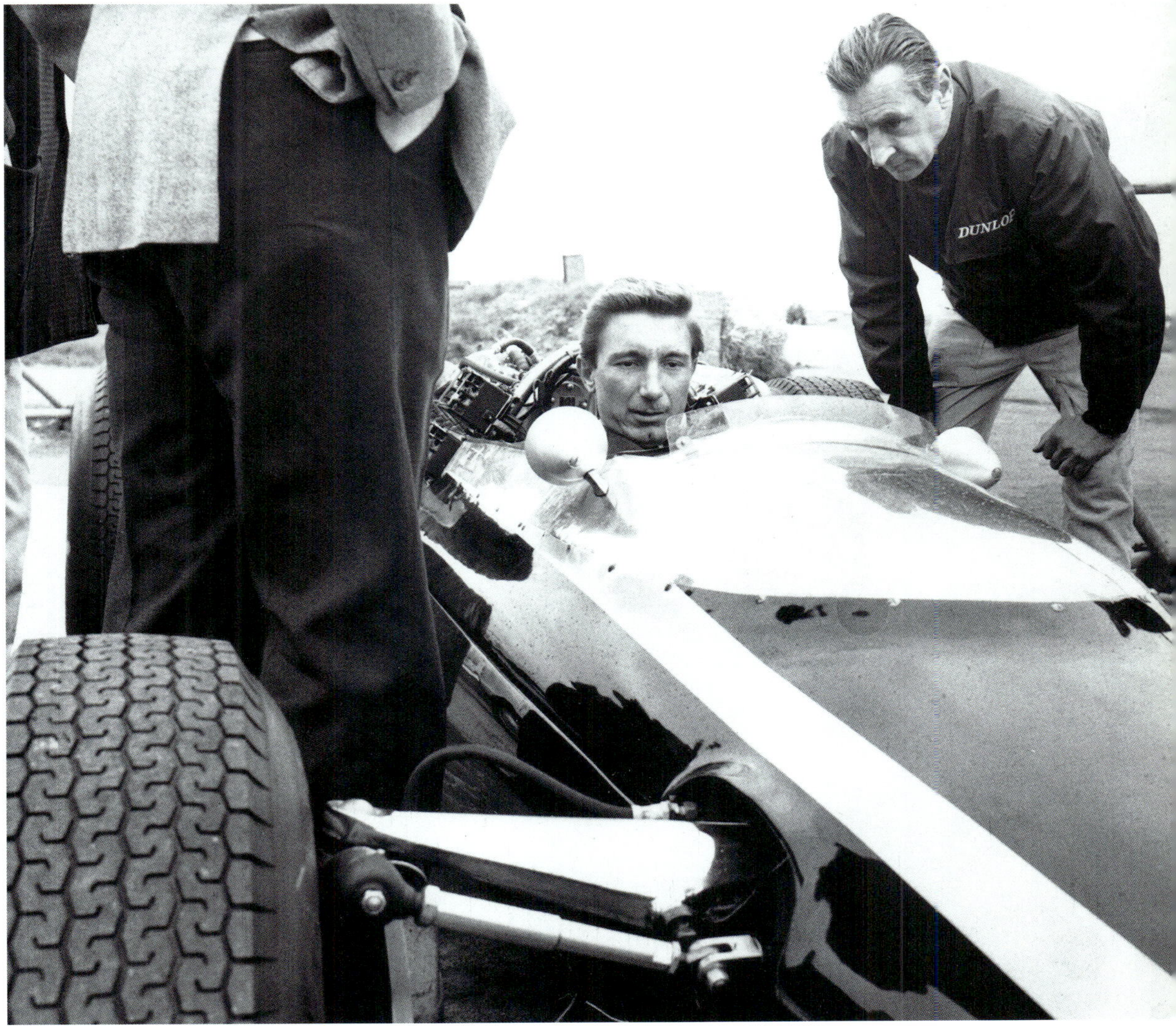

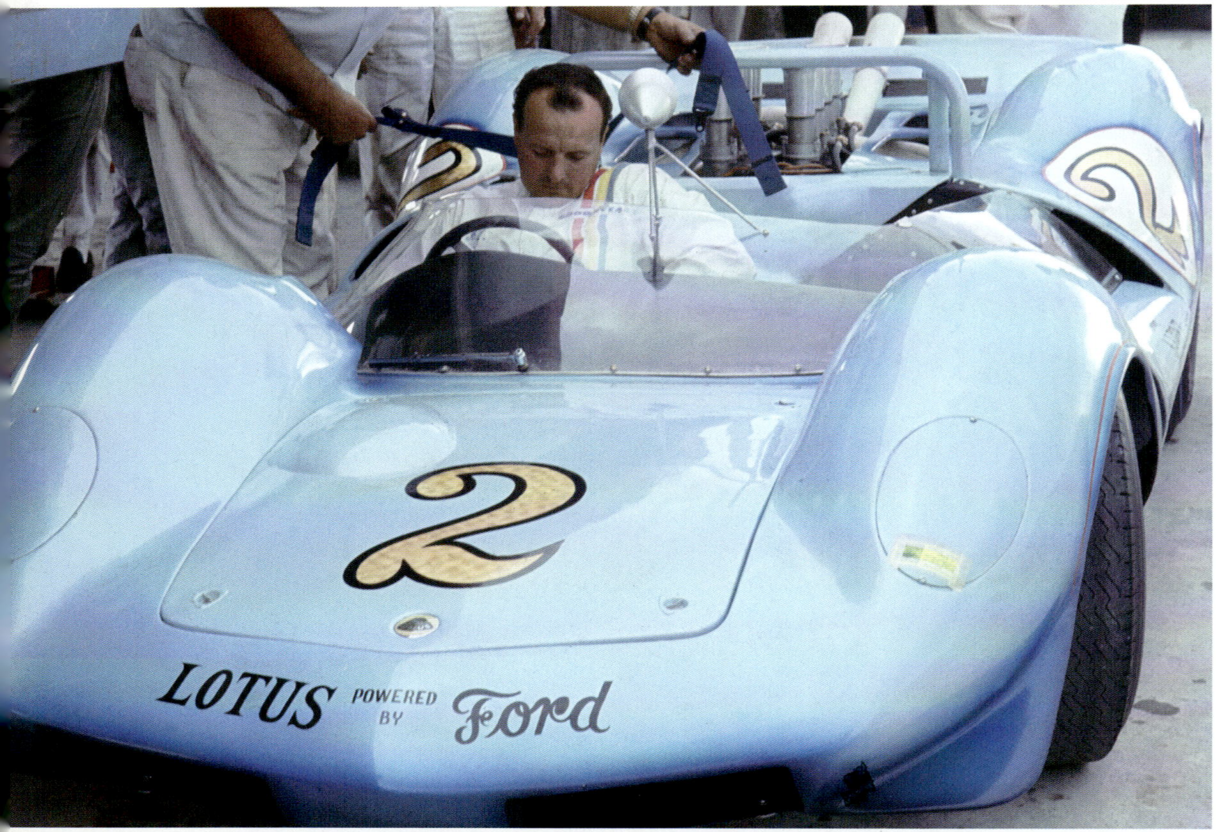

← The Nassau Speedweek was a regular feature of the off season for Americans and various European teams, being set in the sunny Bahamas during late November/ early December. Mike attended the 1965 event which comprised races for sports racers, GTs, and on occasion even Formula Vee. Holman & Moody entered this Lotus-Ford 40 (R3) for the Governor and Nassau Trophy races, but in both cases the legendary A. J. Foyt retired. Sad to say, the Lotus 30 and its type 40 successor were not exactly Chapman's finest creations and usually failed regardless of colour scheme, driver, or entrant.

↓ Another look at the gaudily decorated Lotus 40, and it is a wonder that the exhausts did not set fire to the upswept tail.

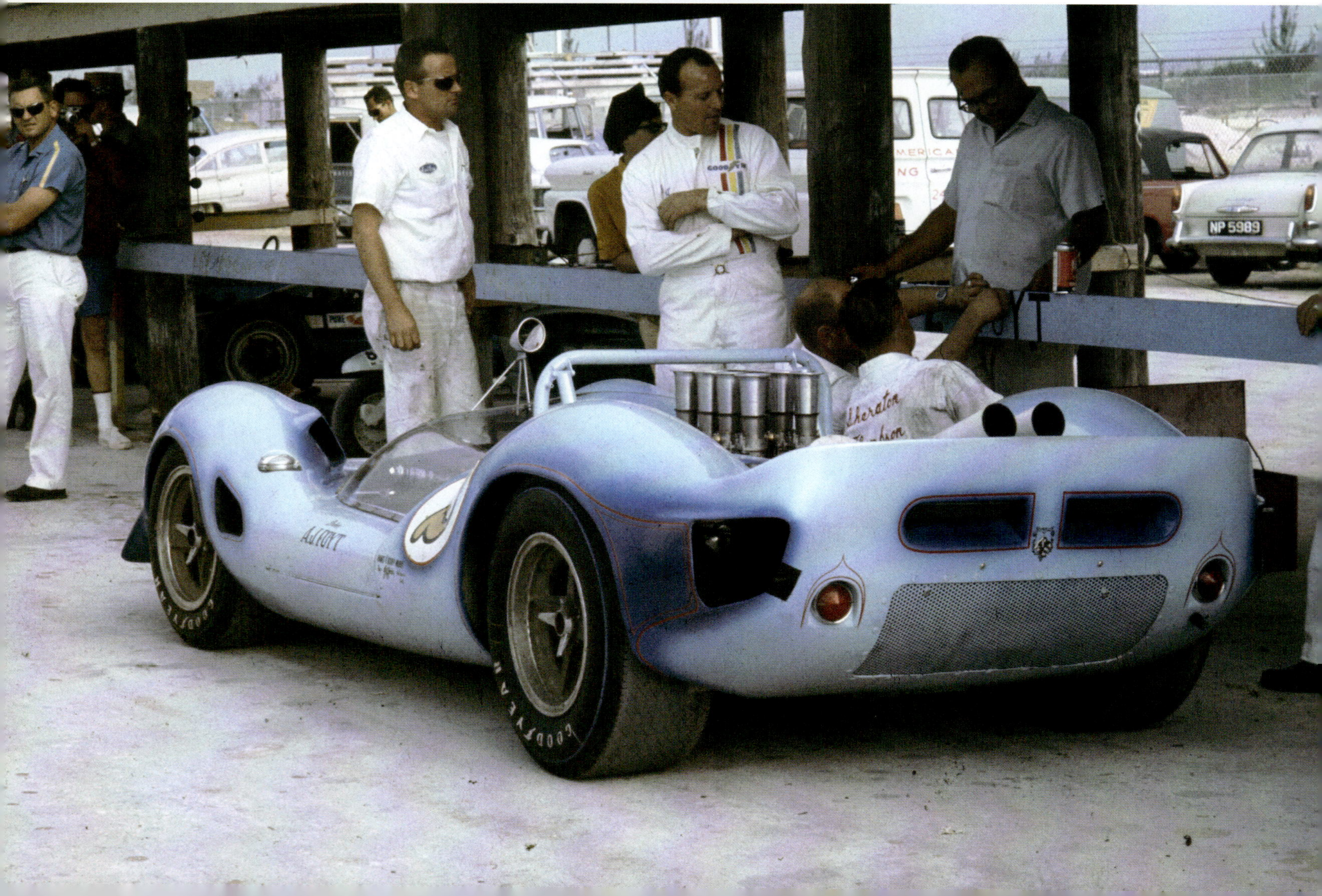

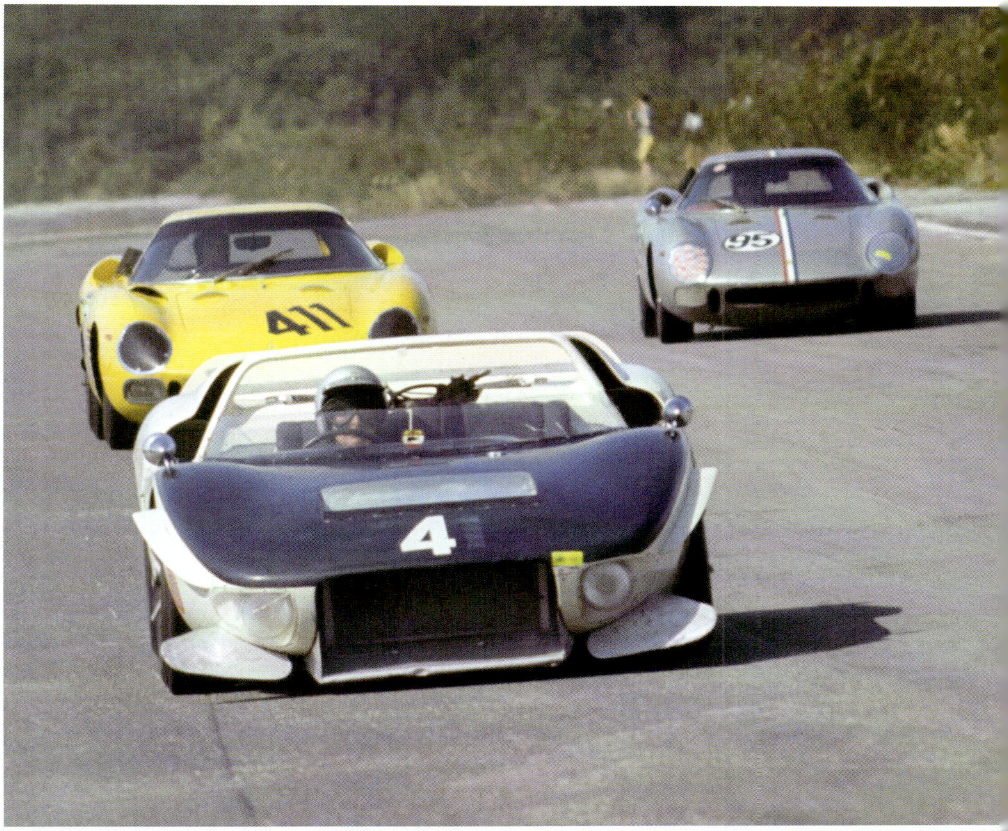

➔ The experimental Ford GTX-1 (110) was originally conceived as a Group 7 challenger, and was built by Bruce McLaren's team at Feltham, but it was far too heavy being GT40-based. Driven by Chris Amon, it retired in both its races at Nassau, but later redeemed itself by winning the 1966 Sebring 12 Hours after reconstruction as a Mk II, only to be scrapped after its Floridian pounding. It was buried at Riverside to avoid the expense of rebuilding it again and the taxes for importing it to Le Mans that year. Following is David Greenblatt's Ferrari 250LM (6047) and the similar Scuderia Bear car (5909) of Richard Holquist, one of the team principals, together with William McKelvy and Bob Grossman. Canadian Greenblatt finished eighth in the Governor's Trophy and seventh in the Nassau Trophy, whilst Holquist was a meritorious fifth in the former, but only survived 11 laps in the latter.

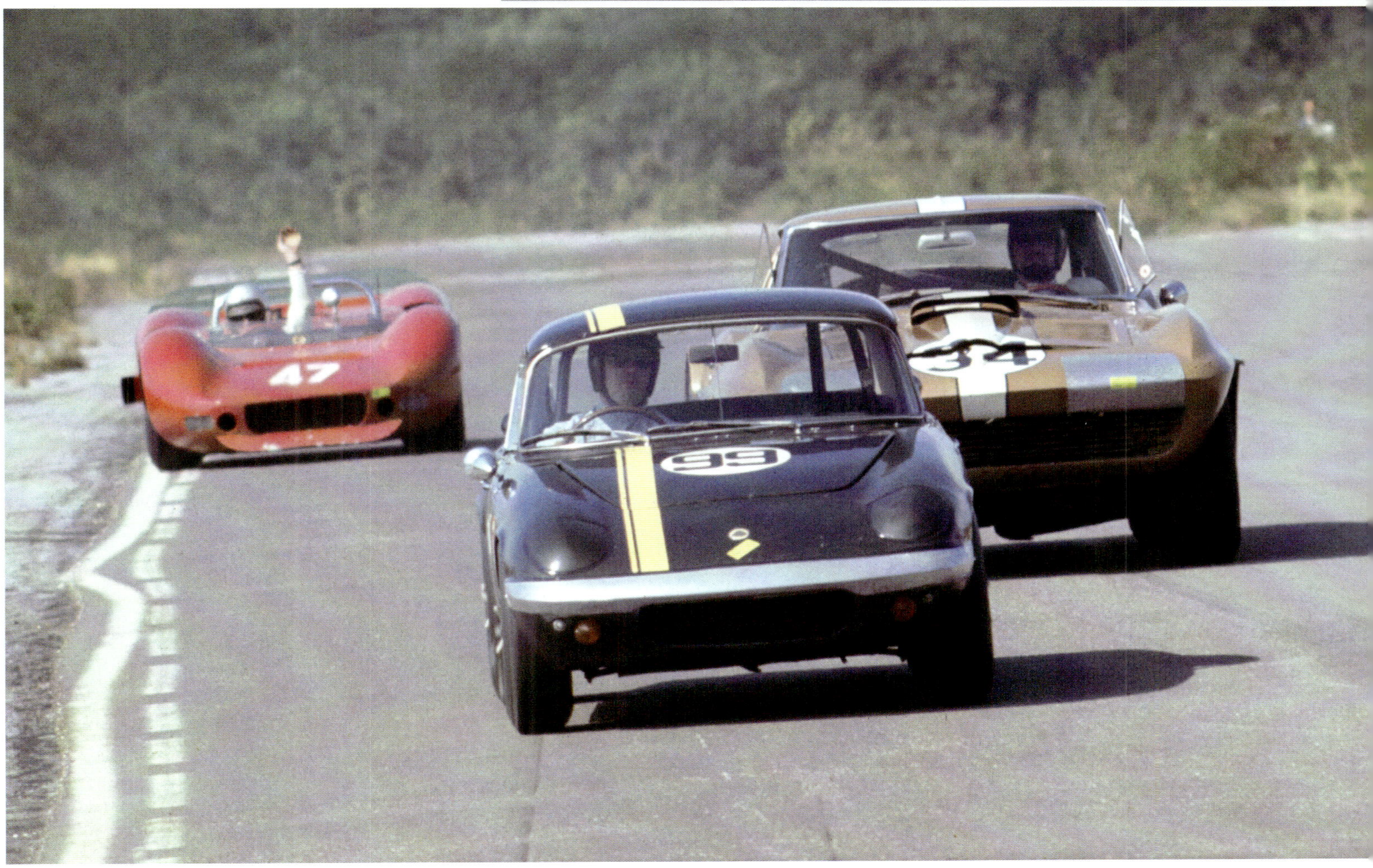

🡓 Mix and match, perhaps, as Bob Leitzinger (Lotus Elan) leads Kenneth Duclos's Chevrolet Corvette Sting Ray, whilst Bruce McLaren (McLaren-Oldsmobile M1B), hand up, retires from the Nassau Trophy race. However, he did win the Governor's Trophy ahead of Hap Sharp's Chaparral 2A.

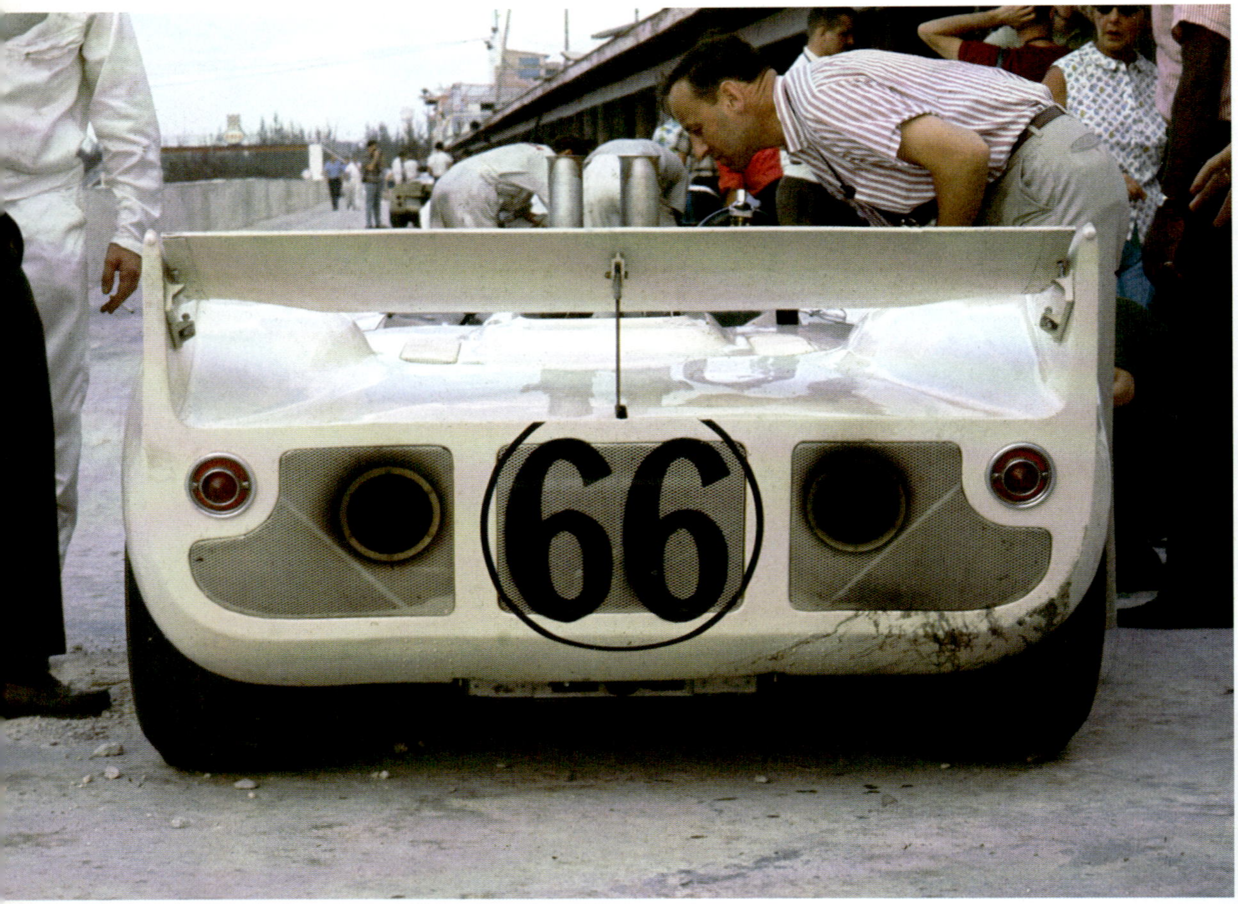

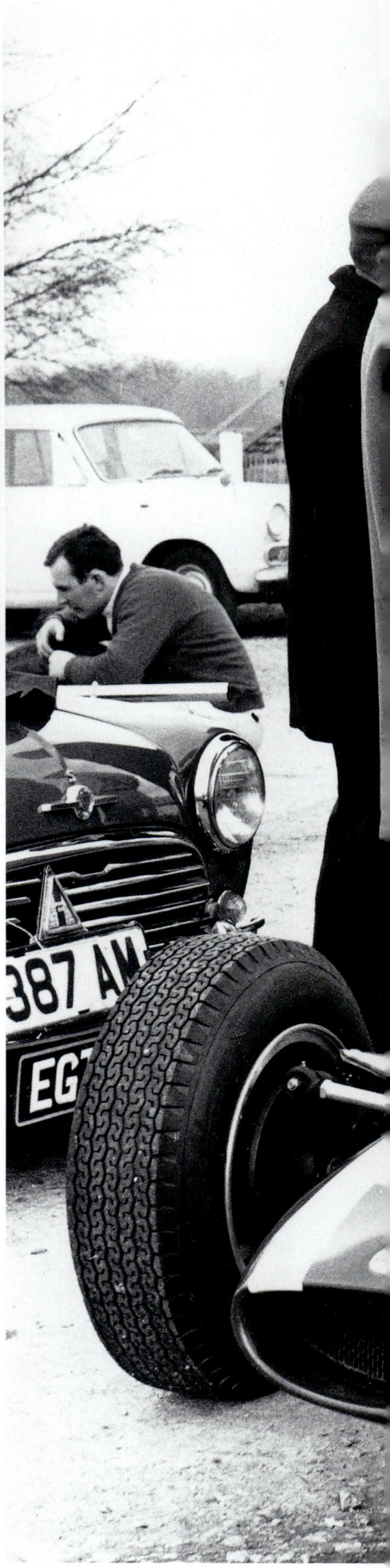

↑ Although Hap Sharp won the 252-mile Nassau Trophy Race and finished second to Bruce McLaren in the Governor's Trophy with the Chaparral 2A, his boss Jim Hall was not so lucky. He retired in the main event when leading by half a lap because his front suspension broke, and finished seventh in the latter after throttle linkage problems lost him two laps. Just imagine the noise coming out of the back of this monster if you strayed too close during a race.

→ Goodwood on a gloomy day and, by the look of the body language, all is not well. The Ford-powered Cooper T83 F3 disproves the old adage that what looks right usually is. In fact the car suffered excessive understeer because of the then little understood concept of lift; too much air was accumulating in the wrong places. As noted by Doug Nye in his definitive book *Cooper Cars*, only seven of these pretty little machines were built, and the bearded John Fenning, along with Stockbridge Racing team-mate Clive Baker, soon gave up on them. An unhappy John Cooper leans heavily over the rear tyre. To the left can be glimpsed the front of a Mini Cooper S with trade plates attached, no doubt a company car with an expired tax disc, which is how things were done in those times.

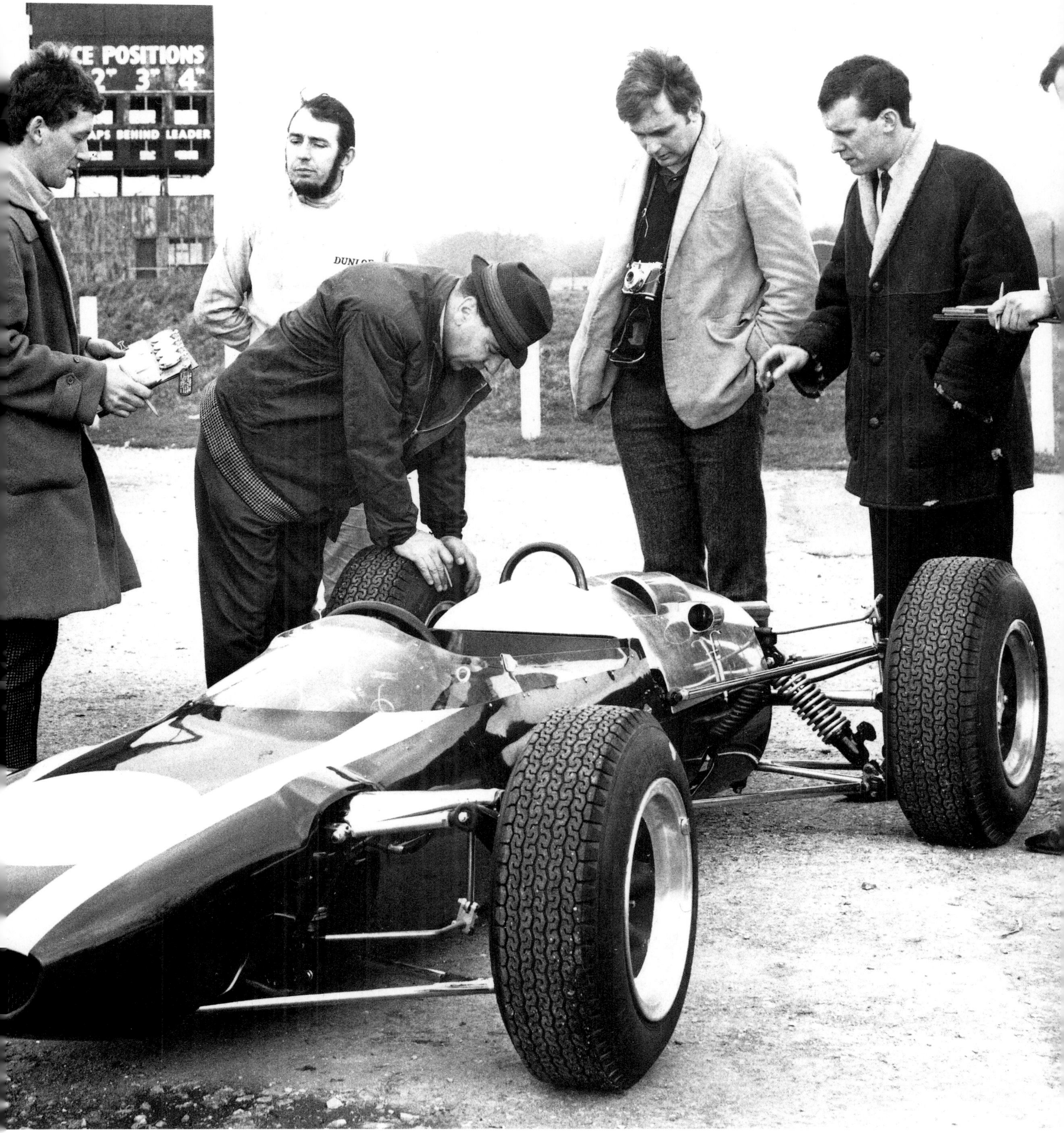
POSITIONS
3 4
BEHIND LEADER

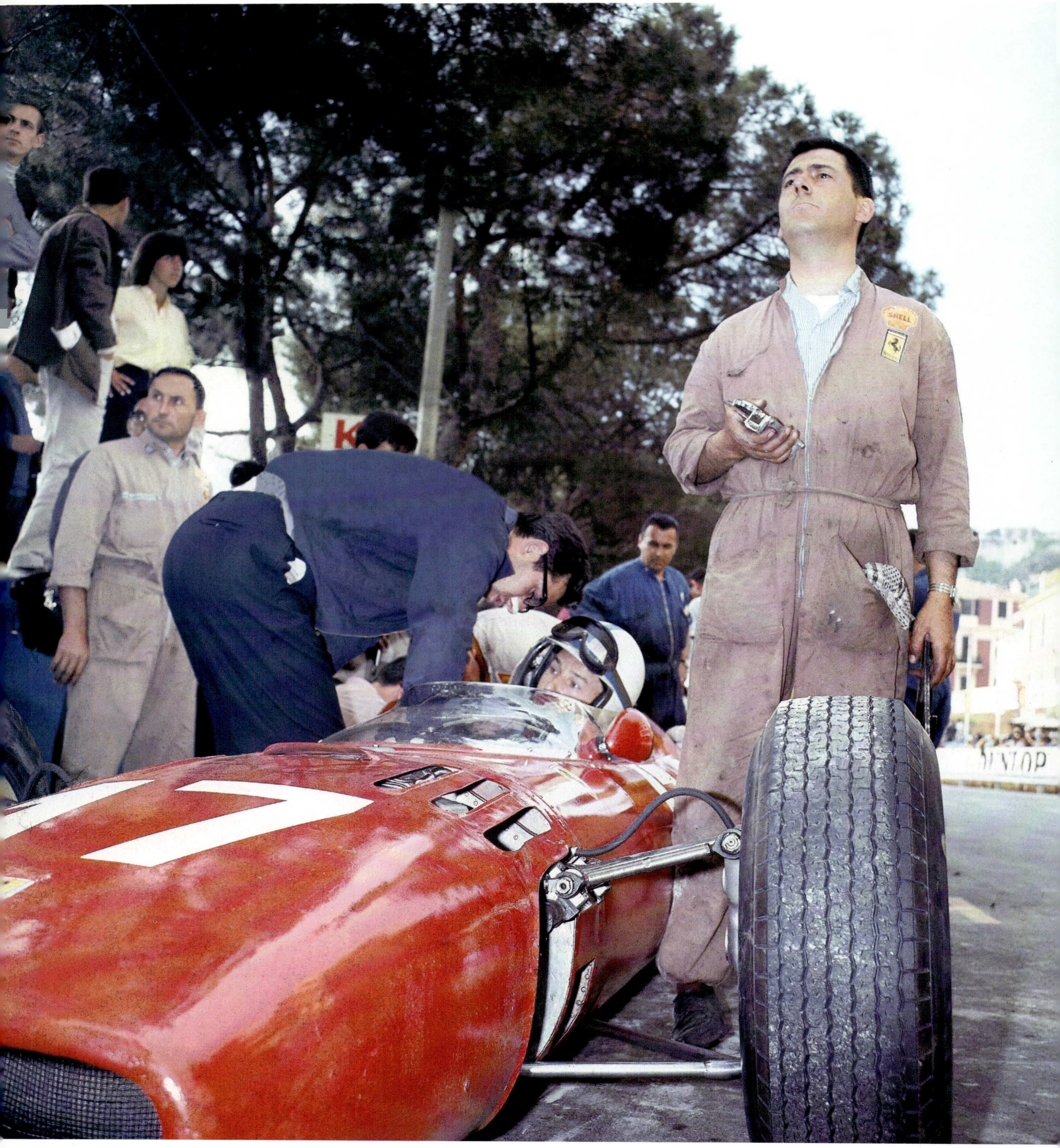

SHELL
DUNLOP

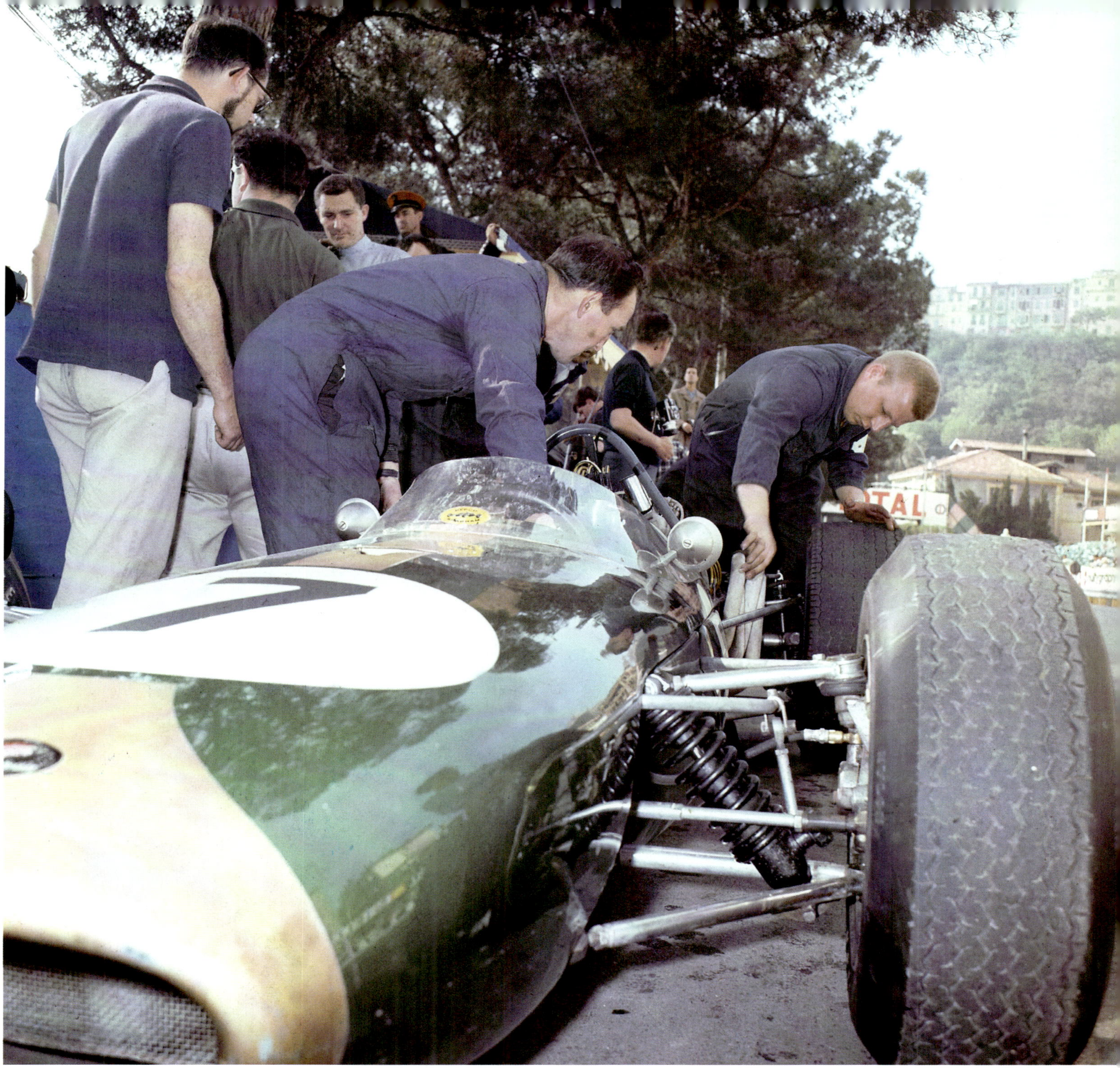

↑ Compared with the Ferrari (left), the Brabham looks altogether much better, this being Jack Brabham's Repco-engined BT19 (F1/1/65), but after only 17 laps it too retired, having started 11th. It was a disappointing GP debut for the BT19 that had convincingly won the International Trophy at Silverstone, but Brabham would go on to win the 1966 World Drivers' Championship at the age of 40. Looking on in the background under the tree is ex-motorcyclist Bob Anderson, who was racing his own private Brabham. The versatile Anderson had been racing in F1 since 1963 and was a former winner of the fearsome North West 200 motorcycle race in Northern Ireland. Sadly, he was very badly injured during testing at Silverstone and died later in hospital on 14 August 1967.

← John Surtees looks slightly unhappy as Mauro Foghieri fiddles in the Ferrari 312 (0010) cockpit and a mechanic strikes a pose at Monaco. Those used to the glass case Pebble Beach concours finish of latter day 'old' racing cars, note the wrinkled panel patina and general air of well-used equipment that so defines period Ferraris.

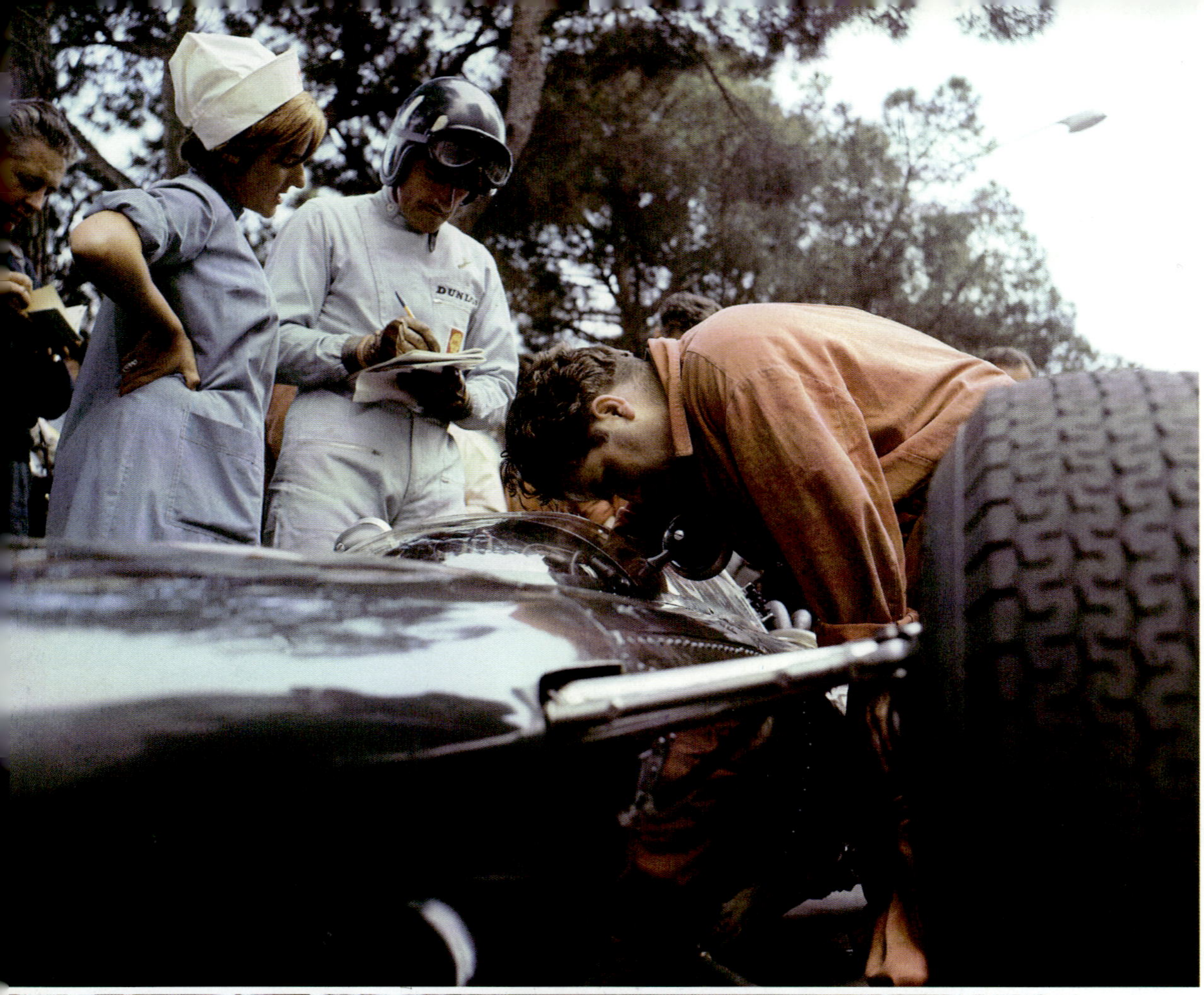

← Perhaps not the best time to ask for an autograph from NGH, who was otherwise engaged, but the nurse got away with it. Hill ultimately finished third at Monaco a lap behind, despite an early problem with the engine cutting out, then later a spin at Mirabeau, and subsequently a slipping clutch.

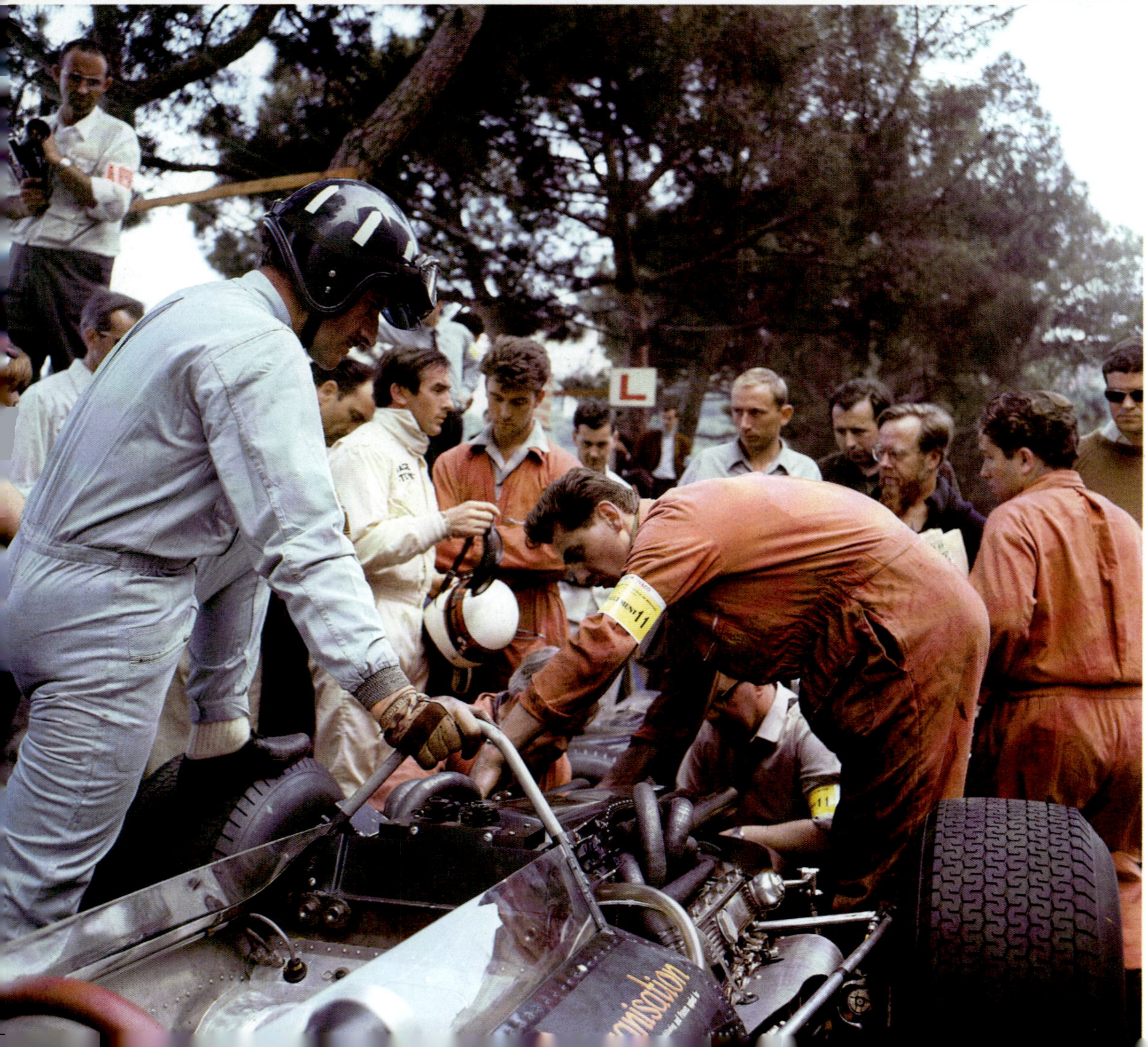

↙ One can easily imagine the imprecations running through Graham Hill's mind as he watches the fiddling and fettling of the P83 H-16 prototype BRM. Graham complained of inadequate, spongy brakes, and drove the car twice being some 8–9 seconds off the pace. In the background JYS is holding his goggles and helmet, Tony Rudd is squatting at the tail, and standing behind him can be seen the bespectacled, bearded 'Jenks'.

→ The BRM team at rest with Jackie Stewart's P261 (2617), complete with tartan seat cover, nearest the camera. Behind is Hill's chassis 2616 with a menacing looking Graham, in a new helmet (having finally ditched his old lid with moth-eaten peak), about to go, and beyond the troublesome H16. Bespectacled Tony Rudd, in pale yellow pullover, looks down from the pit counter whilst the BRM boys go about their business and Jackie Stewart approaches carrying his goggles. As I have observed before elsewhere, the road bears witness to the leaking from every orifice characteristics of period racing cars.

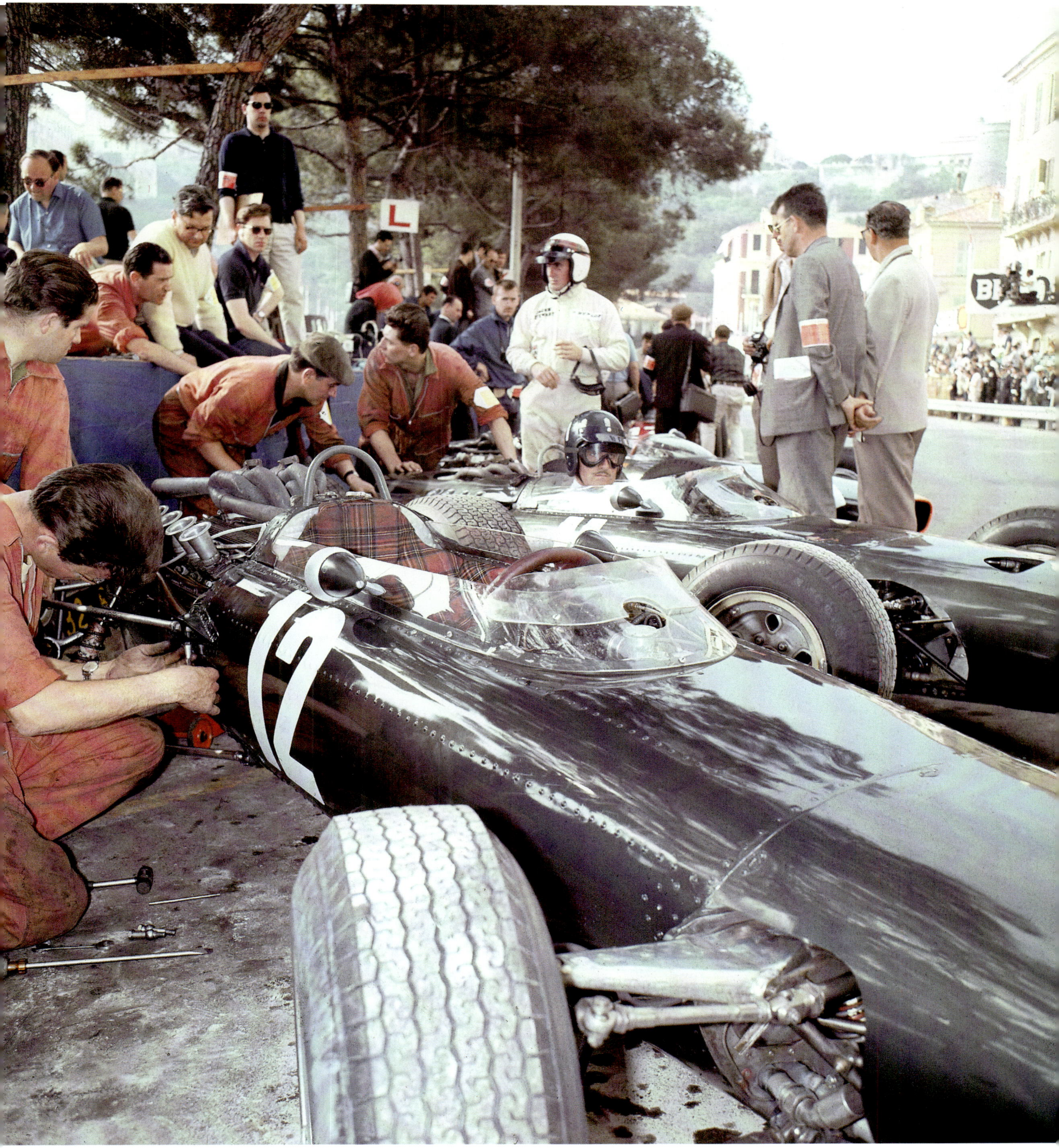

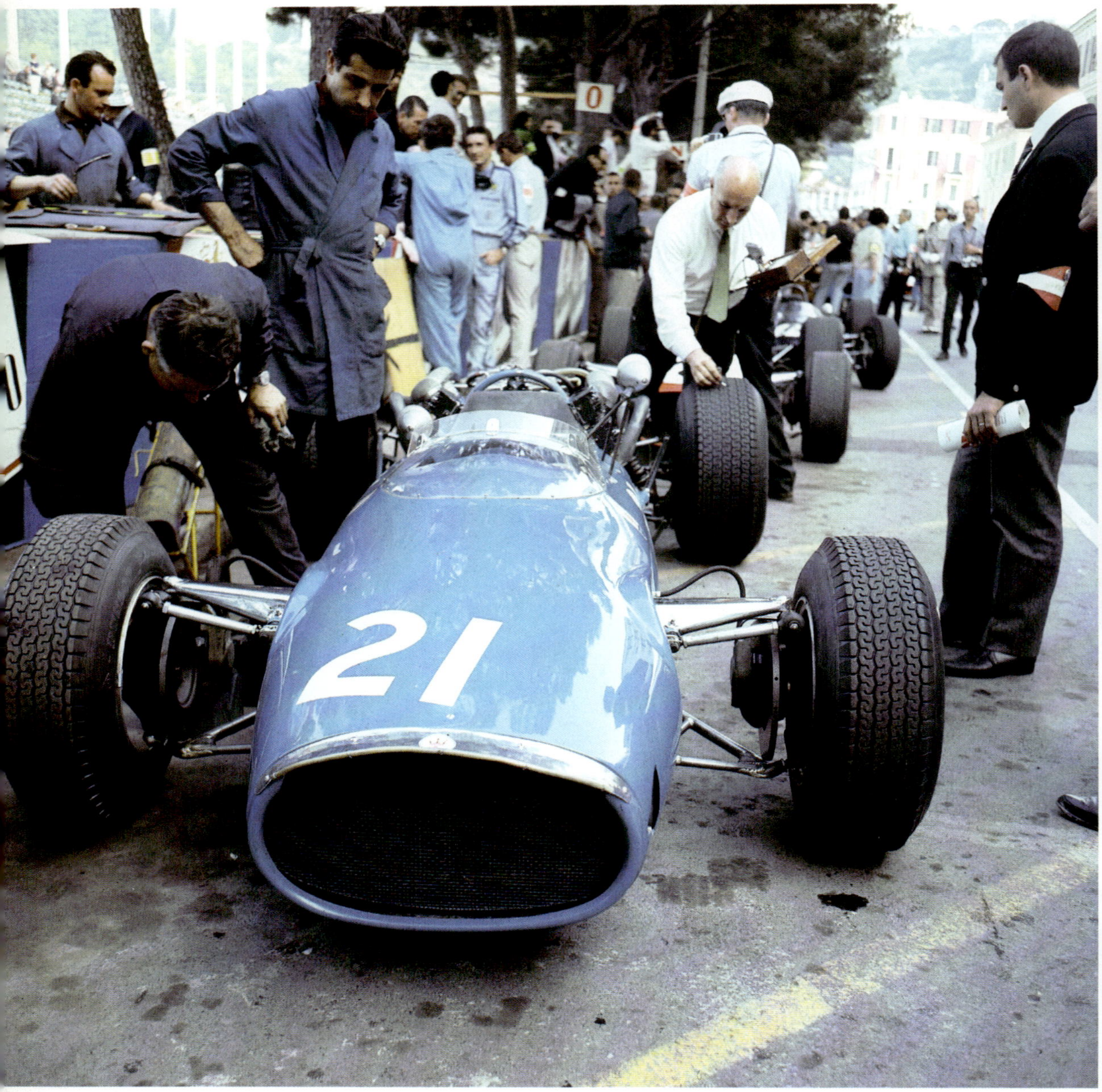

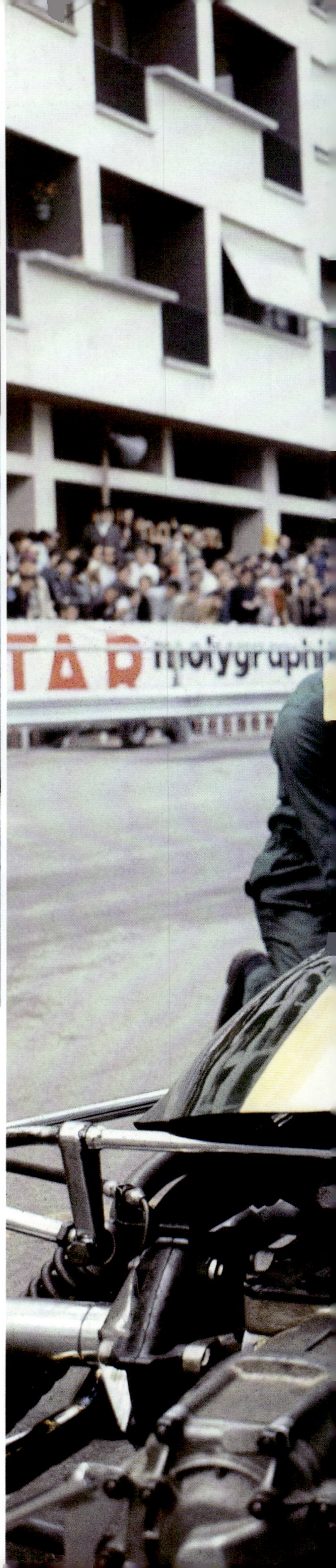

↑ Cooper's V12 Maserati-powered T81 was a popular if rather unsuccessful customer GP car in 1966, and here we see Guy Ligier's example at Monaco, appropriately painted in French blue. A Dunlop technician is taking a temperature reading of the rear tyre. Note that the chrome nose extension has a Maserati Trident decal, and again the front suspension with its distinctive cranked lower front wishbone and exposed disc brakes, which are visually identical to the 1968 BRM V12-powered 86B.

→ Jim Clark, hands on hips, during practice at Monaco 1966, and just as Graham Hill never managed to win the British GP, thus Clark at Monte Carlo. A Lotus technician attends to the left side of the 33 (R11) whilst a Firestone tyre technician busies himself on the right. Standing in the group behind and to the right, in glasses and flat cap, is Gérard 'Jabby' Crombac, renowned Swiss-born journalist and close friend of Colin Chapman and Clark, who started his own magazine *Sport Auto* in France with Jean Lucas, and was editor-in-chief for 20 years. He died on 18 November 2005 aged 76 after suffering from cancer for a number of years.

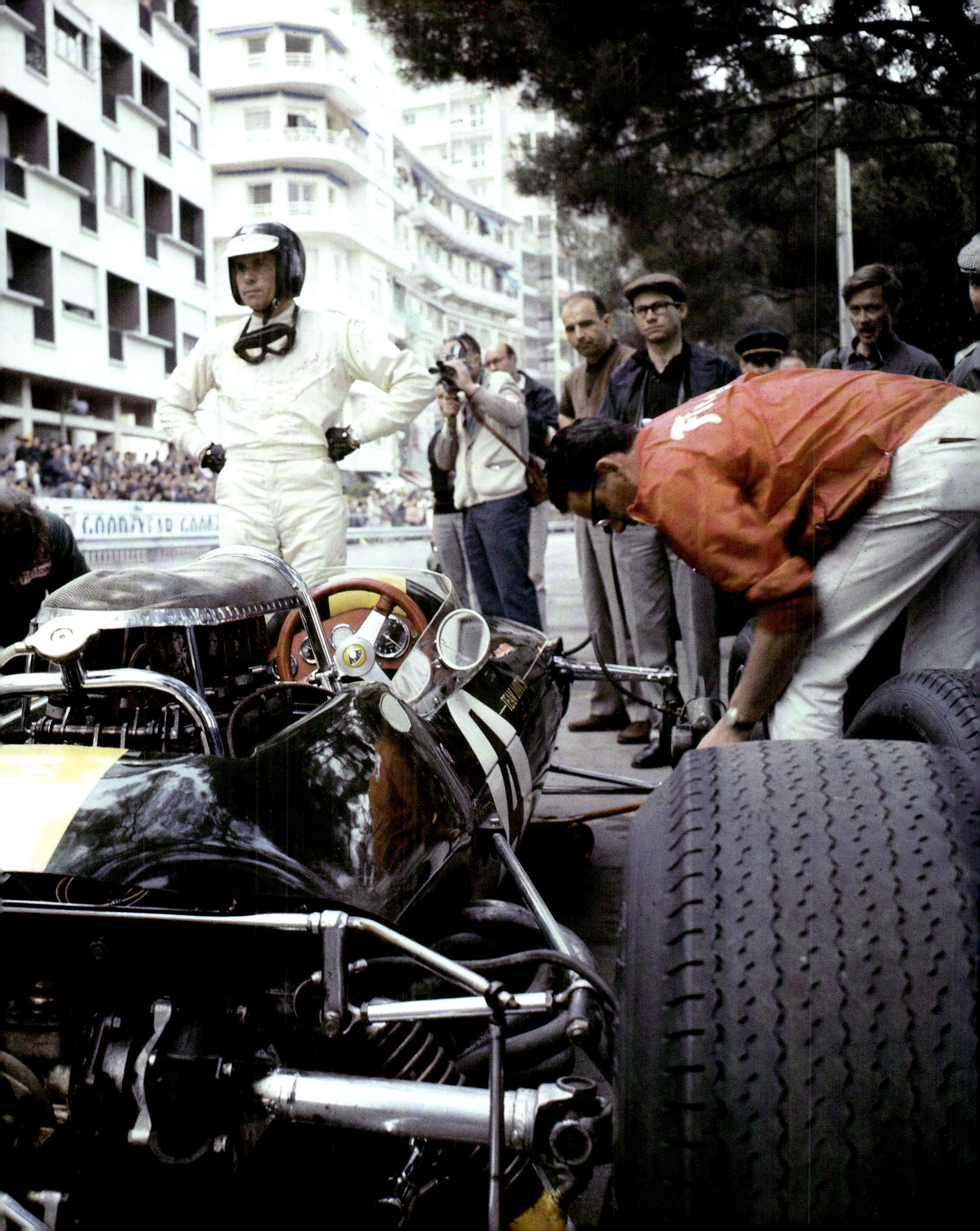

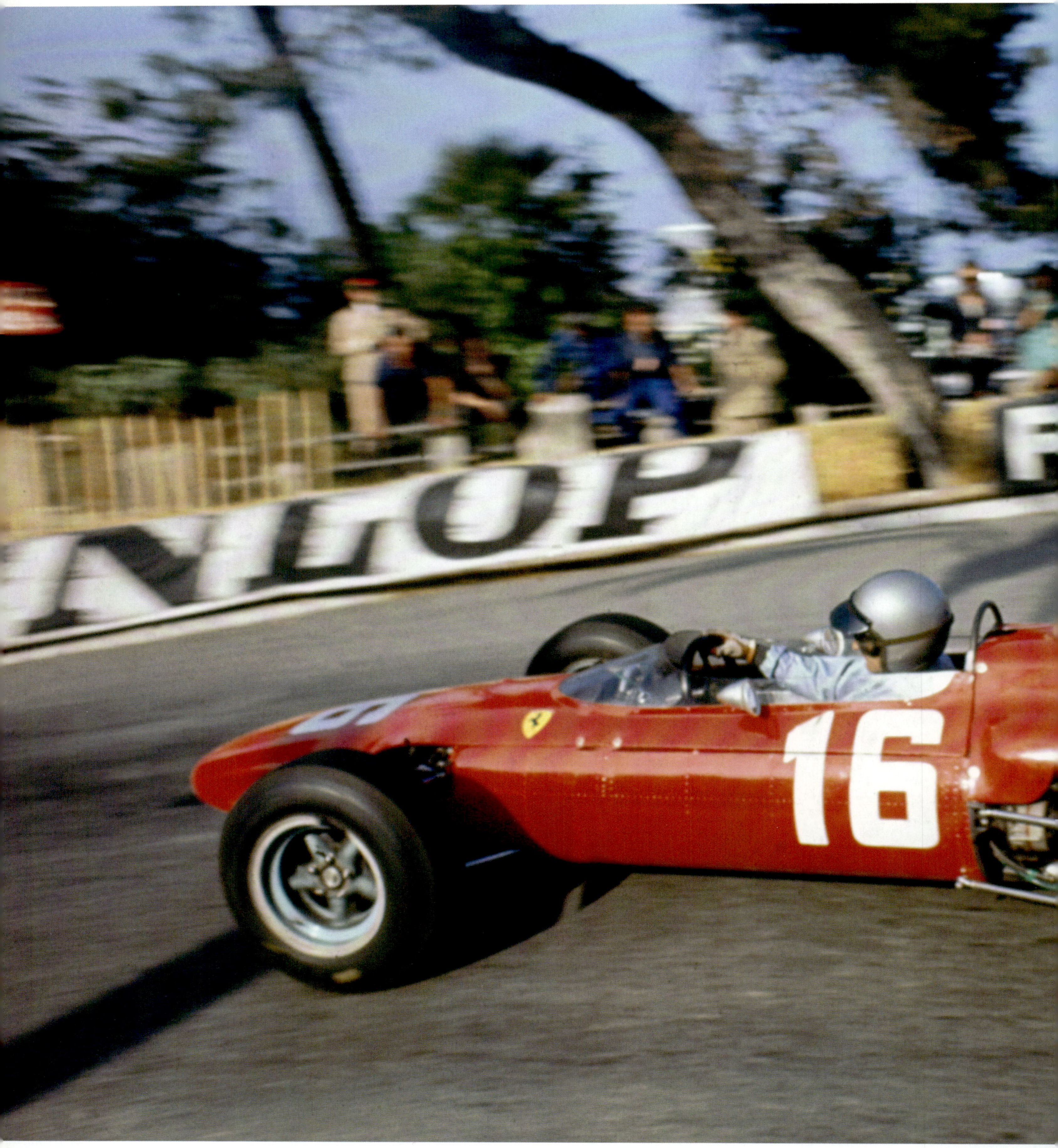
NLOP
16

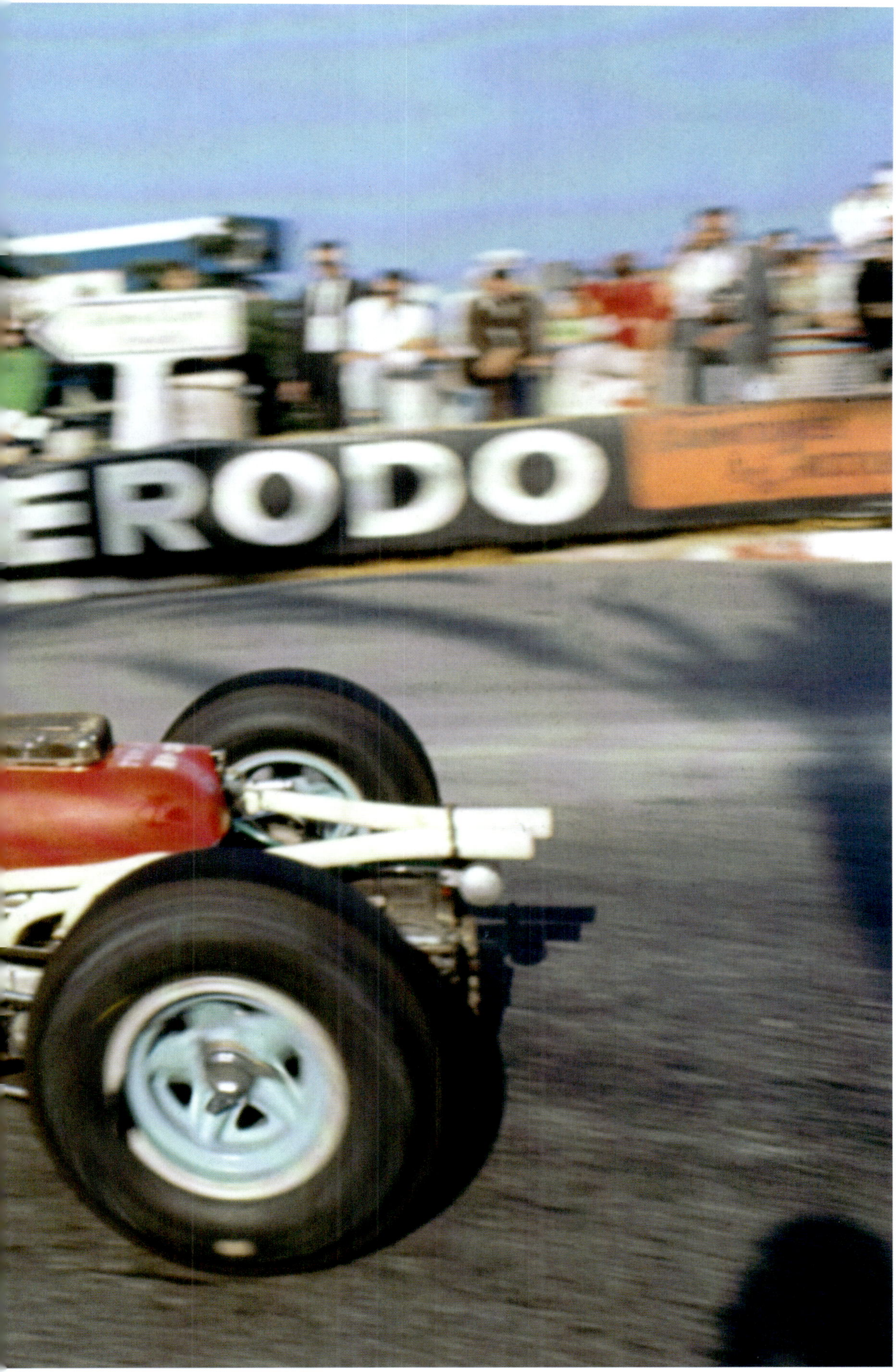

← Monaco 1966, and Lorenzo Bandini is exiting what was then the Station Hairpin and racing to second place in the 2.4-litre Ferrari Dino 158 (0006), after gradually catching winner Jackie Stewart in the BRM until fading front brakes intervened. This is the car that team leader John Surtees should have been driving, but team manager Eugenio Dragoni apparently favoured Bandini. So Surtees had to drive the less wieldy, heavier, and underpowered 312 that nevertheless led until differential failure occurred on lap 16.

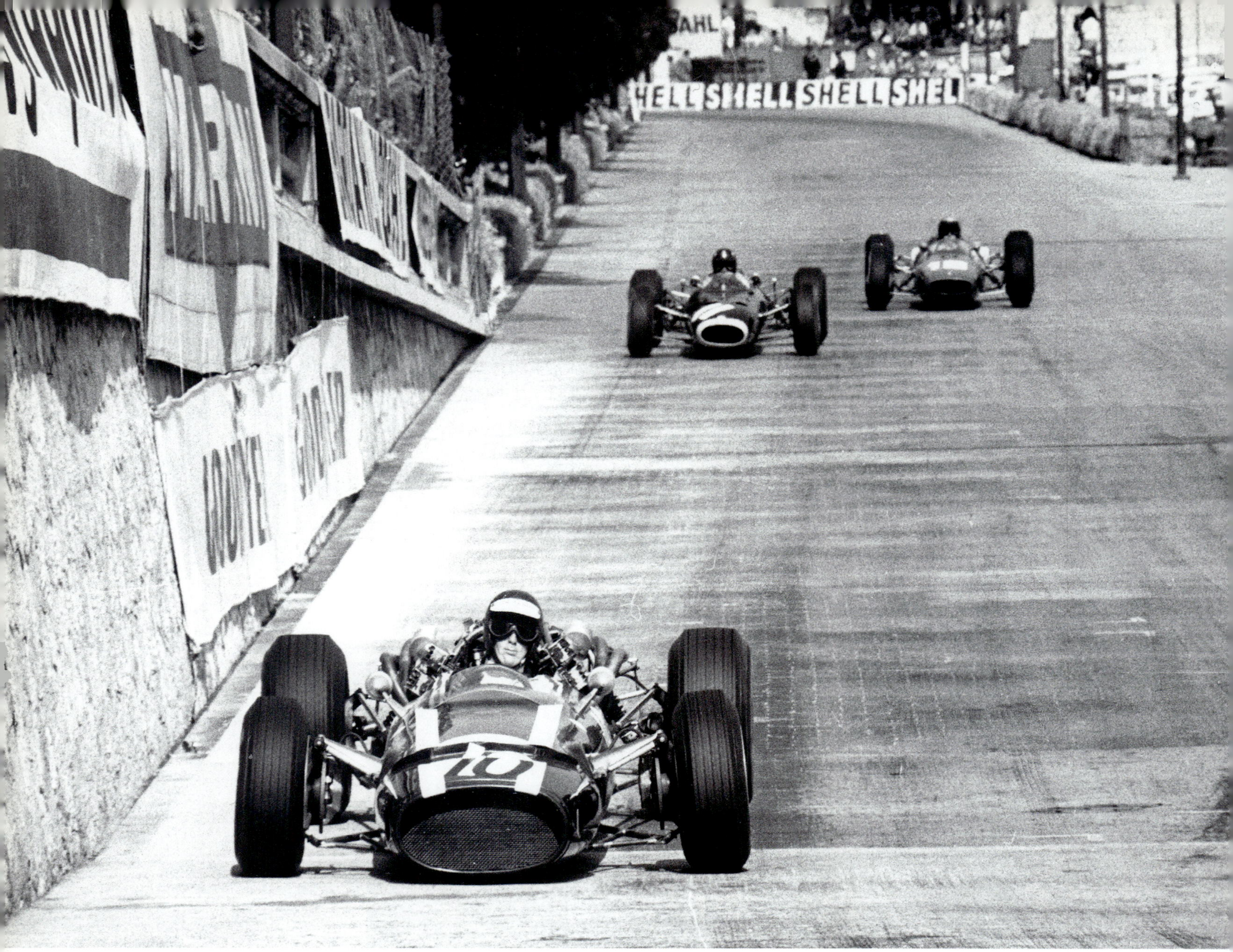

↑ This was a favourite vantage point for photographers at Monaco, the cars racing down towards Tabac with the terrifying left/right flick of the wrists at the old chicane in the background. Jochen Rindt's extremely large looking Cooper-Maserati T81 (F1-3-66), with its über-wide 60° V12 engine seemingly bursting out of the back, brakes heavily, upper wishbones working hard and front wheels displaying considerable negative camber. He is chased by Graham Hill's BRM P261 (2616) and Lorenzo Bandini's Ferrari Dino 158 (0006). Rindt retired on lap 57, whilst Hill finished third and Bandini second.

↗ Following his departure from Ferrari at Le Mans, John Surtees was not unemployed for long, and at Reims for the LIle Grand Prix de l'A.C.F. he became a Cooper works driver for the rest of the season. Starting from the middle of the front row, he was soon in trouble with fuel pump problems, and after losing many laps completed only two more before stopping for good at Thillois. He does not seem too unhappy, however, as he walks back to the pits, and will convincingly outdrive his highly rated team-mate Jochen Rindt for the rest of the season, culminating in a victory in the final round at Mexico. This gave him the runner-up position in the Drivers' Championship and was to be Cooper's penultimate GP victory.

→ Just look over your shoulder, guess who'll be standing there (with apologies to 'The Monkees'). Mike Parkes is all too aware of the presence of Graham Hill's slipstreaming BRM P261 (2616) as he blasts past the Reims pits at circa 180mph in his special long-wheel-base Ferrari 312 (0012). NGH retired on lap 14 with a broken camshaft, whilst MJP finished second, only 9.5sec behind winner Jack Brabham in his Brabham-Repco BT19.

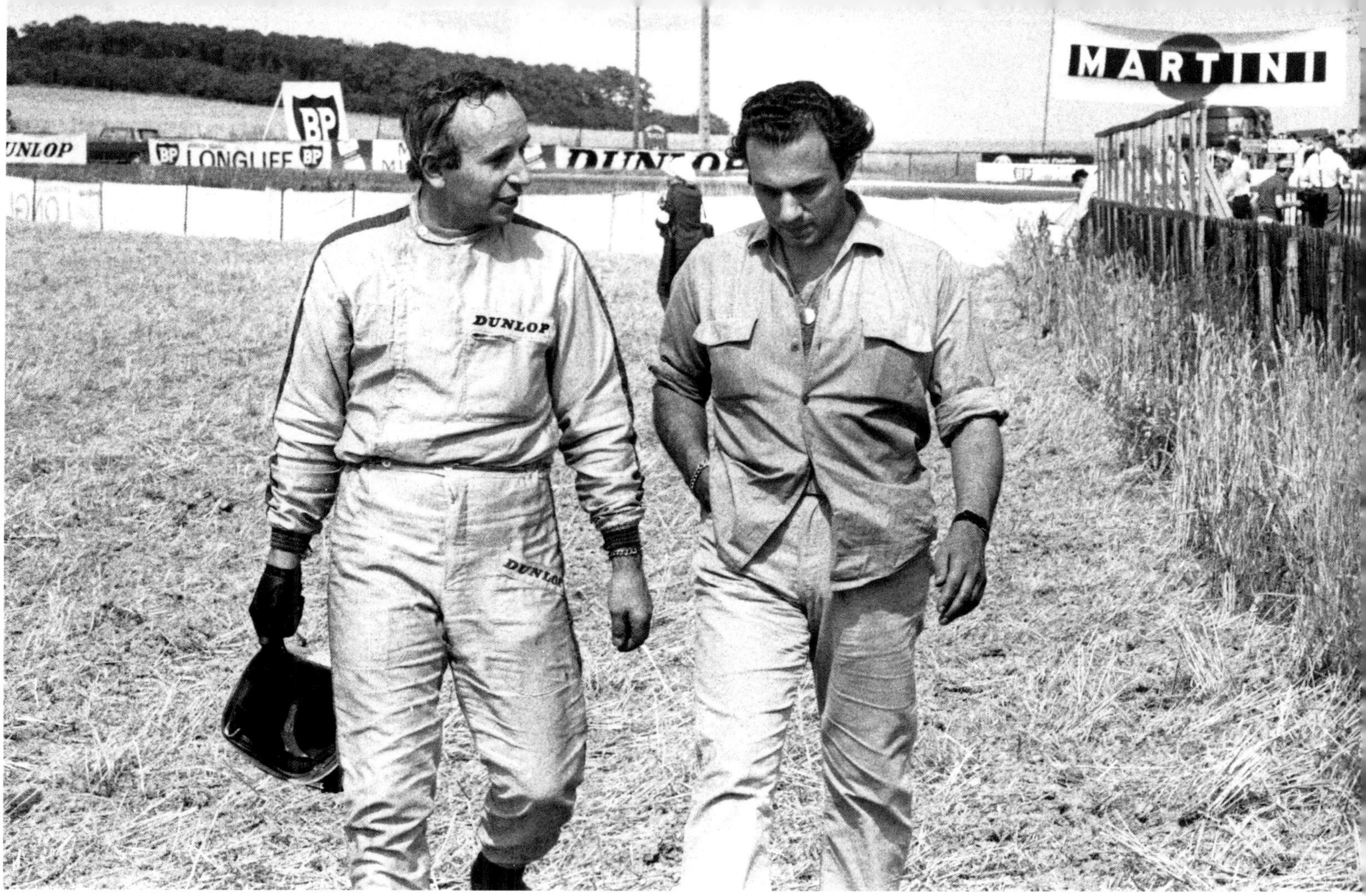
MARTINI
BP
UNLOP
LONGLIFE
DUNLOP
DUNLOP

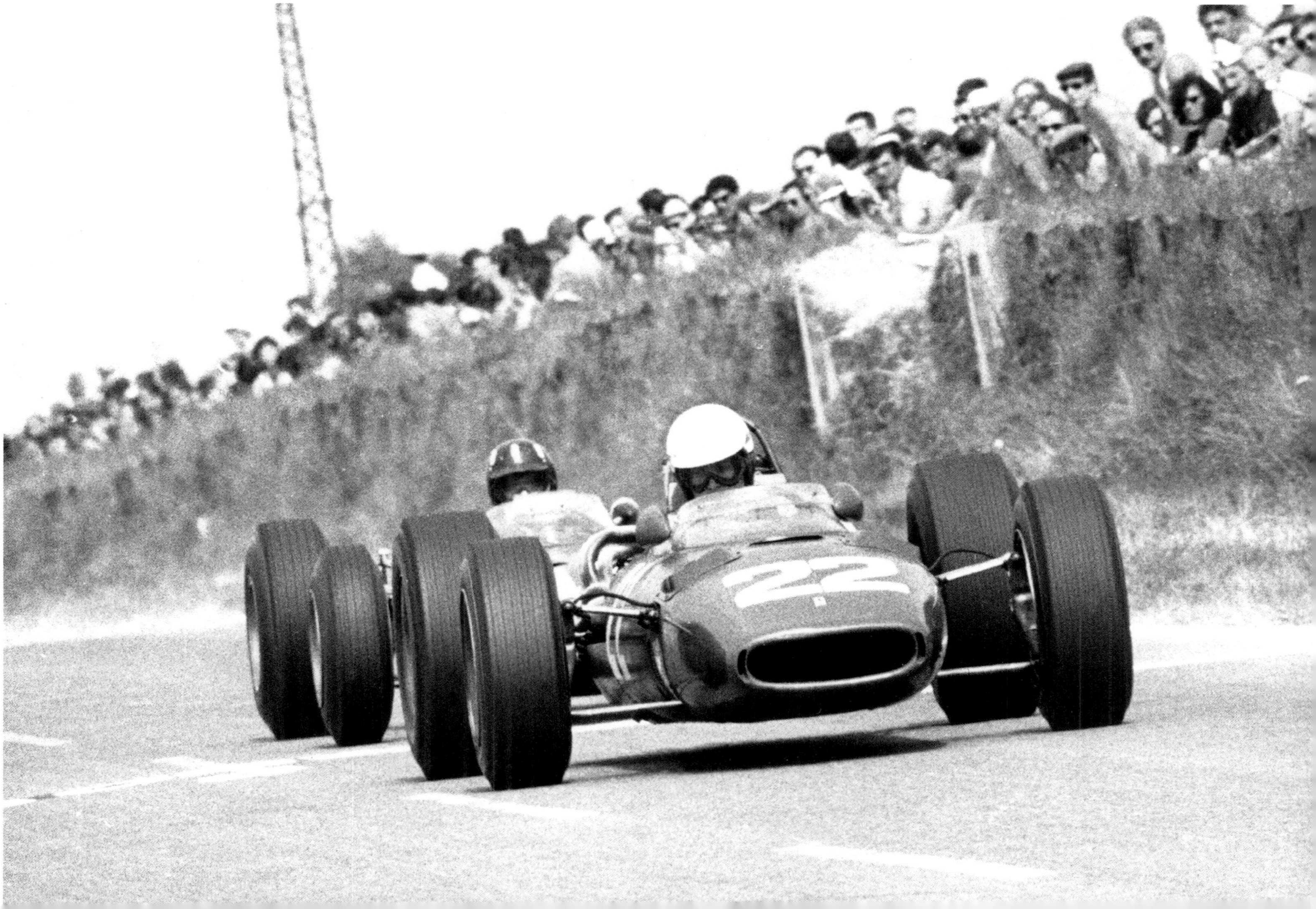
22

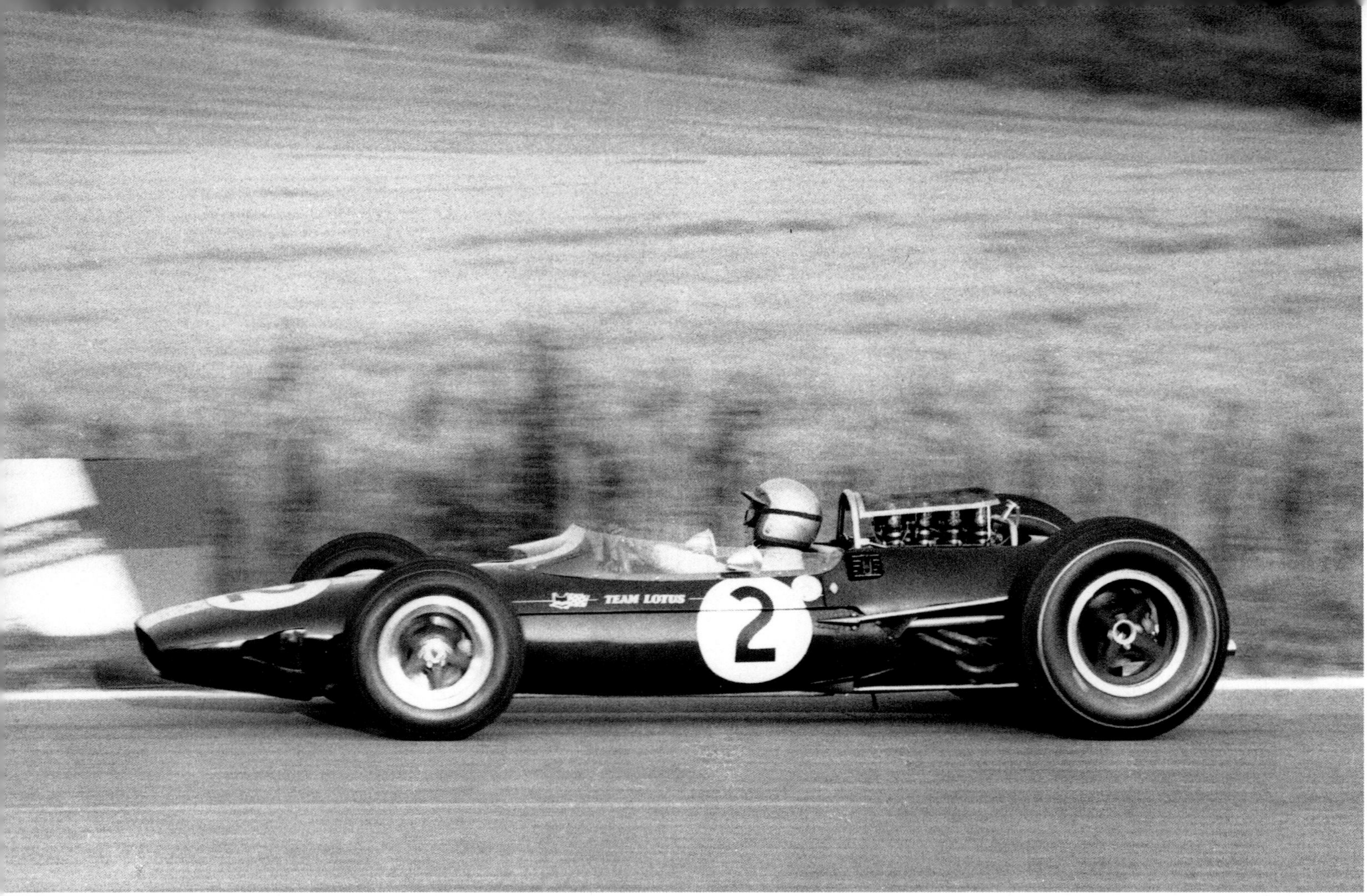
TEAM LOTUS
2

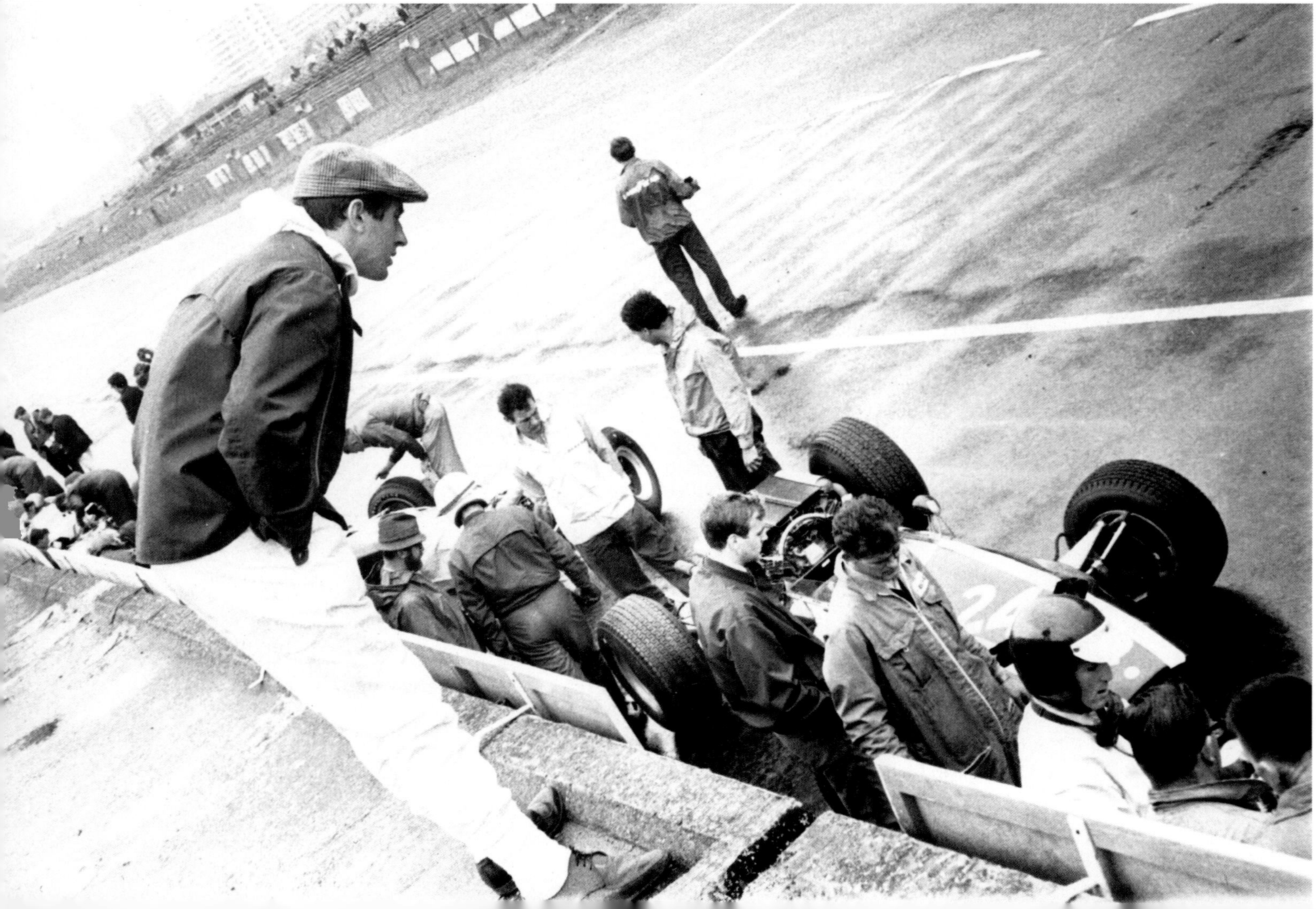

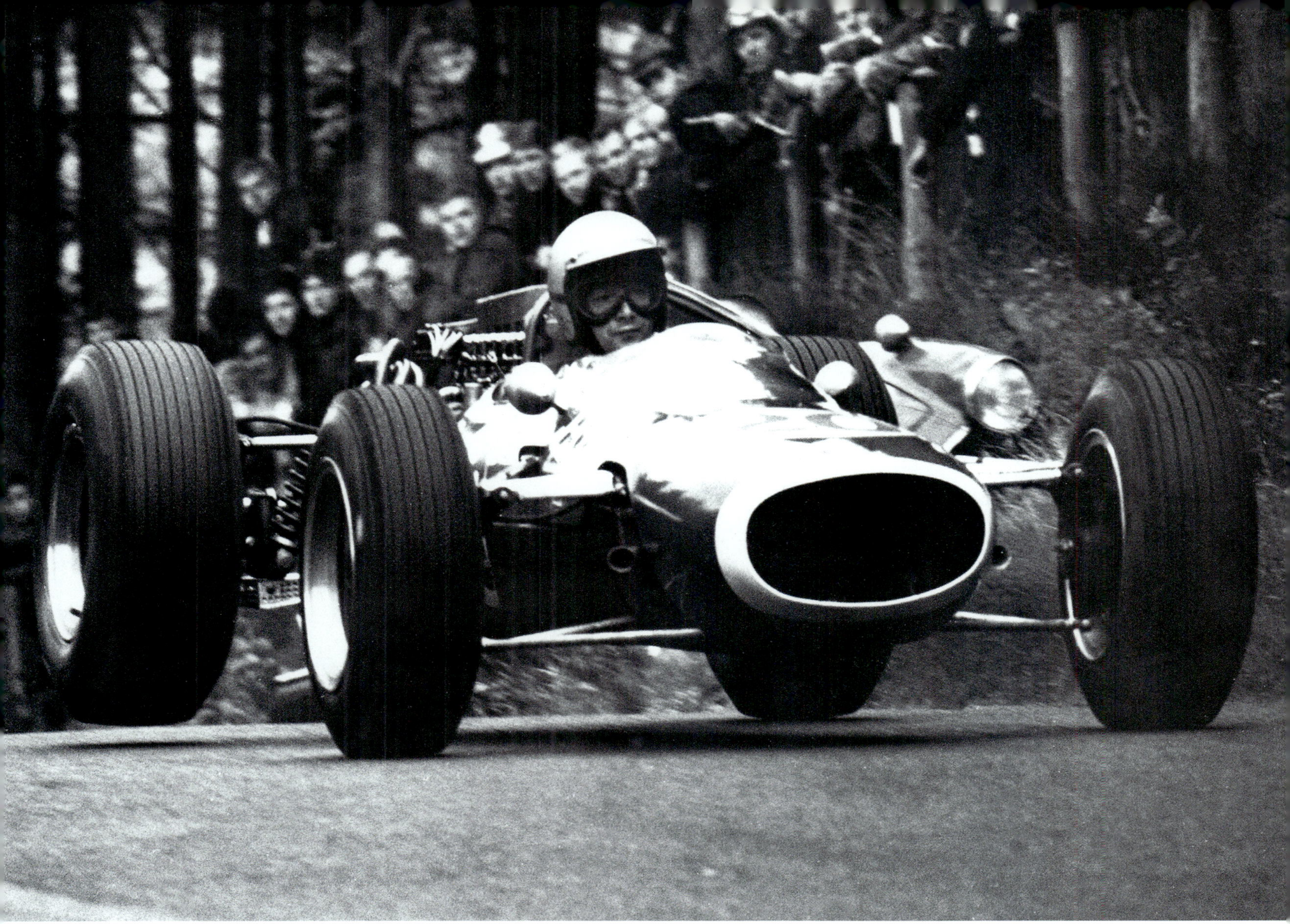

↑ Multi-talented Chris Lawrence is most associated with the Morgan Car Company, but he also started Lawrence Tune, produced the Deep Sanderson racers, worked on the French Monica luxury car project in the 1970s, lived for a while in California, and latterly was heavily involved in the design of Morgan's new Aero 8. He was also a talented racer who won 19 out of 22 races with his Morgan Plus 4 in 1959 and, of course, achieved the now famous Le Mans class win in TOK 258 in 1962. In 1966 he drove this old Cooper T73 (F1-2-64) fitted with a Ferrari V12 engine from the old John Coombs Ferrari 250GTO (3729 GT) entered by J. A. Pearce Engineering at the British and German GPs. He retired here at the Nürburgring where he is passing an abandoned car from an earlier race which has been left on the bank. In those days, and faced with a 14.2-mile circuit, the organisers had little choice, and the best they could do until the meeting was over was to clear the track. But, of course, 'safety' was not really an issue then.

↖ Jim Clark was hit in the face by a bird during practice for the French GP at Reims and his place was taken by the ever-available Pedro Rodriguez in the works Lotus-Climax 33 (R11) but he retired. The rear tyres are truly high profile. Rodriguez had driven for Team Lotus twice before (the 1963 US and Mexican GPs) as well as the NART (but in reality works) Ferraris in Mexico (1964) and Watkins Glen (1965) and went on to race for Cooper (1967) BRM (1968), Reg Parnell Racing BRM (1969), Ferrari (1969) and finally back to BRM in 1970/71. He won Cooper's last ever Grand Prix at Kyalami in 1967 but his true forté until 1970 was sports car racing where his ability behind the wheel of the John Wyer Porsche 908 and 917s was legendary. Alas his race anything, anywhere, anytime attitude finally did for him and he died in a minor sports car race at the Norisring on 11 July 1971 driving Herbert Müller's Ferrari 512M.

← The Zandvoort pits roof made a convenient platform for photography, and during a wet practice session for the 1966 Dutch GP Jackie Stewart looks down on the Cooper team. John Surtees can be seen walking away from the rear wheel of his Cooper-Maserati T81 (F1-7-66), whilst team-mate Jochen Rindt confers with team personnel including Derrick White (far right with crew cut). Is that Henry N. Manney Jr. with hat and beard beside Surtees I wonder?

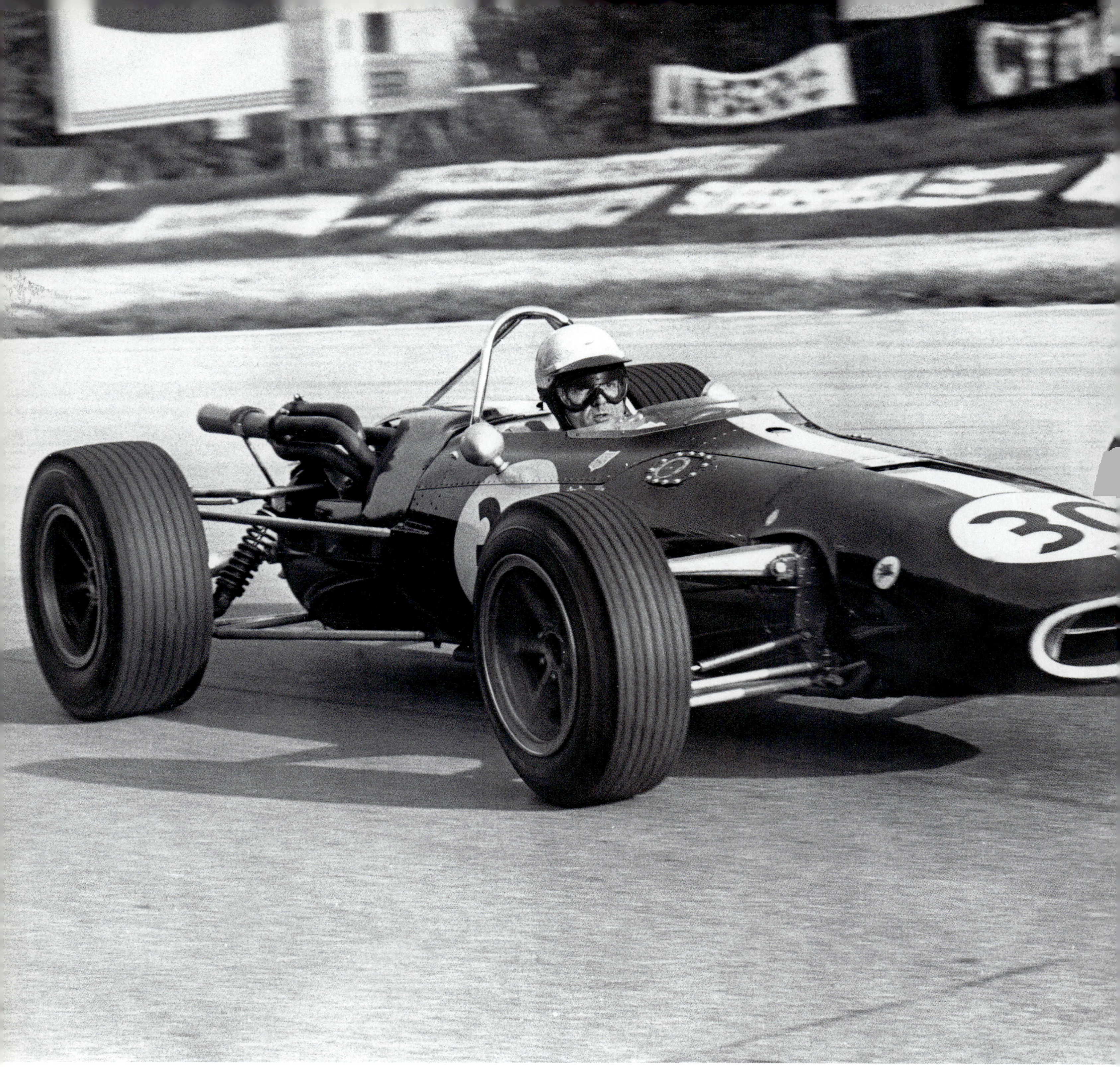

↑ Unsurprisingly, many people think that Phil Hill's F1 career ended at Mexico in 1964, but this is not strictly true. Twice in 1966 he drove a camera car for John Frankenheimer's film *Grand Prix* at the Monaco and Belgian GPs, but for Monza he was actually entered in one of the AAR Eagles. Team leader Dan Gurney had finally received a Weslake V12-powered car, so Phil was left with the Climax FPF-engined T1F-101, but sadly he failed to qualify. There were 20 accepted starters and 22 entries, with Hill being 21st fastest. His tense facial expression and slightly open mouth reveal the extreme concentration and effort required at this level.

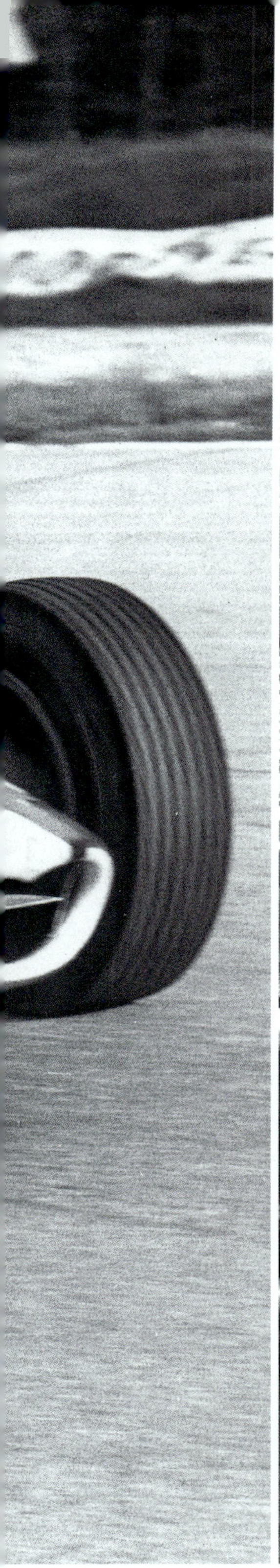

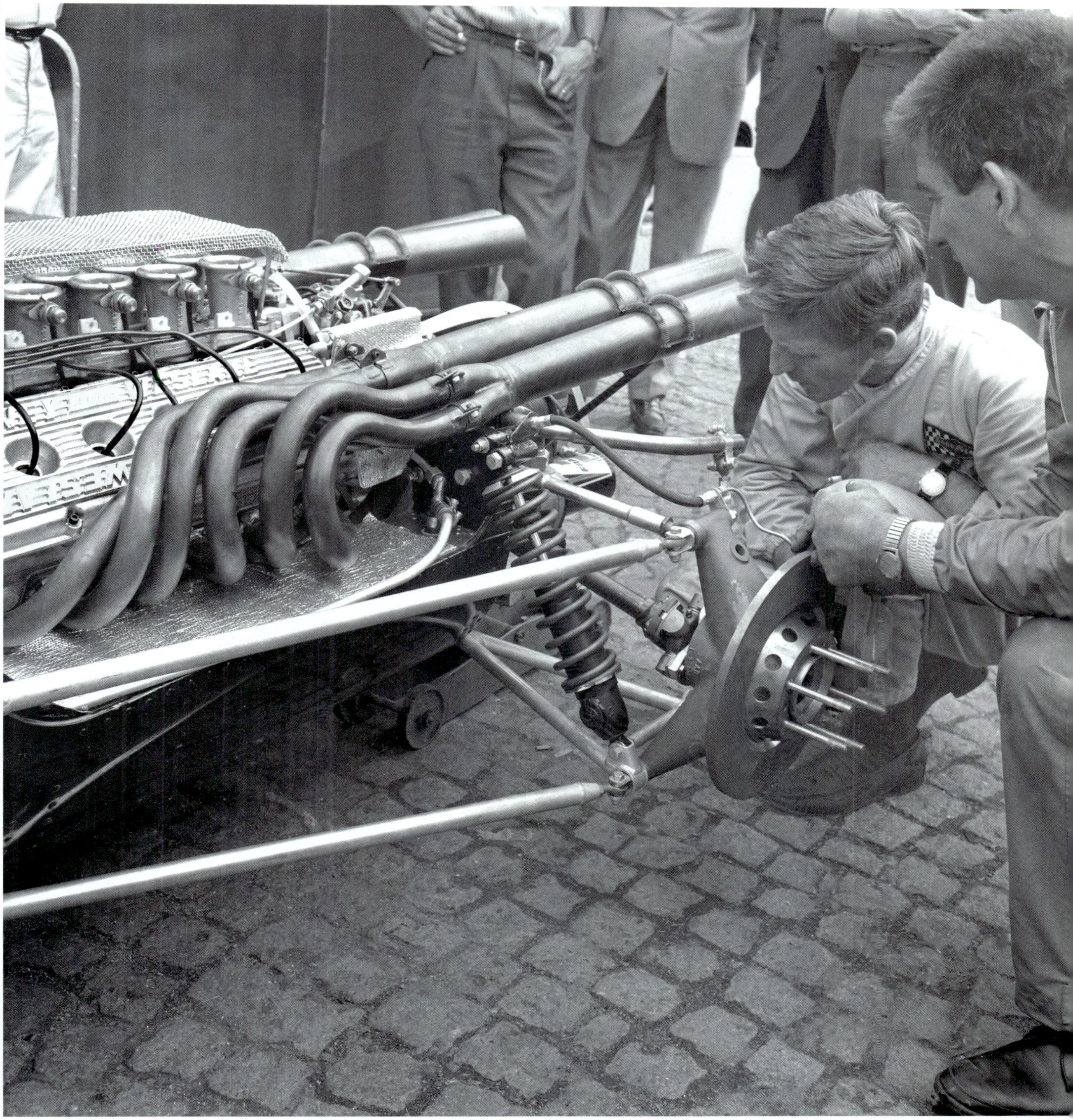

↑ Here is Dan's new Weslake V12-engined Eagle T1G-102 being examined in the paddock at Monza. It almost looks over-engineered, unlike some, and is as ever very nicely presented. In *American Grand Prix Racing: A Century of Drivers & Cars* by Tim Consodine, Gurney is quoted as saying: 'The Weslakes weren't happy with the engine performance on the dyno, but they felt we should put the darn thing in the car anyway so that we'd learn something.' However, the engine was bothered by fuel feed problems during practice, and Gurney retired on lap 8 having started from the last row. Not a good weekend then. T1G-102 was driven just four times by Dan Gurney, including the convincing win at the 1967 Brands Hatch Race of Champions.

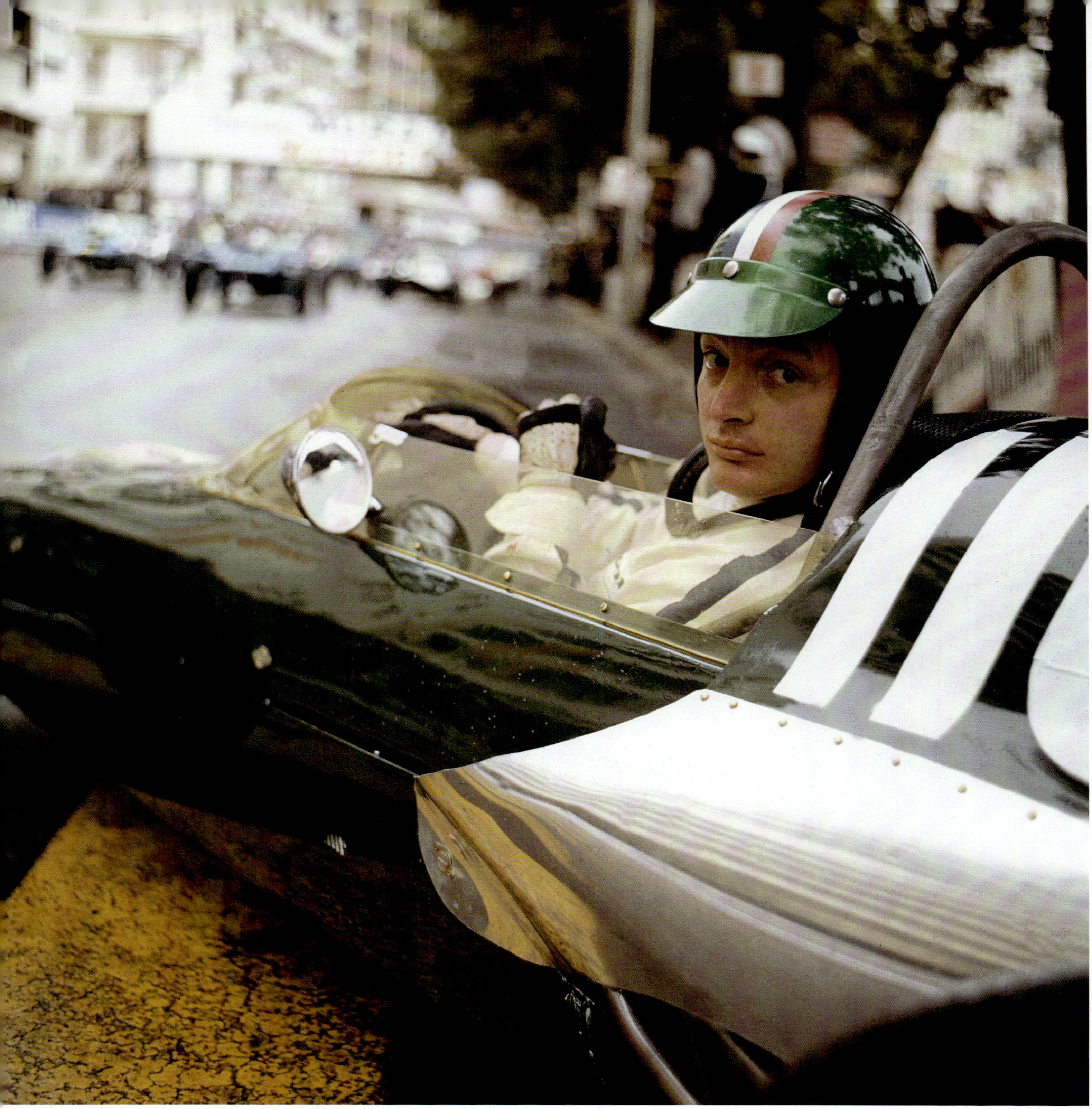

↑ Who remembers 'Green Bean', 'Private Ear', and other such irreverent things? This, of course, is the famous Nick Brittan, whose antics in the 'Green Bean' Anglia, and scurrilous remarks in *Autosport*'s 1970s cartoon strip are forever in our minds. At the 1967 Monaco Formula Vee race, Nick was eliminated when he encountered another car at the chicane on the first lap, apparently rolling but ending right side up without injury.

→ Not much room in any period single-seaters, including Formula Vee, but Nick looks happy enough.

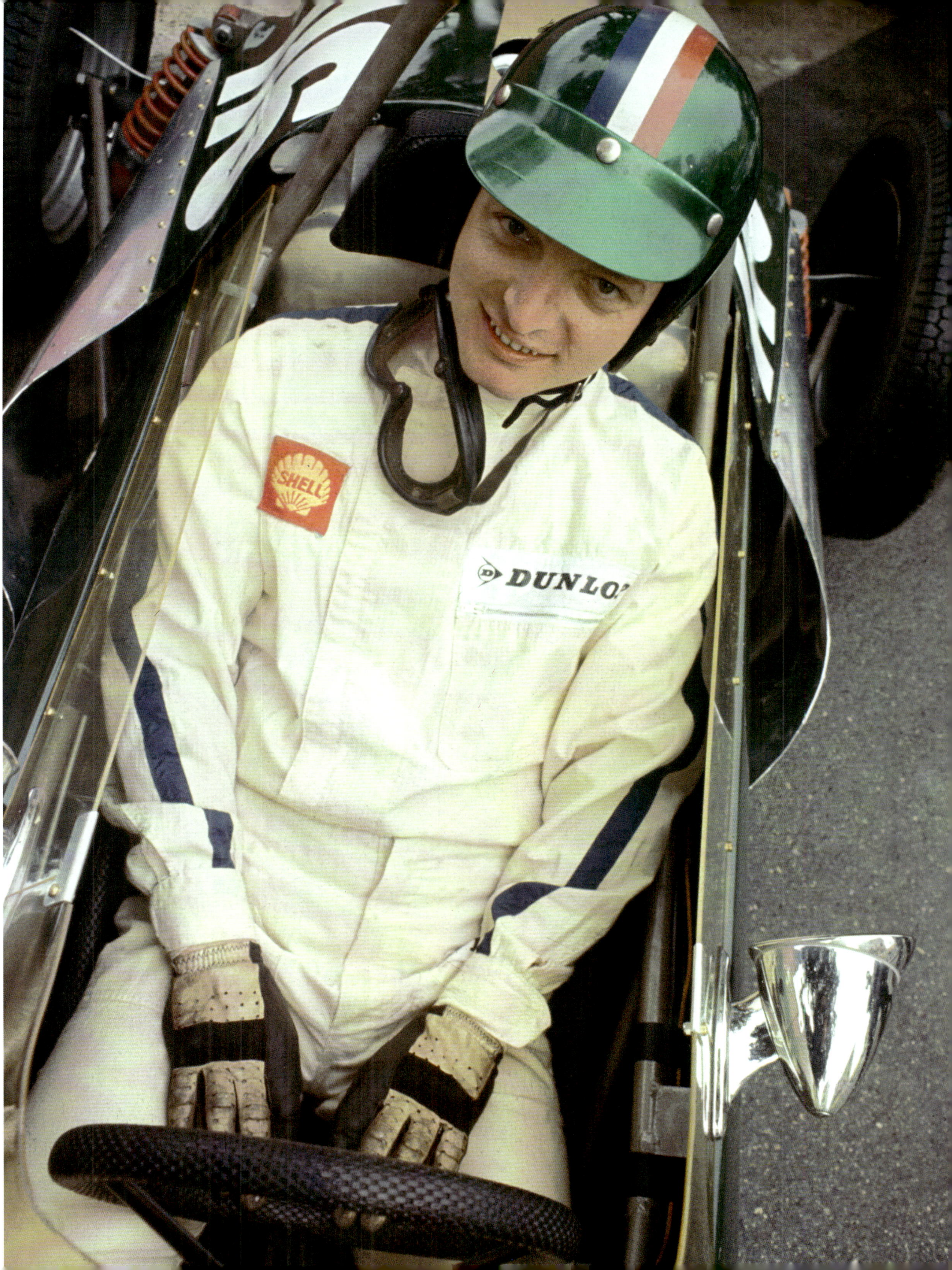
SHELL
DUNLO

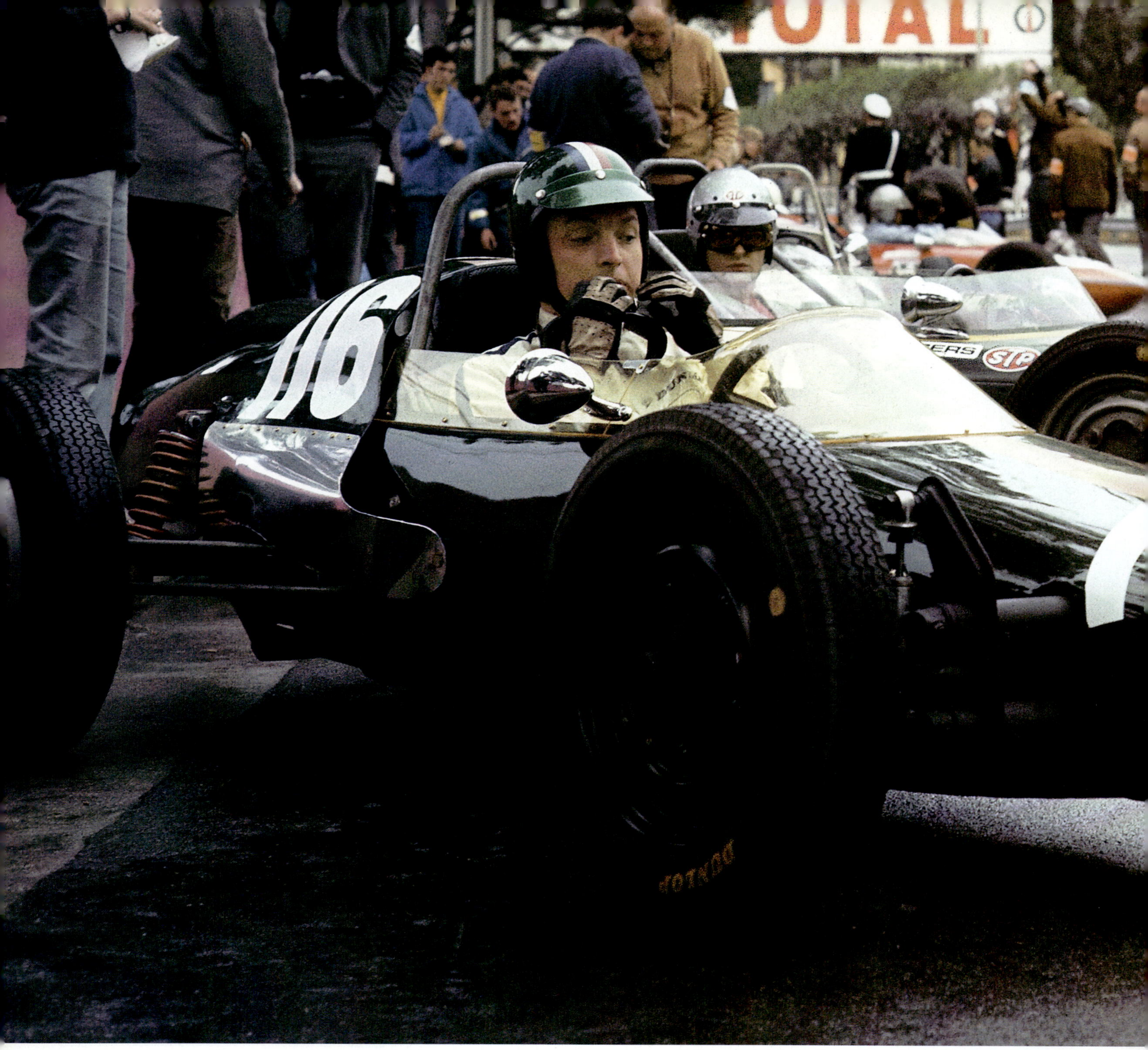

↑ Nick looks slightly surprised by something in his Fuchs (some sources list this incorrectly as an Apal), whilst behind, Willy Segers in his Autodynamic is already goggled and raring to go at Monaco. Brittan won 7 out of 15 races in his first season (1965) with 'Green Bean', being awarded the Peter Collins Memorial Trophy, the Rootes Gold Cup, and the Spring Grove Novice of the Year prize. In 1966 he raced the Alan Fraser Hillman Imp to the Spring Grove Saloon Car Championship, and in 1967 drove a Superspeed Ford Anglia for John Young. He was instrumental in promoting FF across Europe and introducing Formula Vee into Britain during 1967 where he won the inaugural British Formula Vee Championship. He also competed in the 1968 London to Sydney Marathon and was later managing Patrick Depailler's F1 career, amongst others. Space precludes listing his many other interests and achievements. (Nick Brittan 9 July 1936 – 3 November 2006.)

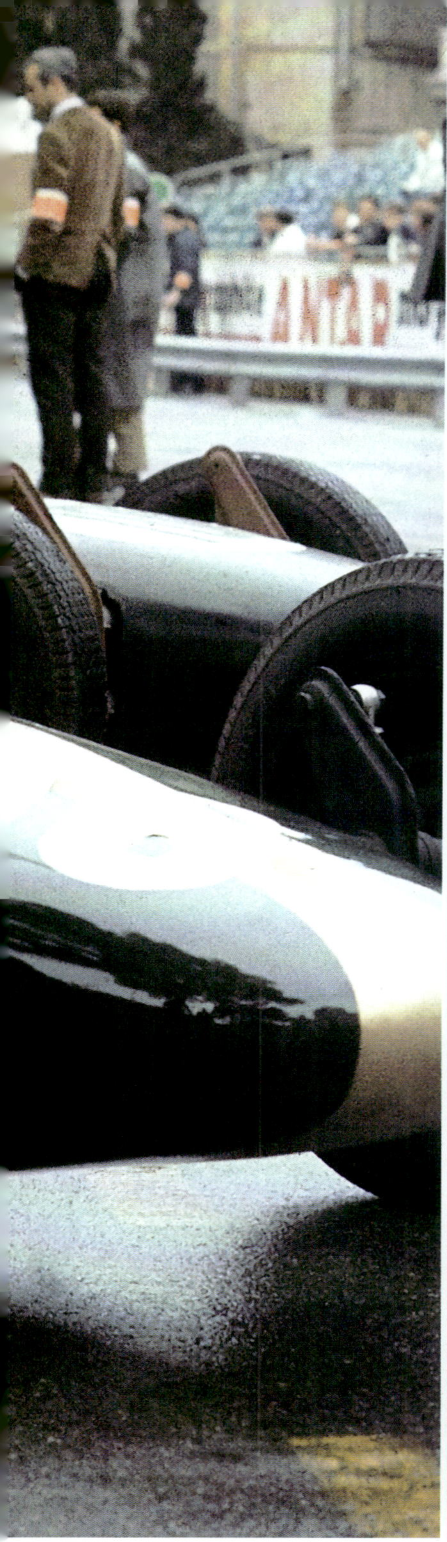

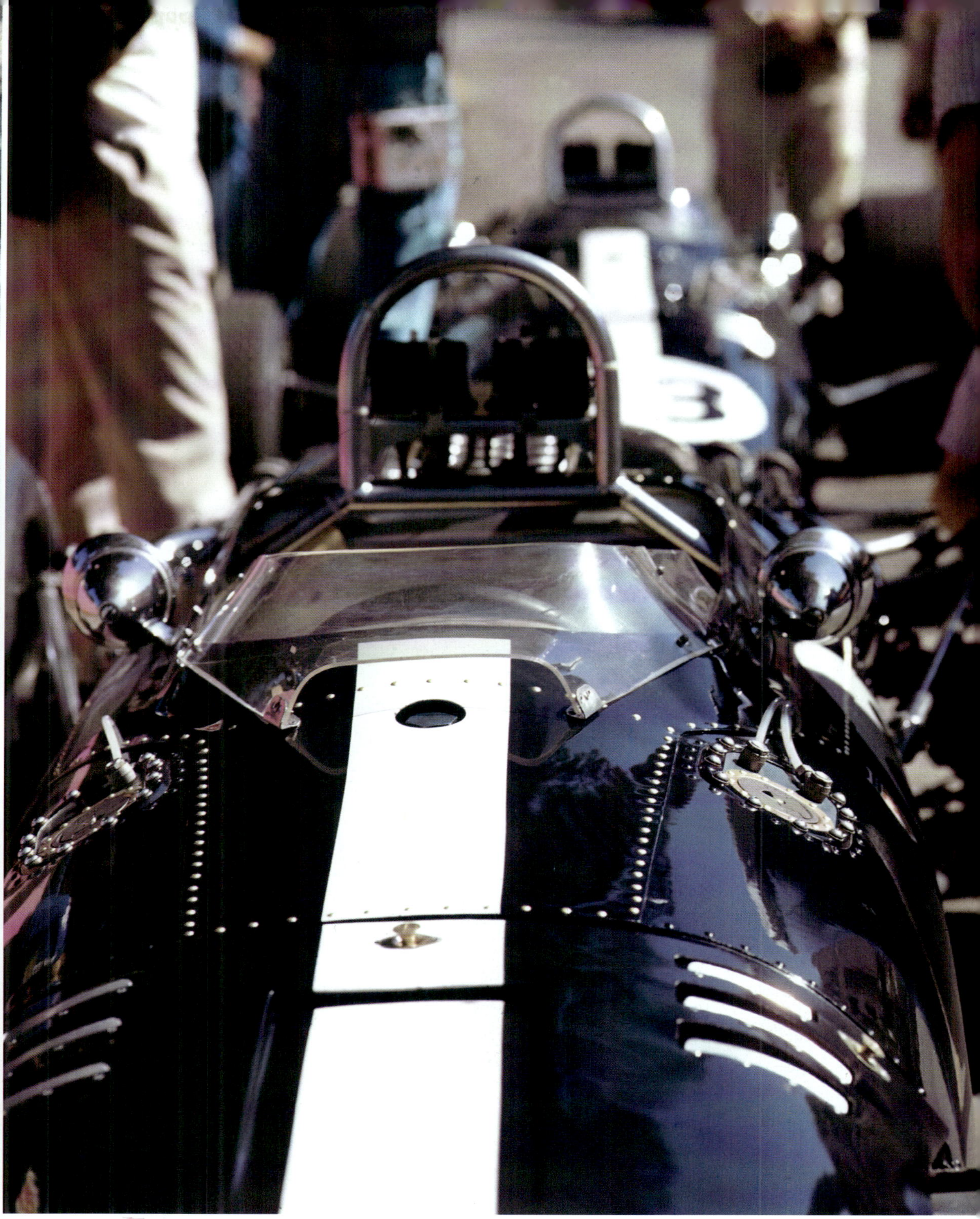

↑ Close-up of one of the Eagle Weslake T1Gs at Monaco 1967. It looks very Indycar like and is beautifully detailed but, alas, looks can be deceptive. Apart from Dan Gurney's Brands Hatch ROC victory and later Spa win, the Eagles were on occasion very quick but mechanically fragile and inconsistent, possibly owing to manufacturing problems. Gurney retired here with fuel pump failure. The number two was Richie Ginther, who having failed to qualify, repeated the trick at Indianapolis and then retired from race driving.

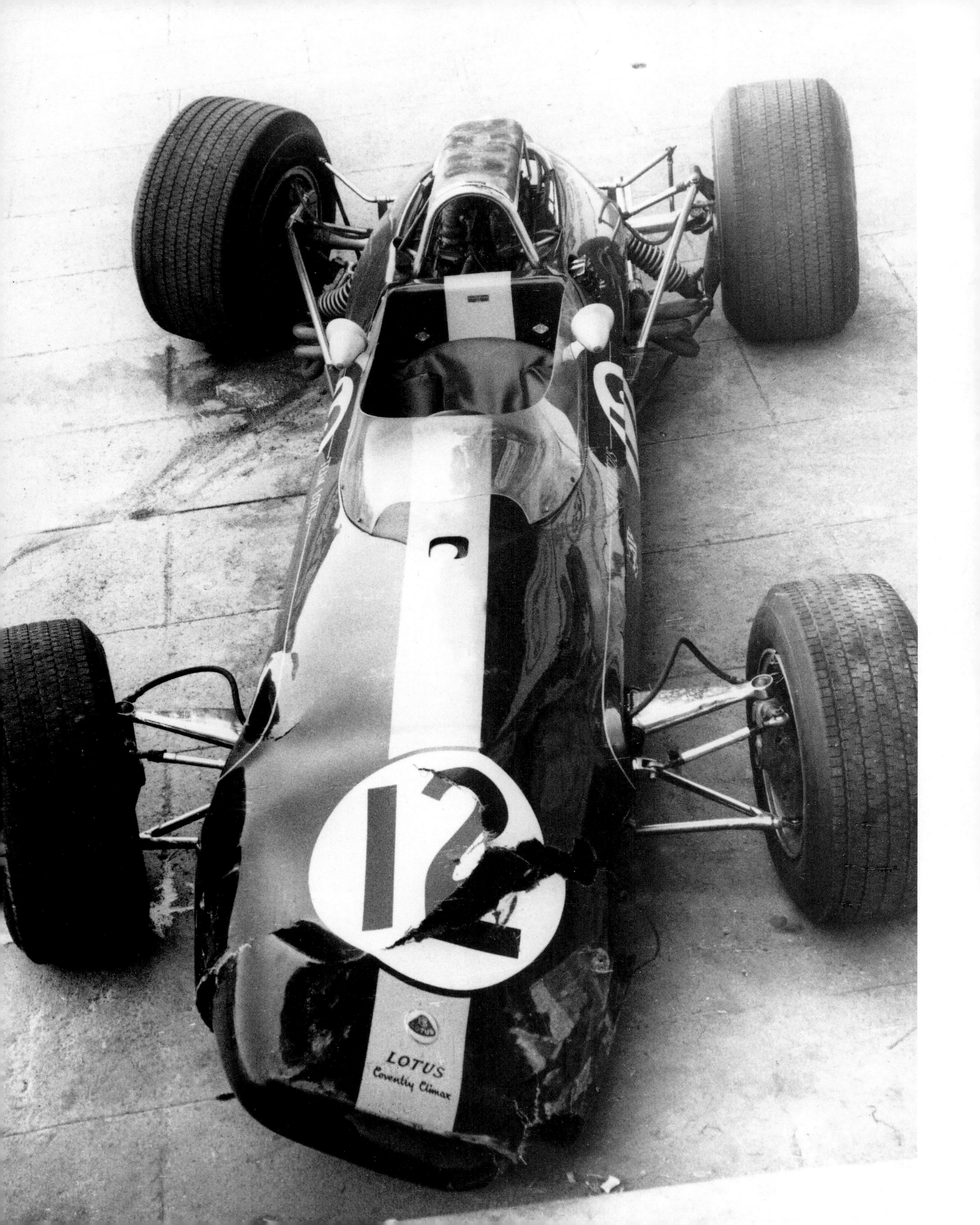
12
LOTUS
Coventry Climax

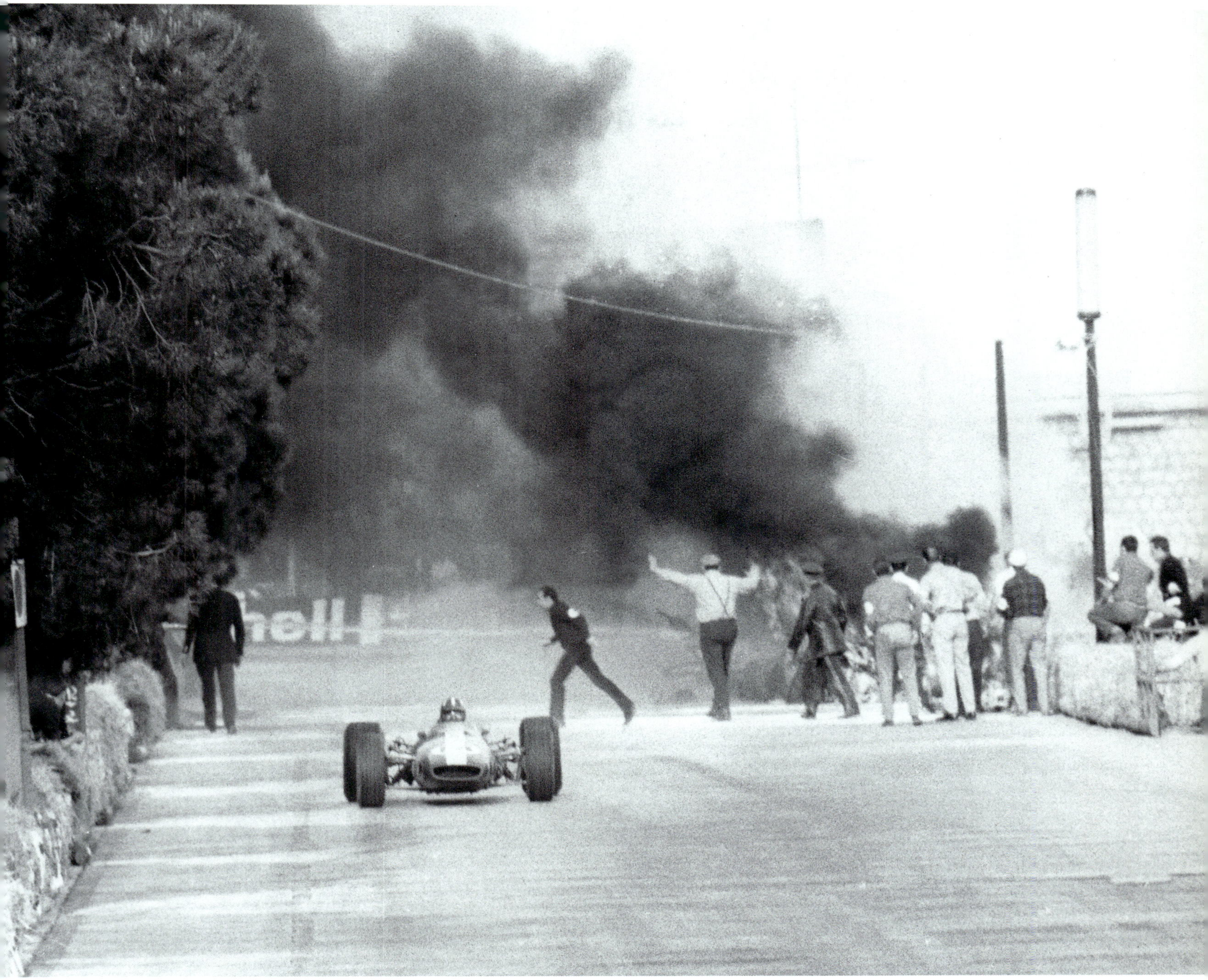

↑ Graham Hill in the Team Lotus Lotus-BRM 33 (R11) exits the chicane past the scene of Lorenzo Bandini's fiery accident at Monaco. As a result of this crash on lap 82, through Bandini's apparent fatigue as he tried to catch Hulme's leading Brabham, the race that was traditionally 100 laps long was thereafter shortened to 80 laps. The terrible conflagration, stoked by the straw bales, fatally burned poor Bandini, who died two days later. Hill finished second.

← Monaco was Jim Clark's bogey track, and in his final appearance here in 1967, having gradually caught Hulme's Brabham, he was poised to take the lead when the offside rear shock absorber failed on lap 43 and he hit the wall at Tabac. Clark had also set fastest lap, but all to no avail. The bent Lotus 33 (R14) awaits collection.

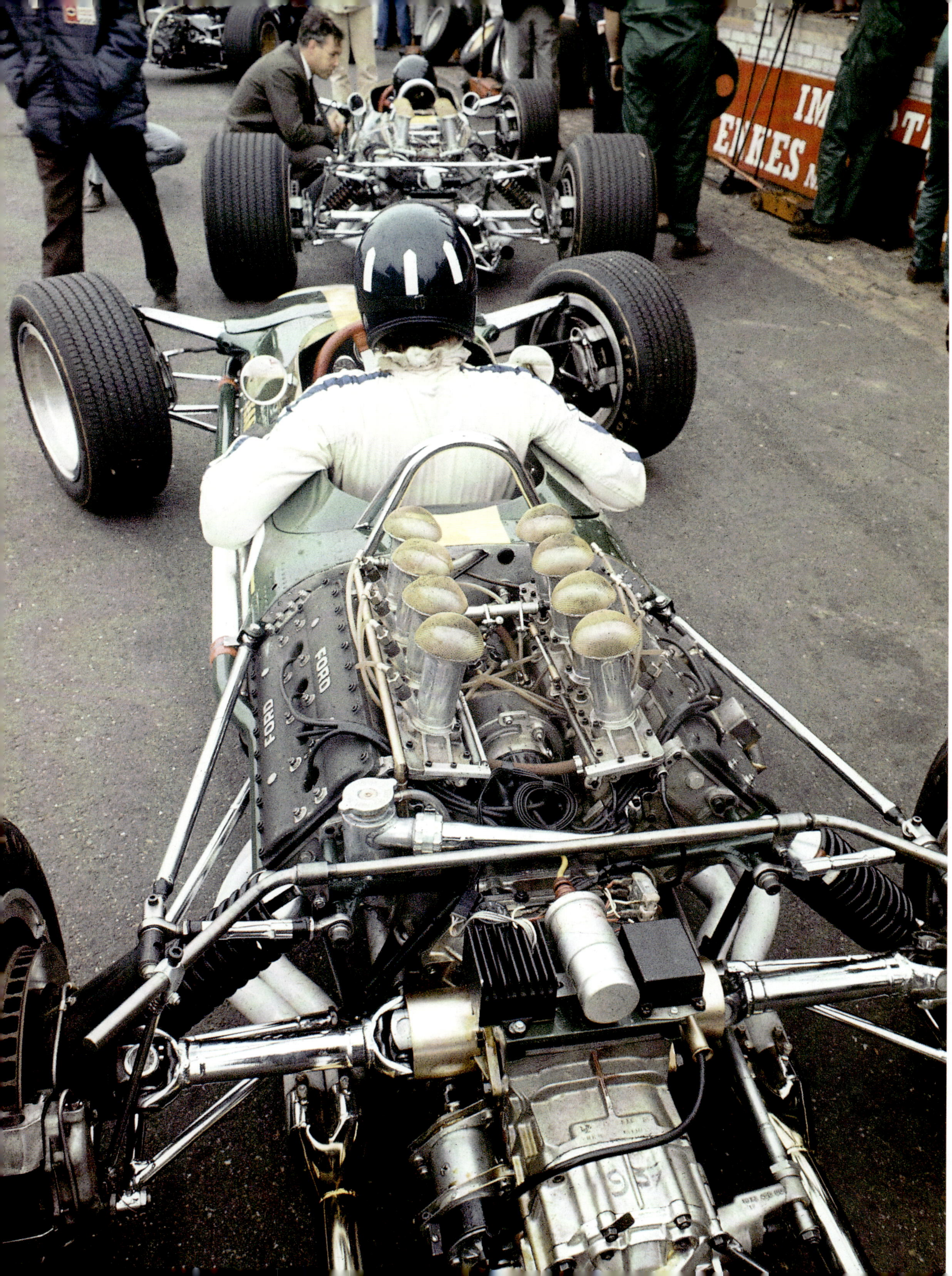
FORD
FORD

← It must have come as something of a relief for both Clark and Hill when the Cosworth DFV-powered Lotus 49 made its race debut at the Dutch GP, especially for NGH, who had been racing the BRM V8-powered 33 that was not as potent as its Climax-engined counterpart used by Clark. Predictably, Graham's car retired after starting from pole, because of cam gear failure, whilst Jimmy's kept going despite the onset of a similar problem, and he won. Graham, who had done most of the development testing as Clark was now a tax exile living in Paris, squeezes himself either into or out of the 49 (R1), whilst Jimmy in R2 is talking to Keith Duckworth.

↓ After finishing second at Le Mans 1961 with Willy Mairesse in a factory Testa Rossa Ferrari, Mike Parkes became a part-time works Ferrari driver for 1962, and full-time in 1963. By 1966 he was driving in F1 following the departure of John Surtees, finishing second in the French and Italian GPs and winning the 1967 International Trophy at Silverstone. Here he is at the 1967 Dutch GP at Zandvoort in his penultimate GP talking with Mauro Foghieri where he will finish fifth in the Ferrari 312, but a horrendous crash in the Belgian GP left Parkes with badly smashed legs and other injuries that ended his F1 career. His helmet carries the BRDC badge on the crown.

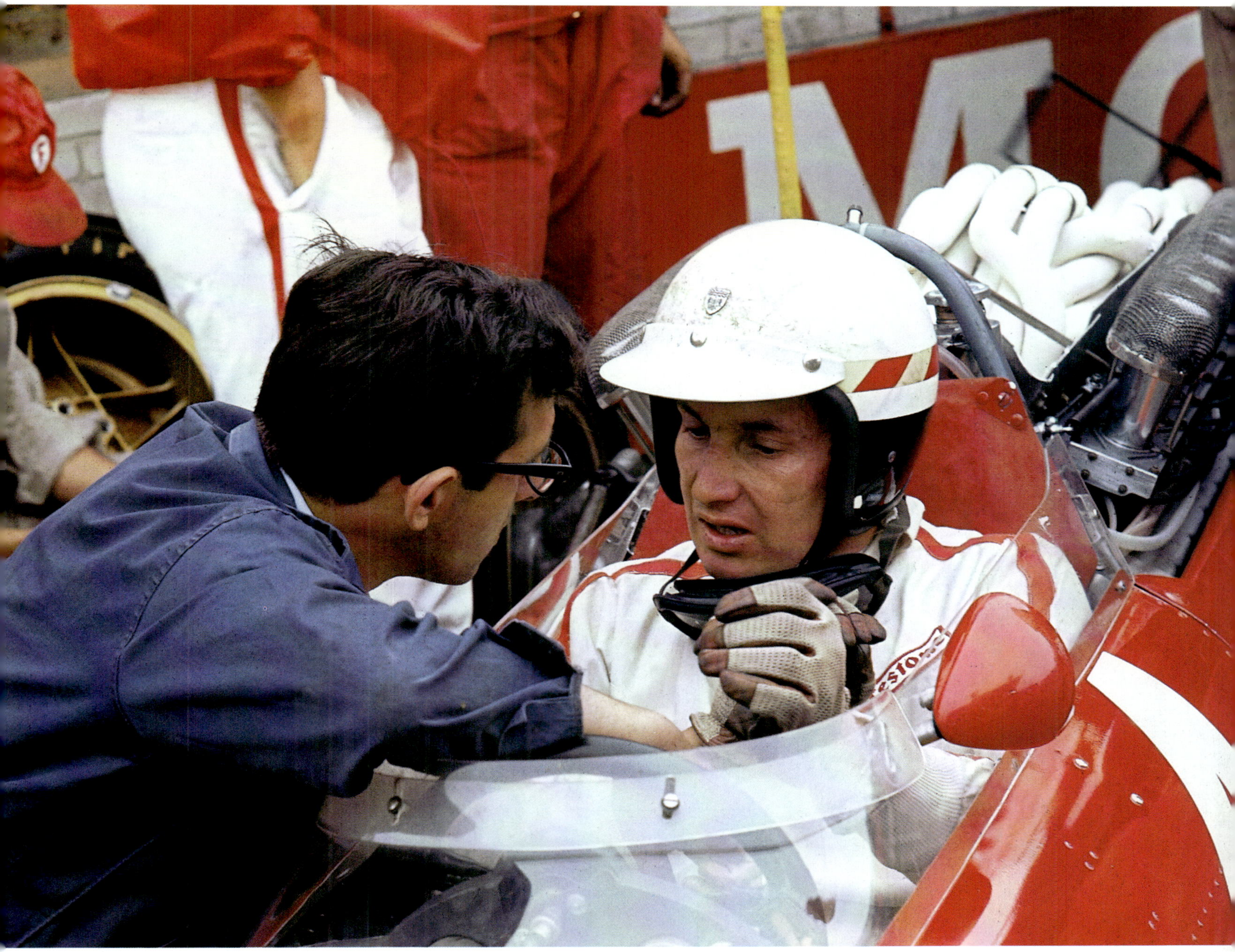

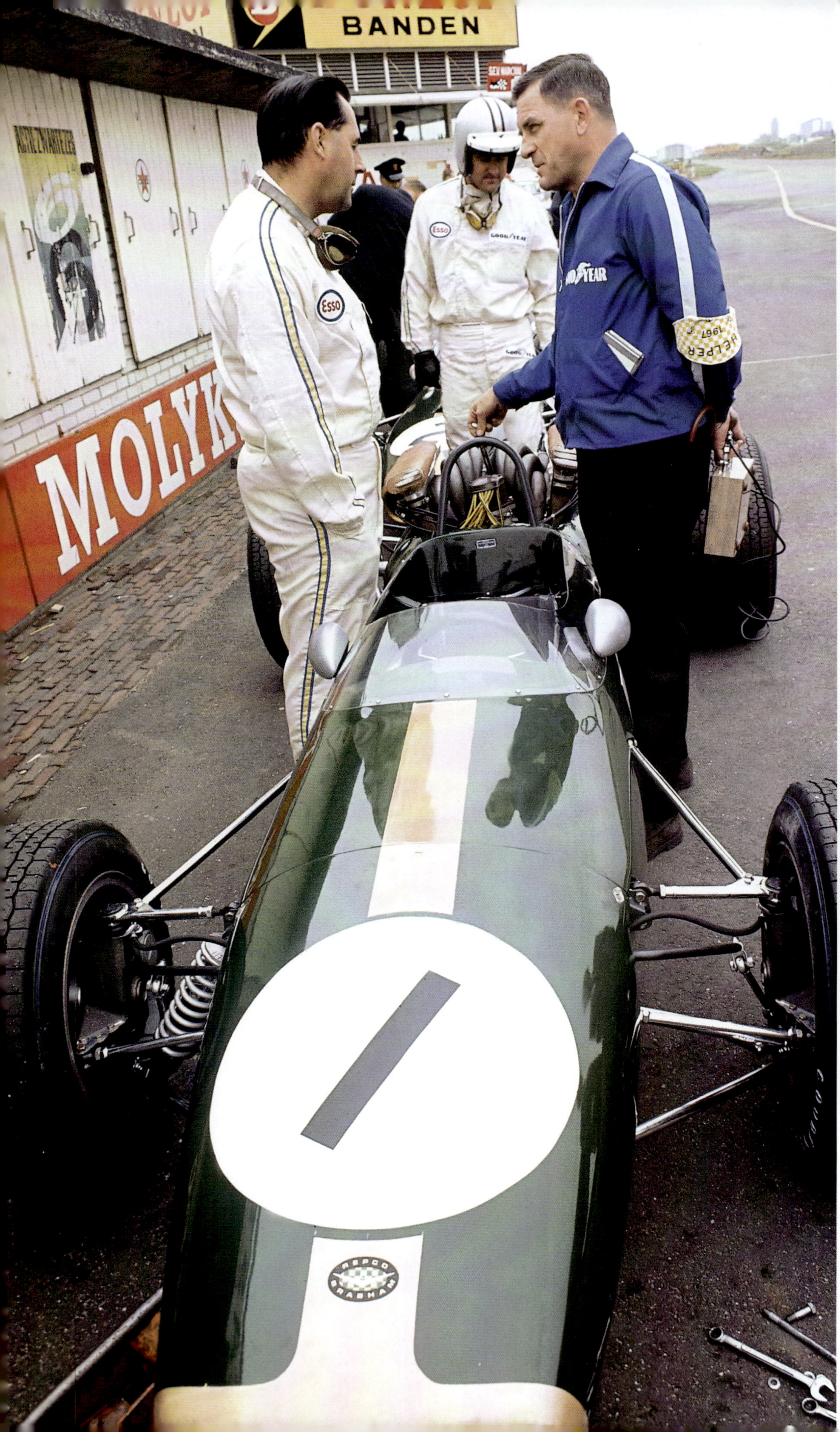
BANDEN
MOLYK
Esso
GOODYEAR
HELPER
1967

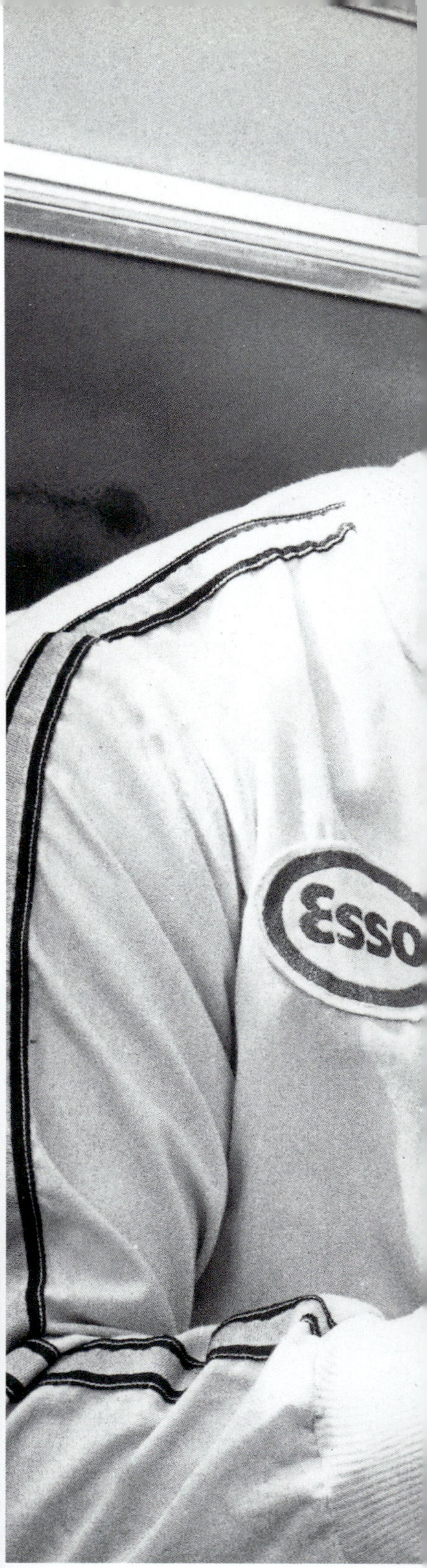
Esso

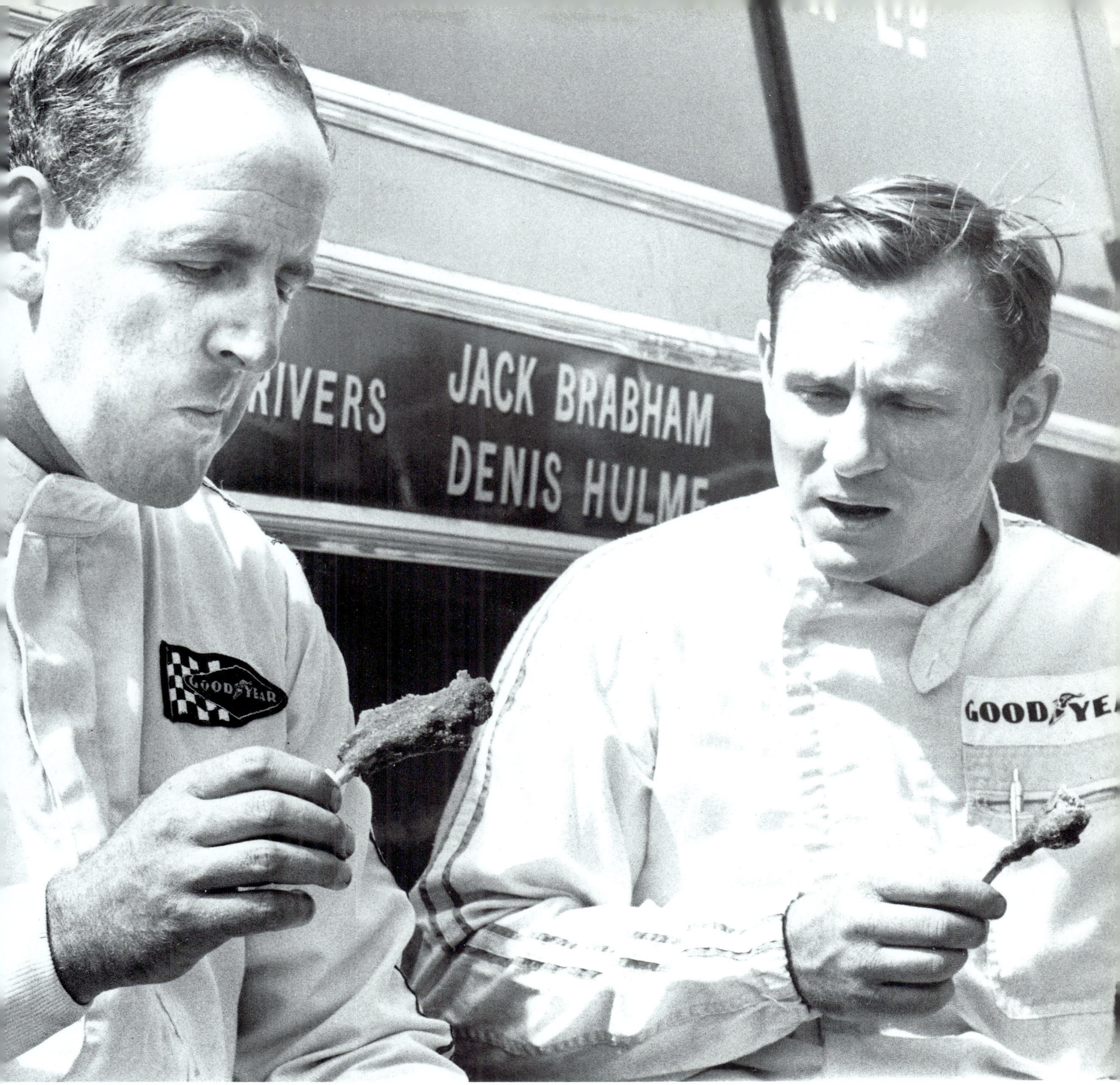

↑ 'I think that's been cloned from the original chicken, Denny.' Bruce McLaren has eaten all of his, but Mr Hulme seems to be regretting that last mouthful.

← Leo Mehl, Goodyear tyre boss, converses with Jack Brabham in the Zandvoort pits, 1967, with team-mate Denny Hulme behind. This was the debut race for the new Cosworth DFV-powered Lotus 49, and suddenly everybody else's cars were just not quick enough. Nevertheless, the canny and always formidable Brabham finished second behind Clark's Lotus, but it would have been third if Hill's similar car had not expired. No. 1 is the old BT19 (F1-2-65), and Hulme's car beyond is the later BT20 (F1-2-66), but the new BT24 will appear at the Belgian GP.

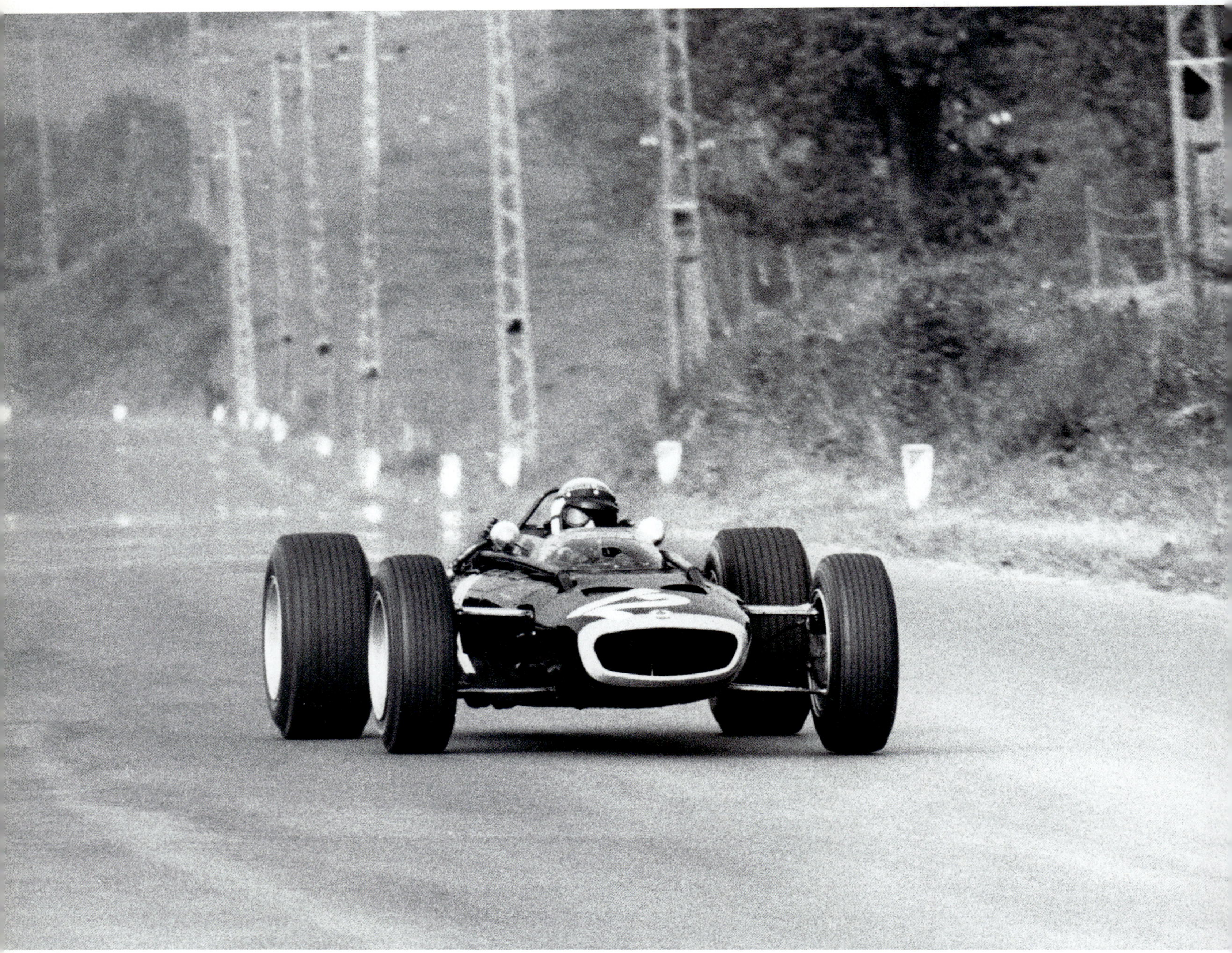

↑ Somewhere on the Masta straight [sic] Jackie Stewart demonstrates his determination during the 1967 Belgian GP at Spa on his way to finishing second, despite gearbox travails, behind Gurney's victorious Eagle Weslake. This is one year on from his very nasty accident here, but he is at full chat with the BRM P83 (03) on tiptoe at about 190mph. Downforce? Never 'eard of it Guv!

↗ Cooper testing at Modena on a hot, still (if the wind sock is anything to go by) day. The works transporter sits behind the pits and Jo Siffert is on the left of the trio at centre, with the Cooper-Maserati in the background. Note how vulnerable the parked light aircraft are to any on-track mishaps as a car exits the final corner.

→ Apparently, Rob Walker's Jo Siffert was driving the works car at Modena, and this appears to be the new magnesium electron skinned T86 (F1-2-67) that Rindt will drive at the British GP. Attending are designer Derrick White (left) kneeling and taking notes, Roy Salvadori leaning over, and John Cooper (right) kneeling, whilst behind Chris Amon ponders.

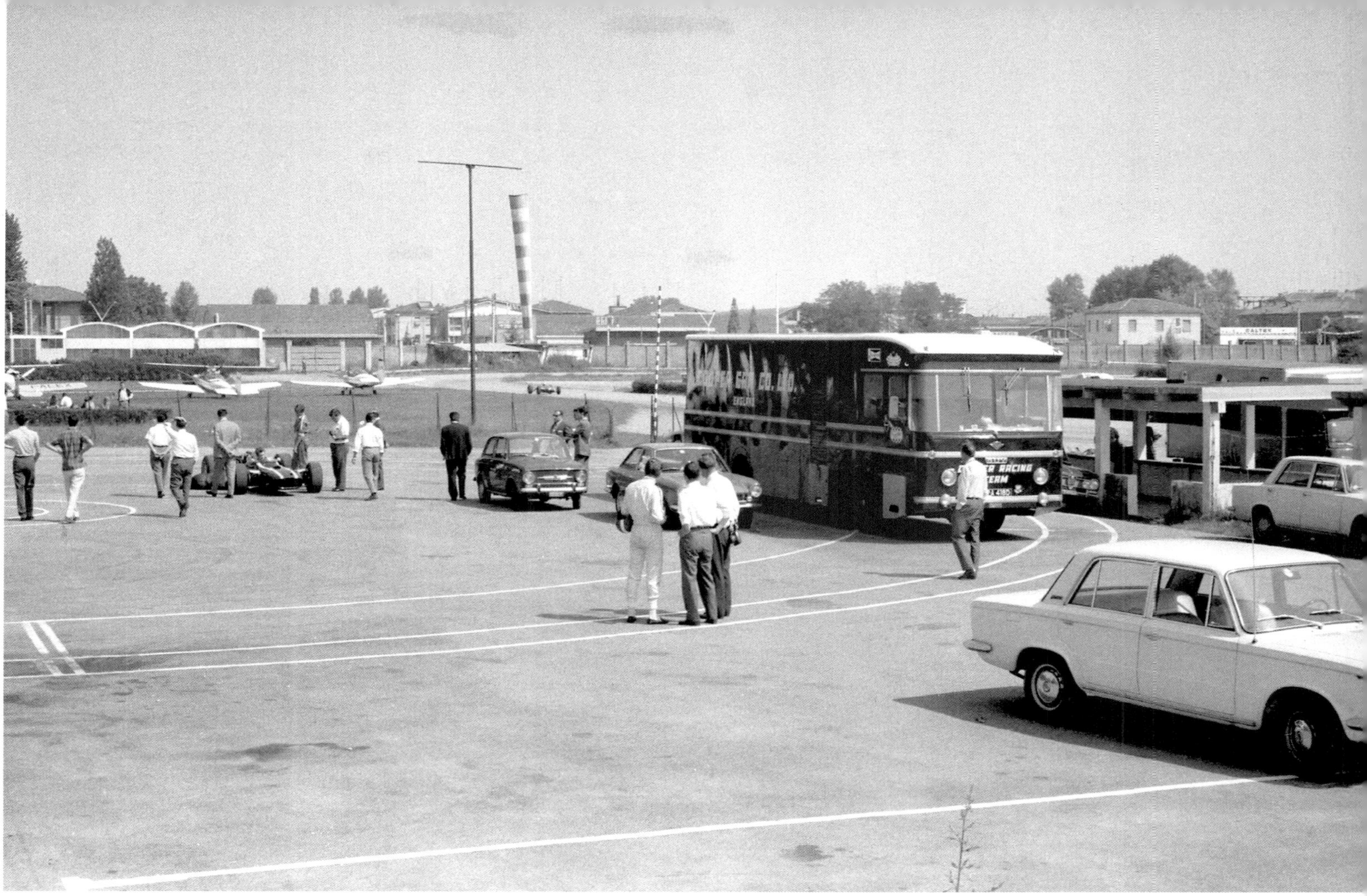

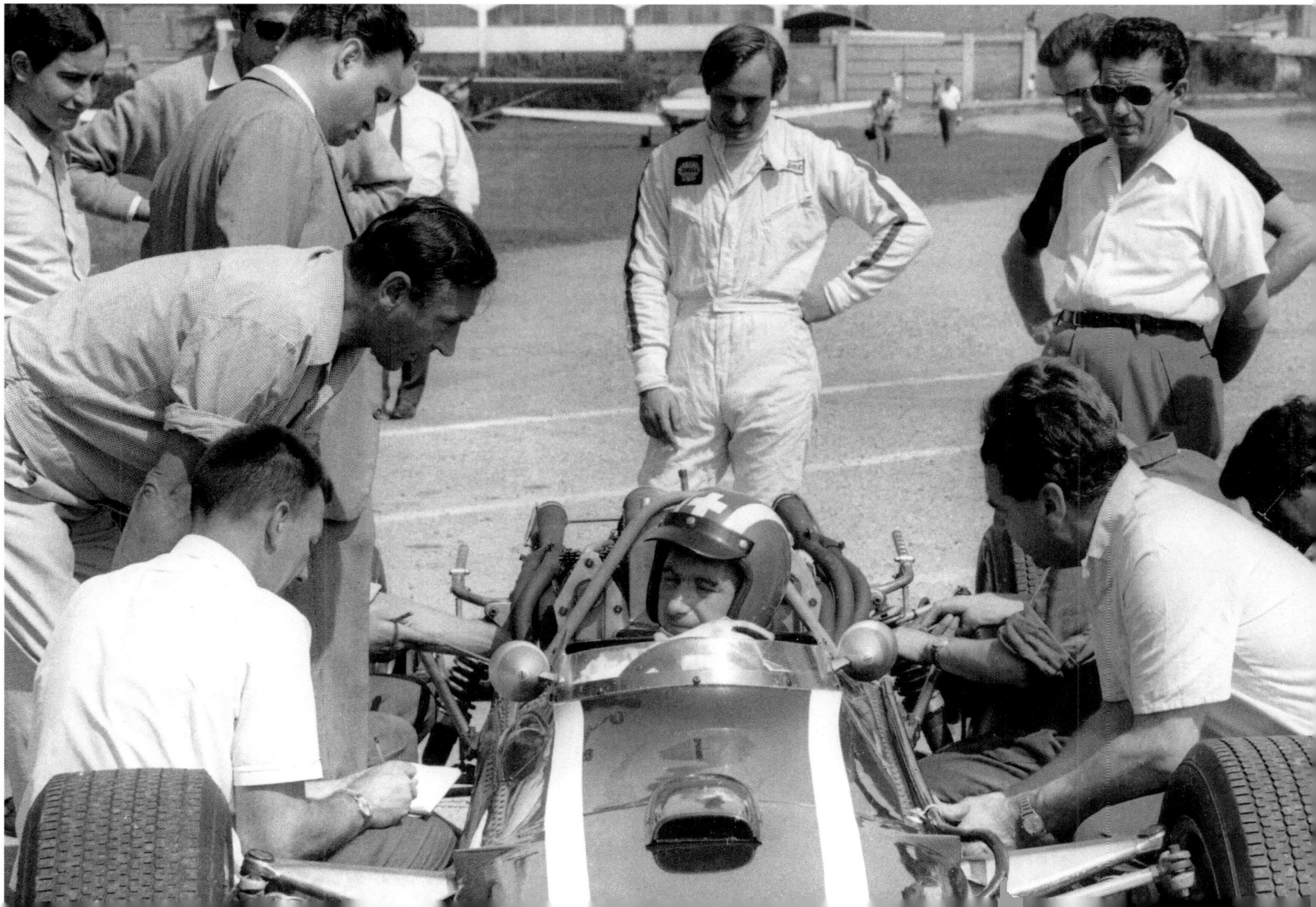

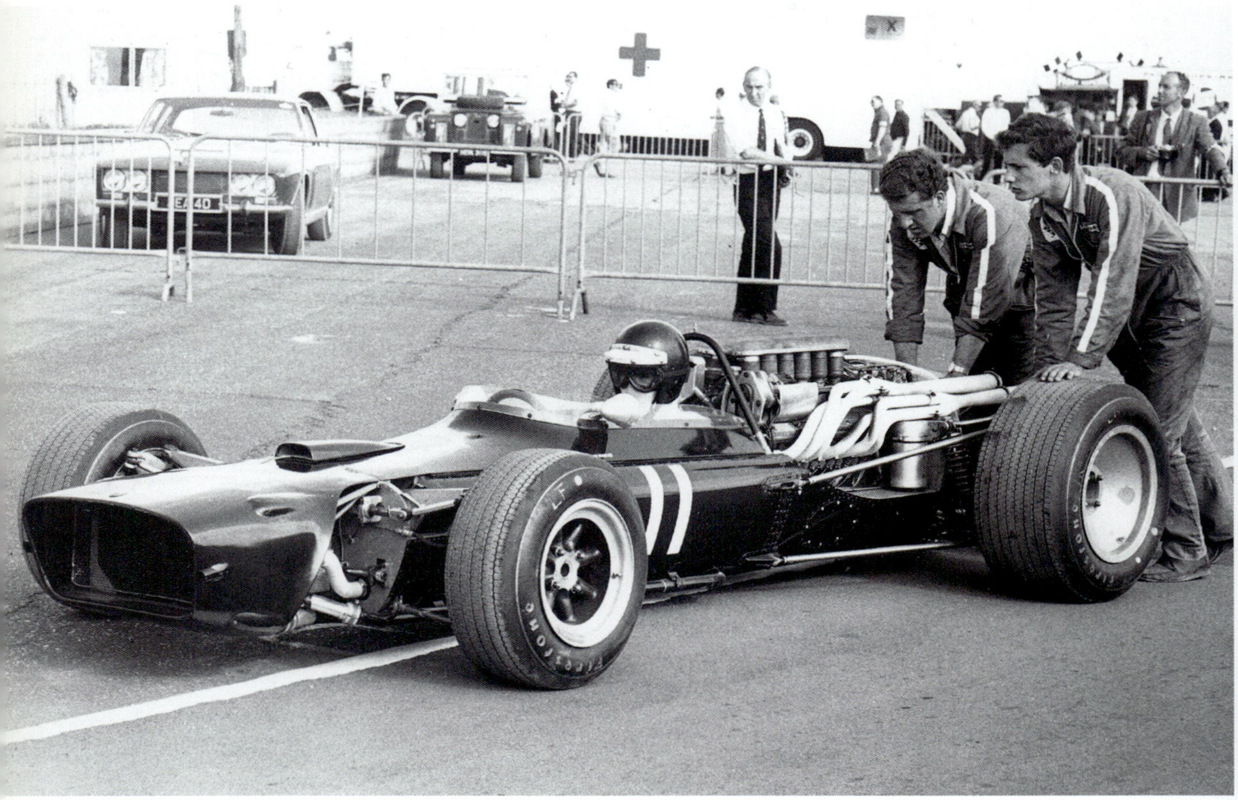

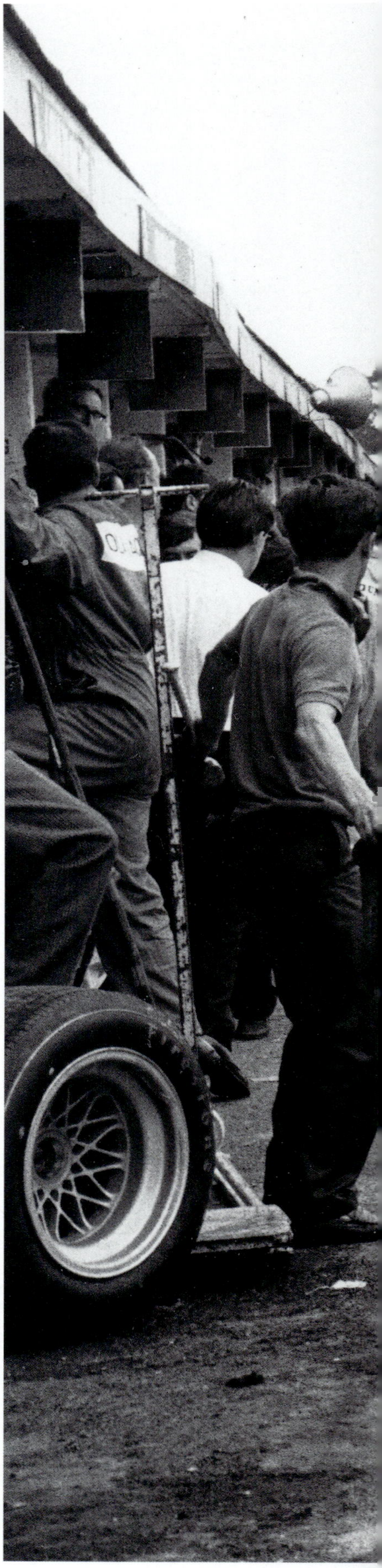

↑ The ugly, unfinished-looking Cooper-Maserati T86 (F1-2-67) with Jochen Rindt aboard at its Silverstone British GP debut being pushed along by the Cooper mechanics, the one on the right being a young Ron Dennis. It was 51kg lighter than the T81, thanks to its magnesium electron monocoque, and was fitted with the 36-valve Tipo 10 motor and Hewland transaxle, but retired here due to engine failure. Its best result was a fourth at Monza that year. Thereafter the T86 made only two more GP starts – at Kyalami in 1968 as a works entry for Ludovico Scarfiotti, and for the last time at Monaco in 1969 driven by Vic Elford for Colin Crabbe.

→ Now that's what you call a wing! The winning Chaparral 2F (001) stops for a drink, change of driver, and shoes at the BOAC 500. Following the retirement of the two Lola T70s (Team Surtees and Sid Taylor Racing) the Chaparral was the quickest car and, despite Phil Hill suffering a puncture during the race, it won. Here, we see the typically overpopulated and narrow Brands Hatch pit lane in all its glory, as the bewinged monster hungrily approaches its aluminium teat.

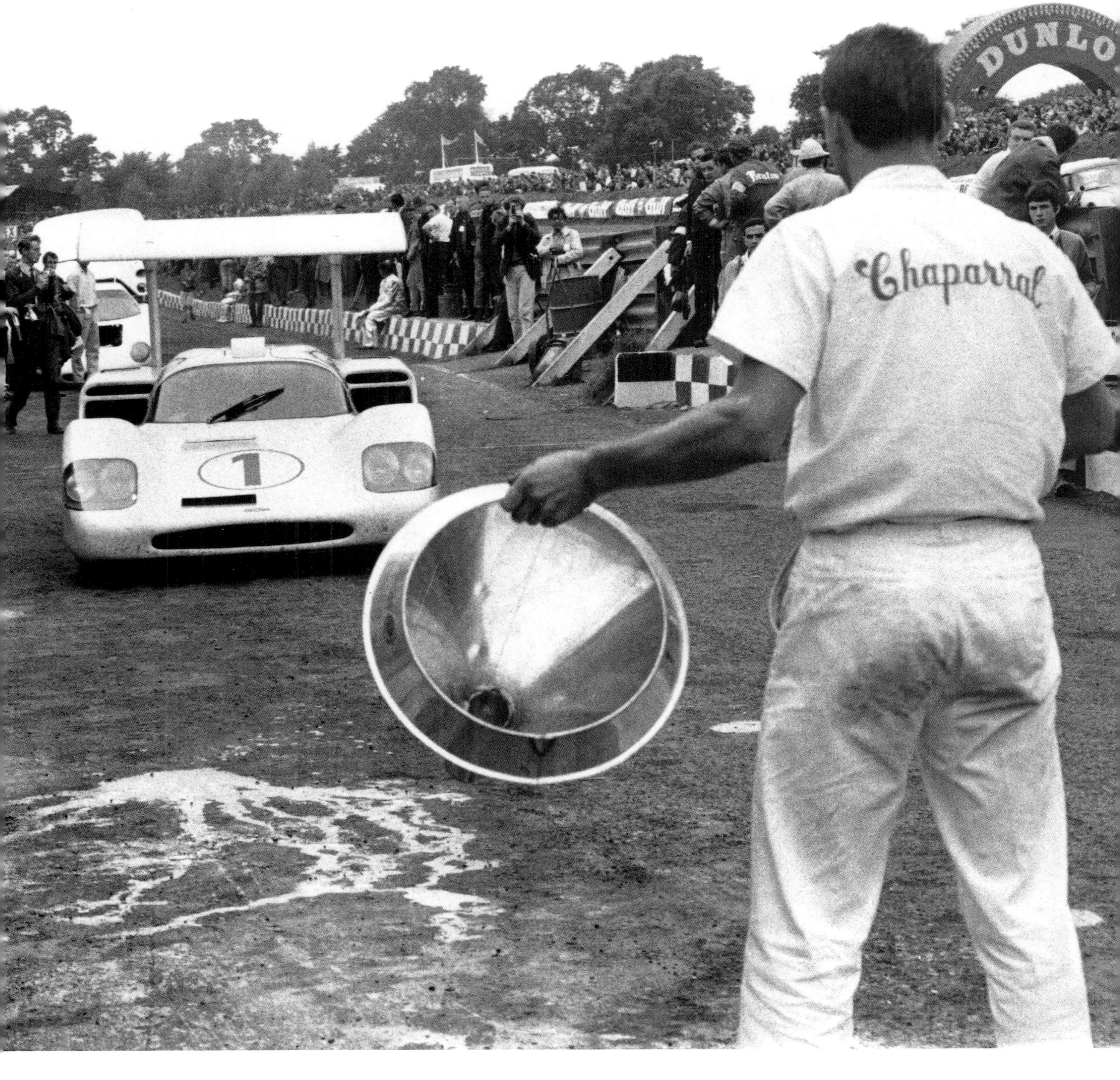
DUNLO
Chaparral
1

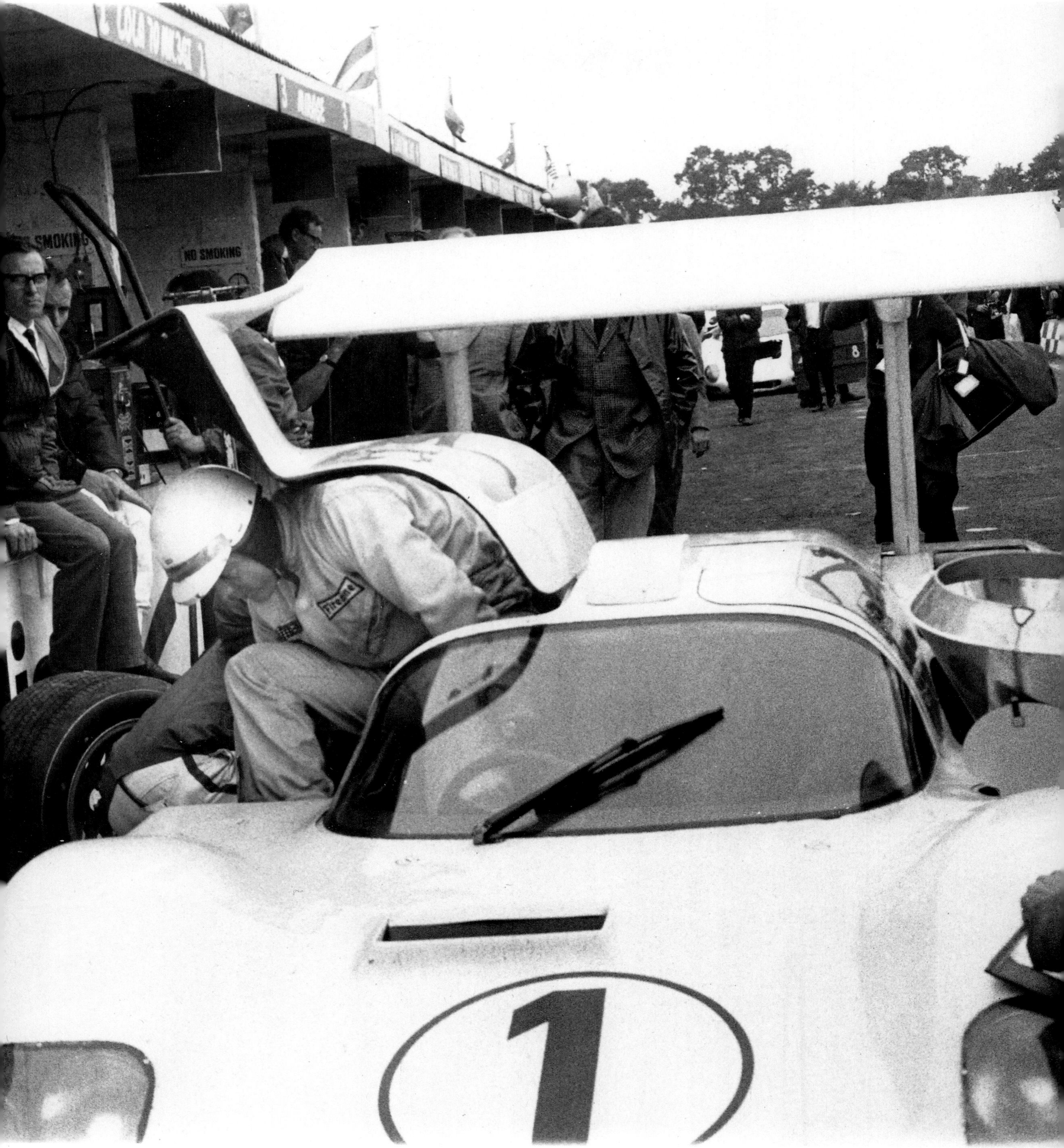
NO SMOKING
NO SMOKING

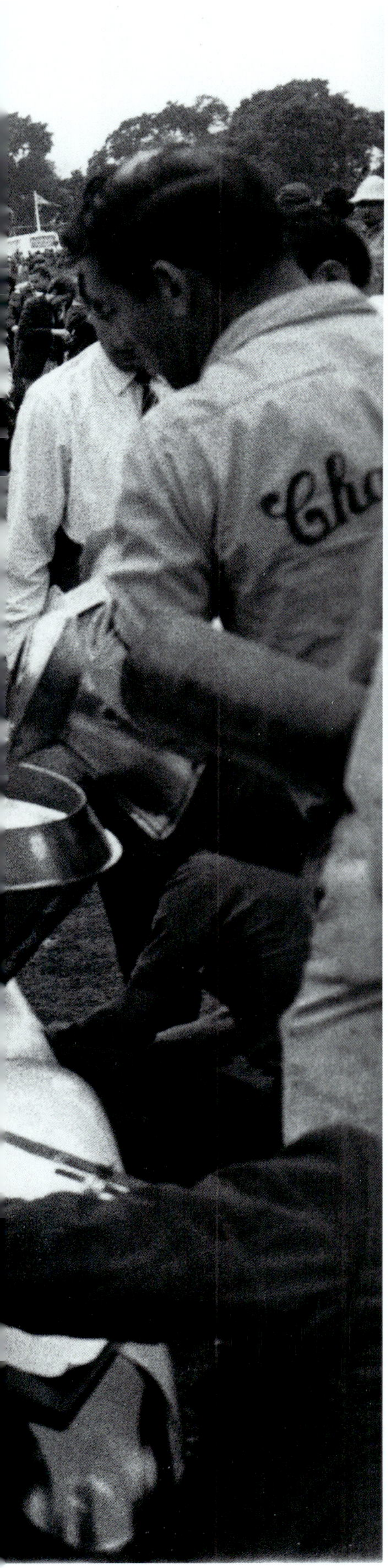

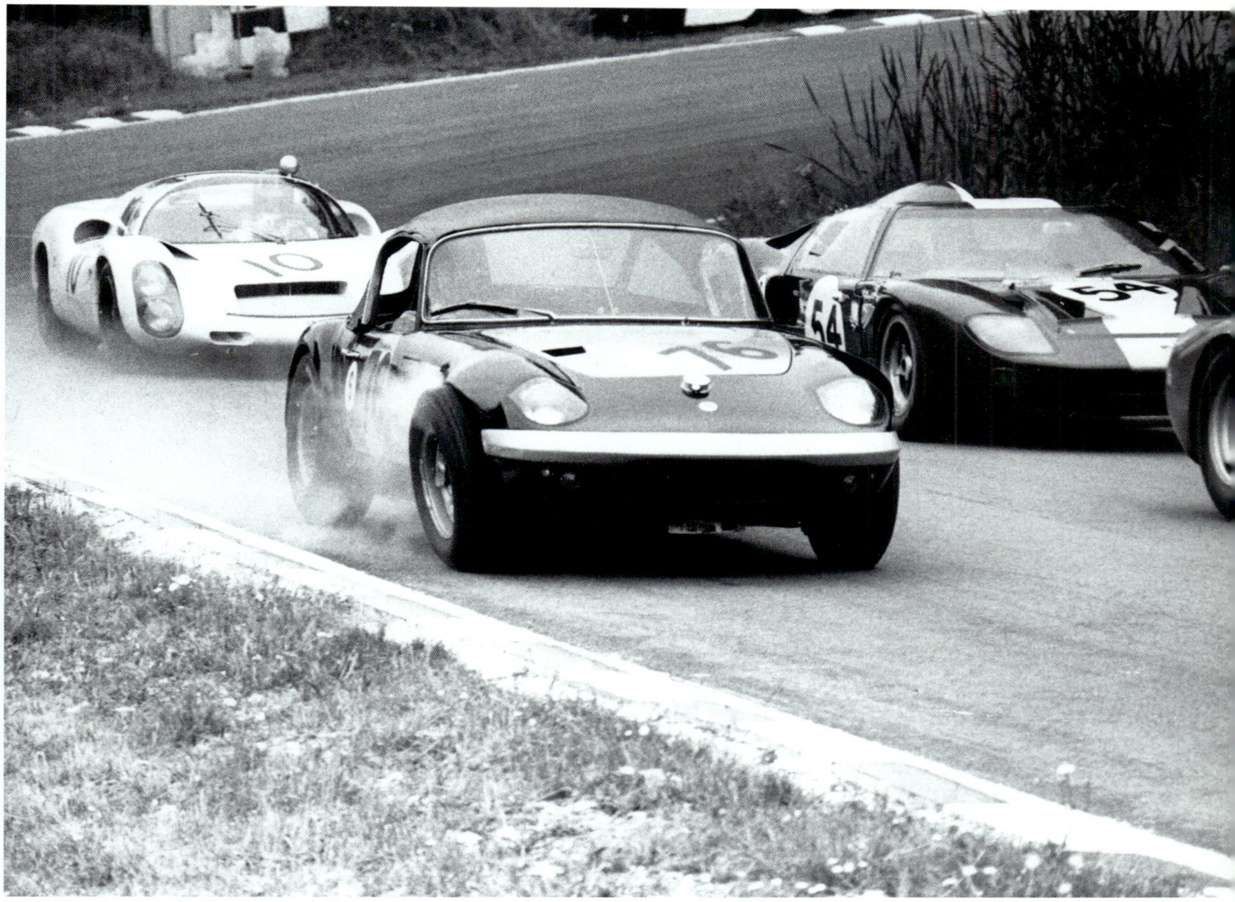

↑ The inaugural BOAC 500, or Brands Hatch 6 Hours as it appears in the stats, was a fascinating race that offered the best of both worlds – GP stars and sports car aces, in many cases one and the same. The Keith Burnard/Peter Taggart Lotus Elan has perhaps just a little too much positive camber on the front as a 906 (possibly Bill Bradley's MRP car), the No. 54 Colin Crabbe's GT40 (1021), driven here by South African F1 racer Dave Charlton, and Graham Hill in the flat 8 Porsche 910 (027), shared with Jochen Rindt (although Hill did not actually drive it as it retired early on), blast by.

← Phil Hill climbs out, fuel goes in, and Mike Spence will take over. They finished nearly a minute ahead of the works Ferrari 330P4 of Jackie Stewart/Chris Amon, the only endurance championship race that the Chaparral 2F ever won.

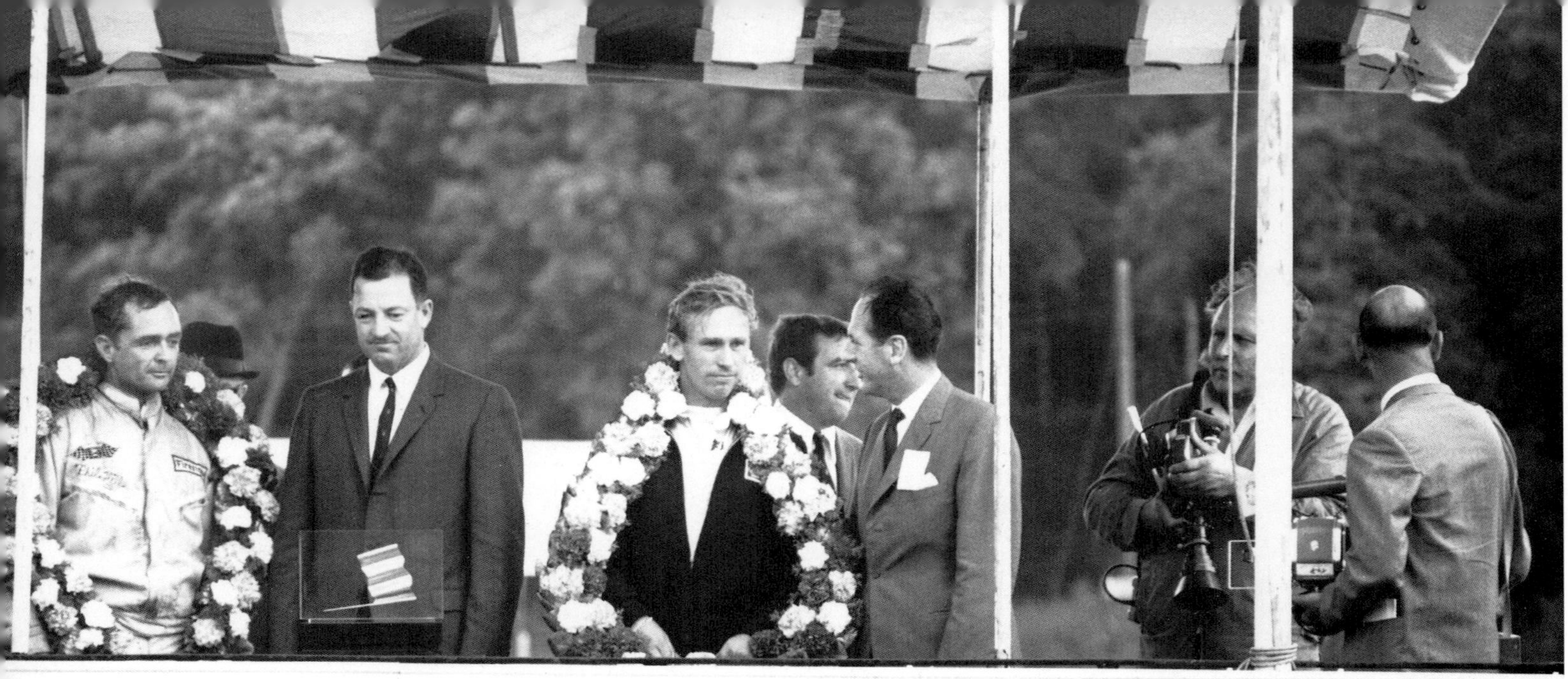

BOAC

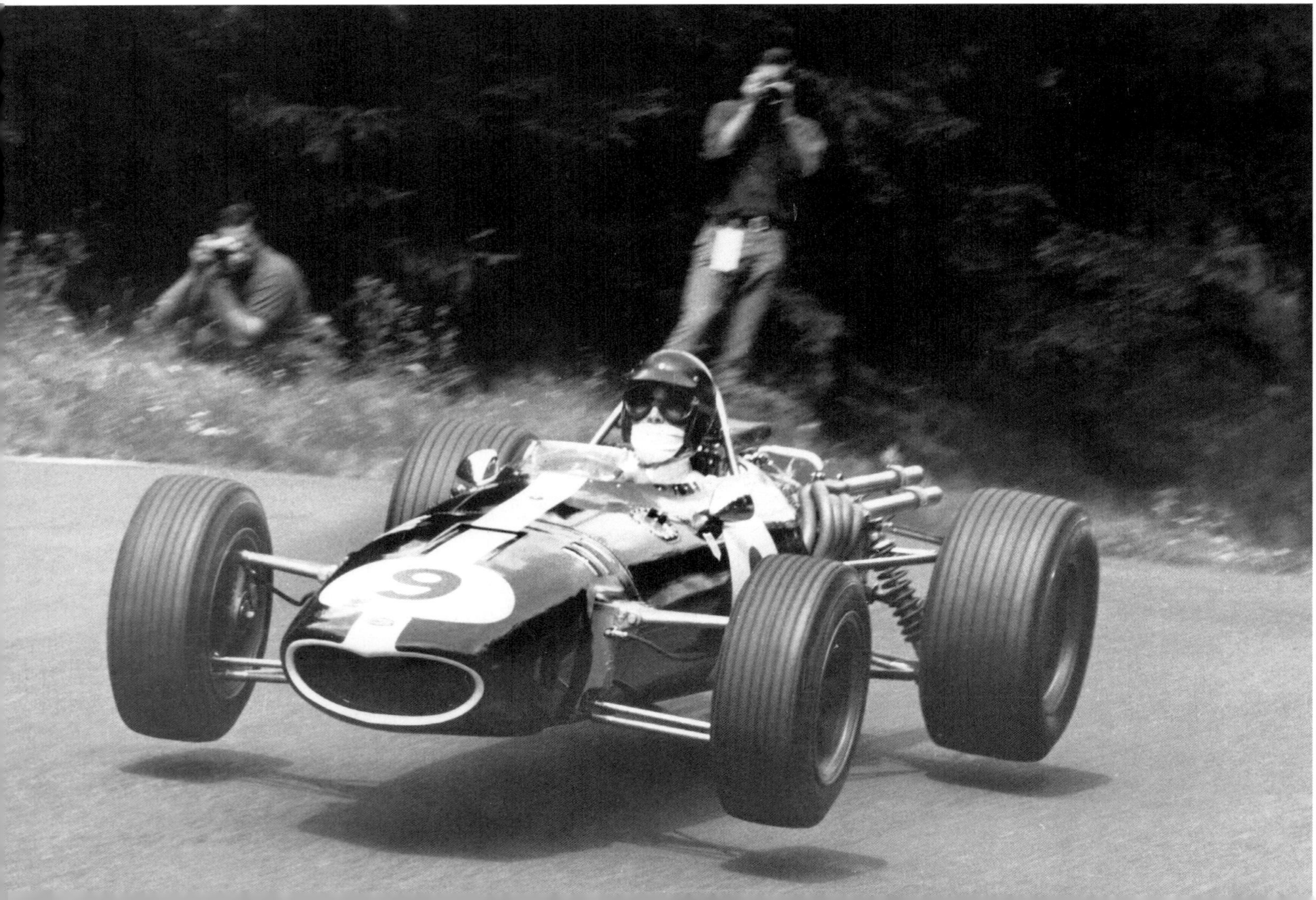

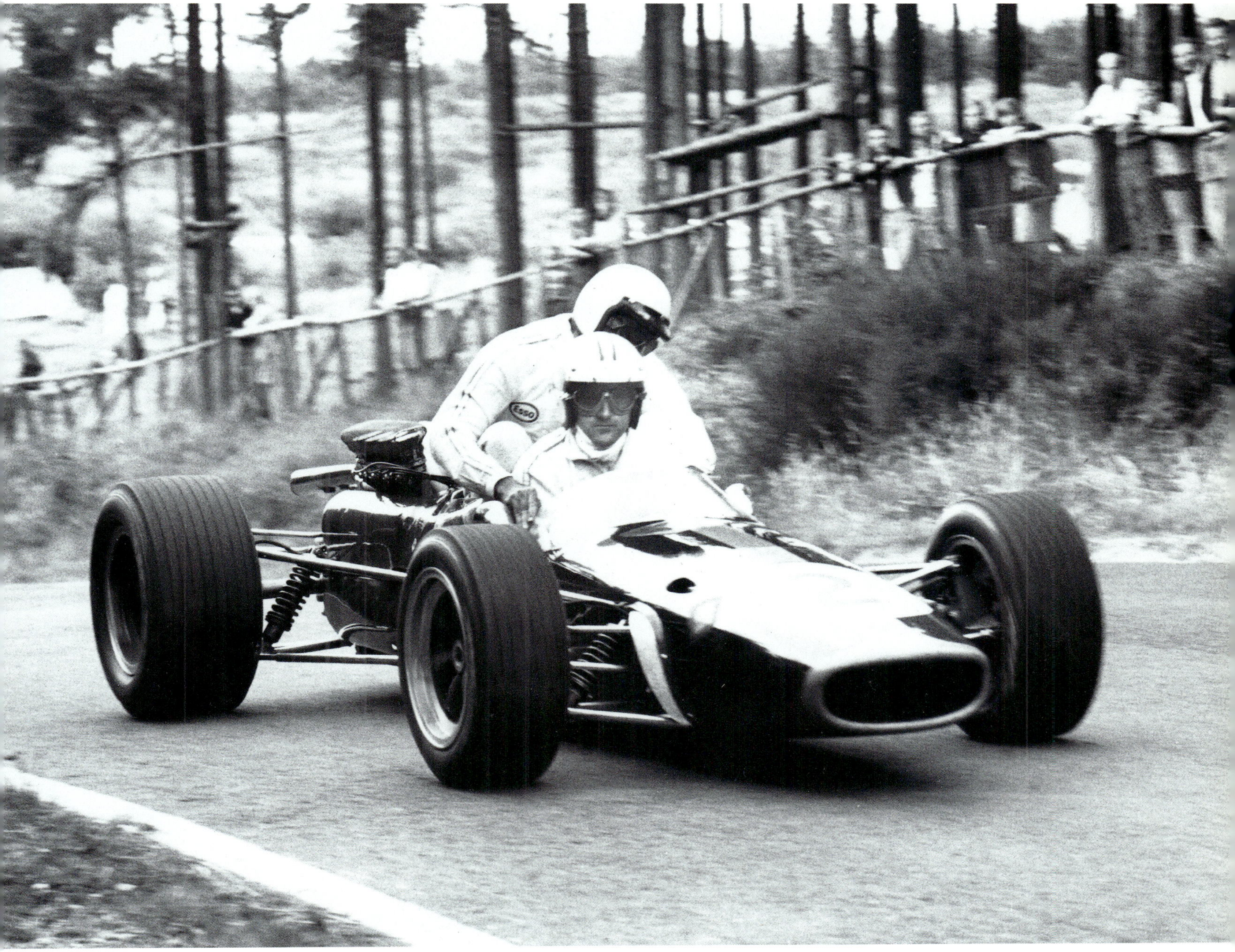

↑ A famous shot by Mike, but one worth repeating if only to show how straightforward and unregulated this era was. Denny Hulme in the Brabham-Repco BT24/2 gives his boss a lift back to the pits during practice for the German GP. Things were better in the race, which Hulme won, but only after Clark's Lotus 49 and Gurney's Eagle suffered front suspension and a drive shaft failure respectively. The icing on the cake was that Brabham finished second and Hulme went on to become 1967 World Champion, just five points ahead of 'Black Jack'.

↖ The 1967 BOAC 500 was Phil Hill's last major victory and he shares the celebrations with Mike Spence. Had the Chaparral's automatic transmission been strong enough to handle the torque of the 2F's Chevy engine, they would surely have won more races. Amongst period travellers and employees the BOAC acronym was said to stand for 'Better On A Camel'.

← Another race that Dan Gurney should have won, the 1967 German GP on the awesome 14.2-mile Nürburgring. Following Jim Clark's retirement, he caught and passed eventual winner Denny Hulme to lead the race, setting a lap record, but alas the Eagle T1G/104 broke a drive shaft late in the race. As he scorns terra firma the snappers enjoy their roadside verge access. Oh happy days!

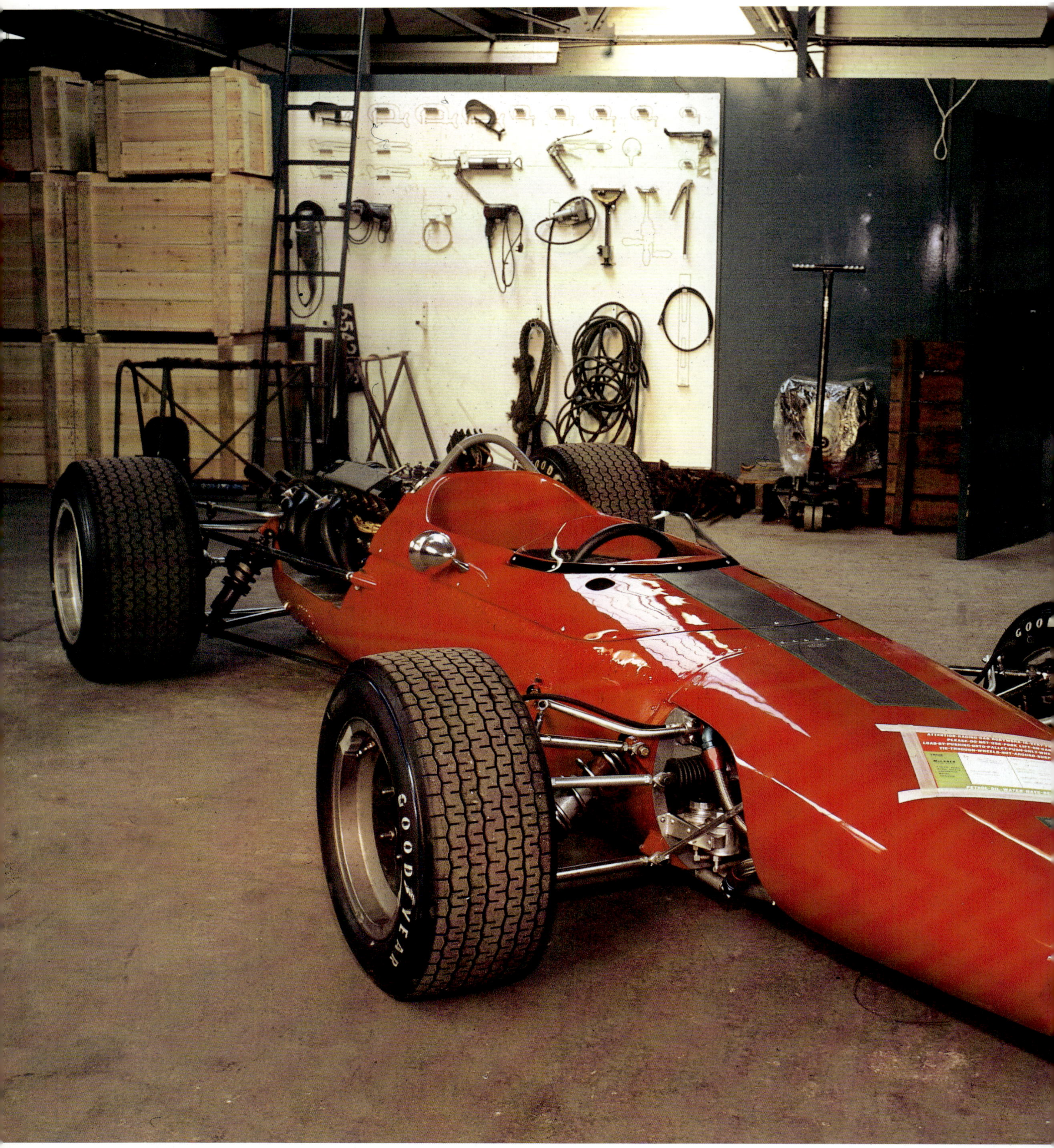
GOODYEAR

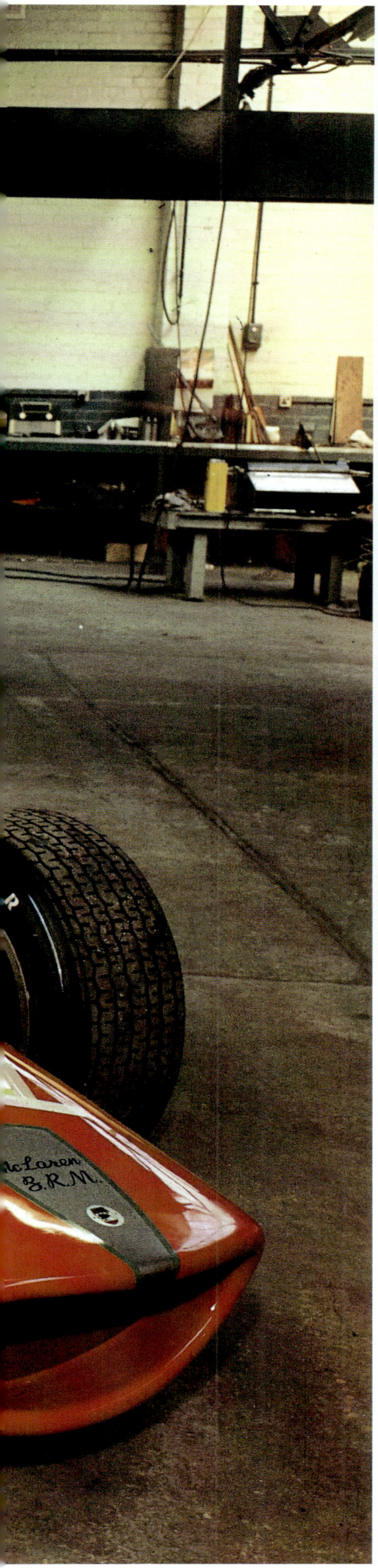

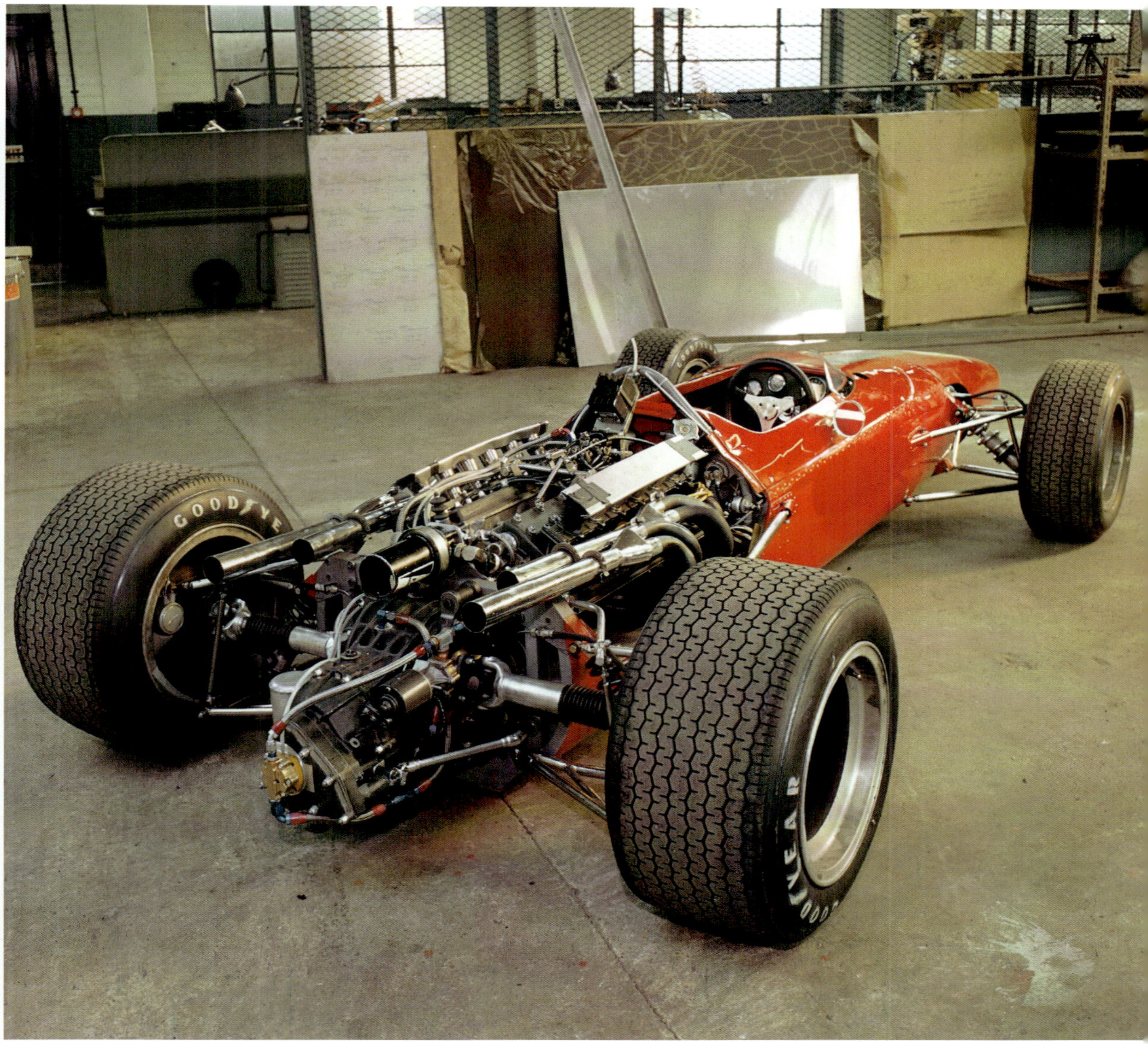

↑ As with all Bruce's cars, the M5A was beautifully prepared and finished (as seen here). BRM's 24-valve 101 V12 supposedly gave 390bhp at 9,750rpm, according to BRM's Tony Rudd, but McLaren reckoned 365bhp (although the team did find another 19 horses during development). The monocoque M5A carried 42 gallons of fuel and used a five-speed Hewland DG gearbox, but retained F2-sized brakes (albeit with slightly thicker discs), Bruce being very light on the stoppers – something that had to be changed for Denny Hulme in 1968.

← The very beautiful McLaren M5A with the BRM V12 engine at the Colnbrook works prior to shipment for the Canadian GP, where Bruce McLaren ran as high as second before a misfire set in, eventually finishing seventh. He was equally competitive at Monza before a cylinder liner disintegrated, posted a DNS at Watkins Glen, and retired in Mexico. Thereafter, the one and only M5A was raced by Denny Hulme in the South African GP at Kyalami (finishing fifth) before being sold to Jo Bonnier, who raced it to the end of 1968. This was the end of Bruce's BRM dalliance, that began with the F2-based M4B, as Cosworth's DFV allied to a new M7A awaited in 1968. Look carefully and you can just read the shipping document taped to the nose.

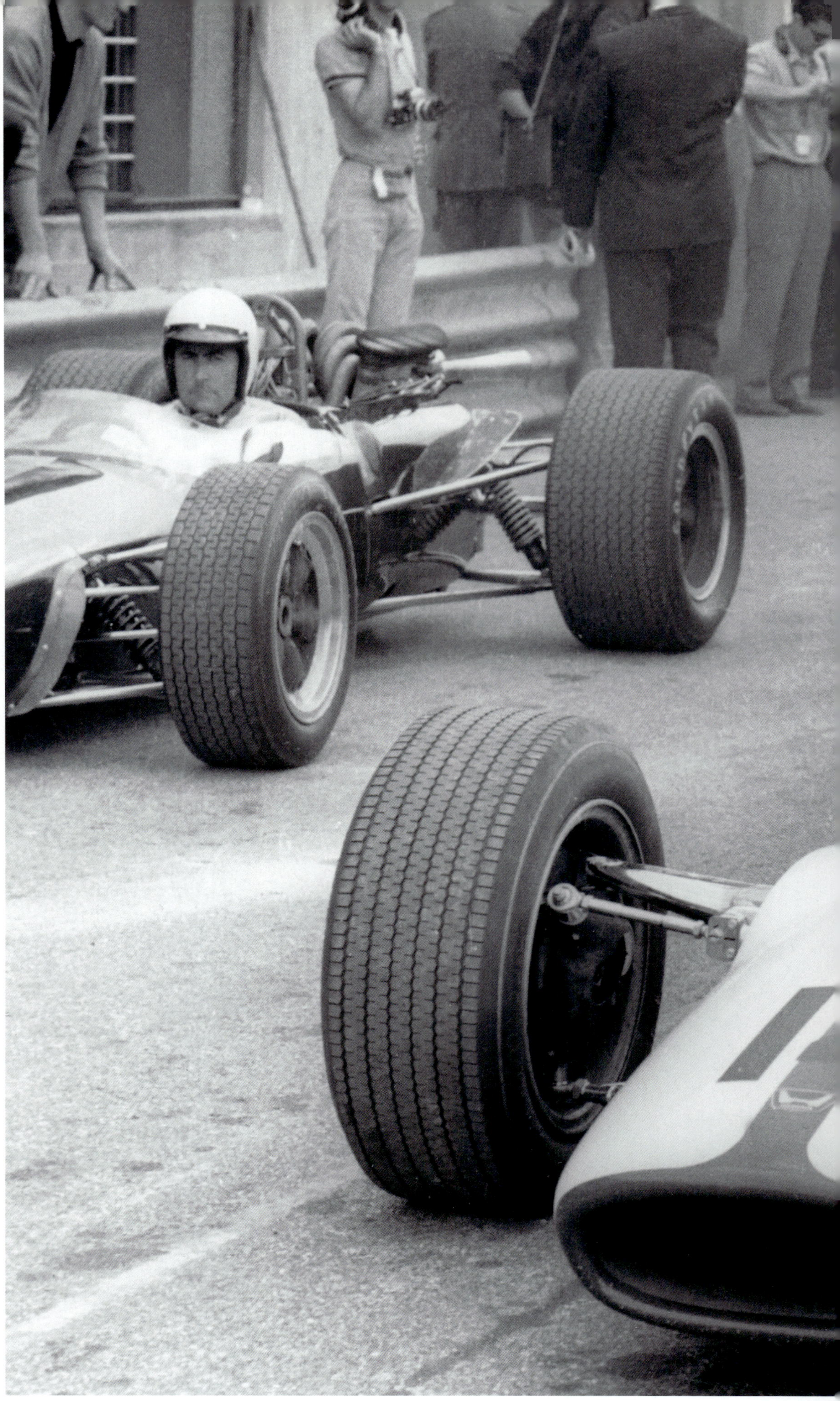

→ The Honda RA300 (aka Hondola) was a purposeful looking machine that was not quite as potent as it should have been. Its predecessor, the RA273, had proven overweight with a narrow power band and tricky handling, and this was the successor that developed 395bhp but weighed over 600kg. However, on this day John Surtees won the Italian GP at Monza after Jack Brabham lost the lead at the Parabolica on the final lap, but only after Jim Clark's Lotus 49 (that had unlapped itself following an earlier delay) took the lead and then ran out of fuel on the last lap. In the pit lane before the off, a pensive Brabham (BT24/1) looks across to Surtees. Behind, Brabham's team-mate Hulme No. 18 (BT24/2), who retired, settles in, and the nose of Mike Spence's BRM P83 (02), who finished fifth, just intrudes.

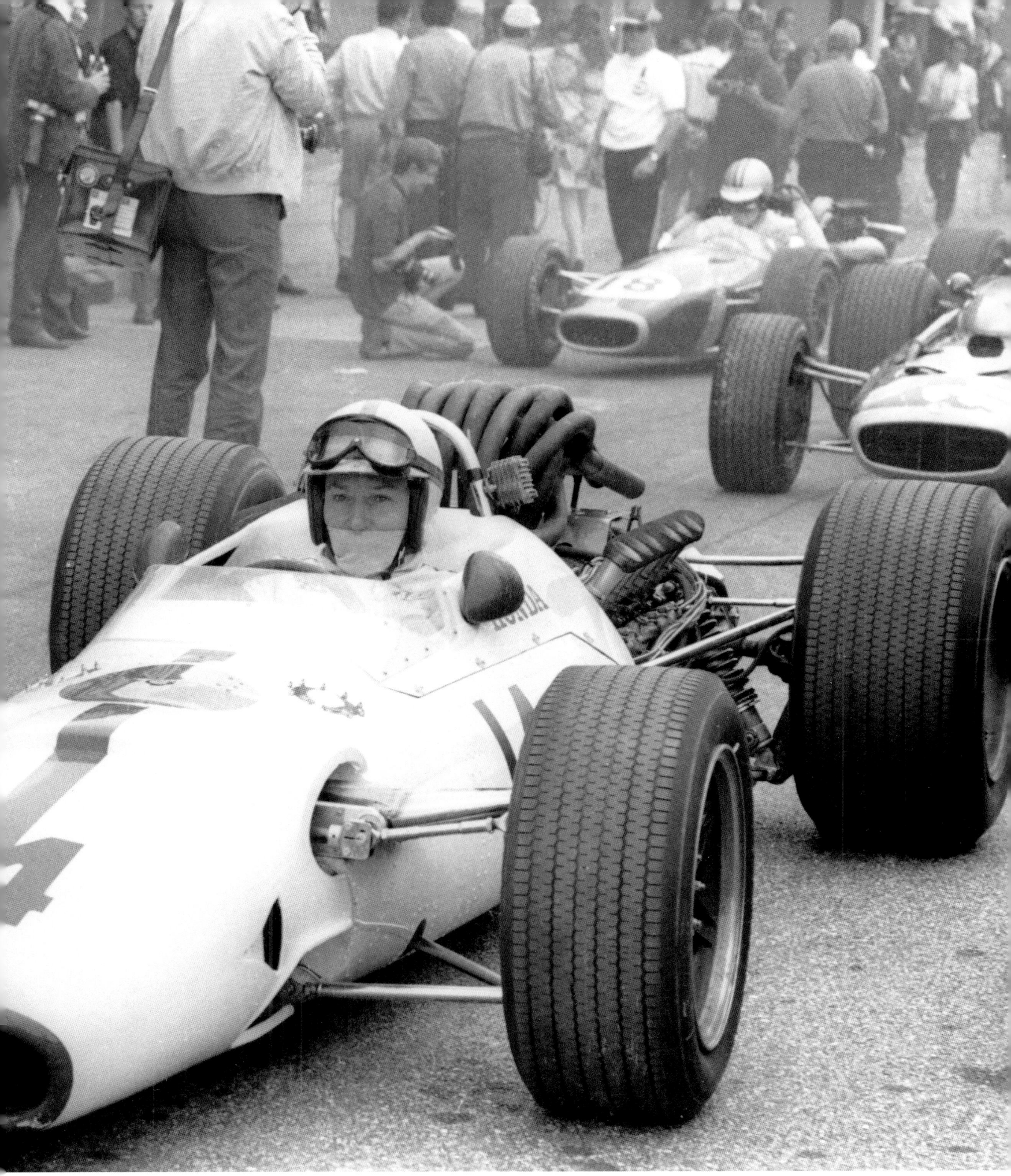
HONDA

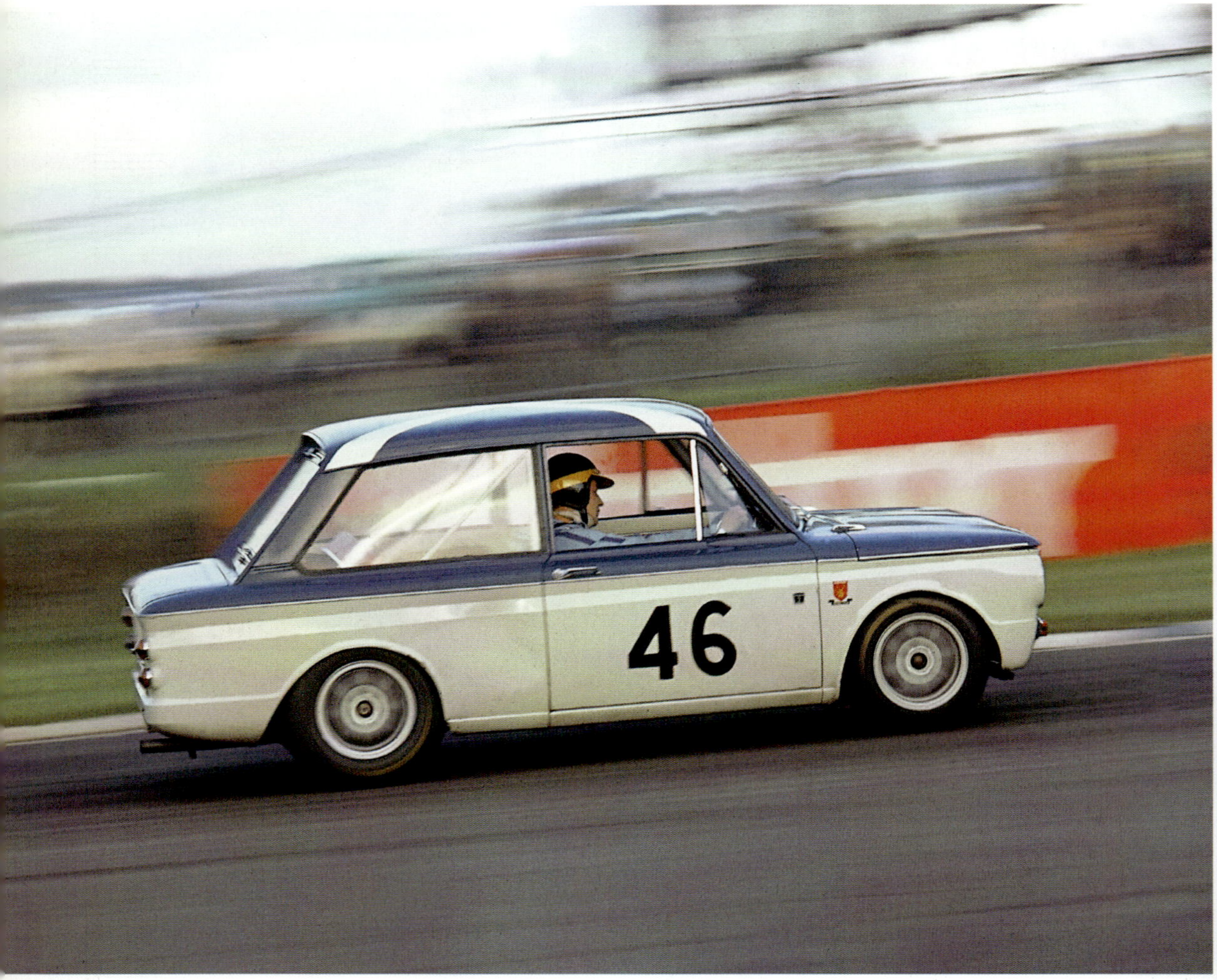

↑ Brands Hatch in October for the Guards Motor Show 200, and the ever-polished, super-fast Tony Lanfranchi in an Alan Fraser Hillman Imp finished third in class, and tenth overall, behind team-mate Bernard Unett and class-winner John Fitzpatrick in the Broadspeed Ford Anglia. He died in October 2004 after a long battle with cancer.

→ In stark contrast to the smooth progress of Lanfranchi's Imp in the preceding picture, John Rhodes is all frenetic action as he utilises the Mini's inherent understeer to scrub off surplus speed. For once Rhodes did not win his class, being beaten by team-mate John Handley at Brands. When John Cooper was asked if there was a Mini driver who stood out from the rest he replied, 'It's got to be Rhodes – Smokey Rhodes was the greatest.' During the period 1965–8, driving the Mini Cooper, he achieved four consecutive 1300cc class Championship titles, three overall race wins, 16 class wins, and won the 1968 Division 2 European Touring Car Challenge. There was also a one-off drive in Bob Gerard's old Cooper T60 at the 1965 British GP that wasted his talent, but success with works MGBs at Sebring and the Targa Floria, a victory in a 1,000-mile race at Brands Hatch, and a class win in a works Healey at Le Mans 24 Hour race. He recalls: 'A highly tuned Cooper Car Co. Mini Cooper, with its fantastic handling and cornering power, gave me the most satisfaction and thrill for my style of driving, even if the tyre temperatures reached 125° centigrade (25° centigrade above boiling water!)'

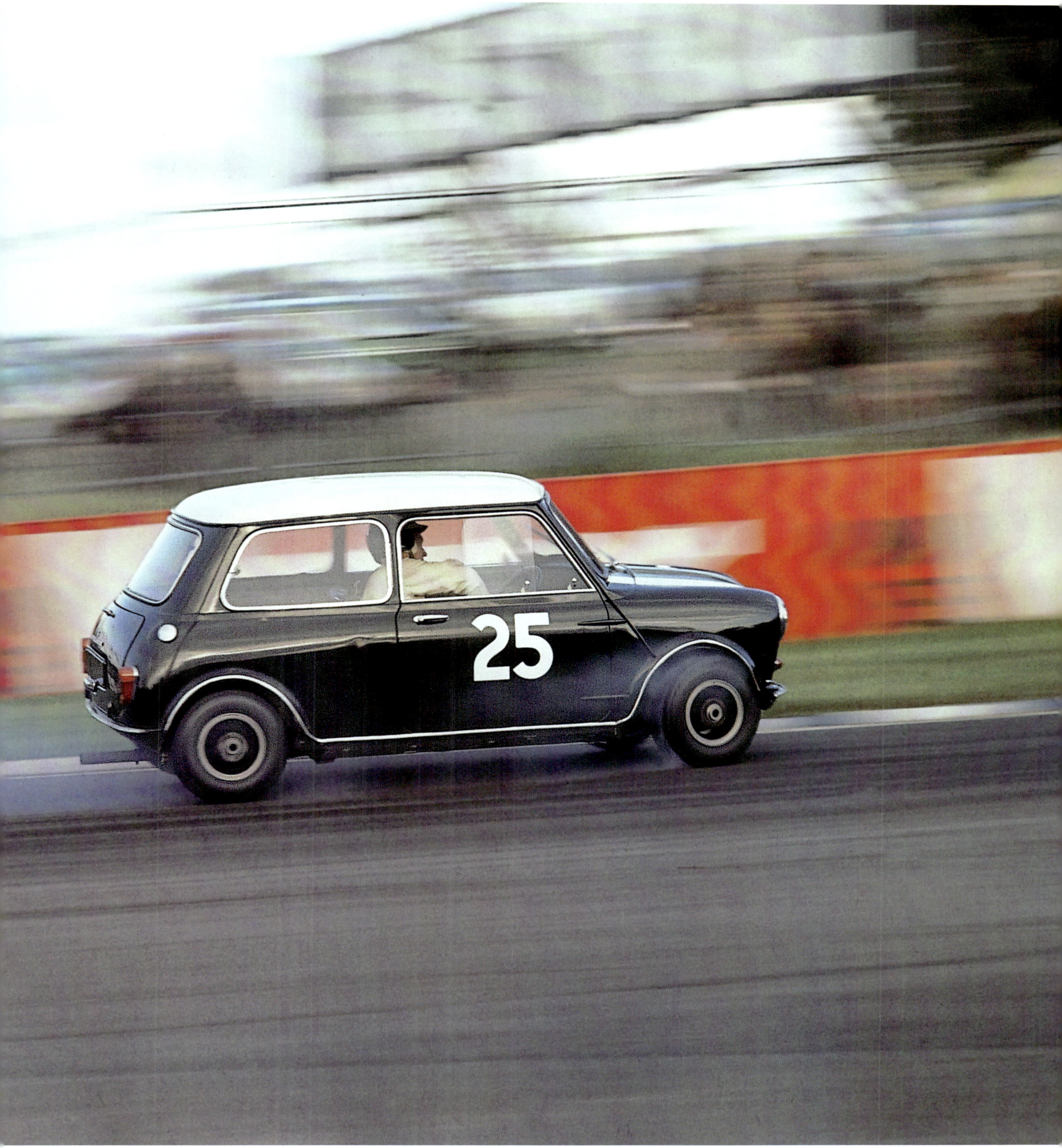
25

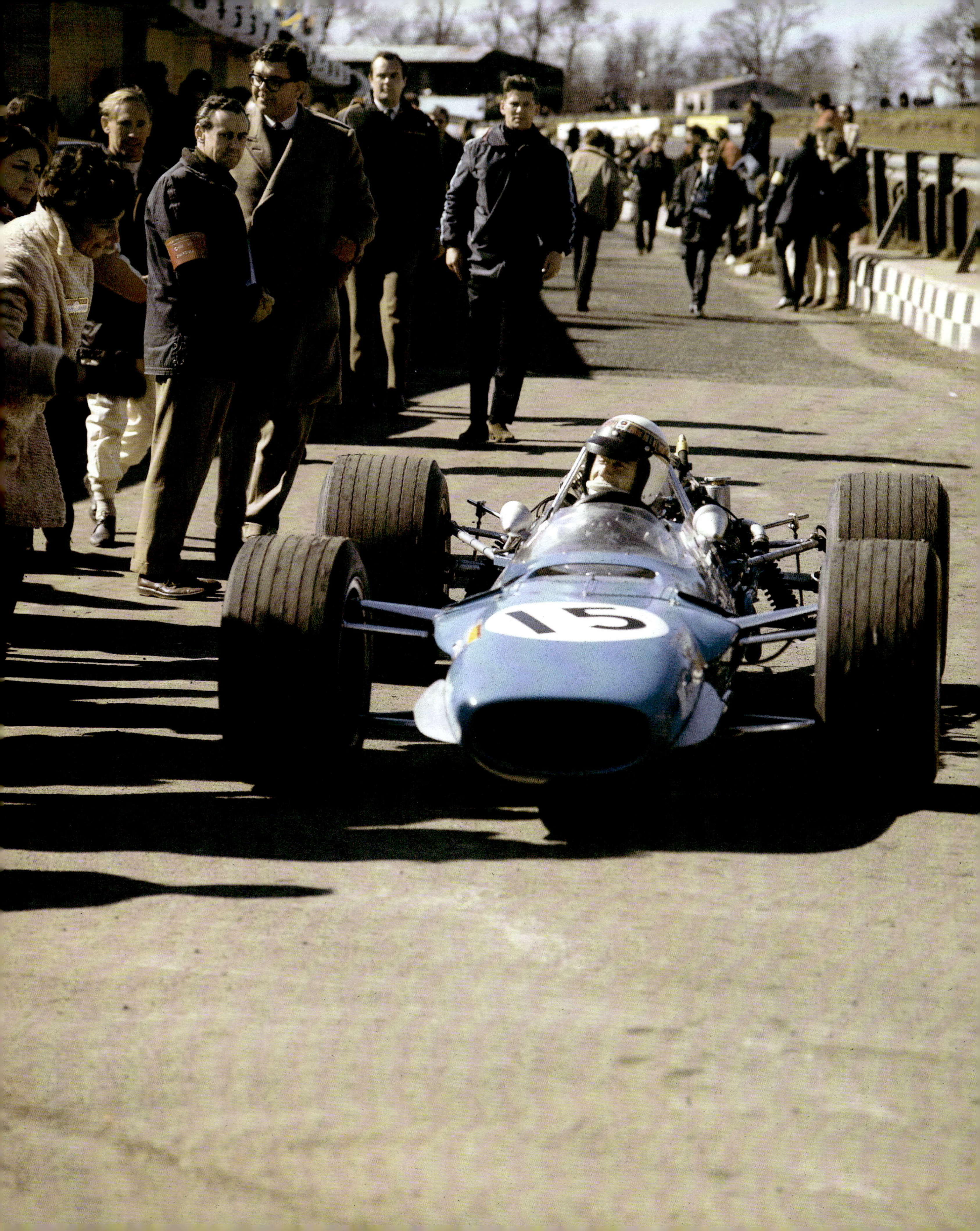
15

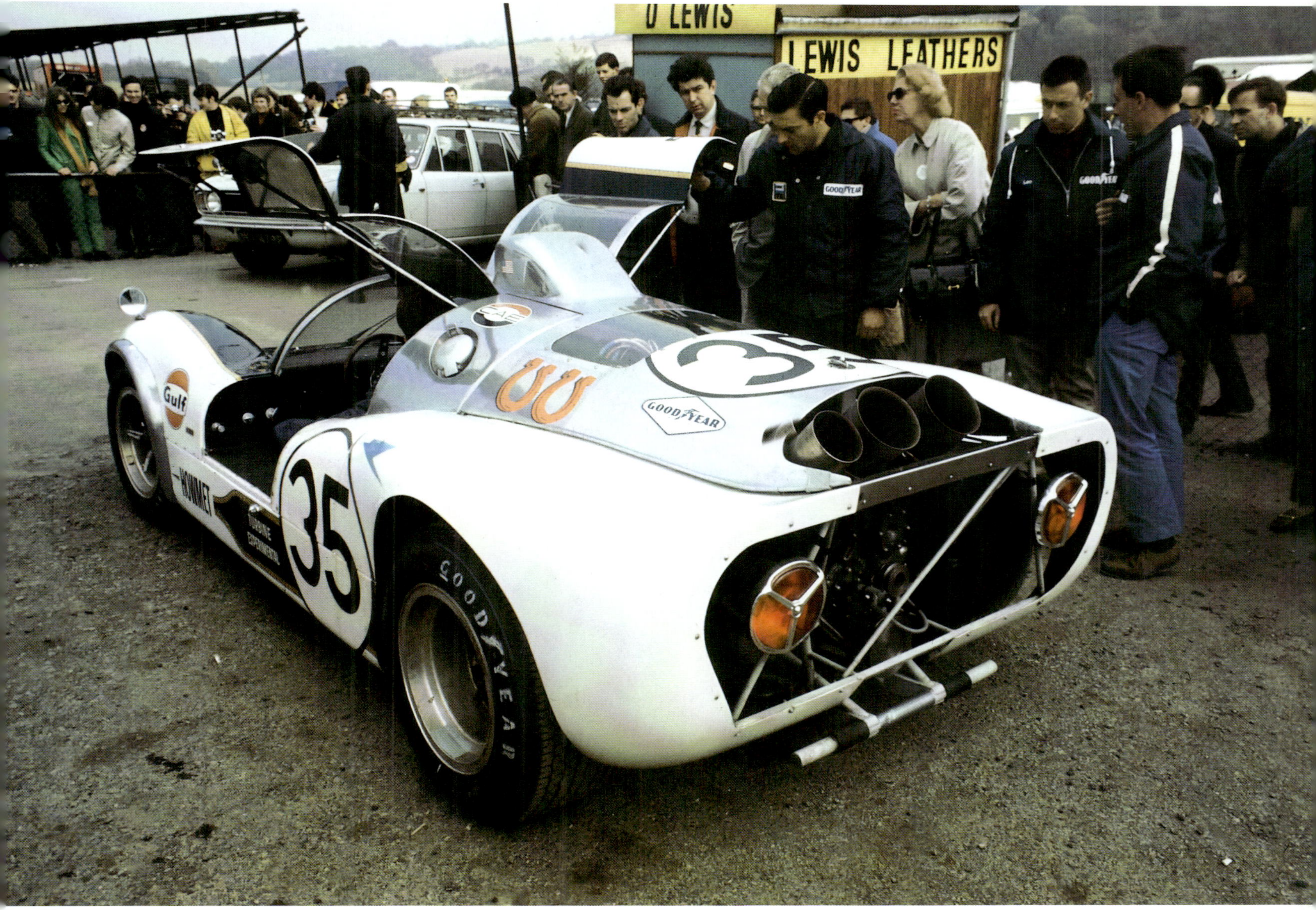

↑ The extraordinary Ray Heppenstal designed and built Howmet TX at the 1968 Brands Hatch 6 Hours. This is the entrance to the paddock, and the TX is displaying its impressive looking mortar launchers and the ubiquitous Ford Cortina Mk 1 rear lights. Note the quick lift jack bar underneath the tail. Powered by a TS325-1 turboshaft unit (originally intended for light helicopter use) that was rated as the equivalent of 2960cc, it developed 325bhp and 650lb ft of torque with a maximum limit of 57,500rpm. It was driven by experienced sports car racer and American dentist Dr Richard Thompson, who qualified it an impressive sixth, but Thompson crashed because of a jammed throttle on lap 7, denying co-driver Hugh Dibley his turn. The nearby booth advertises what was then de rigueur for 'rockers' of all ages, Lewis Leathers.

← A hastily snatched picture by Mike captures Jackie Stewart returning to the paddock after practice for the 1968 Brands Hatch Race of Champions in the Ken Tyrrell Matra-Cosworth MS10/1. He is being congratulated by Bette Hill, behind whom one can see Mike Spence with commentator Barrie Gill and, beyond, BRSCC secretary Nick Syrett in his camelhair overcoat and glasses.

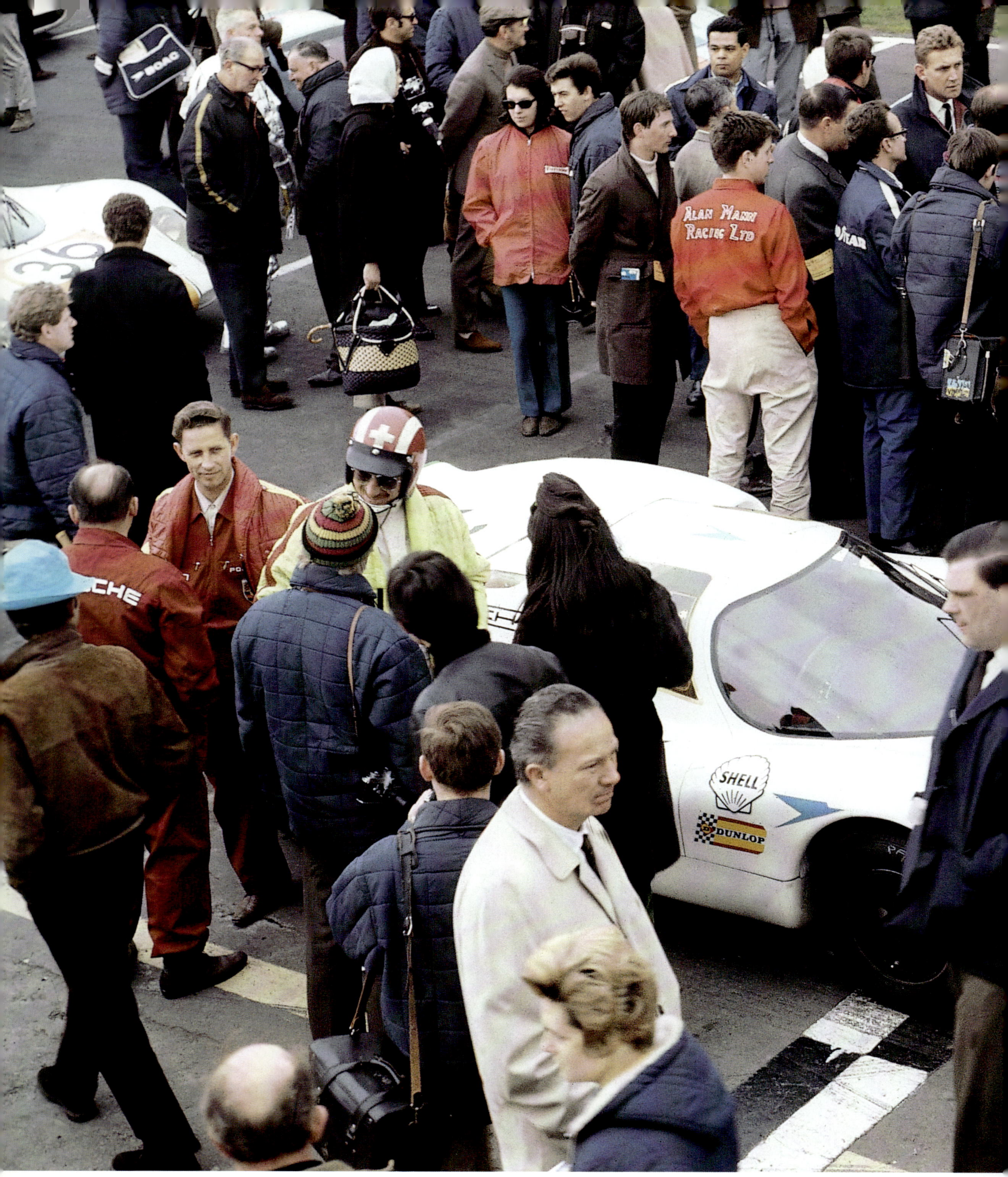
ALAN MANN
RACING LTD
SHELL
DUNLOP

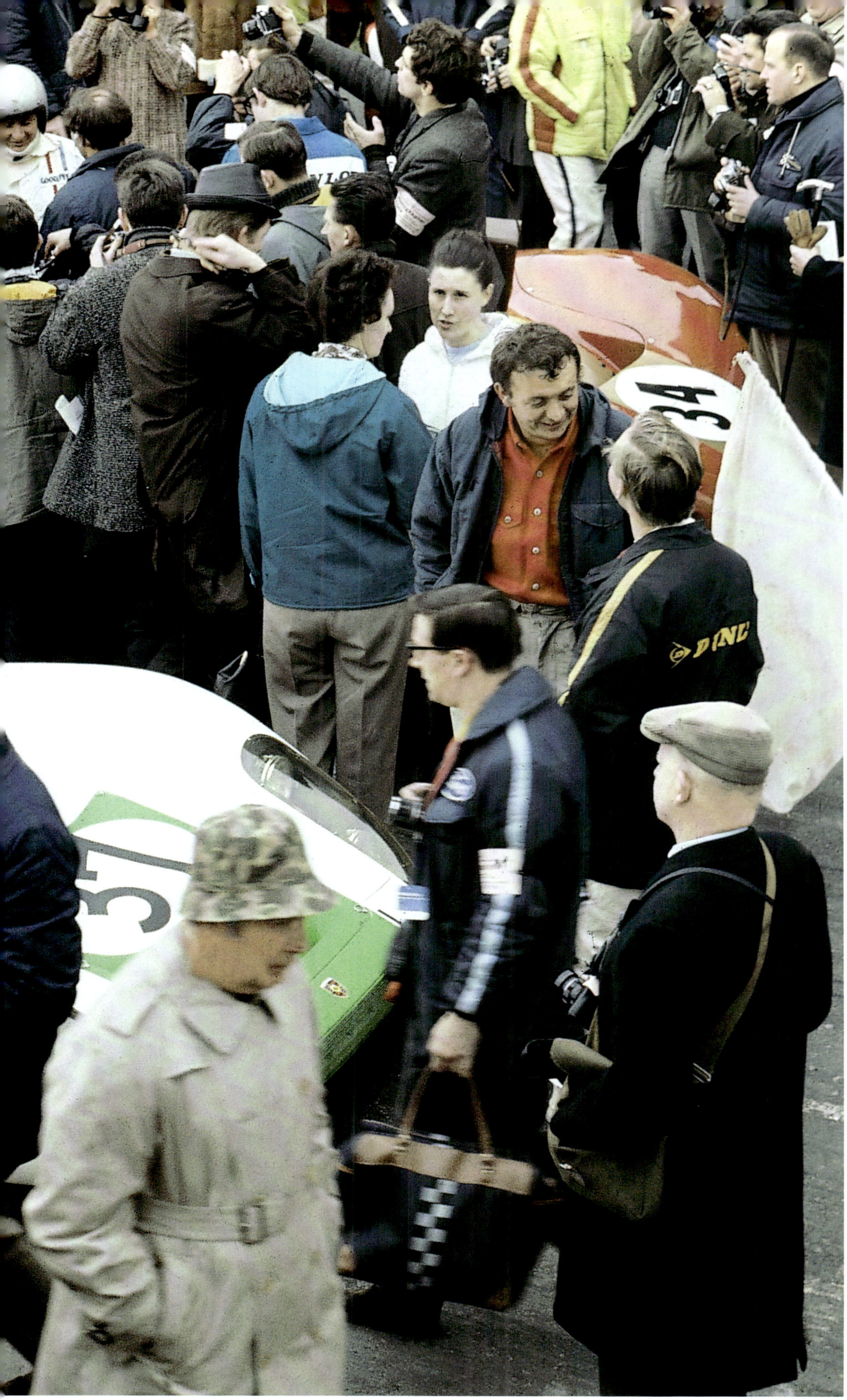

← How many people can you get on the starting grid before a major race? Answer, as many as turn up apparently, at least in those days. The front row at the Brands Hatch 6 Hours is almost buried in bodies, with Bruce McLaren, upper right, holding court having qualified the brand new Ford F3L P68 second fastest, although the car was ultimately flattering only to deceive, and retired on lap 66. Beside him is the pole position Porsche 907 (022) of Jo Siffert, who is seen talking on the left in sunglasses and Swiss national-coloured helmet, shared with Hans Hermann. The Porsche retired because of braking problems on lap 106, and the race was eventually won by the John Wyer Ford GT40 driven by Jacky Ickx/Brian Redman. This, however, was 7 April 1968, and the assembled masses will soon learn of Jim Clark's death at Hockenheim, after which the day was done.

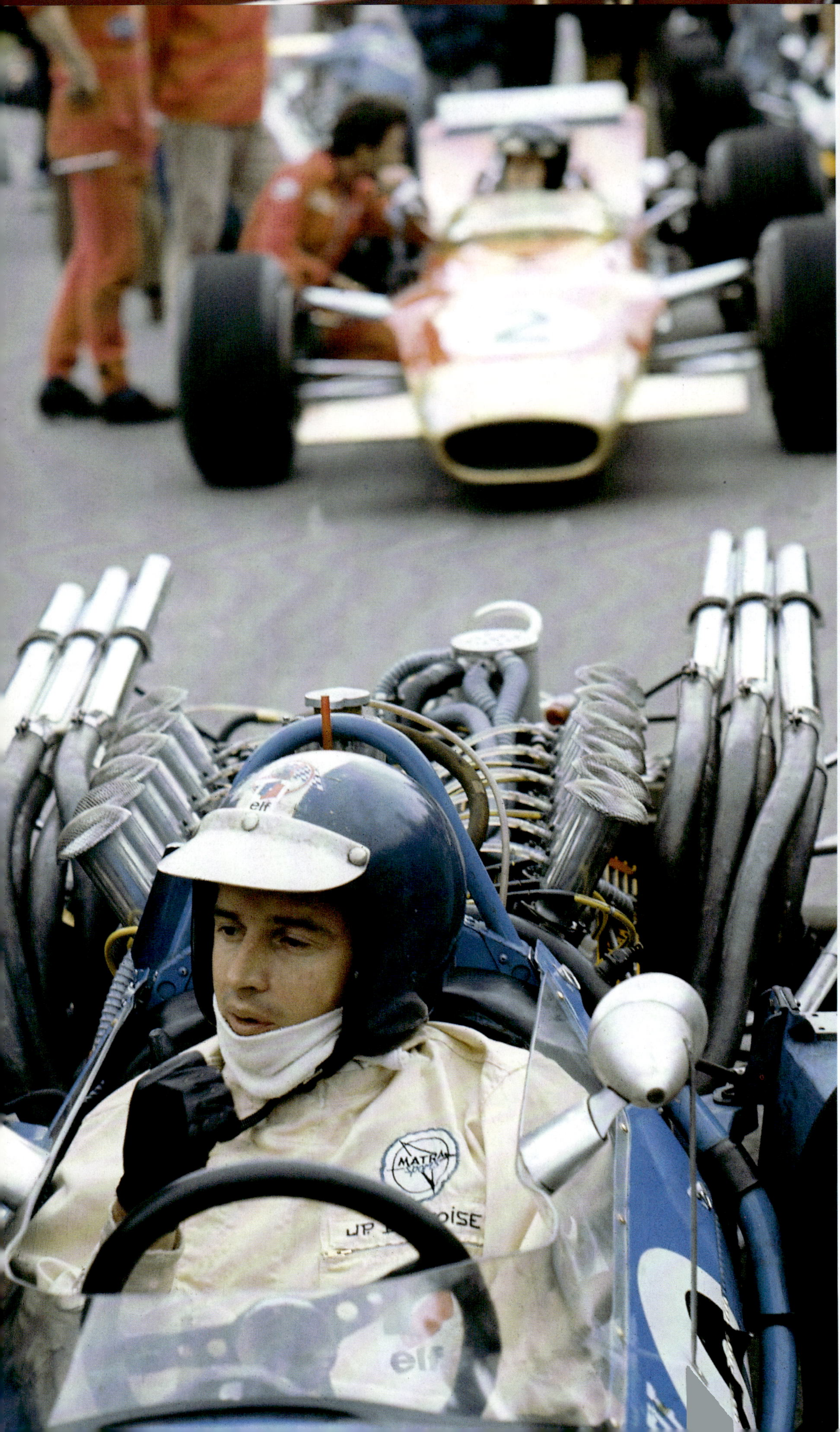
elf
MATRA
elf

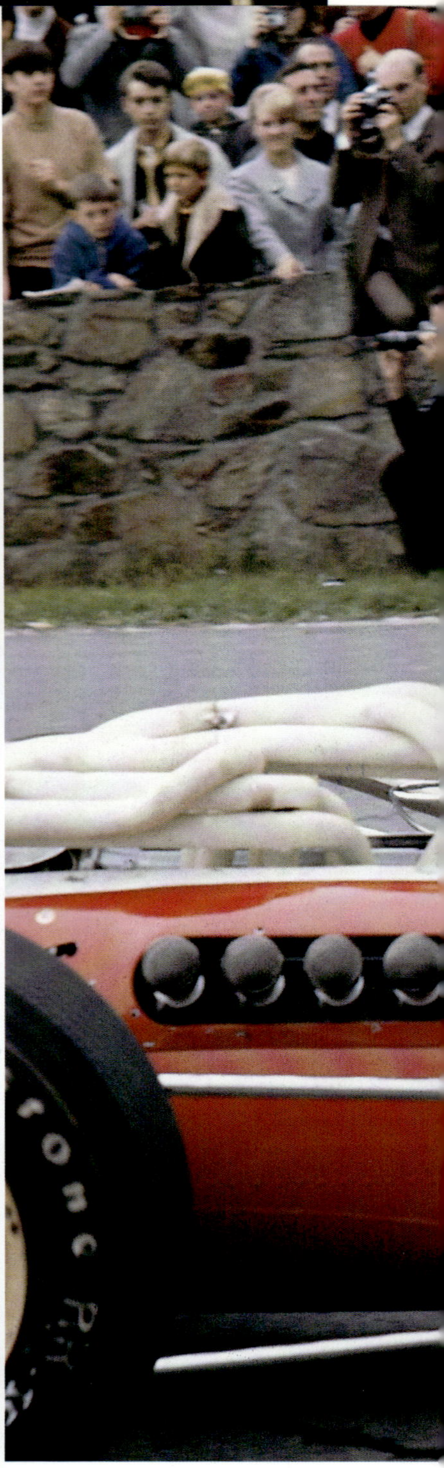

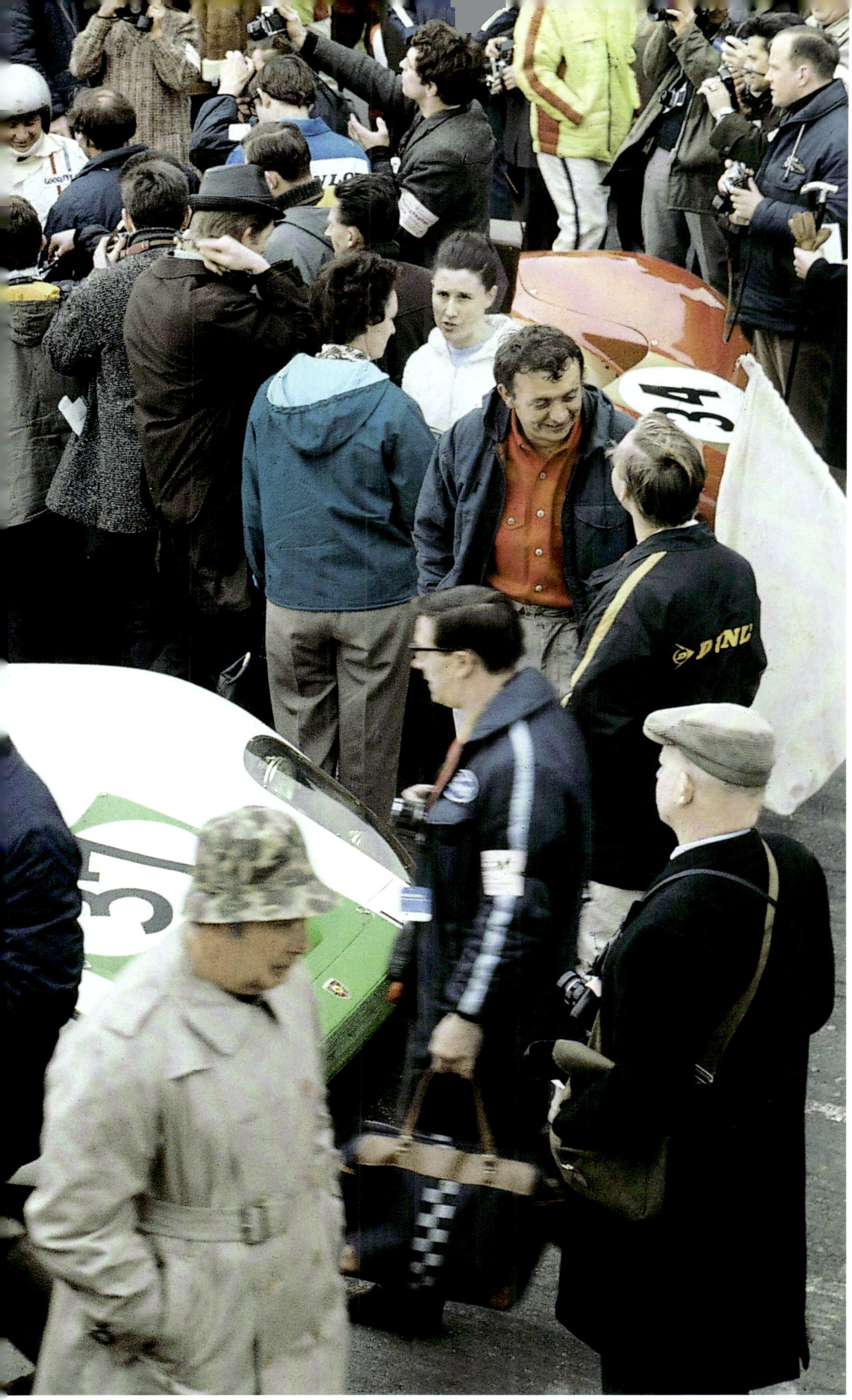

← How many people can you get on the starting grid before a major race? Answer, as many as turn up apparently, at least in those days. The front row at the Brands Hatch 6 Hours is almost buried in bodies, with Bruce McLaren, upper right, holding court having qualified the brand new Ford F3L P68 second fastest, although the car was ultimately flattering only to deceive, and retired on lap 66. Beside him is the pole position Porsche 907 (022) of Jo Siffert, who is seen talking on the left in sunglasses and Swiss national-coloured helmet, shared with Hans Hermann. The Porsche retired because of braking problems on lap 106, and the race was eventually won by the John Wyer Ford GT40 driven by Jacky Ickx/Brian Redman. This, however, was 7 April 1968, and the assembled masses will soon learn of Jim Clark's death at Hockenheim, after which the day was done.

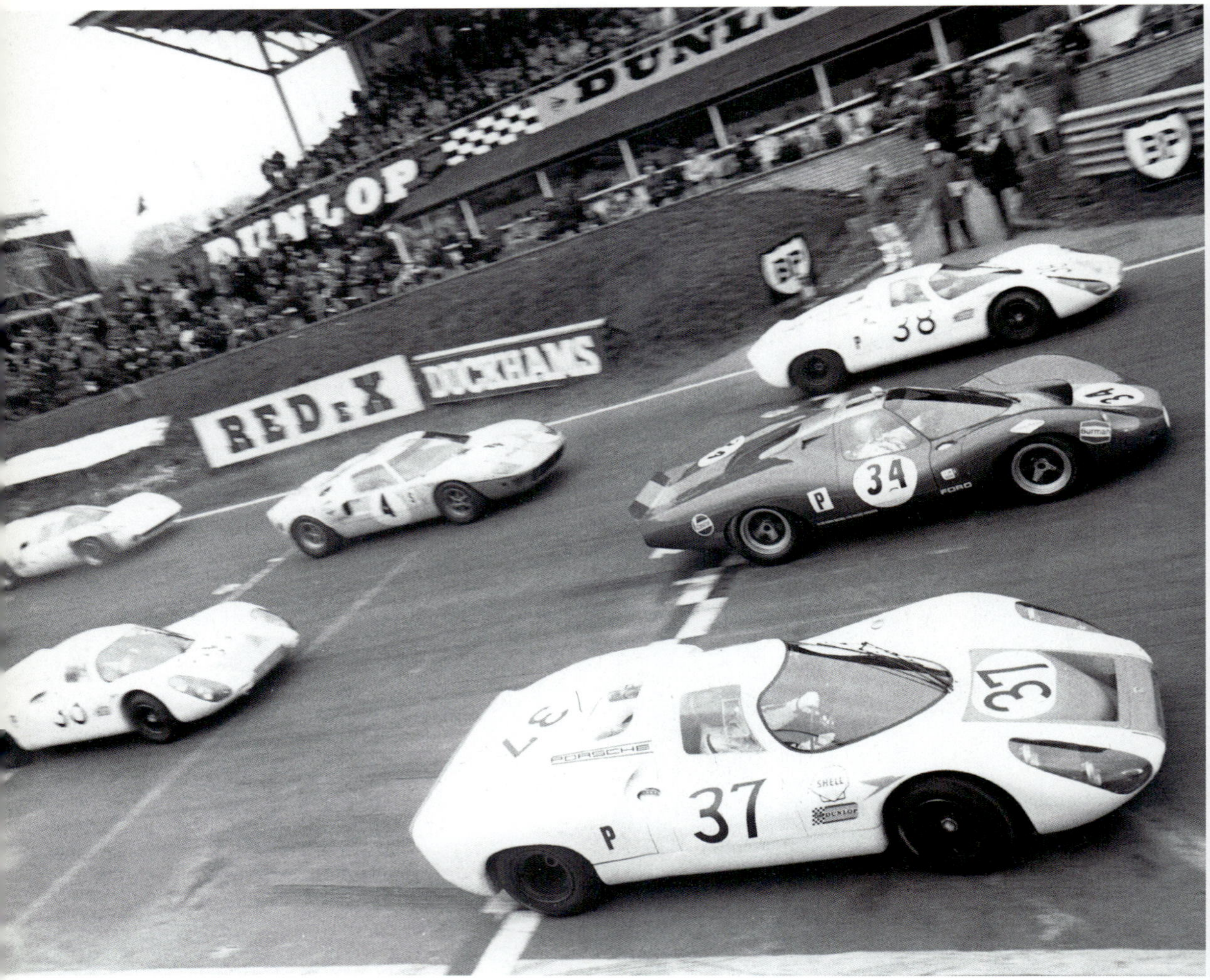

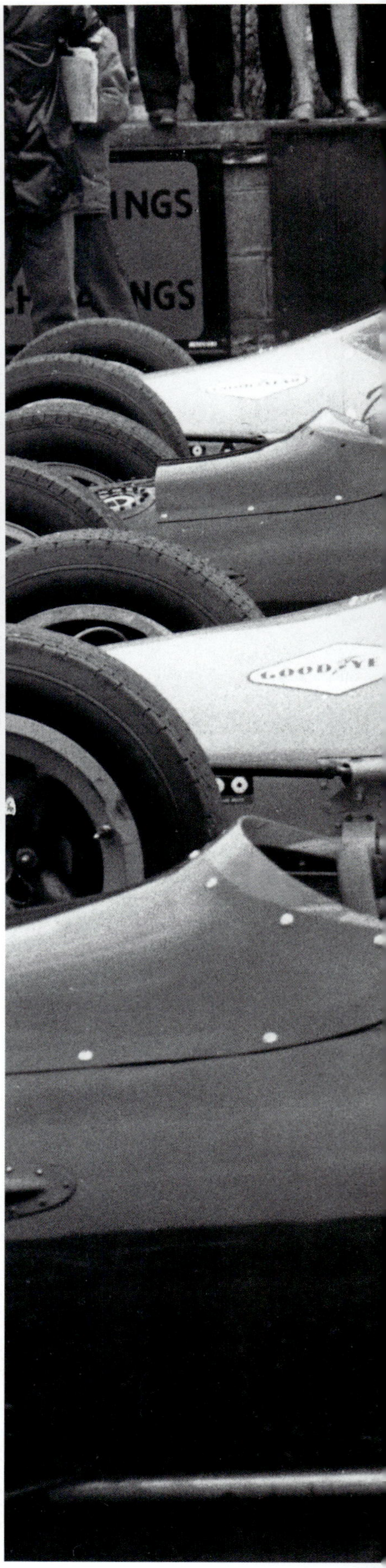

↑ The sort of shot that is no longer possible to take, like so much else these days. Jo Siffert (No. 37), his left hand at 12 o'clock on the steering wheel, applies some opposite lock as he explodes off his marks, leaving some rubber behind in the Porsche 907 (022). Alongside, Bruce McLaren is similarly engaged in the Alan Mann Ford F3L P68 (003), with the Gerhard Mitter/Ludovico Scarfiotti Porsche 907 (028) slightly lagging. Behind is the No. 4 John Wyer Ford GT40 (1075) of Jacky Ickx/Brian Redman, and the third factory Porsche 907 (027) of Vic Elford/Jochen Neerspach. The first two retired, Mitter/Scarfiotti finished second, Ickx/Redman won, and Elford/Neerspach were third.

→ Following the 1/3 debut (McLaren, Hulme) for the new McLaren M7As at the Brands Hatch ROC, the team did even better at the Silverstone International Trophy with Denny Hulme leading Bruce McLaren across the line. This is the front row, with Hulme in M7A/2 furthest from the camera, flanked by Mike Spence in the works BRM P126/03, then McLaren in M7A/1, and right next to Mike (Cooper), Pedro Rodriguez in the other BRM, this one P133/01. Note its elegant radius arm location and perfectly aligned riveting. This was Mike Spence's last race. He was later killed in an Indianapolis testing accident. After hitting the wall, the right front wheel broke loose and struck him a fatal blow on the head. 1968 was a dreadful year for fatalities, and at Indianapolis Spence had been driving the Lotus meant for Jim Clark, who had died at Hockenheim on 7 April.

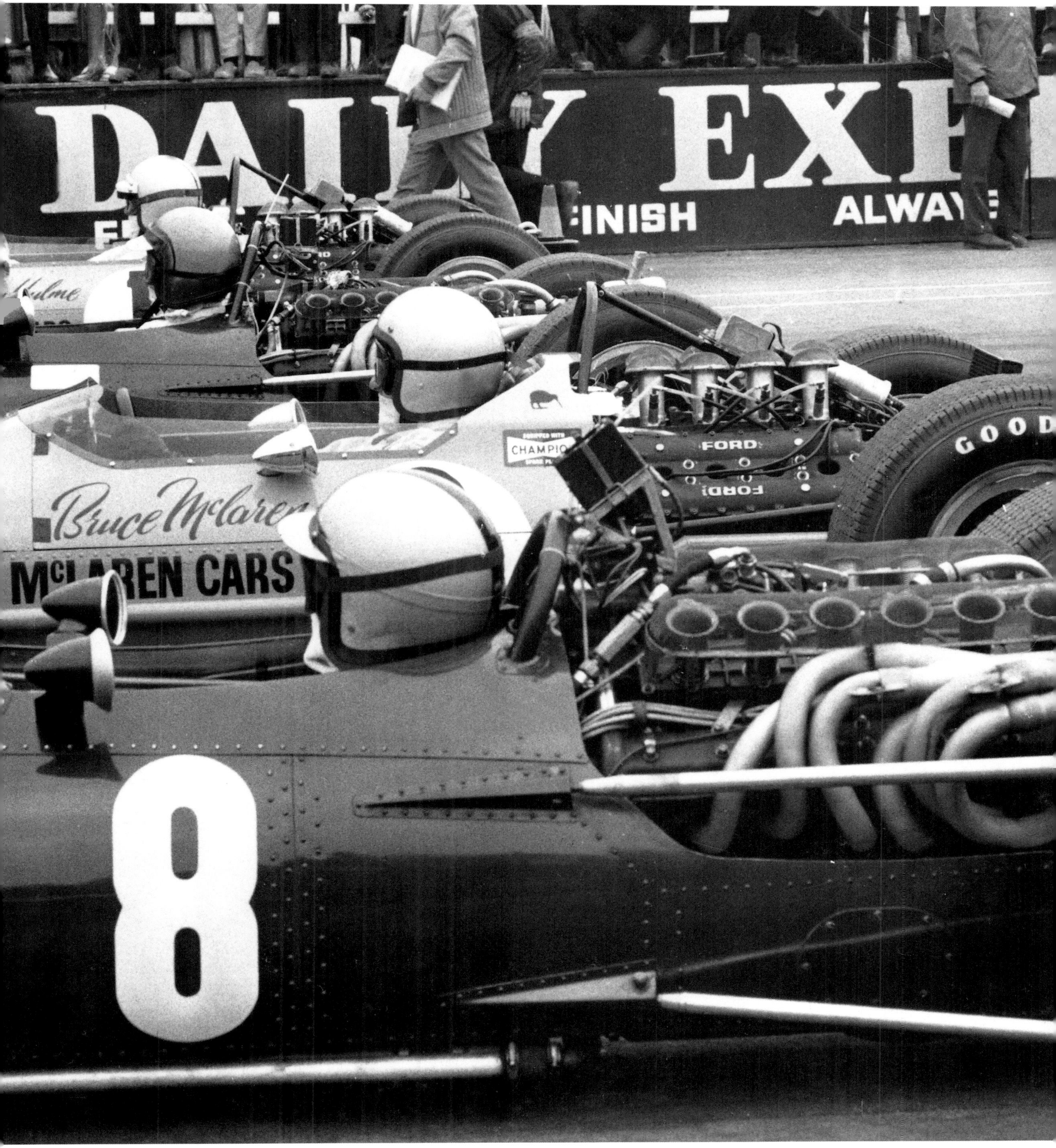
FINISH
FORD
McLAREN CARS
8

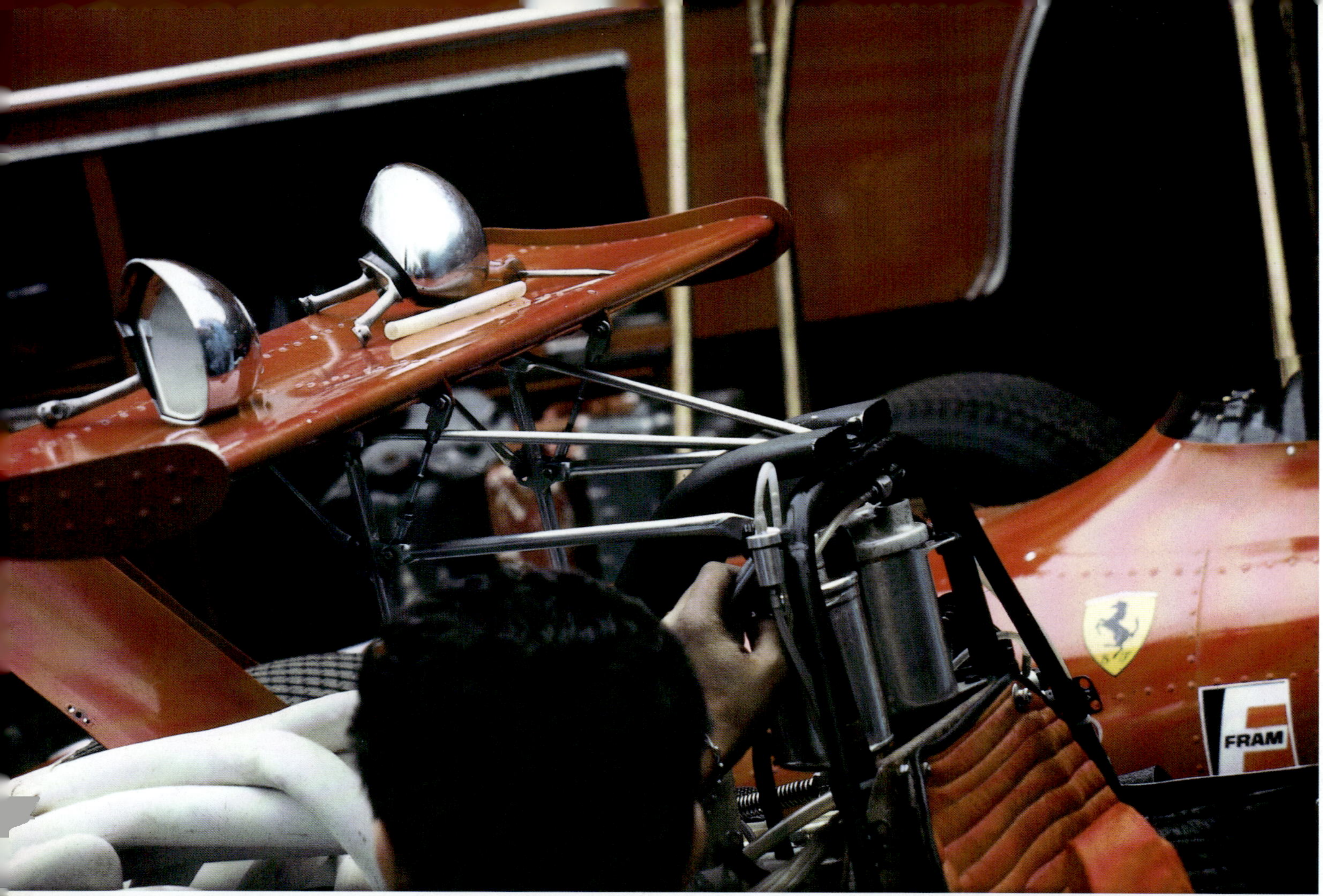
FRAM

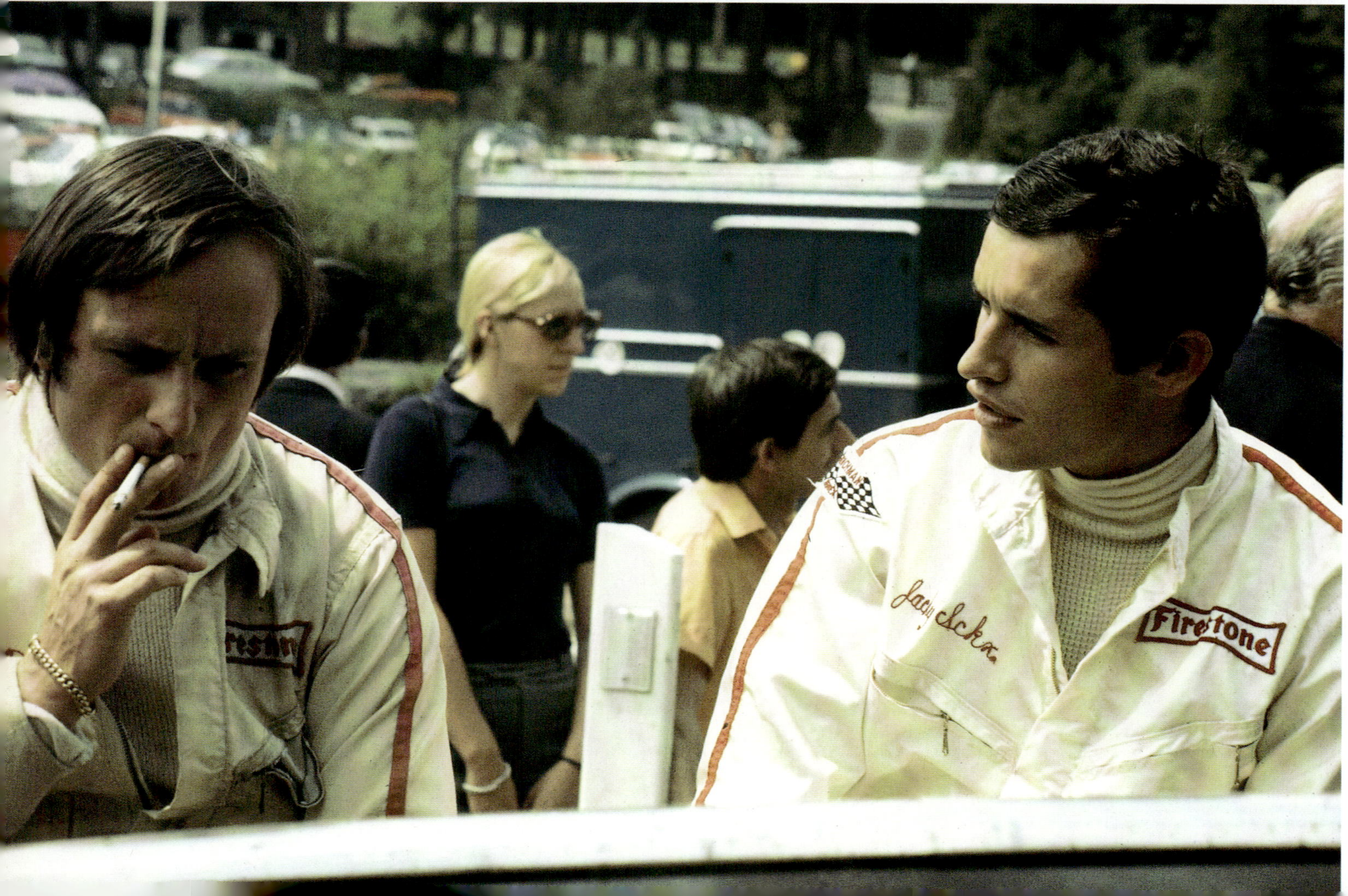
Firestone

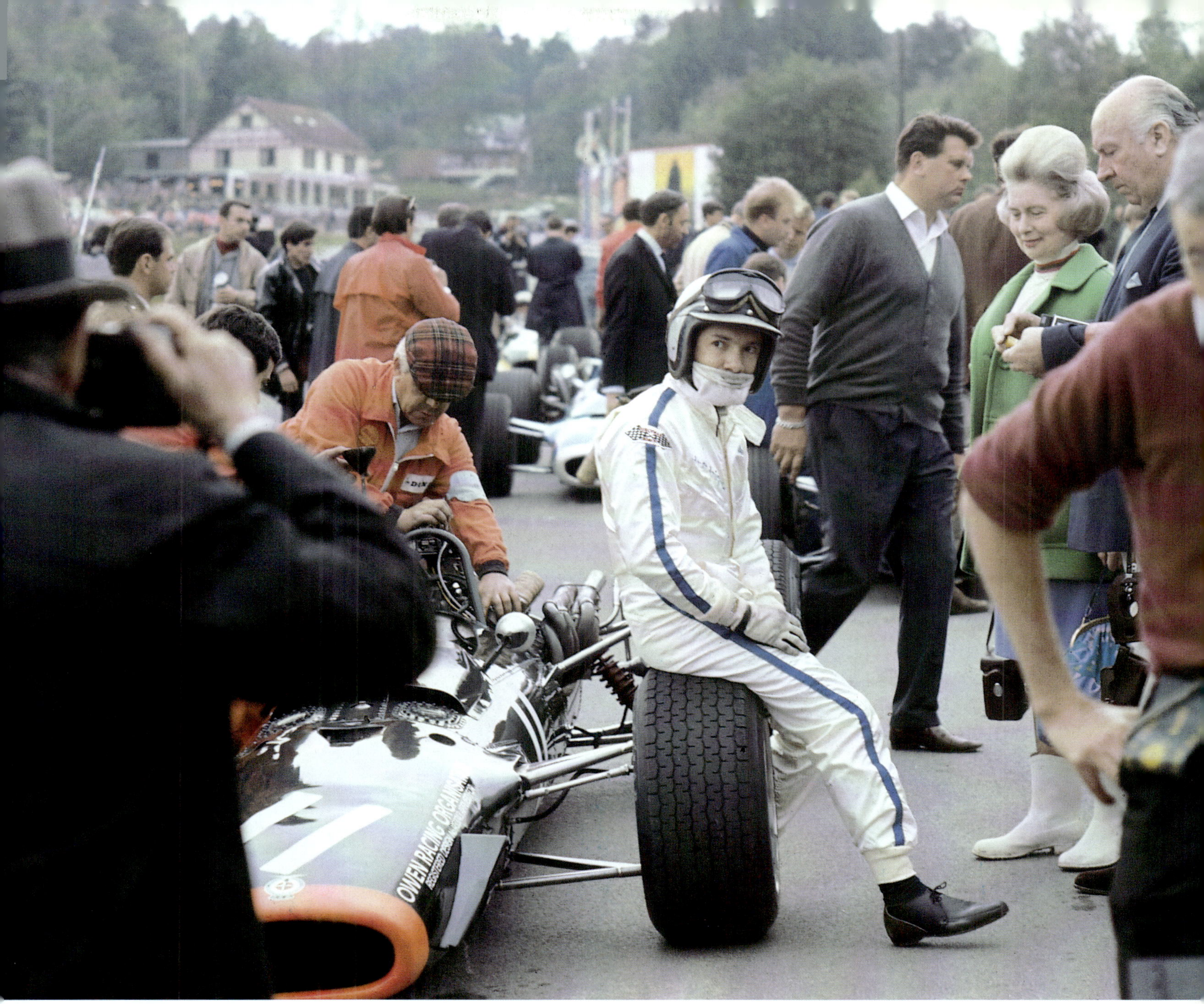

↑ Mike could be quite aggressive when occasion demanded, and was never best pleased by the sudden and unpredictable appearance of the 'I don't care whose shot I'm spoiling' brigade. Fortunately, trilby hat has not blocked Mike's view of an obviously tense Pedro Rodriguez, in his American Hinchman driving suit, sitting on the front wheel (what was it about Mike and front wheels I wonder) of his BRM P133 (01) on the grid of the 1968 Belgian GP. Willy Southcott, in tartan cap, attends to last-minute details whilst, behind, Tim Parnell strides by in cardigan as Jean (look at those white bootettes) and Louis Stanley look on. A blurred Teddy Mayer (right) considers something, possibly Bruce McLaren's M7A that went on to win an eventful race ahead of Pedro. This, of course, is the grid in its original position on the hill leading down to Eau Rouge.

↖ Ferrari was the first team to use a recognisable, functioning aerofoil (or wing, if you prefer) in F1 at the 1968 Belgian GP. Ing. Forghieri's device was mounted high, almost above the rear wheels, improving stability and generating more heat in the rear tyres. Note the period chromed plastic mirrors sitting on the 'wing', a very popular accessory of the period for all boy racers.

← Must you do that Chris? Jacky Ickx in teenage prodigy mode obviously disapproves of Amon's Rothmans habit in the Spa paddock.

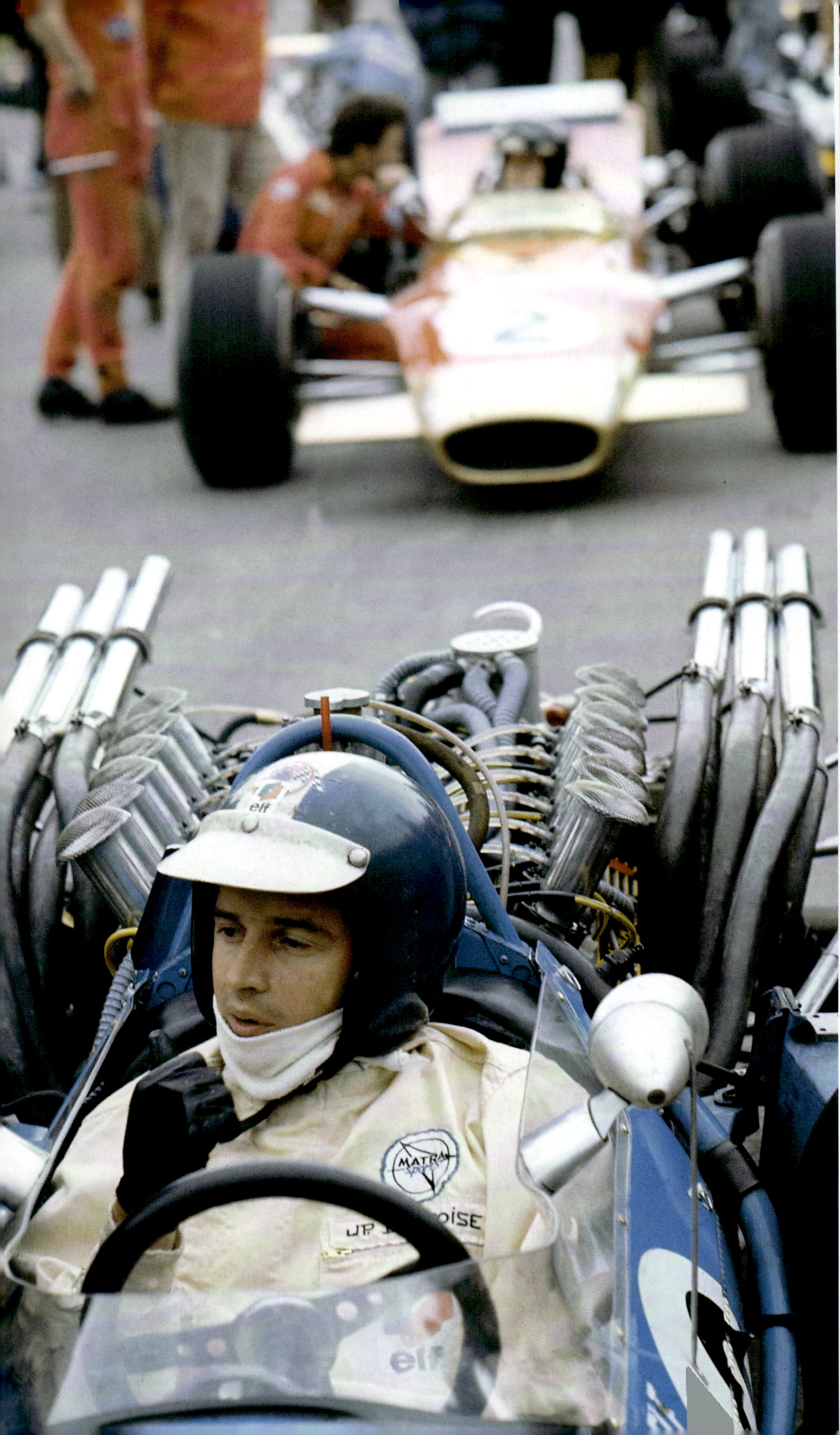
elf
MATRA
elf

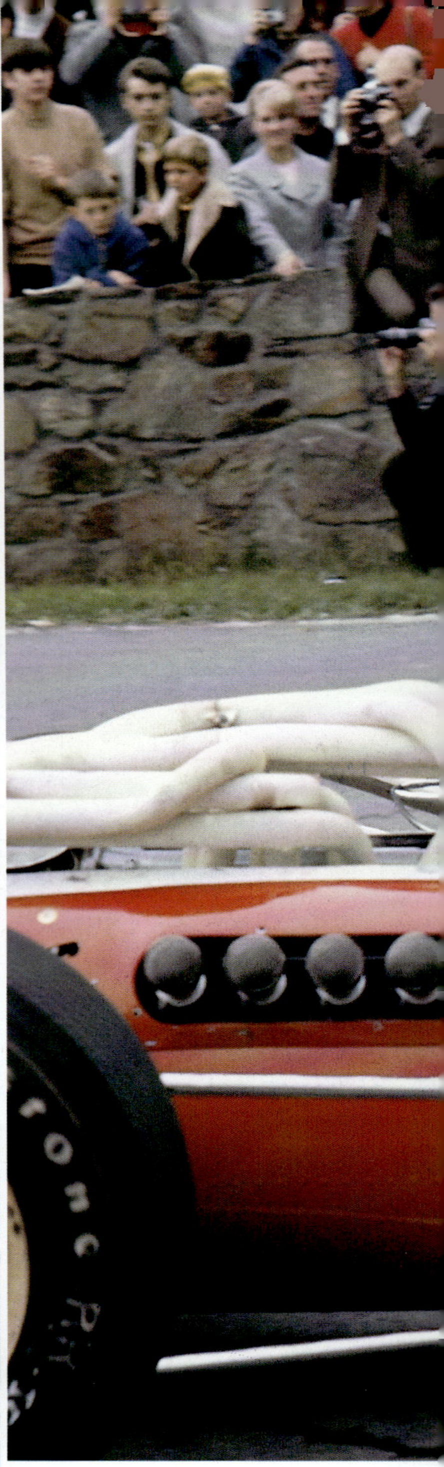

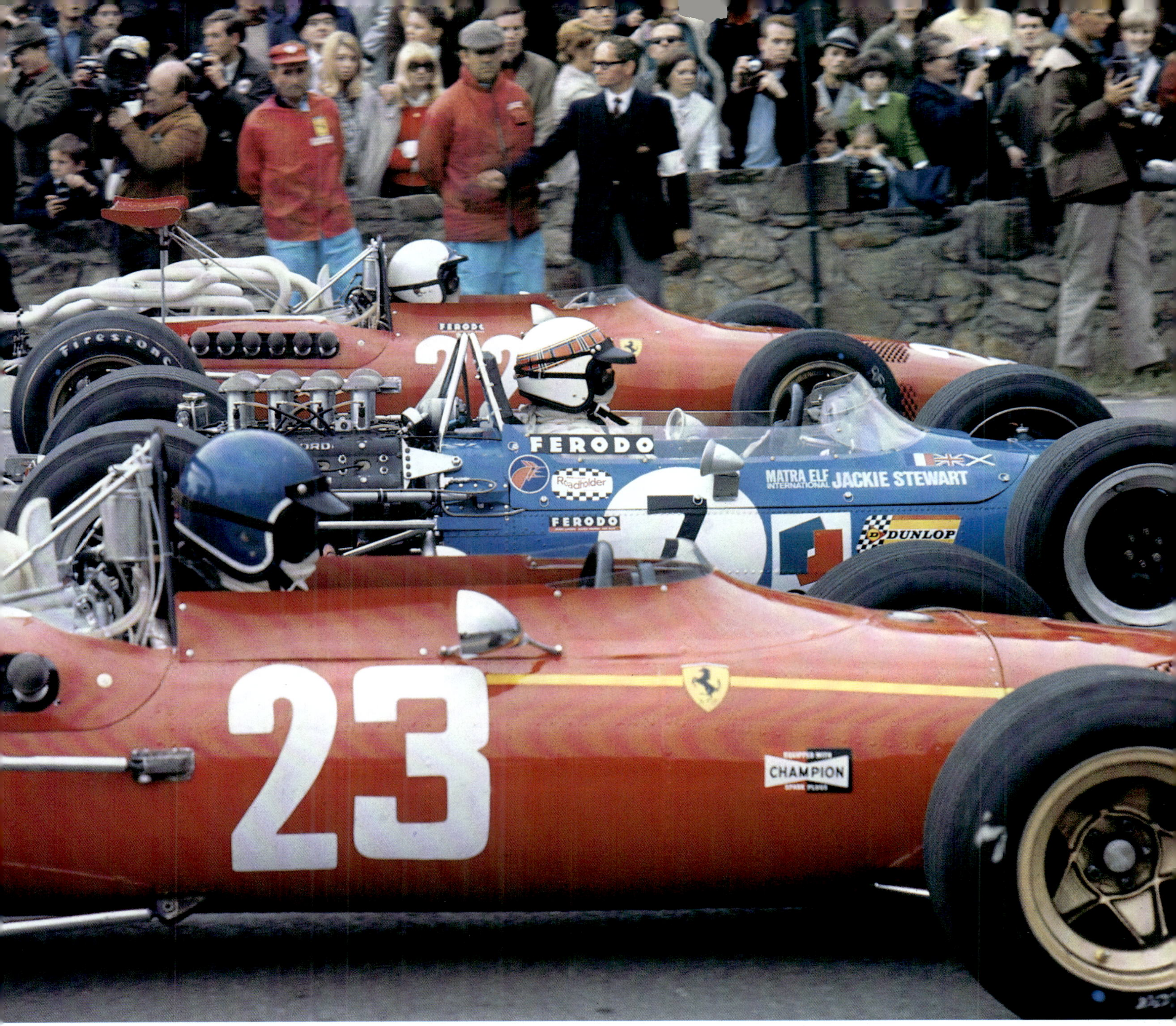

↑ Jacky Ickx, Ferrari 312 (003), Jackie Stewart, Matra-Cosworth MS10/1, and Chris Amon, Ferrari 312 (007) with Forghieri's inchoate aerofoil in profile, at Spa-Francorchamps on 9 June 1968. Amon is on pole by nearly four seconds from Stewart, with Ickx a further two seconds slower. However, Saturday's practice was conducted in a typical Ardennes downpour, so grid positions were not entirely representative. Stewart's time is especially meritorious as he is driving with his right wrist in a plastic support cast following his F2 crash at Madrid earlier in the season. Amon retired with a holed oil radiator after contesting the lead with Surtees (Honda), Stewart led after battling with Hulme's McLaren, but ultimately ended fourth after a delayed stop for more fuel, and Ickx was slowed by a misfiring car, but still finished third.

← Not so much like a racing car engine but more like some kind of huge *Mad Max* multi-barrelled Gatling gun. An unconcerned Jean-Pierre Beltoise, displaying admirable Gallic indifference, sits directly in front of the loudest noise known to man, the Matra V12 in MS11/1. Behind is Jackie Oliver in the second Gold Leaf Team Lotus 49B (R6). Jean-Pierre will finish eighth, three laps adrift after a fuel stop, and Oliver fifth, also stopping for extra fuel (a not unknown phenomenon at Spa) and despite breaking a drive shaft two laps from the finish.

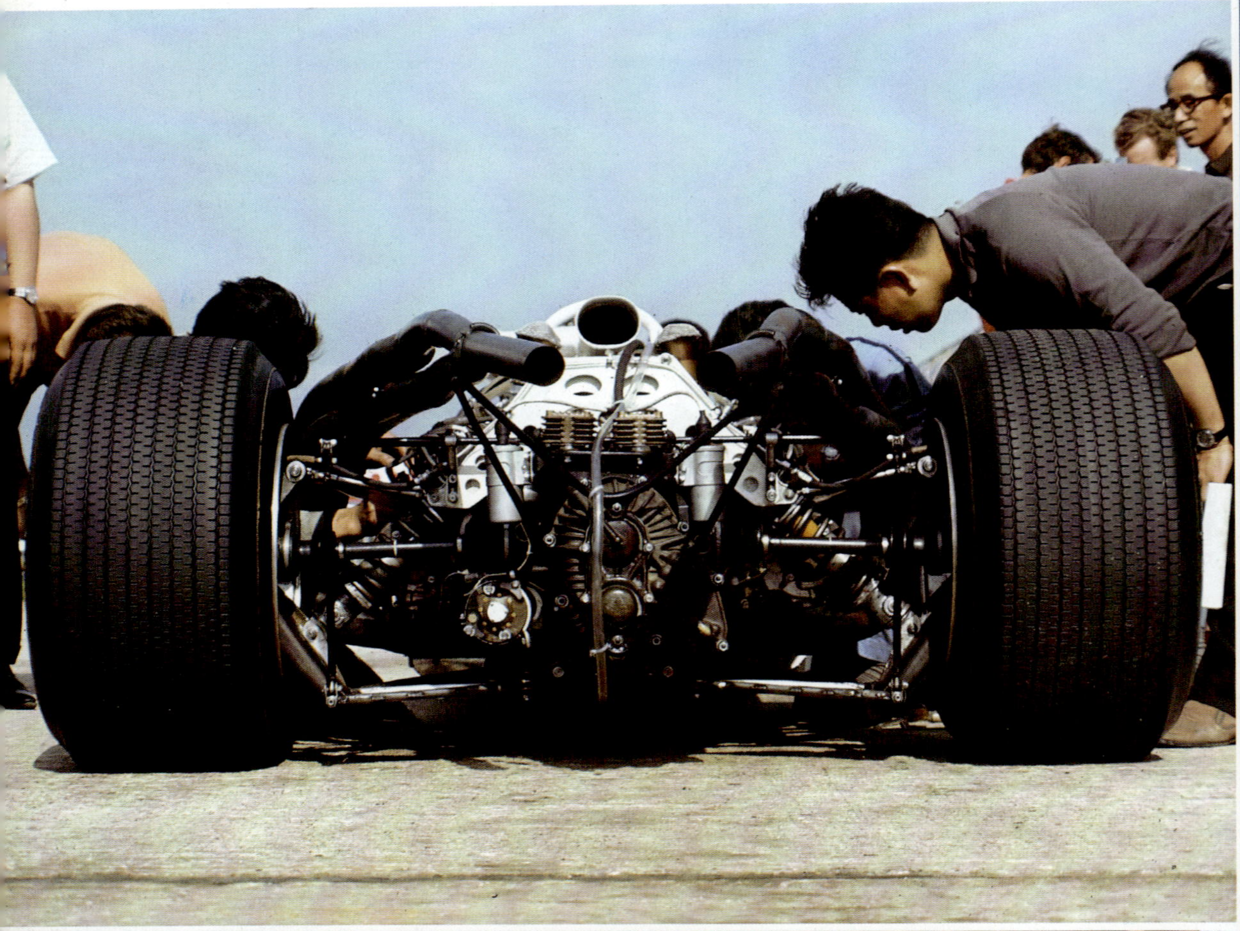

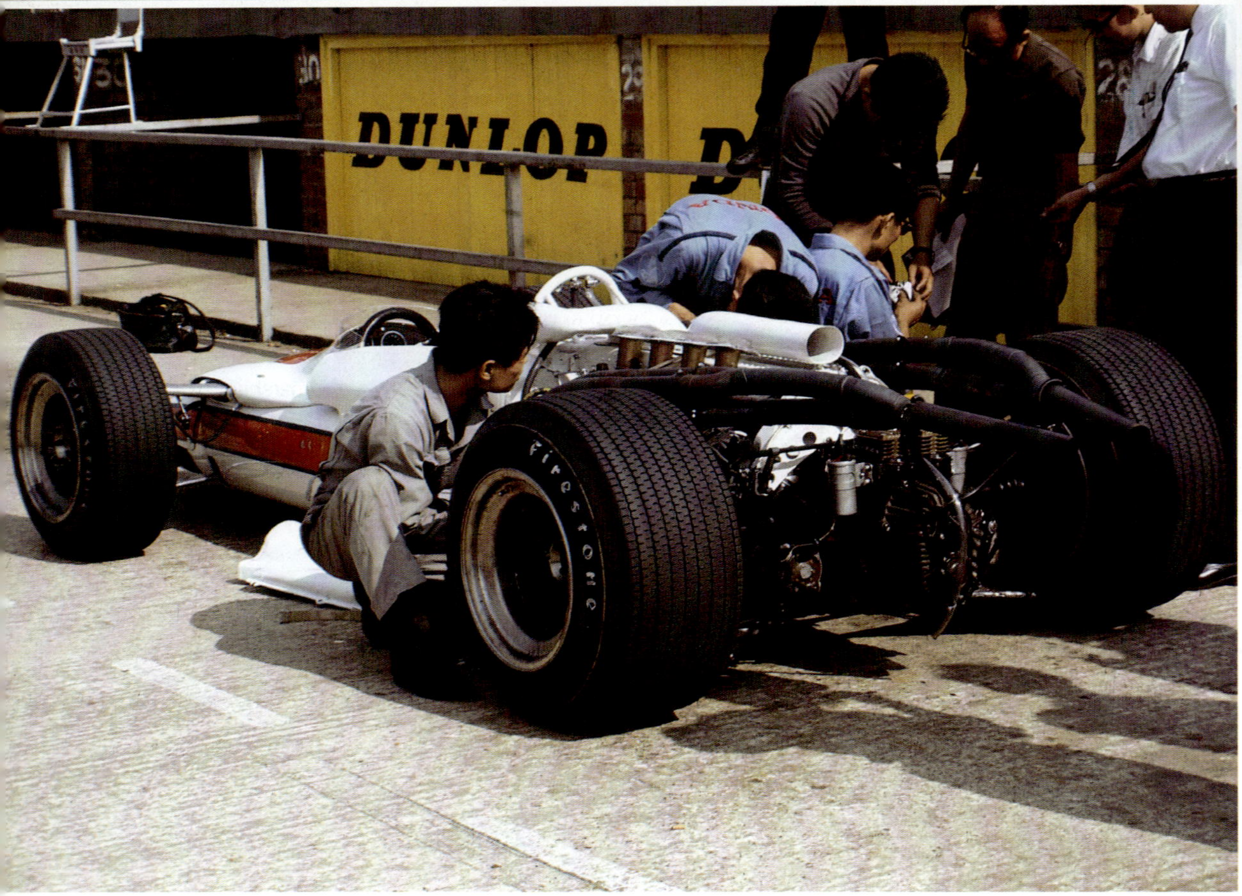
DUNLOP
Firestone

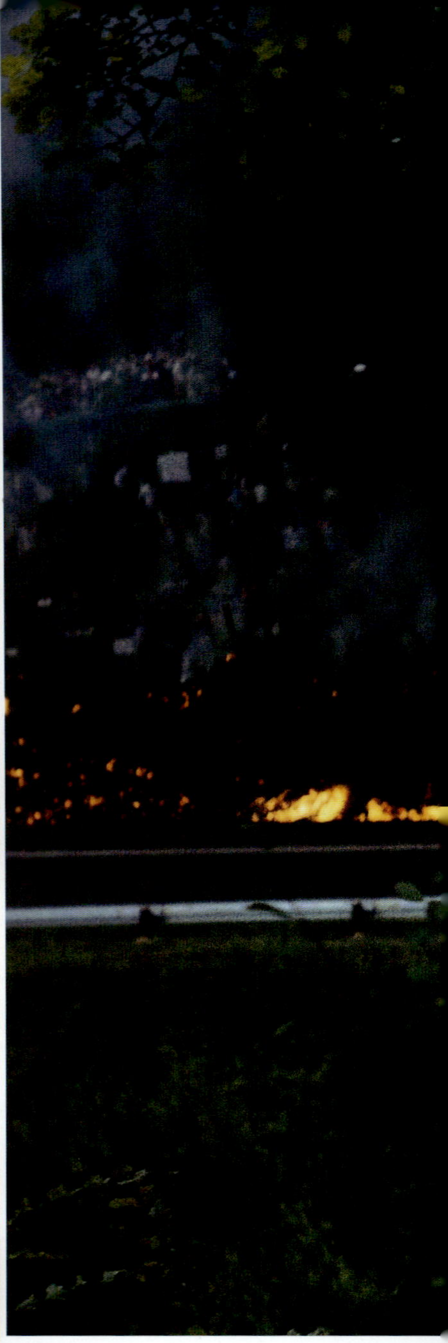

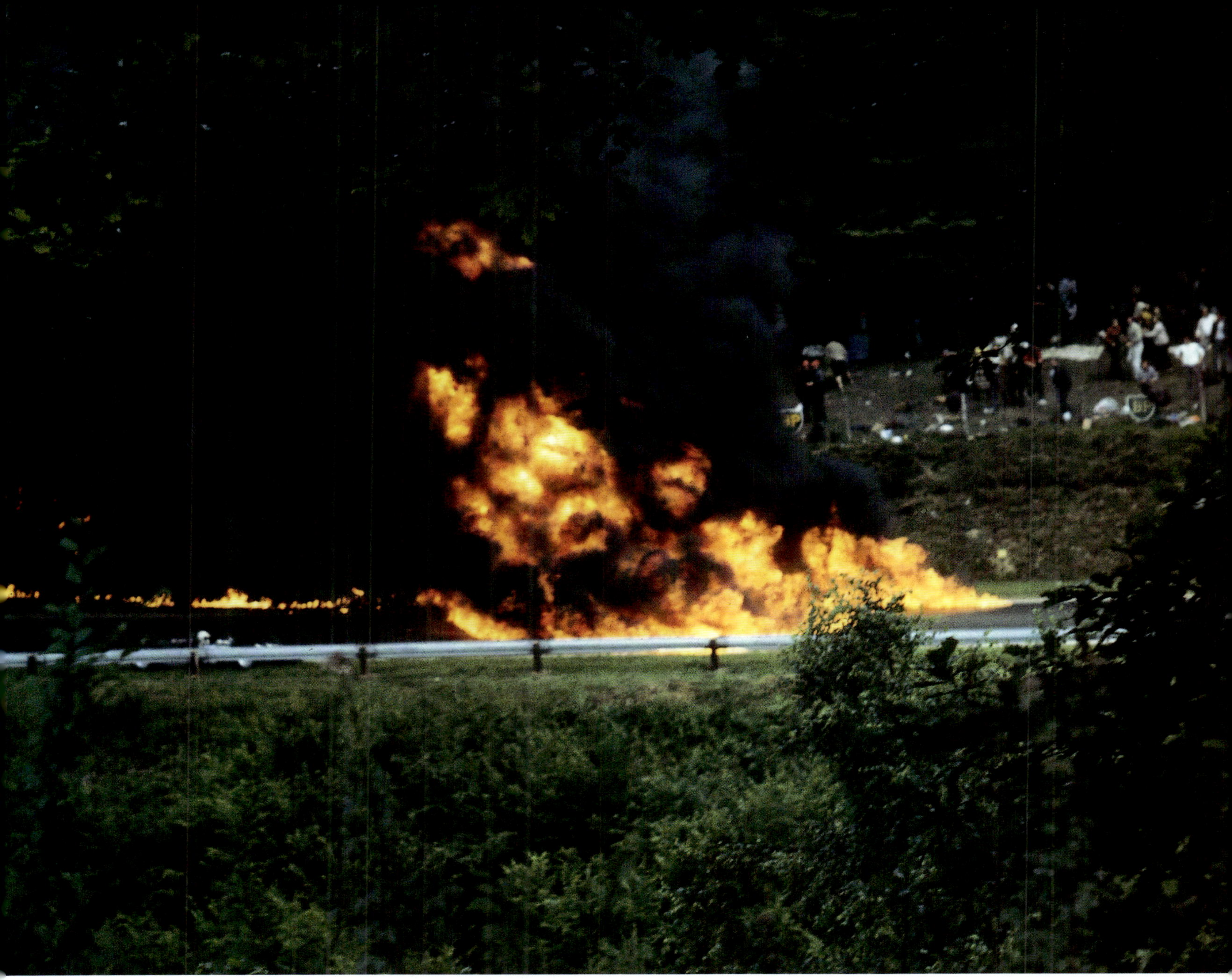

↑ Jo Schlesser started from the back row of the wet French GP at Rouen-les-Essarts and crashed on lap 3. The wretched machine, carrying 40 gallons of fuel, turned over and caught fire with sports car ace Schlesser trapped underneath. It burnt for 20 minutes and, without any chemical fire extinguishers, the marshals apparently attempted to douse the magnesium inferno with water, which of course made it worse and spread the flames right across the track. You can just make out Vic Elford's Cooper-BRM T86B taking to the opposite grass verge to avoid it, and afterwards there was just a pile of ashes and debris left, plus the remains of poor Schlesser. Surtees went on to finish second in the conventional RA301.

↖ The largely magnesium air-cooled (it had no radiator) V8 Honda RA302 was a secret until it suddenly appeared at John Surtees' Slough premises without warning and was subsequently tested at Silverstone. However, it had several serious problems and it was agreed that there was no point in taking it to the French GP. Nevertheless, without anybody's knowledge, the car was removed overnight from the Slough base by representatives of Honda France, and it reappeared at Rouen for French sports car ace Jo Schlesser to drive, with tragic consequences. Additionally this radical new car detracted from the development of the existing R301, and ultimately Honda's F1 programme ceased at the end of 1968.

← Another view, in the Silverstone pits, of the ill-fated Honda RA302, which was claimed to develop 380bhp at 10,500rpm.

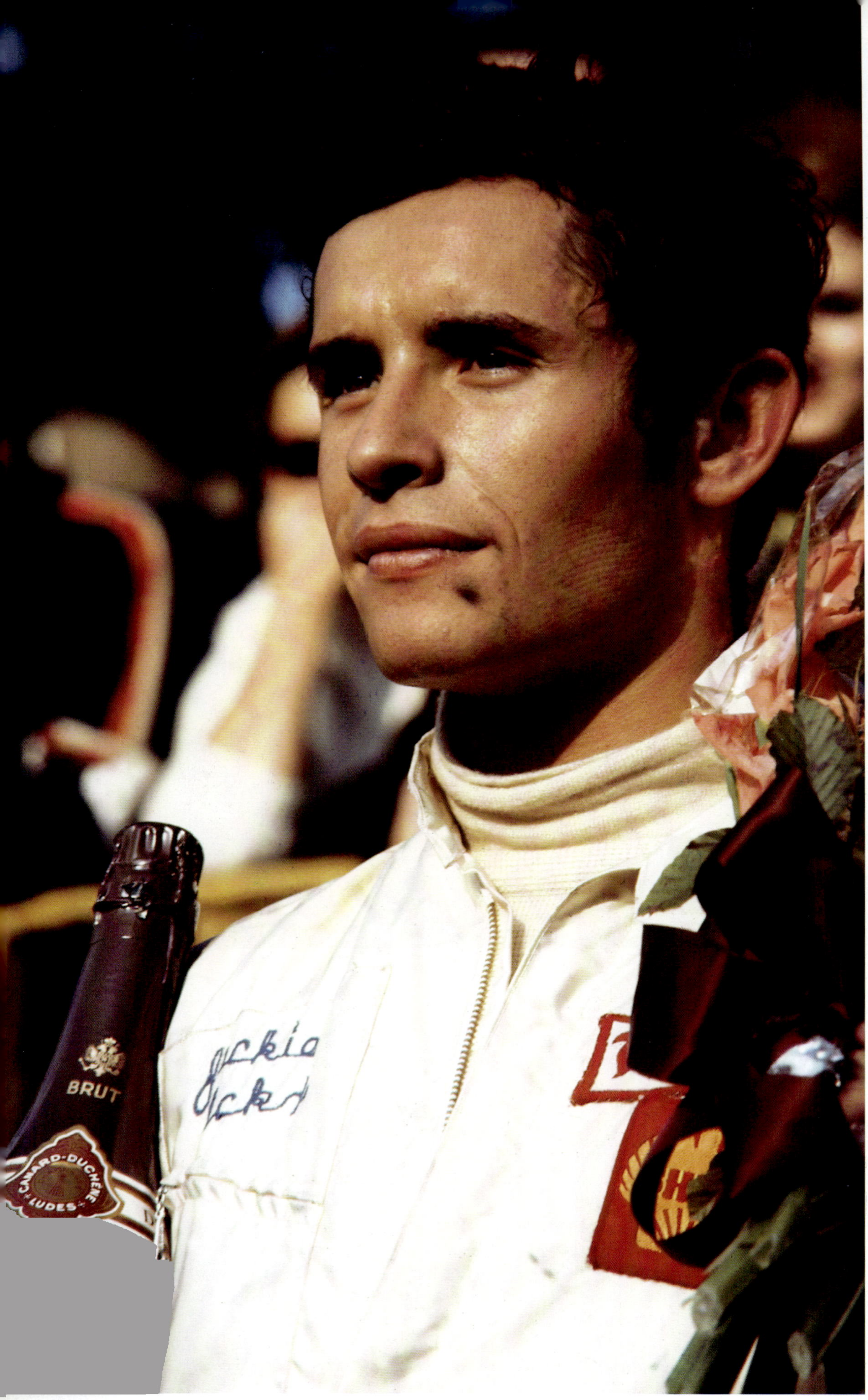

← A thoughtful Jacky Ickx after his first GP victory, at Rouen. His F1 career netted 8 Championship victories, 13 pole positions, and 14 fastest race laps from 116 starts. He drove for Ferrari (1968 and 1970–3), Brabham (1969), once for Yardley McLaren (1973 German GP), Frank Williams Racing (1973, 1976), John Player Team Lotus (1974–5), Walter Wolf Racing (1976), Ensign and Team Tissot Ensign (1976–8), and Ligier Gitanes in 1979. Six of his GP victories came with Ferrari, and the remaining two at Brabham between this race and the 1972 German GP.

→ Not much to smile about here, as Tim Parnell and Piers Courage consider their prospects at the 1968 British GP, Brands Hatch. 16th on the grid, then overheating and several pit stops for eighth place with the Parnell Racing BRM P126 was the answer.

→ A job well done, as a deservedly pleased Jo Siffert savours his 1968 British GP victory at Brands Hatch for Rob Walker in the team's Lotus 49B after a race of constant pressure from Chris Amon's Ferrari 312. Barrie Gill, commentator, broadcaster, and later one of the pioneers of professional sports sponsorship in the UK, shares 'Seppi's' triumph. Gill died in January 2003 aged 68.

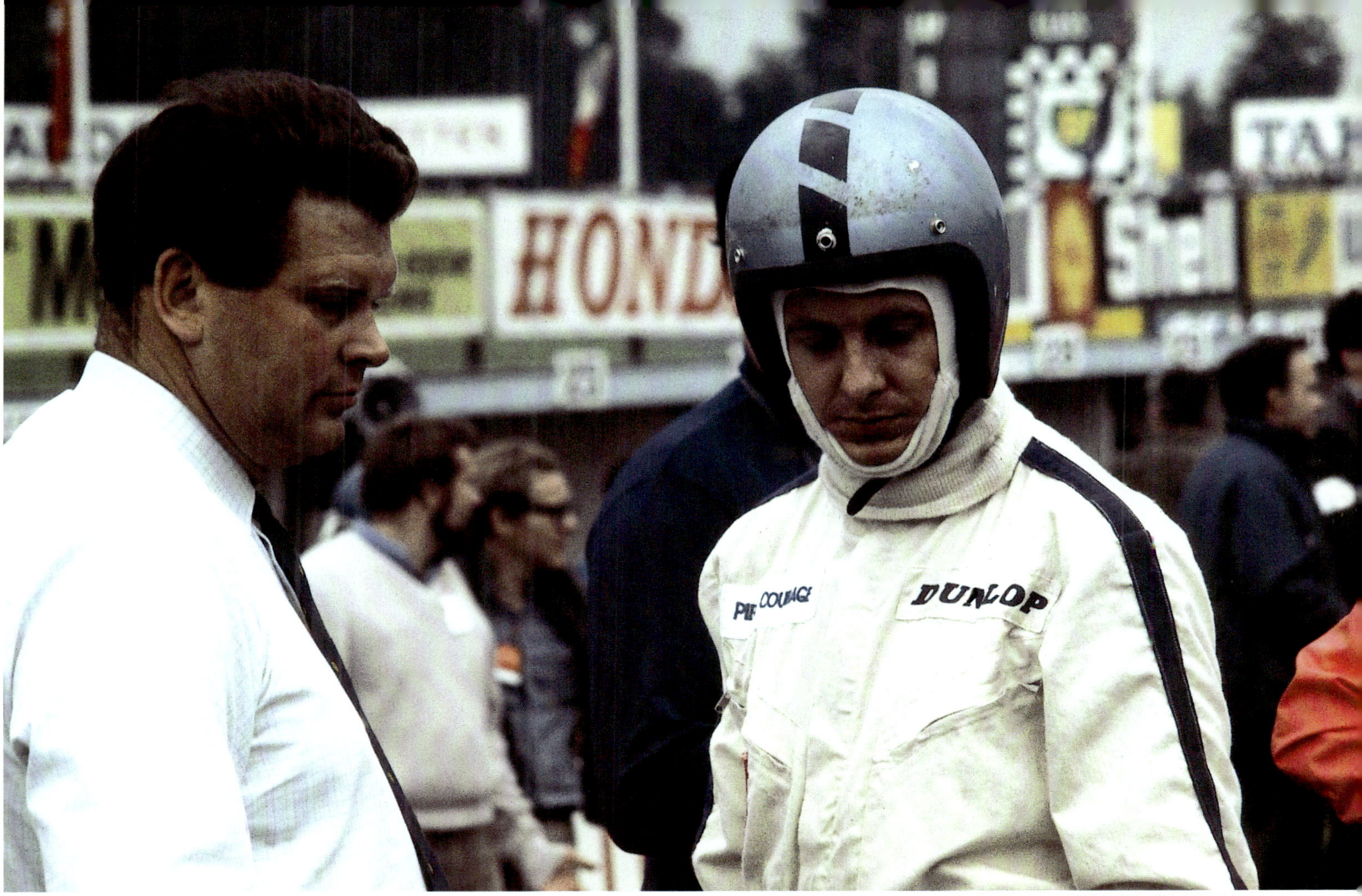
Shell
DUNLOP

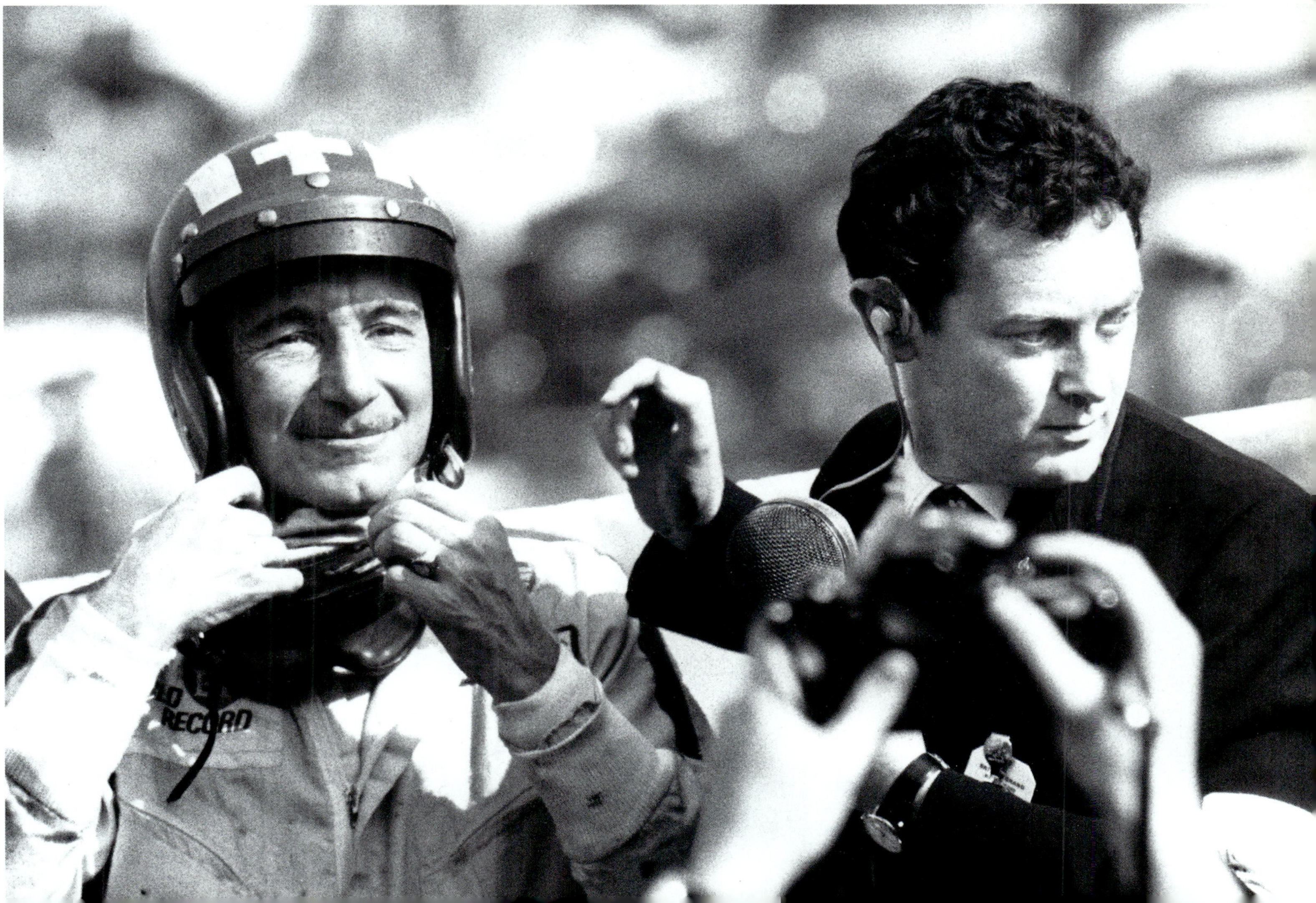
RECORD

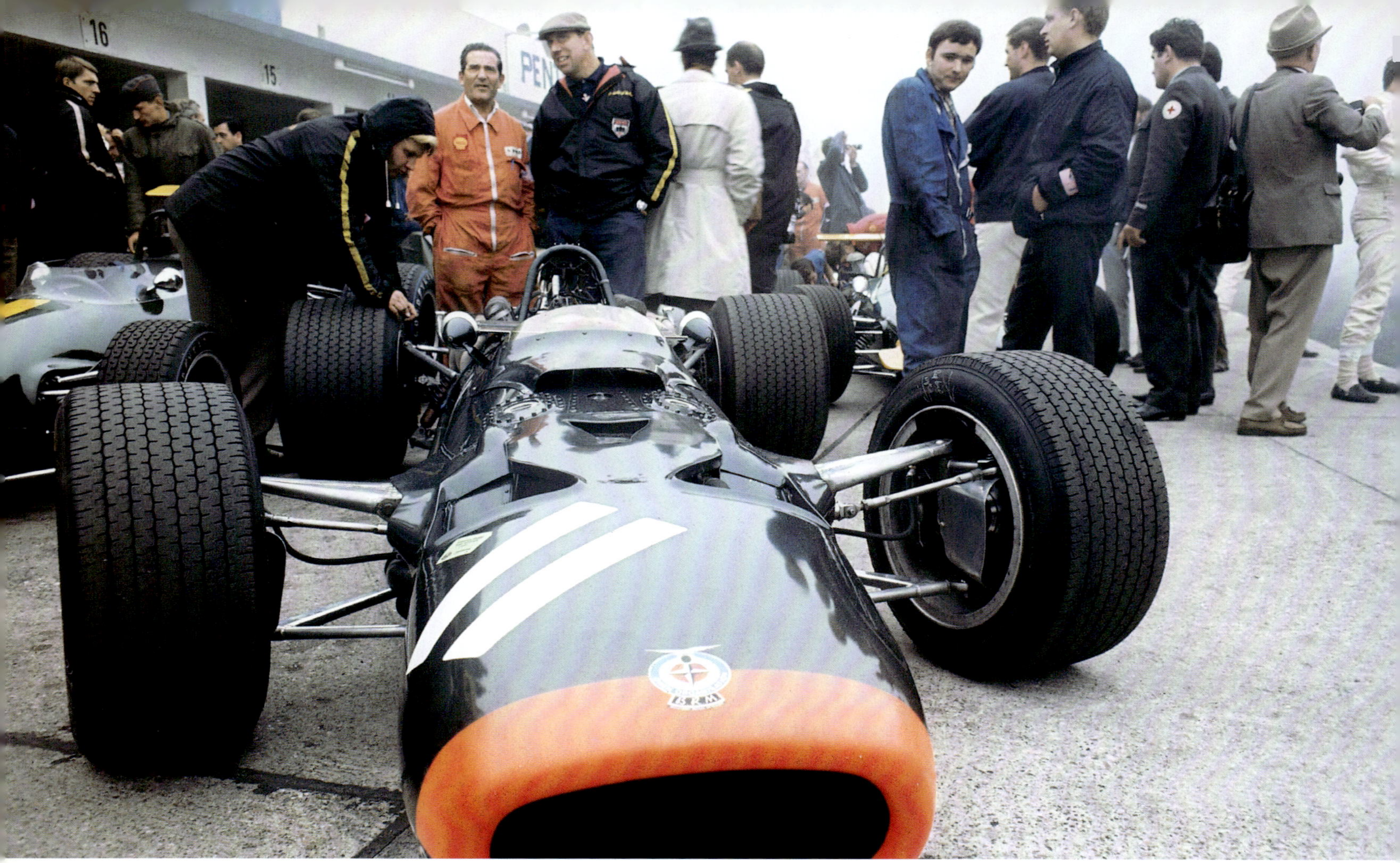
16
15

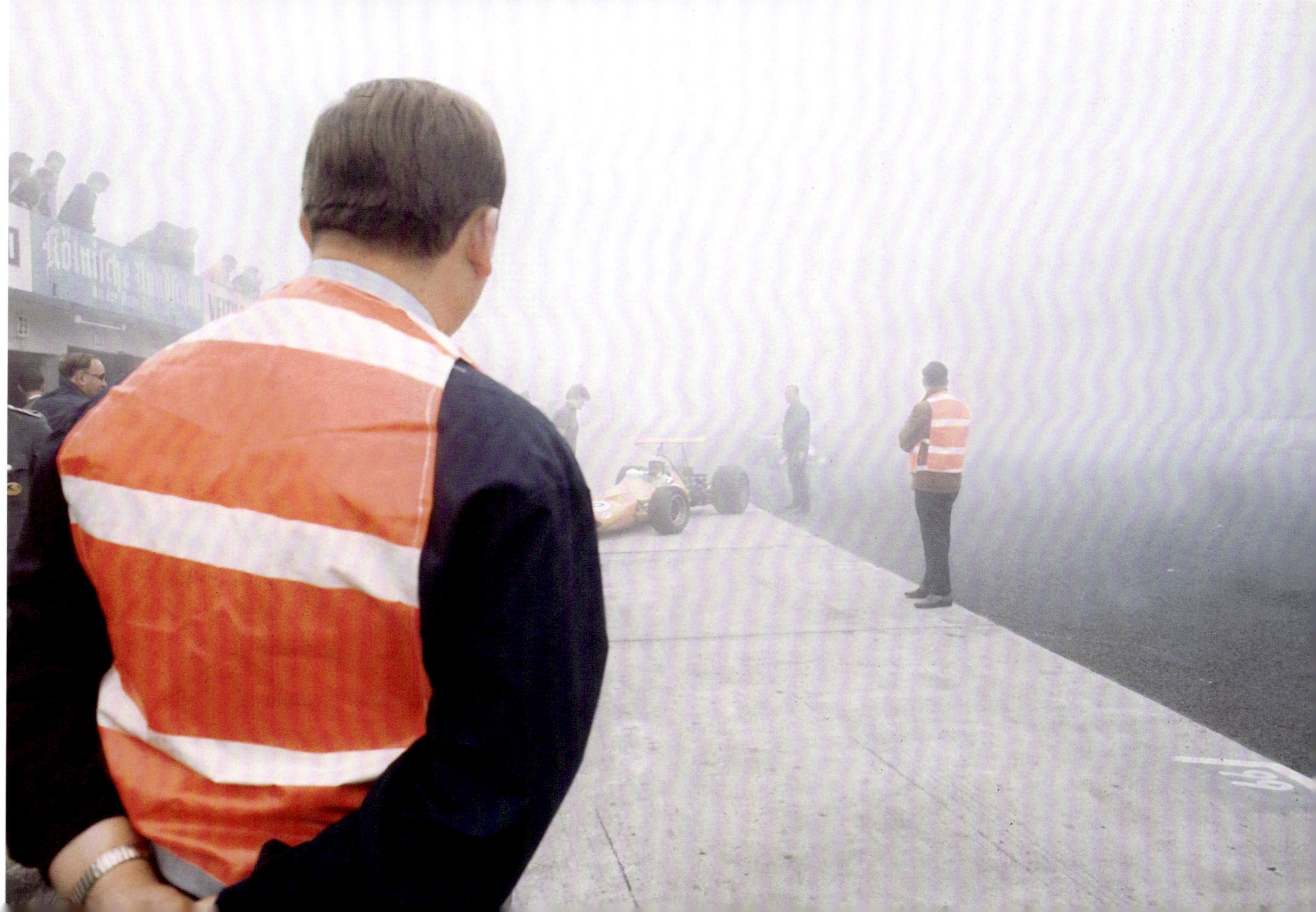

← At the Nürburgring the jolly old weather did its absolute worst, with fog, and then fog and rain combining to really emphasise who was in charge. The 1968 German GP was run in conditions that today would result in a 'no show', but not then. This is Richard Attwood's BRM P126/03 with BRM's Cyril Atkins and Ken Tyrrell standing behind it considering the situation, whilst (far right) Jackie Oliver is peering through the fog pre-race. Attwood's BRM tenure had started very promisingly at Monaco (replacing Mike Spence, who had been killed at Indianapolis), where he set fastest lap and raced to second, only 2.2sec behind Graham Hill, but thereafter his form had seemingly bottomed out and this was his last outing for Bourne.

↙ Come in No. 2, your time is up. Bruce McLaren in the M7A/1 makes it back to the pits at the Nürburgring, no doubt very relieved. Note that the other side of the track is barely visible. Brave, or foolhardy in the extreme? You decide.

→ Piers Courage and Jackie Oliver were the rising stars at this time, although neither fulfilled their true potential. The former tragically perished at Zandvoort in 1970, whilst the latter's debut F1 season was compromised by a difficult first year at Lotus, and thereafter uncompetitive and/or unreliable machinery with BRM, McLaren, and UOP Shadow. Oliver's subsequent career encompassed championship-winning Can-Am racing during 1974, followed by F5000 in 1975–6 before returning to race in F1 with Shadow twice in 1977 (Brands Hatch ROC and the Swedish GP) that ended his F1 racing. Oliver finished 11th here with the GLTL Lotus 49B, whilst Courage will finish eighth in the Parnell Racing BRM P126. Behind, in the Nürburgring murk, is Dan Gurney, whose own F1 career is beginning to fade through no fault of his own.

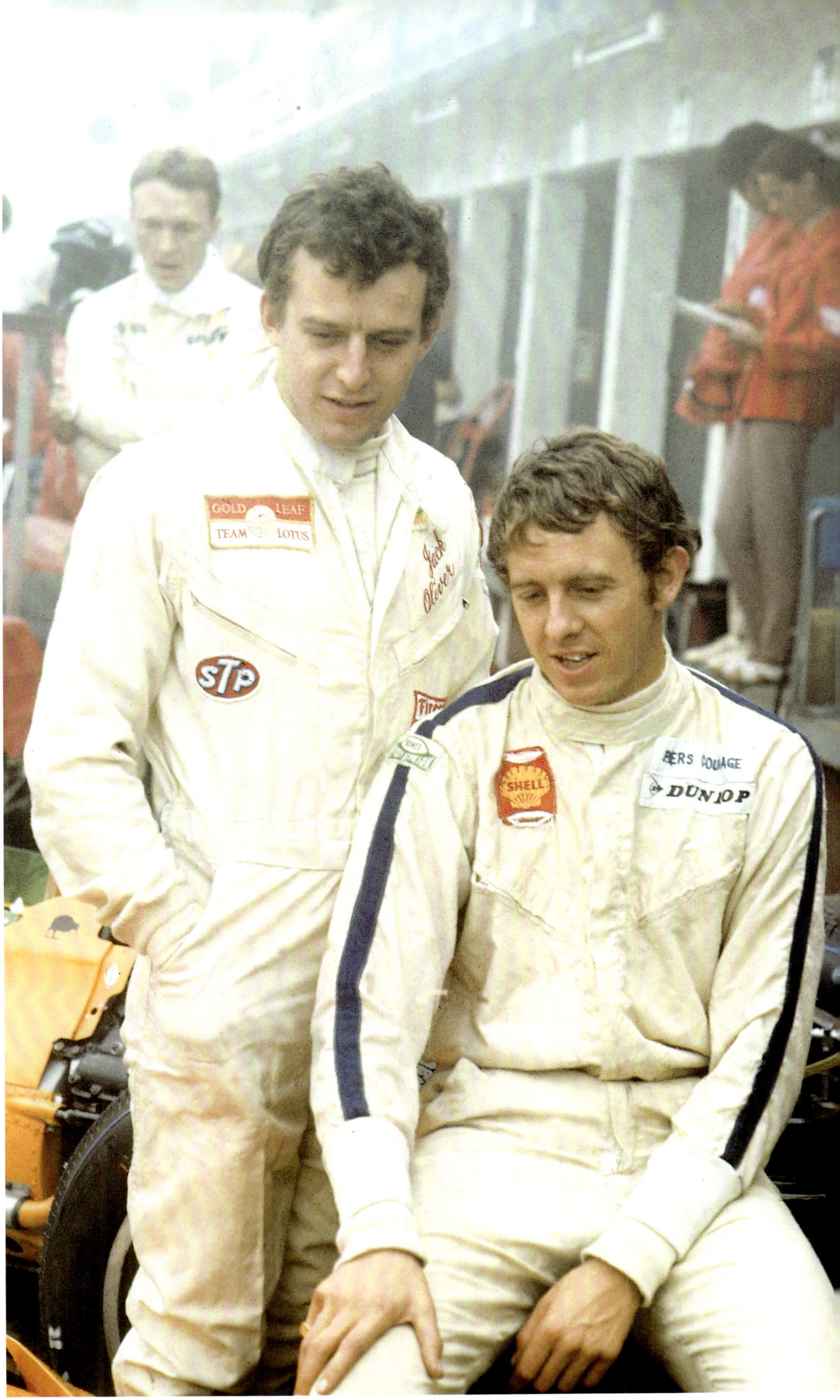

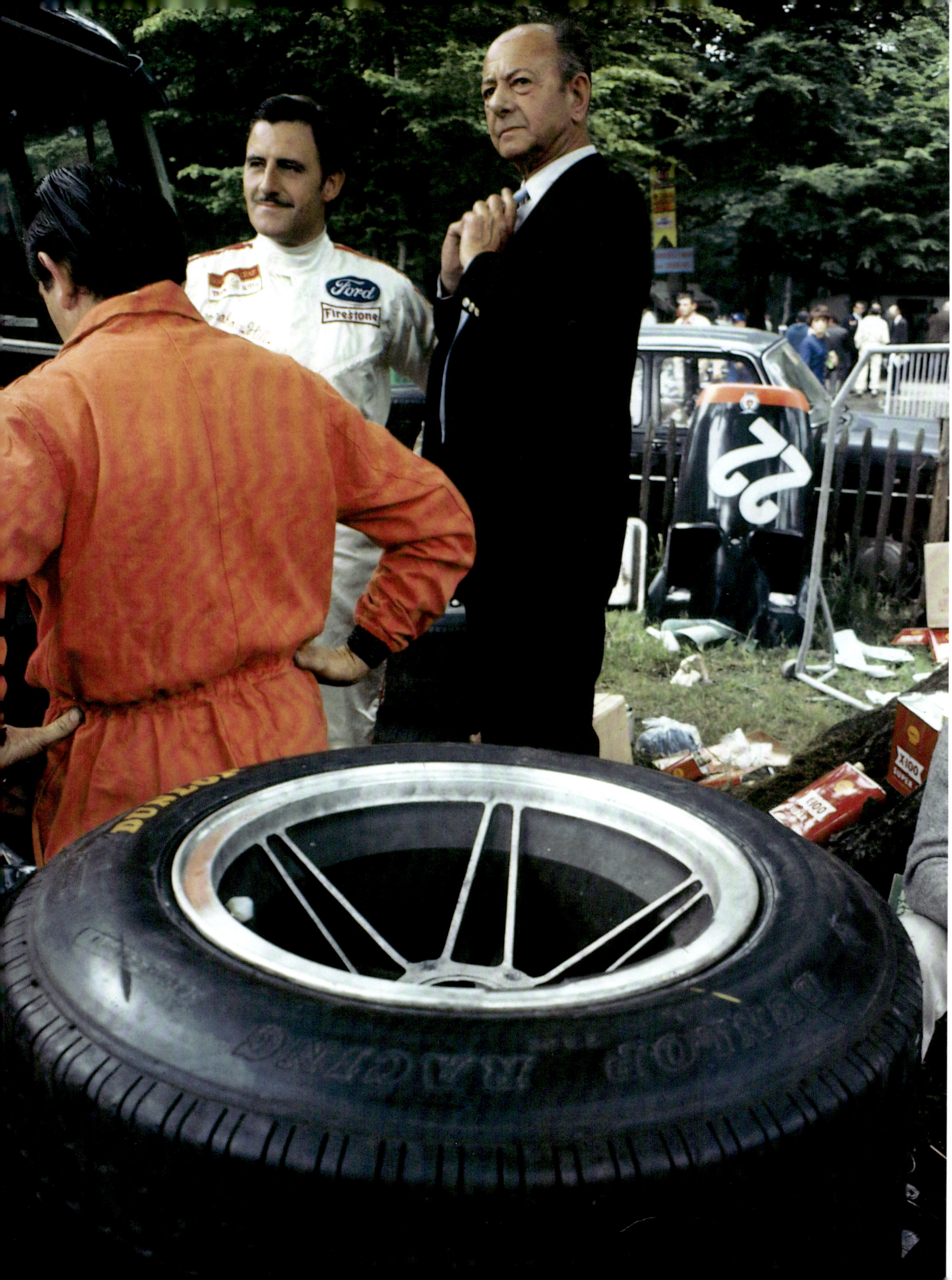
Ford
Firestone
X100
SUPER

← Looking more than ever a matinee idol, Graham Hill (now a Gold Leaf Team Lotus driver) in company with Raymond Mays on the BRM patch in Oulton Park's heavily littered but bucolic paddock at the 1968 Gold Cup meeting. In the background is a P126 nose cone leaning innocently against the fence bearing race number 22. However, the two BRM P126s here were numbered 11 (Piers Courage) and 12 (Pedro Rodriguez), both Reg Parnell Racing entries as the 'works' cars were absent. So this nose cone is possibly a spare from P126/01, which was Courage's car during 1968 that was numbered 22 at the German GP. History – it would be easier to make it up, methinks!

→ Chris Amon and friend relaxing at a minimalist party somewhere in London sometime after the 1968 Belgian GP. The Michael Cooper picture held by the pretty girl shows John Surtees (Honda) being chased by a gaggle of cars, probably including Amon (Ferrari), with whom he contested the lead at Spa, on the approach to La Source.

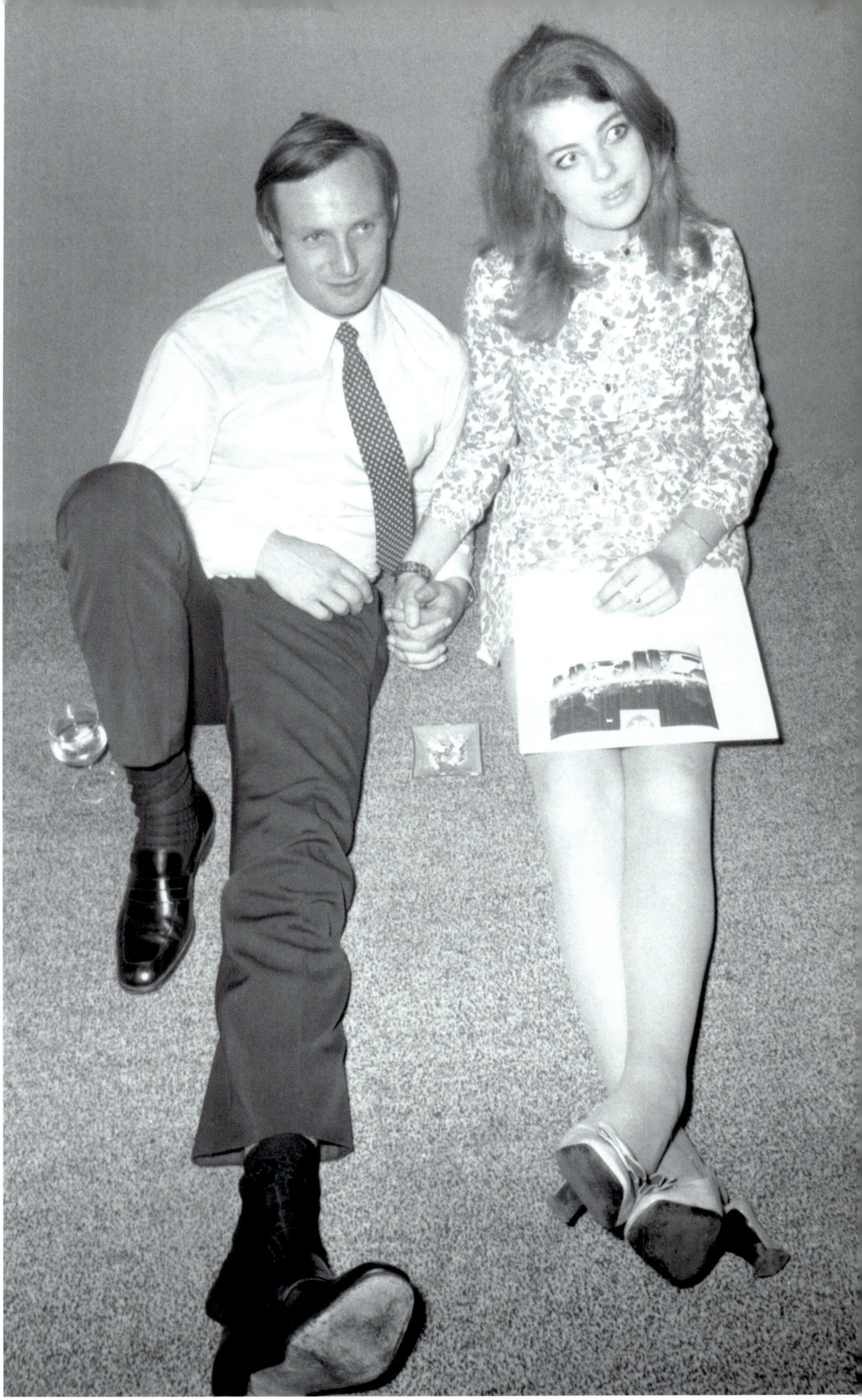

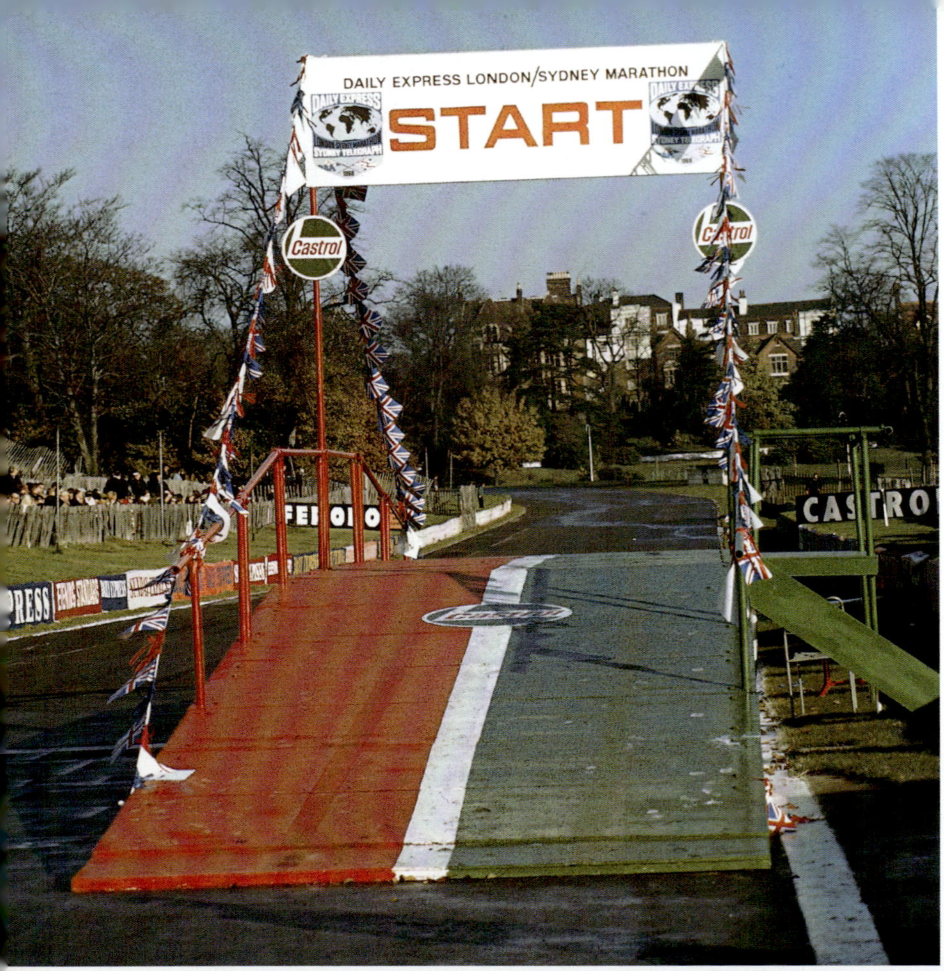

← The start of the 1968 *Daily Express* London to Sydney Marathon was at the Crystal Palace motor racing circuit in South London. The event was the idea of Jocelyn Stevens (creator of *Queen* magazine out of *The Queen* with his friend, famous society photographer Patrick Lichfield) and Tommy Sopwith, erstwhile patron of Equipe Endeavour. Between them they coerced Jack Sears (with Tony Ambrose and Michael Wood-Power) into recceing the route and organising the event. Stevens and Sopwith were friends of Sir Max Aitken, Chairman of the Express Group, and he was persuaded into sponsoring most of the event, with the Australian end covered by Sir Frank Packer. As Jack Sears noted in his official biography *Gentleman Jack* by Graham Gauld, 'Considering how decisions are usually arrived at in major companies today, it is almost beyond comprehension that, in such a short space of time, two guys should come up with a very rough idea, make a firm decision about what it should actually be, and then have it sponsored by two of the largest newspaper groups in the world. No lawyers, no serious costings …'

↓ As part of the show, Australian Penelope Plummer, Miss World 1968, was pressed into service.

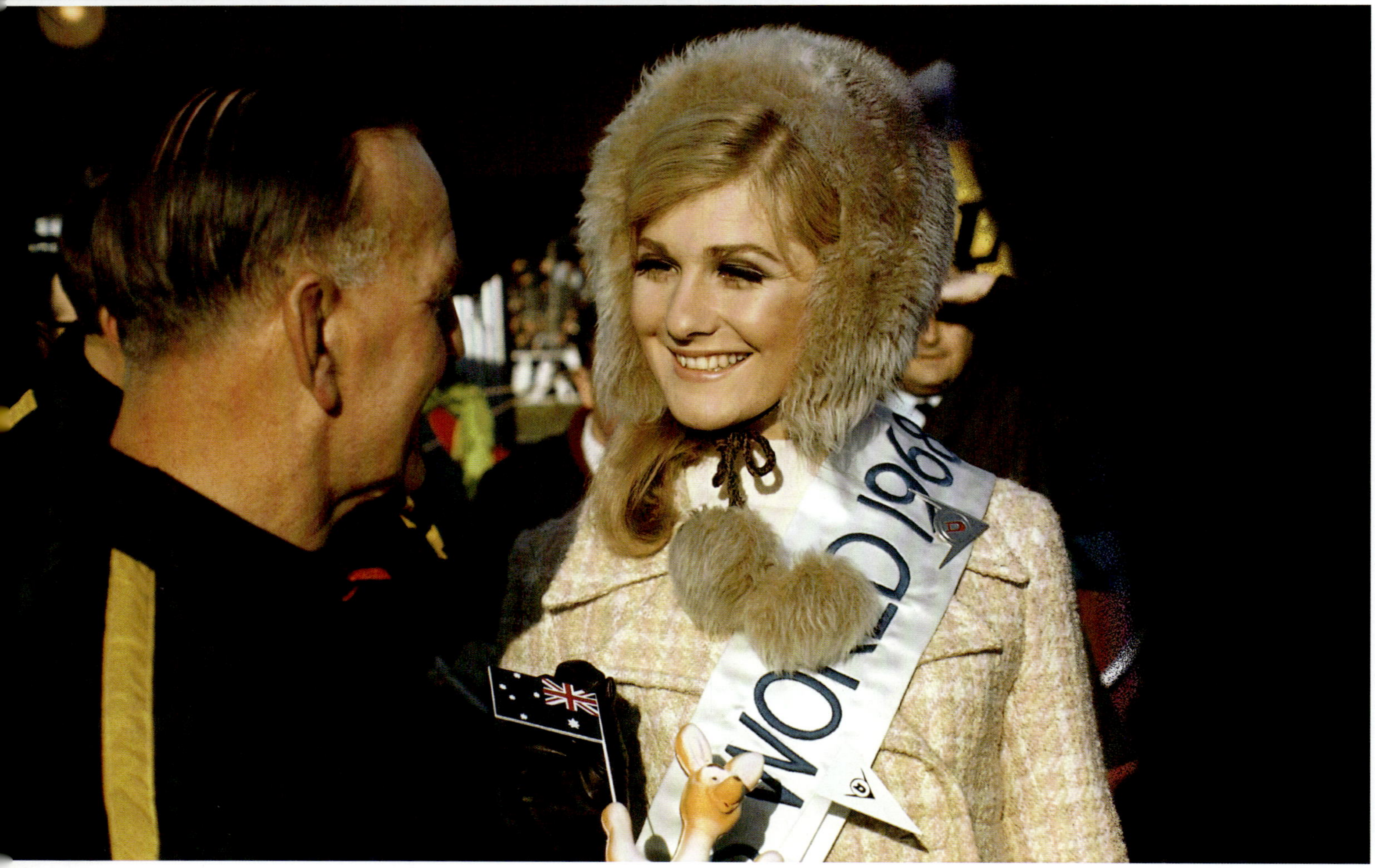

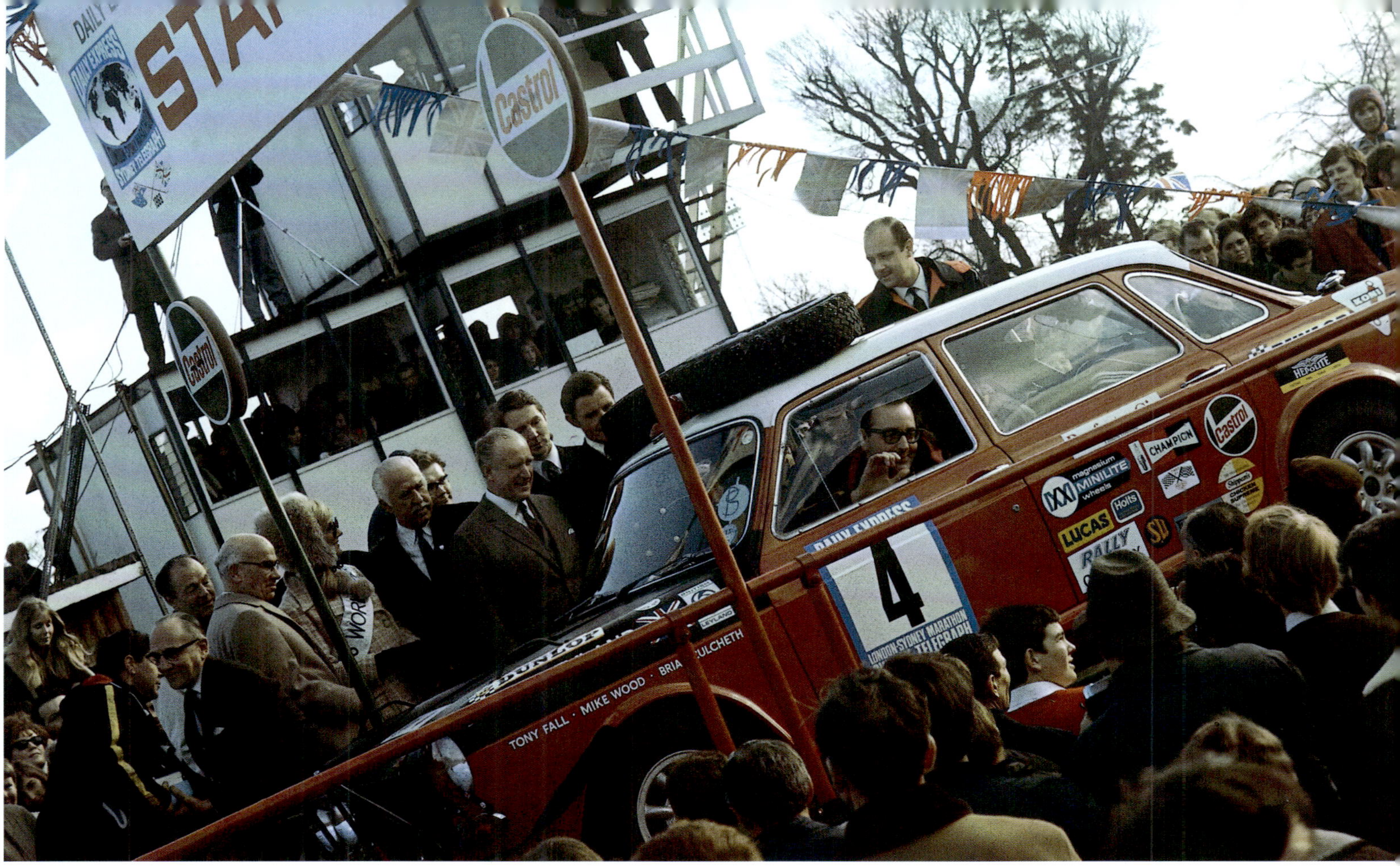

↑ For such a huge and complicated event there were only 100 starters, and the Tony Fall/Mike Wood/Brian Culcheth Austin 1800 seen here came 24th, but their British Leyland team-mates Paddy Hopkirk/Tony Nash/Alex Poole finished second, having lost their chance of winning after stopping to assist the leading Citroën DS19 of Bianchi/Ogier that had suffered a serious collision with an errant Mini. Ultimately the works Hillman Hunter of Andrew Cowan/Colin Malkin/Brian Coyle won, and 56 of the 100 starters were classified as finishing.

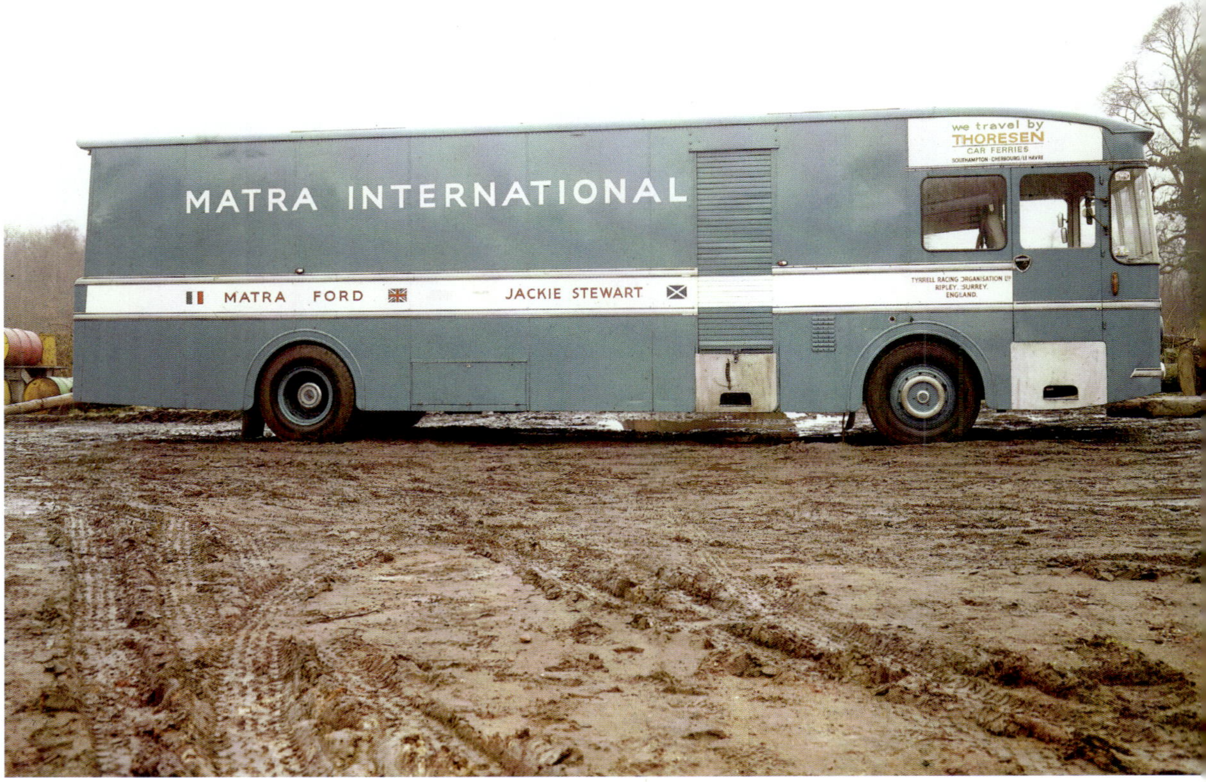

→ The ideal setting for a world-beating F1 team, and the Ken Tyrrell transporter is happily enjoying its mud bath in a woodyard somewhere in deepest rural Surrey. Note that the French flag precedes MATRA, the Union Jack follows FORD, and the Scottish saltire comes after STEWART on the vehicle's flank.

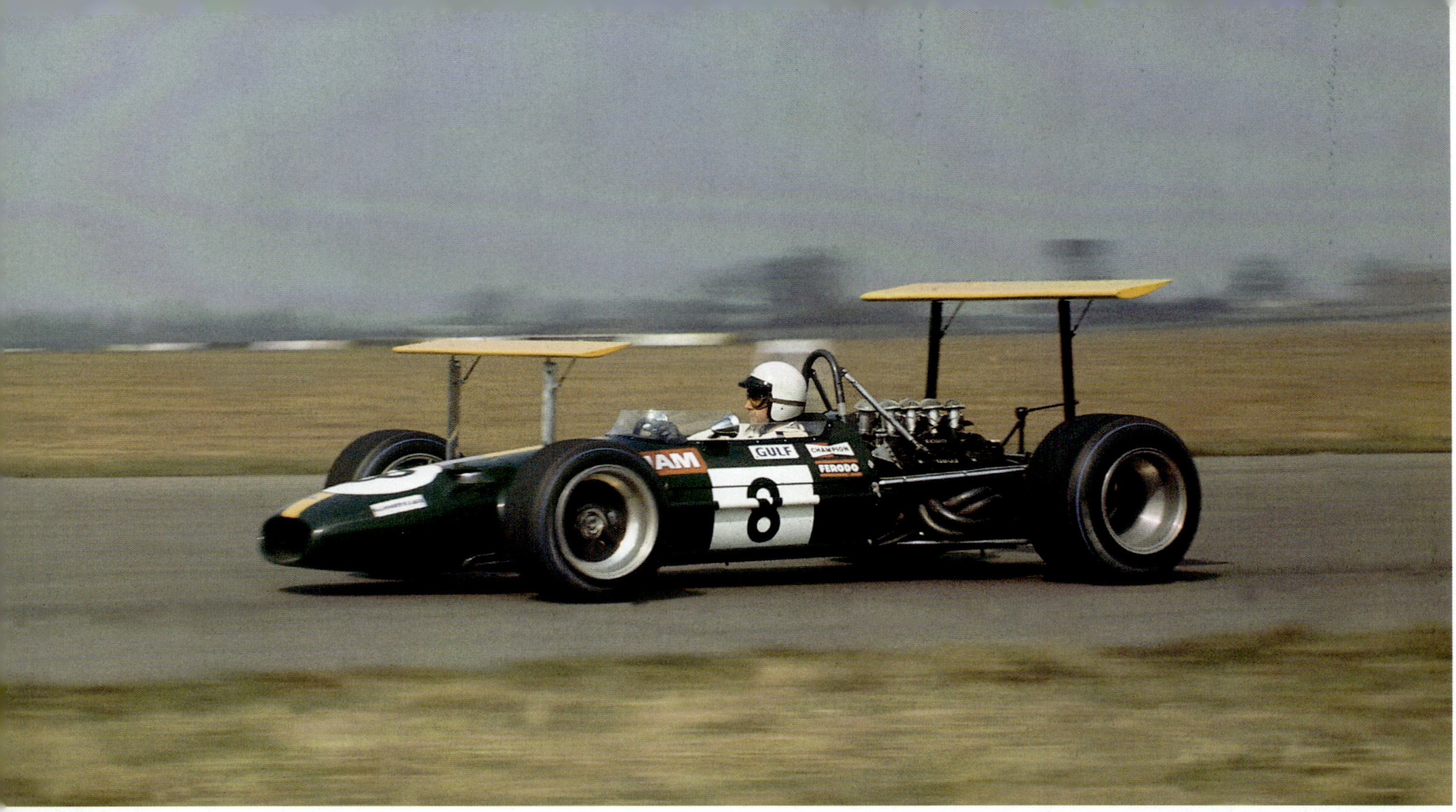
GULF
CHAMPION
FERODO
8

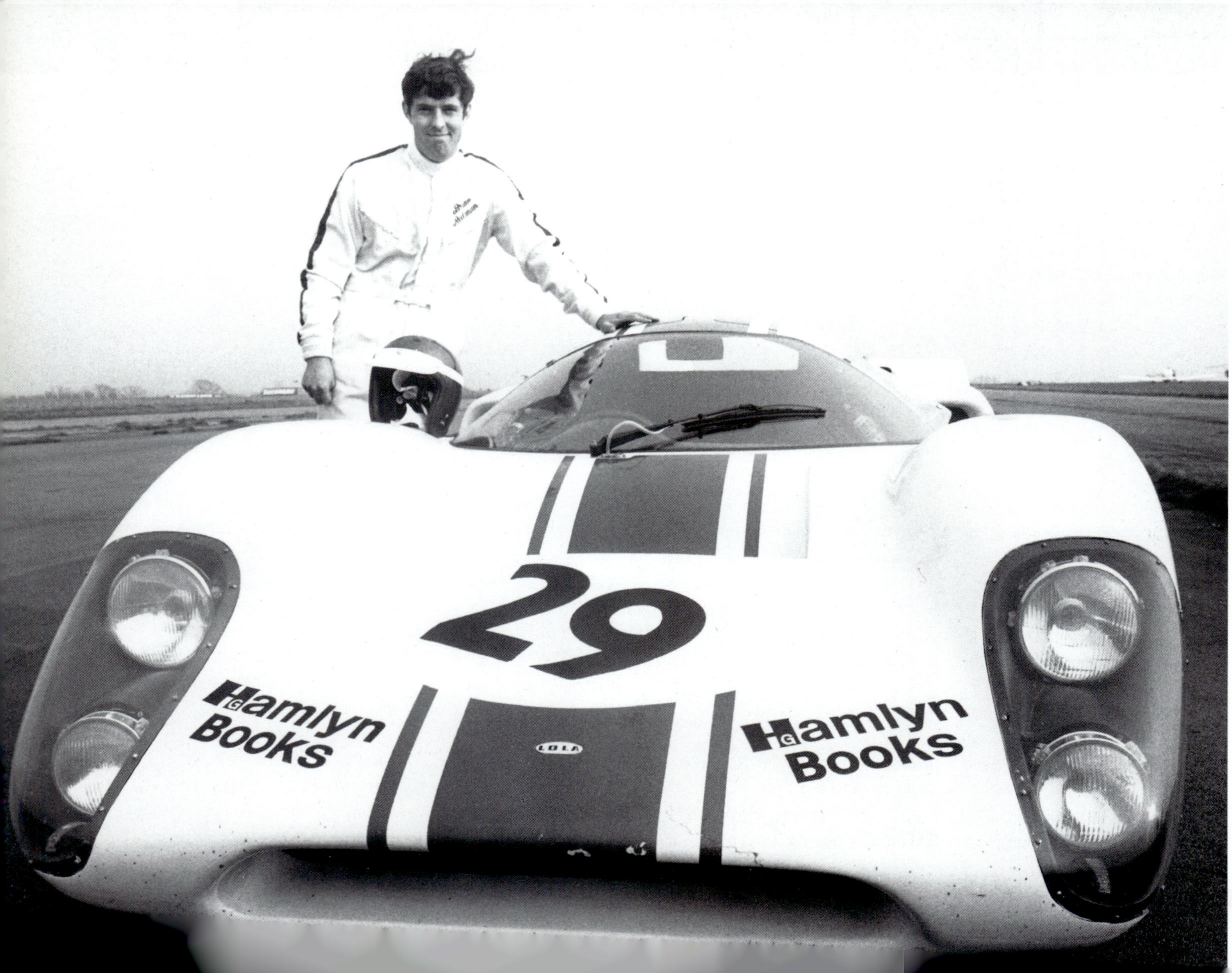
29
Hamlyn Books
LOLA
Hamlyn Books

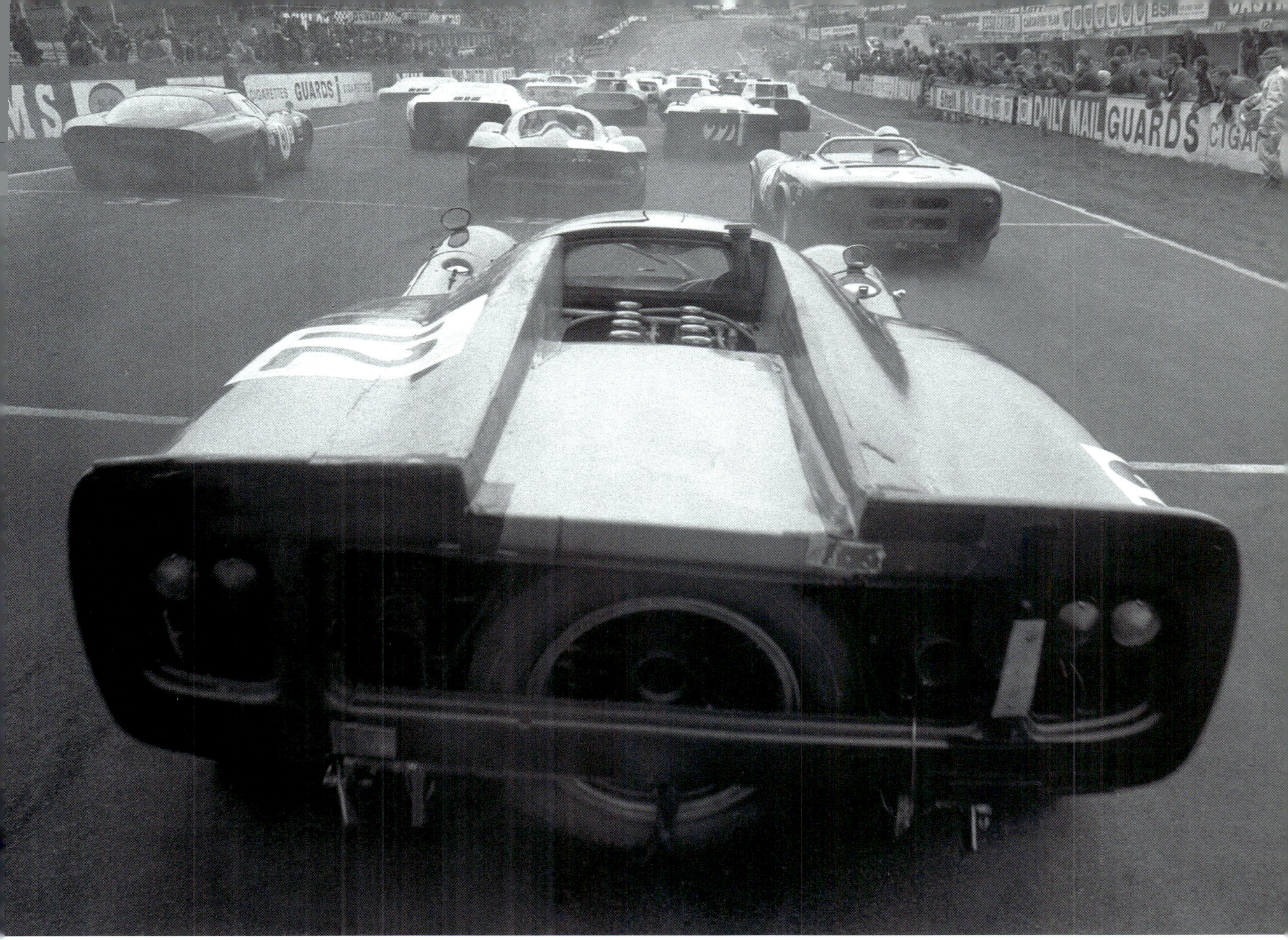

The trademark rear-of-the-departing-grid shot once again as Mike presses the shutter. Motor trader David Prophet's Lola-Chevrolet T70 Mk3 (SL73/105) qualified last and only completed four laps at the 1969 Brands Hatch 6 Hours, thus denying co-driver Edward Nelson his ride. Also visible are the Mike Crabtree/Peter Jackson Nomad-BRM (No. 81 on left) that finished 22nd, Alain de Cadenet's Ferrari Dino 206S (024) that he shared with Tony Beeson to finish 15th, the Ian Tee/Willie Green Ginetta G16A-BRM entered by period *Motor Sport* publisher Wesley J. Tee that also retired early on, so Willie too missed his go. The No. 22 Racing Team VDS Alfa Romeo T33/2 (Gosselin/Bourgoignie) that retired, and the rest of the field are just moving off. David Prophet had raced briefly in F1 (1963 and 1965 South African GPs), F2 during 1964 and 1966–7, but is most associated with sports cars, competing in Ferrari, Ford GT40, McLaren, Lotus, and Lola as here, then later F5000 and finishing fourth in the non-championship 1971 Argentine GP. He was born in Hong Kong on 9 October 1937 and, like so many racers, died in a light aircraft accident when his helicopter crashed shortly after taking off from Silverstone on 29 March 1981.

The 1969 International Trophy at Silverstone was run on 30 March. This, of course, pre-dated the Monaco ban of suspension mounted aerofoil devices that shamed themselves at Montjuich, where both GLTL Lotus 49s crashed. Brabhams favoured the front and rear approach, and the boss duly won the damp/wet race in his updated BT26A/2, beating Jochen Rindt in the Lotus 49 and Jackie Stewart's Matra MS10. Later in the year during testing at Silverstone after the Dutch GP, Brabham will crash and suffer nasty injuries that will keep him out of the fray until Monza in September.

Sid Taylor's Lola-Chevrolet T70 Mk3B (SL76/138) with Barz dry sump engine, and Brian Redman on a grey day at Silverstone before round one of the RAC G4 championship. On a wet track he finished second to Denny Hulme, who was driving John Woolfe's older T70 Mk3, but only because Hulme's gearbox lost a bung and the oil blew out all over Redman's windscreen, which unsurprisingly slowed Brian down a tad!

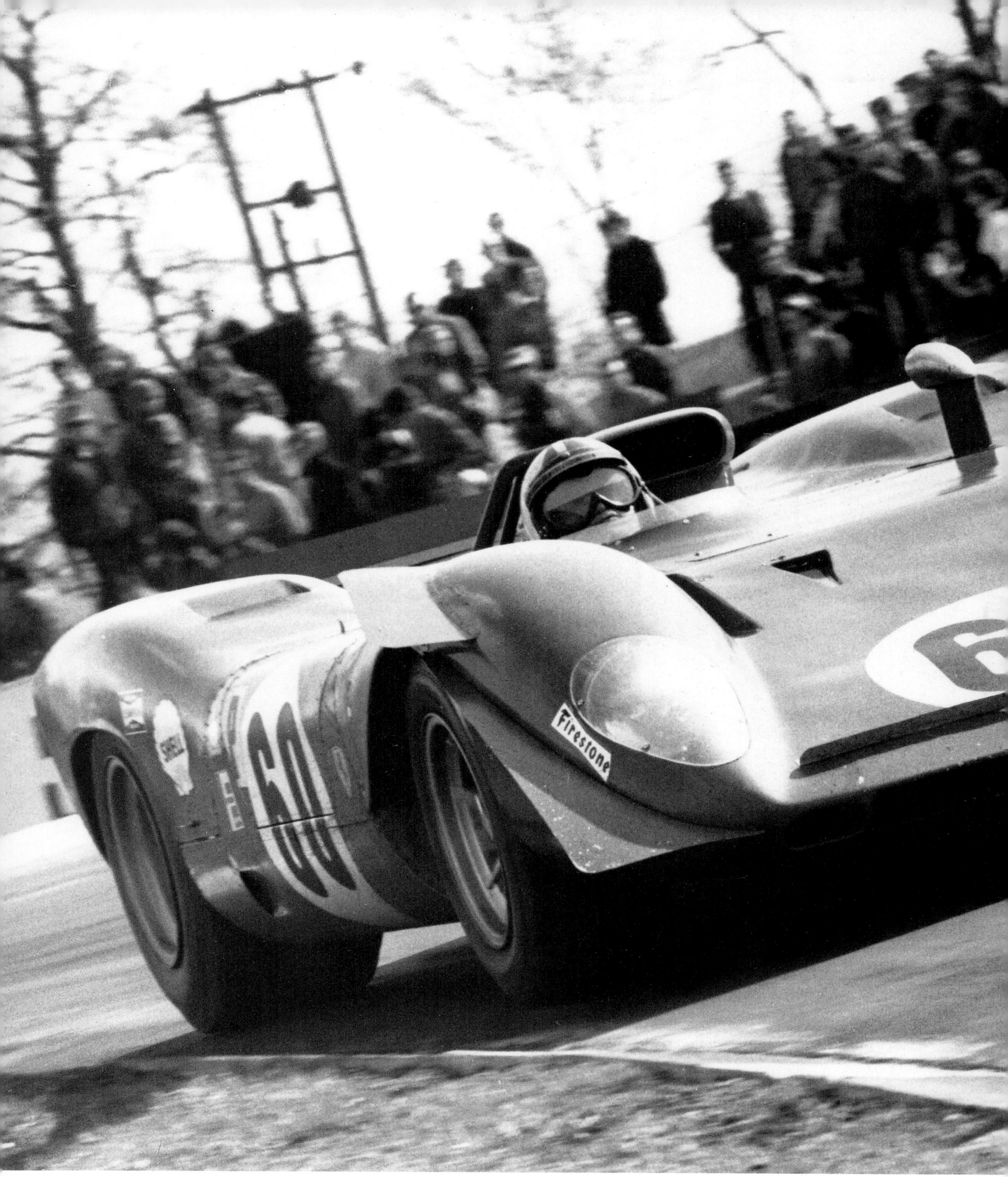
Firestone

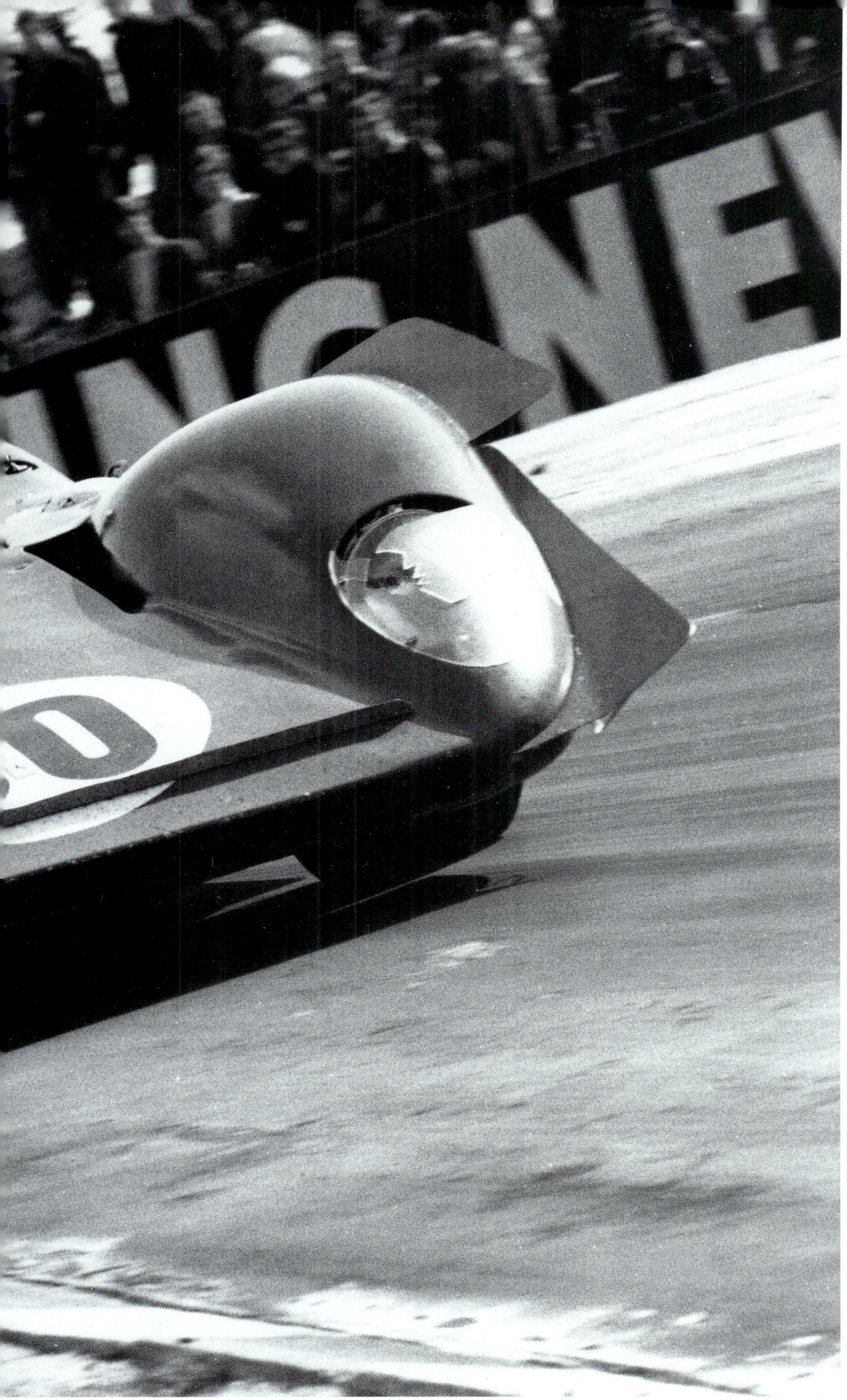

← 1969 was Ferrari's worst year of the decade, with no championship victories in F1 or endurance racing. The main victim in this debacle, the Scuderia apart, was Christopher Arthur Amon, who drove his last race for Ferrari at the 1969 British GP just months before the potent flat 12 312 became available. Amon, seen here, qualified second at the Brands Hatch 6 Hours with co-driver Pedro Rodriguez, but they eventually finished fourth in the Ferrari 312P (0870) behind the three factory Porsche 908s. The 312P is almost Can-Am sized and its clumsy looking adornments reflect the crude and still rudimentary application of aerodynamic devices of that time.

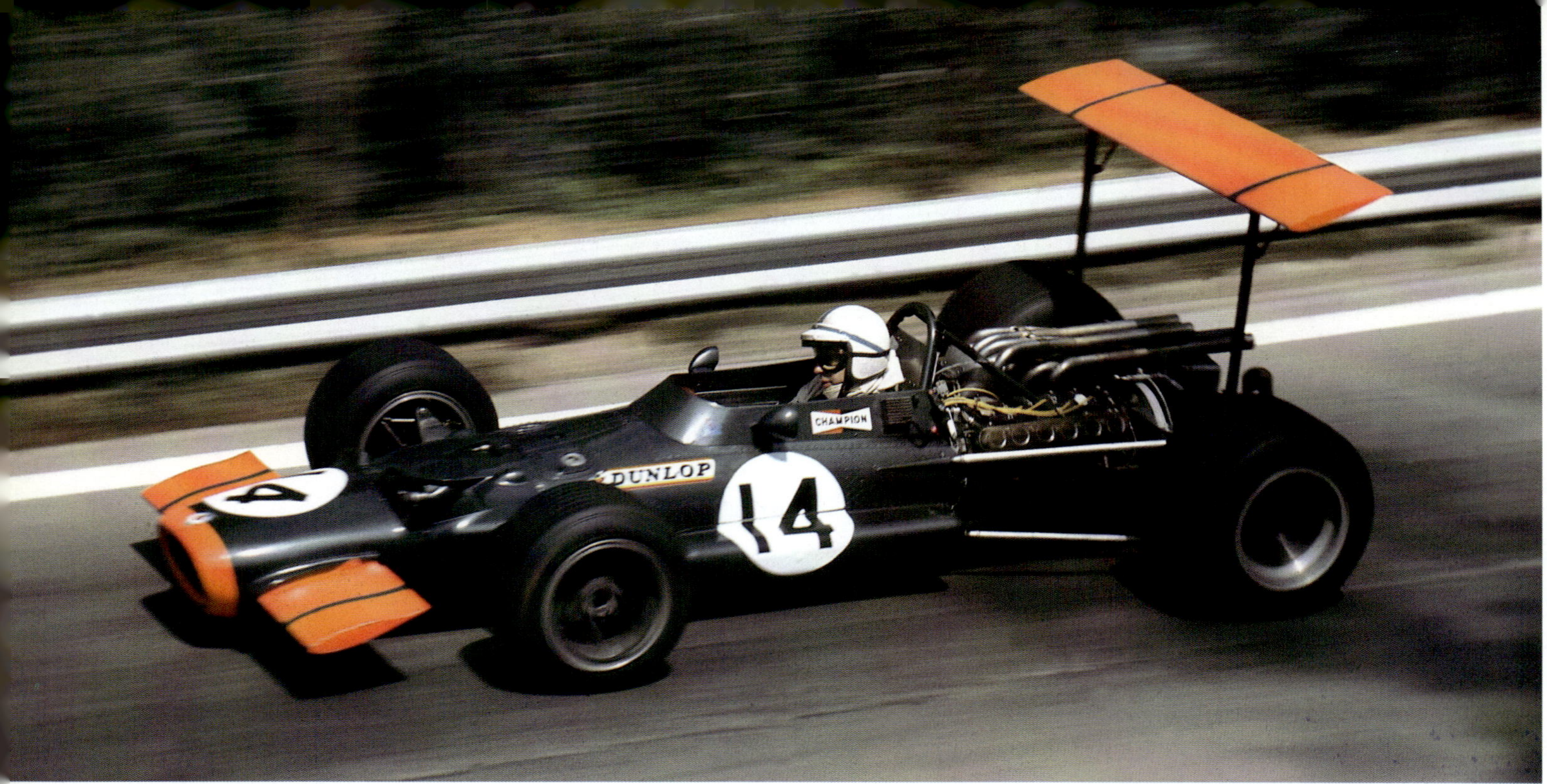
DUNLOP
14
CHAMPION

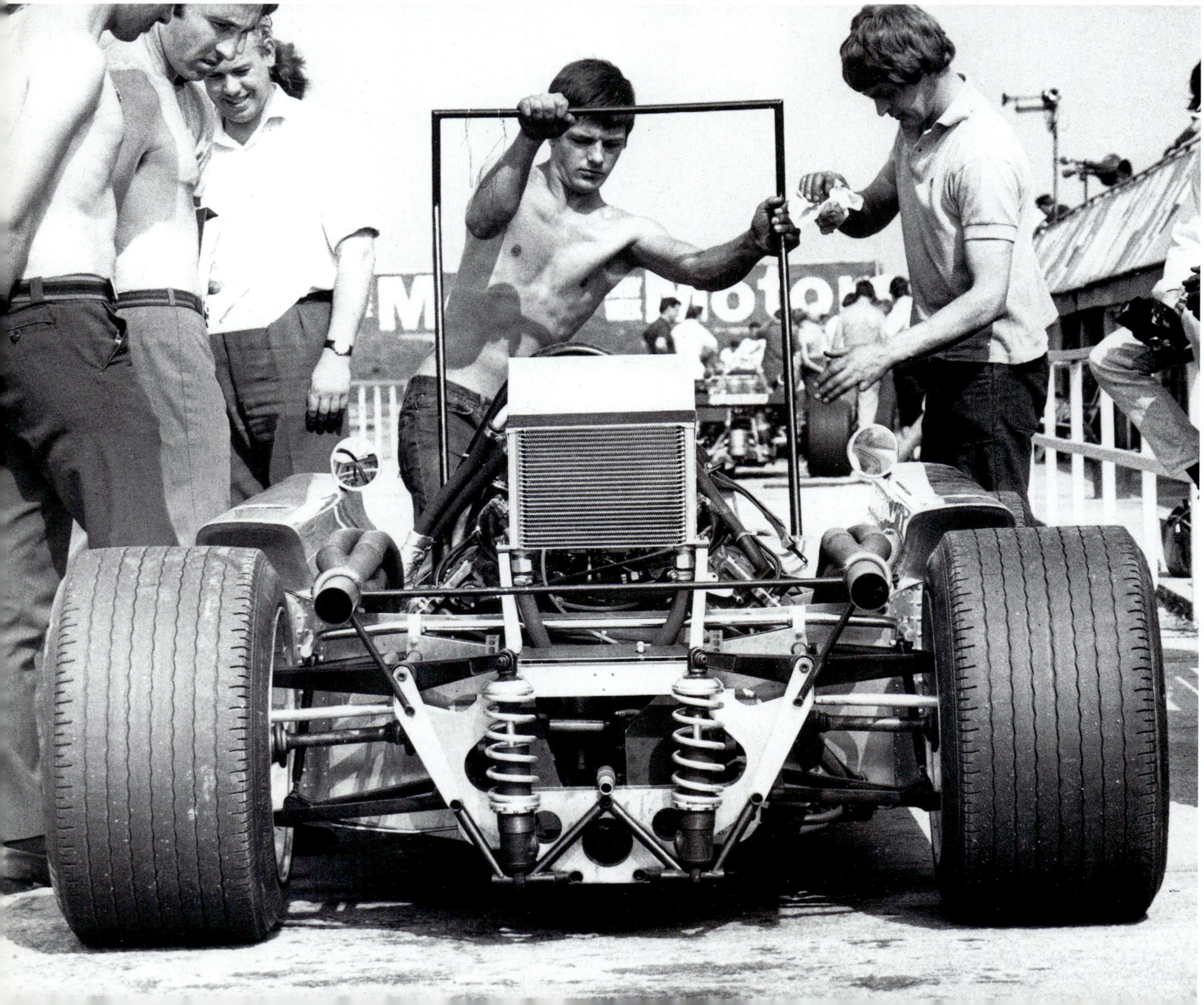

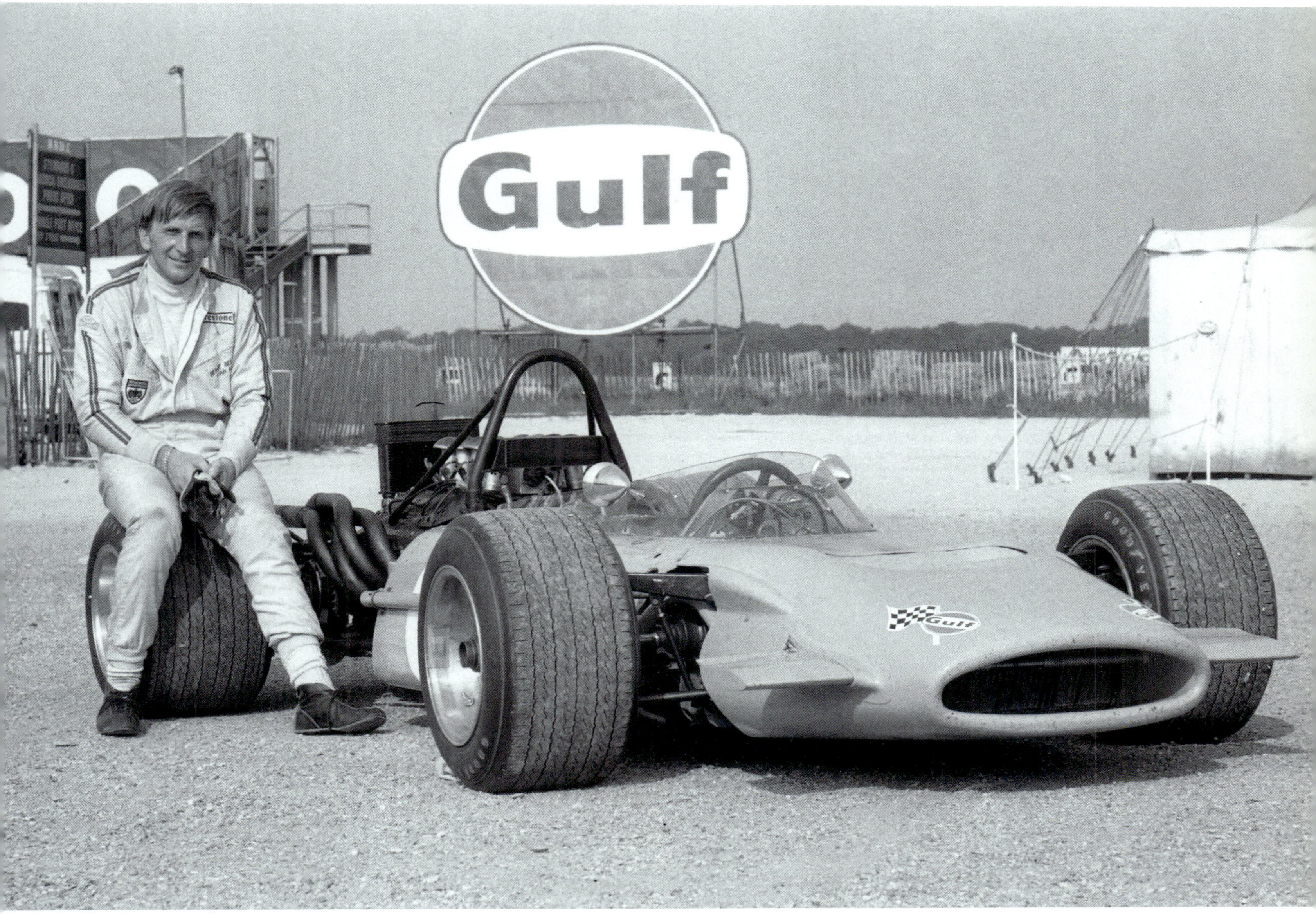

↑ Another technical dead end. The rather oddly proportioned McLaren M9A (see lower caption) was designed by Swiss Jo Marquart, who had been responsible for the triumphant McLaren M8 Can-Am racers. He went on to work for Huron, GRD, Modus, and ultimately Argo. He died in 1993. Derek Bell seems unconvinced by the ungainly device during testing, and he raced it just once at the 1969 British GP, where it retired because of a broken rear suspension carrier. The M9A was not used again.

↖ With Honda withdrawing from F1 at the end of 1968, John Surtees found himself driving for BRM in 1969. It was not a happy experience, and the 48-valve V12 installed in the P138/01 was not giving enough power at Montjuich Park for the Spanish GP. However, Surtees finished fifth despite a faulty ignition coil, and later third in the US GP, but it was otherwise a poor year for one of the world's best drivers.

← One of four such 4WD F1 projects that appeared during 1969, Cosworth's effort was the only one not to be raced. As with the others (Lotus 63, Matra MS84, and McLaren M9A) any putative advantages normally associated with all-wheel drive were negated by the huge advances in aerodynamic and tyre development of the day. Thus, the extra complication, weight, and inherent understeer rendered the concept untenable, and it was best adapted for rallying many years later. Designed by Robin Herd during 1968, the car's Cosworth DFV has been turned round and is fitted with a purpose-built magnesium engine block to save weight. During testing at Silverstone, a shirtless Frank Williams (second from left) and Keith Duckworth beyond, look on. Note the rear suspension with its inboard vertical coilspring/damper assemblies.

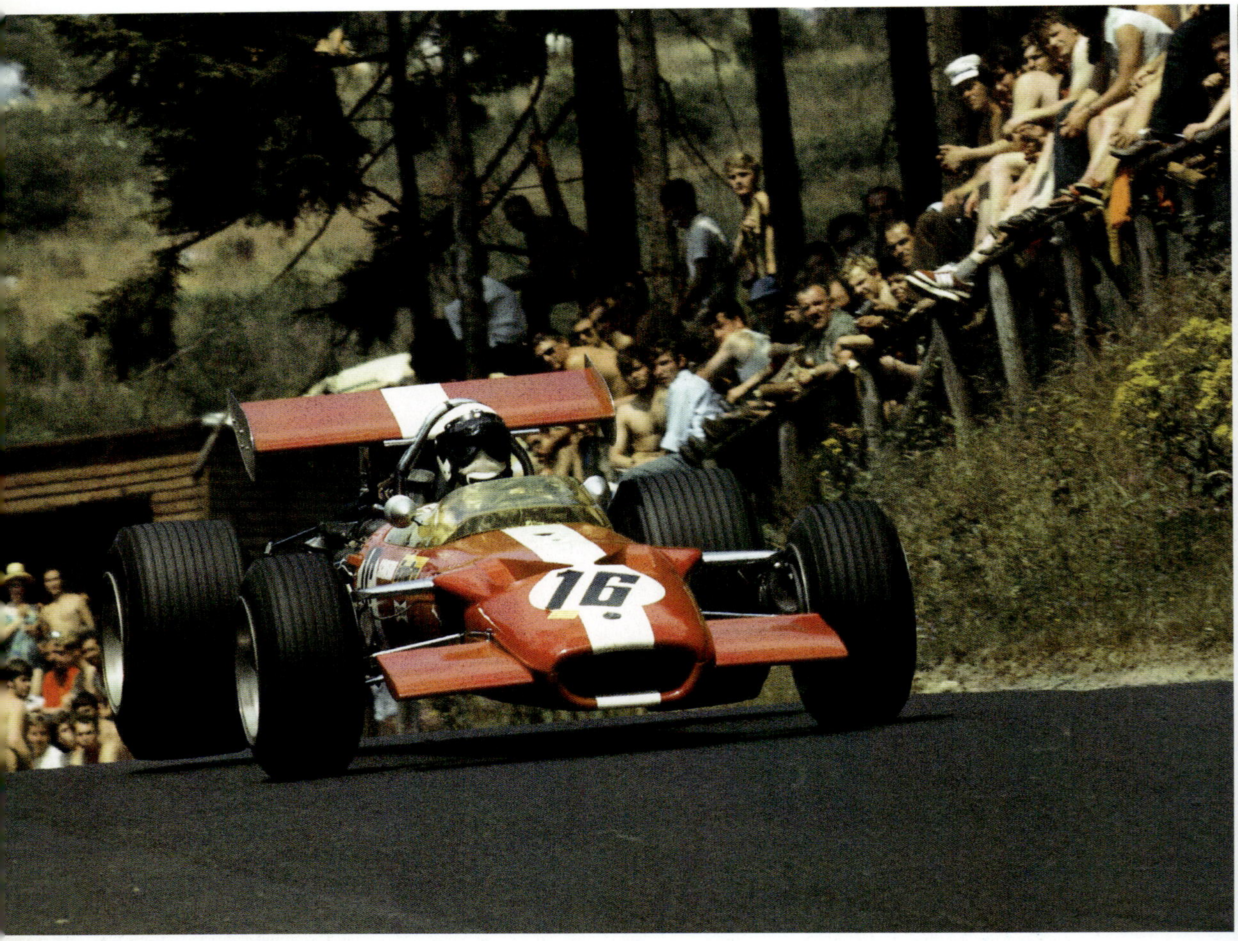

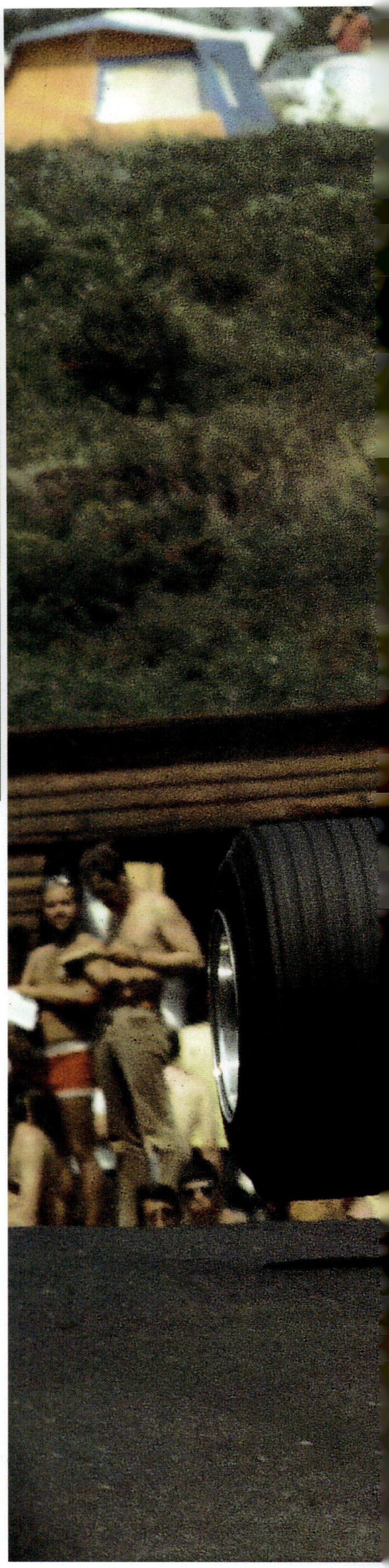

↑ Although still a very competitive sports car driver, Jo Bonnier was really only making up the numbers in F1 after the mid-1960s. In 1969 Colin Chapman was determined to force his drivers into driving the execrable 4WD 63 and sold 49B/R8 to Bonnier, which Graham Hill had to borrow to race in the British GP. However, 'Jo Bo' was back in the very smart looking car at the Nürburgring, but was the slowest of the 13 F1 starters (the remaining eight entries were F2 cars). He only lasted five laps before stopping with a fuel leak. Bonnier went on to enter seven more GPs (two in 1970 and five in 1971) posting two DNQs, one DNS, two retirements, one tenth, and one 16th place) before finally giving up F1.

→ A typical M. Cooper Nürburgring shot, taken during the 1969 German GP as Peter Westbury descends from altitude in the Felday Engineering Brabham-Cosworth FVA BT 30 on his way to fifth in the F2 class. This event traditionally had a separate F2 race within a race. Twice British Hill Climb Champion, the rapid and versatile Westbury was Felday, and he drove in F3, F2, and finally a one-off drive for Yardley BRM at the 1970 US GP that was ended when the P153 blew up during qualifying. He continued on as a F2 front-runner, but as his results began to fade in 1972 he decided to retire in 1973.

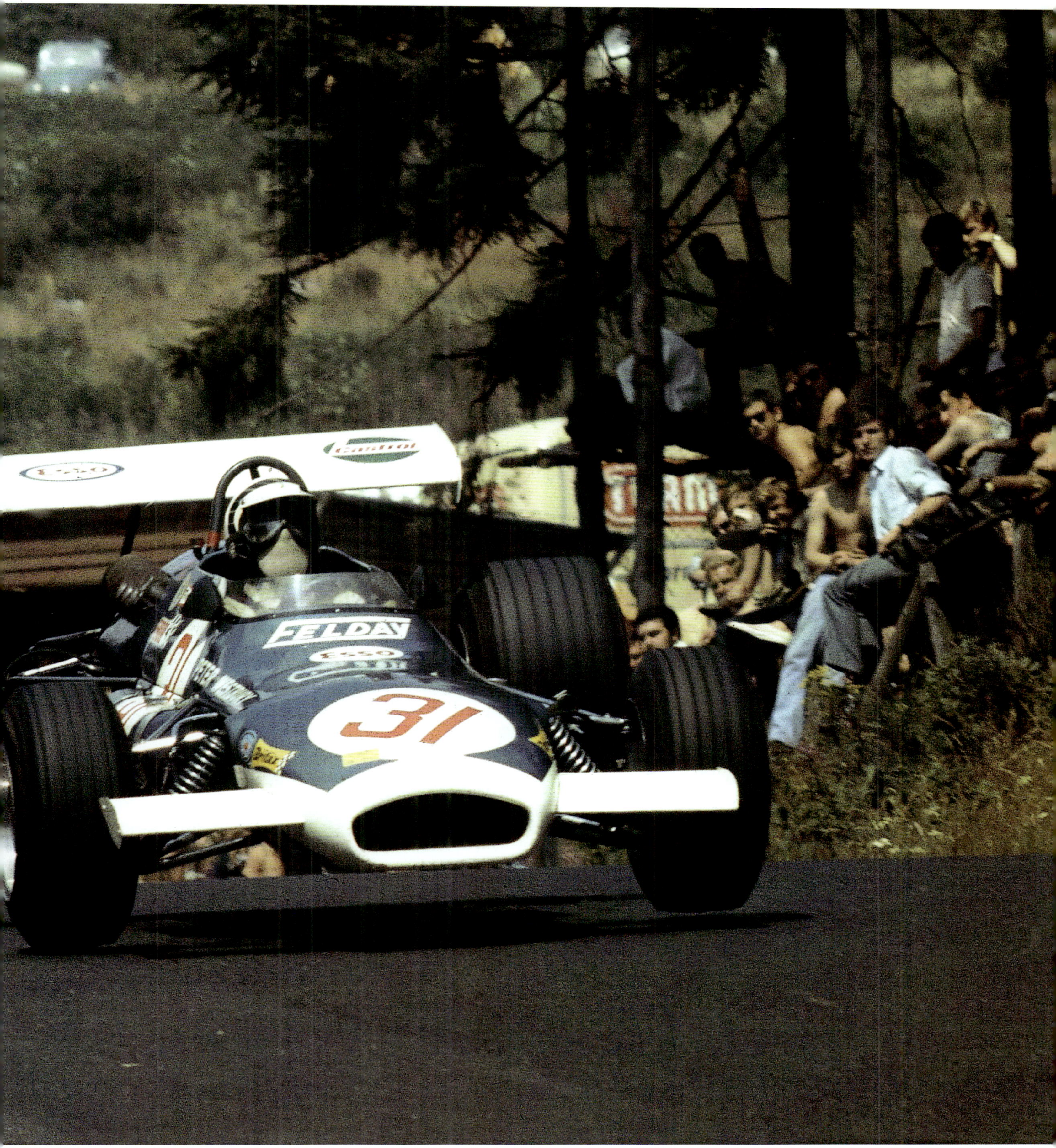
FELDAY
31

↑ Another airborne shot with Jo Siffert defying gravity in Rob Walker's Lotus 49B (R7) as he circulates in third place at the Ring. Note the shadow cast upon the road. However, on lap 13 he suffered a suspension failure and had a hefty shunt into the trees, but escaped unharmed and was still classified fifth overall. R7 was the 1968 British GP winning car and it made 24 GP starts from the 1968 British GP to the 1970 German GP. 'Seppi' first raced for Rob Walker at the 1964 US GP and his last drive was at the final GP of 1969 in Mexico. On the way he had gone from being an always super-fast sports car driver, but only a midfield GP competitor (because of machinery) to being a front-runner in this Lotus 49. Thereafter, a mediocre year at March was succeeded by a very promising 1971 F1 season with BRM that saw him win the Austrian GP, but ended in tragedy at Brands Hatch on 24 October 1971. He was the only driver ever to die at the wheel of a works BRM.

↓ Mike is just a little too close, focal-length wise, but it is still a magnificent shot of Piers Courage, all four wheels clear of the deck, in the immaculate Frank Williams Brabham BT26A/1 at the Nürburgring. Alas, Piers overdid it on lap 2 and crashed out of the race.

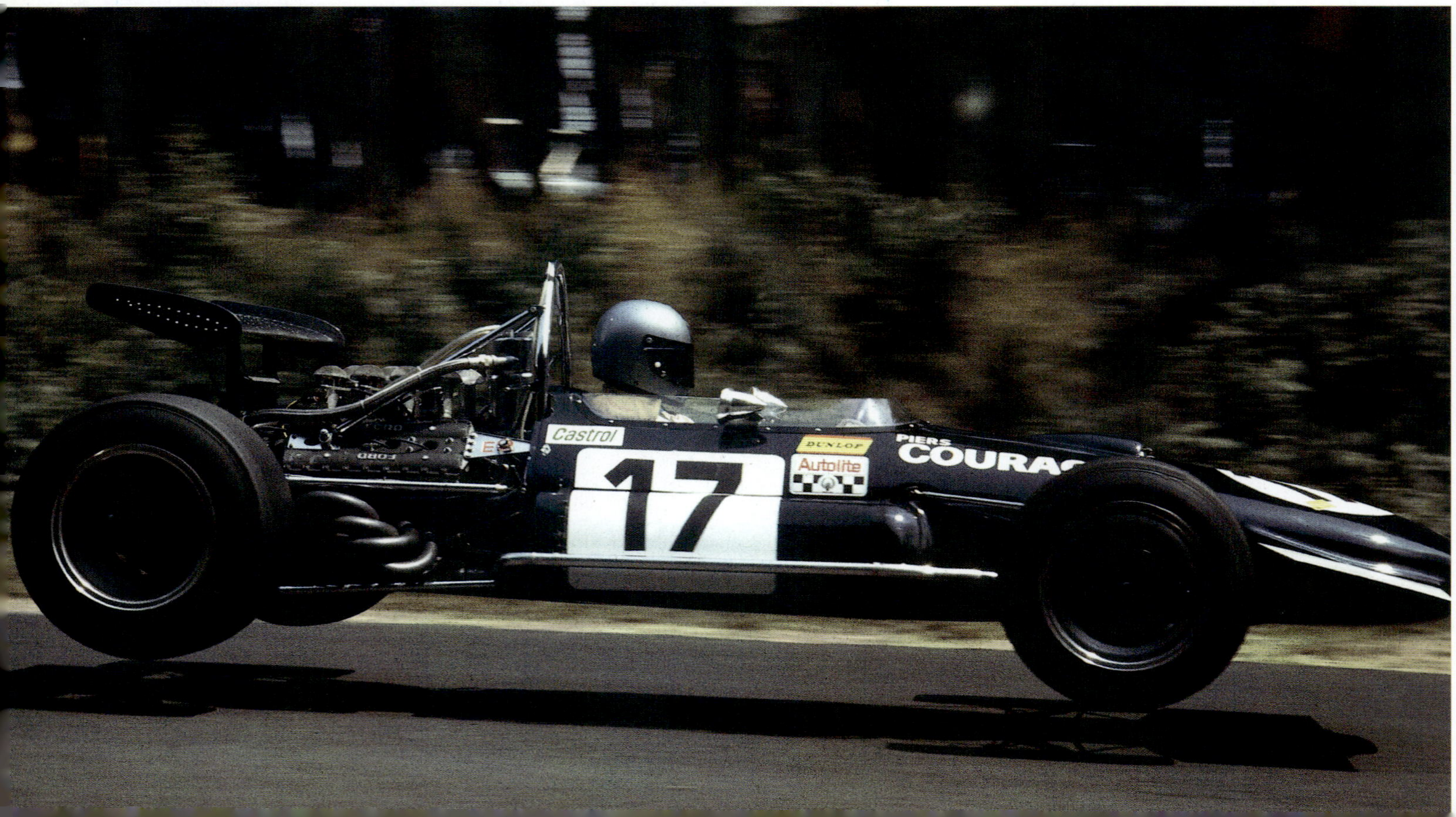

Dexter Brown

Our first meeting was, I think, at the Steering Wheel Club in Mayfair with 'Steady' Barker, in 1965.

Soon after this we went together to Pinewood Studios on to the set of *Chitty Chitty Bang Bang* for *Car* magazine – Mike as photographer, and me to do sketches for a forthcoming article. We travelled down in Mike's Sunbeam Tiger in which I was particularly interested, as I had one too.

Those days of shooting the movie were great. Together we met Dick van Dyke on the set; what a privilege – such a nice man. It felt strange with Mike and I in T-shirts and jeans, whilst everyone else was wandering around in period costume.

Then there were the barbecue days in Mike and Liz's beautiful garden – not forgetting the memorable annual soup/musical evenings, with Liz's wonderful homemade soups courtesy of Mike's bountiful vegetable garden. He was a very keen gardener!

Mike and I teamed up again for the British Grand Prix at Silverstone in 1967, both of us crouched down on the inside of Copse Corner. He was working the Pentax whilst I scribbled away furiously each time the cars came by, so close to us in those days (a 135mm lens was all you needed for a speeding close-up then).

The Earls Court Motor Show was another favourite venue for us both, particularly closing in on the near naked girls draped over the latest cars!

Other remembered days include a time trial around Australian racer Vern Schuppan's garden on a trials bike, on which we all took turns. Mike was always the quickest and most reckless, but frequently finished up in the rhododendrons.

My first painting for Mike was a portrait of Jimmy Clark that I created from snapshots I had, being so moved by his death, which was a shock to us all.

A little known fact is that Mike was an excellent climber of trees! The shot shown of me in my XK120 was taken from the boughs of a large oak for an article in *Autosport* written by Eoin Young (he drove the XK back with the handbrake on for the entire journey – which I still pull his leg about whenever we meet.)

Mike was also very helpful at this time in assisting my son Darin with additional expert advice to help him through a photographic degree course, for which I was always grateful. In return for this I did a sketch of his cottage from the woodshed. It was a wet day, as I recall, with the odd drop of rain dripping down my neck.

The mention of gardens reminds me of Mike and Liz's wedding day held in her parent's garden on a perfect sunny day. In his speech Mike declared, 'I would like to thank my father-in-law for letting us have it on the lawn.' To which Eoin Young shouted from the assembled guests – 'Yes, but just the once!'

During latter years Mike came to many of my exhibitions, and it was really great to see his wonderful shots made into a superb book.

It was a dreadful shock to us all to hear of his death, and even his funeral was particularly moving, being a cold, damp, atmospheric day in March. As we walked in procession from the village church back to his cottage home in its beautiful woodland setting it resembled nothing so much as a scene from a sad film.

R.I.P. Mike.

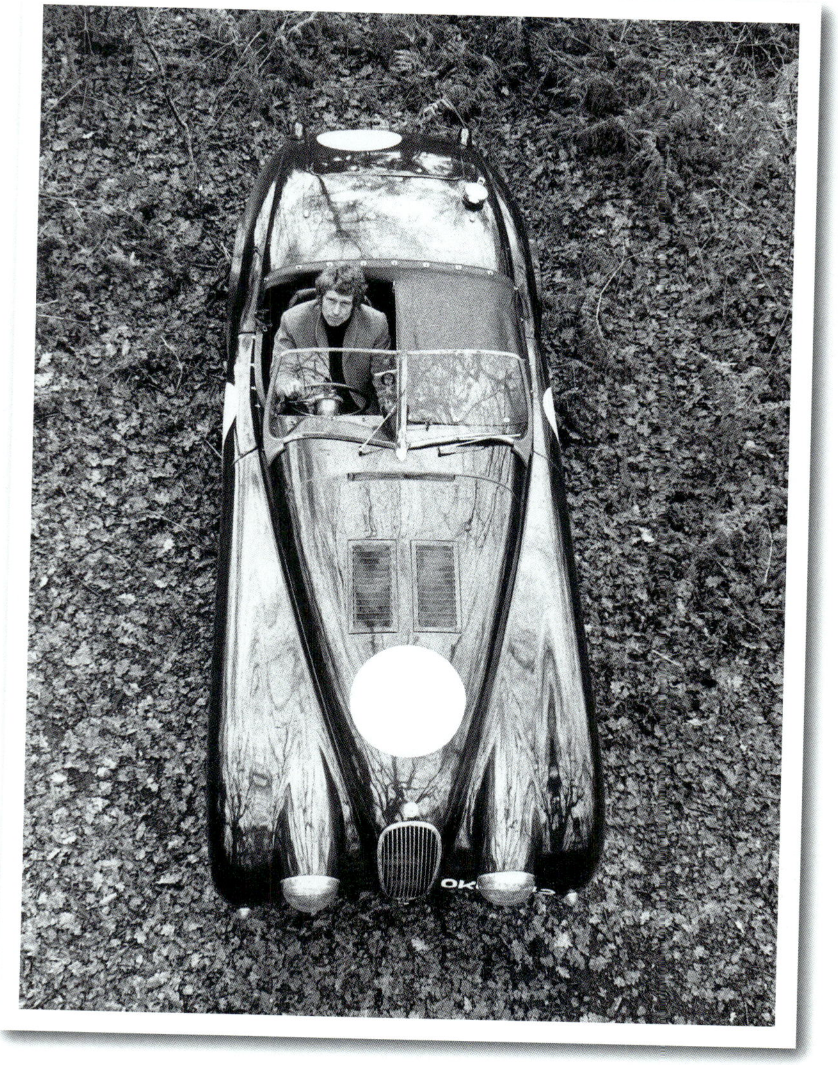

1970s

Mike's racing activities carried on into the new decade but began to wane with the increasing commercialisation of the sport, necessary for its survival but in some ways inimical to the interests of others including the photographers and eventually the punters.

For our man this all reached a head when he attended a Marlboro launch party at Paul Ricard, near Bandol in the south of France, and watched a Marlboro-liveried BRM P160 emerge from a giant cigarette packet. As the decade advanced photo coverage of F1 gradually became a question of access, much of the former vantage points being out of bounds and with it arrived the necessity for ever longer focal length lenses. This in turn robbed us all of the intimate nature of the up close and personal aspect of images taken literally trackside.

Nevertheless Mike was still very active around the circuits for several more years, but the intense and personal contact with drivers, team managers and other personnel of the 1960s was fading away, indeed often no longer possible at the circuits. It was very different back home in Surrey where Mike often shared a jar or three with drivers et al at at the White Horse in Shere whilst playing bar football including James Hunt and Eoin Young, but at the races the 'corporate' approach took control. Some racers gradually evolved into 'stars' and/or businessmen complete with managers and hangers on. Fortunately Mike had alternative interests and commercial contracts and in later years worked for amongst others Honda with whom he enjoyed close relations.

The following images provide a glimpse of this time and are accompanied by a number of overhead shots taken during qualifying for the 1988 British GP at Silverstone. He could still get the appropriate accreditation in Britain via the circuit press officers and made several forays to the British GP at Brands Hatch and Silverstone along with Geoff Goddard and other chums, plus some of the test sessions during which he was almost clobbered by Nelson Piquet's crashing Brabham. These images give a different slant to the variations in design, layout and approach of the class of '88, and during my researches through Mike's archives, appear to be some of his last serial pictures of then contemporary F1.

In an age of very far flung races and locations, the relatively simple life of travelling to and fro to nearby Grands Prix and sports car races in Holland, Belgium, Germany and France by car has also largely departed. However, it had always been a panic rush to get away in time to catch the appropriate ferry, return to base for development of film and printing in time for various publications that week. To facilitate this schedule some photographers actually took many of their pictures during practice and in the first half of the race, making sure they had covered the entire grid thus ensuring that whoever won or lost was on film.

Unlike the highly stage managed artifice and regulatory fascism of latter day professional racing, motor sport was still relatively spontaneous until the mid-1970s, even if it was also potentially lethal. Mike still followed F1 via the media, but that all consuming passion was replaced by the habit of continuity and ultimately he took a greater interest in Indycar racing and also rallying with his friend Chris Rogers.

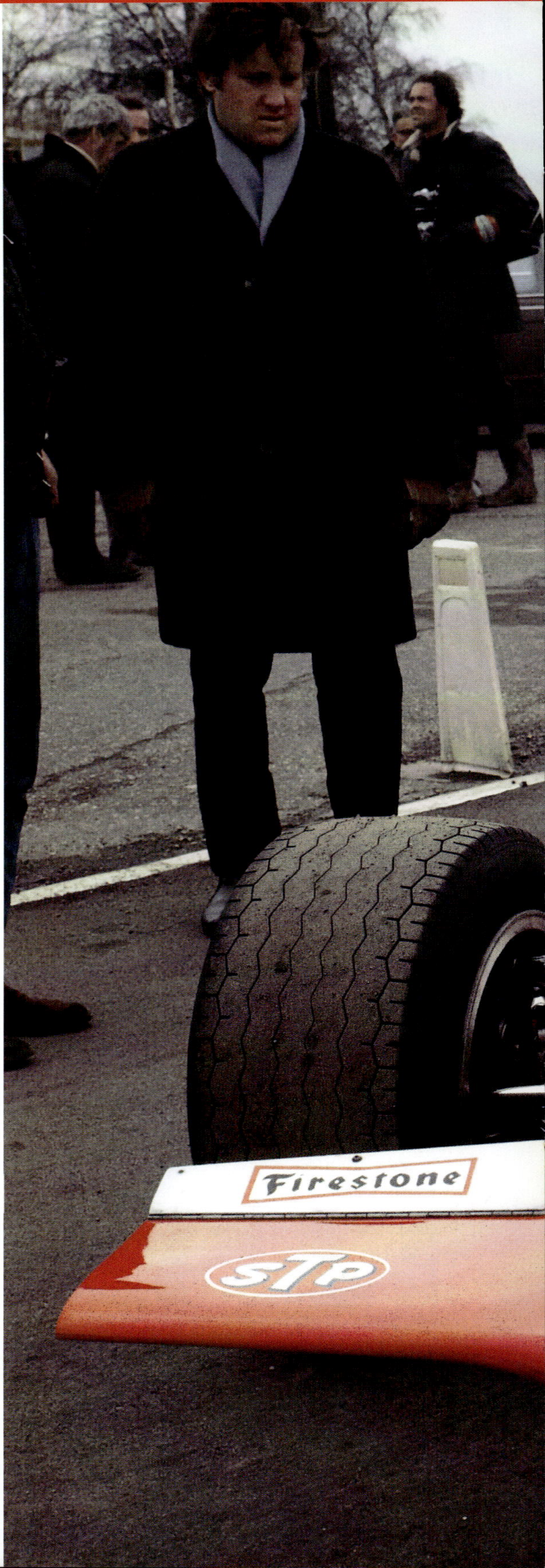

Despite his brilliance and speed, after 96 actual GP starts beginning at Monaco 1963 and ending at the Nürburgring in 1976 (he withdrew from the Canadian GP following a practice collision, his final F1 appearance) Chris Amon is famous for never having won a Championship Grand Prix. He did, however, triumph at the 1970 Silverstone International Trophy, run in two heats, by winning the first in his works STP March 701 by 12.1sec from Jackie Stewart's similar Ken Tyrrell car, and finishing 1.9sec behind Stewart in the second, thus winning on aggregate by 10 seconds. He also won the non-championship Grand Prix d'Argentine for Matra in January 1971. On a cold grey April day, Chris drives 701/1 through the paddock, watched over by March director and ex-racer Alan Rees in overcoat and blue scarf.

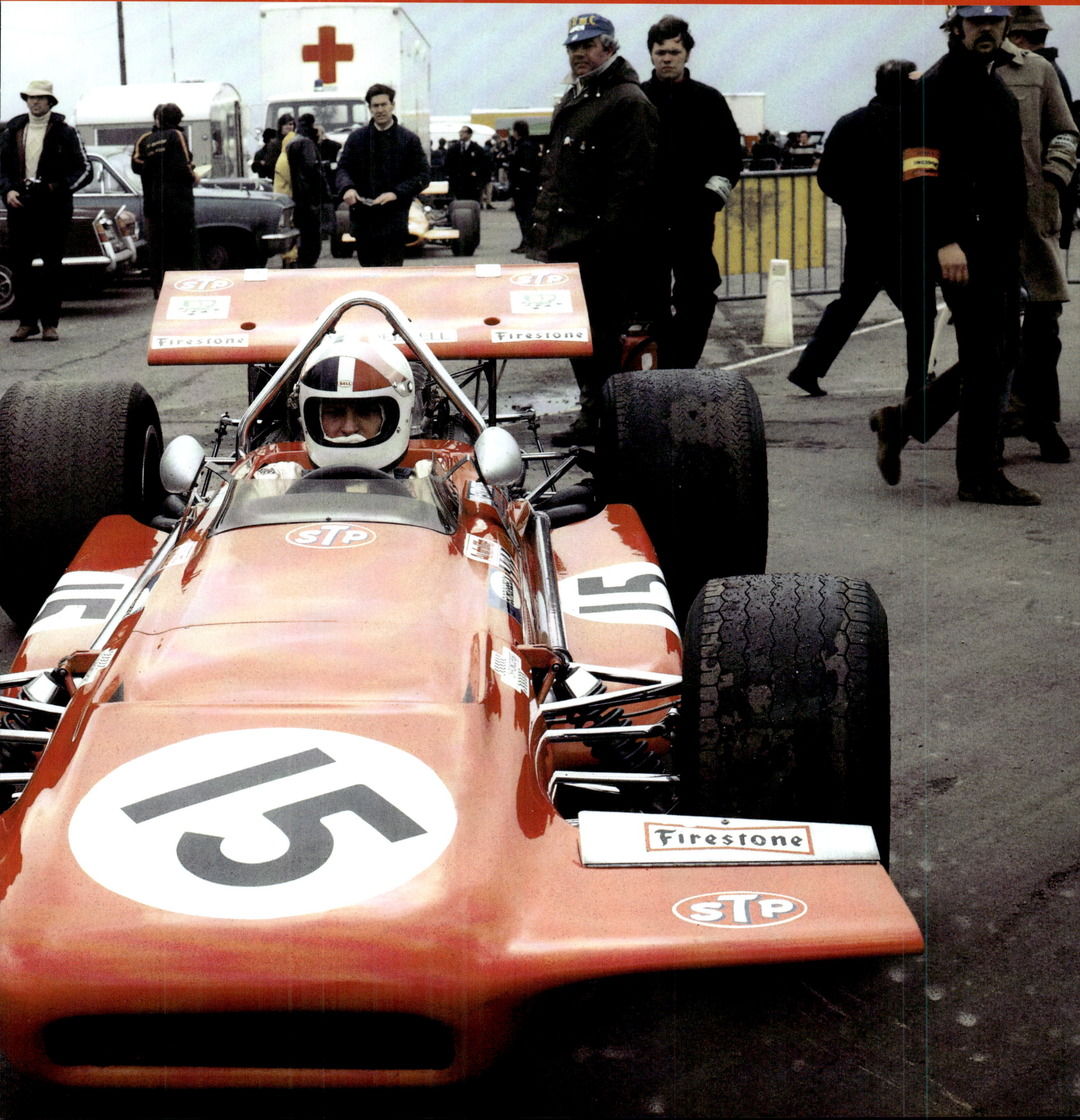

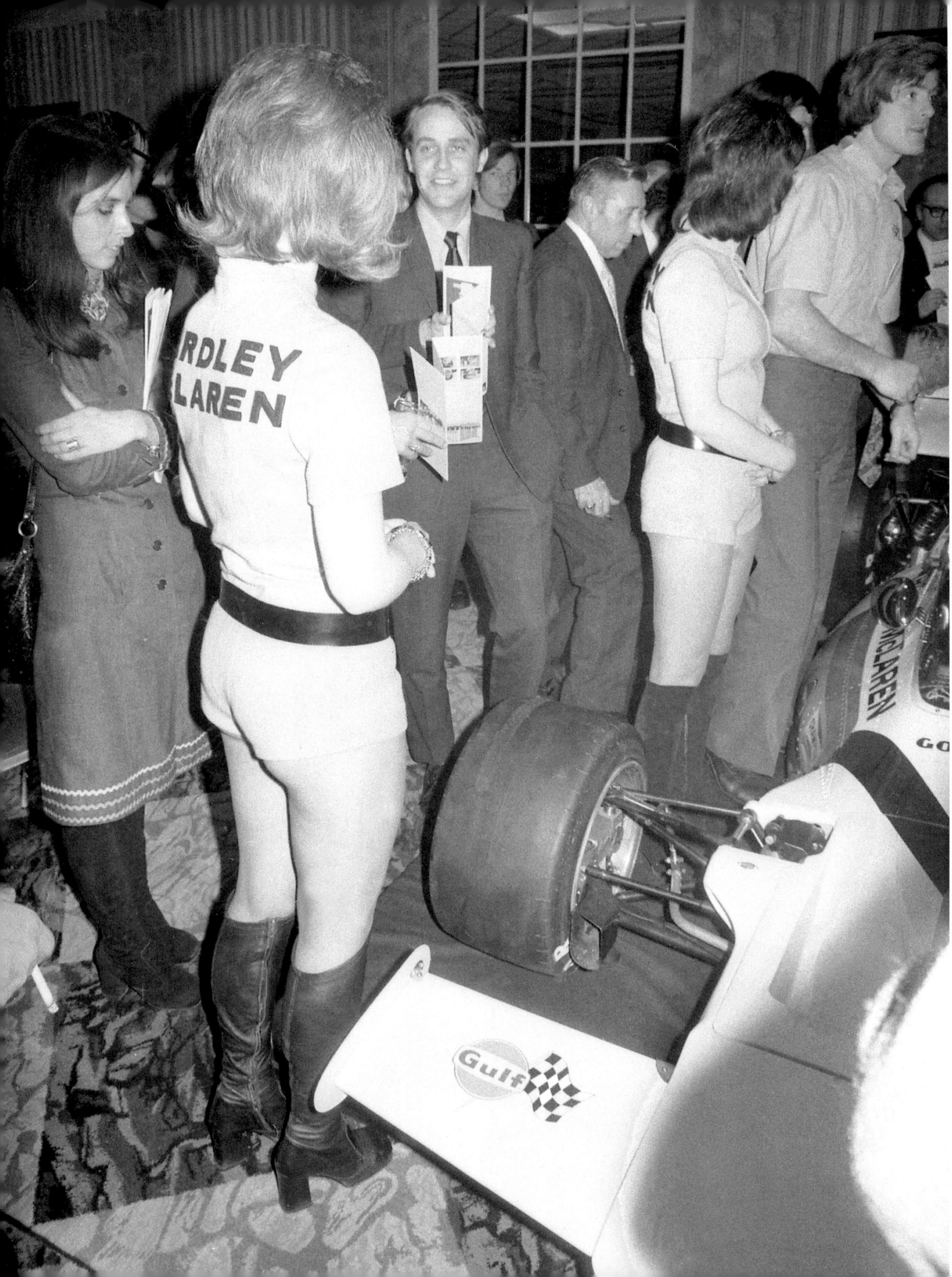
RDLEY
LAREN
McLAREN
Gulf

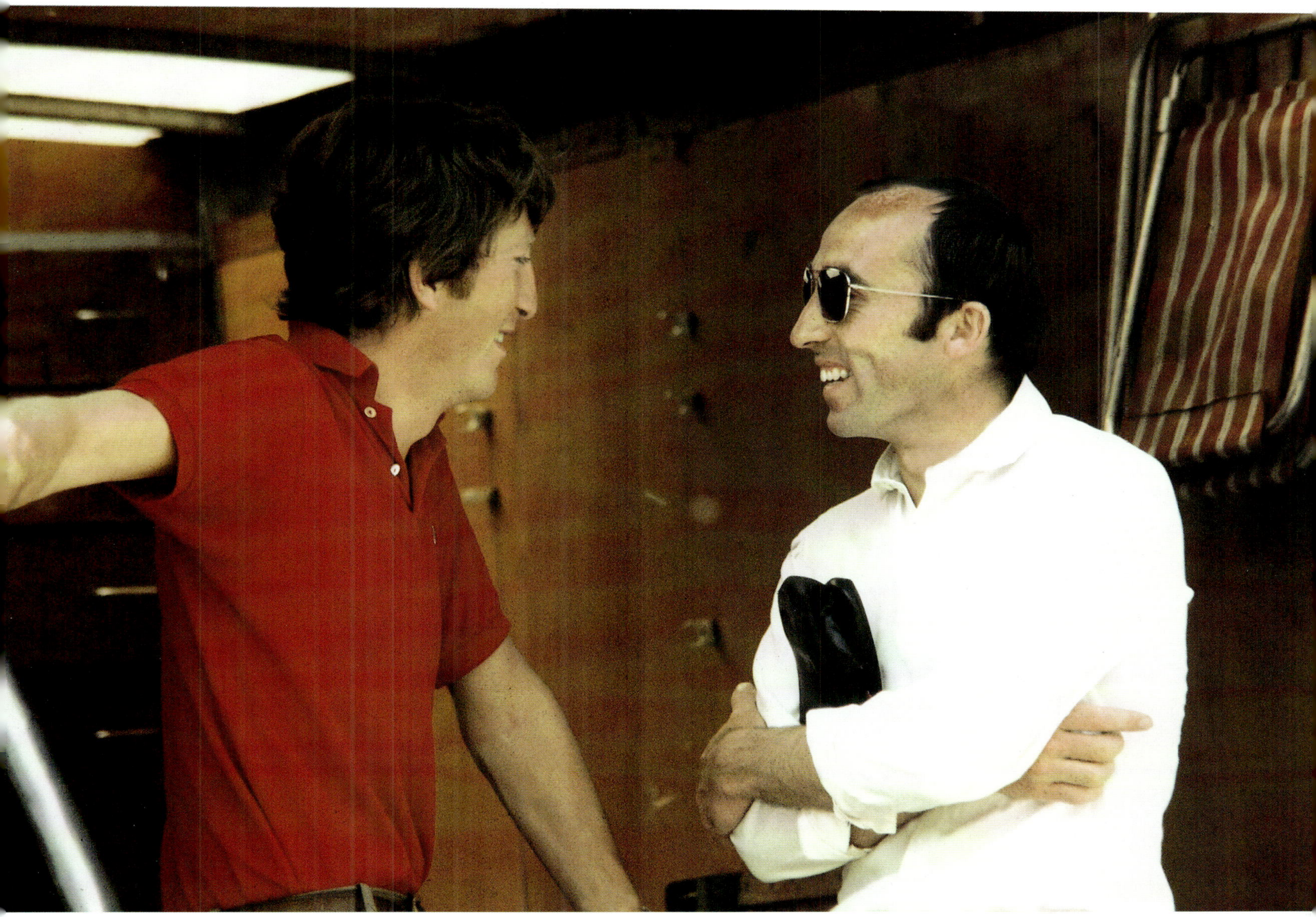

↑ This picture is undated, but it is from *circa* 1970 and shows Jochen Rindt talking to Frank Williams in what looks to be a mutual admiration scenario.

← The Yardley launch party for their sponsorship of BRM in 1970 featured the inevitable provocatively-clad females who are evidently far more interesting to photograph than mere BRMs, and could that be a young Duke of Westminster looking hopeful? The figure far right looks like Alistair Caldwell of McLaren.

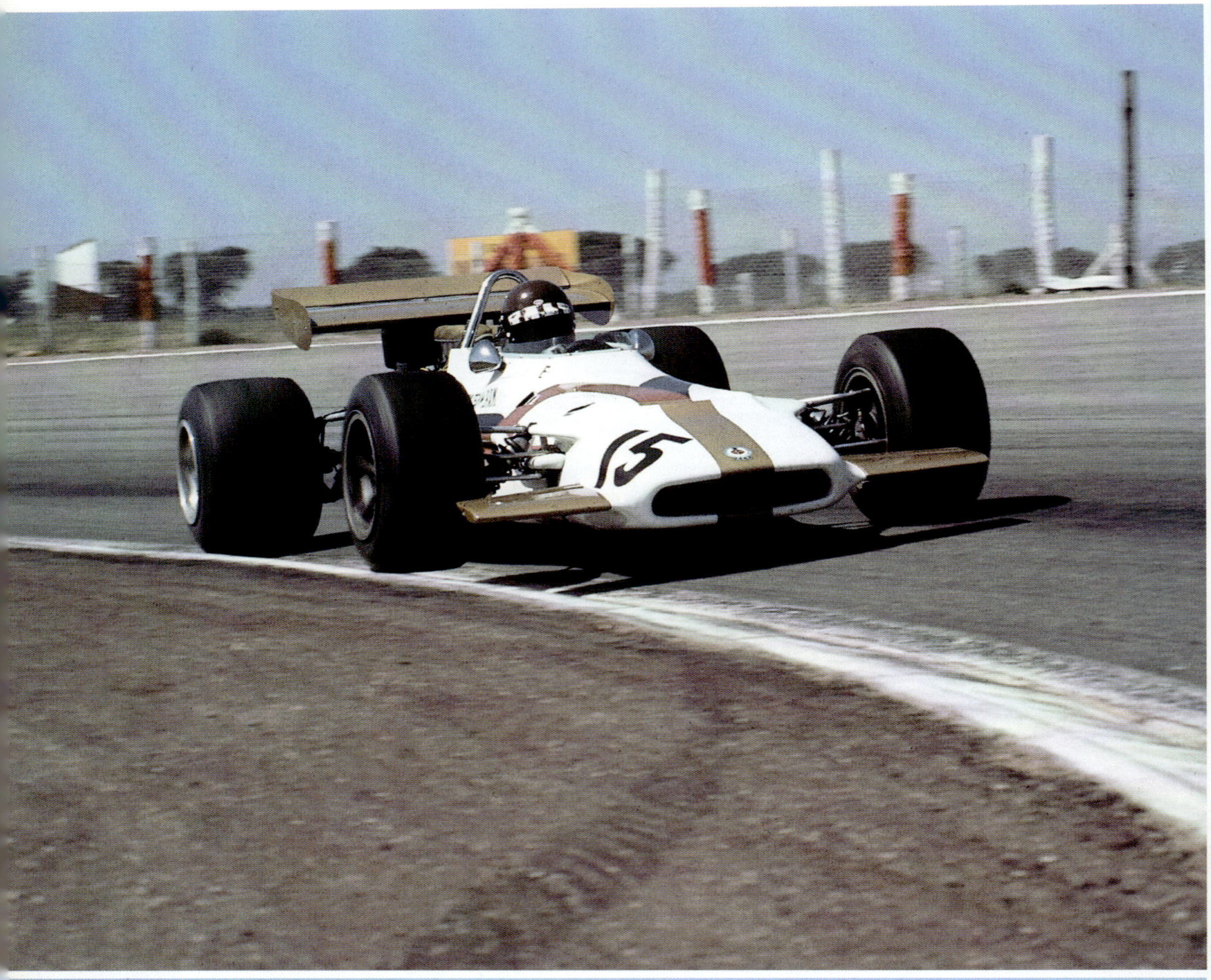
15

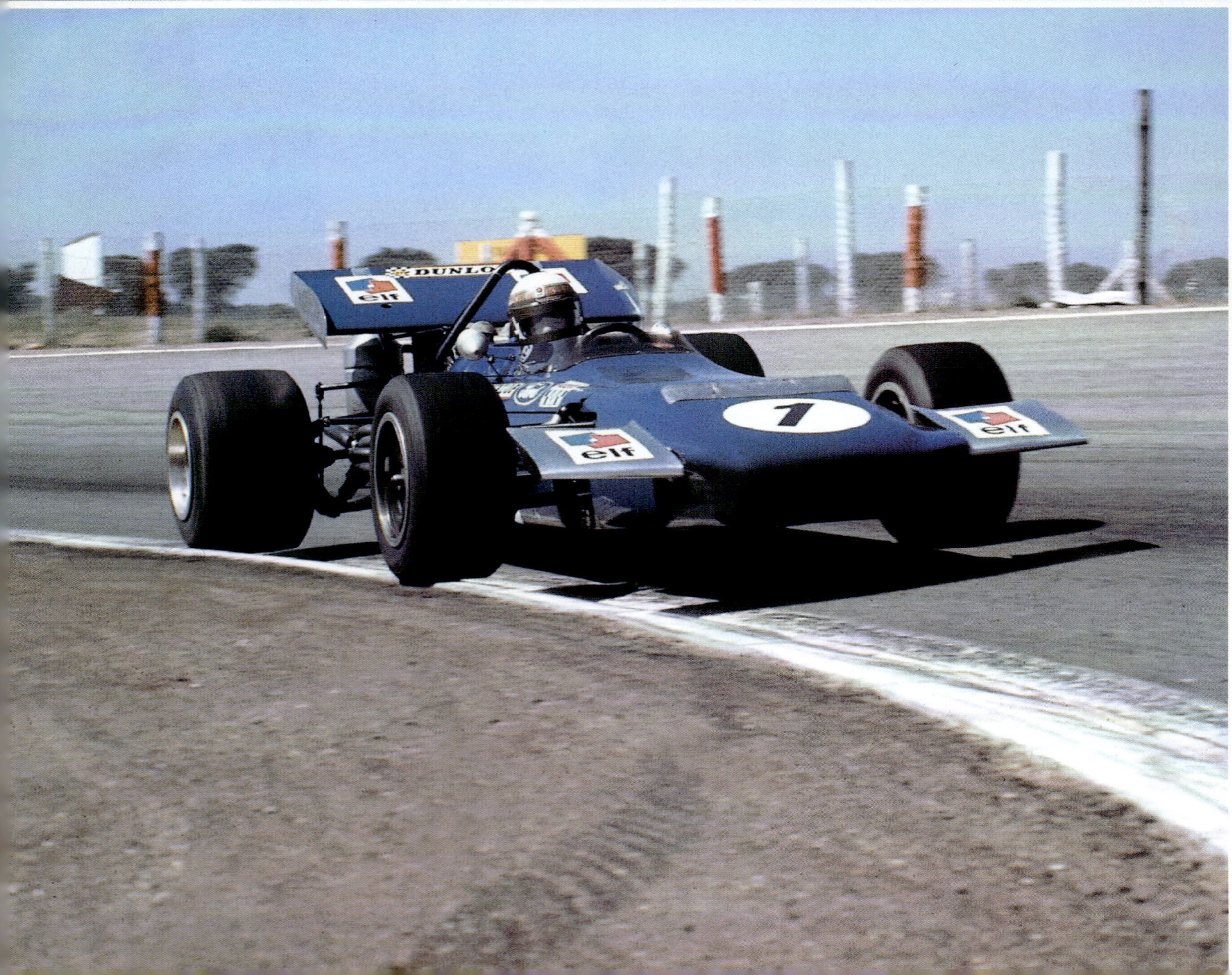
DUNLO
elf
7
elf
elf

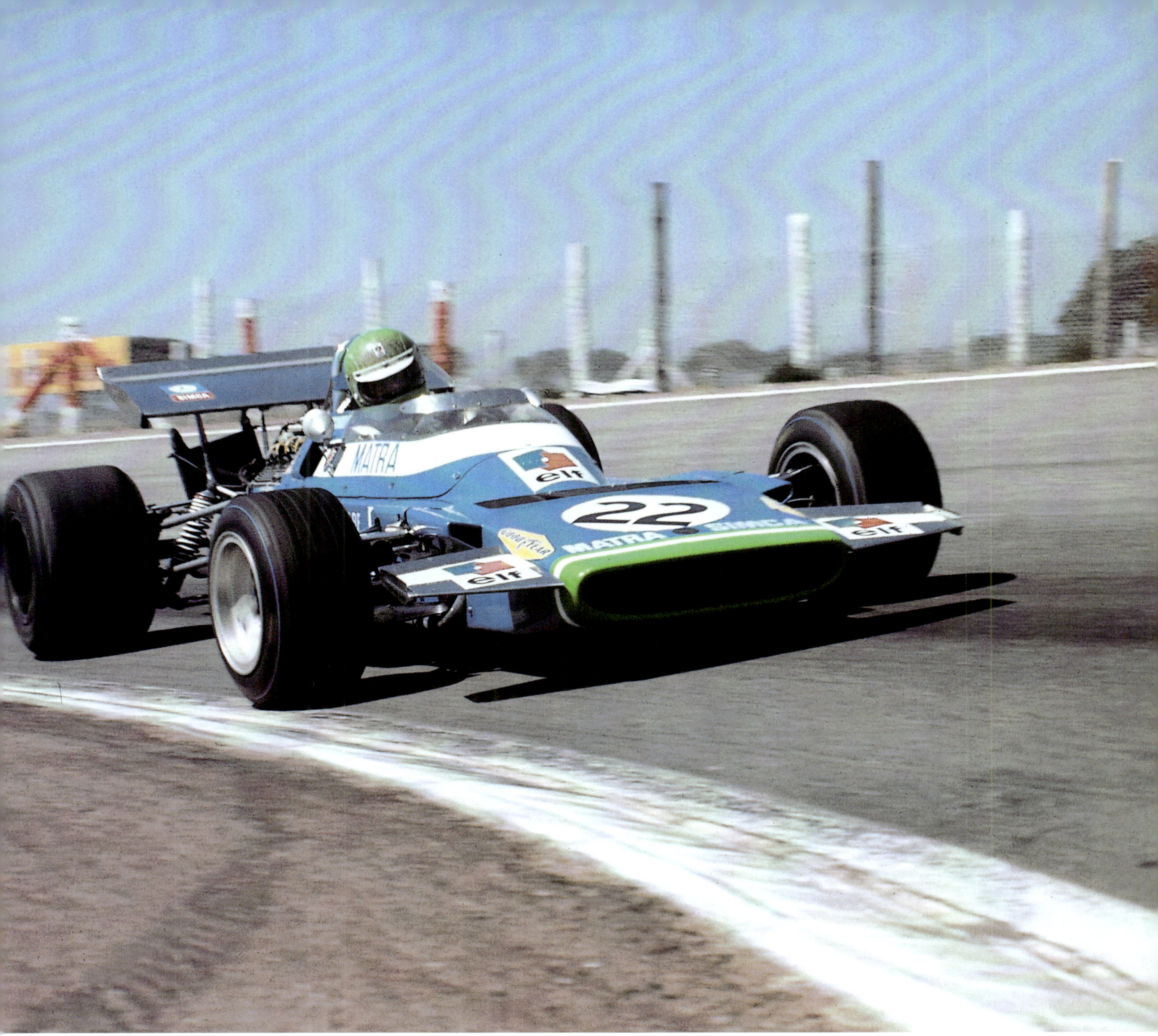

↑ Henri Pescarolo, in his trademark green lid with the wide-nosed Matra MS120/2, applies opposite lock for seventh fastest time. In the race, that was notable for many retirements, he rose to third, but a con rod failed on lap 34.

↖ These shots were taken during practice for the 1970 Spanish GP at Jarama and here is Jackie Oliver, with his distinctive vertically-striped visor, in the BRM P153/01. The arrival of sponsorship from Yardley was undoubtedly very welcome as 1969 had been a dire year, and things were on the up, at least for now. Unfortunately, in the race the BRM broke a stub axle causing Oliver to strike Ickx's Ferrari amidships. Both cars caught fire and burned to a crisp – happily, the drivers escaped with minor burns. As a result of this unexpected mechanical failure, Pedro Rodriguez in the sister P153 was withdrawn on lap 4.

← Jackie Stewart doing what he did best, qualifying well (third) at Jarama, and then leading the race from start to finish after a serious battle with Jack Brabham.

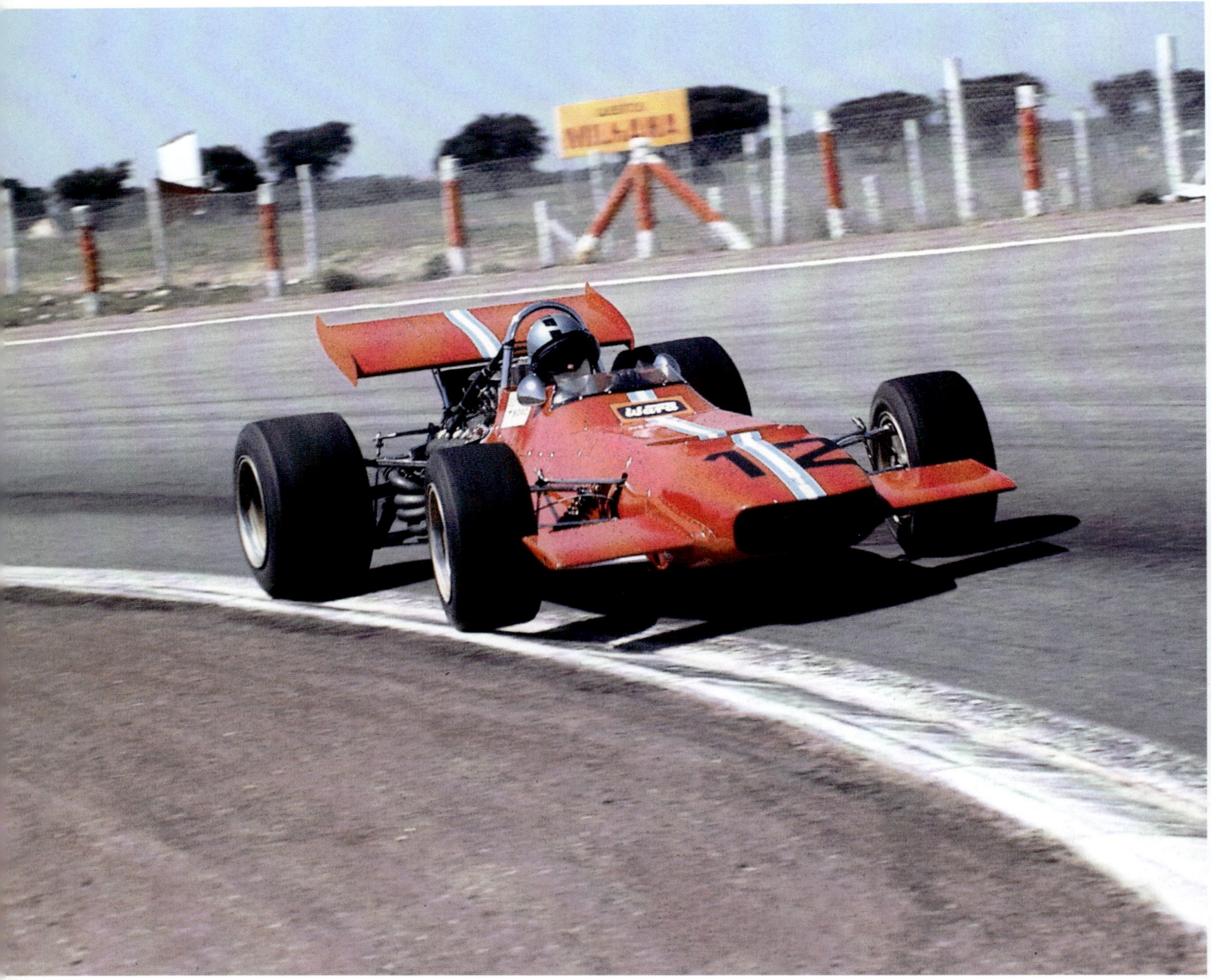

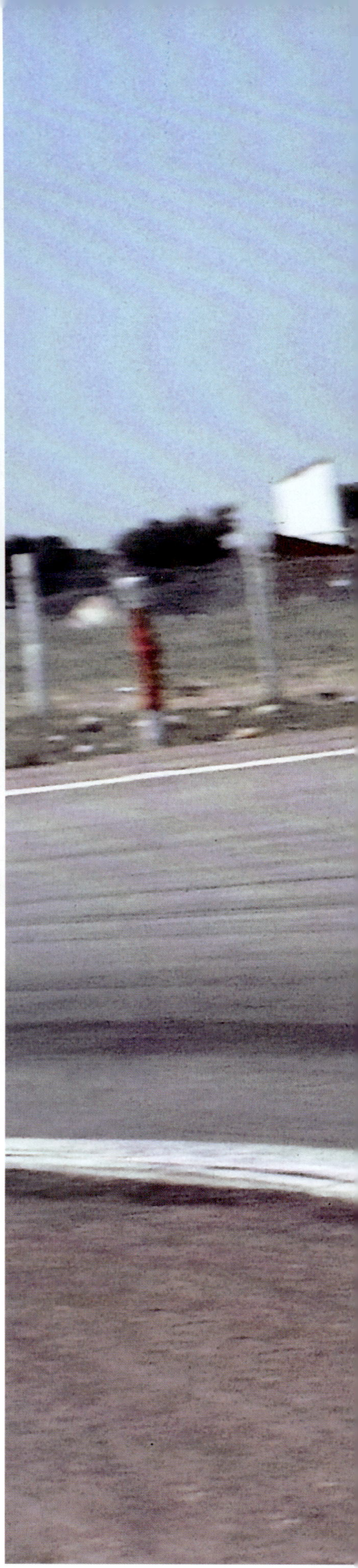

A lovely shot of Piers Courage in the first Frank Williams de Tomaso 505, now enjoying some revisions, well into the kerb before his big shunt ascending the hill behind the pits. In *Piers Courage, Last of the Gentleman Racers*, author Adam Cooper quotes Piers on the accident, 'Going up that corner on top of the hill in fourth, I was headed directly into the sun and I couldn't see anything.'

Jochen Rindt's angle of attack is rather more acute in the Gold Leaf Team Lotus 70 (R2), making its race debut at Jarama. Two were entered (the other one was driven by John Miles) but they were still under development and proving troublesome. Miles failed to qualify, and Rindt's race lasted only ten laps because of ignition problems.

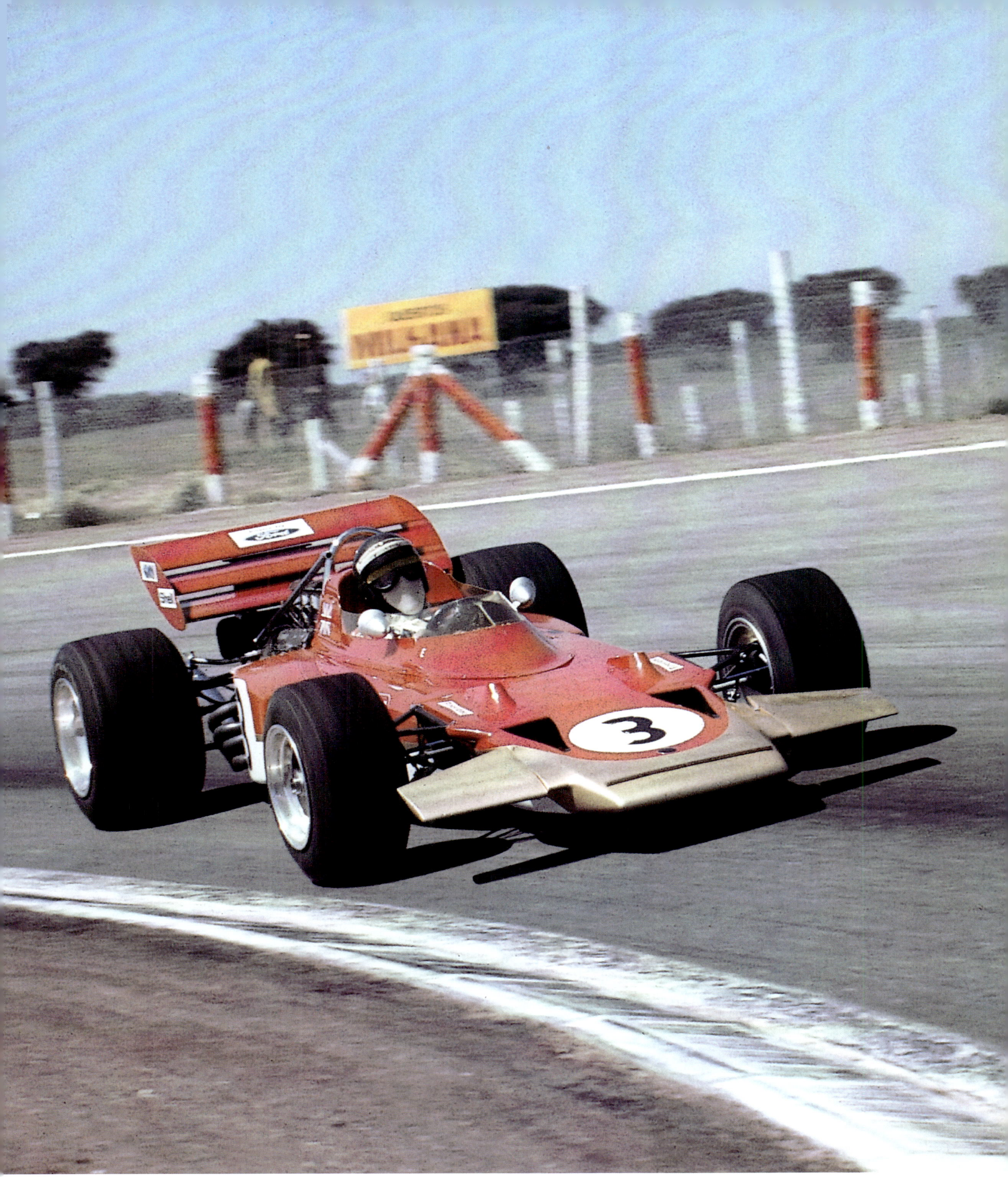

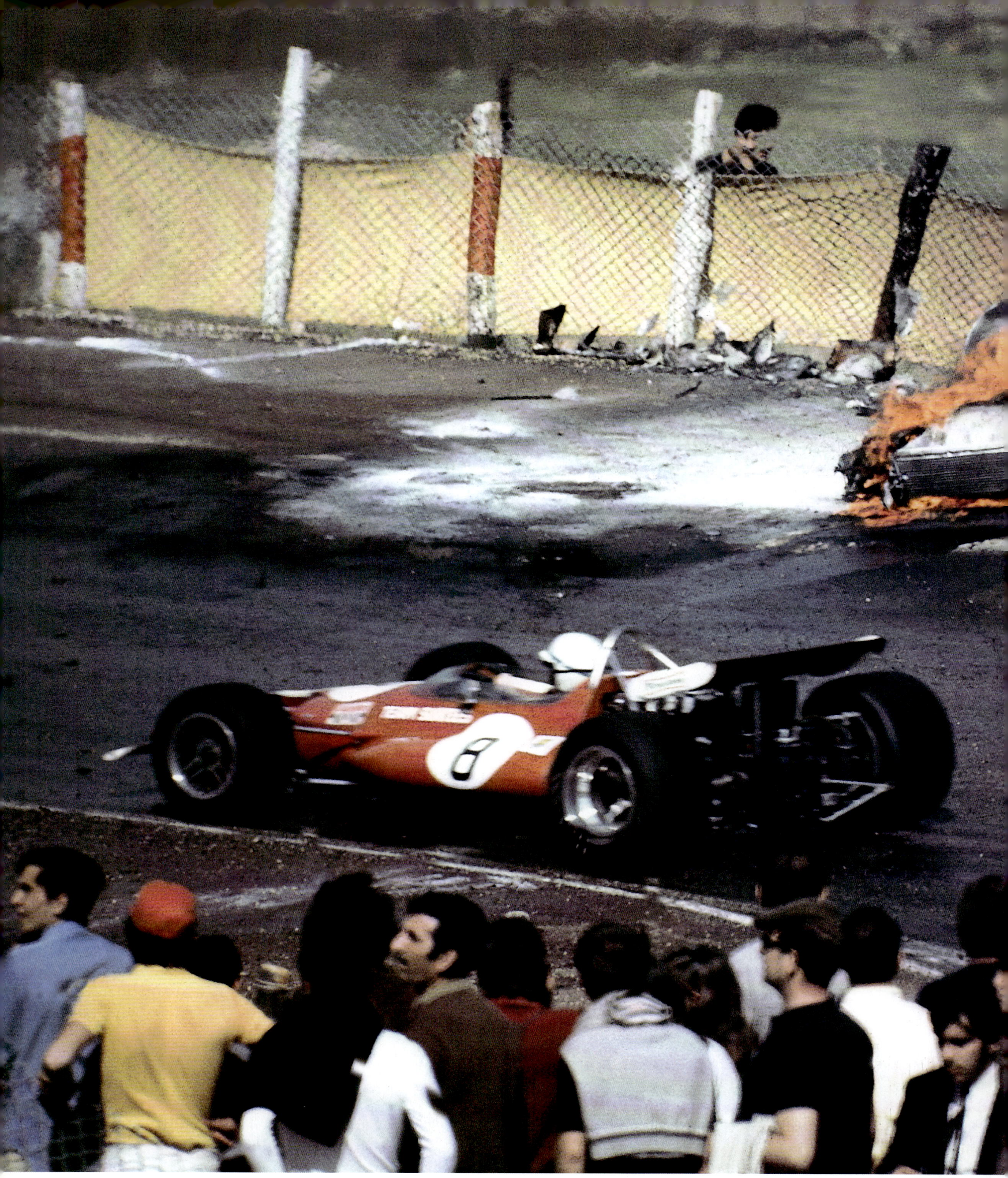

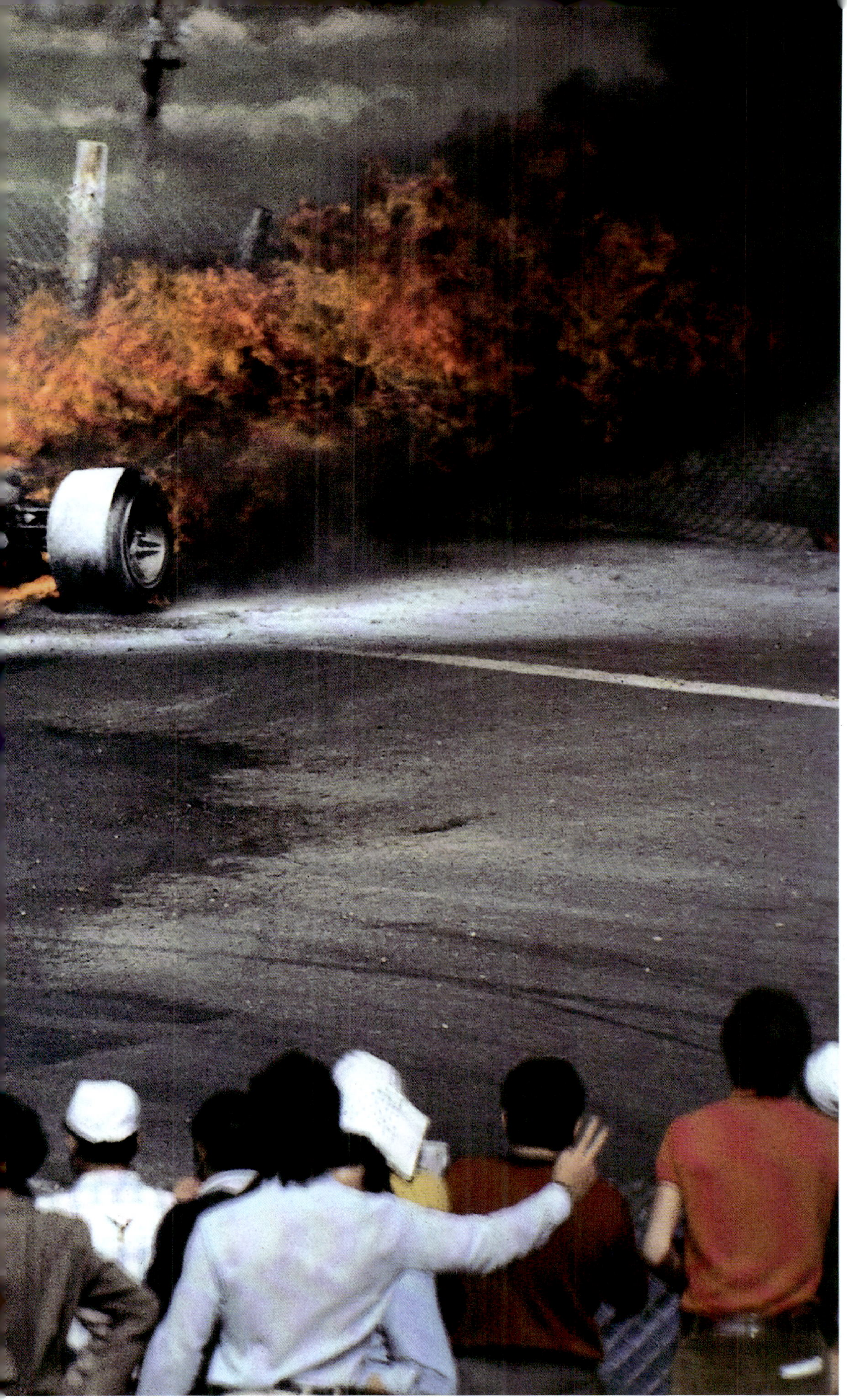

← John Surtees passes by in his stopgap McLaren M7C/1 as Mike focuses his camera on the burning remains of Jackie Oliver's BRM P153/01 after its collision with Ickx's Ferrari during the opening laps of the Spanish GP. No wonder drivers of earlier eras preferred to be thrown clear of their crashing cars.

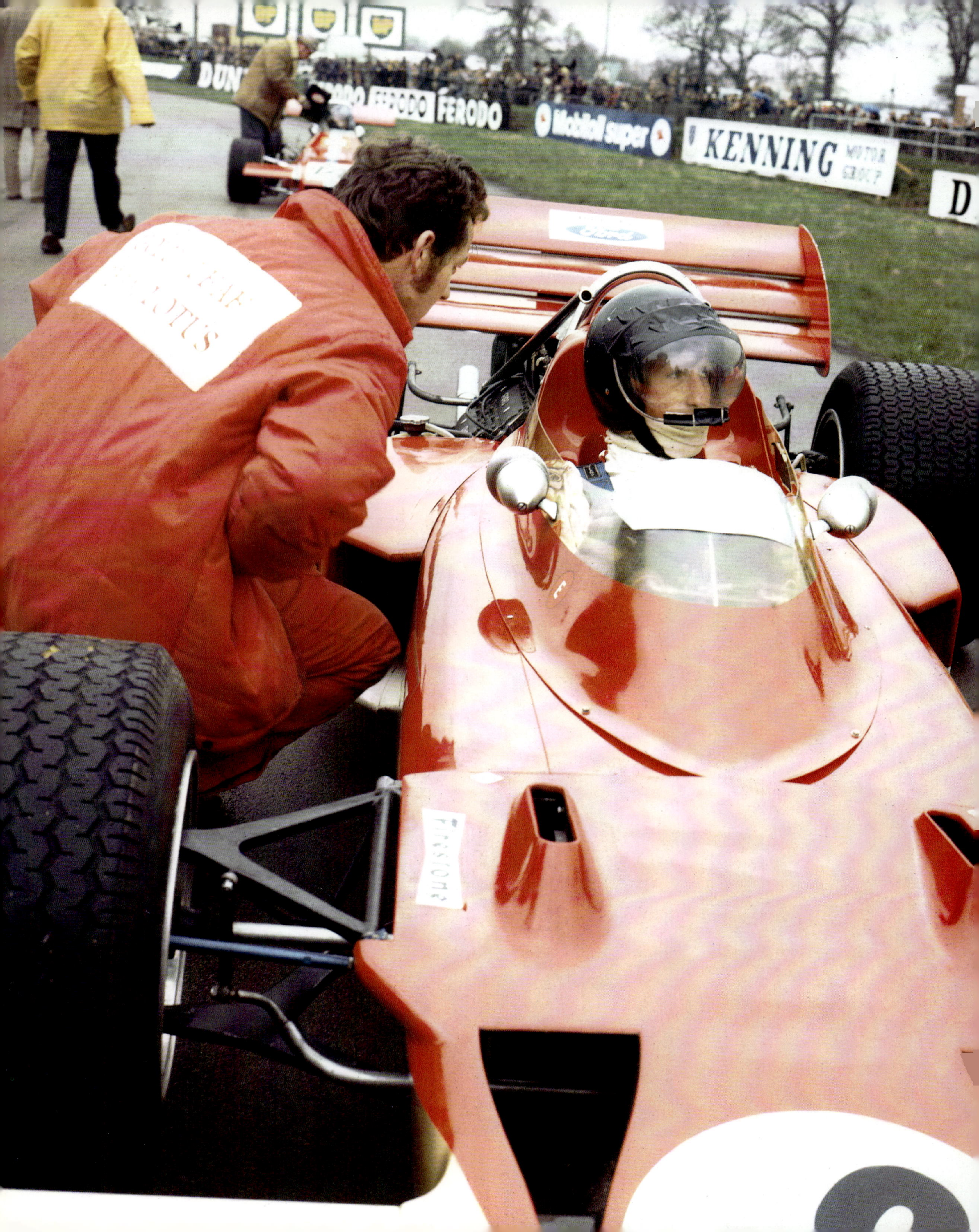
FERODO
FERODO
Mobiloil super
KENNING MOTOR GROUP

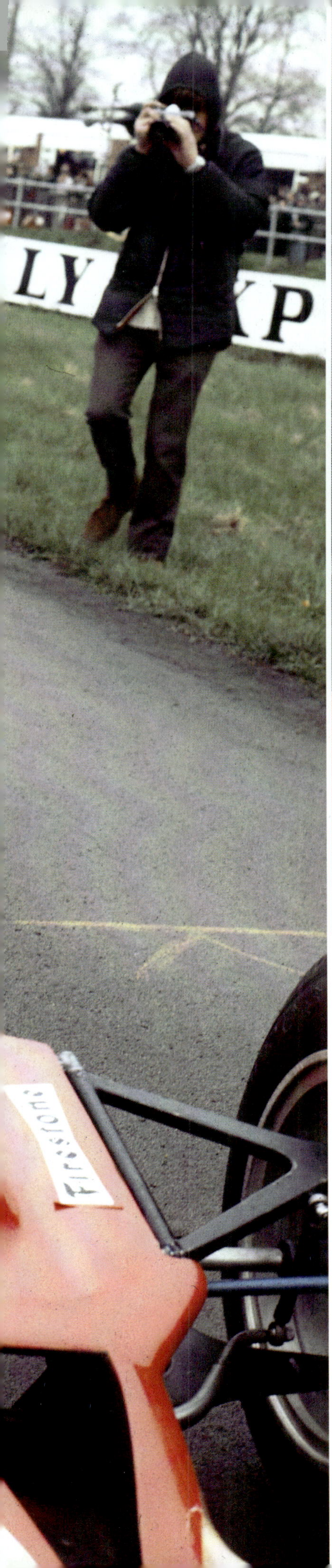

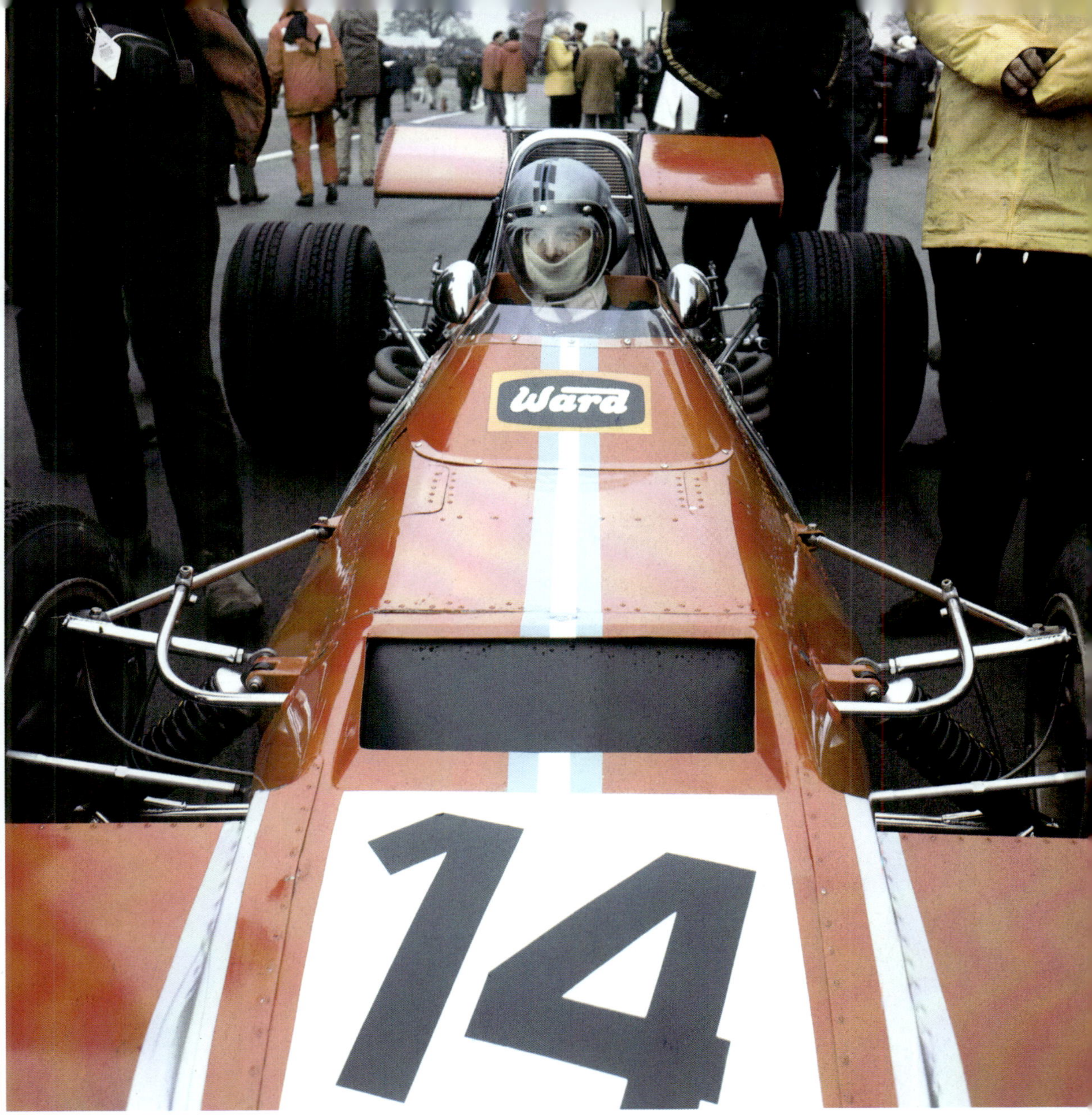

↑ The USAF helicopter pilot helmets were briefly tried by Courage, Stewart, and Brabham in 1970, but the full-face Bell helmets that were already in circulation were about to make open-faced lids redundant. Piers Raymond Courage sits on the grid for the 1970 Silverstone International Trophy in the Frank Williams de Tomaso 505 designed by Gianpaulo Dallara, a new lighter car to replace the one Piers had shunted in Spain. He missed practice because of competing in the Monza 1,000km sports car race and started from the back of the grid in both races, but nevertheless finished a magnificent third.

← Early specification Lotus 72 (R2) at Silverstone with its anti-dive, anti-squat suspension that was removed pre-Monaco where Jochen Rindt won in the old 49C after Brabham crashed at the final corner of the race. The 72 had inboard front brakes, hence the air extractor outlets in the nose. At Silverstone Rindt finished fifth, nearly a lap behind, in heat 1, and quickly retired in heat 2, a disappointing result that, following handling problems, triggered radical changes to the car.

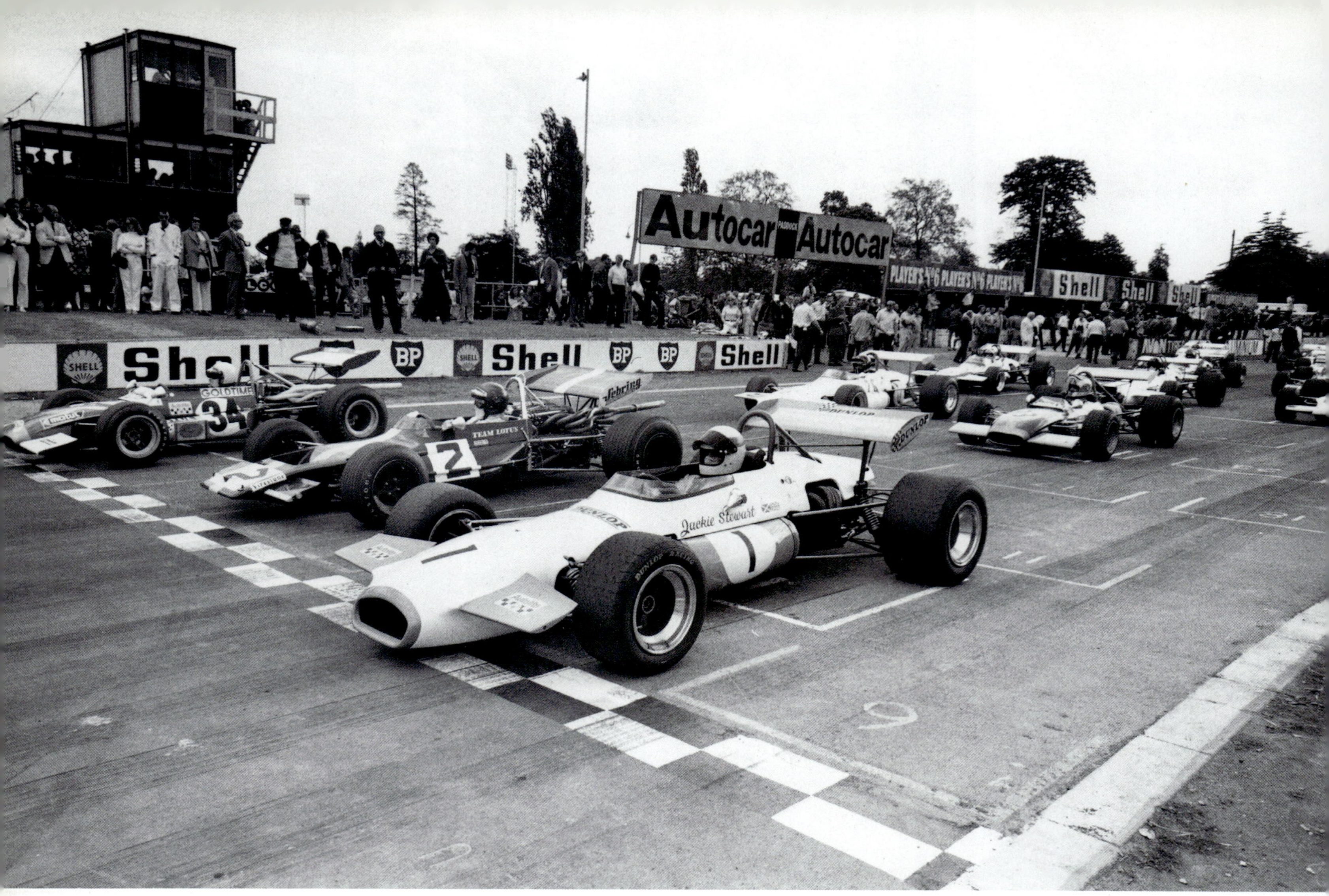

↑ Crystal Palace was only 1.39 miles round, but it was the setting for some of the most wonderful and viscerally exciting races anywhere, before it was closed down by the local authorities in late 1972. Easily accessible by car, bus or train in South London it is still sadly missed by those who knew it. Awaiting the start of the 1970 Alcoa International Trophy and round 4 of the European F2 championship is Jackie Stewart, on pole in the John Coombs Brabham BT30. Alongside are Jochen Rindt in his team's Lotus 69, and the tiny Tecno Racing Team Tecno 69 of Clay Regazzoni. Behind are the second Tecno of François Cevert, and Andrea de Adamich in the Jolly Club Brabham BT30, and the rest of the grid. All are powered by Cosworth's ubiquitous FVA. There are nine current or former F1 drivers in the field, and the race was run over two 20-lap heats (won by Stewart and Rindt) and a 50-lap final, also won by Stewart from Regazzoni and Emerson Fittipaldi. You certainly got value for money in those days.

↗ Just walkin' in the rain, just walkin' in the rain, what a wonderful feeling, we're at Monaco again. The Olivers in company with Yardley's Michael Pitt-Bailey ascend the hill towards Casino Square during the wet Friday morning of the 1970 GP weekend. Jackie Oliver's BRM P153 lasted 43 laps in the race before retiring with that old favourite, engine failure.

→ It was dry on race day at Monaco as a blonde Helen Stewart, Roman Polanski, Jackie Stewart, and Walter Hayes of Ford walk down the hill from Casino Square towards St Devote. Jackie gained pole with the Ken Tyrrell March 701 and led the race until lap 27 when misfiring caused him to stop for a new ignition box, but eventually he retired on lap 58. The man with the pipe, Walter Leopold Arthur Hayes CBE (12 April 1924 – 26 December 2000), ex-journalist and Fleet Street editor (*Daily Mail* and *Sunday Dispatch*), later director of public affairs for Ford, was responsible for providing the initial £100,000 funding that made possible the Cosworth DFV. He was also party to the decision to challenge Ferrari's hegemony in championship endurance racing with the Ford GT40.

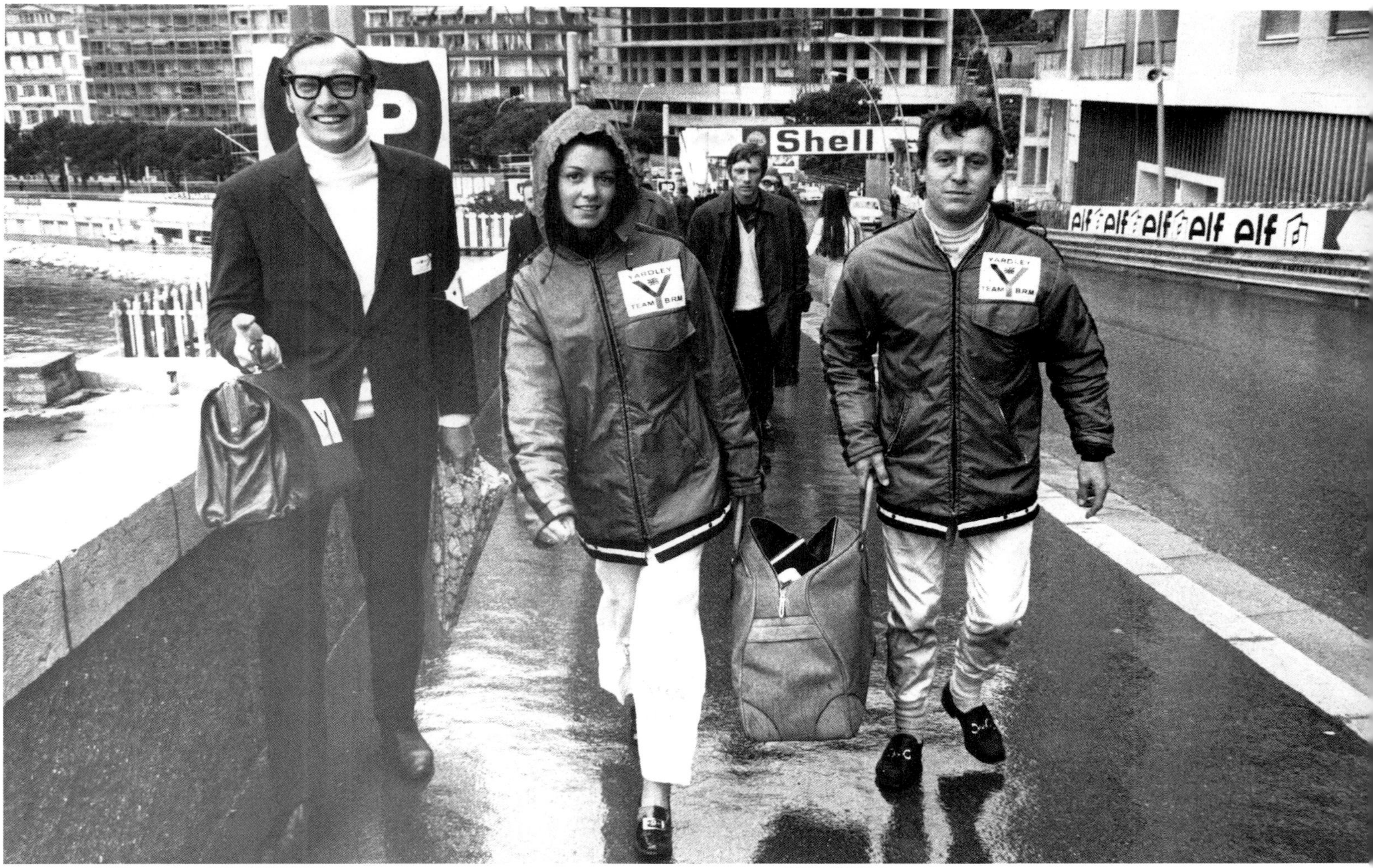
Shell
YARDLEY
TEAM BRM
YARDLEY
TEAM BRM

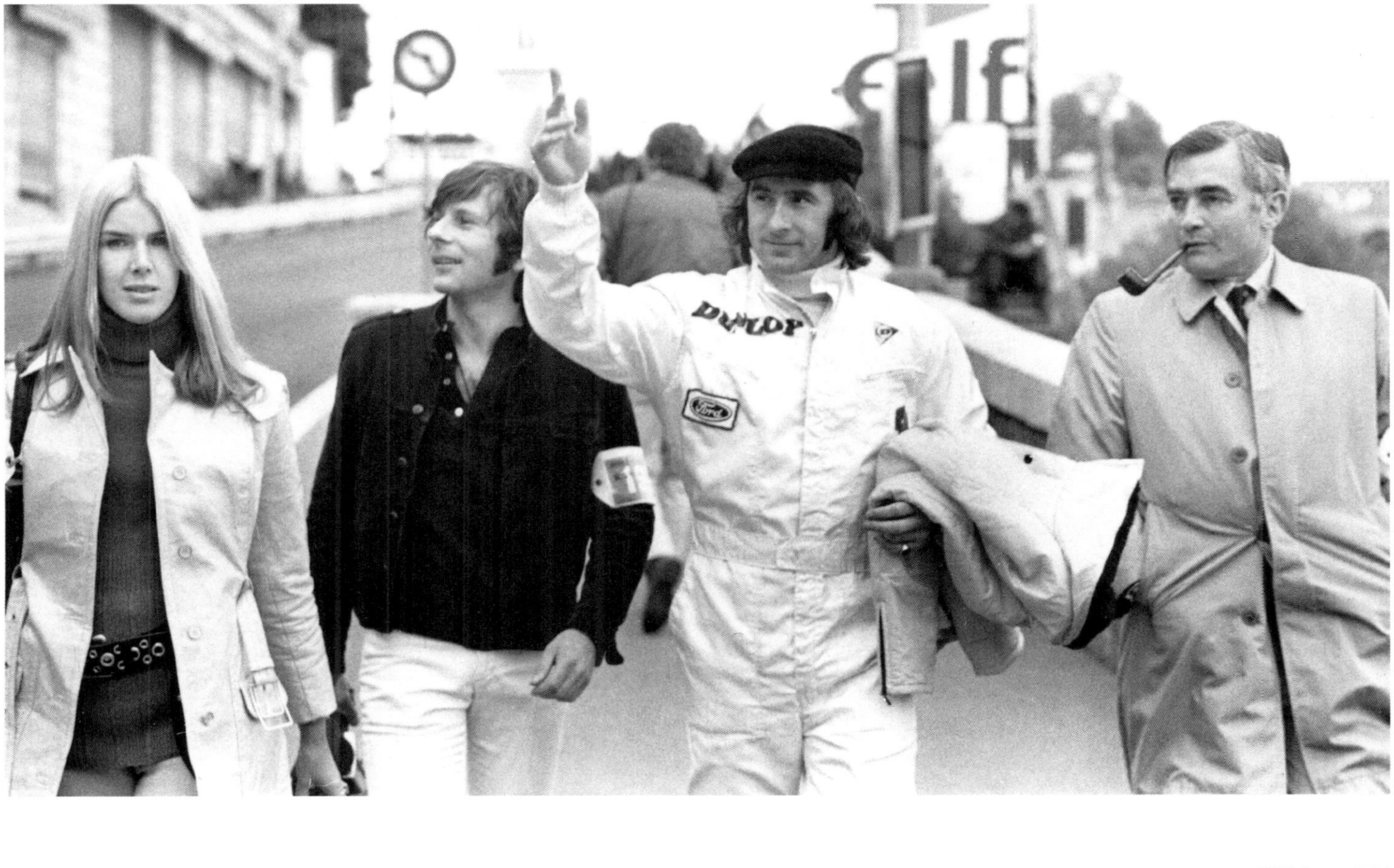
DUNLOP

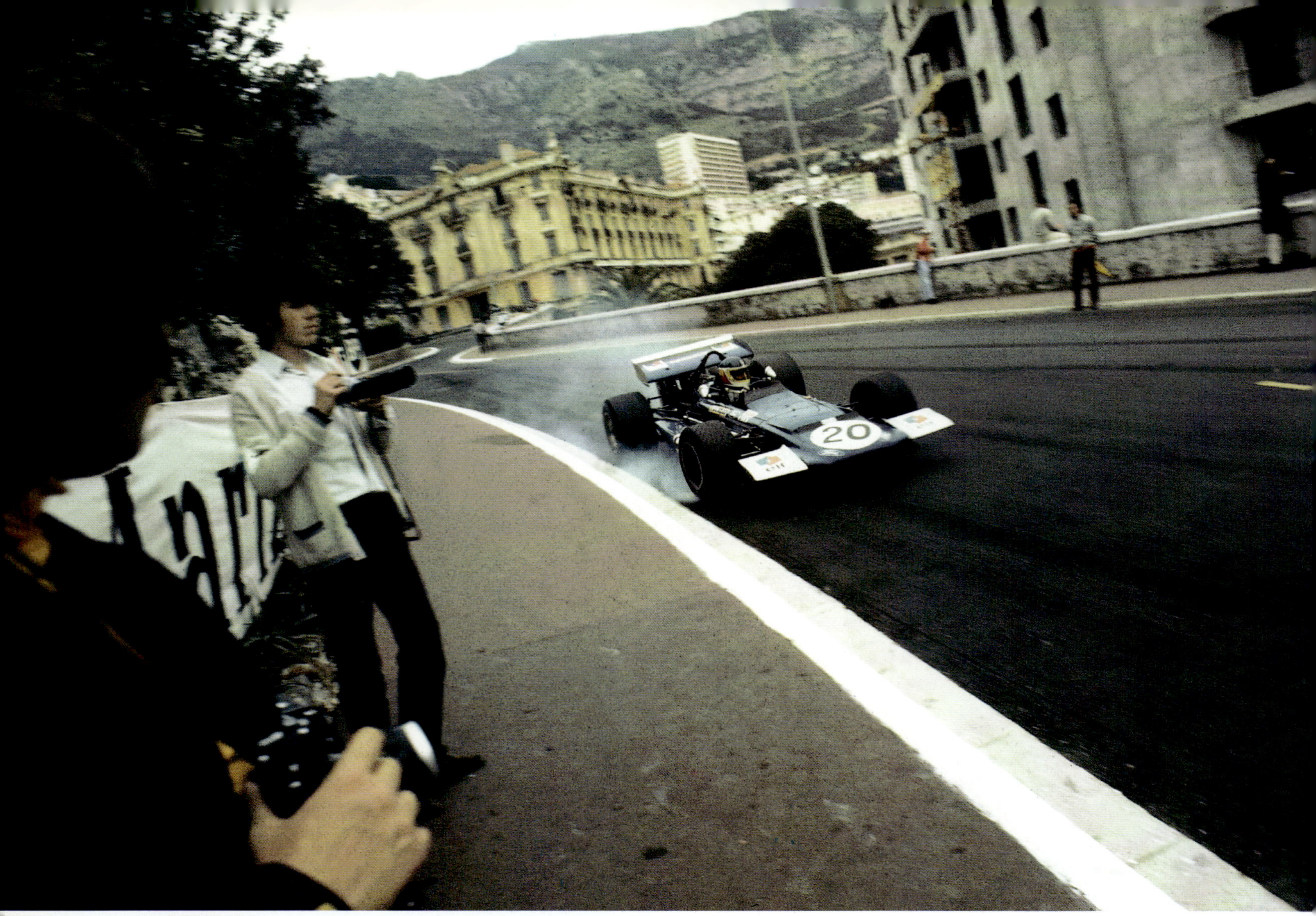

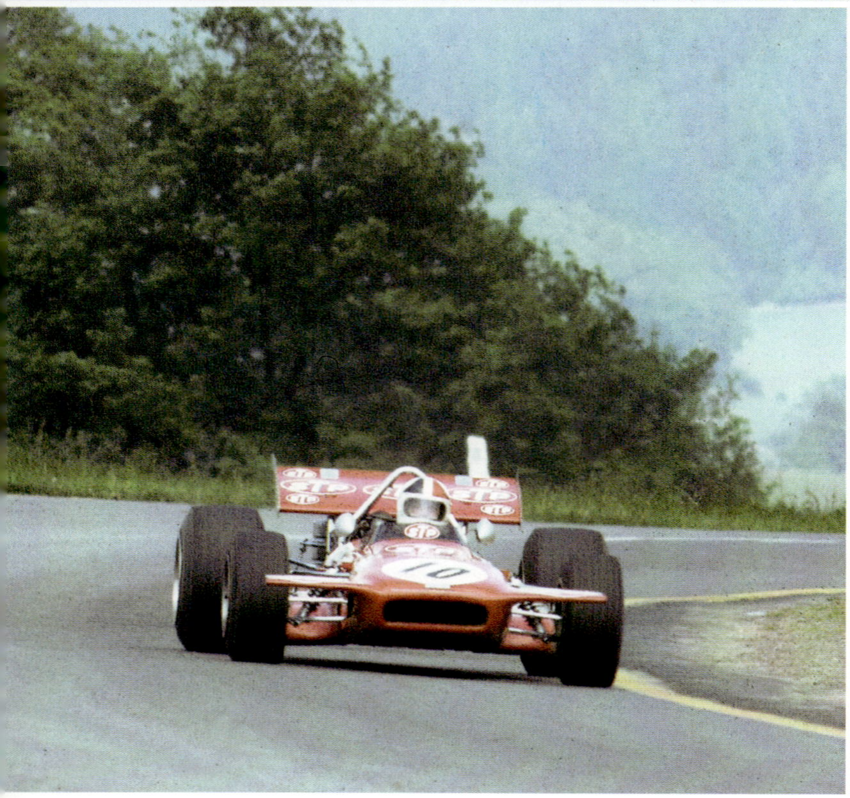

↑ Not the best of shots, but a typical Mike snatched moment that graphically illustrates how close you were to the action. Johnny Servoz-Gavin in the Ken Tyrrell March 701/7 locks up approaching Loew's Hairpin at Monaco 1970. The unfortunate Frenchman had damaged his eyesight in an accident driving an off-road vehicle and he failed to qualify here, bringing his career to an end. He had, in fact, finished fifth in this car at the preceding Spanish GP. During the early 1980s he survived an exploding gas bottle on his boat, despite his heart stopping four times. He died aged 64 on 29 May 2004.

← The new March 701 was competitive straight out of the box, to use a tired cliché, but its potential was limited, and by 1971 it was out of date. At Spa, Chris Amon started on the outside of the front row in 701/1 (Stewart had pole in the Tyrrell 701) but Jackie's car was below par and both were caught and passed by Pedro Rodriguez's BRM P153. Ultimately, despite trying to push the throttle pedal through the bulkhead, Amon could not catch and pass the BRM, and Rodriguez won by just 1.1sec. Chris also finished second at the French GP, fifth at the British, third at the Canadian, fifth at the US GP, and fourth at the Mexican round, all in this car, so it did its best for him. As is so often the case whenever I see a Spa picture, I find myself wondering just where you would end up if you left the road, especially at these speeds.

➔ By 1970 Dan Gurney's F1 career was at an end, and this is the first of three GP races he undertook for Bruce McLaren, at Zandvoort (replacing the injured Denny Hulme) where the M14A/1 suffered timing gear failure. He finished sixth at the French GP, Clermont Ferrand, and retired in his final GP at Brands Hatch on 18 July 1970. Frequently unlucky, he achieved four Grand Prix victories (1962 French GP, 1964 French GP, 1964 Mexican GP, and 1967 Belgian GP) from 86 races, beginning with the 1959 French GP, but should have won many more. He does, however, have the unique distinction of being the only American with his own team in an American car (albeit built in England) to win a World Championship F1 race.

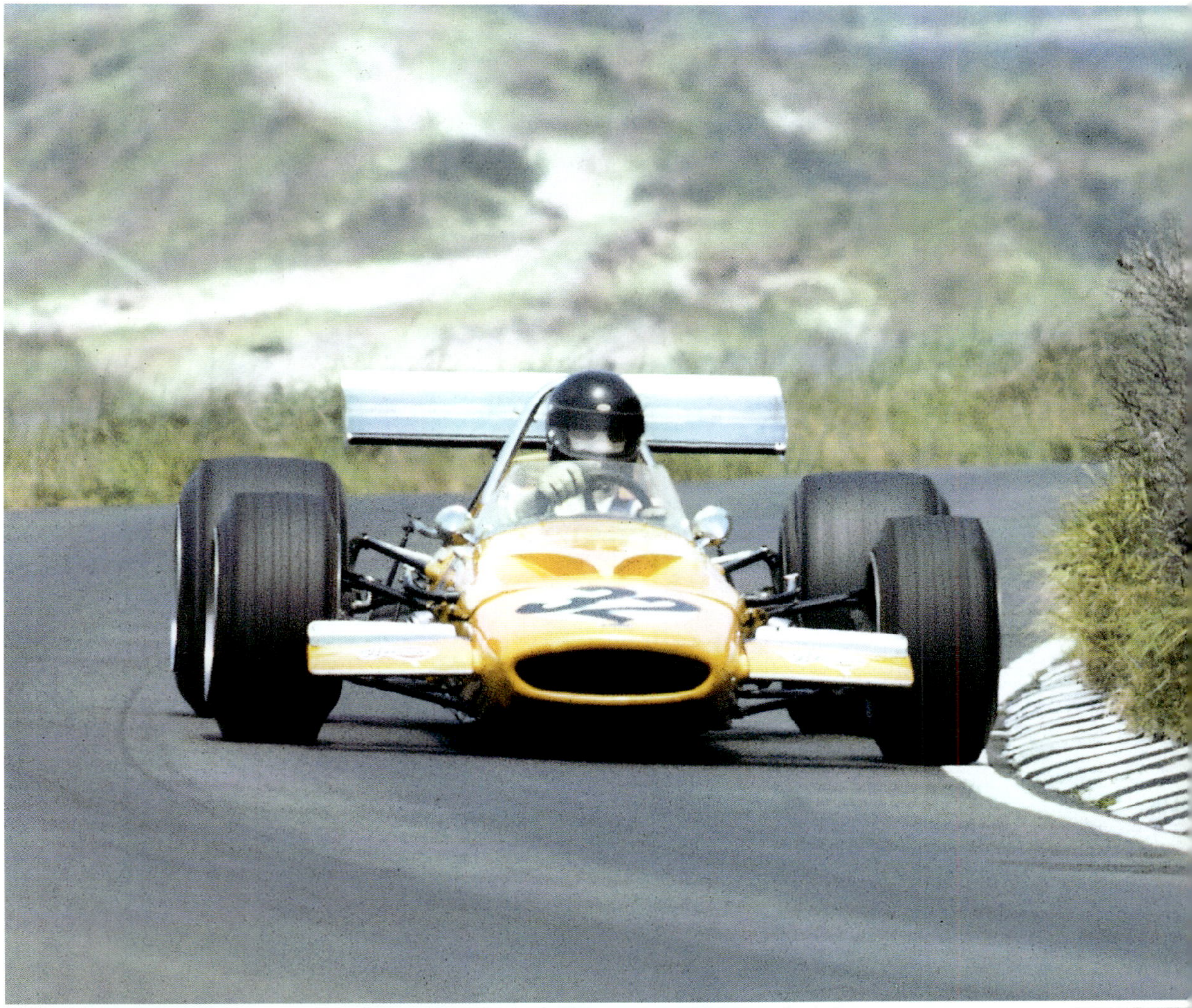

➔ Following his brief and unproductive tenure with BRM in 1969, John Surtees launched his own F1 team in 1970. He is reading the Firestone tyre temperature check at Zandvoort, a feature of the period also used by Goodyear. However, he started off his F1 adventure using an ex-works McLaren M7C/1 up to and including the Dutch GP where he finished sixth, thereafter switching to his own TS7 machine. Note the open face Bell helmet, cotton wool earplugs, and the leather gloves.

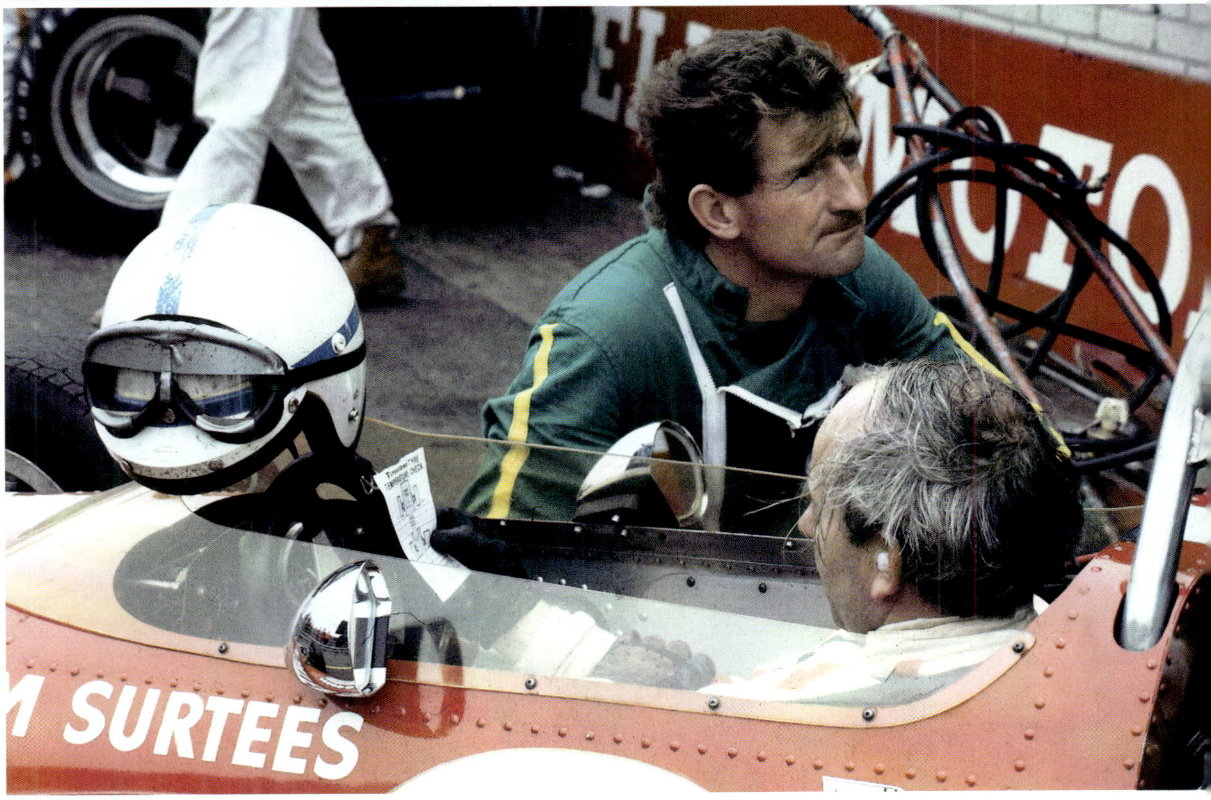

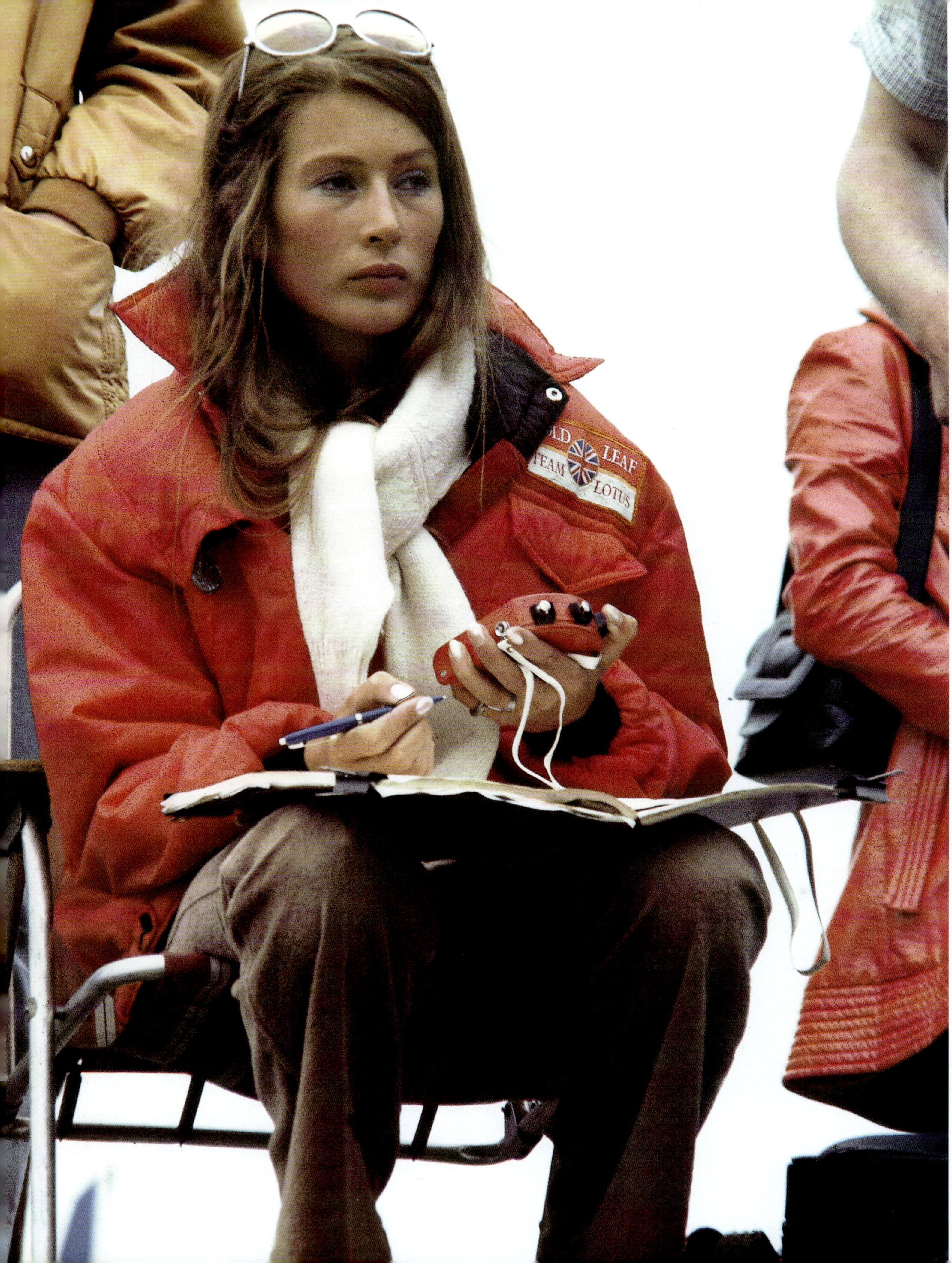
LEAF
TEAM
LOTUS

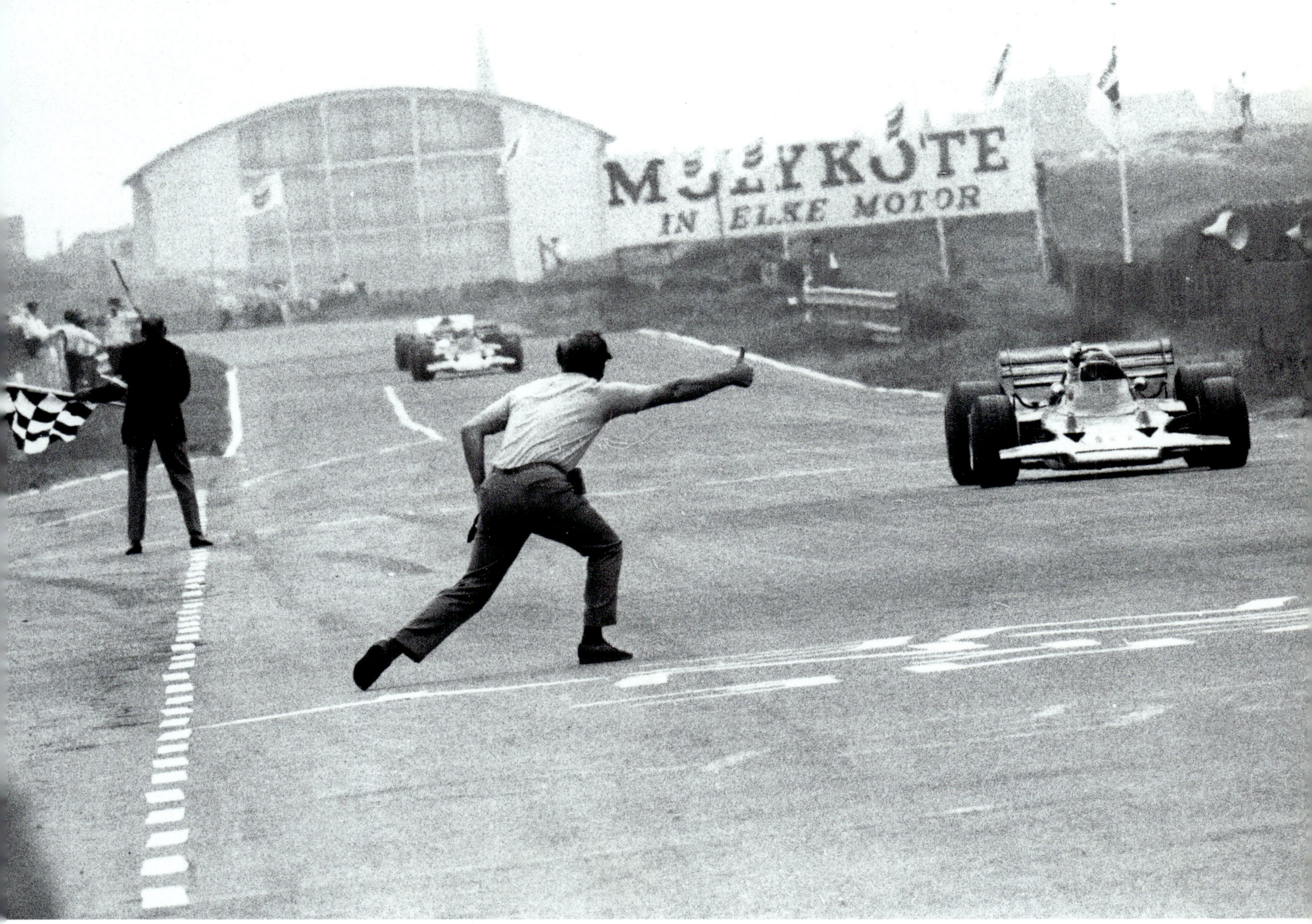

↑ The regulatory fascism and safety concerns of latter times has systematically robbed us of those individual moments and quirky habits that made life more enjoyable. Colin Chapman's always uninhibited response to a victory by one of his cars is well illustrated here as Jochen Rindt wins the Dutch GP in the GLTL Lotus 72/R2. Imagine running onto the track now to do this. Of course, you literally could not, what with mine fields, armed guards, and the Berlin Wall between you and the tarmac.

← Up on the Zandvoort pits roof, Nina Rindt watches her man win the Dutch GP in the GLTL Lotus 72, the first of four consecutive victories for this fated car on a very sad day, as Piers Courage perishes in a fiery accident.

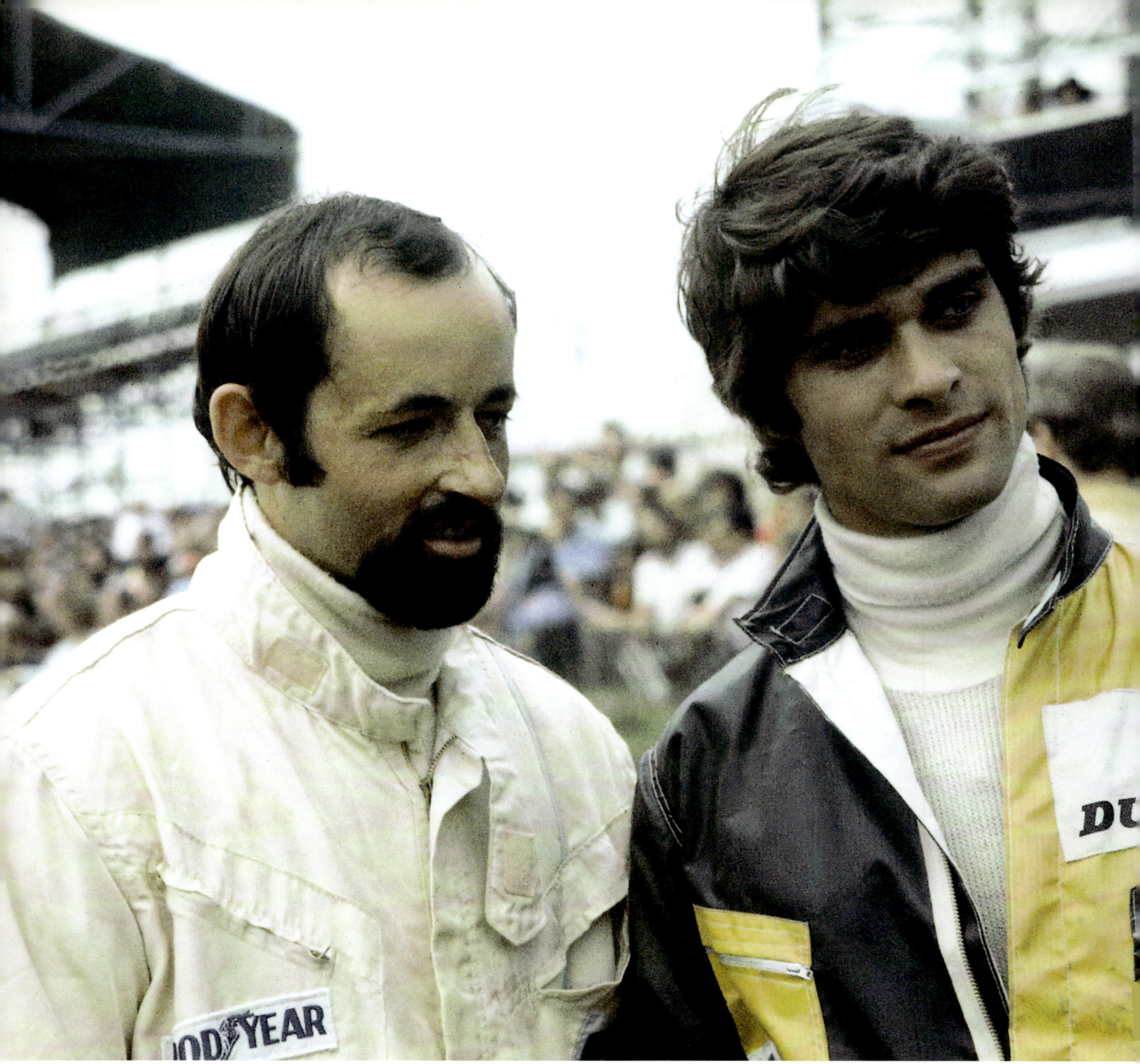

↑ One a driver who had an undistinguished F1 career but became a serial Le Mans winner and surviving sports car champion, the other a brilliant talent carefully nurtured by Ken Tyrrell who was killed just as he was about to take over from Jackie Stewart. Matra's Henri Pescarolo and Tyrrell's François Cevert on the grid at the 1970 British GP, Brands Hatch.

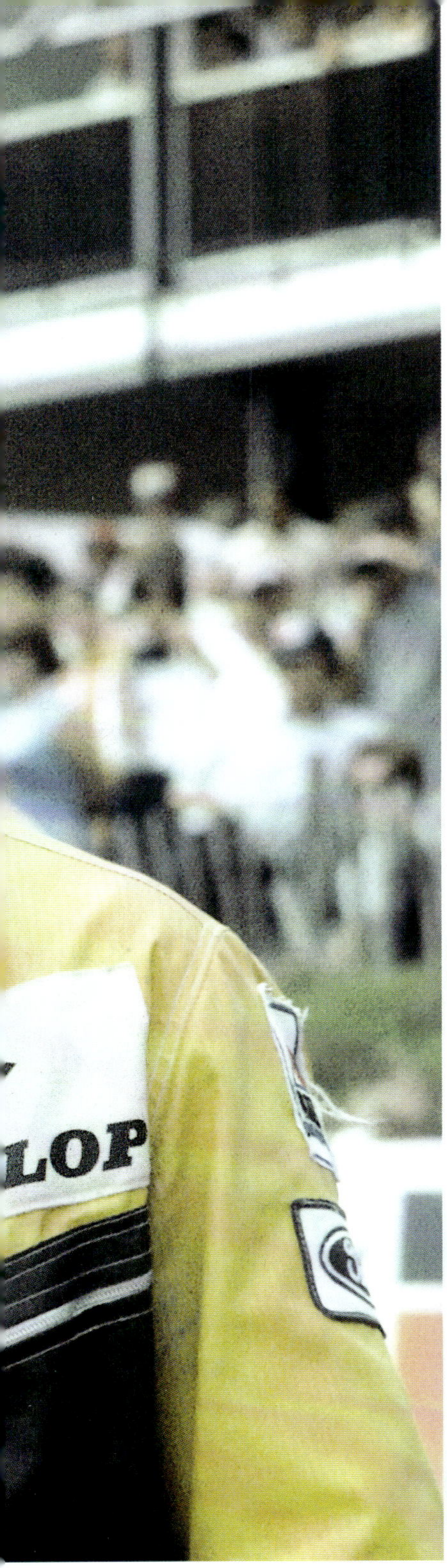

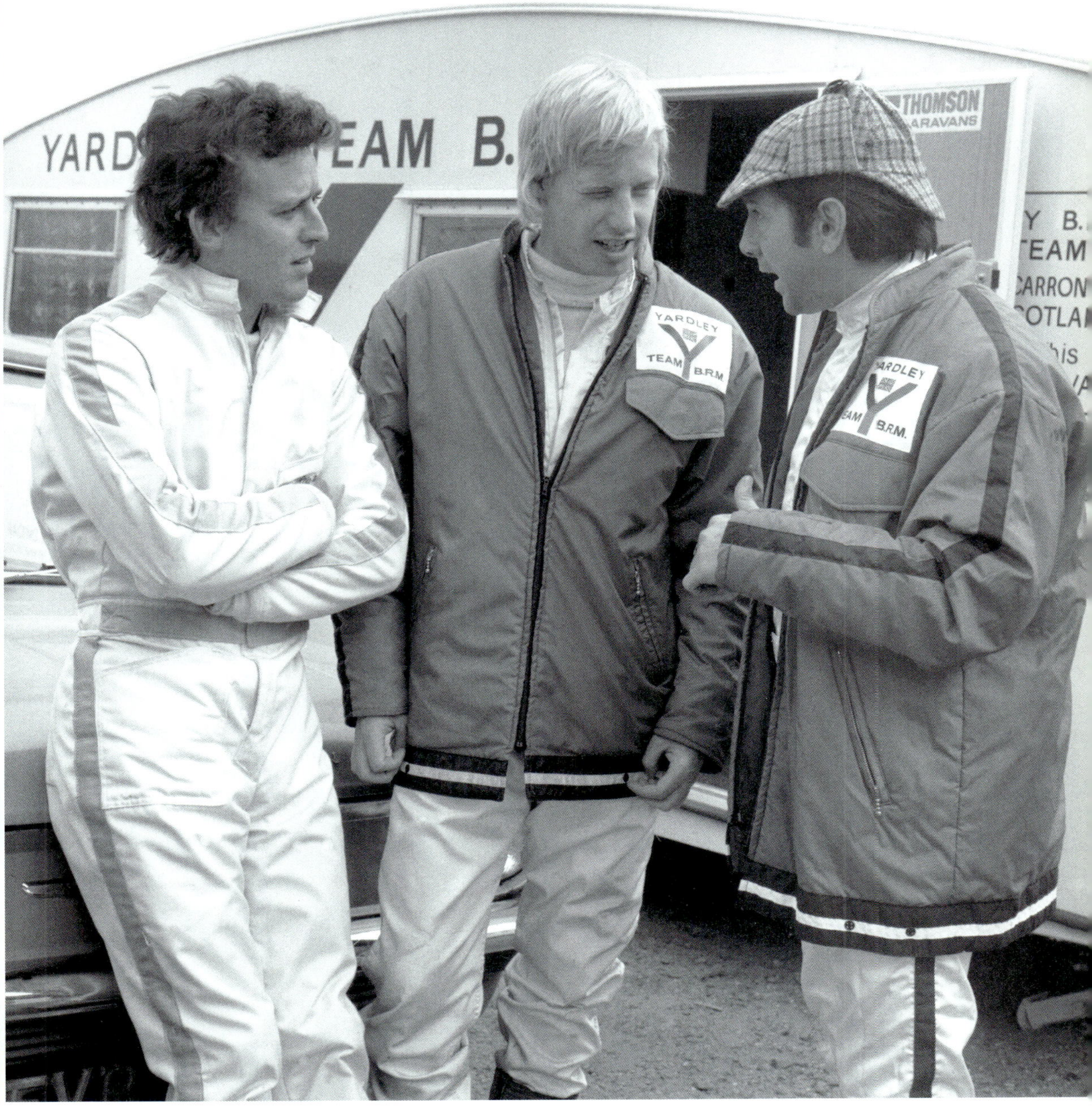

↑ 'So I said to Louis (Stanley), pay me more and I'll go faster.' Pedro Rodriguez in his usual Sherlock Holmes headgear relates something highly unlikely to BRM team-mates Canadian George Eaton and Jackie Oliver in the Brands Hatch paddock during the British GP weekend. Note the sponsor's de luxe caravan.

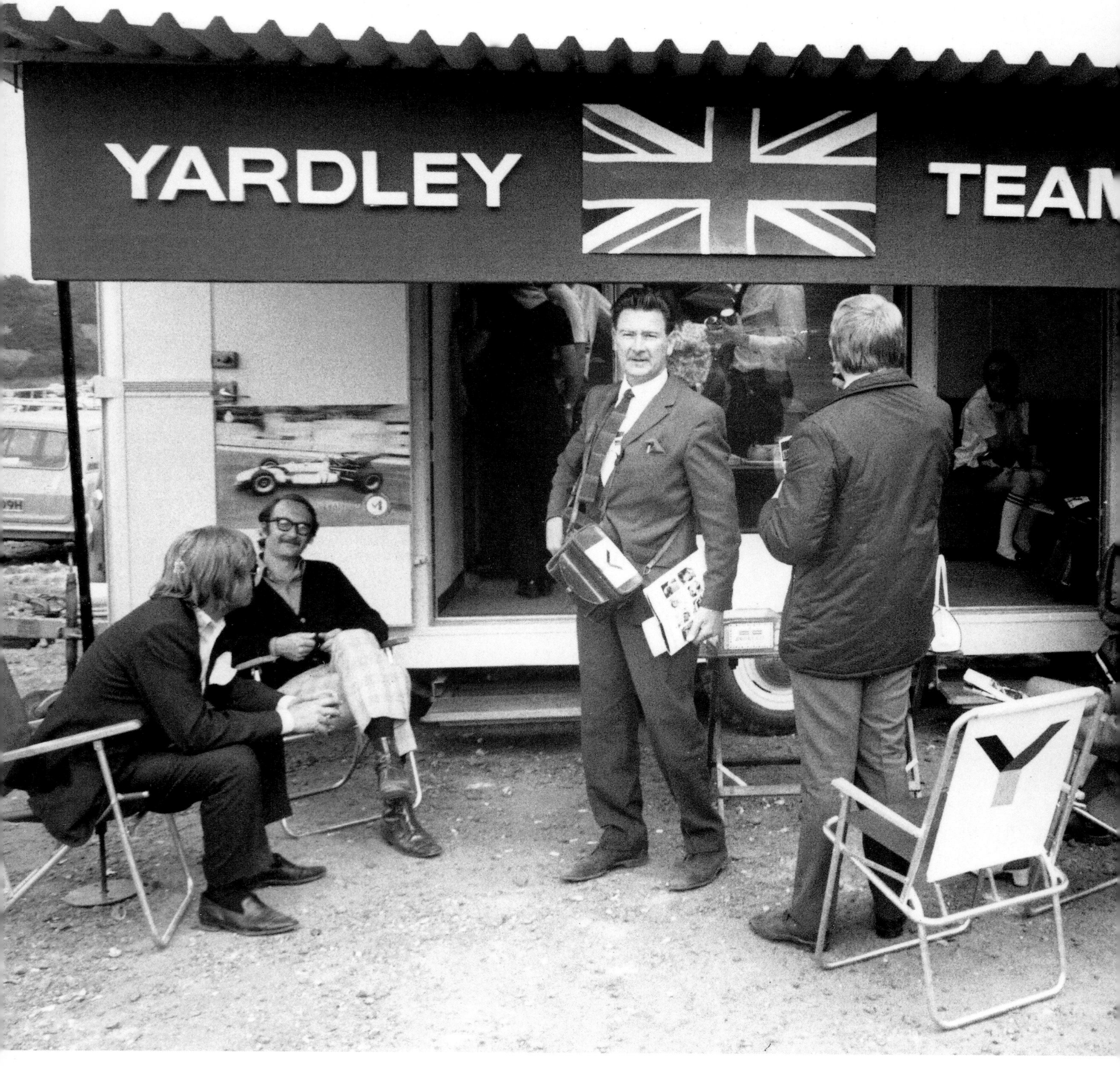
YARDLEY
TEAM

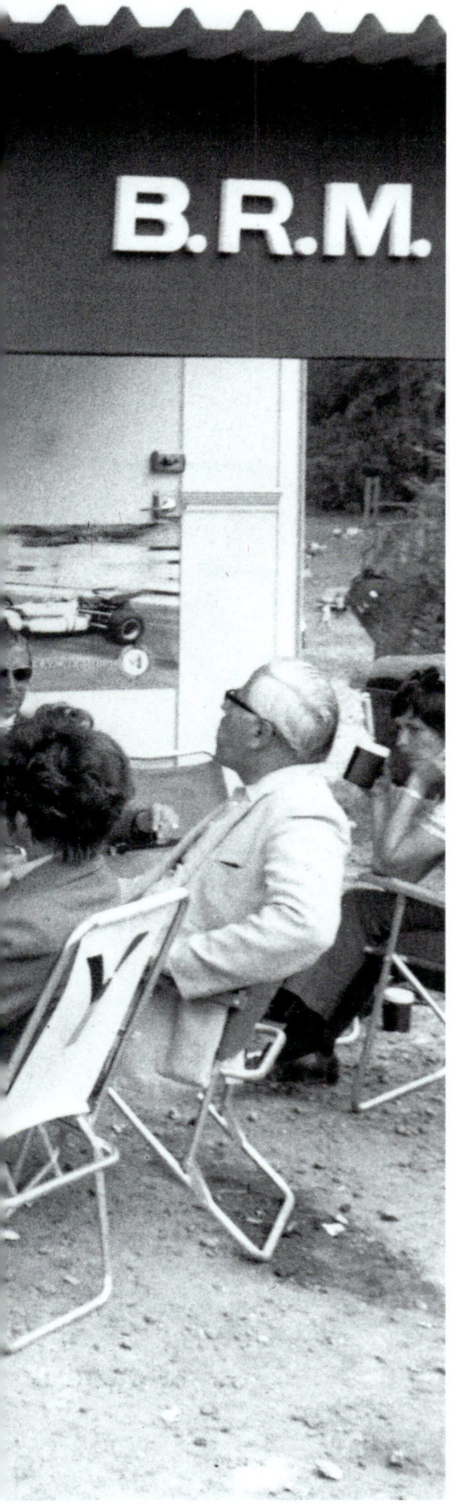

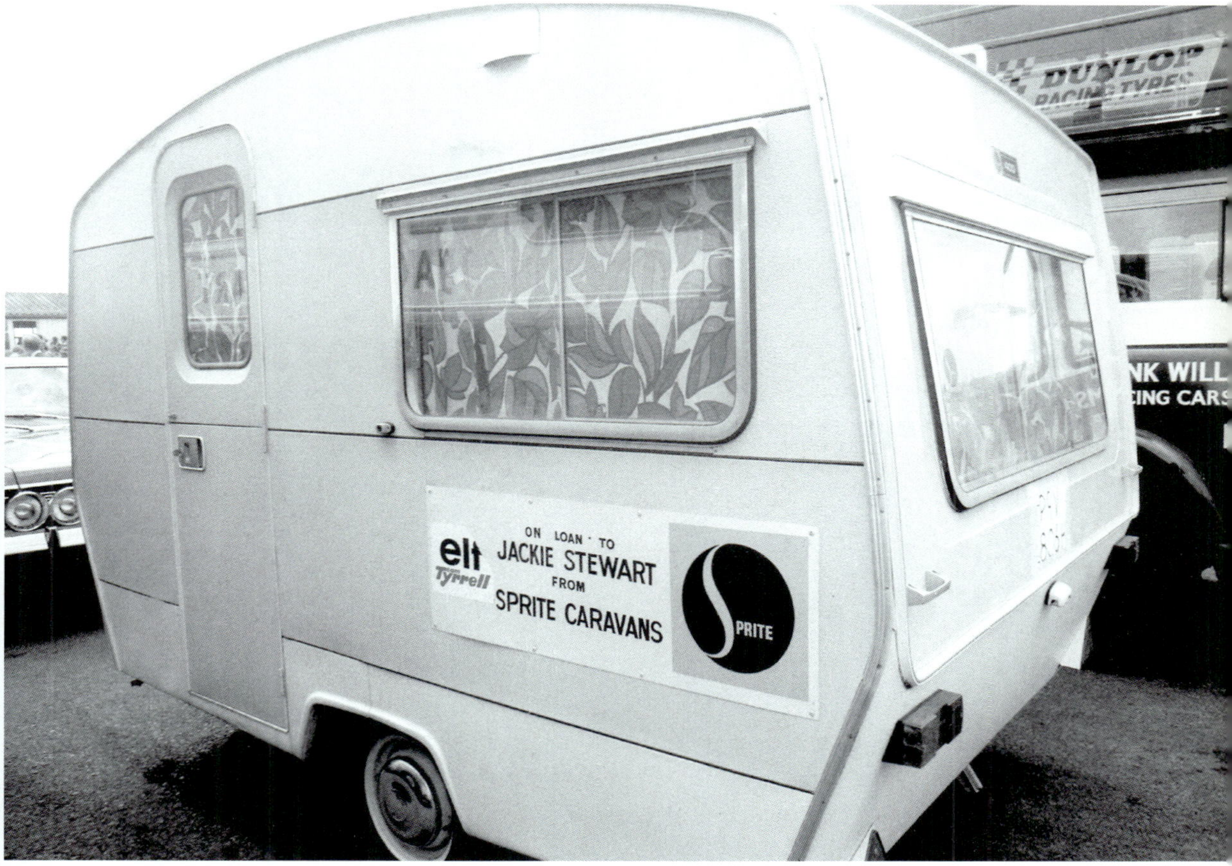

↑ Apparently, small caravans were all the rage at the time, and this is Jackie Stewart's mobile 'dressing room/refuge'. The subtle curtains, so typical of the early 1970s, are just wonderful, are they not? Some things have definitely improved.

← Elsewhere in the paddock, what is presumably Yardley and BRM's hospitality suite, with fold-up sponsor's chairs perched on the specially created *au naturel* gravel surface, plays host to an assorted crew of journos, snappers, and possibly Michael Pitt-Bailey second from left with glasses. Note the 'girlie' in long socks within the hallowed portals. Such style, such aplomb!

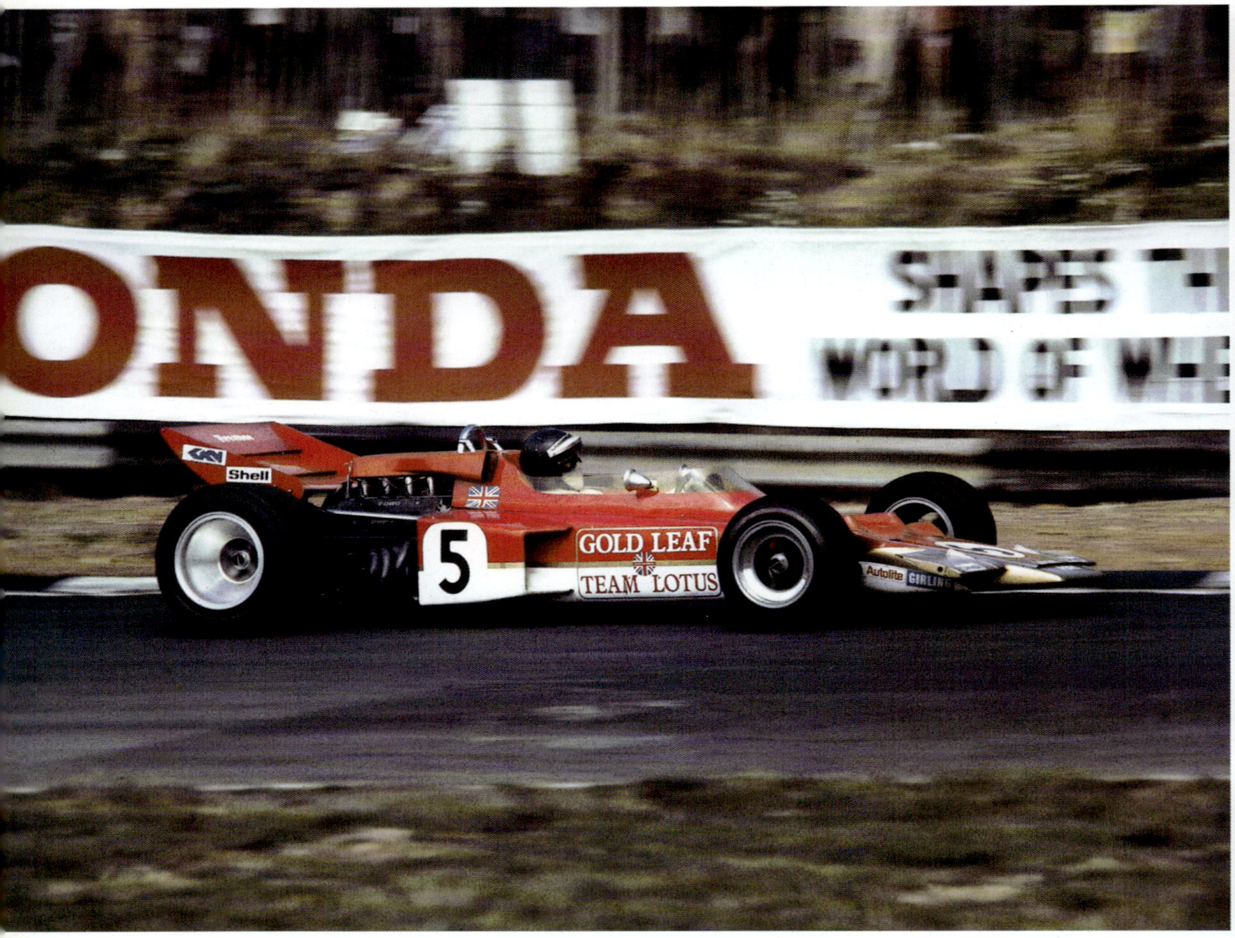

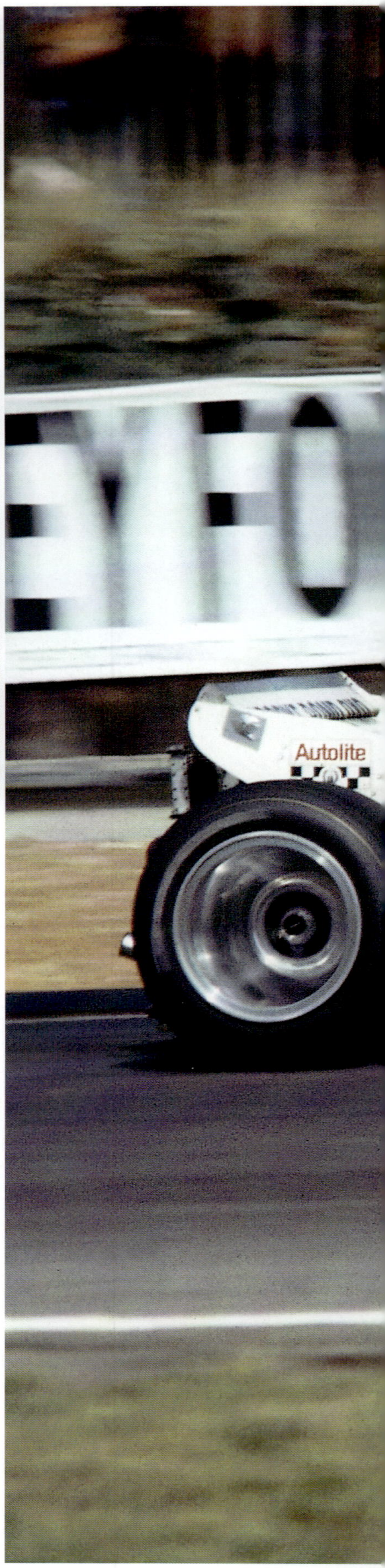

↑ Jochen Rindt winning his penultimate Grand Prix at Brands Hatch in the GLTL Lotus 72 (R2), the car he will suffer his fatal accident in at Monza. The Honda advertising banner was perhaps a tad optimistic, at least in four-wheeled terms. He was lucky, though, just as he had been at Monaco. Brabham, who had shadowed Rindt for 60 laps, took the lead and drew away but disaster struck on the last lap, Jack's BT33 ran out of fuel at Stirling's, and as he coasted towards the finish Rindt blasted by to win. JB immediately suspected what had happened; the setting for the fuel injection had been left on full rich to start the cold engine and not reset before the race. Before a sprinting Ron Dennis could reach the stricken car, JB got out and confirmed his suspicions, merely pointing at the metering unit as Dennis arrived. It was a bitter blow that possibly stopped him from winning a fourth World Championship. In his book *The Jack Brabham Story* with Doug Nye he recalled that for 30 years he had blamed Ron Dennis, but in 2002 Nick Goozee, another of the Brabham mechanics, finally told him, 'Well, that wasn't Ron, it was me ...'

→ Despite his dreadful leg injuries from the 1969 Watkins Glen accident, that left him permanently incapacitated, being unable to apply full pressure to the brake pedal, Graham Hill raced on, courtesy of Brooke Bond Oxo and Rob Walker, and the old faithful Lotus 49 R7, now in C specification. Amazingly, he scored two sixth places (one here at Brands Hatch), a fourth and a fifth, although for a while he could barely walk.

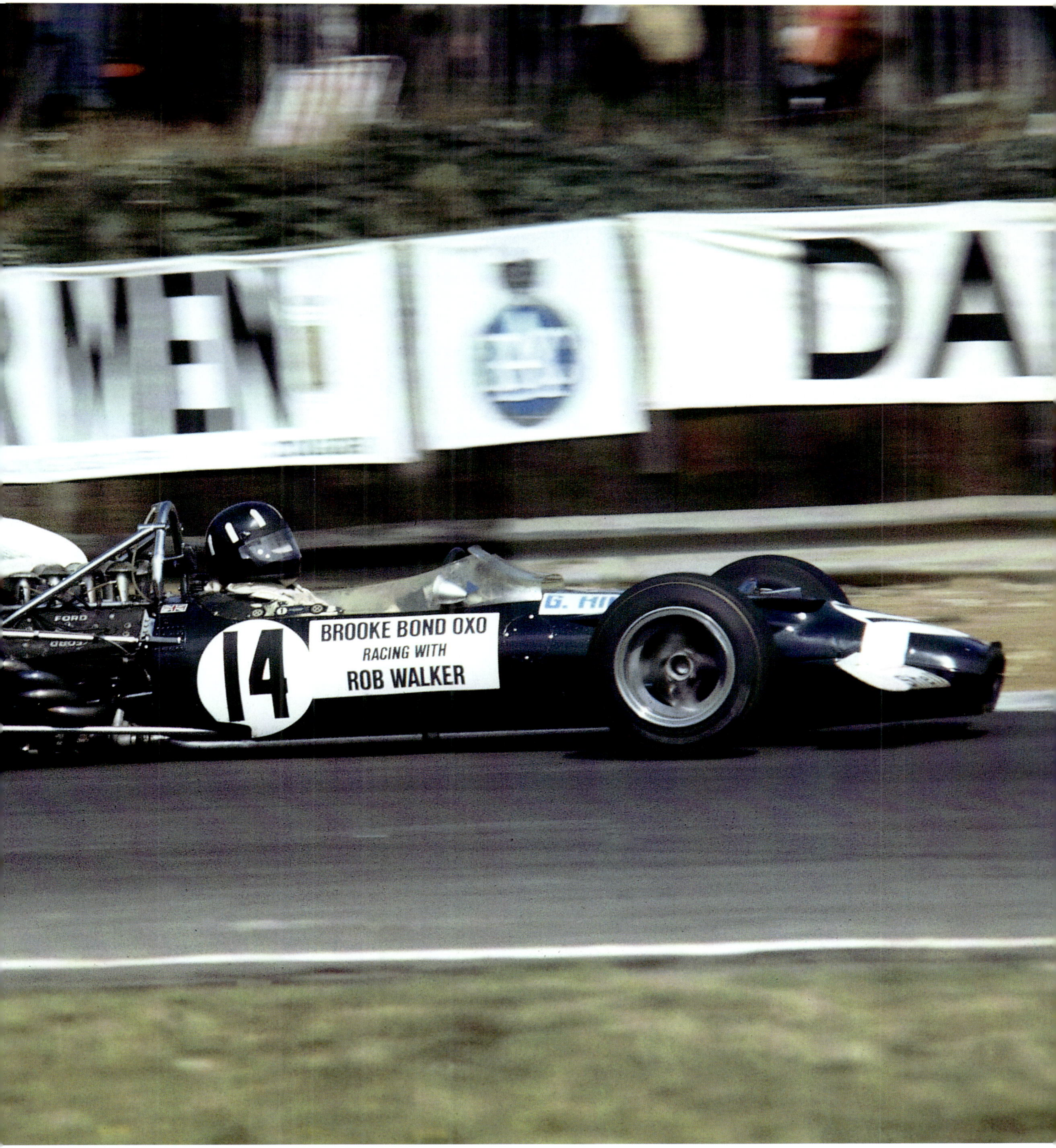
BROOKE BOND OXO
RACING WITH
ROB WALKER
14
FORD

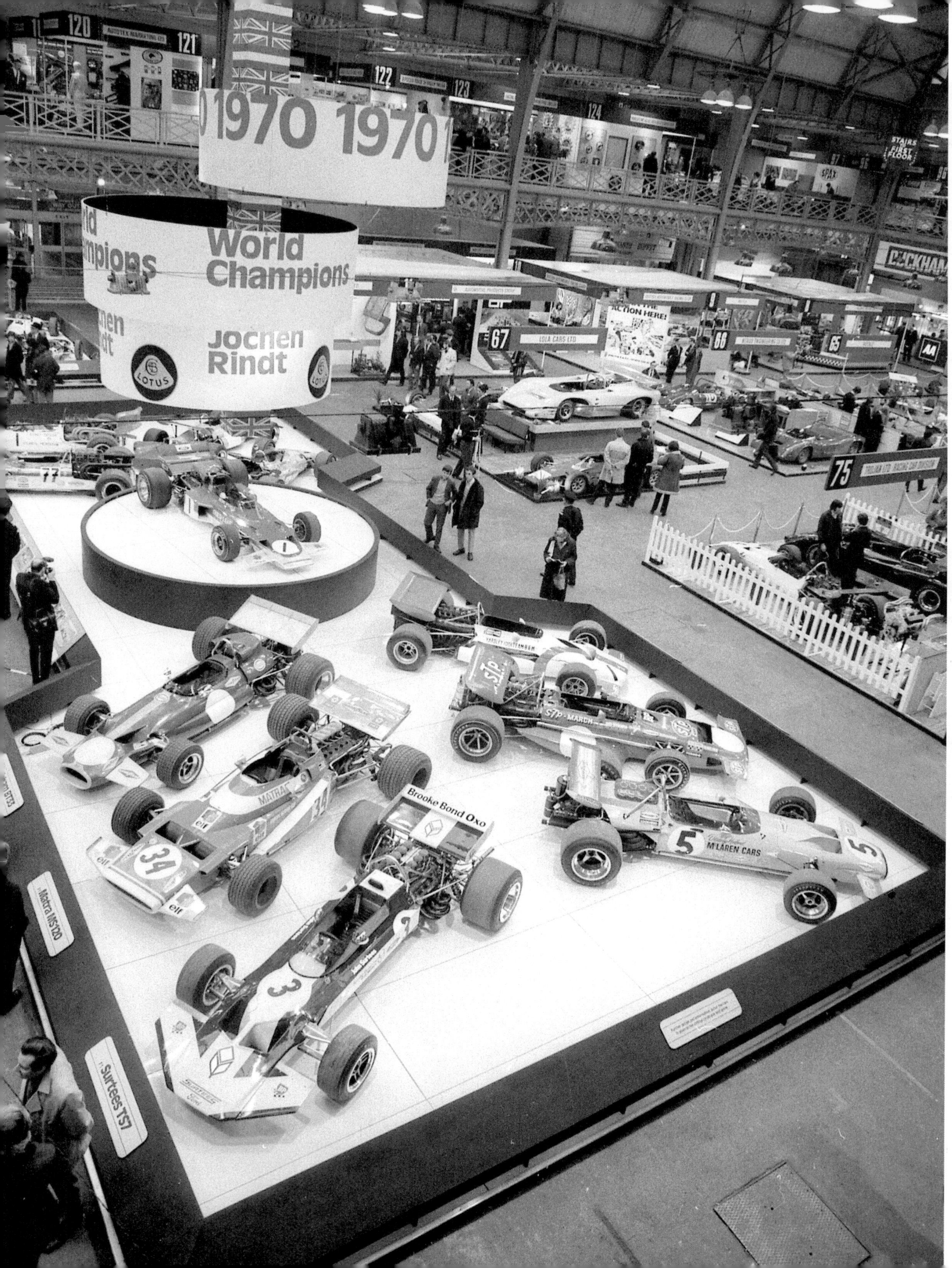

120
121
122
123
124
1970 1970
World Champions
Jochen Rindt
LOTUS
67
LOLA CARS LTD
66
65
75
STAIRS TO FIRST FLOOR
ACTION HERE!
Brooke Bond Oxo
MATRA
elf
34
STP
5
M'LAREN CARS
Matra MS120
Surtees TS7

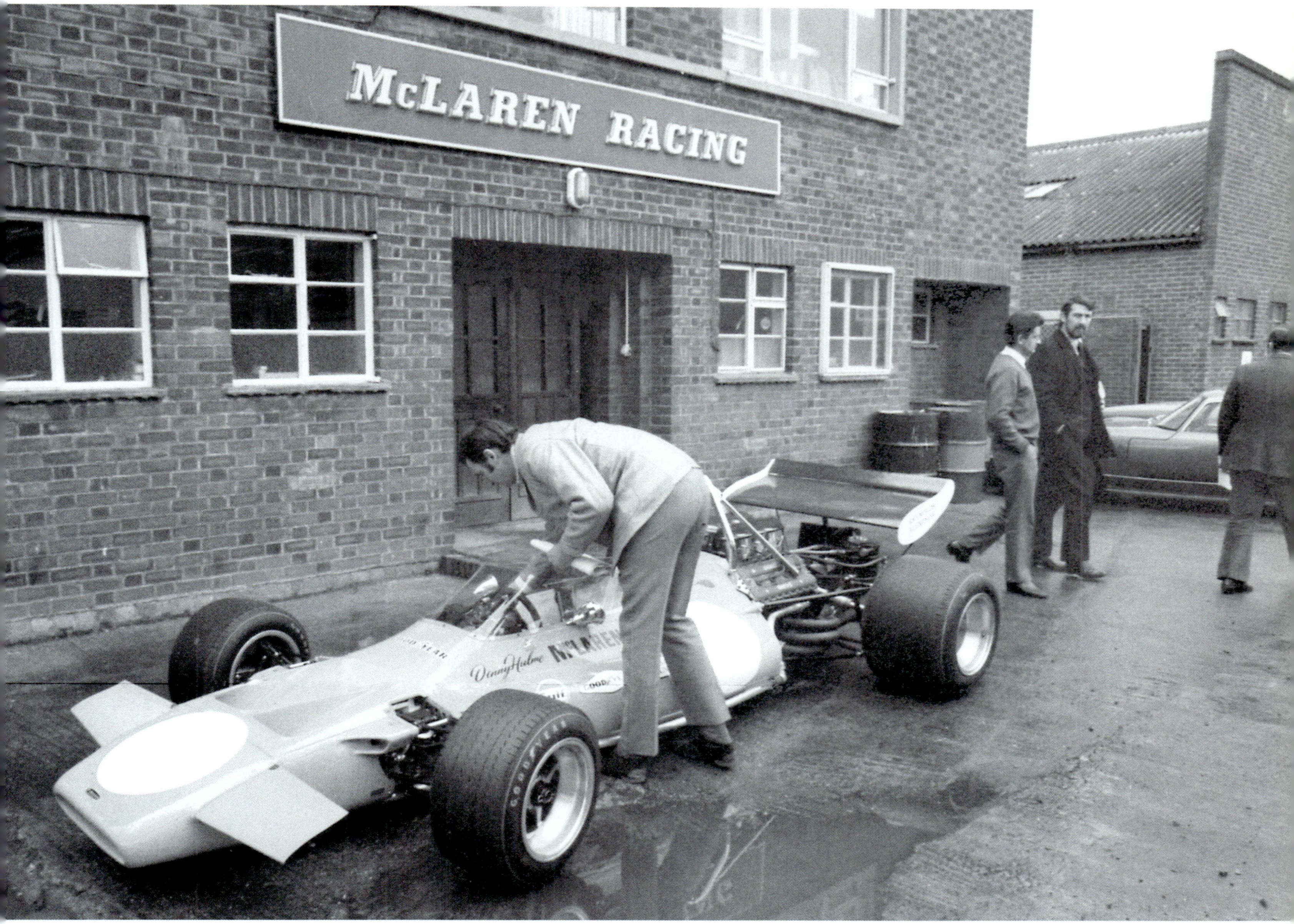

↑ The new McLaren M19A/1 outside 5 David Road, the old McLaren factory at Colnbrook, Slough. Phil Kerr is fiddling with something in the cockpit.

← A poignant picture, the F1 display at the 1971 Racing Car Show with a Lotus 72 denoting Jochen Rindt's posthumous 1970 World Championship title. One cannot imagine this being publicly celebrated in such a way today.

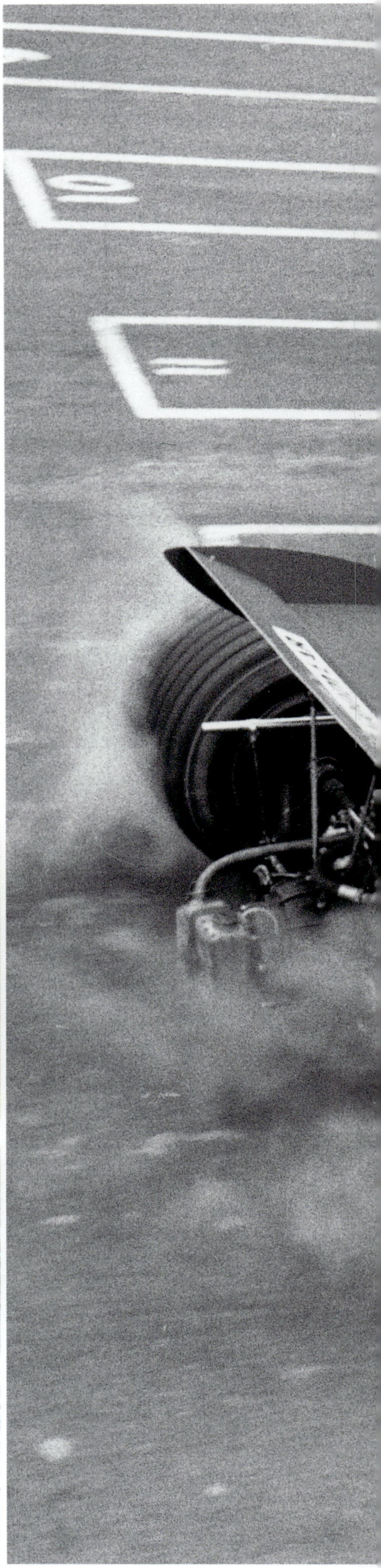

→ Perhaps the most satisfying feeling in the world, letting loose more power than the grip can cope with and a touch of opposite lock before blasting off toward the far horizon. Jackie Stewart and Tyrrell 001 demonstrate what motor racing used to be like.

↓ Another perfect day in paradise for motor racing snappers at the Brands Hatch Race of Champions on 21 March 1971. Emerson Fittipaldi qualified seventh in the Pratt & Whitney STN76 gas turbine powered Lotus 56B, but retired on lap 33. Lotus team-mates Reine Wisell and Dave Walker also drove this 4WD device based upon the 1968 Indy type 56 in 1971, possibly the last of F1's more esoteric offerings. By this time, and in reality even two years earlier, such attempts at extreme innovation were doomed because of ever-improving tyres and the downforce generated by aerofoils, spoilers, etc. Grip, at least in the dry, was no longer a problem, engines were now sufficiently potent and the extra weight and complications of 4WD were redundant. Its best result, and only finish, in a GP was eighth at Monza, but it did manage second at the Rothman's F5000 Championship race at Hockenheim on 12 September 1971, the 56B's last race, both driven by Fittipaldi.

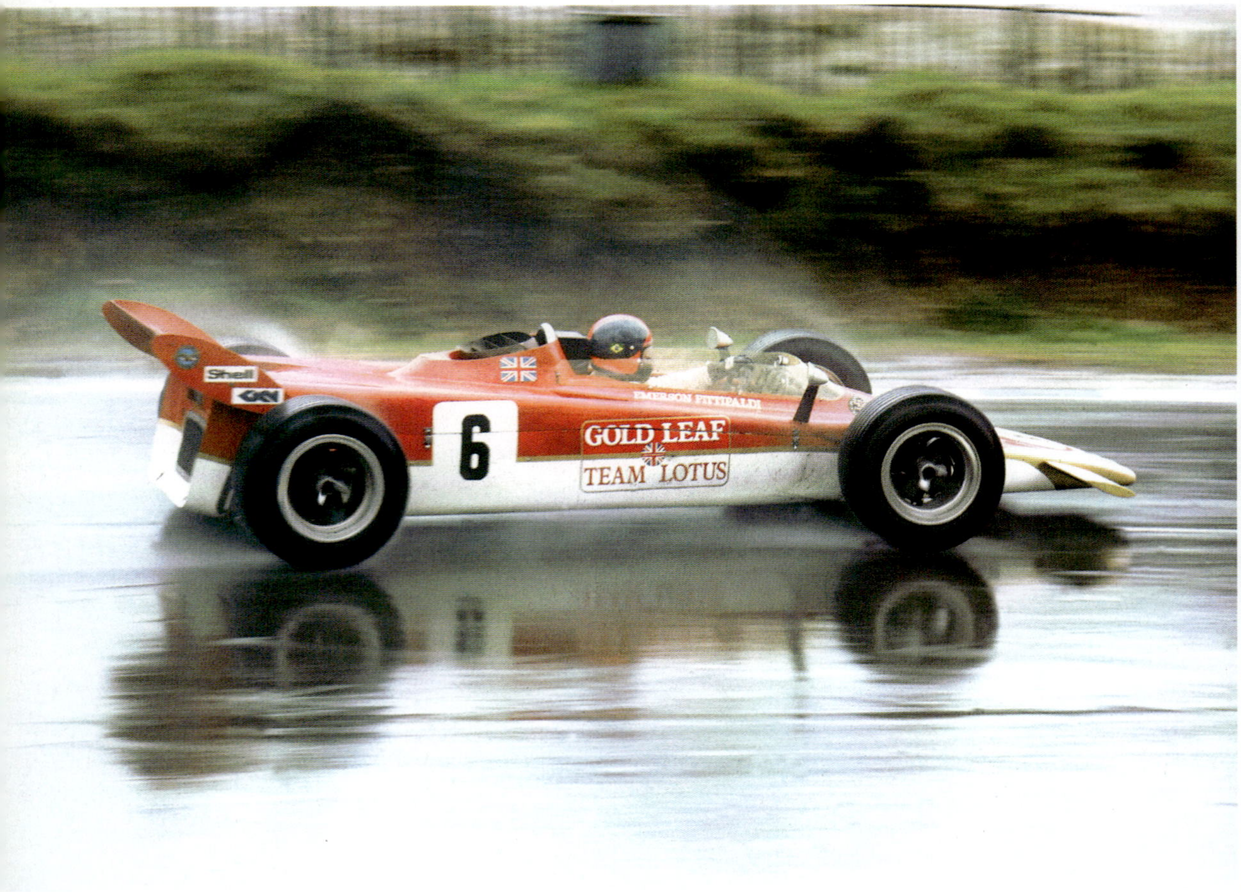

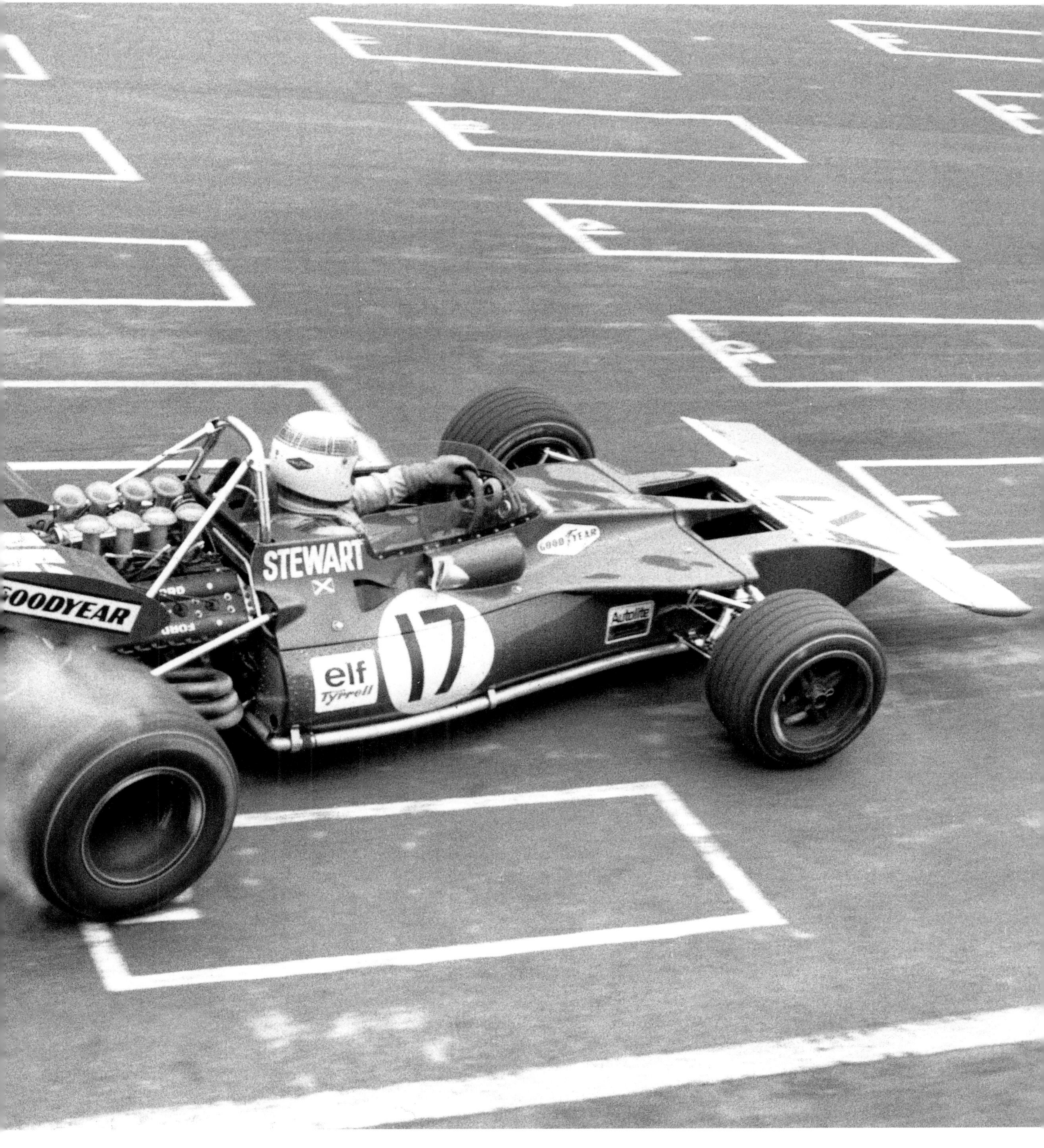
STEWART
17
GOODYEAR
elf
Tyrrell
Autolite
FORD

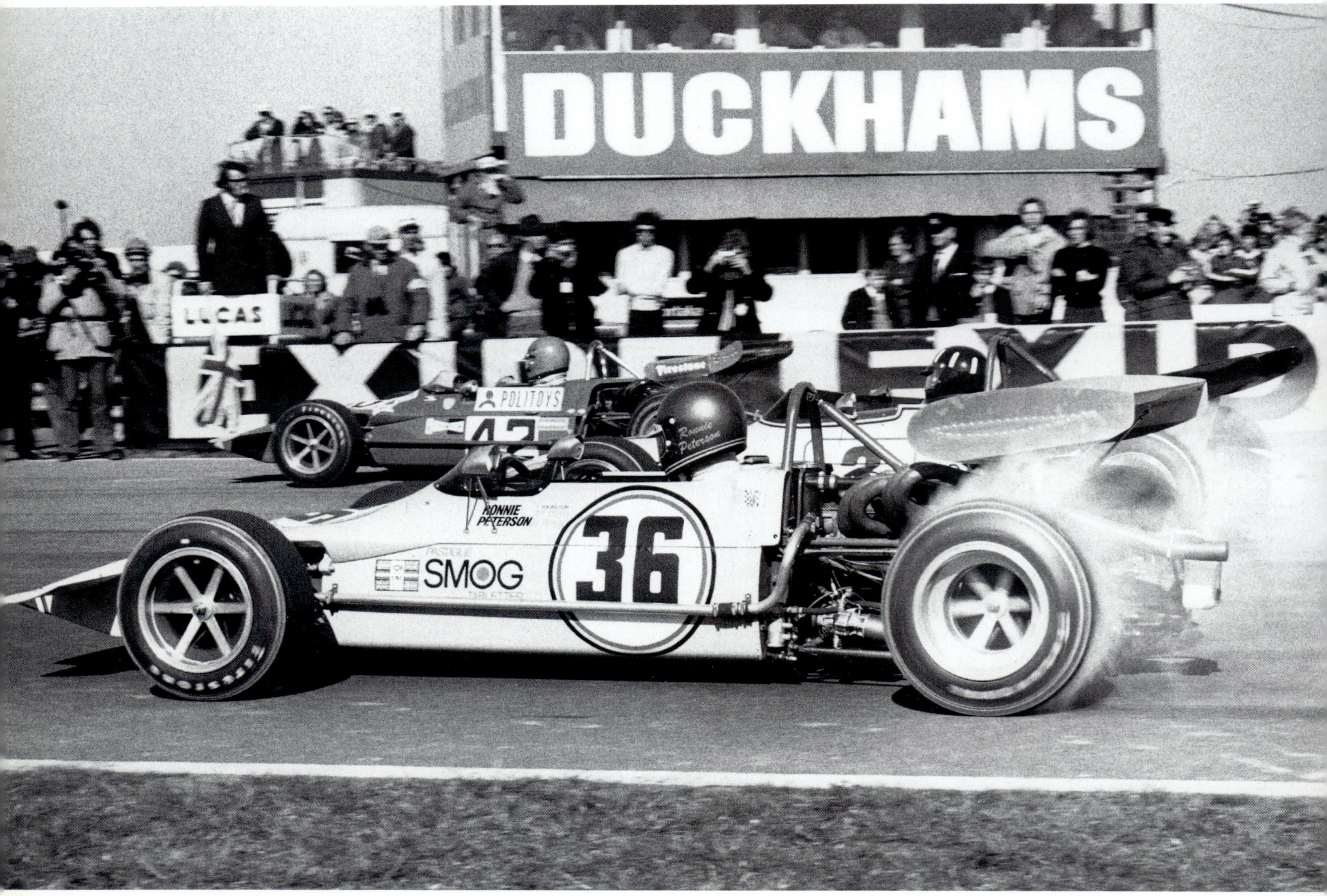

↑ The start of the XXVI BARC 200 *Yellow Pages*-Jochen Rindt Memorial Trophy for F2 cars at Thruxton on 12 April 1971. Ronnie Peterson's SMOG-sponsored works March 712M (7) Cosworth is producing some smog of its own as it briefly lingers on pole position, with Graham Hill in the Rondel Racing Brabham BT36 (2) Cosworth FVA matching Ronnie's wheelspin. On the far side, the Frank Williams Racing Motul March 712M (4) Cosworth FVA of Henri Pescarolo is making a better start, but will only last five laps before his engine breaks. This was a brief and final period where Graham's single-seater skills prevailed and, after winning heat one, he beat Peterson in the final by just 0.6sec, and 26 days later achieved his final F1 victory at the Silverstone International Trophy at Silverstone in the 'lobster claw' Brabham BT34.

→ Montjuich was another street circuit, but longer and faster than the confined spaces of Monaco. Pedro Rodriguez crests the brow in the Yardley BRM P160/01 on his way to fourth place in the 1971 Spanish GP. He had some good finishes in this the original P160, winning the Oulton Park Spring Cup, finishing fourth at the Silverstone International Trophy, and second at the Dutch GP. He retired at The French GP, and then perished in an accident on the Norisring in Herbert Müller's Ferrari 512M.

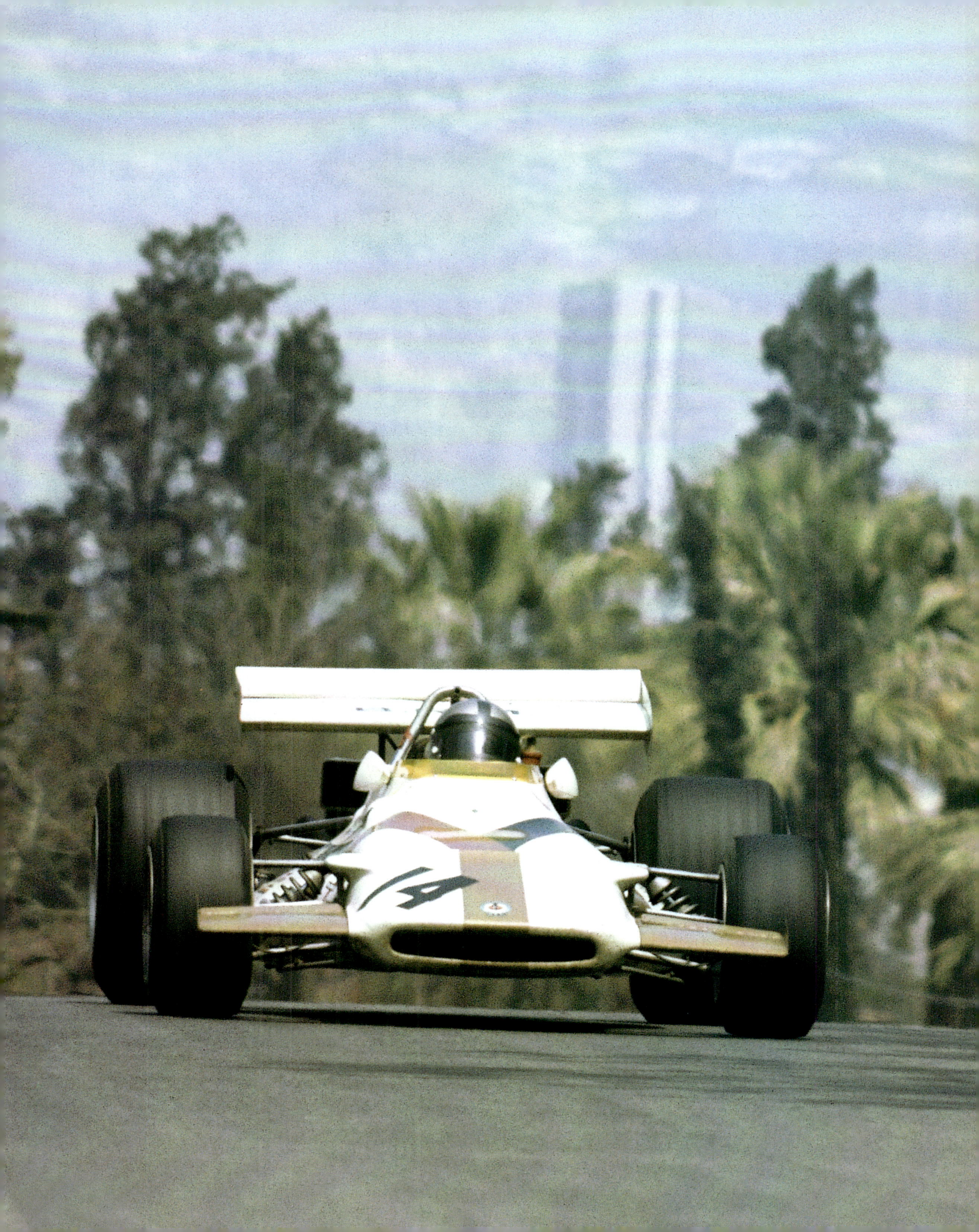
14

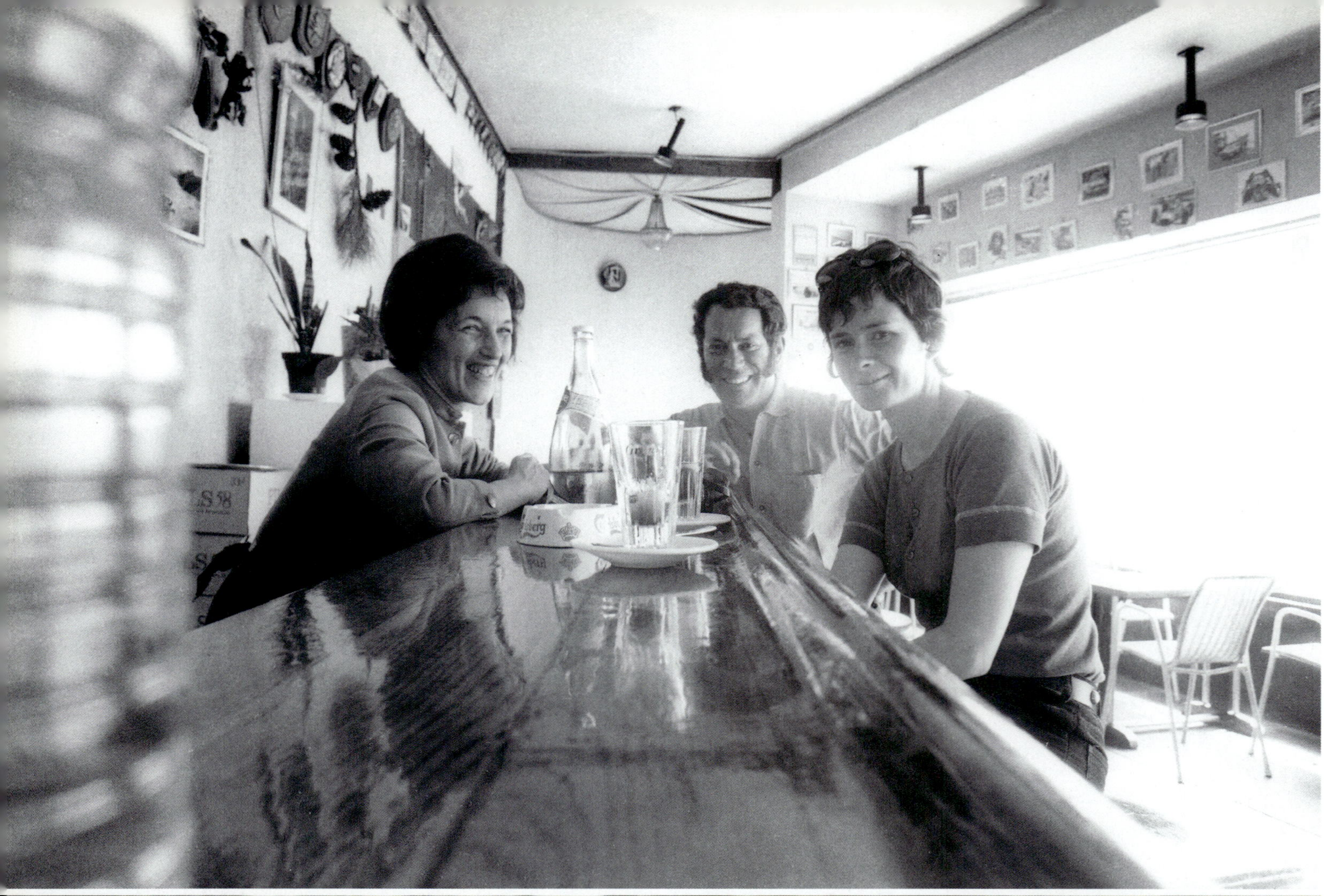

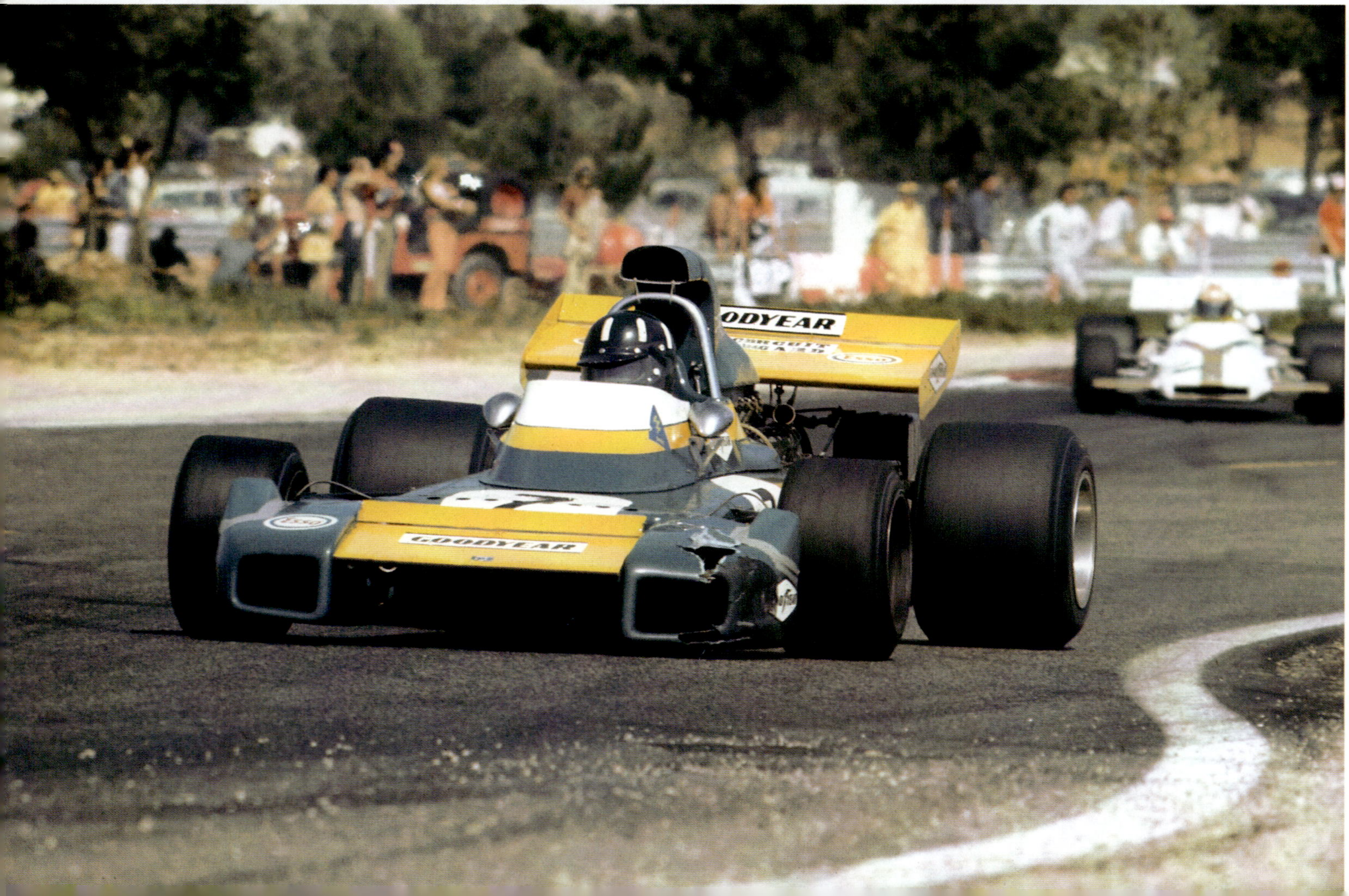
GOODYEAR
GOODYEAR

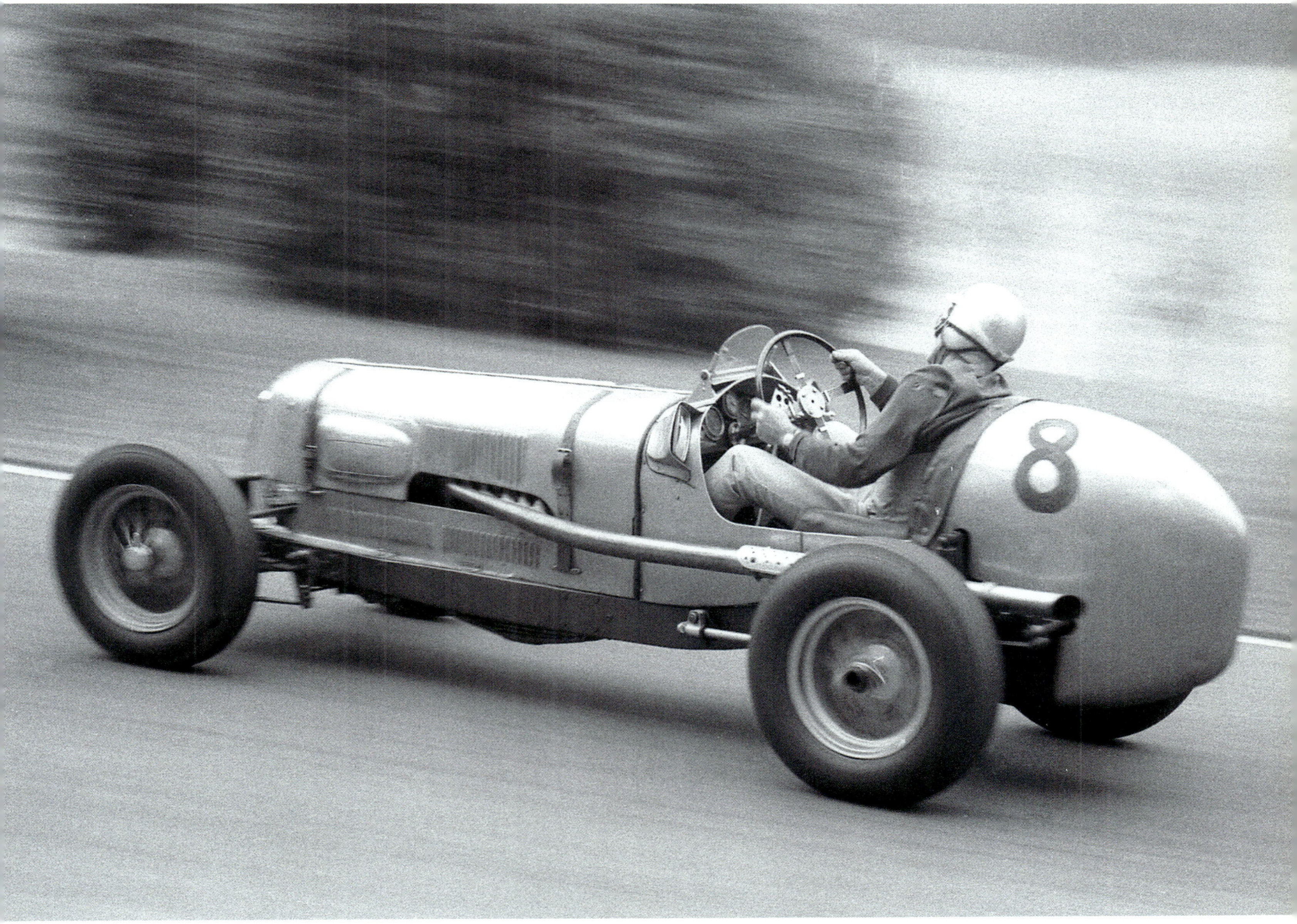

↑ A vintage interlude for Mike came at the *Daily Mirror* Historic Crystal Palace Meeting on 25 September 1971. This is the redoubtable Martin Morris, winner of ten VSCC Seaman Trophies, in his ERA R11B, aka 'Humphrey' (so named by its original 1936 owner Reggie Tongue, who christened it thus after joint ERA founder Humphrey Cook). In 1955 Ken Wharton used R11B, as well as his Cooper-JAP, to win the British Hill Climb Championship. Morris bought the car in 1962 and was one of an elite band of historic racers who were good enough to have been successful professional racers. His very quick, smooth, and relaxed driving style is beautifully illustrated here en route to winning the Seven Seas Fellowship Challenge Trophy. He died in March 2006, and today the car is raced by his son David Morris.

↖ Rosie Bernard of Rosie's bar Monaco in 1971 with Mike and Liz on their honeymoon, a fortnight before the GP. This was halfway up the hill towards Casino Square and was the favoured watering hole for racers, personnel, and aficionados. It was renowned for post-race parties, when tables and chairs would make a bid for freedom out on to the pavement and road. In 1996 the premises were acquired by a nearby clinic, and the bar closed.

← By 1971 Jack Brabham had returned to Australia, leaving Ron Tauranac to run the team. The unique 'lobster claw' Brabham BT34/1, designed by Tauranac, was Graham Hill's mount in 1971, and he won the International Trophy at Silverstone with it. Elsewhere it was not such a happy story, but at Paul Ricard for the French GP Hill qualified impressively, by his then standards, in fourth place. In the race Graham ran fifth but spun off on oil (hence the damage visible here) dropped by Peterson's March, and stopped to change a front wheel, subsequently retiring with a split oil pipe.

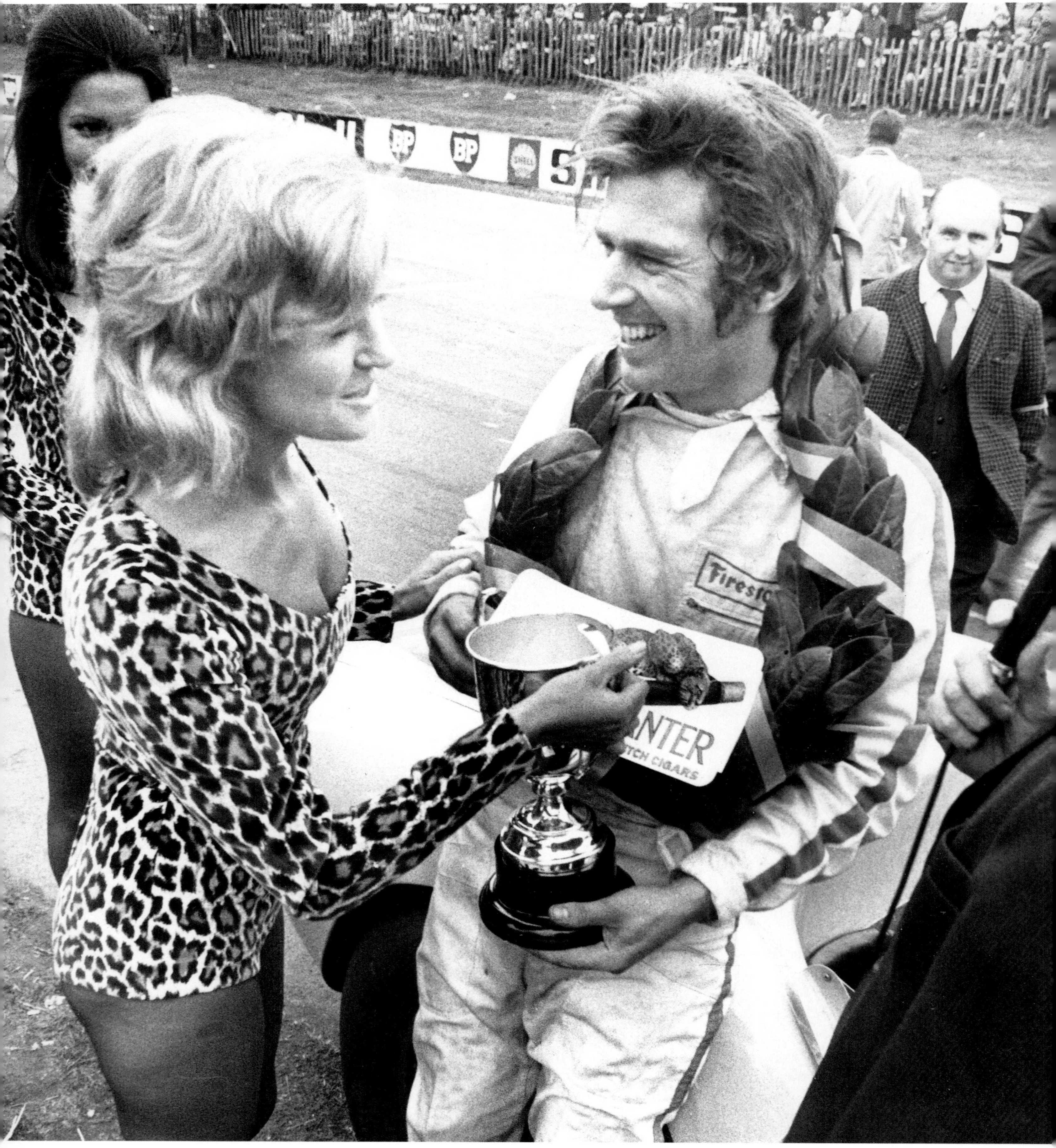
BP
BP

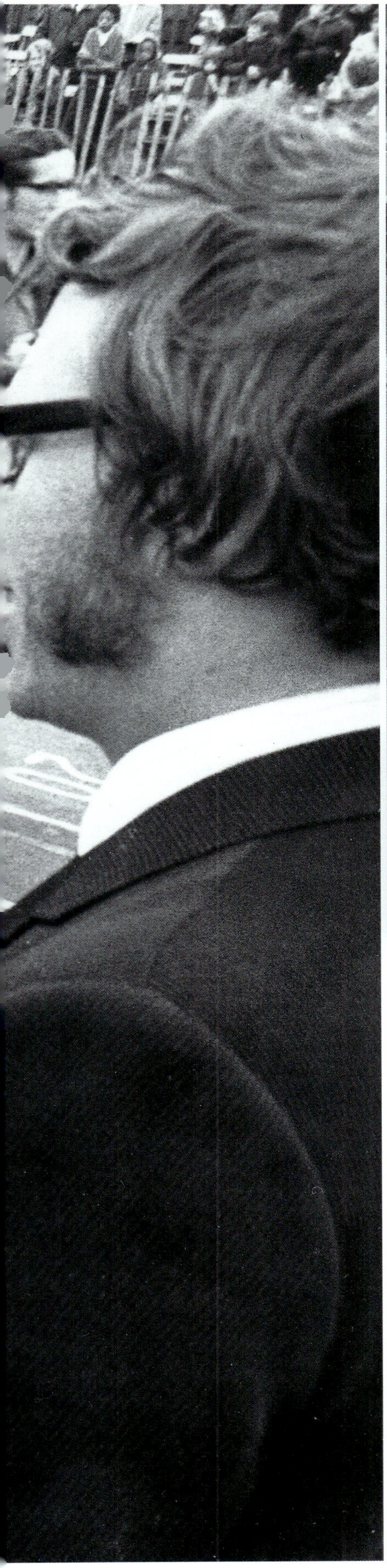

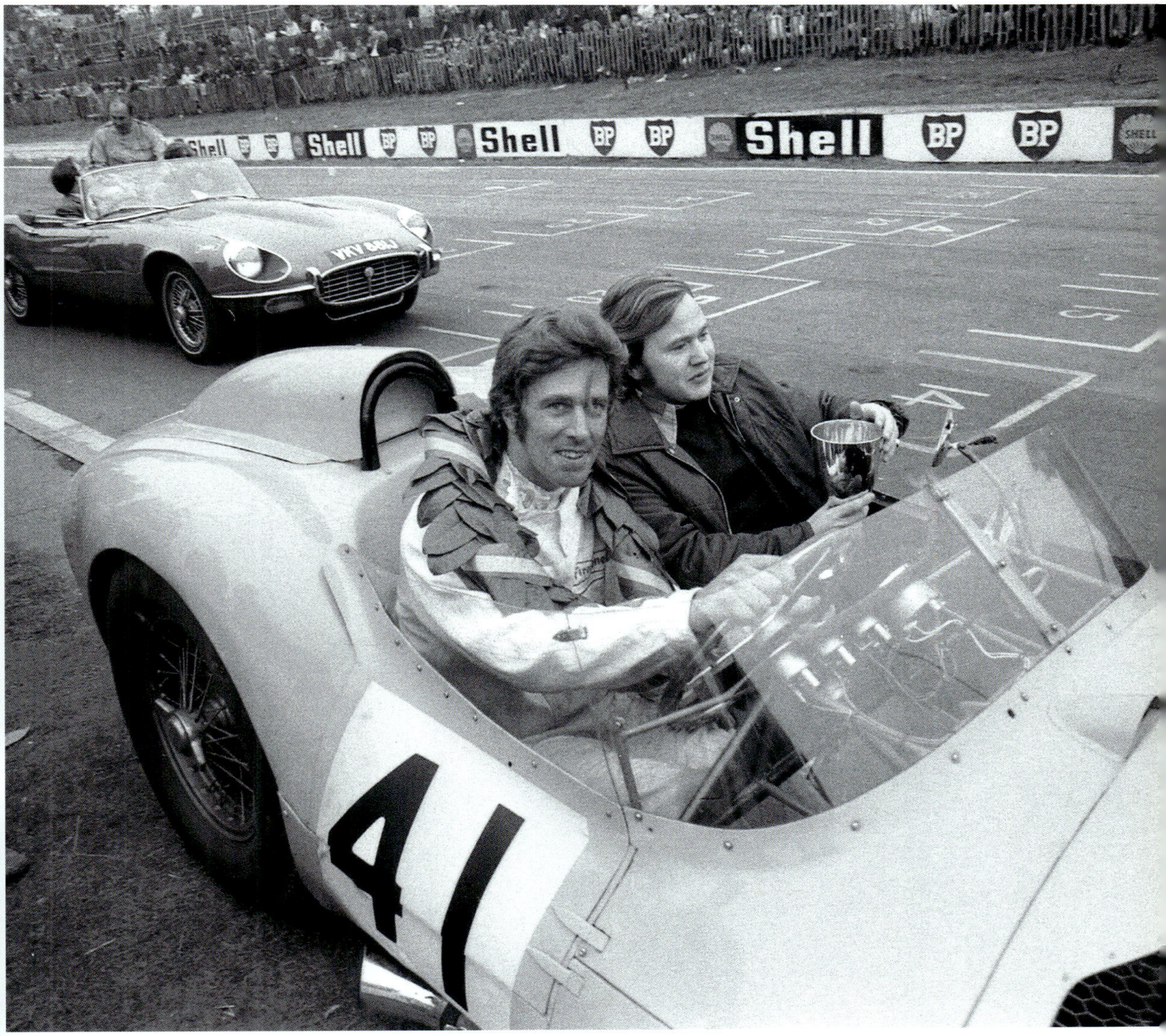

↑ Willie Green has just won the JCB Trophy in the JCB Maserati Tipo 60 'birdcage'. The passenger is Tony Bamford. This is chassis 2457, originally owned by American Dave Causey. Willie recalled to the author that, 'The Birdcage arrived about 1971. It was not very nice to drive, very effective but not enjoyable, a bit like the Lotus 16 or indeed the Vanwall; it did the job but you could not enjoy it like a 250F. And it blew oil all over me for a year until we discovered a hollow dowel that should have been solid! It had a cracked crank when we got it, but we drove it carefully for about three years until Sytner drove it at Thruxton when it gave up and broke the engine in half!'

← You can't change a leopard's spots, but Willie Green would sure like to try! Our ultimate historic racer is being awarded the Panter Cigar Challenge Trophy by June Cooper, with Jennifer Keylock half obscured behind. Others better informed than the author suggest that the commentator might be Neville Haye. When I showed Willie this picture he commented: 'It's frightening looking back over 35 years ago! What awful sideburns!'

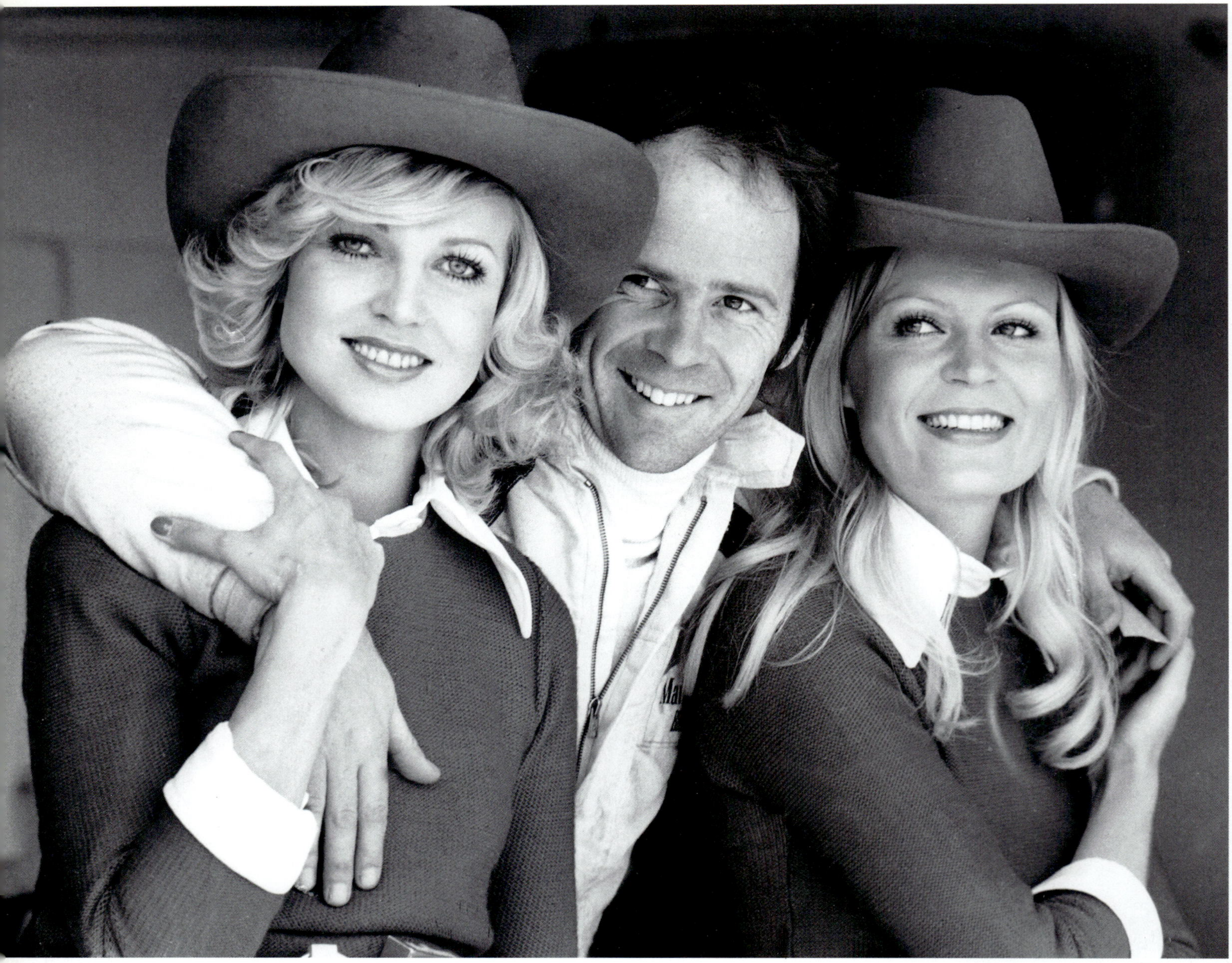

↑ The Marlboro girls and Peter Gethin make friends at the Spanish GP when Peter was a Marlboro-sponsored BRM driver.

→ 'Now listen carefully, I shall say this only once. That is the front of the car Jean-Pierre.' In an obviously posed picture Tony Southgate briefs Jean-Pierre Beltoise on the basics as he sits in the BRM P160/01 during qualifying at the 1972 Spanish GP at Jarama as the Marlboro girls look on sans Mr Gethin. It was all to no avail because the BRM suffered from gearbox problems and failed to finish.

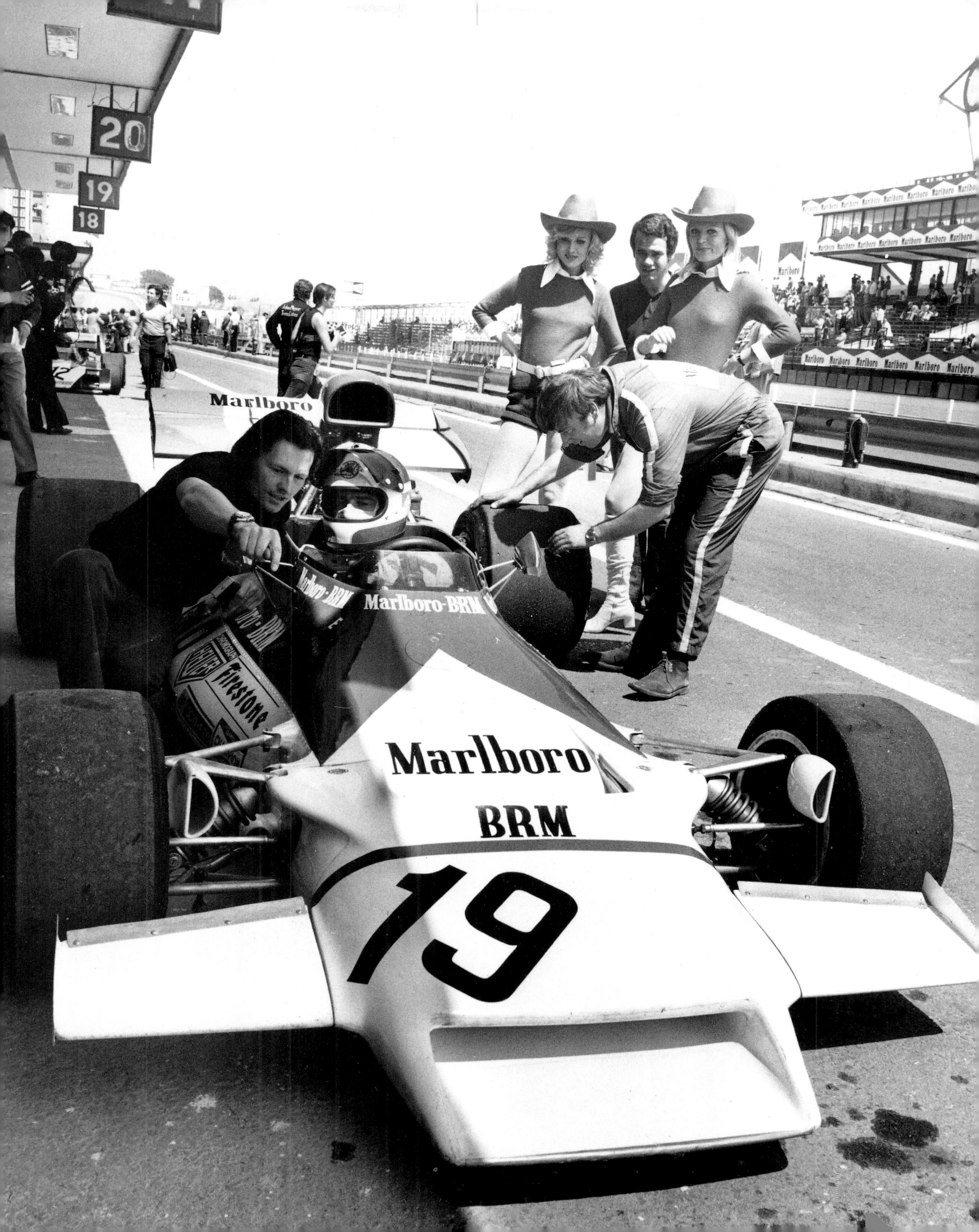
20
19
18
Marlboro
Marlboro-BRM
Marlboro-BRM
Firestone
Marlboro
BRM
19

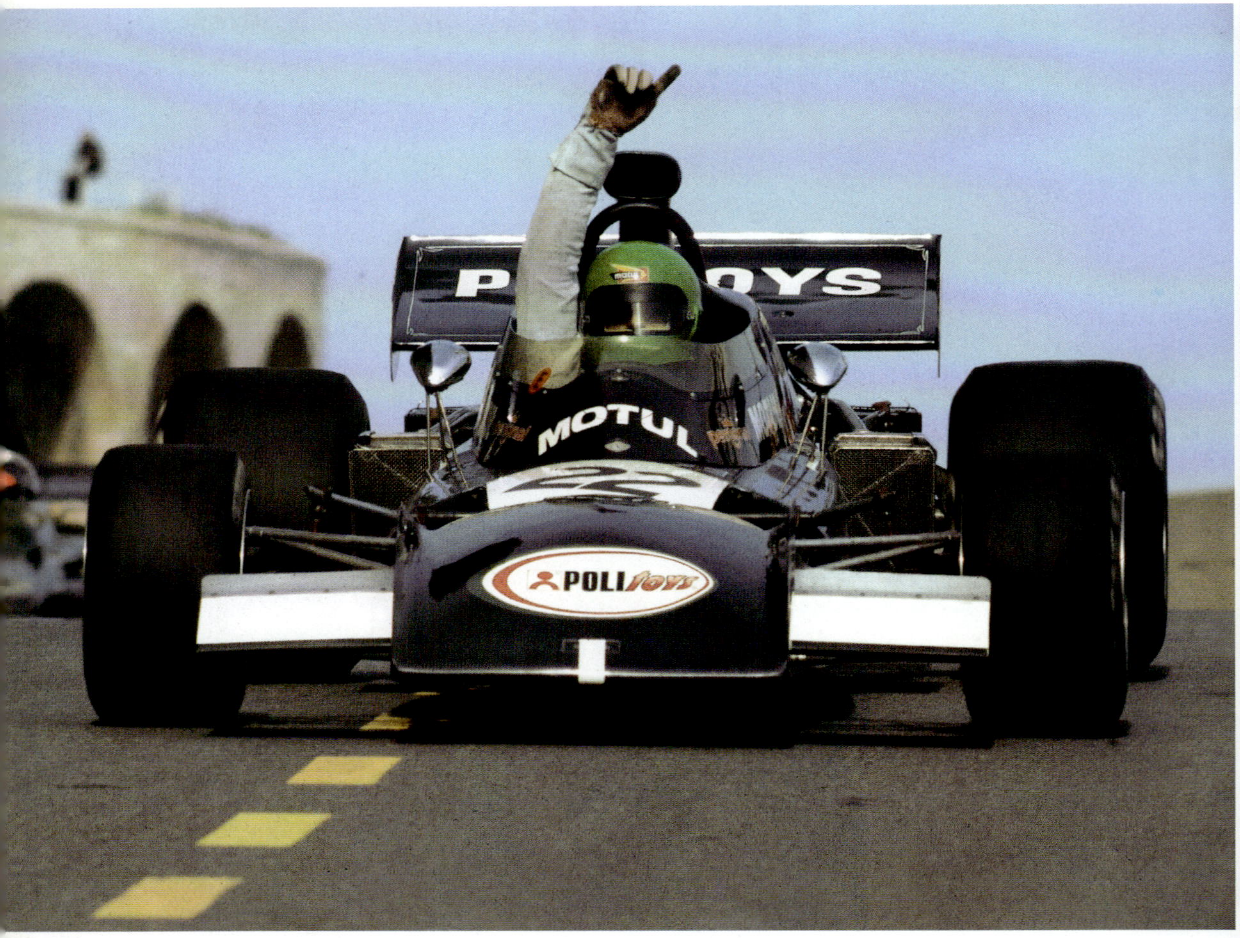

↑There were two notable green helmets in F1 at this time, one belonging to Reine Wisell and the other to Henri Pescarolo. At Monaco in 1972 the Frenchman is driving what has now become the Team Williams-Motul March 721/3, and this is during qualifying as Henri signals his slowing down to the following Emerson Fittipaldi in the JPS Lotus 72. In the very wet race, won by Jean-Pierre Beltoise (BRM's final GP victory), Pescarolo retired after aquaplaning into the barriers near Gasworks on lap 59.

→ In 1971, his second season in F1, Ronnie Peterson had finished runner-up in the World Championship for drivers. However, March's 1972 offering, the 721X, was a real turkey. At Monaco, Peterson exits the tunnel with 721X/2 on a rain-soaked track on his way to an ignominious 11th place, four laps behind Beltoise's victorious BRM.

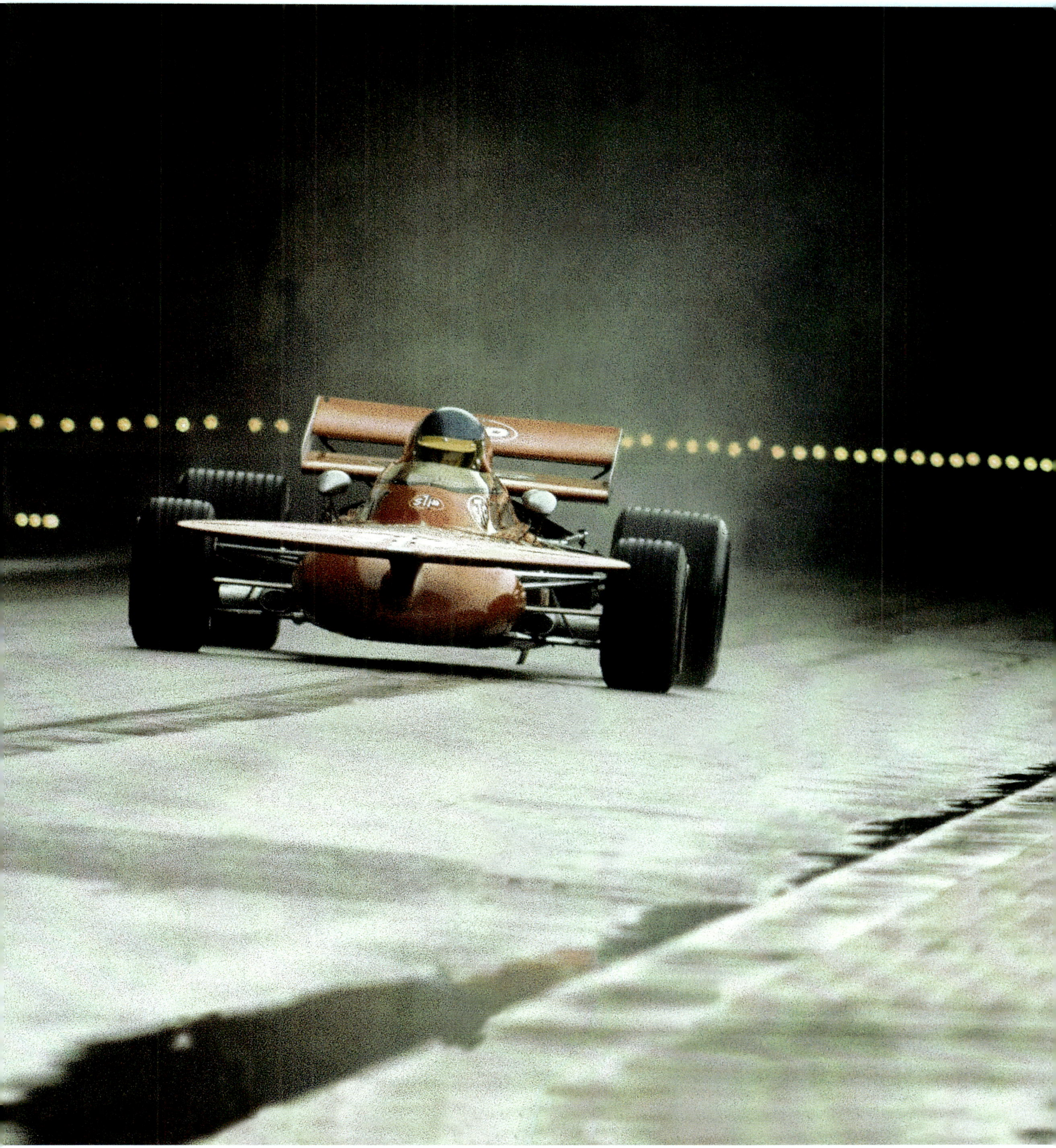

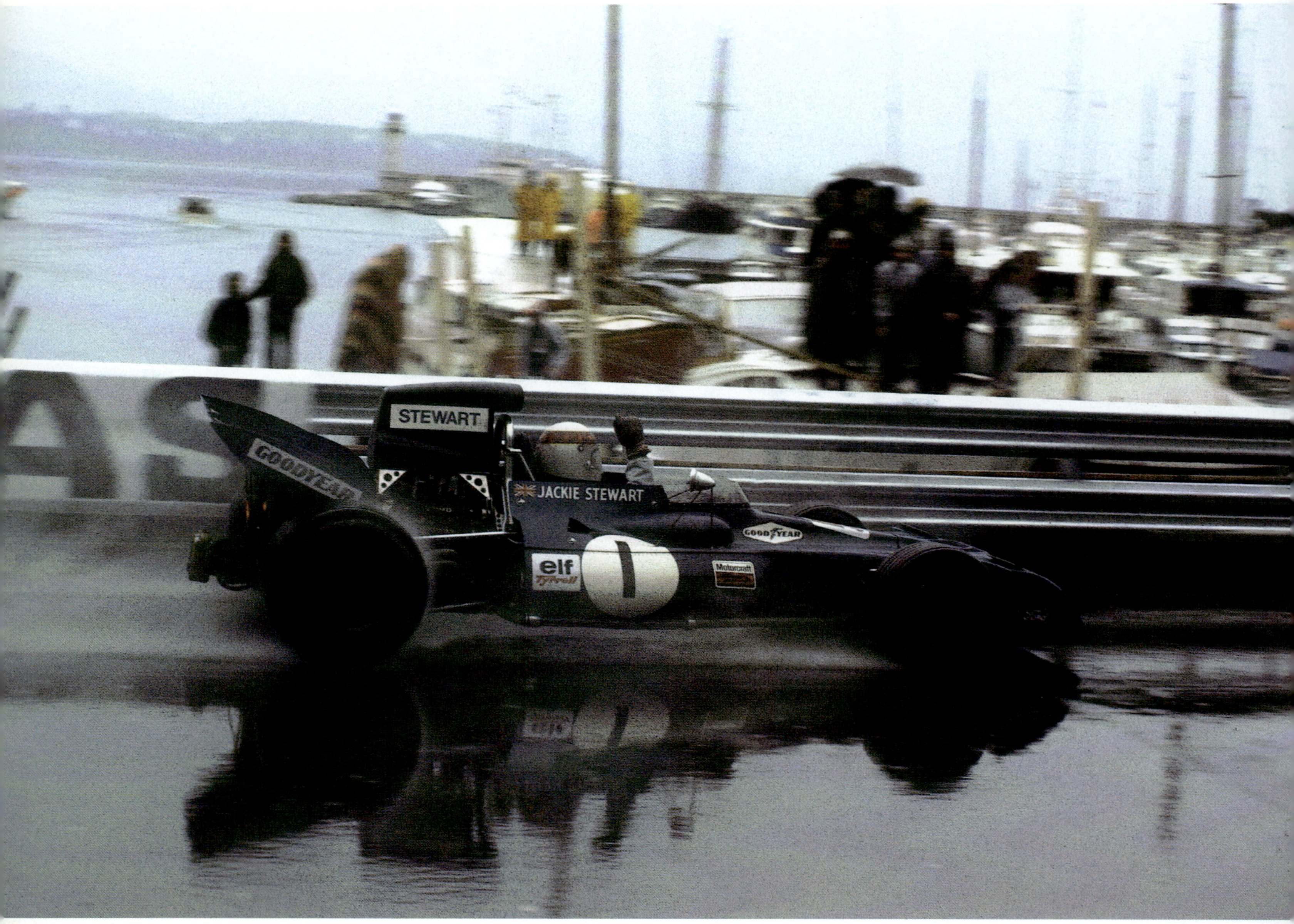

↑ I wonder if Jackie was gesticulating for an umbrella at Monaco? Tyrrell 003 and its skipper are waiting for the tide to go out, and he will ultimately finish fourth, slowed by wet electrics that allowed Fittipaldi (JPS Lotus 72) to catch him late in the race.

→ The International Gold Cup at Oulton Park in 1972 was held in late May and attracted three Marlboro BRM entries, the P180 for Reine Wisell, a P160 for Peter Gethin, and this old P153/06 for Australian Vern Schuppan. He won't be setting any fast times on those tyres! During pre-race testing, Vern talks to Tim Parnell (in raincoat) and BRM designer Tony Southgate. The race was won by Hulme's McLaren, whilst Vern finished fifth and the other two BRMs retired. Schuppan never did drive for BRM in any Grands Prix, although he was entered for the Belgian GP, but Helmut Marko drove instead. Later F1 forays with Ensign, briefly for Graham Hill and Surtees, were unproductive, and he achieved his best single-seater results in America, including finishing third at the 1981 Indianapolis 500. However, his biggest success was winning Le Mans in 1983 with Al Holbert and Hurley Haywood in a Rothmans Porsche 956.

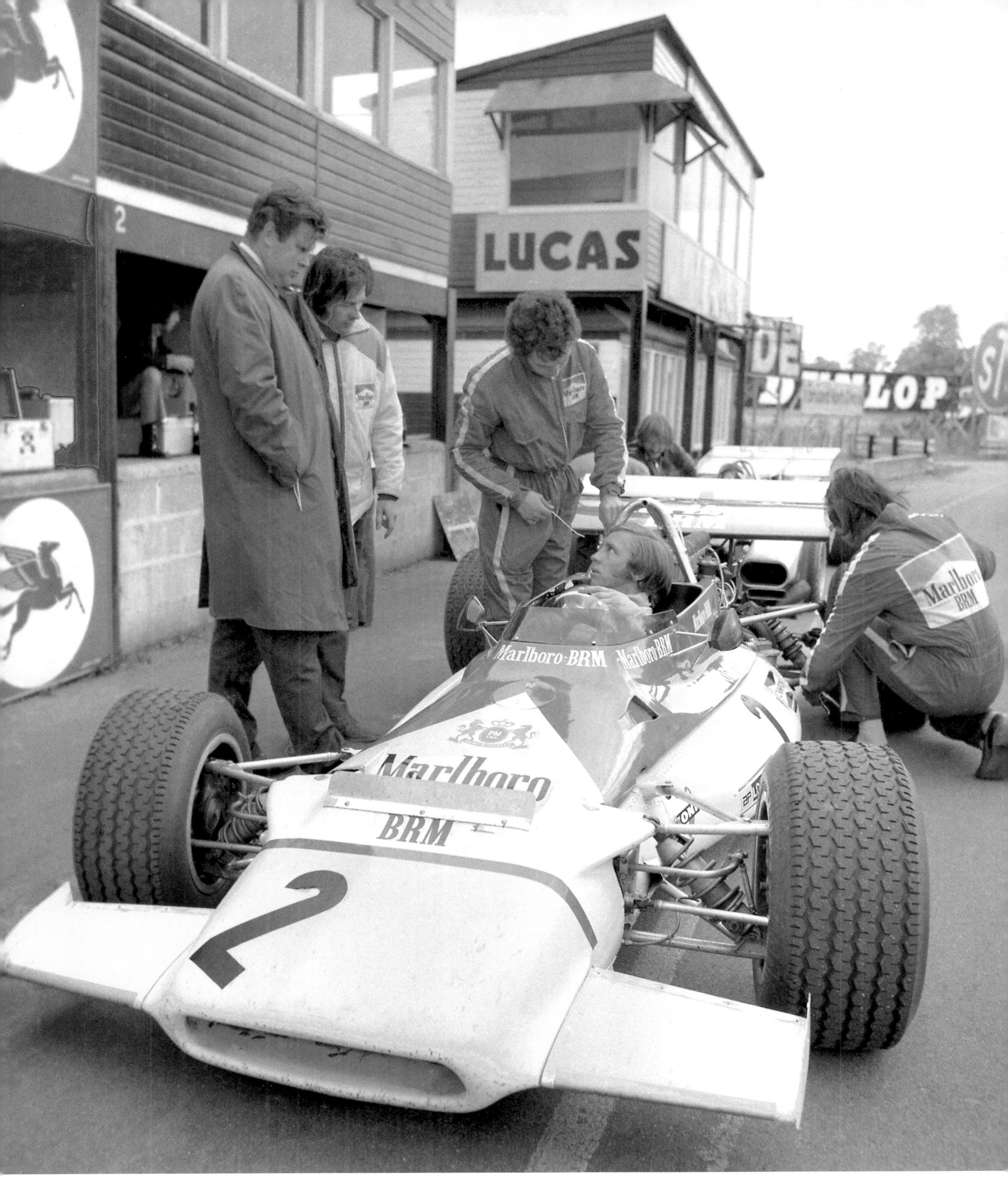
LUCAS
LOP
Marlboro-BRM
Marlboro-BRM
Marlboro
BRM
2
Marlboro
BRM

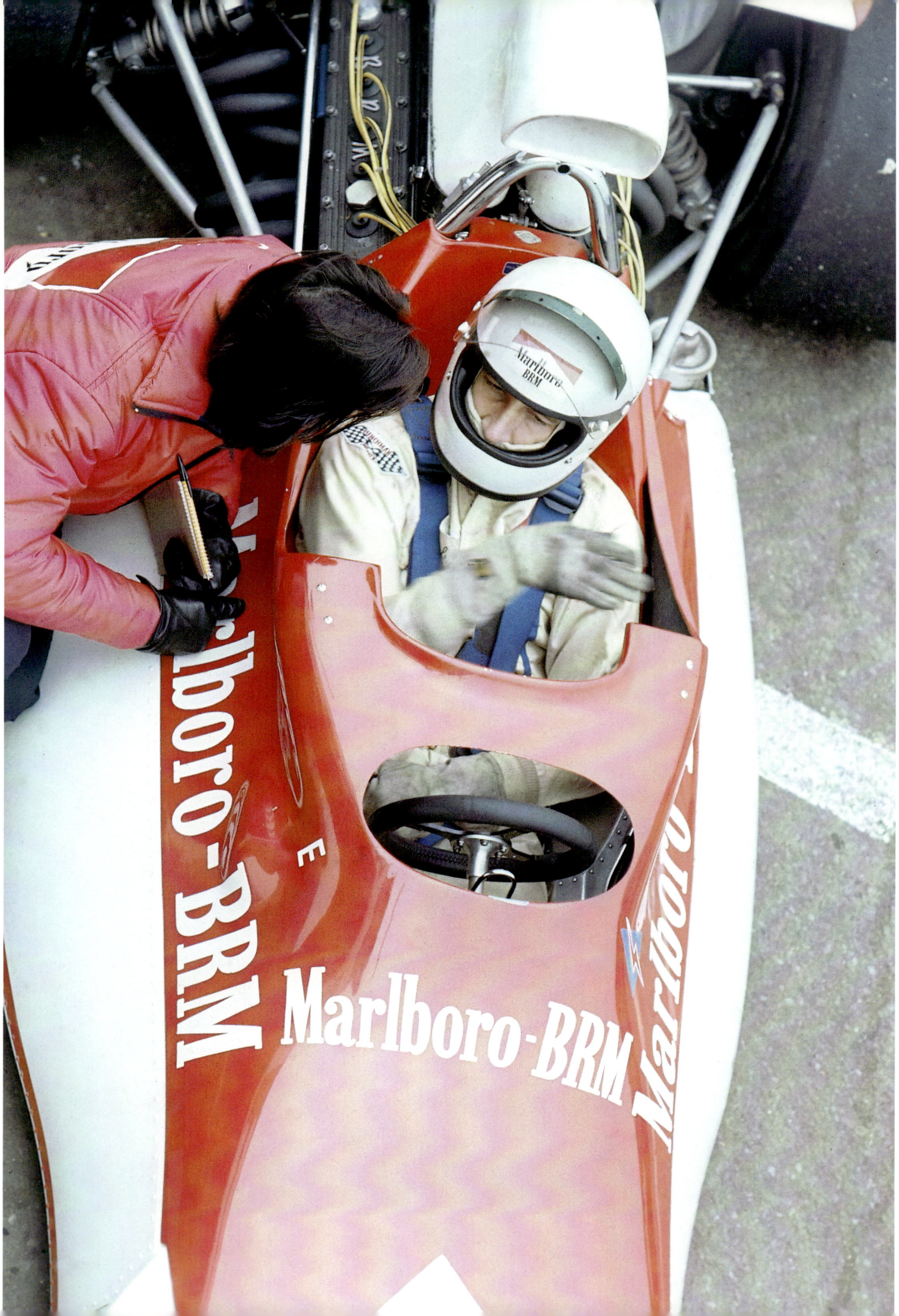
Marlboro
BRM
Marlboro-BRM
Marlboro-BRM
Marlboro

← Howden Ganley adopts the waving arm school of communication as he describes to Tony Southgate the BRM P180's less than endearing characteristics during private testing, perhaps because of its 30:70 rear weight bias. The hole for the steering wheel presumably had something to do with air flow. Two of these machines were built with Southgate-designed so-called 'ladybird sections' and they were not a success, although Beltoise, who had won Monaco for them in a P160, then won the grandly titled World Championship Victory Race at Brands Hatch on 22 October 1972 in P180/02, but this was the last time that either car was used.

→ This is what happens when you let an 'artist' loose on something that is supposed to be a functioning piece of high-performance machinery. Underneath the somewhat esoteric bodywork lies an otherwise fairly normal March 721. Apparently Rolf Stommelen's forward vision was not obscured by the periscope mirror, but let's hope it gave him a good view rearwards. Still, the car's bizarre appearance, courtesy of Lutz 'Luigi' Coloni, certainly gave its sponsors Eifelland Caravans a lot of exposure.

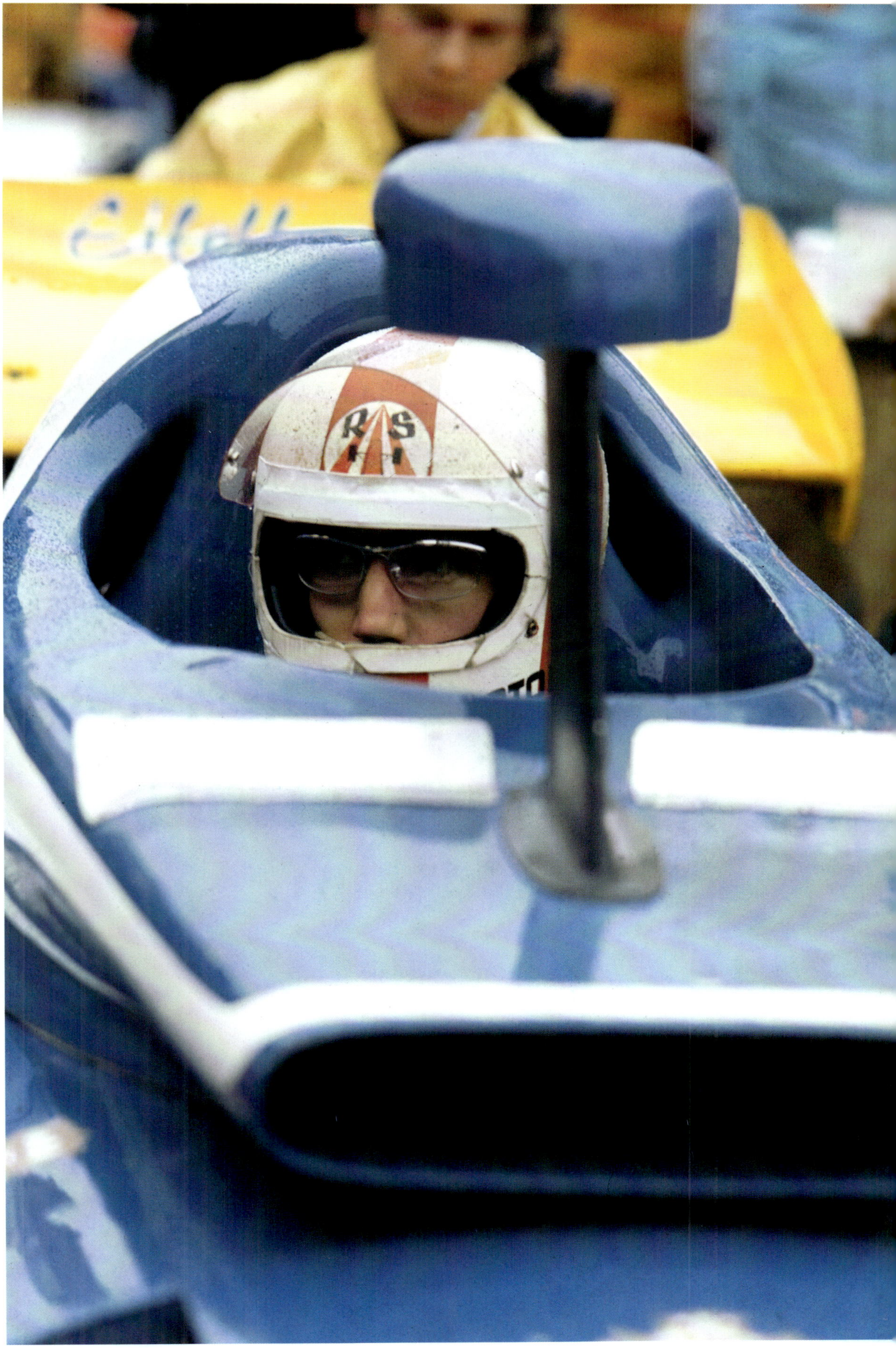

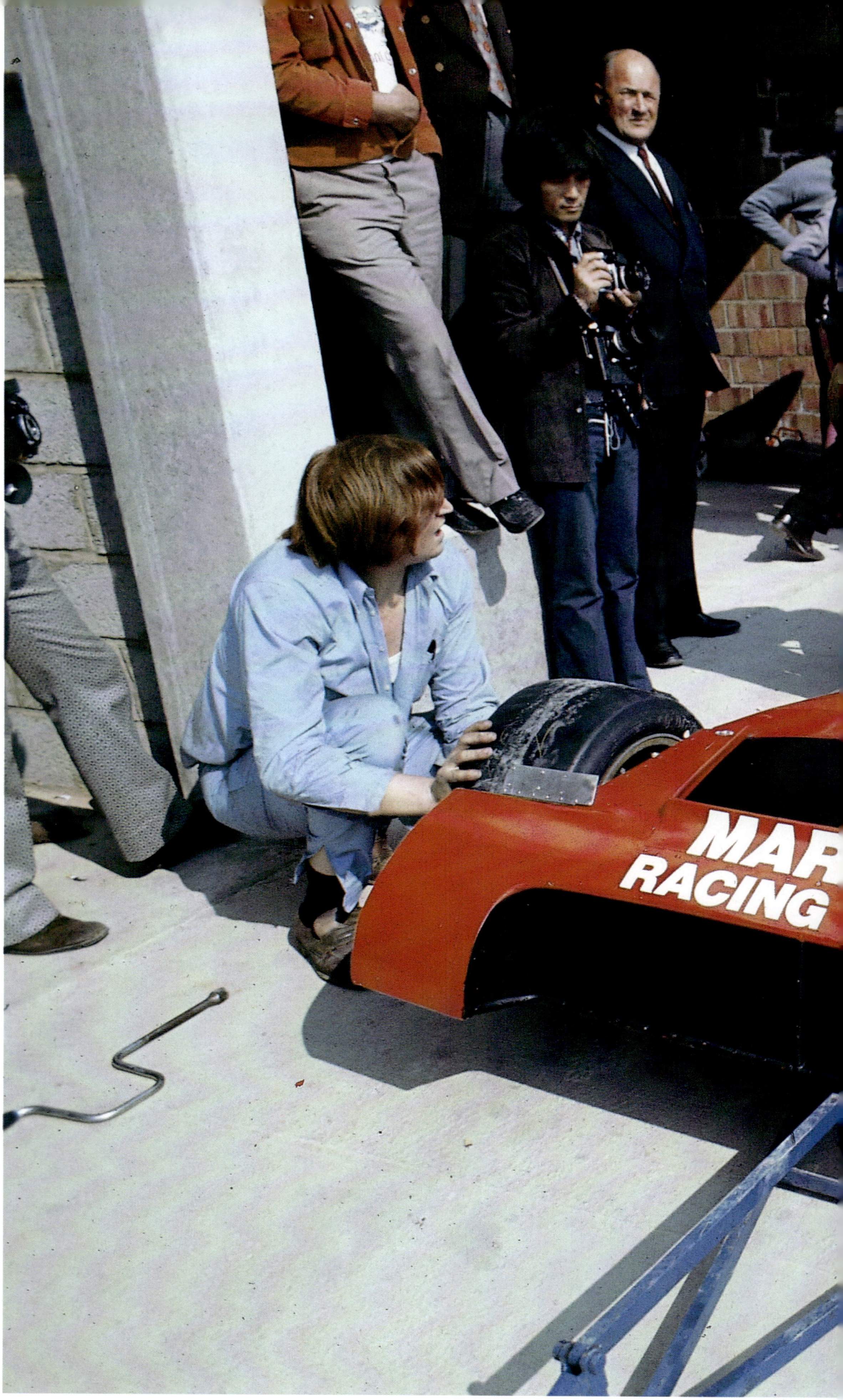

→ By the early 1970s, Mike's interest and participation in GP racing was on the wane, but he was still attending some events. This is Giovanni Galli in the unloved and messy looking Tecno PA123 F12 (T-001) at the 1972 Belgian GP at Nivelles, a sorry if somewhat safer substitute venue for Spa-Francorchamps. Galli at first raced as 'Nanni' to avoid family opprobrium and he eventually became known as Nanni Galli. His GP career began in 1970 with Bruce McLaren, racing an Alfa Romeo-powered M7D at Monza, and ended at Monaco in 1973 for Frank Williams, with a one-off Ferrari drive at the 1972 French GP in between. The Tecno was a woeful failure after the company's successful F2 machines, and their final GP appearance was at the 1973 Austrian GP when the hapless Chris Amon failed to qualify.

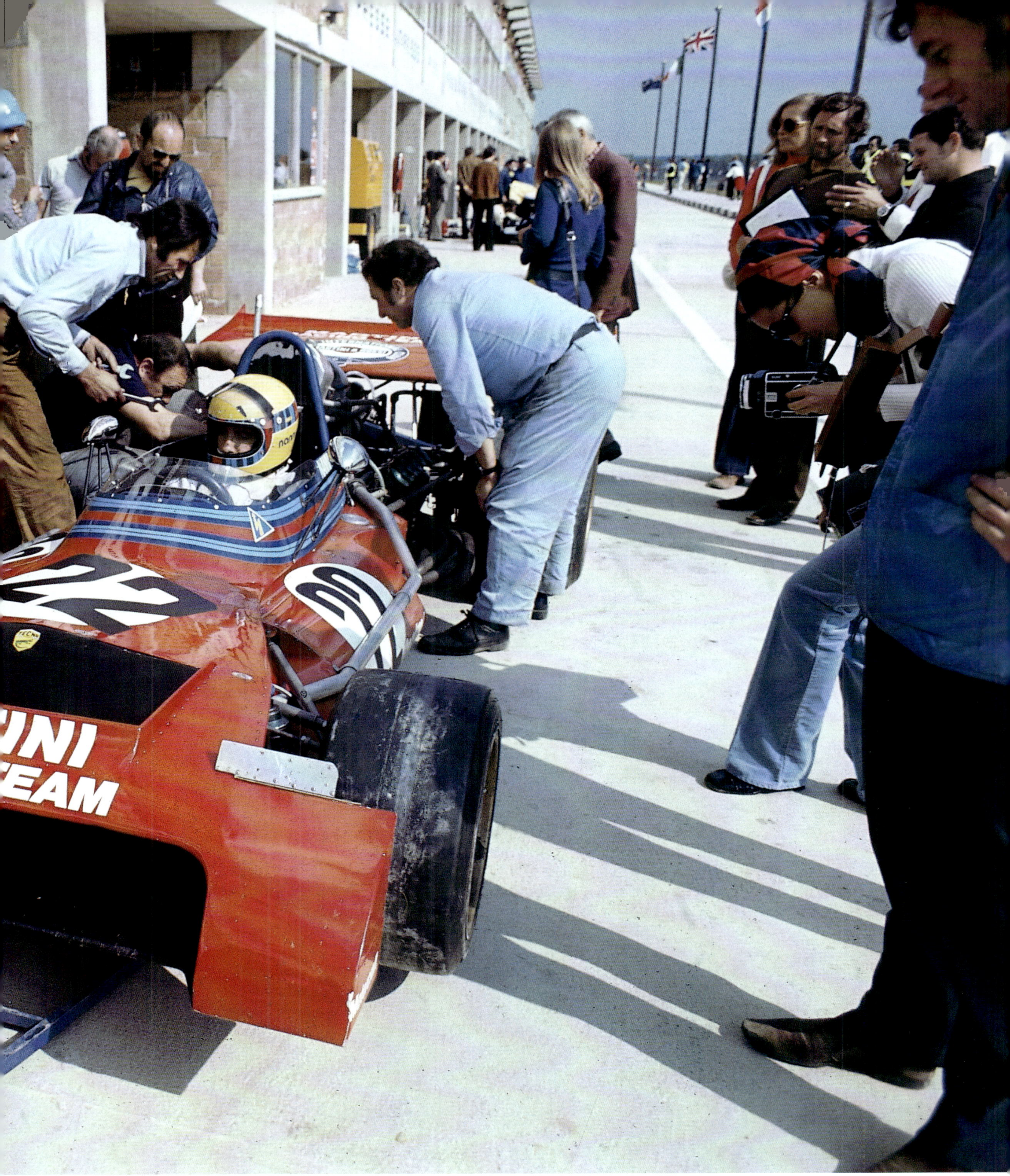

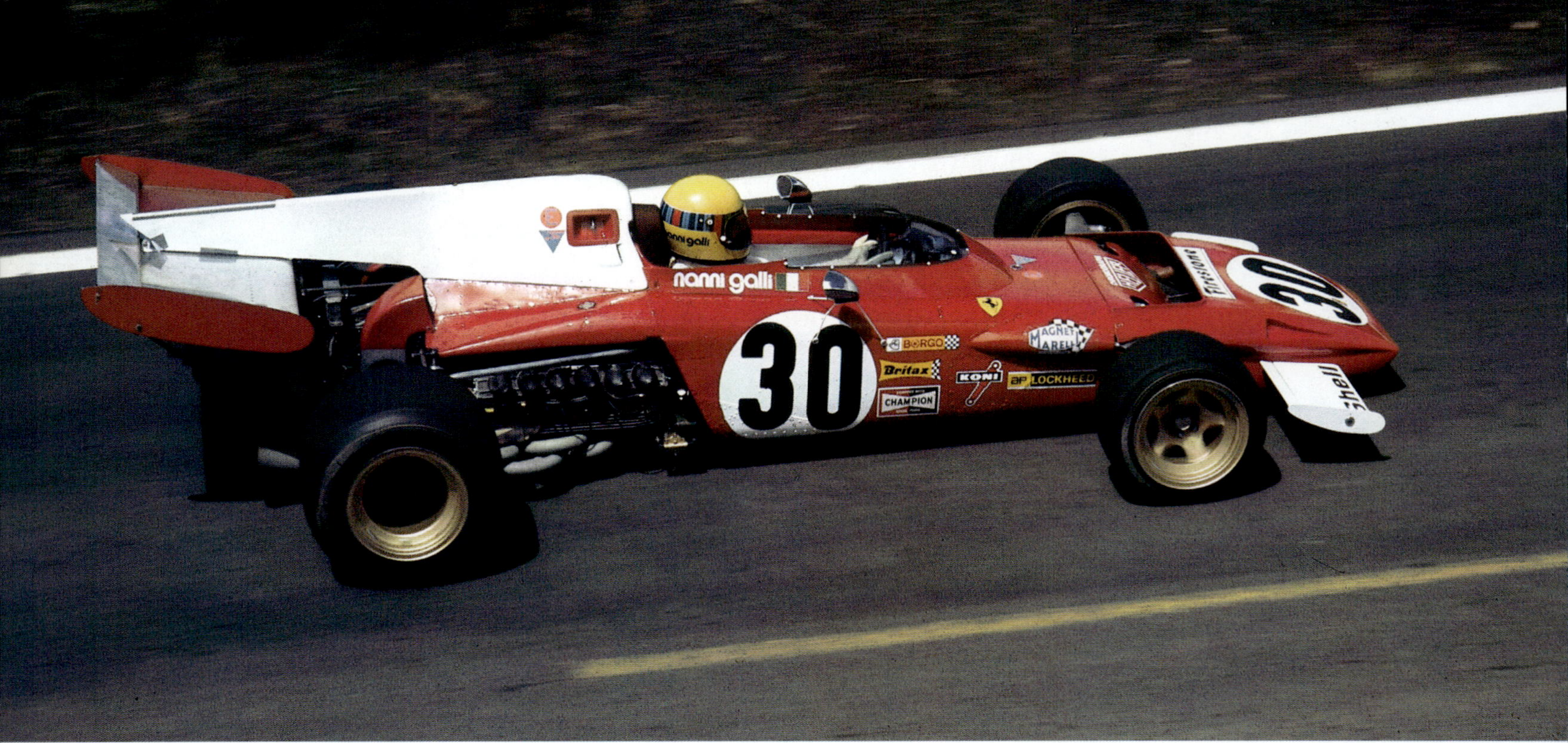

↑ Mike must have liked Nanni Galli because he seems to have photographed him quite often. However, the car is the real subject of this shot. It's the Ferrari 312B2/007 during the 1972 French GP at Clermont-Ferrand, and it looks a proper bit of kit. This was the only time that Galli drove for Ferrari, surely every Italian racing driver's dream, but he finished a lowly 13th.

↗ Twice World Champion Jackie Stewart's exhausting 1972 schedule took its toll of the ever-busy Scot. He was diagnosed with mononucleosis (Glandular Fever) and he developed an ulcer that compromised his form. This is not to detract from Emerson Fittipaldi's championship year, but things might have been different otherwise. JYS enjoys a rare break in the sun at the 1972 British GP at Brands Hatch against the back wheel of Tyrrell 003. He battled with Ickx's Ferrari and Fittipaldi's Lotus 72 for much of the race but, despite setting fastest lap, he could not catch the Brazilian and lost out by just 4.1sec to finish second.

→ During the French GP weekend at Clermont-Ferrand, former rugby player and President of Philip Morris Europe, Ronnie Thomson, is flanked by world-famous automotive and aviation artist Michael Turner (left) and Jean-Pierre Beltoise. The occasion was the presentation of Michael's painting of Beltoise winning the 1972 Monaco GP in the BRM P160B that can be seen on the wall behind his head. JPB began competing in 1959 and was an 11-times French motorcycle champion who worked as a mechanic for René Bonnet. In 1964 he had a serious accident at Reims, suffering multiple injuries, including burns and a very badly broken left arm that thereafter was only capable of restricted movement. Nevertheless, he recovered to become one of the best French drivers of the era, being French F3 champion in 1965, winner of the 1966 Monaco F3 race, and 1968 European F2 champion. He drove for Ken Tyrrell, Matra, and BRM in F1, and also enjoyed success with Matra, Ligier, and Inaltera in championship endurance racing. Blamed for the Ignazio Giunti tragedy at Buenos Aires in 1971, his racing licence was suspended for six months. He ended his career by winning the French Touring Car Championship in 1976/77. A shame that Beltoise's sartorial perfection has been rather compromised by the crookedly sewn on Marlboro patch on his jacket.

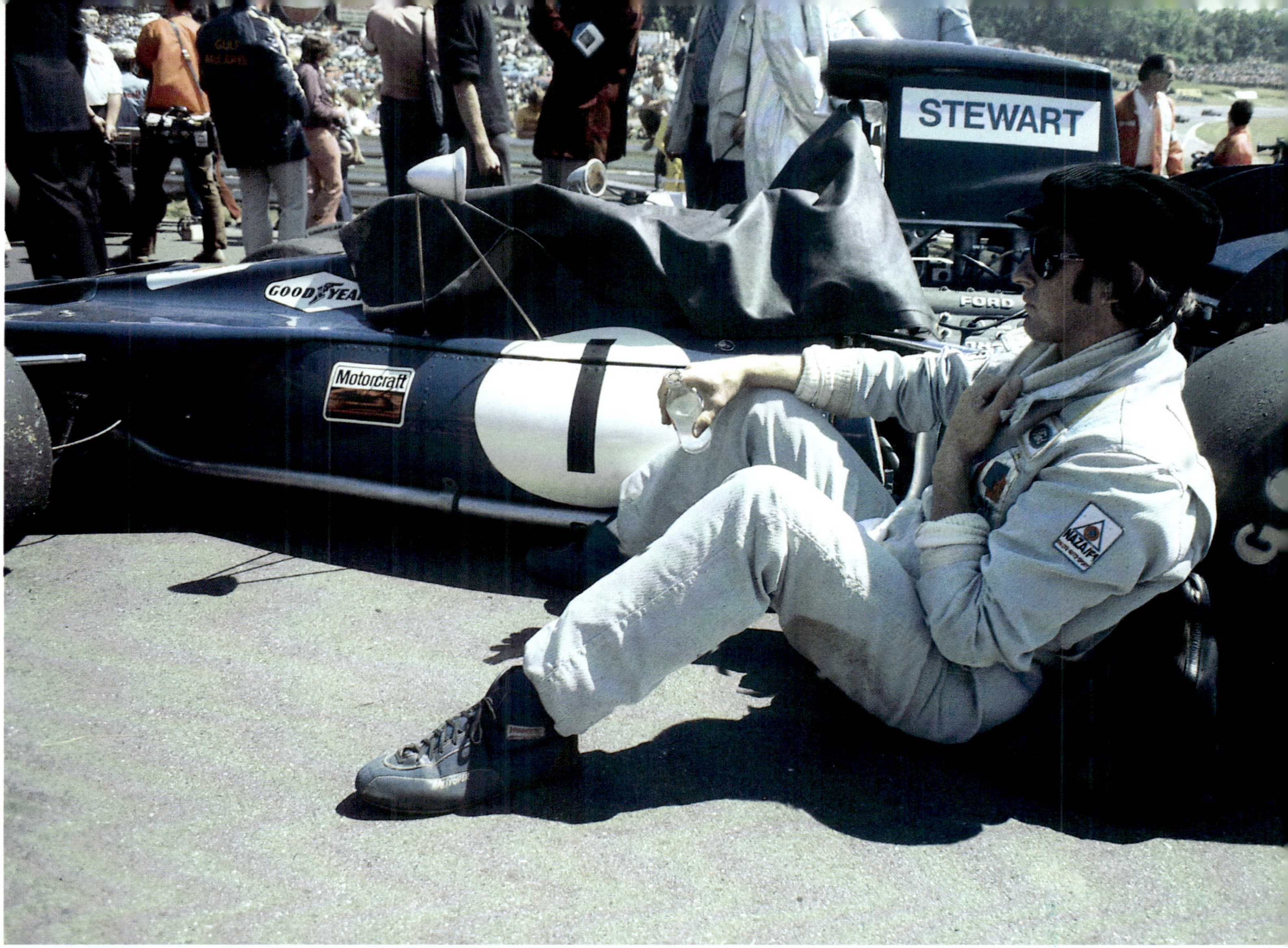
STEWART
Motorcraft
FORD

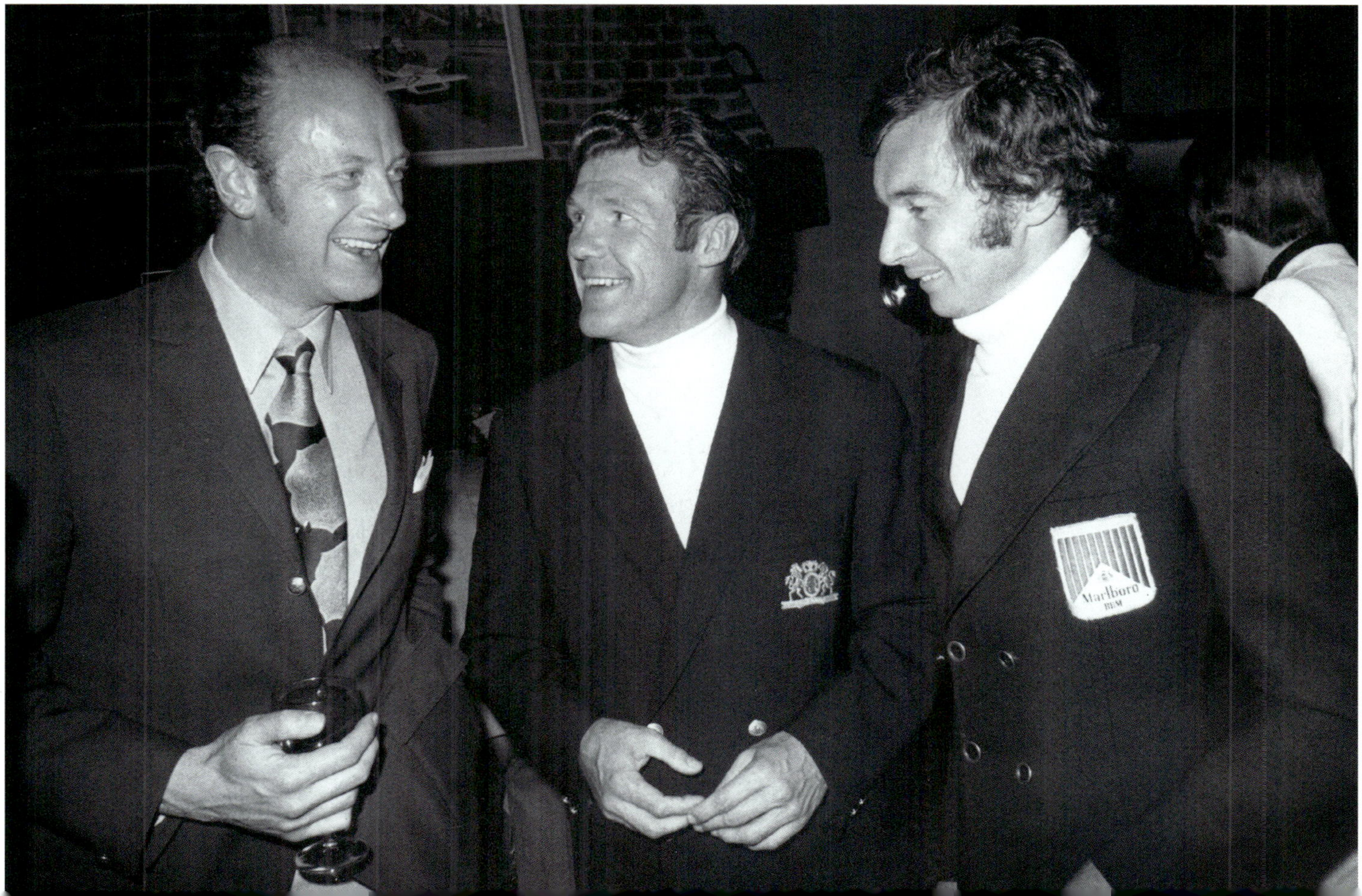
Marlboro

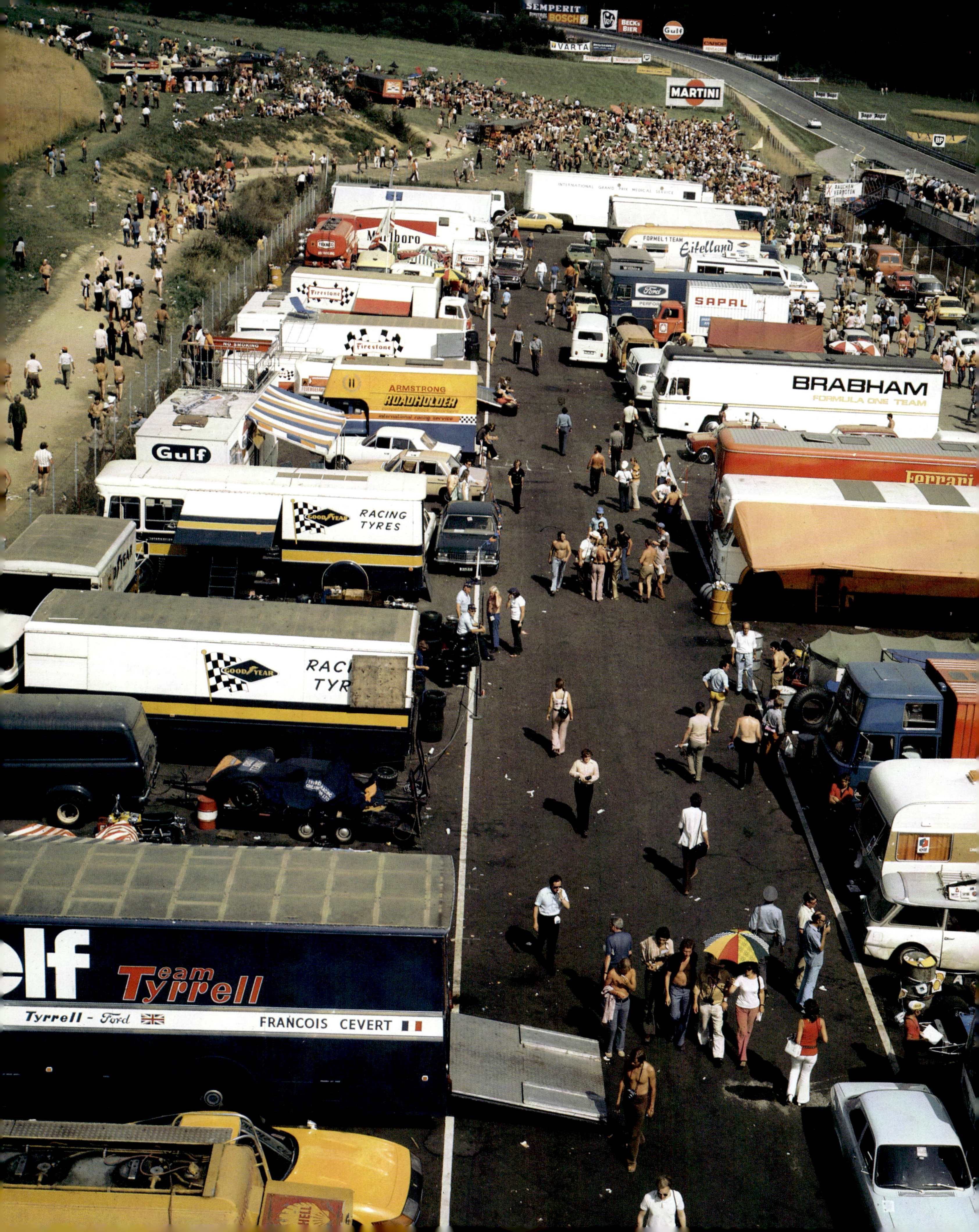
SEMPERIT
BOSCH
BECK'S BIER
Gulf
VARTA
MARTINI
RAUCHEN VERBOTEN
Marlboro
FORMEL 1 TEAM
Eifelland
Firestone
Ford
SAPAL
NO SMOKING
Firestone
ARMSTRONG
ROADHOLDER
international racing service
BRABHAM
FORMULA ONE TEAM
Gulf
GOODYEAR
RACING
TYRES
Ferrari
GOODYEAR
RAC
TYR
elf
Team
Tyrrell
Tyrrell - Ford
FRANCOIS CEVERT

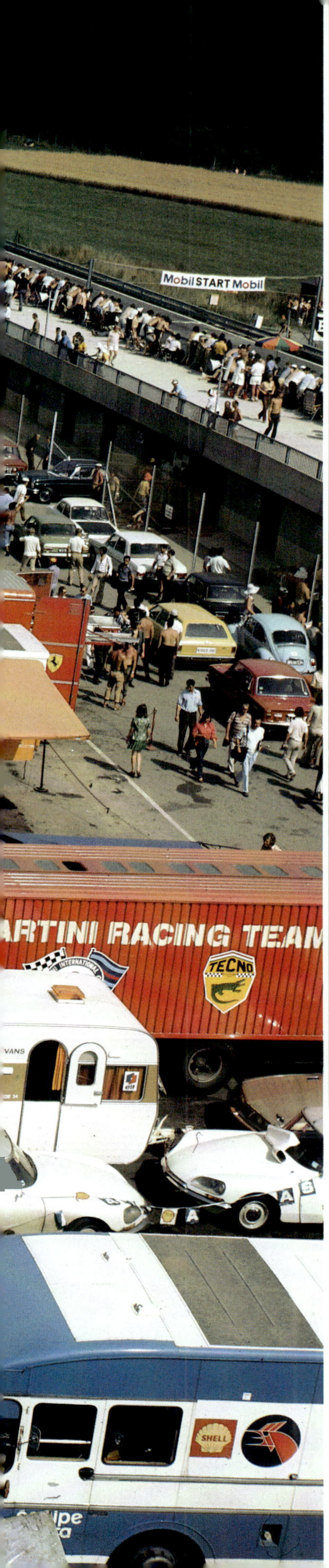

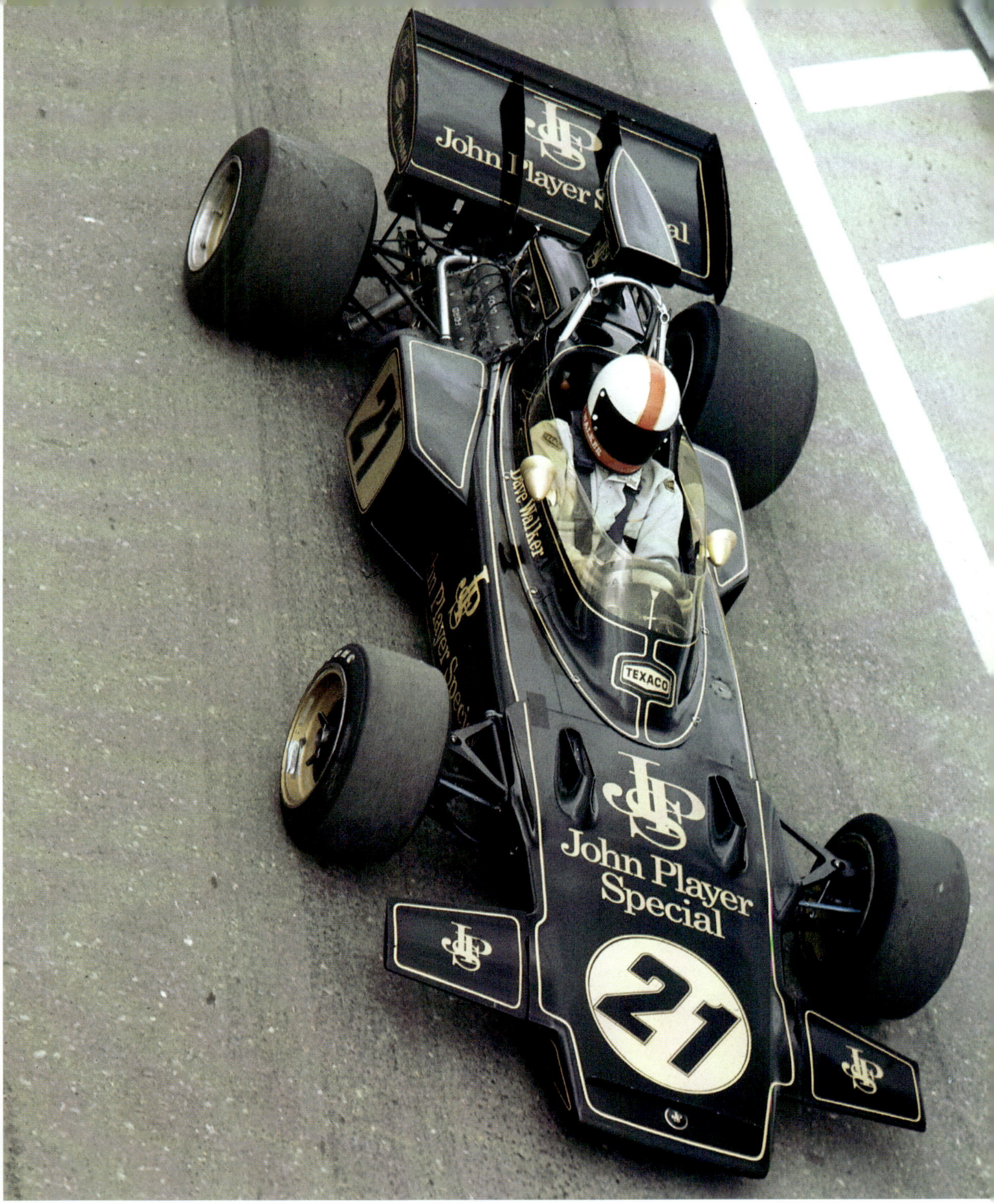

↑ Being number two at Lotus was historically not a happy place to be, as Dave Walker discovered in 1972. Mike catches Walker as he coasts down the pit lane in the JPS Lotus 72D/R6 at the 1972 Austrian GP where he qualified 19th out of 26 and retired in the race. The Australian had won the 1970 Lombank F3 series for Lotus, but his F1 form was disappointing. Lotus blamed Walker, citing his driving and lack of fitness, while Walker blamed Lotus for inadequate machinery in a season when his team-mate Emerson Fittipald won the World Drivers' Championship. He raced the gas turbine 56B at Zandvoort in 1971 but crashed it in the heavy rain, and during his ten GP starts in 1972 he posted one DSQ, one 10th, one 9th (ret), two 14th, one 18th (ret) and four straight retirements. He departed to drive for GRD in F2, but had two nasty road accidents and, after trying 2-litre sports car racing in 1975, returned to Australia.

← F1 paddocks gradually assumed a more structured and ordered appearance during this period, but it is still spectator friendly and accessible. The Austrian GP at the Österreichring in 1972 with the flat-out Bosch Curve in the background but not a single F1 car in sight. Perhaps they raced the transporters?

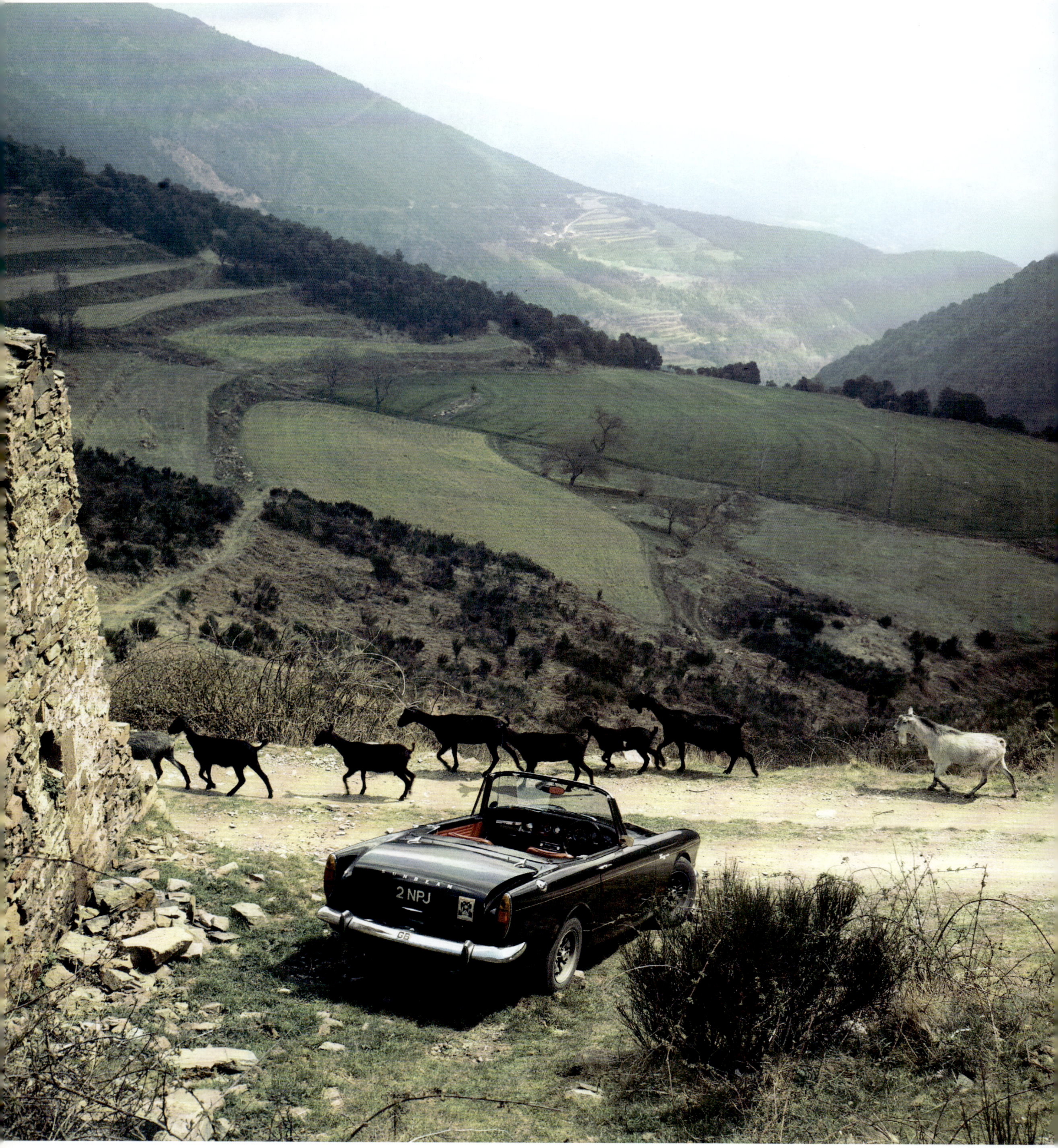
2 NPJ

→ For those who like to see original specification cars in period sponsors' colours, this is the 1973 Williams FW02 (or Iso-FX3) at its launch.

← En route to the 1973 Spanish GP with his wife Liz, Mike has stopped in some far-flung hills in Spain as a herd of goats followed by the billy pass by. The beloved Sunbeam Tiger was bought in 1968 and is bearing Mike's 2 NPJ plate that he transferred from car to car. Happily, the family still own the car today and it is currently being rebuilt.

↓ After his medical problems in 1972 there was no stopping Jackie Stewart the following year, and he won the World Championship with five victories, despite severe opposition from JPS pedallers Emerson Fittipaldi and Ronnie Peterson. He was undoubtedly helped by the fact that Fittipaldi's second half (the championship then was split into two parts) delivered just 14 points, whilst Peterson's first five races produced nothing. At Montjuich Park, however, Stewart in Tyrrell 006/2 was sidelined by brake failure in a race won by Fittipaldi.

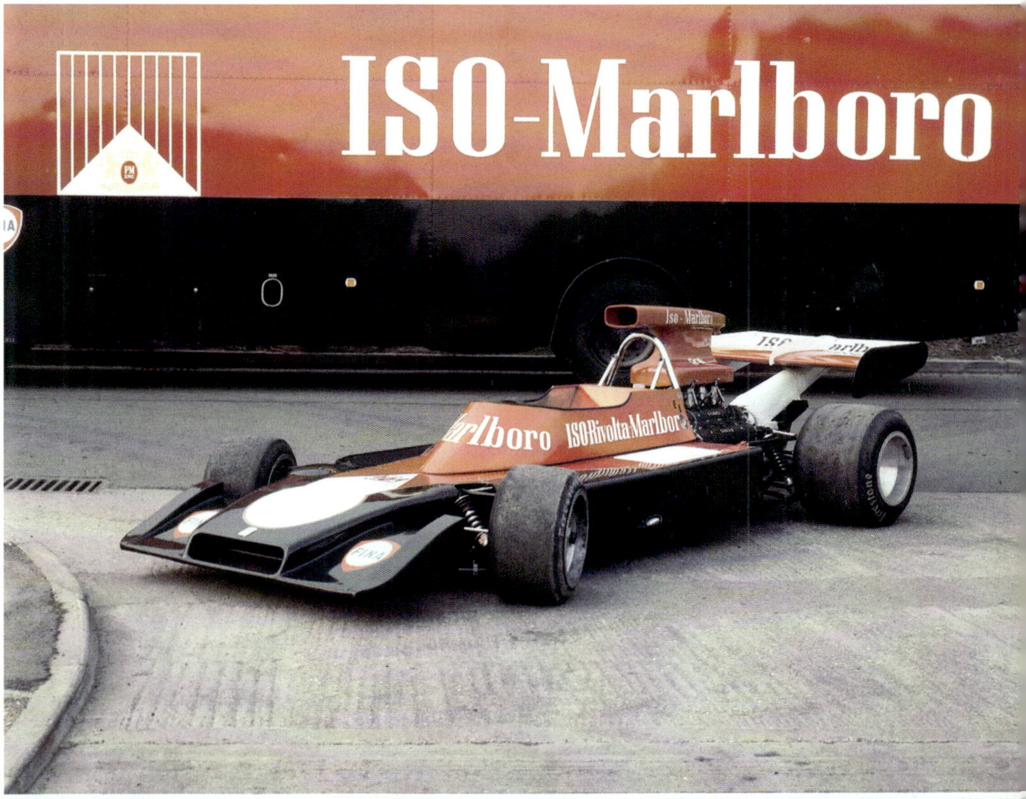

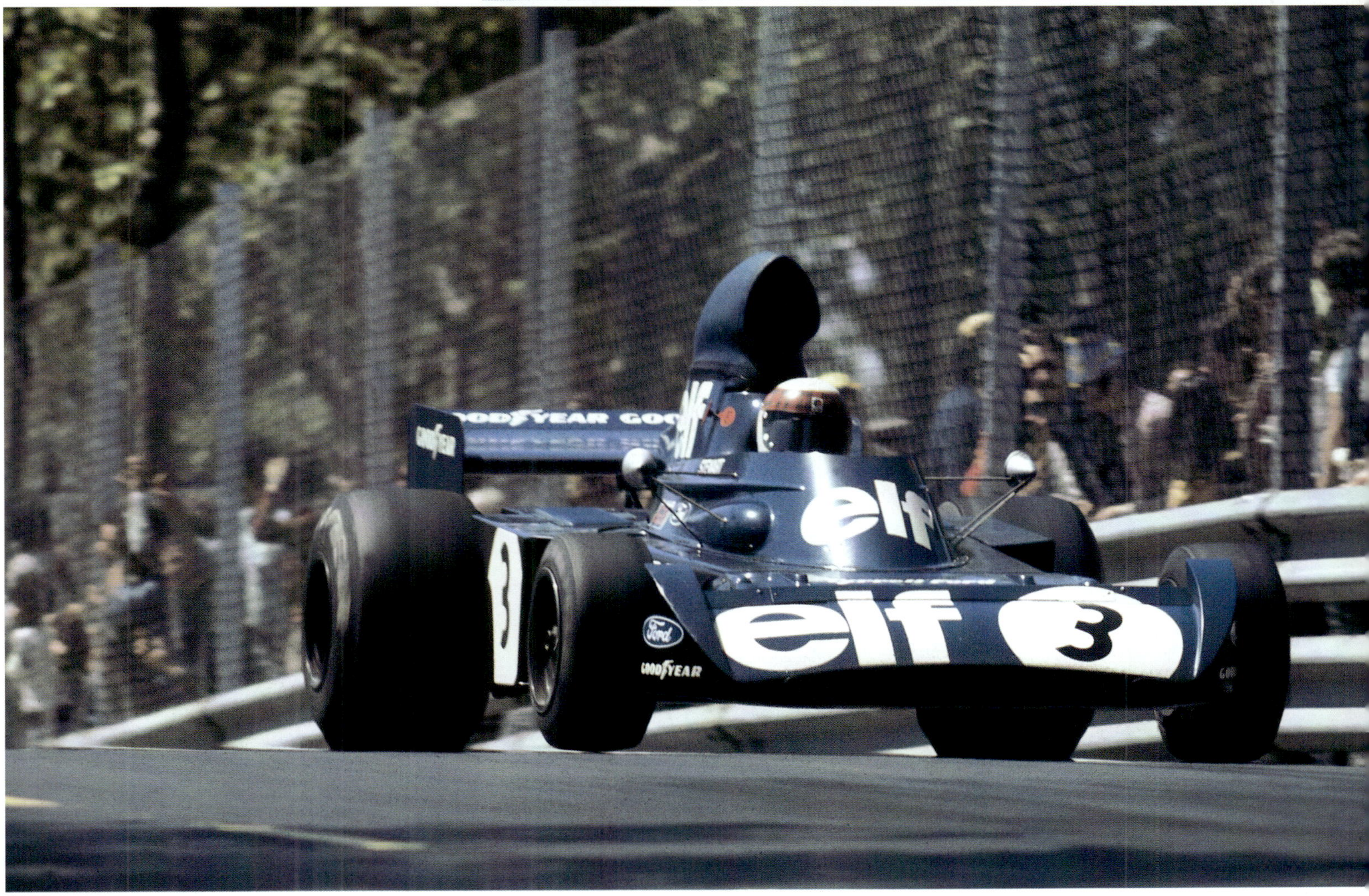

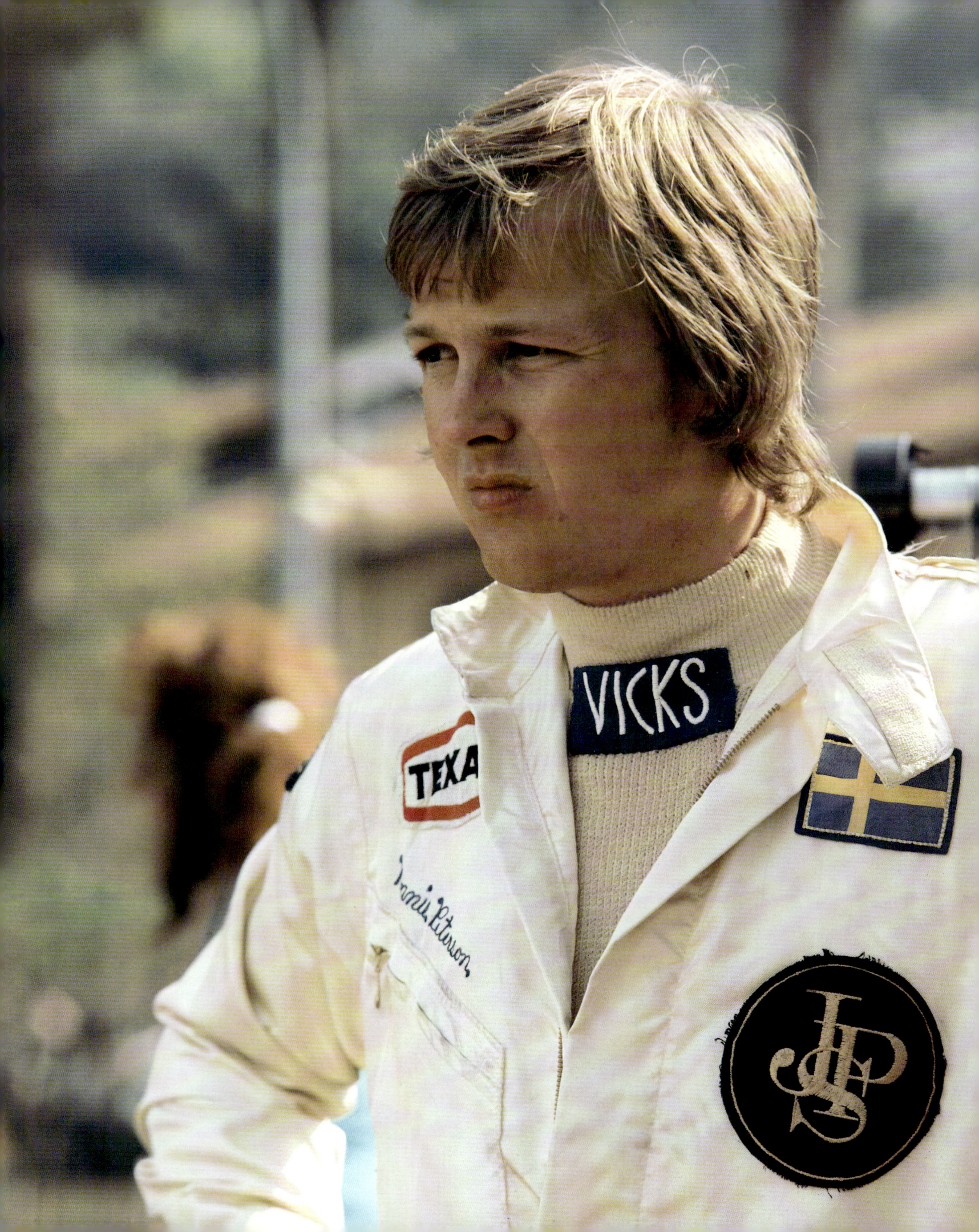
VICKS
TEXA

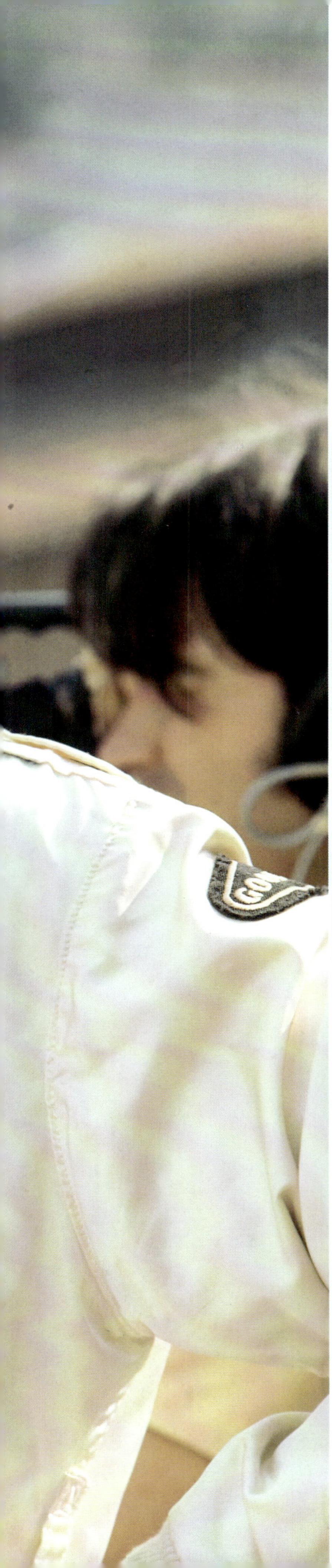

← A very youthful, almost schoolboyish, looking Ronnie Peterson at Monaco. He is 29 years old and in his fourth season of F1, the first with privateer Colin Crabbe (1970), two with STP March (1971/72), and now with John Player Team Lotus. Had it not been for his disastrous start to the 1973 season (four retirements and one 11th place in the first five races) he would have been better than third in the Drivers' Championship, scoring four wins in the last eight races. Fantastically fast in anything and everything he drove, his form at times overshadowed the team's existing star, 1972 World Champion Emerson Fittipaldi. Five years later he would repeat his second placing in the 1971 World Championship, this time in favour of Mario Andretti whom he also overshadowed. Like Jochen Rindt before him, he was to die as a result of an accident at Monza, a track that was ill fated for Team Lotus.

↓ He was just as wiry and spare in 1973, the only difference being that his hair was not yet grey. Arturo Merzario, affectionately known as 'Little Art', at Monaco, and for once no sign of his famous Stetson.

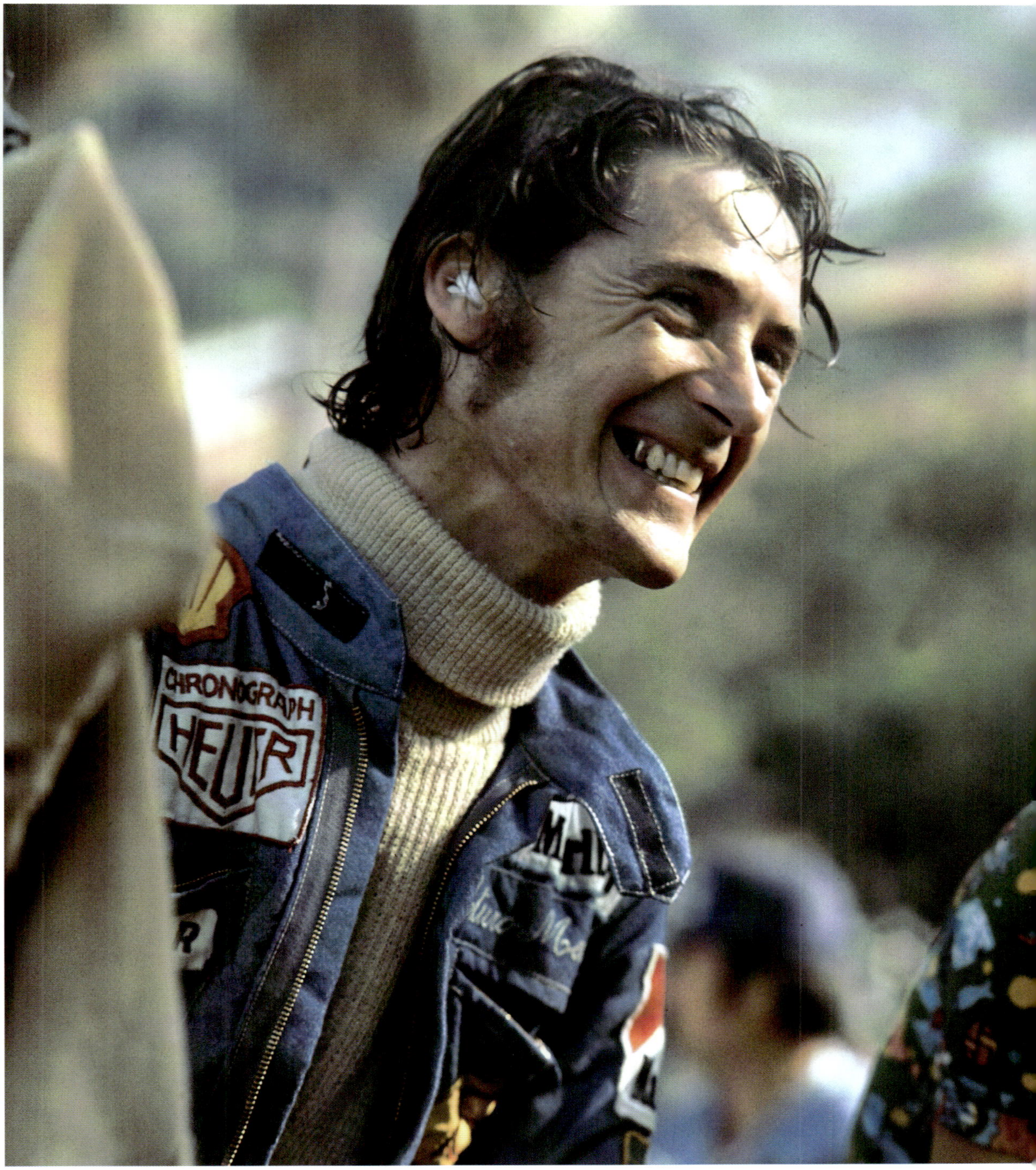

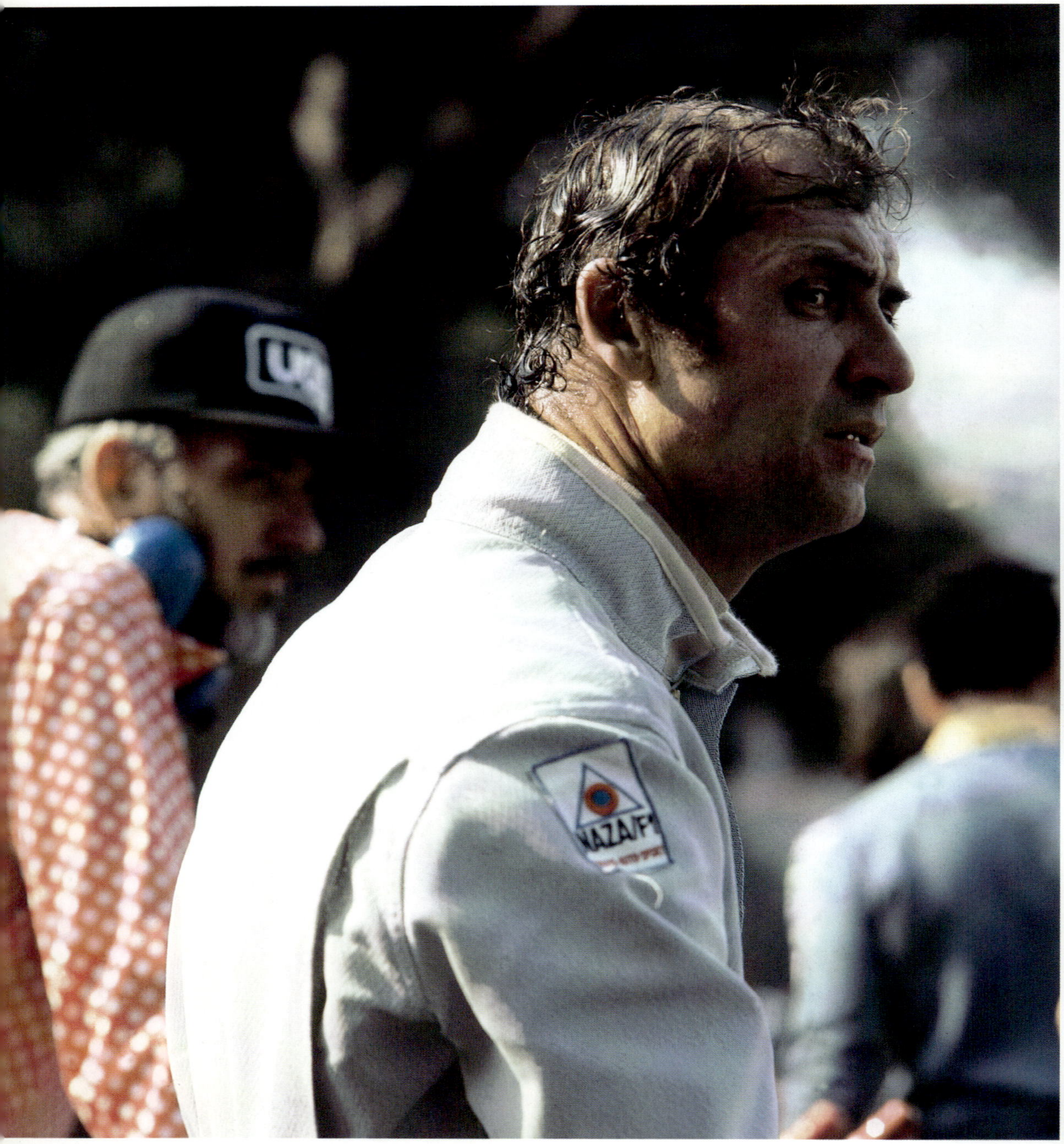

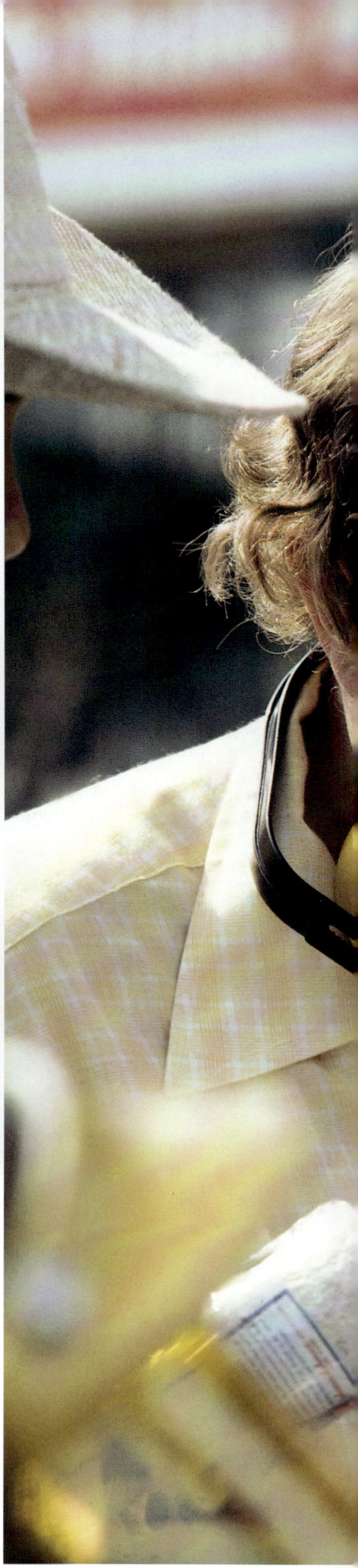

↑ Looking more like a professional boxer, UOP Shadow's novice F1 driver George Follmer, who began his career in 1960, turned out to be quite handy despite his already advancing age at the time (39) and a less than brilliant car. He finished sixth in South Africa and third in Spain, but did not start at Monaco, and after this his season deteriorated. Later he returned to Can-Am and Trans-Am, winning the latter championship in 1976, but he suffered severe injuries in a 1978 Laguna Seca shunt. However, he returned the following year and was still racing a Camaro in Trans-Am into the early 1980s. In the background team patron Don Nicholls concentrates on qualifying.

→ A troubled looking Colin Chapman and a concerned Emerson Fittipaldi confer at Monaco. What is that strange garment Emerson is wearing?

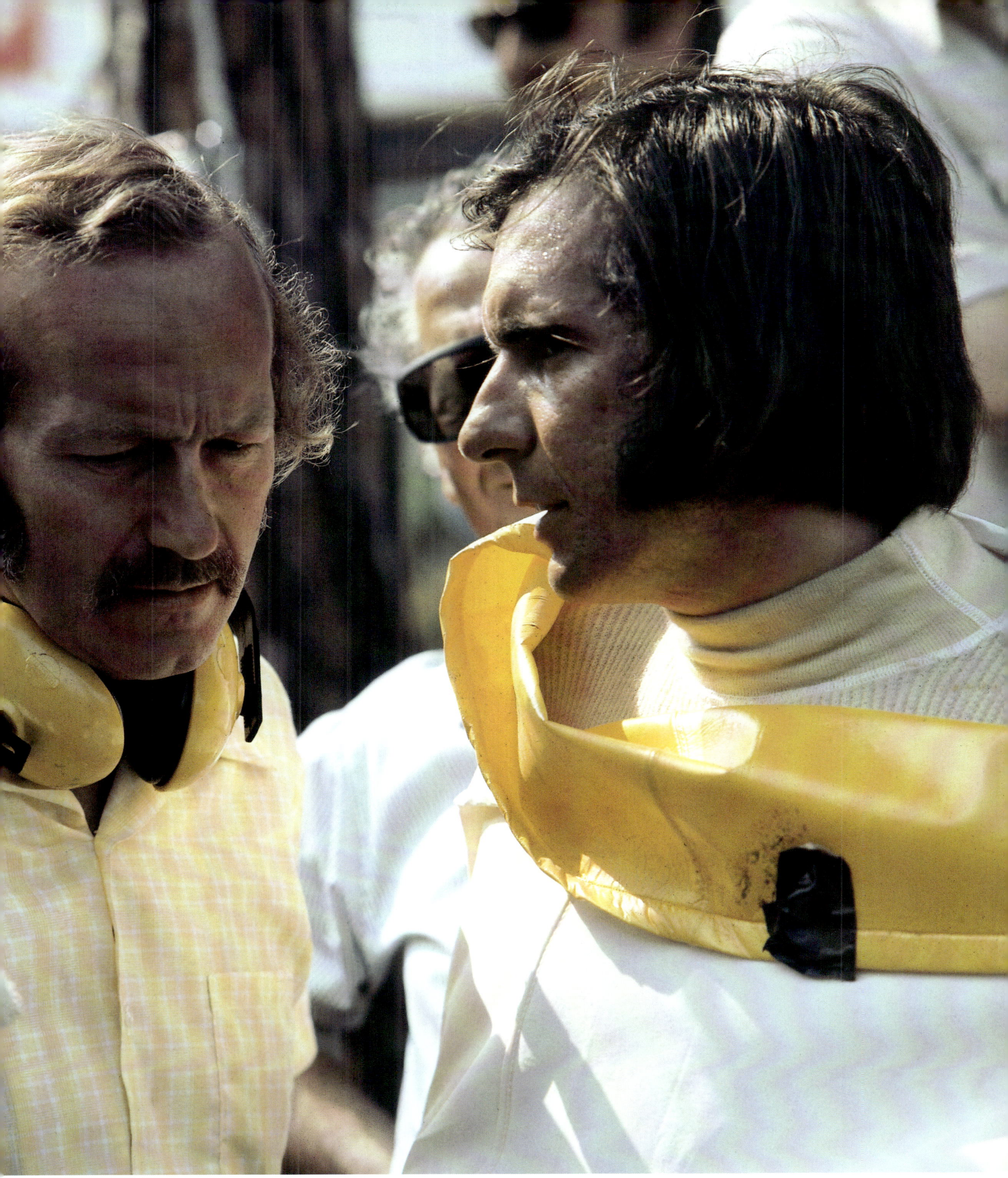

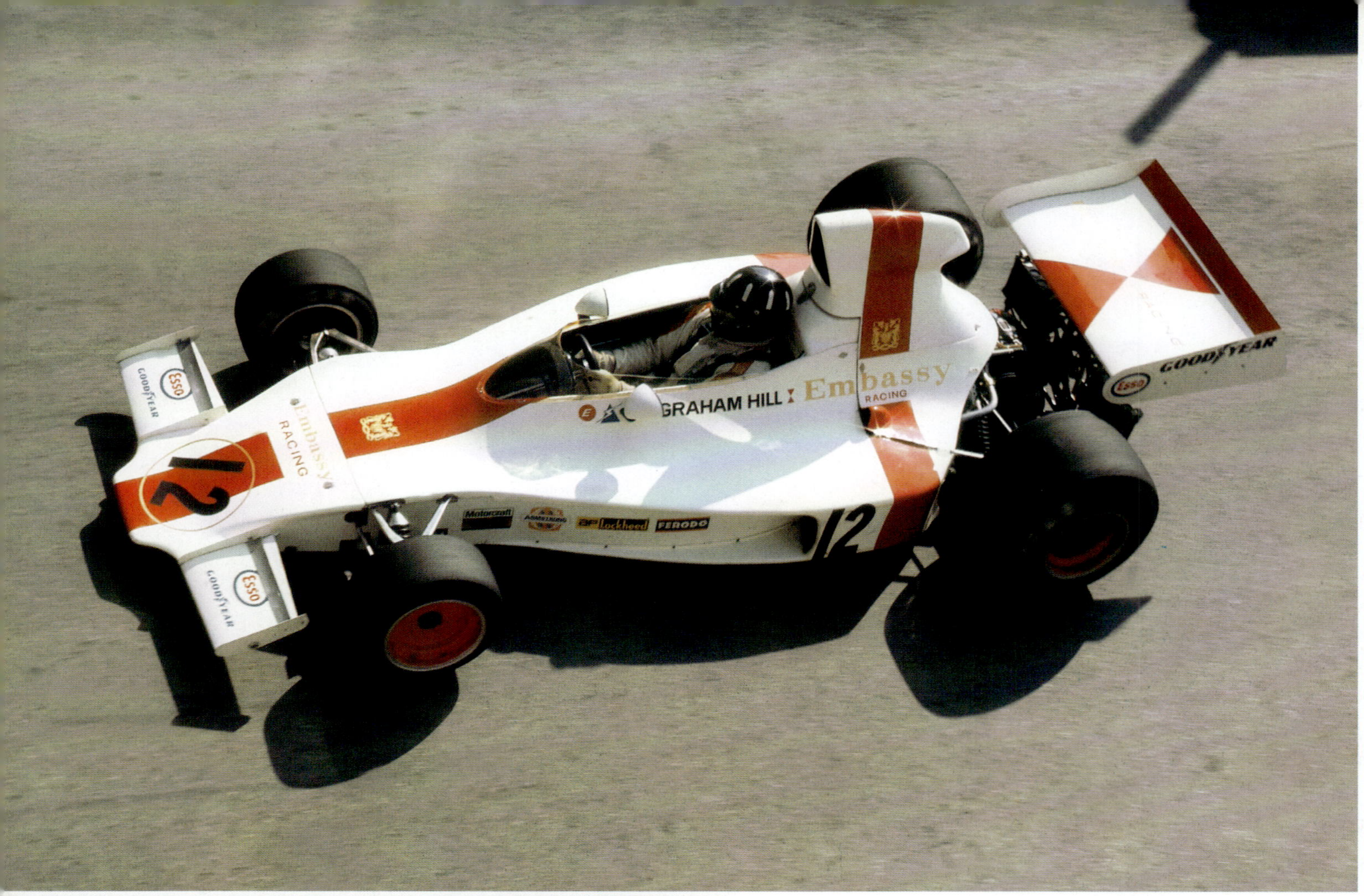

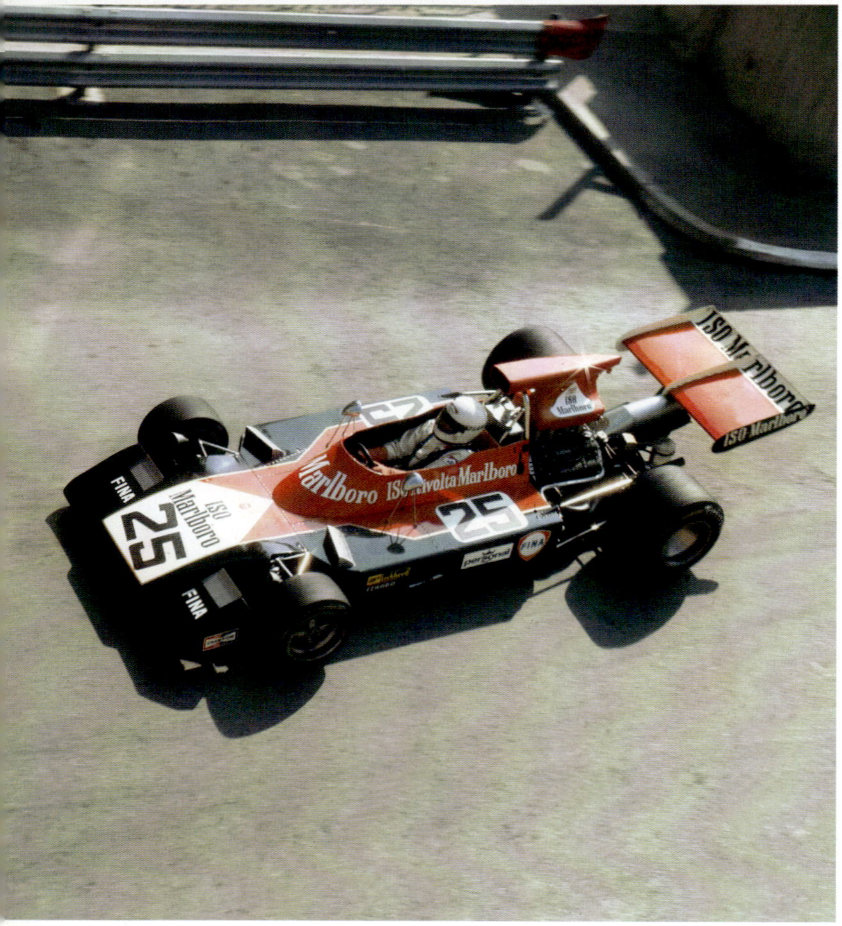

↑ The last two seasons of Graham Hill's F1 career were not a success, starting with the Shadow DN1/3A that he raced under his own Embassy-sponsored team in 1973. This was a sad anti-climax to his former glories. At Monaco, scene of his five victories, poor Graham could only qualify 25th out of 26 starters (a very large number for Monaco), although George Follmer in one of the two works Shadows did not start, and he drove around until lap 62 when the rear suspension failed. The Shadow seems to have been a pretty poor piece of kit regardless of Hill's form.

← Same spot, and Mike captures Howden Ganley in the Iso FX3, or Williams FW02, if you prefer. Ex-BRM racer (1971–2), New Zealander Ganley was another one of those English-speaking drivers whose F1 career and obvious talent were squandered in middle of the grid machinery, and he did very well here to qualify tenth but, alas, drive shaft failure ended his race on lap 41. FW02 first raced at the 1973 Spanish GP, driven by Ganley, and made its final GP appearance for Williams at Kyalami in 1975 in the hands of Jacques Laffite.

→ Hesketh Racing's Harvey Postlethwaite-developed March 731 at Monaco, with James Hunt making his GP debut in what would turn out to be an impressive first season in F1. However, Hunt never really got on with street circuits or, indeed, tracks in close confines, although here he qualified 18th (in itself an achievement for the first time at this tricky circuit) and was running sixth until the engine dropped a valve with five laps to go. Note the lack of anything remotely resembling sponsorship, by now a necessity for every other team in F1.

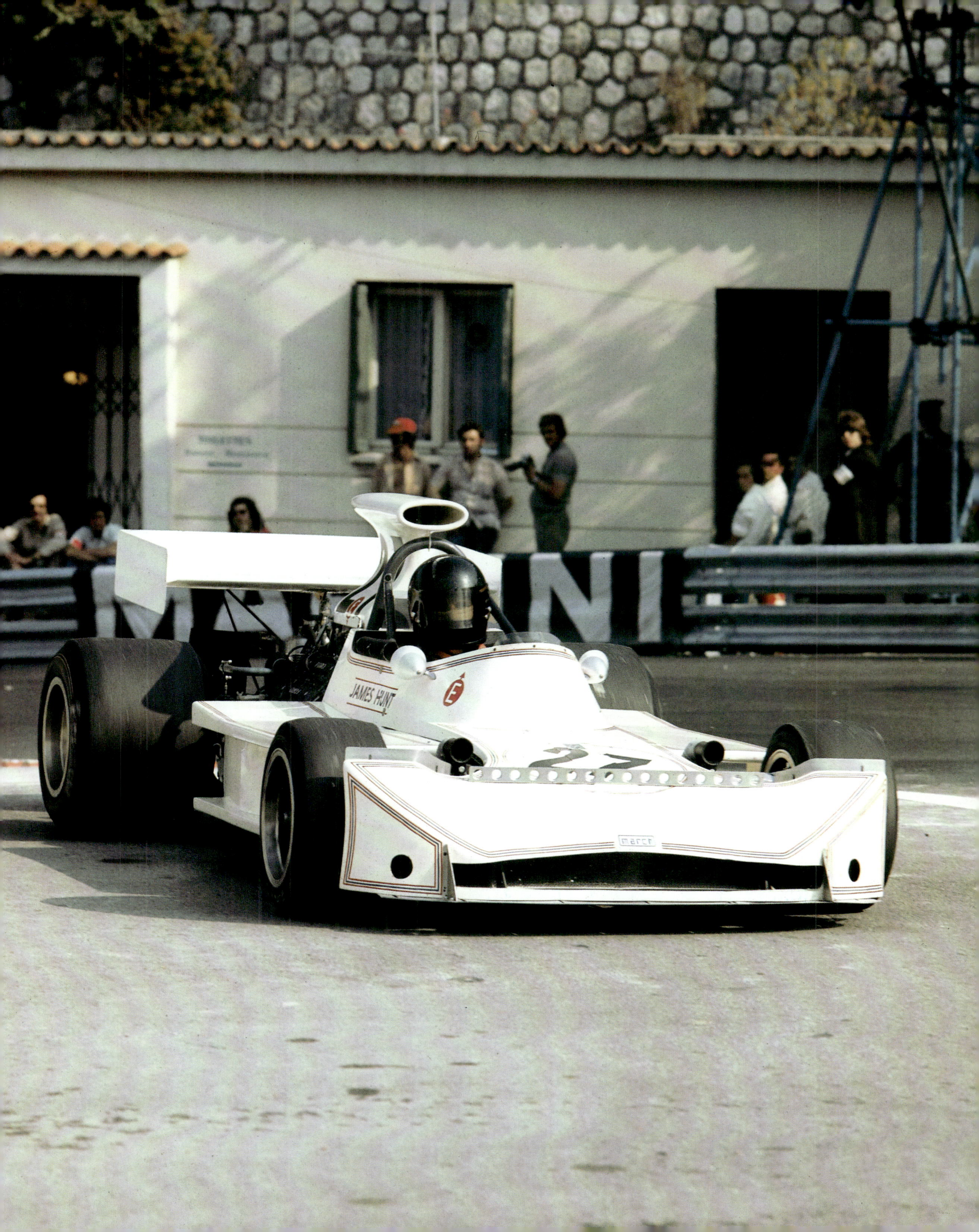
JAMES HUNT

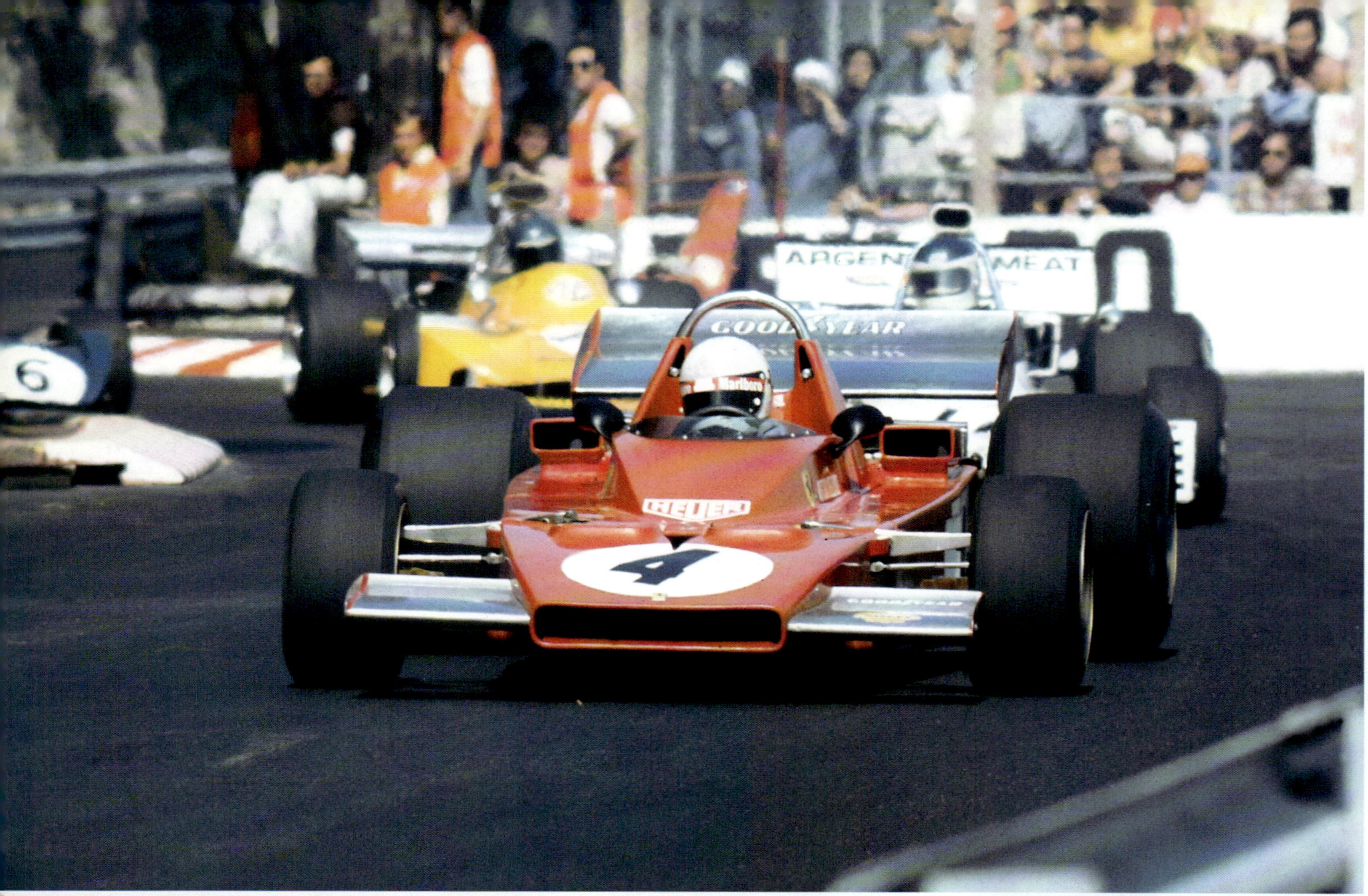
GOODYEAR
4
6

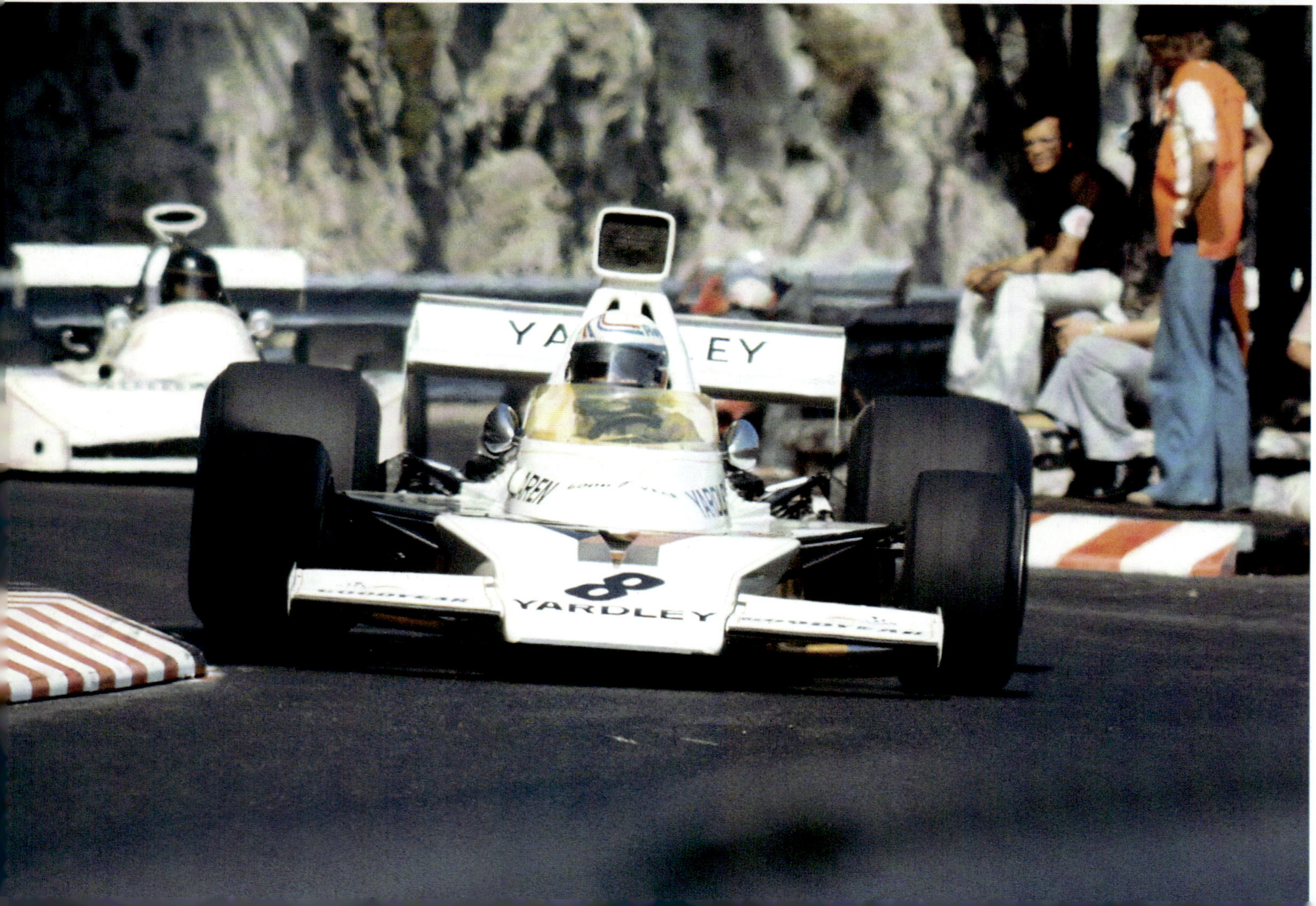
YARDLEY
8

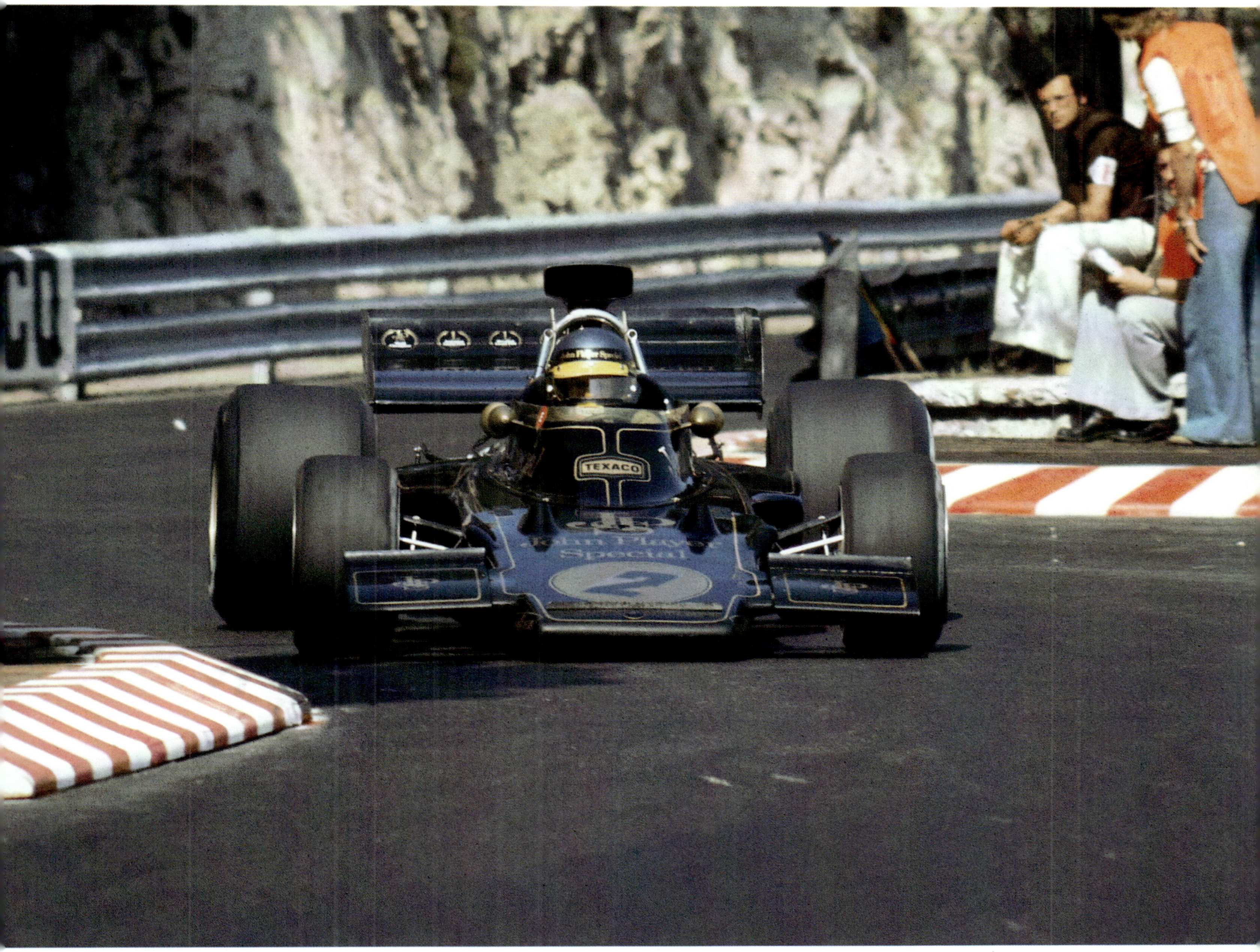

↑ At the same spot, Ronnie Peterson's line is subtly different to that of Peter Revson (see lower caption), and it is noticeable how relatively soft the JPS Lotus 72's suspension is, especially compared to modern practice. 'Super Swede' qualified second, and led the race, pulling away as the others were held up by Regazzoni's BRM. Alas, low fuel pressure then slowed 72 (R6), but he still finished third, a lap behind Stewart's winning Tyrrell and his team-mate Emerson Fittipaldi.

↖ Early in the race Arturo Merzario, in the ugly Ferrari 312B3 F12 (011), leads Carlos Reutemann's Brabham BT42, Mike Beuttler's March 731, and François Cevert's Tyrrell 006 (No. 6) through the chicane at Monaco. The 312B3 was not a success, and later in the season Jacky Ickx left Ferrari, drove a Yardley McLaren to third in the German GP, returned to the Scuderia for Monza, and then finally abandoned ship. They all retired at Monaco, except for Cevert who finished fourth after a puncture on the opening lap.

← Peter Revson (McLaren M23/2) leads James Hunt in the Hesketh March 731 through the chicane at Monaco. This is the first version of the very long-lived M23, and note the angles of the outside wheels and the huge height/width disparity between front and rear tyres, typical of this period. Revson had a successful 1973 season, winning the British and Canadian GPs, although the latter was mired in controversy after some confusion as to who had actually won, before Revson's victory was properly confirmed.

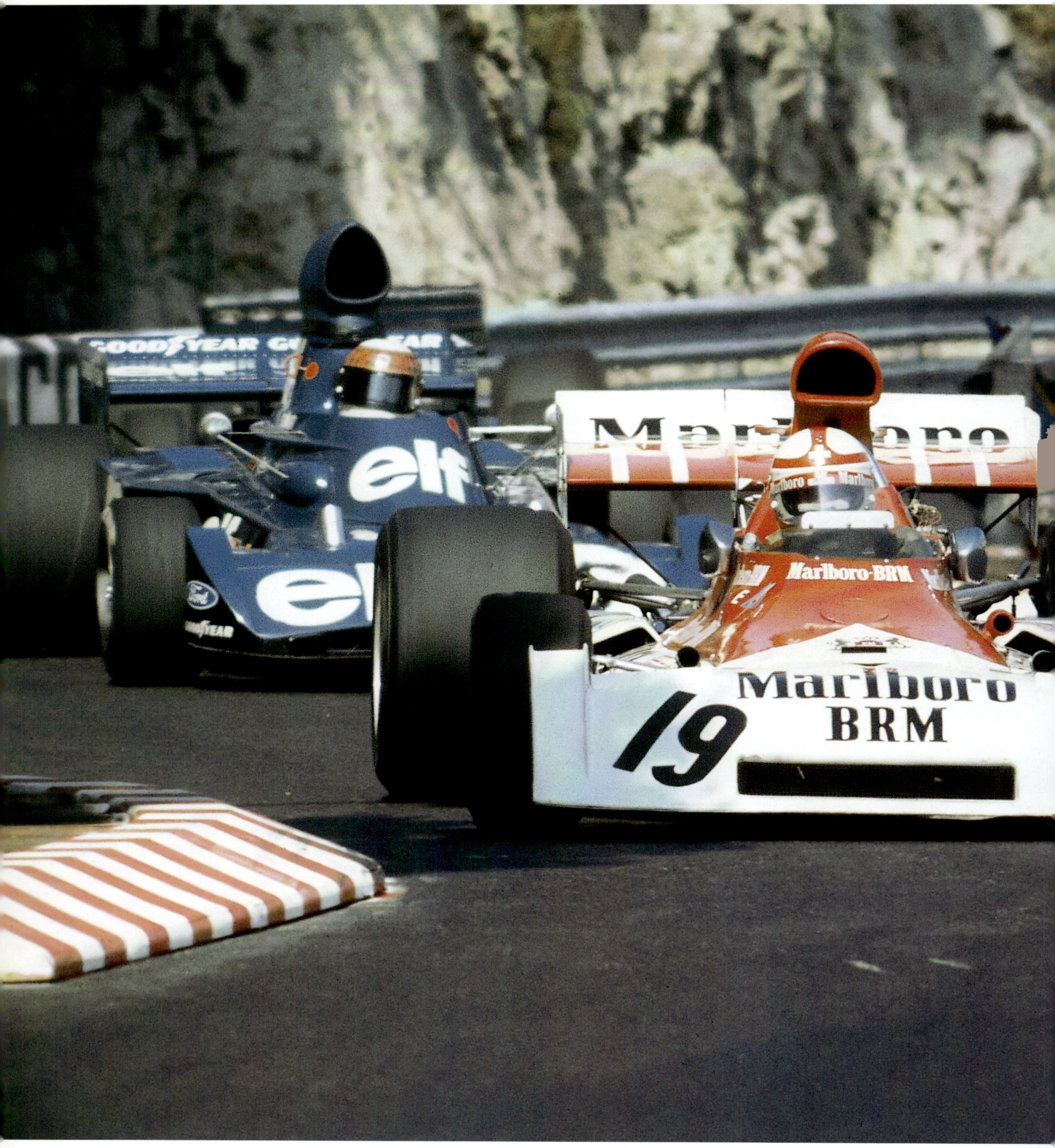
elf
elf
Marlboro-BRM
Marlboro
BRM
19

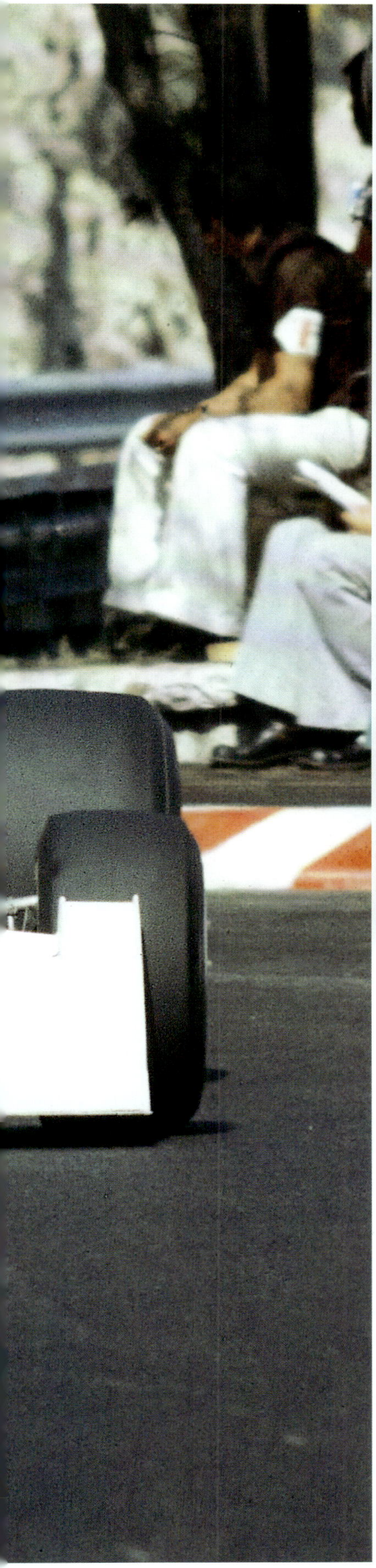

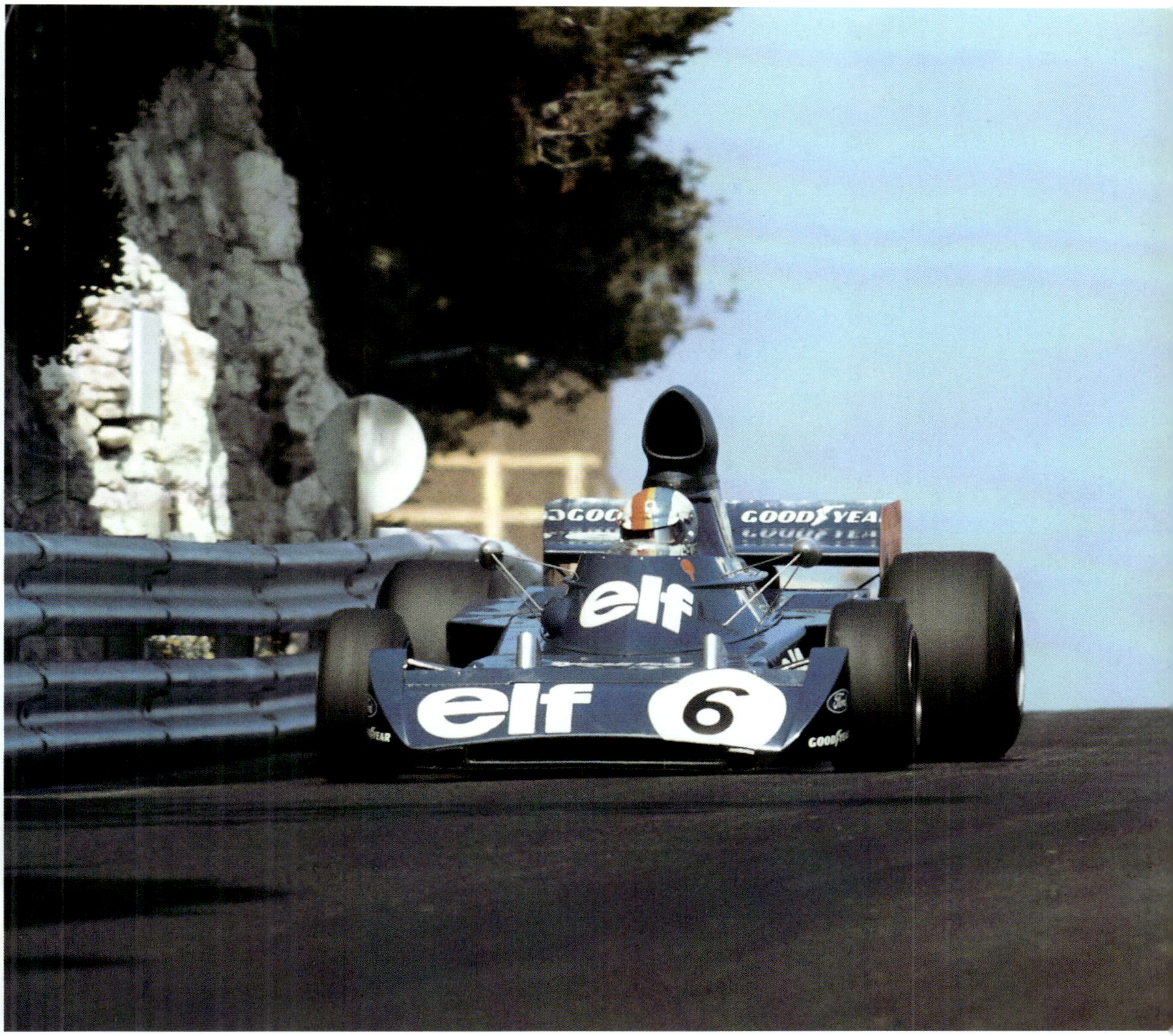

↑ François Cevert is hard on the brakes as he approaches the Monaco chicane in Tyrrell 006, and at this angle the camera catches the significant downhill gradient of the approach.

← Clay Regazzoni signed on as BRM's number one for 1973, and brought some much needed speed and vigour, but the team was in decline. For a while Regazzoni held up the other front runners at Monaco as Ronnie Peterson sprinted away. His BRM P160E/C7 (the latest version now claiming 460bhp) was already suffering severe braking problems and he had to overshoot the chicane on lap 6, and then, after persevering for another few laps, retired with boiling brake fluid. Looking at the full width nose of the Marlboro-sponsored BRM (this was the second and last season of this deal before the ciggies money decamped to McLaren) one is tempted to ask how much air was actually getting to the front brakes, even allowing for the cooling ducts in the front intake. A no doubt frustrated Jackie Stewart in Tyrrell 006/2 follows closely.

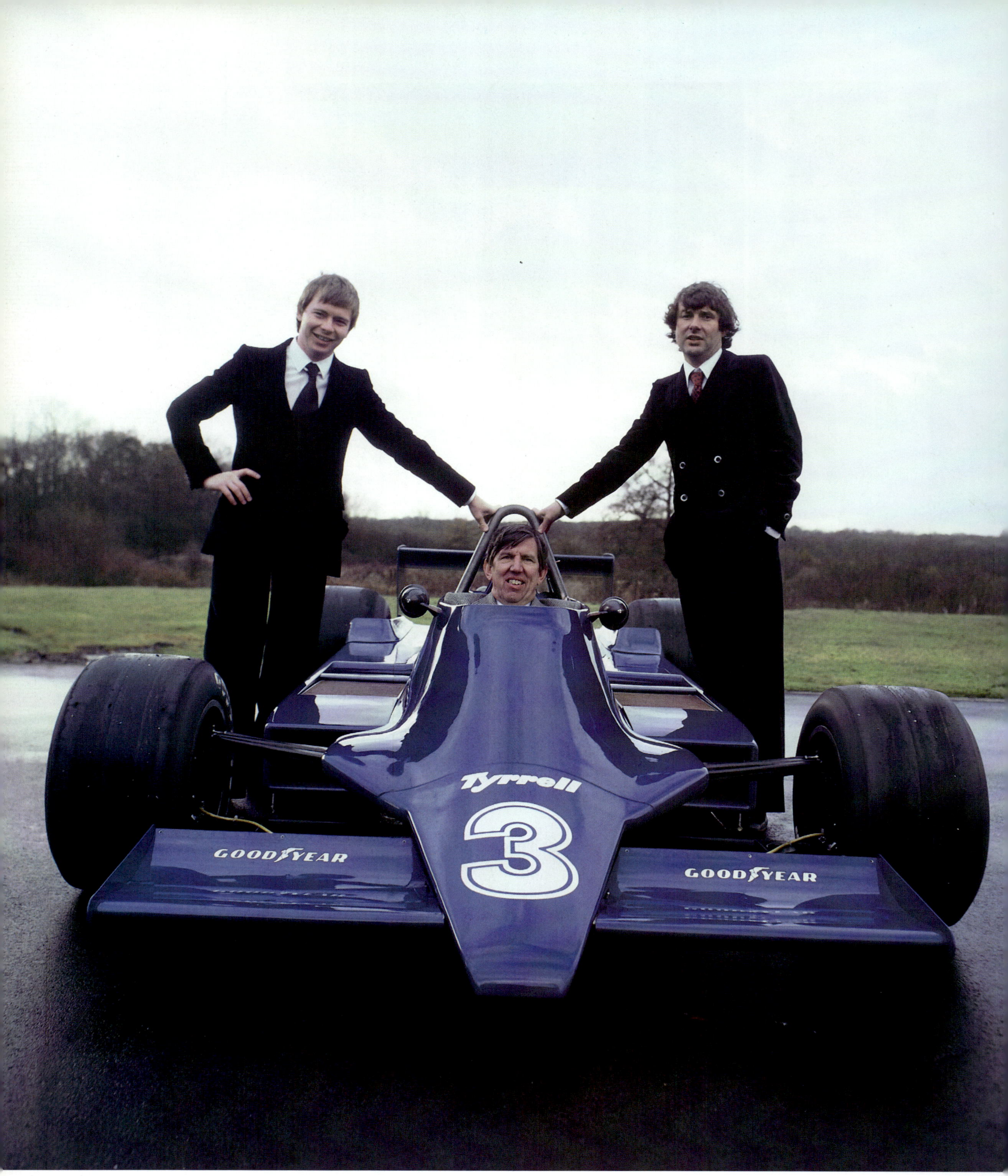
Tyrrell
3
GOODYEAR
GOODYEAR

← Mike was still attending F1 launches in later years, and here is the Tyrrell offering in 1979 with the new Maurice Phillipe (who had replaced Derek Gardner for 1978) designed 009. However, the team had lost their major sponsors, and in turn Tyrrell had to lose one of their boffins, Dr Karl Kempf. Tyrrell 009 was an improved version of the Lotus 79 ground-effect type driven by 1978 signing Didier Pironi (on the left) and newcomer Jean-Pierre 'Jumper' Jarier (on the right). Pironi's best results were two third places (Zolder and Watkins Glen), whilst ex-March, UOP Shadow, and ATS veteran Jarier also managed two third places (Kyalami and Silverstone). Ken Tyrrell grins from the cockpit, but his team had ceased to be a regular race winner, with only Depailler's 1978 Monaco victory to cling on to as the years passed until the team's sale in 1998 to BAR.

→ Fast forward nine years, and Mike took these overhead shots during qualifying for the 1988 British GP. We start with Aytron Senna in the turbocharged Honda V6 Marlboro McLaren MP4/4. This was his first World Championship year, and his win here was one of eight during the season. 1988 was the year that McLaren, with Senna and Prost, should have won all 16 races, but Senna collided with Jean-Louis Schlesser's Williams in the chicane at Monza, so they had to make do with a mere 15.

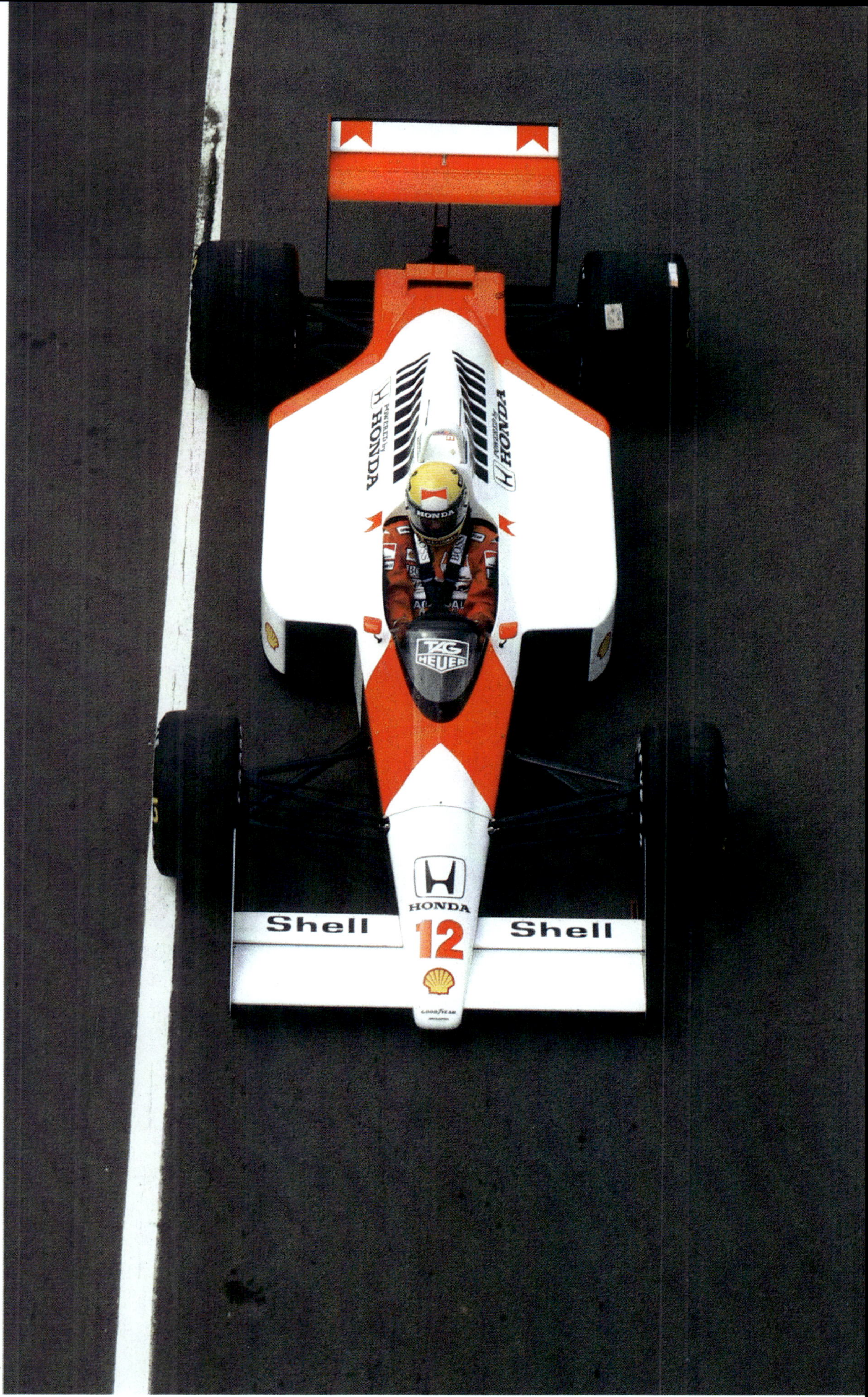

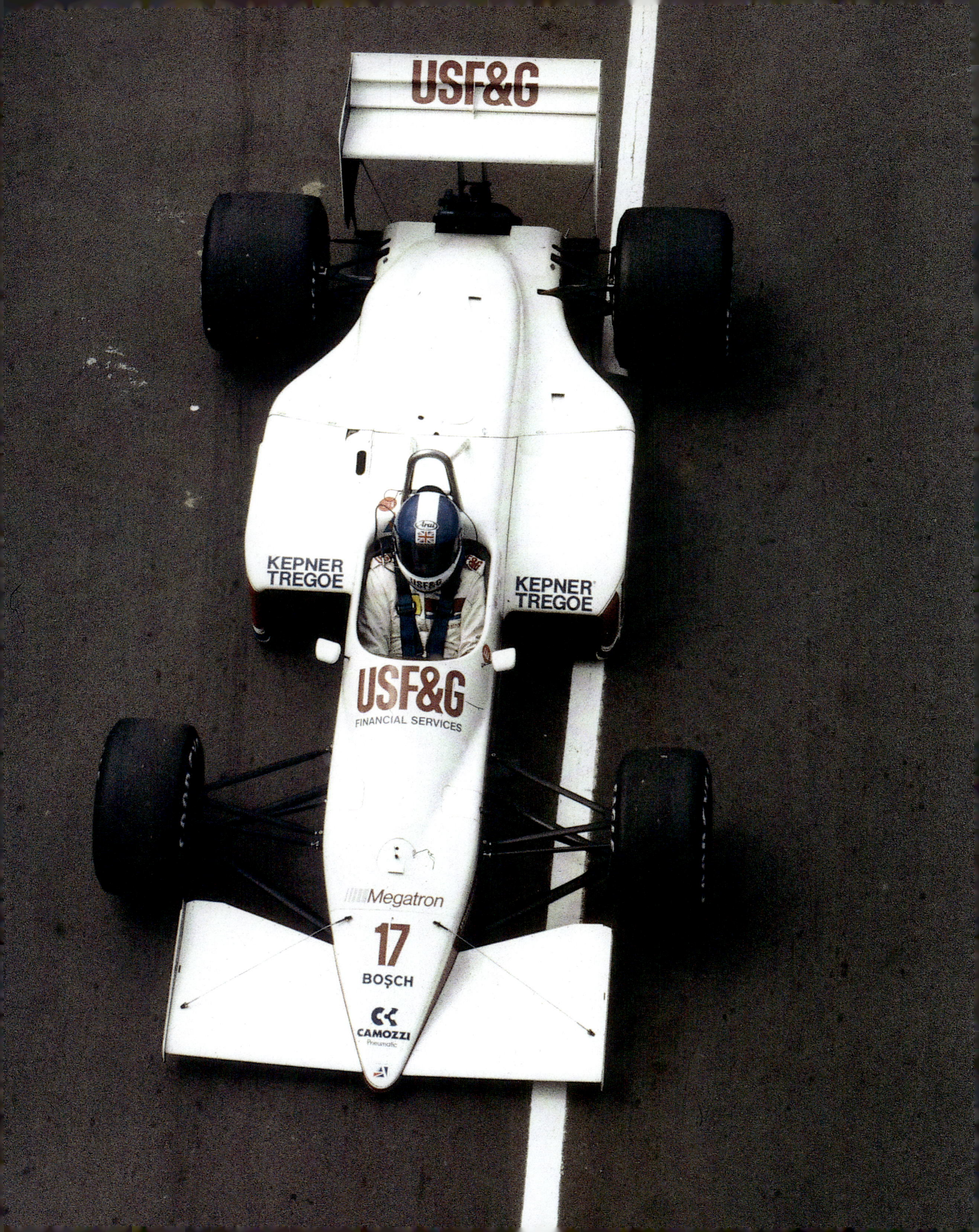
USF&G
KEPNER TREGOE
KEPNER TREGOE
USF&G
FINANCIAL SERVICES
Megatron
17
BOSCH
CAMOZZI
Pneumatic

← Derek Warwick's Arrows A10B-Megatron 4 looks rather different, as well as relatively unadorned. He qualified ninth out of 31 and finished sixth in the very wet race.

→ The Camel Team Lotus T100s were the other Honda-powered cars on the 1988 grids after Williams lost their engine deal. They were driven by Nelson Piquet and Satoru Nakajima, seen here. However, they were never fully competitive, and Piquet finished fifth, his previous form (he was World Champion in 1987) rapidly diminishing, and Nakajima tenth.

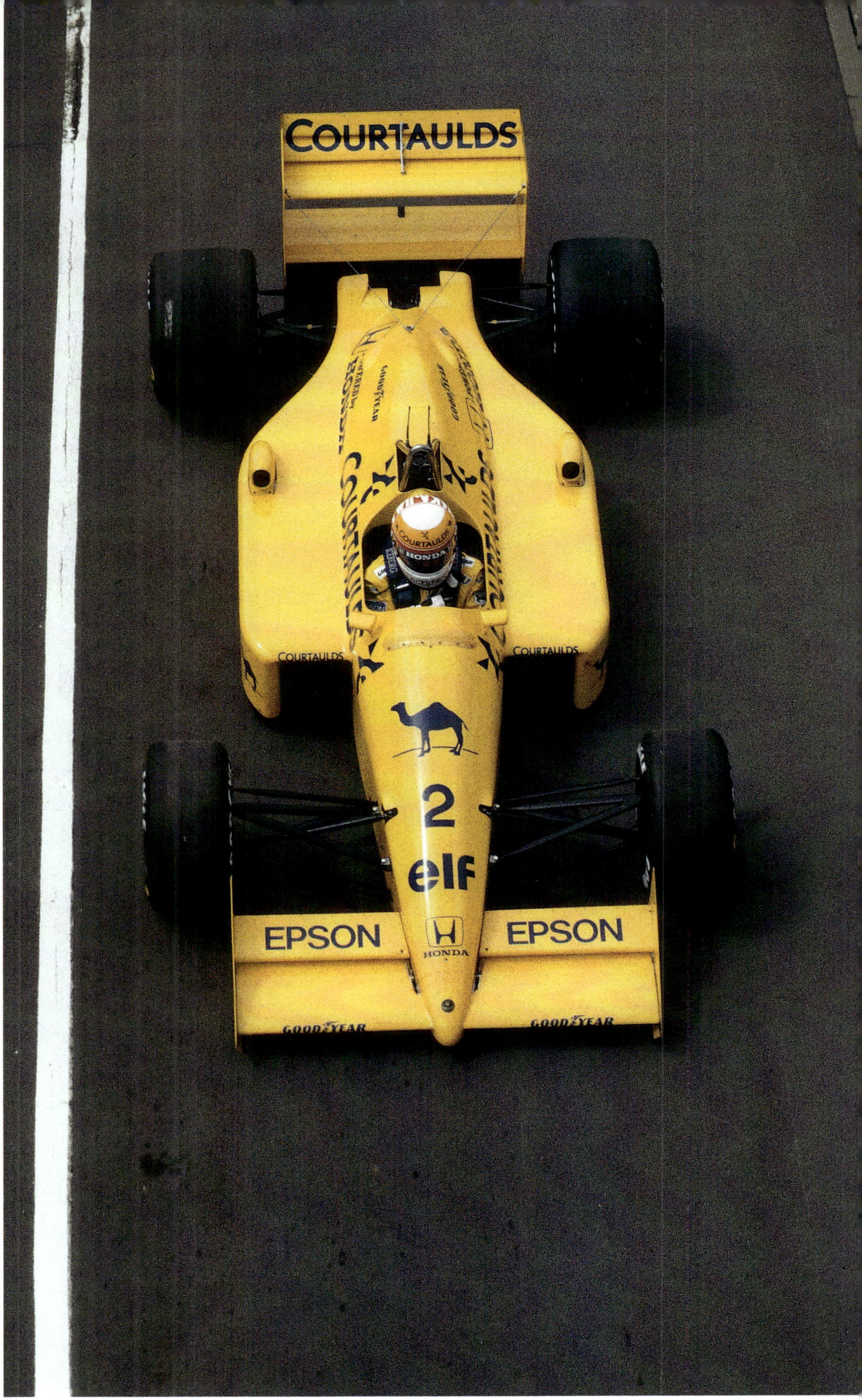

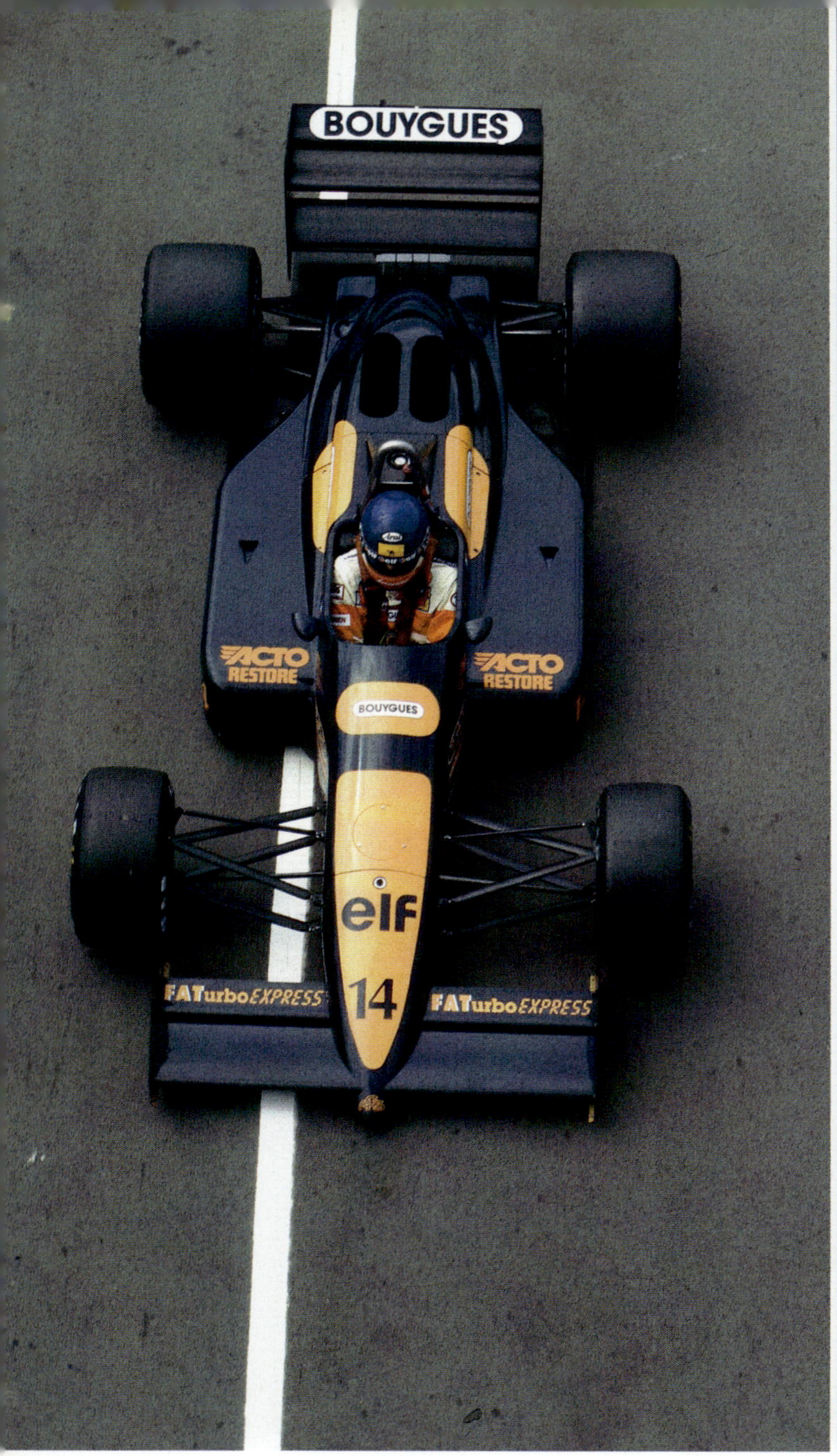

↑ Frenchman Philippe Streiff in the AGS (Automobiles Gonfaronaise Sportive) JH23, powered by a Cosworth DFZ, that started on the eighth row and retired on lap 8 with a broken rear wing. Streiff's career was ended by a horrible accident during pre-season testing in Rio that left him paralysed.

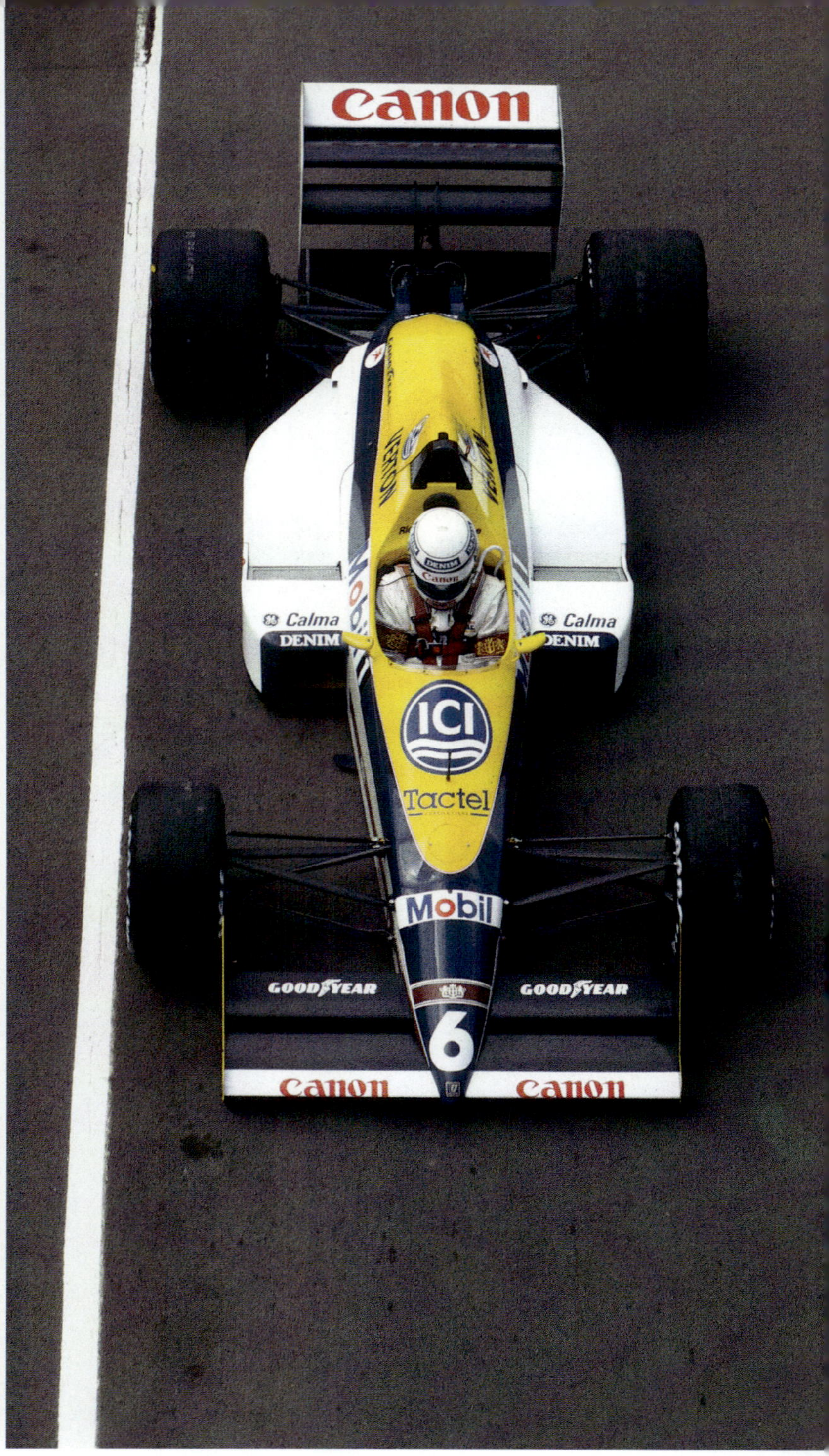

↑ The Canon Williams team made a serious effort not to be totally marginalised when Piquet left them, taking the Honda engine supply with him to Lotus, and much good it did either of them. So, Frank and Patrick used the Judd CV. Ricardo Patrese spent five consecutive seasons with the Didcot outfit, despite having to play second fiddle to Nigel Mansell for three of them. At Silverstone Patrese finished eighth in his FW12, whilst NM finished second and set fastest lap.

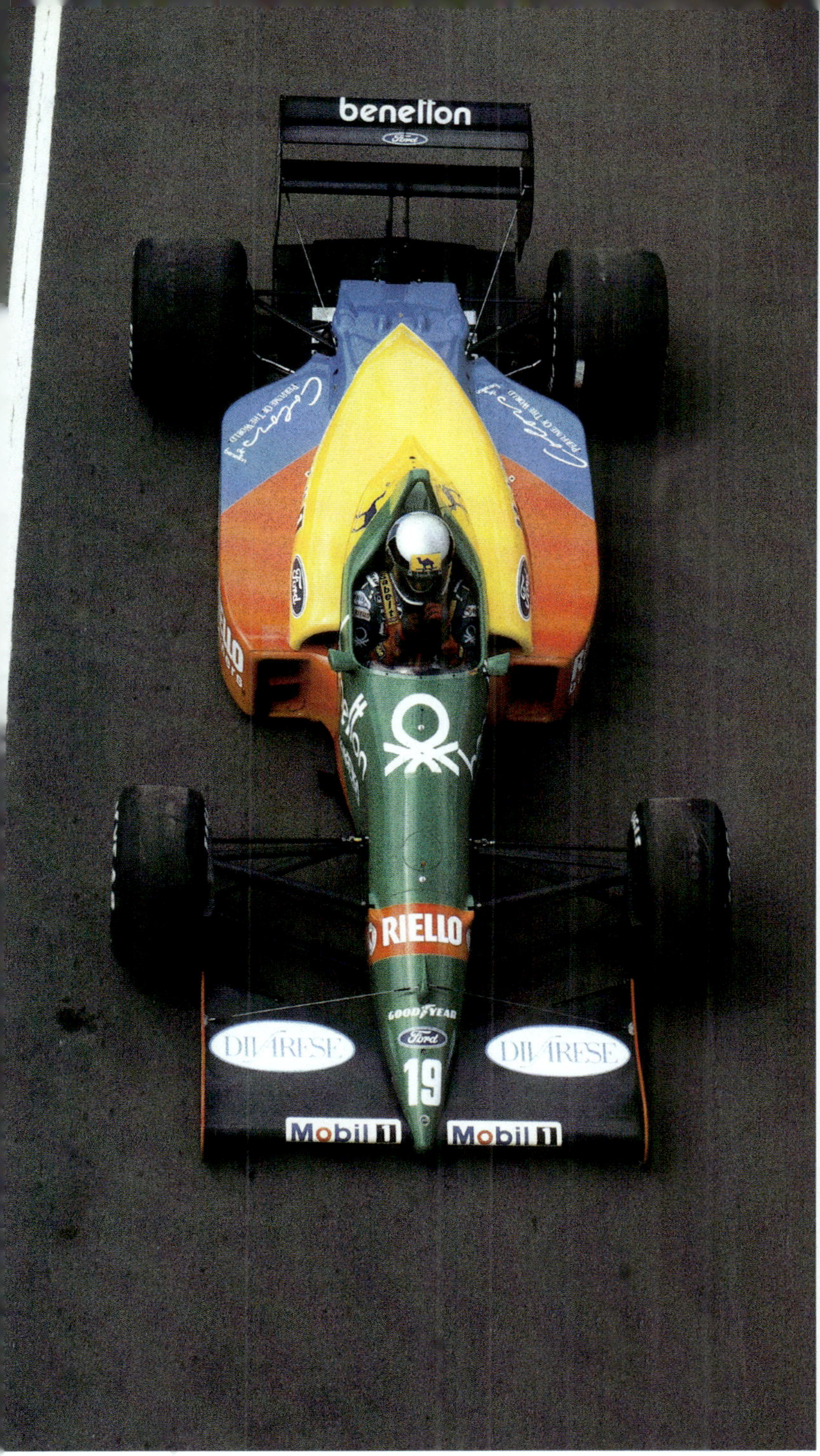

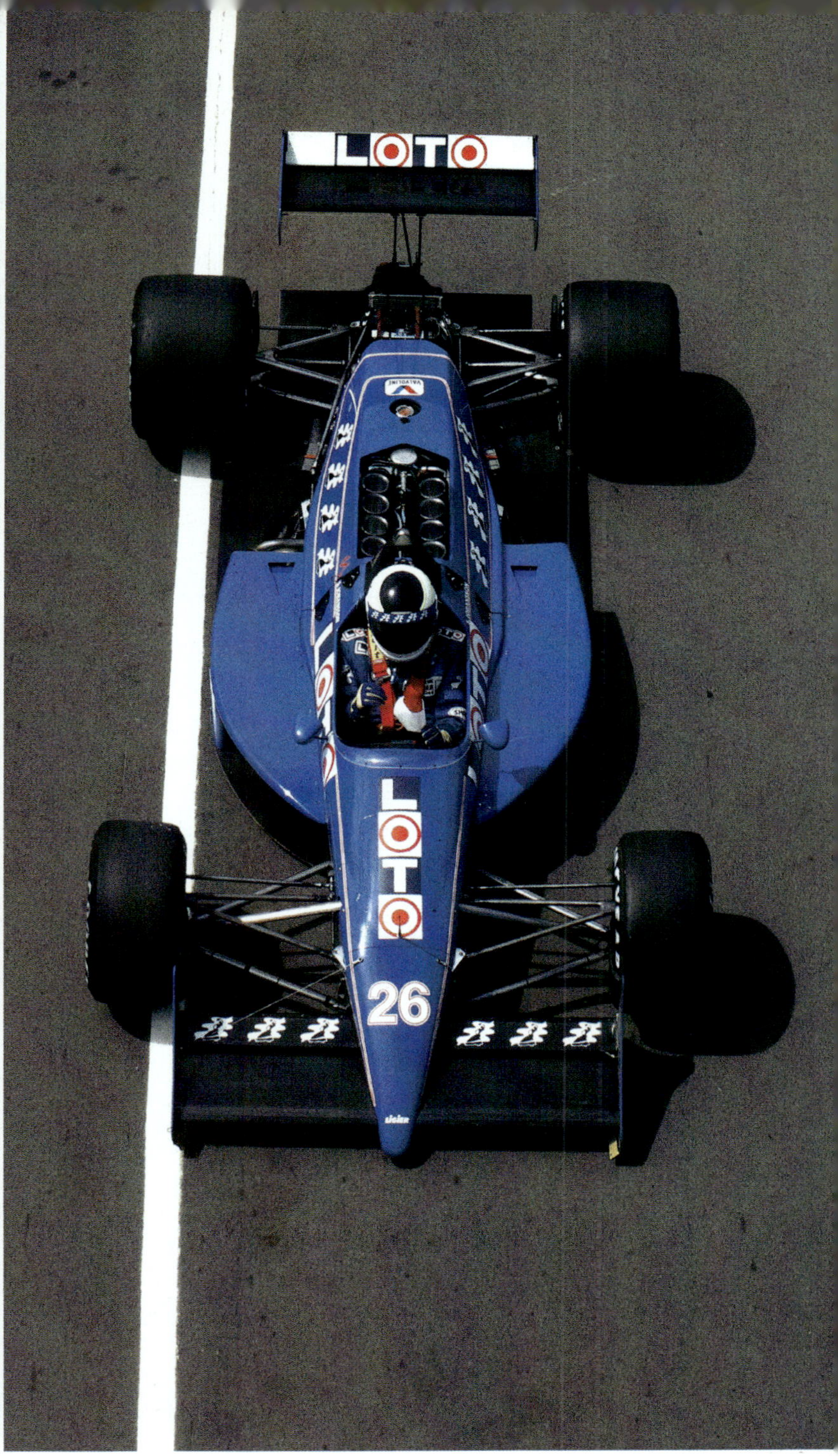

↑ It is hard to believe that Benetton have been in or around F1 for so long, but here they were in 1988 with Alessandro Nannini and Thierry Boutsen in the Ford DFR-engined Benetton B188. Nannini (pictured) achieved a very meritorious third at Silverstone, whilst Boutsen suffered a failed constant velocity joint on lap 38. Alas, a helicopter accident that left him with a disabled arm, ultimately ended Nannini's F1 career.

↑ Having once been F1 stars, Ligier's later attempts were not exactly stellar. Stefan Johansson trundles down the pit lane, but to no avail as he failed to qualify the Judd CV-powered Ligier JS31.

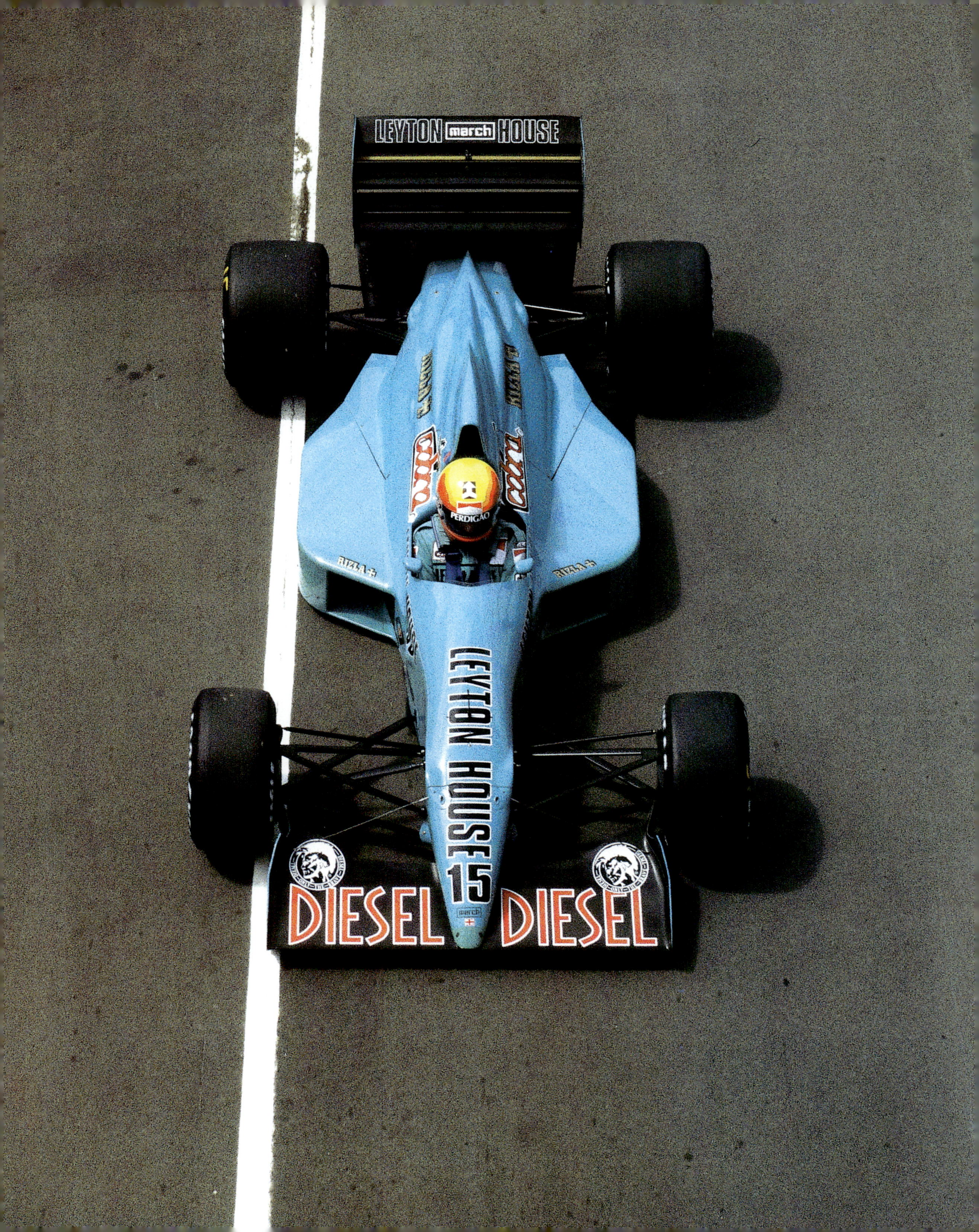
LEYTON march HOUSE
LEYTON HOUSE
15
PERDIGAO
DIESEL
DIESEL

← Mauricio Gugelmin lasted five seasons in F1, the first four sponsored by Leyton House, and his final year, 1992, courtesy of Sasol. At Silverstone, Mauricio outqualified his highly-rated team-mate Ivan Capelli, and both started from the third row in their Adrian Newey designed Leyton House March 881s, again with Judd CV motors. Brazilian Gugelmin finished fourth (he only once bettered this result with a third place in the 1989 Brazilian GP) whilst Capelli's car retired because of electrical problems.

→ Future German touring car ace Bernd Schneider raced the West Zakspeed 881 in 1988 and its Yamaha 891 replacement the following year. It was a truly terrible waste of a sparkling talent, as proved by future performances, but one all too frequent in the quixotic, superficial world of F1. Out of 32 entries in 1988–9 he only managed to qualify six times, and then drove just twice for Footwork Arrows in 1990. At Silverstone the car was nearly 8sec off Gerhard Berger's pole lap!

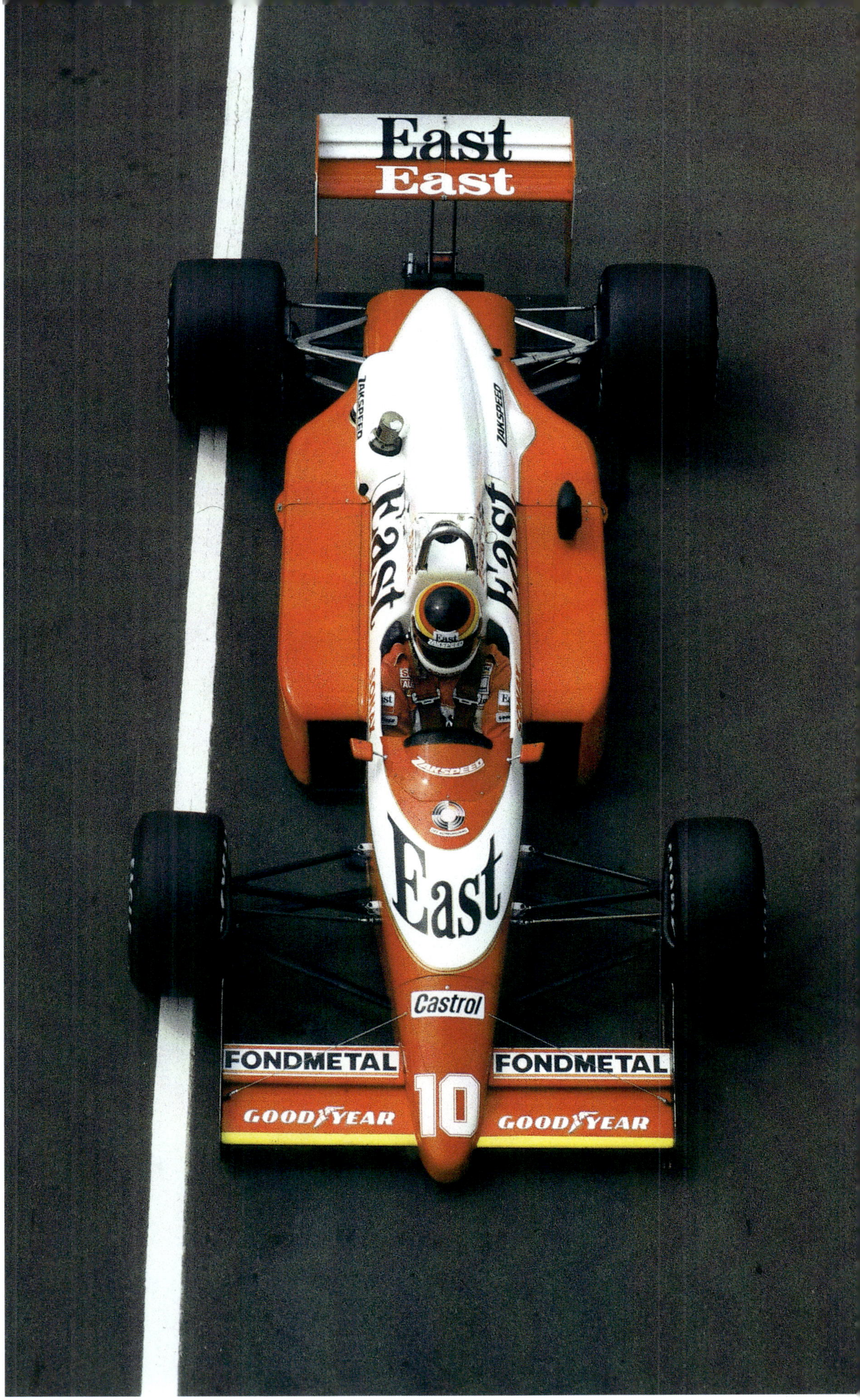

➔ Lola's Larousse Camel Cosworth DFZ-engined LC88 looks very colourful, but its striking appearance was not matched by its performance. Two were entered for Yannick Dalmas (pictured) and Philippe Alliot and they finished 13th and 14th respectively.

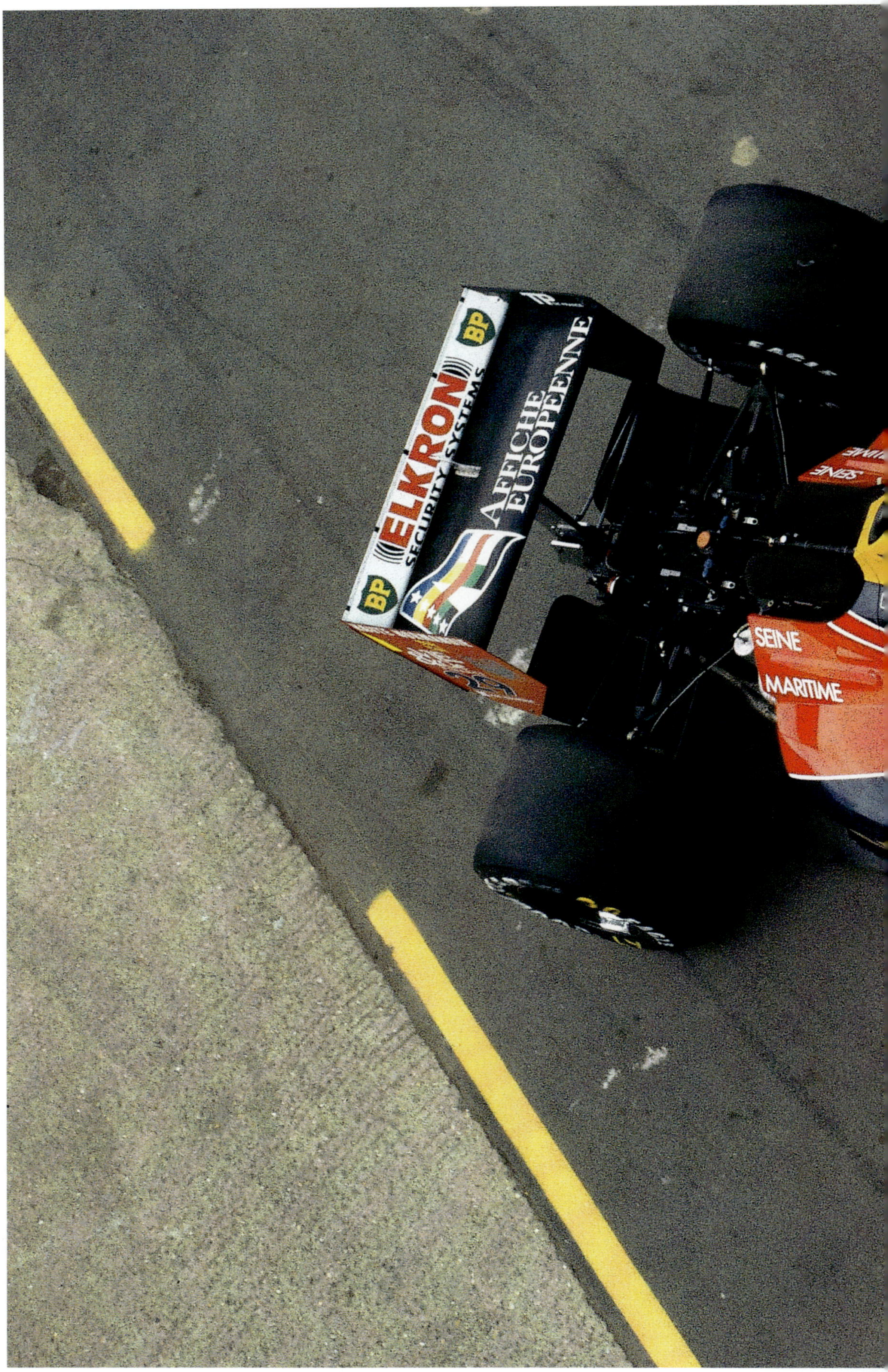

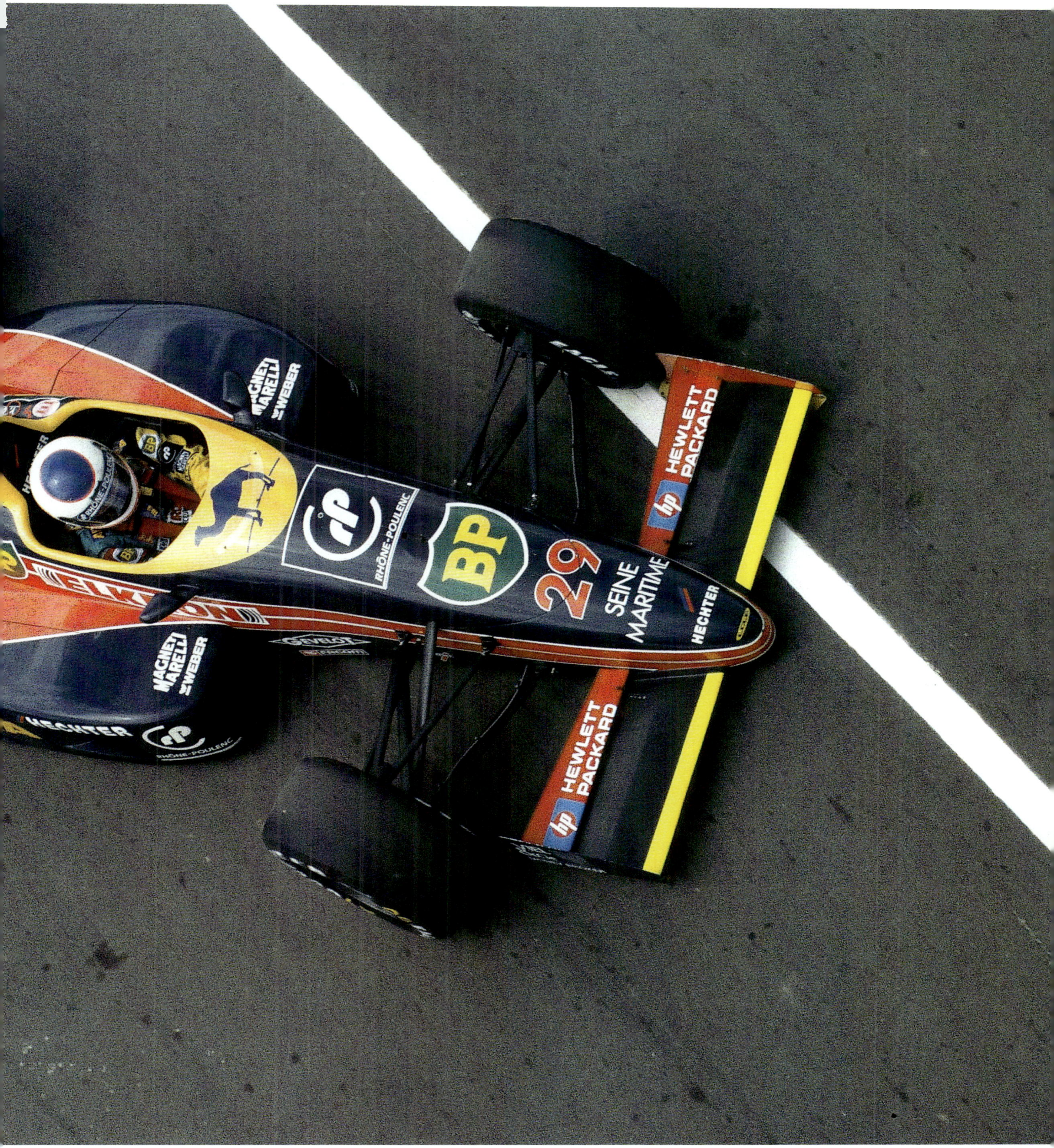
HEWLETT PACKARD
hp
BP
29
SEINE MARITIME
RHÔNE-POULENC
HECHTER
MAGNETI MARELLI
WEBER
HEWLETT PACKARD
hp
HECHTER
RHÔNE-POULENC

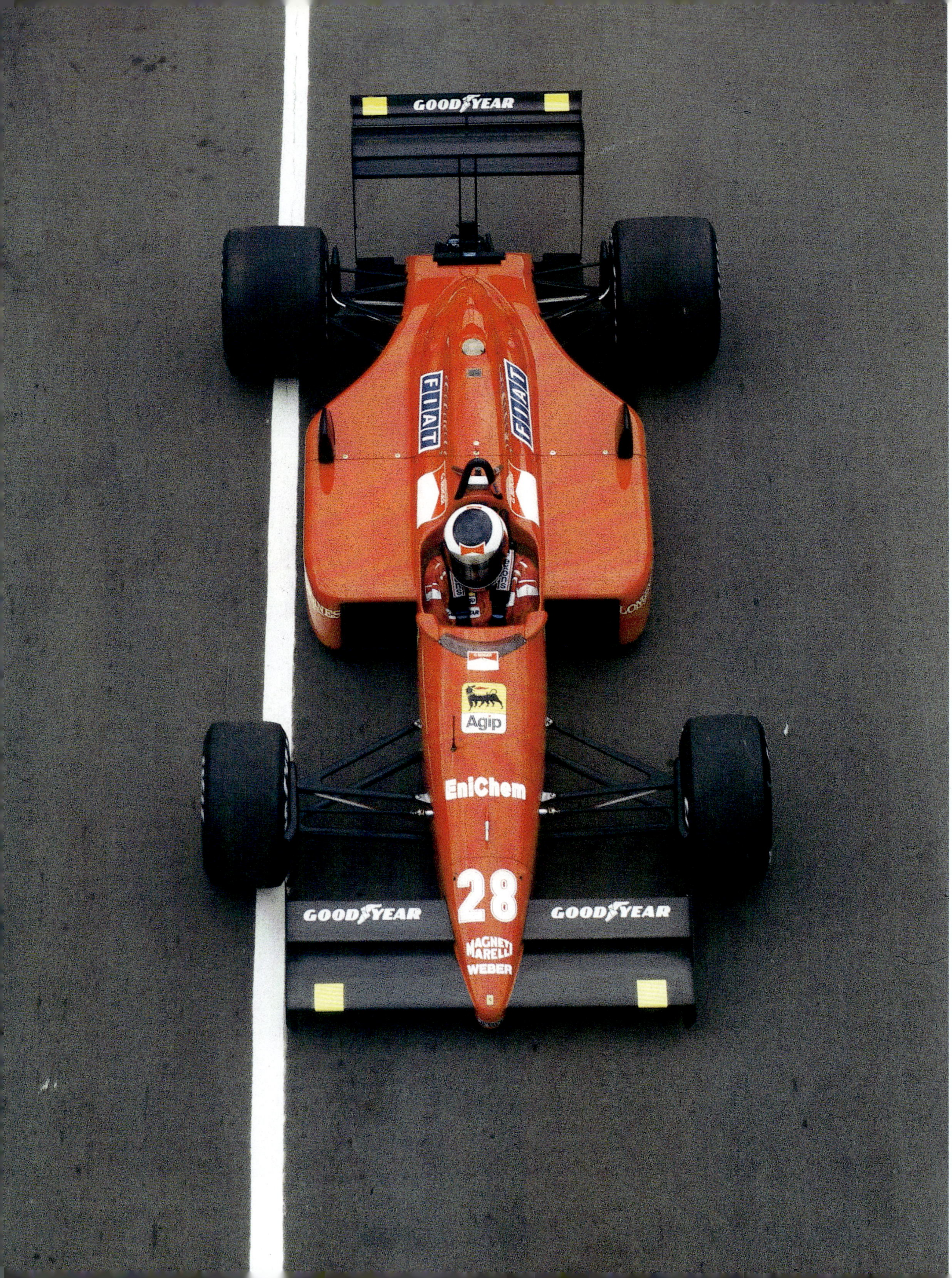
GOODYEAR
FIAT
FIAT
Agip
EniChem
28
GOODYEAR
GOODYEAR
MAGNETI MARELLI
WEBER

Although Gerhard Berger was on pole at Silverstone in the Ferrari F1/87/88C, the Ferraris (Alboreto started second) stood no chance of winning as they were suffering from excessive fuel consumption. Alboreto ran out of fuel on lap 62 and Berger slipped from sixth to ninth as his mount ran dry on the run in to the flag.

Another now almost forgotten F1 racer in the Tyrrell-Cosworth DFZ 017, this is Julian Bailey, who qualified on the penultimate row. He did a full season with Tyrrell, but amongst too many DNQs his best result was a ninth in America. At Silverstone he finished 16th, whilst team-mate Palmer was out with engine failure on lap 14. The following year he had four entries with Team Lotus, resulting in three DNQs and a sixth place in the San Marino GP.

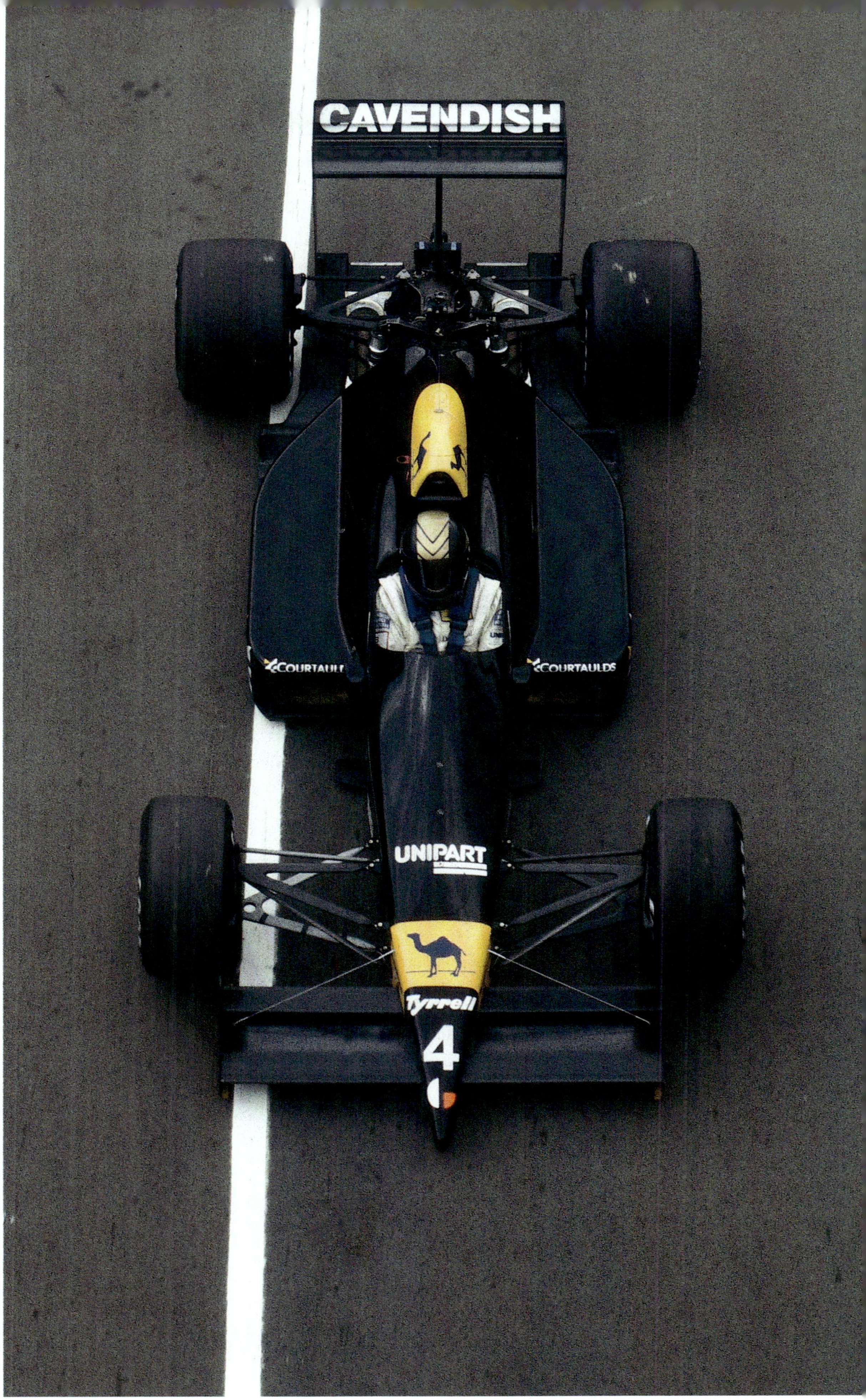

CINEMATIC OVERTURES

Of the three films that Mike became involved in it is John Frankenheimer's *Grand Prix* that stands out.

Frankenheimer very much wanted to have a cast that included genuine racers and associated personnel to lend some reality and gravitas and thus Mike was hired along with other other photographers including Bernard Cahier and Max Le Grand. Liz Cooper recalled that one such was definitely not interested in joining the fun, this being dear Geoff Goddard.

She also remembered that Mike had a speaking part shot from behind whilst interviewing a driver, but his voice was deemed unsuitable so the dialogue was dubbed. Elsewhere Mike appears on screen and all in all it was apparently a lot of fun at various exotic locations including Count 'Johnny' Lurani's palatial home near Monza. Too much in one case when endless retakes resulted in the supporting cast of extras getting more and more inebriated as they waited out the scenes.

Usually the individual race footage was shot the week after a Grand Prix, although some activity occurred during the Monaco race weekend which upset a few people. Apparently, and unsurprisingly, only James Garner could actually drive convincingly and looking at the arrangements for on-board driver shots one can forgive the thespians their fears. Garner it was who famously had to dive into the rather cold Monaco harbour as part of his crash sequence, only to find himself treading water whilst a dispute with a local took place. This eventually erupted into serious threats of violence by a very wet and very cold actor before it was settled.

In stark contrast *Chitty Chitty Bang Bang* was an entirely fantasy film based on an Ian Fleming book and appropriately enough produced by Cubby Broccoli and Harry Saltzman. Mike recorded in his diary of 25 April 1968 that he went to Pinewood Studios on a commission from Howard Vyse, editor of *Autocar* to photograph Ronald Barker's 1908 Napier that was being used in the film.

Steve McQueen's Le Mans was an altogether smaller, tighter production, more narrowly focused and based upon the star's powerful charisma and known driving talent. Mike was tipped off about the film by Jabby Crombac, famous journalist and close friend of Colin Chapman and Jim Clark so he duly joined the cast.

Liz recalls that he was well remunerated and flown back to England every weekend and used to accompany McQueen on off-set jaunts at the purpose built Solar (as in Solar Productions) village about half a mile from the Le Mans paddock where Steve could let rip on his Husqvarna motorbikes in the surrounding countryside.

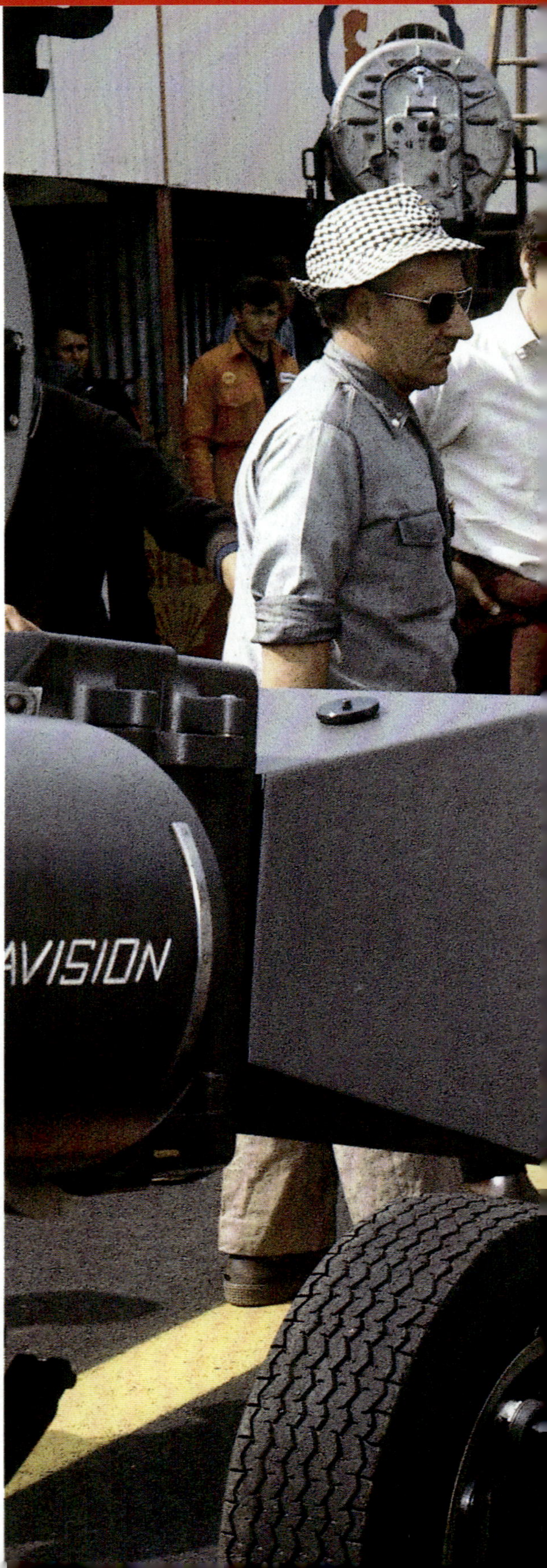

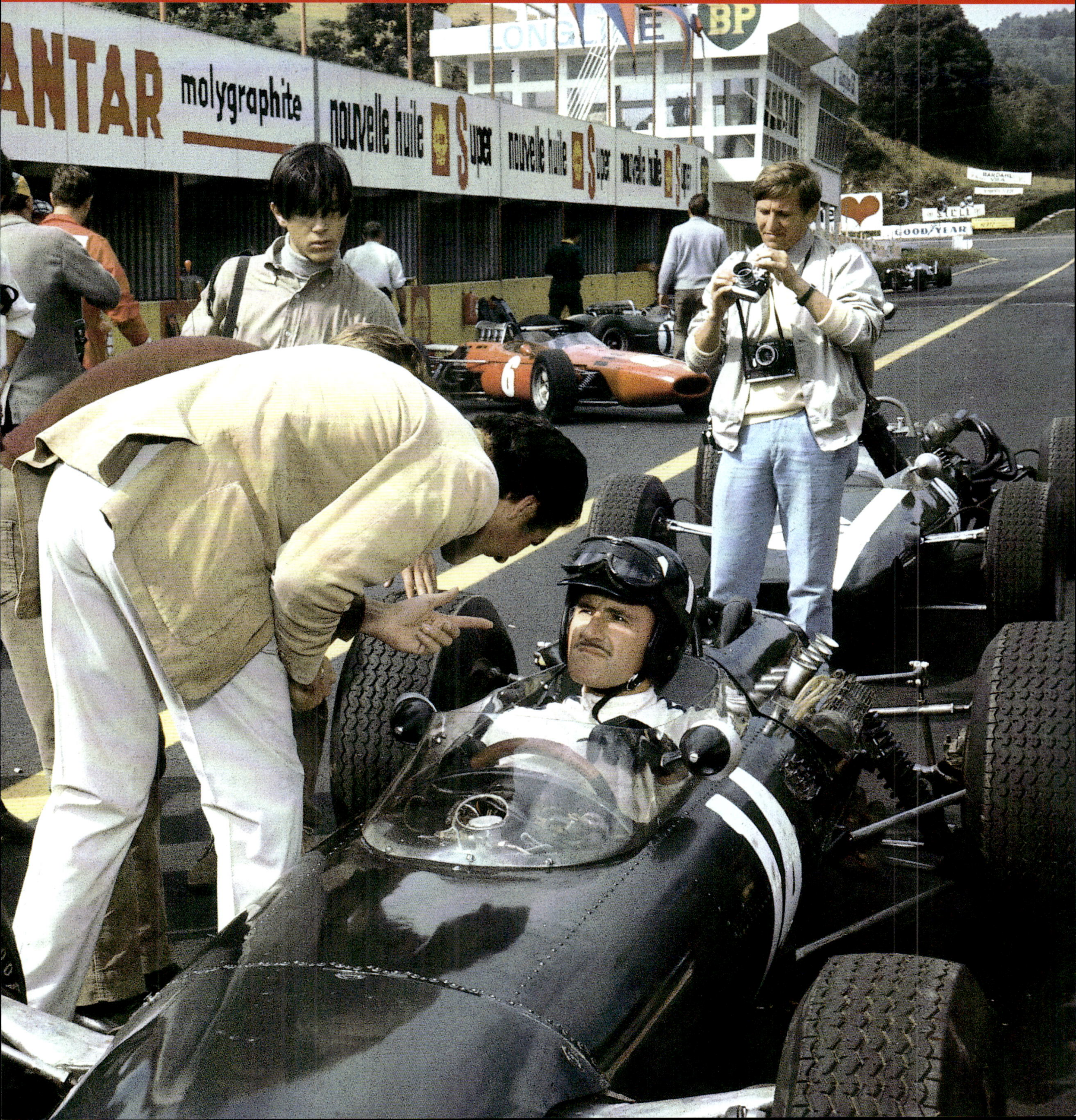

Living dangerously. Graham does not look too happy about something John Frankenheimer is saying, and he particularly does not like fingers pointed at him. At least NGH is sitting in a proper BRM in this shot at Clermont-Ferrand.

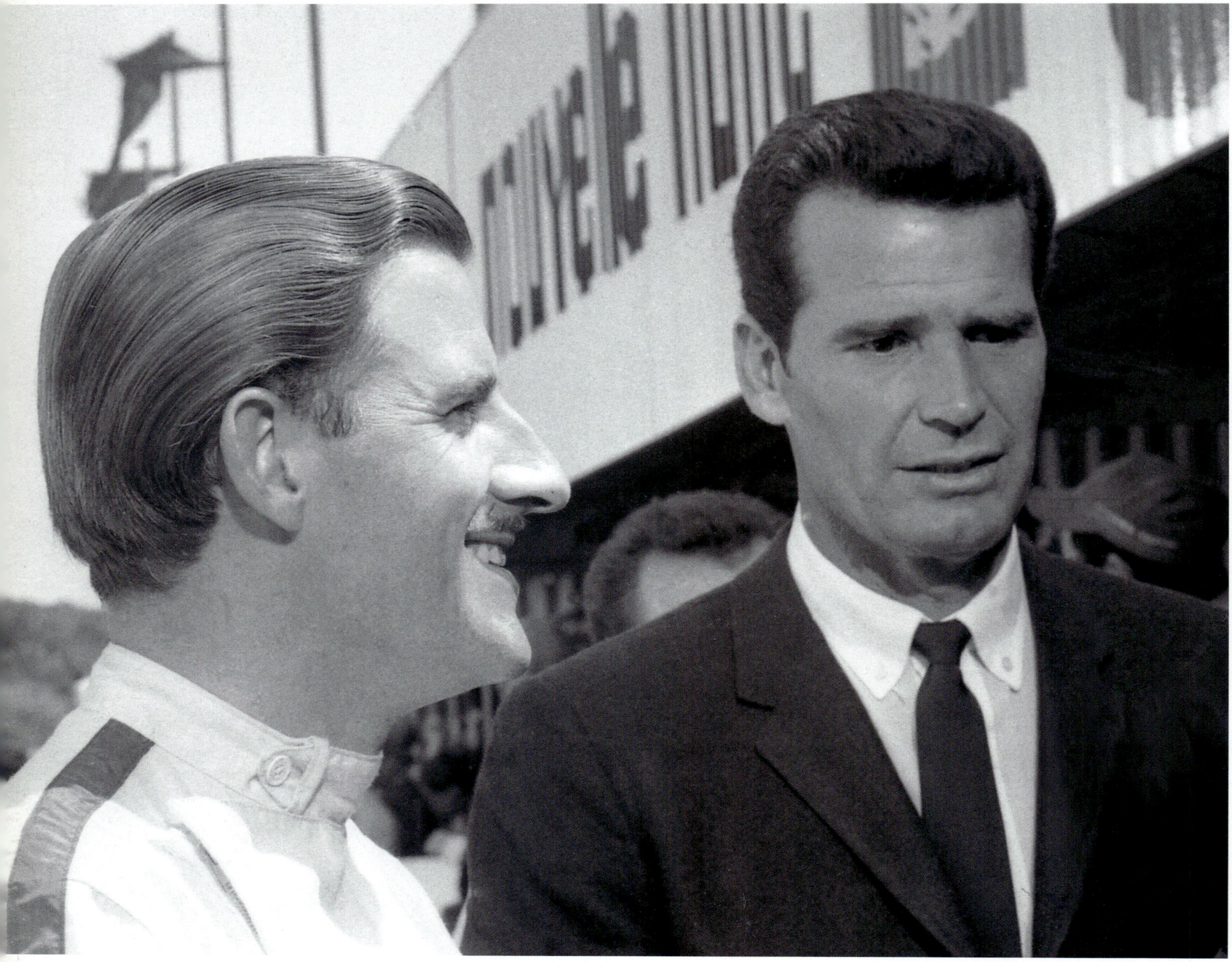

↑ Who is the film star here? Graham looks better groomed than James Garner on the set of *Grand Prix*. Also, if they are both standing on the level, Garner must be a big bloke as he looks at least 2in taller than NGH, who was hardly short.

↗ 'Don't worry Yves (AKA Jean-Pierre Sarti), you are bolted to the car in front and will be towed around this tight, twisty circuit lined with rocky banks and verges in your flimsy Formula Ford car by some racing driver. Legendary lensman Bernard Cahier stands to the right whilst Montand is wearing a (poor) imitation of John Surtees' helmet that later in the film will change to a proper lid bearing the colours of Mike Parkes. Continuity? What's that?

→ Wanted, distinguished male actor with calm disposition to do something very silly. Yves Montand fulfilled his role and survived, at least in real life if not in the film. I wonder what the handling was like? Having a GT40 bolted onto the front must have caused horrendous understeer.

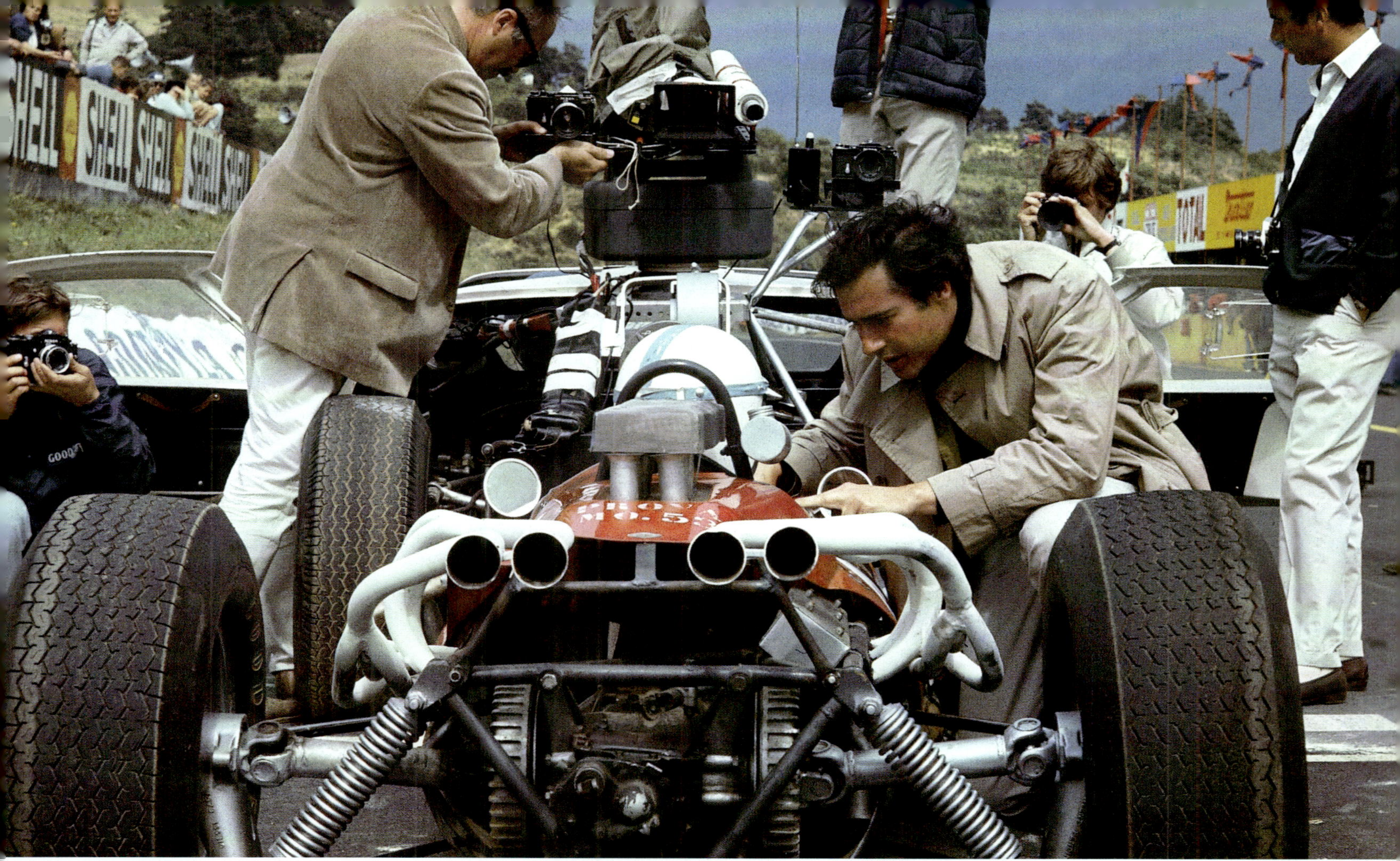
SHELL
SHELL
SHELL
SHELL
TOTAL

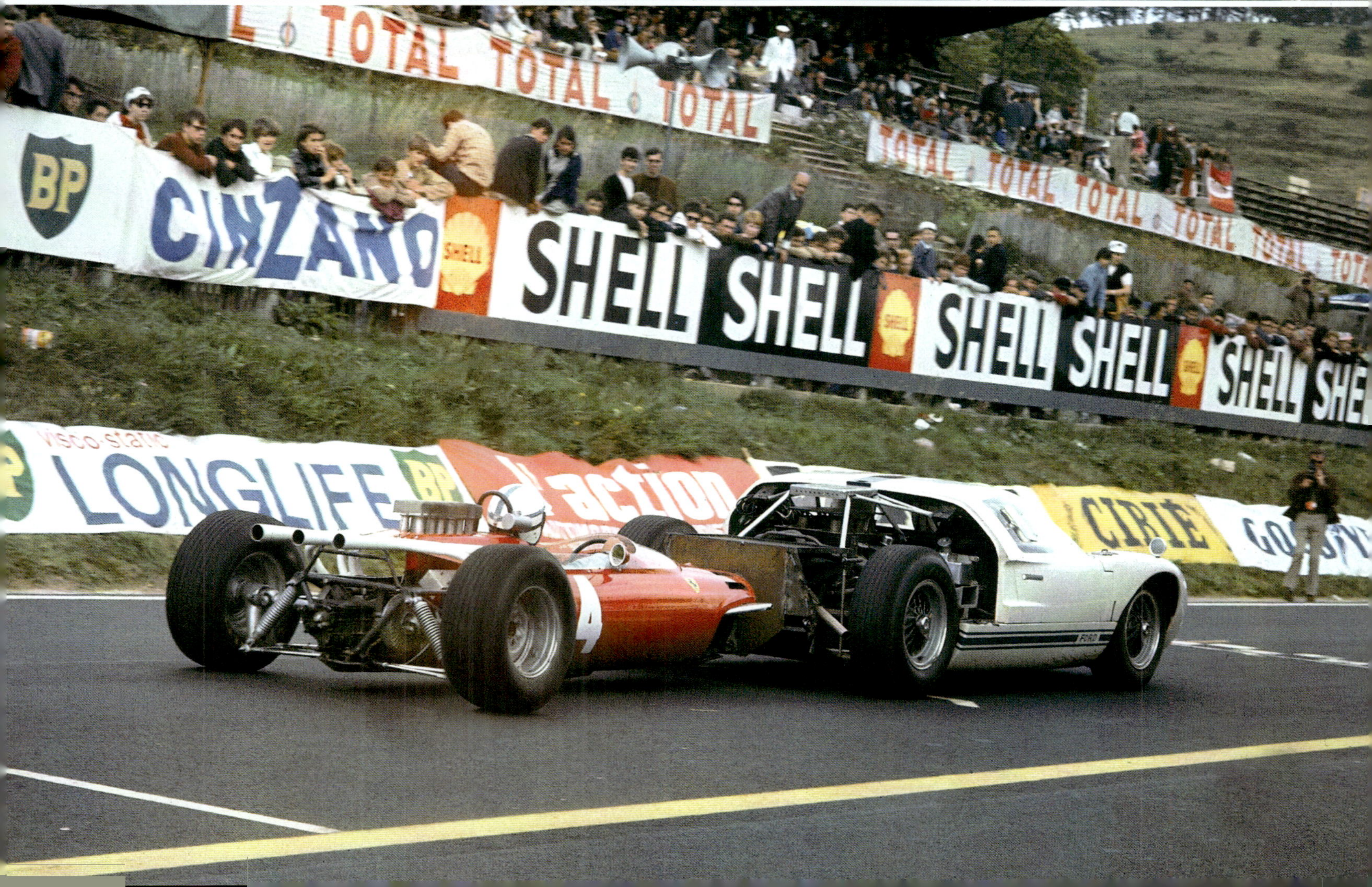
TOTAL
TOTAL
TOTAL
BP
CINZANO
SHELL
SHELL
SHELL
SHELL
SHELL
SHELL
TOTAL
TOTAL
TOTAL
TOTAL
LONGLIFE
BP
action
CIBIE
4

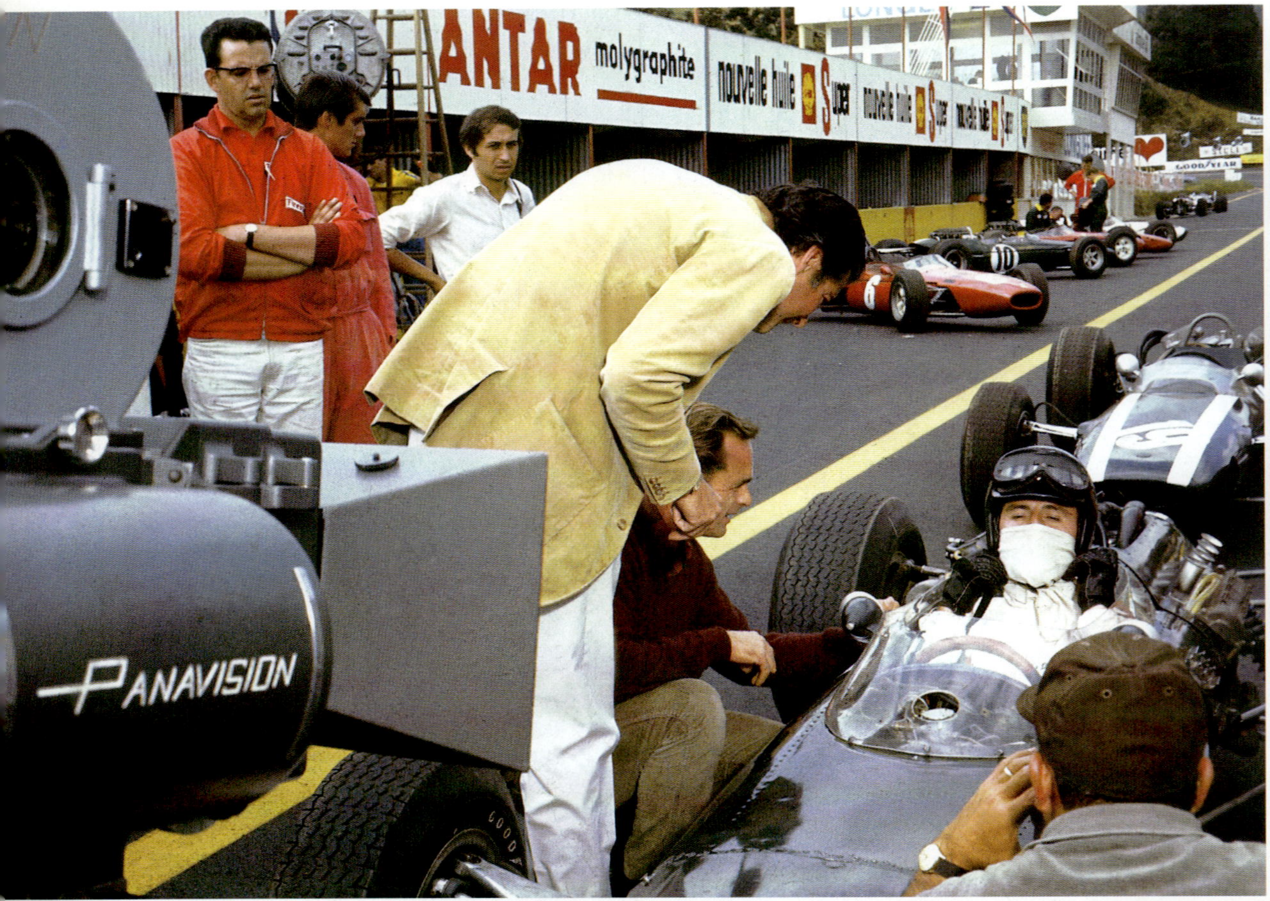
ANTAR
molygraphite
nouvelle huile
Super
PANAVISION

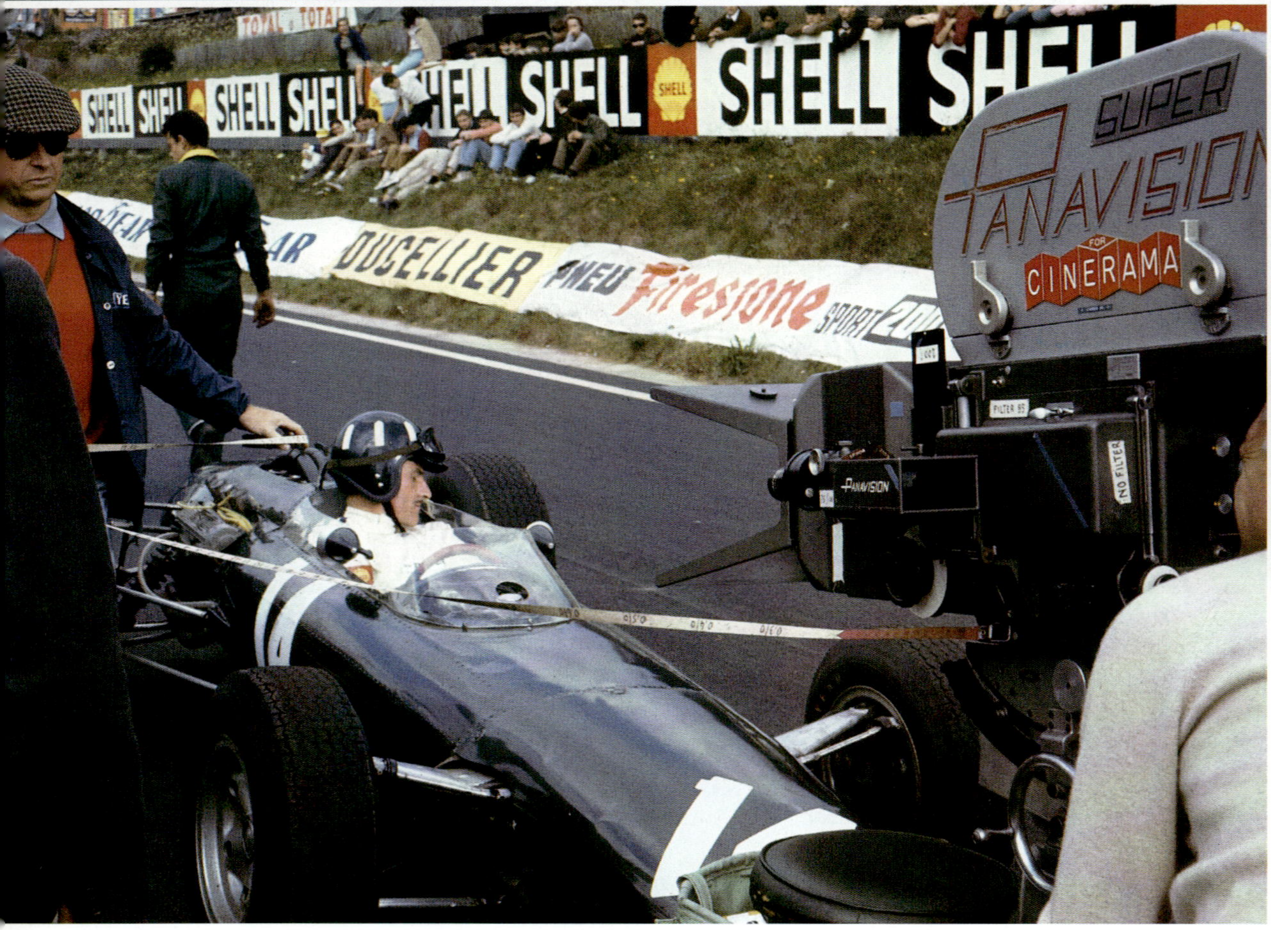
SHELL
DUSELLIER
Firestone
SUPER
PANAVISION
FOR
CINERAMA
PANAVISION
NO FILTER

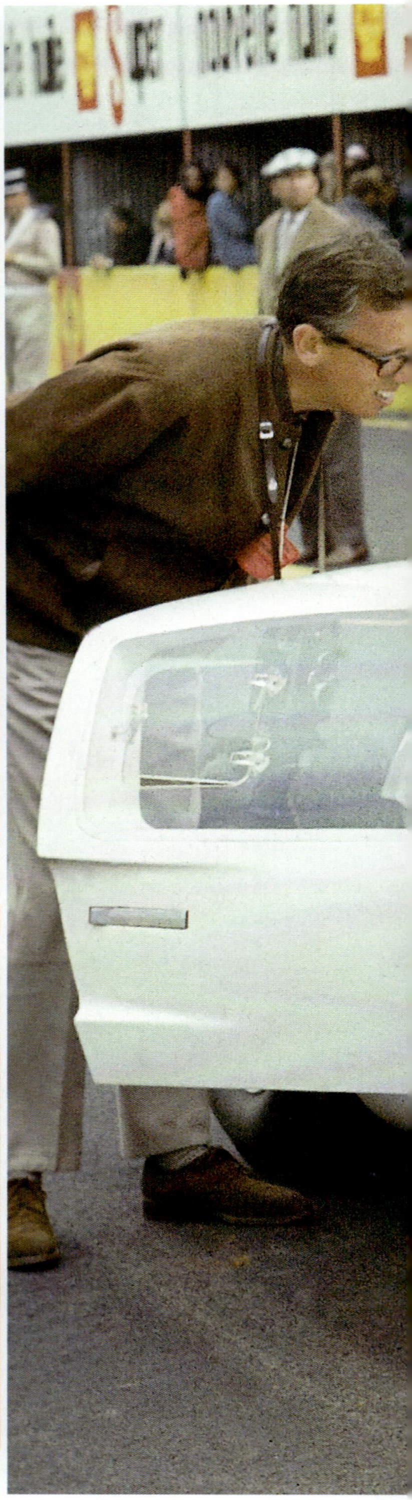
Super
nouvelle huile

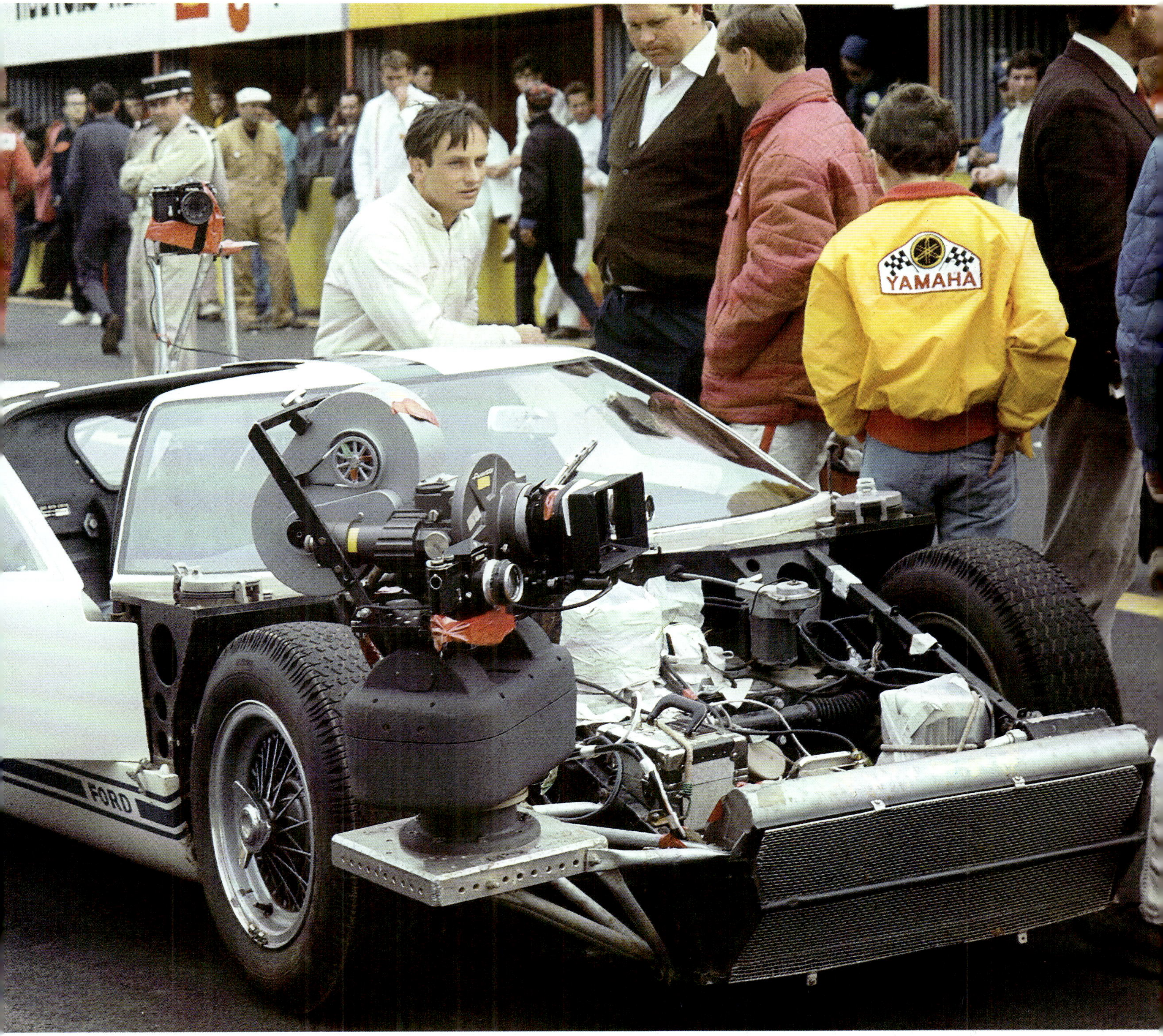

↑Here is the camera car (literally), a Ford GT40 and its distinguished chauffeur Chris Amon, whilst Tim Parnell and could that be Mike Spence look on.

↖A brace of Hills, Phil has just given Graham the facemask, whilst John Frankenheimer is not sucking on his pipe for once.

←The mechanics of filming on show here, and look at that Super Panavision film camera.

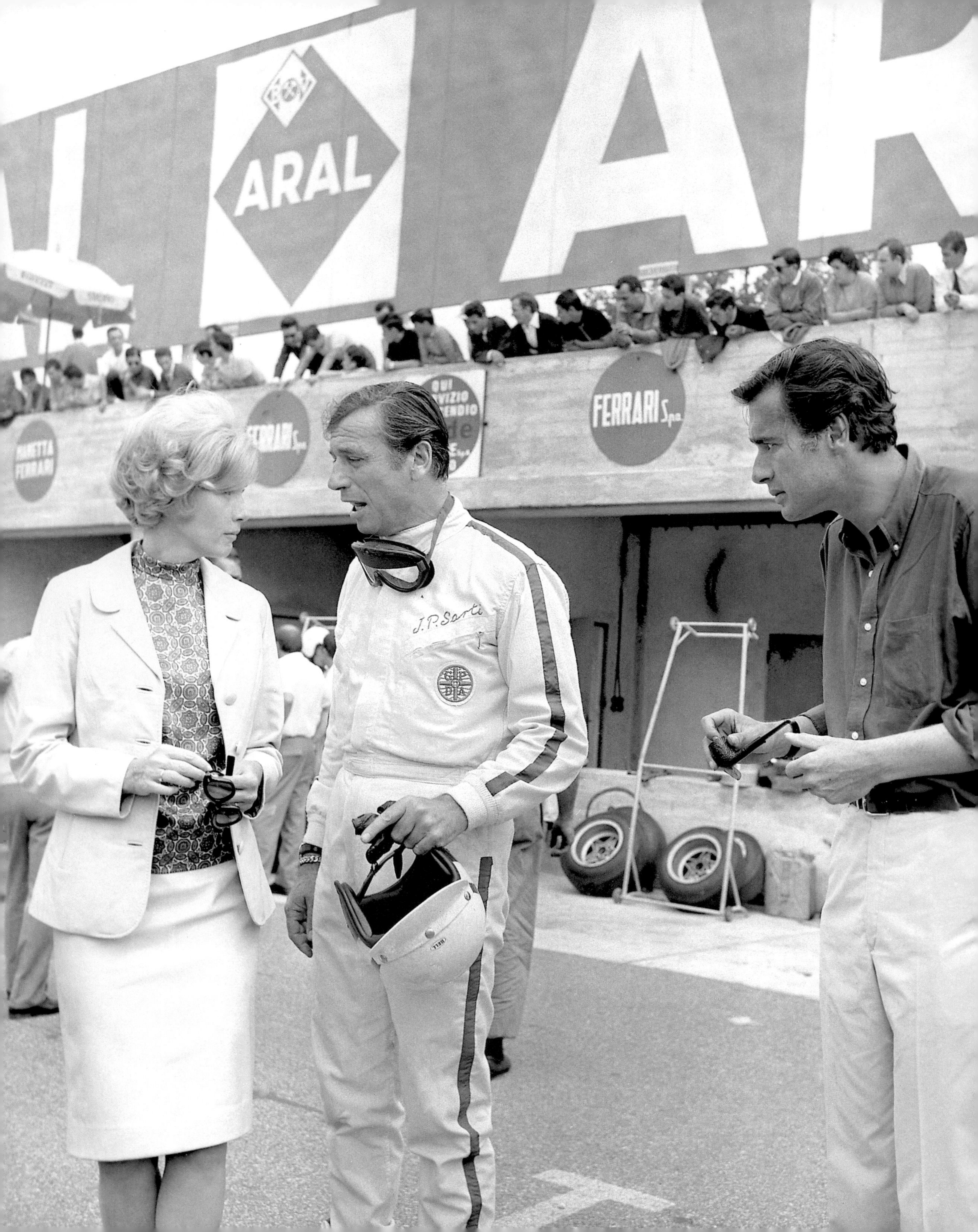
ARAL
FERRARI S.p.a.
J.P. Sarti

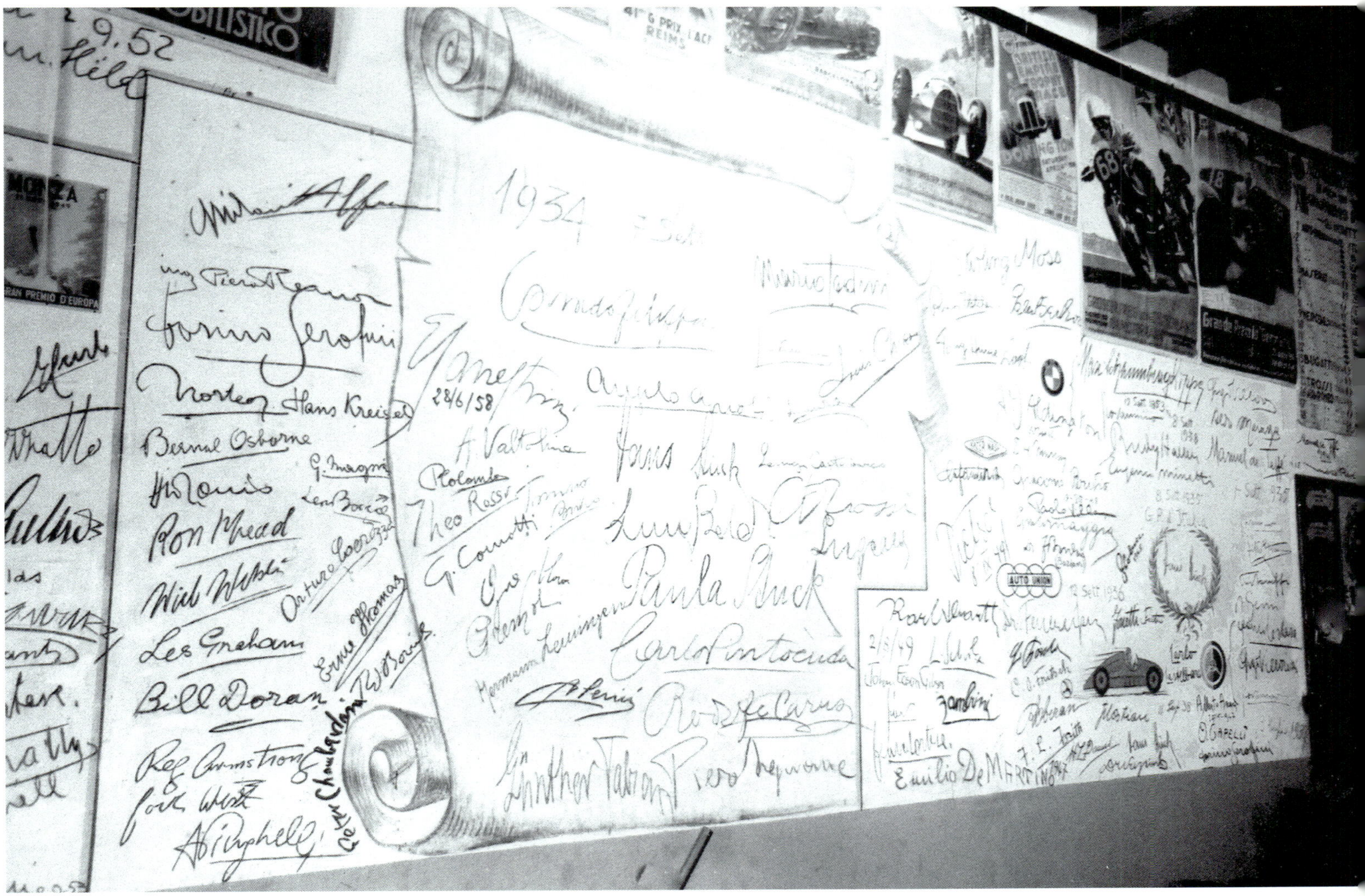

↑ The famous autographed wall in Count Giovanni 'Johnny' Lurani Cernuschi's (1905–95) garage at Castello Cerusco Lombardoni near Monza that was used in the film *Grand Prix*. Lurani was all things motor racing in Italy for decades, and is most famous for having proposed the Formula Junior category in San Remo on 20 November 1956, which was adopted in 1957.

← Eva Marie Saint and Yves Montand (now using the Mike Parkes helmet) receive direction at Monza from John Frankenheimer, who as ever is clutching his pipe. Frankenheimer was heavily involved in television between 1954 and 1960, directing over 150 live shows, and became a friend of Burt Lancaster, who he directed in *The Young Savages*. He was born 19 February 1930 and died from a stroke following complications during spinal surgery on 6 July 2002.

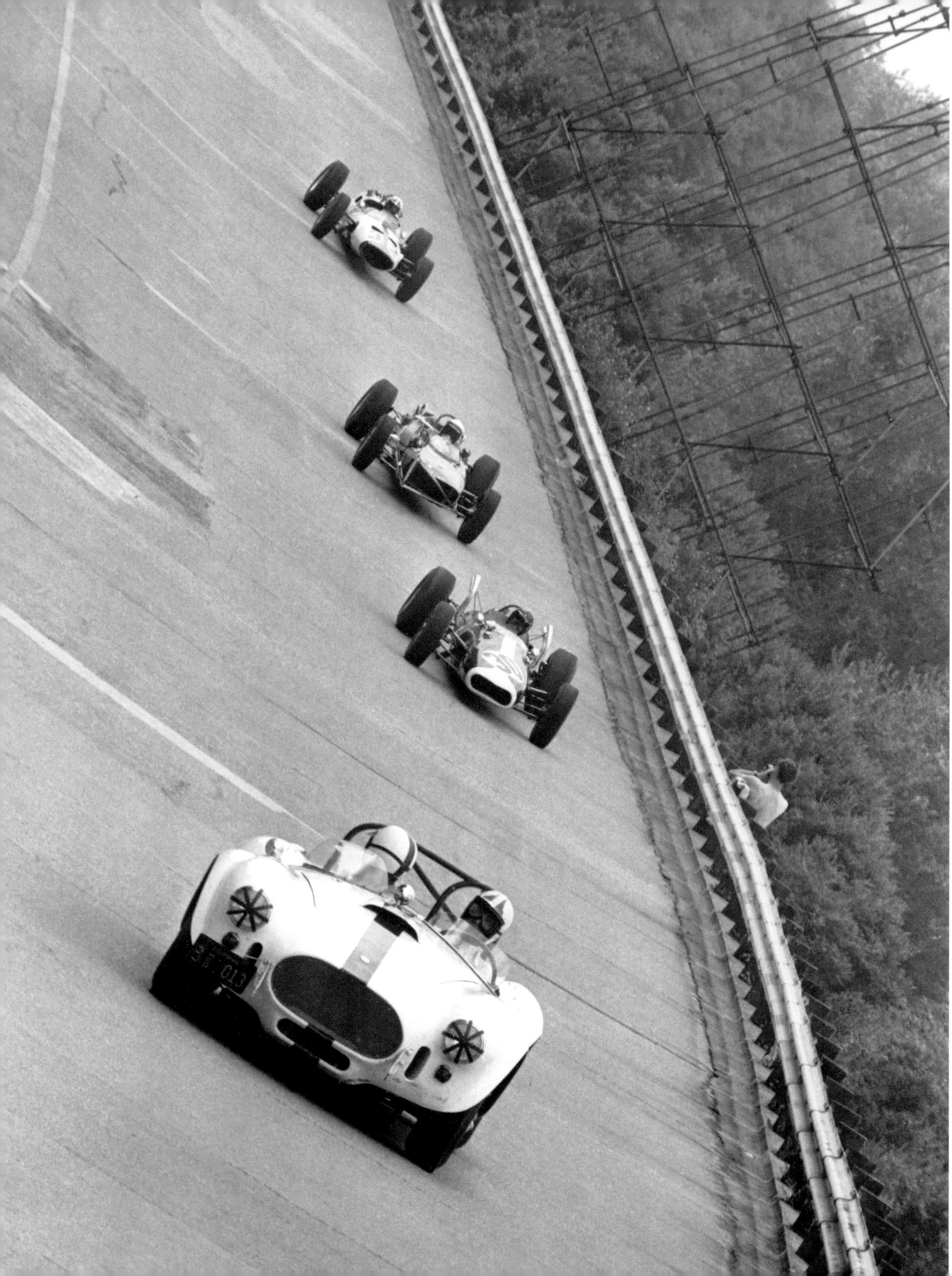

The actors certainly earned their fees on *Grand Prix*, and they dutifully follow Chris Amon in the 7-litre Cobra around the infamous Monza banking in their flimsy, camouflaged FF cars. Rather them than me!

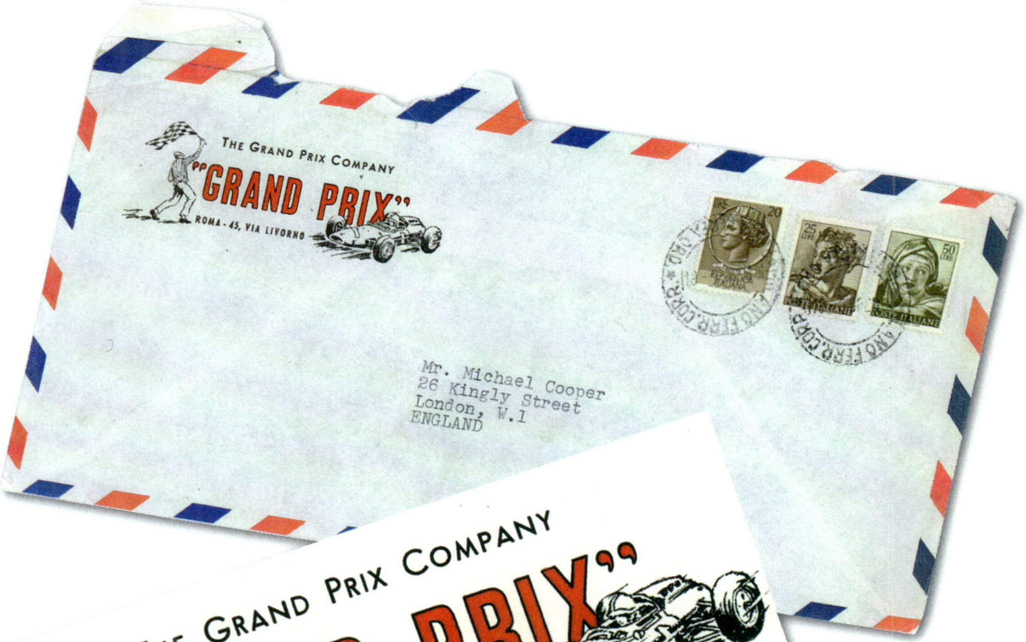

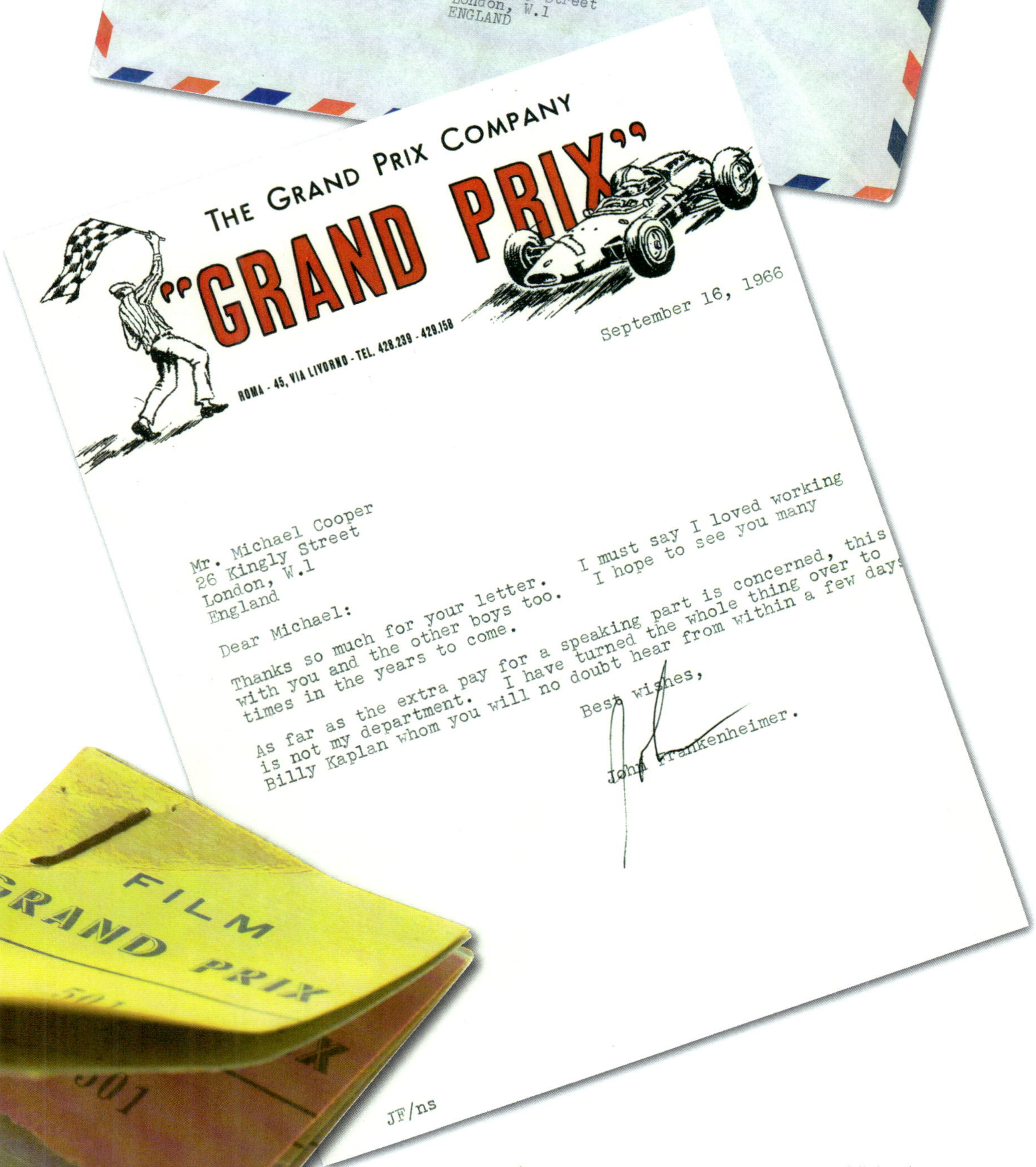

The Grand Prix Company
"GRAND PRIX"
ROMA - 45, VIA LIVORNO - TEL. 428.239 - 429.158

September 16, 1966

Mr. Michael Cooper
26 Kingly Street
London, W.1
England

Dear Michael:

Thanks so much for your letter. I must say I loved working with you and the other boys too. I hope to see you many times in the years to come.

As far as the extra pay for a speaking part is concerned, this is not my department. I have turned the whole thing over to Billy Kaplan whom you will no doubt hear from within a few days.

Best wishes,

John Frankenheimer.

JF/ns

A letter from John Frankenheimer to Michael Cooper, carefully deflecting the issue of extra pay!

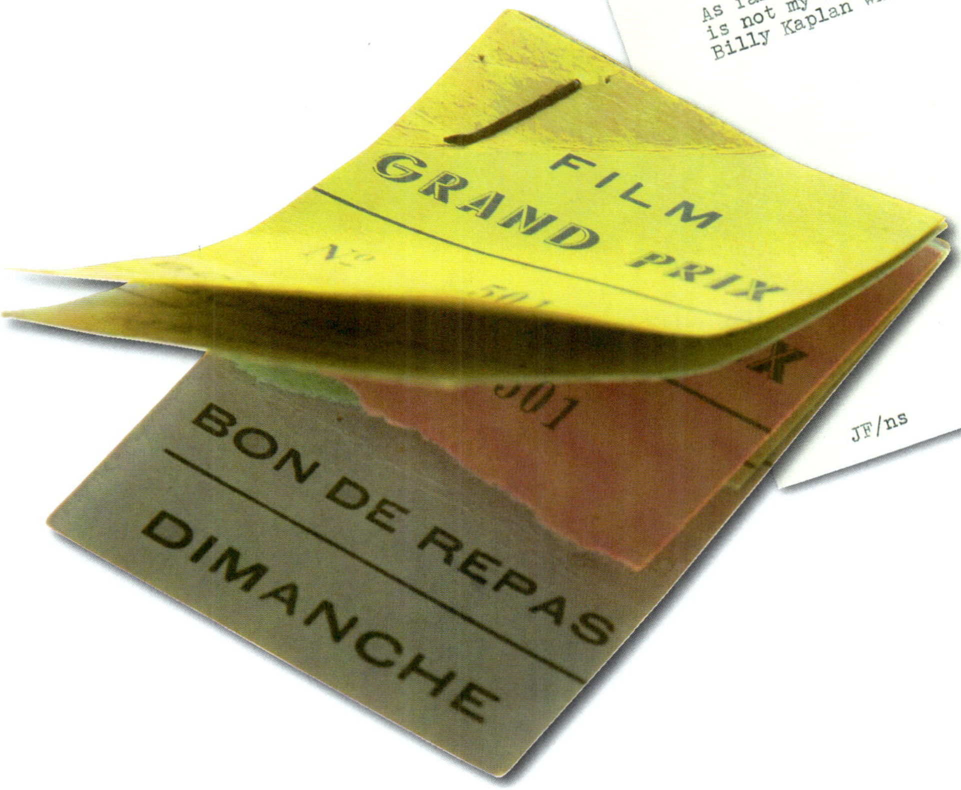

The meal tickets (*bons de repas*) for the film set on *Grand Prix*.

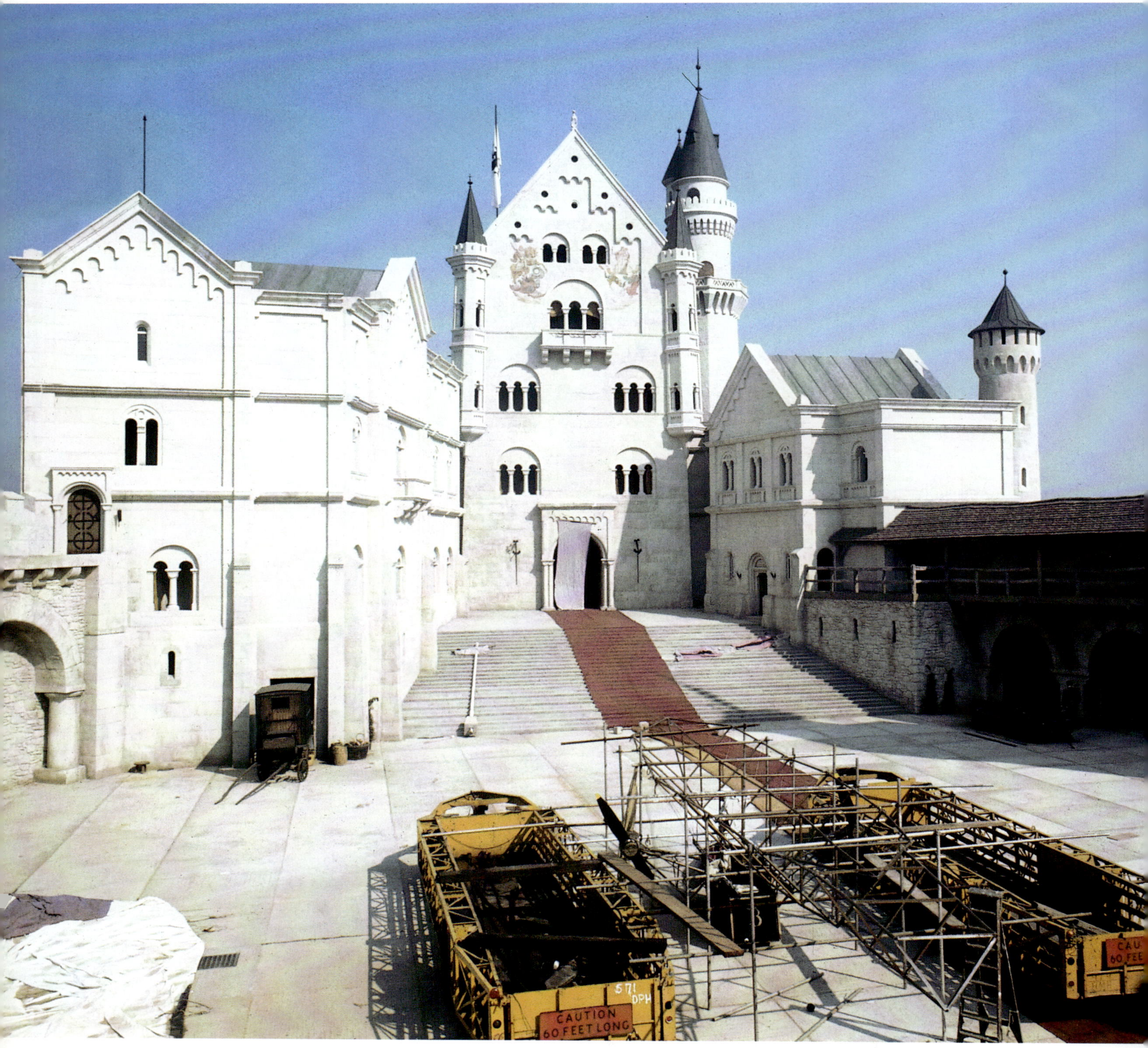

↑The model for Baron Bomburst's castle in *Chitty Chitty Bang Bang* was the fantastic Neuschwanstein in Bavaria, with its crenulated circular turrets and spires. Started in 1869 for Louis II of Bavaria (sometimes referred to as 'Mad King Ludwig') it was still uncompleted when he died in 1886. Mike visited the set and took some revealing pictures that show up the well-disguised two-dimensional aspect of such structures.

→The scaffolding behind the façade, somewhere in Buckinghamshire.

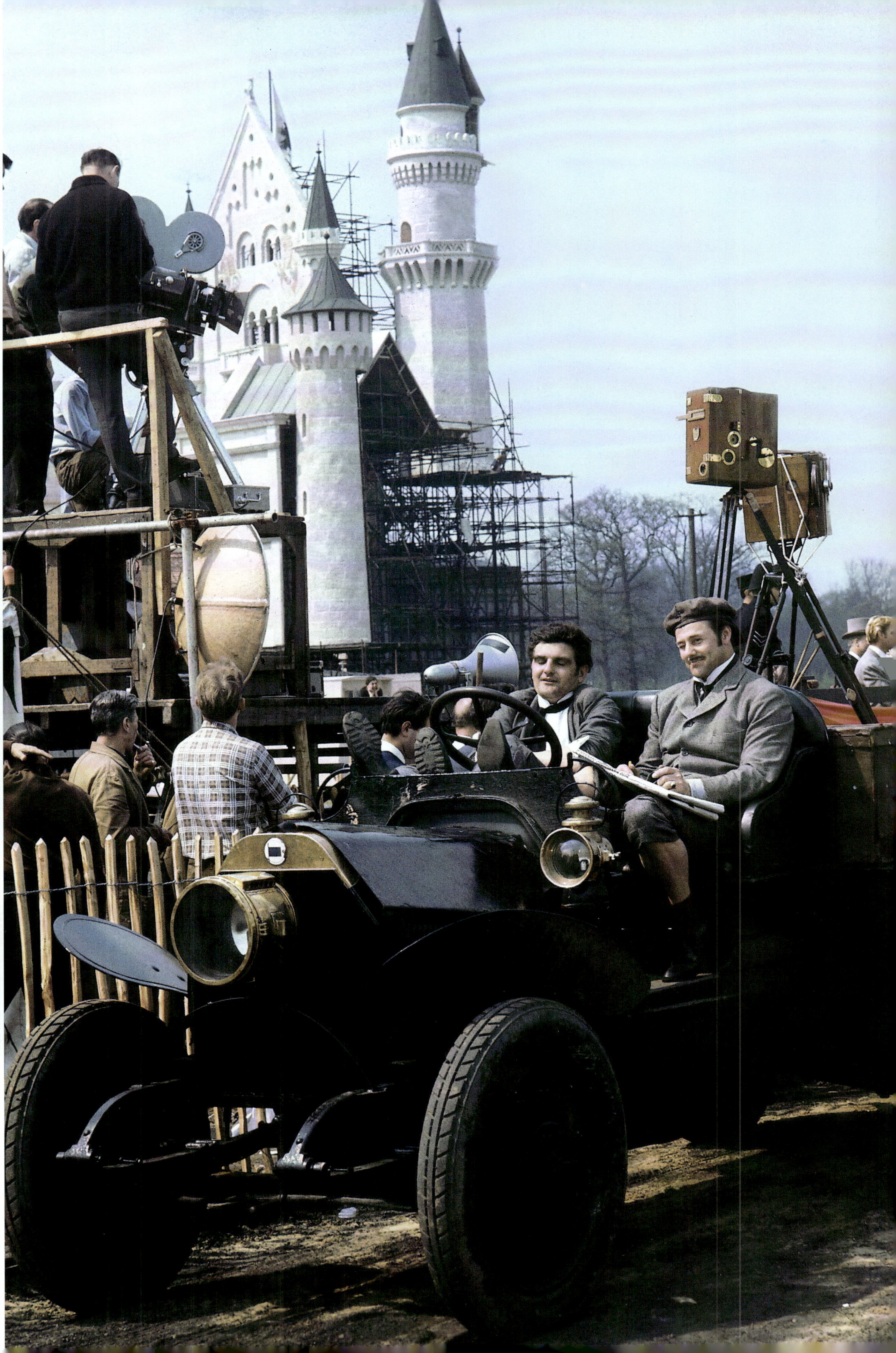

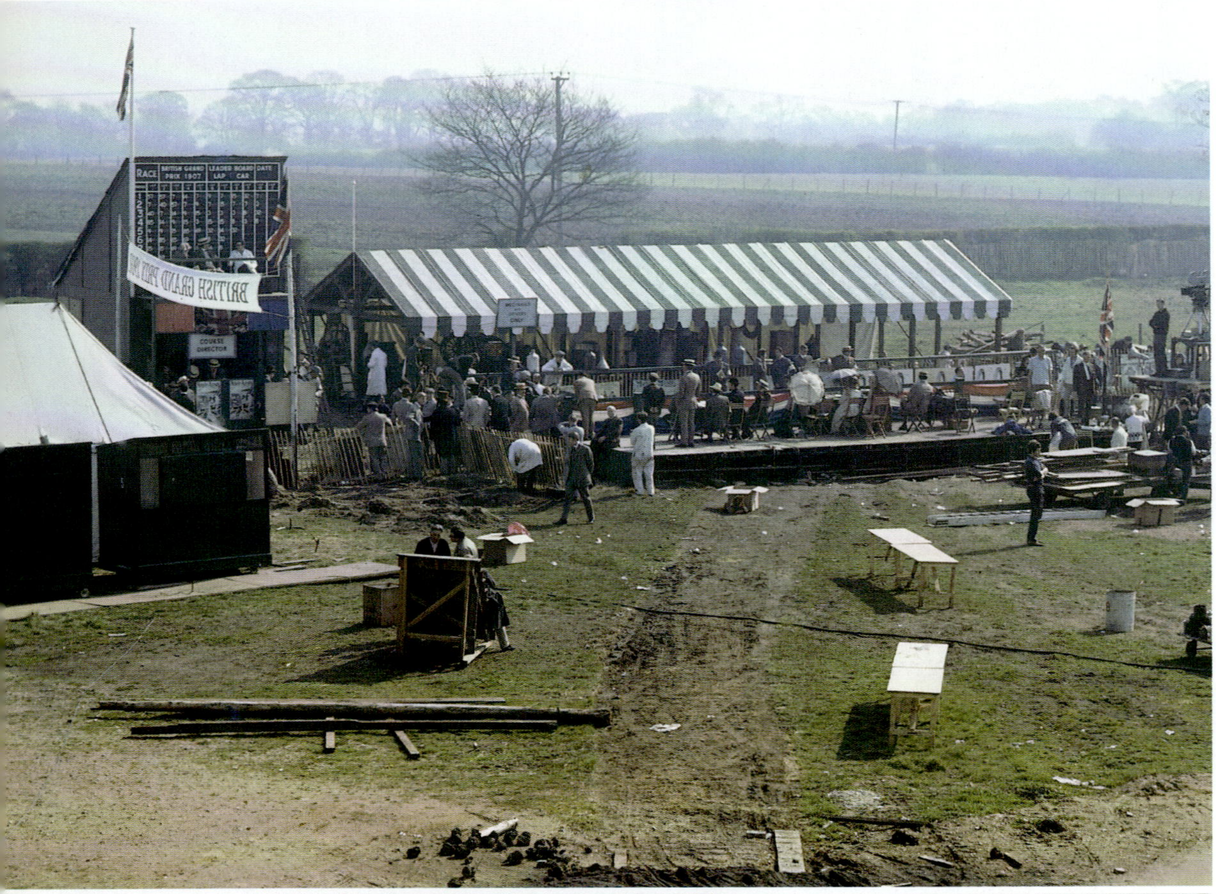

← A muddy field plays host to the starting area of a mythical 1907 and 1909 British GP, its construction as yet incomplete. No doubt the mere fact that no such event existed in period did not bother the studio executives.

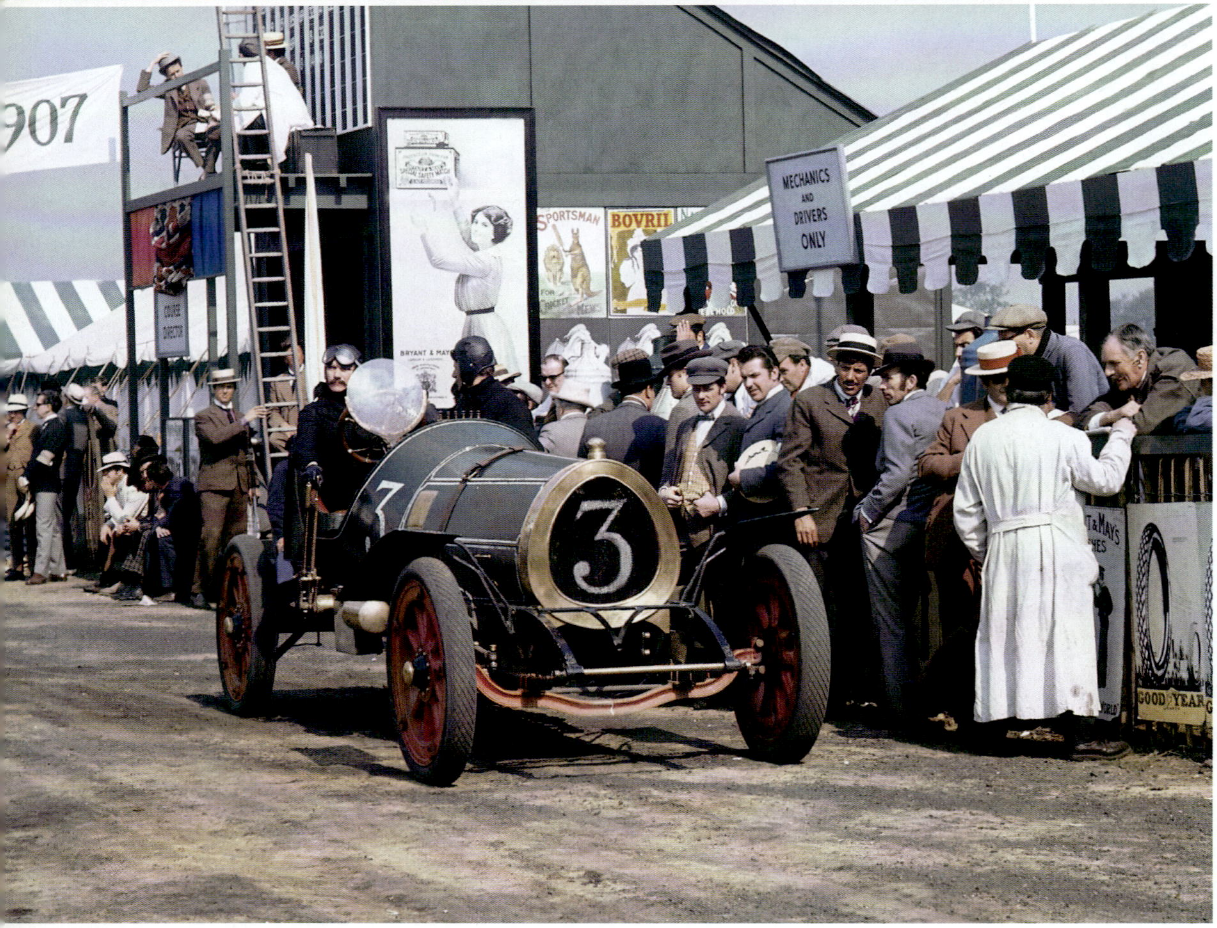

← Based upon Count Louis Zborowski's aero-engined Brooklands racer, the ersatz Chitty was constructed by Alan Man using a 3-litre V6 Ford engine and automatic transmission. The race sequences were part of the film's title footage and the film was based upon a book written by Ian Fleming and produced by Albert 'Cubby' Broccoli, famous co-producer of the James Bond series with Canadian Harry Saltzman.

→ Mike found himself back on a film set in 1970 when Steve McQueen starred in his own production *Le Mans*. Brian Redman and Steve look a trifle posed, whilst young Chad McQueen glares at Mike's intrusion.

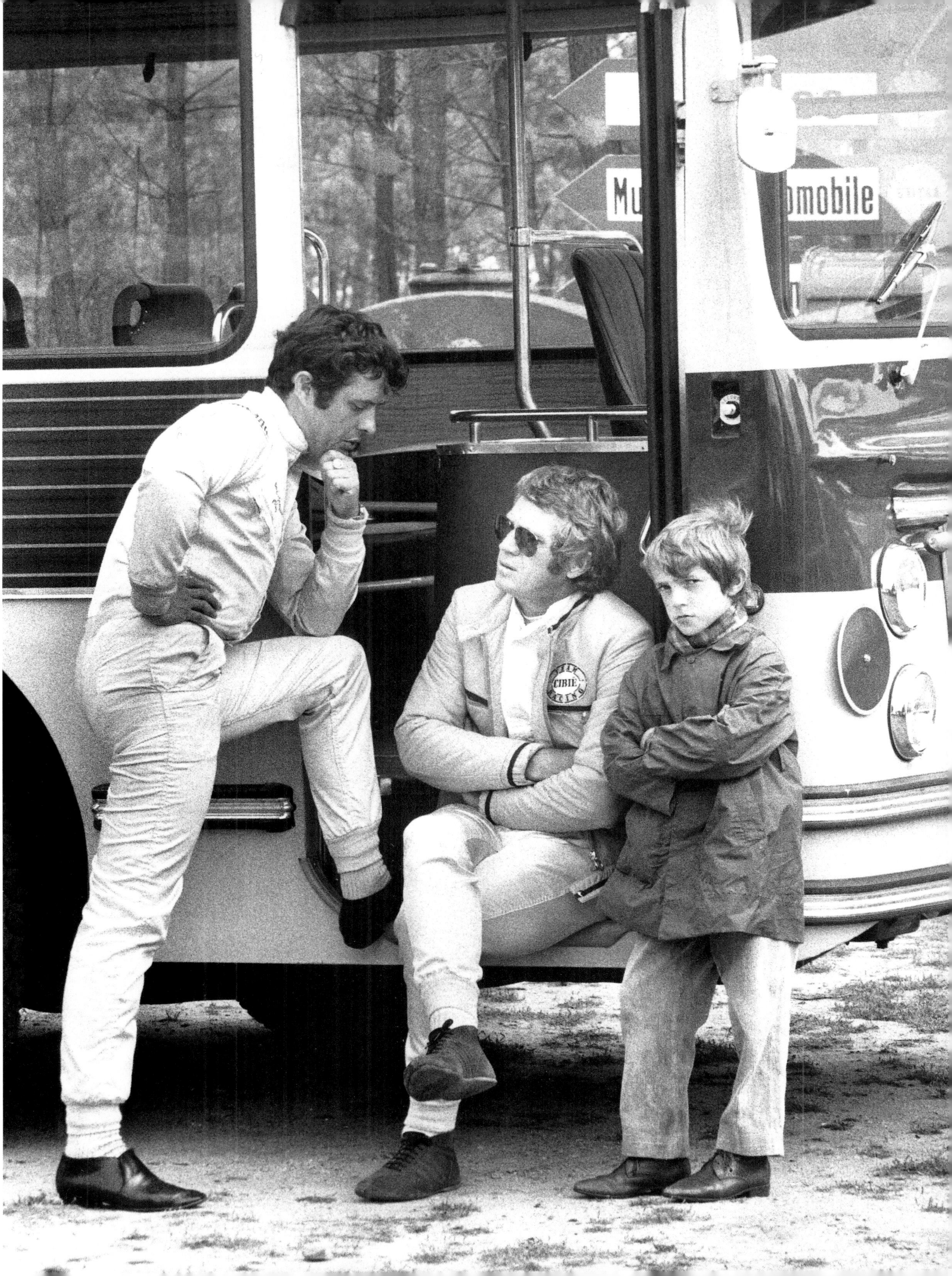
CIBIE

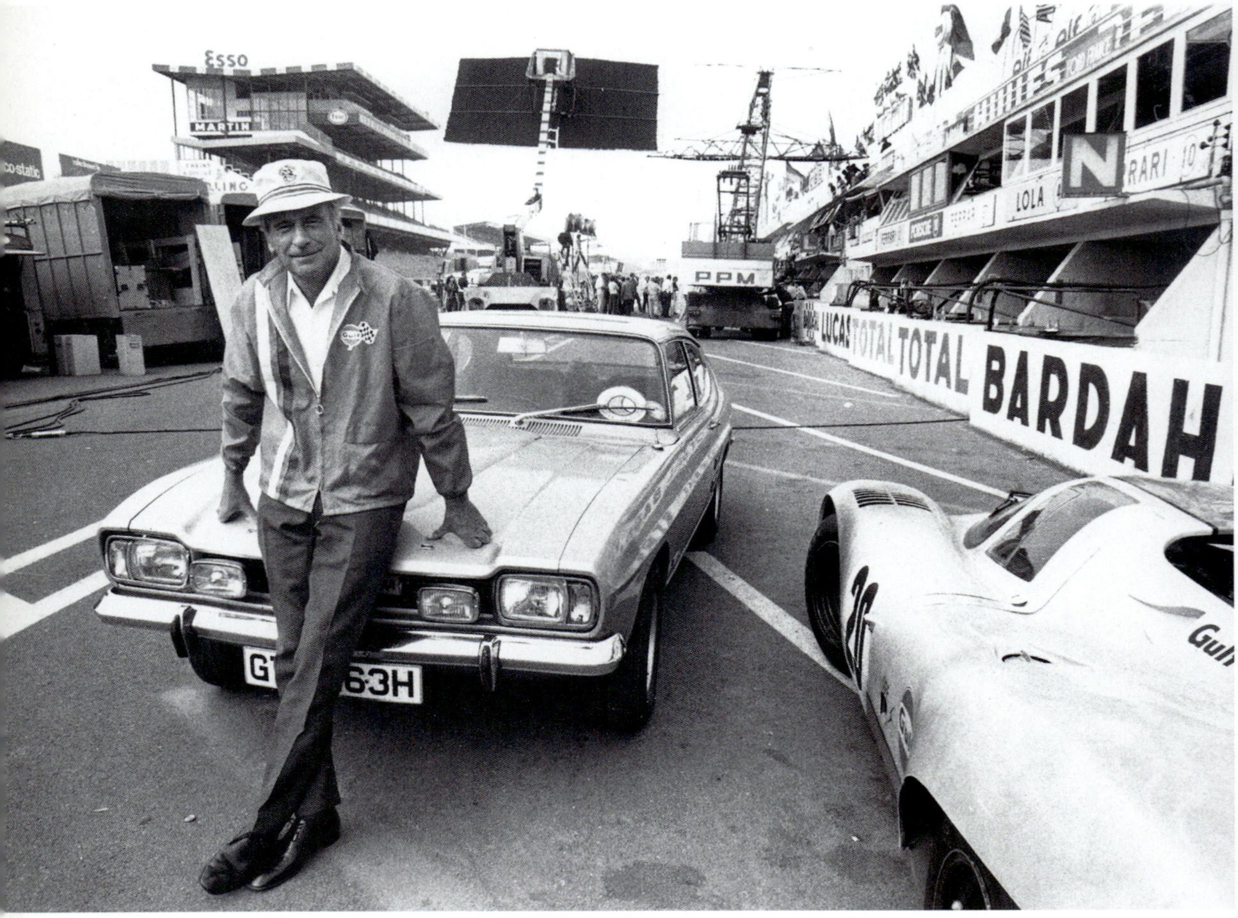

English character actor Ronald Leigh-Hunt (5 October 1920 – 20 September 2005) was a regular performer in all manner of films and TV series, and played David Townsend in McQueen's *Le Mans* film. He is leaning against the fashionable cheap fast car of the era, a Ford Capri 3-litre alongside one of the Porsche 917s, whilst in the background movie personnel and paraphernalia block the track.

The eyes have it. Mike gets the full treatment, and note the Heuer patch on the overalls, a connection that the latter-day TAGHeuer company still uses.

Mike's salary and expenses chit for his work on *Le Mans*.

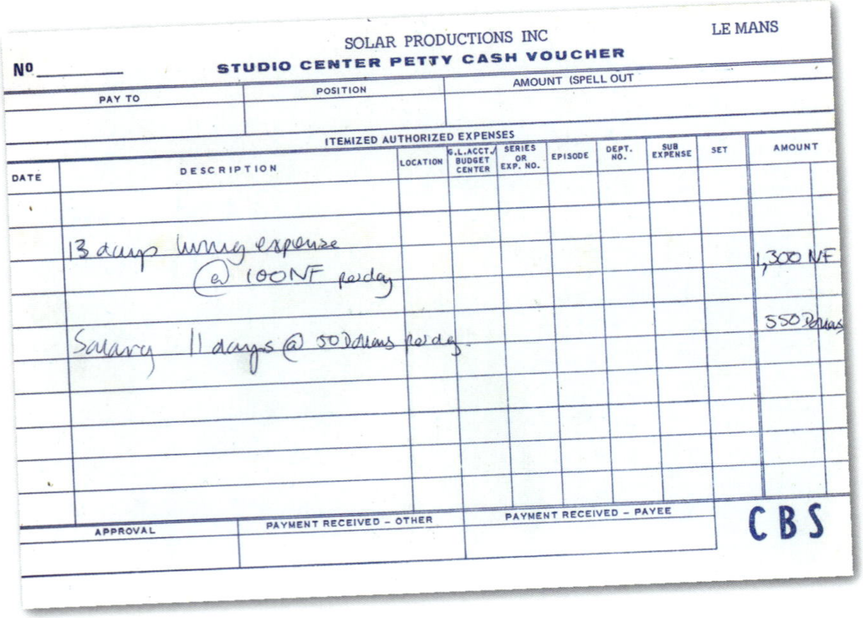
SOLAR PRODUCTIONS INC — LE MANS

No ________ STUDIO CENTER PETTY CASH VOUCHER

PAY TO | POSITION | AMOUNT (SPELL OUT)

ITEMIZED AUTHORIZED EXPENSES

DATE	DESCRIPTION	LOCATION	G.L.ACCT./ BUDGET CENTER	SERIES OR EXP. NO.	EPISODE	DEPT. NO.	SUB EXPENSE	SET	AMOUNT
	13 days living expense @ 100NF perday								1,300 NF
	Salary 11 days @ 50 Dollars per day								550 Dollars

APPROVAL | PAYMENT RECEIVED – OTHER | PAYMENT RECEIVED – PAYEE | CBS

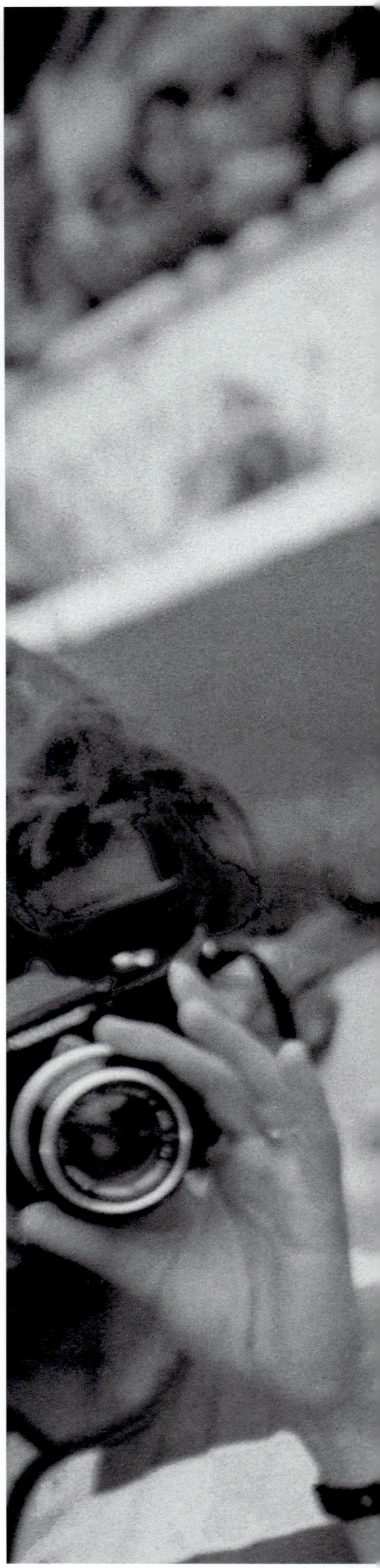

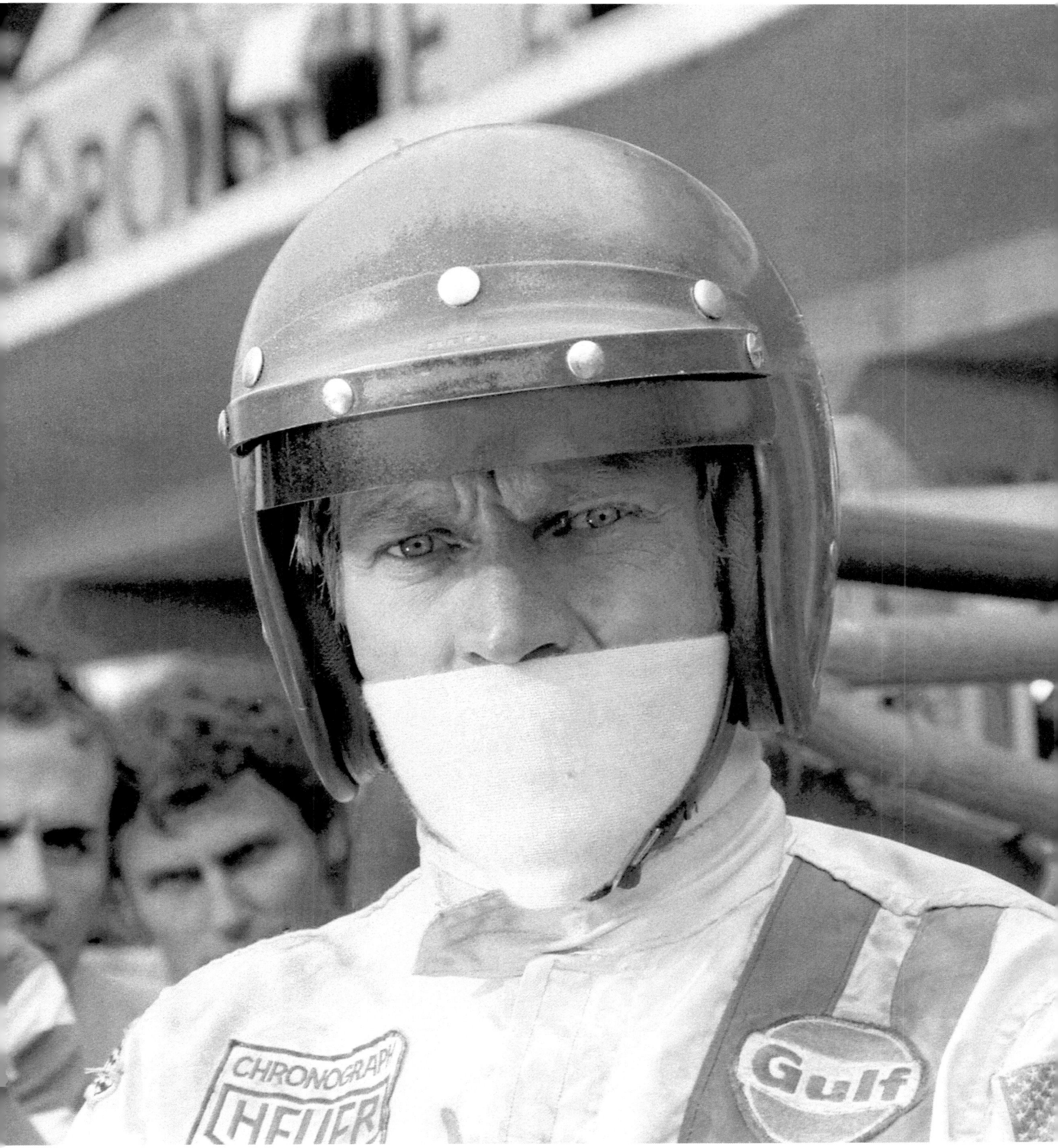
CHRONOGRAPH
HEUER
Gulf

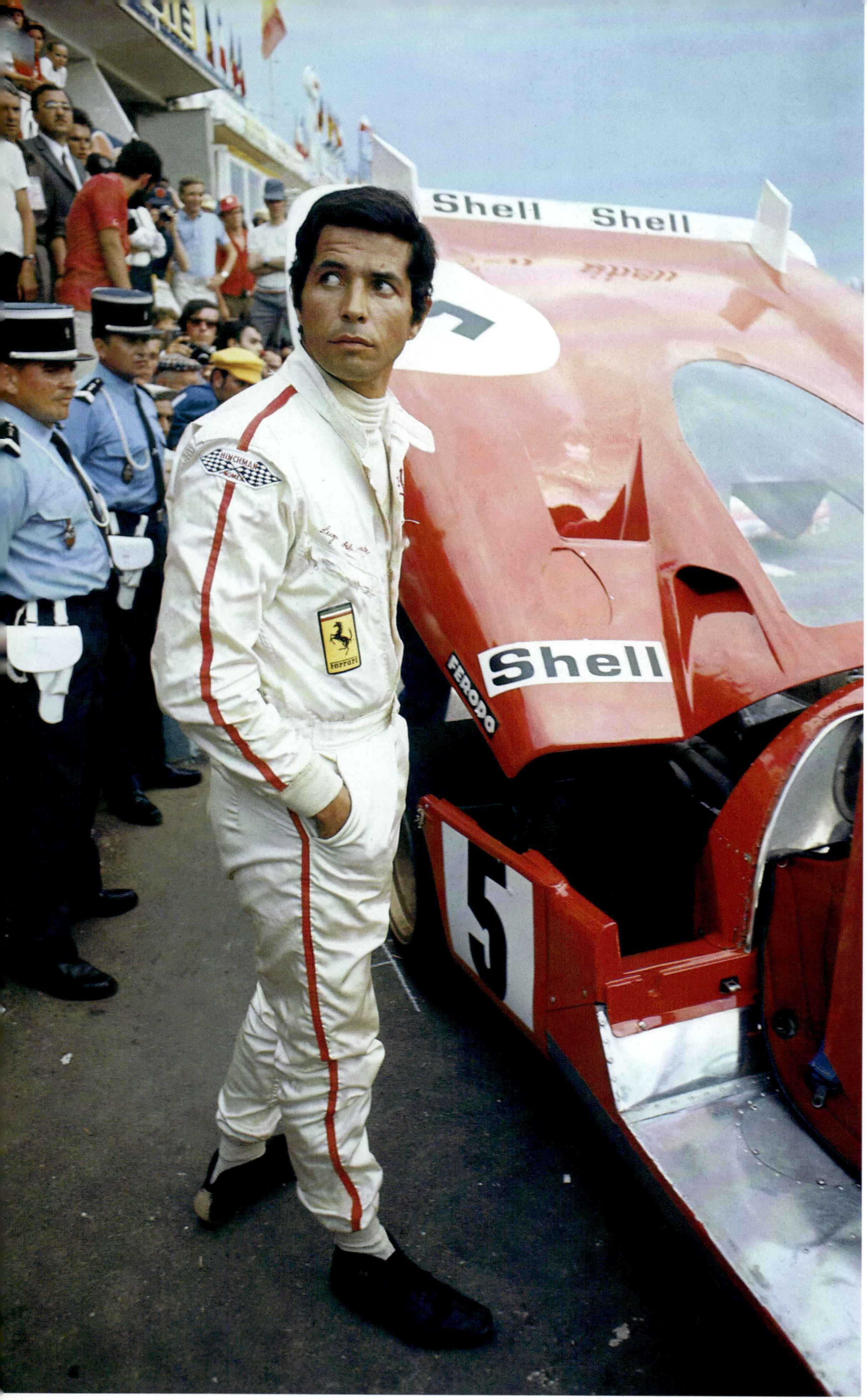

This almost looks like the real thing, but Angelo Infanti, as Lugo Abratte in *Le Mans* is too clean and well kempt for a 1970s racer. Infanti, born in 1939 has enjoyed a long and varied career that has encompassed all manner of roles, including a part in *The Godfather*, and is still working today. Note his American hinchman driving suit, as favoured by Pedro Rodriguez.

Jo Cooper

When asked to put some words together of fond memories of my father, my immediate thought was 'how on earth do I choose which ones?' – there are so many. But I suppose I should try to relate them to the theme!

I was aware from a very early age of the passion for cars that Daddy had, remembering clearly the day he brought home our first new family car – a black Astra GTE, complete with red go-faster stripes! With Ben and I strapped in the back, we experienced an exhilarating demonstration of it's speed and versatility along our narrow country lanes – or was it the driver?

Growing up, I showed little interest in motor sport and often wondered what all the fuss was about, especially the screaming and noise that was generated from the sitting room on Sunday lunchtimes during the F1 season. Then, sometime in the 80s during a day out to a qualifying session at Brands, I began to see some of the merits of motor sport after Dad pointed out Stefan Johansson to me – only then did I join them in front of the TV!

Another memory is of the excitement felt when he was due to be returning from a rally – welcoming him home with a big hug at the door and commenting on his 'rally smell' – something I now know well to be the aroma of a couple of pints in a smoky pub! Then I would eagerly wait the unpacking of his bags to see what gifts he had brought us without fail from his travels – including for me, all the complimentary hotel toiletries from wherever he had been – I built up quite a collection!

Growing up around this passion for cars obviously had its effect on me. I am sure he would have been proud the day I bought my first sports car, a Lotus Elise, although probably not so understanding of the reasons for having to sell it – driving to work on cold winter mornings, scuffed heels and ripped skirts had made me realise why people tend to use them as weekend cars. I am now very much looking forward to the long awaited return, after restoration, of 2 NPJ (now COO 4) – Dad's 1965 Sunbeam Tiger, and to my first drive; for some reason he never allowed me behind the wheel … and Daddy, I promise not to take the first bend into Farley Green quite so fast!

As far as his passion for photography goes, this is something that I was acutely aware of from an early age. I remember the camera being a very prominent part of our lives over the years. At times I found this to be frustrating having to stop what I was doing for a particular moment to be captured, and frequently a little embarrassing, especially during my teenage years! However, looking back I am so grateful for the boxes and boxes of photographs we have, illustrating some very precious family moments.

I miss him terribly; he was a fantastic father and a huge inspiration to me. I am so grateful for these and countless other treasured memories – he is very much still alive in our hearts.

Jo Cooper
February 2009

MORE TO CONSIDER

This last segment of the book features an eclectic assortment of Mike's work, nearly all static and featuring familiar and not so familiar faces.

Like some of his contemporaries and predecessors, Mike was just as interested in or even more concerned with the human aspect or setting of the picture rather than the subject alone. Here are the usually unseen, Amherst Villiers, 'Bunty' Scott Moncrief, Shane Summers and others in sometimes unexpected locations.

What is very apparent are the more relaxed, indeed unaware attitudes of some of the participants, no perfectly honed grooming, no obvious posing (unless asked to do so). This is how people were before media savvy marketing men, personal managers and sponsor priority took over, they could be themselves. The image of an oily faced Bruce McLaren talking with Jim Hall perfectly encapsulates the zeitgeist. Some of it looks almost like a parody (the hot pants garb of the Yardley girls) whilst it is a shock to realise that this was so long ago.

A characteristic feature of Mike's work was his predilection for photographing objects, people and circuits from above and here is a very fine shot of Brands Hatch from the air looking very basic and unspoilt. Other unexpected images include the (in)famous Ray Hannah ground level assault at Goodwood in 1998 and the pictures of Mike's near neighbour, 1960s sports car, F3 and F2 racer Chris Williams at his BMW dealership in Shere near Guilford (no corporate standards bull...then!)

For over 15 years most of the thousands of rolls of film were developed and printed up in a small studio in Kingly Street London W1 between and running parallel to Regent Street to the west and Carnaby Street to the east. This was usually accomplished late into the night/early hours after returning from some far-flung circuit or location as he struggled to supply his prints to the various journals on his list. It was gruelling work after a typically long hard day and much driving to and fro. Latter day snappers can do it all from their laptops even if they do have to tweak and transmit their pictures electronically.

Following his gradual withdrawal from regular F1 and other professional series coverage Mike returned to his career roots as a professional snapper who could be commissioned for any subject or personality. He had strong connections with Honda and was actually allowed to photograph their putative F1 car in 2000 but this material is not available. Nevertheless, every so often he would turn up at a British GP and snap away as the preceding pages illustrate. Every year he would drive to the Geneva Motorshow with Liz and meet up with old friends and colleagues and he always had an active interest in fast road cars. His last two were a 320bhp Subaru Impreza and one of the then new Nissan 350Zs.

Ultimately though his abiding passion after his family was the magnificent garden and orchard of his beautiful home that he lovingly tended against the ravages of rural Surrey wildlife.

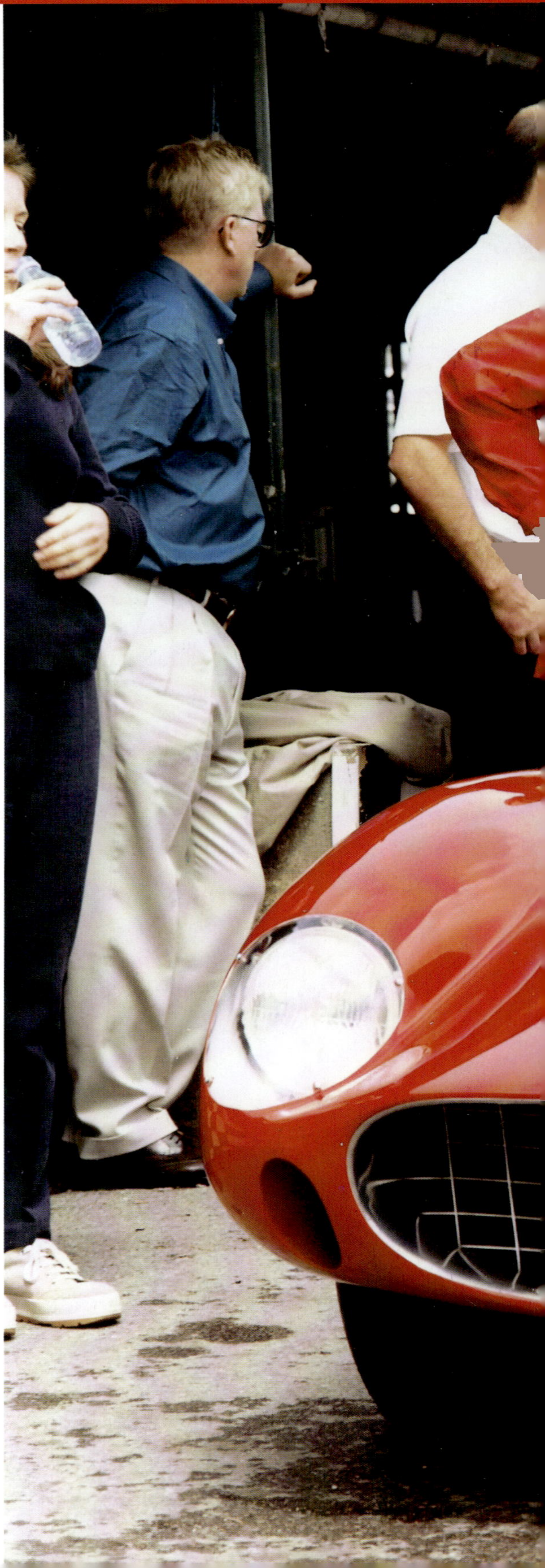

A very dapper gentleman really is the best description of the renowned motor racing photographer Louis Klementaski (12 February 1912 – 24 June 2001). He is almost always dressed thus, blazer, bow tie and slacks from pre-war days when he was one of the few to use colour film. He was born in Harbin, Manchuria which is in northern China, a result of his entrepreneurial father's peripatetic wanderings. The family originated from Poland and 'Klem's' subsequent career included becoming secretary of the pre-war J.R.D.C. (Junior Racing Drivers Club). Famous for his passengering on the Mille Miglia, this is the Ferrari 335S (0700) that he accompanied Peter Collins in during the last ever Mille Miglia (1957) and which the duo would have won easily but for transmission failure after Rome. It also raced at the Nürburgring, Spa, Le Mans, Sweden (2nd Phil Hill/Peter Collins) and the Venezuelan GP at Caracas (1st Phil Hill/Peter Collins). Owner Peter Sachs stands on the driver's side and note the obligatory silencer required for Goodwood test days, this one sometime in 1997.

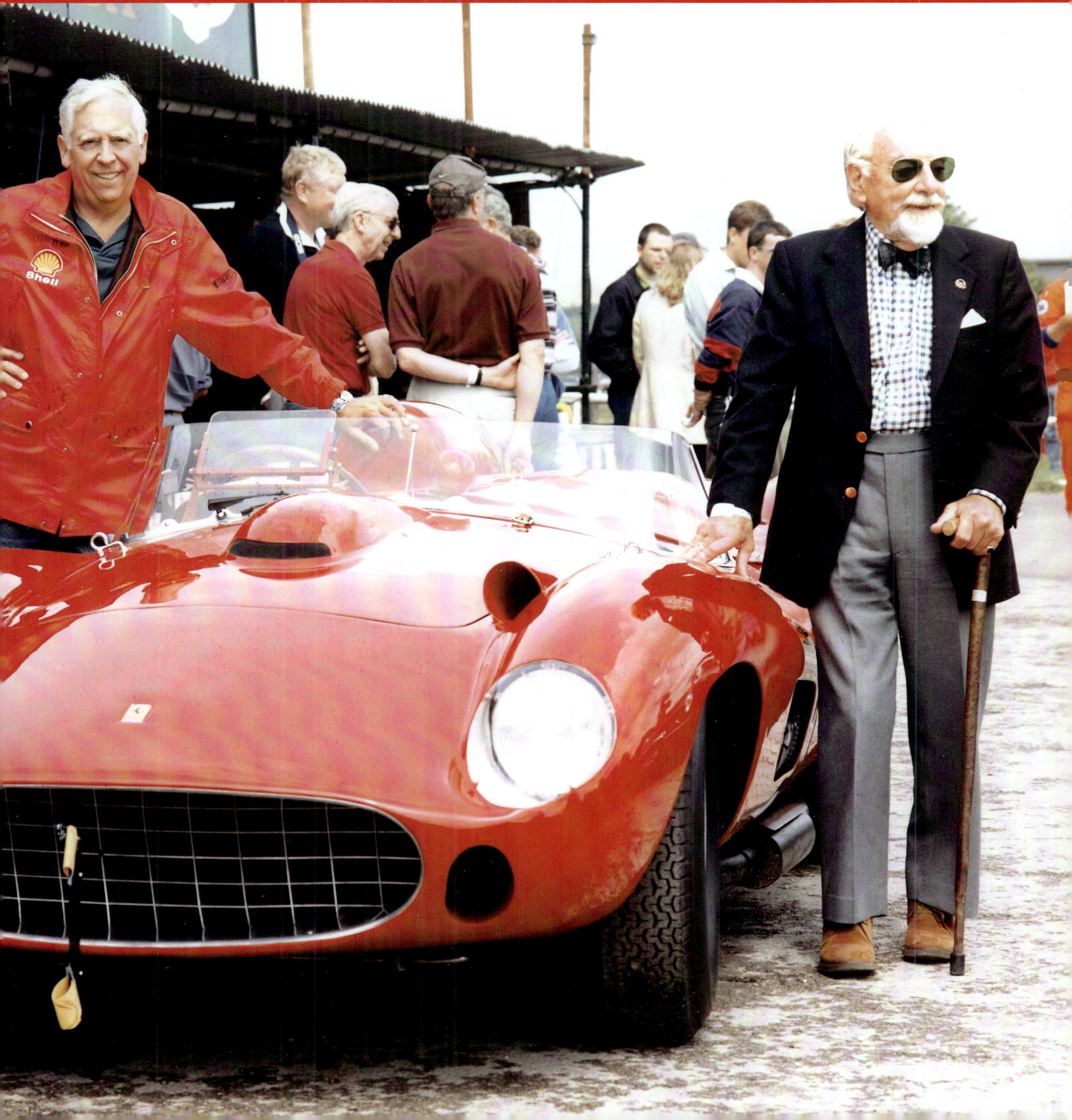

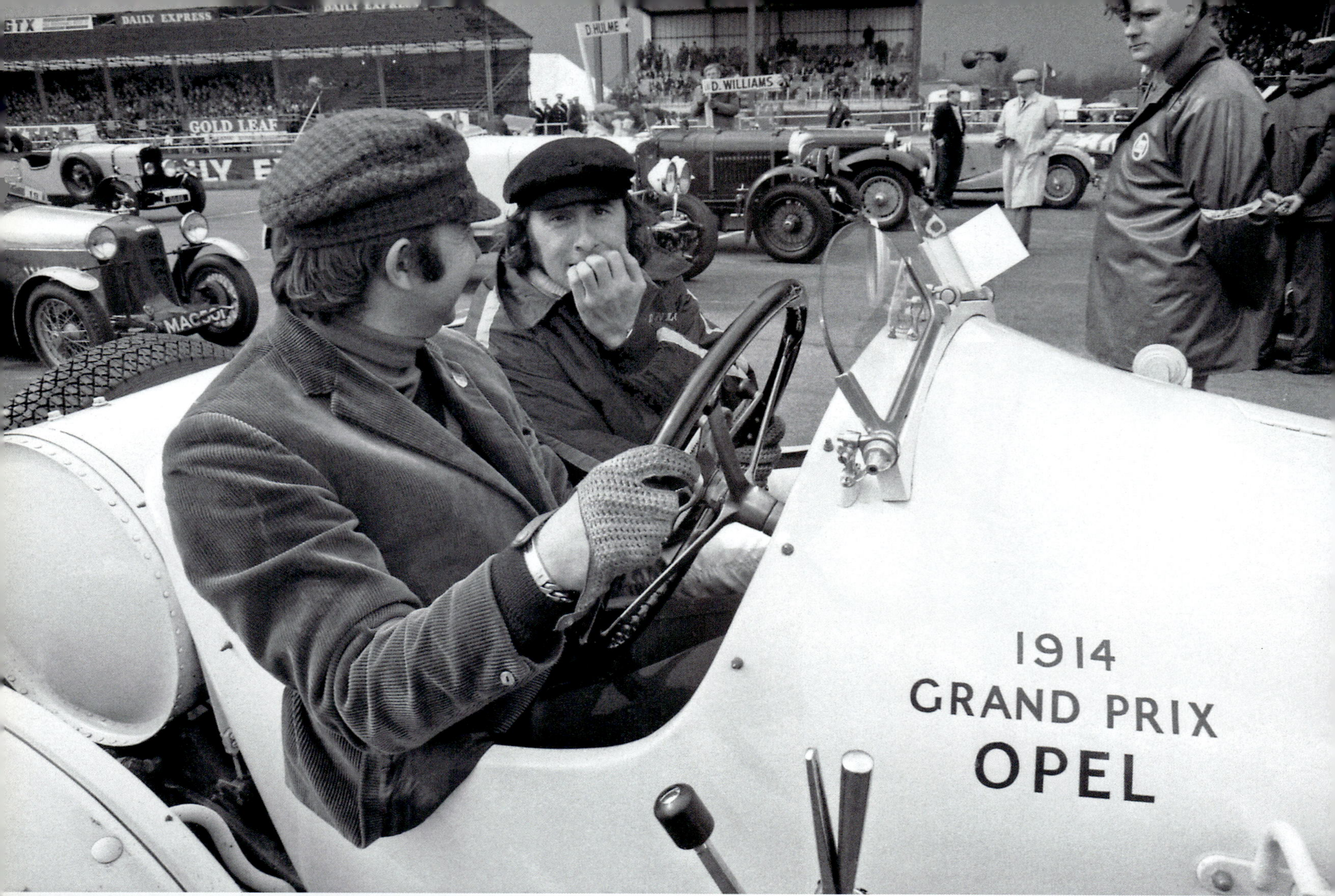

↑ Neil Corner in his 1914 Grand Prix Opel, and an apparently uncertain passenger for a parade at Silverstone.

→ Neil and Freda Corner, Nick Faure, and Willie Green at Silverstone with the inevitable caravan lurking in the background. Perhaps they towed it with the Maserati 250F that is shod with Dunlop RS5 road tyres. The H. J. Mulliner/Park Ward-bodied Rolls-Royce Corniche is apparently courtesy of Avis. In 2009 Willie reminisced to the author: 'The 250F was at its first race at Silverstone in April 1971, but I practised in the other car, the Piccolo 2534, which promptly dropped a valve. Then it snowed and we assumed that the race was off, so a fairly serious party started! Unknown to me the mechanics finished the other car 2525, Moss's 1956 Monza winning 'offset' 250F; it had not turned a wheel since a total rebuild, as you saw it had RS5 road tyres because of the snow, same size front and rear! And running methanol with a serious flatspot at 5500rpm; only discovered when they suddenly called the race back on, at which time I was suffering from some brain fade. I led to Becketts, spun in front of Neil, got back into the lead same lap then spun at Copse, they shortened the race to 5 laps but I nearly got Neil back. There were two inches of snow either side of the track'.

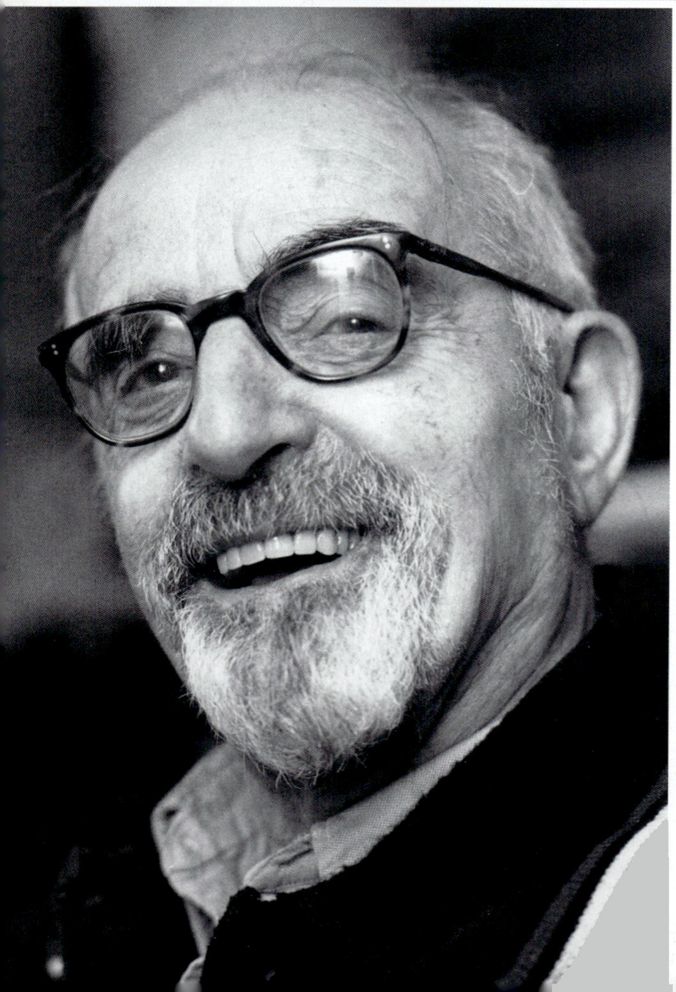

← The remarkable Sydney Charles Houghton 'Sammy' Davis, famous victor of Le Mans 1927 (with Dudley Benjafield) despite the infamous 'White House' crash. He wrote under the pseudonym 'Casque' for *Autocar*, was a recipient of two BRDC gold stars, post-war President of the 500 Club, Vice President of the Vintage Sports Car Club, and much else. Father of 1950s/60s racer and 1964 Targa Florio winner Colin Davis, he was born 9 January 1887 and died on his 94th birthday in 1981.

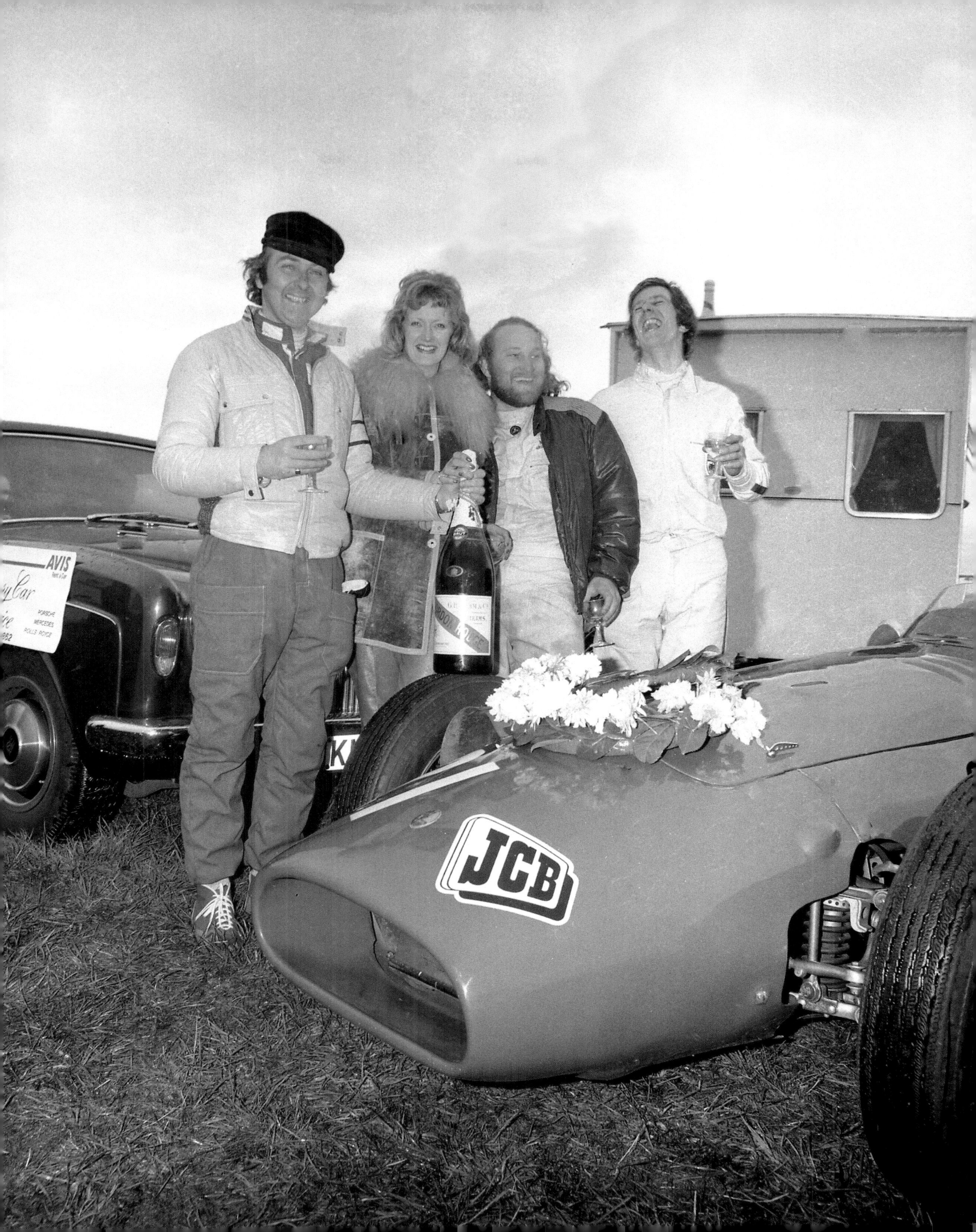
AVIS
JCB

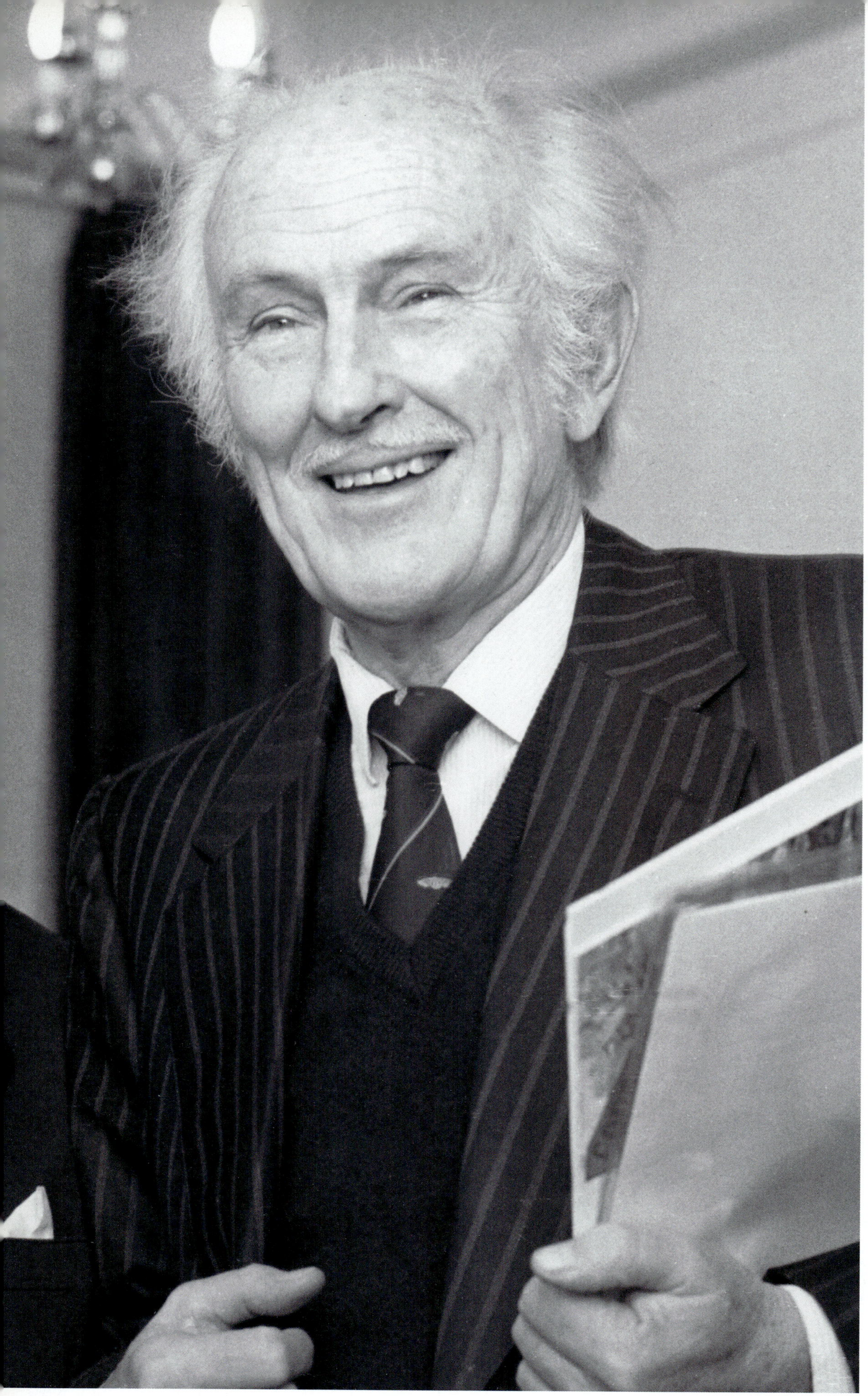

← Charles Amherst Villiers, brilliant engineer and polymath. He was the creator of the famous 'Blower' Bentley supercharger, friend of Raymond Mays (ERA and BRM) who supercharged the Mays 1922 Vauxhall TT in the 1920s, designer of Donald Campbell's first LSR car Bluebird in 1927, cousin of Winston Churchill, consultant for many years on space vehicles in the USA, and for BRM, and self-taught portrait painter (Graham Hill and Ian Fleming – the Hill picture is hanging in the National Portrait Gallery). He was born on 9 December 1900 of Ernest Amherst Villiers and the Hon. Elaine Augusta Guest, and died on 12 December 1991.

→ As recognisable as Big Ben and probably the most photographed racing driver of his era, Graham Hill in ready-to-go mode in his BRM P578, immaculately trimmed moustache and all.

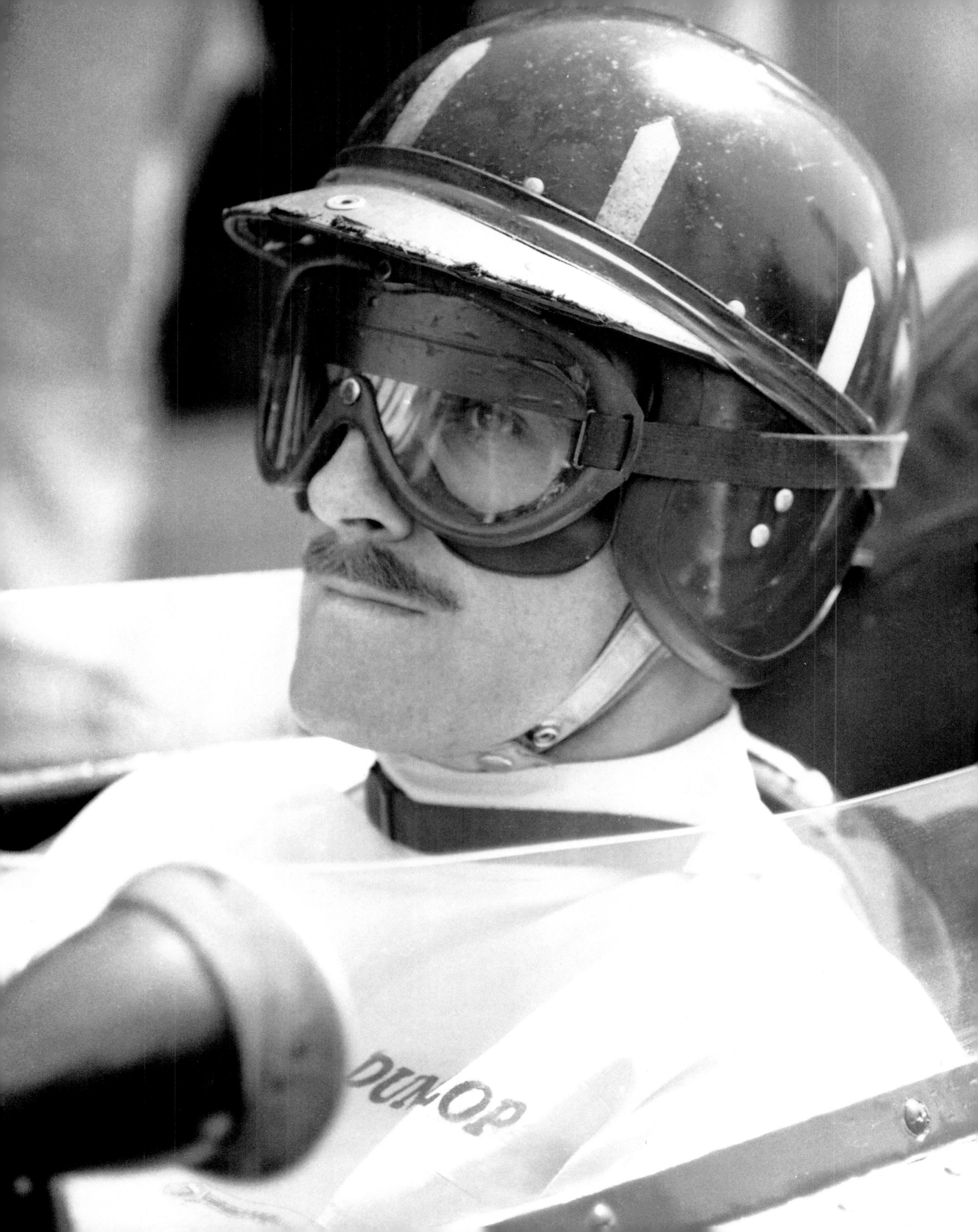
DUNLOP

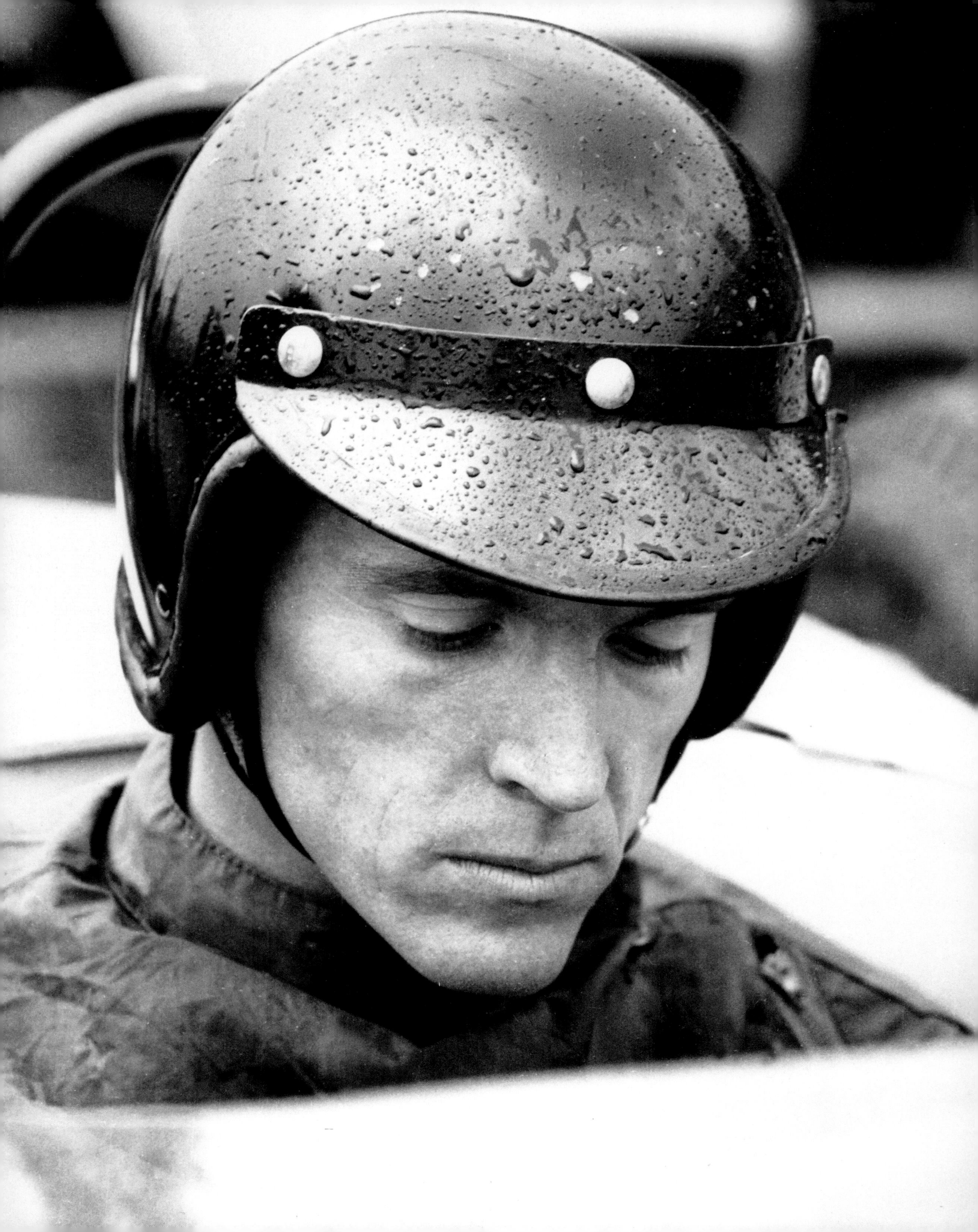

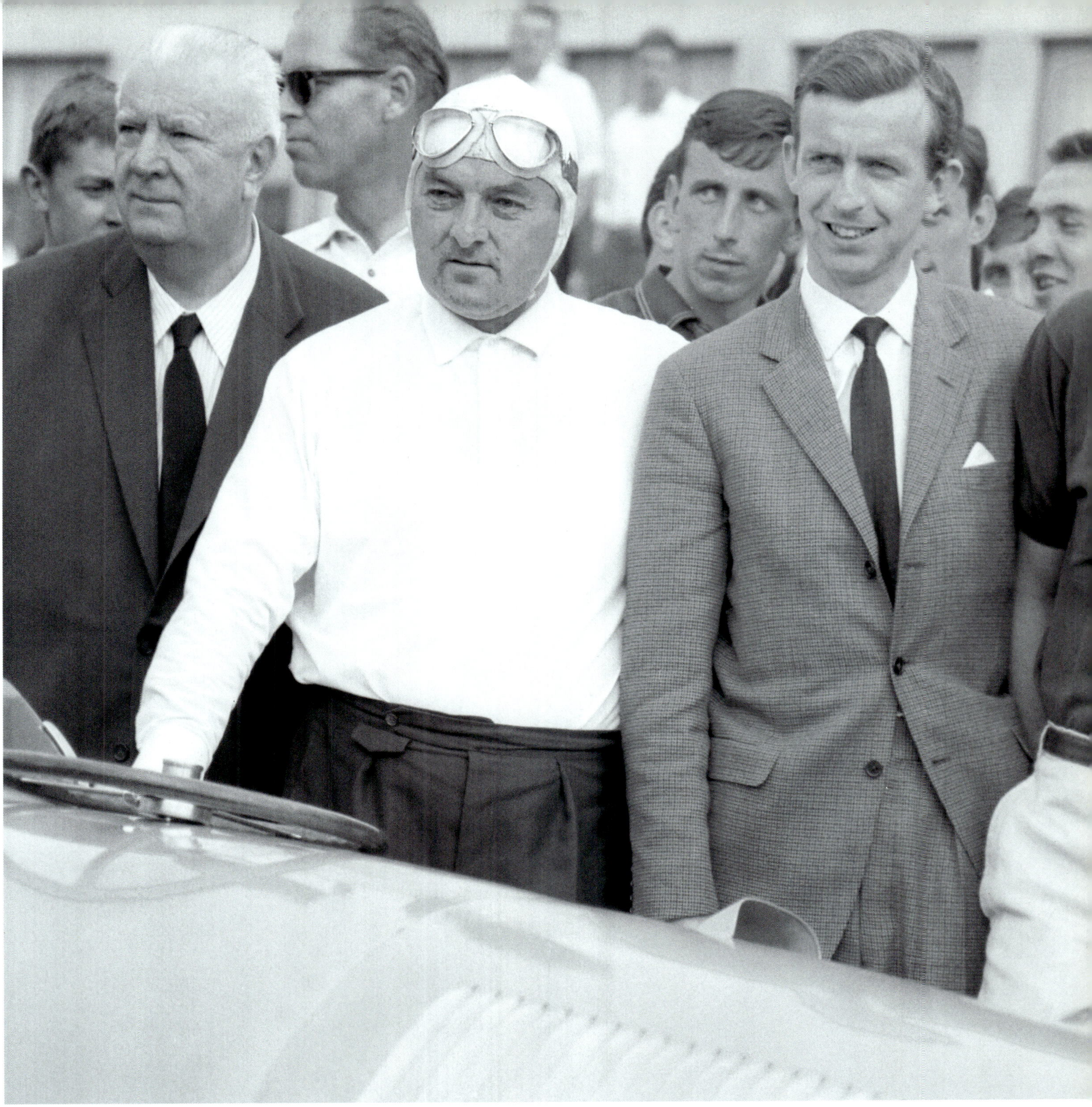

↑ Legendary pre- and post-war Mercedes Benz team manager Alfred Neubauer (29 March 1891 – 21 August 1980) with his 1930s champion driver Herman Lang (6 April 1909 – 19 October 1937) and a very English looking Tony Brooks at the Nürburgring during one of Daimler Benz's frequent PR appearances with their W125 and W154 supercharged 'Silver Arrow' racers.

← A sombre looking Daniel Sexton Gurney somewhere on a rainy day circa 1961, possibly in Louise Bryden-Brown's Lotus 18. Note how less bulky his period Bell helmet is compared to later evocations.

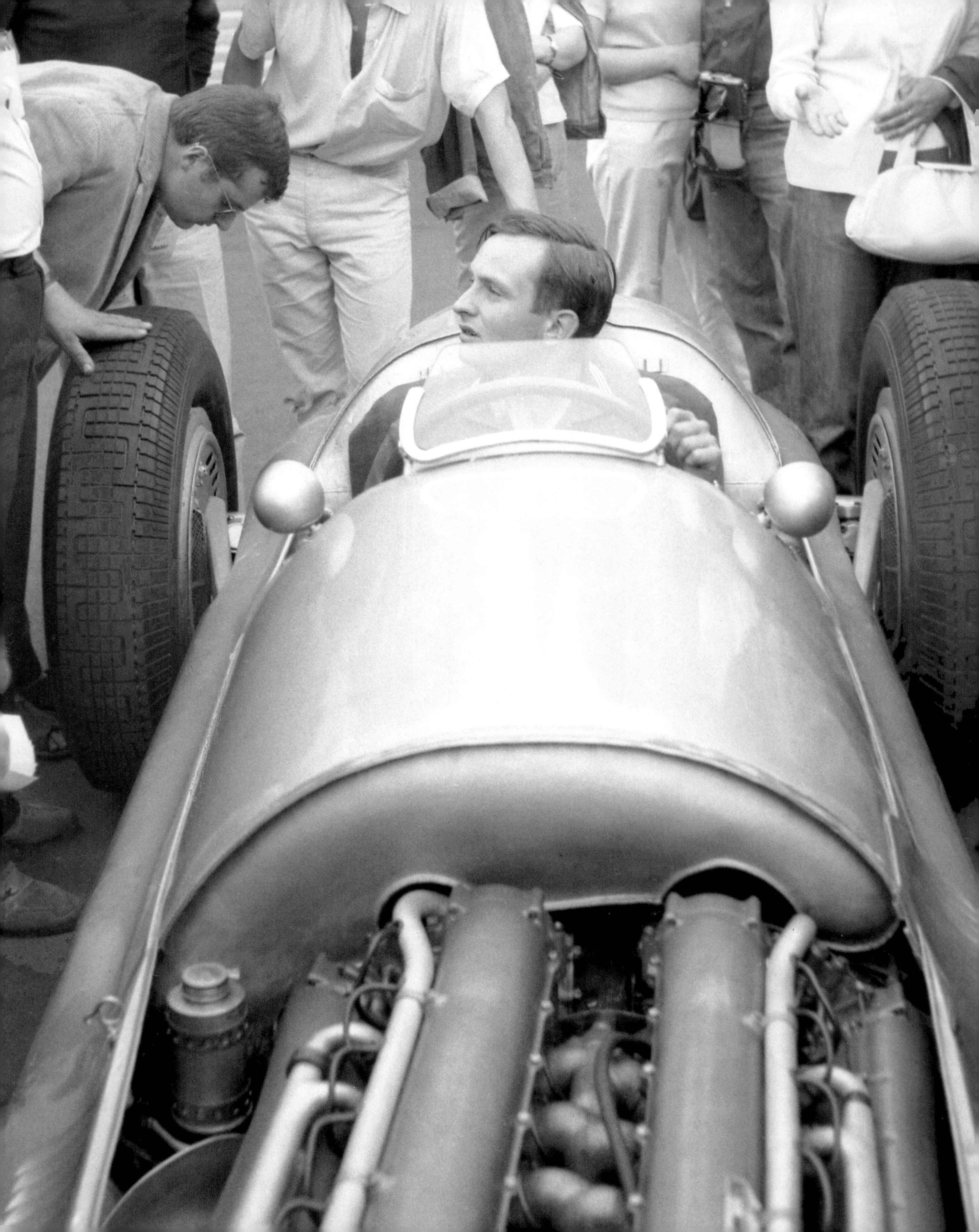

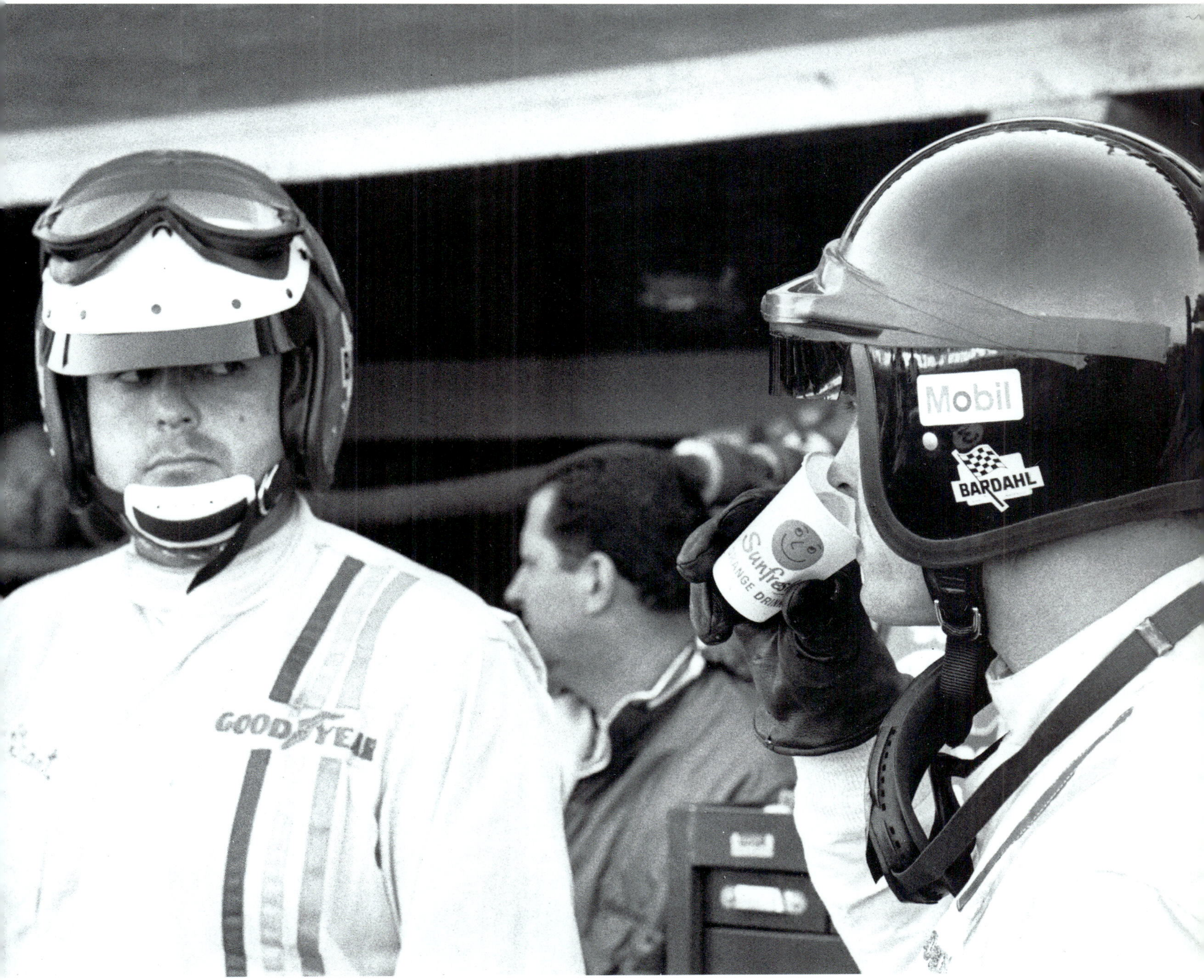

↑ If looks could kill! But Dan Gurney continues supping his *Sunfresh* orange drink at Le Mans 1966, whilst co-driver Jerry Grant seems upset. They led the race until head gasket failure, caused by a holed radiator, stopped them on lap 257. Perhaps that is the reason for Jerry's murderous glare.

← Chris Amon wonders if he can win a GP in the 1939 Mercedes Benz W154. Just look at the size of those rear wheels, and the pukka pre-war Continental tyres with their horizontal tread pattern. The aeroscreens on these cars were reputedly made of bullet proof glass to withstand the stones and assorted detritus thrown up during the continental road races like Pescara where speeds exceeded 180mph on surfaces bordered by grass and rocky verges.

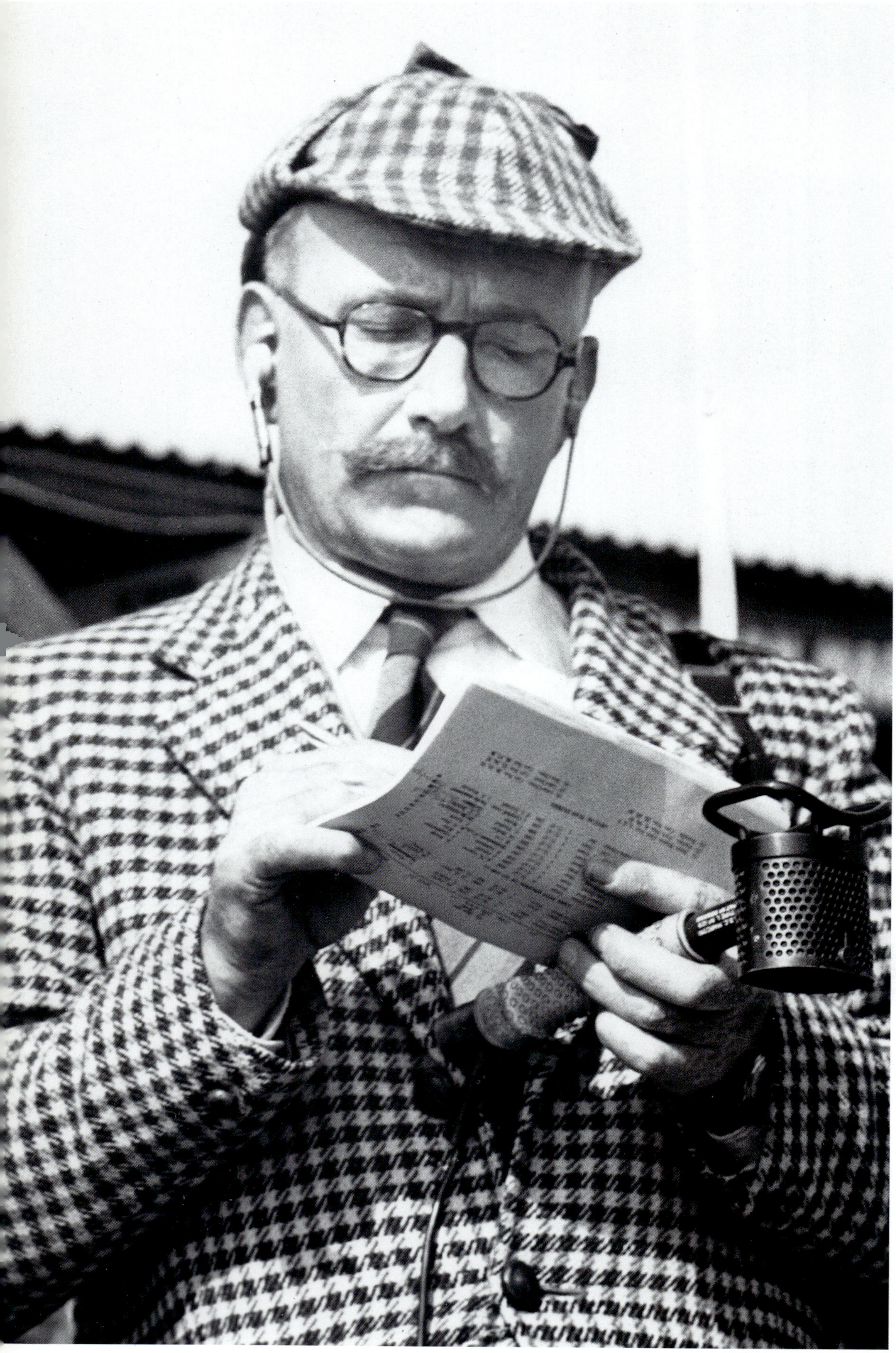

➔ Shane Summers had driven Terry Bartram's Lotus 15 successfully during 1960, and for the following year his mentor had bought a brand new Cooper T53 for his protégé. He had already raced it at the II Grosser Pries von Wien on Aspern airfield and qualified second-quickest to Moss, finally being placed eighth after the steering broke, and at the BARC 200 at Aintree where he finished 12th. Michael captures him sitting in the Cooper (F1-8-61) at Brands Hatch shortly before his fatal accident at Paddock Bend during testing, on Thursday 1 June 1961, for the Silver City International Trophy. Mike had come to know him and was deeply affected by his death.

← John Vary Bolster (24 May 1910 – 13 January 1984), he of the JAP-powered 'Bloody Mary' sprint and hillclimb special, sometime ERA racer, BBC commentator, author and long-time technical editor and road tester for Gregor Grant's *Autosport*. His deerstalker hat, check jackets and collar and tie perfectly complimented his frightfully posh accent, but this masked a character capable of the most outrageous comments and behaviour.

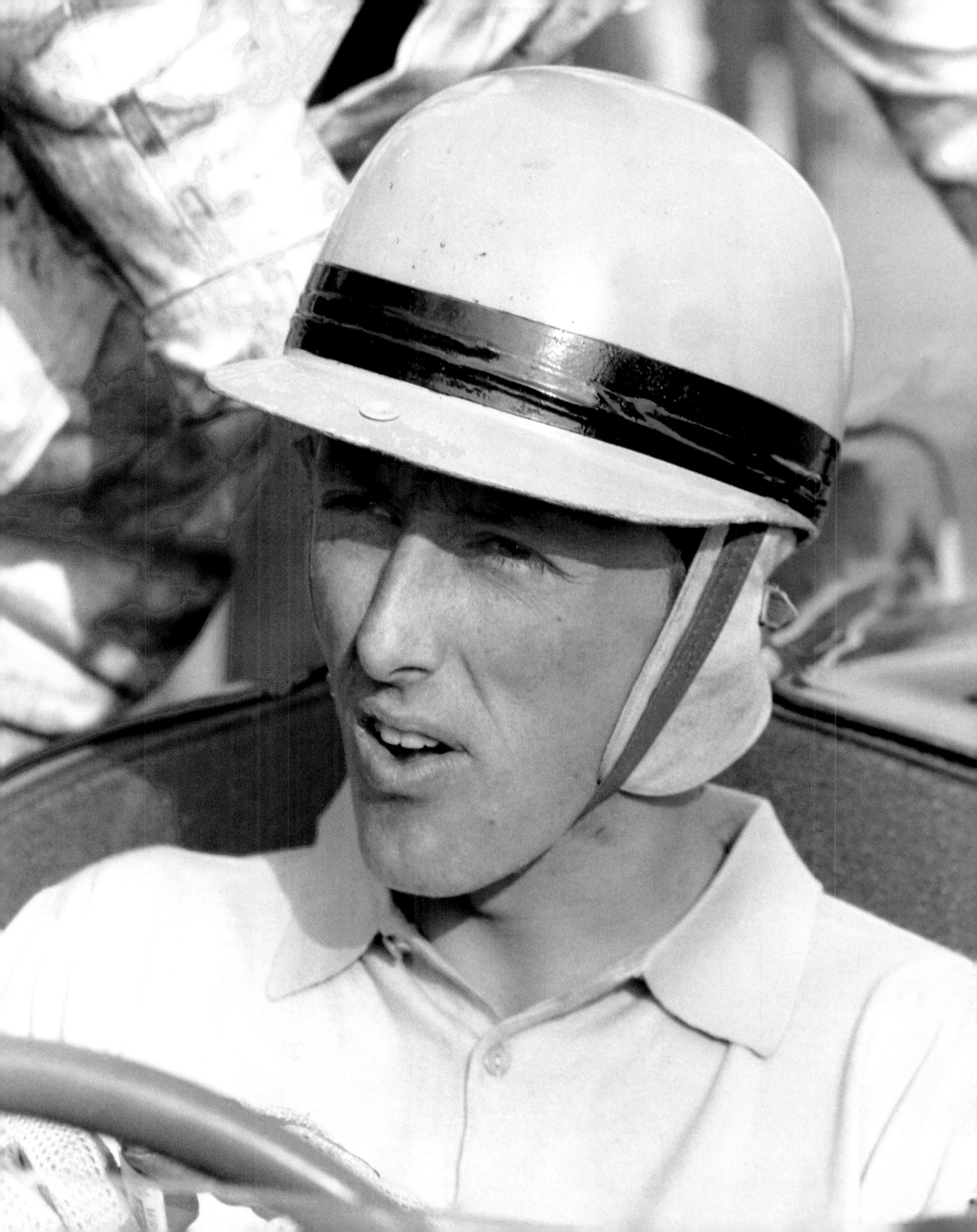

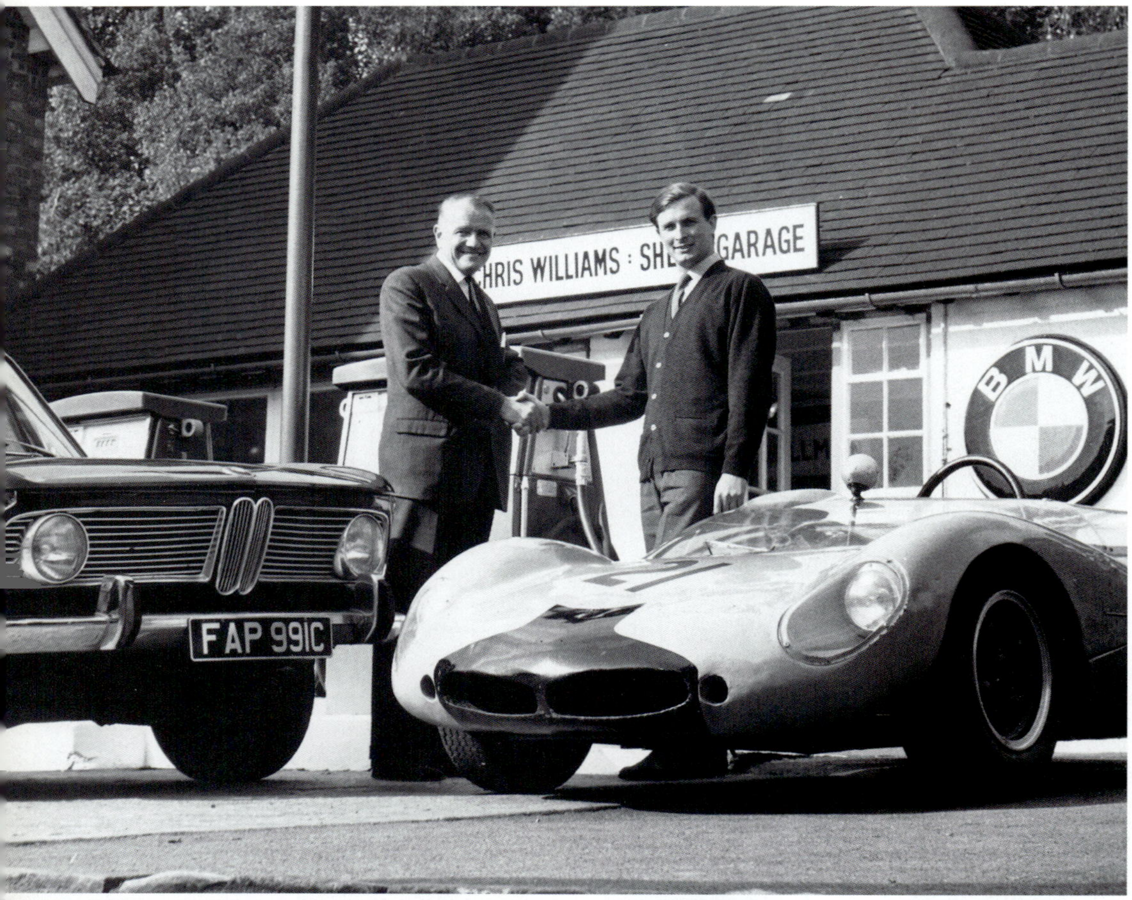

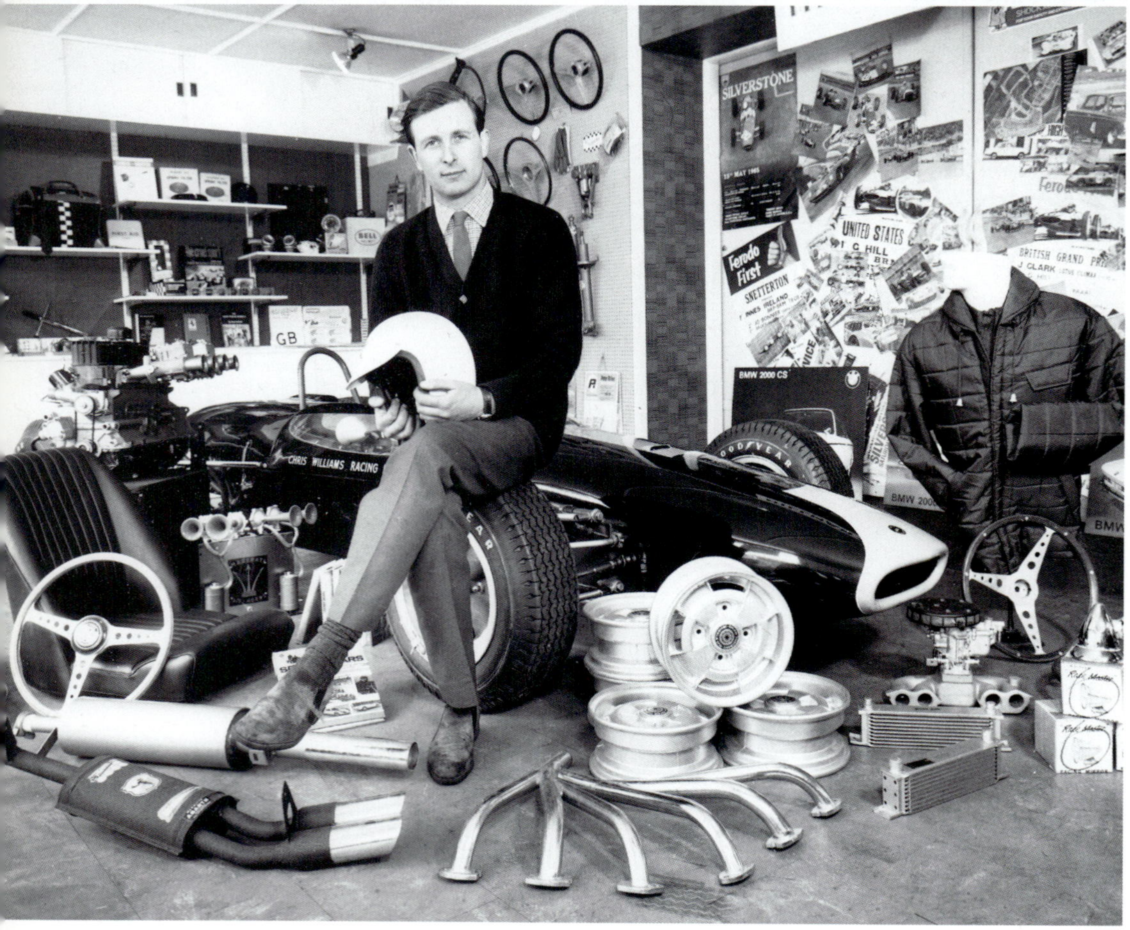

← Christopher Mayo Williams was born in India, educated at Cheltenham, read Engineering at Oxford, and was a near neighbour of Mike who ran Shere Garage, in Shere, near Guildford, selling BMWs. Here, he hands over a BMW to a no doubt happy customer. He started his competition career rallying an Austin Healey Sprite whilst still at University, progressing to a Lotus 7, followed by a successful stint with a Lotus 23B. In 1965 he raced this unique BMW-powered Lotus 23-based machine, that featured Brabham suspension and the distinctive Ferrari-style nostrils, to many wins. For 1966 he raced a F3 Brabham BT18 around Europe, and in 1967 a BT21, winning the East German GP at Schleiz, the Vila Real F3 race in Portugal, and the King Hussein Trophy at Ingliston. During 1968 he joined Alan Rollinson at Red Rose Motors to drive Chevron B9s in F2, but these proved tricky to develop. He had also raced a F2 Lola for David Bridges (finishing fifth in his first F2 race at Hockenheim in 1967), and a Merlyn for Bob Gerard. On 29 March 1969, whilst testing a Merlyn Mk 12 at Silverstone in preparation for a full F2 season with the Gerard-Merlyn team, he crashed at Becketts, dying instantly in the impact.

← A typical assortment of what were known at the time as 'bolt-on goodies' sold by Chris Williams, sitting on his Brabham BT18. Abarth exhaust systems, manifolds, steering wheels, Weber carburettors, alloy wheels, Koni shock absorbers, bucket seats, oil coolers, Bell helmets, rally jackets, driving gloves, Race Master racing mirrors, the whole panoply of such things to make you look better and go faster (you hoped)! It was the automotive form of cosmetics and they frequently promised more than they could deliver, with exception. Look at the back wall and you can see pictures (some taken by Mike) from Silverstone, Brands Hatch, Monaco, Clermont-Ferrand, and Monza in 1965, with McLaren, Surtees, Bonnier, G. Hill, all identifiable, so this probably dates it and the preceding photograph to 1966. Note also the BMW 2000 CS posters (bottom right) and a copy of Robert Daley's iconic book *The Cruel Sport* on the shelving to the left, level with Chris's shoulder.

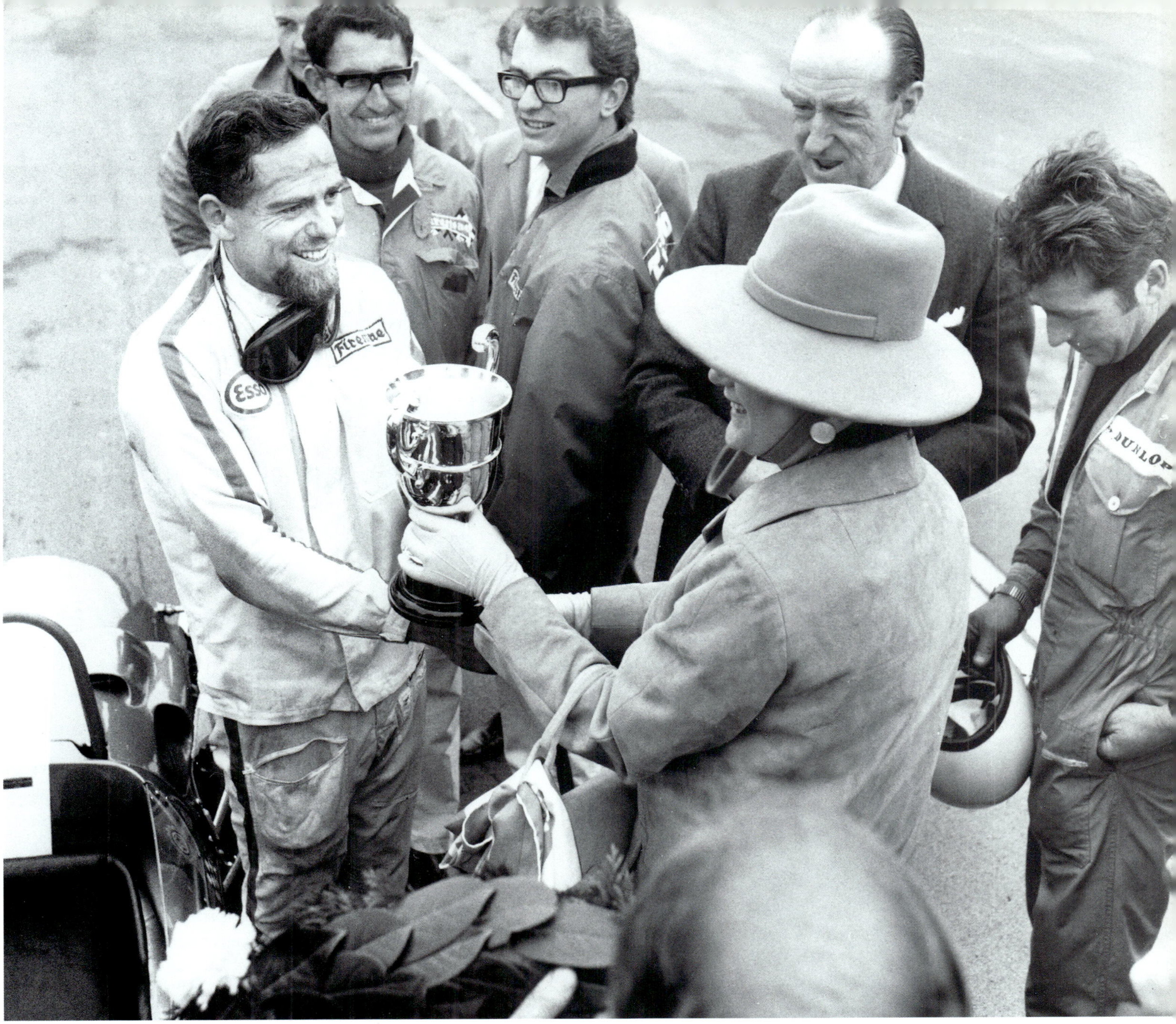

↑ I showed this picture to Peter Westbury in 2009 and he replied: "This is, I 95% believe, me winning the International Caravan Trophy at Silverstone in April 1967. I have no recall as to the two VIPs, but there is me looking very happy having just driven my Felday Engineering's BT21. In the background over my head is John Church, over my left shoulder Peter Moakes, the second man I think is an ex-Brabham/MRD Australian guy, one of many that helped Ron Tauranac to build the cars in Weybridge. Just visible behind him is Ann Marriott, our secretary. Extreme right is Jim Charman, my chief race mechanic all through my career – and still living locally to Forest Green. There is a little story about why I am so happy. In 1966 I still did not circuit race out of deference to my family's wishes. I had two RAC hillclimb championships under my belt (1963 and '64). I had tested the F1 4WD BRM on a few occasions because I was one of a few folk to have experience of 4WD racing cars, the Harry Ferguson Research P99 and the two Felday 4WD sports cars, (1.7-litre V8 BRM and 7 litre Ford V8). One day testing the Felday 4 using a well-known professional driver, I was not getting the feedback I needed so, at Brands club circuit, I drove my car to glean the info. I found I could drive it faster than the paid man and, of course, get the info and have fun. After I retired at the end of 1972, I did not go to a race meeting for three years: it hurt too much. I was also going through a divorce. In 1975 I was introduced to (Sir) George Martin – Beatles arranger. We shared a catamaran, which I sailed from Scotland to Menorca for our use. We kept the yacht for four years." Today Peter Westbury lives happily in Tobago, West Indies with Jenny his second wife.

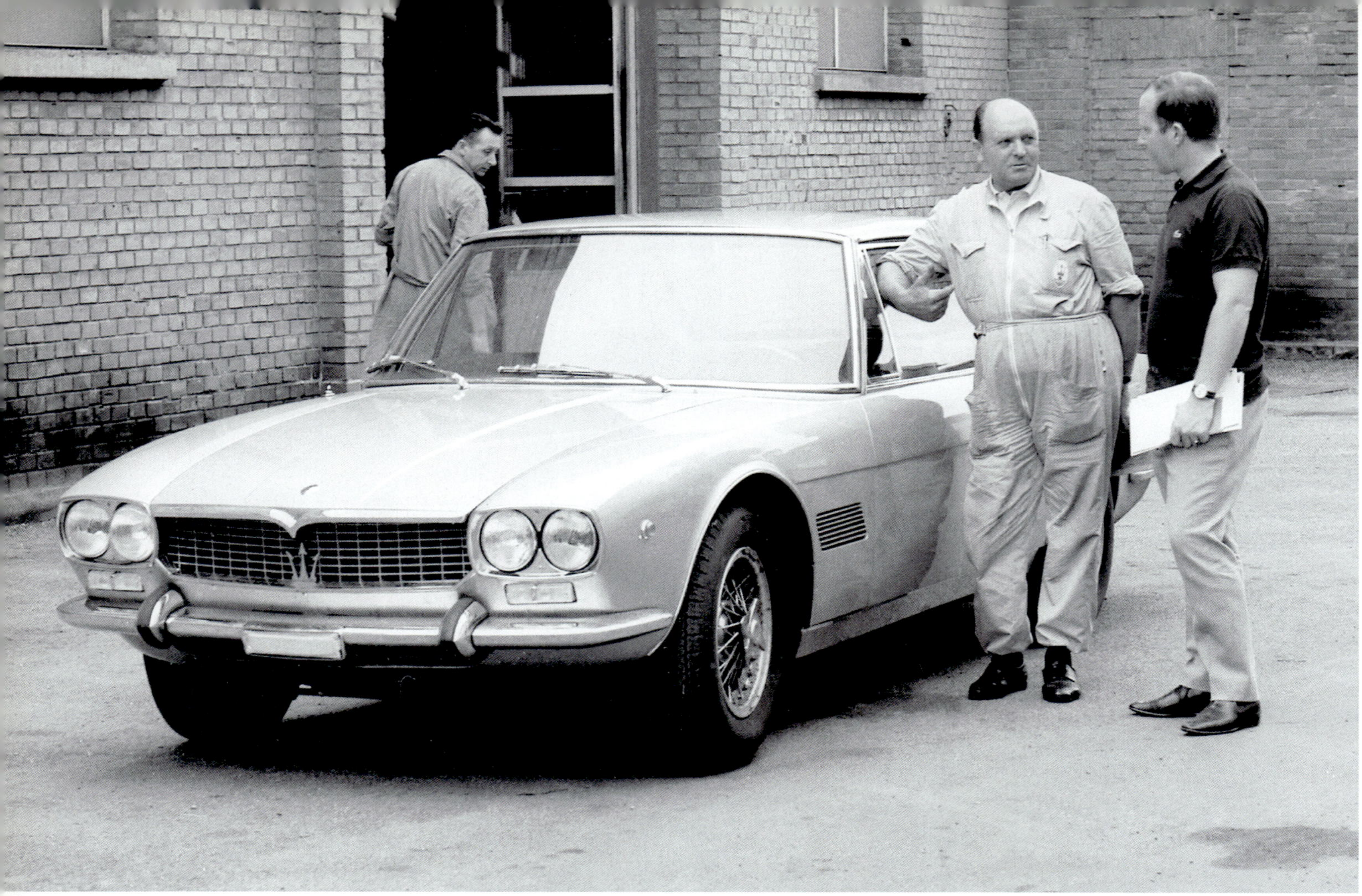

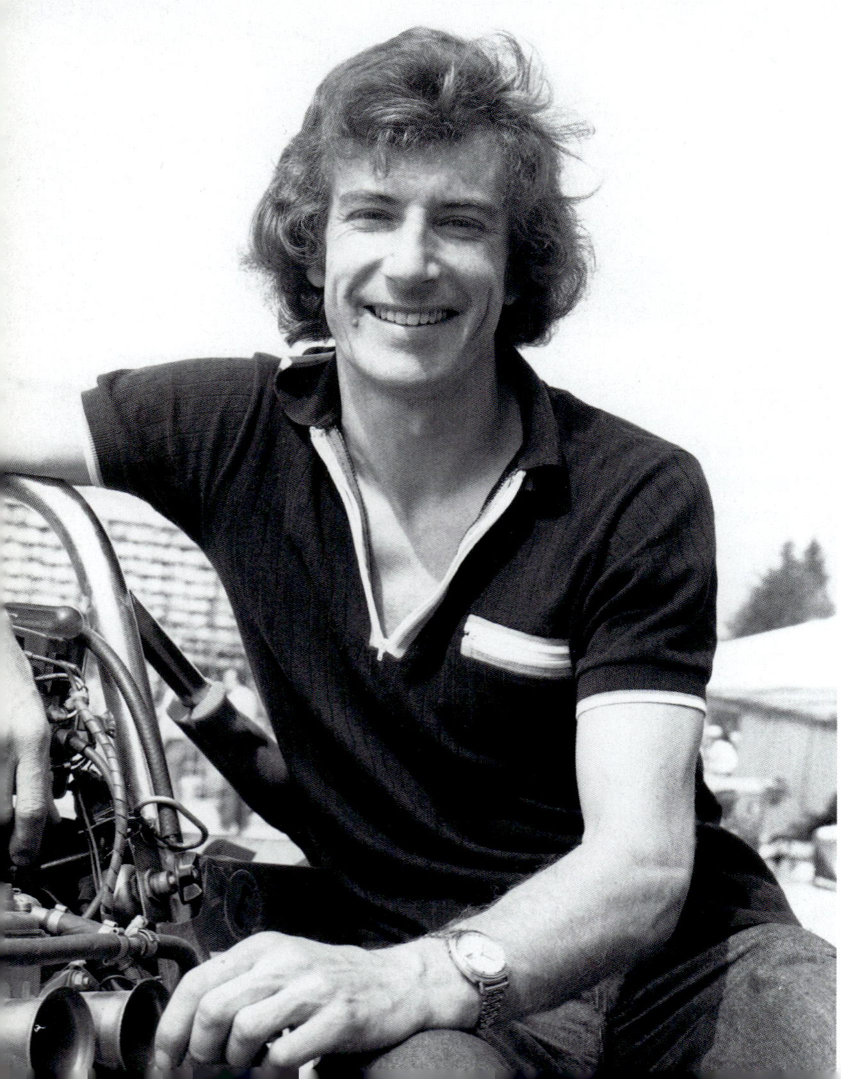

↑ Guerrino Bertocchi, long-time Maserati tester and 'substitute' driver for Maserati, speaks to Eoin Young at the Maserati factory before testing the Quattroporte in the picture. Bertocchi, having survived all those years pounding at record speeds around Modena airport and elsewhere in assorted single-seater and sports racing Masers, was killed aged 74 passengering an errant customer in 1981. Tragically, his son Aurelio also died in a traffic accident four years later.

← Tony Trimmer was another talented but perennially underfunded Brit who had success in FF and F3 in the late 1960s and 1970. He actually drove the works Lotus 72 R5 at the Brands Hatch ROC in 1971, but retired. He finally made it into the F1 World Championship in 1975 but it was a futile struggle with the awful Maki F101 and 102 during 1975–6, and unsurprisingly he failed to make the grid on all four occasions. In 1977 and 1978 he tried to qualify the Melchester Racing Surtees TS19 and McLaren M23 at the British GP, but this too was unattainable. His was very much the fate of many such British racers of the period, whose full potential was never realised because of uncompetitive machinery and inadequate budgets, although he was British F1 champion in 1978.

➔ Graham Birrell, eldest brother of the better-known Gerry Birrell, who sadly died in a crash at Rouen during a F2 race in 1973. Graham, Gerry, and sister Jenny Birrell were all accomplished racers.

🡻 A now retired Innes Ireland drove the Pratt & Whitney gas turbine-powered Lotus 56 Indycar at Silverstone in 1968. As time and tide took its toll he began to resemble a sort of motor racing version of English character actor Trevor Howard.

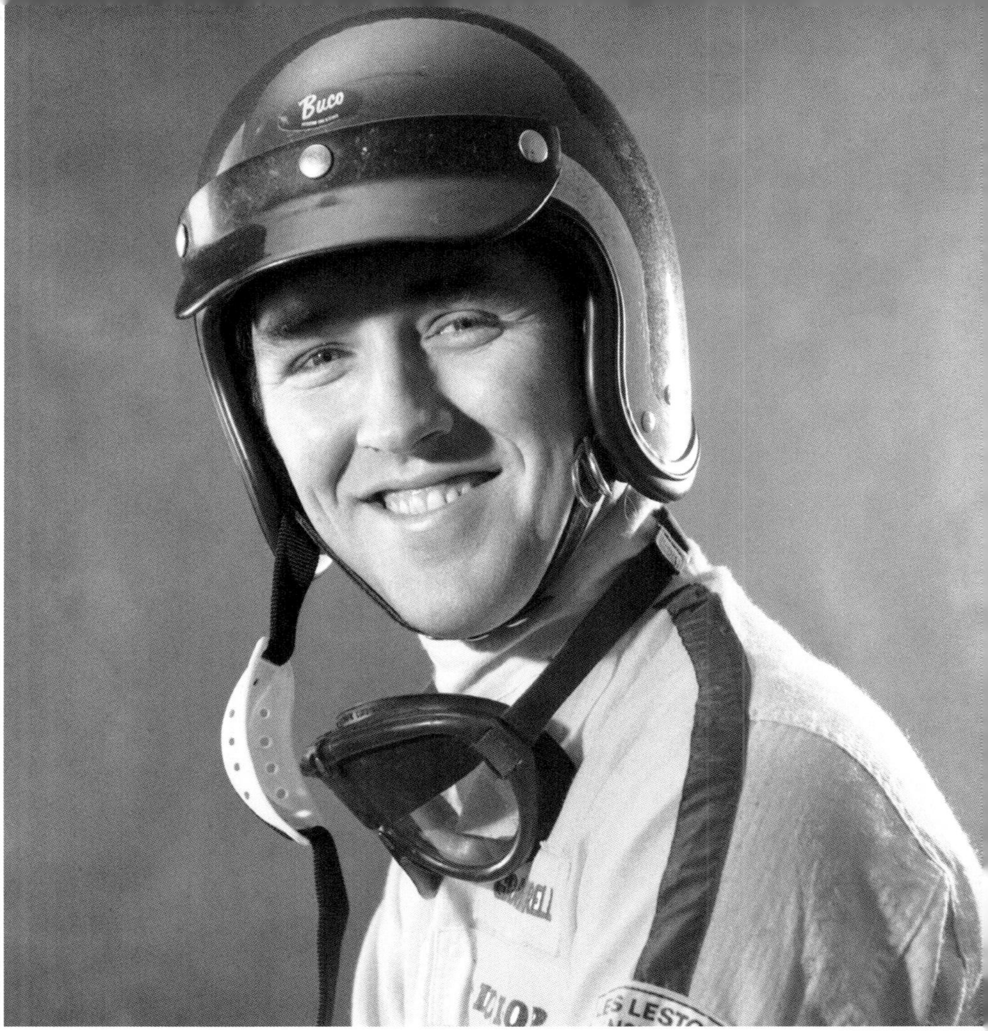

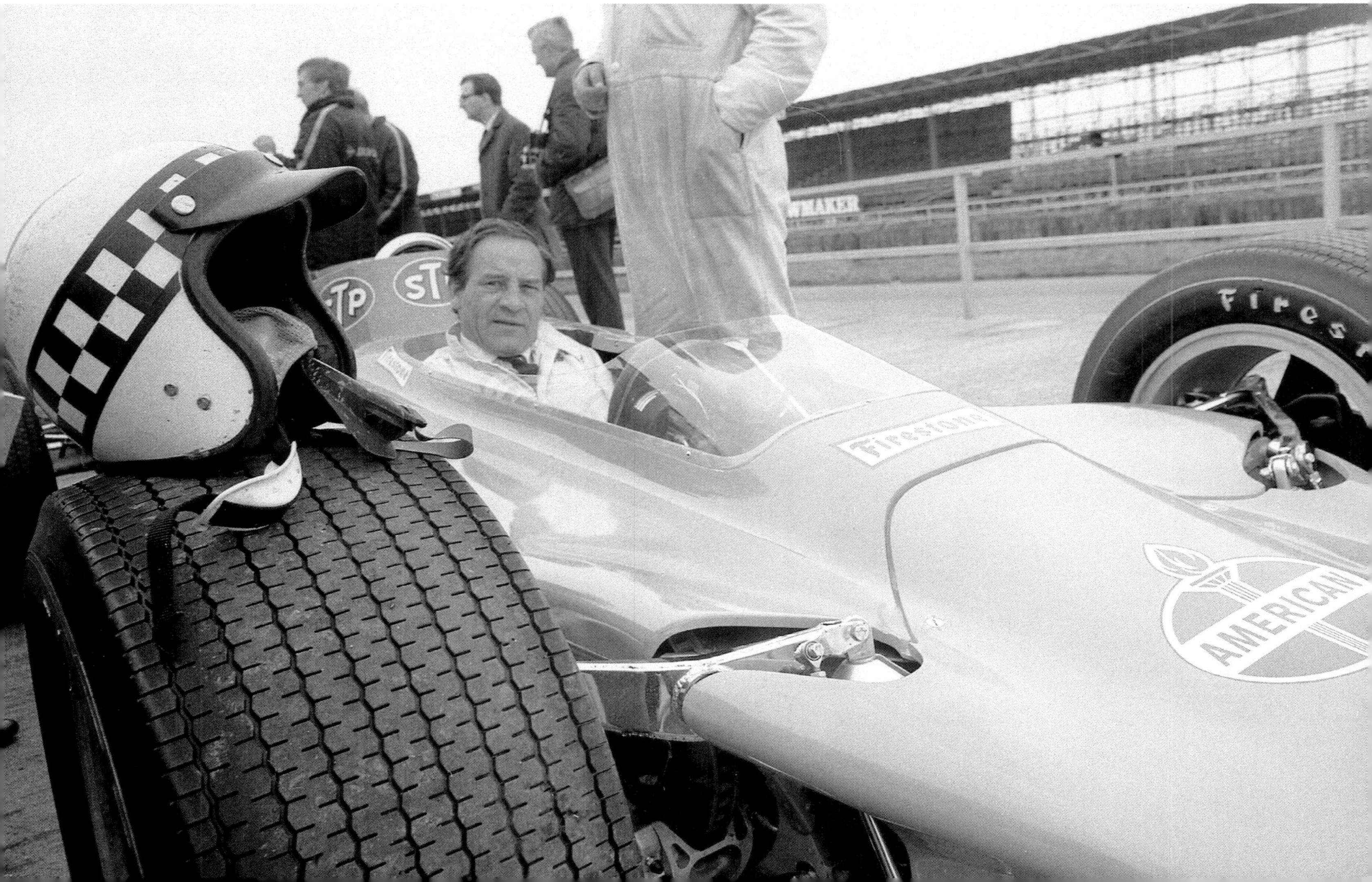

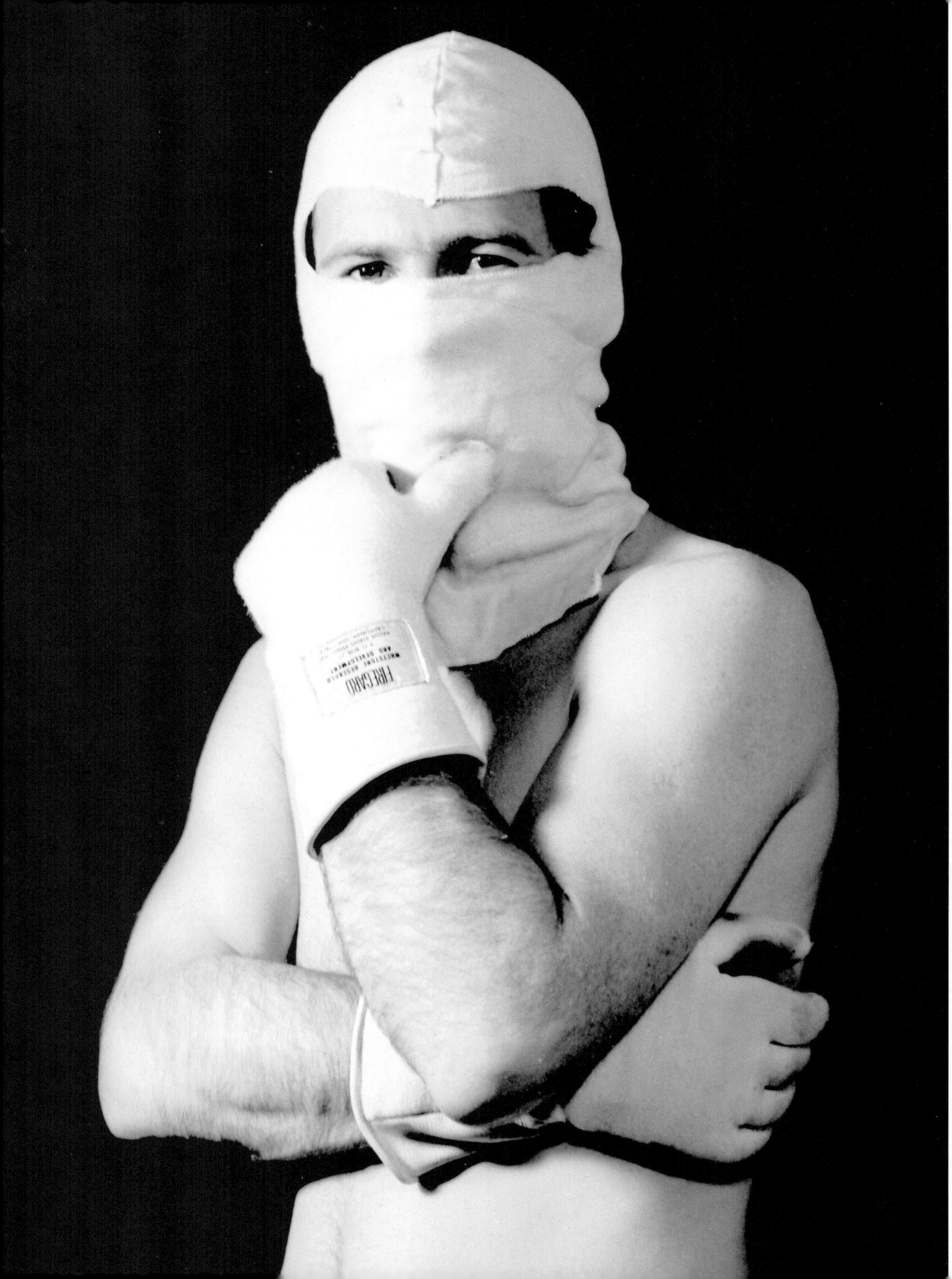

← Vic Elford models this season's fireproof s&m wear somewhere around 1968.

↓ Vic Elford in more orthodox guise, sporting the ever-present cigarette, with David Stone, and a Mk1 Ford Cortina GT at the 1964 RAC Rally, in which they finished third.

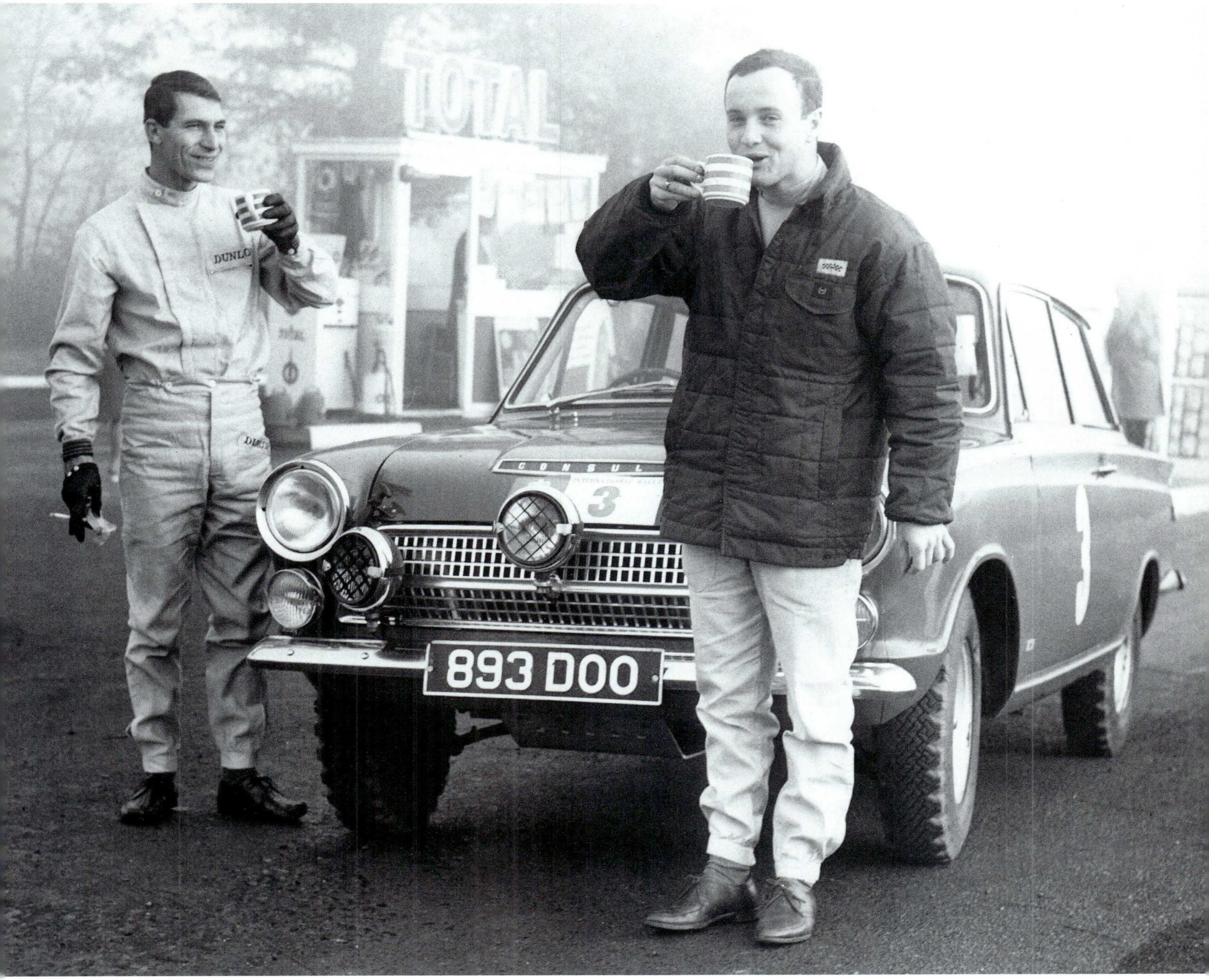

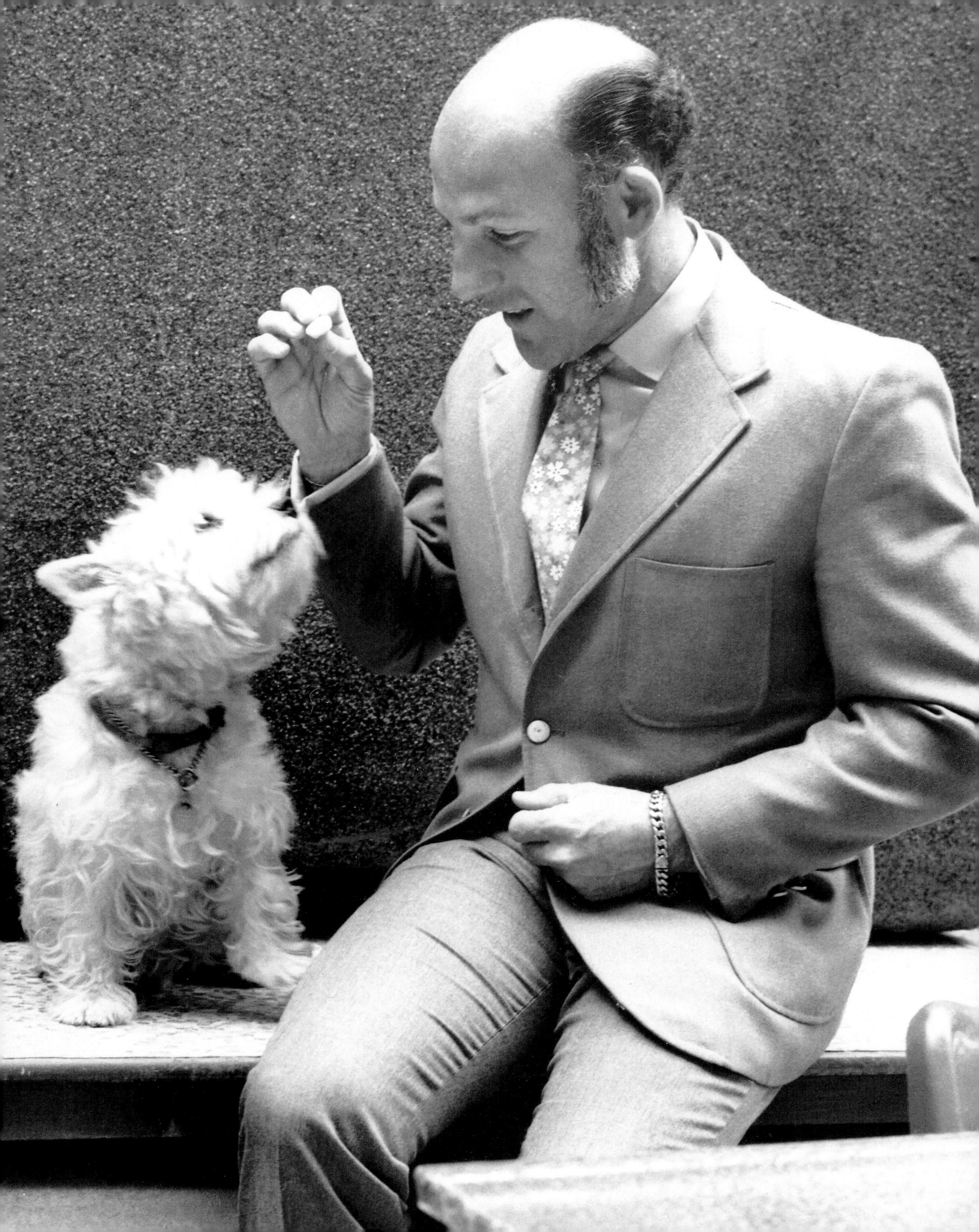

← West Highland white and world famous racing driver in feeding frenzy!

→ Naughty boys at Monaco. Mike's friend Billy Brymon who founded Bryman Airways and ex-McLaren director, famous author and journalist Eoin Young with their photographer passes sitting on a Monegasque wall over 40 years ago.

↓ Would you buy a racing car or three from these men? Alan Rees, Robin Herd, and Max Mosley, with fellow March director Graham Coaker absent.

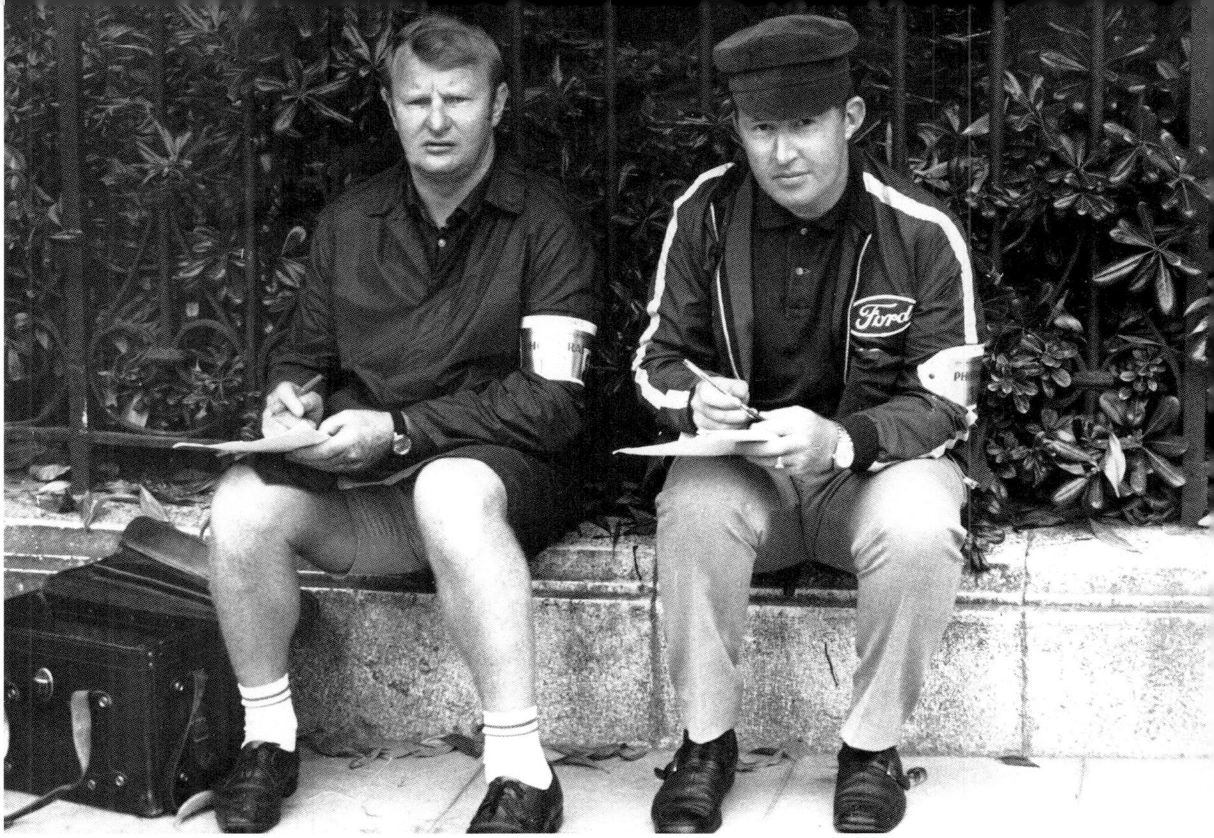

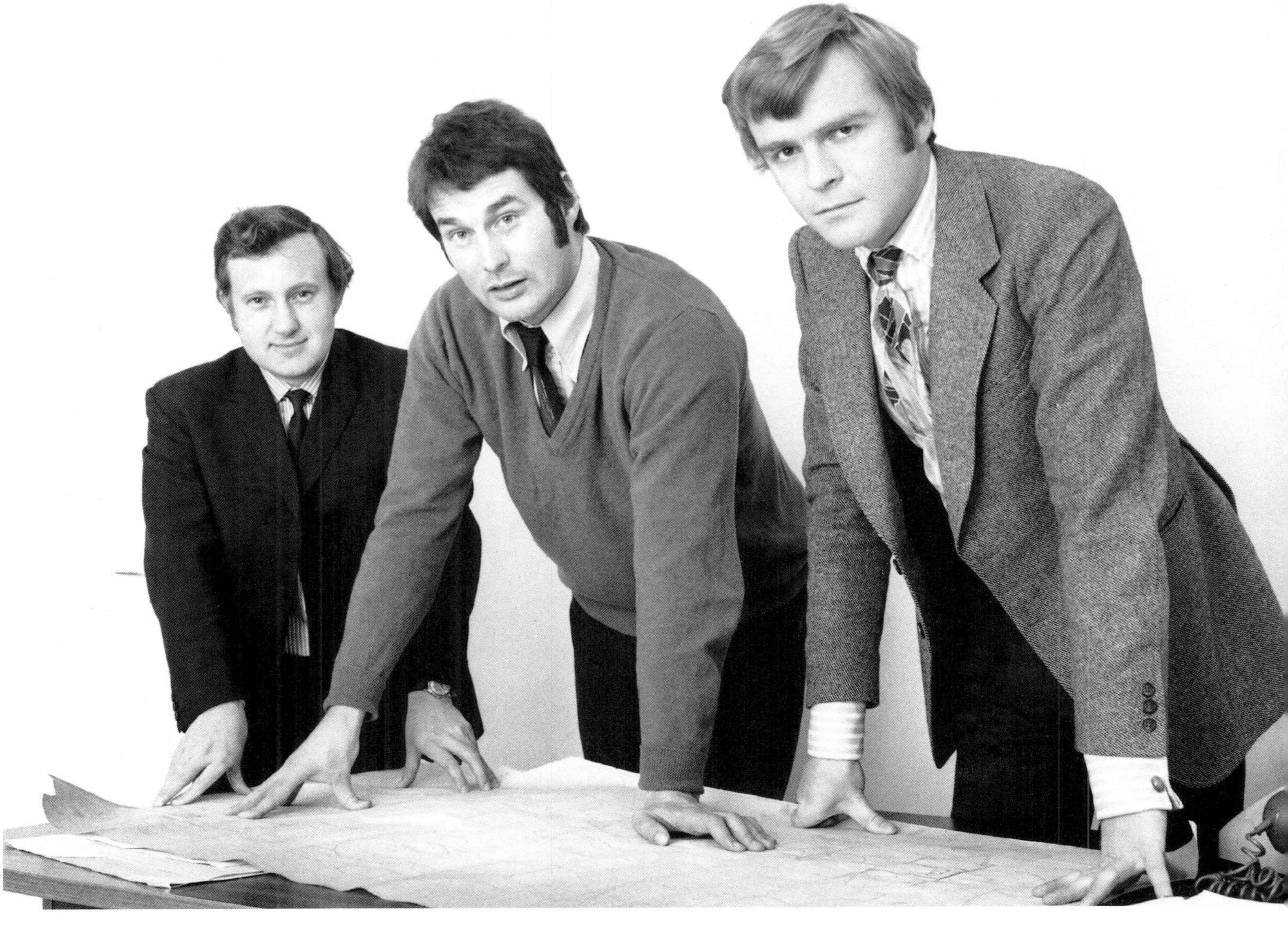

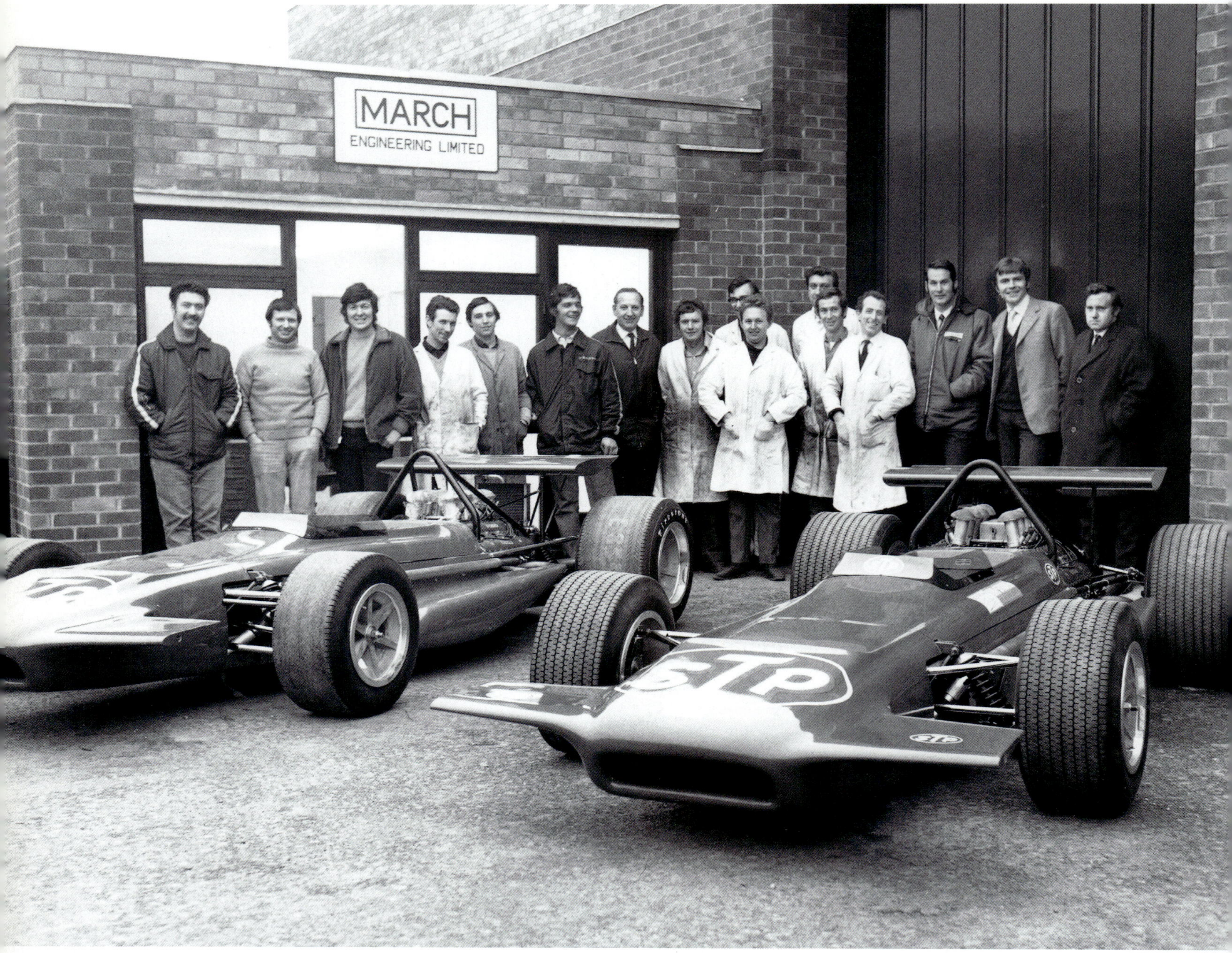

↑ This happy, disparate band of people. The usual suspects, plus those who actually built the cars. I hope that some of them will see this picture. March Engineering and their new March 701s.

→ François Cevert, the man who should have been the first French World Champion driver.

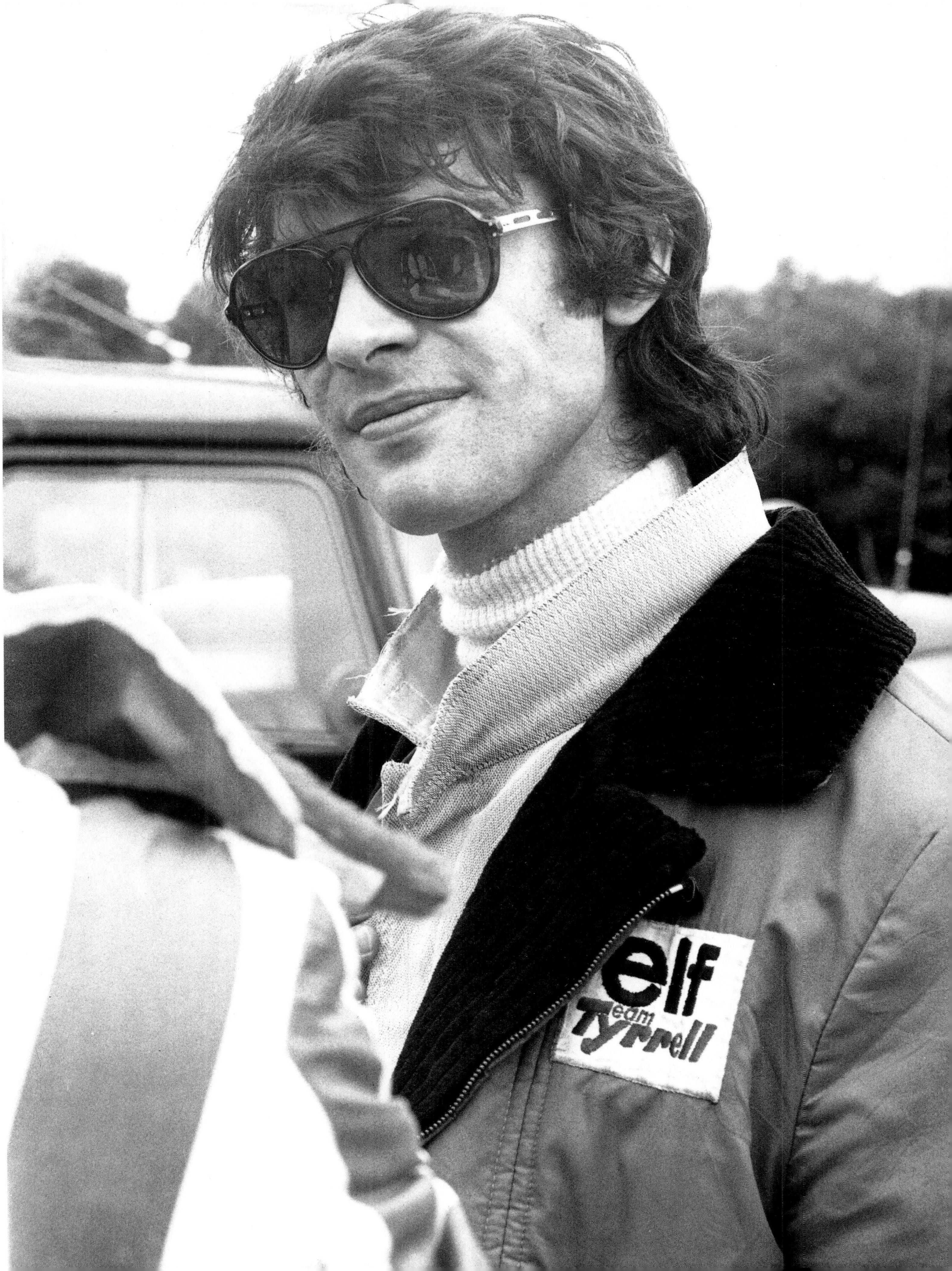
elf
Team
Tyrrell

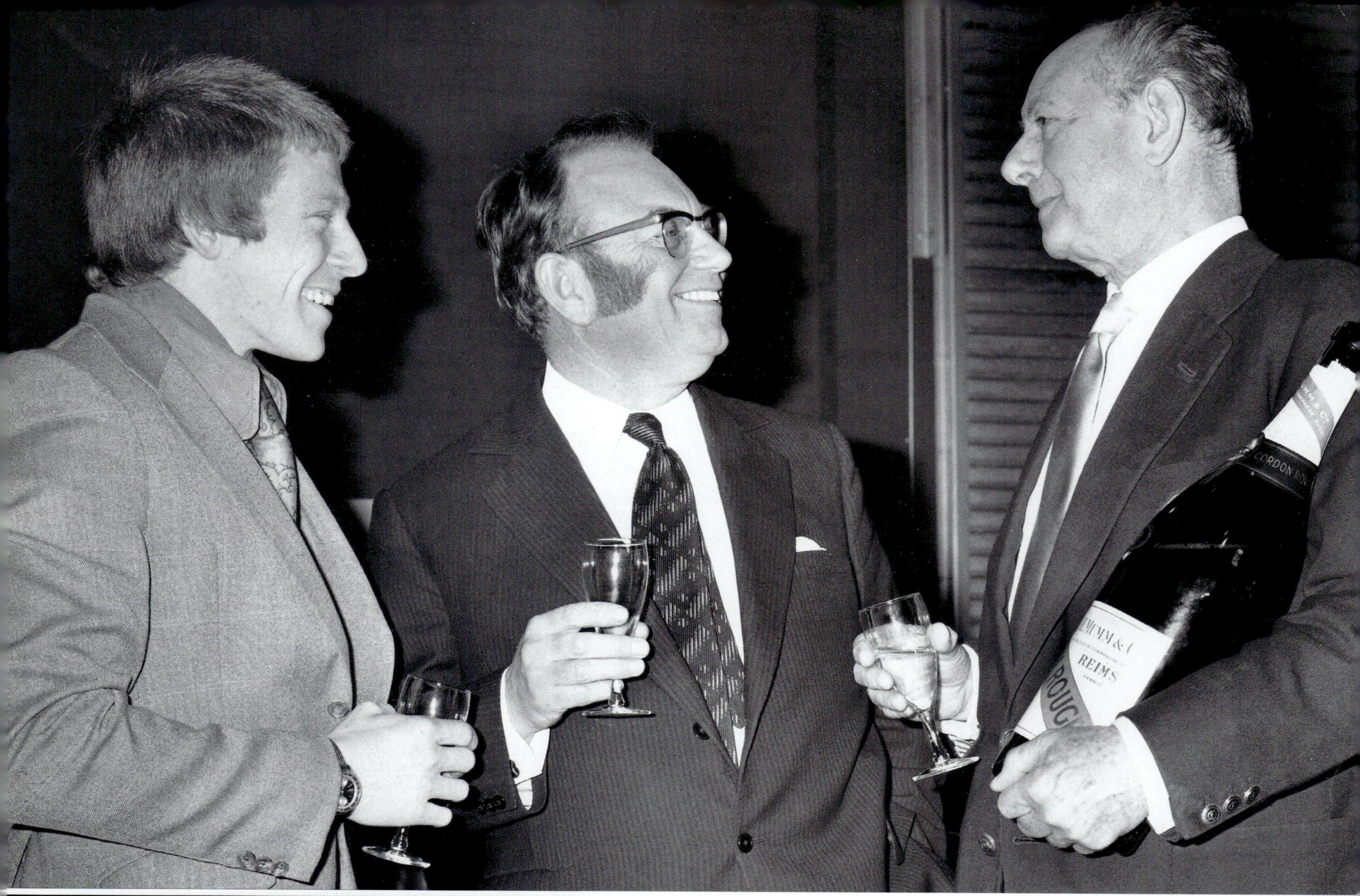

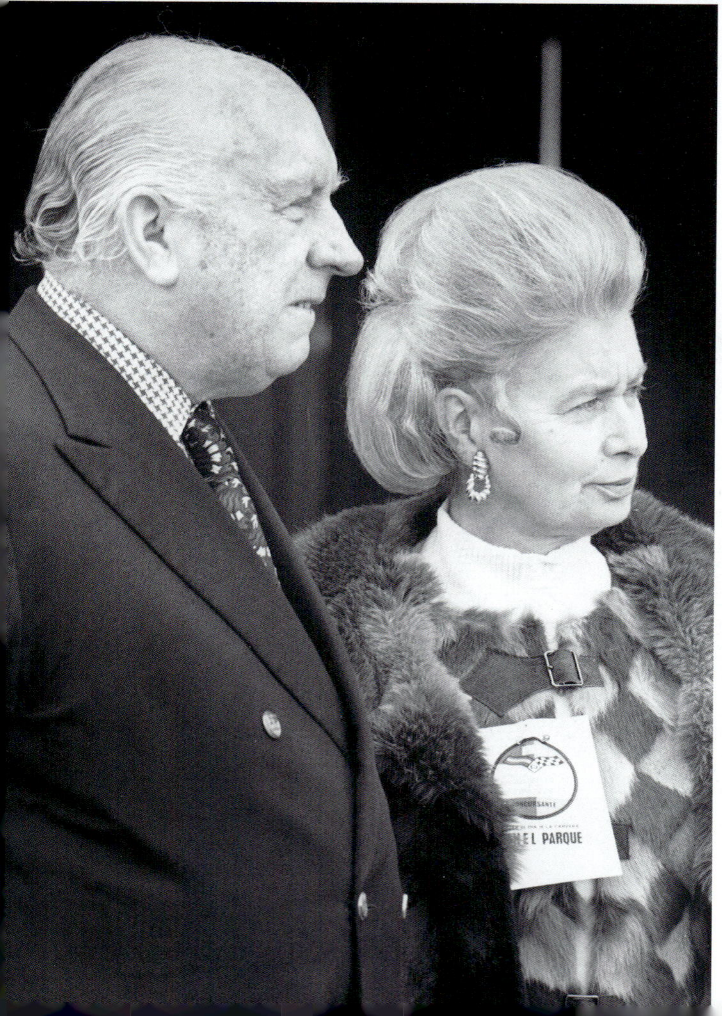

↑ Happier days: Roger Williamson, his mentor Tom Wheatcroft, and Raymond 'I'm in charge of the bottle' Mays. Note Roger's typical early 1970s suit with deep round edged shirt collar and suitably large tie so redolent of the period.

← Louis Stanley was Chairman of BRM (British Racing Motors) and a leading advocate for safety in motor racing. He studied theology at Cambridge and wrote for *Queen* magazine before marrying Jean Barber (née Owen) in 1955, sister of Sir Alfred Owen of Rubery Owen, who had taken over BRM from Raymond Mays. This propelled him straight into GP racing and a role perfectly suited to his authoritative persona. To others he was usually 'Big Lou' and could be rather verbose and at times somewhat pompous. He was Honorary Secretary of the original GPDA (Grand Prix Drivers' Association), creator of the Grand Prix Medical Services (1967), trustee of the Jim Clark Foundation and founder of the Jo Siffert Advisory Council. Born on 6 January 1912, he died two days after his 92nd birthday. His wife Jean passed away in 2002. Here they are during a French GP in typical well-turned-out fashion.

↗ Although the butt of many jokes and criticisms, F1 owed Louis Stanley a great deal. This is the inside of his Grand Prix Medical Unit, a then state-of-the-art mobile facility whose patrons in 1970 included Chris Amon, Jo Bonnier, Jack Brabham, Graham Hill, Colin Chapman, Bruce McLaren, Denny Hulme, Jackie Oliver, Jochen Rindt, Pedro Rodriguez, Jo Siffert, Jackie Stewart, John Surtees, Rob Walker, Jack Durlacher and Frank Williams.

→ John Watson and the late Jean-Marie Balestre, looking suitably unimpressed, at a Michelin promotional event. Love that jacket John!

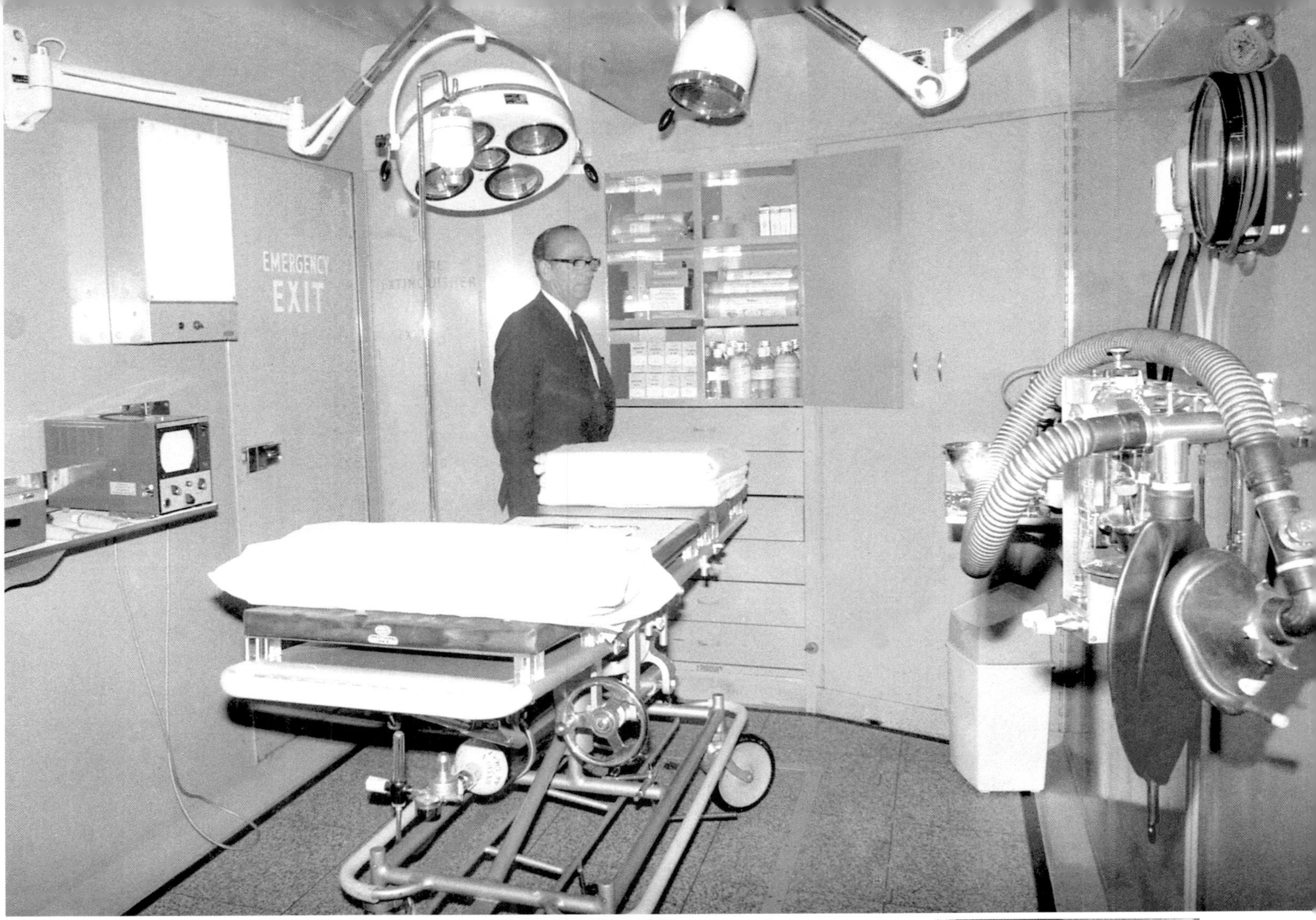
EMERGENCY
EXIT

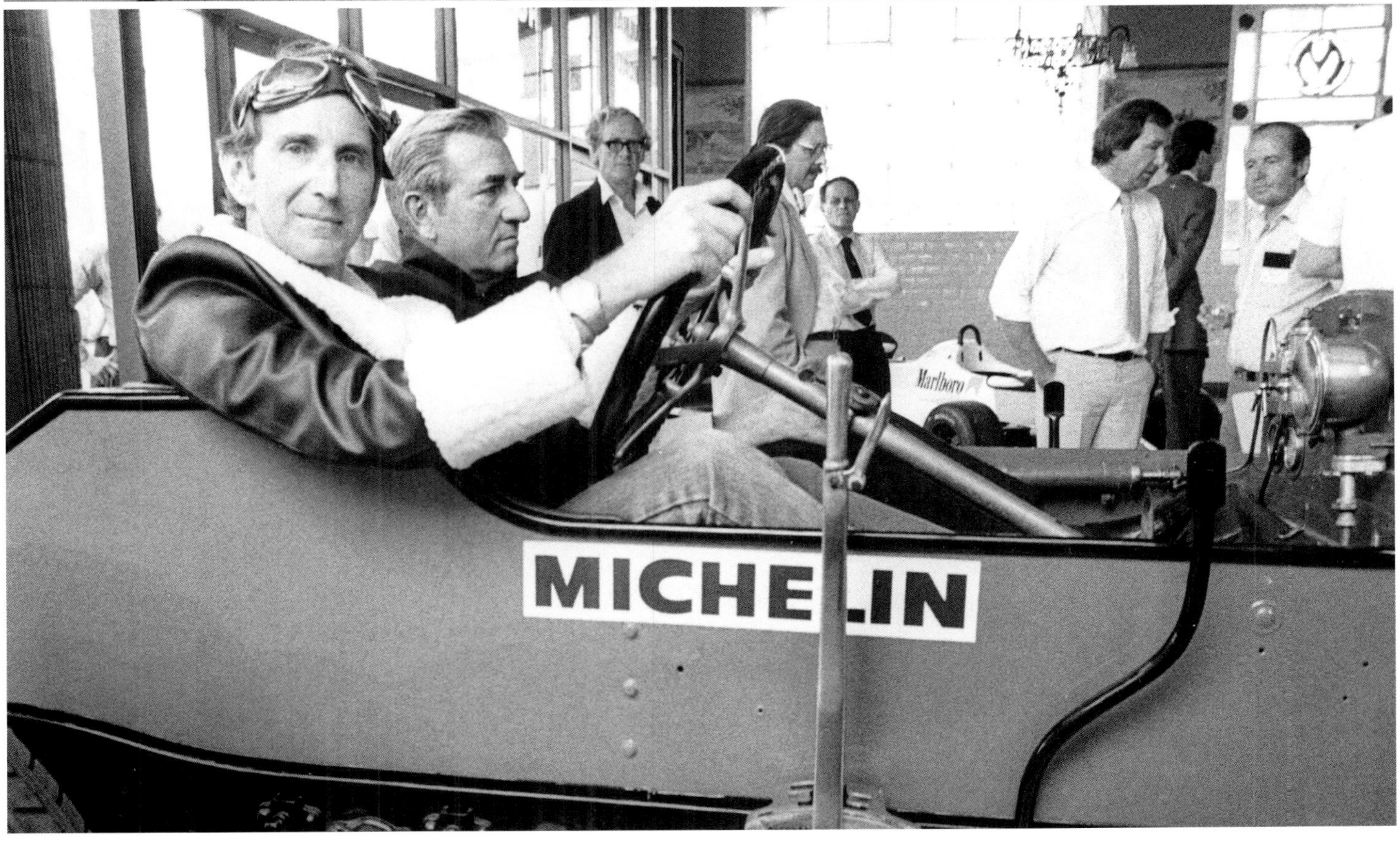
MICHELIN
Marlboro

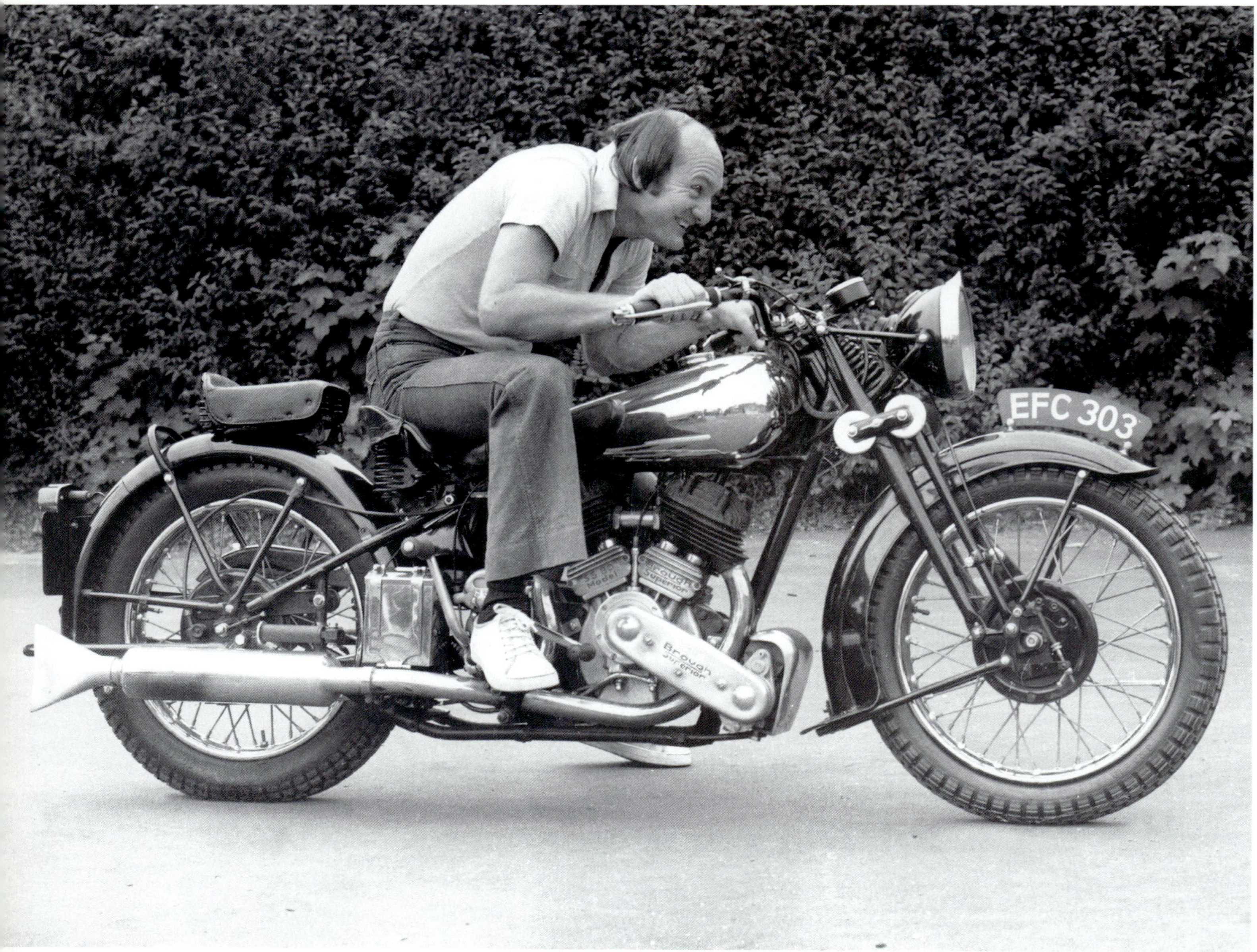

↑ Another famous racer, Mike Hailwood, hamming it up on a Brough Superior SS80 with its period 'fishtail' exhaust end. Unlike many of his bike racing contemporaries, he came from a wealthy background, beginning his career in 1957, and managed to combine both two-wheel and four-wheel racing in 1964–5 with Reg Parnell Racing. When Honda withdrew at the end of 1967, Hailwood returned to motor racing via F5000 and in sports cars for John Wyer. By 1972 he was driving for John Surtees in F1 and displaying race-winning form, but victory eluded him and he joined McLaren in 1974 with Yardley sponsorship. Alas, a crash during the German GP caused him serious ankle injuries that forced him to retire, but in 1978 and 1979 he rode to consecutive TT victories on the Isle of Man, an astonishing comeback after so long away from bikes. In motorcycle racing he won nine World Championships (four with MV Augusta, five with Honda), 76 Grands Prix, and 14 TTs. His 50 F1 championship starts included saving Clay Regazzoni's life at Kyalami in 1973 by pulling him from the burning BRM, for which he was awarded the George Medal. Tragically, he was killed along with his daughter in a traffic accident in 1981 caused by a lorry making an illegal U-turn. Stanley Michael Bailey Hailwood MBE, 2 April 1940 – 23 March 1981.

→ Victor of 52 motorcycle Grands Prix from 125cc to 500cc, plus eight TTs and two 500cc world titles, Phil Read was one of the greatest bike racers of his era. His nickname was 'The Earl' and he was awarded the OBE for his services to the sport in 1979. However, when he raced the 750cc John Player Norton no pillion passengers were allowed. This is taken outside the 1972 Earls Court Motor Show – remember when London had a world famous motor show? Note the omnipresent caravan on far left; what was it about the 1970s and caravans!

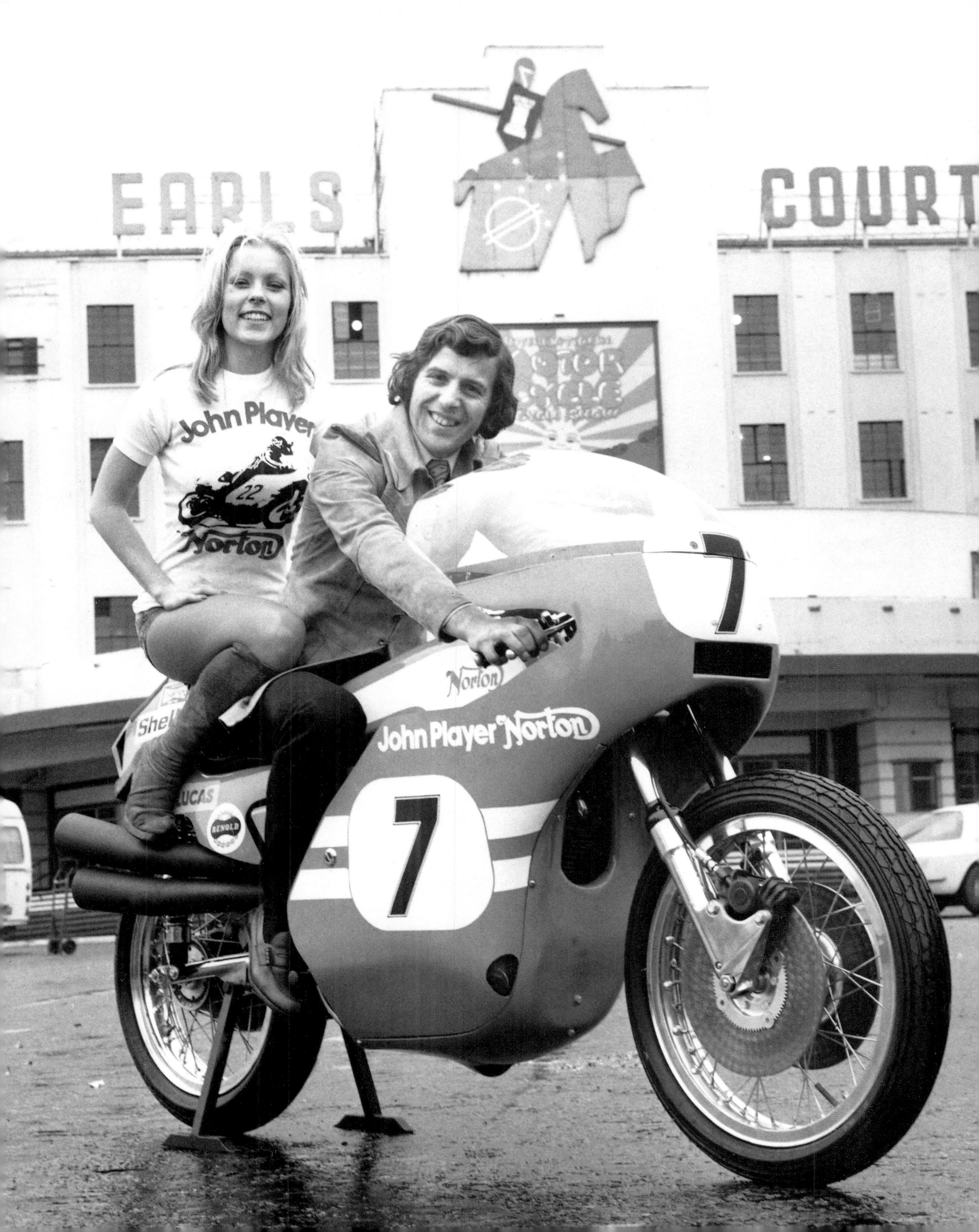
EARLS
COURT
John Player
22
Norton
Norton
John Player Norton
7
7
LUCAS

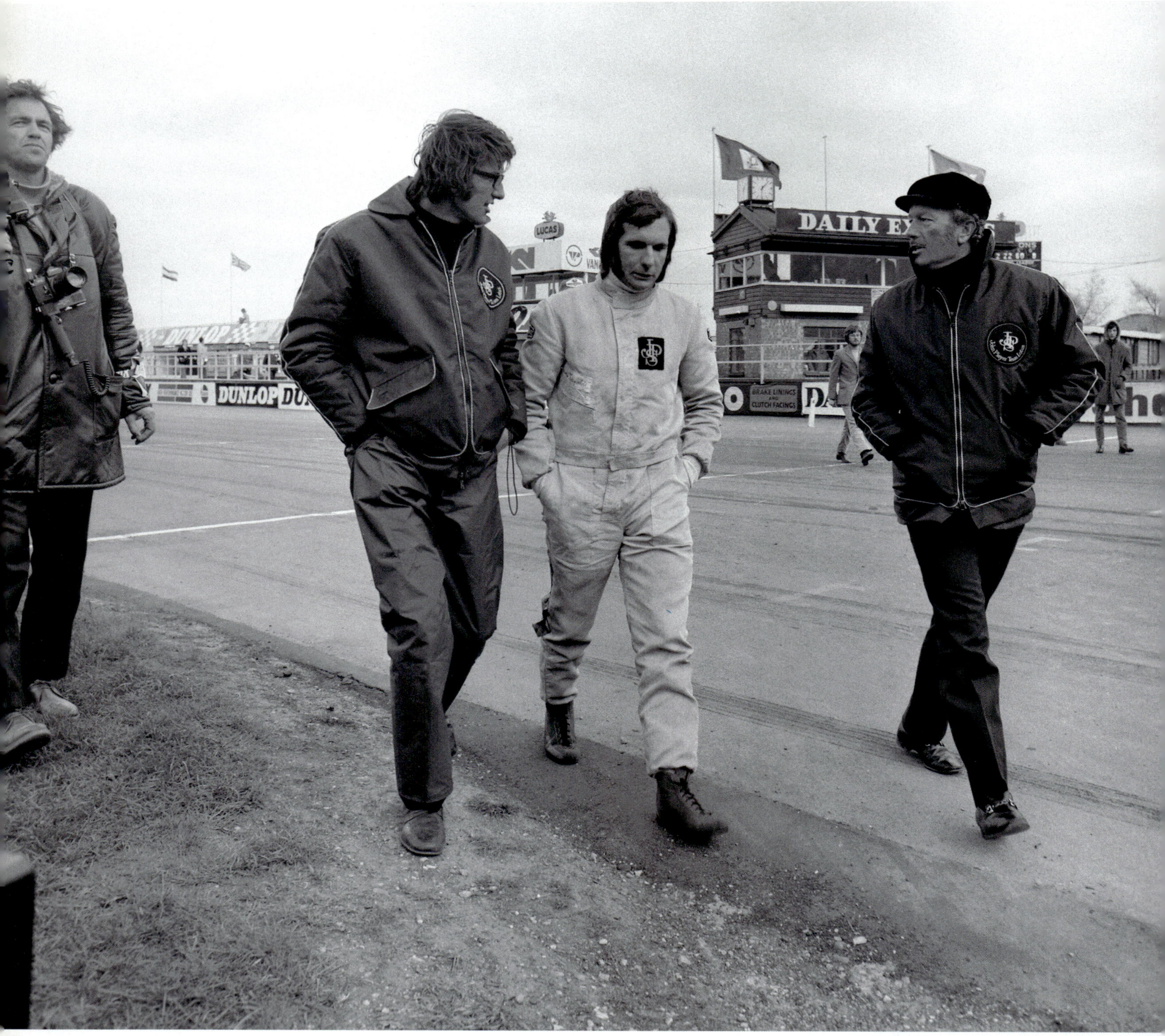

↑ Peter Warr and Colin Chapman are evidently striding along to keep up with an unhappy looking Emerson Fittipaldi at Silverstone, probably at the 1973 International Trophy.

→ Eccentric, legendary purveyor of exotic cars since 1927, David 'Bunty' Scott-Moncrief appropriately posing in front of a Rolls-Royce and a collection of ancient wooden crates, one originally containing, apparently, pure olive oil, and a Kraft margarine cardboard box. He was author of several works, including *The Thoroughbred Motorcar, The Three Pointed Star, and Veteran and Edwardian Cars*. His wife Avril raced a Bugatti, and for decades his distinctive advertisements appeared in *Motor Sport*, but a mere photo caption cannot do him justice.

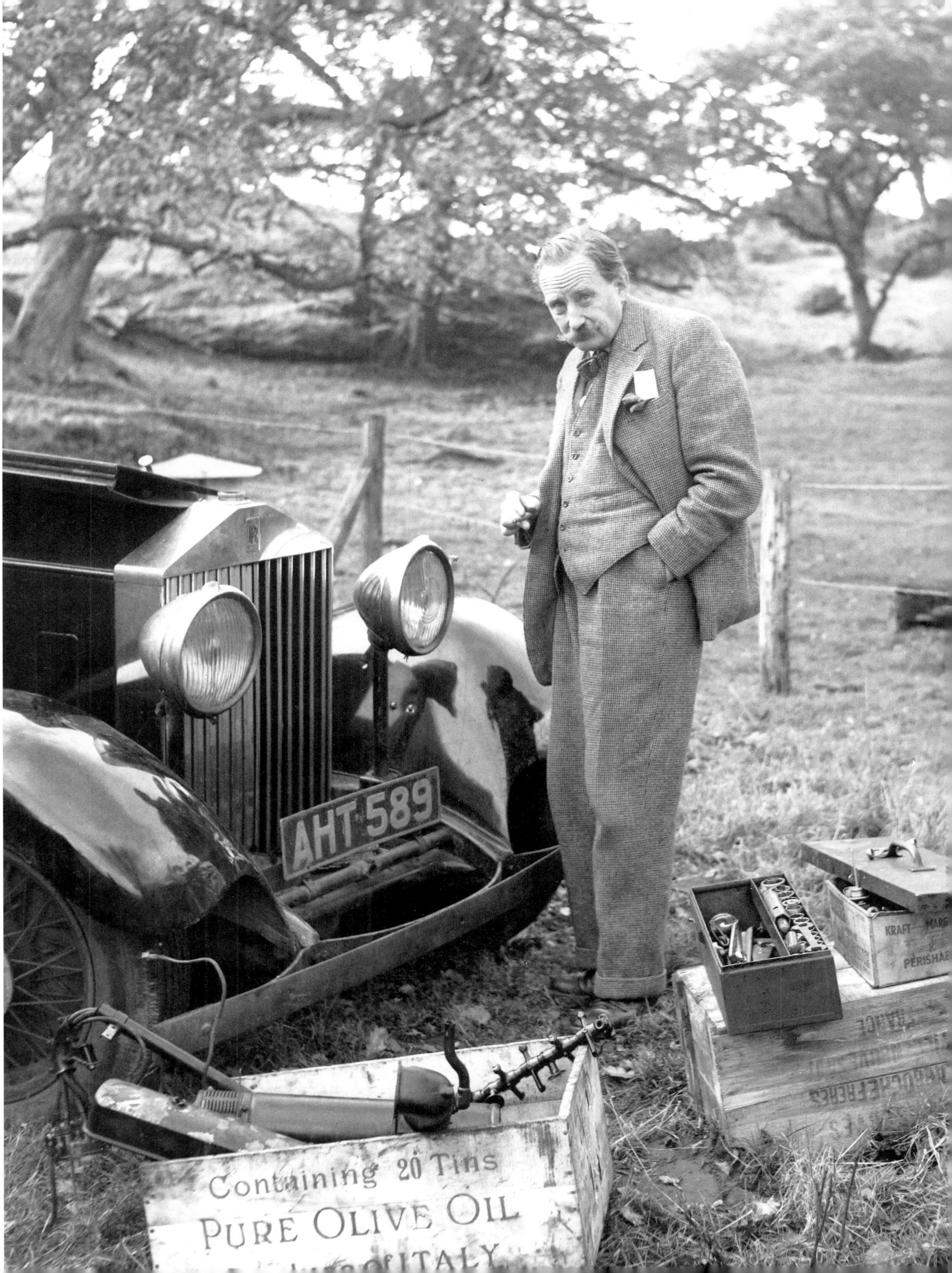
AHT 589
Containing 20 Tins
PURE OLIVE OIL
KRAFT

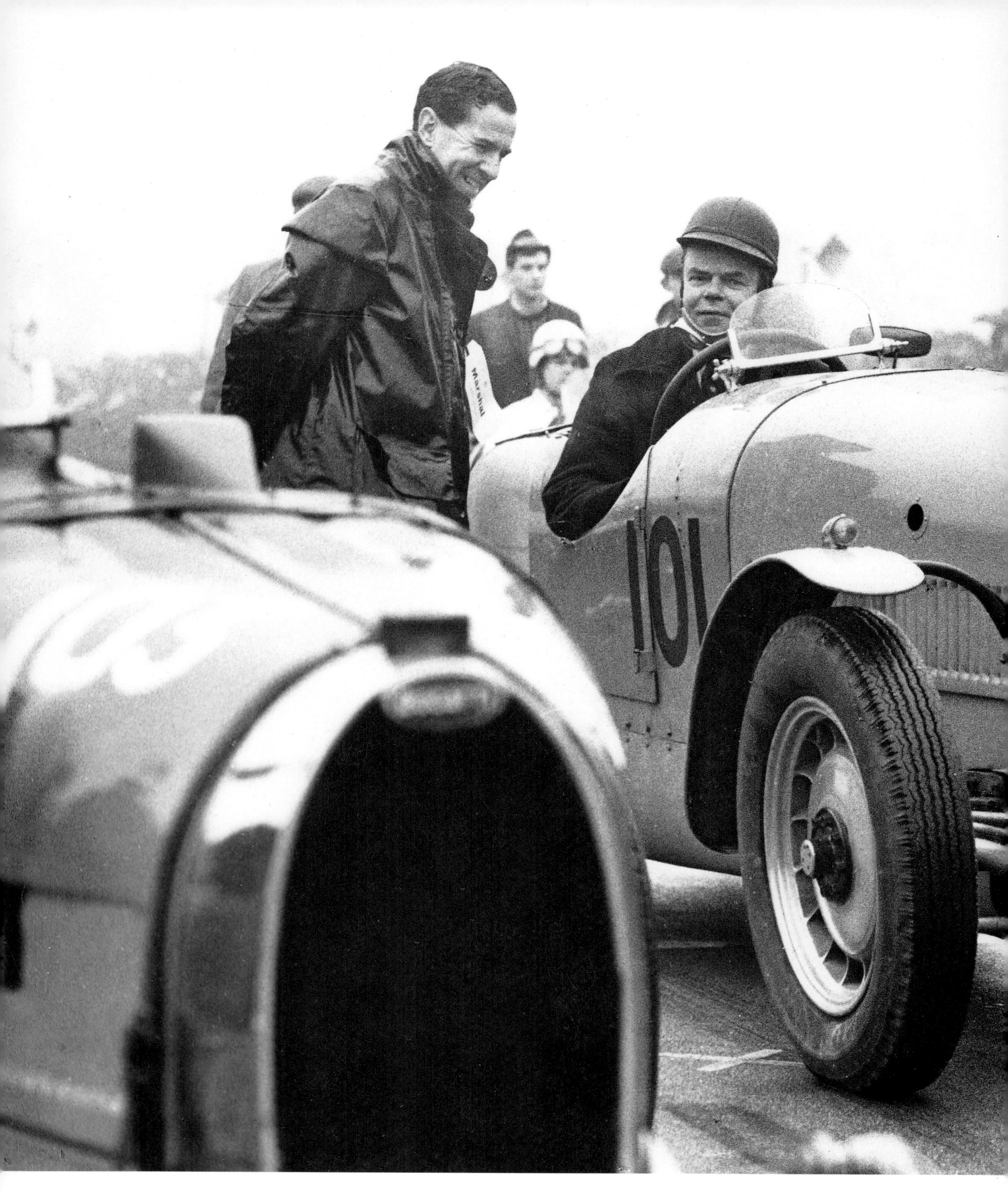
101

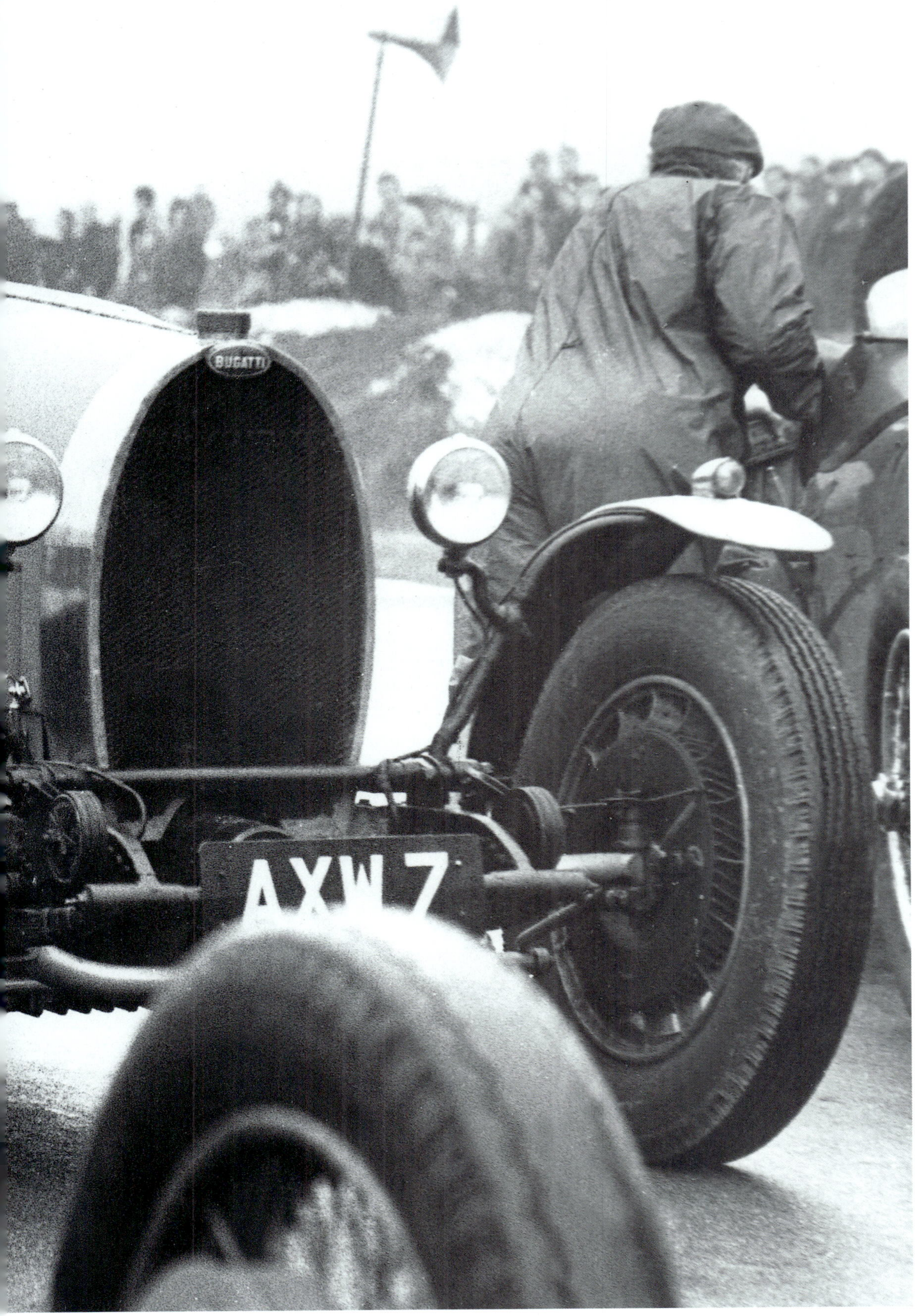

← A. F. (Alec Francis) Rivers Fletcher and then VSCC chairman Cecil Clutton on what appears to be a snowy day somewhere, perhaps Snetterton. As a neighbour and 16-year-old still at school, Rivers Fletcher was once Malcolm Campbell's riding mechanic, being the only person slim enough to squeeze into the GP Delage for the 1928 Junior Grand Prix. Campbell promised (!) Rivers' parents that he would drive carefully and not too fast. Needless to say they won the race. Thereafter, he was a Bentley apprentice until their liquidation, when he joined the motor trade. Rivers raced extensively after the Second World War in a variety of machinery, and he was the long-standing Public Relations Officer for Rubery Owen, who owned BRM. He was in turn assistant clerk of the course at the British GP, chairman of the ERA Racing Car Club, motorsport film-maker, author, journalist, and broadcaster. A very nasty accident at Prescott hillclimb in 1960, left him with slight brain damage and a speech impediment, but he carried on regardless. Born in 1912 he died aged 87 in 2000.

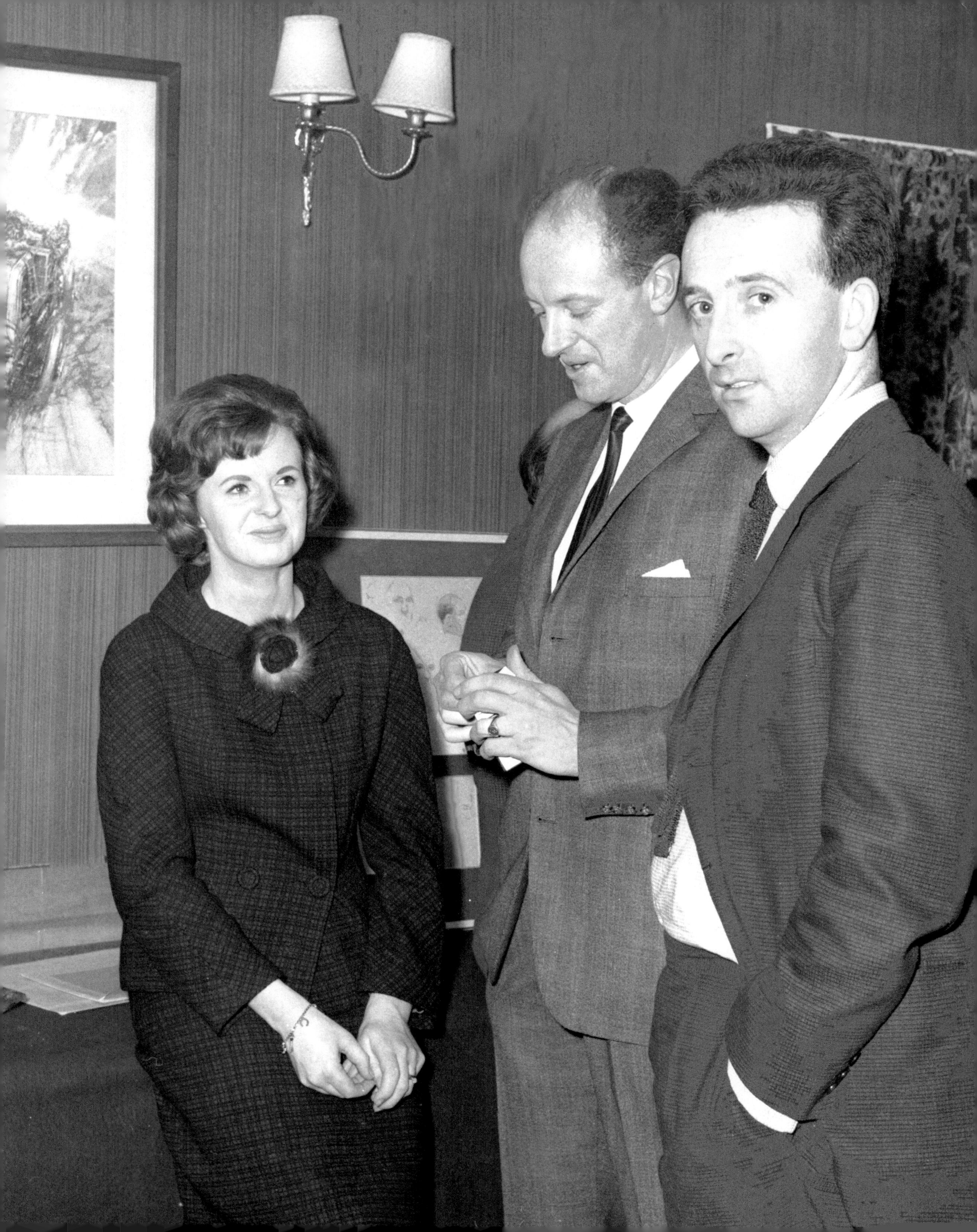

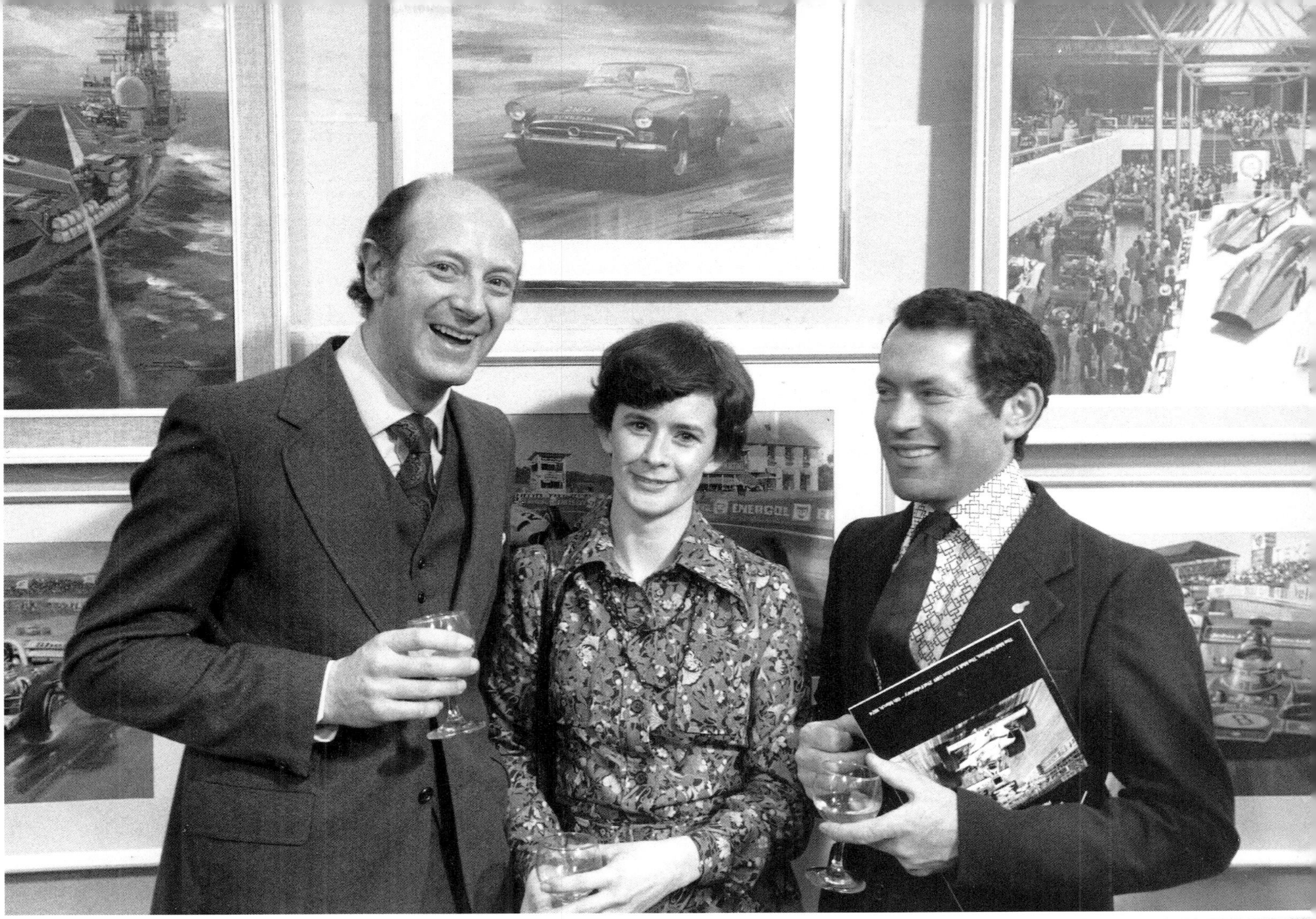

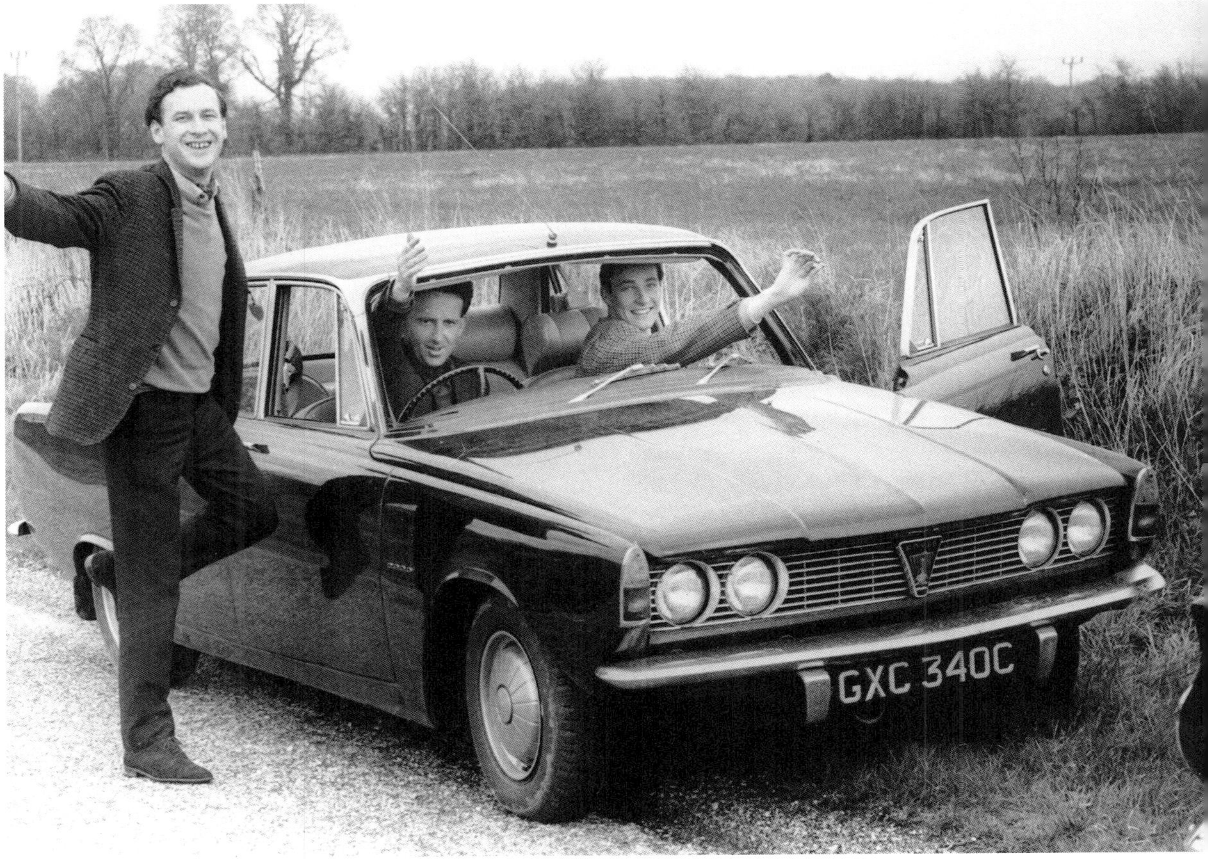

↑ Liz and Mike with Michael Turner at an exhibition of his work during the 1970s.

← Helen and Michael Turner with Anthony Hussey, long time friends of Michael, looking suitably but misleadingly respectable.

→ The missing Rover 2000 windscreen was courtesy of a stone thrown up by Mike's driving in his Cortina, the rear wing just visible on the right. Friend Michael Osborn, driver Anthony Hussey, and Beverly Key, a furniture manufacturer who bought his upholstery coverings from Anthony, who owned Connolly Leather, seem remarkably sanguine about the mishap.

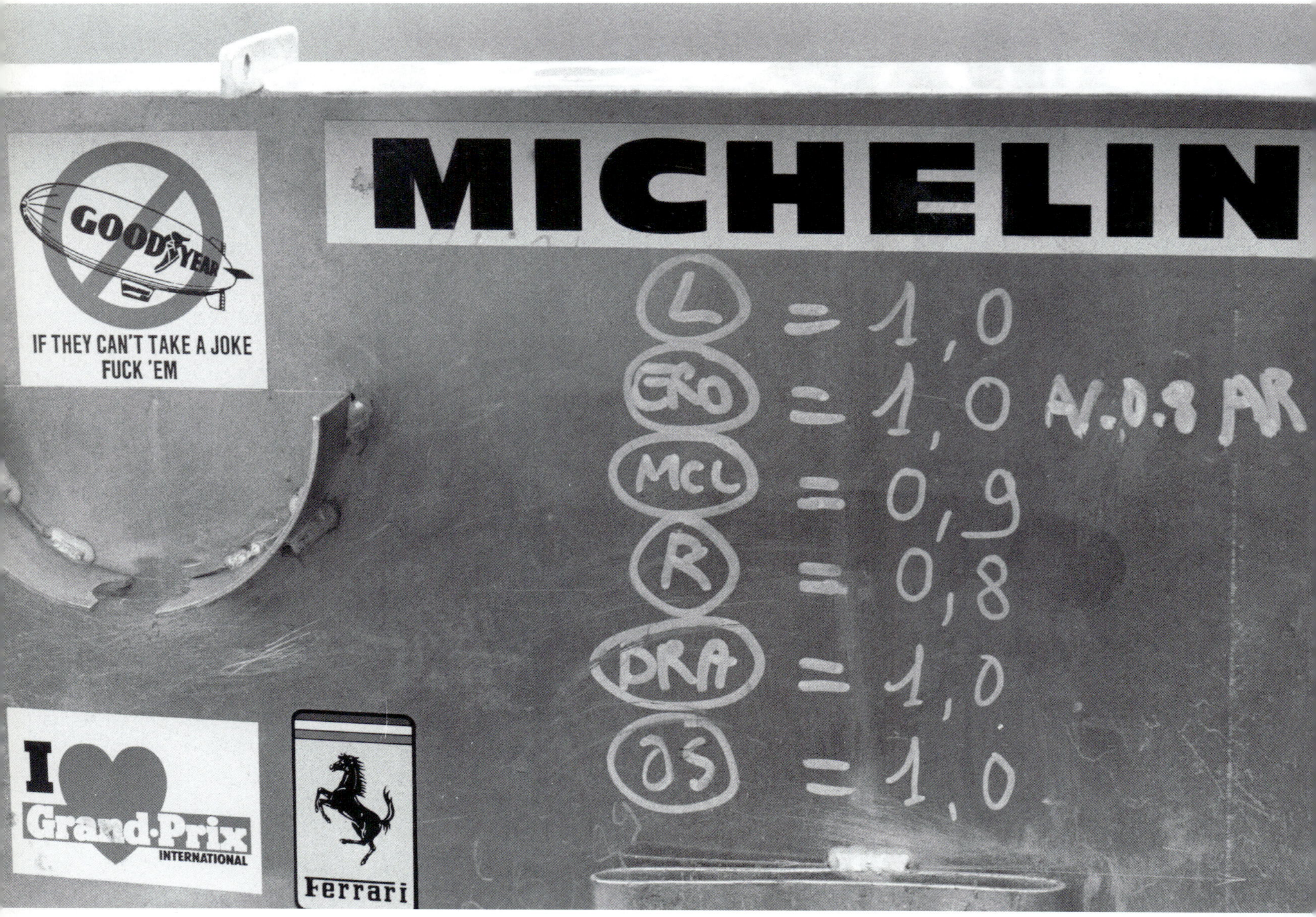

↑ Tyre wars. True sentiments on display here many moons ago; something that would never be allowed publicly now.

↗ Howden Ganley, engineers, and the Williams FW02 (aka Iso Marlboro Williams 1R) before the start of the 1973 GP season.

→ For decades, Hubert Hare and his chums inhabited the infield and environs of Silverstone. Here Hubert leaps to live another day.

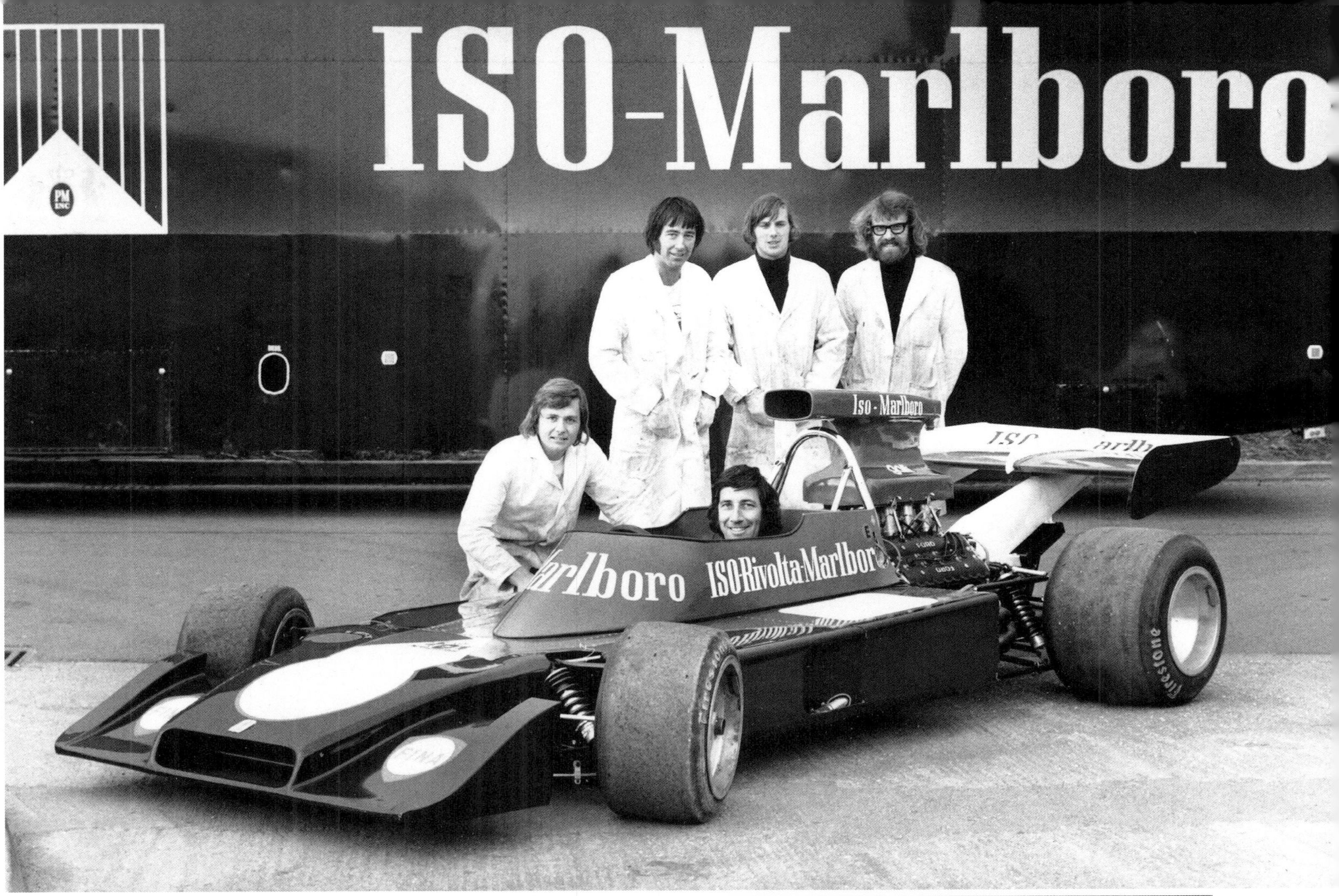
ISO-Marlboro
Iso-Marlboro
Marlboro
ISO Rivolta-Marlboro
Firestone

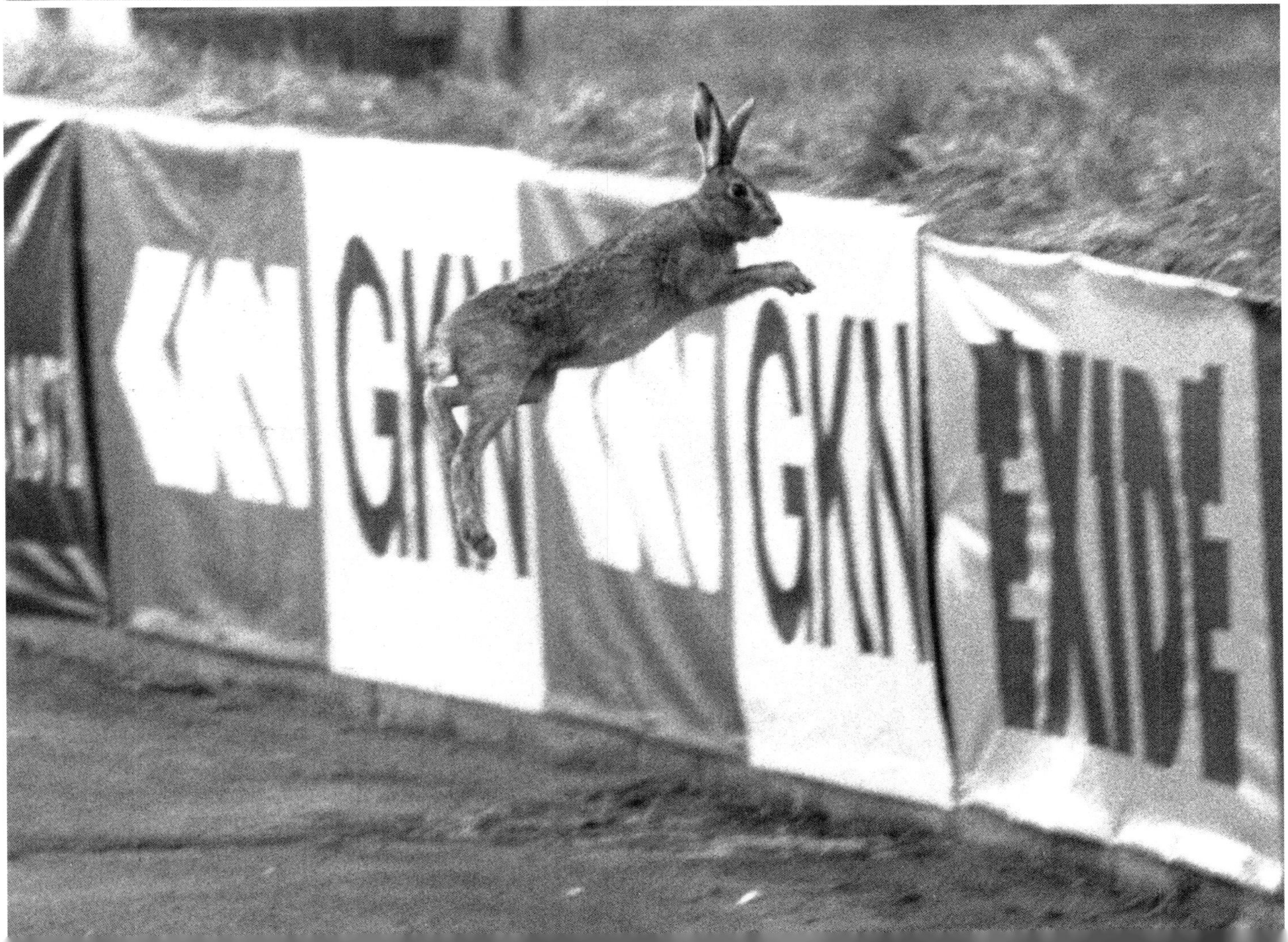
GKN
GKN
EXIDE

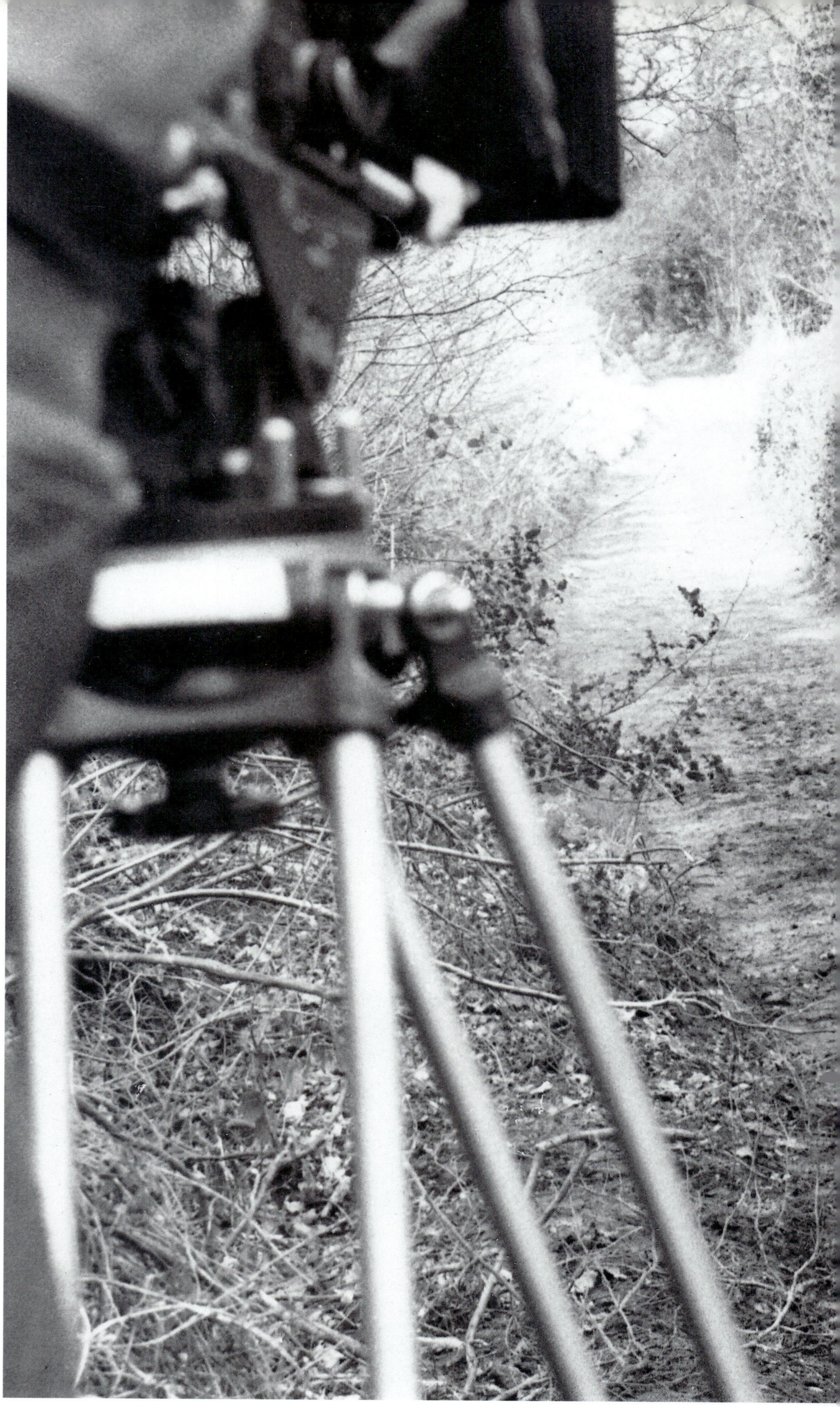

→ Mike and Liz's beautiful cottage, in the background, is hidden in deepest rural Surrey down a forest track, and was used in a scene from the British comedy drama *Rumpole of the Bailey* in April 1983. Liz recalls that they were paid £200 for the use of the house and grounds. The episode was titled 'Rumpole and the Sporting Life', and here are Jeremy Nicholas, as Jeremy Jowling, looking down the barrels of his twelve-bore with Leo McKern, as the lugubrious barrister Horace Rumpole, timing his next line whilst Mike snaps away from behind the camera.

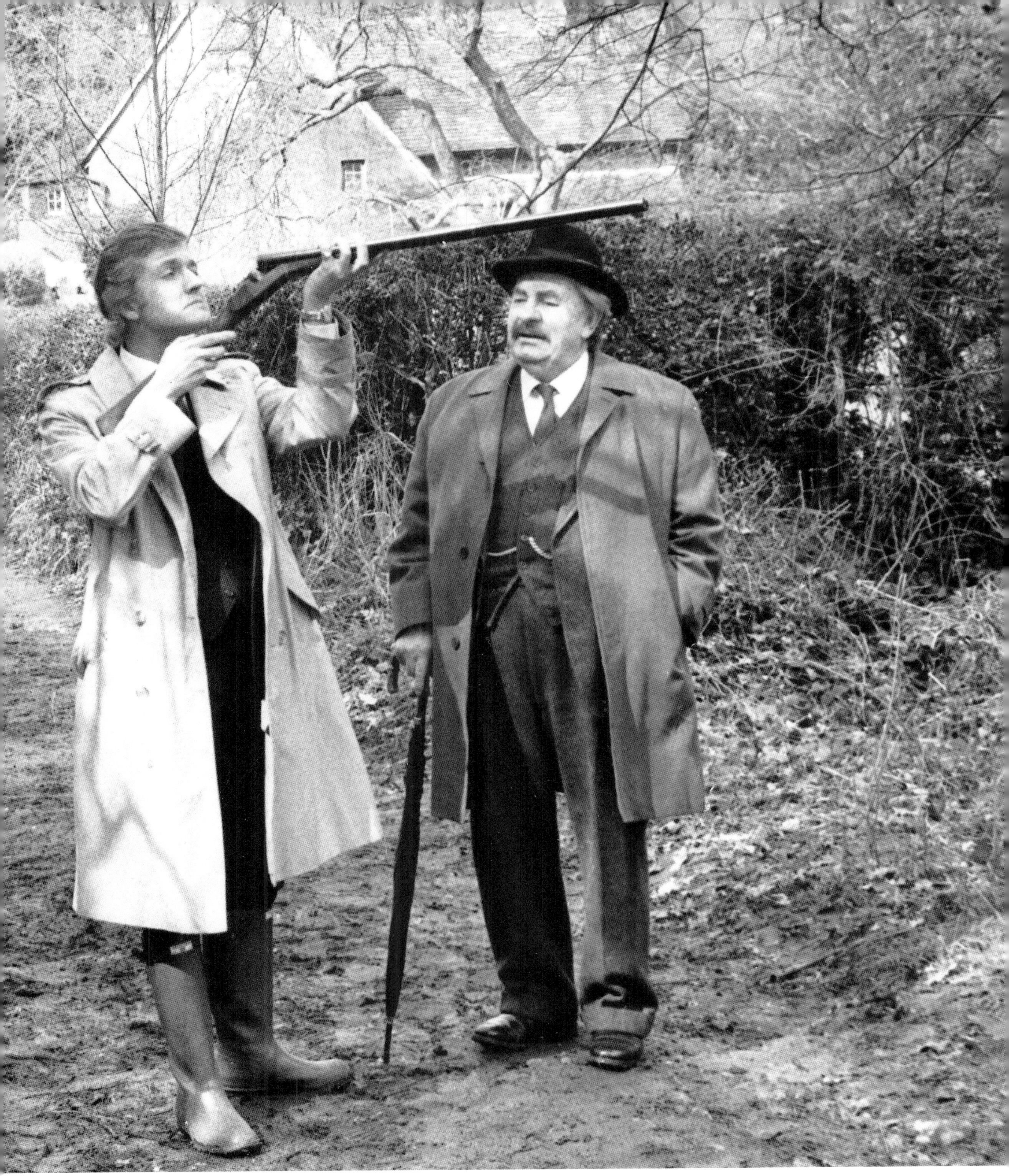

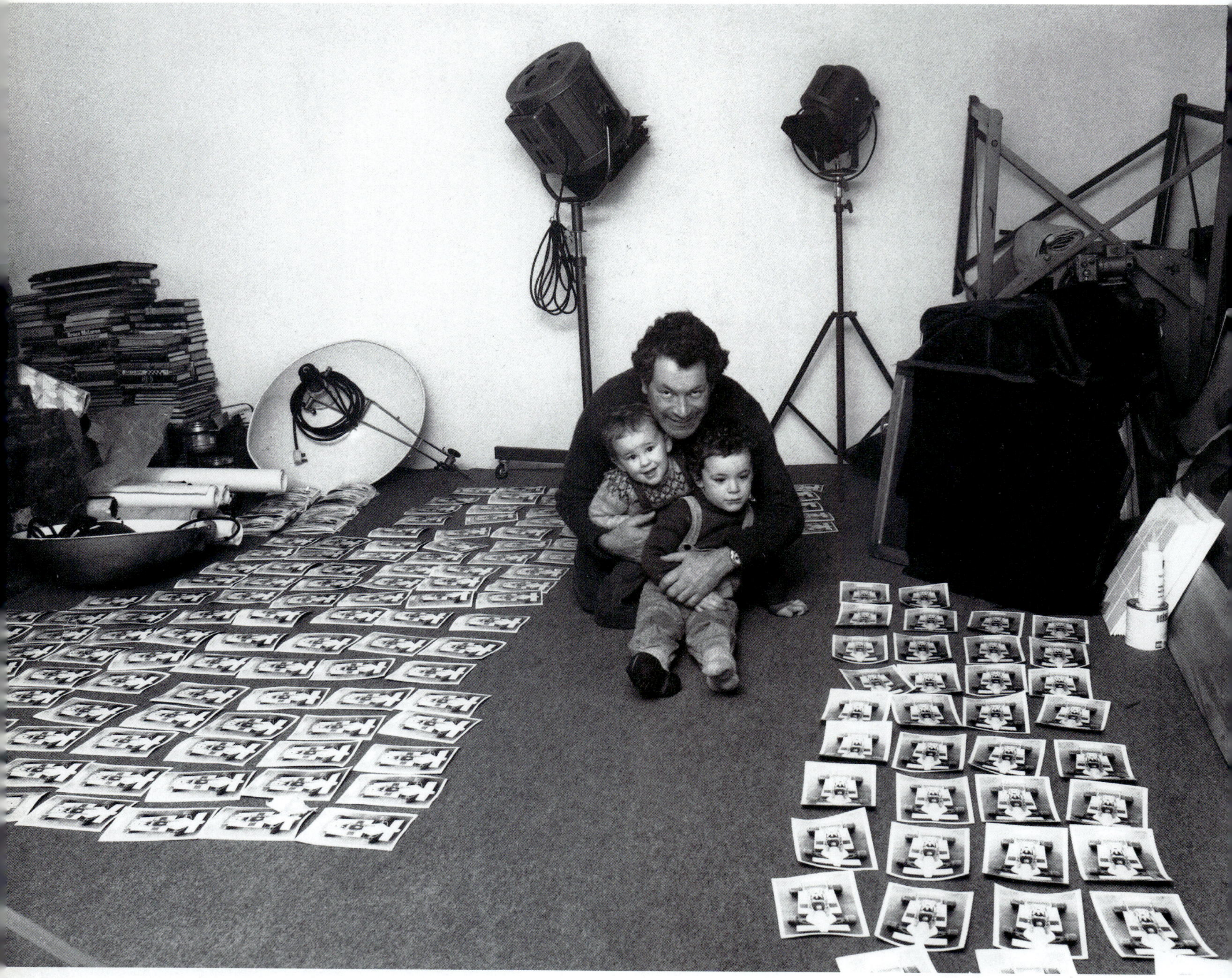

↑ Proud father with Ben and Jo at the Kingly Street (London W1) studio that Mike used for over 15 years.

→ A proper sports car has a long louvred bonnet, shapely tail, 'Monza' filler cap, and bloody great long twin exhaust pipes that can be heard from miles away. Thus, as owned by Dexter Brown, passengering in his very modified 3.8-litre Jaguar XK120 with Eoin Young pressing the pedals for an article in *Autocar* magazine. OKO 242 survived a long period of decline in other hands but, happily, is now being rebuilt.

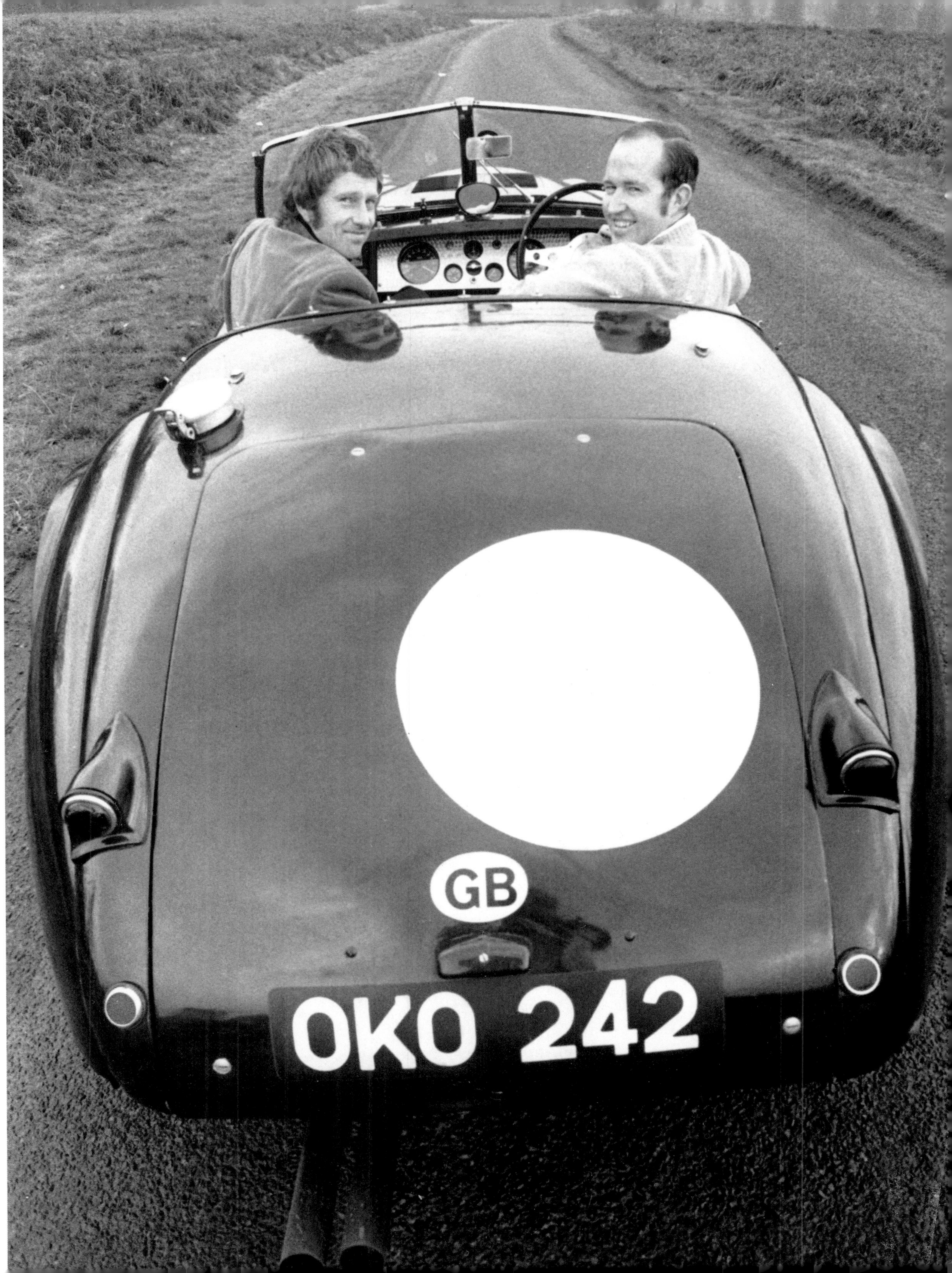
GB
OKO 242

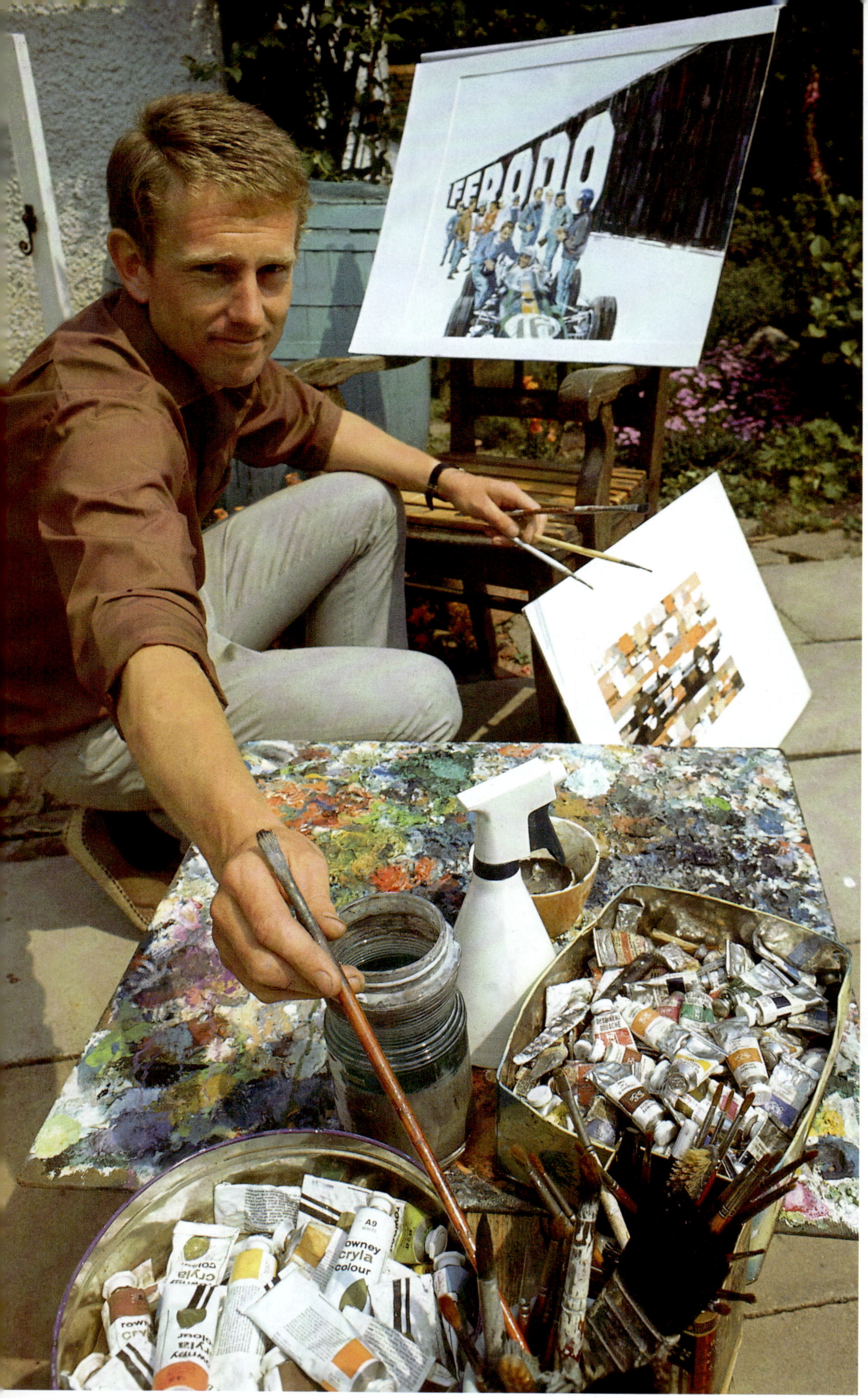

🡐 The works of Dexter Brown with their distinctive style were a favourite of Mike's, and Dexter painted the small portrait that features on the last page, especially for Liz and this book. Dexter works away in his garden on a sunny day over 30 years ago.

🡒 The Earls Court Motor Show was another favourite haunt (on press day) of professional photographers, and Mike has caught the Tory MP Sir Gerald David Nunes Nabarro (29 June 1913 – 29 November 1973) admiring the model on the AC stand. Perhaps he wants to perm his magnificent moustache in the same way. Nabarro, despite his impressive name, came from humble origins. He was elected as Conservative MP for Kidderminster in 1950 and his private members' bill on pollution and smog led to the 1956 Clean Air act. A controversial and baroque figure, he became embroiled in a driving offence when he, or as he claimed, his secretary drove the wrong way on a roundabout. He was convicted but subsequently cleared of all charges at a second trial. During the re-trial he suffered two strokes and he died a few months later aged 60.

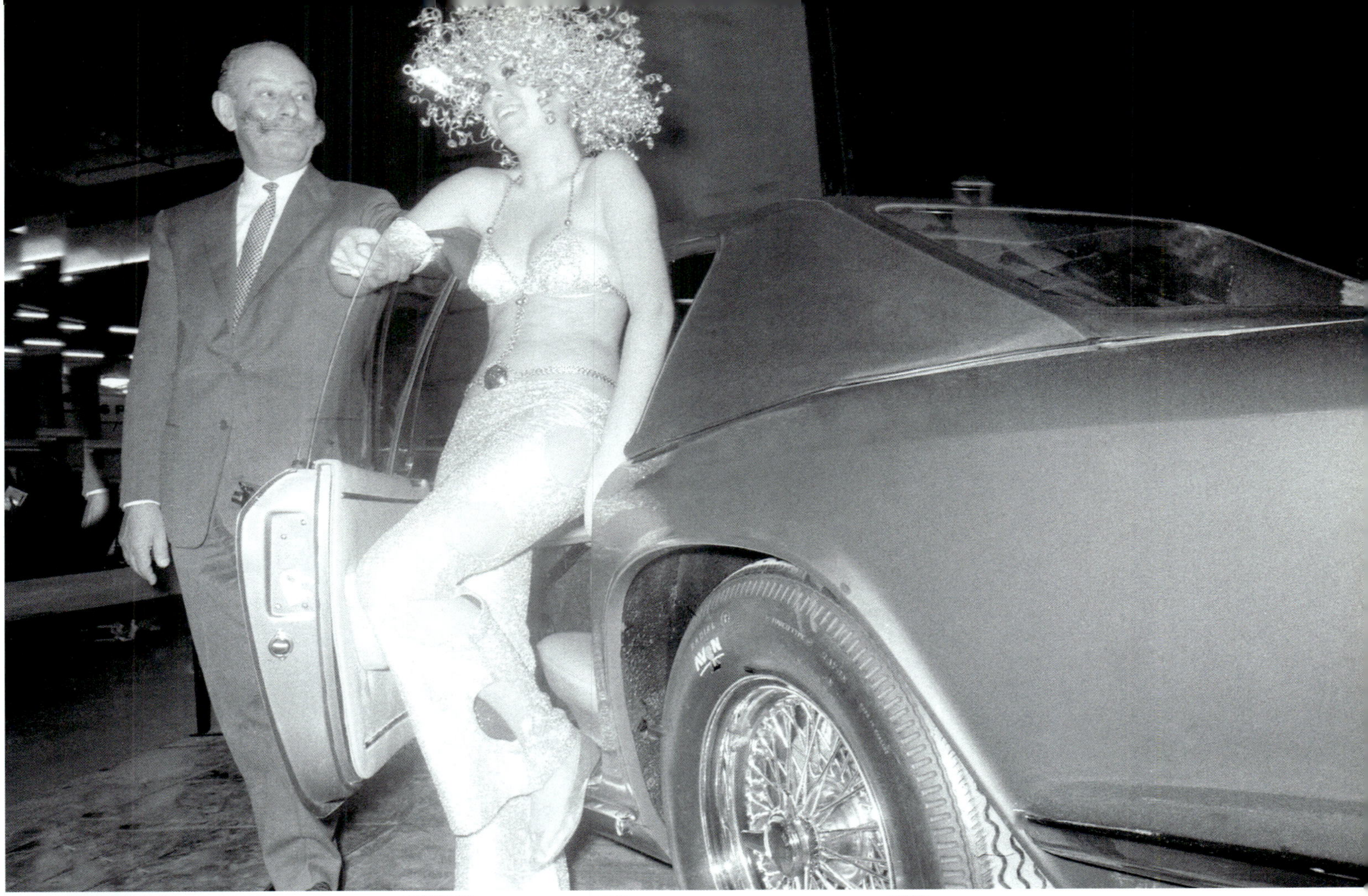

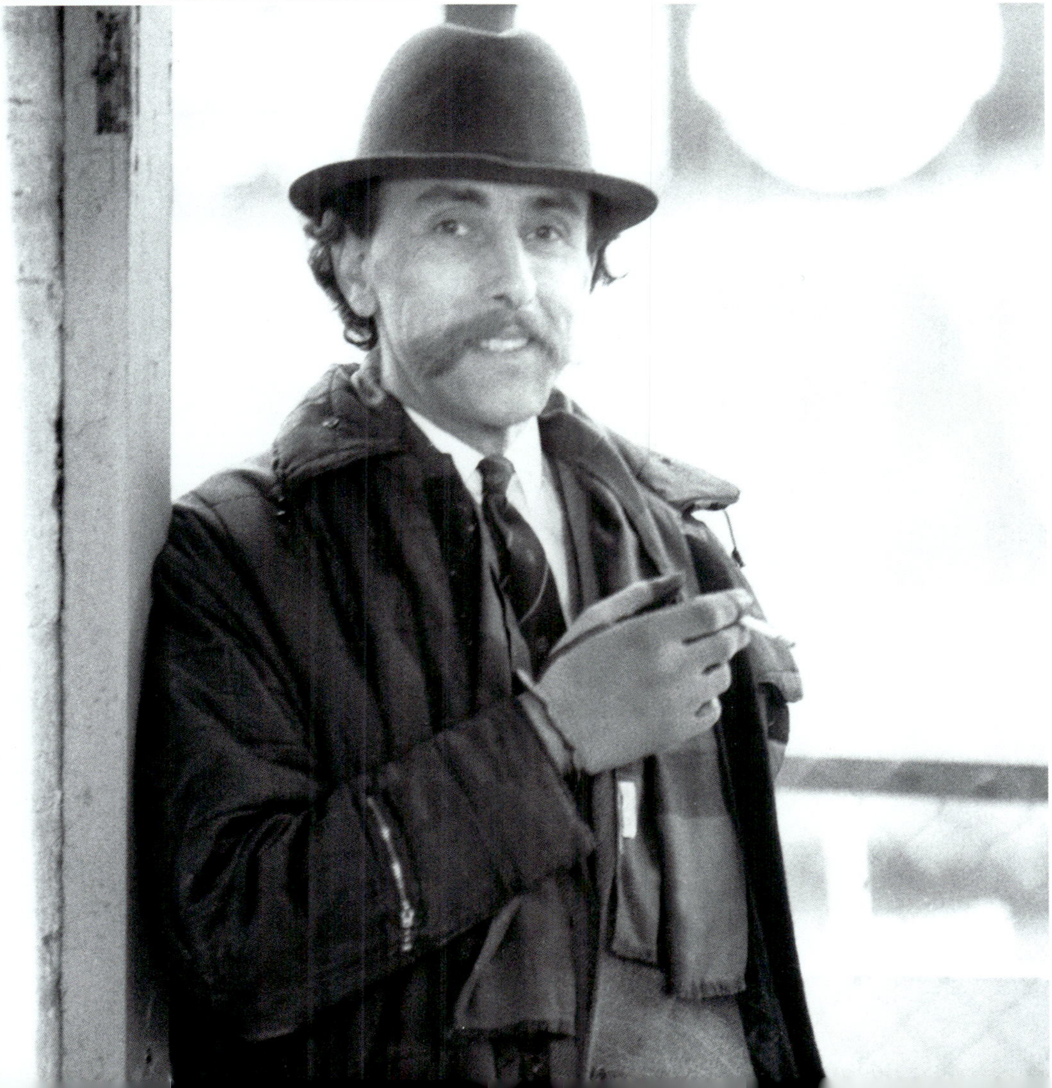

← Scholarly, erudite and pedantic, Leonard John Kensell Setright cut an individual figure for many years around the world of automotive journalism. A devoted Bristol aficionado LJK was author of 12 books (the last published after his death) about cars and motoring. He also wrote for the then trendy *Car* magazine during the 1970s and for many years thereafter. Despite his increasingly patrician demeanour, his parents were Australian although he was born (10 August 1931) in London and was a practising Jew. Noted for his use of Sobranie Black Russian cigarettes, he died of lung cancer on 5 September 2005.

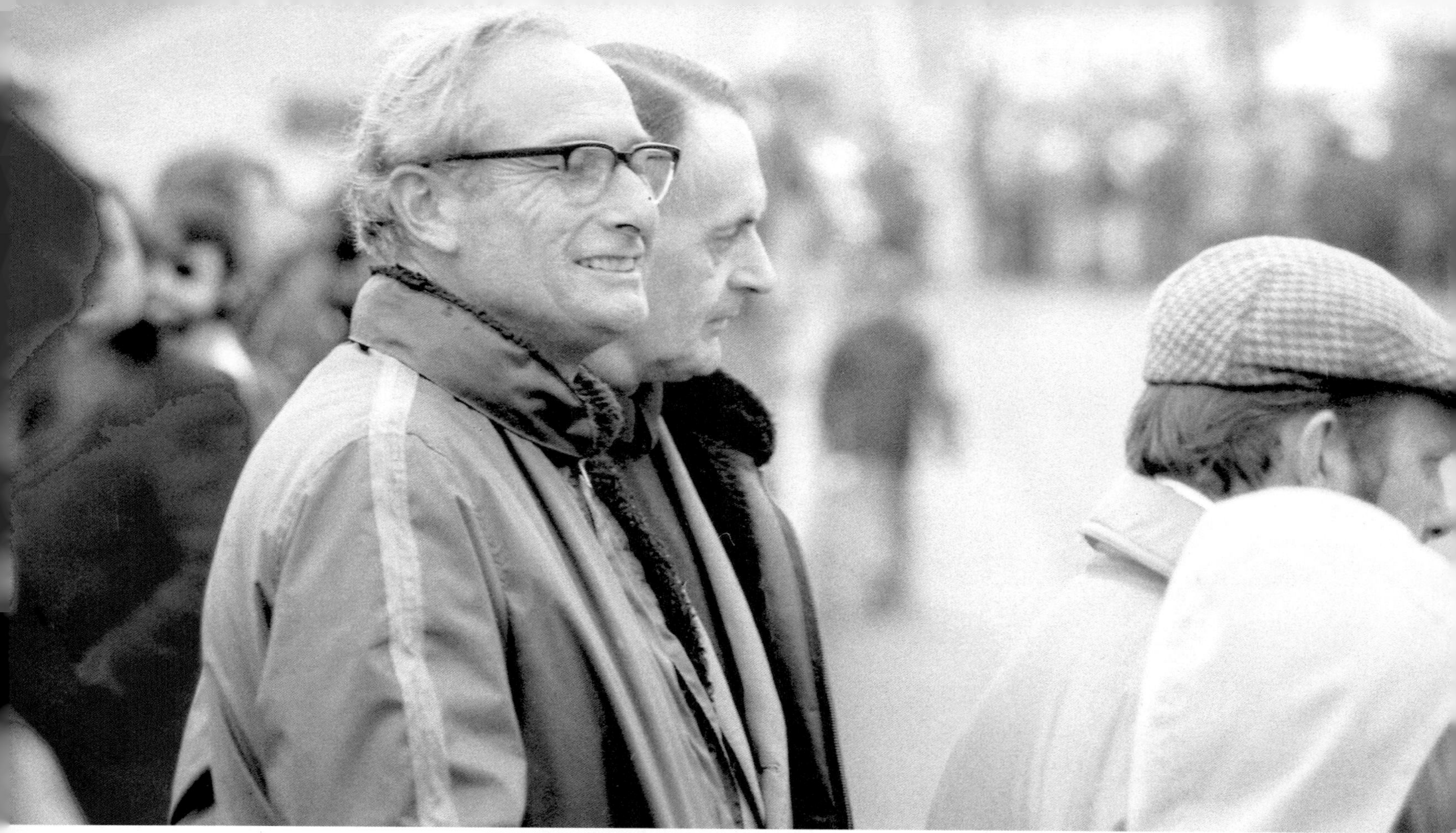

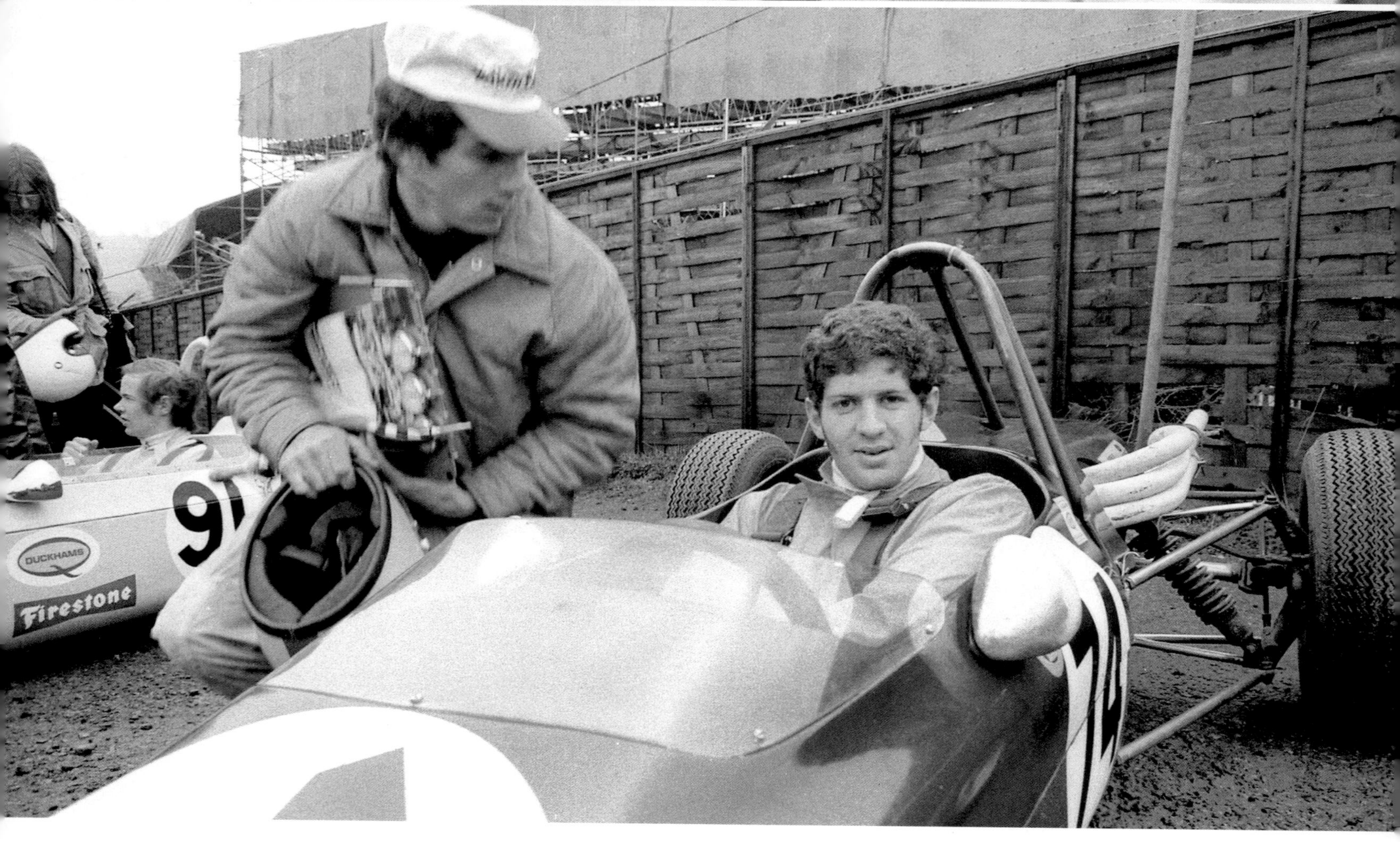
DUCKHAMS
Firestone

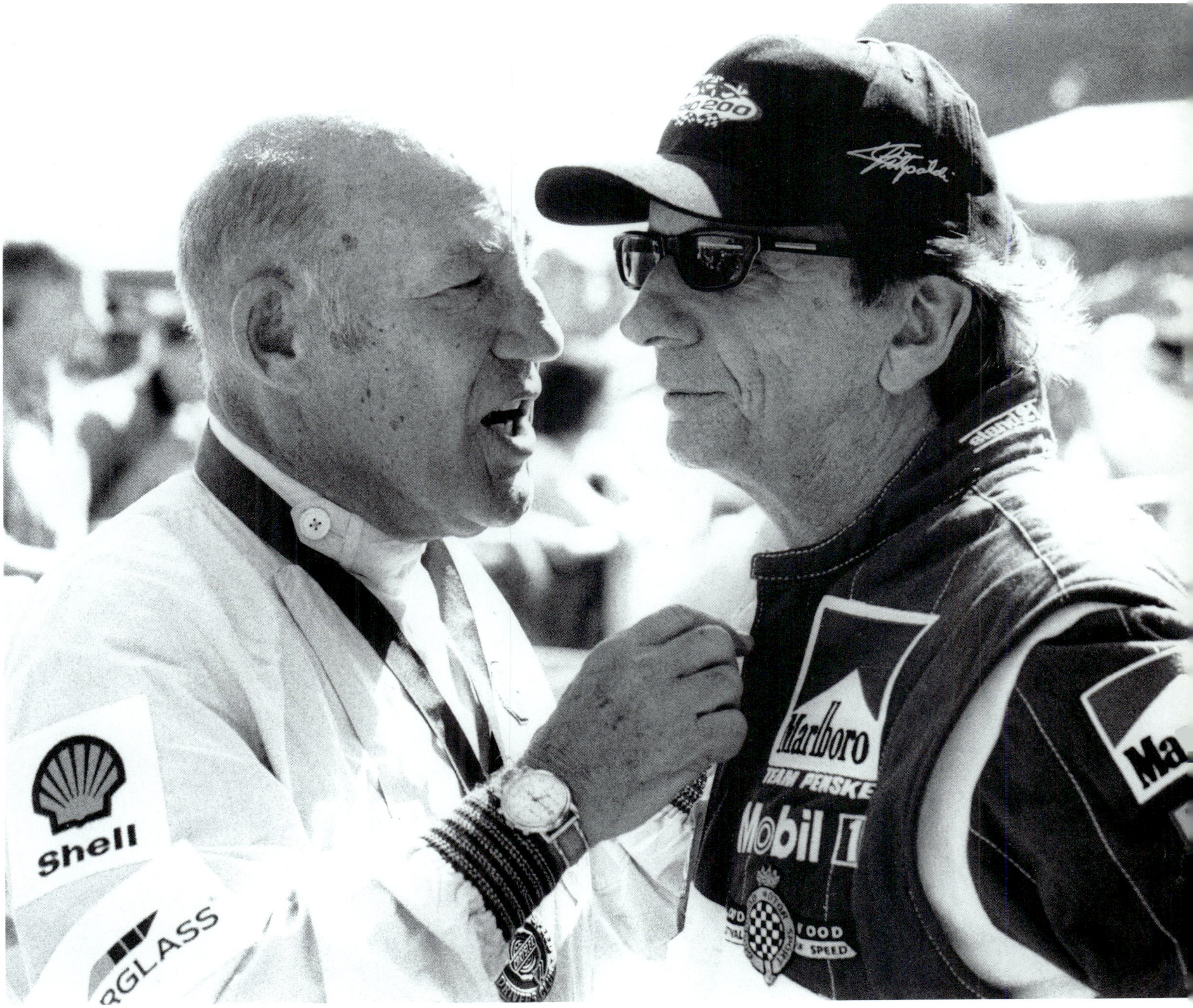

↑ Sir Stirling Moss and Emerson Fittipaldi at the Goodwood Festival of Speed a few years ago. Tempus fugit.

↖ Former team manager for Peter Whitehead during the 1950s, then Vanwall, this is David Yorke, who for years worked with John Wyer, seen here at Brands Hatch. After this, Yorke became involved in the Martini Tecno F1 debacle that finally fell apart in 1973, with Martini decamping to Brabham. He died suddenly in his hotel bedroom in Zeltweg on the night of the 17th August 1984 two days before the Austrian GP.

← A very young Jody Scheckter at Brands Hatch in 1971 during his short foray into Formula Ford. By the end of the year he was racing and winning in F3, despite his sometimes over-the-top driving. He had his first F1 ride at the 1972 US GP at Watkins Glen in a works McLaren M19A, finishing ninth, and the rest is history, culminating in becoming the 1979 World Champion for Ferrari.

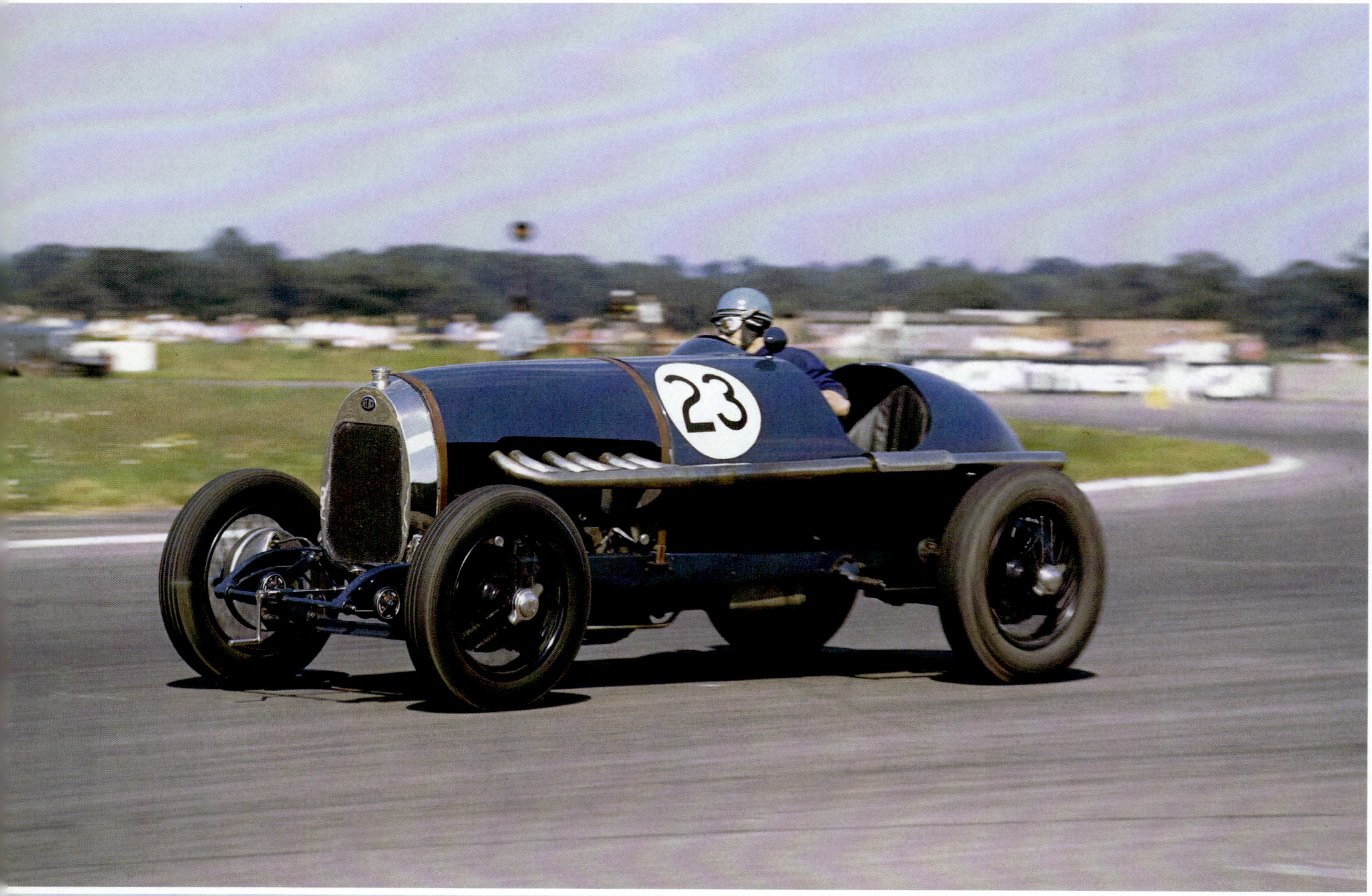

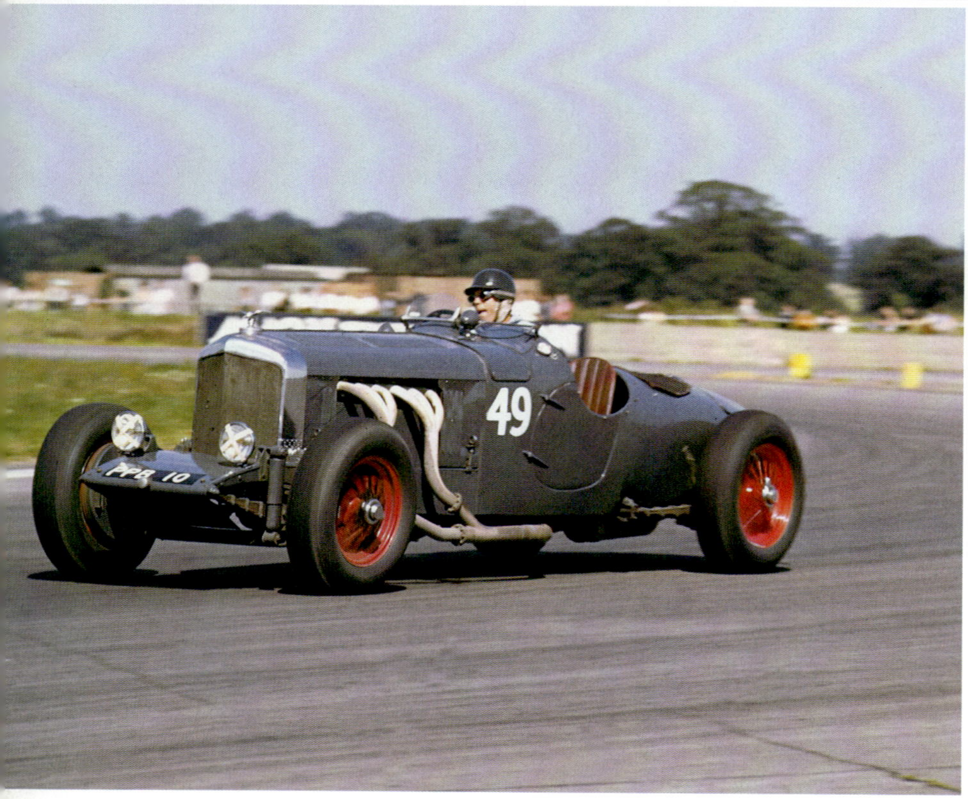

↑ Mike was always keen on most things motor racing, and here are two shots taken at a 1960s Vintage Sports Car Club meeting at Silverstone. This is Nigel Arnold Forster in his 5107cc Delage II that he had rebuilt during the late 1950s/early 1960s. Note his motorcycle style 'pudding basin' helmet.

← Same spot, as Frank Sowden exits Becketts on to the Club straight in his 8-litre Bentley, complete with (almost) matching helmet colours.

→ The Hon. Patrick Lindsay (14 November 1928 – 9 January 1986), chairman of Christies with his Monza Alfa Romeo and Napier Railton, both ex-John Cobb, outside Easton Neston, near Towcester, then estate of his wife, Lady Amabel Lindsay's cousin Alexander, Lord Hesketh, mentor to be of James Hunt. Lindsay was a legendary racer of multiple historic machinery including the famous ERA R5B 'Remus' that was driven by Prince 'B. Bira' during the 1930s and is still owned by the family and raced by his son Ludovic Lindsay to this day.

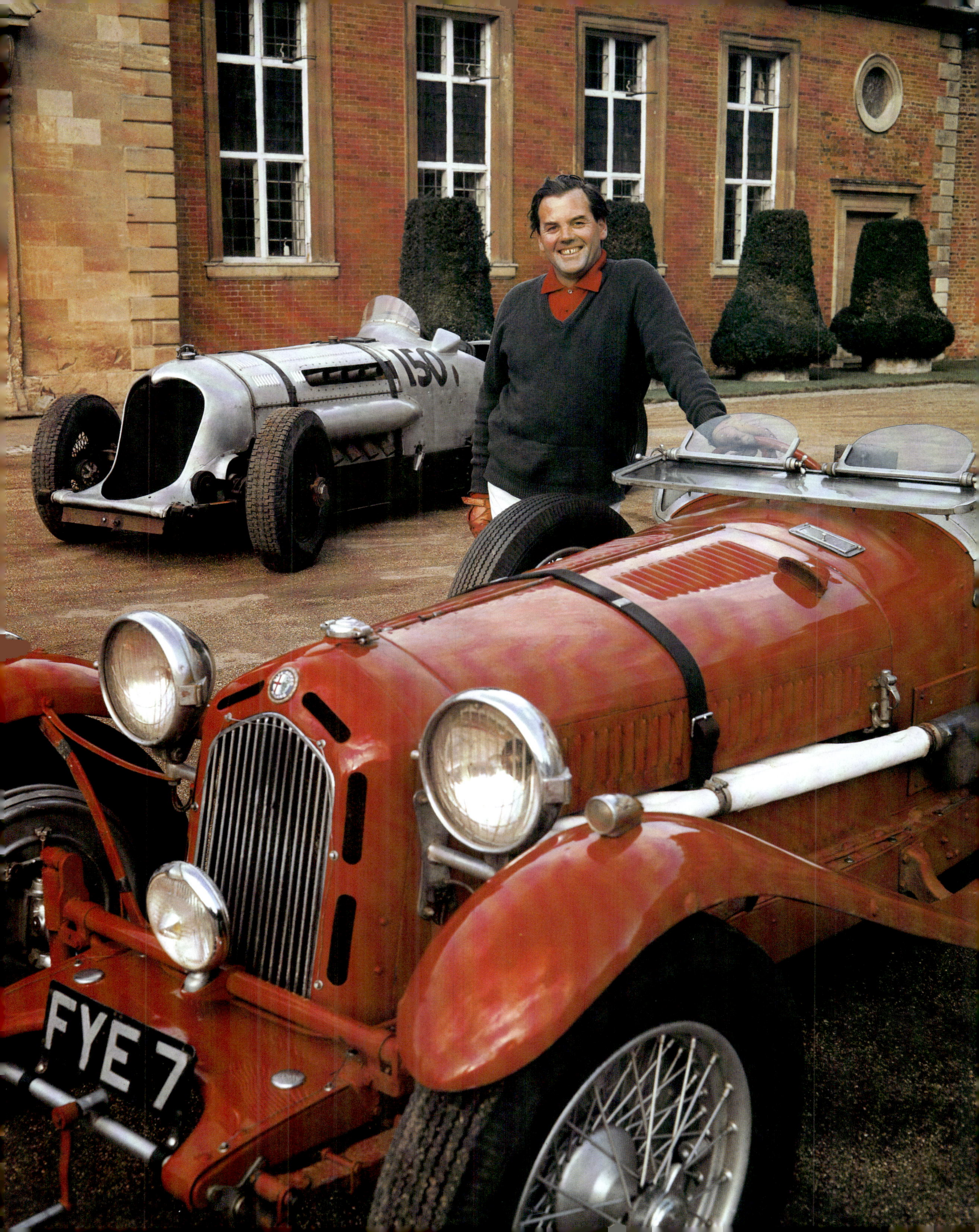
150
FYE 7

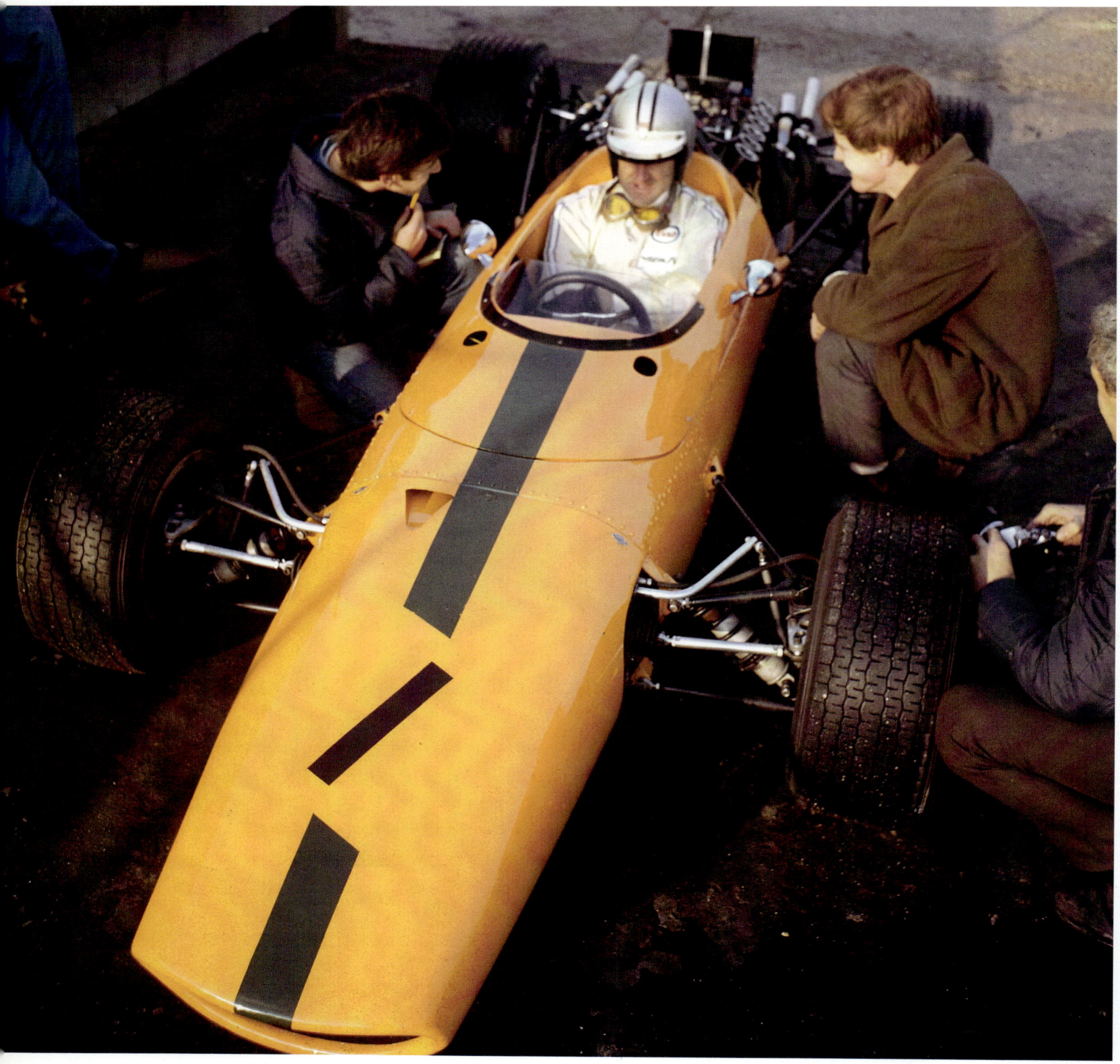

↑Testing at Goodwood during Denny Hulme's first run in the now defunct BRM V12-powered M5A, and he still has the Esso patch on his overalls, a legacy of his time at the Brabham team. Alastair Caldwell is on the right.

→ He was known as 'The Bear', but most pictures of 1967 World Champion Denny Hulme, who died of a heart attack after pulling off the track during the 1992 Bathurst 1,000km, would seem to indicate otherwise. He is wearing Les Leston Nomex overalls and now he is out of the car the Esso patch has been removed from above the Goodyear logo. No doubt in deference to the fact that his McLaren drive was expedited by Gulf Oil and Goodyear, although the team was contracted to Shell and carried their logo on the new M7A. As ever, the period racing driver was not bothered about being photographed in a dirty, chipped helmet.

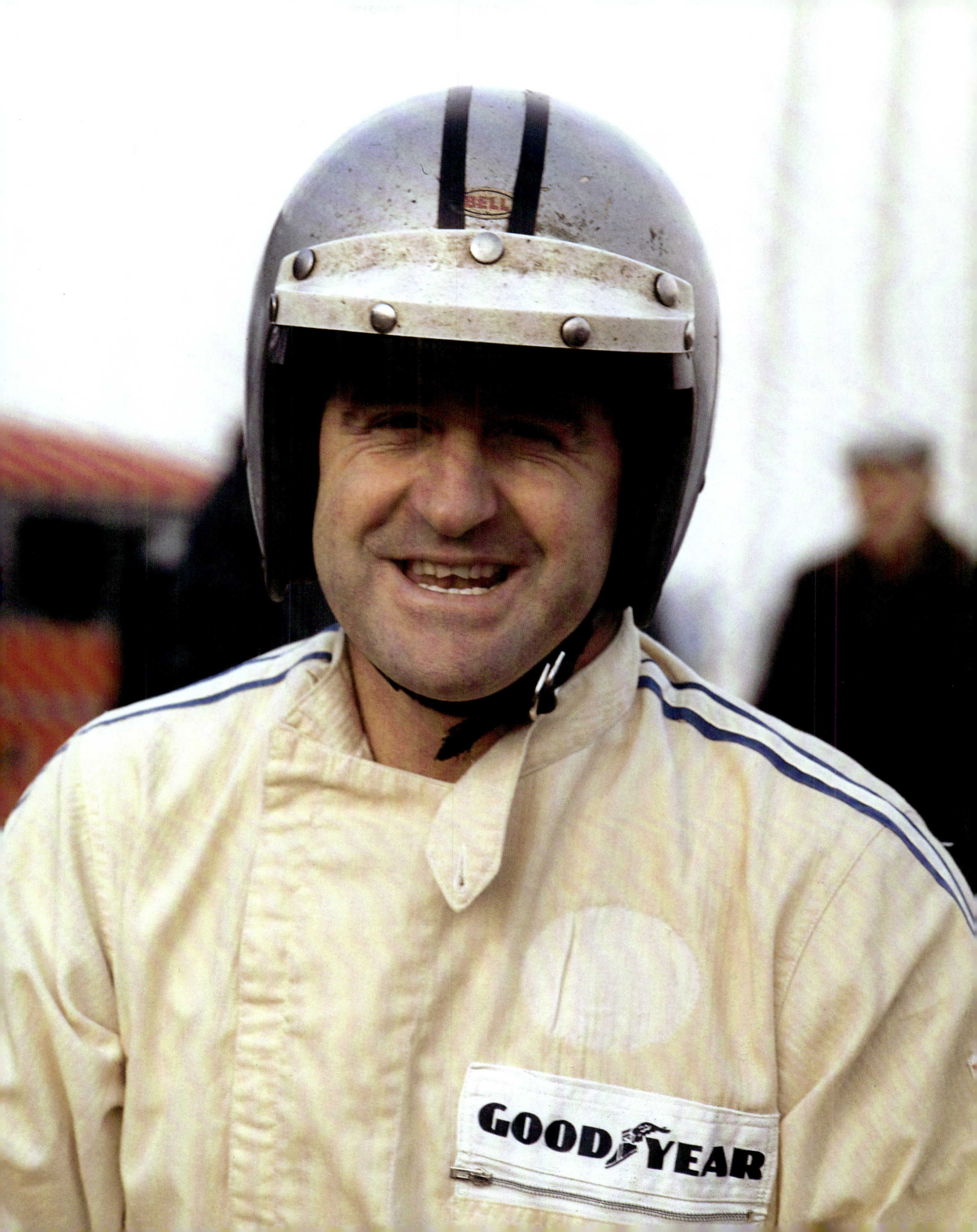
BELL
GOODYEAR

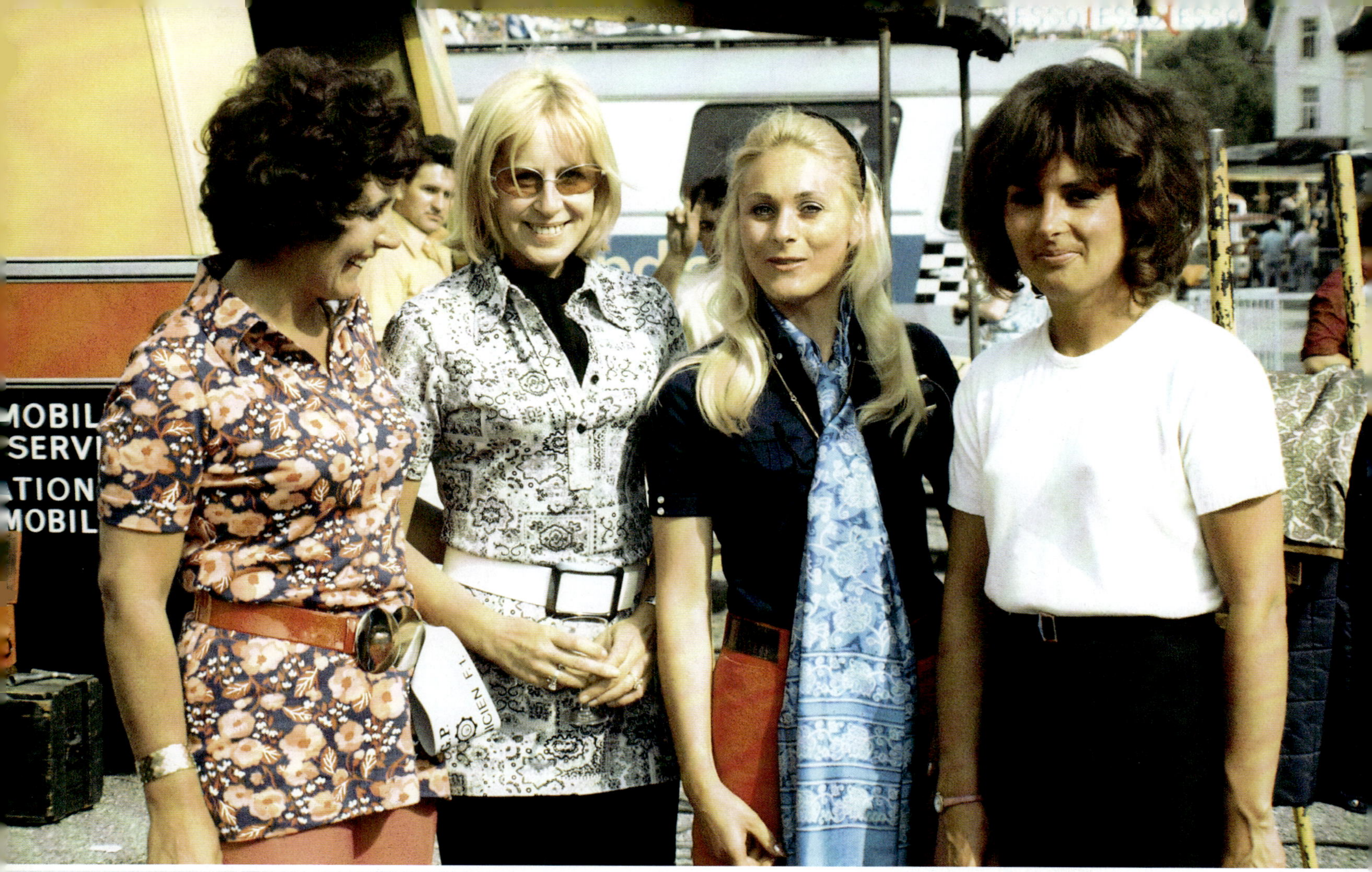

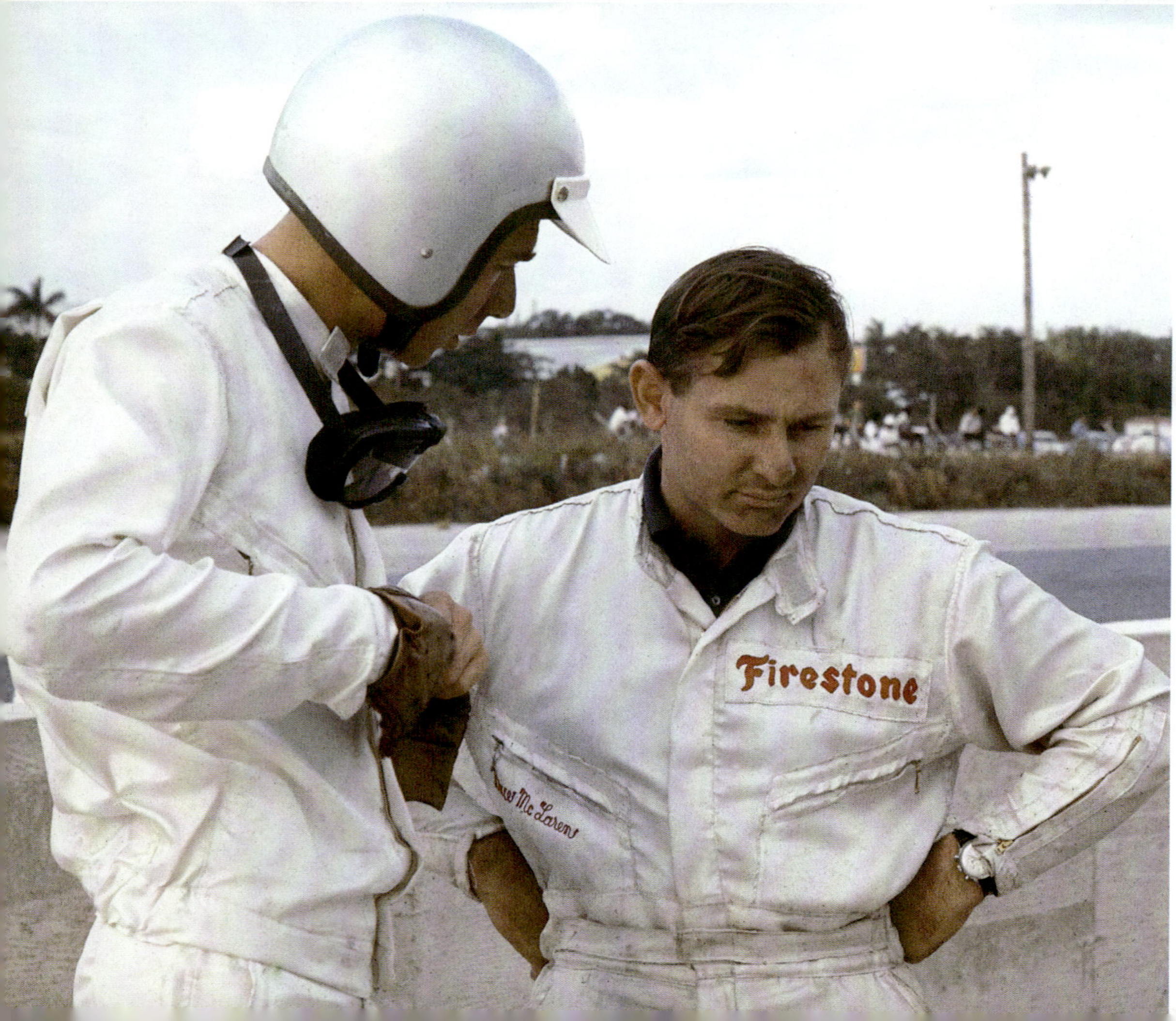

Bette Hill, Norah Tyrrell, unknown and Ginny Parnell in the paddock for the 1968 Belgian GP'. With sincerest apologies to 'unknown'!

The very tall Jim Hall and the rather shorter Bruce McLaren, complete with oil smudge on his nose. Can you imagine any latter-day GP driver even touching anything dirty, let alone appearing in public with the marks of honest toil upon his face?

You don't argue with the Monegasque gendarmerie. This is the centre of Casino Square with the portals of the Hotel De Paris in the background.

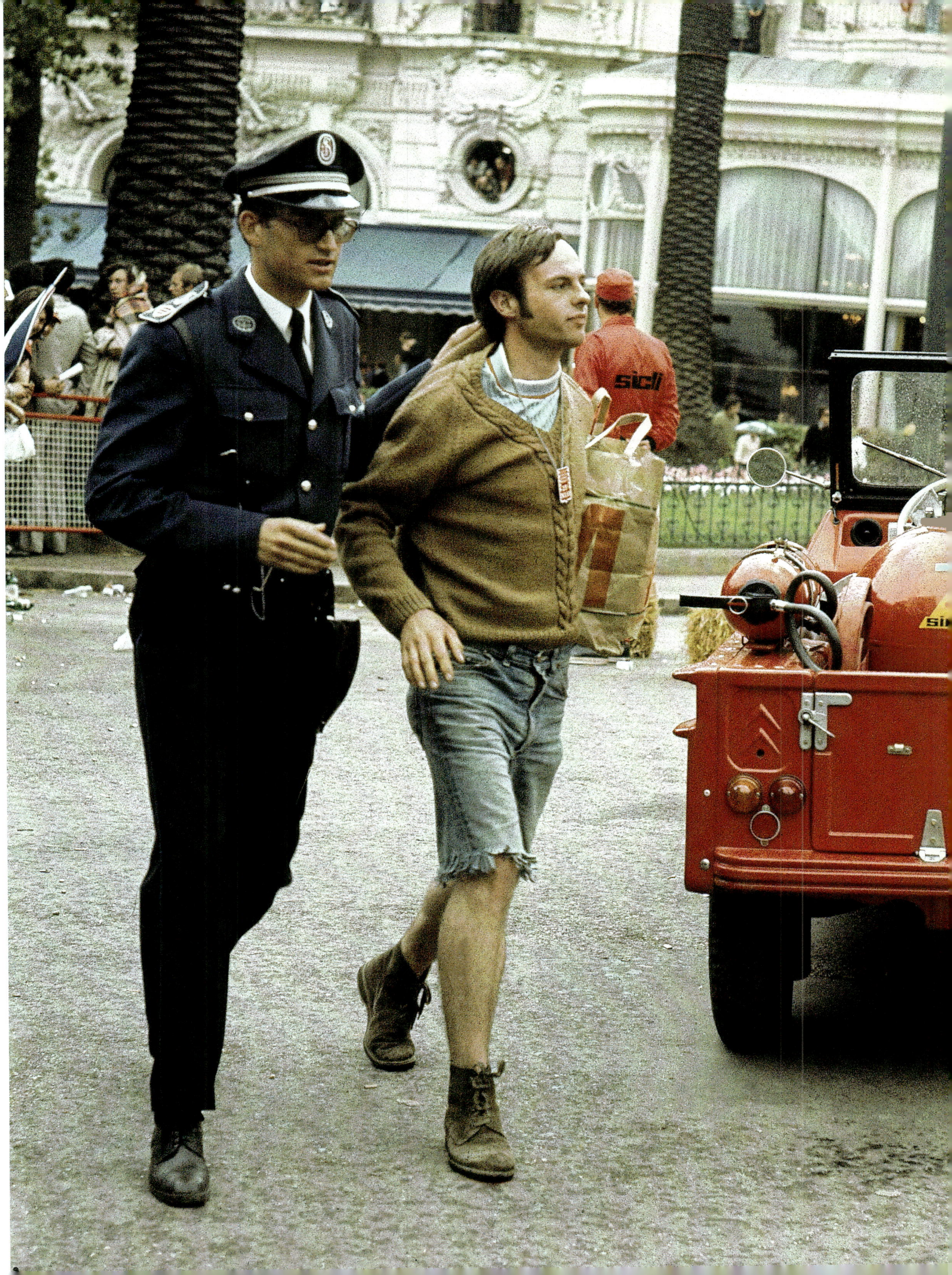
sicli

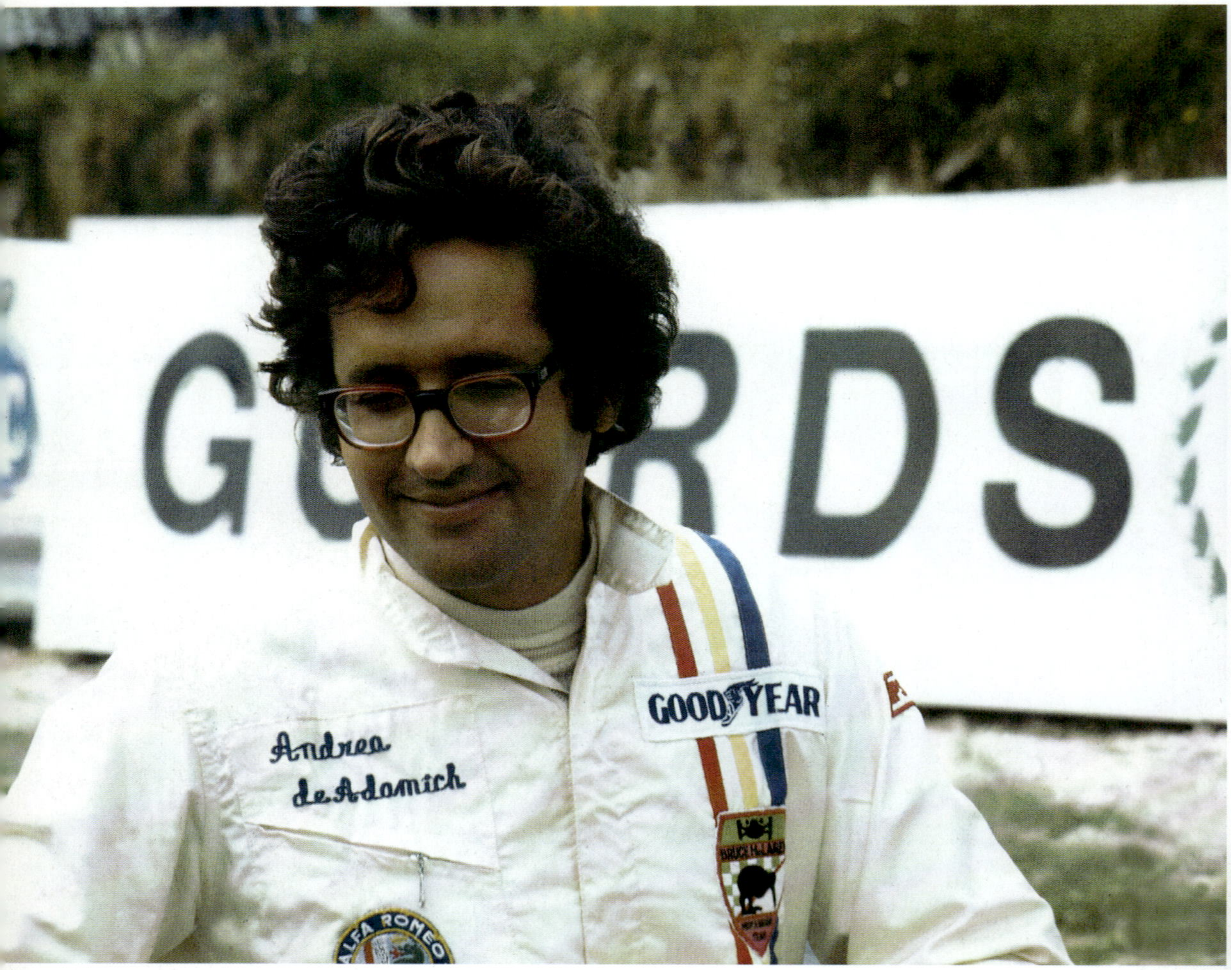

↑ Curly-haired, bespectacled Italian Andrea de Adamich, seen here at Brands Hatch in 1970, had a topsy-turvey career that included F1 and sports car racing. He was a Ferrari works driver, but a crash at the 1968 South African GP, followed by a more serious accident at the Brands Hatch ROC, ended his F1 aspirations at Maranello, even though he won two races for the Scuderia in the 1969 South American Temporada F2 series. For 1970 he found himself driving a third works McLaren M7D and later M14D powered by an Alfa Romeo V8 (he was also Alfa's works sports car driver, which brought him much better results). This proved to be unproductive, and he moved to March the following year, taking the Alfa V8 engine supply with him. This too proved fruitless, and in 1972–3 he drove for Team Surtees in its various sponsor guises before switching to Brabham along with his Ceramica Pagnossin backing. Alas, he was one of the many victims of the notorious Jody Scheckter shunt at the British GP in 1973, which broke his left leg and right ankle, and brought to a conclusion his F1 aspirations, although he continued racing for Autodelta until the end of 1974.

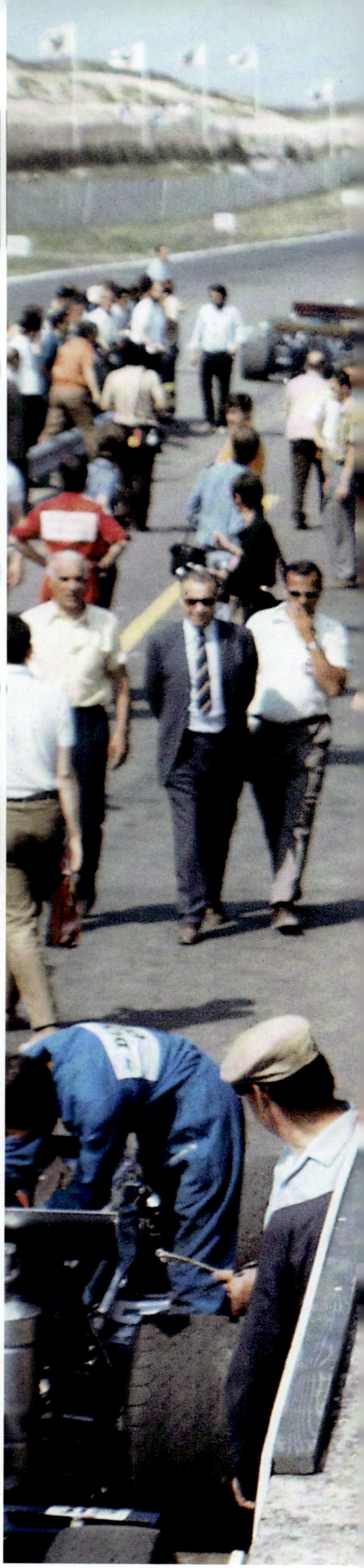

→ The roof of the Zandvoort pits was a perfect place to keep a lap chart and watch proceedings, on a sunny day at least. Denny Hulme says hello to Lyn Oliver as Ginny Parnell looks at something off camera on the Zandvoort pits roof at the 1970 Dutch GP. In the background with her (blonde) head down is Norah Tyrrell. Hulme is not driving after burning the back of his hands in an accident at Indianapolis and he has been temporarily replaced by Dan Gurney in the McLaren team. It was not a happy time as Bruce McLaren had recently died in a testing accident at Goodwood and then during the race Piers Courage perished in a fiery crash.

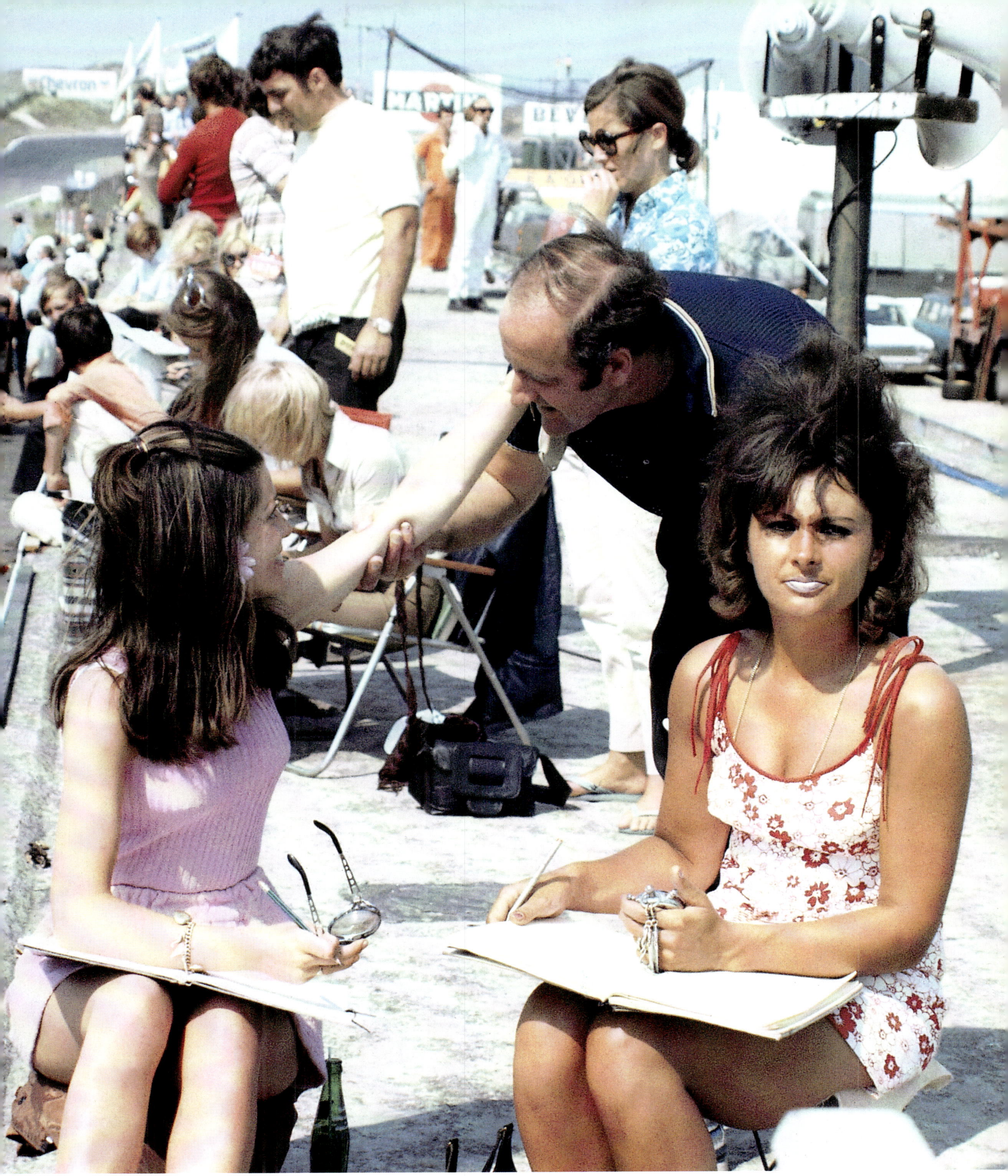
Chevron

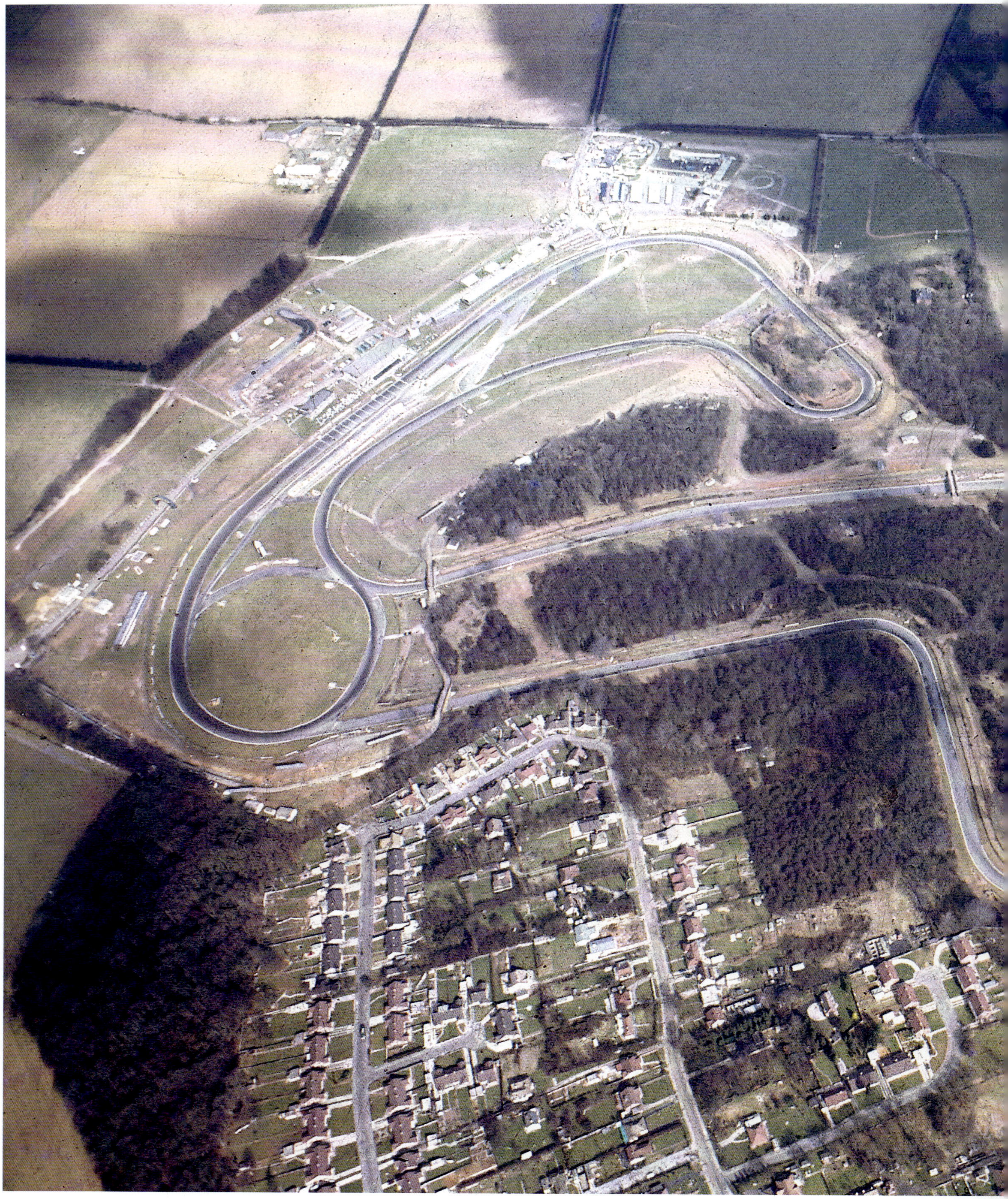

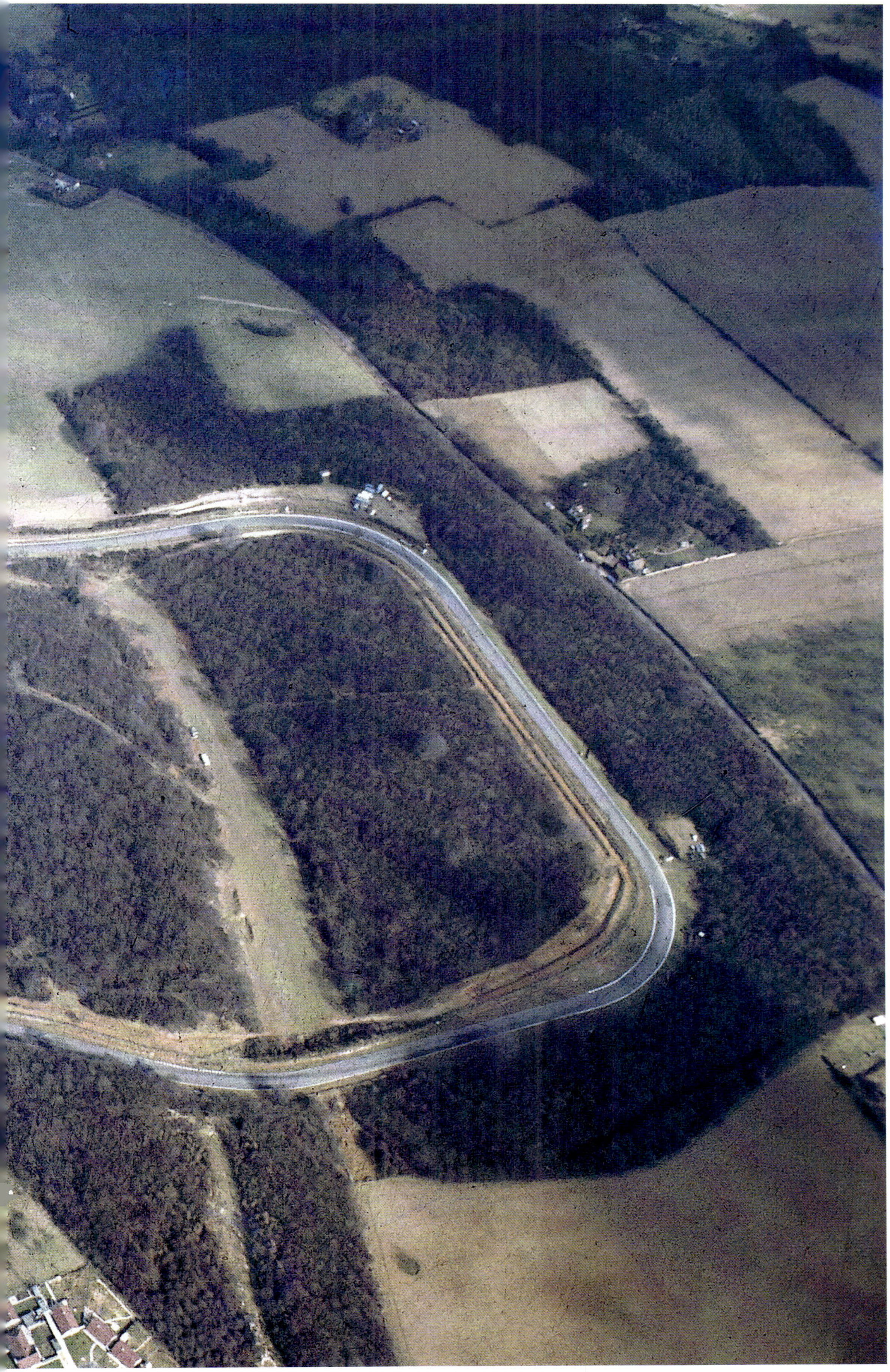

← Brands Hatch long ago, and even then surburbia had encroached upon the circuit.

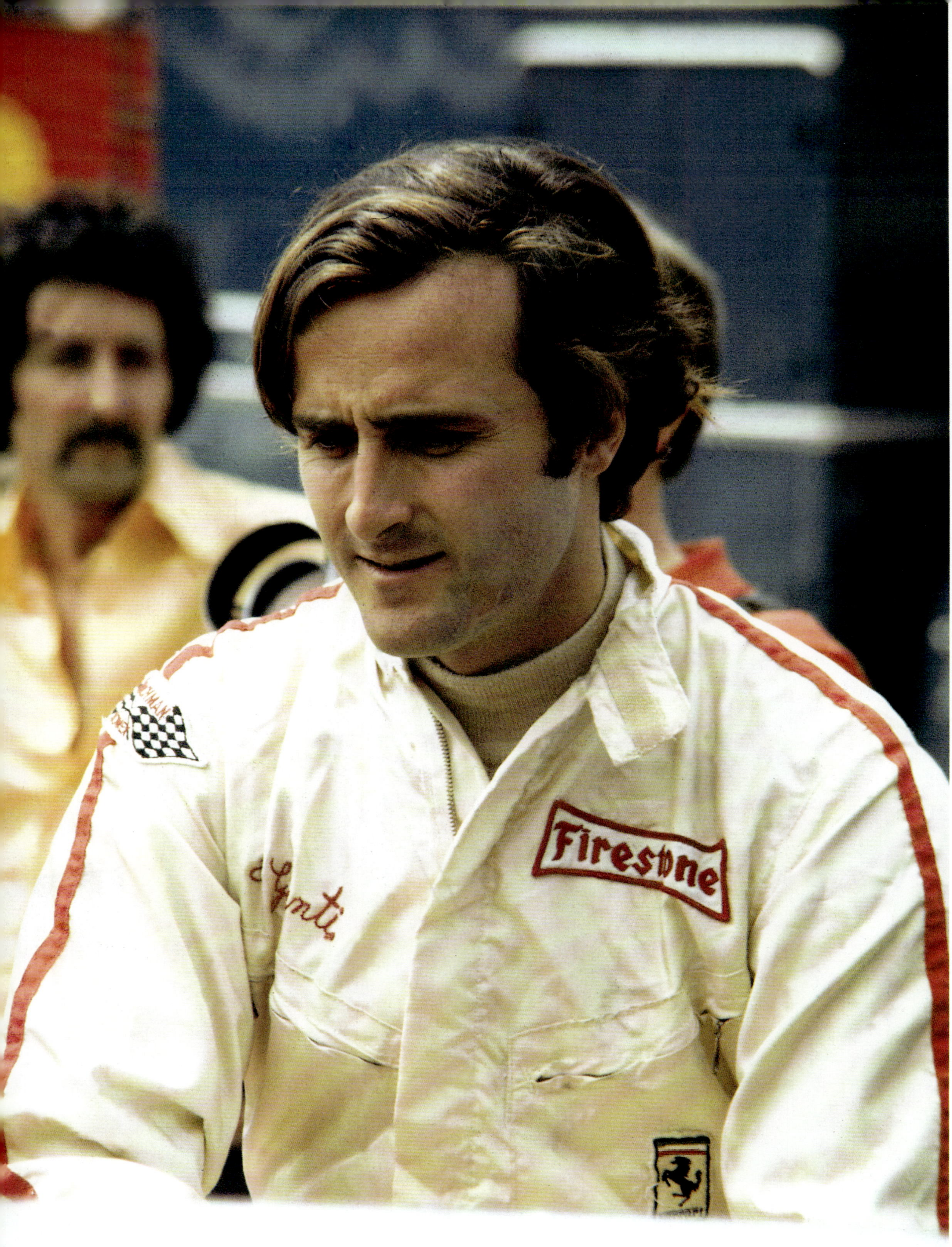
Firestone

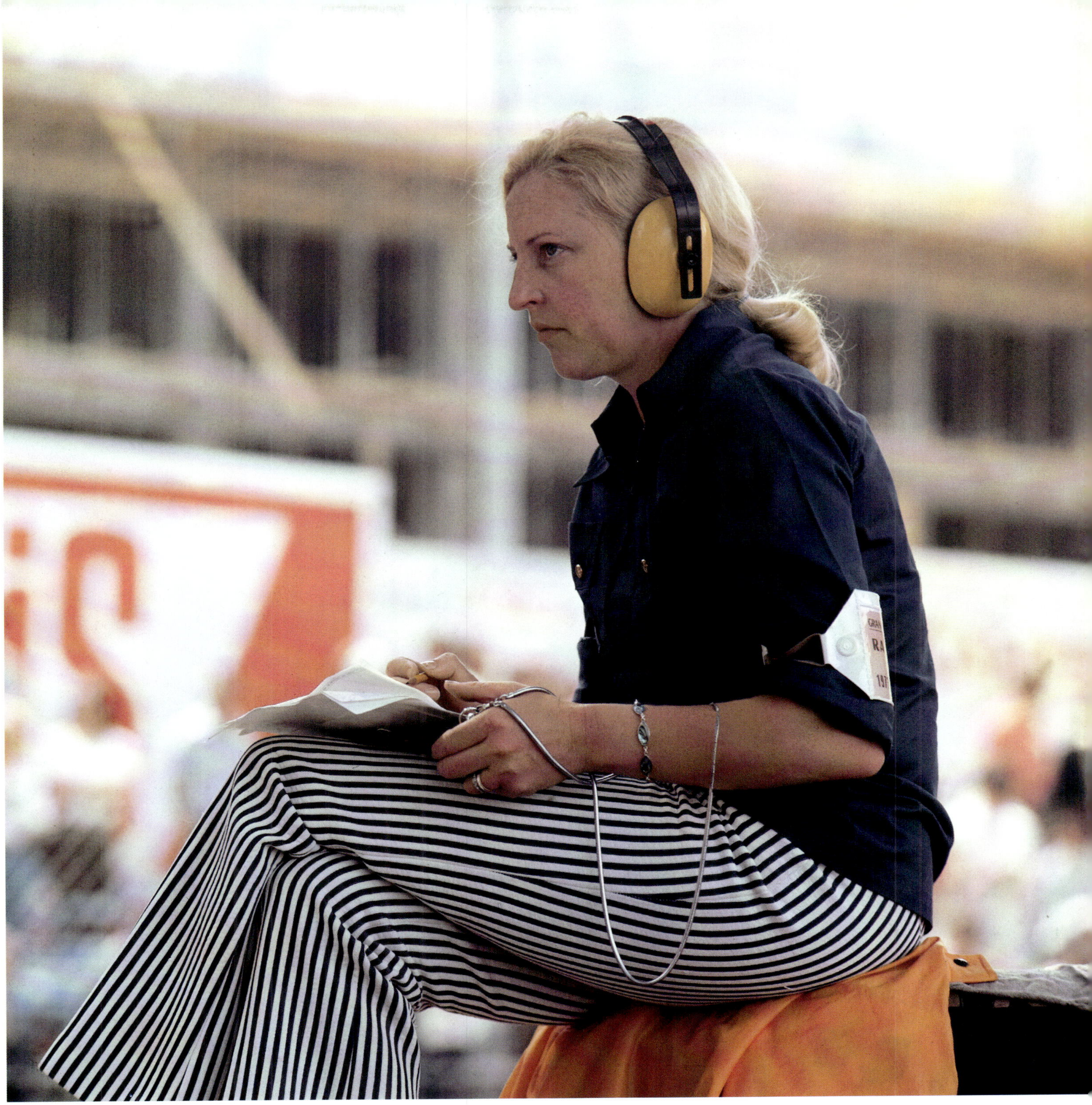

↑ Pat McLaren timekeeping at Monaco.

← Ignazio Giunti's promising career was tragically cut short by the infamous 1971 Buenos Aires 1,000km fatal collision with Jean-Pierre Beltoise's Matra which, having run out of fuel, was being pushed across the track by the Frenchman. Giunti's 1970 outings included four Grands Prix (Belgian, French, Austrian, and Italian – all for Ferrari) and he also raced the factory Ferrari 512S for nearly a complete season that included a (perhaps lucky) win at Sebring after Mario Andretti's fantastic recovery drive.

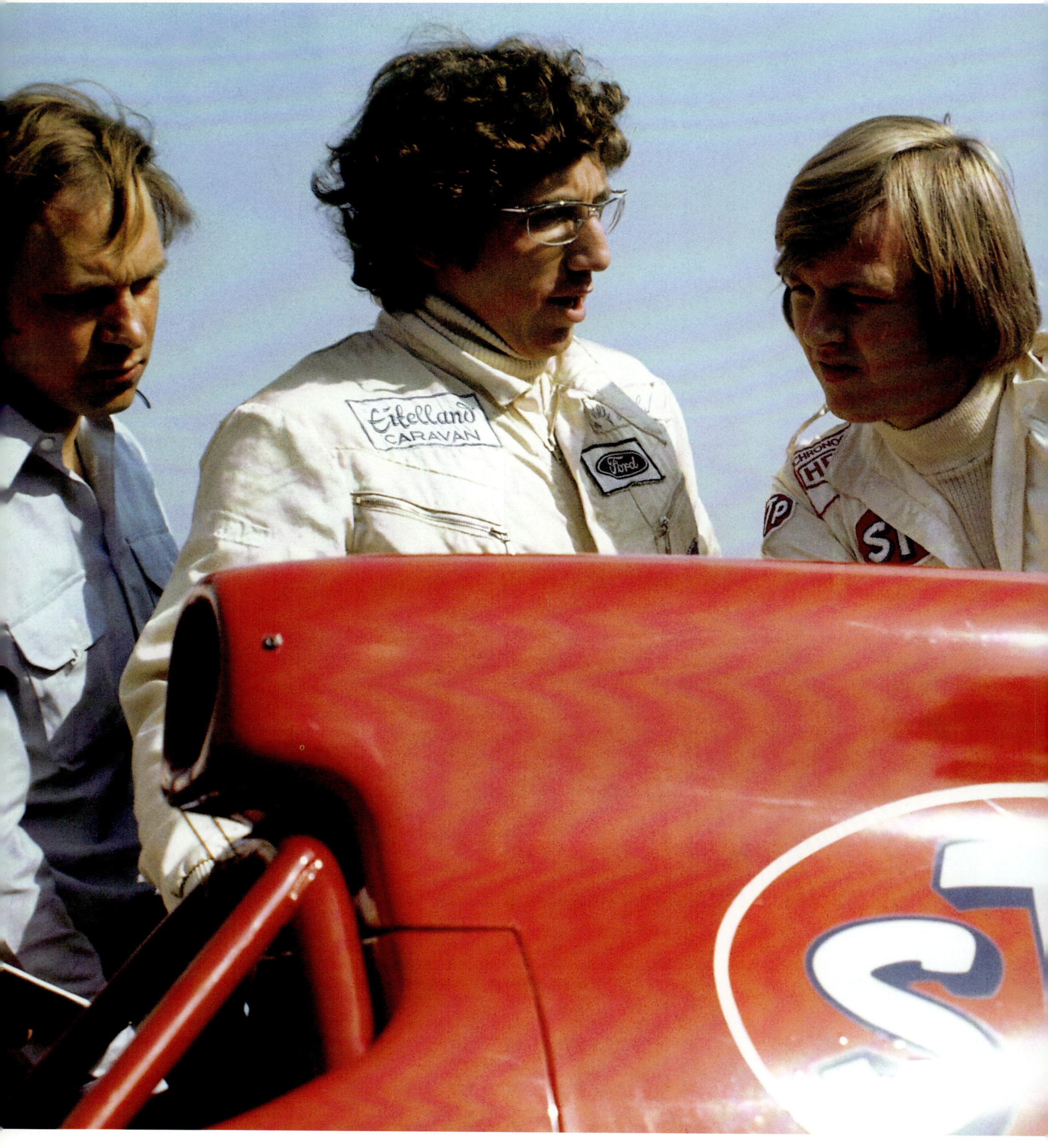
Eifelland
CARAVAN
Ford

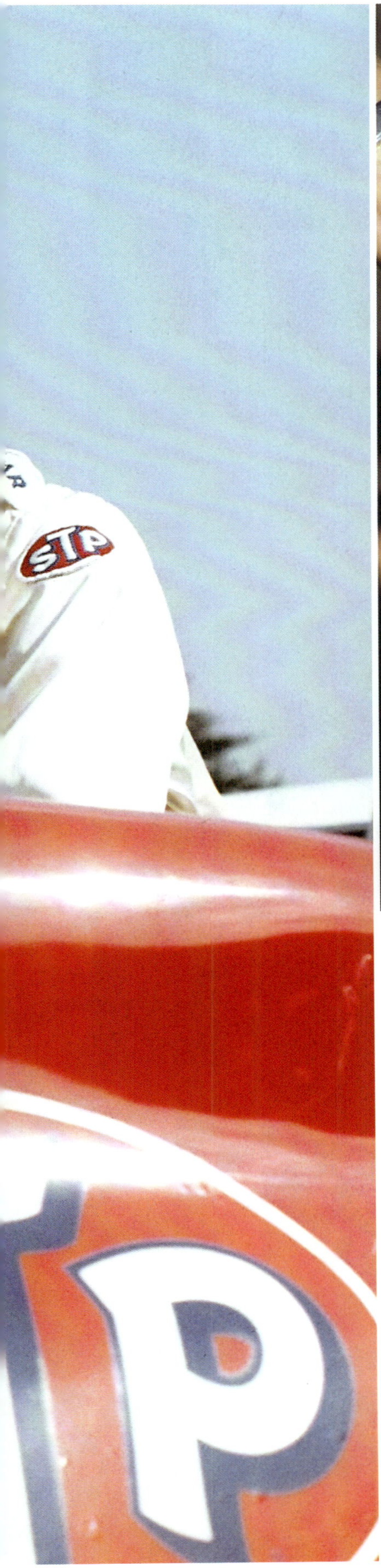

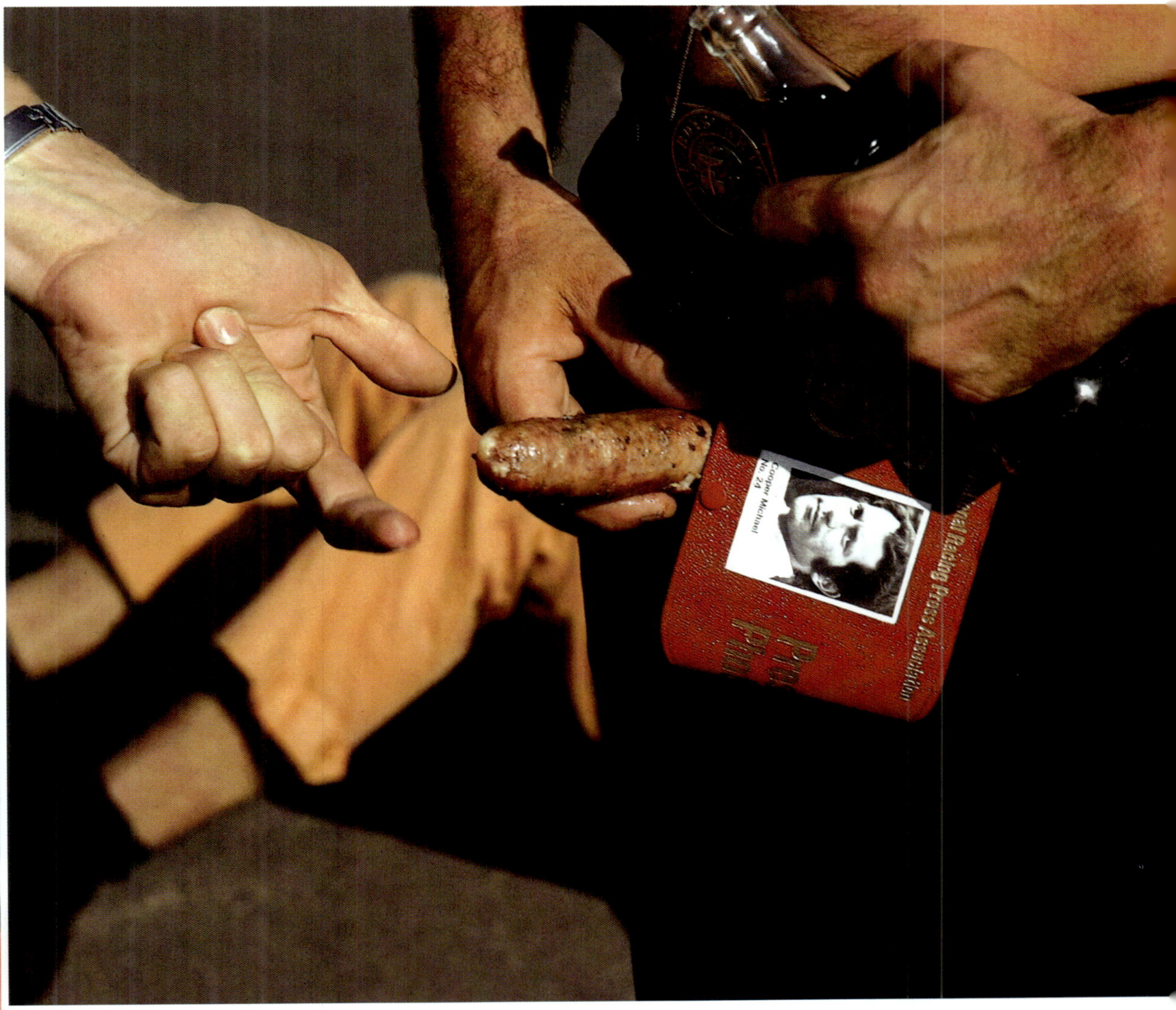

↑ When looking at this image I am reminded of Joyce Grenfell's memorable line to another character in the 1950 Frank Launder and Sydney Gilliat film *The Happiest Days of Your Life*, 'My name is Gossage, but you can call me sausage.' The red leather holder is Mike's International Racing Press Association membership pass. The IRPA was started by the famous photographer, racer, and journalist, Bernard Cahier, who died in 2008. As for the sausage, I am assured that somebody (no names, no pack drill) ate it later.

← Rolf Stommelen and Ronnie Peterson swap notes behind a March 721 airbox.

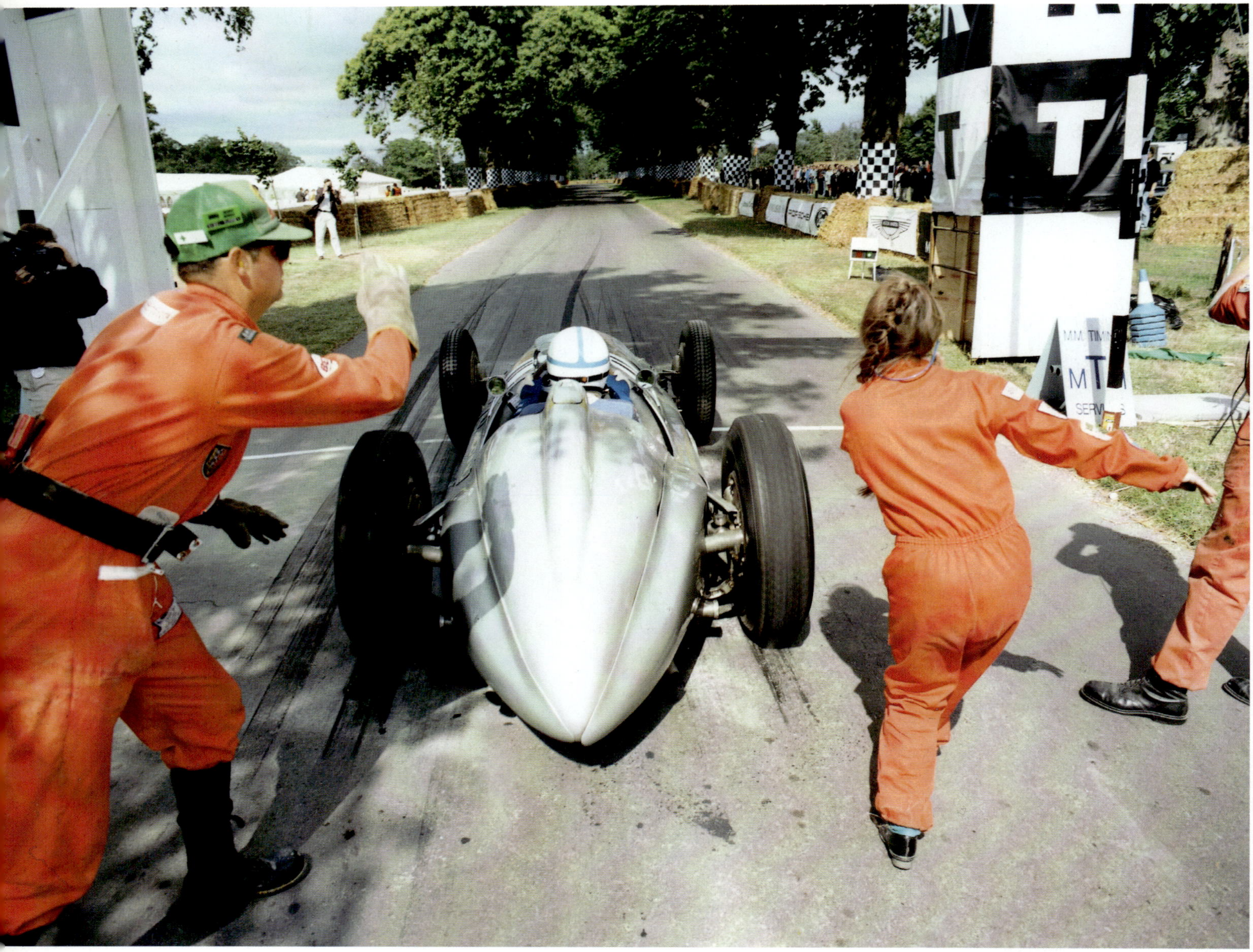

↑ Just occasionally in later years Mike could still indulge his departing shot technique as here at the 1995 Goodwood Festival of Speed. John Surtees gets the rear wheels spinning before the Mercedes Benz W154 actually starts moving forwards whilst Mike receives a lung full of V2 rocket fuel fumes.

→ The other famous Argentinian racing driver of the 1950s, José Froilán González (born 5 October 1922) in the Mk1 BRM V16 at the Goodwood Festival of Speed. Note the large number of holes drilled in his Herbert Johnson helmet, a typical device to get cooling air to the driver's head, favoured by those who raced in hot climes. As to the integrity of the crash hat, well you simply didn't put it to the test. Gonzalez was known as *The Pampas Bull* to most or apparently *El Cabezón* (fat head) to his friends, and finally ended Alfa Romeo's hegemony in post-war Grand Prix Racing by winning the 1951 British GP for Ferrari. Later on he won the Le Mans 24 Hours with Maurice Trintignant and the British GP in 1954, but he was badly affected by the death of his fellow countryman Onofre Marimón during practice for the 1954 German GP. His career gradually declined via drives with Maserati and Vanwall in 1956 then back to Ferrari briefly in 1957 before his final World Championship race at the 1960 Argentinian GP where he finished 10th for Scuderia Ferrari.

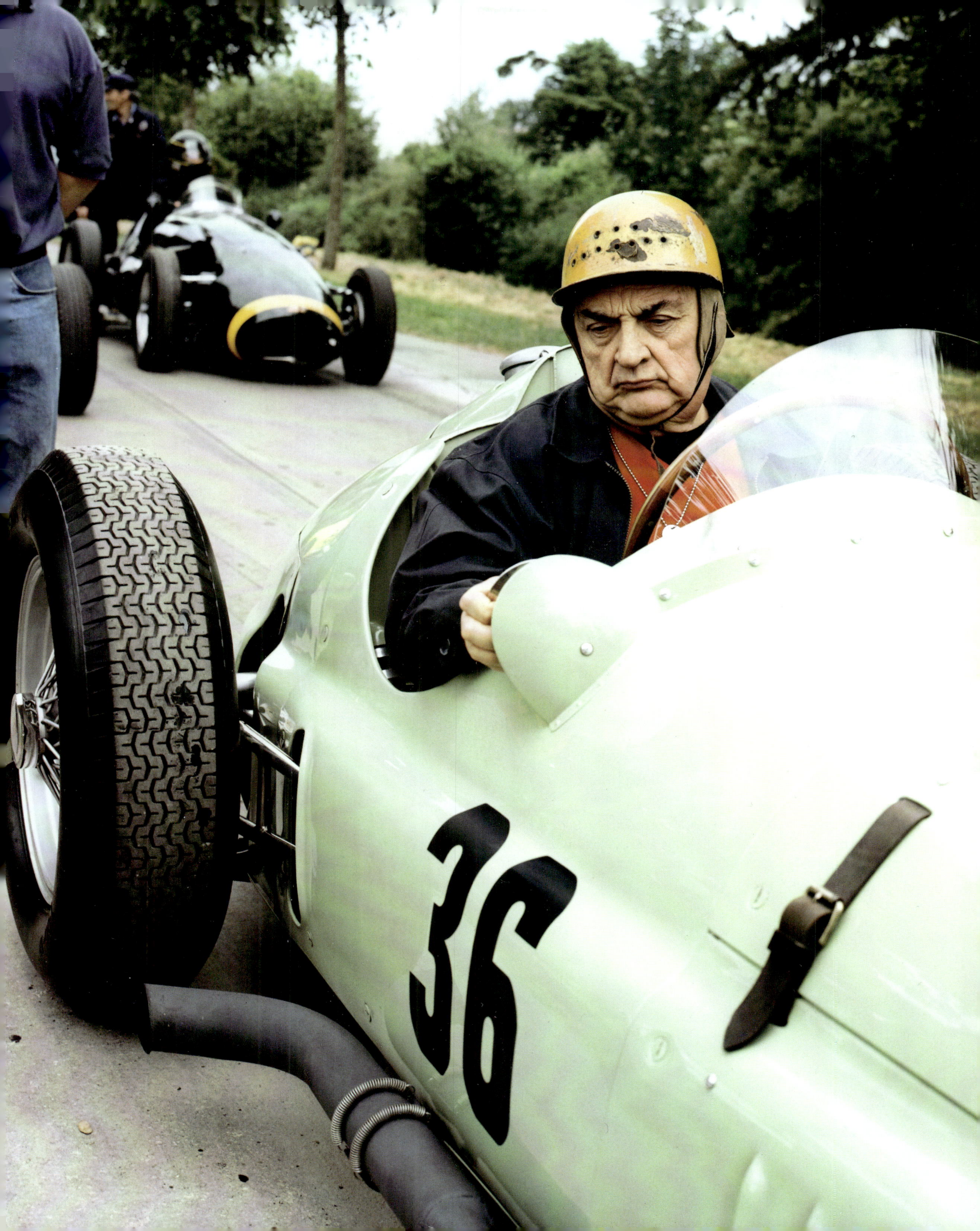
36

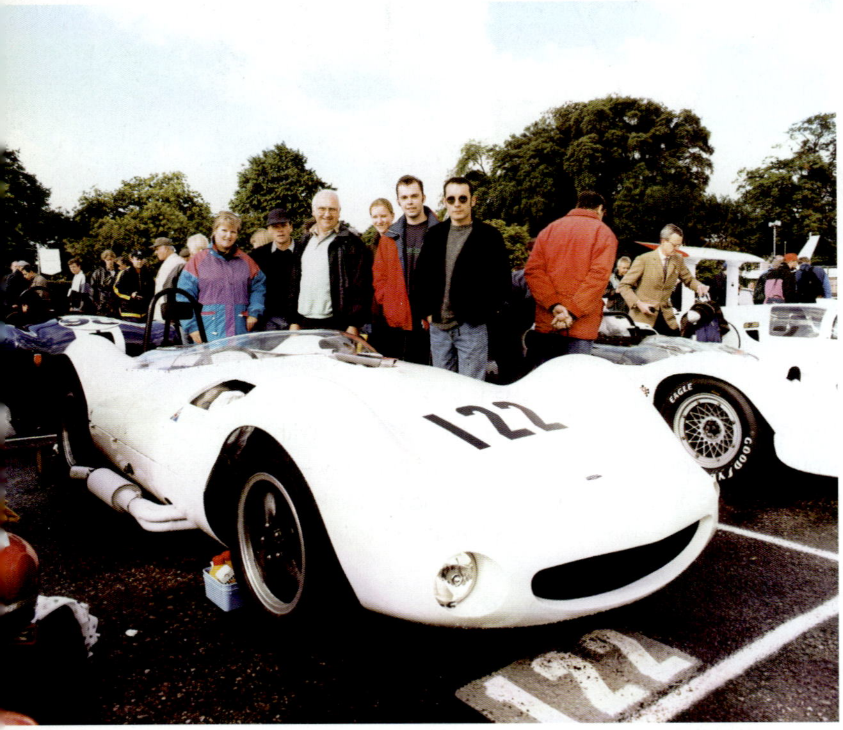

← Jim Hall's Chaparral 1 was built by Troutman and Barnes based upon Lance Reventlow's Chevy-powered Scarabs and raced for three seasons by Hall (1961/62/63). For those of an esoteric bent, Chaparral is a descriptive term for groups of plants and typically densely growing evergreen scrub oaks in parts of California and Lower California, Mexico, dependent upon a Mediterranean type climate. Similar plant communities are found in the Mediterranean basin, Chile, South Africa (Cape region) and Southern and Western Australia. Standing behind the Chaparral with hands in his pockets and wearing dark glasses is Mike's son Ben Cooper.

↓ Here, in the author's opinion, is a fitting end to this anthology of John Michael Cooper's (15 March 1938 – 19 March 2005) varied and sometimes eclectic work. In latter years Mike was a Goodwood regular, and here is another one of those snatched moments in time during the inaugural Revival meeting on 18 September 1998. The unforgettable and intrepid Ray Hannah flies his 1943 Spitfire Mk IXB G-ASJV (formerly OO-ARA) the wrong way up the pits straight at Goodwood less than 20ft above the deck. This got him into serious trouble, but it was worth it – a brief reminder of an earlier, more adventurous, and less proscribed age that Mike understood so well.

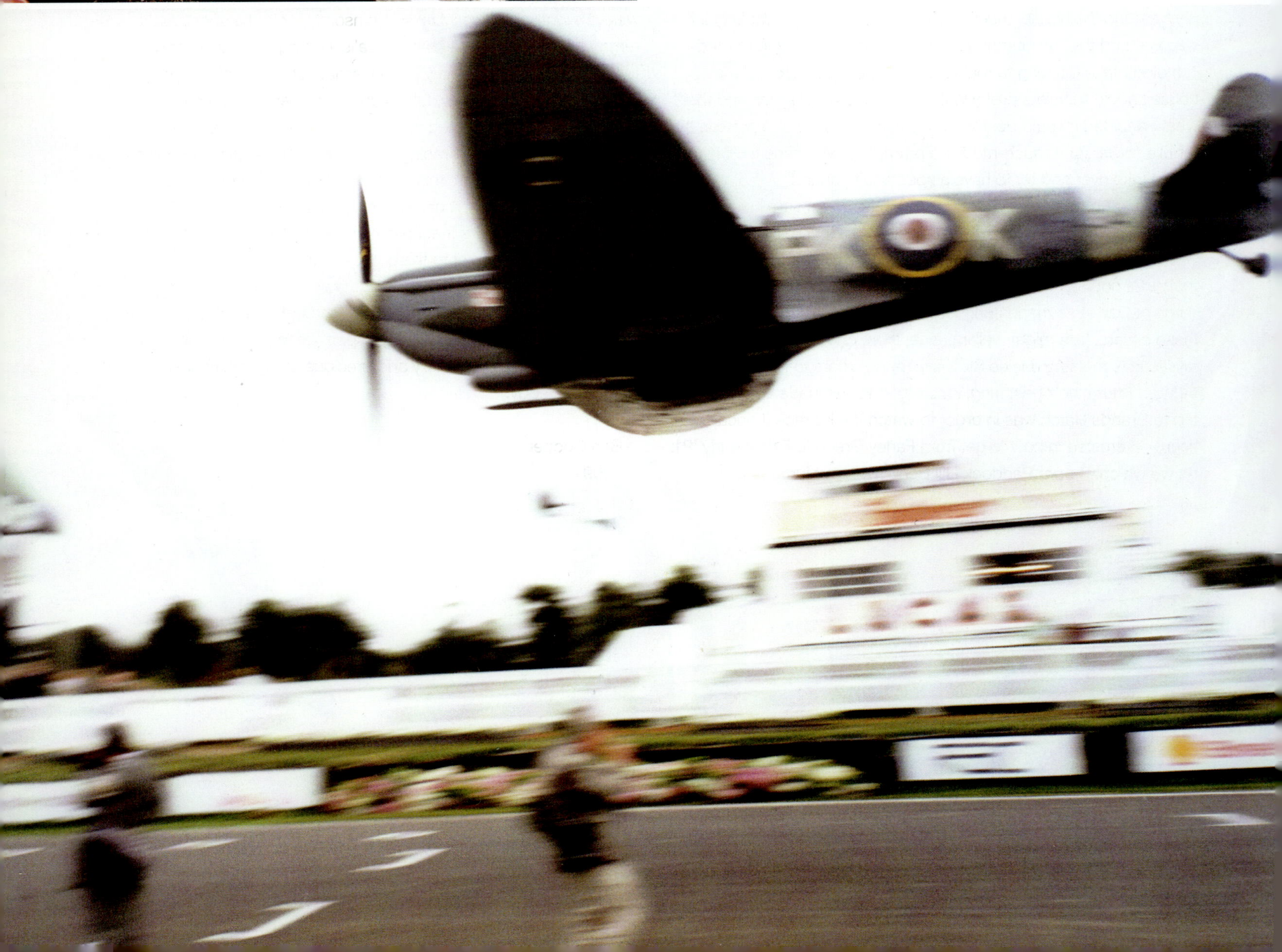

Ben Cooper

I wasn't born with motor racing in my blood, then at the very least I caught the bug very early on. Indeed, my first childhood memory is the sadness I felt watching Villeneuve's accident on the TV.

Dad took me to my first Grand Prix at Brands Hatch in 1985, shortly before my tenth birthday, and the experience didn't disappoint. Watching from Westfield bend, my first real live F1 car roared through, and so began a passion bordering on obsession with both the sport and the driver of that first black and gold car – Ayrton Senna.

Subsequent Sundays were spent in nervous anticipation of the start, and more often than not despair when the BBC decided cricket was more exciting than the unfolding Grand Prix. In the interlude, to release my frustration, I would jump on my bicycle and hare around the house, much to Dad's annoyance, particularly if it was wet and the 'Nürburgring' around our garden turned to mud.

It didn't take me long to realise that my lap times around the house should translate pretty well as a professional racer, and that's what I decided I would do. My poor sister would have to provide the motive power for a much-modified pram, and when she tired I would take over and try to have a spectacular shunt!

Growing up with Dad was an education, and I'm sure I was one of a select few ten-year-olds who knew who Lorenzo Bandini was and what Eau Rouge looked like with Jim Clark sliding through the frame. Of course, this was perfectly normal to me, and meeting some of Dad's old friends only heightened the heroic status of these drivers. You might well imagine, then, one of the highlights of my life was meeting Jackie Stewart. There's more to it than that, though! After much pestering, I managed to persuade Dad that a trip to Brands Hatch was in order to watch the F3 race (I became keenly interested in how to get from Farley Green to F1!) in early '91. As we watched from Paddock Hill Bend my heart jumped as I noticed Jackie Stewart with a small entourage watching just a few feet away. I tugged at Dad's arm, and just as I did so Stewart broke away from his group to say hello! Of course, I was deeply impressed and shyly shook his hand. We met up again later that day in an old grandstand at the back of the circuit. With no one else around, we were introduced to the rest of the party – King Hussein of Jordan and his beautiful wife Queen Noor. I think also a young David Coulthard won that weekend for Paul Stewart Racing. A pretty good weekend all in all.

Such was my immersion in the sport that I was never destined for a 'proper job'. My first employer was Frank Williams, whom Dad had photographed many years before showing empty pockets and no sign of what his future would hold. Dad's interest in F1 had waned slightly with the influx of sponsorship into the sport, and I remember him telling me that he realised things where never going to be the same when a new BRM was launched out of a super-sized packet of cigarettes. Like many of his generation he would lambaste the current breed of cars and drivers, but I wonder if he really meant it. He loved racing, and even with the new technology and increasingly sterile circuits the passion was still there. His enthusiasm for the sport carries on in me, and because of him I've been involved in teams that have won at Le Mans, Monaco, and the Indy 500. I never did get to the bottom of his disapproval of my racing, but I think deep down he was proud, even if he wasn't prepared to live his dreams vicariously through me! What I do have, though, is a whole lot of rainy days spent poring through countless boxes of motor racing history and precious family memories.

Thanks Daddy.

Ben Cooper
2009

Final thoughts

Serendipity was the reason why and how I originally met Michael Cooper and came to know him.

It was at the original Goodwood Revival press day back in 1998 which I very nearly did not attend. At the last moment it became possible and I joined the jostling throng of snappers, journos and suchlike getting in each other's way around one Stirling Moss.

As the melee sorted itself out I found myself talking to Mike about this and that and somehow the conversation turned to his determination to have his best images published to the highest quality in a proper book. He explained to me how horrified he had been at the fate of some of his contemporaries who had their material published by publishers with inadequate production values, limited budgets and not enough content.

Thereafter we quickly discovered that our paths must have crossed several times, especially at the 1962 Goodwood TT, he a 24-year-old professional photographer, me a superannuated schoolboy with an obsession for all things motor racing (as it was then). I already knew Mike's work from John Blunsden's monthly journal *Motor Racing* and the accompanying annual that covered each season.

So to my eternal good fortune he had the faith to collaborate with me on *Sixties Motor Racing* for Palawan Press as at that time I had nothing actually published although I was working on *Jaguar at Le Mans 1950–1995* for Haynes. From such arbitrary beginnings can things be created and now nearly a decade later here I am again wading through Mike's oeuvre for another look at the world of motor sport and other things as he saw them.

Time passed and through numerous visits to Mike and Liz's home I came to know a man who was cultured, eternally optimistic and forward looking, yet paradoxically nostalgic and reflective. It was just as well as I tend to be pessimistic and backward facing and at times Mike probably found me a bit of a chore. However, one of the best things about Mike was that any disagreement was quickly and easily settled with some choice insults and then almost instantly dismissed.

The ability to give and take such remarks and then bear no grudge is the hallmark of a genuine person and Mike was thus in spades. He could also be quite mischievous and the *enfant terrible* was never too far away, but then you need this to be creative. We had a great time sorting through thousands of his images during 1999 and many a laugh as he recalled a scurrilous detail or two. I keep thinking about what he would have made of or said of some of the images in this new book.

He was always happier working in black and white and preferred the human aspect of the subject rather than just concentrating on mere machines. Inevitably there were the black moments in motor sport and Mike was not afraid to capture them on film, but these were an expected price to pay in the full realisation that actions could and sometimes did have serious consequences. He was not at all happy with the changes wrought by the safety campaigns that stopped him from photographing where once he had stood without let or hindrance, or the increasingly sterile and uniform backdrops.

Then there was the once easy, relaxed access to drivers, Mike recalling to me one day that where formerly he could ask a famous driver to take him or a colleague around a circuit after practice he suddenly found himself, courtesy of Mark McCormack's IMG (International Management Group), being asked $4,000 for the privilege.

However, beyond the motor racing, all sound and fury that signifies nothing to quote the Bard, Mike was happiest in his garden, vegetable patch and orchard, forever railing at the montjacs and rabbits and wiring off his precious plants, vegetables and fruits. Every year he would give me enough apples to supply a medium sized greengrocer and famile Cooper were always self sufficient in the fruit and veg department.

Finally came the day that I was testing an ex-Ecurie Ecosse Tojeiro-Buick at Goodwood and I had asked Mike if he would attend and take some pictures of me trying to drive it properly, to which he agreed. He did not appear and I was a trifle disappointed, then two days later Michael Turner rang me up with the awful news. I thanked him, put the phone down, cried a while and remembered all the times I had interrupted his evening meal or viewing of Indycar racing which, God bless, used to irritate him.

Meanwhile, time must be found to print the contents of more rolls of apparently unseen film, as we've barely scratched the proverbial surface so far. Here's to the next one, chin, chin!

Acknowledgements and Bibliography

My sincerest thanks to all those who have assisted me in the production of this book without whom some details would have slipped through the proverbial net:

Liz, Jo and Ben Cooper, Glenda Colquhoun, Anthony Hussey, Michael Turner, Dexter Brown, Alan Cox, David McKinney, Doug Nye, Graham Gauld, Neil Murray, Bill Colson, Robert Barker, Willie Green, Ludovic Lindsay, James Lindsay, David Tremayne and of course my endlessly patient and beautiful wife Sarah Joslin Parker, Helga Oates, the very tolerant Mark Hughes, Christine Smith, my long suffering but always understanding editor Derek Smith and all at Haynes Publishing.

Finally mille grazie Mike for making all this possible.

AUTOCOURSE 1988/89
(Hazelton Publishing 1988) various authors

Autocourse History of the Grand Prix Car 1966-85
(Hazelton Publishing 1986) Doug Nye

BRM – The Saga of British Racing Motors Volume 2 – Spaceframe Cars 1959-65
(MRP 2003) Doug Nye

BRM – The Saga of British Racing Motors Volume 3 – Monocoque V8 Cars 1963-69
(MRP 2008) Doug Nye

COOPER CARS
(Osprey Publishing 1983) Doug Nye

The Jack Brabham Story
(Pavilion Books Limited 2004) Sir Jack Brabham OBE with Doug Nye

MCLAREN: The Grand Prix, CanAm and Indy Cars (second edition)
(Hazelton Publishing 1988) Doug Nye

BRABHAM THE GRAND PRIX CARS
(Hazelton Publishing 1985) Alan Henry

DAN GURNEY THE ULTIMATE RACER
(Haynes Publishing 2000) Karl Ludvigsen

Grand Prix Who's Who 3rd Edition
(Travel Publishing 2000) Steve Small

Gentleman Jack The Official Biography of Jack Sears
(Veloce Publishing 2008) Graham Gauld

Piers Courage LAST OF THE GENTLEMAN RACERS
(Haynes Publishing 2003) Adam Cooper

VIC ELFORD REFLECTIONS OF A GOLDEN ERA IN MOTORSPORTS
(David Bull Publishing 2006) Vic Elford

Formula 1 Register Record Book 1966
(St. Leonards Press 1990) Paul Sheldon with Duncan Rabagliati and Yves de la Gorce

The Formula One Record Book
(Leslie Frewin Publishers 1974) John Thompson with Duncan Rabagliati and Dr. K. Paul Sheldon

Grand Prix Volume 1 1950 to 1965
(Haynes Publishing 1981) Mike Lang

Grand Prix Volume 2 1966 to 1973
(Haynes Publishing 1982) Mike Lang

THE BAHAMAS SPEED WEEKS
(Veloce Publishing 2006) Terry O'Neil

STIRLING MOSS THE AUTHORISED BIOGRAPHY
(Cassell & Co 2001) Robert Edwards

JOHN SURTEES World Champion
(Hazelton Publishing 1991) Edited by Alan Henry

AMERICAN GRAND PRIX RACING A Century of Drivers & Cars
(Motorbooks International 1997) Tim Considine

DAYTONA COBRA COUPÉS CARROLL SHELBY'S 1965 WORLD CHAMPIONS
(Stauffer Publishing 1995) Peter Brock, Dave Friedman, George Stauffer

Maserati Birdcage The marvellous Tipo 60 and 61 sports racing cars
(Osprey Publishing 1980) Joel E. Finn

Formula 1 IN CAMERA 1960-69
(Haynes Publishing 2006) Paul Parker

Formula 1 IN CAMERA 1970-79
(Haynes Publishing 2003) Paul Parker with Rainer Schlegelmilch

Sports Car Racing IN CAMERA 1960-69
(Haynes Publishing 2007) Paul Parker

Sports Car Racing IN CAMERA 1970-79
(Haynes Publishing 2008) Paul Parker

Additionally reference was made to period race reports and obituaries in *Autosport* and *Motor Sport* journals.

Index

AAR (All American Racers) 110, 142
AC 326; Ace 14; Cobra 79, 88, 106 *see also* Shelby Cobra
Aero-Spares Co. 57
AGS-Cosworth JH23 262
Aintree 33, 34, 47, 49, 59, 60
Aitken, Sir Max 186
Alboreto, Michele 269
Aley, John 34
Alfa Romeo 110, 330; T33/2 189; TZ 87
Alliot, Philippe 266
Allison, Cliff 11
Ambrose, Tony 108
American Grand Prix Racing: A Century of Drivers and Cars 143
Amherst Villiers, Charles 288, 292
Amon, Chris 70, 97, 127, 154, 159, 175, 177, 180, 185, 191, 199, 212, 240, 275, 279, 297
Anderson, Bob 131
Arrows A10B-Megatron 4: 261
Arundell, Peter 42, 77, 82, 108
Aston, Bill 62
Aston Martin 49, 52; DB2 14; DB2/4 MkIII 17; DB3S/5 14; DBR1/300 17, 21, 23; DBR4/250 27; Project 214: 54, 102; Project 215: 54
Atkins, Cyril 183
Atkins, Tommy 29, 69, 106
ATS 100: 70
Attwood, Richard 87, 116, 119, 183
Aurora Gear Racing 119
Austin 1800 187
Austin A90 14
Austin-Healey 3000 77, 108
Austrian GP 245
Auto Union 1000S 34
Autocar, The 27
Autodynamic 146
Autosport 34, 144, 197

Baghetti, Giancarlo 70, 88, 93, 109
Bailey, Julian 269
Baillie, Gawaine 62, 69
Baker, Clive 128
Baldyne Engineering 115
Balestre, Jean-Marie 310
Ballisat, Keith 88
Bamford, Tony 231
Bandini, Lorenzo 54, 81, 85, 137, 138, 149, 347
Barker, Ronald 270, 272
Barthel, Dennis 14
Bartram, R. M. (Rick/Terry) 36, 298
Beeson, Tony 189
Belgian GP: 1964 54, 88, 90, 93; 1965 116; 1967 154; 1968 175, 177, 334; 1970 212; 1972 240
Bell, Derek 193
Bell helmets 21, 47, 209, 213, 295
Beltoise, Jean-Pierre 177, 232, 234, 239, 242, 341
Benetton-Ford B188 263
Bentley 8-litre 330
Bentley S2 73
Berger, Gerhard 269
Berman, Monty 112
Bernard, Rosie 229
Bertocchi, Guerrino 302
Beuttler, Mike 255
Birrell, Gerry 109, 303
Birrell, Graham and Jenny 303
Blackbushe aerodrome 106
Blumer, Jimmy 64, 88
Blydenstein, Bill 34
BMW 300
Bolster, John Vary 298
Bondurant, Bob 121
Bonnier, Jo 19, 31, 163, 194
Borgward Isabella TS 34
Boutsen, Thierry 263
Bowmaker 62
Boyd, Maxwell 109
Brabham 110, 229; BT6 77; BT7 97; BT8 99, 111; BT10 115; BT11 90, 93, 97; BT16 119, 121; BT18 300; BT19 131, 138, 153; BT20 153; BT21 301; BT24 161, 164; BT26A 189, 196; BT30 194, 210; BT33 220, 223; BT34/1 226, 229; BT36 226; BT42 255
Brabham, Jack 23, 29, 39, 41, 88, 93, 110, 131, 138, 153, 164, 189, 209, 220, 229
Brands Hatch 9, 62, 99, 100, 198, 287, 288, 329, 339; Anglo-European Trophy 77; Guards Motor Show 200: 166; Guards Trophy 62, 100, 111 JCB Trophy 231; Molyslip Trophy 62; Panter Cigar Challenge Trophy 231; Peco GT Trophy 51, 62; Race of Champions 143, 169, 172, 224; 6 Hour races 64, 110, 156, 159, 161, 169, 171, 172, 189, 191; *see also* British GP: 1968/70/72/85
British GP: 1961 47, 49; 1962 59, 60; 1963 73; 1967 156, 197; 1968 180; 1970 216, 217, 219, 220; 1972 242; 1985 347; 1988 198, 259, 261, 262, 263, 265, 266, 269
Brittan, Nick 144, 146
BRM 10, 54, 110, 219, 271, 347; 4WD F1 car 301; P48 31, 36; P57 36, 88; P83 132, 154, 164; P126 172, 180, 183, 185; P133/01 172, 175; P138/01 193; P153 194, 201, 203, 207, 210, 212, 236; P160 198, 226, 232, 236, 239, 257; P180 236, 239; P261 81, 82, 93, 99, 132, 138; P578 55, 93, 292; V16 Mk1 344
Broadley, Eric 54
Broccoli, Albert 'Cubby' 270, 282
Brooke Bond Oxo 220
Brooks, Tony 11, 36, 295
Brough Superior SS80 312
Brown, Alan 69
Brown, Darin 197
Brown, Dexter 197, 197, 324, 326
Brymon, Billy 307
Buchet, Robert 88
Bugatti 317
Burnard, Keith 159
Byrne, Nicky 34, 62

Cahier, Bernard 10, 270, 343
Caldwell, Alistair 201, 332
Camel 261
Camoradi 24, 47
Campbell, Malcolm 317
Canon 262
Capelli, Ivan 265
Carlsson, Erik and Pat 57
Casner, Lloyd 'Lucky' 23, 47
Centro Sud 88
Cevert, François 210, 216, 255, 257, 308
Chaparral 110; 1: 346; 2A 127, 128; 2F 110, 156, 159, 161
Chapman, Colin 10, 33, 54, 82, 126, 194, 215, 250, 314
Charlton, Dave 159
Charman, Jim 301
Chequered Flag 59, 112
Chevrolet: Corvette 52; Corvette Sting Ray 127; Impala 34
Chipstead Motor Group 122, 125
Chitty Chitty Bang Bang 197, 270, 280, 282
Church, John 301
Clark, Jim 19, 29, 42, 54, 55, 59, 70, 73, 77, 82, 88, 90, 94, 97, 102, 105, 108, 109, 110, 116, 119, 134, 141, 149, 151, 153, 161, 164, 171, 172, 197, 347
Clermont-Ferrand 242, 271, 272, 275
Clutton, Cecil 317
Collins, Peter 289
Coloni, Lutz 'Luigi' 239
Coltman Displays 12
Consodine, Tim 143
Cook, Humphrey 229
Coombs, John 17, 21, 23, 34, 45, 51, 62, 67, 69, 119, 121, 210
Cooper 10, 110, 122, 138, 141; Monaco 23, 33, 67, 77; T51 29; T53 29, 36, 39, 42, 45, 47, 59, 102, 105; T55 41; T56 42; T60 166; T66 73; T73 81, 85, 88, 90, 97, 141; T75 121; T80 122, 125; T81 134, 138, 141; T83 128; T86 154, 156; T86B 179
Cooper, Adam 204
Cooper, Alice 23
Cooper, Ben 109, 287, 324, 346, 347
Cooper, George 14, 17, 27
Cooper, Jo 109, 287, 324, 347
Cooper, John 90, 122, 128, 154, 166
Cooper, June 231
Cooper, Liz 9, 109, 197, 229, 270, 288, 319; cottage 322
Cooper, Margaret 17
Cooper, Michael 7, 9, 12, 17, 27, 53, 54, 67, 109, 197-198, 229, 270, 279, 284, 287, 288, 324, 343, 347, 348; cottage 322; exhibition 319; Kingly Street studio, London W1 288, 324
Cooper Cars 128
Corner, Neil and Freda 290
Cosworth 4WD F1 car 193
Cottam, Alan 69
Coulthard, David 347
Coundley, John 33
Courage, Piers 180, 183, 196, 204, 209, 215
Cowan, Andrew 187
Coyle, Brian 187
Crabbe, Colin 156, 159
Crabtree, Mike 189
Craig, Michael 12
Crombac, Gérard 'Jabby' 134, 270
Crystal Palace 186, 210, 229
Culceth, Brian 187
Cunningham-Reid, Noel 36

Daigh, Chuck 39
Dallara, Gianpaulo 209
Dalmas, Yannick 266
Dangerfield, Neil 113
Davis, Colin 62
Davis, Sydney 'Sammy' 290
de Adamich, Andrea 210, 336
de Beaufort, Carel Godin 49, 75
de Cadenet, Alain 189
de Mortemart, Jean 88
de Tomaso 505: 204, 209
de Villiers Special 49
Delage II 330
Dennis, Ron 156, 220
Depailler, Patrick 146, 259
Derby-Maserati fwd 94
Dibley, Hugh 99, 100, 169
Dickinson, John 77
Dickson, Tom 33
Dors, Diana 12
drag racing 106
Dragoni, Eugenio 81, 137
Dryden, Colin 109
Dubois, Claud 88
Duckworth, Keith 151, 193
Duclos, Kenneth 127
Durnay, Pierre 87
Dutch GP: 1961 41, 42; 1963 70; 1966 141; 1967 110, 151, 153; 1970 213, 215, 336

Eagle-Climax T1F-101 142
Eagle-Weslake 110, 142, 143, 147, 154, 161
Earls Court Motor Show 197, 312, 326
Eason Gibson, John 34
Eaton, George 217
Ecurie Ecosse 19, 33; Ford sports car 99
Ecurie Francorchamps 87
Ecurie Galloise 59
Ecurie Maarsbergen 49, 75
Ecurie Pan American 75
Eifelland Caravans 239
Elford, Vic 156, 172, 179, 305
Ellis, Tony 94
Elva-BMW 100
Embassy 252
Equipe Endeavour 31, 34, 51, 57, 60, 62, 64
ERA R1B/R5B/R9B 94
ERA R11B 229

Fairman, Jack 17, 21, 49
Fall, Tony 187
Faure, Nick 290
Felday Engineering 194, 301; 4WD F1 car 301
Fenning, John 128
Ferguson P99 4WD 49, 301
Ferrari 10, 47, 54, 110, 175, 191, 210; 246SP 62; 250GT SWB 31, 51, 52, 102; 250GTO 54, 57, 62, 69, 77, 79, 88, 113; 250LM 87, 106, 127; 312: 131, 137, 138, 151, 177, 180, 242, 255; 312P 191; 330P 102, 105, 159; 335S 289; 365P2 111; 512M 141; Dino 156: 42, 81, 85; Dino 158: 137, 138; Dino 206S 189; F1/76/88C 269; Testa Rossa (0776R) 11
Fittipaldi, Emerson 210, 224, 234, 236, 242, 245, 247, 250, 314, 329
Fitzpatrick, John 166
Fleming, Ian 270, 282
Fletcher, A. F. Rivers 317
Foghieri, Mauro 90, 131, 151, 175
Follmer, George 250
Ford 110; Anglia 67, 109, 144, 146, 166; Capri 3 litre 284; Cortina 53; Cortina Mk 1 GT 69, 305; F3L P68 171, 172; Galaxie 69; GT40 54, 87, 110, 116, 159, 171, 172, 210, 272, 275; GTX-1 127; MkIV 110; Mustang 64; Zodiac 62
Formula Vee 144, 146
Forster, Nigel Arnold 330
4WD F1 projects 49, 193, 194, 224, 301, 303
Foyt, A. J. 100, 126
Fraissinet, Régis 88
Frankenheimer, John 142, 270, 271, 275, 277, 279
Fraser, Alan 60, 146, 166
French GP: 1961 109; 1964 54, 97, 99; 1966 141; 1968 110, 179, 180; 1971 229; 1972 242
Frère, Paul 17, 21
Fry, Tim 31

Galli, Giovanni 'Nanni' 240, 242
Ganley, Howden 239, 252, 320
Gardner, Frank 77, 100, 113, 119
Garner, James 270, 272
Gauld, Graham 69, 99, 186
Gendebien, Oliver 11
General Motors Styling 53
Gentleman Jack 69, 186
German GP: 1966 141; 1967 161; 1968 183; 1969 194, 196
Gethin, Peter 232, 236
Gilbert, Geoff 113
Gill, Barrie 169, 180
Ginetta G16A-BRM 189
Ginther, Richie 47, 69, 82, 99, 110, 147
Giunti, Ignazio 341
Goddard, Geoffrey 10, 53, 102, 198, 270
Gold Leaf Team Lotus 177, 183, 189, 204, 215, 220 *see also* Lotus; Team Lotus
González, José Froilán 344
Goodwood 11, 14, 57, 36, 109, 128, 288, 289, 332, 348; Sussex Trophy 33, 57, 79; Tourist Trophy 17, 19, 21, 23, 51, 52, 102, 105, 106, 348
Goodwood Festival of Speed 329, 344
Goodwood Revival meeting 346, 348
Goozee, Nick 220
Gordon, Peter, & Co. 14
Gosport Speed Trials 14
Grand Prix 9, 142, 270, 271, 272, 275, 277, 279
Grand Prix Medical Unit 310
Grange Garage 36
Grant, Jerry 297
Green, Willie 189, 231, 290
Greenblatt, David 127
Gregory, Masten 11, 17, 19, 23, 47
Grossman, Bob 88, 127
Gugelmin, Mauricio 265
Gurney, Dan 11, 23, 31, 34, 54, 82, 88, 93, 97, 106, 109, 110, 142, 143, 154, 161, 183, 213, 295, 297
GUY 108

Hailwood, Mike 312
Halford, Bruce 64
Hall, Jim 70, 128, 288, 334, 346
Handley, John 166
Hannah, Ray 288, 346
Hansgen, Walt 100
Happiest Days of Your Life, The 343
Harper, Peter 62
Harris, Ron 77, 119
Hawkes, Douglas 94
Hawkins, Paul 77, 119
Haye, Neville 231
Hayes, Walter 210
Haynes, David 62
Haywood, Hurley 236
Head, Patrick 262
Hegbourne, Tony 77, 119
helmets 21, 47, 55, 209, 213, 295, 344
Heppenstal, Ray 169
Herd, Robin 193, 307
Hermann, Hans 171
Hesketh Racing 252, 255
Hill, Bette 169, 334
Hill, Damon 73
Hill, Graham 23, 31, 34, 36, 51, 54, 55, 62, 67, 69, 75, 79, 81, 82, 88, 93, 99, 102, 105, 110, 119, 121, 132, 138, 149, 151, 153, 159, 185, 220, 226, 229, 252, 271, 272, 275, 292; team 252
Hill, Phil 11, 42, 47, 70, 81, 85, 88, 94, 97, 106, 142, 156, 159, 161, 275
Hillman: Hunter 187; Imp 31, 146, 166; Minx 14, 17
Hoare, Col. Ronnie 31, 57
Hobbs, David 62
Hockenheim 224
Hoeksma, Wim 34
Holbert, Al 236
Holman & Moody 126
Holquist, Richard 127
Honda 54, 198, 262, 288; RA273 and RA300 164; RA301 and RA302 179
Hopkirk, Paddy 108, 187
Howmet Continental TX gas turbine car 110, 169
Hughes, Mike 79
Hulme, Denny 77, 110, 119, 121, 149, 153, 161, 163, 164, 172, 177, 189, 236, 332, 338
Hunt, James 109, 198, 252, 255
Hussein, King of Jordan, and Queen Noor 347
Hussey, Anthony 10, 109, 319
Hutcheson, Alan 34
HWM 1: 14

Ickx, Jacky 110, 171, 172, 175, 177, 180, 203, 255
IMG 348
Imola, City of, GP 49
Infanti, Angelo 286
International Racing Press Association (IRPA) 10, 343
Ireland, Innes 29, 57, 62, 303
Iso FX3 247, 252
Iso-Marlboro Williams 1R 320
Italian GP 143, 156, 164

Jack Brabham Story, The 220
Jackson, Peter 189
Jaguar: 3.8 Mk2 34, 51, 62, 64, 69; D-type 33; E-type 45, 51, 54, 62, 67, 69, 77, 102, 112; Mk 7: 121; SS100 14, 53; XK120 14, 197, 197, 324
Jaguar at Le Mans 1950-1995 348
James, Ken 79
Jarama 203, 204, 207, 232
Jarier, Jean-Pierre 'Jumper' 259
JBW-Maserati 23

JCB 231
Jenkinson, Denis 'Jenks' 102, 106, 132
Jensen 541: 14, 17
Johansson, Stefan 263, 287
John Player Norton 312
John Player Special 234, 236, 245, 255
Johnson, Herbert, helmets 21, 47, 55, 344
Jones, Elizabeth 60
Jopp, Peter 60, 62
Jordan, Chuck 53

Kay Racing 111
Kempf, Dr Karl 259
Kent, Duke and Duchess of 51
Kerr, Phil 223
Kerrison, Chris 102
Key, Beverley 319
Keylock, Jennifer 231
Klementaski, Louis 'Klem' 289

Lancaster, Burt 277
Lanfranchi, Tony 166
Lang, Herman 295
Lanlois von Ophem, Gerard 87
Larousse Camel 266
Lawrence, Chris 141
Le Grand, Max 270
Le Mans 87, 88, 110, 166
Le Mans 270, 282, 284, 286
Leigh-Hunt, Ronald 284
Leitzinger, Bob 127
Leston, Les 21, 57, 59
Lewis, Edward 60
Lewis, Jack 59
Leyton House 265
Ligier, Guy 88, 134
Ligier-Judd JS31 263
Lindner, Peter 64
Lindsay, The Hon. Patrick 94, 330
Lister Jaguar 33
Lola: GT 69; Mk 1 77; Mk3 33; Mk4A 70; Mk6 GT 54, 100; LC88 266; T60 119, 121; T70 110, 111, 156, 189
London to Sydney Marathon, *Daily Express* 186, 187
Lord Mayor's Show 54, 108
Lotus: XI GT 77; XIX (Monte Carlo) 33, 57; 12: 10; 15: 23; 16: 10; 18: 29; 18/21 hybrid 55; 19: 57, 100; 20: 42; 23: 300; 23B 77; 24: 55, 70; 25: 54, 59, 60, 73, 82, 88, 90, 97; 27: 77; 30: 102, 105, 119; 33: 116, 134, 141, 149, 151; 35: 119, 121; 40: 126; 49: 110, 151, 153, 161; 49B 177, 180, 183, 189, 194, 196; 49C 209, 220; 56 4WD gas turbine 224, 303; 69: 210; 70: 204; 72: 209, 215, 220, 223, 234, 236; 72D/R6 245, 255; Elan 127, 159; Elise 287; Elite 57, 59, 87; T100 261; *see also* Gold Leaf Team Lotus; Team Lotus
Lumsden, Peter 102
Lurani Cernushi, Count Giovanni 'Johnny' 270, 277

Maarsbergen 75
Mac, Roger 112
Maggs, Tony 42, 69, 75
Malkin, Colin 187
Mann, Alan 64, 113, 172, 282
Manney Jr, Henry N. 141
Mansell, Nigel 262
Maranello Concessionaires 31, 51, 52, 62, 77, 79, 102, 111
March 308; 701: 199, 210, 212, 308; 712M 226; 721: 234, 239, 343; 731: 252, 255; 881: 265
Marimón, Onofre 344
Markelson, Alan 52
Marlboro 198, 232, 236, 257, 259
Marquart, Jo 193
Marriott, Ann 301
Martin, George 301
Maserati 10; 250F 290; Quattroporte 302; Tipo 60 'birdcage' 23, 231
Matra 110, 187; MS10 169, 177, 189; MS11/1 177; MS120 203, 223
Mayer, Teddy 175
Mays, Raymond 99, 185, 310
McKelvy, William 127
McKern, Leo 322
McLaren 127; Colnbrook factory 223; M1B 127; M5A 163, 332; M7A 163, 172, 175, 183; M7C/1 207, 213; M9A 193; M14A/1 213; M19A/1 223; M23/2 255; MP4/4 259
McLaren, Bruce 23, 51, 73, 81, 88, 90, 94, 97, 105, 127, 128, 153, 163, 171, 172, 175, 183, 288, 334
McLaren, Pat 341
McQueen, Chad 282
McQueen, Steve 270, 282, 284
Mecom, John 100
Mehl, Leo 153
Mercedes Benz: 220SE 62; 300SL 14; W154 297, 344
Merzario, Arturo 249, 255
Mexican GP 54, 110
MG: Midget 77; TF 14; MGA coupé 14; MGB 77, 166
Michelin 320
Midland Racing Partnership 119, 121
Miles, John 204
Mill Garage 77
Mille Miglia 289
Milne, Dick 14
Mini 34, 60, 109; Mini Cooper 166; Mini Cooper S 128
Mitter, Gerhard 172
Moakes, Peter 301
Modena 154
Monaco 54, 79, 115, 144, 146, 307; Casino Square 334; Rosie's Bar 229
Monaco GP: 1964 81, 82, 85; 1966 131, 132, 134, 137, 138; 1967 147, 149; 1968 183; 1970 210, 212; 1972 234, 236; 1973 252, 255, 257
Montand, Yves 272, 277
Monte Carlo Rally 54, 77, 79, 119
Montjuich Park 193, 226, 247
Monza 143, 156, 164, 277, 279
Moore, Roger 112
Morgan Aero 8 and Plus 4: 141
Morley, Don and Erle 77, 108
Morris, David and Martin 229
Morris Minor 14
Mosley, Max 307
Moss, Alfred 49
Moss, Pat 57
Moss, Stirling 17, 21, 29, 33, 39, 41, 45, 49, 51, 52, 54, 55, 57, 100, 116, 307, 329, 348
Motor Racing 348
Motul 226, 234
Murray, David 99
Nabarro, Sir Gerald 326
Nakajima, Satoru 261
Nannini, Alessandro 263
Napier 270
Napier Railton 330
NART (North American Racing Team) 88
Nash, Tony 187
Nassau Speedweek 126, 127, 128
Naylor, Brian 23
Neerspach, Jochen 172
Nelson, Edward 189
Neubauer, Alfred 295
Neuschwanstein 280
Newey, Adrian 265
Nicholas, Jeremy 322
Nicholls, Don 250
Nissan 350Z 288
Nivelles 240
Nöcker, Peter 64
Nomad-BRM 189
Normand 77
Norton, John Player 312
Nürburgring 54, 110, 141, 161, 183, 194, 196, 295; 1,000km race 36, 49, 116
Nye, Doug 128, 220

Ohlsen, John 113
Oliver, Jackie 177, 183, 203, 207, 210, 217
Oliver, Mrs Jackie 336
Opel Grand Prix 290
Opel Styling Department 53
Osborn, Michael 319
Österreichring 245
O'Sullivan, Denis 115
Oulton Park 112, 113; Gold Cup 29, 31, 119, 121, 185, 236
Overton, Alan 14
Owen, Sir Alfred 310

Pabst, Augie 100
Parkes, Mike 31, 51, 52, 57, 62, 64, 69, 77, 111, 138, 151
Parnell, Reg, (Racing) 70, 97, 180
Parnell, Tim 97, 175, 180, 236, 275
Patrese, Riccardo 262
Paul Ricard circuit 198, 229
Pearce, J. A., Engineering 141
Penske, Roger 110
Pescarolo, Henri 203, 216, 226, 234
Peterson, Ronnie 226, 234, 249, 255, 343
Phillipe, Maurice 259
Pierpoint, Roy 64
Piers Courage, Last of the Gentleman Racers 204
Pilsworth, Peter 60
Piper, David 62, 106, 113
Piquet, Nelson 198, 261, 262
Pironi, Didier 259
Pitt-Bailey, Michael 210, 219
Plummer, Penelope 186
Polanski, Roman 210
Poole, Alex 187
Porsche 54, 110; 718: 75; 718RSK 19; 904GTS 88; 906: 159; 907: 171, 172; 908: 110, 141; 910: 159; 917: 110, 141, 284; 956: 236
Postlethwaite, Harvey 252
Procter, Peter 88
Proctor, S. R. 102
Prophet, David 189
Protheroe, Dick 54

RAC Rally 305
Racing Car Show 223
Radford Racing 113
Read, Phil 312
Redman, Brian 171, 172, 189, 282
Rees, Alan 119, 121, 199, 307
Regazzoni, Clay 210, 257, 312
Reims 109, 138, 141
Renault Alpine M64 87
Rene Bonnet Aerojet 87
Reutemann, Carlos 255
Reventlow, Lance 39
Revson, Doug 119
Revson, Peter 111, 255
Rhodes, John 166
Richard, Ted 113
Riley 1.5 14, 34, 60
Rindt, Jochen 110, 119, 121, 138, 141, 154, 156, 159, 189, 201, 204, 209, 210, 215, 220, 223
Rindt, Nina 215
Rodriguez, Pedro 141, 172, 175, 191, 203, 212, 217, 226
Rogers, Chris 198
Rolls-Royce 314
Rolls-Royce Corniche 290
Rondel Racing 226
Rouen-les-Essarts 94, 97, 99, 179, 180
Rover 3-litre 79
Rover 2000 319
Rowe, Maurice 10, 53
Rudd, Tony 54, 132, 163
Rumpole of the Bailey 322

Sachs, Peter 289
Saint, Eva Marie 277
Salmon, Mike 19, 33, 64, 102
Saltzman, Harry 270, 282
Salvadori, Roy 17, 21, 27, 29, 34, 45, 51, 62, 67, 69, 77, 106, 125, 154
Sargent, Peter 102
Scarab 01: 39
Scarab-Chevrolet MkIV 100
Scarfiotti, Ludovico 110, 156, 172
Scheckter, Jody 329
Schegelmilch, Rainer 109
Schlesser, Jo 87, 110, 179
Schneider, Bernd 265
School for Scoundrels 14
Schuppan, Vern 197, 236
Scott Brown, Archie 116
Scott-Moncrieff, David 'Bunty' 288, 314
Scuderia Bear 127
Scuderia Serinissima 62
Sears, Jack 60, 62, 69, 79, 113, 186
Sebring 36, 110, 127
Segers, Willy 146
Senna, Ayrton 259, 347
Servoz-Gavin, Johnny 212
Setright, Leonard John Kensell 327
Shadow DN1/3A 252
Sharp, Hap 127, 128
Shattock, Frank 113
Shelby, Carroll 17, 21, 39, 54, 88, 110
Shelby Cobra 106, 112, 113, 279
Shelby Daytona Cobra 54, 106, 110, 113
Shepherd, 'Doc' 34
Shere, Surrey 109; The White Horse 109, 198
Shere Garage 288, 300
Siffert, Jo 70, 90, 97, 125, 154, 171, 172, 180, 196
Silverstone 69, 119, 179, 189, 290, 303, 330; British Empire Trophy 42, 45; hare 320; International Caravan Trophy 301; International Trophy 34, 39, 41, 172, 189, 199, 209, 226, 229, 314; *see also* British GPs 1963/67/88
Sixties Motor Racing 348
SMART (Stirling Moss Automobile Racing Team) 99
SMOG 226
Snetterton 31, 55, 67, 77
Société Charonnet 88
Sopwith, Tommy 31, 64, 79, 186
Southcott, Willy 175
Southgate, Tony 232, 236, 239
Sowden, Frank 330
Spa-Francorchamps 36, 88, 90, 93, 116, 154, 175, 177, 212, 347
Spanish GP: 1968 193; 1970 203, 204, 207; 1971 226; 1972 232; 1973 247
Sparrow, John 113
Spence, Mike 110, 119, 159, 161, 164, 169, 172, 183, 275
Sport Auto 134
sports car regulations, Appendix C 33
Sprite Caravans 219
Sproat, Stan 99
Stacey, Alan 23
Stanley, Louis and Jean 175, 310
Starting Grid to Chequered Flag 21
Steering Wheel Club 9, 197
Stevens, Jocelyn 186
Stewart, Gwenda 94
Stewart, Helen 210
Stewart, Jackie 99, 110, 121, 132, 137, 141, 154, 159, 169, 177, 189, 199, 203, 209, 210, 212, 219, 224, 236, 242, 247, 257, 290, 347
Stockbridge Racing 128
Stommelen, Rolf 239, 343
Stone, David 305
STP 199
Streiff, Philippe 262
Subaru Impreza 288
Summers, Shane 36, 288, 298
Sunbeam: Rapier 14, 60, 62; Talbot 27; Tiger 9, 88, 197, 247, 287
Supermarine Spitfire Mk IXB 346
Surtees, John 41, 42, 45, 54, 59, 62, 81, 85, 90, 110, 111, 119, 121, 131, 137, 138, 141, 164, 177, 179, 193, 207, 213, 344; team 213
Surtees TS7 223
Sutcliffe, Peter 64, 77, 113
Sutton, John 62
Syrett, Nick 169

Taggart, Peter 159
TAGHeuer 284
Tauranac, Ron 229
Tavano, Fernand 88
Taylor, Dennis and Henry 33
Taylor, Sid 189
Taylor, Trevor 73, 119
Team Lotus 105, 110, 149 *see also* Gold Leaf Team Lotus; Lotus
Tecno 69: 210
Tecno PA123 F12 240
Tee, Ian and Wesley J. 189
Thomas, Terry 14
Thompson, Dr Richard 169
Thomson, Ronnie 242
Thruxton, BARC 200 Yellow Pages-Jochen Rindt Memorial Trophy 226
Tojeiro-Buick 348
Tojeiro-Ford 99
Tojeiro-Jaguar 11, 19
Tongue, Reggie 229
Trimmer, Tony 302
Trintignant, Maurice 17, 21
Turner, Helen 53, 319
Turner, Michael 10, 53, 109, 242, 319, 348
Tyrrell 110, 169, 187, 199, 210, 212; 001: 224; 003: 236, 242; 006: 247, 255, 257; 009: 259; 017: 269
Tyrrell, Ken 42, 183, 216, 259

UDT Laystall 33, 55, 57, 62
Unett, Bernard 88, 166
United States GP 54, 110
Uren, Jeff 69

van Dyke, Dick 197
Vanwall 10, 116
Vanwall VW14 41
Vauxhall: Astra GTE 287; Velox 62; VX 4/90 62
VDS, Racing Team 189
Veuillet, Auguste 88
Villeneuve, Gilles 347
Volvo P544 34
Volvo P1800 112
von Trips, Count Wolfgang 19, 42, 47
Vyse, Howard 270

Waite, Brian 113
Walker, Dave 224, 245
Walker, Ian, Racing 77, 119
Walker, Rob, team 29, 39, 45, 49, 51, 55, 154, 180, 196, 220; Pippbrook Garage 14
Waller, Peter 94
Warr, Peter 314
Warwick, Derek 261
Watkins Glen 54
Watson, John 310
Westbury, Peter 194, 301
Westminster, Duke of 201
Wetherspoons 49
Wharton, Ken 229
Wheatcroft, Tom 310
White, Derrick 125, 141, 154
Whitehead, Graham 23
Whitmore, John 60, 113, 116
Wilkinson, 'Wilkie' 19, 36
Williams 196, 204, 209, 226, 234; FW02 247, 252, 320; FW12 262
Williams, Christopher 288, 300
Williams, Frank 193, 201, 262, 347
Williamson, Roger 310
Willment, John 69, 79, 113
Willment Cobra coupé 113
Winkelmann, Roy, Racing 119, 121
Wisell, Reine 224, 234, 236
Wood, G. 34
Wood, Mike 187
Wyer, John 109, 110, 141, 171, 172

Yardley 201, 203, 219, 226, 288
Yeoman Credit 42, 45
Yield to the Night 12
Yorke, David 329
Young, Eoin 53, 197, 198, 302, 307, 324
Young, John 146

Zakspeed 881 and 891: 265
Zandvoort 75, 183 *see also* Dutch GP
Zerex Special 100, 102

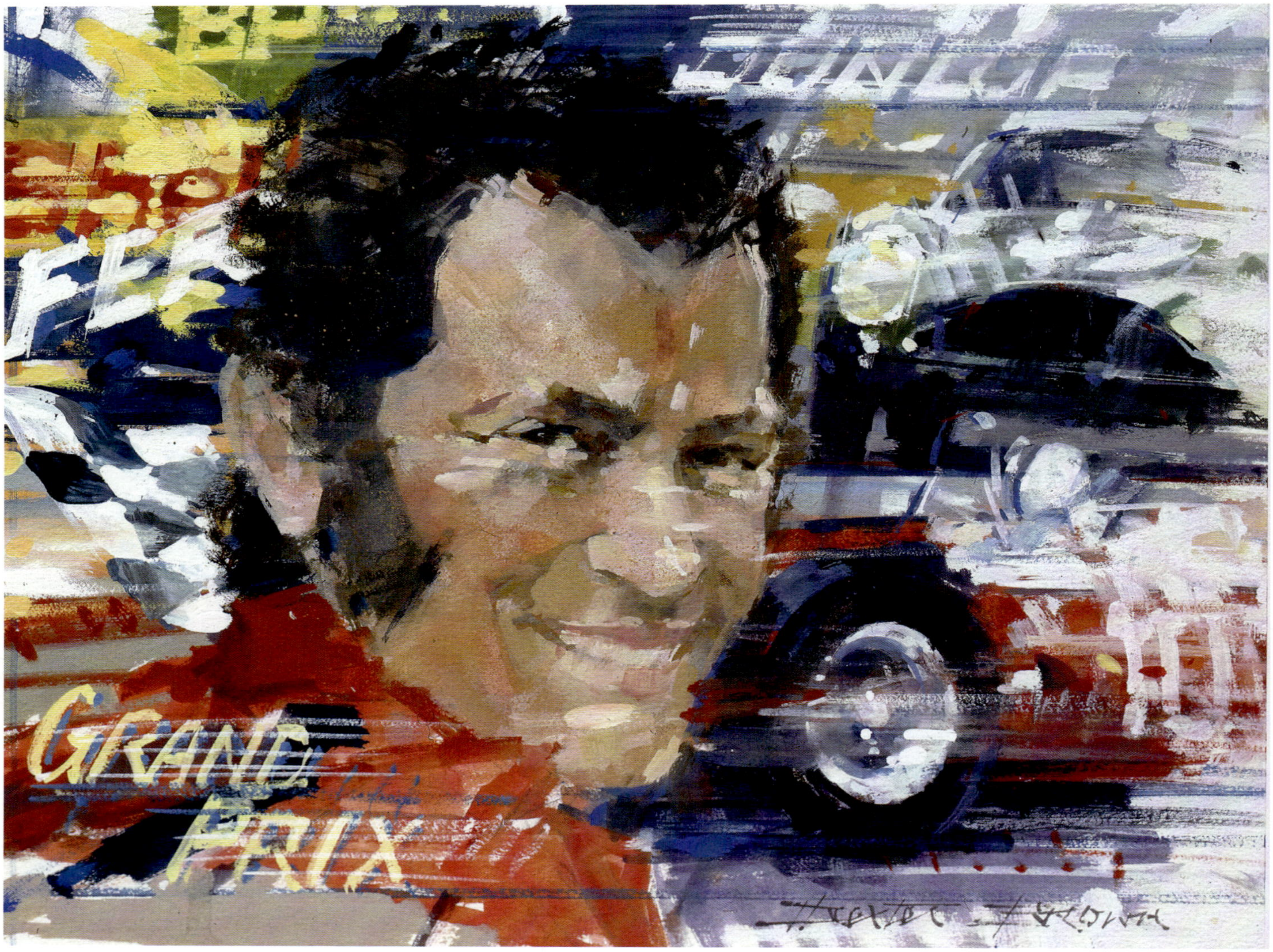
GRAND PRIX

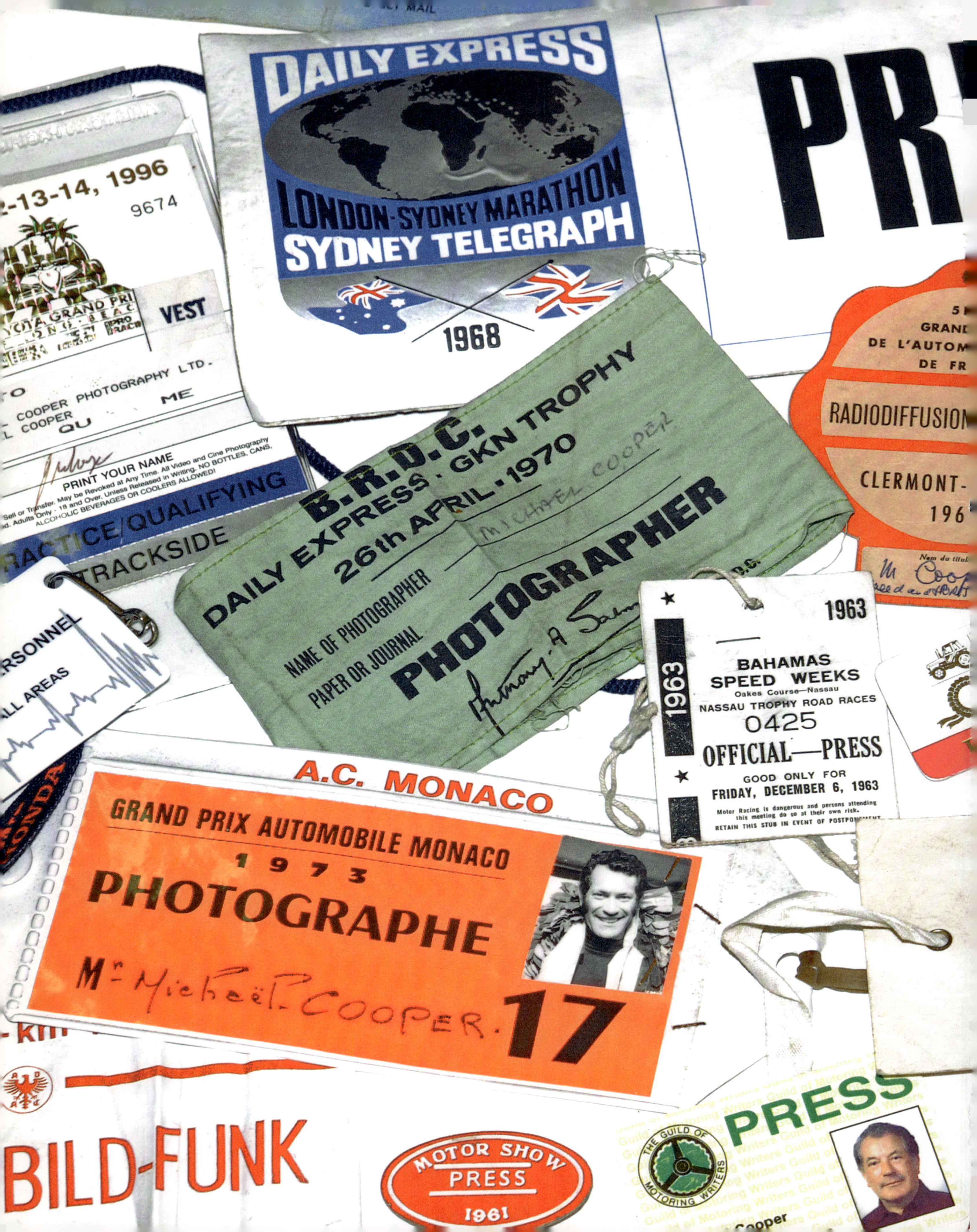
DAILY EXPRESS
LONDON-SYDNEY MARATHON
SYDNEY TELEGRAPH
1968
PR
RADIODIFFUSION
CLERMONT-
2-13-14, 1996
9674
VEST
COOPER PHOTOGRAPHY LTD.
PRINT YOUR NAME
PRACTICE/QUALIFYING
TRACKSIDE
PERSONNEL
ALL AREAS
B.R.D.C.
DAILY EXPRESS · GKN TROPHY
26th APRIL · 1970
NAME OF PHOTOGRAPHER
PAPER OR JOURNAL
PHOTOGRAPHER
1963
BAHAMAS
SPEED WEEKS
Oakes Course—Nassau
NASSAU TROPHY ROAD RACES
0425
OFFICIAL—PRESS
GOOD ONLY FOR
FRIDAY, DECEMBER 6, 1963
Motor Racing is dangerous and persons attending this meeting do so at their own risk.
A.C. MONACO
GRAND PRIX AUTOMOBILE MONACO
1973
PHOTOGRAPHE
Mr Michaël Cooper.
17
BILD-FUNK
MOTOR SHOW
PRESS
1961
PRESS
THE GUILD OF MOTORING WRITERS